Marketing Management
Text and Cases

McGraw-Hill/Irwin Series in Marketing

Alreck & Settle
The Survey Research Handbook
Third Edition

Anderson, Beveridge, Lawton, & Scott
Merlin: A Marketing Simulation
First Edition

Arens
Contemporary Advertising
Ninth Edition

Arnould, Price & Zinkhan
Consumers
Second Edition

Bearden, Ingram, & LaForge
Marketing: Principles & Perspectives
Fourth Edition

Belch & Belch
Advertising & Promotion: An Integrated Marketing Communications Approach
Sixth Edition

Bingham & Gomes
Business Marketing
Third Edition

Cateora & Graham
International Marketing
Twelfth Edition

Cole & Mishler
Consumer and Business Credit Management
Eleventh Edition

Cravens & Piercy
Strategic Marketing
Seventh Edition

Cravens, Lamb & Crittenden
Strategic Marketing Management Cases
Seventh Edition

Crawford & Di Benedetto
New Products Management
Seventh Edition

Duncan
Principles of Advertising and IMC
Second Edition

Dwyer & Tanner
Business Marketing
Second Edition

Eisenmann
Internet Business Models: Text and Cases
First Edition

Etzel, Walker & Stanton
Marketing
Thirteenth Edition

Forrest
Internet Marketing Intelligence
First Edition

Futrell
ABC's of Relationship Selling
Eighth Edition

Futrell
Fundamentals of Selling
Eighth Edition

Gourville, Quelch, & Rangan
Cases in Health Care Marketing
First Edition

Hair, Bush & Ortinau
Marketing Research
Second Edition

Hawkins, Best & Coney
Consumer Behavior
Ninth Edition

Johansson
Global Marketing
Third Edition

Johnston & Marshall
Churchill/Ford/Walker's Sales Force Management
Seventh Edition

Johnston & Marshall
Relationship Selling and Sales Management
First Edition

Kerin, Hartley, & Rudelius
Marketing: The Core
First Edition

Kerin, Berkowitz, Hartley & Rudelius
Marketing
Seventh Edition

Lal, Quelch, & Rangan
Marketing Management Text and Cases
First Edition

Lehmann & Winer
Analysis for Marketing Planning
Fifth Edition

Lehmann & Winer
Product Management
Third Edition

Levy & Weitz
Retailing Management
Fifth Edition

Mason & Perreault
The Marketing Game!
Third Edition

McDonald
Direct Marketing: An Integrated Approach
First Edition

Mohammed, Fisher, Jaworski & Paddison
Internet Marketing: Building Advantage in a Networked Economy
Second Edition

Monroe
Pricing
Third Edition

Mullins, Walker, and Boyd
Marketing Management: A Strategic Decision-Making Approach
Fifth Edition

Nentl & Miller
SimSeries Simulations:
  SimSell
  SimSales Management
  SimMarketing
  SimMarketing Research
  SimCRM
First Edition

Pelton, Strutton, Lumpkin & Cooper
Marketing Channels: A Relationship Management Approach
Third Edition

Perreault & McCarthy
Basic Marketing: A Global Managerial Approach
Fifteenth Edition

Perreault & McCarthy
Essentials of Marketing: A Global Managerial Approach
Ninth Edition

Peter & Donnelly
A Preface to Marketing Management
Ninth Edition

Peter & Donnelly
Marketing Management: Knowledge and Skills
Seventh Edition

Peter & Olson
Consumer Behavior
Seventh Edition

Purvis & Burton
Which Ad Pulled Best?
Ninth Edition

Rayport & Jaworski
Introduction to e-Commerce
Second Edition

Rayport & Jaworski
e-Commerce
First Edition

Rayport & Jaworski
Cases in e-Commerce
First Edition

Richardson
Internet Marketing
First Edition

Roberts
Internet Marketing: Integrating Online and Offline Strategies
First Edition

Spiro, Stanton, Rich
Management of a Sales Force
Eleventh Edition

Stock & Lambert
Strategic Logistics Management
Fourth Edition

Ulrich & Eppinger
Product Design and Development
Third Edition

Walker, Boyd, Mullins & Larreche
Marketing Strategy: A Decision-Focused Approach
Fourth Edition

Weitz, Castleberry & Tanner
Selling: Building Partnerships
Fifth Edition

Zeithaml & Bitner
Services Marketing
Third Edition

Marketing Management
Text and Cases

Rajiv Lal
Harvard Business School

John A. Quelch
Harvard Business School

V. Kasturi Rangan
Harvard Business School

McGraw-Hill
Irwin

Boston   Burr Ridge, IL   Dubuque, IA   Madison, WI   New York   San Francisco   St. Louis
Bangkok   Bogotá   Caracas   Kuala Lumpur   Lisbon   London   Madrid   Mexico City
Milan   Montreal   New Delhi   Santiago   Seoul   Singapore   Sydney   Taipei   Toronto

 McGraw-Hill
Irwin

Marketing Management Text and Cases

Published by McGraw-Hill/Irwin, a business unit of The McGraw-Hill Companies, Inc., 1221 Avenue of the Americas, New York, NY, 10020. Copyright © 2005 by The McGraw-Hill Companies, Inc. All rights reserved. No part of this publication may be reproduced or distributed in any form or by any means, or stored in a database or retrieval system, without the prior written consent of The McGraw-Hill Companies, Inc., including, but not limited to, in any network or other electronic storage or transmission, or broadcast for distance learning. Some ancillaries, including electronic and print components, may not be available to customers outside the United States.

This book is printed on acid-free paper.

1 2 3 4 5 6 7 8 9 0 DOW/DOW 0 9 8 7 6 5 4

ISBN 0-07-296762-5

Editorial director: *John E. Biernat*
Sponsoring editor: *Barrett Koger*
Editorial assistant: *Jill M. O'Malley*
Marketing manager: *Dan Silverburg*
Project manager: *Jim Labeots*
Senior production supervisor: *Rose Hepburn*
Designer: *Mary E. Kazak*
Lead supplement producer: *Cathy L. Tepper*
Senior digital content specialist: *Brian Nacik*
Cover design: *Lodge Design*
Typeface: *10/12 Times New Roman*
Compositor: *GAC Indianapolis*
Printer: *R. R. Donnelley*

Library of Congress Cataloging-in-Publication Data

Lal, Rajiv.
    Marketing management: text and cases / Rajiv Lal, John A. Quelch, V. Kasturi Rangan.
        p. cm. — (McGraw-Hill/Irwin series in marketing)
    Previously published: Homewood, IL: Irwin, c1993.
    Includes index.
    ISBN 0-07-296762-5 (alk. paper)
    1. Marketing–Management. 2. Marketing–Management–Case studies. I. Quelch, John A. II.
Rangan, V. Kasturi. III. Title. IV. Series.
HF5415.13.Q45 2005
    658.8–dc22   2004042585

www.mhhe.com

Contents

Preface

This book is the culmination of a journey that the Marketing unit at the Harvard Business School embarked upon at a faculty retreat in June 2000. At that retreat, several of us teaching the First Year Marketing course took on the challenge of making the curriculum more appealing to a generation of new students enamored by the apparent wealth created by a variety of 'new economy' businesses. But we, like several of our colleagues in other business schools, were continuing to frame the discussions along the well-trodden traditions of the discipline. Simply put, the focus had been on segmentation, target market selection and positioning as the basis of formulating the marketing strategy and the strategy implemented through the elements of the marketing mix, backed up by analyses of consumers, collaborators, and competitors. With the emerging technologies on the horizon and changes in the economy, our students viewed the course to be more about tactics rather than one of central concern to the enterprise. Moreover, the dozen or so 'new economy' cases that were specially written for the course did not help change this perception.

The irony of it all was that the Marketing Concept had won the battle in the corporate world, with "customers" being widely seen as the key asset of a business enterprise. Indeed business after business was realigning themselves around customers, yet in our curriculum we were losing the "war" for students' share of mind. Some of our colleagues at other business schools had responded intuitively by bringing to bear the more systematic and analytical aspects of marketing to class, so it could gain the respectability of other business courses. We refrained from that temptation, because ultimately, as we all recognize, marketing is more than the 'marketing mix,' it is more than 'marketing research' and the quantitative analyses that go with it. It is a blend of rigorous analysis, astute judgments and knowing where creativity matters. Knowing and defining the customer problem is the marketer's #1 job, and then after thoroughly analyzing the situation and assessing the alternatives, bringing to bear a workable set of actions that strategically advances the company's goal, the top priority.

We took this challenge head on and devised a strategy to regain the centrality of marketing to a growing enterprise. The central theme in revamping the course was to adopt a general manager's perspective. Marketing, as we use the word, refers to whatever it takes to grow a business by fostering exchange between the organization and its customers. In general terms, marketing creates value for the firm's customers and extracts a share of the value for the firm. The skill of marketing is the skill to monitor customers, competitors, and collaborators, and to find in each domain a better way to design and deploy the firm's capabilities to serve the customers at a profit. In this way marketing helps to set a firm's strategic direction.

Marketing, thus defined, is a broad general management responsibility and not something to be delegated to marketing specialists. Its skills are required of all careers concerned with the strategy of organizations of every kind. In this way we sought to bring alive the ideas of Peter Drucker when he said: "Marketing is the whole business, seen from the point of view of its final result, that is, from a customers' point of view. . . . There is only one valid definition of business purpose: to create a customer. . . . It is the customer who determines what a business is."

The course and the materials used have several unique features. First, every case in the course now has a business orientation. We very carefully chose the instruments to convey this new overarching approach to marketing. Second, the cases in the first part of the course typically are about new products and capture decisions made by senior managers in the firm, but not limited to managers in the marketing function. The focus on new products allows students to determine marketing's centrality to developing a business. Third, and most importantly, the cases demonstrate the integrative nature of these decisions and do not seek to cover the elements of marketing mix as stand-alone dimensions of the marketing plan. Finally, the logic of the first five modules has an intuitive appeal in developing a business.

The second part of the course is devoted to remaining competitive over time. This segment covers three ways of doing so: the value of developing a brand and how it helps in remaining competitive; managing the marketing costs to maximize profitability; and finally, tracking changes in the environment that call for a change in strategy and challenges in moving away from the status quo.

The students at HBS have responded well to these changes and do indeed perceive the new course to be central to their ability to develop a business.

Structure of the Course

The First Year Marketing course is structured into an introductory class and a series of eight modules. The first five modules focus on creating value, building a business, and capturing value for the firm. The next three modules explore ways for staying competitive over time.

Introduction: The Power of Marketing

We begin by demonstrating the fact that companies can be stunningly successful when they embrace the marketing perspective. The marketing perspective is that customers get to make the rules of the game and companies choose to play the game to create value for their stakeholders. Consumers decide what they will buy and what they won't and the rules they will use to make those decisions. Companies that acknowledge the importance of integrating this customer perspective into their business planning often deliver spectacular results to their shareholders.

Module 1: Creating Value

This module explores the role of marketing in the process of creating value. We look at both Market Driving processes and Market Driven processes and identify the marketing challenges in these contexts. Market Driving processes typically begin with an innovation, often driven by new technology, with virtually little or no input from the customer. The job of marketing is to then help create a demand for the product and translate that into a profitable business. In contrast, the Market Driven processes for creating value begin with a good understanding of the needs of the customers. Marketing therefore provides valuable input into the design of the value proposition and helps realize the full potential of the innovation for its shareholders.

Developing a Marketing Strategy

Module 2: Choosing Your Customers

This is the first step in the process of developing a Marketing Strategy. After having developed a value proposition, the firm has to identify a set of customers, called "the target market," that it wishes to serve. This decision recognizes that customers differ from one another. The marketer exerts some control over the rules governing the games it plays by selecting those customers it wishes to serve. So, we start out by delving into the importance of market segmentation. This is the process of not looking at the set of potential customers as an undifferentiated mass, but rather seeing differences among individuals or segments of the market. We segment the market because the first key decision in marketing strategy is target market selection, i.e., specifying the group of customers you want to serve. From the target market selection decision we move on to "Positioning," i.e., a notion of how you want your target customers to perceive you. Once you have this positioning objective in mind, you can work out the tactical details of how you are going to achieve it with the marketing tools at your disposal. To signify that we use a variety of tools together in a coordinated way, we call these tools the "marketing mix." Bringing these tools into a cohesive package is known as the development of the "marketing plan." A key observation from this module is that the process of developing a Marketing Strategy is iterative because only when you truly understand what it takes to implement the strategy and develop the marketing plan that we can make the right choices about the target market.

The Marketing Plan

Module 3: Communicating the Value Proposition

Having created a product/service and identified a target market to serve, the next step in implementing a Marketing Strategy is specifying a plan for the marketing tools to achieve the desired positioning. So in this module we look at the different options available to a firm for communicating its value proposition to its chosen target market—advertising (TV, radio, and print), promotions, events, public relations, and put it together into an integrated communications plan. We determine which media are most effective for what, how much to spend on these options, and how we pull it all together into a cohesive plan.

Module 4: Going to Market

Having created a value proposition in Module 2, identified the target market and the positioning for the value proposition in Module 3, and developed an integrated marketing communications plan in Module 4, we now have to make the product/service available to the targeted customers. In this module, we explore how to design and manage the network that connects a manufacturer to its customers. There are lots of possible ways to be connected to customers. Obviously, one big question is whether to do this all yourself or find yourself a partner to help. So, we explore how to think through the design of a marketing channel and then the issues in managing it. The management issues get pretty complex because the interests of everybody involved do not naturally line up. In short, each partner who will benefit from a sale wants the other to do more to make it happen. It is generally a situation marked by both cooperation and conflict. An added complication these days is that we usually connect with customers in multiple ways, e.g., both through "bricks" and "clicks."

Module 5: Pricing to Capture Value

All the above modules were focused on creating value for our chosen customers. We do this because if they value it more than our price, they'll buy our stuff. And, if our price is higher than our cost, we make money. And, that's good. So, the other key thing is price. Pricing is the process via which we extract some of the value created for ourselves. We use this to fund future value creation efforts and to contribute to earnings.

Staying Competitive Over Time

Module 6: Brands and Branding

In this module we will explore the meaning of a "brand," the role of brands, and their creation. There is a lot of talk in the public press about "branding" and "creating brands." We attempt to answer these questions and delineate when and how much flexibility might exist in creating brands.

Module 7: Managing Customers for Profits

From markets to segments to individual consumers is the way marketing is evolving. We are increasingly able to determine the profitability of an individual consumer and are therefore better at allocating marketing efforts across consumers. In this module we move away from a transactional mode and approach marketing strategy from this new perspective. As we move to an individual level, firms will have to make a new set of choices beyond what we have seen up until now—does the company wish to have a transactional relationship or a long term relationship with the customer? Are these choices compatible with the consumer's desires to have or not to have a relationship with the firm? Given the differences in customer segments along this dimension, a firm's management of their portfolio of customers to maximize profits is the central issue in this module. We also witness the use of customer loyalty programs and database marketing to achieve these goals.

Module 8: Sustaining Value

Every profitable product/service attracts competitors who desire to benefit from the opportunity identified by you. Over time, as the market develops, consumer needs change and new entrants offer competing and sometimes even better products/services; the original value proposition and the marketing strategy lose their edge and need to be reconsidered. This module explores how the marketing strategy needs to be modified in light of such new developments in the marketplace.

Throughout the course, most interesting cases involve multiple mix elements, e.g., some of our "going-to-market" cases will present product policy dimensions. Marketing does not divide itself up as neatly as, say, mathematics where an addition problem is an addition problem; division is a division, etc. Thus, our module names suggest a focus but we recognize that other mix elements are necessary in the picture because in the end we have to have a coordinated overall plan.

Marketing Management: Text and Cases is the result of the efforts of many who have contributed to this venture in a variety of different ways. In particular, we would like to thank Dean Kim Clark, the members of the division of research and Professor David Bell, as Marketing Area Unit Head, for his support of our efforts. We also want to thank members of our teaching group over the last four years: Rohit Deshpande, Anita Elberse,

David Godes, Sunil Gupta, Doug Holt, Nirmalya Kumar, Gail McGovern, Youngme Moon, Elie Ofek, Kash Rangan, Tom Steenburgh, Marta Wosinska, and Jerry Zaltman.

We would like to thank many colleagues who have allowed us to include their materials in the book. In addition to the teaching group colleagues, these include David Bell, Robert Dolan, John Gourville, Das Narayandas, Susan Fournier, and Luc Wathieu. We are also indebted to our assistant, Judy Tully, and Marketing Unit Area Coordinator, Kathy Randel, for all her help in making the First Year Marketing experience such a wonderful one for all of us.

Part 1

Introduction

1

Marketing Strategy—an Overview

E. Raymond Corey

A **strategy**[1] is a plan of action designed to achieve certain defined **objectives.** In business firms, objectives may be stated in such terms as sales volume, rate of growth, profit percentages, market share, and return on investment (ROI), among others. The importance of defining objectives to give purpose and direction to strategies cannot be overestimated. How can we formulate useful strategies in any domain unless we know what we are trying to accomplish?

Strategies are developed at multiple levels in the organization—corporate, divisional, business unit, and departmental. Taken together, they form an integrated plan for the enterprise as a whole. Thus, corporate strategies are the sum of business unit strategies plus any plans for new business initiatives.

At the heart of any business plan is its **marketing strategy.** Businesses exist to deliver products and services to markets. To the extent that they serve this purpose well and efficiently, they grow and profit. Other components of a business unit strategy (e.g., finance, production, and R&D) must support the business's marketing mission. By the same token, marketing objectives and strategies have to be formulated to take account of the firm's core competencies as well as its resource limits.

Elements of Marketing Strategy

A marketing strategy is composed of several interrelated elements. The first, and most important, is **product/market selection.** What markets will we serve with what product lines? A second critical element is **price.** What prices will be set for individual products; how will

---

[1] Words and phrases often used in marketing are noted in bold letters when they first appear.

Professor E. Raymond Corey prepared this note as the basis for class discussion.

products in the line be priced relative to each other; will we offer quantity discounts, deferred payment plans and/or rental options; what kinds of price promotions will be needed to compete effectively?

Another is **distribution systems:** the **wholesale** and **retail channels** through which our products and services move to the ultimate users. These may include such business entities as the company's salesforce, independent distributors, agents, and franchised outlets. **Market communications,** a fourth element in marketing strategy, includes such components as print and television advertising, direct mail, trade shows, point-of-sale merchandise displays, sampling, and telemarketing.

Depending on the nature of the business and its markets, the marketing strategy may include other elements. A company whose products need repair and maintenance must have programs for **product service.** Such programs are often business units themselves with extensive repair shops, service personnel, and spare parts inventories. The product service program is usually expected to make a profit, but in addition, its cost, quality, and availability are usually a part of what the buyer would evaluate in making the purchase decision. It serves, then, as part of the overall marketing program to differentiate the product offering. **Technical service** may be part of the ongoing buyer/seller relationship. Done well, this and the supplier's viability can be important elements of its competitive advantage.

In many enterprises, **plant location** is a critical strategic component. If the product can be economically shipped only within a limited distance of the plant and/or if the product is **customized** to buyers' specifications, plant location may effectively define the geographic market boundaries. Metal containers and corrugated boxes are examples. Or if government regulations require local manufacturing, plant location choices amount to country-market selection decisions.

The combination of these several factors, and others, and the relative emphasis on each in a marketing program is called the **marketing mix.**[2] It varies considerably from one product/market to another and over different stages of market growth. Some firms, for example, may rely primarily on heavy **television advertising,** others on **direct mail,** and still others on a technically trained **salesforce.** The marketing mix may vary even among competitors selling the same products in the same markets. **Consumer packaged goods** manufacturers, for example, such as Kellogg or Proctor & Gamble, advertise extensively to move their products through distribution channels and off supermarket shelves. By comparison, many retailers, such as Osco Drug, Wal-Mart, or A&P, sell the same products at much lower prices under their own **private brand labels,** with little or no advertising.

The discussion that follows considers four primary elements in any marketing mix: product/market selection, pricing, distribution, and market communications. A final section presents a model for strategic planning.

Product/Market Selection

The most important choice made by any organization, whether a business, school, hospital, or government agency, is deciding what markets it will serve with what products. Product/market selection decisions commit the firm to particular customer groups, specific fields of technology, and a certain competitive milieu.

By way of definition, a product is the total package of attributes the customer obtains when making a purchase. Product benefits might include what the product does, manufacturer and retailer **warranties,** repair service, technical assistance, the value of the **brand**

---

[2] The concept of the marketing mix is credited to Professor Neil H. Borden, a member of the Harvard Business School faculty. See Neil H. Borden, "Concept of the Marketing Mix," HBS Case No. 502-004, Harvard Business School Publishing, Boston, MA 02163.

name in terms of implied product quality and reliability, assurance of ongoing product availability, and the personal relationships that may develop between the buyer and the seller. A watch, for example, is an instrument for telling time. It is also a piece of jewelry, and some watches—Rolex, for example—may serve as status symbols. In addition, part of the product's meaning may be convenience and/or the pleasure of the shopping experience.

Any list of product attributes may include negatives, as well. In the case of cars, repair frequency and cost may, indeed, be negative factors. A family on a vacation tour inevitably takes risks on the tour provider's performing to the expectations it created in the advanced billing, and often on the weather. Industrial buyers may run the risk of poor product performance or the supplier's going out of business. Thus, product meaning must be defined in terms of the full range of benefits, risks, and disadvantages the buyer obtains with purchase and use, including the buying experience.

Regardless of what the seller thinks of the product, what counts for strategic planning purposes is the prospective purchaser's opinion and the value he or she places on the seller's product versus competitive offerings. It is important to distinguish, however, between **perceived value** and **potential value.** The first is the customer's existing perception of the product. The latter is what the buyer can be educated to recognize. The realization of potential value is accomplished through **market communications.**

As for the term **market,** it may refer to a place where buyers and sellers meet, or to a **retail outlet,** or to a set of potential customers. For purposes of this discussion, a market is a pocket of latent demand. It may be likened to a vein of ore in the ground, available to be mined. New market opportunities may arise from a wide range of exogenous factors. A major source of new market opportunities is new technology in such fields as electronics, aerospace, and the medical sciences. Population growth and increases in national and personal incomes also create new markets and expand existing ones. Societal needs such as crime prevention, health care, and population control also create new markets. Shifts in culture, style, and public tastes in food, clothing, entertainment, the arts, and travel lead to new market opportunities, as well.

Market Segmentation

Markets can be delineated in terms of segments. A **market segment** is a set of potential customers alike in the way they perceive and value the product, in their buying behavior, and in the way they use the product. Defining relevant market segments is the first step in product/market selection. It creates a framework for developing market strategy. Markets may be segmented along several dimensions:

Demography

Demographic segmentation relies on such factors as family income, age, sex, ethnicity, and educational background as explanatory variables for differences in taste, buying behavior, and consumption patterns. For example:

> When Population Services, Inc., a not-for-profit organization, undertook the marketing of condoms and oral contraceptives in Bangladesh, it found significant differences in buying behavior among males and females and among rural and urban dwellers. Based on these differences, PSI used as a strategic framework a four-quadrant matrix, as depicted in **Figure A,** to address distinctions among these segments in product meaning and the buying influences to which each responded. Different communication strategies were developed for each one.[3]

In industrial markets, the size of the enterprise, its nature (e.g., for-profit, government, nonprofit) and type of industry (e.g., manufacturing, services, defense, construction)

[3] V. Kasturi Rangan, "Population Services International: The Social Marketing Program in Bangladesh," HBS Case No. 586-013, Harvard Business School Publishing, Boston, MA 02163.

FIGURE A

	Male	Female
Rural		
Urban		

are demographic variables. They tend to explain patterns of **buying behavior.** For example:

> IBM, in selling mainframe computers, organized its marketing programs in terms of such customer categories as Health and Education, Banking and Finance, Government, Manufacturing, Distribution, and Airlines. Computer usage, buying behavior, and service needs were deemed to vary enough among these segments as to justify specially trained IBM sales and service units serving each one.

Geography

Geographic segmentation frameworks are useful in both consumer and industrial markets. Different areas of the country and different parts of the world may vary significantly in terms of market potential, competitive intensity, product-form preferences, and government trade regulations.

Another geographic variable is economical shipping distance. In the case of high weight- or bulk-to-value products, plant location, as noted earlier, will define the market area. Similarly, the desire of the customer to be close to the supplier, as in the case of customized products and services—such as health services or restaurants—may effectively limit the market geographically.

It should be noted, however, that with the increasing globalization of markets, geographic segmentation variables have declined somewhat in importance versus others. Product uses and preferences and buying behavior across the world are coming to exhibit greater commonality. Advances in communication and transportation have also eased geographic market limits.

Psychographic Variables

So-called psychographic typologies attempt to segment markets according to individual lifestyles and attitudes toward self, work, home, family, and peer-group identity. "Senior citizens," for example, may vary markedly from the "baby-boomer" generation, and from "teenagers" in their needs for products and services, political persuasions, and residential preferences and, thus, comprise a distinct and very high-potential market segment. Working women and homemakers, "couch potatoes" and "exercise freaks," people of different ethnic origin exhibit such significant differences in product wants and responsiveness to different buying influences as to comprise different market segments.

The comparable segmentation variable in industrial sectors might be **corporate culture.** Some enterprises are greater risk takers than others and may have more to gain as **early adopters** of new products and technologies, while more risk-prone firms are found among the followers. Some firms focus intensely on price factors in making purchasing choices while others give priority to developing long-term relations with suppliers based on technical and service contributions.

Product Application and Use

The way industrial purchasers use the product and how it fits into their processes and systems may provide the basis for market segmentation. For example, the technologies for manufacturing nylon carpet, or hosiery, or cordage, or synthetic fabrics vary considerably one from the other, accounting for significant differences in product specifications and in technical service needs.

A consumer who buys tableware for his or her own use or as—say—a wedding gift may well have different preferences with regard to price levels, retail source, and brand name for each of these purchases. Thus, any one consumer may exhibit different purchasing behavior in buying comparable products if they are intended for different purposes.

It is also important to recognize that the market segmentation scheme appropriate at one stage in the development of a market may become obsolete with market growth and maturation. Customers become educated in buying, evaluating, and using the product. Demand increases, and new competitors enter. New product forms are introduced, and new distribution channels emerge. Such events change the way people buy and lead to much more elaborate market segmentation structures. Not to continually revisit the task of segment delineation and look for new market opportunities is to lose touch with the market and to risk significant loss in competitive position.

Market segmentation is an art, not a science. Its purpose is to delineate groups of potential buyers according to their needs, market potential, and buying behavior. In the context of a firm's overall strategy, some segments may be defined demographically, some geographically, some in terms of lifestyle and corporate culture, and some in accordance with product application. Some may be defined as subsets of other variables. Having developed a segmentation scheme, strategic planners may select from among these those markets the firm may serve most creatively and profitably, and to develop strategies for each. **Figure B** lists useful segmentation variables.

Product/Market Selection Criteria

In making product/market choices, a number of factors must be considered:

Product Value

First and most important, market entry and development efforts must focus on those segments that value the product most highly. Target those applications in which the product or service makes its greatest contribution. If markets are veins of latent demand, marketing

FIGURE B
Segmentation Variables

Demographic

Consumer
- family income, age, sex, ethnicity, education level

Industrial
- enterprise size, type, buying processes

Geographic

Product preferences, trade regulations, market potential, competition
Economical shipping distance, customers' source-proximity needs

Psychographic

Consumer lifestyle
- attitudes toward self, work, family; peer-group identity

Corporate culture
- tolerance for risk-taking, buyer/supplier relationship values

Product use and application

Consumer
- purchase purpose

Industrial
- application technology

resources are best spent on "digging where the dirt is softest" (e.g., where the product is most highly valued).

Long-Run Growth Potential

Ultimately market size and profit potential is key. Growth potential estimates should factor in any follow-on market opportunities as well as the one at hand. As in the case of computers and microchips, new technologies often move rapidly from one application to another, and early market entrants may ride the wave of technological progress in the development of new applications.

Resource Commitments

Product/market choices often commit firms to heavy financial drains not only in marketing costs but also in production facilities and R&D. Can the resources be made available to compete in some high potential market, and does the estimated return on assets justify the investment?

> At one point, early in the development of the computer market, General Electric had entered the race. It soon withdrew, however. Having undertaken other major enterprise initiatives in fields such as aircraft engines, aerospace and defense products, and up against IBM's already massive marketing, manufacturing, and product development programs, GE could not support a major commitment in computers.

Company–Product/Market Fit

New product/market opportunities need to be assessed in the context of existing business operations. This raises such issues as these: Will the firm's reputation and brand name be of value? Can the new venture utilize existing manufacturing capacity and distribution systems? Will the proposed offering enhance the company's position with existing customers and its strength in dealing with its distributors and retail outlets? On the other hand, might the new product obsolete or cannibalize the sales of existing product offerings without increasing total profitability? But if we don't obsolete our own products, won't our competitors do it for us? A case in point:

> U.S. car manufacturers dragged their feet considerably in adding compact cars to their product lines out of concern for cannibalizing the sales of their very profitable full-size models. Only after foreign competitors made significant inroads on their markets in the United States and abroad did the domestic manufacturers bow to the pressure of significant losses in **market share** and began making small cars.

In product/market selection it is useful to think of the market as a chessboard, with the squares representing different market segments. Competitors are arrayed over the playing area, each seeking to occupy certain spaces with particular product offerings. It may be that some spaces, previously unrecognized as market opportunities, lie vacant and would be easy to occupy. Some may be filled by weak competitors; they can be attacked. But other squares are solidly dominated by strong competition with superior product lines; proceed at risk. In the race to take segment positions, the advantage often lies with the **first-mover,** the one to get there first. It has the chance to develop **market recognition,** gain customer access, lead technology and end-product development, and achieve **scale economies** in its manufacturing and marketing operations. As primary demand builds, new market entrants succeed to the extent that they "bring something to the table," usually in the form of differentiated products and services.[4]

[4] The concept of scale economies relates size to cost efficiency and operational effectiveness. The theory is that increases in, say, plant size or such marketing investments as the field sales force or advertising will result in lower costs per unit and greater effectiveness up to some optimal point. Beyond that point, both cost efficiency and effectiveness decline.

The Art of Pricing

Basically, the prices of products and services are determined by the interplay of five factors:

1. Supply/demand conditions
2. The firm's production and overhead costs
3. Competition
4. Buyer bargaining power
5. Product value to potential customers

In the following section, these are considered separately, although in operation they are interrelated.

Supply/Demand

The extent of **supply** relative to **demand** for a product or service is the most basic determinant of price. The greater the supply of a good, the lower the price. The number of barrels of oil being produced, or the total plant capacity for making a synthetic fiber, or the number of hotel rooms in an area interacts with market demand to set basic price levels.

In general, basic levels of supply and demand are beyond the control of individual players . . . but the major players will try to influence total supply relative to demand. They may seek to limit market demand through lobbying government for trade restrictions such as imposing high import tariffs on a particular product or simply closing the country's borders to foreign producers. Depending on the nature of the product, large companies might also pressure the government to close down surplus production capacity or to buy up and stockpile excess quantities of the product. Government involvement in such initiatives is usually predicated on there being a public interest such as the health of the country's defense industries, levels of domestic employment, or the buildup of a domestic manufacturing infrastructure.

Another way to control supply is by acquiring all sources of supply or forming **cartels** such as the OPEC oil cartel or the DeBeers diamonds group and imposing production quotas on member companies. These tend to be precarious coalitions at best. For DeBeers, for example, the major threat may be the diamond mines in northern Canada and for OPEC, the large oil reserves in Russia. The possibility of either one putting significant amounts of product into the market would threaten price stability.

> Rockefeller, founder and president of the gargantuan Standard Oil Company, used every possible means to control the supply of oil being produced and refined. These included buying up newly discovered oil fields, acquiring all the refineries in major centers, forming oil cartels, and lobbying state legislatures to grant him exclusive pipeline rights. Such initiatives sought to prop up and stabilize oil prices in the face of recurrent crude oil gluts and yield to Standard Oil immense monopoly profits.[5] By the late 1870s, Standard Oil controlled 90% of the oil refined in the United States.[6]

Competitive signaling can serve, as well, to discourage other companies from building new production capacity. For example, one firm, learning that a competitor is planning to add production capacity, may announce a price cut to make the proposed expansion less attractive.

---

[5] At the same time, it must be noted, Standard Oil's predatory practices raised public ire and demand for antitrust controls. Widely cited as an example of destructive competition, the Standard Oil model gave reformers considerable ammunition in passing the Sherman Antitrust Act of 1890.

[6] Ron Chernow, *Titan, the Life of John D. Rockefeller, Sr.* (New York: Random House, 1998).

Cost Factors

In pricing, cost sets the floor. A supplier cannot for long continue to sell below the costs of making and marketing a product and still stay in business. But what should be counted as cost for strategic purposes will depend largely on the firm's pricing objectives. A company may elect, for example, to sell its product at a price that covers the direct costs of labor and materials, but not fixed overheads such as plant depreciation. Its purpose in doing so may be to keep a workforce employed in the event of a decline in sales or to thwart a competitive threat. Or seeking to quickly penetrate some new market, the firm may base its pricing strategy on estimated future costs, anticipating the realization of scale economies as production volumes increase.

The relative levels of **fixed** and **variable costs** also affect pricing strategy. If such fixed costs as depreciation, R&D, sales, and advertising are high relative to variable costs (labor and materials per unit), maximizing sales volume becomes an important strategic objective in order to spread fixed charges over as many units as possible. This explains, for example, why hotels and airlines offer substantial off-season price cuts to try to fill rooms and seats, respectively. Any income represents a **contribution** to their high **overheads.**

In contrast, if variable costs (i.e., those costs that vary directly with the number of units produced), are a relatively high portion of the total, maximizing unit margins is critical to profitability. In the packaged foods business, for instance, materials and packaging per unit represent such a large part of total costs that profitability depends on increasing as much as possible the spread between these variable costs and unit selling price, not on cutting price to build sales volume.

In all cases, low-cost producers have a substantial competitive edge. Not only does low cost mean high profits, but it may also mean survival in periods of price warfare. Efficient manufacturing and distribution processes and the realization of scale economies are often the foundation for market success.

Competition

If cost factors ultimately set the floor for prices, competition establishes the ceiling. The competitive milieu varies, however, by geographic area and often by stages of market development.

Firms may legally respond to competitive price pressures in three ways: (1) by **differentiating** their products, (2) attempting to dampen **intrabrand competition** among their resellers, and (3) exercising **price leadership.** The first, **product differentiation,** yields some degrees of freedom in pricing against competitive offerings. Any unique benefits the product offers in terms of functions, or services, or availability that are of value to users may be translatable into **price premiums.** In effect, a differentiated product may enjoy quasi-monopoly status if it is in demand and comparable competitive offerings are not available. For example:

> To the extent that some significant percent of the population insists on eating Cheerios brand breakfast cereal, General Mills may command premium prices, that is, up until the point at which price differences between this product and closely similar **store brand** or **generic brand** cereals cause shoppers to settle for some second-choice offering.

Intrabrand competition, the competition among the firm's resellers, tends to put pressure on price levels. Price competition at this level soon generates **interbrand competition,** and market price levels decline. Intrabrand competition is more likely to be intense if the number of resellers in an area is relatively high. Accordingly, the fewer the number of resellers the firm **franchises** in an area, the less pressure on resale prices.

A strong field salesforce working with resellers may also monitor **resale prices** and discourage price cutting. In so doing, field sales personnel have strength in their relations with resellers to the extent that the firm's product line represents a significant source of reseller revenue and enjoys strong end-user demand. Seeking to influence resale prices does have legal implications, however, and should be carried out only with a clear understanding of the laws that apply to **resale trade.**

The mantle of price leadership typically falls on the industry's largest firm, respected for its leading-edge technology, strong distribution, and low production costs. Price leaders seek to set price levels in response to changes in supply and demand, product cost factors, and perhaps the intensification of competition. If competitors recognize the leader's moves as beneficial to the industry and to their own **bottom lines,** they are likely to conform. If not, the leader must usually retract announced price changes or risk losses in market share. Or, an announced price increase may fail to stick as smaller competitors chip away at industry price levels to gain market share. As price cutting becomes widespread, the price leader may formally recognize the new lower levels by publishing revised price schedules.

Pricing in any industry is usually characterized by **conscious parallelism,** following the moves of the market leader to maintain uniform prices across the market. As long as competitors do not communicate with each other directly and pricing moves cannot be construed as predatory (intended to drive smaller competitors out of business), price parallelism is legally acceptable and often essential for survival.

Buyer Bargaining Power

In price negotiations, buyers have strength to the extent (1) that they account for a significant portion of the seller's sales, and (2) that they have multiple options for meeting their procurement needs. Buyers are in strong negotiating positions if they have multiple supply sources competing for their business and/or if **self-manufacture** is an option. The first creates a high degree of dependency on the firm's largest buyers and leads, often, to the seller's willingness to offer price reductions rather than lose sales volume. Sears Roebuck, and the large automakers were notorious for putting its suppliers in this position, then demanding to audit their costs, and setting prices at some small margin over cost. Home Depot is also a quintessential example of driving its suppliers hard to reduce product purchase costs. This company has continued to expand its market coverage by requiring its suppliers to stock and maintain their alloted **shelf space** on credit—as much as 130 days. It has been known as well to call suppliers collect. "Playing hardball" with suppliers may significantly reduce supply costs. Long run it may well have an adversary affect on the willingness of new suppliers to bid on Home Depot's business and ancillary services.

Sellers have negotiating strength to the extent that they offer differentiated products. In addition, they are in strong bargaining positions in serving existing accounts if these customers are satisfied with the seller's product and if switching to another supplier would be disruptive and costly. **Switching costs** may include obsoleting inventories, reengineering manufactured parts, and establishing new personal working relationships.

Product Value

The worth of a thing is the price it will bring.

This old English saying gets to the heart of pricing strategy, that is, pricing to **product value.** But customer value, as we learned earlier, may vary considerably across market segments and from one buyer to another, depending on the priority each buyer may give to the product's several attributes.

How do sellers cope with the ever-present necessity of adjusting prices to reflect differences in product value to different market segments or in geographic variations in competitive intensity?

In the case of physical goods, sellers may attempt, and often successfully, to implement differentiated price strategies through cosmetic differences in the product. A manufacturer of heavy duty cleaner, for example, might sell in janitorial supply houses at one price, supermarkets at a higher price, and yachting supply stores at a still higher price, using different packaging designs for each market segment. Such a scheme may work well until users discover that functionally the cleaners are all the same whether used to clean floors, ovens, or bilges. In the long run, successful price differentiation by market segment has to be based on functional product differentiation. Thus, in the case of a heavy-duty detergent, the product line might include cleaners of different strengths for different uses.

The risk in any price differentiation strategy, however, is that low-priced products sold in one market will make their way across segments into markets where higher prices would normally prevail. This is the so-called **black-market** phenomenon,[7] often a factor in the case of physical goods such as computers or industrial equipment or cigarettes. Black markets are non-franchised resale outlets which typically acquire the excess stock of **authorized dealers** or users and sell at a price lower than that of the authorized dealers.

Skimming v. Penetration Pricing

In entering new markets or introducing new products, sellers may elect to price high to reach those segments for which the product has the greatest value (**skimming**) and then bring the price down over time to tap other pockets of demand. New books, for example, are often introduced in hard cover at one price and then brought out in a paperback edition at a much lower price. New electronic devices are typically put on the market at relatively high prices with dramatic price cuts following over one or two years. For another example, the manufacturer of a new chemical product may offer the product at a high price to the user for which it has the greatest value and then lower the price for other applications to other customers.

A skimming price approach is used largely to maximize unit profits in the early stages and, sometimes, to gain market experience at low market volume levels. Such an approach can also be justified by the need to recoup heavy product development costs. Alternatively, the strategy may be to price low to achieve high market share before competitors can react or to break into some existing market (**penetration pricing**).

> When *USA Today* sought to enter the highly competitive daily news market in 1982, newsstand copies sold for a quarter, and large numbers of papers were given away free in hotels, airline terminals, and other public places. Then when readership became widespread, prices were quickly raised to that of the leading daily papers.

In contrast, penetration pricing preempts competition and allows the firm to gain **learning curve**[8] experience so as to quickly achieve scale economies in manufacturing and marketing to create end use demand. The cost of penetration pricing is the profit sacrificed by charging some market segments much less than they would be willing to pay. The potential gains are large market share and a dominant competitive position.

Penetration pricing is also generally regarded as the higher-risk strategy. If it is to succeed, several conditions have to be met:

- The product must be free of any defects that might create consumer dissatisfaction and incur large costs for repair, recall, or retrofitting.
- Production capacity must be in place to satisfy anticipated demand.
- Distribution channels must be available for reaching potential buyers.
- Product adoption does not require long testing periods by potential customers; lags between product introduction and general market acceptance would give competitors time to react.

[7] Frank V. Cespedes, E. Raymond Corey, and V. Kasturi Rangan, "Gray Markets: Causes and Effects," *Harvard Business Review*, July–August 1988.

[8] Learning curves are used to forecast reductions in cost with increases in volume.

FIGURE C
Factors Affecting
Firm Price Levels

Price Depressors	Price Lifters
Excess supply relative to demand	Controlled supply
Intense brand competition	High product value
Intrabrand competition	Product differentiation
High buyer bargaining power	High buyer dependency on suppliers
Penetration pricing	Skimming
Black markets	Effective price leadership

Figure C summarizes the factors which tend to lift individual product prices and those which depress them.

Channels of Distribution

Distribution systems include the firm's **personal salesforce,** with **wholesale distributors** and **retail outlets** providing geographically structured market coverage. In recent years, **electronic commerce** channels, in particular the Internet and EDI (Electronic Data Interchange), have grown rapidly, adding new dimensions to a worldwide distribution infrastructure.

In structuring sales channels, firms face a myriad of options. Among the key choices are (1) whether the business will sell through a field salesforce direct to its user-customers or rely largely on **middlemen,** (2) if the latter, what kinds of resellers will be needed to reach the firm's markets, and (3) will they be recruited **selectively** or **intensively** in any given geographic area? Most distribution systems comprise a mix of intermediaries based largely on the nature of the product, market demographics, and buyer behavior. The discussion that follows considers the several basic channels options and the choice factors that tend to shape the firm's distribution strategy.

Elements in the Distribution System

The primary components of any distribution system would include **direct sales reps, sales agents, distributors,** and **retail dealers.** Direct sales reps are employees of the firm and call directly on its customers. They are particularly economical and effective in serving accounts that buy in large quantities and need extensive product service, technical support, and product customization. Sales agents are independent operators who generally carry the lines of several (say, 8 to 10) suppliers. Their customer profile is very much like that of a direct salesforce, but because they are on commission, they represent a variable cost. Agents are the channel of choice if the firm does not have the resources to support an **in-house sales organization.** In addition, they are often used as first-stage **intermediaries** in entering new and unfamiliar geographic or product markets.

Distributors buy from many suppliers and have wide product lines. Their role is to serve customers who purchase relatively small amounts of a number of different items at any one time and want ready and reliable availability. Most distributors are independent businesses operating as single outlets or chains, but some, such as W.W. Grainger, serving industrial customers, are large national organizations. Some are **captive branches** of a parent organization, set up often as vehicles for moving the output of business units in some parent organization but carrying the lines of outside suppliers, as well. GESCO, operating as a profit-center in General Electric, is an example.

Retail outlets, such as pharmacies, restaurants, gas stations, hardware stores, and supermarkets, comprise a vast **infrastructure** supplying end-products and services to both consumers and business buyers. Most are **independent chains** (e.g., Wal-Mart). Some are captive—Goodyear Tire stores, for example. In some product areas, retail outlets are often **franchised.** The franchisees are required to purchase some or all of their supplies from **the franchisor** and to conform to certain standards of store design, service quality, and product presentation. McDonalds, Dunkin' Donuts, and Exxon gas stations are examples.

The emergence of **electronic commerce** channels warrants special attention. The **Internet** provides both consumer and industrial buyers exceedingly convenient access to many thousands of product offerings. It may be used to gain product information, place orders, and make payment by credit card, funds transfers, and electronic cash. The Internet can also deliver **digital products** such as publications, graphs and pictures, software, and audio and video tapes. It offers sellers market exposure unlimited—say—by the number of catalogs in circulation, flexibility in changing price and product information, and opportunities to present product offerings over the computer through print, graphics, animation, and sound. The Internet may serve, as well, as a source of after-sale product support. As an alternative to multilevel physical distribution, the Internet yields significant savings in such transactions costs as dealer margins, catalogs, **point-of-sale** display materials, inventory investments, storage, and shipping.

There are some drawbacks. The accessible market is limited; the majority of Web users are in the United States, and as of 1995 only an estimated 10% of U.S. households had online service subscriptions. This cohort tends to be younger, relatively affluent, and more educated than the population as a whole. Hence, less-educated, older, and lower-income segments in this country are inaccessible through electronic channels. But this constraint will ease over time. It is predicted that volume of trade through electronic channels will grow from $3 billion in 1996 to about $100 billion in the year 2000.

Another deterrent to the growth of electronic commerce is security concerns. Sellers face problems in qualifying buyers and verifying the legitimacy of orders. Buyers are nervous about submitting credit card numbers over public networks and providing information that may be used to profile their purchasing patterns. Understandably, a major concern of Web access providers is how to develop means of assuring data integrity.

Electronic data interchange (EDI) actually preceded the emergence of the Internet. It is an open standard used to conduct business-to-business transactions. EDI is used almost entirely by large companies for the automated exchange of transaction data among suppliers, their customers, and banks. It facilitates order entry, reduces order and fulfillment errors, optimizes inventory levels, and improves procurement cycle times to yield significant reductions in procurement and production costs.

Proprietary value-added networks (VANs) are used for EDI data interchange and provide such services as data recovery, tracking, and auditing. While these services come at a cost, VAN systems offer greater security than the Internet.[9]

Cost Factors

For firms with supply sources and resale outlets cutting distribution costs is a high priority. Any savings there drops to the bottom line.

Cost efficient distribution systems typically depend on having state-of-the-art logistics systems in moving product from point of manufacture to point of resale or use. WalMart, for example, transfers products directly from inbound vehicles to storebound vehicles, enabling goods to be delivered continuously to warehouses, repacked, and dispatched to stores often without ever sitting in inventory. Dell Computer serves its commercial and consumer PC markets with **custom** and standardized computers without having parts or

[9] The source of this discussion of electronic commerce is Raymond S. Bamford and Robert A. Burgelman, "Internet-Based Electronic Commerce in 1997: A Primer," #SM-36, September 1997, Board of Trustees of the Leland Stanford Junior University, Palo Alto, CA.

finished units going through its accounts payable. For each company, leading-edge logistics systems has given it a significant competitive advantage in competing for markets worldwide.

Channels Support

Successful distribution depends on how effectively suppliers support the channels through which their products move to markets. In working with intermediaries, the supplier seeks to assure that (1) its products are stocked and available at the resale level, (2) resellers actively display, advertise, and promote the product to end-customers, and (3) resale prices and margins do not deteriorate. The supplier's interest in preserving resale price levels comes out of a concern for sustaining reseller interest in marketing the product. If there is intense intrabrand price competition at the resale level, sales volume will increase for the most aggressive price cutters; other intermediaries may drop the line; still others may continue to carry the line but give it little attention. At the least, the outcome is likely to be a decline in market coverage. In addition, intense intrabrand competition will lead to waves of interbrand price competition as competitors seek to hold market share.[10]

In dealing with the channels environment, suppliers gain strength under these conditions:

Selective Rather Than Intensive Distribution The fewer the number of intermediaries in a given geographic area, the less incentive resellers have to cut **resale prices,** and the more interest they are likely to have in promoting the product line to build sales volume. How intensive the supplier's resale representation should be will depend, of course, on the nature of the product and how people buy. For an item like toothpaste, adequate market coverage may mean having the brand on every drugstore and supermarket shelf in the community. In selling cars, however, one dealer in the community is likely to suffice, except for large metropolitan areas. Toothpaste is a convenience item; people shop for cars. Further, to justify the investment required on the part of the car dealer, car manufacturers must offer the potential for large sales volumes undiminished by intense local intrabrand competition.

Superior Product Line Breadth and Quality This factor gives the reseller a competitive edge in his local market.

A High Degree of Supplier/Reseller Interdependency The greater the share of the dealer's sales the supplier's line accounts for, the more dependent each is on the other, and the greater the pressure to work together to maximize sales volume and profits. Interdependency is also enhanced to the extent that computerized systems link supplier/reseller order entry, delivery, and billing processes, and provide useful purchasing data.

A Supplier Salesforce Presence at the Resale Level In business-to-business marketing, the supplier's field salesforce plays an essential role in training dealer personnel in **product presentation** and **after-sale service,** calling on key end-customers, monitoring inventory levels, gathering **market intelligence,** and discouraging resale price cutting. In consumer goods marketing, the supplier's field salesforce may be concerned with **in-store display, shelf space,** and the implementation of **promotional programs.**

End-Market Demand Development Depending on the nature of the product and buyer behavior, advertising and promotion may serve effectively to build product line demand and create **brand pull** in end markets. Heavy advertising to consumers of such products as cars, health and beauty aids, and beer and soft drinks is often the primary element in what is called a **pull strategy.** (A discussion of **push** v. pull strategies follows in the next section on market communications.)

[10] Das Narayandas and V. Kasturi Rangan, "Dell Computer Corporation," HBS Case No. 596-058, Harvard Business School Publishing, Boston, MA 02163.

A prime example of effective channels support is the Du Pont Stainmaster marketing program:

> Du Pont's position as the world's leading supplier of carpet fiber has been built on product innovation and strong marketing presence at every level in the distribution chain. In developing the market for Stainmaster carpet fiber, Du Pont representatives worked with carpet mills to assure carpet quality. At the retail level, Du Pont supplied dealers with **product training manuals, in-store displays,** and carpet-identification medallions. In addition, Du Pont supplied its dealers with **cooperative advertising** materials and funding, and directed advertising messages to consumers through **print media,** television, and radio. **Consumer advertising** expenditures significantly exceeded those of competing fiber producers. A toll-free 800 number could be used by carpet mills and dealers to request product information and promotional materials. Consumers, too, could call in with questions on product performance, carpet cleaning, and dealer locations. Large by industry standards, the Du Pont Fiber Department's field salesforce worked extensively with its dealer network to implement these initiatives.[11]

As at Du Pont, a major concern is protecting and enlarging the **installed base** that comes from, year in and year-out loyal accounts. Not only does this group yield essential revenues, it provides guidance for allocating such marketing expenditures as **local advertising** and promotion and **field sales support.**

Pressures For Change

Of all the elements of a marketing program, distribution systems are hardest to build and hardest to change. Products can be redesigned, prices can be raised or lowered overnight, advertising programs can be revised, but changes in distribution usually generate tremendous forces of resistance. Nevertheless, change is often essential as markets grow and evolve. New product technologies, advancing market education, the intensification of competition, the emergence of new ways of going to market (e.g., the Internet), warrant the constant revisiting of distribution strategy.

Standing in the way of change, however, might be the strong relationships that may build up among producer personnel and those resellers who stand to lose by channels restructuring. A high degree of uncertainty may also be a factor. Will we lose customers who may prefer sourcing through current channels? Will competitors take over our disaffected dealers and with them our key accounts? Will we lose market share and profits in the short run? the long run? Will we have to write off system investments such as our **physical distribution centers** and our highly trained field salesforce? In particular, change comes hard because of psychological commitments to previously successful but now obsolete strategies and an inability to assess objectively the costs of taking no action. Changes Goodyear made in its distribution strategy in the early 1990s is a case in point:

> As of early 1992, Goodyear sold through 4,400 independent dealers, 1,047 **company-owned stores**, and 600 **franchised dealers.** Its distribution network did not include **garage/service stations, warehouse clubs,** or **mass merchandisers.** Company-owned stores sold only the Goodyear brand as did about half its independent dealers. In comparison, Michelin, Goodyear's largest competitor, sold through 7,000 independent dealers, most of which were **multibrand outlets,** 125 company-owned stores, as well as almost 600 warehouse clubs, mass merchandisers such as Sears and Montgomery Ward, and service stations. The latter were growing much more rapidly than company outlets and independent dealers.

If Goodyear was to hold market share, it became evident that this largest of the American tire makers had to expand its distribution network. Such a move, however, was fraught

---

[11] Bette Collins, James D. Cullen, and Paul W. Farris, "Stainmaster," #UVA-M-0357, Rev. 9/90, University of Virginia Darden School Foundation, Charlottesville, VA.

with risks. Goodyear's independent dealers, irritated by increased low-price competition, might take on and promote other brands. Selling through **discount channels,** Goodyear would be likely to suffer depressed prices and profits. But Goodyear's new president, Stanley Gault, supported those managers who felt it essential to be represented in resale outlets accounting for an increasing percentage of replacement tire sales. In 1992, Goodyear broadened its distribution to include Sears, Kmart, and Wal-Mart for a total increment of 1,500 new outlets to the distress of many of Goodyear's independent dealers. With this change and innovative new product offerings, however, Goodyear experienced steady increases in earnings, and realized a modest growth in market share.[12]

Market Communications

Any list of communications channels available to marketers would include **print media** (i.e., newspapers, magazines, and trade journals), **television, direct mail, telemarketing** (i.e., telephone calls to customers), **trade shows, point-of-sale displays, personal sales-forces,** and **third-party influencers** (e.g., doctors, consulting engineers, and sales clerks). Putting these together effectively in a communications mix requires an understanding of how buyers make purchasing choices, that is, the **decision-making process (DMP),** and the **decision-making unit (DMU).**

The decision-making process typically moves through several stages depending on whether this is a **repeat purchase,** like a household supply item, or a **new buy** such as a family residence. Stages may include (1) an awareness of need, (2) search for information, (3) identification of options, (4) **source qualification** and **short listing,** (5) selection, and (6) **post-purchase affirmation** of the buy decision. The process will be shaped by the nature of the product, the purchaser's previous buying and product use experience, and whether one or more people are involved in the buy decision. A key point for marketers is that the communications vehicles needed to influence purchasing decisions are likely to be different at different decision-making stages. Television and print advertising may create an **awareness of need,** but talking to friends, visiting stores, and reading relevant publications may serve better in gathering information. The final selection might be strongly influenced by a store clerk or a field sales person.

The DMU may be composed of a complex of players. For a major household purchase such as a car or a vacation, it may include husband and wife plus children. In business firms, purchasing managers, engineers, production managers, controllers, financial officers, marketing representatives, and general management often interact in making major procurements. **Routine rebuys,** however, might be the responsibility of the purchasing department alone.

The various participants in the DMP are likely to have different concerns and give different priorities to the product's multiple attributes. The marketer's task is to treat these needs individually, addressing each DMP member's interests with relevant information and assurances.

Understanding these needs begins with a comprehension of the influences to which the prospective buyers are most likely to respond. Some may rely heavily on the examples and advice of friends and neighbors. Some may turn to authoritative sources such as doctors, product testing organizations (e.g., *Consumers Union*), or store personnel. Others may find the kind of visual presentations and product information available in catalogs and

---

[12] Bruce Isaacson and John Quelch, "Goodyear: the Aquatred Launch," HBS Case No. 594-106, Harvard Business School Publishing, Boston, MA 02163; E. Raymond Corey interview with John Montgomery, Goodyear Director of Advertising, July 22,1997.

magazines to be most relevant. The buying stimulants to which the several members of DMU respond are likely to vary within the group. For example:

> Population Services International, in marketing birth control devices in Bangladesh, found that husbands and wives varied significantly in the kinds of concerns about family size and the buying influences to which they gave credence. To males, birth control meant fewer mouths to feed, but also fewer sons and a threat to the sense of masculinity. They were most influenced by radio and TV commercials. For women, contraception meant more food and clothing per family member, greater opportunities for children's education, and preserving their own health. But negative **product attributes** included possible health problems and a fear that birth control contravened the will of God. Their cues came from husbands, doctors, rural medical practitioners, pharmacists, spiritual doctors, and social workers.[13]

Other factors, in addition to an understanding of **buying influences,** will shape the market communications strategy. A primary one is cost. Communications cost calculations take into account such factors as advertising rates and effectiveness in reaching a **target audience** with a persuasive message. For example:

> In launching credit card services in Singapore, Citibank considered for promotional vehicles (1) **direct mail,** (2) **take-ones,** applications placed in stores, (3) **direct sales,** and (4) **bind-ins,** newspaper and magazine inserts. For each one, Citibank marketing managers were able to estimate the unit cost, the number of prospects reached, and the **response rate.** Bind-ins, for example, reached the greatest number of prospects at the lowest unit cost per insert, but it also generated the lowest response rate, 1%. Direct sales was by far the most expensive approach and reached the smallest number of potential customers, but the response rate was 50%.[14]

As seems obvious, different communications tools serve different purposes. Compare, for example, **media advertising** with **personal selling.**

Media advertising may be an effective low-cost way to

- Provide product and price information.
- Inform prospective purchasers where to buy.
- Suggest product-use ideas.
- Establish brand and package familiarity to facilitate **product identification** at the point-of-sale.
- Identify the brand with its **target market** segment.
- Develop reseller interest and brand support.

Personal selling can accomplish the same communications purposes but at a higher contact cost. In addition, it can be used effectively to

- Identify prospective customers.
- Develop solutions tailored to buyer needs.
- Deal with customer problems such as late deliveries, product failure, and the need for technical assistance.
- Provide **market feedback** on **product performance,** user demand, and competitive activity.

Personal selling is usually preferable to media advertising when relevant information is difficult to communicate through **mass media,** or when the number of prospective buyers is too few to justify the cost of media advertising.

[13] V. Kasturi Rangan, "Population Services International: The Social Marketing Program in Bangladesh," HBS Case No. 586-013, Harvard Business School Publishing, Boston, MA 02163.
[14] V. Kasturi Rangan, "Citibank: Launching the Credit Card in Asia Pacific," HBS Case No. 595-026, Harvard Business School Publishing, Boston, MA 02163.

FIGURE D   **A Push-Pull Strategy for Stainmaster Carpet Fiber**

Pull	Value Chain	Push
Brand advertising	Du Pont	Technical support
	Carpet mills	Sales training
		In-store training
800 number	Distributors	In-store display
		Coop. advertising
	Retailers	High resale margins
		Selective franchising
	Consumers	

Push v. Pull Strategies

A particular choice some marketers may have to make is whether the communications strategy should be designed primarily to create end-market demand and, thus, pull the product line through its distribution channels, or offer resellers extensive incentives to promote—push—the product to end-users. Such incentives would usually include high dealer margins, sales aids, cooperative advertising, and sales contests.

In consumer marketing, the choice will rest on what kinds of **buying influences** (e.g., advertising messages or sales clerk recommendations) are likely to be most persuasive. Pull strategies, because of the scale of upfront advertising investments, are often costly, justified only by large potential markets.

Push and pull are also relevant concepts in business marketing. Using a pull strategy, a manufacturer of aircraft engines, for example, may focus on persuading airlines to specify its engines in placing orders for new equipment on airframe manufacturers.

The fact is that marketing communications programs, such as those for Du Pont Stainmaster carpet fibers or Goodyear tires or aircraft engines, contain both push and pull elements working together to create and fulfill market demand. The problem is in knowing how to balance these initiatives in any communications mix to achieve cost effectiveness.

Figure D diagrams the push-pull elements in the Stainmaster marketing program. Extensive brand advertising aimed at consumers and an 800 number served to create end-use demand, pulling Stainmaster through the value chain. Working in the other direction, DuPont technical support for the carpet mills, cooperative advertising, in-store display material, and sales training at the retail level stimulated reseller interest in promoting Stainmaster carpeting. Other important trade incentives included attractive resale margins and selective franchising to make Stainmaster profitable for the dealers.

Pull elements in the marketing program are effective if the brand name is meaningful to the buyer and if product benefits can be effectively communicated through mass media. Push elements are needed in a marketing strategy if the way the product is presented at the point-of-sale is important, if sales clerks' recommendations are meaningful to buyers, and if buyers count on reseller after-sale service.

A Model for Strategic Planning

Figure E presents a model for marketing strategy formulation. It may be used both in screening opportunities, developing strategies for new product/market ventures and for reviewing and reformulating existing strategies. It places marketing strategic planning in the context of overall strategy formulation for the firm. The following explains the model.

FIGURE E **A Model for Marketing Strategy Formulation**

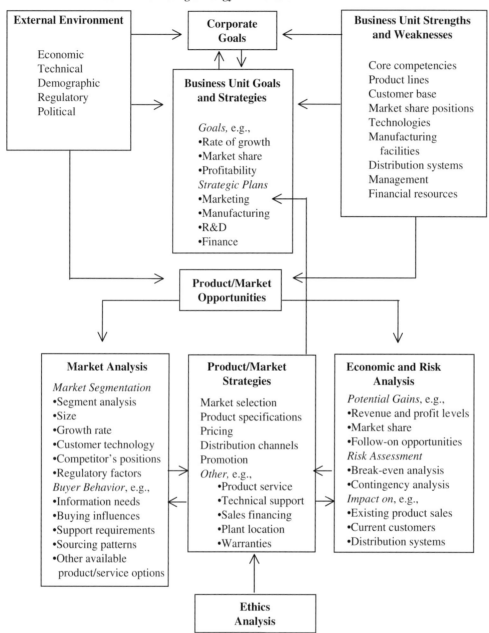

Corporate Goals

The firm's objectives establish directions and goals for strategic planning at the business unit level. Such objectives are typically oriented toward corporate growth and the maximization of stockholder value. They may also reflect the firm's strong interest in maintaining employment, providing a safe work environment, and serving national interests, among others. At the same time, the summation of bottom-up planning on the part of its strategic business units (SBUs) establishes limits on what is possible in setting goals for the enterprise in its entirety.

External Environment

This area of analysis contemplates an examination of the exogenous factors which create a favorable climate for business growth, yield new product/market opportunities, or put limits and conditions on business ventures.

Business Unit Strengths and Weaknesses

An assessment of the SBU's core competencies (i.e., the unique skills and assets that comprise the foundations for sustainable competitive advantage) serves to focus the SBU on those things it can do well. It also helps to identify weaknesses that would jeopardize the chances of success in certain kinds of ventures. For example, a manufacturer of heavy construction equipment, with no skills in advertising and retail distribution, would not be likely to succeed in a consumer package-goods business. An identification of weaknesses must also take account of the firm's limiting commitments, that is, any investments in manufacturing resources, distribution systems, technology, and an existing customer base that preclude undertaking certain ventures or that would have to be written off.

Product/Market Opportunities

These arise out of exogenous factors ranging all the way from new technology to income growth to shifts in fashion preferences. New product/market opportunities also come out of new ideas generated internally by—say—personnel in R&D, or marketing, or manufacturing. The pool of opportunities is grist to be run through the mills of market analysis and economic analysis.

Market Analysis

This begins with market segmentation, with the initially more attractive segments screened for market potential, competitive intensity, and regulatory conditions. Also essential is an understanding of buyer needs, the factors that influence their purchase decisions, where and how they buy, and what perceived advantages some new brand or product form might have over what it is intended to replace.

Economic and Risk Analysis

It is essential at some point in marketing strategy formulation to quantify, to the extent possible, potential revenues and profits and to assess market risks. Break-even analysis[15] estimates upfront R&D, manufacturing, and marketing investments and also factors in assumptions regarding price and variable costs to calculate how many units must be sold to recoup the sum of initial outlays. Contingency analysis forces a consideration of what could go wrong (e.g., market price declines, lack of demand, higher-than-estimated costs) assesses the likelihood of these events, and sets forth contingency plans for dealing with such uncertainties. Impact analysis addresses such issues as product/market/firm fit: how does the proposed initiative fit in the context of the firm's ongoing business? Are the ongoing business and the new venture compatible and mutually supportive? Is there a risk that the new product/market initiatives will have a negative impact on sales of existing product, on distribution channels, and on relations with current customers?

Ethics Analysis

It is important that marketing managers identify ethical issues that may arise in marketing operations and understand the firm's position in dealing with them both in domestic markets and abroad. There are certain areas of concern that typically surface in dealing with customers. One is bribery, the offering of money, gifts, and/or personal services, such as

---

[15] See E. Raymond Corey, "A Note on Marketing Break-even Analysis," HBS Case No. 578-072, Harvard Business School Publishing, Boston, MA 02163.

vacation trips, to those who significantly influence purchase decisions. Another form of bribery is paying off local government officials charged with, say, clearing imported goods or setting import duties. This is a difficult area of ethical choice because accepted practice varies significantly in different countries. Ethical issues also arise around false and misleading advertising and bait-and-switch tactics, that is luring buyers into a store by cut-price promotions, declaring the item out of stock, and switching the buyer to some higher-priced model. Ethical issues are involved, as well, in product design and manufacture: compromising on product quality, or safety, or environmental compatibility to cut costs. This discussion touches on major ethical issues but does not exhaust the list.

Product/Market Strategies

The planning process culminates in developing strategies by product/market segment. The ultimate purpose is to assess feasibility and fit, and given limited resources, to prioritize new opportunities in terms of long-term revenue and profit potential. The strategic architecture is then in place for carrying out those initiatives that seem most promising.

Chapter

Callaway Golf Company

Rajiv Lal   Edith D. Prescott

Ely Callaway, Callaway Golf Company's (CGC) 80-year-old founder, chairman, and chief executive officer, sat in the conference room one sunny day in fall 1999 contemplating his company's remarkable story. He wondered how that story might continue in light of some recent internal and external challenges. In the span of a decade, Callaway had built CGC into the dominant player in the golf equipment business, despite charging premium prices. CGC sales had increased steadily from $5 million in 1988 to over $800 million by 1997 (see **Exhibit 1** for income statements). He accomplished this with the clarity of his vision:

"If we make a truly more satisfying product for the average golfer, not the professionals,

and make it pleasingly different from the competition, the company would be successful."

Established in 1982, the publicly traded company designed, developed, manufactured, and marketed high-quality, innovative golf clubs, in addition to golf bags, accessories, and balls (CGC golf balls were to be launched February 2000). (See **Exhibit 2** for CGC products, **Exhibit 3** for CGC products' contribution to net sales, and **Exhibit 4** for a general explanation of golf club types and functions.) These clubs were sold at premium prices to both average and skilled golfers and were known for their high performance and skill forgiveness. Best known of the company's products were the Big Bertha line of clubs and their subsequent updated versions, which originally revolutionized the golf industry in 1991. By 1998, 69% of all professional golfers worldwide played with a CGC driver.

In 1998, the magic began to fade when sales dropped 17% and CGC experienced a loss of $27 million. Admittedly, CGC had "gotten away with murder" with its retail partners

Research Associate Edith D. Prescott prepared this case under the supervision of Professor Rajiv Lal. HBS cases are developed solely as the basis for class discussion. Cases are not intended to serve as endorsements, sources of primary data, or illustrations of effective or ineffective management.

EXHIBIT 1 **CGC Income Statements**

Source: CGC 1998 Annual Report, p. 20 and CGC 1997 Annual Report, p. 28.

	1998	%Sales	1997	%Sales	1996	%Sales	1995	%Sales
Net sales	$ 697,621	100%	$ 842,927	100%	$ 678,512	100%	$ 553,287	100%
Cost of goods sold	401,607	58%	400,127	47%	317,353	47%	270,125	49%
Gross Profit	296,014	42%	442,800	53%	361,159	53%	283,162	51%
Selling expenses*	147,022	21%	120,589	14%	80,701	12%	120,201	22%
General & admin expenses	98,048	14%	70,724	8%	74,476	11%	N/A	
R&D	36,848	5%	30,298	4%	16,154	2%	8,577	2%
Restructuring costs	54,235	8%	N/A		N/A		N/A	
Litigation settlement	N/A		12,000	1%	N/A		N/A	
(Loss) Income from Operations	(40,139)	−6%	209,189	25%	189,828	28%	154,384	28%
Interest and other income, net	3,911		4,586		5,804		4,017	1%
Interest expense	(2,671)		(10)		(37)			
(Loss) Income before income taxes	(38,899)	−6%	213,765	25%	195,595	29%	158,401	29%
Income tax (benefit) provision	(12,335)		81,061		73,258		60,665	
Net (Loss) Income	(26,564)	−4%	132,704	16%	122,337	18%	97,736	18%

*In 1995, includes General and Administrative Expenses.

because demand for its products was historically so strong. While the changes initiated in 1998-99 had begun to bear fruit (sales in first half of 1999 were $415 million contributing $38 million to net income), Callaway wondered if CGC would have to revise the way it approached retailer relationships to make them more mutually beneficial? To address possible market confusion, should the communication strategy shift? And how should CGC balance the catch-22 of new product development as both the company's lifeblood and its burden? In fall 1999, Callaway faced these questions; the answers would guide him in refocusing CGC's retail channels, new product development, and marketing strategies.

Company History

CGC was led by Ely Callaway (pronounced E-lee), a powerful motivator who defined the company's culture. People described the LaGrange, Georgia, native as charming, feisty, optimistic, energetic, and inspirational. A distant cousin of golf legend Bobby Jones, Callaway was a golf club champion at 20 and a three-handicap golfer at 40. In recent years he found that he did not have much time to play golf. He said, "I spend my time trying to put myself in the place of the average hacker and see how they will react to our new woods and irons."[1]

The Start of CGC

The day after he sold his winery in 1982, Callaway received a cold-call from the cash-strapped founders of a small golf manufacturing company named Hickory Stick USA, Inc. Callaway saw potential in the antique-looking, yet modern clubs, and decided to invest $435,000. He changed the name of the company to Callaway Hickory Stick, Inc. and focused on expanding the product mix. The designs were essentially knock-offs of existing companies' clubs (the only difference lay in the hickory shafts); thus, Callaway's first priority was to develop original products. Callaway put in $2 million of his own money over the first three years, thinking it would take the company eight to ten years to break even.

[1] Glenn Sheeley, "Callaway led golf's charge out of the woods," *The Atlanta Journal-Constitution*, June 27, 1999.

EXHIBIT 2   CGC Products

The company's primary golf club offerings included the **metal woods, irons,** and **putter** categories, which covered six major product lines.

Metal Woods

In 1997, the Biggest Big Bertha Titanium Drivers (BBBT) became available. This product line had the largest titanium clubheads of any CGC club ever produced, provided the maximum forgiveness, and had long, ultralight graphite shafts. Although these clubs were long and large, they were lighter than those in the Great Big Bertha series. The BBBT drivers were offered in lofts ranging from 6 to 12 degrees.

In 1998, CGC introduced the Big Bertha Steelhead Stainless Steel Drivers and Fairway Woods (BBSS). The BBSS line was designed to replace the Big Bertha Stainless Steel Drivers and Fairway Woods with the War Bird soleplate. BBSS had a large, forgiving clubface with a weight chip that had a low center of gravity. The BBSS drivers were available in lofts ranging from 6 to 12 degrees, and the associated woods were offered in a 2-wood (The Deuce), Strong 3-wood, 3-wood, Strong 4-wood, 4 wood, 5-wood, 7-wood (Heaven Wood), 9-wood (Divine Nine), and 11-wood (Ely Would).

In 1999, CGC introduced the Great Big Bertha Hawk Eye Titanium Drivers and Fairway Woods (GBBHE), which were designed to replace the Great Big Bertha Titanium Drivers and Fairway Woods (GBBTD). The GBBHEs had a new oversized clubhead that included a thin, titanium crownplate, a strong, lightweight titanium body, and a tungsten gravity screw. The tungsten gravity screw was inserted into the sole of the clubhead, producing a low center of gravity. The GBBHE drivers were available in lofts ranging from 6 to 12 degrees, and the GBBHE woods were available in a 2-wood (The Deuce), Strong 3-wood, 3-wood, Strong 4-wood, 4-wood, 5-wood, 7-wood (Heaven Wood), and 9-wood (Divine Nine).

Irons

In 1997, the company offered the Great Big Bertha Tungsten Titanium Irons (GBBTT). These clubs had the same primary design characteristics as the Big Bertha Irons, but had a larger clubhead and a tungsten inset. The tungsten piece enabled the weight to be concentrated low and deep in the clubhead, thereby giving an increased sweet-spot surface. These clubs were available in irons 1-9, pitching, approach, sand, and lob wedges with either graphite or steel shafts.

In 1998, CGC introduced the Big Bertha X-12 Irons (BBX), which had a low center of gravity to get the ball airborne more easily with the desired trajectory and spin. The clubs also had a unique, multilayer design in the cavity that allowed for forgiveness with off-center hits. This line was available in irons 1-9, pitching, approach, sand, and lob wedges with either graphite or steel shafts.

Putters

CGC had two lines of putters, the Odyssey brand and the CGC series. CGC acquired Odyssey in 1998 for $129 million, and it became the best-selling putter on the market. Odyssey putters were known for their better feel and forgiveness, as compared to other manufacturers' putters. Included in the Odyssey line were the TriForce series, introduced in 1999, which had "better ball roll" than other clubs due to the center of gravity being pushed back away from the clubface, Rossie Mallet Putters, and Dual Force blade-style putters.

The second line of putters was the Callaway series, which included the Carlsbad, Tuttle, Tuttle II, and Bobby Jones putters.[a]

[a] Callaway Golf's 10-K Report, December 31, 1998.

Richard Helmstetter

CGC's transformation from a niche producer to an innovation powerhouse came with the arrival of Richard Helmstetter, who Callaway met on a California golf course in 1985. As a highly successful manufacturer of Japanese billiard cue sticks since the 1970s, Helmstetter's knowledge of woodworking made him the target of a concerted recruitment campaign by Callaway. After a full year of pursuit, which culminated in thrice-weekly

EXHIBIT 3 **CGC Products' Contribution to Net Sales**

Source: Callaway Golf's 10-K Report, December 31, 1998.

Product Type	1998		1997		1996	
Metal woods	$389,900	56%	$544,258	64%	$479,127	71%
Irons	$229,112	33%	$233,977	28%	$168,576	25%
Putter, accessories, and other[a]	$78,609	11%	$64,692	28%	$30,809	4%
Total:	$697,621	100%	$842,927	100%	$678,512	100%

[a]1998 and 1997 net sales include $49.2 and $20.5 million, respectively, of Odyssey putters and wedges.

EXHIBIT 4 **The Golf Clubs**

Source: Callaway Golf Company information.

The Driver	**No. 1 wood.** The longest-hitting wood club, most often used on the tee in an attempt to achieve the greatest distances. The strongest and most accomplished players may occasionally choose to use a driver off the fairway on holes requiring the longest second shots.
The Fairway Wood	**Fairway Wood—Nos. 3, 4, 5**—Exactly as the designation suggests—are played off the fairway. Some golfers choose to use the No. 3 wood, which has a smaller, more lofted head than the driver, off the tee for greater accuracy. This is also common and accepted practice among Tour pros.
The Utility Woods	**Utility Woods—Nos. 7, 9, and 11.** This category is fairly new and growing rapidly. The No. 5 wood is occasionally included. For many golfers, especially seniors, women, and beginners, the high-lofted fairway, or trouble, woods are replacing hard-to-hit long irons. Trouble woods, because of the built-in loft, are adept at extricating a ball from the difficult lies in the rough. They are also used to hit the ball high and land softly on shots requiring carry over hazards and demanding parachute-style landings.
The Irons	**Long irons—Nos. 1, 2, 3, 4 irons.** For shots requiring at least 180 yards. Effective use of these clubs is normally associated with better players.
	Middle irons—Nos. 5, 6, 7 (sometimes 8) irons. With these clubs, the target is the green from a range of between 130 and 170 yards. At that distance, golfers will almost always go for the green.
	Short irons—No. 9, Pitching Wedge, Sand Wedge, Lob Wedge (sometimes 8 iron)—A.K.A. Scoring Clubs. When you get these clubs in your hands, you're thinking only about getting it on the green and hopefully, relatively close to enable you to post a good "score" on the hole. The short shaft length makes them easier to use and a favorite among most golfers.
	These clubs also can fall into a second category known as specialty clubs. They have the versatility to be used for all manner of shots around greens—chips, pitches, lobs, sand shots—including awkward situations anywhere on the golf course.
The Putter	**The putter** is used on the greens or from areas very near the green where the path to the cup is relatively smooth and straightforward, unfettered by unusual terrain or longer grasses.

calls to Helmstetter's office, the billiard cue stick expert had finally agreed to move to California as CGC's vice president and chief of new products in 1986.

S2H2

In 1988, CGC introduced the first of three revolutionary new club designs. The new design was a unique clubhead model called S2H2 (short, straight, hollow, hosel). (The hosel was the small piece that had formally connected the shaft to the clubhead.) The idea was to redistribute the weight of the hosel—that is, nearly eliminate it to free up precious weight to be used elsewhere in the club, and instead push the shaft straight through the clubhead. (See **Exhibit 5** for a glossary of golf terms and **Exhibit 6** for diagram of S2H2.)

EXHIBIT 5
Glossary of Terms

Source: Callaway Golf Company information.

Golf Term	Definition
Clubface	The front, flat side of the clubhead. Makes contact with the ball.
Clubhead	Located at the bottom of the shaft. Makes contact with the ball.
Flex	The degree to which the shaft is flexible. Each club has about four flexes. (Similar to one pair of pants coming in six different sizes.)
Lie	Describes the grass on the golf course. A golf course is composed of many different kinds of grasses.
Loft	The degree to which a ball is airborne after making contact with the club.
Rough	Overgrown grass—makes for more difficult hitting.
Shaft	Tall, skinny piece between the handle and the clubhead.
Short Game	Describes the short distance between a ball's course location and the hole.
Soleplate	Part of the golf club that glides along the turf.
Tee	The small piece of wood that is stuck into the ground to rest one's golf ball on. The tee is only used for the first shot of the game.

Helmstetter said, "We had discovered, purely by accident, a better mousetrap." And every club the company made since then incorporated the S2H2 concept. Helmstetter continued, "We continue to refine the idea of transferring weight from a place where it is not very efficient to where it is very efficient."

This technology led to the introduction of S2H2 metal woods in 1989. (Although wood clubheads were originally made of wood, metal provided better performance, and the original product name was retained.) Both S2H2 irons and woods were available with steel or graphite shafts instead of the heavier hickory shafts. By the end of 1990, the S2H2 driver was number two on the Senior PGA Tour, and company sales had reached $22 million.

Helmstetter had a unique approach to research and development. Instead of spending his day trying to figure out how to build a better iron, he had teams working on an ongoing project called "RCH Tough Questions." RCH were Helmstetter's initials, and he had about 400 unanswered questions, such as "where does backspin come from?" and "why does a shot on the club toe hook left instead of right?" Helmstetter said, "If we can understand where backspin comes from, then maybe one of us will have a bright idea." He believed strongly in intuition and even more strongly in informed intuition. What he tried to do was hire scientists, engineers, and golfers and throw them into the mix of trying to answer these questions. While trying to identify the perfect launch conditions to hit a ball the farthest possible distance if one's headspeed was 80 miles per hour, the engineers found that the clubhead needed to be bigger, which led to the development of Big Bertha.

Big Bertha

Named after a World War I cannon, the second revolutionary new design by CGC was the introduction of the Big Bertha oversized metal woods in 1991. Big Bertha metal woods provided a larger "sweet spot" and, despite their unprecedented high price of $250, they were wildly popular with millions of golfers worldwide. The Big Bertha clubs were critical to CGC because they reshaped golf, forever changing the way clubs were manufactured and the way customers purchased them. One golf analyst said, "If you're a golfer, CGC has changed almost everything in your bag, whether you own Big Bertha or not. If you're a Tour player, you can't afford not to try Big Bertha because everybody else is doing it and you don't want to be left behind."[2]

Prior to the Big Bertha, the driver was golfers' least favorite club—many would even avoid using it at all because average players were not skilled enough to hit the club

[2] Mike Purkey, "Great Big Empire," *Golf Magazine*, May 1998.

28

EXHIBIT 6 The "S2H2" Concept

Source: Company publication

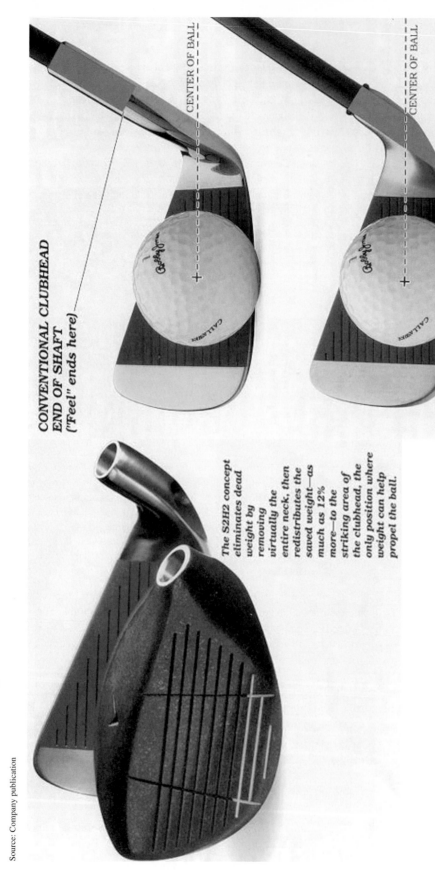

CONVENTIONAL CLUBHEAD
END OF SHAFT
("Feel" ends here)

"S2H2" CLUBHEAD
END OF SHAFT
("Feel" ends here)

CENTER OF BALL

CENTER OF BALL

The S2H2 concept eliminates dead weight by removing virtually the entire neck, then redistributes the saved weight—as much as 12% more—to the striking area of the clubhead, the only position where weight can help propel the ball.

with accuracy. The Big Bertha changed this sentiment, and even reversed it for many golfers. This was possible because the clubs combined S2H2 technology with an oversized head that was more forgiving on mis-hit shots. In response to the change in driver sentiment, one golf analyst said, "Thanks to the Big Bertha, we can hit it in the heel and the ball will go straight. We can hit it in the toe and it will go straight. The game is easier and more pleasurable for those of us who don't play golf for a living."

After the Big Bertha, one year went by before competitors had an oversized metal wood and six years before their performance really began to challenge CGC. By 1999, the competition had had eight years to catch-up technologically, closing the performance gap between CGC and its competitors.

In 1994, CGC introduced Big Bertha irons and Big Bertha metal woods with the Warbird soleplate, and CGC sales reached $449 million. Helmstetter had contributed so significantly to the success of CGC by this time, that Callaway honored him by opening a state-of-the-art club test center in his name the same year.

Titanium

By 1995, titanium was on the scene and was the third of CGC's primary technological breakthroughs to date. Helmstetter and his team had figured out that clubs were more forgiving as golfers hit the balls at increasing moments of inertia. Because the total weight of the clubhead was somewhat fixed, the moment of inertia was increased by moving material away from the clubhead center. Thinner shells of a heavy material, such as steel, or a material of equivalent strength but lower density could have accomplished this, but Helmstetter knew he could not get there with stainless steel. Switching to titanium required re-tooling the facility, but his thought about research and development was:

> If you can make something sufficiently good, what it costs doesn't matter. You can't be bound by typical business school practices of "let's discover how big the market is and then how much can we spend to develop the product so that it can have a specific minimum margin." R&D is really a misnomer because between the "R" and the "D" is the lightning bolt. There are scientists, technicians, and designers who individually do not come up with new products. It is when they are taken together that someone will have a spark. This talent is very expensive and developing an R&D budget is extremely difficult. You sort of pick a number—maybe 5% of sales. If you're spending less than that, you're not making enough mistakes.

In 1995, Big Berthas were replaced with Great Big Bertha titanium drivers. These clubs had an extended shaft and a larger clubhead, but were lighter in weight. The Great Big Bertha was introduced at $500, and although some deemed it marketing suicide, a primary competitor, Taylor Made, introduced a club in the same price range. Thus began the "clubs as a status symbol" phenomenon.

Don Dye became CEO in 1996, and the following year, CGC introduced another series of new products—the Biggest Big Bertha Titanium Driver and the Great Big Bertha Tungsten Titanium Irons. The Biggest Big Bertha was a better driver than the Great Big Bertha because it was more forgiving, hit the ball farther, and felt better, but it did not live up to expectations in the market. It was overpriced at $600 (versus $500 for the Great Big Bertha), and CGC continued selling both. Incrementally, consumers did not perceive the product to be 20% better.

In 1997, CGC year-end sales were $843 million. The company also purchased Odyssey Golf for $130 million. Odyssey had the number-one-selling line of putters, and CGC admired Odyssey's commitment to technology. Big Bertha X-12 Irons were introduced in 1998, and subsequently became the best selling irons in history. CGC also introduced the Big Bertha Steelhead Metal Woods and Little Bertha golf clubs for kids. Also in 1998, Ely Callaway reassumed CEO leadership after the departure of Don Dye.

Product Development

CGC sold more units of more equipment at the highest prices than any other company in the golf business. To achieve that, CGC had to consistently be on the leading edge of technology and to continually exceed customers' expectations. Producing products that were equal to that of competitors was not good enough; thus, research and development was a critical focus for the company. (CGC had also continually added capacity over the past ten years, having sold 500,000 units in 1988 and six million units in 1998.)

CGC's biggest challenge therefore, was to have products that were not only differentiated from competitors' products, but also differentiated from its own. If a product stayed in the pipeline too long, even if it was the best product, its sales would begin declining. (See **Exhibits 7** and **8** for prices and sales of CGC and Taylor Made woods respectively.) This decline occurred because the people who really wanted the product would buy it within the first two years of its introduction. Sales, and prices, typically declined after two years, forcing CGC to continually make its own products obsolete. Besides declining sales, another reason to continually introduce technologically superior products was to prevent existing CGC golf club users from switching to another brand. CGC had developed a great brand and consumers knew that CGC always delivered a high-quality product, but Chris Holiday, senior vice president of U.S. sales, said:

> The bottom line is that the real loyalty when it comes to golf clubs, is to the club that works the best—to the club that golfers think will help them play better. As soon as a manufacturer comes out with a golf club that's better than ours, the brand name won't save us—it will only give us some time to react. We have to continue to make the best golf clubs in the world, otherwise golfers who played our clubs for 15 years will drop us in a minute if they think there's a golf club that they can play better with.

Being on the cutting edge had a price, however, as the company's R&D spending had gone from $6 million in 1994 to $37 million in 1998. CGC expected this upward trend to continue since R&D had always been the lifeblood of the organization.

CGC had, in essence, created a whole new category with oversized metal woods. (See **Exhibit 9** for CGC new product introductions by year.) What this created, however, was the feeling among golf manufacturers that, "if CGC can succeed, then we can succeed," which brought more manufacturers into the golf arena. One retailer described the development environment in 1999:

> Everyone is trying to beat each other to the punch by coming out with new products at any time. It used to be that there were two major golf merchandise shows per year; one in September in California (later changed to Las Vegas) and the other in January in Florida. Manufacturers used to save all of their new introductions for those shows, but that is no longer true. Products now come out at a fast and furious pace, and life cycles are too short. I think it's too much.

Sometimes, depending on golfer acceptance, products did not even last an entire season. The same retailer continued, "I think manufacturers should slow down the pace of new product introductions. The products need more time to be given a chance and to get out to the public before the clubs are discontinued." These shorter product life cycles also contributed to the growth in closeout programs. In the last two years, several manufacturers spent millions of dollars getting rid of excess inventory through traditional channels of distribution.

Consumer Behavior

Golf was a difficult game whose participants' emotions ranged from frustration to addiction, with passion and fun mixed in. Even when played in teams, golfers were very competitive with themselves. Golfers often blamed their equipment for their poor play, and thus

EXHIBIT 7 CGC Woods' Sales (in units per 1,000 woods and selling price)

Source: Golf Datatech Representative, March 2000.

		1997				1998				1999			
		Q1	Q2	Q3	Q4	Q1	Q2	Q3*	Q4	Q1	Q2	Q3	Q4
Biggest Big Bertha	Units	10.15	45.35	53.27	30.96	20.84	39.12	34.10	20.52	12.32	17.26	14.20	9.13
	Price	$ 462.89	$ 479.98	$ 467.19	$ 451.89	$ 443.53	$ 407.45	$ 374.08	$ 364.31	$ 345.76	$ 318.21	$ 278.80	$ 252.27
Great Big Bertha	Units	68.74	137.69	116.66	82.58	53.26	109.29	98.20	51.92	26.48	51.65	66.40	27.94
	Price	$ 365.25	$ 370.81	$ 368.98	$ 367.54	$ 363.97	$ 337.49	$ 309.02	$ 298.93	$ 286.49	$ 246.93	$ 227.22	$ 220.52
Great Big Bertha Hawkeye	Units	N/A	N/A	N/A	N/A	N/A	N/A	N/A	N/A	21.07	73.38	74.03	57.98
	Price	N/A	N/A	N/A	N/A	N/A	N/A	N/A	N/A	$ 392.95	$ 380.58	$ 375.14	$ 372.41
Big Bertha Steelhead (Graphite Shaft)	Units	N/A	N/A	N/A	N/A	N/A	N/A	11.78	47.01	47.91	88.03	82.21	62.30
	Price	N/A	N/A	N/A	N/A	N/A	N/A	$ 240.20	$ 231.03	$ 224.24	$ 213.40	$ 212.12	$ 212.85
Big Bertha Steelhead (Steel Shaft)	Units	N/A	N/A	N/A	N/A	N/A	N/A	4.30	11.22	12.91	24.69	23.85	17.31
	Price	N/A	N/A	N/A	N/A	N/A	N/A	$ 157.03	$ 156.38	$ 153.79	$ 150.89	$ 148.45	$ 148.68

EXHIBIT 8 Taylor Made Woods' Sales (in units per 1,000 woods) and Selling Price

Source: Adapted from Golf Datatech reports, March 2000.

		1997				1998				1999			
		Q1	Q2	Q3	Q4	Q1	Q2	Q3	Q4	Q1	Q2	Q3	Q4
Titanium Bubble 2 Graphite	Units	N/A	16.32	26.05	29.07	33.49	76.92	72.97	41.59	29.92	31.82	22.18	10.78
	Price	N/A	$ 473.58	$ 460.53	$ 356.89	$ 302.62	$ 292.88	$ 289.99	$ 286.91	$ 250.28	$ 236.49	$ 216.33	$ 213.45
Titanium Bubble Graphite	Units	49.51	109.22	94.05	56.14	31.93	51.80	38.04	16.27	5.69	5.89	3.57	1.02
	Price	$ 291.65	$ 285.57	$ 276.91	$ 270.44	$ 229.75	$ 206.94	$ 204.77	$ 199.60	$ 192.35	$ 205.80	$ 195.18	$ 186.46
Burner Bubble Graphite	Units	35.15	65.38	57.03	45.28	35.45	53.64	51.61	33.23	23.76	36.00	33.37	27.59
	Price	$ 196.30	$ 194.56	$ 189.31	$ 167.67	$ 176.61	$ 190.87	$ 190.69	$ 183.32	$ 179.08	$ 171.74	$ 160.59	$ 146.28
Burner Bubble Steel	Units	9.00	16.65	14.89	8.64	6.86	11.61	14.29	9.80	7.65	11.95	6.94	5.85
	Price	$ 135.55	$ 161.55	$ 144.33	$ 126.19	$ 119.80	$ 133.22	$ 138.45	$ 137.48	$ 137.49	$ 131.73	$ 119.35	$ 120.20

EXHIBIT 9   **CGC—New Product Introductions by Year**

Source: CGC Public Relations Department.

Woods		Irons	
1991	Big Bertha Metal Woods	1991	N/A
1992	N/A	1992	N/A
1993	N/A	1993	N/A
1994	Big Bertha War Bird Metal Woods	1994	Big Bertha Irons
1995	Great Big Bertha Driver	1995	New Big Bertha Irons
1996	Great Big Bertha Fairway Woods	1996	Big Bertha Gold Irons
1997	Biggest Big Bertha Titanium Drivers		Big Bertha Tour Series Wedges
1998	Big Bertha Steelhead Stainless Steel Drivers	1997	Great Big Bertha Tungsten Titanium Irons
	and Fairway Woods	1998	Big Bertha X-12 Irons

often wanted to update their clubs. Although one's mental state and skill level had much to do with on-course achievement, in golf, unlike almost any other sport, the equipment also had a significant effect on a user's performance. Even though highly skilled golfers would play well no matter what type of club they used, average golfers were able to see noticeable improvements in their game when they used premium equipment. Beginning golfers also benefited because the more forgiving clubs allowed them to make ball contact sooner, frustrating them less so they would not quit the sport prematurely. Golfers were, therefore, always looking for an edge that would help lower their score and enable them to enjoy the game more.

In making a purchase, most golfers accepted word-of-mouth recommendations. This form of advertising worked because of the way golf was played, in groups of four people who spent several hours together on the golf course. One salesperson compared it to the old Flex Shampoo TV commercial tag line—"and they told two friends, and so on, and so on." The foursome also provided a convenient way to demo a new club. When one player had hit a particularly good shot with a new club, others in the group were able to try it for themselves.

Average golfers (defined as playing ten rounds minimum per year) were CGC's target market, generally had handicaps above 18, and bought new equipment every two to three years. This buying cycle was only an average, for some golfers kept clubs for eight years or more. One avid golfer (defined as playing 30 rounds minimum per year), who owned Ping irons since 1987 and CGC woods since 1997 said:

> I've had the same irons for 13 years. I play 60 rounds of golf a year and have successfully achieved consistent distance and control with them. They work for me, I see no reason to change. Woods are a different story—I have gone through several sets. The problem is that everything is so confused now. It is not clear to me which clubs are the best. I would love to update my woods, but at $300 per club, I'm not willing to make the $1,000 investment.

The remaining golfing population consisted of beginner (played first round in a given year) and occasional (played one to seven rounds per year) golfers. For a beginning golfer, buying new clubs was a daunting task. Retail shops offered a wealth of options that forced beginners to rely on the advice of salespeople. Beginners, however, viewed the golf retail experience as fun because it was a whole new consumer world for them. At the same time, beginners were price-sensitive, reluctant to invest large sums until they knew that they enjoyed the game and stood a reasonable chance of improving. They often purchased "starter sets," lower-priced options at $100 to $250 for a bag, five irons, two woods, and a putter. The lighter clubs were easier to swing, giving the user a better chance of lofting the ball— which was of critical importance to beginners. Beginners also tended to purchase second-hand premium clubs, or previous year's models that had been discounted.

For more experienced players, reasons for buying new clubs ranged from the desire for the latest and greatest, to one's brother-in-law saying "you have to have it," to golfers who held clubs for so long that they were at a technological disadvantage. Once they made the decision to purchase new clubs, most golfers went by brand name—it was all about who had what. One average golfer said, "If someone looks in my bag, I want it to say that I'm affluent, that I'm a 'player.' I want to look good."

When deciding where to purchase new clubs, most golfers chose off-course retailers for their wide selection and convenient locations. (Over 90% of off-course retailers had hitting bays or swing simulators where consumers could try out equipment.) Conversely, avid golfers, who tended to be members of country clubs, would opt to purchase new clubs at their on-course pro shop. These golfers preferred to demo the clubs first-hand on the course or driving range and also felt a loyalty to their pro and his pro shop. An on-course consumer could shop and demo clubs at the pro shop and then comparison shop, but one golfer said, "but then you're screwing the pro."

Although woods and irons were expensive purchases, putters were relatively inexpensive at around $100 each. Because putting was viewed as the most critical aspect to the game and because most golfers were weak putters, they tended to update their putters fairly frequently and with less product research. In fact, many golfers owned five or more different putters, and when one putter "stopped working," they would change to another.

Sales and Marketing

Helmstetter stated that his group had to come up with products that consumers did not know they wanted, even if it cost triple the price. He believed that if customers knew what they wanted, then it was too late. Helmstetter said:

> After you create the product and get it to work, then you convince the consumers that they have always wanted and needed it. We start with the central idea that the product is better, and we can prove to them that it's better. Then we get the professional endorsements, get enough consumers to test it, and figure out what the advertising should look like.

Sales

CGC derived sales from both the United States and abroad. (See **Exhibit 10** for sales history of CGC.) Within the United States, the company sold to on-course and off-course golf retailers who sold professional quality equipment, and no one customer accounted for more

EXHIBIT 10   Sales History of CGC (in thousands)

Source: CGC 1995 and 1998 Annual Reports.

	1991	1992	1993	1994	1995	1996	1997	1998
Worldwide Sales in Dollars	$ 54,753	$ 132,058	$ 254,645	$ 448,729	$ 553,287	$ 678,512	$ 842,927	$ 697,621
U.S. Sales in Dollars	44,896	102,323	188,099	331,493	367,359	466,517	527,407	437,628
U.S. Sales of Woods in Dollars	31,730	80,851	155,355	236,446	247,372	324,466	352,708	241,842
U.S. Sales of Woods in Units	258	503	1,050	1,514	1,433	1,581	1,501	1,220
U.S. Sales of Irons in Dollars	10,524	16,918	20,455	69,976	91,938	118,366	153,052	141,810
U.S. Sales of Irons in Units	204	304	354	841	1,036	1,576	1,703	1,826
Net Income	$ 6,416	$ 19,280	$ 42,862	$ 78,022	$ 97,736	$ 122,337	$ 132,704	$ (26,564)

than 5% of revenues in 1998. About 65% of CGC business was done in off-course retail shops. The number of on-course retail stores had increased from 5,000 to 7,000 over the past five years, whereas off-course retail stores increased from 1,500 to 2,000 over the same period. Although an additional 1,000 off-course shops were also added during this time, they had failed and closed their doors. Of the estimated 2,000 off-course shops, CGC serviced 1,500 of them in 1999, versus 1,000 five years prior. In general, about one-third of off-course shops sold two-thirds of products, and two-thirds of on-course shops sold one-third of products.

Although on-course retailers were considered vital to CGC, the company relied more heavily on off-course shops because they were generally better financed than on-course shops. In addition, pros in on-course shops did not have the time to sell products properly because they were running the course, giving lessons, selling shirts, and renting golf clubs. Despite tremendous variation in size between the two types of retailers, CGC maintained a "one price" policy with all customers. Thus, it provided no volume discounts, whether a customer did $10,000 or $40 million of business a year.

Through its subsidiary, Callaway Golf Sales Company, CGC sold products wholesale to customers via regional field representatives (outside sales), in-house telephone salespeople (inside sales), and customer service representatives. Salespeople divided their customers into three groups, "A," "B," and "C," which they visited weekly, once a month, and four times per year, respectively, depending on their importance as an account. During visits, outside salespeople tended to spend one to two hours at a customer's store.

Outside salespeople had many responsibilities in the field, including running "demo days," maintaining physical inventory, straightening-up CGC's displays, taking customer orders, providing product seminars, and getting to know the salespeople. "Demo days" were conducted on weekends at on-course retail shops 30 to 40 times a year by each outside salesperson (totaling more than 2,500 per year). These events allowed golfers to try CGC clubs against their own at the clubs' driving ranges.

Another outside sales task was to determine holes in the individual store's inventory and suggest a fill-in order using knowledge of sales trends. (New products were on "allocation" so that stores would pre-order up to their allocated amount, and not get more product once the inventory was depleted.) Retailers did not have sophisticated inventory management; thus, CGC relied on its outside sales group to do physical counts. Outside salespeople also spent time educating salespeople about CGC products because salespeople would gravitate to the products they knew the most about, and the more they knew, the more convincingly they could sell.

Outside of the United States, foreign subsidiaries and international golf club distributors made most of CGC sales. The company distributed products in more than 50 countries, and sales to these countries received an export-pricing discount to alleviate the expense of distribution, advertising, and selling costs. (See **Table A** for country breakdown by 1998 sales.)

Marketing

CGC's marketing program was critical for two reasons. First, the key to making money in the golf business began with the product, and it had to be a product that differentiated itself

TABLE A
1998 CGC Sales Breakdown by Country

Source: Callaway Golf Company's 1998 Annual Report.

Country	Sales (in thousands)	% of Sales
United States	$437,628	63%
Japan	61,460	9
United Kingdom	64,077	9
Other foreign countries	134,456	19
Total	697,621	100

enough so that the company could charge a premium. Second, as CGC achieved product differentiation via continuously updated technology, it became increasingly important for the end consumer, as well as retail salespeople, to understand the product well enough to make educated buying decisions or sales pitches.

CGC used television, golf magazines, trade publications, and word-of-mouth as its primary forms of advertising. The company also endorsed professional golfers in all five major Tours (PGA, LPGA, Senior PGA, European PGA, and Nike) as a vehicle to promote its products. Notably, many professional golfers throughout the world used CGC products, even though they were not under contractual obligations, and CGC rewarded this voluntary usage with shared cash "pools."

CGC planned to spend $25 million on worldwide Pro Tour endorsements in 1999, but this program was likely to be scaled back in the future. (In 1999, Tour player Colin Montgomerie had contracted with CGC for $1 million, the highest amount the company had ever paid a professional golfer.) The goal was to assemble a portfolio of quality pros who signed for a reasonable price and who believed in the products. (Pro contracts generally had three-to-four-year terms.)

In choosing pro players, one CGC executive said, "We don't want to pay a zillion dollars for a super-prestigious pro—it's not worth it, given we're the market leader already; but we also don't want a bunch of players who will never get on television either. We want pros who are going to be on leader boards and who will win some tournaments." Some CGC pros in 1999 were Rocco Mediate, Colin Montgomerie, Annika Sorenstam, Jim Colbert, Bruce Fleisher, and Carlos Franco.

CGC used endorsements more as a validation, rather than as a cornerstone, of its product marketing campaign. Comparatively, acceptance and use by the pros was the absolute core of the Titleist marketing strategy, whose management pursued pros aggressively. A Callaway spokesman commented, "We develop clubs for average golfers, but it just so happens that pros use them too. That validates our products' quality and technology."

Media

When it launched Big Berthas in 1991, CGC ran three consumer print ads and three ads in trade magazines. Ely Callaway said, "Not a minute of television—all word of mouth based on the performance of the product."[3] Television was later used, and CGC's advertising had changed over time from using cartoons, to celebrities, to company spokespeople describing the technological advantages of CGC's clubs. CGC wanted to demonstrate that it was serious about R&D, but it did so in a lighthearted way.

CGC ads were aired primarily during golf tournaments, and also on CNN and ESPN. The company never used prime time air because of the high cost. In 1998, CGC's advertising budget was $33 million, up from $20 million in 1997 and $18 million in 1996. See **Table B** for total spending on advertising, promotional, and endorsement related expenses.

[3] Ibid.

TABLE B
CGC's Total Advertising, Promotional, and Endorsement Related Expenses

Year	Dollar Amount
1998	$79 million (Advertising = $33 million)
1997	$62 million (Advertising = $20 million)
1996	$45 million (Advertising = $18 million)

Source: Callaway Golf Company's 1998 10-K Report.

EXHIBIT 11

Approximate Average Wholesale Prices of Callaway Products

Source: Company information.

	1997	1998	1999
Woods			
Warbird	$150	$140	$85
Big Bertha Steelhead*		158	150
Great Big Bertha	290	245	140
Biggest Big Bertha	340	295	190
Great Big Bertha Hawkeye			290

*Steel and graphite combined.

Pricing

Setting wholesale prices of innovative products like the Big Bertha Metal Woods was not easy. Ely Callaway explained the process as follows:

> We relate the new product to existing products on the market, we relate it to the impact we are going to have on the consumer, how rare is the product, how much money did it take to create it, and how long did it take. We throw all these things in together and our internal staff consisting of the merchandising, product and R&D personnel get together and decide on the price. There is no set formula.
>
> Since it is difficult to predict a consumer's willingness to pay for such innovative products, it is a matter of "judgment" and "speculative courage." The Big Bertha Metal Woods introduced in 1991 sold for $400, which was probably twice as much as anybody had ever paid for a driver. But when we have a product like the Big Bertha and we know internally what benefits it is going to bring to the golfer, there is no way the golfer can help you judge it until you offer it and until they hit it. So the experience itself has to be anticipated.

Callaway adjusted the wholesale prices of woods and irons rather infrequently. The wholesale price was typically maintained over the life cycle of the product and was reduced only at the end of 2 or 3 seasons when a new product was likely to be an improvement over the existing product. (See **Exhibit 11** for recent wholesale prices of the Callaway product line.)

Industry/Competitive Analysis

In 1986, there were 20 million active golfers on 13,353 courses in the United States, and by 1998, there were 26 million golfers on 16,365 courses (70% were open to the public). These numbers were expected to increase by two million players and 300 to 400 new courses annually. (Of the 448 courses opened in 1998, 54% were nine-hole courses.)[4] The largest increase was among golfers who played between eight and 24 rounds per year, increasing 56%, from 5.4 million to 8.4 million. At the same time, avid golfers declined from 5.6 million to 5.4 million participants, and occasional golfers remained steady at 10 million.[5]

Some golf industry analysts, however, disputed the new participant growth numbers. Between 1988 and 1998, golf attracted between 1.5 and 3.0 million beginning golfers per year, but most quit because of what the National Golf Foundation called, "the inability of the industry to deliver an experience that stimulates more golfers to stay with the game or that motivates the average golfer to play more often."[6] Reasons for this included the time involved in playing (18 holes of golf could take four hours to complete), the unavailability of courses (difficult to get desired tee times), and the increasing cost to play (the average cost per round had risen 5% per year since 1996).

Between 1986 and 1998, golf expenditure in the United States on fees, equipment, and merchandise increased from $7.8 to $15 billion. In 1998, golfers spent $2.2 billion on clubs, $5 billion on merchandise, and the remainder on playing fees—nearly 50%. The average

[4] National Golf Foundation Web Site, http://www.ngf.org.

[5] AG Edwards Analyst Report, "Callaway Golf Company," September 28, 1999, p. 2.

[6] Ibid.

U.S. golfer spent $1,152 on all golf-related purchases, with avid golfers spending twice as much and other golfers spending less.[7]

Although worldwide interest in golf was growing, the worldwide premium equipment market was declining. Demand in the United States had decreased in 1998, and worldwide sales had been negatively affected by the Asian economic turmoil. Another reason for the decline was the saturation of product in the marketplace. By 1998, 18 types of "oversized head" clubs from 13 manufacturers shared the market that CGC had created in 1991. As new, technologically superior clubs were introduced on a regular basis, golfers began to have difficulty justifying the advantage of the clubs in the store versus the clubs in their bags. Another issue was that many golfers had "traded-up" earlier than their normal buying cycle dictated, making it difficult to warrant a new purchase.

Competition

The highly competitive golf equipment industry was marked by many well-established and well-financed companies with popular brand names, as well as new companies with trendy products. In the late 1980s and early 1990s, manufacturers were not well-financed and were unwilling to gamble on new, radically designed clubs—with the exception of Ping, which was very innovative and, in fact, dominated the world's iron market until 1995. By 1999, however, manufacturers were more willing to introduce unique designs. In the iron and metal woods categories, CGC's most significant competitors were Taylor Made, Titleist, Cobra, and Ping. In the putter category, CGC competed with Titleist and Ping. (See **Exhibit 12** for retail sales of woods per quarter.) Additional challenges came from some Japanese companies with leading edge products threatening to enter the U.S. market. One industry insider said:

> The biggest problem in golf is coming up with Act II. There are many companies that introduce a club and can get reasonable market share, but then as that product cycle expires and it's time for a new club, the company cannot come up with something better or something that matches the promise of the initial club.

Taylor Made Golf

Taylor Made had been acquired by the German multinational Adidas-Salomon in 1997, and thus had deep resources to aid its efforts. Taylor Made's commitment to R&D was strong and produced the revolutionary Bubble Shaft in 1994, which used perimeter weighting to make it possible to swing the club with more power and less effort. Taylor Made marketed itself to the average golfer, and its 1998 sales were $321 million. More than 51% of its sales were derived from the woods category, followed by irons (38%), accessories (10%), and putters (1%).[8] The company sold to both on-and-off-course golf shops, but had discontinued selling to all eTailers, such as Fog Dog, as of 1999. Management felt it was too difficult to maintain its standards of price and image via that distribution channel. The company was also known to have made consistent efforts to support its retailers through a variety of programs, such as rebates on sales targets and cooperative marketing programs. As of 1999, Taylor Made management did not know in which direction they were taking the company; thus, new products were released every year to try and maintain some market share. One retail manager said:

> Last year Firesole was the best thing since sliced bread, but this year it's Supersteel. How can I stay consistent with my customers and try and promote with them that it's the best club and that they're going to stay with it for a long time if there is a new product coming out every year?

---

[7] Ibid.

[8] Adapted from Golf Datatech reports.

EXHIBIT 12 Woods Retail Sales in Dollars and Units

Source: Adapted from Golf Datatech reports, March 2000.

Woods	1997				1998				1999		
	Q1	Q2	Q3	Q4	Q1	Q2	Q3	Q4	Q1	Q2	Q3
Industry Sales (in millions)	$ 107.80	$ 226.43	$ 205.14	$ 138.45	$ 96.25	$ 197.39	$ 188.11	$ 118.95	$ 93.56	$ 190.12	$ 180.20
Dollar Share:											
Callaway	45.7%	47.6%	48.5%	46.9%	42.6%	36.8%	32.9%	36.3%	38.7%	38.6%	39.7%
Cobra	9.9%	9.6%	9.2%	8.1%	7.2%	7.7%	7.4%	6.8%	5.5%	4.5%	4.1%
Taylor Made	21.4%	24.2%	25.0%	24.8%	25.6%	22.9%	21.8%	19.1%	17.2%	18.4%	18.7%
Titleist	1.2%	0.7%	0.5%	1.6%	2.7%	3.9%	3.7%	3.8%	4.1%	7.0%	8.1%

Woods	1997				1998				1999		
	Q1	Q2	Q3	Q4	Q1	Q2	Q3	Q4	Q1	Q2	Q3
Industry (in thousands)	485.78	965.78	872.04	605.04	434.94	909.07	877.96	592.42	468.67	941.16	893.56
Unit Share:											
Callaway	37.4%	37.9%	38.6%	36.3%	31.7%	27.8%	26.7%	29.4%	30.1%	30.3%	31.8%
Cobra	10.0%	10.3%	9.8%	8.8%	7.3%	7.6%	7.4%	6.8%	6.1%	5.2%	4.4%
Taylor Made	20.3%	22.2%	22.4%	23.3%	25.0%	21.6%	20.4%	17.2%	16.0%	16.6%	17.2%
Titleist	1.7%	1.0%	0.8%	1.3%	1.8%	2.4%	2.3%	2.2%	2.4%	4.8%	5.4%

Inventory Share:	Q1	Q2	Q3	Q4	Q1	Q2	Q3	Q4	Q1	Q2	Q3
Callaway	29.9%	32.7%	31.6%	29.8%	25.9%	24.2%	20.7%	23.3%	26.8%	27.1%	25.7%
Cobra	12.2%	13.2%	11.2%	9.1%	9.3%	11.1%	9.3%	9.4%	7.6%	7.1%	6.6%
Taylor Made	18.8%	21.7%	22.1%	24.2%	23.7%	20.6%	20.1%	18.5%	17.1%	17.4%	16.9%
Titleist	1.9%	1.7%	1.3%	1.6%	2.1%	2.3%	1.8%	2.2%	2.3%	4.1%	3.8%

Titleist Golf/Cobra Golf

Titleist and Cobra were owned by Fortune Brands. Unlike CGC, which wanted to market itself as the premium, average players' product, Titleist marketed itself as the professional or very good players' product. This was the company's strategy because management felt that all golfers aspired to classify themselves in that category. Titleist spent twice as much money as CGC did on endorsements and also had the number-one shoe (Foot Joy) and golf ball in 1999. This type of marketing paid off. As one avid golfer who was on the market for new woods said, "I know that Tiger hits with Titleist, so I'll probably give those a try in the pro shop."

Cobra was founded in 1973 and later became a public company before it was acquired by Fortune Brands in 1996. As opposed to Titleist, which focused on the highly-skilled golfers, Cobra was dedicated to the average golfers, especially ladies and seniors. Like many companies, Cobra was first a "wood company" with its initial product, the Baffler wood. The company later built-up its iron business, and its winning product was the King Cobra oversized irons in 1993. Combined sales and employees totaled $963 million and 4,650, respectively, in 1998.[9]

Ping Golf

Ping was one of the few privately owned golf companies, went head-to-head with CGC in irons, and, like CGC, had started out as a putter company. Management was keenly focused on research and development, and Ping was most famous for heel-toe and perimeter weighting, as well as custom fitting innovations.

Ping distributed almost exclusively to on-course retailers where management felt consumers could be properly fitted. Another reason the company built its business at on-course shops was that there was no way that off-course shops could simulate ball flight, which management viewed as a critical process to proper fitting. Realizing that fewer and fewer golfers were members of golf clubs, Ping began to sell to off-course retailers to make its products accessible to more people. Ping did not participate in any endorsement program with professional golfers.[10]

Regulatory Pressure

In November 1998, the United States Golf Association (USGA) set forth another challenge for CGC when it announced the adoption of test protocol to measure the so-called "spring-like effect" in driver clubheads. Callaway said:

> We are working to overcome the attitude of the USGA, which makes rules governing equipment. They threw a big scare into the industry after their announcement. They said that people were hitting the ball too far off the tee, and they wanted to take the Big Berthas away from them. We held a PR campaign where we asked golfers, "you don't want them to do this, do you?" There was a temporary victory in that the USGA approved the Big Berthas and all clubs in the market like them. We have some new club designs that we're going to want to make, but we know that some of them will be turned down. This is a significant challenge for both CGC and the industry.

This USGA protocol, which applied only in the United States, concerned both recreational and professional golfers. In reality, only 20 golfers in the world might, at some point, hit the ball too far—and the club was only one factor; players were getting stronger and courses were better developed. CGC products conformed to the regulations as of 1999; however, this would guide future product development for CGC and for the entire golf industry.

---

[9] 1998 Fortune Brands annual report.

[10] Adapted from Ping Golf website (www.pinggolf.com) and speaking with retailers and club users.

Retail Channels

Retail stores existed at both on-and-off-course sites. On-course shops, usually small and with limited selection, were located at golf courses, including a variety of both private and public facilities. Conversely, off-course shops were located outside of "green grass" locations; they were larger, offered a greater selection, and were generally categorized by size of store. Some off-course shops competed on the basis of service and expertise levels, while others were attractive because of the convenience of their locations, but all were priced competitively. As one retailer said, "You're either in the ballpark, or you're not in the game."

All sizes of off-course stores actively used advertising as part of their marketing strategies. Price advertising was prominent in newspaper advertising, but less so in television. In the industry, most manufacturers allowed their customers to advertise price, and many had minimum advertised price policies. Only in 1999 did CGC allow its wholesale customers to advertise price. Prior to that, customers could advertise price only by using flyers or catalogues in direct mail campaigns.

Retail Staff

Retail stores offered varying levels of sales assistance. Depending on a customer's skill level, salespeople spent between 15 minutes to an hour-and-a-half with each customer. On the one hand, beginning golfers needed a high level of service and personal care, and the retail goal was to get them into a good-fitting set of clubs at a price they could afford. Average or avid golfers, on the other hand, generally entered a store already knowing exactly what they wanted. These higher-skilled golfers tended to spend their time in the hitting bays and based their purchase decisions, with little help from salespeople, on which clubs within their price range felt the best. Salespeople did, however, make suggestions if they felt that a golfer's swing and skill level were not a good match for the clubs they were trying. Salespeople could also influence a sale by giving a golfer a $450 set of clubs to try in addition to the $700 set of clubs that the golfer was currently trying out in the hitting bay. One salesperson said, "The more expensive clubs might be a hair easier to hit on certain shots, but most people can't tell the difference."

In-depth knowledge of the sport was critical in enabling the staff to speak intelligently with the customers. In general, golf salespeople were well educated, polite, displayed a passion for golf, and did not adopt a "hard sell." Despite this, CGC management sometimes felt that product knowledge was not always reaching the point-of-sale. This stemmed from the high turnover, low salaries, and non-career status of salespeople.

To aid point-of-sale product knowledge, CGC supplied the retailers with equipment brochures, informational CD ROM's, televisions with informational videocassettes, pocket-sized product guides, and product training by its outside salespeople. Not all of these aids were equally effective. Some retailers also resisted the product training because store managers often did not want to pay salespeople to spend time talking to manufacturers' representatives. One retailer's comment was, "We don't need it, the products sell anyway." Another retailer had an alternative view. He said, "We're all in this together, I welcome the product training here. The better educated my staff is, the better they can sell the products and increase my bottom line—as well as the manufacturer's."

Some retail salespeople who welcomed training complained that when a CGC field representative visited them in the store, that he stayed only briefly, checked inventory, and did not instill in them any wisdom about CGC products. As a result, salespeople said they often felt undereducated about CGC technology and, therefore, could not justify the high prices to their customers. Sometimes they would steer customers to the retailer's private label products, or to other manufacturers' products that they felt were "more for the money," that they "believed in" and understood well. (Traditionally, name brand products yielded 15% to 25% margins, and private label products yielded 40% to 50% margins.)

In addition to product training and educational aids, CGC provided other means of support for its retailers, including product advertising, endorsements, demo days, warranty programs, 800 numbers, terms of payment, and closeouts. Closeouts generally occurred when existing equipment was discontinued to make room for new products or when CGC had too much inventory itself and wanted to get rid of it. At the time of a new product introduction, for example, if a retailer had eight of the previous clubs left in inventory, CGC would supply the store with one more new club for free, which brought down the average cost of the remaining inventory. Once a new product was introduced, the retailer had the discretion to mark down the remaining inventory to a price at which it would sell. In 1999, CGC held its own closeout and sold $40 million of excess inventory of Great Big Bertha, Biggest Big Bertha, and Great Big Bertha irons to the market at a lower price.

As a result of these support mechanisms, retail surveys consistently placed CGC in the top three for everything from advertising, to quality of products, to excellence in customer service. CGC was always dead last, however, in margins. Reasons for this included CGC's "no volume discount" policy and credit terms of 2% 30 net 60 (2% discount if paid within 30 days, otherwise pay in full within 60 days), which was considered a tight payment schedule within the industry—some manufacturers offered up to 120 days. One CGC insider said, "If you get to 60 and don't pay, the credit department comes down on you like a ton of bricks." It was the company's view that a bank, and not CGC, should finance their customers' businesses. CGC management felt its only responsibility was to provide its customers with the best products that would create the most demand and sell through, enabling the customers to pay their bills within 30 to 60 days.

Inventory

The CGC brand was so powerful that retailers had to carry CGC clubs in order to validate their stores as legitimate golf equipment shops. Stores also often used CGC equipment to develop their price image because shoppers would choose key CGC products to price compare from shop to shop.

There was no magic to how much inventory retailers carried. In general, they carried two-to-three months of inventory at a time, which varied in size during the busiest middle two quarters. Many on-course shops sold only "soft goods," such as shirts, caps, and balls, and sold clubs by mail order only. Off-course stores, conversely, focused on offering the biggest name brands with the largest market share.

It was impossible for retailers to carry all variations of every club because there were an overwhelming number of SKUs (a large retailer could have up to 10,000 SKUs in inventory). This was because there were right-handed clubs, left-handed clubs, ladies' clubs, and clubs with various lofts and shafts. (There were 24 different styles of clubheads and 10 different available shafts for the Great Big Bertha Hawkeye club alone.) Limited physical space and cost prevented retailers from carrying everything; thus, retailers tried to build inventories to fit the maximum number of people.

Retail Challenges

The golf retail business had become more difficult over the last 20 years. In the 1970s, virtually all golf clubs were sold through on-course golf shops, and in the entire United States, there were only 50 off-course shops—most of which were family-owned, "ma and pa"-type retailers. As off-course shops exploded in number, there were too many retailers "sharing the pie." This was a problem because, relative to other industries, the golf business was not very large. One senior executive said, "It's not like the pharmaceutical business where everybody needs some."

In the 1970s and 1980s, name brand merchandise was not as important to golfers as it was in 1999, so retailers had more of an opportunity to sell their private-label, higher-margin products. In the retailers' opinion, margins had steadily decreased over the years, but CGC believed that the cause was actually a higher percentage of the retailers' business being made up of name brand (i.e., lower margin) products.

Another retail challenge for CGC was its future role in the Internet. As of 1999, CGC had online retailers selling its products on the Internet (it did not sell direct), but this channel accounted for less than 1% of CGC's business. Management did not believe that it would replace the retail channel in any significant way because golfers wanted to touch, feel, hit, and swing golf clubs, and they did not like the delayed satisfaction in having product shipped.

In fall 1999, CGC management was doing some serious thinking about ways to draw itself closer to its biggest customers, but one executive said, "It won't include tiered pricing, I can tell you that." When asked if manufacturers realized that they needed the retailers more than ever, one retail manager replied, "If they don't they'll be out of business because we support the products."

What to Do Next?

Looking out the conference room window, Ely Callaway admired a Porsche in the company parking lot with a license plate that read, "THX ELY." A small symbol of CGC's success, the license plate embodied the culture that permeated the company. CGC had enjoyed many years of positive growth, followed by a down year in 1998. To alleviate some problems and to help rebuild, Callaway had already made several changes. After Don Dye's departure, the workforce was reduced, underperforming accounts were closed, and non-core businesses were discontinued. Callaway wondered; What products should be developed? How should CGC approach its retail partner relationships? And, should CGC's marketing campaign be refocused?

Despite these questions, Callaway remained confident in his organization. When asked if CGC could stay ahead of the competition, he said, citing Newton's First Law of Motion, "No problem. Bodies in motion tend to remain in motion." He continued, "It's a hell of a story, and it's not over yet."

Chapter 3

Tesco Plc.

David E. Bell

Our strategy is to take a successful U.K. company and make it a world leader in an industry we think will become an international industry. Neither of these things is proven yet: we haven't made the transition, and the industry hasn't yet become international.
—*Terry Leahy 2002*

We will have more space overseas than in the U.K. by 2003/04.
—*Tesco Interim Report 2002*

The 1990s had been a successful decade for Tesco, the British supermarket chain. The early 1990s found Tesco staggering under the effects of the recession that had hit the United Kingdom. Sainsbury's, Tesco's number one competitor and archrival, was announcing yet another record year. Marks and Spencer, another vaunted food rival, was still one of the world's most admired retailers. By the end of the decade, things were a bit different. Tesco was the number one food retailer in the United Kingdom, Sainsbury's was scrambling to recover and had been rumored as a takeover target, and Marks and Spencer had stumbled at home and internationally. So successful had Tesco been at almost everything it had touched, even Tesco.com, its Internet/home delivery service, was profitable, probably the only such example worldwide.

At the start of 2002, Terry Leahy, CEO since 1997, had reason to be pleased. Not only had the company's stock price more than doubled, from 89 pence[1] in April 1996 to 206 pence in October 2002, he had personally been recognized by the Queen for his services to food retailing, and was now a knight, Sir Terence. At the tender age of 46, Leahy was not

---

[1] One pound (£1) was worth $1.57 in December 2002. £1 = 100 pence.

This case was prepared by Professor David E. Bell with assistance from Senior Researcher Cate Reavis of the Global Research Group. HBS cases are developed solely as the basis for class discussion. Cases are not intended to serve as endorsements, sources of primary data, or illustrations of effective or ineffective management.

about to sail into the sunset. For one thing, at his accession to the role of CEO he had announced an aggressive ten-year growth plan for the company: (i) develop a strong core U.K. business, (ii) be as much in the non-food business as in food, (iii) develop a profitable retailing services business, and (iv) be as strong internationally as domestically. For another, competition showed no signs of weakening. One of his main competitors, Asda, had been bought by Wal-Mart, the American retail giant. Asda, along with Morrisons and Tesco, occupied the value segment of U.K. supermarket retailing. With a recovering Sainsbury's together with another grocery competitor, Safeway, at a slightly higher price point, and continuing vigorous competition from European discounters such as Aldi, Netto and Lidl at lower price points, Tesco would not be number one for long if it grew complacent. What would the story be at the end of the next ten years? Had Tesco deserved its success, or had it merely survived against inept competition? And if it had deserved its success, was that success transferable to Tesco's small but thriving international ventures?

Company Overview

In 2002, Tesco operated 1023 stores in ten countries (750 in the United Kingdom), employed 260,000 people worldwide, and had access to a population of 280 million people. Since 1999, turnover had increased 38% and net profit 37%. (For more financial information see **Exhibits 1–4.**) Tesco's main competitors included Sainsbury's, Safeway, Asda, and

EXHIBIT 1 **Tesco—Income Statement (millions of pounds)**

Source: Company reports and Schroder Salomon Smith Barney estimates.

Year to February	1999A	2000A	2001A	2002A	2003E	2004E	2005E
Sales—U.K.	15,835	16,958	18,372	20,052	21,461	23,049	24,708
–Europe	1,167	1,374	1,756	2,203	2,614	3,026	3,554
–Asia	156	464	860	1,398	2,343	3,573	4,955
Group sales	17,158	18,796	20,988	23,653	26,418	29,649	33,218
UK gross margin	*25.4%*	*25.3%*	*25.3%*	*25.4%*	*25.4%*	*25.4%*	*25.4%*
Operating profit—U.K.	919	993	1,100	1,213	1,308	1,409	1,516
–Europe	48	51	70	90	145	180	214
–Asia	(2)	(1)	4	29	70	125	190
Group operating profit	**965**	**1,043**	**1,174**	**1,332**	**1,523**	**1,714**	**1,920**
Group operating margin	*5.6%*	*5.5%*	*5.6%*	*5.6%*	*5.8%*	*5.8%*	*5.8%*
Income from associates	6	11	21	42	58	72	88
Net interest payable	(90)	(99)	(125)	(153)	(190)	(206)	(218)
Adjusted PBT	**881**	**955**	**1,070**	**1,221**	**1,390**	**1,580**	**1,790**
Exceptionals/amortization	(39)	(22)	(16)	(20)	(10)	(10)	(10)
Reported PBT	842	933	1054	1,201	1,380	1,570	1,780
Tax charge	(237)	(259)	(333)	(371)	(427)	(485)	(550)
Tax rate	*28.1%*	*27.8%*	*31.6%*	*30.9%*	*30.9%*	*30.9%*	*30.9%*
Net profit	605	674	721	830	954	1,085	1,230
Minority interest	1	0	1	0	(2)	(5)	(8)
Net attributable profit	**606**	**674**	**722**	**830**	**952**	**1,080**	**1,222**
Dividends	(277)	(302)	(340)	(390)	(435)	(491)	(551)
Retained profit	**329**	**372**	**382**	**440**	**517**	**589**	**671**
FRS3 EPS (p)	9.1	10.1	10.6	12.0	13.7	15.4	17.3
Adjusted, diluted EPS (p)	**9.4**	**10.2**	**10.7**	**12.1**	**13.6**	**15.3**	**17.2**
Total dividend (p)	4.12	4.48	4.98	5.60	6.25	7.00	7.80

EXHIBIT 2   **Tesco—Balance Sheet (millions of pounds)**

Source: Company reports and Schroder Salomon Smith Barney estimates.

Year to February	1999A	2000A	2001A	2002A	2003E	2004E	2005E
Intangible fixed assets	112	136	154	154	134	124	114
Tangible fixed assets	7,441	8,391	9,884	11,349	12,774	14,117	15,381
Inventories	667	744	838	929	1,000	1,091	1,188
Debtors	151	252	322	454	477	521	570
Investments	201	258	255	225	225	225	225
Cash	127	88	279	445	445	445	445
Total assets	**8,699**	**9,869**	**11,732**	**13,556**	**15,054**	**16,523**	**17,923**
Shareholders' funds	4,382	4,769	4,978	5,530	6,097	6,735	7,457
Minority interest	(5)	29	36	36	36	36	36
Provisions	17	19	402	440	440	440	440
Long-term debt	1,218	1,559	1,925	2,741	3,320	3,753	3,991
Short-term debt	830	847	1,413	1,489	1,489	1,489	1,489
Trade creditors	1,100	1,248	1,538	1,830	2,053	2,304	2,580
Other short-term creditors	1,157	1,398	1,440	1,490	1,619	1,766	1,930
Total liabilities	**8,699**	**9,869**	**11,732**	**13,556**	**15,054**	**16,523**	**17,923**

EXHIBIT 3   **Tesco—Cash Flow Statement, 1999–2005E (millions of pounds)**

Source: Company reports and Schroder Salomon Smith Barney estimates.

Year to February	1999A	2000A	2001A	2002A	2003E	2004E	2005E
Operating profit (EBITA)	965	1,043	1,174	1,332	1,523	1,714	1,920
Depreciation	401	428	468	524	585	657	736
EBITDA	**1,366**	**1,471**	**1,642**	**1,856**	**2,108**	**2,371**	**2,656**
EBITDA margin	*7.98%*	*7.83%*	*7.82%*	*7.84%*	*7.98%*	*8.00%*	*8.00%*
Interest and taxes	(366)	(344)	(433)	(555)	(542)	(605)	(670)
Working capital	(19)	48	295	182	130	115	130
Net cash flow from operations	981	1,175	1,504	1,483	1,696	1,880	2,117
Dividends	(238)	(262)	(254)	(297)	(325)	(363)	(405)
Capital expenditure (net)	(1,005)	(1,211)	(1,910)	(1,835)	(2,000)	(2,000)	(2,000)
Exceptional items	(26)	(6)	0	0	0	0	0
Acquisitions/disposals	(274)	1	(76)	(96)	0	0	0
Other	0	(18)	(58)	(85)	0	0	0
Free cash flow	**(562)**	**(321)**	**(794)**	**(830)**	**(629)**	**(483)**	**(289)**
Shares issued	42	20	88	82	50	50	50
Noncash movements	(9)	(39)	(38)	(8)	0	0	0
Opening net debt	(1,191)	(1,720)	(2,060)	(2,804)	(3,560)	(4,13)	(4,573)
Closing net debt	**(1,720)**	**(2,060)**	**(2,804)**	**(3,560)**	**(4,139)**	**(4,572)**	**(4,810)**
Gearing	*33.7%*	*37.3%*	*48.7%*	*56.4%*	*60.1%*	*60.6%*	*58.2%*

Morrisons supermarkets. Since the mid-1990s, Tesco's stock had outperformed its competitors as well as the industry index (see **Exhibit 5**).

In addition to its traditional supermarket format, Tesco operated Tesco Metro (urban convenience stores targeted toward office workers who wanted ready made meals), Tesco Express (a convenience store often near Esso gas stations), and Tesco Extra Hypermarkets. Tesco had achieved a 4% share of the non-food market[2] in the U.K. and was well on its way

[2] Non-food includes clothing, music and appliances and the like, but not normal grocery items like shampoo, and not automobiles.

EXHIBIT 4   Tesco—Key Data, 1999–2005E

Source: Company reports and Schroder Salomon Smith Barney estimates.

Year to February	1999A	2000A	2001A	2002A	2003E	2004E	2005E
Dividend cover	2.3	2.3	2.1	2.2	2.2	2.2	2.2
Interest cover	7.7	7.1	6.6	6.2	5.9	6.1	6.5
Book value per share (p)	77.0	82.6	84.7	91.7	99.0	107.5	117.1
ROCE	15.3%	14.5%	14.5%	14.4%	14.6%	14.8%	15.2%
Asset turnover	1.95	1.88	1.82	1.77	1.75	1.79	1.85
Payment period (days)	31.4	32.5	35.8	37.8	38.0	38.0	38.0
Collection period (days)	2.1	3.5	4.5	5.2	5.0	5.0	5.0
U.K. store numbers	639	659	691	728	792	827	882
U.K. sales area ('000 sq. ft)	15,975	16,895	17,949	18,822	20,076	21,106	22,136
Sales (ex VAT) per sq. ft/wk (£/wk)	19.56	19.95	20.39	21.09	21.24	21.52	21.97
U.K. profit per sq. ft (£)	1.14	1.17	1.22	1.28	1.29	1.32	1.35

TABLE A
First Six Months of 2002

	Sales	Operating Profit
United Kingdom	£10.5 bn	£537 m
International	£2.3 bn[3]	£59 m

to achieving its goal of a 6% share. Worldwide non-food sales had increased to £7 billion. The company offered a number of retail services through the Tesco Personal Finance division.

In addition to the United Kingdom, Tesco had operations in Ireland, Hungary, Poland, Czech Republic, Slovak Republic, Thailand, South Korea, Taiwan, and Thailand. Tesco's international business accounted for 42% of the company's total floor space, but only 10% of its net income.

Company History

In 1919, Jack Cohen invested his serviceman's gratuity worth £30 in a grocery stall in London. In 1924, he introduced Tesco Tea, his first private label product. (The name Tesco came from the initials of his tea supplier, T. E. Stockwell and the first two letters of Cohen's name.) The first Tesco store was opened in 1929 in London and by the end of the 1930s there were over 100, mainly in London. After a visit to the United States in the mid-1930s, where he discovered the U.S.'s self-serve supermarket model, Cohen decided to adopt the same "pile it high and sell it cheap" format. The first American-style Tesco was opened in 1947, the same year the company (Tesco Stores Holdings) went public. Cohen's emphasis on self-service led to his paying more attention to his suppliers, and, in effect, ignoring his customers.

The fortunes of the once-thriving chain declined so much in this period that "doing a Tesco" became British jargon for snatching defeat from the jaws of victory. As a final insult, the Imperial Tobacco Company, Britain's major player in the tobacco industry, having considered an acquisition of Tesco as part of a diversification strategy, eventually declined on the ground that Tesco might damage Imperial's brand image.

---

[3] £1 billion in Asia, £1.3 billion in Europe.

EXHIBIT 5   **U.K. Competitors' Stock Prices**

Source: Graph based on data from Commodity Systems Inc. via Yahoo!

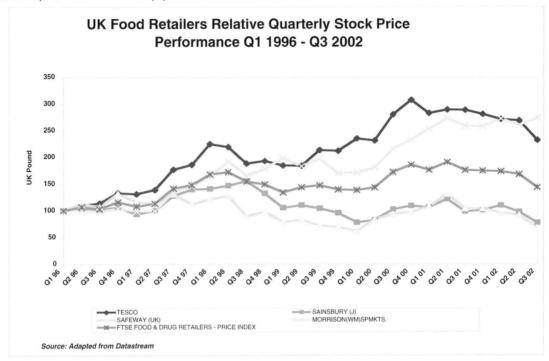

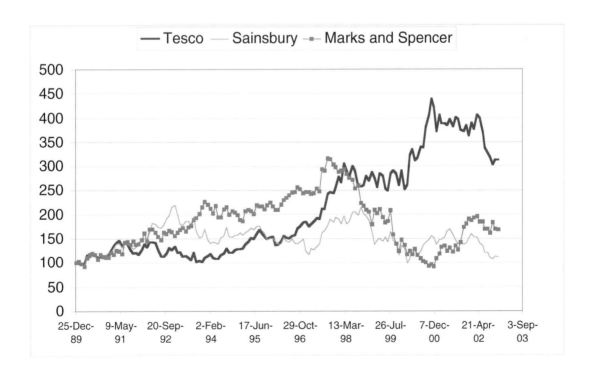

Recovery—Improving Operations

In the early 1980s, Ian MacLaurin became the first non-family CEO. MacLaurin reputedly had great charisma; he would lift the morale of any store just by entering it. But coming from the operations side of the business he realized that the company needed to be streamlined to have any hope of survival. He closed many of Tesco's smaller stores and built larger, more economic, 30,000 square foot stores in the suburbs. His aggressive expansion into a core business of over 200 superstores, a centralized distribution system which left Sainsbury's trailing, and advances in fresh food and its own label, set Tesco up well strategically. As for the merchandising side of things, innovation was fairly straightforward—copy whatever Sainsbury's was doing.[4]

The economic boom of the 1980s provided some breathing space for Tesco, but it also permitted them the (complacent) luxury of higher margins through higher prices. The recession of the 1990s exposed this copycat merchandising strategy; the lower priced continental discounters attracted the value conscious and Sainsbury's did a better job at attracting the quality conscious. Tesco had no differentiated offer to maintain the loyalty of its customers. Just at this time, as Tesco's fortunes again plummeted, the newspapers were rubbing it in with headlines announcing Sainsbury's most profitable year yet, and the election of Marks and Spencer as "Britain's most admired retailer."

Recovery—Focus on the Customer

In 1992 Terry Leahy, by then director in charge of fresh foods, was elevated to the board with responsibility for marketing. He realized that if Tesco continued to lose 1–2% of share per year, as it was then doing, the company would be in dire shape very quickly. As a good marketer should, he began to investigate a basic question: why, exactly, were customers leaving? Based on focus groups, Terry concluded that Tesco had squandered a lot of goodwill with its core customers because they were angry with the company. The anger had less to do with a rational comparison of what the company had to offer, but rather that Tesco had so obviously been chasing Sainsbury's, copying them on this, copying them on that, instead of trying to satisfy its own customers. By March 1993, Leahy was able to make a report to the board. He summarized what he thought Tesco needed to do:

1. Stop copying Sainsbury's as a merchandising strategy;
2. Institutionalize listening to customers;
3. Build a merchandising offer based on responding to what Tesco's own customers wanted.

Tim Mason, now Marketing Director, coined the phrase "bricks in the wall" to describe this incremental approach to merchandising; no sweeping innovation, just patient responses to customer needs. Describing the strategy internally, Leahy used the slogan "Tesco: The Natural Choice for Ordinary Shoppers," indicating that the chase for the upscale customer was over. Externally the slogan was "Every Little Helps," an expression that resonated with the people that had accused the company of deserting them.

In the fall of 1993 the first customer-driven innovation occurred with the introduction of a "value line," a low-priced no-frills range of basic items. The investment community was aghast at the move. Critics said this would cheapen Tesco's image and no one would "lower" himself or herself to buy such things. But they were wrong. Some customers did buy them, but perhaps more importantly, the rest saw the value line as an indication that Tesco was trying to help. In the fall of 1994 Tesco introduced "One in Front," a commitment

---

[4] One of the young up-and-coming managers in charge of doing the copying was one Terry Leahy, hired in 1979.

to keep lines short at the checkout counter. Cashiers were to signal for help if they saw more than one person waiting in line. As Leahy recalled:

> In the busy days of the 1980s, stores were so crowded, long lines were the norm. Customers accepted that waiting was a necessary part of shopping, and management accepted that acceptance. But it didn't mean customers liked it. A consequence of "One in Front" was that we needed more cashiers, at least, more people who could be cashiers. So we progressed to have more staff—more multitasking staff—in our stores.
>
> It wasn't long before I noticed a pattern in our focus groups. No matter what the focus group was talking about, whether being critical or not, there was always a point where somebody would stand up and praise the staff at Tesco. And the group would nod in agreement. So we made our staff the heroes of our "Every Little Helps" advertising campaign. We had a constant character "Dotty," an elderly, difficult-to-please customer. Everyone in the U.K. got to know and love Dotty. And our staff were the heroes.

In February 1995 Tesco introduced the "Clubcard" which offered a penny back per pound spent (1%). Leahy thought of the rebate idea while sitting on a train. "I recalled shopping at the Co-op store when I was a boy. You gave your Co-op number when you bought something and at the end of the year got a dividend based on your purchases. The Co-op stopped doing it years ago, but in the fifties, when times were hard, it meant a lot to their customers." The Clubcard concept was tested in a few stores for a few months, with great success, and then rolled out nationally. The Clubcard was immediately productive in that it got a lot of people to try Tesco again. The Clubcard also offered an opportunity to use direct mail to target customers. The best customers, those spending in excess of £600 per quarter, were given special offers, like flights not available to all, or cash coupons.

Observers were not impressed with this innovation either, one critic referring to it scornfully as "electronic Green Shield stamps,"[5] but Tesco management credited the Clubcard, now with 10 million members, as a major contributor to the Tesco turnaround. One manager commented, "A loyalty card is a 'must have' these days for a retailer. Some have suggested that a loyalty card can be used as a device to merchandise to the best customers, but that's not how retail works. Once you've opened a store, you want everyone in your store, not just the big spenders. We don't think there is such a thing as a bad customer. Success in retailing comes from the last 3% of customers."

Telephone operators and the Tesco website together fielded over 100,000 customer queries per week, many relating to the Clubcard program (lost cards, enquiries about point accumulation), but also comments about the quality of products. All managers had on-line access to these customer comments. The company credits knowledge of customer needs derived from Clubcard data with adding three points to its in-stock percentage.

And the focus groups continued. Tim Mason observed:

> We learn things all the time. We discovered that people didn't like our stainless steel refrigerators. They reminded people of a hospital. So now we install refrigerators that are colored. We also learned the importance of clean toilets. We all know they ought to be clean; what we didn't fully appreciate is that customers relate the hygiene of the toilets with the hygiene of the store as a whole.

Recovery—Focus on Employees

Tesco's focus on customers soon extended to employees. Leahy began meeting with "focus groups" of employees: "I would ask each group what Tesco stood for. A typical response would be 'Caring for customers.' Then I asked what they would *like* Tesco to stand for, and they would use words like teamwork, praise and trust. These are part of our core values

[5] Green Shield stamps was a widely-used "money-back" scheme, popular in the 1960s and 1970s, in which customers collected stamps at various participating retail stores and, after suitable accumulation, traded them in for gifts.

today. People want to enjoy being at work. The goodwill of the staff is the main productivity lever that you have."

Leahy knew that reenergizing the staff would require an attitude of respect, meaningful work, and training—throughout the organization. "Too many people at high levels had vaguely defined roles; too many people in the stores were performing elementary tasks." During 1996–1998, all managers were put through a training program designed to teach fundamental aspects of management; how to run a meeting, how to identify the causes of a problem and, perhaps most importantly, how to spot resistance to change and to learn methods for dealing with that resistance. Treating employees with respect extended to job security. So far as possible, employees whose positions were eliminated were found jobs elsewhere in the company.

Recovery—Focus on Growth

When Terry Leahy became CEO in 1997 he was satisfied that Tesco had become a stable, competitive player in the U.K. supermarket business. But growth was only keeping up with inflation. The company he envisioned in 2007 would derive much of its revenue from non-food, and international business would be as important as the U.K. business. Leahy also announced the ambition of making Tesco an "essential part of the landscape" in the United Kingdom. He wanted the company to be a British institution, like the BBC or Marks and Spencer had been in their prime.[6]

Leahy's ambitious growth goals could be achieved in three ways:

- by increasing the effectiveness of the existing U.K. business;
- by finding new ways to deliver value to U.K. customers;
- by expanding the pace of international expansion.

But in order to be able to execute his strategy, Leahy knew that he would need an organization that would work hard, and effectively, in pursuit of the goals he had laid out. The organizational strategy was to communicate very clearly where the company was headed, and empower everyone to make it happen. To make the empowerment succeed, Leahy ensured that each person had a set of quantifiable objectives, relevant to the employees' situation, and a set of incentives for achieving them.

The approach, described as "The Tesco Way," was summarized in a widely distributed brochure (see **Exhibit 6**). One of the core values was "simplicity." Dido Harding, now a director of food procurement, who joined Tesco after a stint at Woolworth's, noted that Tesco was run rather differently: "There was a clear message that bright people weren't supposed to use their intellect to make things more complicated, but rather to make things simpler." Tesco's Corporate Affairs Director, Lucy Neville-Rolfe, said the notion of simplicity extended to communications: "We have a message of the week that is sent by e-mail

---

[6] This latter goal was accomplished not only through being an increasingly important part of customers' retail lives, but also by touching their daily lives too. Tesco had spent £77 million on a "Computers in Schools" program whereby customers could donate till receipts to a local school that in turn could trade those receipts for computer hardware and software. Tesco organized a running event, "Race for Life," which had attracted a quarter of a million women and had raised £12M to support cancer research. Other programs integrated retail objectives as well as entering the fabric of peoples' lives. About 500,000 Tesco customers were members of a "baby club." A woman would be a member during pregnancy and until the baby was two years old. Every three months a member would receive a brochure appropriate to the age of the infant providing information about health, development of the child, and tips about the concerns mothers typically faced. The brochure also contained coupons for relevant products.

EXHIBIT 6 **The Tesco Way**

Source: Graph based on data from Commodity Systems Inc. via Yahoo!

Introduction

The Tesco Way

Over the years we've developed an approach to doing business and this has become known as the Tesco Way. We have drawn together the five elements of that approach and this booklet summarises them. They are:

- **Our Core Purpose**   the reason for all that we do
- **Our Goals**   what we have set out to achieve
- **Our Values**   the way we want to behave
- **Our Principles**   Better, Simpler and Cheaper
- **Our Steering Wheel**   which measures progress against our priorities and provides a visual reminder of our plans

This booklet is a reminder of the key messages, first delivered at the company conference in 1999. Understanding and managing the Tesco Way is a key ingredient for success at Tesco. The Tesco Way is a way of working which is:

BETTER, SIMPLER and CHEAPER

The Core Purpose

Our core purpose is all about customers:

To create value for customers to earn their lifetime loyalty

For us customers are at the heart of all that we do. The purpose, values and goals work together to create the culture and clarity of direction which enable us to achieve success.

Our strong UK core business has increased its market share and we are successfully expanding overseas because we understand better than others what our customers want - and how best to provide it. We create value for our customers because we understand them and improve our business for them.

The expansion of our non-food, e-commerce and Tesco Personal Finance businesses are all examples of our Core Purpose in action - delivering products, which delight customers and increase their loyalty to us.

53

EXHIBIT 6 (Continued)

Our Goals

Our goals provide a key framework for us all.

Tesco is a successful growth company and our success has come from focusing on the goals:

- **Tesco will be a growth business**
- **Tesco will become the business people value more than any other**
- **Tesco will have the most loyal and committed staff**
- **Tesco will be a global retailer**
- **Tesco will be as strong in non-food as in food**

In any business, direction is crucial and in Tesco it is our goals that provide it. For example, by developing a personal strength in non-foods we can enable our goal of being as strong in non-food as in food. Later in this booklet we show how our goals are reflected in the Steering Wheel and in our various one year plans.

Our Values

Our Values are our code of conduct - they are the way we have chosen to work at Tesco and drive the whole way we do business. They are:

NO ONE TRIES HARDER FOR CUSTOMERS

- *Understand customers better than anyone*
- *Be energetic, be innovative and be first for customers*
- *Use our strengths to deliver unbeatable value to our customers*
- *Look after our people so they can look after our customers*

These customer values reflect that in Tesco everything starts with the customer and that our passion to provide customers with value and service overrides all else.

TREAT PEOPLE THE WAY WE LIKE TO BE TREATED

- *All retailers, there's one team ... The Tesco Team*
- *Trust and respect each other*
- *Strive to do our very best*
- *Give support to each other and praise more than criticise*
- *Ask more than tell and share knowledge so that it can be used*
- *Enjoy work, celebrate success and learn from experience*

We want our people to be well managed and to work in an environment that is based on trust and respect. We have learnt over the years that well motivated and managed staff will give customers great service: by living the people values we create a good place to work and one where great service is delivered.

EXHIBIT 6 (Continued)

Our Principles –
Better, Simpler and Cheaper

Better, Simpler and Cheaper are our guiding principles and underpin the Tesco Way.

As we about our work and, most importantly when we are making changes, we have an unwavering commitment to make Tesco Better, Simpler and Cheaper.

Our senior managers have been applying these principles for some time as they seek to improve the business. They were inspired by three business writers:

- **Better**   (from Reichheld's "The Loyalty Effect")
- **Simpler**   (from de Bono's "Simplicity")
- **Cheaper**   (from Jones & Womack's "Lean Thinking")

The combination of these three principles provides a powerful tool which we must all understand and employ when making decisions.

The adoption of Better, Simpler, Cheaper principles leads us to change which is:

BETTER for CUSTOMERS

SIMPLER for STAFF

CHEAPER for TESCO

BETTER

Successful businesses grow by retaining their existing customers whilst attracting new ones; creating lifetime loyalty is part of Tesco's Core Purpose. In the Loyalty Effect, Reichheld explains that there are six core approaches to loyalty based management.

- **Grow the business** by attracting and retaining customers
- **Improve productivity** by recruiting the right people, developing them, ensuring loyalty and managing their careers
- **Measure value** by tracking the behaviour of customers, employees and investors - and measuring their impact
- **Create intellectual capital** by attracting and retaining the right people
- **Maximise shareholder value** by attracting and retaining the right investors
- **Build strategic advantage** by designing business systems on the principles of value, loyalty and partnership between customers, staff and shareholders

The virtuous circle of loyalty is illustrated below:

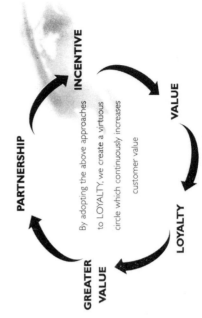

By adopting the above approaches to LOYALTY, we create a virtuous circle which continuously increases customer value

Continued investment in customers is enabled by investment in employees who deliver better service and higher productivity. This in turn can be reinvested in creating value for customers.

EXHIBIT 6 (Continued)

Our Plans

Like any successful business we have a long term plan. It is owned by the PLC Board and its purpose is:

to create value for customers to earn their lifetime loyalty

On an annual basis we produce a series of integrated business plans - one each for Customers, Operations, People and Finance. Each of these plans engages our people and focuses effort where it will deliver the best return.

The **Customer Plan** contains projects which deliver real improvements in the year for our customers - to build their loyalty.

The **Operations Plan** focuses on making Tesco simpler and more cost efficient so that we are able to reinvest savings in our customers and our people.

The **People Plan** focuses us on developing the capability and commitment of people so we are able to make Tesco better, simpler and cheaper.

The **Finance Plan** ensures that the output from the Customer, Operations and People Plans delivers value for our shareholders.

The Steering Wheel

The **Steering Wheel** is the tool we use to help us to manage in a balanced way. It has an important role in communicating both our strategy and our performance. The four quadrants are interdependent - and we give equal emphasis to each of them.

It is based on Kaplan and Norton's "Balanced Scorecard" and provides a very visual indication of our progress against our plans.

The segments within each quadrant show those objectives we've set and how we perform against them.

The highest level Steering Wheel is the corporate Steering Wheel. Each of the major functions in Tesco has their own Steering Wheel which feeds off the corporate one. All UK stores have had an individual Steering Wheel since 1997 and it has become the centre of management, measurement and motivation.

In this way, the business strategy comes to life in every major operating unit. The PLC Board's vision is translated into visible objectives and measures which are tracked using the Plan-Do-Review cycle. In stores and distribution centres this cycle may be as frequently as weekly; in the Boardroom it is quarterly.

The Steering Wheel diagram with four quadrants: OPERATIONS, PEOPLE, FINANCE, CUSTOMER. Operations segments: SUPPORT FOR THE BUSINESS, REPLENISHMENT, BUYING & RANGING OF PRODUCTS, SERVICE PRODUCTIVITY, BUILDING, REFITTING & MAINTAINING. People segments: LIVE THE VALUES, APPOINT THE BEST, DEVELOP PEOPLE TO BE THE BEST, WIN COMMITMENT. Finance segments: MANAGE OUR INVESTMENT, MAXIMISE PROFIT, GROW SALES. Customer segments: RETAIN CUSTOMER LOYALTY, INCREASE CUSTOMER SPEND, ATTRACT NEW CUSTOMERS.

to our top 2,000 managers, any of whom can reply directly if they have a question. They in turn pass it on, perhaps translated appropriately. No one in management has a private secretary—even Terry sometimes picks up his own phone—which makes for good communication. It's the same on the outside. We don't use lobbyists because it is easier to communicate if we do it in person."

Another cornerstone of The Tesco Way was the "Steering Wheel," which laid out the objectives that managers would be judged by. Each quarter a manager would be shown the wheel and how his or her performance rated against those objectives, color-coded for impact: green indicated good progress, yellow a caution, and red declared a problem. A store manager's steering wheel included objectives such as shrinkage, and the results of visits by mystery shoppers. The store manager was also measured on how well the store's employees understood the store's performance on key measures. As a result, employee back rooms were plastered with graphs on which key indicators were updated daily.

Increasing the Effectiveness of U.K. Stores

Logistics

According to industry observers, Tesco's U.K. stores had one of the best distribution networks in the world. This was in spite of Tesco's reputation of being "obsessed with stores" rather than operations. Tesco spent £200–300 million per year on its logistics systems, mostly on upgrading existing facilities.

The emphasis was on using existing resources more efficiently. For example, the distribution centers were increasingly using cross-docking, a system by which goods flow directly from in-bound trucks to waiting store-bound trucks. Adoption of this technique was hampered by the lack of loading bays, which meant some doors needed to be used for loading and unloading. The critical bottleneck at the warehouses led to a number of creative initiatives designed to increase the ability to coordinate arrival and departures of trucks. One initiative was to use Tesco's own trucks to collect goods from suppliers, a technique known as primary distribution. Another initiative had store managers visiting the distribution centers to see at first hand the problems created if a truck was not unloaded at a store promptly.

Most stores currently received two deliveries per day: a "fill-up" delivery and a "top up" delivery, though the goal was to move to two main deliveries per day, thus increasing turns and reducing out-of-stocks.

Procurement

The Steering Wheel for buyers included performance objectives such as delivered cost, product quality, and delivery reliability, but, said Dido Harding, "We are mainly measured on gross margin because that's the only cost measure that is unique to the buying function. Even though we are held to account on gross margin, the attitude is to deliver for the customer: in our case, the store manager. That permeates everything. The customer really is king."

Negotiations with key suppliers usually occurred once per year. A pricing system would be agreed upon that laid out the price Tesco would pay as a function of the quantity it ultimately ordered, and the reliability with which it was delivered. Tesco's goal was to hold as little inventory as possible so flexibility was a key component of vendor selection.

Tesco had followed a trend in the industry by encouraging some vendors to dedicate themselves, or one of their factories, exclusively to their needs. "In part, we were forced to do this by competitors, like Marks and Spencer and Sainsbury's, who were tying up suppliers." Harding went on to describe Tesco's relationship with vendors:

> There are a lot of relatively small vendors who supply us with Tesco branded merchandise. We are an important customer to them so we have to make sure that our contracts are win-win. Dealing with larger vendors is a different story. With dedicated suppliers we need to think of cost in terms of total operations. With large vendors we like to concentrate on calculating their *marginal cost*. When a supplier has many customers some will be more profitable than others. We want to be their most demanding customer. But even though we may fight like cats and dogs over the price we need, we also cooperate about increasing sales in their category. This isn't an easy adjustment to make. Sometimes when we hire people from other companies they cannot understand the notion of cooperating with vendors.

The Tesco spirit of simplicity in communication extended to suppliers. They had access to the company's sales data, though not necessarily in real time. Twice a year, Terry Leahy made a presentation to assembled vendors where he laid out exactly what Tesco was up to in the coming months.

The Stores

Though promotions were not unusual, the general pricing philosophy at Tesco was that of EDLP (Every Day Low Pricing). There was a strong push to give more authority to store managers. A manager hot line was set up. A new program dubbed TWIST (Tesco Week in Store Together) required all corporate managers to spend a week in a store working on a specific store task. Phillip Clarke, the board member in charge of logistics and IT, spent a week stocking shelves, and Terry Leahy had worked a cash register. Tim Mason, the Director of Marketing, indicated that plans were afoot to use technology to permit store specific Plan-o-grams that would allow store managers to modify buyer-designed core offers. He continued:

> The Tesco brand has been transformed over time from being cheap, down market and distressed, to that of market leader and most admired. We did that by simply thinking of ourselves as being in "the shopping business." We aimed to provide the "Best Shopping Trip for Everybody." We recognize that Sainsbury's attempts to justify higher prices by being aspirational, but we find many customers with children are reluctant to shop there because they are afraid their children will misbehave. Asda is proud of its low prices, but they are perceived by many as a bit too cheap. We hope no one can complete the sentence, "I don't shop at Tesco because . . ."

Extending the Retail Offer to U.K. Customers

Alternative Formats

Building on its core supermarket business, Tesco had three additional store formats. Metro stores were small convenience supermarkets located in busy downtown areas, having a particular emphasis on sandwiches and casual food. Express stores were smaller convenience stores often located next to Esso gas stations. Finally, Tesco's hypermarket format, called Extra, was the major vehicle by which Tesco could fulfill Leahy's objective of growing rapidly in non-food. **Table B** summarizes Tesco's store formats.

Retailing Services

In 1997 Tesco began offering financial services; by 2002 it had 3 million registered customer accounts. The goal was to provide customers with convenient financial products during their shopping trip. Customers could open a bank account enabling them to deposit

TABLE B
Tesco Retail Formats,
U.K. Only, 2002

Store Format	Number	Average sq. ft.
Express	100	2,000
Metro	180	10,000
Superstore	408	35,000
Extra	62	90,000

checks as part of a register transaction; £6 million was deposited in a typical week. Money could be withdrawn from any ATM. Tesco also sold car insurance and by 2002 had 600,000 policies outstanding. Travel insurance could be bought as a routine register transaction and loan applications could be filled out and handed in on the spot. Tesco's profits from these services were £20m in the 2002 financial year.

Tesco.com

In December 1995 five people were assigned to study the idea of home shopping. Microsoft developed a website, and 12 stores were selected to act as shipment points. Orders were to be taken by phone, fax or over the Internet. Launched in December 1996, the project soon foundered. Taking orders by phone and fax proved prohibitively expensive. Moreover, as John Browett, now CEO of Tesco.com (a legal subdivision of Tesco Plc) observed, "We discovered that the 5% of the British population who had Internet access didn't buy groceries."

For a year the operation was held in a limited number of stores until it could be executed properly. John Browett recalled the analysis that followed:

> Around this time the belief spread that the best way to do home shopping was from a dedicated warehouse, but we studied the economics with great care and decided that was not correct. A lot of companies are afraid to do the numbers. They either don't want to, or can't. But doing the numbers allows you to make the right call. For example, when we lower prices we know exactly how low we can go. Our analysis suggested that a given store would get no more than 500 orders per week. People argued that if we were filling online orders in the store we'd be crowding out our traditional customers. But our stores have an average of 40,000 customers per week. The online orders, which could be done at off peak times, weren't going to bother anyone.
>
> On the idea of dedicated warehouses, there is no way you could afford to stock all of the skus you'd need to give a full assortment. The fact is, a lot of our early customers were shopping online precisely to find obscure items they couldn't find in their local store.

Tesco.com was relaunched with orders taken over the web and fulfilled from the stores. Logistics were improved in two ways, one by reducing the flexibility of delivery windows and the second by improving the order picking process. Customers could select one of two delivery windows, either 7:00–9:00 P.M. or 8:00–10:00 P.M. It was believed most people would be home on a weekday evening. The evening delivery times permitted more flexibility about when the orders could be picked, and improved the delivery scheduling. Each store had several specially designed shopping carts with six containers to hold different orders. A touch screen on the cart informed the picker, who was a regular store associate and who followed a set path around the store, when to pick an item off the shelf and which container to put it in. In that way shopping for six took not much more time than shopping for one.

Store managers were happy with the presence of Tesco.com; the store was credited with the sales as if they had been made to a conventional shopper, the sales were largely made in off-peak periods, and, as an added bonus, the picker would notice irregularities such as out-of-stocks that could then be corrected.

As of 2002, Tesco.com covered 95% of the United Kingdom and was filling 100,000 orders per week worth nearly £10 million, or about 2% of Tesco total sales. Commenting on the kinds of customers that Tesco.com was attracting, Browett said:

> Tesco.com appeals to the cadre of people who have been doing it for a while and have become very adept; for them they can do an entire week's shopping in 10 minutes. Another group of regular users are people with small children at home for whom a trip to the supermarket can be a nightmare. A third group is the single professional for whom a trip to the store is a poor use of time. For them a £5 delivery fee is well worth it even if they buy only a few items.

Browett believed that in-store delivery would continue to be the most sensible system even if online sales became as much as 10% of store sales. Not only had Tesco.com reported a profit in 2001, as a further indication of the prospects for this channel, Tesco had exported the model to the Republic of Ireland, and to Korea, and via a joint venture to Safeway, Inc. in the United States.

International Expansion

Like many retailers facing a zero sum game in their domestic markets, the lure of potentially fast growth foreign markets was strong. In the mid-1990s, as its cash flow began to recover, Tesco made some decisions about what its international strategy should be. Leahy recalled:

> There were no texts on how to be successful at international retailing. It worked in our favor that we didn't start out believing we had all the answers. We thought about how we could add value for us and for customers. We needed countries where we would be early entrants, countries that were stable, and countries with sufficient spending power per capita, and with growth potential. We also recognized that our skill set involved opening networks of stores rather than integrating pre–existing chains. This thinking led us to identify the former Communist countries of Eastern Europe, and a few emerging overlooked countries in Asia.

David Reid, Vice Chairman of Tesco, and the person in charge of the international venture, described how Tesco selected the hypermarket as the correct vehicle for Tesco abroad:

> We knew that we did not have a ready-made international format. We had no hypermarkets in the U.K. at that time, but it became obvious that it was the right format. It was the only format that would help us achieve our goals for non-food growth. It also helped that tastes are more international in non-food than in food. It was also the right choice logistically. It didn't make sense to build distribution centers to service many small stores, at least not in the early stages. And finally, it seemed to us that no matter how we started, we'd end up opening hypermarkets, so it made sense to skip the first step and open hypermarkets to begin with.

Tesco recognized the advantages that local partnerships could provide. In Asia, Tesco found partners in the CP group (Thailand) and Samsung (South Korea), but in Eastern Europe there was a dearth of possibilities. Tesco instead identified small thriving retailers and bought them to obtain the managements, who were then given the task of building the number one retailer in their country. The first foreign country was Hungary, in 1994, quickly followed by Poland, the Czech Republic, and Slovakia. Later in the 1990s Tesco established a presence in Thailand, South Korea, Taiwan and Malaysia.

Since Tesco had no experience with hypermarkets, and no knowledge of the local customers, they gave great autonomy to the local management. According to Leahy:

> Even today, with 65,000 employees overseas there are only 70 of our U.K. managers living abroad. And they are trainers not operating managers. We've told the local managers that they are to be the number one in their country, but we don't tell them how to do it. As a result, their enthusiasm is sky high.

The role of the trainers was to be sure the values of the local teams were in keeping with those of the parent. The Tesco Way, with its emphasis on simplicity, on the customer, and on steering wheels, was a constant, but not the retail solutions. David Reid believed the Tesco Way had been absorbed and understood by senior management, but less so as one went lower down in the organization. Foreign managers had problems understanding the notions of empowerment and promotions based on merit; indeed some actively resisted it.

The international strategy seemed to be working. By 2002, Tesco claimed market leadership in six out of the nine countries it had entered, and profitability in eight, with a combined contribution to operating profit well in excess of £100 million. The company believed it was the most profitable international retailer in both Asia and Central Europe. Tesco had 150 hypermarkets overseas and had plans to start introducing other of its domestic formats, such as Express stores. As Tesco opened its 62nd hypermarket in the U.K., it was clear that Tesco's overseas investments were paying off in more ways than simply providing operating profit.

Terry Leahy reflected on the success of its strategy:

> You could say that we had pursued a "pull" strategy overseas by letting the local market dictate what we offer. A "push" strategy would have presumed we knew what could work and would have proceeded by rolling out store after store. I think there are very few economies of scale across countries in food retailing; what's important is not to lose any local economies of scale. That is why it is important to be number one within a country, rather than simply to build sales across countries. There are some cross-border synergies like IT and sourcing, but the main advantage we have is by exporting our culture. Global retail brands won't be the norm in my generation. After all, consumer goods companies have taken 100 years to achieve an 8% share. I doubt if it will be much different in retail. Most of our overseas customers think they are shopping in a local store.

The Next Five Years

At the end of 2002 Tesco was on track to achieve the goals Terry Leahy had set out in 1997. Tesco was nearing his goal of being 50% international, and perhaps most incredibly of all, it had become the most admired retailer in the United Kingdom, "an essential part of the landscape."

A lot had happened to Tesco since the early 1990s. But despite that success, it could be argued that Tesco faced stronger competitors in 2002 than it had in 1992. Domestically, Asda had become a formidable foe under the ownership of Wal-Mart; Sainsbury's had begun revitalizing its stores and internationally, Carrefour and Wal-Mart were being increasingly aggressive. Tesco International still benefited significantly from the strong financial condition of Tesco in the United Kingdom.

In the 1970s "doing a Tesco" was a characterization of failure. In the 1990s "The Tesco Way" was a symbol of retail revival. The new decade would reveal whether the Tesco Way was purely a local solution or a formula for international retail success.

Creating Value

Chapter 4

Creating Value

Rohit Deshpandé

The fundamental objective of marketing is to create value. It does this in two ways, within the organization by making a contribution at different levels of the firm. And outside of the organization by creating value for customers. Marketing plays this role by bringing the voice of the customer into the organization. This note describes each of these aspects of marketing beginning with how marketing makes a contribution within the firm.

Creating Value within the Firm

Creating Value at the Corporate/Business Unit Level

If we begin by thinking at the level of the entire organization, we can see that marketing creates value in terms of corporate culture. Many organizations are concerned about their extent of customer focus. They are trying to instill in the corporation a shared sense of values about the primary importance of the customer relative to other stakeholders. Johnson & Johnson Company's much-lauded handling of the Tylenol poisoning crisis in 1982 is often credited to their corporate values enshrined in their credo at the time of the crisis. This credo had as its first statement: "We believe our responsibility is to the doctors, nurses and patients, to mothers and all others who use our products and services."[1] Interestingly, the very last of the 24 statements in the J&J credo reads: "When we operate according to these principles, the stockholders should realize a fair return." This prioritization of cultural values by putting the customer first clearly involves more than a simple listing of values in a credo. In order for the culture to guide action it must not only be reinforced, it must be measured. Such measurements involve assessments of both employees and customers and come from using a set of tools including consumer and customer research, customer visit programs, and market orientation assessments.[2] The common purpose here is to devise mechanisms for bringing the voice of the customer into the organization so that the firm gets closer to its customers (see **Figure 1**).

[1] James Burke, *A Career in American Business,* written in 1989, HBS No.389-177.

[2] Rohit Deshpandé, *Developing a Market Orientation,* Thousand Oaks, CA: Sage Publications, 1999; Edward F. McQuarrie, *Customer Visits,* Thousand Oaks, CA: Sage Publications, 1998.

FIGURE 4.1   **The Contributions of Marketing within the Firm**

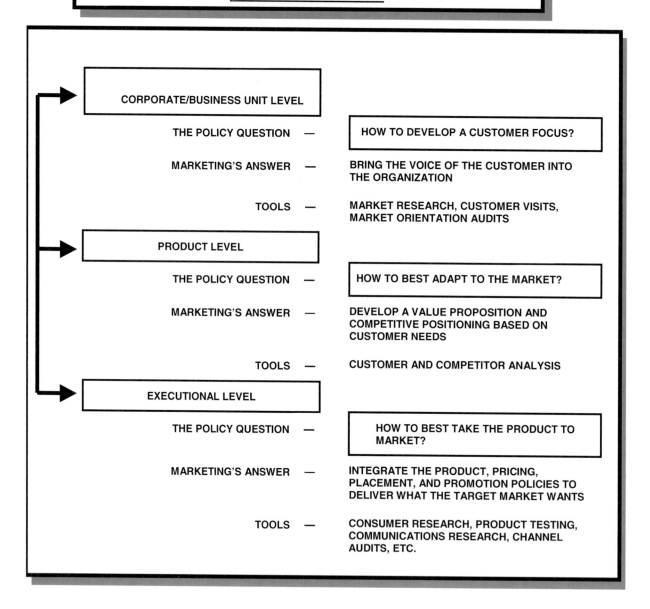

Creating Value at the Product Level

The Note on Marketing Strategy (9-598-061) describes the marketing process as beginning with a 5 C's analysis, i.e., an understanding of customer needs, company skills, competition, collaborators, and context. This information is essential in trying to answer the policy question of how a product or service should be best adapted to a market. A key role for marketing at this stage is to help shape the value proposition for the product which can then be explicitly described in a positioning statement. The importance of a positioning statement cannot be overstated since it establishes the foundation for the executional level of the marketing mix (described below). A simple form of a positioning statement is:

For (**Target Market**), (**Our Product/Brand**) is (**Single Most Important Claim**) among all (**Competitive Set**) because (**Single Most Important Support**).

A hypothetical example might be:

"For business people who rent cars, Acme is the company that will give you the best service among all rental car companies because the employees own the company."

Note that in this example, marketing input is key in understanding both the product benefits desired by the target market as well as how the product is differentiated versus the competition.

Creating Value at the Executional Level

As described in **Figure 1,** the next step for marketing is to detail the tactical elements of the product, its pricing, the advertising and promotional support, and the distribution channel arrangements. Effective execution involves an integration of these four marketing mix elements so that they flow seamlessly from the positioning. Once again this implies careful assessment through consumer research, product testing, channel audits, and so on so that each executional element is working both independently and in unison with the others (see *Note on Marketing Strategy* HBS Case 9-598-061 for an elaboration of the four marketing mix activities). There are many examples of brilliant strategy with poor execution leading to publicized failures. The Walt Disney Company's initial attempt at using a skimming pricing policy in the launch of its Euro Disney theme park on the outskirts of Paris is one such illustration of inadequate modification of marketing mix elements in scaling a successful U.S. model to Europe.[3]

Creating Value for Customers

It is obvious that marketing cannot deliver value within the firm if it has not created value for customers. Understanding how marketing does this can be best described within the context of new product development.

We think of the traditional new product development process as a sequence of phases from idea generation through product commercialization (see **Figure 2**).[4] Brainstorming for new product ideas should come from as many sources as possible. These might include customer complaints about existing products, improvements on competitors' technologies, and internal R&D laboratories. These ideas are then screened to eliminate those that are outside of the firm's interest or resources. The smaller set of ideas is then translated into a concept that customers can understand and evaluate. This is typically the first stage at which samples of consumers are asked to provide concept ratings. Those concepts that are considered viable are then further elaborated in terms of likely pricing, distribution, and marketing communications. A business feasibility analysis is performed with revenue and profit projections. Those products that survive through this stage of the development process are then manufactured in a limited quantity for the purpose of testing in a real

---

[3] Robert F. Hartley, "Euro Disney," in *Marketing Mistakes,* New York, NY: John Wiley, 1995, Chapter 9.

[4] Philip Kotler, *Marketing Management,* Englewood Cliffs, NJ: Prentice-Hall, 1997, Chapter 11.

FIGURE 4.2
The New Product
Development Process

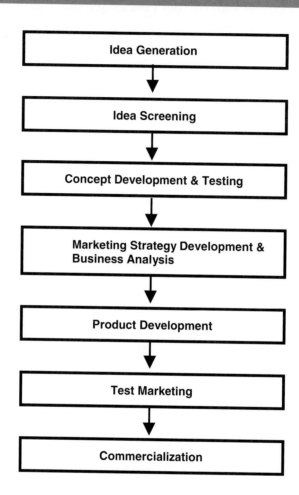

THE NEW PRODUCT DEVELOPMENT PROCESS

Idea Generation

Idea Screening

Concept Development & Testing

Marketing Strategy Development &
Business Analysis

Product Development

Test Marketing

Commercialization

market, typically regional. Finally, the successful product is commercialized for a full-scale launch (for a detailed discussion of market research tools and their applicability see Vincent P. Barabba, "The Market Research Encyclopedia," *Harvard Business Review,* January–February 1990, Reprint 90103).

Two things should be immediately apparent—this is often a laborious and expensive process, and it depends a great deal on the ability of consumers to readily evaluate the potential success of the product (at concept stage, test market stage, or even right after full commercialization). The first factor often leads firms to skip steps in the product development process and bring the product to market faster. Although this saves money in the short term, it can frequently be far more expensive in the long term when mistakes are made that might have been avoided with careful consumer research. But how about the second situation? What happens when the product is a breakthrough innovation that might be difficult for consumers to easily evaluate? How does traditional market research work when attempting to predict the success of the first fax machine or the first VCR? In order to answer these questions, we need to make a distinction between two very different approaches to new product development—Market Driven and Market Driving strategies.

Market Driven strategies begin with an unmet customer need. An example would be to add internet-enabling technology to a Palm PDA. The traditional new product development process described above is perfectly suited for this kind of situation. Customers are known, they can be easily surveyed, their needs are explicit, and we can test customer satisfaction with the new product. These types of product innovations are frequently described as being "incremental" (where consumers do not need to be educated about the use and functionality of the new product). The role of marketing is not only to carefully research the unmet customer needs but also to devise a marketing plan that effectively communicates the availability of the incremental innovation at an acceptable price point and at a convenient distribution place. Although this seems quite simple to state, it is much harder in practice as evidenced by Motorola's experience in cellular telephones. By focusing on building the best analog phone in the world and ignoring customer interest in digital technologies, Motorola saw its market share halved in the late 1990s as competitors like Nokia, Ericsson, and Qualcomm entered the market.

Market Driving strategies begin with a new technology. An example might be the original Palm PDA. Here we cannot rely on the traditional new product development process. Who are the customers likely to be? A horizontal slice of the general public or a vertical slice of specific professions (e.g., physicians, sales representatives) where a hand-held computing device might be useful? And if we were to simply survey potential customers, how clearly might they be able to articulate their need for a product that they have never seen or considered? These types of product innovations are frequently described as being "breakthrough" (where consumers need to be educated about not only where the product might be purchased but also why they might need such a product). In such situations, the nature of market research tends to be more qualitative than quantitative. A small sample of "lead users"[5] (i.e., those who have characteristics of being "Technology Enthusiasts," see Geoffrey Moore, *Inside the Tornado,* HarperCollins Publishers, 1995) is observed in its usage of product prototypes in a beta test. Sometimes this involves a cross-functional team of engineers, design experts, and marketing managers visiting such lead user sites to observe the product being used.[6] The role of marketing in such a situation is to create customers rather than simply satisfy current customers in order to build an entirely new product category. This can be a very difficult task as evidenced by the failure of the Palm's category predecessor, the Newton PDA developed by Apple, which was eventually taken off the market only a few years before the Palm's incredible success. It is very important in a Market Driving strategy not to be so technology-obsessed that the firm pushes the product at its customers. Such a technology-push is referred to as feeling "superior to the market" and can lead to the dangerous situation of entirely ignoring all customer input (see George Day, *The Market Driven Organization,* New York, NY: Free Press, 1999, chapter 2).

Summary

This note outlines the role of marketing in creating value both within and outside of the firm. In order to make a contribution within the firm in terms of building a customer-focused corporate culture, developing the value proposition and positioning, and detailing

---

[5] Eric von Hippel, "Lead Users: A Source of Novel Product Concepts," *Management Science* 32, no. 7, July 1986, 791–805.

[6] Edward McQuarrie and Shleby McIntyre, "Implementing the Marketing Concept through a Program of Customer Visits," in Rohit Deshpandé, *Using Market Knowledge,* Thousand Oaks, CA: Sage Publications, 2000.

FIGURE 4.3

	Market-Driven Strategy	Market-Driving Strategy
Nature of Product/Service	Incremental Innovation	Breakthrough Innovation
Creates	New Product, Line Extension	Truly New Product Platform, New Category
Customer Goal	Satisfy/Delight Current Customers	Create Customers
Nature of Customer Needs	Expressed	Latent
Nature of Market Research	Quantitative Research Methods (e.g., customer surveys, test markets)	Qualitative Research Methods (e.g., lead-user observations, focus groups)

the 4 P's of the marketing mix (product, pricing, place or channel, and promotion); marketing needs to research customers and their expressed or latent needs. This voice of the customer can then be heard in the new product development process either in a Market Driven strategy (to serve expressed customer needs) or Market Driving strategy (to create customers) as seen in **Figure 3.**

Chapter  5

FreeMarkets OnLine

V. Kasturi Rangan

As Glen Meakem and Sam Kinney, the two co-founders of FreeMarkets OnLine, Inc., grabbed their sandwiches on the way to the conference room, their thoughts focused on how to position their company, both with clients and the capital markets. Finally, by January 1998, nearly three years after starting their business, they had something that was working—their company's monthly revenues were sufficient to cover its $300,000 monthly burn rate. The company had achieved 1997 revenues of almost $1.8 million, and was aiming for over 200% growth in 1998 to $6 million. The two founders were already looking beyond that to when the company's revenues and valuation would allow them to raise a large amount of growth capital and provide investor liquidity through an IPO. But before that might happen, they knew they needed to lay out a clear and compelling strategy which would create the most value.

Founding

FreeMarkets OnLine was founded in Pittsburgh in 1995 by three entrepreneurs. The founders chose Pittsburgh to take advantage of the city's unique blend of industrial and high-technology infrastructure. Important were its location close to major manufacturing centers, a hub airport, and a strong local skill base in both software and manufacturing. Having purchased the interests of the third founder, for all practical purposes Glen Meakem and Sam Kinney constituted the firm's founding team: their equity, combined with other equity investments, launched the company's technology and business development efforts.

By the end of 1993, it had been clear to Meakem that he had stumbled on a very big opportunity. Having worked on purchasing studies for clients while a member of McKinsey's Houston office, he knew that industrial buyers faced tough challenges sorting through the variety of suppliers available for any given purchase. His impression was that the average

Professor V. Kasturi Rangan prepared this case as the basis for class discussion rather than to illustrate either effective or ineffective handling of an administrative situation. The author would like to thank Professor Kannan Srinivasan for his input in developing this case lead.

skill level of buyers in a wide range of manufacturing companies was low and the information available to help them make decisions was very limited. For a wide range of industrial input components and materials, identifying truly high quality suppliers while also establishing fair market prices (including total acquisition costs) was extremely difficult. Because of these challenges, industrial buyers were unaware of the savings opportunities still lurking beneath their decisions, Meakem had concluded. So it was only natural that when he left McKinsey to join a *Fortune* 500 company's corporate business development group, he began working on purchasing improvement projects.

Even before Meakem arrived at the company, it was experiencing success by conducting supplier negotiations as "silent auctions." A group of suppliers would be assembled in a hotel ballroom surrounded by flip charts. On each flip chart was the most recent price bid by a supplier on a component like a casting or a machined part. Over the course of the day, prices dropped as suppliers participated in this open price discovery process. But the logistical difficulties of bringing together all of the suppliers made these events difficult to replicate.

Network technology could change all this, thought Meakem, who remembered an article he had read in the May–June 1989 issue of *Harvard Business Review*, "The Logic of Electronic Markets," by Thomas Malone, Joanne Yates, and Robert Benjamin:

> That's where electronic markets come in. Electronic markets offer cross-company electronic connections, just as single-source sales channels do, and therefore give customers the same convenience. But they include offerings from competing suppliers. Not only do customers have electronic connections to their suppliers but they can also choose which suppliers they want to use. From the customers' perspective, then, electronic markets are more desirable than single-source sales channels. If the technology exists to create electronic markets and customers want them, it is just a matter of time until services arise to meet that need. Making an unbiased electronic market is a potentially profitable business in its own right.

Working with another manager in this *Fortune* 500 company, Meakem led the development of a rudimentary interactive bidding system. They fielded this version in September 1994. And it worked—interactive bidding among competing suppliers generated price savings.

All the while, however, it became clear to Meakem that in order for such a bidding system to work, some important groundwork had to be put in place. First, the bidding was only as good as the product specifications. The suppliers needed a precise understanding of the components or materials on which they were bidding, including related services like delivery and inventory management. Second, results depended upon having the right suppliers involved. When these "lower tech" issues were not addressed, electronic markets failed. When he approached the company about backing a full-service approach, he found that managers were focused on the technology itself. Meakem concluded that he would have to make this happen on his own. Consulting legal counsel, he was advised that he needed to make an absolutely clean break, take nothing—no presentation documents, no supplier names, no software or documentation.

Meakem set up shop in his basement with his vision of what network technology would do to industrial markets. According to Meakem:

> It's an interesting challenge, starting a business in an industry that has yet to be created. I like to use the term "going to the basement" to describe early entrepreneurial ventures like ours. You start with very little—no team, no cash, no market, no technology, no product, no customers, and no business model. Fortunately, I did have four critical assets: an idea, experience, my Rolodex of contacts from my previous experiences, and about $75,000 of savings. I also had my wife Diane. Despite the fact that we had two children under three years of age, she was very supportive.

Sam Kinney, like Glen Meakem, had several years of experience under his belt, including five years of consulting at Booz-Allen and then McKinsey, and two years as a budget director at Lucas Aerospace. Sam Kinney described the genesis of the firm:

> Glen and I had been colleagues at McKinsey after he graduated from the Harvard Business School and I from Tuck (Dartmouth). After two years, Glen left McKinsey and I, too, was itching to leave to start a company. When Glen came up with the electronic bidding idea, I jumped at it, because it was a very good fit. We knew each other and liked working together and had similar entrepreneurial aspirations.

Meakem explained how they arrived at the name:

> You have to balance multiple objectives. The name must evoke in potential clients and investors a sense of what the business does. But to be acceptable as a trademark, you typically have to invent new words or new uses of words because you cannot trademark obviously descriptive names. We also felt that with the pace of Internet startups, there would be a land grab for good names in this field.

They settled on "FreeMarkets OnLine" to satisfy a number of objectives. First, it seemed to portray the essence of what the business would do—create a fair and open exchange. Second, it appeared to be available for trademark registration. Third, it would signal to investors through "OnLine" that this was a business that could partake in the venture capital and IPO boom emerging around the Internet.

Software Development

Creating the software necessary for bidding became the most time-consuming early challenge. By mid-1995, when FreeMarkets had to commit to technical design decisions, the Internet was just beginning to be recognized as a powerful new medium. Netscape's IPO, one of the milestone events in publicizing the Internet, was still three months away. Internet service providers were in the throes of upgrading to 28.8 modem speed and meeting demand—few were able to offer any technical assistance.

FreeMarkets wanted the system to be fast, allowing real-time interaction. Although a few relatively static bid boards for industrial components existed, most stayed open for days before closing. The company wanted to create a truly interactive market to close not after days, but in only a few hours. That presented some technical challenges. According to Vincent Rago, Vice President of Information Technology:

> Our needs have always been one step ahead of the development tools. As a result, we have had to solve problems before ready-made solutions have been available. People speak about the costs of being on the "bleeding" edge of technology. While we haven't cut any arteries, we've clearly had to absorb some nicks and bruises.

Despite the lack of tools, FreeMarkets tested its BidWare and BidServer software by October 1995. On its maiden voyage in November 1995, the software conducted a live bid for about $3.2 million worth of injection-molded plastic appliance parts.

"It was a thrilling feeling," recalled Meakem.

> At the end of that first Competitive Bidding Event (CBE), Sam, our whole team, and I were screaming and cheering as though we had just put a man on the moon. Seeing real suppliers bid across a network for real business using our BidWare technology was electrifying. It was a resounding validation of our concept.

See **Table A** below for a brief description of an online Competitive Bidding Event:

TABLE A

> It's 1:00 P.M. EST. The purchasing team from one of the world's largest manufacturers of air-conditioning equipment has gathered in a headquarters conference room to watch as 12 companies from across the United States and Canada engage in a live Internet bidding event in competition for new business.
>
> The stakes are high: nearly $2.5 million worth of precision-machined parts in eight categories, or "lots," will be awarded as a result of this bidding event. During the preceding weeks, both the manufacturer's purchasing staff and prospective suppliers have been preparing for this moment with the help of FreeMarkets OnLine, the leading provider of on-line industrial market-making services. Now all sides are ready. The buyer and 12 suppliers log in to a secure private network with FreeMarkets OnLine's BidWare software, and the bidding begins.
>
> Within minutes, the buyer has saved thousands of dollars from its historic spending level. New bids come in every couple of minutes, driving the unit price lower and lower. By 1:45, the buyer has saved tens of thousands of dollars below its historic costs—and there are still more than two hours remaining before the bidding concludes.
>
> Excitement in the room continues to build, as expectations for significant savings increase. By 3:45, the bidding intensifies as time begins to run out. The total savings now stands at more than $300,000, and bids are becoming even more frequent.
>
> Shortly after 4:00 P.M., the bidding ends. More than 250 interactive bids were received. All told, this air-conditioning equipment manufacturer saved more than $400,000—a 16% savings below its historic spending level of $2.5 million—thanks to FreeMarkets OnLine's innovative approach to on-line industrial market making.

The first CBE was also a resounding confirmation of the company's ability to design, build and ship user-friendly commercial software. According to Meakem,

> I am passionate about the need for software to be self-trainable and easy to use for "normal" people. I am very much a follower of Scott Cook at Intuit in this regard. From the early versions of BidWare right through to the present, we have proven that we can understand a market need, then design, build, and test complex, wide area networked, client-server applications. In what has been a capital constrained environment, our software development team has not wasted any money.

Addressing the issue of how to successfully build software, Vincent Rago, Vice President of Information Technology, offered this perspective:

> Money is not the key issue in software development. Yes, if you can't pay really talented software designers and engineers, you don't have a development effort. But the bigger issue is focus—focus by the development team on a real set of customer needs, including high level market or business needs, detailed functionality, and usability. You can spend $50 million and completely fail in a software development effort. You can also spend $500,000 and create great software. Small teams fueled by intense senior management focus build great software. Large teams without focus fail.

In addition to proving out new software, early pilot CBEs thrust FreeMarkets into the operational elements of building Requests for Quotation (RFQs), identifying and recruiting potential suppliers, and supporting the bidding as suppliers participated from their place of business. "This was the moment of truth," declared Meakem, "where we had to put into practice the full-service vision. In addition to achieving excellence in operational tasks, we needed to become at least as knowledgeable as our clients about the industries in which we made markets, and we needed to get there fast." According to Kinney:

> At that point, we thought of ourselves as being in the competitive bidding business—selling Competitive Bidding Events to buyers and running our technology in ways they never could. We were successful at developing reasonable expertise and market knowledge, and what became apparent was just how much of this was "art" rather than "science." The dynamics of

each CBE—who was hungry, how hard the parts were to make, what was happening to material prices—made each CBE a very unique experience. That's when we began to see ourselves in broader terms—as "market makers" in industrial products.

The imagery of "market making" stuck, and became a powerful influence on the development of the company. Project managers are known in FreeMarkets as Industrial Market Makers. Their job is to lead the art and science of making markets for custom products, where each buyer in the market has his own set of objectives and issues.

The Market

"Unglamorous as it may sound, industrial purchasing is big, big businesses," wrote *Investor Relations* magazine (May 1997, pp. 75–77):

> In the U.S. alone, some $600 billion worth of industrial intermediate components are sold each year. The average U.S. manufacturer spends some 55 percent of sales on direct material purchases. And with labor downsized to the bone, but Wall Street still clamoring for ever higher margins and continual earnings growth, purchasing would seem to be a logical place to look for efficiencies.

According to Kinney there were many reasons why buyers should find value in a service which helps assemble suppliers into electronic bidding sessions:

> First of all, many supply industries are very fragmented. For example, in the $20 billion U.S. market for injection molded plastic parts, there are 3,000 suppliers. Second, in some of these industries the productivity variance between suppliers in the top quartile and the bottom quartile is simply enormous. In industries like plastic materials and metal stampings, the top quartile is 80–100% more productive than the bottom quartile. Some suppliers are really that much better. Third, in the face of this fragmentation and variation, buyers are left with an information problem—too many potential alternatives and no good way to sort them out. Buyers have had to rely on supplier sales representatives, themselves not disinterested parties, to educate them about the markets.

Meakem and Kinney knew that some degree of focus was necessary to ensure early success and prevent diluting the effort across too many fronts. They knew that in the industrial markets, some products were truly so sophisticated or rare as to require tight partnerships between buyers and suppliers. Other products had already become commodities—where market prices were reasonably easy to discover using published sources or quick telephone solicitations. The team decided to concentrate in the middle—those components which were not commodities, but for which competitive supply markets existed. According to Meakem, "The technique is most successful when the product is specifiable, when competition among suppliers is sufficient, and when the buyer's purchase is large enough to stimulate that competition." **Table B** describes the types of components which made up the target market. Using a couple of different estimating techniques, FreeMarkets concluded that this market was still huge—over $300 billion in the United States alone.

TABLE B

No-tooling Custom Components	Low-tooling Custom Components	Transferable-tooling Custom Components
Fasteners	Machined parts	Stampings
Service center metals	Metal fabrications	Castings
Specialty chemicals	Corrugated packaging	Plastic moldings
Electronic components	Printed circuit boards	

The target market decisions would emerge as an early source of differentiation for FreeMarkets. "What many observers of electronic commerce fail to realize," offered Kinney, "is that industrial purchasing is dominated by 'custom' products—those made by a supplier to the buyer's blueprint. Most electronic commerce applications are for standard products like light bulbs and gloves." This distinction was made clear in an *InformationWeek* article (November 13, 1997):

Catalogs, which involve one buyer and one seller at a time, is the largest [market] segment, accounting for 60% of the $8 billion market [for business-to-business electronic commerce]. Noted examples include companies such as AMP, Cisco Systems, Dell Computer, and National Semiconductor selling to corporate buyers, resellers, and distributors via the Web. Intermediaries such as GE TPN that post sellers' catalogs, also fit into this category.

The [upward price] *"auction"* model also involves an on-line bidding event, but buyers compete for a successful bid from a single seller. Web startups such as FairMarket in Boston and FastParts in Chicago are testing this model, which has seen success in the business-to-consumer market through OnSale Inc. and more recently Internet Shopping Network's FirstAuction site.

The [downward price] *"bid"* model, which involves real-time bidding [by] multiple suppliers [to sell to a buyer], is the only one of the models that will increase its market share [of business-to-business electronic commerce] in the next five years, according to Forrester [Research].

But all three approaches [*"catalog," "auction,"* and *"bid"*] will grow dramatically as the overall business-to-business E-commerce market more than doubles annually to reach $327 billion by 2002.

The Organization

Exhibit 1 shows the company's organization structure. According to Meakem:

Our business requires an eclectic blend of skills. We have a very high speed software development team, a network operations group, senior level client sales, a laser targeted consulting ability, an information agency, and a back office all in one company. We have grown up this way from the beginning so we do not have the organizational integration problems characteristic of so many information, software, and consulting companies. We work in cross functional teams both to make markets and to develop and build software and information products.

The fact is we are in the business of selling and delivering a complex conceptual service. This service is made possible by people, process, software products, and unique information. The fact that our service is difficult to deliver, requiring a blend of organizational skills, is our second most important competitive advantage. Our most important competitive advantage is the fact that we serve our clients very well, and they trust us in return.

The Sales Model

Another important decision with long-term ramifications was how the company would sell its services. Convinced from the start that the message needed to reach senior executives and purchasing decision makers, it began to build a direct sales model. This direct model consisted of high bandwidth "client developers" networking into and establishing relationships with senior level Purchasing, Operations, and Finance executives at large targeted corporations.

By January 1998, the company had two full-time senior "client developers." Everyone else on the eight member senior leadership team also had a direct role in client development. In particular, Meakem and Executive Vice President and COO David Becker spent significant amounts of their time pursuing client development activities. According to Meakem,

EXHIBIT 1 Organizational Structure

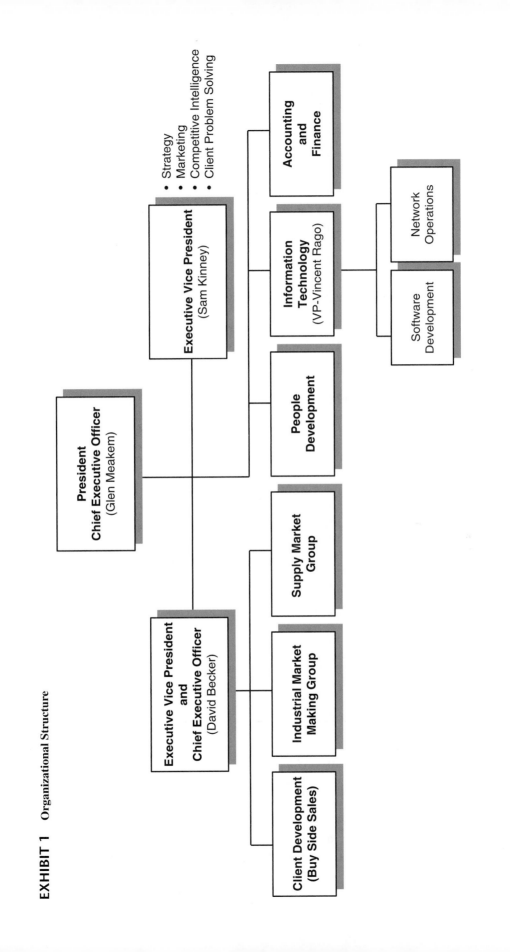

"old fashioned senior level sales will always be the life blood of our business. No one ever tells you this in business school, but without people who can sell a concept, ask for money, and close deals, you are dead."

Shunning the popular practice among Internet startups of "press-release marketing," FreeMarkets operated under a media silence policy from its founding until January 1997, fully 21 months into its existence. It put up a single-page Web site with the company's address and phone number. Kinney explained:

> We were trying to find multimillion-dollar negotiation projects for purchase of mission-critical parts. We were doing this by convincing senior level executives to take a chance with us on millions of dollars of their purchasing spend. We didn't then believe, nor do we now, that this true industrial-strength commerce will happen as a result of a passive Web presence. Further, so much of the value of market making is off-line that it really would have confused matters to have solicited business directly via the Web.
>
> Too many people give away too much competitive intelligence through the press and on their web sites. We didn't want to open ourselves up to copying before we had established our presence. Now, however, as recruiting has become a bigger part of our challenge, we've sought publicity and built a real Web site (http://www.freemarkets.com). At this point, the risks of silence far outweigh the risks of publicity.

The client development effort was aimed at finding those opportunities where the buyer would be likely to engage FreeMarkets to use its technique in sourcing a basket of products. Typical situations were supplier consolidations, annual negotiations, or when corporate-wide purchasing savings projects were underway.

The Market-Making Process

The company's core service was to provide Online Industrial Market Making services which culminated in real-time Competitive Bidding Events, also known as CBEs. In these events, a single industrial buyer used the FreeMarkets BidWare software and a secure, private network to allow a number of potential suppliers to simultaneously submit price bids against one another, as they attempted to win a buyer's purchase order. The on-line auction process used by the company created a level of competitive intensity among suppliers that was more intense than sealed bidding or face-to-face negotiations.

The key enabling technology was FreeMarkets's proprietary BidWare software for buyers and suppliers and the company's proprietary BidServer software which ran CBEs from its server in Pittsburgh. On either end of the network were user-friendly software applications which ran in the Microsoft Windows 95 and 97 environments. BidWare for Suppliers contained the functionality that allowed suppliers to monitor "market" prices, submit bids, and print valuable market benchmarking reports. BidWare for Buyers contained the functionality to monitor the bidding and print detailed results reports.

The five steps in the FreeMarkets OnLine® Industrial Market Making process are shown and described below:

Phase 1: Identify Savings Opportunities

Phase 2: Prepare Total-Cost RFQ

Phase 3: Identify, Screen, and Support Suppliers

Phase 4: Conduct On-Line Competitive Bidding Events

Phase 5: Provide Post-Bid Analysis and Award Support

Phase 1: Identify Savings Opportunities FreeMarkets worked directly with buyers, analyzing spending and applying FreeMarkets's market-making experience to help buying organizations identify potential savings.

Phase 2: Prepare Total-Cost RFQ Since a detailed understanding of *all* requirements including logistics and quality levels was required by all competing suppliers, RFQ preparation involved much more than just providing drawings and volume forecasts. Working with client buyers and engineers, the FreeMarkets Industrial Market-Making Team created a comprehensive RFQ which defined all elements of total cost.

Phase 3: Identify, Screen, and Support Suppliers The FreeMarkets Supply Markets Team took the lead in identifying and contacting suppliers. Throughout this process, the Market-Making Team, along with the buyers they serviced, screened potential suppliers, narrowing the field to those whose capabilities best matched the buying organization's needs. FreeMarkets also provided extensive RFQ support to suppliers, answering questions and gathering feedback.

Phase 4: Conduct On-line Competitive Bidding Events Those suppliers selected by the buyer prepared their quotes with the support of the FreeMarkets team. All suppliers participated in training sessions to learn every aspect of BidWare, FreeMarkets's proprietary software used by suppliers, to submit real-time bids. On the bidding day, suppliers dialed into a secure global network. Buyers, meanwhile, watched the on-line bidding event from their facility.

Phase 5: Provide Post-bid Analysis and Award Support FreeMarkets followed up CBEs by collecting cost breakdowns from suppliers to validate quotes. FreeMarkets also supported final supplier analysis and qualifications to achieve optimal award decisions.

As indicated in the above description, the Online Industrial Market Making process was characterized by several stages. It usually started with interviews with the buyer and appropriate manufacturing and quality personnel, during which all the specifications—technical, commercial, logistical, and quality—were spelled out. FreeMarkets's industry experts assisted, drawing on their knowledge of the relevant manufacturers' processes and supply market conditions. This initial step was laborious and detailed, but was absolutely necessary in developing the Requests For Quote required for dissemination to the various potential suppliers.

According to Executive Vice President and Chief Operating Officer David Becker (a business school classmate of Meakem's):

> Our market-making staff works as a cross-functional team. In addition to the Industrial Market Maker who leads the team, we engage an Associate Market Maker who handles much of the supplier screening, and a Market Making Engineer who performs detailed part and drawing analyses to ensure drawings are correct and suppliers obtain complete, consistent technical information. The team is supported by our Supplier Support Group that handles RFQ questions and BidWare training. For this particular event, team members spend a number of days at the buyer's site, collecting the RFQ information, developing the lot-setting strategy, and selecting suppliers.
>
> The buyer also provides the technical documents and other requirements that become part of a solid RFQ. However, we try to take as much of the preparation workload off the buyer as possible. The time spent in preparing a great RFQ pays off on the back end, both in the quality of the bids and also because buyers can really implement the savings we obtain in the online marketplace. Suppliers understand exactly what they are bidding on, so the bids are real.

The next step consisted of grouping the various components (or part numbers) into several independent "all-or-nothing" lots. According to FreeMarkets OnLine's Jason Reneau:

> While a number of factors are important, it comes down to solid judgment and experience. First, the lots must make sense from the suppliers' point of view; that means, to the greatest extent possible, grouping parts with similar process requirements, sizes, volumes, materials, or tooling. It also means understanding differences in the buyer's quality, delivery, and technical support requirements. When the lots are properly set, we typically achieve a solid competitive outcome.

Simultaneously, FreeMarkets worked with the buyer to determine which suppliers to include for the bid, invariably introducing the buyer to several new suppliers who were capable of manufacturing the requested components. This was possible because of the up-front research done by them to unearth a larger pool of suppliers than traditionally used by the buyer. FreeMarkets prescreened every potential supplier. A detailed 10- to 15-page questionnaire was completed by each supplier. In addition to seeking general company information, the survey sought information on the supplier's marketing and sales, manufacturing, logistics, quality, and administrative systems. The most detailed part of the questionnaire was reserved for the targeted parts.

According to Glen Meakem:

> Buyers choose which suppliers they want to bid on their business. Incumbent suppliers are included if they're not already on the list, of course. And we've found that we introduce buyers to aggressive, world-class suppliers that they may not have known about before. So without incurring the cost of identifying and qualifying these new suppliers, buyers can allow them to bid on their business.

Finally, FreeMarkets uses its proprietary Bidware software and a global private network to hold an online Competitive Bidding Event (CBE) at a previously chosen time. According to Meakem:

> We help buyers create fair, open, and aggressive competition—that's what results in large purchasing cost savings. On average, we save our buyer clients 15%. The CBE enables the right pool of high-quality suppliers to take part in an online, interactive competition for business.

CBEs took place in real time, over a 90-minute to two-hour time period. Suppliers submitted electronic bids on various lots of goods using their BidWare software. Suppliers watched the other bids come in—and counterbid—but they didn't know the identity of their competitors. The buyer saw both the bids' dollar value and which suppliers were submitting the bids.

Exhibit 2 shows two buyer side screens during different auctions in process. Benchmarks to evaluate the bidding were built in. One tracked the savings compared to "historic" costs and the other tracked savings compared to the buyer's goal, called "reserve." An automatic "overtime" functionality meant that "lots" of business only closed when new low bids on each lot were no longer submitted by suppliers. Even after the close of the bidding event, winners were not necessarily the lowest bidder. The buyer considered factors such as the results of final quality audits in making the awards, and multiple awards were not uncommon. The key ground rules were that the "lots" were the absolute lowest unit of award, the buyer had to award the business only to suppliers who participated in the online market, and no follow-on negotiations were permitted. Approximately 50% of awards had gone to low bidding suppliers and approximately 35% had gone to second place bidders. **Exhibit 3** shows a bid history graph and results information from an actual lot.

EXHIBIT 2

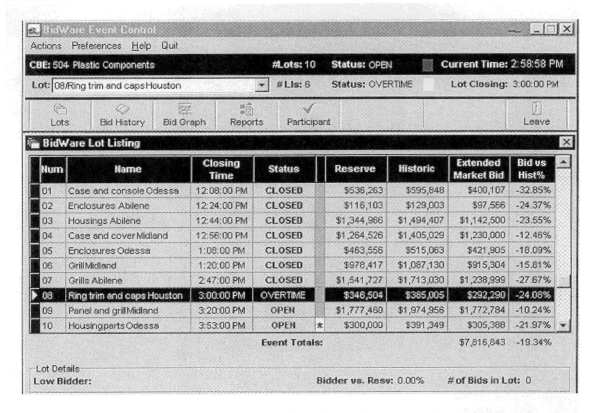

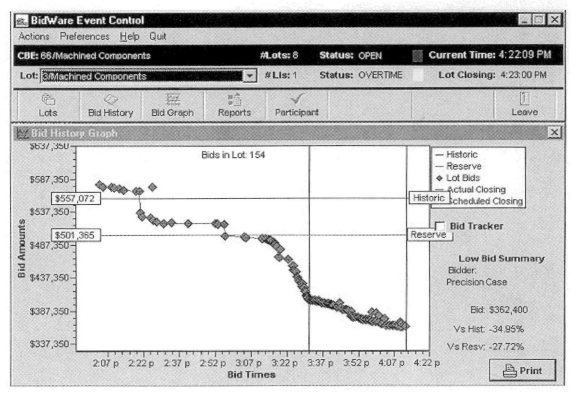

EXHIBIT 3 **Aggressive Lot Level Bidding Drives Buyer Savings**

Sample bid history from January 25th CBE - Lot 1: Strains & Reliefs

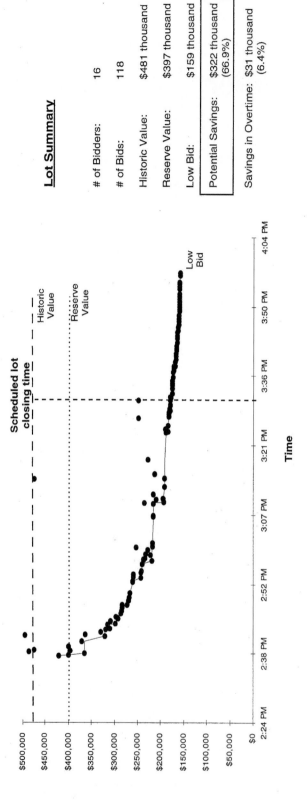

Lot Summary

# of Bidders:	16
# of Bids:	118
Historic Value:	$481 thousand
Reserve Value:	$397 thousand
Low Bid:	$159 thousand
Potential Savings:	$322 thousand (66.9%)
Savings in Overtime:	$31 thousand (6.4%)

Source: FreeMarkets OnLine, Inc. 1997

Note: Each dot represents a distinct bid for the lot by an individual supplier

The Revenue Model

"The revenue-generation model is at the heart of our new business development process," stated Kinney. He explained:

> We had a range of options available to us and only a few examples to follow. In 1995, all Internet businesses seemed to be built around a model of advertising revenue and site traffic. Popular focus was to build "content" and drive traffic to the site by registering with search engines. This type of model just wouldn't work for us—we add much of our value "off-line."

Meakem and Kinney knew from their consulting days that corporations to some degree would pay fees for the kind of value-added—big savings—that the electronic bidding technique could bring. Cash flow could be attractive using a consulting model, and that would make it much easier to build the business on a pay-as-you-go basis. But such a model could not deliver the equity upside that seemed possible in the Internet IPO market, an upside necessary to attract risk capital and risk-takers as employees.

A higher aspiration, they thought, would be to turn the electronic bidding technique into a completely new channel in the industrial markets. Creating a new channel brought with it a number of challenges, not the least of which was the articulation of the value model. But the channel idea had strong appeal. Kinney explained:

> We had always been intrigued by the transformation of consumer markets by the likes of Wal-Mart, Sam's Club, and category killers like Best Buy. The quality of products sold by traditional consumer brand marketers like P&G and Magnavox had never been higher, but the pricing pressure brought down upon them by powerful channel intermediaries was intense. No comparable channel intermediaries existed for many industrial products.

The obvious direct channel comparison in industrial markets was the manufacturer's representative. Many of the suppliers ultimately targeted for CBEs were accustomed to paying commissions to these representatives. But in the case of manufacturers' reps, each representative was tied to one particular supplier's offerings—there was no channel that stimulated a direct price comparison between two or more independent offerings. In essence, there was no channel designed from the buyer's perspective, only channels designed around the needs of suppliers.

In the end, the company chose a pricing model that was a hybrid of service fees and sales commissions. To make a competitive market for a basket of purchased components, FreeMarkets charged buyers a monthly service fee based on the size of the market-making team dedicated to the event. Typically, that fee was a fraction of the fee that a major consulting firm would charge. A typical project with a fair complement of engineering work would cost the buyer $75,000 per month for two to three months. Expenses such as travel and lodging were extra charges. In addition to the fee, buyers agreed that the winning supplier would pay sales commissions to FreeMarkets in lieu of the commission they might pay to a manufacturer's representative. The sales commission varied by supply industry. In general, though, FreeMarkets set the commission level at about one-half of the prevailing rate in order to provide the buyers a built-in level of savings off the current channel cost embedded in prices. For the industrial intermediate supply industries the company currently served, these commissions were generally 2.5% of purchase price. Commissions were paid in installments as suppliers shipped products to buyers. Most contracts the company placed were annual contracts which could be renewed; therefore, commissions resulting from any particular Competitive Bidding Event could flow for two or three years.

Under normal circumstances, suppliers would have paid manufacturers' representatives a 4%–7% commission for effecting the sale of their products to the buyers. Manufacturers' representatives usually carried many lines of complementary but noncompeting products.

That is, they represented many suppliers across a wide range of markets. FreeMarkets On-Line effectively disintermediated the manufacturers' reps by "repping" all of the competing suppliers in a given bid at once.

The fee plus commission pricing model had its benefits and challenges. According to Meakem:

> Industrial buyers do not really understand channels that well. To them, the channel is the sales rep—the same channel that prevailed in Henry Ford's day. Channel evolution has been so glacial in industrial markets that we are forced to sell a very new concept. At times, buyers have a hard time understanding why the commission is a fair compensation model for us. But we persevere in making this sell, because we are confident in the value we add. Our sales commission and the industrial purchasing channel we represent is the right answer for buyers, suppliers, and our investors. In the end, the commission cost is typically trivial compared to the savings we generate for buyers.
>
> In addition to the selling challenges, the commission presents cash flow hurdles for us. A typical bid is for the annual quantity of products a buyer will purchase. The commission is only due from suppliers after the product ships, so the revenue stream from commissions amounts to a small monthly payment that does not begin until months after the bulk of the service costs have been incurred. We also face the administrative costs of tracking commissions and the chances for yield loss. On the benefit side, commissions usually last well beyond the first year. Currently, we have a little less than two years' experience collecting these commissions, but we believe our average commission stream will run for over two years.

A Successful Start

From the time of its founding in 1995 until the end of 1997, the company had handled 38 different CBEs for 15 buying clients, resulting in purchase awards totaling approximately $70 million over 40 different suppliers. The savings over historical costs to the buyers ranged from 1% to 43%, with the weighted average being 15%. Four of the company's 15 buying clients were repeat customers, and the company believed it would serve virtually all of its buying clients again. **Table C** provides a brief overview of the company's performance through 1997, and **Exhibits 4** and **5** provide detailed financial statements.

On the buyer side, the company's client base consisted of 15 *Fortune* 500 companies who had engaged FreeMarkets to make one or more industrial markets. Four of these companies had emerged as stable ongoing users of the service. On the supplier side, over 300 companies ranging from *Fortune* 500 conglomerates to small manufacturing houses had signed the company's Supplier Representation Agreement and participated in online bidding. Overall, its clients represented a wide cross-section of industries. Buyers were from both North America and Europe, while suppliers were from across the globe. See **Exhibit 6** for a summary of actual online market results through January 1998.

Importantly, of the company's 1997 revenues of $1.8 million, over $350,000 was from supplier sales commissions. The company's plans were for achieving $6.0 million in 1998 revenue, with over $200 million of new business being awarded to suppliers. "By the year 2000, suppliers will win over $500 million per year worth of purchase contracts through our online market channel," predicted Meakem.

TABLE C

$000s	1995 (9 months)	1996	1997
New Annual Purchase Awards	$249	$23,424	$46,831
Revenues	16	409	$1,783
Profits (losses)	($922)	($1,431)	($1,016)

EXHIBIT 4   Statement of Operations

Source: FreeMarkets OnLine.

	Actual FY 1995	Actual FY 1996	Actual FY 1997
Revenues			
Buyer fees	$ 10,000	$ 270,500	$ 1,425,000
Supplier commissions	6,512	138,320	358,179
Total revenues	16,512	408,820	1,783,179
Cost of Service—Market Making			
Payroll	11,372	327,108	801,601
Payroll taxes	1,105	28,727	60,583
Health benefits	278	18,163	36,645
Bidware cost and amortization	4,010	31,083	42,894
Other direct costs and office allocations	7,331	100,610	166,906
Total cost of services	24,095	505,691	1,108,629
Gross profit	(7,583)	(96,871)	674,550
Operating Expenses Technical Operations			
Payroll	40,837	59,408	97,019
Payroll taxes	3,520	5,226	8,045
Health benefits	1,074	3,234	5,186
Network expense	—	70,772	60,890
Other direct costs & office allocations	29,187	4,851	49,363
Total technical operations	84,618	143,491	220,503
Technical development			
Payroll	178,610	253,704	208,663
Payroll taxes	15,911	19,793	15,74
Health benefits	4,515	8,714	7,597
Other direct costs & office allocations	133,814	112,055	63,849
Total technical development	332,850	394,266	295,883
Client Development and Marketing			
Payroll	25,164	198,042	325,200
Payroll taxes	2,070	1,134	18,290
Health benefits	697	3,003	6,618
Travel and meals	—	53,252	91,143
Marketing and printing	—	43,349	62,057
Other direct costs & office allocations	31,455	17,155	42,066
Total client dev. and marketing	59,385	320,935	545,374
General and Administrative			
Payroll	152,383	207,030	275,173
Health benefits	4,173	10,425	14,889
Payroll taxes	12,598	23,110	20,310
Professional fees	69,713	81,239	160,034
Other direct costs & office allocations	198,499	153,821	158,467
Total general and administrative	437,366	475,625	628,882
Total Operating Expenses	914,219	1,334,317	1,690,642
Net Income/(Loss)	$(921,802)	$(1,431,188)	$(1,016,092)

The company had just shipped out its second-generation proprietary global bidding system, BidWare 2 and BidServer 2, but it would need to constantly keep at the cutting edge of software development. Depending on the technical development agenda the company chose to pursue, at least $5 to $10 million would be needed over the next five years to develop new, improved, and expanded software products for the industrial marketplace. As the company expanded, its current staff of 43 people would also need to grow, especially because of the heavy upfront customization work needed in the early stages of the bidding process. The current market making team consisting of 23 people was capable of handling

EXHIBIT 5 Balance Sheet

	Dec-95 Actual	Dec-96 Actual	Actual Dec-97
ASSETS			
Current Assets			
Cash and cash equivalent	$ 106,496	$ 557,648	$1,925,008
Accounts receivable	7,579	148,787	1,052,337
Other current assets	7,125	5,550	8,001
Total current assets	$121,200	$711,985	$2,985,346
Office furniture and equipment			
Office furniture and equipment	94,930	172,151	263,850
Accumulated depreciation	(11,680)	(36,861)	(74,384)
Net furniture and equipment	83,250	135,290	189,466
Other assets	101,825	137,572	91,149
Total assets	$ 306,275	$ 984,847	$3,265,961
LIABILITIES AND STOCKHOLDERS' EQUITY			
Current Liabilities			
Accounts payable	$ 185,112	$ 118,650	$ 88,360
Accrued liabilities	17,539	39,348	83,540
Current portion of debt	—	14,000	—
Total current liabilities	202,651	171,998	171,900
Long-Term Liabilities			
Long-term debt	—	21,000	58,332
Stockholders' Equity			
Preferred stock	—	85	187
Common stock	171	175	184
Additional paid in capital	1,025,255	3,144,580	6,404,441
Retained earnings (deficit)	—	(921,802)	(2,352,991)
Current year loss	(921,802)	(1,431,189)	(1,016,092)
Total stockholders' equity	103,624	791,849	3,035,729
Total Liabilities and Equity	$306,275	$985,847	$3,265,961

about four CBEs per month. Recruiting and training additional market making and software development staff would be of utmost priority, especially at a time when the company was attempting to rapidly ramp up to scale.

Going Forward to Scale

As Meakem and Kinney entered 1998, the fundamental question of how to position the company with buyers, suppliers, and investors was as important as ever. What kind of company should FreeMarkets make itself into in order to maximize its return to shareholders and make a lasting impact on industrial market making? This question was complicated enough but, making it even more difficult to tackle was the range of options which were now available to the company as it molded a business strategy going forward.

During their offsite meeting in early January, the eight member senior team had debated three critical strategic opportunities, but had failed to come to any solid conclusions.

1. Horizontal Market Expansion or Vertical Market Dominance?

Impressed by the savings that FreeMarkets had generated for its buying clients, both existing and potential buyers had suggested new supply markets. Some of these new supply markets were near commodities like chemicals, pulp, coal, freight, and reinsurance. But even as these opportunities were coming in, there was internal momentum toward

EXHIBIT 6 FreeMarkets OnLine Marketplace History (US $000s—Unless Otherwise Noted)

CBE Number	CBE Date	Buying Client Number	Supply Industry	Historic Cost	New Market Cost	Potential Savings	(%)	Actual Commissioned Awards to Suppliers
1.	Nov-95	1	Plastic molded parts	$ 3,542	$ 2,837	$ 705	20%	$ 249
2.	Nov-95	1	Plastic molded parts	844	802	43	5	0
3.	Jan-96	2	Plastic molded parts	1,494	1,359	134	9	1,655
4.	Apr-96	1	Plastic molded parts	706	475	231	33	446
5.	Apr-96	1	Plastic molded parts	1,836	1,421	414	23	1,192
6.	Apr-96	3	Metal stampings	700	608	92	13	608
7.	May-96	2	Plastic molded parts	1,387	1,073	314	23	105
8.	May-96	2	Metal stampings	3,629	3,178	451	12	3,035
9.	Jun-96	4	Plastic molded parts	2,667	2,159	507	19	2,170
10.	Jun-96	4	Plastic molded parts	5,725	4,913	812	14	5,611
11.	Aug-96	5	Plastic molded parts	3,348	2,967	382	11	266
12.	Aug-96	1	Plastic molded parts	633	486	147	23	505
13.	Aug-96	1	Plastic molded parts	1,278	996	282	22	0
14.	Sep-96	1	Plastic molded parts	1,245	1,200	45	4	0
15.	Oct-96	2	Metal stampings	1,062	1,049	13	1	802
16.	Oct-96	6	Metal castings	1,055	923	132	12	0
17.	Nov-96	6	Metal machinings	4,014	2,862	1,151	29	2,798
18.	Dec-96	7	Chemicals	4,941	4,311	629	13	4,090
19.	Dec-96	8	Plastic molded parts	2,131	1,822	308	14	141
20.	Apr-97	6	Plastic molded parts	3,631	3,187	444	12	3,187
21.	Apr-97	6	Service center metals	19,048	18,859	188	1	6,290
22.	May-97	9	Plastic molded parts	7,878	7,684	194	2	0
23.	Jun-97	10	Metal machinings	2,743	2,590	153	6	1,202
24.	Aug-97	11	Metal fabrication	723	632	92	13	580
25.	Aug-97	1	Plastic molded parts	2,197	1,712	485	22	1,900
26.	Sep-97	6	Plastic molded parts	9,691	7,649	2,043	21	5,500
27.	Sep-97	6	Plastic molded parts	7,200	6,300	1,000	14	5,000
28.	Sep-97	12	Metal fabrication	5,653	3,261	2,391	42	2,772
29.	Oct-97	13	Pole line hardware	1,169	1,095	74	6	570
30.	Oct-97	13	Pole line hardware	1,625	1,607	18	1	800
31.	Oct-97	12	Metal machinings	6,102	3,473	2,629	43	3,600
32.	Oct-97	12	Specialty metals	3,375	3,010	365	11	3,100
33.	Nov-97	12	Service center metals	11,048	9,740	1,308	12	9,800
34.	Nov-97	12	Metal machinings	1,681	1,180	501	30	1,200
35.	Dec-97	14	Metal fabrication	4,213	3,920	292	7	NA
36.	Dec-97	15	Metal machinings	1,017	913	104	10	800
37.	Dec-97	15	Metal machinings	593	374	219	37	350
38.	Dec-97	6	Commercial valves	10,564	8,353	2,212`	21	NA
39.	Jan-98	14	Metal fasteners	535	399	136	25	NA
40.	Jan-98	16	Corn sweetener	31,200	30,000	1,200	4	30,500
41.	Jan-98	6	Printed circuit boards	24,500	14,000	10,500	43	16,000
42.	Jan-98	12	Metal machinings & fab	11,000	9,130	1,870	17	9,300
Totals				$209,620	$174,407	$35,213	17%	$126,304

seeking vertical market dominance in selected supply industries. It was argued by the supporters of this strategy that only through dedicated marketing efforts, including brand identity creation and tailored sales and pricing approaches, could FreeMarkets truly differentiate itself and showcase the huge value it brought to its clients. But this would involve a focused industry domination strategy which increased risk in the minds of some team members. "Given our current success," said Meakem, "there is no doubt that the path of least resistance is to follow the purchasing needs of our clients and not to focus too narrowly." But even as the team debated, new opportunities for horizontal market expansion were pouring in.

2. Technology and User Support Subscription Licensing?

Some buyers and third parties had requested that FreeMarkets license the bidding technology for their own use. Some had counter-proposed with buyer fees only—no commission. Based on direct customer requests, Meakem knew that there was a market for industrial bidding software similar to the BidWare/BidServer system exclusive of full-service Online Industrial Market Making. But, because the very nature of the technology and the benefits it provided required best practice purchasing skills and execution, there were strong feelings in the group that buyers who tried to use the bidding technology without high quality front end market making would tarnish the whole concept of online real-time industrial market making. This group felt that poorly executed markets would not yield real (and ethical) business results for buyers or suppliers. There was strong anecdotal evidence of this from suppliers who had dealt with Meakem's old employer. This group argued passionately that if FreeMarkets did license the technology, it should ensure that any resulting "marketspace" and support services (telephone training, etc.) be branded separately from FreeMarkets OnLine. "Pursuing this strategy will compromise our core business," Kinney had warned. But supporters had argued, "By having a strong position in the software and related services portion of the industrial on-line bidding space, the company could enhance its core full-service on-line industrial market-making business."

3. Networked Purchasing Information Systems?

In the course of working with its buying clients, the company had realized that buyers within large industrial companies had limited access to information about certain purchases. This lack of information extended within their companies as well as to the external market environment. Meakem wondered if it was possible to develop a Worldwide Web-based information system and service which met both the internal communications needs and the external information needs of buyers. A colleague had argued that FreeMarkets might be better off simply selling the information to information management companies. For example, the supplier survey done in support of various market-making events would be very valuable to many clients he had suggested. It was clear that any major business and technology development effort in support of these ideas would require major incremental external investment in the company.

What Next?

The senior team at FreeMarkets was convinced they had identified a set of real market needs and were at the leading edge of an important set of business applications and services to meet these needs. Recruiting at a furious pace to keep up with core market-making growth, they debated the direction and pace they should be taking to maximize the opportunity. "Euphoria is one thing, but it has to be based on sound business strategy," said Kinney. "So let's figure it out," urged Meakem.

Chapter

6

Xerox: Book-In-Time: The New Way to Market, Order, Print, and Fulfill Books One at a Time, Just in Time, Worldwide

V. Kasturi Rangan

Ranjit Singh, senior V.P., Internet and Software Solutions, and Frank Steenburgh, senior V.P. and General Manager, Graphic Arts, pondered the possibilities for commercializing what some considered a breakthrough printing process. Xerox's Book-In-Time (BIT) system could produce one 300-page book for $7, which was an enormous business advantage in a market where such economies were available to printers only when lot sizes exceeded 1,000 copies. A printing system, consisting of a document printer, color cover printer, and a binder, could add up to as much as a $1.5 million sale for Xerox, and open new business segments at printers who already owned Xerox equipment. Naturally, some senior executives viewed

Professor V. Kasturi Rangan prepared this case with research assistance from Jay Sinha. HBS cases are developed solely as the basis for class discussion. Cases are not intended to serve as endorsements, sources of primary data, or illustrations of effective or ineffective management.

BIT as a terrific opportunity to expand the company's copying and printing equipment portfolio. Michael Ruffolo, President, Document Solutions Group, had instructed Singh and Steenburgh to craft a commercialization plan in three months, in time for a divisional review by June 1, 1999. According to Ruffolo:

> We would like to approach it with an open mind and consider the full gamut of opportunities. We could offer a service to authors, publishers, wholesalers/retailers, and book printers, or we could also be selling selected components and modules to different players in the book value chain. Successful commercialization is the challenge. We know that the technology works and will only get better as we shape our marketing plan in the next year.

Singh had spent 10 years turning around software/solutions-related initiatives for businesses big and small, and Ruffolo 10 years with computing and telecommunications giants NCR and AT&T, before they had converged at Xerox in the past 18 months. Among his responsibilities, Michael Ruffolo had worldwide profit responsibility for developing, marketing and delivering document products, services and solutions through global industry businesses dedicated to Manufacturing, Financial Services, Graphic Arts and the Public Sector. Xerox recorded over $7.0 billion in annual sales to these four industries in 1998. Stated Ruffolo, "The sales resources to successfully commercialize Book-In-Time lies in our Graphics Arts Business, which calls on the publishing and printing market. What we need is a successful start-up plan and a way to transition it to scale." Frank Steenburgh, head of Graphic Arts, was a Xerox veteran with over 25 years of sales, marketing, and product development experience in the printing and publishing marketplace.

Xerox Corporation

Xerox, with 1998 revenues of $19.4 billion, a net income of $1.69 billion before a restructuring charge, and an operating profit margin of 13.6%, was one of the great comeback stories of the decade. Whereas in the 1980s it was a stand-alone, black-and-white, analog copier company, by 1999 it had transformed itself into a networked, color, digital company that sold document solutions to its customers worldwide.

In 1998, the company's operations were organized by four business groups:

Office documents The largest of Xerox's four business units, with worldwide sales of $10 billion in 1998, this group sold black and white digital and light lens copiers and color copiers/printers to offices.

Production systems With worldwide revenues of $5 billion in 1998, this group manufactured and sold large production publishing and printing systems. The company had made a decisive move in the nineties to embrace the digital world. Indeed, its future thrust was on document technology enabled by computers and digital printers in a networked environment. The company had launched the highly successful DocuTech Production Publisher in 1990, which accounted for over $2 billion of its 1998 revenues.

Channels group Given the rapid explosion of the SOHO (Small Office Home Office) market segment in the eighties, Xerox chose to approach this fragmented market through conventional retail channels (office supply stores like Staples, Office Max, and Office Depot, mass merchandisers like Sears, and superstores like Wal-Mart) and value added resellers (e.g., Pinacor, Tech Data). This unit, with 1998 sales of $1.4 billion, was one of the fast growing businesses within Xerox. It essentially sold the lower end of the Office Document product line through retail and reseller outlets.

Document services group This $3 billion group provided industry consulting, systems integration, network services and outsourcing to major accounts. This fast-growing Xerox business (approximately 40% growth rate in 1998) served over 6,000 client companies in 40 countries.

Until 1998, Xerox's Customer Operations, with approximately 15,000 sales reps and 20,000 service technicians, sold the products and services of the four business groups. But in January 1999, Xerox announced a series of initiatives designed to allow the company to better capitalize on growing digital market opportunities and create greater value for customers and shareholders by aligning by industry rather than geography.

"We believe these changes will better align Xerox to serve its diverse customers, increase the effectiveness, efficiency, and breadth of our distribution channels, and provide an industry-oriented focus for global document services and solutions," stated Xerox President and Chief Operating Officer G. Richard Thoman. "This migration to an industry global account and solutions focus will evolve over the next couple of years. Our goal is to have our large customers view us as "strategically relevant" to their businesses, he added.

As a result of the 1999 changes, the Document Solutions Group, headed by Ruffolo (see **Figure A**), was not only responsible for the sales of all products, services, and solutions to the Graphic Arts, Manufacturing, Financial Services, and Public Sector businesses, but also had accountability for the three business units that comprised the former Document Solutions Group.

FIGURE A   Document Solutions Group

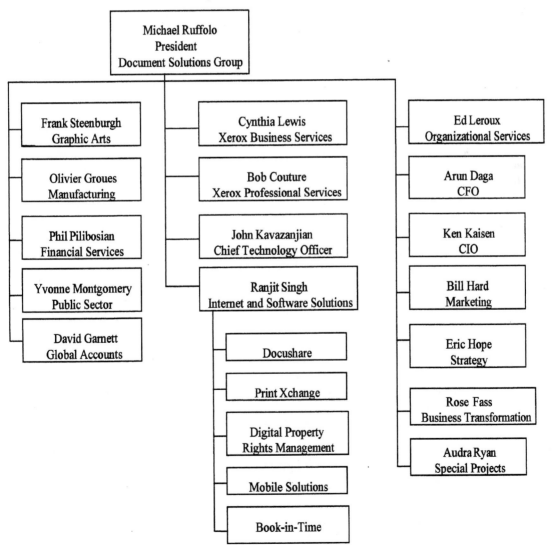

The Book-In-Time project reported to the Internet and Software Solutions unit headed up by Ranjit Singh. This group was charged with commercializing PARC-developed (Palo Alto Research Center, Xerox's in-house research lab) technology and building software platforms across various industry segments. Book-In-Time was one among a handful of promising new projects such as Docushare and Print Xchange. John Stempeck had headed up the Book-In-Time project from 1996–1998, before moving on to a different job. He was instrumental in moving the project through its incubation to its current commercialization phase. Ranjit Singh was brought in from a different business unit of Xerox to guide the commercialization of the various new project ideas.

Xerox's group of research laboratories, especially PARC, was highly reputed for its breakthrough inventions. According to an authoritative book:

> Highly visible contributions in information technology from PARC gave rise to a new computing paradigm that became populated by an amazing array of techniques and technologies, including personal computing, client-server architecture, graphical user interfaces, local area networks, laser printing, bit maps, page description languages, and object-oriented programming. It was also true, however, that some of these technologies were better exploited commercially by other entrepreneurs. The most famous example is the Graphical User Interface (GUI) system that launched Apple Computer as a serious personal computer player.[1]

Xerox had sold GUI to Apple for what many managers at Xerox and Apple now consider "a song." GUI was only one among several inventions that Xerox licensed out in the 1970s and 1980s for little return. Its inability to seize on certain commercial opportunities during this period was explained by its managers:[2]

- Investment was technology focused but failed to consider how the customer would evolve into the technology's use.
- Insulated [ourselves] from rapidly emerging markets because of commitments to existing markets.

At that time, many within Xerox considered its strength to be in Sales and R&D, with its workforce of 15,000 sales reps and 20,000 service technicians respected as one of the best in the business; its weakness, as a lack of ability to envision changing market needs and influence its evolution. Xerox had considerably altered its new product commercialization process to address a number of these problems.

Xerox followed a rigorous phase-gate process in evaluating new projects and bringing them to market. Called TTM (time to market), the process broadly had 5 phases, starting with the idea-generation stage where usually a white paper was prepared regarding the technology/business opportunity, followed by prototyping and initial announcement. Depending on the success of the project through the first three stages, the fourth step was broad commercialization. The final phase involved the implementation of an after-sales service and customer satisfaction plan. From phase to phase, a senior management team thoroughly evaluated the technology and business parameters for ultimate success. The Book-In-Time project was one of a dozen in Michael Ruffolo's portfolio, having consumed about $5 million of R&D and an operating budget of $1 million/year during the last two years in phases 2 and 3. The project had reached the initial announcement stage and would soon need a firm business plan before broad commercialization.

Ranjit Singh interpreted the phase-gate review process as follows:

> The structured process was designed for big pieces of equipment involving considerable engineering and tooling up. In reality, for internet- and software-type products, we whip the project through only three steps. Prototyping and commercialization go hand-in-hand. We need to think big, start small, and scale up fast.

[1] "Research and Change Management in Xerox," by Mark B. Myers, Chapter 4, *Engines of Innovation,* edited by Richard S. Rosenbloom and William J. Spencer.
[2] Ibid.

TABLE A
U.S. Book Sales by Segment ($millions)

Source: Association of American Publishers.

	1992	1995	1996	1997
Adult trade, Total	3,484.2	4,234.1	4,195.4	4,095.2
Hardbound	2,222.5	2,646.9	2,586.0	2,410.2
Paperbound	1,261.7	1,587.2	1,609.4	1,685.0
Juvenile, Total	1,177.4	1,326.7	1,447.6	1,358.0
Hardbound	850.8	836.6	867.7	887.7
Paperbound	326.6	490.1	579.9	470.3
University press	280.1	339.7	349.3	367.8
Religious, Total	907.1	1,036.9	1,093.4	1,132.7
Bibles, hymnals, & prayer books	260.1	293.0	294.8	285.4
Other religious	647.0	743.9	798.6	847.3
Mass market paperbacks	1,263.8	1,499.6	1,555.1	1,433.8
Book clubs	742.3	976.1	1,091.8	1,145.3
Mail order	630.2	559.5	579.5	521.0
Professional, Total	3,106.7	3,869.3	3,985.0	4,156.4
Business	490.3	617.6	721.4	NA
Law	1,128.1	1,400.4	1,429.8	NA
Medical	622.7	809.3	815.8	NA
Technical & scientific	865.6	1,042.0	1,018.0	NA
College texts & materials	2,084.1	2,324.8	2,485.8	2,669.7
El-Hi texts & materials	2,080.9	2,466.2	2,619.1	2,959.6
Standardized tests	140.4	167.3	178.7	191.4
Subscription reference	572.3	670.8	706.1	736.5
Other	449.0	476.0	493.2	510.0
Total net sales	16,918.5	19,947.0	20,780.0	21,277.4

NA—Not Available.

According to Singh, scale-up was crucially dependent on the robustness of the technology. "It is a constant juggling game," added Singh. "Say I have $50 million for seven projects. This year I know we will kill two or three and replace them with new projects with better business potential. The trick is to make those decisions fast and decisively and move to commercialize hot prospects."

Book Industry Overview

In 1997 the book market was valued at $92 billion in worldwide sales (at the end user/consumer level); printing expenditures amounted to about $20 billion. A total of 8.5 billion books were printed worldwide.[3] The U.S. accounted for 2.4 billion books valued at $21 billion in retail sales. The book market was growing at approximately 5% per year, of which 68% of titles were in paperback format and 32% in hard cover; 69% of titles were non-fiction and 31% were fictional.

Products within the U.S. book publishing industry could be divided into the following six major categories: adult trade, juvenile trade, mass market, professional, college, and ELHI (elementary and high school). Trade books, representing the largest share of the book market, encompassed all general interest publications, such as adult and juvenile fiction, nonfiction, advice, and how-to books. See **Table A** for book sales by market segment.

As the U.S. economy began to recover in the mid-1990s, the outlook for the book publishing industry also began to improve. Shifting demographics pointed toward higher enrollment levels in schools and colleges, while the federal government appeared likely to increase funding for libraries and the arts. Many publishers expected growth among medical and healthcare-related titles to correspond with the concerns of the aging U.S. population,

[3] Source: Xerox.

FIGURE B
U.S. Book Channels
System (1997)

Source: Xerox.

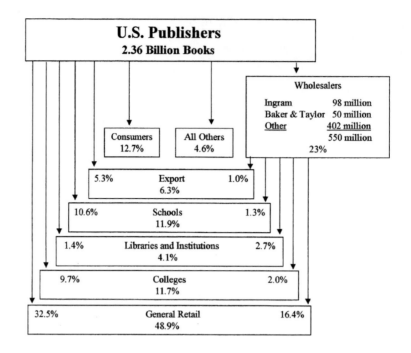

as well as growth in professional and technical titles to support rapid changes in office technology. In general, industry analysts expected the U.S. book market to grow at 6% to 8%.[4]

Market research by Xerox revealed that:

- 53% of books were selected by subject, only 22% due to author's reputation.
- Publisher name/imprint was simply not a factor in the consumer's reason for purchase of a particular book.
- 55% of books were planned purchases and 45% were bought on impulse.
- 81% of books were bought for oneself, whereas 19% were purchased as a gift.

While Xerox did not break up its research by professional and scientific versus popular books, a wide dispersion was believed to exist on the above numbers between the two groups.

The Distribution Value Chain

Nearly 77% of all book sales in the United States were made to customers, institutions, or retail chains, and 23% were routed through wholesalers. **Figure B** sketches the flow of products from publishers to channels to markets. **Exhibit 1** provides further detail on units sold and average price points by channel category.

Publishers

The book publishing industry faced many changes entering the mid-1990s. Observers noted that the industry, once characterized as gentlemanly and literary, had quickly become more cutthroat and businesslike. *National Review* cited as evidence the trend for large publishing houses to replace long-time chief executives, best known for their "literary sensibilities," with industry outsiders steeped in "modern management techniques." As a result, many employees within the publishing industry shifted focus from building relationships with authors and carefully tailoring manuscripts to cutting costs and analyzing profit and

[4] U.S. Industry Profiles, Printing and Publishing.

EXHIBIT 1 **1996 Distribution Channel Analysis**

Source: Company documents.

	Dollars	Units	$/Unit	Dollar Share	Unit Share
Sales to retail/consumer					
Publisher sales to general retailers	$5,379,200,000	766,400,000	$ 7.02	27%	32%
Publisher sales to consumers	2,855,900,000	298,700,000	9.56	14	13
Wholesaler sales to general retailers	1,754,300,000	386,200,000	4.54	9	16
Total	$9,989,400,000	1,451,300,000	$6.88	50%	61%
Sales to other channels					
Publisher sales to colleges	$2,855,900,000	228,000,000	$12.53	14%	10%
Publisher sales to libraries & institutions	780,700,000	33,600,000	23.24	4	1
Publisher sales to schools	2,714,500,000	251,000,000	10.81	13	11
Publisher sales for export	1,291,100,000	125,100,000	10.32	6	5
Publisher sales to all other	217,400,000	107,600,000	2.02	1	5
Wholesaler sales to colleges	348,000,000	47,100,000	7.39	2	2
Wholesaler sales to libraries & institutions	1,379,300,000	62,800,000	21.96	7	3
Wholesaler sales to schools	341,100,000	30,400,000	11.22	2	1
Wholesaler sales for export	201,300,000	23,200,000	8.86	1	1
Total	$10,129,300,000	908,800,000	$11.15	50%	39%
Total sales by channel (from either publisher or wholesaler)					
General retail	$7,133,500,000	1,152,600,000	$6.19	35%	49%
Consumers	2,855,900,000	298,700,000	9.56	14	13
Colleges	3,203,900,000	275,100,000	11.65	16	12
Libraries & institutions	2,160,000,000	96,400,000	22.41	11	4
Schools	3,055,600,000	281,400,000	10.86	15	12
Export	1,492,400,000	148,300,000	10.06	7	6
All other	217,400,000	107,600,000	2.01	1	5
Total	$20,118,700,000	2,360,100,000	$8.52	100%	100%

loss statements.[5] An industry insider noted that an increasing trend among modern day publishing houses was to move the profit targets higher and higher, from the historical 8% to 10% to 12% to 15%.[6]

Over 40,000 companies participated in the book publishing industry in the mid-1990s. However, the industry was dominated by several giant publishing houses. According to *Trade Book Publishers, 1996: Analysis by Category,* the top 12 trade book publishers accounted for nearly 85% of the overall U.S. book publishing market. These large publishers consolidated many of the smaller imprints in the early 1990s in order to cut costs and reposition themselves for the onset of electronic publishing. However, this concentration of power among relatively few publishers led to criticism from some quarters regarding the quality and diversity of materials published. Industry observers saw an increasing role for smaller presses to publish works of literary quality that did not necessarily have enormous sales potential. (See **Table B** for the world's leading book publishers.)[7]

Printers

According to industry sources, the worldwide printing market was worth about $20 billion. The industry had been relatively stable through the 1990s, with modest increases in revenue. Employment in the industry had been decreasing slowly as more and more aspects of the

[5] Ibid.

[6] Ibid.

[7] Ibid.

TABLE B **World's Leading Book Publishers (1997)**

Source: Compiled from public sources by casewriter.

Company	Sales $ (B)	World Share (%)	Brief Description
1. Bertelsmann	$5.0	5.4	Bertelsmann publishing was part of Bertelsmann AG of Germany, the 3rd largest media company in the world, with interests in publishing, music, television, online, film, and radio. In March 1997, it had finalized a $1.5 billion deal to acquire Random House (#6).
2. Warner Books	$4.0	4.3	Warner Books, the publishing arm of the media giant Time Warner, Inc., also had interests in film, television, and publishing.
3. Simon & Schuster	$2.4	2.6	Simon & Schuster, one of the world's largest educational book publishers and publishing arm of media blockbuster Viacom, was heavily involved in the Internet, published books under imprints such as Macmillan, Prentice Hall, and Scribner.
4. Pearson	$2.0	2.2	Pearson Books, a publishing unit of Pearson, the United Kingdom media group, published books under the imprint of Penguin and Ladybird.[8]
5. Readers Digest	$1.7	1.8	Readers Digest Assn. engaged in publishing and direct marketing, creating and delivering products, including magazines, books, recorded music collections, home videos, and other products.
6. Random House	$1.6	1.7	Random House Inc. was the world's largest English-language general trade book publisher.
7. Groupe de la Cite	$1.5	1.6	Groupe de la Cite was France's #1 book publishing house and one of France's leading CD-ROM publishers.
8. Grupo Planeta	$1.4	1.5	Grupo Planeta was a Spanish company involved in publishing and sales of reference books and important works.
9. Hachette Liure	$1.4	1.5	Hachette Liure was a French book publisher and distributor.
10. Reed Books	$1.3	1.4	Reed Books, the publisher of Reed Illustrated Books, which produced *The Joy of Sex,* Marks & Spencer cookery books, and Sir Terrance Conran's *The Essential Garden Book,* had been sold in a £33 mill. management buyout. The creation of the new company Octopus Publishing Group ended Reed Elsevier's foray into consumer publishing.
11. Harcourt Brace	$1.2	1.3	Harcourt Brace was the publishing and educational services subsidiary of Harcourt General, Inc., a premier global provider of educational products and services.
12. HarperCollins	$1.0	1.1	HarperCollins was owned by News Corp. Ltd., a giant media company based out of Australia.
Total	$23.1	25.0	

printing process were being automated and computer controlled. See Table C below for the leaders in this market.

R.R. Donnelley, Quebecor, and Banta were the leaders in book printing. The industry was fragmented, with as many as 40,000 printing presses in the United States alone. According to Jack Klasnic, an industry consultant, the top 25 accounted for about 25% of industry volume. Of the remaining, 500 printers accounted for another 25% of industry volume and the rest for the remaining 50%. Small presses (less than 20 employees) usually focused on brochures, pamphlets, and the like because they did not have the appropriate offset printing machinery (35" × 23" press) to gain production economies for book printing. A large percentage, 95% or more, of all print jobs were accomplished by the offset printing process, machinery for which was supplied by industry giants like Heidelberg from Germany. The printing machinery industry was consolidated with Heidelberg,

[8] Pearson Books also owned Simon & Schuster. It bought the company from Viacom for $4.6 billion in 1998.

accounting for nearly 50% of worldwide marketshare, followed by Mitsubishi (from Japan) and MAN-Roland (also from Germany). The market size for printing machines was estimated to be about $10 billion worldwide in 1997. The cost of a 35" × 23", 4-color web press (i.e., paper fed in rolls) was between $1 million and $2 million, but when one added the cost of all the ancillary equipment on the printing line, costs could run upwards of $5 million.

Among the other printers shown in **Table C,** some such as Hallmark and American Greetings were specialized in-house support for the company's greeting card operations. World Color Press was heavily into magazine covers. Others like Deluxe Corporation specialized in printing checks, and Moore Corporation in business forms. But with the advent of electronic cash and advanced word processing software, the check printers like Deluxe and form printers like Moore were considering alternate markets. A large percentage (95% and more) of all print jobs were accomplished by the offset printing process, which involved developing the text on a metal plate for imprinting on paper. This required printers to buy printing presses from suppliers like Heidelberg. Xerox's digital printers like DocuTech served a complementary market, mainly office printing of documents. Xerox, IBM, and OCE (a Dutch-based operation partly owned by Siemens) were the three main providers of equipment to this nearly $5 billion worldwide market. Xerox was the clear leader, with a 50% share.

Wholesalers

Ingram, the largest wholesaler, traded close to 100 million books in 1997. Its nearly half a million titles in stock was the most extensive of any book wholesaler in the world. Ingram was renown for its superb 24 hour to 48 hour shipping service to its retailers. It received most of its orders electronically and operated warehouses in seven locations. Ingram was the logistics backbone behind Internet retailer Amazon.com's rise to fame. In November 1998, however, it was announced that the $600 million (in sales) wholesaler was acquired by the retail chain of Barnes & Noble for $600 million in cash and stock. Industry commentators speculated that this must have been a welcome deal for both. Net margins at the wholesale level were rumored to be at 1% to 2%, and that combined with inventory turns of only 4 to 5, made it a very difficult business in which to make money.

The #2 wholesaler, Baker & Taylor, operated two business units. The first was Baker & Taylor Books, which supplied books, books on tape, calendars, and other information services to more than 100,000 libraries, schools, and bookstores in the United States and abroad. It sold some 50 million books a year from about 25,000 publishers. The second unit, Baker & Taylor Entertainment, supplied videos, CDs, cassette tapes, interactive games, CD-ROMs, and software to some 25,000 libraries and retailers in the United States. It offered more than 50,000 video titles and 70,000 audio titles. The company had recently launched Replica Books, a unit that published and sold licensed out-of-print titles—to both

TABLE C
Printing Companies with the Highest Sales, Ranked by Sales in 1996 ($millions)

Source: *American Printer,* American Printer's 100 + (annual), July, 1995, p. 28+.

1. R. R. Donnelley & Sons (Chicago, IL), with $6,599.0 million
2. Hallmark (Kansas City, MO), $3,600.0
3. Quebecor Printing Inc. (Quebec, Canada), $3,110.3
4. Moore. Corp. Ltd. (Ontario, Canada), $2,517.7
5. American Greetings Corp. (Cleveland, OH), $2,172.3
6. Deluxe Corp. (St. Paul, MN), $1,895.7
7. World Color Press Inc. (New York, NY), $1,641.4
8. Banta Corp. (Menasha, WI), $1,083.8
9. Quad/Graphics (Pewaukee, WI), $1,002.1
10. Treasure Chest Advertising Co., Inc. (Glendora, CA), $900.0

the parent company and other wholesalers—at a premium of about $5 over the original price.[9] All Replica Books were produced on Xerox DocuTech production systems.

Retailers

Even though the U.S. market was served by nearly 12,000 independent retailers, the top four retail chains—Barnes & Noble, Borders, Crown, and Books-A-Million—accounted for over 75% of market share. The top two, Barnes & Noble (sales $2.5 billion, 700 stores) and Borders (sales $1.8 billion, 300 stores), dominated the market. A unique aspect of the Barnes & Noble and Borders strategy was their extensive network of 25,000- to 30,000-square feet superstores. Unlike mall-based bookstores, many of these superstores were stand-alone, aimed at the destination shopper. Superstores offered comfortable browsing areas, coffee bars, and special events such as book signings, author readings, and children's story hours. They were usually open longer hours (9 A.M. to 11 P.M.), and generally provided for a variety of customer conveniences.

Barnes & Noble and Borders reported pre-tax net margins of 3% to 5% and inventory turns of about two. The independent bookstores fared worse, and many were barely profitable. Many independents believed that the big superstores were able to eke out a 3% to 5% additional rebate from publishers for a variety of promotional and merchandising activities that the smaller stores could not match.

Apart from retail consolidation and the growth of superstores, the other major buzz in the industry was online retailing. Amazon.com with 1998 sales of about $540 million (and net losses of about $50 million) had created a distribution model whereby it offered readers nearly two million titles from its wholesalers' and publishers' stock, even though it carried only about 2,000 of the fastest-moving titles in its own inventory. By eliminating retail margins, Amazon was able to offer deep discounts of 20% to 30% on many titles. Shipping was effected from its distribution facilities and was usually fulfilled within two to five days of receiving the order, depending upon which books it had in stock and which it had to order from wholesalers. Customers paid shipping charges. Amazon was renown, not only for its excellent customer service, but also for its unique ability to assemble a database of a community of customers with similar reading tastes. Thus, as part of selecting a book, a customer would be able to access peer comments on a book and also Amazon's recommendation for similar books. Both Barnes & Noble and Borders copied Amazon's popular model. Bertelsmann had paid $200 million for a 50% equity stake in Barnes & Noble's online spin-off.

Economics of the Value Chain

On a typical 300-page paperback book, retail-priced at $25, a 48% margin would be paid to the trade. Of the publisher's selling price, nearly 20% covered manufacturing costs (paper, printing, and binding), 20% covered author royalties, rights, and permissions, overhead was about 30% including sales and marketing costs, and when the 25% costs of book returns were factored in, publishers could earn about a 5% margin at best. The practice of accepting unsold books in the pipeline had long been an industry tradition, and while the return percentage varied over book categories (nearly 40% for mass market paperbacks to 15% for profession texts), the cost of accepting the returned books and disposing of them at discount prices added a huge cost burden to the publishing industry. By comparison, internet retailers like Amazon.com returned less than 2% of their wide selection, giving publishers a reason to consider alternative models of production and distribution.

[9] "Leadership Online: Barnes & Noble vs. Amazon.com," by Pankaj Ghemawat, HBS case No. 798-063, May 26, 1998.

Cost per book was a function of print run size. For example, per-unit fixed costs for mass-market paperback publishers were low because the number of copies printed was large—often more than 500,000 in the first run. By contrast, a specialized professional book printed in a small quantity incurred the same composition and plant costs that would be required to print a general interest title expected to sell many copies. For a book with a short run, these fixed costs were spread over a smaller number of books, raising the per-unit cost.

The following example for a typical 300-page book from an offset printing process details the up-front cost elements. After the text was composed on a word processor, a film was made as an intermediate process, usually 16 pages to a sheet. At a cost of $50 to $75 a sheet, that meant a $1,000 cost. The films were then converted to plates for mounting on the printing rollers, which added an additional $1,500 cost. On top of it, if one included $1,000 for the labor involved in mounting the plates on the print roll and the depreciation cost of the machinery to make the film and the plates (about $500,000 to $750,000 capital cost), the first book carried with it an overhead of $3,500 to $5,000.

The cost of acquiring the paperback rights to a successful hardcover title or buying the rights to an unreleased book by a popular author could run into the millions of dollars. When these costs were spread over a high-volume output, the author's fee was within a range that enabled publishers to eke out a profit. But when books flopped, the publishers took a beating. By comparison, authors of professional books were usually paid a flat royalty rate (10% to 15% of retail selling prices) only after the books were sold.

Trade and paperback publishers generally printed far more copies than they expected to sell to the book buying public. They permitted retailers to return all unsold books for a full refund. This was costly to the publishers because returns entailed handling, freight, processing, and disposal at a lower price through alternative channels. On average, roughly 25% of all publishers' book shipments were returned by retailers in any given year, although the actual percentage varied widely by category. Millions of dollars were spent by both publishers and retailers to ship unsold books back and forth. Other variables affecting the return rate were the relative sizes of a publisher's backlist and frontlist. A publisher with many backlist nonfiction titles usually had much lower returns than a publisher that emphasized new fiction, because a frontlist title by definition was new to the market, while a backlist title such as *Tom Sawyer* was tried and true. On average, about 25% to 30% of a publisher's sales came from titles on its backlist.[10]

Book Acquisition

The books that made up a publisher's list arrived in a variety of ways: some as completed manuscripts, either by an author or through a literary agent; others were "commissioned," whereby a contract was signed before the author started writing the work.[11]

When a finished manuscript arrived, its initial destination was the editorial department. Here it was usually allocated to an editor who was responsible for judging its merits for publication. In some cases, the editor did not independently evaluate the manuscript but sent it to outside experts.[12] This was usual for highly specialized or technical works. After the manuscript had been read and evaluated, a decision was made on its acceptance, rejection, or revision. If accepted, it took between nine months to a year for the book to appear in print.

[10] *Standard & Poor's, Industry Surveys—Publishing*, April 23, 1998.

[11] I. See R. Escarpit, *The Book Revolution* (London: Harrap, UNESCO).

[12] M. Lane, *Books and Publishers* (Lexington Books, 1970).

Commissioned works followed a somewhat different course. A contract for them was usually signed on the basis of a proposal agreed to between the publishing house and the writer. It was rare for a house to decline to publish a commissioned book, unless the completed manuscript did not meet the terms of the proposal.

Book-In-Time Project at Xerox

Book-In-Time was a digital, low-cost, order-to-fulfillment system for the on-demand printing of books. Xerox's unique technology had been optimized for custom lengths of as low as one but could economically handle up to 1,200 or more as **Table D** below shows:

The biggest advantage of the Book-In-Time system was the cost for run lengths of 1,000 and below. **Table D** presents the approximate costs of four types of offset printing and a comparison of Xerox's Book-In-Time system. At run lengths of less than 25 books, other printing methods would have to incur a minimum cost of $5,000 or so, whereas Book-In-Time could conceivably deliver at a cost of $6.90 per book.

Beyond a run length of about 1,200 copies, the traditional printing method was extremely efficient because of the tremendous speeds at which the printing presses were able to print the multiple copies. Moreover, Xerox's Book-In-Time was a sheet-fed rather than a web- (or roll) fed operation, thus limiting the possibilities for binding and finishing. But sheet-fed presses were more flexible, especially with respect to changeover and set-up time between operations.

Over the years, Xerox engineers had perfected a system whereby any book transcript that was digitally stored in a central server could be downloaded to a DocuTech production printer, resulting in a high quality printed book block. The multicolored (laminated) cover would be simultaneously printed on a DocuColor machine and would come together with the book-block at the binding machine. The system was capable of printing a 300-page book at the rate of one book per minute. In order to facilitate the printing of books that were out of print or which did not have a digital input file, Xerox engineers had designed a system where the material could be accurately scanned to yield a digital starting point. This usually cost about $150 for a 300-page book, and an additional $100 for the cover. This step was followed by a "mastering" phase that enabled an optimal set-up for the printing process to follow. Currently it took Xerox technicians close to a full, 8-hour shift to master one book, but process development was underway to cut it down by at least half or more. Even though the system was not currently configured to provide hardbound books, developers at Xerox thought it was only a matter of time before the feature would be built in. The production process is shown in **Exhibit 2.**

TABLE D   **Unit Cost versus Run Lengths (300-page softcover book)**

Bookrun Lengths	38" Web Press	40" Sheet Fed Press (or roll fed)	28" Sheet Fed Press	Short-run Digital Printer	Book-In-Time
Less than 25					$6.90
25	$179.42	$169.64	$228.29		$6.90
50	90.07	85.29	114.70		$6.90
100	45.39	43.12	57.89	$11.47	$6.90
250	18.59	17.82	23.82		$6.90
500	9.66	9.38	12.46	$3.85	$6.90
1,000	5.19	5.16	6.78		$6.90
2,000	2.95	3.06	3.94		$6.90
3,000	2.21	2.35	2.99		$6.90
4,000	1.84	2.01	2.51		$6.90
5,000	1.62	1.80	2.23		$6.90

Sample Implementation Scenario

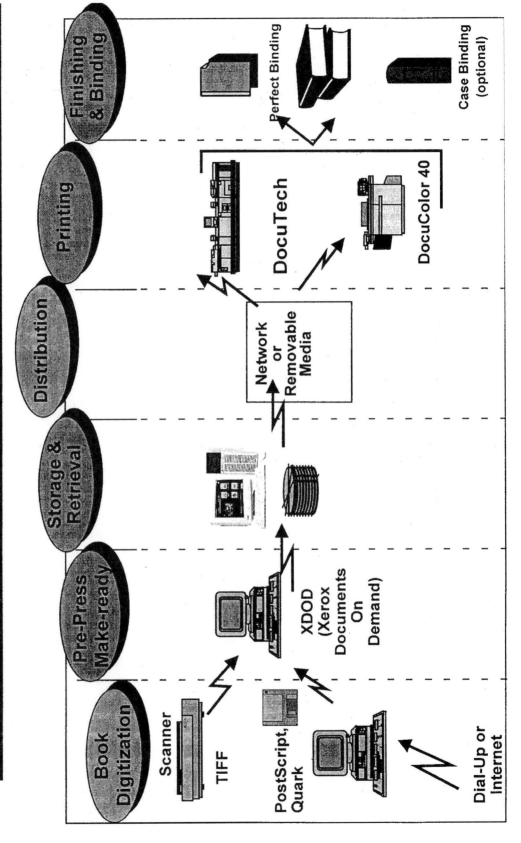

The typical list price of the main components of the production process were:

1. Xerox DocuColor 40 (with front end) $195,000
2. DocuTech 6180 Production Printer $330,000
3. Horizon Binder $80,000
4. Scanner and related software/hardware $150,000
5. Server/glue software $140,000

John Stempeck and his team of about 15 engineers operating out of Xerox facilities in Burlington, Massachusetts attempted to estimate the size of the market for Book-In-Time. "The market is enormous," offered Stempeck:

> In the United States alone, about 50,000 new titles and about 1.5 million repeat titles were printed last year. But the real interesting statistic for us is the 1 million titles that were out of print. Of course, worldwide (including the United States) that number turns out to be 1 million new titles and 25 million repeat titles printed last year and a whopping 20 million titles out of print. One has to only ask the question—Why were these titles out of print? Obviously because the demand was too low. Here is where our low volume technology can be a big boon for the industry.

Added Ranjit Singh: "In the digital world, the market becomes instantaneously global, so the potential market is about twice as big. Currently, small runs are usually sent out to the Far East because of the lower costs, but that means a 8 to 12 week lag time. We are talking about 24-hour shipment."

The market for on-demand, short-run books was not confined to the tail end of a typical book lifecycle alone. Even at the front end, review copies, complimentary copies, and galley proofs were usually printed in lots of less than one thousand. Even before the books went out of print, each subsequent edition was for small lots as well.

An internal Xerox study had projected the following estimates of U.S. volume that could be converted to "on demand" (see **Table E**):

John Kavazanjian, Chief Technology Officer, offered this perspective:

> We are up against entrenched ways of doing business, all the way from production to distribution, sales, and marketing. Breaking this traditional mindset requires a paradigm shift in the way in which we approach the market, and that is not easy. It is not whether the digital revolution will occur; it will and, indeed, ten years from now, the world will be a very different place. Our dilemma is to spot that window in the next three to seven years when the real change will take place. We have to be ready to move when the window opens.

TABLE E
On Demand Conversion Potential

Category	Market Share %	Number of Books (millions)	On Demand Conversion Potential (%)
Trade	36	864	2
Textbooks			
Subscription reference	1	24	100
College	7	168	50
Elementary—high school	10	240	4
University press	1	24	50
Professional	7	168	50
Subtotal:	26	624	37
Mass market paperbacks	23	552	n/a
Religion	7	168	n/a
Book club	5	120	n/a
Mail order	4	96	n/a
TOTAL	**100**	**2,400**	—

Xerox's two big challengers in the digital printing industry were IBM and OCE. IBM's equivalent digital printing equipment would cost the user about $3 million (compared to $1.5 million for Xerox). IBM's equipment was roll fed and according to Stempeck "occupied much more space." In terms of print quality, there was no apparent difference between IBM and Xerox. In terms of costs, experts thought Xerox had an advantage in small runs (less than 1,000) and IBM in long runs. Ingram, the largest book wholesaler in the United States, had leased IBM equipment and had entered into an exclusive agreement with IBM to operate a press by the name of Lightning Print. The main function of Lightning Print was to provide support for Ingram's wholesaling operation by reducing its inventory of infrequently ordered books. Lightning Print, however, sold its excess capacity in the open market. OCE, on the other hand, was not as active in the United States as it was in Europe. But IBM's printing division was rumored to be up for sale. The printing division, with $2 billion in 1997 sales, was up for sale at about $2.5 billion.[13]

A Lightning Print publicity release claimed that 140 publishers had used its services to print and distribute books. Ingram had placed Lightning Print's On Demand titles in its Advance Plus systems, which provided information of availability of its books to 13,000 bookstores and 9,300 libraries.

Meanwhile, Xerox in Germany had struck an arrangement with Georg Lingenbrink GMBH, the leading German book wholesaler, which marketed under the name Libri. System infrastructure and system operations were based on newly developed software by Xerox and Deutsche Telekom. This was to ensure customer-oriented data administration and the protection of electronic files against charges and access of third parties. Customer-related print releases and invoicing based on orders entered were guaranteed. Monthly statistics about the electronic title stock as well as the number of books ordered gave the publisher and Libri important economical control data. Libri obtained the simple reproduction rights for the Book on Demand titles from the publisher. The calculation and fixing of the retail price was carried out by the publisher on the basis of the usual trade margins and the production costs offered by Libri. After the editing of the print master, Libri produced two samples for acceptance by the publisher. After that the publisher generally had very little to do. At the end of the month, Libri credited the publisher's account with the margin based on actual customer offtake. **Exhibit 3** provides a line drawing of the Book-In-Time concept.

Xerox also ran a document technology center (DTC) in Waltham, Massachusetts. Modeled after the German operation, the Waltham facility was completely equipped with the full array of digital scanning, printing and building equipment. The National Academy Press had entered into an arrangement with DTC to transfer 500 titles to its operations. The Libri and DTC facilities served as prototyping centers for the Book-In-Time team. The pure operating costs (omitting R&D) at each center could be covered at a production volume of 250,000 books at 25% margin. While the Libri facility was managed as an "outsourcing" operation, the Waltham DTC was owned and operated by Xerox.

Options

Michael Ruffolo did not wish to leave any opportunities unexplored, including the option of setting up a chain of technology centers to get into the actual book production business. This could involve work on behalf of publishers, printers, wholesalers, retailers, or even direct customers and consumers. Stempeck envisioned the upside potential of the Book-In-Time brand value, "Imagine, we will be able to deliver a book that will look the same as the original, be delivered in the same timeframe, and be reasonably priced to any market around

[13] "IBM Seeks Buyer for Global Network," *Wall Street Journal*, September 1, 1998, p. A3.

EXHIBIT 3

Source: Company documents.

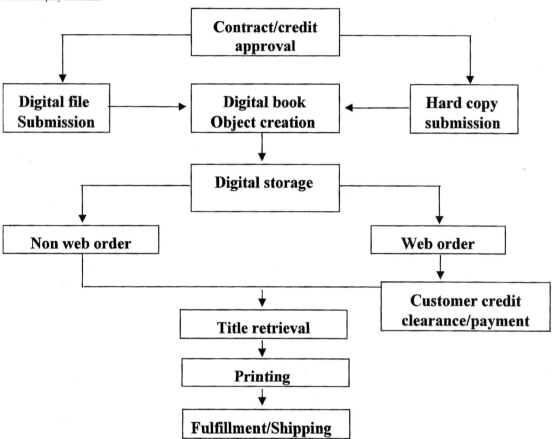

the world. In other words, we are striving to create a can of Coca Cola!" Stempeck had even toyed with the idea of service franchising, as well. But for the time being, senior managers at Xerox were actively evaluating two options:

1. The Graphic Arts salesforce had already expressed an interest in undertaking the task of selling the Book-In-Time system of equipment to all potential buyers in the value chain, from publishers and book printers to retailers. Of course, there always was the possibility that customers would ease into the production operations by buying system components first. Indeed, many commercial printers already owned many of the parts of the BIT system. It appeared to be a matter of integrating many of those pieces into a system, combined with software and services that leveraged Xerox's present organization. Frank Steenburgh had expressed, "If this is the way we want to do it, I believe we have real synergy."

2. The other option under active consideration was best articulated by Ranjit Singh, "We could expand our chain of document technology centers to get into the book production business. In essence, we would provide this as an "on-demand" service. Naturally, we would have to consider the channel implications for our Graphic Arts customers."

Chapter  7

Freeport Studio

Rajiv Lal   James Weber

We never lost confidence in Fran. But when you miss forecasts by 70%, you've got some problems. Our bet was Fran would find the solutions so we'd break-even by year two.

—Leon Gorman, President L.L. Bean, Inc. Freeport, Maine, October 1999

In November 1999, Fran Philip (HBS '83), senior vice president and general manager, faced some tough choices. Either she came up with a credible plan to make Freeport Studio profitable in the next year or risk having the business closed by its parent—retailer and catalog powerhouse L.L. Bean.

Freeport Studio was a new brand of women's clothing sold through a catalog. L.L. Bean created the brand in an effort to revive stagnating sales and reduce seasonal sales swings. After an intensive review of internal needs and external opportunities, L.L. Bean decided that a women's catalog clothing brand both fit well with the company's existing operations and had great potential in the marketplace.

Freeport Studio was launched with great excitement in January 1999. The excitement soon faded when sales for the first few months were below expectations. The business seemed to recover in the spring, but then the bottom fell out—results for July fell short of plan by some 70% and total fall demand (July–November) was off by 60%. First year sales estimates, which had been reduced from an initial $80 million to $66 million after the slow launch, were reduced again to $43 million after the fall catalog drop in early August. Any hope of a profitable year had also disappeared. Projections were revised from an estimated $6 million profit at the time of the launch to a $2 million loss by November. Compounding these problems was a troubling unsold inventory that was approaching $12 million.

James Weber, Senior Associate, Center for Case Development, and Professor Rajiv Lal prepared this case as the basis for class discussion rather than to illustrate either effective or ineffective handling of an administrative situation. While this case describes real events, certain data have been disguised.

Philip was devastated. She knew she had little time to make changes to the spring catalog, which would be mailed in January. As soon as the catalogs had started under-performing, the market research department had conducted extensive customer research. Philip, a seasoned cataloger, knew she would need that information. "I don't know if it's the clothes or the creative or the customers who're getting the catalog," Philip said to herself, staring out into the dark Maine night, "but by the time the spring book goes out, I'll have done everything I know how to do." If she failed and the catalog was closed, staff members would be forced to find other positions within L.L. Bean and the company would lose a great opportunity to jumpstart its growth.

L.L. Bean

Leon Leonwood Bean founded his company in Freeport, Maine in 1912 to make a better hunting shoe by attaching leather uppers to rubber bottoms. Bean then mailed circulars to a list of non-resident Maine hunting license holders guaranteeing his Maine Hunting Shoe to give "perfect satisfaction in every way." When 90 out of the first 100 shoes he manufactured were returned because they fell apart, Bean stood by his promise, fixed the problem, and replaced the shoes.

The business took on Bean's personality and values: dependable, honest, friendly, and personally interested in the customers. Bean, known for his thrift, encouraged his customers to send their Maine Hunting Shoes back for repair when they became worn, rather than discarding them. During discussion of a production incentive system, Bean, concerned about maintaining quality, reportedly stated he "would rather see an employee do a good job than hurry, and anyway, I eat three good meals a day and couldn't eat a fourth."[1] Throughout its existence, the company strove to meet Bean's values and what he referred to as the Golden Rule: Sell good merchandise at a reasonable profit, treat your customers like human beings, and they will always come back for more.

L.L. Bean specialized in outdoor related products such as clothing and equipment for hunting, fishing, and camping, but also sold dog beds, tote bags, travel items, and other "interesting" goods and gadgets. Given its heritage, clothing products were typically designed to keep a body warm and dry in the often harsh conditions of the Maine woods. Bean continuously added products to his line as long as he had thoroughly tested them and believed they were the best available.

For many years, the business consisted of the catalog, a manufacturing plant, and a single, but large, store in Freeport. Since 1951, the store was open 24 hours a day—365 days a year to better serve its customers. Bean himself could often be found in the store shaking hands and talking with customers, and he seemed to be as happy offering outdoor advice as making a sale. Bean remained active in the business until his death at age 94 in 1967. By that time, sales had reached nearly $5 million.

Leon Gorman, Bean's grandson, became president of L.L. Bean shortly after Bean's death. Gorman's efforts to modernize the business, combined with a greater interest in outdoor leisure activities in the 1970s and 1980s, led to a period of rapid growth. By the early 1990s, sales had reached $1 billion. Throughout this period, L.L. Bean's business strategy and product focus had not changed significantly. One factor contributing to the growth in the late 1980s and early 1990s was increased sales to Japan. L.L. Bean had long mailed its catalogs internationally, but such sales had been modest. In the early 1990s, surging catalog sales to Japan spurred L.L. Bean to open nearly 20 retail stores in that country as part of a joint venture.

---

[1] Historical material from "L.L. Bean, Inc.," HBS No. 366-013, by Charles Leighton and Frank Tucker.

By 1999, under Gorman's continued leadership, L.L. Bean, long a Maine institution, had become an internationally known brand. The "flagship" store was still located on its original site and had grown to over 140,000 square feet in area. With 3.5 million visitors per year, it was Maine's second most popular destination behind only Acadia National Park. L.L. Bean had also opened 10 outlet stores. These stores, located primarily in the northeast, sold discontinued items, seconds, and overstocks. The company's primary business was its catalogs which earned some 80% of total sales. L.L. Bean offered 16,000 products in over 70 different catalogs, and mailed over 200 million catalogs per year to the six million active customers in its master file. It manufactured 5% of the products it sold, including the Maine Hunting Shoe, and used outside vendors located worldwide for the remainder. Overall, L.L. Bean employed 4,000 people year round and an additional 6,000 during the Christmas shopping period, nearly all in the Freeport area.

Challenges in the 1990s

Despite its success, L.L. Bean faced several challenges. The most pressing were stagnant sales and a heavy dependency on the 4th quarter, or holiday season. Sales, which had grown 15% per year for the three years ending in February 1995, had grown less than 2% per year since then. The lackluster sales were caused by falling demand for many of L.L. Bean's core products and poor performance overseas.

L.L. Bean had long been a seasonal business with slow sales in January through October and a huge jump in November and December. This led to an unproductive use of company resources and had L.L. Bean typically running at a loss for its first three quarters of the year. The problem was becoming more severe as the company grew larger. L.L. Bean needed to find and hire some 6,000 seasonal workers yearly. Many of these were telephone representatives, but in recent years, several large companies in other industries had moved their customer service operations to Maine and seasonal workers that L.L. Bean had trained began to find permanent positions elsewhere.

The Search for Answers

In the fall of 1997, L.L. Bean hired the Boston Consulting Group (BCG) to work with a team of L.L. Bean employees to come up with solutions to the sales growth and fourth quarter dependence problems. Fran Philip was selected to lead this group and would report directly to Gorman and his top team (which later became known as the Office of the President, or O.O.P.).

Philip was an experienced cataloger. After graduating from the Harvard Business School in 1983, she held management positions at two catalog companies, Williams-Sonoma and The Nature Company, before joining the startup team at Calyx & Corolla in 1988. There, she and her partners created an innovative system of sending flowers directly from the growers to the consumer. At Calyx & Corolla, she was the vice president of operations and in that role was responsible for customer service, communication with growers, systems development, and finance and accounting. The business sent out 11 million catalogs per year and was earning $15 million in sales by 1994 when Philip was lured away by L.L. Bean. At L.L. Bean, Philip conceived of and merchandised several new catalogs. She was selected to head the BCG/L.L. Bean team partly because she was the newest member of the L.L. Bean senior management group and Gorman felt it was important to have someone less tied to the traditional thinking of the company.

Gorman had asked the BCG/L.L. Bean team to come up with several new sizable concepts to drive demand and profit to the off-peak months. The team considered many ideas in their search; both extensions to existing lines and categories totally new to L.L. Bean. Concepts considered included women's sportswear/casual clothing, plus or large-sized clothing, home lines, and travel lines. The women's sportswear/casual clothing included items such as dresses, jumpers, pants, and other garments that women might wear shopping, to dinner, or to a professional job on casual Friday. The casual clothing segment, often referred to as updated sportswear, was a bit dressier than weekend shorts and T-shirts, yet not formal. L.L. Bean had an existing women's apparel line that tended to be less dressy than the updated sportswear segment. Home lines was a broad category and covered items such as bedding and bath linens, indoor and outdoor furniture, and garden accessories. L.L. Bean had previously launched a home line and it had become one of the company's fastest growing and most profitable segments.

The team soon focused on updated sportswear because it seemed to address the key problems facing the company, and it was an attractive market. Women tended to buy clothing for themselves evenly throughout most of the year, but there was a slow period during the holiday buying season. (See **Exhibit 1.**) A large portion of these sales were through catalogs. The segment was large and growing faster than the overall women's apparel market. (See **Exhibit 2.**) This was due to women wearing updated sportswear type clothing in more situations and an increase in the number of companies with casual dress codes five days a week. In response to this market opportunity, two large catalog companies, Lands' End and Eddie Bauer had expanded in the segment by creating new brands. Other competitors, such as J. Jill, Coldwater Creek, and Nordstrom, were growing rapidly in this segment as well; both in terms of sales and in their 12 month buyer files (those who had purchased within the past year). (See **Exhibit 3.**) Finally, a large potion of individuals who bought from L.L. Bean, bought also from companies that focused on updated sportswear. (See **Exhibit 4.**)

The BCG/L.L. Bean team created several charts to further clarify their thinking on how L.L. Bean might compete in the market. The first chart looked at where many women's apparel companies positioned themselves in terms of the clothing's style/fashion and its

EXHIBIT 1　**Seasonality**

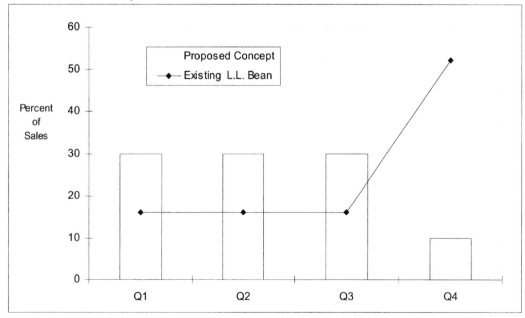

EXHIBIT 2 **Industry Segment Growth**

Source: Company document.

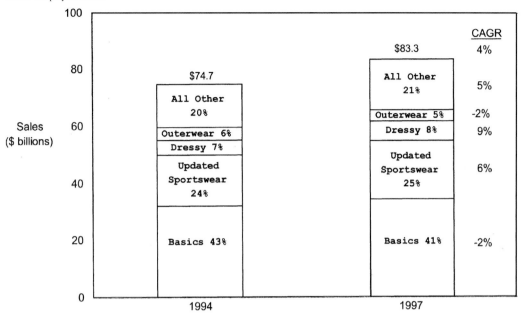

EXHIBIT 3 **Buyer File Growth Rate**

Source: Company document.

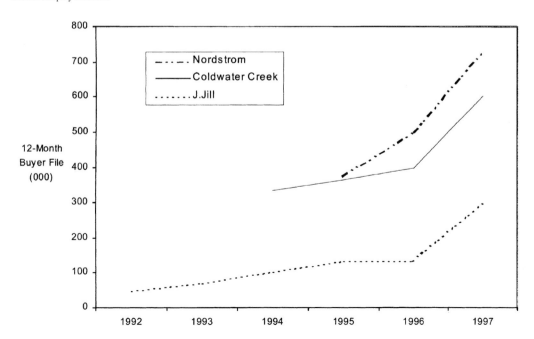

EXHIBIT 4 **Customer File Overlap**

Source: Company document.

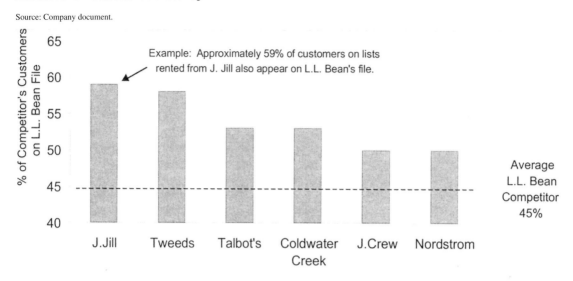

intended end use (See **Exhibit 5**). The team also looked at the product mix of likely competitors and the price point range within those offerings (See **Exhibit 6**).

The Catalog Industry

Catalog retailing had several key characteristics not found in other forms of retailing. First, customers only saw what was in the catalog and many aspects of the catalog were fixed several months to a year prior to its arrival in the home. Quick changes in merchandising and price, common in store and internet-based retailing, were not possible in catalogs.

Second, catalog retailers' lifeblood was its customer file and mailing lists. The single best potential buyer for a catalog was someone who had bought from that catalog in the past—the more recent, or more often, or more money the individual spent, the better. Thus, a new customer not only improved today's sales, but also increased the likelihood of future sales as well. At the same time, there was a high attrition rate among customers. The catalog industry had a historical attrition rate of some 50%. L.L. Bean's experience was no different from the industry average—fully half of this year's customers would not be customers next year. This meant that it was necessary to constantly find new customers to survive in the industry. Maintaining and growing the 12-month buyer file was a key performance criteria.

A catalog company found new customers by more efficiently converting names on its existing mailing list to customers, and by obtaining new lists from list brokers. Lists brokers typically rented out lists of names on a one-time use basis. Because catalog shoppers tended to buy from more than one catalog company, it was valuable for a catalog company to rent the buyer files of other catalog companies. This "sharing" of lists was facilitated by list brokers. Thus, L.L. Bean would both rent its list to a broker and rent other lists from the broker. Sharing of customer data, not common in other forms of retailing, was the norm in catalog retailing. Extensive data about a list was readily available prior to its rental. (See **Exhibit 7** for a copy of a list data card describing J. Jill's list.)

"One of the things I loved about the catalog industry," Philip stated, "was all the numbers. Buying habit data existed that you just didn't get in other channels. With my training, it was great to be able to make decisions based on quantitative analysis and not just intuition."

EXHIBIT 5 Brand Positioning

Source: Company document.

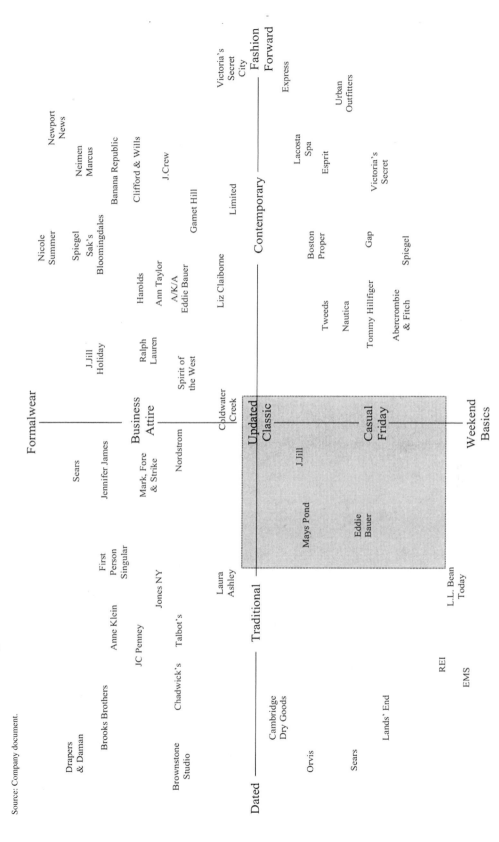

EXHIBIT 6 Product Depth and Price Range

Source: Company document.

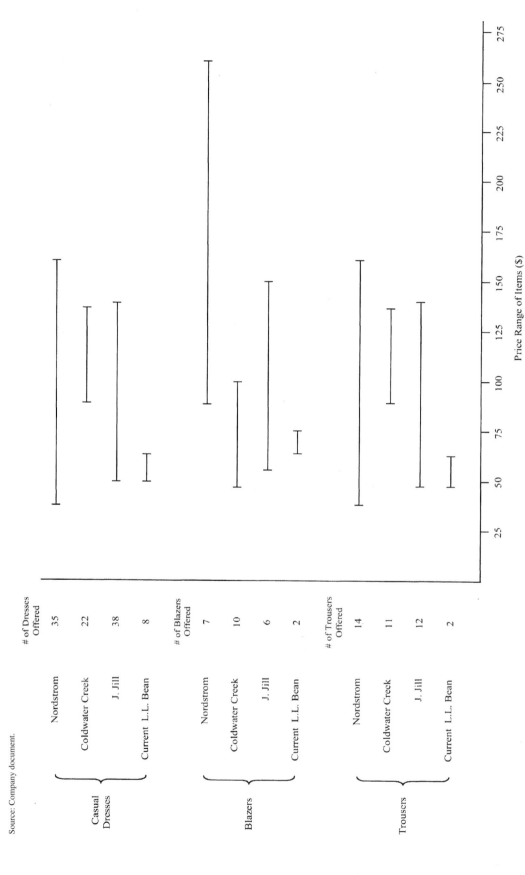

	# of Dresses Offered
Nordstrom	35
Coldwater Creek	22
J. Jill	38
Current L.L. Bean	8

Casual Dresses

	# of Blazers Offered
Nordstrom	7
Coldwater Creek	10
J. Jill	6
Current L.L. Bean	2

Blazers

	# of Trousers Offered
Nordstrom	14
Coldwater Creek	11
J. Jill	12
Current L.L. Bean	2

Trousers

Price Range of Items ($)

25   50   75   100   125   150   175   200   225   250   275

EXHIBIT 7   **Rental List Data Card**

Source: Millard Group, Inc.

```
J. Jill                                    09/07/99  37040
                                           Page 1 of 1
```

```
      346,076   LAST 3 MONTH BUYERS       95.00/M    NAMES THRU:  07/24/99
      591,756   LAST 6 MONTH BUYERS       95.00/M
      945,800   LAST 12 MONTH BUYERS      95.00/M    -----UNIT OF SALE-----
      303,146   LAST 13-24 MONTH BUYERS   95.00/M    $150.00 AVERAGE
                FUNDRAISERÕS RATE         50.00/M
                PUBLISHERÕS RATE          60.00/M    ---------SEX----------
                FOOD RATE                 50.00/M    100% FEMALE
```

THE J. JILL CATALOG FEATURES SIMPLE, UNIQUE, AND
NATURAL STYLE IN APPAREL, ACCESSORIES, SHOES, AND
GIFTS. WITH AN EMPHASIS ON NATURAL FIBERS AND
CREATIVE DETAIL, J. JILL OFFERS RELAXED CAREER
AND WEEKEND WEAR FOR THE WOMAN WHO IS CASUAL IN
HER APPROACH TO DRESSING. J. JILL OFFERS MISSES'
SIZES 4-20, PLUS AN EXTENSIVE ASSORTMENT OF
PETITE AND WOMEN'S SIZES. THE MAJORITY OF THESE
BUYERS ARE AGE 35-45, HAVE INCOMES OF $50,000+,
AND SPEND AN AVERAGE OF $150 PER ORDER.

SELECTS: RECENCY: LAST 3 MOS. $21.00/M, LAST 6
        MOS. $16.00/M, Last 12 Mos. $11.00/M
        DOLLAR: $50+ $21.00/M $75+ $31.00/M
        $100+ $41.00/M, $150+ $51.00/M, $200+
        $56.00/M. STATE, SCF, ZIP: $6.00/M
        PRODUCT, SIZE, INCOME: $16.00/M AGE
        SELECT: $16.00/M, CANCEL FEE $50.00/L

SOURCE: 100% DIRECT MAIL

CUMMULATIVE DOLLAR

@COMMISSION: 20% TO RECOGNIZED BROKERS
** RFM PARTICIPANT **
****
PRODUCT SELECTION GROUPS
SPORTSWEAR
DRESSES & SUITS
SWIMWEAR
FOOTWEAR
ACCESSORIES
GIFT & HOME
****

** FUNDRAISERS & PUBLISHERS WILL RECEIVE 50% OFF
SELECTION CHARGES FOR ALL ORDERS PLACED.
** ALL SPECIAL OFFERS/INCENTIVES SHOULD BE
APPROVED IN ADVANCE BY DM MANAGEMENT

-------MATERIAL-------
4-UP CHESIRE
MAGNETIC TAPE
9-TRACK 1600 BPI
PRES SENS $8.50/M

------KEY CODING------
$3.00/M

----MINIMUM ORDER-----
5,000

---UPDATE SCHEDULE----
LAST: 08/02/99
NEXT: 08/23/99
UPDATE: 10 TIMES/YR

---NET NAME POLICY----
85% + $8.00/M
RUNNING CHARGES
50,000 MINIMUM

----MAG TAPE INSTR----
$25.00 NON-
REFUNDABLE CHARGE
DO NOT RETURN TAPE
DOES NOT APPLY ON
EXCHANGE ORDERS

----RECOMMENDED BY----
HEIDI THIBODEAU
MILLARD GROUP, INC.

Freeport Studio

In December 1997, the BCG/L.L. Bean team finalized the business concept of what later became known as Freeport Studio. Leon Gorman and the O.O.P. approved the concept and asked Philip to create a business plan. Philip's first hire was Cindy Marshall, an L.L. Bean marketing manager with prior experience at J. Jill. Philip and Marshall wrote the plan over a weekend and it was approved by late January 1998. The business plan called for the first catalog to be mailed in January 1999. Philip called the schedule aggressive, but attainable. For L.L. Bean, she noted, it was like going into "warp drive."

Philip spent early 1998 forming her key management team. She knew that to successfully launch Freeport Studio in such an aggressive timeframe she needed the best possible talent. In particular, she was looking for individuals with a combination of L.L. Bean tenure and significant outside experience with other retailers. Philip also wanted like-minded entrepreneurs who could share her vision for Freeport Studio and be comfortable with the risk and ambiguity involved in a new startup. In addition to Marshall, the marketing manager, Philip hired Deb Snite, a seasoned merchant as product manager, Jill Gravel, a strong buyer to manage inventory and sourcing, and Kristina Boissonneault, a systems specialist known for her project management skills as operations manager.

Concept Overview

Freeport Studio would offer "high quality, well designed sportswear (updated sportswear) for the active busy woman." The line would include "dresses, jumpers, skirts, slacks, jackets and other related separates that are versatile, easy to wear, and easy to care for." Comfortable yet easy-care and wrinkle-free fabrics, such as Tencel lyocell (a form of rayon), were emphasized. While Freeport Studio planned to offer styles and colors more fashionable than L.L. Bean's traditional look, it did not plan to stray so far as to not fit with the L.L. Bean image.

Freeport Studio would be an affiliated brand of L.L. Bean: a clothing line sold under the name Freeport Studio, but with the subtle inclusion of the L.L. Bean name in catalogs and advertisements. In 1997, the dressier women's clothing category was a highly profitable business for L.L. Bean with $30 million in sales. Sales had been flat, however, and there was concern that the category detracted from the overall L.L. Bean image and that that image did not do justice to the category's potential. With Freeport Studio, most updated sportswear type clothing would be removed from the L.L. Bean catalogs. This would both focus and strengthen the core brand, as well as allow Freeport Studio to focus its own message to its customers. Freeport Studio would be marketed through its own catalog mailed 10–12 times per year, yet avoiding the peak holiday season.

Freeport Studio planned to rely on L.L. Bean for all operational tasks, such as receiving and storing stock, shipping products to customers, and order processing and other aspects of customer service. Within each of these operational groups, however, Freeport Studio formed sub-teams to focus on the unique requirements of the Freeport Studio business. Kristina Boissonneault set up a separate call center staffed with specially trained Freeport Studio "consultants" who could advise customers and help them match various products to create complete outfits. She also worked with the fulfillment center to create the special packaging the new brand required to achieve a high quality delivery presentation. "Special touches" used to reinforce the quality image of the product and the service were shipping clothing on hangers or wrapped in tissue.

Market Overview

Trends

The women's apparel market was estimated to be approximately $80 billion, with nearly $7 billion sold through catalogs. While the market had been growing at some 4% per year, the updated sportswear segment was growing faster at 6%. The segments where L.L. Bean traditionally competed—the basics category and the "all other" category which included sleepwear—were growing at 3%. These trends were driven by increased casual dressing in both work and social situations.

Competition

Freeport Studio intended to position itself in a segment with relatively few existing catalog competitors—the casual Friday, updated classics, and relaxed weekend niche. (See shaded box in **Exhibit 5.**) Its primary competitors were J. Jill ($136 million total net sales), Coldwater Creek ($247 million) and Nordstom ($4.4 billion). All three of these companies had grown the women's updated sportswear catalog portion of their businesses rapidly in recent years. Other competitors were J. Crew, Tweeds, and a new Orvis spin-off; May's Pond. Industry leaders, such as Eddie Bauer, Lands' End, Spiegel, and Talbots, were also considered competitors. Finally, several gift and home catalogs were adding casual clothing to their lines.

Product Strategy

Vendor Base

Freeport Studio expected to source some 80% of the line from a handful of key local suppliers which were also current L.L. Bean vendors. The Goodman Group, based in Brockton, Massachusetts, was an instrumental vendor to the startup. It supplied a number of competitors in the industry and was very eager to work with Freeport Studio. Goodman provided design assistance and expertise that lowered Freeport Studio's overhead needs. Two other Massachusetts based vendors, Susan Bristol, Inc. and KGR, were key partners as well.

Pricing

Philip and Snite, the product manager, believed Freeport Studio could price its products 10% or more below that of its key competitors while offering equal or better products. This was achievable because its product line would be completely private label and because it planned to enter the market at large volumes by leveraging the assets of L.L. Bean, (namely mailing lists and financial backing). Gross margins were expected to be approximately 55%.

Marketing Strategy

Philip was confident that Freeport Studio could offer high-quality products, an unbeatable guarantee of complete customer satisfaction, and, with the experience of L.L. Bean, outstanding customer service. What would determine the success of the business, she felt, would be creating the right presentation of the products (Creative Plan) and reaching the right potential customers (Circulation Plan).

Creative Plan

Freeport Studio planned to "communicate its brand personality through copy, photography, and other creative elements." It would attempt to differentiate its catalog through "creative imagery, positioning, layout, and voice." To align Freeport Studio with the core strengths of L.L. Bean, the catalog would show its products were suited for "women who enjoy the outdoors and need clothes for the rest of their busy active lives." This meant that the clothing would typically be shown being worn by women engaged in an activity such as working professionally, shopping, preparing a meal, playing with children, or visiting with friends. Often, the settings were outdoors. The visual imagery was supported by copy writing touting the comfort and easy care nature of the garments. (See **Exhibit 8** for selected catalog pages.)

Circulation Plan

Freeport Studio planned to produce four different catalogs; one per season. Each of the four catalogs would be followed by 1 or 2 remails: a catalog identical to its predecessor except with a different front and back cover. As had been standard practice in the industry, catalogs would be sent several months in advance of the season. The reasoning behind this was that people like to have the clothes at the start of the season, and that, historically, it had taken several weeks from the time an order was placed to the time it was received by the customer. Thus, Freeport Studio would mail its spring catalog in January, followed by remails in February and March. Similarly, April–June mailings covered the summer season, July–September the fall season, and October and November for the winter. The last regular catalog of the year would arrive in homes during the first week of November—no catalogs would be mailed in December. The first mailing of each catalog would be the largest with later mailings being progressively smaller and focused on the best customers.

A total of 20–25 million catalogs, all to U.S. customers, were planned for the first year. Larger mailings yielded higher sales, but with diminishing response rates, did not necessarily mean higher profits. The overall response rate for the catalogs was expected to be 2%–5% during the first year and the average order value was estimated at $100. The catalog would primarily be mailed to existing L.L. Bean customers; particularly those customers who had purchased L.L Bean's women's apparel products. Philip believed that the extensive L.L. Bean master file would be a sufficient base on which to build the Freeport Studio business.

In order to rapidly build the 12-month buyer file, Freeport Studio would test segments of the L.L. Bean customer database as well as test small numbers of rented mailing lists. Tests generally involved mailing small numbers of catalogs, say 10,000, to each of several different customer segments, and then using sophisticated regression and other modeling techniques to identify the best potential buyers. Philip and Marshall planned to send such test mailings to a very broad range of potential customers. Such tests were expensive, but could potentially uncover valuable customer segments that later could be targeted with larger mailings.

Initial financial performance estimates for Freeport Studio are shown in **Exhibit 9.**

Overall, the Freeport Studio concept satisfied Leon Gorman's requirement that any new business must fit with L.L. Bean's business model. Key criteria included meeting the L.L. Bean Golden Rule, a high overlap with existing customers, a highly productive category, primarily direct mail, and taking advantage of the company's operational strengths. (See **Exhibit 10** for further details.)

The Launch

The startup team spent 1998 hiring the remaining staff, selecting vendors, designing the clothes, selecting mailing lists, and creating the catalog. Much of this work involved overseeing and coordinating with outside service providers who helped in areas such as the selection of fabrics, determining clothing design specifications, and producing the creative elements of the catalog. The Freeport Studio name, product offer, and catalog design had been shown to various focus groups and received positive feedback. By the end of the year, they were ready to go.

Freeport Studio mailed its first catalog on Friday, January 15, 1999, with an in-home arrival date of the following Monday and Tuesday. Almost immediately, Philip and her

EXHIBIT 8A   Catalog Page

G-H. Taking a relaxed approach, our unstructured jacket and skirt in buttery Tencel®/acetate twill. Machine washable. Raisin, Midnight or Plum. USA. Misses XS-XL; Petite XS-L.

G. Notched-collar jacket with seaming detail and shell-buttoned patch pocket. Back yoke with button and pleat detail.
2C30685 Tencel® Twill Jacket $98

H. Long skirt has back slit with three shell buttons. Elastic waist. Misses, 36" long; Petite, 33" long.
2C30475 Tencel® Twill Skirt $68

E. Tencel®/rayon skirt set feels soft as suede and wears with total ease. Top features pintuck detailing on the sleeves; matching elastic-waist skirt has pintucked hem. Hand washable. Storm Blue or Dark Plum. USA. Misses XS-XL, 36" long; Petite XS-L, 33" long.
2C30397 Pintucked Tencel® Skirt Set $148

F. Stretch faille slingbacks are a super season-spanning style. Breathable fabric uppers and cushioned insoles for comfort. Chunky 1¾" heels and lightweight lug soles. Black, Grey or Brown. Imported. Whole and half sizes 6-10; 11M.
2C31384 Faille Slingback $65

Working Assets 17

EXHIBIT 8B   **Catalog Page**

B. Soft and seasonless—the cardigan-style jacket and easy, long-sleeved dress. Both, of resilient ribbed cotton knit with satin trim. Machine washable. Black Marl. Imported. Misses XS-XL, 51½" long; Petite XS-L, 47½" long.
2D30402 Marled Knit
Dress and Cardigan $112

C. Crafted of ultrasoft, pebble-grain leather, our beautifully proportioned zip-top bag has a comfortable, ¾"-wide shoulder strap with silver-tone buckle detail. Outside snap pocket, inner zip pocket. Nylon lining. Black or Brown. Imported. 10¾"H x 11½"W x 2¾"D.
2D31686 Scoop Shoulder Bag $59

D. We call this our "accessory dress." Simple and flattering on its own, it's a great backdrop for your favorite scarves or jewelry. Styled with double princess seams and a full, sweeping skirt. Cotton/polyester knit. Machine washable. Charcoal. Imported. Misses S-XL, 52" long; Petite XS-L, 48" long.
2D30447 Princess-Seam
Knit Dress $95

E. Whimsically patterned neckerchief softens the neckline on a shirt or dress, adds a shot of mellow color. Shadow-striped silk chiffon. By Echo®. Dry clean. Charcoal Multi. Imported. 21" square.
2D31431 Flower Box Neckerchief $24

Working Assets 31

EXHIBIT 8C   Catalog Page

garment-washed linen

Forget old ideas about linen. Ours is soft, comfortable and completely machine washable. We love its natural ease and crinkled texture which means you can forgo ironing. Perfect now, and right into autumn. Berry, Straw, Eucalyptus or Black. USA. Misses XS-XL; Petite XS-L.

EXHIBIT 9A
Initial P&L Forecast
($000)

	1999		2000	
Gross demand (sales)	79,953		127,092	
Returns, outs & cancellations	22,755		36,170	
Net sales	57,198	100.0%	90,922	100.0%
Cost of goods sold	25,739	45.0%	40,915	45.0%
Gross margin	31,459	55.0%	50,007	55.0%
Catalog costs	10,256	17.9%	12,849	14.1%
Variable operating expenses	6,162	10.8%	9,794	10.8%
Other operating expenses	4,025	7.0%	4,700	5.2%
Contribution	11,016	19.3%	22,664	24.9%
Interest costs	515	0.9%	818	0.9%
Pre-tax income	10,501	18.4%	21,846	24.0%
Revenue per catalog circulated ($)	3.43		4.35	

EXHIBIT 9B
Forecast
Assumptions

	1999	2000
Catalog circulation	23,310,000	29,202,558
Average response rate	3.5%	4.4%
Average order size	$100	$100
Units per order	2.9	2.9

team knew there were problems. The 80 specially trained phone reps received only half the calls expected. Catalog sales followed predictable patterns with 40% of sales typically occurring in the first 10 days a catalog was in the home.

January 28th Demand Assessment

Ten days after the customers received their catalogs, Philip and her team began to conduct an early demand assessment. A number of key issues were identified:

Catalog Delivery Issues

The catalogs were slow to arrive in homes because they were mailed over a three-day holiday weekend and there was bad weather throughout much of the country. As of Thursday of the delivery week, three states had not received the catalog and five major states had received only partial deliveries. Compounding this problem, the delivery tracking service with which Freeport Studio had contracted functioned poorly making it difficult to know which areas had received the catalogs and which had not. In response, Philip decided that future mailings would avoid three-day weekends and a new tracking system would be developed.

Prominence of L.L. Bean Logo

There was evidence that the location and prominence of the L.L. Bean logo was a problem. After much debate during the initial catalog planning sessions, it had been decided to place the logo in the lower right-hand corner of the front cover. This would, the team believed, let customers know this was an L.L. Bean affiliated brand, yet not make too strong a connection so that customers would think Freeport Studio and L.L Bean were one and the same. Anecdotal feedback after the mailing indicated that some felt the logo was not visible enough. Further, when catalog recipients who called to request their names be removed from the mailing list were asked if they knew it was an L.L. Bean brand, many responded they did not. Three steps were taken to address this issue. A telephone survey was used to further probe the connection between the Freeport Studio and L.L. Bean brands. A "Dot Whack" would be placed on the cover of the March mailing catalog announcing a "new L.L. Bean

EXHIBIT 10 Concept's Fit with L.L. Bean

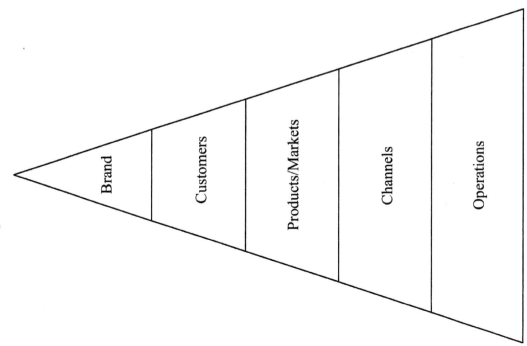

Brand

L.L. Bean Golden Rule and company values
Affiliated brand
- Freeport Studio by L. L. Bean
- Distinct brand personality, pricing, products
- Distinct creative

Customers

L.L. Bean's women's apparel customers
Active women who enjoy the outdoors and need clothes for the rest of their busy active lives
Age 35+, average L.L. Bean household income

Products/Markets

Versatile wardrobe essentials: casual dresses, trousers, blazers, skirts, jumpers, accessories, footwear
- Easy to wear silhouettes, soft colors, florals, prints
- Easy care fabrics

Channels

Direct mail
- Specialty books, not carried in L.L. Bean full books
- Distinct direct marketing, customer acquisition

Operations

Best service
Current L.L. Bean operations

brand." Dot Whacks were simple sticker labels that could be added to a catalog cover after it was otherwise completed. It was too late to make any changes to the February mailing, and only a Dot Whack was possible for the March mailing. For the summer catalog, first mailed in April, the L.L. Bean Logo would be placed directly under the Freeport Studio name at the top of the cover page.

Lack of "Wear Now" Merchandise/Sale Merchandise

Freeport Studio had apparently overestimated the willingness of consumers to buy spring clothes in January. This trend had been declining in recent years as faster delivery allowed purchases to be made closer to the season of use. Further hurting sales was the abundance of fall/winter merchandise on sale in January. L.L. Bean's Women's Book, mailed at about the same time as the Freeport Studio catalog, had a prominent sale Dot Whack on the cover, and competitors had placed a greater emphasis on sales items in their January catalogs as well. The team decided to increase the number of catalogs mailed in March because the merchandise would be wearable on receipt and the Dot Whack would increase response rates. The first fall catalog (mailed in July) would be repaginated to place lightweight fabrics and sleeveless items near the front. Further, they considered reversing the circulation plan in general so that early mailings would be small and later mailings would grow larger as it gets closer to the season. Finally, the spring 2000 catalog would include a sale section of fall/winter goods.

Initial Merchandise Learnings

Early sales patterns indicated some positive results as well. While Philip and Snite had created the first product line to be purposefully broad, they were now able to see clear trends of what the customer wanted. Snite noticed that Tencel coordinates were selling strongly, as well as prints and two-piece sets. She and her product developers immediately added more of these styles to the fall '99 and spring '00 lines in development. Jill Gravel, the inventory and sourcing manager, realized that petite sizes were selling out causing her to reorder more quickly than anticipated. On the front line, Boissonneault, the operations manager, reported many customer requests for Tall and Plus sizes, which had not appeared in the catalog. This led to extended sizes being built into the plan for the next year.

Other Issues

With early performance figures in, Philip lowered the estimate of sales from the January catalog from $10.2 million before it was mailed to $7 million based on the 10 day results. (See **Exhibit 11.**) Further, net sales for year 2 were dropped from $91 million to $65 million. Philip took this step in January 1999 because budgeting was due for the next fiscal year. On a positive note, individual customers of Freeport Studio were spending 50% more than individual customers of L.L. Bean's Women's catalog. The average order size at Freeport Studio was $150 compared with $100 for L.L. Bean.

EXHIBIT 11
Performance Data as of January 28, 1999

	Original Plan for January	Performance as of January 28	Adjusted Plan for January
Average unit value	$63	$63	$63
Units per order	2.0	2.4	2.15
Average order	$126	$149	$135
Response rate	2.62%	0.4%	1.6%
$ per book	$3.30	$0.61	$2.27
Total demand (000)	$10,218	$1,881	$7,014

March–June

The situation at Freeport Studio improved after the poor launch. Performance of the spring catalog picked up in March largely, it was believed, due to the Dot Whack and timeliness of the clothing. Results from the summer catalog, first mailed in April and followed by May and June remails, met forecast. Freeport Studio's 12-month buyer file had reached a respectable 122,000 names after only five months of operations. During the spring performance review in June, Philip and her team felt optimistic that their hard work was beginning to pay off.

Summer Disaster

The optimistic mood disappeared the following month. Freeport Studio mailed its first fall catalog in July and the phones did not ring. Ten days later it held its first review. Sales were forecasted to be $2.87 million, 73% behind the plan of $10.47 million. Reasons cited for the shortfall included the busy vacation period, delivery problems in several key states, and mailing at a time when most catalogs were focused on price reductions on summer items. Further putting pressure on Philip and her inventory manager Gravel, were rising levels of unsold merchandise.

The August mailing performed only slightly better than July: 60% below plan. This led to Freeport Studio cutting its total fall (July–Sept) sales projection from $37 million to $20 million, decreasing first year sales projection, for the second time, from $66 million to $43 million, and reducing first year contribution from a gain of $5.7 million to a loss of $2.2 million. Gravel now estimated year end inventory figures at $12.5 million.

November

Philip, desperate to discover what was holding the business back and how to turn it around, reviewed the market research she had commissioned over the previous months. In July, L.L. Bean's market research department had conducted a telephone survey of those who received the July mailing; had sent a written survey insert out with the August catalog mailing; had placed a survey inside the packages of products ordered by customers in August and September; and had conducted focus groups in October. The data indicated that consumers' awareness of the catalog was high and it was easy to shop and order products. Customers also liked the selection of fabrics, and the perceived quality of the products had improved since an earlier survey conducted in January. They ranked the catalog poorly on "Fit my Lifestyle" questions. The research also indicated the customers wanted more color, and a review of what was selling showed customers were in fact buying the brighter colors. (Details from the survey mailed with the catalogs appear in **Exhibit 12.**)

Participants from several focus groups, who were generally favorable towards the catalog, made a number of interesting comments. Many participants felt Freeport Studio clothing was either of the classic style, or a mix of classic and trendy. One participant stated, "It is a very conservative, classic look. The woman depicted in the catalog thinks she is still hip, but is growing more conservative with age." Another stated, "It is a classic style, but still trendy enough where you can show your own personality." Others commented on the lifestyle. One woman stated, "I really like the clothes a lot, but when I take my kids to the playground I would not wear them." Another woman described the models as showing women living the "good life—a professional job, good income, two kids, a husband, and a nice house in the suburbs." Another added, "They (Freeport Studio) are trying very hard to appeal to that type of person, almost too hard. It is more of an ideal, what our lifestyle should be like." In a conversation about colors, a participant explained "There is not a lot of variety in the colors, you just get a lot of those same (earth) tones. I, personally, am a

EXHIBIT 12 Survey of Catalog Recipients—Satisfaction with Catalog Creative Attributes (percent very satisfied)

	Jan 1999[a] Freeport Studio Catalog	Aug 1999[b] Freeport Studio Catalog	Top 10%[c] of Freeport Studio Customers	Top 10%[c] of L.L. Bean Customers	Next 10%[c] of L.L. Bean Customers
Quality of products	40	45	52	35	43
Value for the price	15	14	18	10	14
Order information	41	48	52	39	52
Variety of merchandise offered	19	18	20	15	20
Selection of colors/patterns	21	16	17	16	16
Merchandise relevant to your needs	16	15	22	7	12
Sizing and fit information	26	26	26	23	28
Selection of sizes	33	30	33	21	35
Information provided in item description	37	35	38	29	33
Ease of finding a specific item	22	23	21	23	27
Clarity of product in photographs	40	34	32	31	41

[a]Results from survey inserted in January Freeport Studio catalogs.
[b]Results from survey inserted in August Freeport Studio catalogs.
[c]Further breakdown of results from survey inserted in August Freeport Studio catalogs.

color person. I like the basic colors for some things, like skirts, but I like peppier looking sweaters." However, another felt that the type of woman attracted to Freeport Studio "is not going to buy a lot of loud colors."

The market research data led to a proposal for a new creative focus in the catalog. The new design called for placing more emphasis on the clothes, and reducing the clutter by toning down the "lifestyle" look—what was going on in the pictures. Thus, women would be shown posed simply, with few, if any props, and seldom shown engaged in activities. By highlighting details such as fabric and trim, Philip and her team hoped to be able to bring out the quality of the clothing itself. They believed that by refocusing on their original "studio" idea, which they had embedded in the name Freeport Studio, and moving away from the outdoor theme of the traditional L.L. Bean look, they would attract a broader customer base looking for casual clothing. Finally, more brightly colored items were added to the product line. (See **Exhibit 13** for selected proposed catalog pages.)

Philip and Marshall, the marketing manager, also reviewed the results of the circulation plan for the year to devise their circulation strategy for the upcoming year. Freeport Studio had mailed nearly 25 million catalogs in 1999, which was near the high end of the initial plan. (See **Exhibit 14** for monthly circulation figures.) It cost $0.44 to print and mail a catalog in 1999 and this cost was not expected to change in the coming year. Most of the catalogs were sent to people in the top deciles (10% increments) of the L.L. Bean master file, which contained some six million names. The best buyers were sent up to 14 Freeport Studio catalogs per year while less lucrative buyers might only receive four catalogs.

Roughly 5% of catalogs were sent to names from rented lists. Marshall had selected these lists on an experimental basis. The likely sales per book of rented lists could not be accurately estimated in advance, though it was expected to be lower than the top deciles of the L.L. Bean master file. Total sales for the year were expected to be $44.6 million from a customer file that had grown steadily to approximately 217,000 buyers. These buyers placed an average of 1.4 orders with an average order size of $145. The 1.4 orders per customer reflected the fact that while 75% of customers ordered only once, another 16% ordered twice and the remainder ordered more than twice.

In order to better understand where demand was coming from, Freeport Studio divided sales into first time sales and repeat purchases (see **Exhibit 15A**). Of first time sales, $31.3 million came from the 19.6 million catalogs sent to the "F2+ 1–3" customers—L.L. Bean

EXHIBIT 13A   Proposed Catalog Page

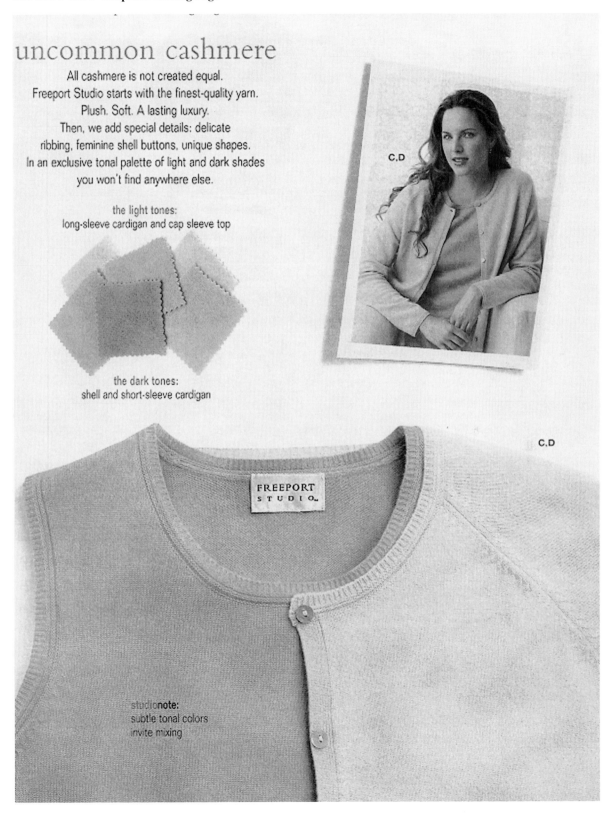

uncommon cashmere

All cashmere is not created equal.
Freeport Studio starts with the finest-quality yarn.
Plush. Soft. A lasting luxury.
Then, we add special details: delicate
ribbing, feminine shell buttons, unique shapes.
In an exclusive tonal palette of light and dark shades
you won't find anywhere else.

the light tones:
long-sleeve cardigan and cap sleeve top

the dark tones:
shell and short-sleeve cardigan

C,D

C,D

FREEPORT
STUDIO.

studionote:
subtle tonal colors
invite mixing

EXHIBIT 13B Proposed Catalog Page

A-B. Quilted Silk. Boxy, hip-length jacket and cropped vest—two key items that give your wardrobe an instant update. We went to great lengths to assure superb quality in every detail, from the sandwashed silk shell and contrast silk lining to the unique channel quilting. Dry clean. By Freeport Studio. Imported. Black/Lead, Hydrangea/Sky, Meadow/Aloe, Smokey Pearl/Aluminum or Geranium/Melon.

A. Quilted Silk Vest. Zip-front with mandarin collar. Side-seam pockets.
2A34019
Misses XS-XL $78

B. Quilted Silk Jacket. Luminous, durable encased shell buttons and patch pockets.
2A32426
Misses XS-XL $128

B

EXHIBIT 13C   **Proposed Catalog Page**

studio**choice:** pastel
skimmer for a kick of color

key trends: Soft color. Very pretty. Very wearable.
Simple basics in shades of Pear, Buttercup, Pale Pink, Sky and Orchid.
Give your wardrobe a lift.

D. Silk Shell. Luxurious layer that's sleeveless without being too bare. Easy fit with straight hem and side slits. Hand washable. By Freeport Studio. Imported. Black, Sky, Cream or Pale Pink.
2A28507
Misses XS-XL $32

E. Leather Skimmer. Simple, versatile slip-on adds a new note to pants and skirts in cool pastels or pearlized Champagne. Super comfy Lite Flex sole. Imported. Pale Pink, Pale Blue or Champagne Pearl.
2A33782
Whole and half sizes 6-10; 11; M and W $54

F. Silk Mandarin-Collar Tunic. Easy and elegant in a mini herringbone weave that feels luxurious and is hand washable! Button front and cuffs. Slightly shaped fit with side slits. By Freeport Studio. Imported. Pale Pink, Cream or Sky.
2A32519
Misses XS-XL $68
Petite XS-XL $68

FREEPORT
S T U D I O

EXHIBIT 14 Catalog Circulation[a]—1999 (millions)

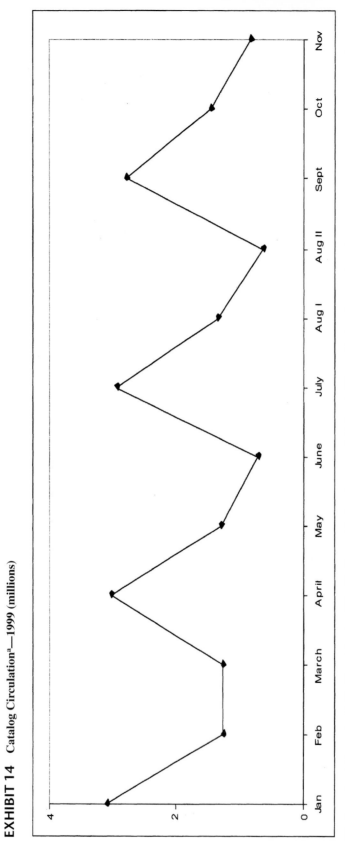

[a] The figures above total approximately 21 million catalogs. An additional 1 million catalogs were sent as package inserts and special mailers over the course of the year for a total of 24.77 million catalogs in 1999. Sale catalogs were produced to liquidate inventory and Freeport Studio might not need to send so many in 2000.

EXHIBIT 15A
Customer Segment Performance—1999

Source of Customer[a]	Circulation (thousand)	Gross Demand per Book[b] ($)	Gross Demand ($ thousand)
F2+ 1–3 years	19,639	1.59	31,289
Outside rentals	1,309	0.98	1,281
Past Freeport Studio customer	1,769	4.08	7,211
Package inserts	450	6.50	2,925
Catalog requests	810	1.39	1,122
Other sources	795	0.94	750
Total	24,772	1.80	44,578[c]

[a]F2+ 1–3 buyers were those who had purchased at least twice from L.L. Bean within the past three years. Outside Rentals were those buyers from rented lists. Past Freeport Studio Customers were those who had previously purchased from Freeport Studio (not including Package Insert buyers). Package Inserts were catalogs placed inside packages of products mailed to buyers. Catalog Requests were individuals who called/wrote to request a catalog. Other Sources were largely other past L.L. Bean buyers.
[b]Gross Demand per Book is defined as Gross Demand (sales) divided by circulation.
[c]Includes an estimate of December sales.

EXHIBIT 15B
F2+ 1–3 Sales by Decile

Decile	Demand/Book ($)	Response Rate (%)
Decile 1 (Top 10% of L.L. Bean buyers)	2.40	1.66
Decile 2 (2nd 10% of L.L. Bean buyers)	1.05	0.72
Decile 3 (3rd 10% of L.L. Bean buyers)	0.94	0.65
Decile 4 (4th 10% of L.L. Bean buyers)	0.94	0.65

buyers who had purchased at least twice from L.L. Bean within the previous three years. Another $1.3 million in first time sales came from the 1.3 million catalogs sent to people from rented lists. All repeat purchases from these two segments were reported as sales to past Freeport Studio customers, except those credited to package inserts. (Freeport Studio sent a package insert catalog with nearly every package it shipped.) A breakdown of the demand per book for customers in the F2+ 1–3 category shown in **Exhibit 15A** is shown in **Exhibit 15B.** The demand data revealed some key differences. Customers who had purchased from Freeport Studio in the past were by far the best customers. Further, while rented lists ranked among the lowest levels of sales per book, surprisingly, such lists were doing better than some L.L. Bean deciles.

From the data gathered in the first year, Freeport Studio could determine the profile of its better customers. Therefore, it could, for example, rent lists that met more specific demographic and buyer behavior criteria. By doing so, Freeport Studio expected the rented lists to perform at $1.30 per book next year versus the $0.98 per book in 1999. The cost of rented lists in 1999 was $0.11 per name. If Freeport Studio rented names that met the additional demographic or behavioral criteria it desired, the rental cost was estimated to be $0.15 per name.

As Fran Philip reflected on the issues facing Freeport Studio, she recalled the trust Leon Gorman placed in her to lead the business to profitability by year two. But Philip also knew that the high attrition rate of customers meant that to be viable beyond year two, Freeport Studio must attract 200,000 new customers in the coming year. Philip estimated that the Freeport Studio yearly attrition rate would be comparable to the L.L. Bean historical rate of 50%. This rate was expected to decrease with increasing loyalty (measured as number of orders per year) in the customer base.

Philip's immediate tasks were clear. She first needed to decide whether she should follow the creative strategy that had been proposed. Then she had to determine how many catalogs Freeport Studio should mail in 2000, to whom they should be sent, and whether the customer file could be built from internal sources. Finally, she needed to produce a pro forma financial statement that would convince Gorman that Freeport Studio's circulation strategy would result in a profitable business next year.

Chapter 8

Omnitel Pronto Italia

Rajiv Lal   Suma Raju

Our vision at Omnitel is to position the cellular phone in a manner akin to the positioning of the wristwatch. We want the cellular phone to be personal and indispensable. Like the wristwatch, it will be a possession that stays close to you from morning to night, and even at night, it won't be too far away from you. At Omnitel, we want to dramatically change the rules: cellular phones are going to be the primary mode of communication. There is going to be a paradigm shift in the perception of the cellular phone.

—Omnitel's Vision Statement

In early June 1996, Fabrizio Bona, Omnitel's marketing director, prepared for his meeting the next morning with Francesco Caio, Omnitel's CEO, to discuss his proposal for a new pricing strategy for Italy's second mobile phone service provider. He leafed through the folder containing the results of Omnitel's recently conducted market research. The survey indicated that customers were very happy with Omnitel's customer service. The results had also overwhelmingly indicated that the Italian consumers viewed the monthly usage fee as a tax and resented it deeply. They didn't even want to pay an activation fee. Instead, they wanted to pay a fee only when they used the phone.

The results not only excited Bona, but also made him a little nervous. On this basis, he had drawn up an innovative but radical proposal that he felt would enable Omnitel to compete effectively with Telecom Italia Mobile (TIM). The state-owned and operated TIM had had a monopoly over the Italian telecommunications market until Omnitel's February 1995 entrance into the market.

Senior Researcher Suma Raju prepared this case under the supervision of Carin-Isabel Knoop, Executive Director, Global Research Group, and Professor Rajiv Lal. HBS cases are developed solely as the basis for class discussion. Cases are not intended to serve as endorsements, sources of primary data, or illustrations of effective or ineffective management.

Bona's plan, christened "LIBERO," eliminated the monthly fee completely from "Free Time," and let customers only make a payment when they used their cellular phones. The plan would charge Lit. 1,595 ($1 = Lit. 1,603) for calls made during the peak hours and Lit. 195 for calls made during off-peak hours. Bona anticipated average usage to be 193 minutes per month consisting of 93 minutes of outgoing calls (13 minutes at peak and 80 minutes at off-peak) and 100 minutes of incoming calls (25 minutes at peak and 75 minutes at off-peak). The total revenue per customer per month would also include the set up charges that amounted to Lit. 10,000. Bona realized that his new proposal was radically different from anything that had been offered previously, not only in Italy but also in the rest of Europe. Enticing customers with highly subsidized handsets in exchange for their agreeing to sign a contract for a year or two seemed to be the accepted method for acquiring new customers, especially in countries that had more than one cellular phone operator. In fact, in 1995, dealers in the United Kingdom had been very successful in acquiring new customers (an increase in the customer base of almost two million from the previous year) by offering attractive handset subsidies to their customers when they signed up for access to cellular service. But the customers were required to pay a minimum monthly fee for a fixed period of time.

Bona wondered how he could convince Caio to continue to sell phones at full price, but drop the monthly fee. He knew Caio would have several objections and raise more than a few questions. He could already hear Caio telling him, "If we do not charge a recurring monthly fee, we will never be able to get high-quality customers. Customers will just buy the phone and hold on to it without making any calls, and we will end up with very low-end customers." Caio had been especially impressed with the success that several other cellular operators in Europe had had when they offered subsidized handsets. Bona knew that Caio was definitely considering replicating their techniques. At their last meeting together, Caio had stated:

> I think it's a great idea to offer our customers handset subsidies in exchange for their signing a contract with us. Not only will more people sign up because of the subsidy, but we will also be guaranteed a constant revenue stream from the monthly fees. Best of all, it's not too risky for us to replicate this strategy because it has already been tested and proved successful in several countries.

Bona also wanted to support his proposal through an advertising campaign, with a budget of Lit. 40 billion ($25 million) that he intended to spend in less than three months, two times higher than TIM's budget for the same period. His vision was to completely blanket Italy with LIBERO posters and billboards. The ambitious campaign would stimulate usage as well as completely change the customer's mindset regarding cellular phones.

Underlying all these issues was the main concern that TIM should in no way view Omnitel's proposal as a price cut, and risk setting off a price war. Would it be possible to convince Caio that the new proposal would not lead Omnitel into a price war with TIM? Would Caio even take his radical plan seriously, Bona wondered, or would he think that his plan was too risky to implement, especially for such a young company as Omnitel, which had a loss of Lit. 128 billion in 1995 ($79.8 million). Omnitel would definitely be treading on uncharted territory if it completely eliminated its monthly fee. Although Bona had heard Caio state at many a meeting about the need for Omnitel to be different from other cellular companies, he wasn't sure if Caio would agree to so radical a change. Bona felt he was right. Now he had to convince Caio.

The Mobile Telephony Market in Italy

In 1987, the European Commission had completed a study on the $150 billion European telecommunications industry, dominated at the time by 12 state-owned telecom behemoths. In 1993, the Commission declared that by January 1998, all member states would have to open their markets and guarantee competition in the telephony markets. Under pressure from business interests, the EC liberalized cellular telephony by January 1994, but liberalization was subject to interpretation by the country involved.[1] Omnitel was only able to obtain a GSM[2] license in December 1994. Further, while Italy's Telecom Italia, the state-owned telecom monopoly, did not have to pay for a license, the second provider, Omnitel, had to purchase a GSM license. Omnitel paid Lit. 750 billion ($469 million) for a GSM license in December 1994.

Omnitel's entrance not only increased competition, but also enhanced awareness about cellular products among Italians.[3] Cellular penetration in Italy was 7.5% by the end of the first quarter of 1996, and was expected to increase to 22.8% by the end of 2000.[4] Although Italy's cellular penetration was lower than that of several European countries (see **Exhibit 1**), analysts were predicting strong growth in the Italian cellular market for the next few years.

Telecom Italia Mobile (TIM)

TIM was formed in July 1995 when it divested from Telecom Italia and began to be listed separately on the Italian stock exchange. With over four million customers by the end of the first quarter in 1996, TIM enjoyed a strong hold over the Italian cellular market. TIM offered two types of tariffs. (See **Exhibit 2** for TIM's tariffs.) The first, Eurofamily, charged a very high rate of Lit. 1,524 per minute during its peak hours between 7:30 A.M. and 8:30 P.M. and a very low rate of Lit. 170 per minute during its off-peak hours, in addition to a monthly fee of Lit. 10,000. TIM particularly benefited from the calls made by Eurofamily subscribers as well as from calls made to Eurofamily subscribers[5] from fixed lines at peak times since revenue from calls made during the peak hours was essential to TIM if it were to profit from this tariff system.[6] The second, Europrofessional, targeted towards business customers, had rates ranging from Lit. 663 per minute during peak hours to Lit. 206 per minute during off-peak hours, in addition to a monthly fee of Lit. 50,000. Europrofessional was structured in a complicated manner, with different rates over five small time periods.

Since TIM had enjoyed a monopoly over the Italian telecommunications market until Omnitel's recent entrance (generating 97% of Italy's 7.5% penetration), its marketing costs had been lower than its European counterparts.[7] Further, because of the lack of competition, TIM had not felt the need to offer handset subsidies to attract customers. The handsets cost between Lit. 700,000 and Lit. 1.20 million depending on the model.[8] With Omnitel's entrance, TIM expected its marketing costs to increase substantially.[9] TIM also expected to see an increase in its customer acquisition costs, as it would have to compete with Omnitel for every subscriber.

When TIM had a monopoly, its distribution included the "Il Telefonino" chain of stores including 20 TIM-owned shops and 150 Telecom Italia stores.[10] In addition, it had 1,500

---

[1] For more details, see HBS Case No. 800-297, "Telecommunications and Privatization in Europe and Italy," by Professor Michael Watkins and Ann Leamon.

[2] GSM (Global System for Mobile Communications) was a digital cellular radio network. Since GSM was a wireless platform, GSM users were fully mobile, and could do wireless data computing anywhere, without worrying about adapters, telephone jacks, cables, etc.

[3] IMI Sigeco, "Italy-Telecoms," Research Report, April 15, 1996.

[4] Salomon Brothers European Equity Research, Analyst Report, May 17, 1996.

[5] The party that initiated the call paid charges, but the caller paid the rate that was applied to the party that received the call.

[6] A local call at the pay-phone cost Lit. 200.

[7] IMI Sigeco, "Italy-Telecoms," Research Report, April 15, 1996.

[8] Ibid.

[9] Ibid.

[10] Salomon Brothers European Equity Research, Analyst Report, May 17, 1996.

EXHIBIT 1 Overview of Mobile Communications History in North American and Western Europe, 1990–1995

Source: Extracted from MTA-EMCI, 1996.

	1990			1991			1992			1993			1994			1995		
	Subscribers (000s)	Subscriber Growth (%)	Penetration (%)	Subscribers (000s)	Subscriber Growth (%)	Penetration (%)	Subscribers (000s)	Subscriber Growth (%)	Penetration (%)	Subscribers (000s)	Subscriber Growth (%)	Penetration (%)	Subscribers (000s)	Subscriber Growth (%)	Penetration (%)	Subscribers (000s)	Subscriber Growth (%)	Penetration (%)
North America:																		
United States	5,283	51	2.11	7,557	43	2.98	11,033	46	4.31	16,009	45	6.19	24,134	51	9.24	33,737	40	12.79
Western Europe:																		
Finland	226	47	4.53	287	27	5.72	354	23	7.06	480	36	9.53	650	35	12.81	1,024	58	20.12
France	284	55	0.50	374	32	0.66	437	17	0.76	564	29	0.98	870	54	1.50	1,371	58	2.36
Germany	274	74	0.45	532	94	0.66	772	45	0.96	1,771	129	2.19	2,442	38	3.01	3,471	42	4.26
Italy	266	309	0.46	568	114	0.98	781	38	1.35	1,207	55	2.08	2,362	96	4.06	3,794	61	6.50
Norway	203	17	4.81	234	15	5.50	283	21	6.61	371	31	8.63	607	64	14.07	1,090	80	25.14
Sweden	483	43	5.68	589	22	6.91	681	16	7.84	844	24	9.67	1,392	65	15.85	2,066	48	23.41
United Kingdom	1,140	36	1.99	1,230	8	2.14	1,399	14	2.42	1,999	43	3.45	3,509	76	6.04	5,416	54	9.27
Total Western Europe	3,471	50	0.85	4,667	34	1.09	5,885	26	1.36	8,911	51	2.00	14,490	63	3.24	22,525	55	5.02

Note: Projections include PCS/PCN/PHS for United States, France, Germany, and the United Kingdom.

134

EXHIBIT 2   TIM and Omnitel Tariffs

Source: Company documents.

	Monthly	Min Incl.	Traffic (Lit/min)		
			Monday–Friday	Saturday	Holidays
TIM GSM Tariffs					
EuroFamily	10,000	0	1,524	170	170
Hours			7.30–20.30	0.00–24.00	0.00–24.00
			170		
			20.30–7.30		
EuroProfessional	50,000	0	412 663 412 256 206	412 206	206
Hours			8.00–8.30 8.30–13.00 13.00–18.30 18.30–22.00 22.00–8.00	8.00–13.00 13.00–8.00	0.00–24.00

	Monthly	Min Incl.	Traffic (Lit/min)		
			Monday–Friday	Saturday	Holidays
Omnitel GSM Tariffs					
Free Time	10,000	0	1,524	170	170
Hours			7.30–20.30	0.00–24.00	0.00–24.00
			170		
			20.30–7.30		
Night/day	20,000	0	795	265	265
Hours			8.00–20.00	0.00–24.00	0.00–24.00
			265		
			20.00–8.00		

exclusive dealers all over Italy.[11] But with Omnitel's entrance, TIM became more aggressive in acquiring customers. At a shareholders meeting in early 1996, TIM proposed purchasing up to 30 million of its ordinary shares, to distribute to dealers, as a reward for meeting certain sales targets. In addition, TIM was planning to launch its first prepaid card in September 1996, named "Ready to Go." TIM was planning to target this card towards low-end customers, customers who would not qualify for subscription service because of their credit histories and customers who did not have regular sources of income. This new card would be valid for a period of three months, and calls would be charged at Lit. 2,016 during peak-hours, and Lit. 224 during off-peak hours.[12]

TIM's marketing strategy was to cater primarily to the upper echelons of Italian society, touting the cellular phone as a status symbol, an item of indulgence. "TIM's message through its advertising is, 'you have a cellular phone, and you are somebody'," Vittorio Colao (HBS 1990 and then consultant to Omnitel Pronto Italia) explained.

Omnitel Strategy

After Omnitel received its license to become Italy's second GSM mobile telecommunications operator, it launched its commercial service in December 1995, with network coverage of 40% of Italian territory. (See **Exhibit 3** for a history of Omnitel and **Exhibit 4** for Omnitel's launch advertising.)

During its initial six months of operations, Omnitel offered plans similar to TIM's (see **Exhibit 2** for Omnitel's tariffs) but had focused primarily on its high-quality customer service. As a new entrant into the telecom market, Omnitel had no intention of reducing prices; instead, its initial strategy had been to position itself as a telecom company that provided high-quality customer service. The company felt that its superior customer care would be its competitive advantage over the former Italian monopoly, TIM.

However, by May 1996, Omnitel had only signed up 180,000 subscribers, and Omnitel was dissatisfied with its market share of 4%. Though customers were very pleased with the quality of customer service that they received, it had not resulted in a corresponding increase in market share as Omnitel had hoped it would. Omnitel charged its customers a monthly fee of Lit. 10,000 in addition to charging Lit. 1,524 for calls made during the peak hours and Lit. 170 for calls made during off-peak hours. All customers also paid a set up fee per call that resulted in additional revenue of about Lit. 10,000 per customer per month.

The average usage rate was 188 minutes per month per subscriber, and consisted of 88 minutes of outgoing calls (13 minutes at peak and 75 minutes at off-peak) and 100 minutes of incoming calls (25 minutes at peak and 75 minutes at off-peak). How could Omnitel differentiate itself from TIM in a meaningful way without getting into a price war? "We cannot afford to get into a price war with TIM since they are financially so much stronger than we are," Bona's associate, Margherita Della Valle, Marketing Analysis Manager, had cautioned. "If we give TIM the impression that we are trying to undercut its prices, it will result in TIM slashing its prices too, and we will end up in a no-win situation."

Customer Service

From the outset, Omnitel strove to use its customer service as its major competitive advantage over TIM. Customer service focused on three main areas. First, the operator's approach: a polite operator always answered the customer's call. Bona explained: "We have taken a very American approach: 'Hi, I am so and so. How may I help you, or what can I do for you today?' In contrast, TIM's operators say, 'This is operator number 25367.' It's very impersonal."

[11] Ibid.

[12] IMI Sigeco, "Italy-Telecoms," Research Report, April 15, 1996.

EXHIBIT 3 **History of Omnitel**

Date	Event
1990:	
June	Omnitel Sistemi Radiocellulari Italiani established
December	Omnitel presents to the PTT Ministry its request to run a GSM cellular license in Italy
1994:	
January	Omnitel and Pronto Italia agree to form Omnitel Pronto Italia
November	PTT Ministry considers request
1995:	
January	An extraordinary shareholders' meeting agrees to increase capital from Lit. 650 billion to Lit. 1,450 billion
February	A presidential decree officializes agreement between Omnitel and Ministry
May	First advertising campaign for Omnitel
	Agreement with Telecom Italia on carrier charges/usage of fixed network
July	"Preoperation" announcement
October	Agreement with TIM on national roaming
November	Raises fund for project financing
December	Public service begins on December 7 on 40% of territory or 60% of Italian population; 1.3% of market
1996:	
January	Omnitel has 60,000 clients in its first month of service
May	Coverage extended to 50% of territory

Second, the company tried to minimize a customer's waiting time during a call—85% of Omnitel's customer service calls were answered in less than 20 seconds, and the company goal was to have zero waiting time. Third, Omnitel tried to offer one-stop calling. Operators were trained to answer all of a customer's questions and tried to avoid transferring a call to another operator.

Furthermore, Omnitel endeavored to maintain a low churn rate of 10%–15% per year.[13] The average churn rate in the United States, in contrast, was in excess of 30% in 1995 and was expected to be over 40% by the end of 1996.[14] "Omnitel is built around customer satisfaction, so the company was obsessed about churn. A high churn is a bad indication. It means customers are dissatisfied," Colao stated. Churn also resulted in additional hidden costs. Colao explained:

> Churn is a killer in our industry. One point of churn was then worth almost $10 million. The real problem with churn is that it's even worse than it appears. When you lose a customer, you first try to convince him not to go away, then you have to disconnect his or her service. You have to pay the commissions to the trader, and the trade is upset because we keep producing customers without really seeing a [net] increase. In addition, we also have to go through administrative procedures with the closing of each account.

Subscriber Acquisition Costs

Omnitel's shareholders, especially the American shareholders,[15] were comfortable with the idea of incurring high customer acquisition costs and believed it was an essential investment. One of its American shareholders commented, "A customer is very valuable over his lifetime; you can afford to spend a lot of money acquiring high-quality customers; it will pay for itself very quickly." Offering handset subsidies increased customer acquisition

[13] Churn rate for the given time period is defined as the number of customers disconnecting the service divided by the average number of customers enrolled in the service.

[14] Kris Szaniawski, Mobile Communications, 1996 Pearson Professional Ltd., September 5, 1996.

[15] Bell Atlantic International Inc., Air Touch International Inc., Cellular Communications International Inc., and Lehman Brothers Holding Inc.

EXHIBIT 4 Omnitel's Launch Advertising

English Translation

1995 was just the warm-up for an explosive 1996.

It has been a sparkling year. We covered 40% of Italy with our GSM network. Another 2,000 dealers are ready to advise you and provide speedy account activation. Our three plans satisfy every need. Our technical support is thorough and efficient. Our customer service listens, and resolves all problems with maximum speed and courtesy, 24 hours a day. You need but call a single number, once. To top it off, our experimental service has been very successful (11,500 subscribers in under two months), and we started commercial services in December. But believe us, this is only the start.

Vi diamo acolta — Omnitel — We listen to you.

Note: The Translation is approximative and designed to give a sense of general themes.

costs. Della Valle, however, remained unconvinced that incurring higher acquisition costs through subsidies in order to get the "high-quality" customer was relevant to the Italian market. She felt that subsidizing cell phone costs would not substantially increase subscriptions, as Italians were willing to pay full price for their handsets:

> It's not as simple as Omnitel just making a significant investment in each customer in the beginning, and reaping its benefits later. The Italian market is different. Here, people seem quite willing to pay for the access. People like to show off to their friends that they have the most fancy, most expensive, most technologically advanced handset available, and they are willing to pay the price for it. People here would be embarrassed to be seen with some of the phones that are sold in the U.S. and Germany because they are so fashion conscious. The kind of phone one uses is an expression of one's personality.

Colao agreed:

> You have to understand the Italian mindset: Italians are far more impulsive in their purchases than Americans, for example. Americans are more rational in their purchases. They will set aside a Saturday afternoon to go to the mall to make a purchase. In Italy, the layouts of the cities are such that you are constantly passing by a lot of stores where you can see these phones displayed. If people see something they like in a store window, they will be more inclined to make an impulse purchase.

Cellular Phone Distribution

Omnitel sold its handsets through 2,000 shops that sold consumer electronics goods and telecommunications goods and services. Both TIM and Omnitel paid the cellular phone distributors Lit. 40,000 commission for each account that they activated, and neither made any profit on the handsets sold. When Omnitel was encountering difficulties in expanding its customer base, some distributors had approached Omnitel and said, "Give us more commissions, and we will promote your product over TIM's." Both Bona and Della Valle opposed this idea. "What's the point? If we increase commissions, tomorrow TIM will also increase its commissions. Only the dealers will win out, while we get into a war with TIM about dealer commissions," Bona explained. Rather, Bona felt that the key to solving Omnitel's distribution problem was the customer. "It is the customer who needs to go into a store and say, 'You don't sell Omnitel phones, I am looking for an Omnitel phone.' But we first need to create that desire in the customer to own an Omnitel phone."

Exploring Options

Market Research

In an effort to increase its market share, Omnitel decided to conduct market research, interviewing more than 5,000 current and potential customers. We wanted to better understand the minds of the customers," Bona explained. "What their expectation was from a new entrant like Omnitel and what they thought about our positioning in terms of customer service." The results indicated that the customers were very happy with Omnitel's customer service.

However, an overwhelming majority of those surveyed resisted paying the monthly fee. One customer seem to speak for many:

> I like the way Omnitel has positioned itself because I have never heard a polite word from TIM's customer service. But what I'd really like to have in terms of cellular phone service is not to have to pay a monthly fee. Why should I have to pay a tax every month to use the phone? I want to pay for the service when I use it; I don't want to spend money when I am not using it. With a monthly fee, I am charged a minimum whether or not I use the cellular phone.

The above statement was in direct contrast to consumers' experience in the United Kingdom. Bona related what he had heard a U.K. customer say:

> When I first signed up for a cellular phone, I got the phone for free, but I had to sign a contract for a year, which seemed all right at that time. But I was shocked to see my bill at the end of the first month. It was so very high. It included the connection fee, the activation fee and the monthly fee. I felt duped because of all these other charges. I discontinued the service as soon as the contract was up.

As the results were compiled, it was clear to both Della Valle and Bona that the monthly fee was an issue of contention. But eliminating it would not be an easy task. Della Valle explained:

> First, if Omnitel eliminates the monthly fee, TIM will view it as a price cut, and the last thing we want to do is give TIM the impression that we want to engage in a price war. Second, how will the economics work? Only if customers start using their phones a lot more will eliminating a monthly fee not hurt us. It is after all, the monthly fee that saves our economics when customers buy the phone, and never use it. Third, there is the issue of dealer commissions. We pay the dealers a commission for each phone that they sell. This system works well if there is a monthly fee, because the customer is bound to a contract to pay us a minimum each month for a certain period of time. However, if we eliminate the fee, we will pay dealers up front, without any guarantee of future revenue from a customer because the customer can buy the phone, and not make any calls on it. All three issues are big risks for us.

However, Bona believed that by eliminating the fee and implementing several of the strategies that he had charted out in his proposal, Omnitel could increase both the number of subscriptions and the volume of usage.

The market research results also indicated that customers liked to talk on their fixed-line phones in the morning until they got in their cars. In the evenings, since the off-peak period for cellular phones did not start until 8:30 P.M., they were using their fixed-line phones to make their calls. Indeed the peak period on fixed lines was in the early evening. The market research further revealed the perception of the Italian people towards cellular phones. Since TIM had always marketed the cellular phone as a status symbol, it was exactly how the Italian consumer perceived it: the cellular phone was a possession that was both expensive and exclusive, something that only people of a certain stature had the right to own. Bona and Della Valle felt that this perception was obvious throughout in the market research. "Customers seem to have a psychological barrier against cell phones because of the image that TIM has created in the market," Bona stated, "Omnitel is going to completely alter that perception."

Conjoint Analysis[16]

Omnitel also conducted a conjoint analysis. Conjoint analysis was a research tool used to uncover consumer preferences for alternative product designs and pricing options. With this methodology, Omnitel analyzed the relative importance of different attributes to current users of cellular services. Individuals taking part in the analysis were given a set of product descriptions in terms of cellular services attributes such as tariffs, service, and peak/off-peak rates, and were asked to rank these product profiles in order of preference. Next, using cluster analysis,[17] the individuals studied were divided into four value-based

[16] Conjoint analysis information has been extracted from HBS Case 590-059; *Conjoint Analysis: A Manager's Guide* by Professor Robert J. Dolan.

[17] Cluster Analysis is a procedure by which the data matrix containing the value system of each individual can be clustered: HBS Case 590-059; *Conjoint Analysis: A Manager's Guide* by Professor Robert J. Dolan.

EXHIBIT 5
Random Sample
Structure
(percentage)

Source: Omnitel market
research.

	Base[a]	Research Sample
Age:		
18–24	8	18
25–34	34	24
35–44	25	18
45–54	15	20
55–64	18	20
Sex:		
Male	59	45
Female	41	55
Education:		
Elementary degree	3	22
Junior high school degree	23	29
Senior high school degree	60	38
University	14	10
Social Class:		
High	11	18
Medium/High	32	23
Medium	57	59
Occupation:		
Professionals	14	5
Employees	38	34
Self-employed	21	18
Housewives	13	18
Students	5	10
Retired	6	10
Others	3	6

[a]Base: 18–64 years old, social class at least medium, living in 10,000+ towns, excluding blue collars.

segments—brand loyal, those sensitive to service, cost sensitive, and finally those sensitive to the monthly charge and peak rates. The relative importance of the different attributes for these four segments, segment size and segment-specific characteristics are available in **Exhibit 6.** A similar exercise was repeated for prospects as well as for those who had considered but rejected cellular services recently. (See **Exhibits 5** through **8** for details.)

The results of the conjoint analysis also indicated that customers wanted a different set of tariffs for local calls and long-distance calls and international calls. At the time, TIM offered its customers Lit. 170 per minute regardless of whether the call was local, long-distance, or international. The analysis also indicated that customers did not mind paying more than Lit. 170 per minute up to Lit. 200 per minute.

Trends in Europe

For Omnitel managers, analyzing mobile trends in Europe was another way to generate and evaluate options. The European cellular industry was still at its infancy at year-end 1995. Overall penetration was at 5.0%, with 22.5 million customers. (See **Exhibit 1** for penetration rates.) The Scandinavian countries led the pack with an average penetration of over 20% while France, Belgium, and Spain had penetration levels at 2.1%.[18] Analysts expected

[18] The Analyst Forum, Goldman Sachs Global Research, December 12, 1995.

EXHIBIT 6 Value-based Segmentation—Personal Users (deviation from sample average)

Source: RI Data—Cluster analysis on conjoint data.

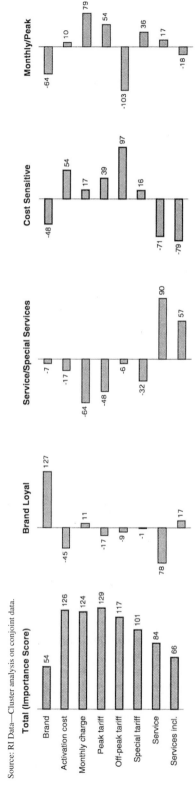

Total (Importance Score)

	Score
Brand	54
Activation cost	126
Monthly charge	124
Peak tariff	129
Off-peak tariff	117
Special tariff	101
Service	84
Services incl.	66

Brand Loyal

	Score
Brand	127
Activation cost	-45
Monthly charge	11
Peak tariff	-17
Off-peak tariff	-9
Special tariff	-1
Service	-78
Services incl.	17

Service/Special Services

Brand	-7
Activation cost	-17
Monthly charge	-64
Peak tariff	-48
Off-peak tariff	-6
Special tariff	-32
Service	90
Services incl.	57

Cost Sensitive

Brand	-48
Activation cost	54
Monthly charge	17
Peak tariff	39
Off-peak tariff	97
Special tariff	16
Service	-71
Services incl.	-79

Monthly/Peak

Brand	-64
Activation cost	10
Monthly charge	79
Peak tariff	54
Off-peak tariff	-103
Special tariff	36
Service	17
Services incl.	-18

Description of Segments—Personal Users

Source: RI Data tables; Omnitel market research.

Size—Percent		Satisfaction with TIM	OutgoingCalls/Total Calls	Segment-specific Characteristics
Brand loyal	25%	• More satisfied than average (in particular by cost and additional services)	38%	• Younger profile (18-34 years) • Late adopters • Less sophisticated users (post office payment) • Use mainly off peak • Less willing to switch to private operator
Service sensitive	19%	• Very unsatisfied by cost • Unsatisfied by additional services technical assistance and plan flexibility	38%	• Mainly 25-44 years old • Calls equally distributed P/OP • Unwilling to switch to private operator
Peak charge and fixed costs	35%	• More satisfied than average (in particular by cost and plan flexibility)	36%	• Mainly 25-34 years old • Early adopters • Willing to switch
Cost Sensitive	21%	• Average satisfaction	30%	• Almost 60% employees • Mainly off peak calls

142

EXHIBIT 7 Value-based Segmentation—Prospects (deviation from sample average)

Source: RI Interim Data—Cluster analysis on conjoint data.

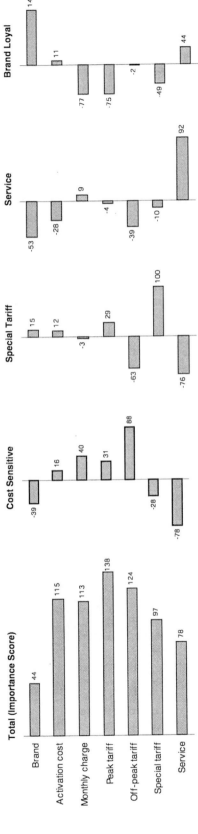

Total (Importance Score)

Brand	44
Activation cost	115
Monthly charge	113
Peak tariff	138
Off-peak tariff	124
Special tariff	97
Service	78

Cost Sensitive

Brand −39, Activation cost 16, Monthly charge 40, Peak tariff 31, Off-peak tariff 88, Special tariff −28, Service −78

Special Tariff

Brand 15, Activation cost 12, Monthly charge −3, Peak tariff 29, Off-peak tariff −63, Special tariff 100, Service −76

Service

Brand −53, Activation cost −28, Monthly charge 9, Peak tariff −4, Off-peak tariff −39, Special tariff −10, Service 92

Brand Loyal

Brand 143, Activation cost 11, Monthly charge −77, Peak tariff −75, Off-peak tariff −2, Special tariff −49, Service 44

Description of Segments—Prospects

Source: RI Data tables; Omnitel market research.

Size—Percent		Segment-specific Characteristics
Cost Sensitive	30%	• Mainly 25-54 years old • More professionals • Good attitude toward private operator • Strongly agree on having cellular phone to be always reached
Special tariff	22%	• Mainly 25-34 years old • Higher social class with smaller families • More informed about GSM technology • Pro-Telecom Italia
Service	33%	• Mid age (25-44 years) • Mid class • Unsatisfied by Telecom fixed and positive on private operator
Brand loyal	15%	• Mainly 25-34 years old • More educated • Handset costs as big of a barrier as service cost • Unsatisfied by Telecom fixed

143

EXHIBIT 8 Value-based Segmentation—Rejectors (deviation from sample average)

Source: RI Data—Cluster analysis on conjoint data.

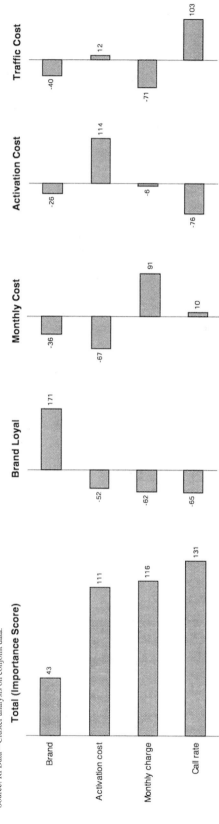

Total (Importance Score)

Brand 43
Activation cost 111
Monthly charge 116
Call rate 131

Brand Loyal

171
-52
-62
-65

Monthly Cost

-36
-67
91
10

Activation Cost

-26
114
-6
-76

Traffic Cost

-40
12
-71
103

Description of Segments—Rejectors

Source: RI Data tables; Omnitel market research.

Size—Percent		Segment-specific Characteristics
Monthly cost	33%	Mid class, more employees and retired people, mainly in smaller towns
Traffic cost	26%	Younger profile, more educated, more self-employed
Activation	25%	More males, more self-employed, mainly in larger towns
Brand loyal	17%	More females, larger share of non working individuals, more employees and housewives, mainly in larger towns

EXHIBIT 9   Country and Market Statistics

Source: Extracted from *European Cellular Industry Overview*, Goldman Sachs, October 23, 1995.

	Mobile Launch Date		Population (million)	(US$) GDP per Capita	Mobile Subscribers	
	Analog	Digital			2004E ('000)	1994–2004E CAGR
Finland	1982	1992	5.1	$19,250	2,162	13%
France	1985	1992	58.1	$23,050	11,455	29%
Italy	1985	1995	57.0	$18,070	17,350	23%
Norway	1981	1993	4.3	$27,020	2,093	14%
Sweden	1981	1992	8.8	$22,290	4,046	11%
United Kingdom	1985	1992	58.3	$17,550	20,433	18%

strong growth in the European cellular market for the next several years. (See **Exhibit 1** for subscriber growth.) A Research Analyst[19] explained at an Analyst Forum:

> First, cellular penetration rates are relatively modest both in absolute terms and relative to GDP per capita. Second, "value for money" of the service continues to increase due to the combination of reduced cost of the service and improved quality of service. Third, all cellular operators in Europe have adopted the GSM digital standard, which allows customers to use their cellular phones throughout Europe and many other parts of the world. Fourth, many European countries are beginning to have more than one mobile operator—leading to increased marketing of cellular services, which should improve customer awareness and help stimulate demand.

"The issues facing Europe are similar to those elsewhere in the world," Birdt continued:

> As overall penetration rates increase, average revenue per customer should continue to decline due to lower revenues per marginal customer. In order to achieve the projected penetration rates, cellular operators will increase their overall marketing efforts, which could increase subscriber acquisition costs. Also, the emergence of additional mobile operators and a more competitive market could place downward pressure on prices and upward pressure on costs. However, we remain very positive on the growth prospects for cellular services in Europe.

The Omnitel managers also had their eyes on the specific European countries where several strategies and trends were emerging in the mobile phone market. (See **Exhibit 9** for country and market statistics.)

Scandinavia

All three Scandinavian countries had very high penetration rates primarily due to their highly educated and wealthy populations (see **Exhibit 9** for GDP per capita) who had always been early adopters of technology. Mobile phones were also more cost-effective than fixed-line phones in Scandinavia because of the countries' vast size and low population density.[20] Also, because of a high standard of living, many Scandinavians had second weekend homes and preferred to just use a mobile phone at their second home.

Finland

The telecommunications market in Finland was the most sophisticated in Europe with a high degree of liberalization starting in 1985, which lead to increased competition and a high-quality infrastructure. The increased competition forced players to offer new and innovative products to its customers. Two operators dominated the cellular market in Finland. The first, Telecom Finland, had roughly two thirds of the market. The second, Finnet Group, through its associate company Radiolinja, had the remaining share of the market.

[19] Stuart Birdt, Goldman Sachs.

[20] Survey: Telecommunications: To the Finland Base Station, *The Economist*, October 9, 1999.

EXHIBIT 10

Source: European Cellular Industry Overview, Goldman Sachs, October 23, 1995.

Consumer Plan	Telecom Finland	
	With Tax	Without Tax
Connection fee[a]	$29.00	$23.75
Basic fee (per 6 months)	28.50	23.36
Airtime peak (7:00 A.M.–5:00 P.M.)	0.83	0.68
Airtime off-peak (5:00 P.M.–7:00 A.M.)	0.20	0.16

Note: Exchange rate: US$1 = FIM4.21.

[a]One-time fee charged to subscribers to initiate service.

Cellular operators had reached a penetration rate of 20% by year-end 1995. In addition to the reasons mentioned above, Finland's high penetration rate was also attributed to presence of the popular mobile phone operator, Nokia, which had its base in Finland.[21] Market penetration was expected to increase to 41.3% by the year 2000. Cellular operators in Finland competed primarily on service quality rather than prices. The average usage rate per subscriber in Finland was much higher than the average usage rate for Europe. Finnish operators were different from other European cellular operators because unlike the other European operators, the Finnish operators offered negligible dealer commissions and no handset subsidies (offering a handset subsidy was illegal in Finland).[22] Fixed charges, connection fees, and monthly charges were low in Finland, largely due to the lack of subsidies.[23] In addition, Finland's churn rate, at 12%, was one of the lowest in Europe. Analysts expected to see continued expansion of the customer base, although they expected the proportion of lower spending customers to increase primarily due to increasing volumes among existing customers.[24] (See **Exhibit 10** for tariffs.)

Sweden

The Swedish telecommunications market had a penetration rate of 23.4% by year-end 1995 and was expected to increase to 55% over the next 10 years. Sweden's usage rate was between 100–110 minutes per month per subscriber.[25] Sweden had very high acquisition costs because of high dealer commissions and handset subsidies as well as a high churn rate of 20.5% during 1995. Both handset subsidies and dealer commissions had been instrumental in attracting new customers.[26] Handset prices were expected to fall and analysts predicted that operators would be able to reduce their dealer commissions without restraining subscriber growth.[27] In addition, analysts expected to see significant reduction in prices of lower-end services as opposed to regular mobile services as cellular phones slowly replaced fixed-line phones.[28]

Liberalization in Sweden enabled the entrance of a large number of cellular operators. The country had three prominent players in its mobile telecom market. The first, Telia, the dominant telecom company with a market share of 71.6% at year-end 1995, started in 1981. In an effort to stay competitive, Telia was looking at international expansion as well as vertical expansion. The second, Europolitan, had a market share of 7.3%. The third, Comviq, commenced operations in 1981 as an analogue operator and began digital operations in September 1992. Comviq had the remaining share of the market. The three

[21] Ibid.

[22] Cellular Growth Analyser: SBC Warburg Dillon Read, October 23, 1997.

[23] Telecom Finland: Annual Report, 1996.

[24] Helsinki Telephone: Handelsbanken Markets, January 1998.

[25] NetCom Systems AB: Telecommunications Sweden, SBC Warburg, June 11, 1997.

[26] Ibid.

[27] Ibid.

[28] Telia: Handelsbanken Markets, October 1997.

EXHIBIT 11
Sweden Tariff
Comparison

Source: Extracted from *NetCom Systems AB: Sweden Research*, Goldman Sachs, September 10, 1996.

Consumer Plan	Comviq	Telia Mobiltel	Europolitan
Connection fee[b]	$30.00	$0.00	$0.00
Monthly subscription[a]	18.80	22.46	22.46
Airtime peak	0.66	0.72	0.72
Airtime off-peak	0.12 to 0.24	0.24	0.24

Note: Exchange rate: US$1 = SEK6.68.
[a]Monthly subscription fee covers call costs up to the amount of the monthly fee.
[b]One-time fee charged to subscribers to initiate service.

EXHIBIT 12
Norway Tariff
Comparison

Source: Extracted from *NetCom GSM: Norway Research*, Goldman Sachs, April 1, 1996.

Consumer Plan	NetCom asa	Telenor Mobil
Connection fee[a]	$57.00	$40.72
Subscription	8.14	8.14
Airtime peak	1.14	1.14
Airtime off-peak	0.49	0.49

Note: Exchange rate: US$1 = NOK6.14.
[a]One-time fee charged to subscribers to initiate service.

operators had different strategies. Telia capitalized on its significant financial resources and long-standing relationships with large business users.[29] Europolitan primarily focused on high-end business users and, as a result, had less subscribers, but higher revenue per subscriber than Comviq.[30] Comviq viewed its wireless business as a mass-market product and attempted to attract both business and private users.[31] (See **Exhibit 11** for tariffs.)

Norway

The Norwegian mobile phone market had a penetration rate of approximately 25.1% at the end of 1995. Norway had two key players competing in the mobile telecommunications market: TeleNor and Netcom Asa. TeleNor began its operations in 1982 and had a majority market share of 65%. Netcom Asa, which launched its service in 1993, had the remaining market share of 35%. A majority of Netcom's customers were private or non-business customers whom Netcom attracted through aggressive marketing efforts.[32] Netcom also targeted its marketing efforts towards small and mid-sized companies with up to 500 employees. TeleNor, on the other hand, had considerable control over the market for large companies.

To increase traffic, both operators had begun to reduce their tariffs. (See **Exhibit 12** for tariffs.) Both operators, like most of their European counterparts faced a high churn rate of 22% during the early 1996. To combat this problem, the operators were focusing on creating loyalty among their high-end customers through quality service, rather than offering further price reductions to their low-end customers.[33] The low-end customers were much more sensitive to changes in prices, and often chose and changed subscriptions according to the prices they offered.[34] The operators marketed their services directly to the end user through dealers whom they controlled or with whom they had close relationships.[35] The operators

[29] NetCom Systems AB: Sweden Research, Goldman Sachs, September 10, 1996.

[30] Ibid.

[31] Ibid.

[32] Ibid.

[33] Netcom ASA, Enskilda Securities, August 18, 1997.

[34] Ibid.

[35] Netcom GSM: Norway Research, Goldman Sachs, April 1, 1996.

paid the dealers responsible for selling the handsets a commission to encourage sales. Operators also offered subsidies on handsets, but expected subsidies to decline since phone prices were also expected to fall over the next few years.

United Kingdom

In the United Kingdom, the mobile market had a penetration of 9.3% by December 1995, with continued strong growth expected in the next 10 years. The cellular companies hoped to stimulate demand by offering lower handset prices and continued subsidies. The usage rate ranged from 160–170 minutes per month per subscriber.

Vodafone and Cellnet were the dominant players in the United Kingdom's mobile market, with 43.0% and 42.3%, respectively. Along with two other companies, Orange with a 7.3% market share, and Mercury One2One with a 7.4% market share, they had a total of 5.4 million subscribers among them by year-end 1995.[36] Both Vodafone and Cellnet had a geographic coverage of over 89% within the United Kingdom and roaming access to over 120 networks in 70 countries. Neither of the other two competitors came close to offering this breadth of coverage.

The emergence of Orange caused a significant change in the pricing, usage and growth in the U.K. wireless industry.[37] Vodafone introduced a series of new tariffs, which included "bundled" minutes, with lower prices, in response to the success Orange had in attracting customers; other operators offered special promotions, including a fixed number of free minutes of airtime per month for a specified number of months.[38] (See **Exhibit 13** for tariffs.) Although cellular phones were mostly used by high-end business customers,

[36] Orange plc: U.K. Research, Goldman Sachs, January 19, 1996.

[37] Ibid.

[38] Ibid.

EXHIBIT 13   **U.K. Tariff Comparison**

Source: Extracted from *Orange plc: U.K. Research,* Goldman Sachs, January 14, 1996.

Operator/Consumer Plan	Connection Charge[a]	Monthly Charge	Inclusive Minutes	Call Charges[b] Peak	Call Charges[b] Off-peak	Charge Period[c]
Orange						
Talk 15[d]	$47.40	$23.70	15	0.40	0.30	1 second
Talk 60[d]	$47.40	$39.50	60	0.32	0.16	1 second
Vodafone (GSM)						
Personal World[b]	$39.50	$23.70	None	0.55	0.24	60 sec/30 sec
Personal World Extra	$47.40	$35.55	50	0.47	0.16	1 second
Cellnet (GSM)						
Frequent Caller-Plus	$79.00	$39.50	None	0.40	0.16	60 sec/30 sec
Regular Caller-Plus	$39.50	$23.70	None	0.55	0.24	60 sec/30 sec
Mercury One2One[e]						
Bronze Service	$47.40	$23.70	None	0.40	0.08	1 second
Silver Service	$47.40	$39.50	None	0.24	0.08	1 second
Gold Service	$47.40	$55.30	None	0.24	0.08	1 second

Note: Exchange rate: US$1 = £0.63.

[a]A one-time fee charged to subscribers to initiate service.

[b]These tariff schemes provide loyalty discount of 5% after one year and 10% after two years.

[c]Initial minimum charge period and billing increment thereafter.

[d]Number of free minutes included in the fixed monthly charge.

[e]Mercury One2One tariff schemes include weekend free local calls.

companies were beginning to target the less wealthy business community.[39] The subscriber acquisition costs were high in the United Kingdom because of the huge subsidies on handsets. The top-of-the-range handsets received subsidies of up to £250[40] (£1 = $1.58). In addition, a study by Andersen Consulting in early 1996 indicated that the United Kingdom had the highest churn rate in Western Europe at 28%.[41]

Telecommunications in the United Kingdom was regulated; therefore, it had a special structure where dealers purchased airtime at wholesale rates from the cellular operators, and retailed the cellular service to their subscribers.[42] These dealers sold not only their own service, but also branded services like Vodafone's and earned commissions for signing up new customers and retained a percentage of the revenues generated by the customers. In addition to selling services to customers, they also sold handsets, and were responsible for the billing of the service (and assumption of the risk of bad debt and fraud) as well as all customer service functions.

LIBERO: The New Proposal

Armed with results of the market research and conjoint analysis, Della Valle and Bona were very conscious of the fact that they needed to avoid getting into a price war with TIM under any circumstance. Rather, they wanted to focus on building Omnitel's market share through segmentation and pricing innovation. Since TIM offered only two different plans (Eurofamily & Europrofessional), Della Valle saw a definite opportunity for Omnitel: "If we can further segment the market in terms of needs, attitudes, pattern of usage, demographics, and certain other characteristics," Della Valle explained, "we can achieve greater penetration by creating customer loyalty." The new proposal that Bona had prepared with Della Valle's help would not only be a major commercial launch for Omnitel, but also its first step towards pricing innovation.

Della Valle and Bona wanted an Italian name for Omnitel's next new plan, and LIBERO seemed like the perfect name. LIBERO meant, "free" in Italian, and they wanted to market the name to mean that it was a plan "free of taxes and monthly fees."

No Monthly Fee

By eliminating the fee, Omnitel would be able to increase not only the number of subscriptions, but also the volume of usage. The per minute charge of Lit. 195 would be higher than TIM's rate of Lit. 170 per minute. Bona and Della Valle did not want to focus on the price of the plan, but on the concept of no monthly fees.

Advertising and Distribution

Bona's proposal included opening shops in strategic locations like downtown Milan and the Milan airport as well as through franchising. Bona explained:

> If we are able to create a demand for the Omnitel cellular service, then the rest of the distribution will need to carry Omnitel phones because otherwise they will lose sales. So, instead of offering dealers increased commissions to promote our services, we are going to put that money into our advertising campaign to create this incredible demand for Omnitel's cellular phones. With LIBERO, we will not offer any handset subsidies nor will we increase commissions to dealers, even though some dealers have been asking us for more commissions. With the no monthly fee concept, we will greatly increase our customer base, because that's what

[39] Vodafone Group: Smith Barney Analyst Report, September 9, 1996.

[40] Telecom Italia Mobile: SBC Warburg Analyst Report, September 25, 1996.

[41] Kris Szaniawski, Mobile Communications: 1996 Pearson Professional Ltd., September 5, 1996.

[42] Orange plc: U.K. Research, Goldman Sachs, January 19, 1996.

customers want. So, even though dealers won't be making large commissions, they will be making more of them. This increase in our customer base is also going to build traffic in the dealers' stores. They are going to thank us one day for the tremendous volume we will bring them if we implement the LIBERO plan.

Next Steps

Bona wanted to dramatically change the rules. He believed that cellular phones would become the main mode of communication. To accomplish this goal, Omnitel could pursue one of two options. The first option, which Bona supported, would include eliminating the monthly fee, but charging full price for the handset. The other option, which Caio seemed

EXHIBIT 14 **European Mobile Markets**

Source: Extracted from Société Générale Strauss Turnbull Securities Ltd., October 1996.

	Subscribers Prior to Competition (000s)	Subscribers June 1996 (000s)	Net Change (000s)	Subscribers of New Operators (000s)	New Operator Market Share
Denmark	210	1,254	1,044	461	44%
Finland	356	1,335	979	230	24
France	170	1,961	1,791	744	42
East Germany	840	2,140	1,300	700	54
West Germany	2,140	4,953	2,813	390	14
Italy	3,800	5,220	1,420	502	35
Netherlands	480	846	366	140	38
Portugal	27	451	424	237	56
Sweden	675	2,328	1,653	712	43
United Kingdom	1,900	6,198	4,298	1,067	25
Total/Average	9,758	25,847	16,089	5,183	32

EXHIBIT 15 **Estimated European Cellular Subscribers Growth, 1995–2004E**

Source: Extracted from Mobile Communications, November 30, 1995.

Country	Year-end 1995		Year-end 1998E		Year-end 2000E		1994
	Subscribers	Penetration	Subscribers	Penetration	Subscribers	Penetration	2004E CAGR
Belgium	212	2.1%	573	5.6%	1,603	15.5%	29%
Denmark	659	12.7	1,049	20.0	1,869	35.1	14
Finland	1,024	20.1	1,462	28.4	2,162	41.3	13
France	1,371	2.3	4,125	7.0	11,455	19.2	29
Germany	3,471	4.2	7,613	9.3	18,333	22.2	22
Italy	3,794	6.5	8,050	14.1	17,350	30.4	23
Netherlands	503	3.3	1,261	8.1	3,361	20.8	26
Norway	1,090	25.1	1,633	37.4	2,093	47.4	14
Portugal	293	2.8	658	6.7	1,323	13.2	23
Spain	871	2.2	2,832	7.2	6,932	17.5	33
Sweden	2,066	23.4	2,911	32.6	4,046	44.5	11
United Kingdom	5,416	9.3	11,988	20.3	19,765	32.7	18

partial to, but one that Bona thought was not the appropriate path for Omnitel and the Italian market, would include offering a heavily subsidized handset to customers in exchange for signing a contract for a certain period with Omnitel, and paying monthly fees.

Bona knew that if he wanted Caio to seriously consider his proposal, he would have to convince Caio of three things. First, eliminating the monthly fee would not lead Omnitel into a price war with TIM. Second, eliminating the much-detested monthly fee would increase Omnitel's customer base far more than if it were to offer handset subsidies. Third, even without the minimum monthly fee from its customers, Omnitel would be able to receive more revenues because of the sheer increase in the overall call volume. Finally, even if he could find satisfactory answers to these questions, he still had to worry about how to communicate this plan to the end users and get the support of the dealer network. With these thoughts in mind, Bona leafed through **Exhibits 14** and **15** and began wondering if he needed any last-minute modifications to his plan: LIBERO.

Part 3

Choosing Customers

Chapter  9

Target Market Selection and Product Positioning

Miklos Sarvary

We have seen that after marketing analysis, the next phase in the marketing process consists of the following three steps:

- market segmentation
- target market selection and
- product/service positioning

These steps are the prerequisites for designing a successful marketing strategy. They allow the firm to focus its efforts on the right customers and also provide the organizing force for the marketing mix elements. Product positioning in particular, provides the synergy between the 4Ps of the marketing plan.

In this note we will elaborate in more detail on how to perform these steps. The objective is to show you a few tools that are used in practice by marketing professionals. You have seen some of these tools in detail in the module addressing customer analysis. Here, we will recall how to use them for strategy setting.

1. Market Segmentation

Market segmentation is a logical next step to customer analysis. It consists of clustering the firms' potential consumers in groups (called market segments) that clearly differ from each other but show a great deal of homogeneity within the group. In other words, the objective

Professor Miklos Sarvary prepared this note as the basis for class discussion rather than to illustrate either effective or ineffective handling of an administrative situation. Professor John Deighton provided part of the material.

is to find groups of consumers who share the same (or similar) preferences. However, it is also important that the so-created groups be sufficiently different from each other.

One needs to distinguish between two (related) types of segmentation: (i) benefit segmentation and (ii) segmentation based on observable characteristics. Benefit segmentation is really what marketers are trying to achieve (i.e. to group consumers based on their needs). Take the example of nonprescription drugs treating pain, inflammation and fever. Market research has revealed that people evaluate these drugs along two dimensions: effectiveness and gentleness. There are two basic segments, each valuing one of these dimensions more than the other. Thus, there is a segment that prefers an effective drug even if it has side effects while the other segment prefers a less effective drug provided that it is gentler, i.e. without side effects. These two segments represent benefit segments because they are based on differences in consumers' preferences.

In practice, we can typically observe segments based on some observable characteristics. We have seen that most often, marketers use consumer demographics[1], consumers' geographic location and their lifestyle to create segments. The motivation is clear. Segments created in such a way are easy to identify and address with a marketing message. It is important to realize however, that *such segmentation only works to the extent that it is correlated with benefit segments.* In the previous example about nonprescription painkillers, it happens to be the case that older people tend to belong to the benefit segment that values the drugs' gentleness while younger consumers prefer potent drugs even if they have side effects. As such, age is a good variable to segment the market in this case. Age groups are easy to target and, in this case, age strongly correlates with distinct consumer preferences.

The analytic tool to perform the task of market segmentation is **cluster analysis.** Cluster analysis does exactly what segmentation is about. It finds groups of people based on how far they are from each other in a multi-dimensional space defined by many characteristics. Furthermore, it also computes measures to inform the researcher how "good" the grouping is, where a "good grouping" is defined as one where people are close to each other when they belong to the same group but each group is situated relatively far from the others. Again, the characteristics used by the procedure can be of two types: they can relate to benefits and they can relate to observable variables. As we have discussed, segmentation should start with benefit segmentation. Therefore, the first step is to identify clusters of customer needs. Such analysis is usually preceded with the measurement of customer needs for a representative sample of consumers using **conjoint analysis.** Once preference data is collected with this procedure, the marketer can apply cluster analysis to find prototypical consumer groups. A good example, is the study we have seen in the Omnitel case (501-002). Exhibit 6 in the case shows that there are 4 benefit segments based on consumers' preference profiles: "brand loyals," "service sensitives," "cost sensitives" and people who are sensitive to peak tariffs. Once such groups have been established, the next step is to identify what consumer demographics-based categorization correlates to this benefit segmentation. In other words, what demographics would discriminate best between these benefit segments? **Discriminant analysis** helps the marketer to find such variables. Discriminant analysis is a statistical tool that orders a set of variables based on how good they are at discriminating between two or more groups of observations. Besides providing an ordered list of variables, the procedure also provides statistics that help assess the discriminating ability of the variables. Using discriminant analysis, the marketer obtains a suggestion on what

---

[1] "Demographics" is also often used to segment business markets. In this case, demographic variables used to identify segments include the Standard Industrial Classification (S.I.C.) code, the organization's size and geographic location. Beyond these demographic variables type of organization (e.g. profit, non-profit), organizational structure (e.g. hierarchical, connected etc.) and the type of buying situation are also often used for segmenting business markets.

observable variables to use for segmentation and how good those variables are in describing the benefit segments. Exhibit 6 in the Omnitel case also shows the demographic characteristics of the four benefit segments.

In summary, segmentation requires the following steps from the marketer:

- measure customer needs with conjoint analysis on a representative sample of potential consumers
- Find prototypical consumer profiles (benefit segments) using cluster analysis on conjoint data.
- Find the observable variables (demographics) that are most likely to discriminate between the so-created benefit segments using discriminant analysis.

This process seems quite straightforward, but in practice it requires quite a bit of experience and creativity. There can be multiple acceptable benefit segmentations suggested by cluster analysis for example. In general, these procedures require multiple iterations and informed compromises from the marketer in order to provide a "good," actionable segmentation for the product. This is why customer analysis and segmentation are also referred to as "data mining," a term often used by database marketers.

2. Target Market Selection

Target market selection is the next logical step following segmentation. Once the firm understands the structure of consumer demand it has to decide which segments it wants to serve and how. Thus, in this phase, customer analysis is complemented by two additional analyses—competitive and company analyses—to perform the task of target market selection. The objective is to select segments in such a way that the firm maximizes its profit. In the case of over-the-counter painkillers discussed above, there are two basic types of drugs competing on the market. One is based on aspirin (e.g. Bayer) and the other is based on acetaminophen (e.g. Tylenol). It turns out that aspirin is more effective but has side effects causing minor stomach irritation. Thus, it is natural for firms producing these different drugs to focus on the segments that best fit their products. In this case, target market selection is relatively simple. In other cases, more elaborate analysis is required to choose the appropriate segments to serve.

The key analysis for target market selection is called **differential advantage analysis.**[2] It is a systematic way to collect and compare data on potential competitors *and* your company to evaluate who is most likely to succeed serving each of the identified segments. The method starts by data collection on each competitor (including your firm) in five areas:

- Ability to conceive and design
- Ability to produce (quality and quantity)
- Ability to market
- Ability to finance
- Ability to manage/execute

Each of these general areas need to be subdivided to more concrete questions/items. In the first category for example, "ability to design" the marketer needs to evaluate competitors' R&D capability (size and experience of the design group and R&D budget), existing

---

[2] See *Product Management*, chapter 5, by Lehmann, D. R. and R. S. Winer, Irwin, 1997 for more details and examples on this method.

patents and copyrights, access to new technologies through third parties, etc. Similarly, to assess "ability to produce" competitors' production technology and capacity as well as flexibility need to be evaluated. Once the data are collected, the next step is to synthesize the data in so-called *competitor capability matrices,* one matrix for each segment. In each matrix, the detailed items of the evaluation areas are listed in the rows and the competitors—including the firm itself—are listed in the columns. Each entry consists of a rating (say on a 10-point scale) of the competitor on the item corresponding to the entry. This format allows the marketer to recognize obvious patterns and identify the segments where his/her firm is likely to be the strongest player. If there are too many items in the rows (as it is often the case), it is useful to replicate the matrix by only listing the items that represent critical success factors in the product category. This allows a more parsimonious evaluation of the situation.

Differential advantage analysis only helps in target market selection by pointing out the strength and weaknesses of the firm in addressing each of the market segments. Once these are identified, the firm needs to consider an additional factor, namely the competitive reactions it might face if it decides to compete for a segment. This includes a careful analysis of competitors' overall corporate strategies and their reputation/history for competitive behavior.

3. Product Positioning

As we have seen before product positioning is the marketers' effort to identify a unique selling proposition for the product. A good positioning statement answers three questions to the public:

(i) Who are the customers,

(ii) What is the set of needs that the product fulfills and

(iii) Why is the product the best option to satisfy those needs?

The positioning statement is primarily directed to potential customers and has a guiding role in defining every element of the marketing mix. It provides the organizing force between the marketing mix elements to ensure synergy among them. However, it is also important for internal communication within the firm. It provides the identity to the firm. For example, the famous positioning statement by IBM, *"The solution to your problem is IBM"* helped change the firm's internal culture by teaching employees to be problem solvers for the customer.

What tools do marketers have to perform the task and evaluate the output of product positioning? The tools in question are **perceptual maps.** They tell the marketer which product dimensions are important for customers and how does the product fare compared to competitors and consumers' ideal point.

As you recall (see note Analyzing Consumer Perceptions, 599-110), there are two very different approaches for creating perceptual maps: (i) compositional and (ii) decompositional. **Compositional** perceptual maps are based on product attributes pre-defined by the marketer. To create such a map the marketer needs to follow three steps:

(i) Obtain "important" product attributes

(ii) Obtain ratings on these attributes

(iii) Compose map based on "relevant" attributes

The result of the first step should be already available from cluster analysis, which also starts with a careful collection of product attributes. As you recall, this step is usually done in a focus group, which is a structured but typically open-ended conversation between a marketer and a small group of (potential) consumers. The objective is to understand which product attributes are important for consumers. In this phase it is usually a good idea to include as many attributes as possible. The second step is typically done by survey methodology, where a questionnaire is sent to a large population of carefully selected potential consumers who rate products on each attribute. The final step consists of a statistical procedure (typically **factor analysis**), which clusters the attributes into groups called "factors." Within each group, the attributes are highly correlated but each factor is independent from each other. Conceptually, factor analysis is the "segmentation" of the attributes. The so-obtained factors are assumed to be the relevant dimensions along which consumers evaluate products. Marketers usually "name" the factors based on the "holistic evaluation" of the variables that they contain. This creative process is quite subjective but has an important implication for later marketing action. It is essentially the interpretation of consumers' perceptions. A nice example of a perceptual map can be seen in the L.L. Bean case. There, the researchers decided that the two key attributes to position all clothing apparel stores are (i) how formal their assortment is and (ii) how fashionable it is.

Decompositional perceptual maps are created without the pre-definition of product dimensions. Advocates of this methodology argue that people are not really good at expressing what attributes are important for their choice decisions. Rather, people tend to evaluate products "holistically".[3] Decompositional maps are created in two steps:

(i) Obtain perceived distance measures between products

(ii) Compose map that best fits the reported distance measures

The first step is done in a survey where consumers are asked to rate (say on a 10-point scale) how "similar/dissimilar" a set of products in the same category are from each other. The second step is based on a statistical procedure called **multidimensional scaling.** Interestingly, most of the time people's distance ratings provide relatively consistent maps. The final step consists again of interpreting the dimensions of the map. This step is even more subjective than naming the factors in factor analysis and requires far more creativity.

Both compositional and decompositional perceptual maps have advantages and drawbacks. Compositional maps are easier to interpret because they are based on real product attributes. However, they often miss key attributes that consumers have a hard time to articulate. For this reason, decompositional methods are better suited for the evaluation of entirely new product concepts. They are also easier to administer because consumers are only asked to rate a single distance between products, rather than filling out a lengthy questionnaire.

4. Product Differentiation

Product differentiation is an important part of product positioning. As we have seen, one role of the positioning statement is to clearly articulate to consumers the benefits that the product fulfills. However, the firm does not want to introduce products targeted at needs that are already served by competitors. In such situations consumers simply choose the cheaper firm and competitors have an incentive to undercut each other's price. This leads

---

[3] An often-sited example is a marketing study performed about electric cars. The car market being well-understood marketers have created a perceptual map based on consumers' ratings of cars on traditional attributes. A subsequent simulated test market gave completely inconsistent results. It turned out that a major attribute, "whether the car was electric or not" explained almost all the discrepancy between the results. People simply disliked the fact that the car was electric even if it matched traditional cars on all "important" attributes.

to intense price competition and leaves no profit to the firm. To avoid price competition the product needs to be clearly **differentiated** from other offerings. We distinguish two types of differentiation labeled **horizontal** and **vertical,** respectively.

Horizontal Differentiation

Horizontal differentiation is a positioning strategy that makes use of the fact that consumers differ in their *tastes*. In the category of passenger cars for example, some consumers like small cars, others like sedans while still others like sport cars. Each of these groups consists of a relatively homogeneous set of people with similar needs. The idea of horizontal differentiation is to identify the group(s) whose need(s) are not served by a competitor.

Perceptual maps can be also used to identify possible un-served needs. It is relatively easy to spot on the map empty areas, i.e. a combination of attributes not covered by other products. These represent opportunities for new, differentiated product introductions. It is not clear however, that these opportunities can be explored. The attribute combinations in question may not be technically feasible (supply-side constraint). Alternatively, the identified area may represent an insufficient number of consumers (demand-side constraint). The goal is to select un-served needs that can be *profitably* realized.

Vertical Differentiation

Vertical differentiation also exploits the fact that consumers are different. However, it takes advantage of a different source of consumer heterogeneity, namely that consumers differ in their *willingness to pay for quality*. In a pure vertical differentiation problem, consumers agree on a unique relevant dimension driving their preferences. We call this dimension "quality." Quality may be the combination (e.g. the weighted average) of many complementary attributes. In the case of passenger cars for example, it can be a combination of speed, comfort and reliability. All consumers agree that these are the relevant dimensions contributing to quality and they all prefer more quality to less. They only differ in their *valuation* of quality. Staying with the example of passenger cars, most consumers prefer a BMW to a Ford, but few can (or would be willing to) pay the price for the BMW. Vertical differentiation amounts to positioning products to consumers with a specific willingness to pay for quality un-served by a competitor.

Perceptual maps can also provide guidance for vertical differentiation. In product categories where preferences are taste driven, perceptual maps exhibit "ideal points" representing segments of consumers with distinct tastes. In product categories where quality is the key determinant of preferences, the perceptual map often produces an "ideal direction," which essentially represents consumers' perception of quality. Successful products tend to line up along this direction. In the Tweeter case for example, most consumers would categorize Tweeter as a higher quality store than Circuit City because of its service as well as its product assortment. Which attributes and to what extent contribute to the perception of quality is itself an important question for the marketer. Also, it is easy to spot empty segments on the quality dimension indicating possible opportunities for the introduction of new products.

Differentiation in Practice

In most product categories, marketers have the option to differentiate their products both along quality as well as in terms of customer tastes. Creativity again, plays an important role in this task. New product dimensions can be discovered that are important to segments, which have not been thought of as consumers before. IBM for example was taken by surprise with the emergence of the PC category, which appealed to the individual consumer rather than businesses and corporations. It turned out that this new segment of the market was interested in ease of use and an affordable price. The firm can sometimes change the

FIGURE 1
The Augmented Product[4]

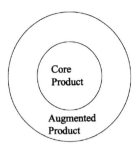

entire paradigm of differentiation. Product categories where preferences are largely performance driven may be differentiated horizontally (examples include Apple's iMac or Swatch's redefinition of the watches category).

The primary time for thinking about differentiation for existing products is in the phase of product concept development. The firm should strive to develop products that are differentiated from competitors'. However, other elements of the marketing mix also have an important role in differentiation. Advertising is an obvious tool to communicate to consumers to what extent and along what dimensions the product is different from other alternatives. Price can be an important signal of quality and thus it is a tool for vertical differentiation. Packaging can be key for differentiation (think of the importance of packaging for "green" consumers, for example).

One of the most important tools of differentiation is customer service. As products mature, all competitors can efficiently deliver the same core product attributes. Then, the only way to create a sustainable differentiated offering is through special customer services. This leads to, what we call the **augmented product** (see **Figure 1**). Car dealerships for example, offer roughly the same core products (similar selection of cars) but they differentiate themselves on the type and amount of services that they offer to customers. Services are an efficient tool for differentiation because they are relatively hard to copy by competitors compared to other marketing mix elements. In contrast to physical products, it is hard to quantify the additional profit generated by services. However, it is relatively easy to see the extra expenditures that they represent. Because to most firms, services appear to be a risky investment, competitors are reluctant to match services in the short run.

The Role of Brands in Product Differentiation

It helps to start to think about brands simply as nouns that marketers have introduced into consumers' language to make product differentiation concrete. At a minimum, we want to assert that our offering is not like our competitors' offerings. When we call something Snapple for instance, we are asserting that it is worth noting some special distinctions between Snapple and all other fruit juices. Some of these assertions can be viewed as promises or pledges about attributes of the product that cannot be verified before buying. Other assertions may have to do with how Snapple users are differentiated from Cola users, or how Snapple usage occasions are differentiated from other beverage usage occasions. Most ambitiously, a brand can assert that it *is* the category. Perhaps the highest goal to which a brand builder can aspire is to have the noun that he/she has imposed on the language displace the natural language word. For example, facial tissue was displaced by Kleenex, acetaminophen became Tylenol, online book buying became Amazon and we speak of Fedexing a package or Xeroxing a document.

Rich meanings accumulate around brands, as they do around all the nouns in language. Some of these meanings derive from the marketer's assertions, pledges and promises, but not all. Brands come to mean things the marketer may not have intended, as for example

[4] Theodore Levitt (1980), "Marketing Success Through Differentiation—of Anything," *Harvard Business Review* (January–February).

when Perrier came to mean "polluted with benzene." It is often the case that consumers co-create the meanings of brands, taking the marketer's efforts and turning them to their own purposes, as for example motorcycle gangs did with Harley Davidson. Building a brand is a complex meaning-making negotiation. It takes time, costs money, and often fails. But if it succeeds, the sum of the meanings attached to the brand constitutes an asset, called brand equity that may be among the corporation's most valuable properties. Brands, like all nouns, *denote* and *connote*. That is, they point to things (denotation) and convey the signification of those things (connotation). To a builder of brands, it is important to note that unless the brand is useful for denoting, it will not survive long enough to connote anything.

How can we ensure that a brand denotes something useful? It may help to think of the consumer as navigating an unfamiliar landscape, and turning to the brand as a navigation aid or signpost. We do not want to create more signposts than the customer needs, and certainly not fewer. As an illustration, you may find that your credit card carries as many as three brands. It may bear a bank or affinity group's brand, an issuer like First USA or Associates, and a network like Cirrus or Plus. These are all attempts at service differentiation through brand building. Will they all succeed? Do consumers care for so many signposts? If you need to draw cash in a distant city, you may need the Cirrus brand. If you want to avoid intrusive telemarketing from an aggressive card issuer, you may need the issuer's brand. In all likelihood, every experience differentiating this card from the others in your wallet will, however, accrue to only the dominant brand. Many financial service brands struggle to denote anything that the consumer finds worthy of notice.

When you have solved the denoting problem, you can confront the connoting problem. A brand's connotations are, in effect, its *reputation*. And like all reputations, they are partly the result of being inherently good or bad, and partly a matter of grandstanding. In a perfect world, a strong brand would be simply the reward for being a good product. However there is a great deal of stage management in brand building. We shall pick up that discussion in the note on integrated marketing communication.

Chapter 10

Warner-Lambert Ireland: Niconil

John A. Quelch   Susan P. Smith

Declan Dixon, director of marketing for Warner-Lambert Ireland (WLI), examined two very different sales forecasts as he considered the upcoming launch of Niconil, scheduled for January 1990. Niconil was an innovative new product that promised to help the thousands of smokers who attempted to quit smoking each year. More commonly known simply as "the patch," Niconil was a transdermal skin patch that gradually released nicotine into the bloodstream to alleviate the physical symptoms of nicotine withdrawal.

Now in October of 1989, Dixon and his staff had to decide several key aspects of the product launch. There were different opinions about how Niconil should be priced and in what quantities it would sell. Pricing decisions would directly impact product profitability as well as sales volume, and accurate sales forecasts were vital to planning adequate production capacity. Finally, the product team needed to reach consensus on the Niconil communications campaign to meet advertising deadlines and to ensure an integrated product launch.

Company Background

Warner-Lambert was an international pharmaceutical and consumer products company with over $4 billion in worldwide revenues expected in 1989. Warner-Lambert consumer products (50% of worldwide sales) included such brands as Dentyne chewing gum, Listerine

Research Associate Susan P. Smith prepared this case under the supervision of Professor John A. Quelch as the basis for class discussion rather than to illustrate either effective or ineffective handling of an administrative situation.

TABLE A
Incidence of
Cigarette Smoking in
Ireland (1988–1989)

Of adult population (16 and over)	30%	(100%)
By Gender		
Men	32	(50)
Women	27	(50)
By Age		
16–24	27	(17)
25–34	38	(14)
35–44	29	(12)
45–54	29	(9)
55+	27	(19)
By Occupation		
White collar	24	(25)
Skilled working class	33	(30)
Semi- and unskilled	38	(29)
Farming	23	(17)

Note: To be read (for example): 27% of Irish citizens aged 16–24 smoked, and this age group represented 17% of the population.

mouth wash, and Hall's cough drops. Its pharmaceutical products, marketed through the Parke Davis Division, included drugs for treating a wide variety of ailments, including heart disease and bronchial disorders.

Warner-Lambert's Irish subsidiary was expected to generate £30 million in sales revenues in 1989:[1] £22 million from exports of manufactured products to other Warner-Lambert subsidiaries in Europe and £4 million each from pharmaceutical and consumer products sales within Ireland. The Irish drug market was estimated at £155 million (in manufacturer sales) in 1989. Warner-Lambert was the sixteenth-largest pharmaceutical company in worldwide revenues; in Ireland, it ranked sixth.

Dixon was confident that WLI's position in the Irish market would ensure market acceptance of Niconil. The Parke Davis Division had launched two new drugs successfully within the past nine months: Dilzem, a treatment for heart disease, and Accupro, a blood pressure medication. The momentum was expected to continue. The Irish market would be the first country launch for Niconil and thus serve as a test market for all of Warner-Lambert. The companywide significance of the Niconil launch was not lost on Dixon as he pondered the marketing decisions before him.

Smoking in the Republic of Ireland

Almost £600 million would be spent by Irish smokers on 300 million packs of cigarettes in 1989; this included government revenues from the tobacco sales tax of £441 million. Of 3.5 million Irish citizens, 30% of the 2.5 million adults smoked cigarettes (compared with 40% of adults in continental Europe and 20% in the United States).[2] The number of smokers in Ireland had peaked in the late 1970s and had been declining steadily since. **Table A** presents data from a 1989 survey that WLI had commissioned of a demographically balanced sample of 1,400 randomly chosen Irish adults. **Table B** shows the numbers of cigarettes smoked by Irish smokers; the average was 16.5 cigarettes.

Media coverage on the dangers of smoking, anti-smoking campaigns from public health organizations such as the Irish Cancer Society, and a mounting array of legislation restricting tobacco advertising put pressure on Irish smokers to quit. Promotional discounts and coupons for tobacco products were prohibited, and tobacco advertising was banned not

[1] In 1989, one Irish pound was equivalent to US$1.58.

[2] *Adults* were defined as those over the age of 15, and *smokers* as those who smoked at least one cigarette per day.

TABLE B
Number of Cigarettes Smoked Daily in Ireland: (Based on 400 Smokers in a 1989 Survey of 1,400 Citizens)

More than 20	16%
15–20	42
10–14	23
5–9	12
Less than 5	4
Unsure	3

EXHIBIT 1   **Cigarette Advertisement from an Irish Magazine**

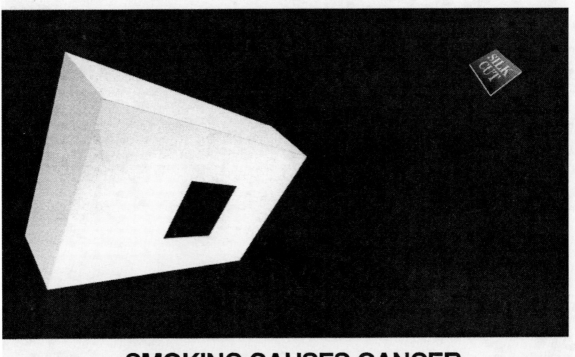

SMOKING CAUSES CANCER
Irish Government Warning

only on television and radio but also on billboards. Print advertising was allowed only if 10% of the ad space was devoted to warnings on the health risks of smoking. **Exhibit 1** shows a sample cigarette advertisement from an Irish magazine.

Smoking as an Addiction

Cigarettes and other forms of tobacco contained nicotine, a substance that induced addictive behavior. Smokers first developed a tolerance for nicotine and then, over time, needed to increase cigarette consumption to maintain a steady, elevated blood level of nicotine. Smokers became progressively dependent on nicotine and suffered withdrawal symptoms if they stopped smoking. A craving for tobacco was characterized by physical symptoms such as decreased heart rate and a drop in blood pressure, and later could include symptoms like faintness, headaches, cold sweats, intestinal cramps, nausea, and vomiting. The smoking habit also had a psychological component stemming from the ritualistic aspects of smoking behavior, such as smoking after meals or in times of stress.

Since the 1950s, the ill effects of smoking had been researched and identified. Smoking was widely recognized as posing a serious health threat. While nicotine was the substance within the cigarette that caused addiction, it was the tar accompanying the nicotine that made smoking so dangerous. Specifically, smoking was a primary risk factor for ischaemic heart disease, lung cancer, and chronic pulmonary diseases. Other potential dangers resulting from prolonged smoking included bronchitis, emphysema, chronic sinusitis, peptic ulcer disease, and for pregnant women, damage to the fetus.

Once smoking was recognized as a health risk, the development and use of a variety of smoking cessation techniques began. In *aversion therapy,* the smoker was discouraged from smoking by pairing an aversive event such as electric shock or a nausea-inducing agent with the smoking behavior, in an attempt to break the cycle of gratification. While aversion therapy was successful in the short-term, it did not prove a lasting solution, as the old smoking behavior would often be resumed. Aversion therapy was now used infrequently. *Behavioral self-monitoring* required the smoker to develop an awareness of the stimuli that triggered the desire to smoke and then to systematically eliminate the smoking behavior in specific situations by neutralizing those stimuli. For example, the smoker could learn to avoid particular situations or to adopt a replacement activity such as chewing gum. This method was successful in some cases but demanded a high degree of self-control. While behavioral methods were useful in addressing the psychological component of smoking addiction, they did not address the physical aspect of nicotine addiction that proved an insurmountable obstacle to many who attempted to quit.

Niconil

Warner-Lambert's Niconil would be the first product to offer a complete solution for smoking cessation, addressing both the physical and psychological aspects of nicotine addiction. The physical product was a circular adhesive patch, 2.5 inches in diameter and containing 30 mg of nicotine gel. Each patch was individually wrapped in a sealed, tear-resistant packet. The patch was applied to the skin, usually on the upper arm, and the nicotine was absorbed into the bloodstream to produce a steady level of nicotine that blunted the smoker's physical craving. Thirty milligrams of nicotine provided the equivalent of 20 cigarettes, without the cigarettes' damaging tar. A single patch was applied once a day every morning for two to six weeks, depending on the smoker. The average smoker was able to quit successfully (abstaining from cigarettes for a period of six months or longer) after three to four weeks.

In clinical trials, the Niconil patch alone had proven effective in helping smokers to quit. A WLI study showed that 47.5% of subjects using the nicotine patch abstained from smoking for a period of three months or longer versus 15% for subjects using a placebo patch. Among the remaining 52.5% who did not stop completely, there was a marked reduction in the number of cigarettes smoked. A similar study in the United States demonstrated an abstinence rate of 31.5% with the Niconil patch versus 14% for those with a placebo patch. The single most important success factor in Niconil effectiveness, however, was the smoker's motivation to quit. "Committed quitters" were the most likely to quit smoking successfully, using Niconil or any other smoking cessation method.

There were some side effects associated with use of the Niconil patch, including skin irritation, sleep disturbances, and nausea. Skin irritation was by far the most prevalent side effect, affecting 30% of patch users in one study. This skin irritation was not seen as a major obstacle to sales, as many study participants viewed their irritated skin areas as "badges of merit" that indicated their commitment to quitting smoking. WLI recommended placement of the patch on alternating skin areas to mitigate the problem. Future reformulations of the nicotine gel in the patch were expected to eliminate the problem entirely.

Niconil had been developed in 1985 by two scientists at Trinity College in Dublin working with Elan Corporation, an Irish pharmaceutical company specializing in transdermal drug delivery systems. Elan had entered into a joint venture with WLI to market other Elan transdermal products: Dilzem and Theolan, a respiratory medication. In 1987 Elan agreed to add Niconil to the joint venture. Warner-Lambert planned to market the product worldwide through its subsidiaries, with Elan earning a royalty on cost of goods sold.[3]

Ireland was the first country to approve the Niconil patch. In late 1989 the Irish National Drugs Advisory Board authorized national distribution of Niconil, but stipulated that it could be sold by prescription only. This meant that Niconil, as a prescription product, could not be advertised directly to the Irish consumer.

Health Care in Ireland

Ireland's General Medical Service (GMS) provided health care to all Irish citizens. Sixty-four percent of the population received free hospital care through the GMS, but were required to pay for doctor's visits (which averaged £15 each), and for drugs (which were priced lower in Ireland than the average in the European Economic Community). The remaining 36% of the population qualified as either low-income or chronic-condition patients and received free health care through the GMS. For these patients, hospital care, doctor's visits, and many drugs were obtained without fee or co-payment. Drugs paid for by the GMS were classified as "reimbursable"; approximately 70% of all drugs were reimbursable in 1989. Niconil had not qualified as a reimbursable drug; although WLI was lobbying to change its status, the immediate outlook was not hopeful.[4]

Support Program

While the patch addressed the physical craving for nicotine, Dixon and his team had decided to develop a supplementary support program to address the smoker's psychological addiction. The support program included several components in a neatly packaged box which aimed to ease the smoker's personal and social dependence on cigarettes. A booklet explained how to change behavior and contained tips on quitting. Bound into the booklet was a personal "contract" on which the smoker could list his or her reasons for quitting and plans for celebrating successful abstinence. There was a diary that enabled the smoker to record patterns of smoking behavior prior to quitting and that offered inspirational suggestions for each day of the program. Finally, an audio-tape included instruction in four relaxation methods which the smoker could practice in place of cigarette smoking. The relaxation exercises were narrated by Professor Anthony Clare, a well-known Irish psychiatrist who hosted a regular television program. The tape also contained an emergency-help section to assist the individual in overcoming sudden episodes of craving. A special toll-free telephone number to WLI served as a hot line to address customer questions and problems. Sample pages from the Niconil support program are presented as **Exhibit 2.**

While studies had not yet measured the impact of the support program on abstinence rates, it was believed that combined use of the support program and the patch could only increase Niconil's success. It had proven necessary to package the Niconil support program separately from the patch to speed approval of the patch by the Irish National Drug Board.

[3] A royalty of 3% on cost of goods sold was typical for such joint ventures.

[4] None of the products in the smoking-cessation-aid market was reimbursable through the GMS. Reimbursable items excluded prescriptions for simple drugs such as mild painkillers and cough and cold remedies.

EXHIBIT 2 Sample Pages from Niconil Support Program

The first step

Fill in the contract in your own words. Write down all the reasons that are most important to you for beating the smoking habit.

Then write down how your life will be better and more enjoyable without the smoking habit.

Finally, write down how you will reward yourself for your courage and hard work. You will deserve something very special.

Choose the day

Decide when to stop and put a ring round that date on your calendar.

Try to find a time when you are not going to be under pressure for a few days. The start of a holiday is good for two reasons. You will not have the stress of work and you will be free to change your routine.

Countdown

1. In the days leading up to your stop date see if you can get your partner or a friend to stop smoking along with you.
2. Ask a local charity to sponsor you or join a non-smoking group. Having other people to talk to who have kicked the habit can be a lifeline when your willpower gets shaky. They will know and understand what you are going through. Your doctor will be able to tell you what groups are running in your area.
3. The evening before your stop date, throw away **all** your cigarettes and get rid of your lighters and ashtrays. You will not need them again.
4. Read over your smoker's diary entries. Know your habit.
   - What are the most dangerous times?
   - Where are the most dangerous places?
   - What are the most dangerous situations?
   - Who do I usually smoke with?

CONTRACT

1. I, ... HAVE STOPPED SMOKING BECAUSE I WANT:

2. MY LIFE WILL BE BETTER WHEN I AM FREE OF SMOKING BECAUSE:

3. AFTER BEATING SMOKING FOR A MONTH I WILL CELEBRATE BY:

SIGNED:

DATE:

WEEK ONE   THE WINNER'S DIARY

DAY

1. Today is the greatest challenge. If you succeed today, tomorrow will be easier. You can do it.
2. Well done. The first 24 hours are over. Your lungs have had their first real rest for years.
3. Remember: smoking is for losers. If you find yourself getting tense, use your relaxation tape.
4. Read your contract again. See how much better life is getting now that you are freeing yourself from this unpleasant addiction.
5. Your body says "thank you". It's feeling fitter already.
6. Don't forget to distract yourself at key cigarette times.
7. Well done. You're through your first week. Give yourself a treat. Go out for a meal or buy yourself something you've always wanted.

COUNT DOWN TO D-DAY   DAY 1

Cigarette	Time of day?	Where were you?	Who were you with?	What were you doing?	How did you feel?
1					
2					
3					
4					
5					
6					
7					
8					
9					
10					

A combined package would have required approval of the complete program, including the audio-tape, which would have prolonged the process significantly. If separate, the support program could be sold without a prescription and advertised directly to the consumer. Development of the support program had cost £3,000. WLI planned an initial production run of 10,000 units at a variable cost of £3.50 per unit.

The support program could serve a variety of purposes. Several WLI executives felt that the support program should be sold separately from the nicotine patches. They considered the support program a stand-alone product that could realize substantial revenues on its own, as well as generating sales of the Niconil patches. Supporting this position, a pricing study completed in 1989 found that the mean price volunteered for a 14-day supply of the patches and the support program combined was £27.50, and for the patches alone, £22.00. The mean price for the support program alone was £8.50, suggesting a relatively high perceived utility of this component among potential consumers. There was a risk, however, that consumers might purchase the Niconil support program *instead* of the patches, or as an accompaniment to other smoking cessation products—thus limiting sales of the Niconil patches.

Another group of executives saw the support program as a value-added point of difference that could stimulate Niconil patch sales. This group favored wide distribution of the support programs, free of charge, to potential Niconil customers. A third group of WLI executives argued that the support program was an integral component of the Niconil product which would enhance the total package by addressing the psychological aspects of nicotine addiction and improve the product's success rate, thereby increasing its sales potential. As such, these executives believed that the support program should be passed on only to those purchasing Niconil patches, at no additional cost.

Two options, not necessarily mutually exclusive, were under consideration for the distribution of the support programs. One option was to distribute them through doctors prescribing Niconil. A doctor could present the program to the patient during the office visit as he or she issued the Niconil prescription, reinforcing the counseling role of the doctor in the Niconil treatment. Supplying the GPs with support programs could also serve to promote Niconil in the medical community. A second option was to distribute the support programs through the pharmacies, where customers could receive the support programs when they purchased the Niconil patches. A disadvantage of this option was that a customer might receive additional support programs each time he or she purchased another package of Niconil. However, these duplicates might be passed on to other potential consumers and thus become an informal advertising vehicle for Niconil.

Pricing

Because all potential Niconil customers would pay for the product personally, pricing was a critical component of the Niconil marketing strategy. Management debated how many patches to include in a single package and at what price to sell each package. In test trials, the average smoker succeeded in quitting with Niconil in three to four weeks (i.e., 21 to 28 patches); others needed as long as six weeks.[5]

As Niconil was essentially a tobacco substitute, cigarettes provided a logical model for considering various packaging and pricing options. The average Irish smoker purchased a pack of cigarettes daily, often when buying the morning newspaper. Fewer than 5% of all cigarettes were sold in cartons.[6] Because the Irish smoker rarely purchased a multi-week

---

[5] Smokers were advised not to use the patch on a regular basis beyond three months. If still unsuccessful in quitting, they could resume use of the patch after stopping for at least a month.

[6] A carton of cigarettes contained 20 individual packs of cigarettes; each pack contained 20 cigarettes.

cigarette supply at once, he or she was thought likely to compare the cost of cigarette purchases with the cost of a multi-week supply of Niconil. WLI thus favored packaging just a 7-day supply of patches in each unit. However, Warner-Lambert subsidiaries in continental Europe, where carton purchases were more popular, wanted to include a six-week supply of patches in each package if and when they launched Niconil. Managers at Warner-Lambert's international division wanted to standardize packaging as much as possible across its subsidiaries and suggested as a compromise a 14-day supply per package.

Following the cigarette model, two pricing schemes had been proposed. The first proposal was to price Niconil on a par with cigarettes. The average Irish smoker smoked 16.5 cigarettes per day and the expected retail price in 1990 for a pack of cigarettes was £2.25. WLI's variable cost of goods for a 14-day supply of Niconil was £12.00.[7] Pharmacies generally added a 50% retail mark-up to the price at which they purchased the product from WLI. A value-added tax of 25% of the retail price was included in the proposed price to the consumer of £32.00 for a 14-day supply. In addition, the consumer paid a £1.00 dispensing fee per prescription.

Under the second pricing proposal, Niconil would be priced at a premium to cigarettes. Proponents argued that if the Niconil program were successful, it would be a permanent replacement for cigarettes and its cost would be far outweighed by the money saved on cigarettes. The proposed price to the consumer under this option was £60.00 for a 14-day supply.

Competition

Few products would compete directly with Niconil in the smoking cessation market in Ireland. Two small niche products were Accudrop and Nicobrevin, both available without a prescription. Accudrop was a nasal spray that smokers applied to the cigarette filter to trap tar and nicotine, resulting in cleaner smoke. Anticipated 1990 manufacturer sales for Accudrop were £5,000. Nicobrevin, a product from the U.K., was a time-release capsule that eased smoking withdrawal symptoms. Anticipated 1990 manufacturer's sales for Nicobrevin were £75,000.

The most significant competitive product was Nicorette, the only nicotine-replacement product currently available. Marketed in Ireland by Lundbeck, Nicorette was a chewing gum that released nicotine into the body as the smoker chewed the gum. Because chewing gum in public was not socially acceptable among Irish adults, the product had never achieved strong sales, especially given that its efficacy relied on steady, intensive chewing. A second sales deterrent had been the association of Nicorette with side effects, such as mouth cancer and irritation of the linings of the mouth and stomach.

Nicorette was sold in 10-day supplies, available in two dosages: 2mg and 4mg. Smokers would chew the 2mg Nicorette initially, and switch to the 4mg gum after two weeks if needed. In a 1982 study, 47% of Nicorette users quit smoking, versus 21% for placebo users. A long-term follow-up study in 1989, however, indicated that only 10% more Nicorette patients had ceased smoking, compared with placebo users. The average daily treatment cost to Nicorette customers was £0.65 per day for the 2mg gum and £1.00 per day for the 4mg gum. Nicorette, like Niconil, was available at pharmacies by prescription only, so advertising had been limited to medical journals. Anticipated 1990 manufacturer sales of Nicorette were £170,000; however, the brand had not been advertised in three years.

[7] This cost of goods included Elan's royalty.

TABLE C	Year 1	100,000 units
Estimated Unit Sales	Year 2	125,000 units
of Niconil in Western	Year 3	150,000 units
Europe	Year 4	175,000 units
	Year 5	200,000 units

Forecasting

Although Nicorette was not considered a successful product, WLI was confident that Niconil, with its less-intrusive nicotine delivery system and fewer side effects, would capture a dominant position in the smoking cessation market and ultimately increase the demand for smoking cessation products. Precise sales expectations for Niconil were difficult to formulate, however, and two different methods had been suggested.

The first method assumed that the percentage of smokers in the adult population (30% in 1990) would drop by one percentage point per year through 1994. An estimated 10% of smokers attempted to quit smoking each year, and 10% of that number purchased some type of smoking cessation product. WLI believed that Niconil could capture half of these "committed quitters" in the first year, selling therefore to 5% of those who tried to give up smoking in 1990. Further, they hoped to increase this share by 1% per year, up to 9% in 1994. Having estimated the number of customers who would purchase an initial two-week supply of Niconil, WLI managers then had to calculate the total number of units purchased. Based on experience in test trials, WLI anticipated that 60% of first-time Niconil customers would purchase a second two-week supply. Of that number, 20% would purchase a third two-week supply. About 75% of smokers completed the program within six weeks.

A more aggressive forecast could be based on WLI's 1989 survey, which showed that of the 30% of [the 1,400] respondents who were smokers, 54% indicated that they would like to give up smoking, and 30% expressed interest in the nicotine patch. More relevant, 17% of smokers indicated that they were likely to go to the doctor and pay for such a patch, though a specific purchase price was not included in the question. A rule of thumb in interpreting likelihood-of-purchase data was to divide this percentage by three to achieve a more likely estimate of actual purchasers. Once the number of Niconil customers was calculated, the 100%/60%/20% model used above could then be applied to compute the total expected unit sales.

Production

Under the terms of the joint venture with Elan and using current manufacturing technology, production capacity would be 1,000 units (of 14-day supply packages) per month in the first quarter of 1990, ramping up to 2,000 units per month by year-end. WLI had the option to purchase a new, more efficient machine that could produce 14,000 units per month and reduce WLI's variable cost on each unit by 10%. In addition, if WLI purchased the new machine and Niconil was launched in continental Europe, WLI could export some of its production to the European subsidiaries, further expanding its role as a supplier to Warner-Lambert Europe. WLI would earn a margin of £2.00 per unit on Niconil that it sold through this channel.[8] Estimated annual unit sales, assuming a launch of Niconil throughout Western Europe, are listed in **Table C.** Warner-Lambert management aimed to recoup any

[8] Warner-Lambert's European subsidiaries were likely to consider purchasing this new machine themselves as well.

capital investments within five years; the Niconil machine would cost £1.2 million and could be on-line within nine months.

Marketing Prescription Products

Prescription products included all pharmaceutical items deemed by the Irish government to require the professional expertise of the medical community to guide consumer usage.[9] Before a customer could purchase a prescription product, he or she first had to visit a doctor and obtain a written prescription which specified that product. The customer could then take the written prescription to one of Ireland's 1,132 pharmacies and purchase the product.

The prescription nature of Niconil thus created marketing challenges. A potential Niconil customer first had to make an appointment with a doctor for an office visit to obtain the necessary prescription. Next, the doctor had to agree to prescribe Niconil to the patient to help him or her to quit smoking. Only then could the customer go to the pharmacy and purchase Niconil. This two-step purchase process required WLI to address two separate audiences in marketing Niconil: the Irish smokers who would eventually use Niconil and the Irish doctors who first had to prescribe it to patients.

Niconil's potential customers were the 10% of Irish smokers who attempted to give up smoking each year (2% of the total Irish population). Market research had shown that those most likely to purchase Niconil were aged 35–44 and in either white-collar or skilled occupations (18% of Irish smokers). Smokers under the age of 35 tended to see themselves as "bullet proof": because most were not yet experiencing the negative health effects of smoking, it was difficult to persuade them to quit. Upper-income, better-educated smokers found less tolerance for smoking among their peers and thus felt greater pressure to quit. Research had also indicated that women were 25% more likely to try Niconil as they tended to be more concerned with their health and thus more often visited the doctors from whom they could learn about Niconil and obtain the necessary prescription.

The most likely prescribers of Niconil would be the 2,000 General Practitioners (GPs) in Ireland. The average GP saw 15 patients per day and eight out of ten general office visits resulted in the GPs writing prescriptions for patients. Although 10% of Irish doctors smoked, virtually all recognized the dangers of smoking and rarely smoked in front of patients. A *Modern Medicine* survey of 780 Irish GPs indicated that 63% formally gathered smoking data from their patients. GPs acknowledged the health risk that smoking posed to patient health, but they were usually reluctant to pressure a patient to quit unless the smoker was highly motivated. Unsolicited pressure to quit could meet with patient resistance and result, in some cases, in a doctor losing a patient and the associated revenues from patient visits. Smoking cessation was not currently a lucrative treatment area for GPs. Most would spend no longer than 15 minutes discussing smoking with their patients. To the few patients who asked for advice on how to quit smoking, 92% of GPs would offer "firm, clear-cut advice." Fewer than 15% would recommend formal counseling, drug therapy, or other assistance. GPs were not enthusiastic about Nicorette due to poor results and the incidence of side effects.

WLI was confident that Niconil would find an enthusiastic audience among Irish GPs. As a complete program with both physical and psychological components, Niconil offered a unique solution. In addition, the doctor would assume a significant counseling role in the Niconil treatment. It was anticipated that the GP would initially prescribe a 14-day supply of Niconil to the patient. At the end of the two-week period, the patient would hopefully return to the doctor for counseling and an additional prescription, if needed.

[9] Drugs and other pharmaceutical products that did not require a written prescription from a doctor were called "over-the-counter" or "OTC" drugs.

Marketing Communications

WLI intended to position Niconil as a complete system that was a more acceptable alternative to existing nicotine replacement therapy for the purpose of smoking cessation. Niconil would be the only smoking cessation product to address both the physical dimension of nicotine addiction through the patch and the psychological dimension through the support program. Compared with Nicorette gum, Niconil offered a more acceptable delivery system (Niconil's transdermal system vs. Nicorette's oral system) and fewer, less severe side effects. WLI planned to promote these aspects of the product through a comprehensive marketing program. The Niconil launch marketing budget, detailed in **Exhibit 3,** followed the Warner-Lambert standard for new drug launches. Several WLI executives felt that this standard was inadequate for the more consumer-oriented Niconil and pressed for increased communications spending.

Advertising

Because Irish regulations prohibited the advertising of prescription products directly to the consumer, Niconil advertising was limited to media targeting the professional medical community. Three major publications targeted this audience: *Irish Medical Times, Irish Medical News,* and *Modern Medicine.* WLI planned to advertise moderately in the first year to raise awareness of Niconil in the medical community. After that it was hoped that the initial momentum could be maintained through strong public relations efforts and personal testimony to the product's efficacy. **Exhibit 4** summarizes the proposed 1990 media advertising schedule for Niconil.

EXHIBIT 3
Niconil First Year Marketing Budget (£'000)

Advertising	
Ad creation	£ 4
Media advertising	28
Total advertising	**32**
Promotion	
Development of support program	3
Production of support programs	35
Training/promotional materials	44
Direct mailing to GPs	2
Total promotion	**84**
Public relations	
Launch symposium	5
Roundtable meeting	2
Press release/materials	1
Total public relations	**8**
Market research	3
Sales force allocation	23
Product management allocation	50
Total budget	**£ 200**

EXHIBIT 4
1990 Niconil Media Advertising Schedule

Publication	Frequency	Circulation	Cost/1.000	Placements
Irish Medical Times	Weekly	5,200	£154	13
Irish Medical News	Weekly	5,100	137	11
Modern Medicine	Monthly	3,700	176	5

WLI's advertising agency had designed a distinctive logo for Niconil that would be used on all packaging and collateral materials such as "No Smoking" placards. These would feature the Niconil logo and be distributed to doctors' offices, hospitals, and pharmacies to promote the product. Ideally, the logo would become sufficiently well recognized that it could be used eventually on a stand-alone basis to represent Niconil to the end consumer without the brand name. This would allow some flexibility in circumventing Irish advertising restrictions to reach the end consumer. Sample logos and packaging are illustrated in **Exhibit 5.** The agency had also developed the following four concepts for a Niconil medical journal advertisement:

- "Day and night I crave cigarettes. I can't stop. I'm hooked." When they ask for help, give them the help they need—new Niconil nicotine transdermal patches.
- Where there's smoke, there's emphysema, throat cancer, angina, lung cancer, sinusitis. Now a way to break this deadly addiction. Introducing Niconil nicotine transdermal patches—all they need to succeed.
- Emphysema, lung cancer, peptic ucler, angina, sinusitis, throat cancer. Help end their deadly addiction. One-a-day instead of a pack-a-day. Introducing Niconil nicotine transdermal patches.
- "How many of your patients are dying for a smoke?" Help them break the cycle of addiction. Introducing Niconil nicotine transdermal patches. A better way to stop.

Direct Mail

A direct mail campaign to Ireland's 2,000 GPs was planned in conjunction with the Niconil product announcement. Two weeks prior to launch, an introductory letter would be mailed with a color photo of the product, a reply card offering a support program, and additional product information. The support programs would be mailed in response to the reply cards, arriving just prior to the launch. A response rate of at least 50% was anticipated based on past direct mail campaigns.

Public Relations

The formal Niconil product announcement was scheduled to occur in Dublin at a professional event that WLI had dubbed the "Smoking Cessation Institute Symposium." The symposium would be chaired by Professor Anthony Clare (the narrator of the Niconil audio-tape), Professor Hickey (an expert in preventive cardiology), and Professors Masterson and J. Kelly from Elan Corporation. Open to members of the medical profession and media, the event was intended to focus attention on the dangers of smoking and to highlight Niconil as a ground-breaking product designed to address this health hazard.

WLI had sought endorsements from both the Irish Cancer Society and the Irish Heart Foundation, two national health organizations that actively advocated smoking cessation. Because both nonprofit institutions relied on donations for financing and were concerned that a specific product endorsement would jeopardize their tax-exempt status, they refused to endorse Niconil directly. Representatives from each institution had, however, stated their intention to attend the launch symposium.

In advance of the symposium, a press release and supporting materials would be distributed to the media. Emphasis would be placed on the role that Niconil would play in disease prevention. It would also be noted that Niconil had been developed and manufactured locally and had the potential for worldwide sales. Other planned public relations activities

EXHIBIT 5   Sample Niconil Logo and Packaging

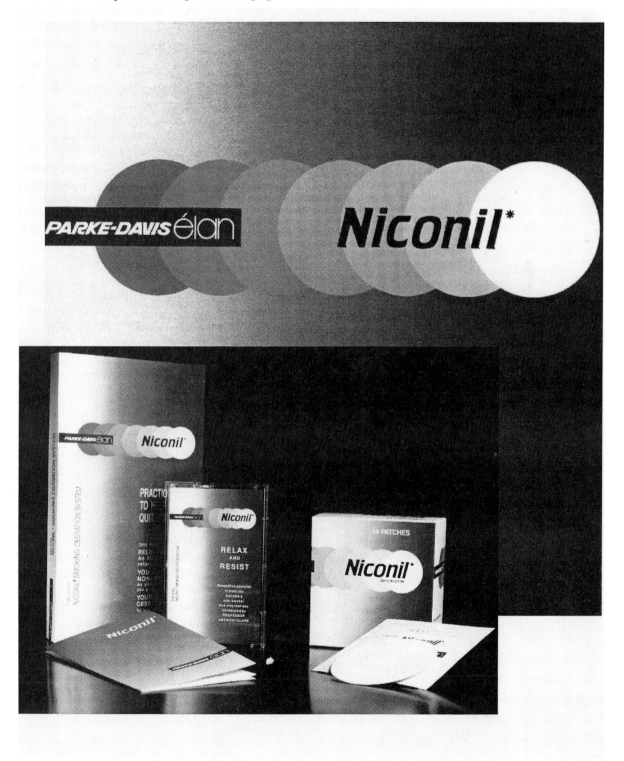

included a round-table dinner for prominent opinion leaders in the medical community. Publicity in the media was planned to coincide with key "commitment to change" times such as New Year's and Lent.[10]

Sales Strategy

WLI Ireland had a sales force of 16 representatives whose average annual salary, bonus, and benefits amounted to £25,000 in 1988. They focused their selling efforts on 1,600 Irish GPs who were most accessible geographically and most amenable to pharmaceutical sales visits. The sales staff was divided into three selling teams of four to six representatives. Each team sold separate product lines to the same 1,600 GPs. The team that would represent Niconil was already selling three other drugs from Elan Corporation that were marketed by WLI as part of their joint venture. These four salespeople would add Niconil to their existing product lines. Sales training on Niconil would take place one month prior to the product launch.

The pharmaceutical salesperson's challenge was to maintain the attention of each GP long enough to discuss each item in his or her product line. Because Niconil was expected to be of great interest to GPs, the salespeople were keen to present Niconil first during the sales visit, followed by the less exciting products. Normally, a new product would receive this up-front positioning. However, Dixon argued that Niconil should be presented last during the sales call to maximize the time that a salesperson spent with each GP and to prevent the sales time devoted to the other three Elan products from being cannibalized by Niconil. Based on revenue projections for all four products, salespeople would be instructed to spend no more than 15% of their sales call time on Niconil. On average, each WLI salesperson called on six to seven doctors per day. The goal was for each sales team to call on the 1,600 targeted GPs once every three months. In the case of Niconil, all 16 sales people would present the new brand during their calls for six weeks after launch.

Critical Decisions

With just three months to go before the launch of Niconil, Dixon felt he had to comply with the international division's suggestion to include a 14-day supply of patches in each Niconil package, but he debated whether to price the product on a par with or at a premium to cigarettes. Equally important, he had to decide which sales forecast was more accurate so that he could plan production capacity. And finally, he needed to make decisions on the communications program: which advertising concept would be the most effective, what other efforts could be made to enhance product acceptance, and was the current budget adequate to support Warner-Lambert's first national launch of such an innovative product?

---

[10] Lent was an annual penitential period during spring of the Roman Catholic religious calendar that was still observed by many of the 95% of the Irish who were Roman Catholic.

Chapter 11

TiVo

Luc Wathieu   Michael Zoglio

"Look at these guys . . . They decide what we watch and when we watch it . . . " "Network programmers—who needs them? Program your own network. TiVo. TV your way."

Between these two lines, the TiVo commercial showed a pair of burly men throwing a TV network's chief programmer out of the window of a tall office building. Brodie Keast, TiVo's vice president of marketing and sales, had replayed the ad a dozen times on that morning of May 2000, and he still found it to be as hilarious as the first time he saw it. The TiVo digital video recorder, beyond its many advanced features, made a big idea real—if you owned the TiVo black box and subscribed to the TiVo service, you could really control what you watched and when you watched it. TiVo's marketing team intended to get that big idea across through a catchy communications campaign, with a boldly humorous tone that would help consumers envision how TiVo restored the fun of television.

Fourteen months into the launch, TiVo had signed up 42,000 subscribers, with a current rate of 14,000 new subscribers per quarter. With 102 million TV-watching households in the U.S., that was only about .04% penetration, despite availability in most major consumer electronics stores across the nation. Yet, everyone who owned TiVo seemed satisfied with it, with 72% of owners even claiming that TiVo had made TV viewing "a lot more enjoyable." Ninety percent said they would recommend it to family and friends. Early adopters were raving deliriously in the online forums of TiVo's website.

TiVo's marketing team argued that a lack of awareness was a key cause of the discrepancy between the love for TiVo and its lackluster sales. The provocative TV and print campaign, including the "Network Executive" commercial, was conceived with this problem in mind. But would people get it? Or would they just be confused? And was it too controversial? Keast had his share of last-minute doubts.

Research Associate Michael Zoglio prepared this case under the supervision of Professor Luc Wathieu as the basis for class discussion rather than to illustrate either effective or ineffective handling of an administrative situation.

A major problem with the digital video recorder category was that its many functions (which involved pausing and replaying live TV as well as an array of flexible recording services) were not as easy to explain as they were to experience. The "Network Executive" ad just substituted any explanation with the phrase "Program your own network." But maybe it would be better to just try something completely straightforward, that is, to explain TiVo for what it did. Why not simply show a stream of satisfied customers reporting their experiences with TiVo: "TiVo allows me to pause live TV when I am interrupted by the phone . . . With TiVo you can record 30 hours of programming without the hassle of videocassettes . . . And TiVo is intelligent: it automatically detects and records the shows that you love . . . TiVo will make suggestions just for you . . ."? And then a voice-over would tie it together: "Pause. Rewind. Fast-forward. Pause again. Look at it in slow motion. With TiVo's features, you are in control. With TiVo, you watch anything you want when you want to watch it. And it's available at your favorite electronics store, for just a little more than a VCR."

Keast knew that things were not that simple, and that he had to account for TiVo's best strategic interests, and to integrate the new television campaign with other marketing decisions. However, before okaying the "Network Executive" ad (and three other equally amusing commercials based on the "Program your own network" theme), Keast decided to step back and review the company's situation one more time.

Early Days

When TiVo founders Jim Barton and Michael Ramsay left Silicon Graphics, a leading provider of 3D graphics hardware and software, in August 1997, their idea was to equip homes with a "home network" that would integrate all household communication devices. Both Barton and Ramsay had been involved in the development of an interactive television system (the "Full-Service Network Project") that Silicon Graphics installed with Time Warner in 4,000 homes in Orlando, Florida. Although that project was deemed successful, its initiators recognized that the internet, not television, was quickly becoming the key home interactive instrument. However, when the project was cancelled, Barton and Ramsay felt that its key ideas could be converted into a congenial and affordable "home network" technology.

After a few months, it became apparent that devising a meaningful and user-friendly home networking system was overly ambitious. Consequently, the two entrepreneurs decided that instead of allowing consumers to command the whole house, they should focus on the television. Relying on fast-improving hard disk technology, the device would provide an easy-to-use interface between the confusing hundred-plus channel lineup and what people would actually want to watch on their TV, at any given time of the day. (If executed properly, this concept was sure to reach immediate popularity, they thought.) A cute brand identity would give a gracious face to the machinery, whose technological sophistication would remain hidden in a black box next to the TV set. It would get a friendly-sounding name: TiVo. The first TiVo was shipped on March 31, 1999.

The physical TiVo unit was a set-top box that interfaced between the broadcast feed (be it cable, satellite, or antenna) and the television (see **Exhibit 1**). The TV signal passed through a digital encoder that compressed it using the MPEG-2 format.[1] After being digitized, the signal was recorded on a hard drive. The number of hours that the unit could record depended on two factors: hard drive capacity and recording quality. The TiVo box

---

[1] 'MPEG' stands for Moving Picture Experts Group, and MPEG-2 is the standard digital audio and video compression format for products such as digital television set-top boxes and DVD.

EXHIBIT 1
The TiVo Unit and
Remote Control

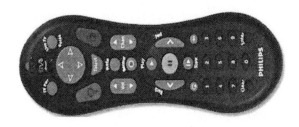

EXHIBIT 2
Recording Quality
and Recorder
Capacity

	Best	High	Medium	Basic
"14 Hour" box	4 hours	~7 hours	~10 hours	14 hours
"30 Hour" box	9 hours	14.5 hours	19 hours	30 hours

came with four quality pre-sets, ranging from "best" to "basic." "Best" compressed the signal least whereas "basic" compressed the signal the most, taking up less space on the hard drive (see **Exhibit 2**).

What happened to the digitized content next depended on whether the viewer was watching live TV or previously recorded programming. Viewers who watched live TV received it with a few-second delay, because TiVo recorded the signal before sending it to the television set. In order to have the ability to pause and rewind live TV, TiVo always kept a 30-minute cache of digitized feed of the live program being watched.

When the viewer was using TiVo to record television, the digitized program was just recorded on the drive (up to its full capacity). When the viewer subsequently watched a recorded program, the MPEG-2 data was decompressed, decoded, and passed into the television, where it then appeared in the normal fashion. The compression, encoding operation, decoding operation, and the user interface were all controlled by a Power PC processor. The TiVo unit operated on a proprietary operating system.

In order to ensure product reliability and effective distribution, Barton and Ramsay sought the partnership of consumer electronics superstar brands Sony and Philips. TiVo subsidized[2] the two companies so that they would manufacture the black box, distribute it, and promote it to retailers. After initial shipments through regional dealers, TiVo became nationally available through Best Buy, an electronics chain, in September 1999. In October 1999, Circuit City and Sears were added, and a national distribution was in place.

[2] See the item "Sales and Marketing-Related Parties" in the quarterly results reported in **Exhibit 3**.

EXHIBIT 3 **TiVo Results**
(quarterly data, in thousands)

	Sep-99	Dec-98	Mar-99	Jun-99	Sep-99	Dec-99	Mar-00	Jun-00*
Subscribers (approximate)	0.0	0.0	0.0	1.0	2.5	18.0	32.0	48.0
Revenues	—	—	—	$8	$33	$182	$424	$719
Costs and expenses:								
Cost of services	—	—	(689)	(636)	(749)	(1,993)	(4,168)	(4,988)
Research and development	(1,659)	(2,146)	(1,596)	(1,859)	(2,327)	(3,945)	(4,678)	(5,679)
Sales and marketing	(354)	(567)	(2,168)	(1,847)	(5,323)	(15,164)	(9,180)	(11,384)
Sales and marketing— related parties	—	—	—	(382)	(4,946)	(9,844)	(4,547)	(5,349)
General and administrative	(706)	(1,337)	(1,125)	(1,057)	(1,757)	(3,088)	(2,691)	(3,631)
Stock-based compensation	—	—	—	(187)	(501)	(842)	(969)	(919)
Other operating expense, net	—	—	12	(201)	(4,808)	(2,213)	—	—
Loss from operations	(2,719)	(4,050)	(5,566)	(6,161)	(20,378)	(36,907)	(25,809)	(31,231)
Interest income	46	55	53	224	614	2,022	1,824	1,907
Interest expense and other	(7)	—	(2)	(176)	(281)	(7)	(70)	(112)
Net loss	($2,680)	($3,995)	($5,515)	($6,113)	($20,045)	($34,892)	($24,055)	($29,436)

*Projected.

With production and sales outsourced, Barton and Ramsay could emphasize the company's true nature as an entertainment service. TiVo was priced as a distinct service not included in the cost of the hardware. The black box was priced $499 for a model with up to 14 hours of recording capacity and $999 for a model with up to 30 hours, and the TiVo service came at an additional charge of $9.95 per month, $99 per year, or $199 for the lifetime of the unit. Without the service, TiVo could be used to pause, replay and fast-forward live TV, but recording (and accessing TiVo's system of personalized suggestions and automatic recording of favorite shows) required payment of the additional fees.

While the hardware manufacturers took control of retail distribution and in-store communications, TiVo's promotional activities were restricted to public relations, animating the TiVo.com website (which featured both a service demonstration and the opportunity to buy the system online), and a very limited mass media campaign (see **Exhibit 4** for an example of an early print ad). Sample black boxes were sent out to the press around the time of the launch. Although this led to a fair amount of publicity for the device and the TiVo brand, there was some confusion in the press as to how the new product category should be introduced. TiVo was indiscriminately referred to as a personal video recorder (PVR), digital video recorder (DVR), personal digital recorder (PDR), intelligent video recorder (IVR), or on-demand TV. Oftentimes the press discussed the features of the device, but it was not always to the advantage of the company, as the first-generation product was not free of problems. For instance, the review of personal technology columnist Walter Mossberg in *The Wall Street Journal* was lukewarm:

> In my tests, TiVo's Personal Television displayed some serious glitches, which the company says it is fixing, and it is designed as much for advertisers as for users. . . . I also thought TiVo's onscreen program guide was confusing, as is the process of navigating around the unit's menus. . . . changing channels caused the TiVo picture to break up or freeze briefly.[3]

[3] "Personal Technology: Two Companies Offer TV-Viewing Options for the VCR-Challenged," *The Wall Street Journal*, April 8, 1999.

EXHIBIT 4   **Early Print Ad**

Introducing TiVo.
Now you can pause live TV and never miss a minute of the action again.

Pause live TV. Or rewind it. Even slo-mo it. Record your favorite shows without videotape. Automatically. Every time they're on. Teach it what kind of shows you like and it will search out and suggest others. It's TiVo. The first Personal Television Service. And it's available on the Philips Personal TV Receiver. It's about to change the way you'll watch TV. Forever.

Changing Habits on a Mass Scale

TiVo's marketing problem went well beyond the usual task of inserting a product within preexisting preferences and lifestyles of targeted consumers. Indeed, the company was faced with the more challenging task of inviting people to change their consumption habits altogether, in a domain (TV viewing) that was deemed one of the most ritualistic elements of contemporary American life. Keast explained:

> Typically, with television, changes in technology have been slow. First, things went from black and white to color—a major technological change, mind you, but this wasn't a major change in the way television was consumed. Then the remote control came along. Now people could flip from channel to channel, and this made consumers less captive. Networks were nervous and competition intensified, but the industry's structure and basic viewing habits remained unchallenged. Then cable and the satellite dish appeared, together with a proliferation of targeted channels that gave consumers even more choice. Yet, none of these changed the way you watch television. When we introduce TiVo in the household, it changes the balance of power overnight. It's truly a revolution, one that changes the way television is watched. So we were faced with the ultimate marketing challenge of changing human behavior on a mass scale—a behavior that was ingrained over a period of 50 years.

Life before TiVo

In 1999, more American households had television than telephone service, with the average American household owning 2.4 television sets. The average household spent 7.4 hours per day watching TV, with the average adult spending about 4.3 hours per day in front of the screen. Americans regularly intensified their experience by purchasing larger television sets. Advanced home audio systems complemented their viewing. In 1999 the number of families owning a 25-inch or larger TV set and a surround-sound audio system reached 20 million. This number had increased by 300% since 1995. When buying consumer electronic equipment, 71% of consumers were influenced by friends or relatives, 56% by publications and advertising, 40% by store staff, and 30% by television advertising.[4]

Television viewing was a rather passive activity, and avid consumers were often ironically called "couch potatoes." Dependence was sometimes so extreme that it created problems in the household. Getting children to do their homework was a constant fight, and television was often used as a reward to encourage children to do various tasks. An estimated 68% of Americans complained that they felt "widowed" by their loved one during the Fall television season. Couch potatoes spent less time with their children, and they were frequently accused of housework avoidance, mood swings, and work neglect.

Networks would schedule their most popular shows in "Prime Time," the broadcast time between 8 P.M. and 11 P.M., with season premieres typically drawing audiences larger than 25 million viewers. Advertisers attempted to take advantage of this audience, spending much of the $52 billion 1999 expense in television advertising in the United States for prime time space.

Life with TiVo

The basic idea behind TiVo was that it would take control away from the networks and put it directly into the hands of the consumer. To empower consumers, the TiVo service provided them with a variety of specific features. Accessing these required a connection to a telephone line, so that the unit could call TiVo headquarters nightly to download feature upgrades and update programming schedules.

[4] Data cited in "Can Anybody Help," *The Wall Street Journal*, June 26, 2000.

The electronic program guide (EPG) was the user's interface with the device. The EPG, a menu of options, included the option to watch live TV. Another option was to view "Now Playing," a system that accessed all previously recorded programming. Additionally, the EPG gave access to (1) previews for shows that could be scheduled for recording with one push of a button, (2) a TiVo-produced video magazine, (3) a set of network showcases where networks promoted their best shows, and (4) an on-screen TV guide.

Among the most popular features was the **season pass** that allowed users to specify their favorite show, so that TiVo would automatically record all its episodes. TiVo would track and record the show without help from the viewer, regardless of when it was on, and accounted for scheduling changes. Moreover, the TiVo remote was equipped with a **"thumbs up"** and a **"thumbs down"** button (see **Exhibit 1**). With these buttons, viewers could indicate how much they liked or disliked what they were watching, effectively revealing their preferences to the service. Subsequently, TiVo would suggest television programs that viewers might want to watch. By pushing a button, these suggestions could then be scheduled for recording. Keast explained:

> Within the four walls of the box, there is a preference engine that runs inside the recorder, and it keeps track of what shows you have chosen to record, and of the shows you have been watching. Then there are also, on the remote, the two thumb buttons. As you are watching, you can offer feedback to the service, in the form of up to three thumbs up or three thumbs down. It keeps track not only of the shows themselves, but also of the featured topics and actors. Over time, the suggestions get better and better.

Envisioning this service was perhaps more difficult for non-users. However, pressing the thumb buttons was so rewarding in terms of useful programming suggestions, that TiVo owners became extremely addicted to it after a while. Not only did the thumb buttons lead to programming suggestions: TiVo would also proactively record programs that agreed with the viewer's preferences, if sufficient hard drive space was available. Keast recalled an amusing anecdote:

> I came home and my TiVo was full of episodes of *The Brady Bunch*. One of my children had gone through and given all of these *Brady Bunch* reruns three thumbs up, so TiVo just kept recording them. So I had to go through the archive of shows and delete them, all the while changing the three thumbs up rating to three thumbs down so the unit would stop recording the *Brady Bunch* episodes.

According to an independent study, 62% of TiVo owners watched more TV with the service than without, and 31% of the owners said that TV was their primary source of entertainment (as compared to 16% before ownership). Fifty-nine percent said that they watched programs that were once unavailable to them because of inconvenient scheduling, and there was a 31% decrease in channel surfing. Children's programming and dramas were the most recorded programs, with situation comedies following closely.

While "pause live TV" was deemed as having the most significant "Wow!" factor, this feature was used less and less over time, simply because live TV was watched less (70% of owners were watching recorded materials every day). Moreover, it appeared that "pause" was used more to conveniently handle interruptions (phone calls, etc.) than to stop an image that needed to be scrutinized.

TiVo's data showed that subscribers were fast-forwarding through 90% of commercials (thanks to digital technology, TiVo could fast forward three times, 18 times, or 60 times the normal speed). "We don't believe it necessarily mean that consumers don't like advertising in general, but it proves that they don't like 30 second commercials that are not specifically relevant to them," said Keast.

Despite the apparent high satisfaction of current owners ("TiVo is the best thing since sliced bread!" "TiVo has turned my Super VHS VCR into a $500 clock and paperweight! If only I'd known then what I know now—the glory of TiVo!" said fans on TiVo's website), non-users sometimes held opinions that concerned the company. For instance, a *New York Times* reader wrote:

> I've been thinking about buying a . . . TiVo. But . . . I've decided to wait until someone invents a complementary and equally subversive device—one that prevents . . . TiVo from packaging my viewing habits for resale. Why pay to be spied on? I'd sooner let some network suit go through my trash.[5]

Pandora's Box[6]

TiVo's ability to shift programming and skip advertisements was a source of concern for both television networks and the advertising industry. History, however, had shown that both industries had survived a number of supposedly fatal threats. When the remote control was invented, there was a concern that people would just change channels when commercials aired. However, various studies later showed that less than 5% of commercials were zapped. Then, when cable TV and dish systems led to channel proliferation, conventional networks feared audience fragmentation and a decrease in advertising revenues. Indeed, the market share of the big three networks (ABC, CBS, and NBC) dropped from 91% of the national audience in 1978 to 45% in 1999; yet, the three networks' revenues from advertising grew from $4 billion to $14 billion over the same period. Finally, the popularity of the VCR, despite its time shifting potential and the ability to watch rented movies instead of live TV, did not prevent the $50 billion television advertising industry from flourishing.

TiVo as a Threat

Brodie Keast summed up the dilemma for the networks:

> Early on the networks and advertisers couldn't decide whether to sue us or buy the company. And now they're just kind of somewhere in between. And TiVo certainly raises big questions for the networks, who essentially are aggregators of programming content. And if at some point, consumers can choose, "I want this specific show. I like *Will and Grace*, and I want this off the Discovery Channel, and I want that off of HBO . . ." They're making their own personal TV line-up. Will consumers care about who's aggregating shows? What is the value of must-see TV on Tuesday nights or whenever it's on? With TiVo, commercial space at 2:45 A.M. might be just as valuable as commercial space at 8:15 P.M. On top of that, networks lose the ability to position a popular show at prime time, and then count on enough consumer inertia to put a new show behind it to promote it. I mean all those rules just kind of go away.

The rules went away for advertisers as well. Using conventional viewer panel data to predict audience size and characteristics as a function of the airing time of a commercial became impossible. Consequently, the conventional way that advertising agencies sold media space to marketers, on the basis of reach, would be jeopardized. And if viewers were going to skip the ads anyway, the questions became more complex. How was P&G going to sell soap in a TiVo-ed world? TiVo was determined to uphold at least two principles that

---

[5] *The New York Times*, September 3, 2000.

[6] Pandora, an extremely beautiful woman created from dirt and water, was blessed with all kinds of talents given to her by each of the Greek gods. Zeus offered her a box full of disasters that she was supposed to keep closed. Pandora could not resist curiosity, and when she opened the box all kinds of calamities were released. As she quickly closed the box, the only thing that remained trapped in it was hope.

constrained the degrees of freedom for advertisers: consumers should remain in control at all times, i.e., they should only be exposed to commercials on an opt-in basis, and data about individual viewing patterns would remain inaccessible except in aggregate format.

Even though TiVo had sold a limited number of units by May 2000, industry experts were predicting that category sales would range between 350,000 and 800,000 units by year end 2000, and anywhere between 30 million and 55 million units in use by 2005. These forecasts were fueling the concerns of networks and advertisers.

TiVo as an Opportunity

TiVo never claimed that it had set out to revolutionize television by ruining the networks and eliminating television advertising. After all, the TiVo remote control could have enabled the viewer to skip commercials altogether, but it didn't. Said CEO Ramsay:

> Network psychology is to have a line in the sand mentality. If you're on one side of the line, you're their friend. If you're on the other side of the line, you're their enemy. Advertising the ability to skip commercials is on the other side of the line. We designed the technology so that it doesn't infuriate the networks.[7]

Ramsay sought the partnership of the industry, claiming that the growth of personal television would benefit both viewers and the industry. Network leaders, such as CBS, NBC, Discovery, and The Walt Disney Company were equity investors in the company, with NBC and Discovery represented on the board of directors. These and other networks were also involved as "programming partners" so that they could be featured in the different services TiVo offered. On the advertising side, P&G and General Motors were actively working with TiVo on defining the advertising formulae of the future.

Opportunities for Advertisers

TiVo's marketing team believed that TiVo created an enormous opportunity for what they humorously called "couch commerce," claiming that "couch commerce will have the convenience of the internet with the emotional motivation of the television." The process to make this vision happen was already initiated, said Keast:

> The advertising piece is something that we'd like to let evolve with advertisers, rather than us trying to come up with all the answers. Most television advertising nowadays is not relevant to people, when they're watching something, with such a very large and diverse national audience. So that's why people skip over ads when they have a chance to do so. All we're assuming is that with this technology, there should be greater message personalization and targeting, to make advertising more relevant and interesting. It is still very early to claim that anyone has completely figured it out. For now, we're working with charter advertisers to try to adapt our service so that more personalized and more targeted advertising can be delivered. In any case, we will allow consumers the choice to opt into it or not get in at all.

An obvious advantage was that TiVo could keep track of what shows were being watched, and of how many people were planning to record a particular show. TiVo could thus help advertisers to both track and predict the television audience. Moreover, advertisers could be informed of how many people fast-forwarded through their commercials, and learn about the aggregate profile of those who did not. Old marketing techniques were good at identifying successful shows, but the actual viewing pattern of commercials inserted in those shows remained largely a mystery.

Early ideas that TiVo offered to advertisers included shipping TiVo's hardware with pre-loaded advertisements that viewers would watch while the unit was setting itself up during installation. Another idea was to have the networks (or TiVo directly) air a number of

[7] Quoted in "Boom Box," by Michael Lewis, *The New York Times*, August 13, 2000.

different versions of the same commercial (for instance, there could be three different versions of the same car brand promoted at the same time), and the unit's preference engine would retain only the one that best applied to the viewer.

TiVo's most inventive concept was that of **telescoping ads.** Instead of 30-second commercials, ads could be made up of a sequence of many shorter screens which users could select, based on specific categories or even on the basis of brand names, on an opt-in basis. TiVo's fast-forward and rewind features would make it easy to find the relevant part of any telescoping ad.

Opportunities for Networks

Networks could benefit from TiVo's ability to track how many people were scheduling a show for future recording. Network showcases would prove particularly useful in that respect. Before TiVo, if a new sitcom was advertised, the network had to wait until the day after the premiere to verify the effectiveness of its promotions. With TiVo, networks could adjust their launch strategy as they monitored the behavioral response to their campaign. Networks could also establish audience size and characteristics in advance, in order to market advertising slots more effectively.

Virtually all service features of TiVo were supposed to bring new opportunities to television networks. The season pass, for instance, guaranteed that viewers would not miss any episodes of their favorite show, increasing regular network viewership and loyalty. The thumbs buttons could provide networks with aggregate feedback on their shows' degree of success. The network showcases were potentially more effective than monthly pamphlets sent in the mail, and they made it easy for viewers to commit to a show immediately, on impulse. Movie channels would not need to schedule movies at different times of the day to maximize their chance to meet interested viewers. TiVo's viewing suggestions based on the preference engine would give the networks additional chances to match their shows with the most interested audiences.

Competition

When TiVo was launched in March 1999, it was alone in its category. However, over time, competition developed. A device called ReplayTV emerged as a strong competitor. And software industry leader Microsoft announced that UltimateTV was to be launched in Fall 2000.

Replay Networks

The Replay Networks company was created in August 1997 by a *Star Trek* fan who was seeking a way to record *Star Trek* episodes automatically, whenever they would air. The resulting device, named ReplayTV, started shipping in April 1999. As Replay Networks was manufacturing its own hardware, initial distribution was very limited. National distribution started in April 2000, after a contract was signed with Panasonic to build and market the units.

ReplayTV was also a black box, similar to the TiVo units manufactured by Philips and Sony. The hard drive was capable of recording for the same amount of time, with comparable quality settings. ReplayTV shared many features with TiVo, such as pause live TV, search tools, and the ability to record programs through an electronic program guide.

ReplayTV's remote control had no thumbs buttons like TiVo's. But it did include a distinctive button marked "Quickskip." Quickskip was able to time shift the recorded program by 30 seconds instantaneously, which was exactly the length of a typical commercial.

When ReplayTV was launched nationally in May 2000, it was touted as a digital VCR. The price of the unit was $200 higher than TiVo's unit, but the service was included in the price, without requiring an additional fee. For the salesperson in the electronics store, this guaranteed a higher commission. Replay's marketing efforts largely concentrated on newspaper advertising and on educating the salespeople, providing them with standardized key catchphrases ("You can skip commercials with the 30 second Quickskip button," "You don't need to pay a monthly fee for service"). ReplayTV also produced a set of television commercials focused on the pause feature. For instance, in one of them, a viewer paused a boxing match to get more pizza, and the boxers were shown standing around as if waiting for the viewer to allow them to resume.

Microsoft's UltimateTV

In March 2000, Microsoft announced that it would augment the services of its one-million subscriber WebTV subsidiary with a digital video recording device called UltimateTV. WebTV's existing set-top boxes allowed TV viewers to send email and surf the internet on their TV screen. The UltimateTV box, made by Thomson as well as by Sony, would furthermore be bundled with satellite television thanks to leading provider DirecTV. This was meant to provide consumers with a unique combination of access to electronic mail, internet surfing, interactive television, as well as personal video recording.

Launch was expected in Fall 2000, in time for Christmas. Microsoft claimed to be offering more technologically advanced features, including watching or recording two shows simultaneously, recording pay-per-view movies, 30 second skip, and fast-forwarding at up to 300 times normal speed. WebTV's personal television service would be subscription-based, priced around $10 per month, like TiVo's. The price of the UltimateTV box, bundled with DirecTV or sold separately, was not yet announced. Microsoft's product announcements and marketing communications emphasized UltimateTV's technological advances.

Other Competitors

Since its creation, the personal television category had ignited the imagination of a number of entrepreneurs. For instance, Jovio, a start-up from Pittsburgh, PA, had announced its intention to launch a free service that would be similar to TiVo's, but additional advertising inserts would be appended onto the recorded programs. Individual profiles and behavioral data about viewing patterns would be captured and sold to potential marketers who would advertise on Jovio.

Seagate and Thomson had announced a joint venture to put their own personal television hardware inside the television set.

Conventional VHS video recorders, despite their shortcomings and the competition of digital video disks (DVD) players, continued to sell well: 60 million units per year, sometimes at a price below $100.

Making It Happen

Lessons after Christmas 1999

In addition to the accelerating pace of change in the competitive environment, the lessons learned from the disappointing sales results of Christmas 1999 were an important trigger for TiVo's new communications campaign.

Retail Execution

Marketing TiVo at the point of purchase appeared to be more challenging than expected. In contrast to most other consumer electronics goods distributed under the Philips and Sony brand name, selling TiVo often appeared to require extensive explanations and an in-store demonstration. The manufacturers' reps could not give TiVo the amount of support it required. It was hard to convey a sense of urgency to TiVo's distribution partners. Moreover, a 50% salesperson turnover rate in consumer electronics stores made training efforts ineffective. There was a lot of variance in the way TiVo was sold. "I pitch it as a super VCR," said a salesman in a high-end electronics store in the Boston area:

> There is no tape to buy, no tape to put in before you record, no tape to store in the family room. That's because there are 30 hours available on the hard drive. Moreover, because it is recorded digitally on a hard drive, the recording quality is superior to a VCR, and there is no degradation over time. Our demo unit is not hooked to TiVo, but you need the subscription, and I always recommend buyers to go for the $200 lifetime subscription. These things are here to stay. When buyers are in doubt I tell them to take it home and return it if they don't like it. Very few people return these boxes after trying them.

A salesman from another store said:

> I just acquired a TiVo, so for me the sale is easy. First, I show the pause feature. Many people ask me about skipping commercials, so I also show the incredible speed of fast-forwarding. And as you won't be able to stop the fast forwarding on a dime, TiVo automatically rewinds about 10 seconds once you stop it. This is very cool because it works out just right. Programming the recordings is very easy. And the thumbs up and thumbs down really gets you programming that you didn't know about. I heard that Microsoft is going to bundle TiVo with WebTV,[8] but you can safely buy TiVo now, because that's not going to happen before Spring 2001 and getting TiVo that way will require a satellite dish.

Pricing

"We came to the conclusion that the price was too high," said Keast:

> A $1,000 ticket meant that TiVo was more expensive than most TV sets, and more than twice the price of a good satellite system. With this service being so new there was no reference point. If you take DVD, it always had the VHS tape as a reference point. It had much better quality and sound. And the way it fits in your life was pretty well understood right from the start. Here we start with a completely blank sheet of paper. We thought TiVo would be worth $1,000 for early adopters, but it simply wasn't clear what the reference point would be to get this price accepted.

Awareness

Despite public relations efforts, the degree of awareness, both for the brand and for the category, remained negligible. The marketing team realized that TiVo needed a demo; it was difficult to explain and difficult to understand. Co-branding with Philips and Sony certainly brought an image of reliability, but it didn't seem to contribute to awareness. Moreover, the company realized that there was "a tremendous amount of inertia: no matter how great TiVo is, improving television viewing is not on the top of anybody's priority list, unless they really experience the benefits."

Cookbook Won't Work

When marketing new products, conventional marketing wisdom suggested that (instead of a mass-market approach) marketers should focus their resources on targeting early adopters. In theory, early adopters could be expected to share some common traits that would make them, as a segment, directly addressable in an economical fashion. They also tended to be opinion leaders, and initially targeting them (if that translated into sales) would kick off a viral effect.

TiVo, as a small company, did not want to waste marketing money on unlikely prospects. Thus, much of the pre-Christmas 1999 campaign was conceived with the early adopter theory in mind.

Of all the features of TiVo, the one that possessed the single most important "wow" factor was the ability to pause live TV. Just as earthquakes grabbed our senses by shaking things up that were supposed to stay fixed, TiVo stunned first-time users by stopping

[8] Sic.

something that had always been assumed to be streaming. Those who were price-insensitive enough to consider spending $1,000 for the unit on the basis of that "wow" factor were rare. Indeed, focus group research showed that even early adopters required at least seven points of exposure for an awareness of TiVo to mature into an actual purchase. Thus it was not clear that there existed a segment of consumers who would be particularly easy to target first. Moreover, early adopters did not fulfill their role as effective advertisers of TiVo. A TiVo team asked early adopters to invite friends over for an evening to demonstrate TiVo, only to learn what those early owners told their friends was extremely fragmented. Some described TiVo as a super VCR, others would focus exclusively on the season pass, and others emphasized live TV features, etc. The only consistent element was that TiVo was liberating their daily life.

How should TiVo now segment the market and which segment would it be most efficient to target most aggressively at this stage? What positioning statement could they use as a guide for action, to bring TiVo ahead of the competition?

Elements of a Plan

Despite the ongoing uncertainty about the best way to approach the market, the marketing team at TiVo had started to craft the elements of a marketing plan. Even though each individual element had its own rationale and sounded promising, the team had to ensure that the elements were strategically consistent. It was agreed that quarterly marketing and sales expenses could be tripled if the marketing plan was deemed capable of capturing a leading market share in the upcoming Fall and Christmas selling season, while building brand equity for the long run.

Product

DirecTV had approached TiVo, apparently intrigued by TiVo's dedication to a congenial concept of personal television. There was a possibility that DirecTV would become an equity partner. If TiVo was bundled with the DirecTV receiver, consumers would probably face a choice between a DirecTV-Microsoft and a DirecTV-TiVo bundle at some point in the near future. Internet provider and entertainment company AOL was also entertaining discussions with TiVo, but it was not clear at this point what product implications this partnership could have at this point.

Price

The TiVo team was determined to let the price of the 30 hour recorder drop from $999 to $399. There was a question whether production of the 14 hour recorder should be interrupted, in which case they could give away the units in inventory for free.

Communications

The prevalent idea was to use different media for different purposes. Keast depicted the thoughts of the marketing team:

> TV ads would introduce the notion that you can have your own personal TV network and you don't need to rely on the networks in terms of deciding what you watch, and when you are going to watch it. And then in the print ads where you have a little more space to get into more details, there may be some features and benefits. These get described, but in a different way than technology. We don't want to look like a computer company. Then there is the website, Tivo.com, which offers a deeper educational experience, in terms of what the service is about, how does it work, what do you need to get, where can you get it, what it is going to cost—all those kinds of things. Television advertising would be used to raise awareness, interest, curiosity, and to promote the TiVo brand identity.

EXHIBIT 5   Proposed Print Ad

TiVo helped cure my road rage.

I'm embarrassed to say...I was a mess. Every Thursday I'd leave work early so I could watch my favorite law show. I'd be sailing along, humming the theme song, which I absolutely love, when all of a sudden, gridlock traffic. And...I'd lose it. I, and this is hard to admit as a PTA member, wanted to throw my SUV into low and crush every living thing in front of me. Then my husband got me TiVo, which lets me watch the shows I want whenever I want to watch them. I especially cherish Season Pass, which automatically retrieves my favorite show week in and week out for the entire season. I'm fine now. And you'll be too if you go to **tivo.com** or your local electronics store.

TiVo, TV your way.™

TiVo is available on recorders from Philips or SONY at Best Buy and Circuit City. ©2000 TiVo, Inc.

The "Network Executive" ad was only one of a group of four targeted television commercials under consideration. The other three commercials were described as follows:

"Sports Education" A sports-obsessed father has a "class" for his son and daughter. He effortlessly skips from sporting event to sporting event, showing his son "icing," the "7-10 split," and the "slamma-jamma." For his daughter, he highlights "the lob" and the "the triple-axle." His son starts imitating the twirling of the triple-axle, and the father says "No, Bobby stop that! Jenny, triple-axle . . . Bobby! Stop that!"

"Cop" A bumbling police officer voices over scenes of him dropping his gun, getting in a car accident. He claims that "I'm in a high stress occupation; when I get home, television is my salvation. TiVo let me create my own TV network." When asked what he watches, he replies, "Mostly cop shows."

"Kids" "Ahh . . . the joys of parenting . . ." Scenes of children knocking over vases, destroying houseplants, throwing tantrums. "Sometimes kids and parents need a break. Why not create a TV network just for the kids?" Then the camera shows kids watching TV; now they are calm, passive, and happy. "TiVo. TV your way."

Two print ads were also under review (see **Exhibit 5** for an example).

A CBS executive, who had heard of the "Network Executive" commercial, had warned TiVo that his network would certainly refuse to show the ad.

Both ReplayTV and Microsoft were taking another path, emphasizing the amazing features of the digital video recorder. Did that mean that TiVo was trapped in the wrong lane? How would competitors adjust to TiVo's marketing plan?

Chapter 12

The New Beetle

Rajiv Lal   Neela Pal

While the first few cars will fly out of dealerships—some nostalgic Beetle buffs have already put down deposits—the long-term picture for the car is dicey. VW has only vague notions of who might buy it, and a puny ad budget to tout it. . . . For the agency [and marketing team] creating the ad campaign for the New Beetle, there's the added challenge: following in the tread marks of the old Beetle ads of the 1960s and 1970s; which are widely regarded as some of the best in history. Put it all together and it seems like a marketer's version of "*Mission: Impossible.*"

—*Daniel McGinn, "New Legs for a Bug,"* Newsweek, *January 12, 1998*

On March 10, 1998, with an hour to prepare before her marketing strategy meeting, Liz Vanzura (HBS '90), marketing director for Volkswagen, reflected on the challenge confronting her—one that had been so aptly described in a recent *Newsweek* article as "Mission: Impossible." By the end of the day, a team including Vanzura, Charlie Waterhouse, director of product development, and Steven Keyes, director of public relations, would have to finalize the marketing plans that would position the Volkswagen's New Beetle with one foot in the past and the other on the accelerator heading directly into the future.

Just a few weeks earlier, on January 5, 1998, Detroit's Cobo Hall had housed the 1998 North American International Auto Show—the country's leading automotive press event where Volkswagen (VW) had unveiled a dynamic multi-level stand that featured its new line-up of cars. Throngs of journalists and visitors had crowded the lower level of the display to catch a glimpse of the show's unexpected star, the New Beetle. Six brightly

Research Associate Neela Pal, HBS 2000, prepared this case under the supervision of Professor Rajiv Lal. HBS cases are developed solely as the basis for class discussion. Cases are not intended to serve as endorsements, sources of primary data, or illustrations of effective or ineffective management.

colored cars smiled out at onlookers from under the spotlights. One popular model with heat sensitive paint even invited visitors to press its flesh and make different patterns appear on the body.[1] As people walked by, they smiled and touched the characteristic curves of the car, reminisced about how they had named and painted their "Bug"[2] many years ago, and marveled at how the icon of the 1970s and "flower power"[3] had been transformed into a car for the new millennium.

While VW had much to celebrate with the recent success of the show, the company knew that the success of the New Beetle was still far from guaranteed. From its heyday as the automotive icon of the 1960s counter culture, VW had seen sales in the United States decline precipitously from over half a million cars in 1970 to less than 50,000 cars by 1993. However, with the support of a new advertising campaign targeted to a younger generation of car drivers and product introductions such as the New Passat, VW of America had steadily rebounded with an annual sales growth of 29% over the 1993 to 1997 period. In 1998, Volkswagen of America had targeted sales of 200,000 units, a 45% increase over the 1997 sales of 137,885 cars. To propel the company to this sales level, VW expected the New Beetle to contribute to at least 25% of the 1998 goal by selling its entire first year production quota of 55,000 cars. The VW marketing team knew that meeting this challenge would rely on their ability to successfully define a target audience, position the product, and develop an innovative advertising and media campaign—all in time for the New Beetle's arrival at dealers' showrooms in late spring.

With the car in production for nearly four years, VW of America had had time to conduct research to aid in developing the New Beetle marketing strategy. Initial research had indicated that the New Beetle appealed to a number of different consumer segments. While targeting a single segment such as Baby Boomers would be a more focused strategy, Vanzura wondered whether the full potential of the car would be realized if it were sold to such a narrow customer base. Once the target audience had been determined, there was still a question of how to position the New Beetle. Vanzura knew from qualitative research that many consumers perceived the New Beetle as a "toy car" and so a key element of the car's positioning would be to communicate it as a "real, driveable car." Beyond this message, the marketing team had been debating about the car's unique selling proposition. Discussions both internally and at Volkswagen's advertising agency, Arnold Communications, had focused on how much of the car's heritage the new positioning should leverage. While the body—"rounded shape, distinct fenders, single head and tail lamps, and a face that looked like it smiled"—played to the nostalgia of the original Beetle, the new car was no replica.[4] Vanzura asked herself, "how retro should we go" in our marketing efforts?[5] The answer to this question would impact not only the image of the New Beetle but also how consumers would perceive the broader Volkswagen product line-up.

The team's marketing strategy was also important to the company's senior management in Germany. There was concern that the choice of brand positioning would either define the New Beetle as another faddish, niche product, or again define Volkswagen as the Beetle car brand. Dr. Ferdinand Piech, Chairman Volkswagen AG Board of Management, had succinctly summed up his perspective on the New Beetle's role in the VW universe: "Despite all the high expectations we have for the New Beetle, one thing is for sure, Volkswagen will never be again the one-car company."[6]

---

[1] Matt Delorenzo, *The New Beetle*, Wisconsin, MBI Publishing Company, 1998, p. 55.

[2] A nickname given to the Beetle for its shape and insect-based name.

[3] A movement among hippies in the 1960s and 1970s, expressing counterculture or antiestablishment beliefs and ideals. Dictionary.com.

[4] Delorenzo, p. 58.

[5] Daniel McGinn, "New Legs for a Bug," *Newsweek*, January 12, 1998.

[6] Delorenzo, p. 54.

The Rise and Fall of Volkswagen in America

Volkswagen faced significant challenges in creating a presence for itself when the company sold its first two cars, Type 1—VW's model name for the Beetle—in the United States in 1949. With the end of World War II, most Americans were cautious about buying imported cars. With a shortage of parts and costly repairs, foreign cars were a luxury few could afford.[7] In addition, products from Germany had an additional image problem that limited demand. Despite these pressures, Volkswagen's sales grew and by the end of 1954, a total of 8,913 Volkswagens were traveling America's streets.

In 1955, the company was incorporated and officially became Volkswagen of America, a subsidiary of Volkswagen AG. Dr. Carl H. Hahn, then head of Volkswagen of America, decided that the company needed a unified corporate image and began an advertising campaign to market the Volkswagen brand. The first advertisement appeared in the *New York Times* in the spring of 1959. The full-page photo depicted a scene from a New York Volkswagen dealership: a customer, sitting in an armchair with a cup of coffee in hand, watching his Beetle being serviced.[8] The ad became distinctive for its message—not about selling cars but rather, its focus on the quality of service a Volkswagen owner could expect from his dealer. The print copy marked the inception of a unique and effective advertising campaign, produced by Doyle, Dane, Bernbach, Inc.,[9] which would help Volkswagen eventually become one of the best known car brands in the United States.[10]

In addition to his marketing initiatives, Hahn, after visiting VW dealers nationwide, decided to organize nationally rather than within smaller geographic regions.[11] By 1962, a new national Volkswagen of America organization was created and dealerships expanded into a national network.[12] On October 18th of that same year, the company opened its headquarters in Englewood Cliffs, New Jersey, and the one-millionth Volkswagen arrived in the United States.[13]

Beginning in the late 1950s, Volkswagen experienced a string of single-product successes in the U.S. market. The Beetle, which achieved almost cult status among U.S. consumers in the 1960s, was followed by the Rabbit (which ultimately became the Golf) a fuel-efficient car that enjoyed instant popularity among energy-conscious American consumers (**Exhibit 1**).[14] By 1968, with the help of other models such as the Volkswagen "Microbus" and the Karmann Gia sport coupe, Volkswagen was selling over a half million cars annually in the United States.

Over the next several years, a series of events brought the company's booming sales to a halt. During the 1970s, the appreciation of the Deutsche Mark against the dollar threatened to price VW's cars—most of which were low or mid range models—out of the market. In early 1975, VW was losing money on nearly every car sold in the United States and falling sales threatened to break-up the company's U.S. distribution network as dealers began defecting, particularly to new Japanese brands.[15] To insulate its prices from further exchange

---

[7] "Volkswagen Celebrates 50 Years on American Roads," VW Company Press Release.

[8] Ibid.

[9] Doyle, Dane, Bernbach, Inc (DDB) was the predecessor to New York advertising agency DDB Needham which was Volkswagen's agency in the United States until 1995.

[10] "Volkswagen Celebrates 50 Years on American Roads," VW Company Press Release.

[11] Ibid.

[12] Ibid.

[13] Ibid.

[14] The two sentences preceding footnote lifted from HBS Case—Hanson, Gordon, and Shapiro, Helen. "Volkswagen de Mexico's North American Strategy (A)," HBS Publishing Case 9-794-104, 1994, p. 2.

[15] Steven Tolliday, "Rethinking the German Miracle: Volkswagen in Prosperity and Crisis, 1939–1992," unpublished paper, Harvard Business School, 1991, p. 29–30.

EXHIBIT 1   Volkswagen Rabbit

Source: Volkswagen company documents.

1975 Volkswagen Rabbit VW 3134-75

rate volatility, the company acquired an unfinished manufacturing facility in Westmoreland, Pennsylvania, from Chrysler in 1976 and the first U.S. manufactured Rabbit appeared on the market in 1978. Predating Japanese transplants, the new subsidiary represented the first modern attempt by a foreign automaker to produce cars in the United States. But the Rabbit's fortunes proved to be short-lived. The 1982 recession, the drop in oil prices, and the declining popularity of hatchbacks[16] contributed to declining sales. During the same period, VW also experienced problems with the Beetle. Unable to comply with the requirements of new environmental legislation, VW had stopped selling the Beetle in the United States. Finally, by the mid-1980s, facing stiff competition from the onslaught of Japanese brands, VW saw its sales, for the first time since 1958, dip below 100,000 units.[17]

Maryann Keller, an auto industry analyst, summarized VW's rise and fall as a failure to keep in step with American consumers' ever-changing demands. "VW had a generation of lovers and lost them. They allowed the Japanese to seduce this generation. The VW product line is tired and old."[18] By the early 1990s, Volkswagen's sales had fallen to 20% of its 1970 peak (**Exhibit 2**). By 1993, with sales of 49,533, trade magazines even began reporting rumors of a Volkswagen pull-out from the U.S. market.[19]

[16] A car having a sloping rear door that is lifted to open. Dictionary.com.

[17] Paragraph taken from: Hanson, Gordon, and Shapiro, Helen. "Volkswagen de Mexico's North American Strategy (A)," HBS Publishing Case 9-794-104, 1994, p. 2.

[18] *Automotive News*, November 30, 1987.

[19] Gordon, Paul. "VW Updates Classic Beetle." *Peoria Journal Star*, November 29, 1994, C1.

EXHIBIT 2
Volkswagen Sales History

Source: Volkswagen company documents.

	Type 1	Total VW
1949	2	2
1950	328	330
1951	367	417
1952	887	980
1953	1,139	1,214
1954	8,086	8,913
1955	32,662	35,851
1956	42,884	49,550
1957	54,189	72,555
1958	61,507	85,985
1959	96,892	129,315
1960	127,159	162,037
1961	162,960	186,260
1962	194,508	226,649
1963	232,550	270,788
1964	276,187	313,426
1965	314,625	357,144
1966	318,563	411,956
1967	339,971	443,510
1968	423,008	569,292
1969	403,016	551,366
1970	405,615	569,696
1971	354,574	522,655
1972	358,401	485,645
1973	371,097	476,295
1974	243,664	334,515
1975	92,037	267,730
1976	27,009	201,670
1977	19,245	260,702
1978	9,932	239,300
1979	10,681	292,019
1980	4,572	293,595
1981	33	278,513
1982		171,281
1983		166,915
1984		177,709
1985		218,042
1986		217,231
1987		191,705
1988		168,800
1989		133,650
1990		136,357
1991		96,736
1992		75,873
1993		49,533
1994		97,043
1995		115,114
1996		135,907
1997		137,885

Relaunching Volkswagen in America

In fall of 1994, VW's marketing team including Waterhouse and Keyes met to discuss the lackluster performance in the U.S. market and began laying out a "strategic recovery" plan to reinvigorate the Volkswagen franchise. Waterhouse recounted the situation:

> In 1993, sales were at an all-time low for Volkswagen. Although sales volume was expected to pick up once car supply constraints were lifted with our new plant in Mexico operating at full capacity, it still would not be enough to get back to selling the number of cars we did in the '70s and '80s. We asked ourselves how Volkswagen could bring back the excitement it once had in the marketplace while still updating the brand's image to appeal to a new generation of consumers. We knew we would have to do things differently.

Arnold Communications

One of the most significant changes VW made was hiring a new advertising agency. After a hotly contested agency review, VW ended its 35-year relationship with DDB Needham, one of Madison Avenue's most prominent agencies. Volkswagen surprised many in the industry by hiring a small Boston-based firm, Arnold Communications. The Volkswagen team explained the challenge facing their new agency:

> When we hired Arnold, we gave them the task of making the Volkswagen brand important again and relevant to the '90s car buyer. We knew that the heritage of German engineering and the car's more fun, pleasurable driving experience were powerful strengths of the brand. Surely, these strengths could be better leveraged with consumers. However, we also knew the brand had some serious weaknesses to overcome. Despite our continuous marketing efforts, the brand's image had been slowly eroding, and there was a perception in the minds of consumers of poor quality and reliability. Even our recent Farfegnugen campaign had done very little to strengthen our brand equity. And our weak sales had also eroded confidence among our dealer organization.

To obtain a more in-depth understanding of consumer and dealer perceptions, the Arnold team undertook its own research and conducted extensive consumer interviews, visited 95 of the top 100 dealers, and drove Volkswagens for over 50,000 miles to experience the cars for themselves. Fran Kelly (HBS '83), chief marketing officer at Arnold Communications, summarized what they uncovered about the Volkswagen consumer:

> From a standard demographic analysis, we found that Volkswagen consumers were younger, slightly more affluent, and more educated than the average car purchaser. But more interesting were the attitudes of these consumers. We found that Volkswagen owners enjoyed a more *active* role in driving. They enjoyed driving on challenging winding roads, didn't always obey speed limits, and saw the car as more than just a way to get from place to place. We also found that these consumers had a unique attitude towards life. Well-informed, more adventurous, creative, confident, self-sufficient, experimenters, Volkswagen drivers seemed to want to make and take the most out of their lives.
>
> Our interviews also highlighted how the brand was perceived versus the competition. In comparison to other European brands such as BMW and Mercedes, Volkswagen was perceived as its namesake the "people's car" and found appealing for its affordability. It also offered a more unique, individualistic, driving experience versus Japanese cars such as Honda and Toyota.

With this fresh insight about the target market, the Arnold team recommended a new product positioning and brand essence that would become the foundation for the Drivers Wanted campaign. Kelly recalled the presentation:

> The brand essence statement captured the rational and emotional benefits that Volkswagen provided its consumers. We knew that to be distinct and appealing in a highly competitive marketplace, we had to take advantage of how people both *thought* and *felt* about the brand.

The rational benefit of Volkswagen was that it was the only brand that offered the benefits of German engineering *affordably*. Emotionally, the car represented a completely different driving experience—more connected to the road—and a different way of living—more connected to the world.

And as we thought about our positioning, we gave consideration to not only what we wanted to stand for but also what we did *not* want to stand for. For example, we wanted the Volkswagen brand to be invitational and approachable *not* exclusionary like some of the other European car brands. We wanted to sell our consumers on VW's unique driving experience *not* just on the car's ability to get people from one point to another, faster or cheaper—a focus of several Japanese competitors (**Exhibit 3**).

In June 1995, Arnold launched the first of its new advertising under the Drivers Wanted campaign (**Exhibit 4**). One of these early ads featured young executives trapped in their busy workday, escaping into Jettas and Golfs for after-work exhilaration.[20] The voiceover "On the road of life, there are passengers and there are drivers," and the tag line, "Drivers Wanted" aptly captured the spirit that Volkswagen wanted to convey to its consumers. With no new product introductions planned, the objective of the advertising campaign for the balance of 1995 and 1996 became to "get Volkswagen back on the consumer's shopping list."

Initial measures indicated that the advertising was proving successful and Volkswagen's unaided awareness and loyalty numbers began to improve. More importantly, sales began to rebound as 1995 and 1996 both experienced an annual 16% increase versus their respective previous years. With this momentum, in 1997 Volkswagen of America turned their attention to extending the Drivers Wanted platform to a younger generation of consumers. Under the new objective to "invite in new and different drivers," the marketing team launched its first co-branding effort. Public relations director, Keyes explained:

> The Trek/K2 promotion came to us opportunistically. We had an availability of models with sunroofs, spoilers, and alloyed wheels and we were thinking of implementing an aftermarket price promotion to push these cars out. But we knew that this price promotion would go against the very image we were trying to build. So, Arnold suggested that we approach Trek—a mountain bike company—and K2—a ski products company—about a co-marketing opportunity. In our initial conversations, both Trek and K2 expressed some hesitancy in working with us. They didn't think that Volkswagen had the image they wanted to be associated with. But we finally convinced them and in April '96, we introduced the "Jetta Trek" and it was a hit. We decided that instead of putting a monetary incentive on the car, we would put a total package around the car that would help reinforce the lifestyle image of the drivers we were targeting. By giving away a Trek mountain bike or K2 snowboard with a specially designed vehicle, we were able to expand the brand's consumer base and invite in a younger audience of drivers.

In addition to innovative promotions, Arnold Communications also developed advertising that would appeal to the hip Gen-X driver. In April 1997, Arnold debuted the acclaimed spot in which two young men drove aimlessly in a Golf as a narrator told how VW "fits your life, or your complete lack thereof."[21] The commercial became so popular that its theme music *Da Da Da*, from an obscure German song, was released as a single and its quirky plot parodied by television shows such as *Spin City*. Along with attractive lease-financing deals, this effort enabled the company to achieve its sales target, and more importantly, begin a relationship with a new generation of VW drivers.

While the marketing organization of Volkswagen of America had been busy with their efforts to reinvigorate the brand, the product development and engineering group had been working on a completely redesigned product line consistent with the new platform strategy

---

[20] Daniel McGinn, "New Legs for a Bug." *Newsweek*, January 12, 1998.

[21] Ibid.

EXHIBIT 3 Volkswagen Competitive Position

Source: Volkswagen company documents.

Volkswagen is:

- more approachable
- more likeable
- more value
- more human

Drivers wanted.™

Volkswagen is:

- more driveable
- more substantial
- more individual
- more spirited

EXHIBIT 4   **Volkswagen Drivers Wanted Advertisement**

Source: Arnold Communications.

developed and articulated by Dr. Ferdinand Piech, Chairman Volkswagen AG Board of Management. With the launch of the New Passat in November 1997, the company finally had some real product news and the focus of the brand's advertising shifted to supporting the launch. The reviews for the New Passat praised the car's styling and heralded the brand as a real contender in the mid-size car market, although many questioned whether Volkswagen had the image to market a car that was priced over $20,000. But despite a limited marketing budget and the higher price tag, the New Passat helped to strengthen VW's image while improving profits for both the manufacturer and dealers—who sold more cars at a higher margin.

By the end of 1997, Volkswagen was selling 137,885 cars, a 178% increase from its nadir of 1993 sales. It appeared that VW was back on track in the U.S. market. But the events of the first few months of 1998 would test the sustainability of this comeback and answer the question of whether the '90s would be the start of a new era for Volkswagen in the United States.

The Beetle Phenomenon

The Original Beetle

The Volkswagen Beetle was born in the mid 1930s, when Ferdinand Porsche began drawing up plans for "Volksauto," a people's car.[22] Built in a plant located in Wolfsburg—a town midway between Berlin and Hamburg—the car was conscripted into World War II and served as Germany's equivalent to the Jeep during the late 1930s and early 1940s. Although originally named the *Kraft durch Freude* or "Strength through Joy" car, people quickly adopted the car's more endearing appellation, the Beetle, when one of the prototypes was so dubbed by the *New York Times* in 1938.[23]

From its humble beginnings, the Volkswagen Beetle would soon become the most successful car model ever, selling over 21 million automobiles (**Exhibit 5**).[24] Americans first saw the car in 1949 and the Beetle quickly began to attract a cult-like following. With its distinctive round shape, face-like front end, and low price, the car stood out from the cookie-cutter stylings of the over-sized over-priced domestic cars and appealed to a new generation of Americans. For many, the Beetle was their first car. It was particularly popular with students who were budget-minded as well as drivers who sought to express their individuality and personal style through the car.[25] And despite the inconvenience of an air cooled engine that could not generate enough heat to keep the windows from frosting inside, or the choice between cooling off the car or climbing hills, Beetle owners were intensely loyal to their "bugs."[26] These owners found the car's flaws to be endearing. And stories about "Beetle-stuffing" contests—to see how many people could fit into a Beetle—and cross-country road-trips where "Herbie"[27] served as car, home, and friend, were abundant. As one owner once described, "[The car is] a member of the family that just happens to live in the garage."[28]

A large part of the car's success in the United States was also attributable to the memorable advertising campaign created by Doyle Dane Bernbach, which captured the unique essence of the Beetle in simple and humorous ads. "Buy low. Sell high." recommended one print ad, suggesting the Beetle as a solid investment as it required "very little upkeep" and retained its value over time (**Exhibit 6**). Another famous advertisement pictured a Volkswagen over the word "Lemon"[29] and went on to explain how VW refused to ship the car because of some blemished chrome (**Exhibit 7**). By 1970, Beetle sales had peaked at 405,615 units and the car had become a true American icon (**Exhibit 8**).

In 1979, the Beetle's run in America came to an abrupt stop. Volkswagen's inability to meet the requirements of two pieces of legislation—the National Highway Safety Act of 1966 and the Clean Air Act of 1970—forced the company to stop selling the car in the United States. However, America's love affair with the Beetle did not end.

---

[22] Thurow, Roger. "Post Script: Volkswagen Beetle: The Ubiquitous Bug Turns 5." *The Wall Street Journal*, October 18, 1985.

[23] Delorenzo, p. 18.

[24] Thurow, Roger. "Post Script: Volkswagen Beetle: The Ubiquitous Bug Turns 50."

[25] Meredith, Robyn. "Beetle-juiced Volkswagen Hopes to Recapture Love of Original Bug," *The Fort Worth Star-Telegram*, January 4, 1998.

[26] Ibid.

[27] Name of the magical Beetle featured in a series of Disney movies, "Herbie the Love Bug."

[28] Thurow, Roger. "Post Script: Volkswagen Beetle: The Ubiquitous Bug Turns 50."

[29] Vernacular description for something that is unsatisfactory or defective. Dictionary.com.

EXHIBIT 5 **Volkswagen Beetle—1958**

Source: Volkswagen company documents.

EXHIBIT 6
Beetle, "Buy Low, Sell High," Print Advertising

Source: Arnold
Communications.

Buy low. Sell high.

The day you sell your car could very well be Black Tuesday.

Which is why we'd like to let you in on a good thing.

A common Volkswagen Beetle.

According to the Official Used Care Directory,* a 1969 Beetle that sold new for only around $2,000 still sells used for around $1,550 in 1971.

Our tip really isn't much of a revelation.

Seasoned traders have known that since a Beetle requires very little upkeep, you don't have to make a big investment in oil and gas issues.

And every Beetle is sealed underneath so the bottom won't suddenly fall out of your market.

And what other 3-year-old car can be sold honestly with the words: "It looks just like new."

When we introduced the Beetle in 1949, a lot of car makers did sell us short.

Now they're trying to make their own.

We'd guess after 23 years and 18 million Volkswagens, somebody out there has spotted a trend.

The Reincarnation of the Beetle

More than ten years after the last Beetle was sold in the United States, J. Mays, then head of Volkswagen's newly established Simi Valley California design center, and Freeman Thomas, chief designer, with the full support of Helmut Warkuss, Director of Design Center for Excellence, Volkswagen, began toying with the idea of designing a new Beetle as a way to revive slumping sales of the VW franchise.

EXHIBIT 7   Beetle, "Lemon" Print Advertising

Source: Arnold Communications.

This Volkswagen missed the boat. The chrome strip on the glove compartment is blemished and must be replaced. Chances are that you wouldn't have noticed it; Inspector Kurt Kroner did.

There are 3,389 men at our Volkswagen factory with only one job: to inspect Volkswagens at each stage of production. (3,000 Volkswagens are produced daily; there are more inspectors than cars.)

Every shock absorber is tested (spot checking won't do), every windshield is scanned. VWs have been rejected for surface scratches barely visible to the eye.

Final inspection is really something! VW inspectors run each car off the line onto the Funktionsprüfstand (car test stand), tote up 189 check points, gun ahead to the automatic brake stand, and say "no" to one VW out of fifty.

This preoccupation with detail means the VW lasts longer and requires less maintenance, by and large, than other cars. (It also means a used VS depreciates less than any other car.)

We pluck the lemons; you get the plums.

The designers' vision for the car combined the equity of the past with the design geometry of the future.[30] By reinterpreting the original Beetle using the classic elements and basic shapes that made the car so popular, and adding cutting-edge technology and modern detail, the designers hoped to create something that would capture the Beetle's spirit and sense of history while still being a distinctively new model for the 1990s.[31] Trying to reflect the Beetle philosophy, the team identified four design principles—honest, simple, reliable, and original—for the new concept.[32] But even with all the attention to design, Mays and Thomas knew that the only way to sell the car to German management would be for the New Beetle to include the most up-to-date elements of German engineering and to offer superior driving performance. By 1993, their final designs convinced the company to move forward with what was now called Concept 1.

[30] Delorenzo, p. 24.

[31] Ibid.

[32] Ibid, p. 35.

EXHIBIT 8 Beetle—1975
1975 VW Beetle VQ 3170-75

Source: Volkswagen company documents.

For its first public showing, the manufacturer decided to display the car at the 1994 North American International Auto Show in Detroit. On the last press day of the show, journalists received their first glimpse of the new concept as a banana-yellow car rotated proudly on the display stand. An emotional video developed by the car's designers played in the background:

> It's funny the things we remember. The things we hang on to. The first day of school. A first dance. A first kiss. A first car. Some things are simply unforgettable. . . What if quality never went out of style? What if originality still meant something original? What if simplicity, honesty, and reliability came back again? Imagine a new Volkswagen. A concept that defines the automotive icon. Imagine a vision of high technology and advanced engineering. An expression of innovation, safety, and performance. Imagine the descendant of an enduring original. Different, unmistakable, yet true to its heritage in style and in spirit. Every line, every curve, every memory. Not just the evolutions of a cherished classic, but the continuation of a worldwide love affair that began 21 million cars ago. Innovation embodied in tradition. A new Volkswagen concept. One look, and it all comes back. But then, it never really left. The legend reborn. A friendship rekindled.[33]

Following the show, *Chicago Tribune* automotive reporter, Jim Mateja, wrote a letter to Dr. Ferdinand Piech in his February 13, 1994 column that appropriately captured the enthusiastic reception the car had received and directly called for the car's prompt production.

> Dear Dr. Piech,
>
> What are you waiting for Doc? Bring back the Beetle. And hurry.
>
> In case you haven't noticed, VW has been in the latrine since you stopped selling the Beetle in the United States. Unless you come up with a new, small, dependable, inexpensive car like the old Beetle real quick, you're going to find that Volkswagen, once a household word, is soon going to be the answer to a Trivial Pursuit question.
>
> You have the opportunity to get what most people in life don't—a second chance to regain the fortune you once enjoyed when the VW Beetle was one of the most popular cars in the universe despite being butt-ugly, cramped, and lacking most of the essentials of vehicle motoring, from gas gauge to radio.
>
> So take a close look at the Concept 1 car that was shipped from your Simi Valley, California design studios. Then let the board of directors give it a glance before you call for the formal vote—All in favor say "jawohl!" and get on with it. People are waiting.[34]

Waterhouse too remembered the strong reactions from the public and press:

> This was a car that was never meant to be. But from the day it debuted, consumers really linked emotionally to the car and were the force in bringing it to the market. In Detroit, it was touted as the automotive darling of the show. At the same time, the industry press *did* question if this was a "real" driveable car and whether the retro look would be totally passe by the time the car came to market. We took all the feedback and made some significant changes to the original design. We knew we had to get it right because the New Beetle would be crucial to turning around the company's image in the world's largest automotive market.

With this introduction, there was no turning back. The outpouring of emotion and the enthusiastic reception from press, dealers, and the general public was most encouraging. Volkswagen of America executives and the board member in charge of the North American region, Dr. Jens Neumann, a visionary who recognized the power and potential of the car, convinced VW's management in Germany to make a real car out of the concept.

By the time Concept 1 had transformed into the New Beetle, the car had been thoroughly overhauled from its original older brother. Based on the recently re-engineered top of the line Golf platform, the New Beetle housed an engine that was now in front and water-cooled,[35] offered front and side airbags and air-conditioning in the standard package,

---

[33] Ibid, p. 13.

[34] Ibid, p. 15.

[35] In the original Beetle, the engine was rear-mounted and air-cooled.

EXHIBIT 9   **The New Beetle**

Source: Volkswagen company documents.

and emitted music from a six-speaker sound system. Access to the 12 cubic feet of storage space in the rear hatch was hidden beneath a large VW badge on the back.[36] The change to the Golf platform also meant that the New Beetle would be larger and more spacious than the Concept 1 design. Finally, the brakes were up-graded from drum brakes to four-wheel disc brakes to ensure that in all aspects of the car, the New Beetle would handle as well as the VW Golf. Yet the shape, although more refined and modern than its predecessor, was instantly recognizable. And in a tribute to the original Beetle, Volkswagen had mounted a bud vase on every dash. "The new car puts the original seat in a modern package (**Exhibit 9**)."[37]

Marketing a Classic

With the design work complete and initial positive reactions from the market, VW now faced the daunting task of turning the excitement surrounding the car into actual sales. Vanzura, Waterhouse, Keyes, and Arnold Communications knew that their first step in identifying a target market and developing a compelling value proposition for the car would be to talk to consumers. Arnold Communication's Kelly explained the research process:

> We went across the country and conducted man-on-the-street interviews with men and women, young and old, rich and struggling, highly educated to life educated, and hip to conservative—a very diverse group of people. Our conversations centered on exploring the relationship people had with the original Beetle and the potential relationship they could have with the new model. In our quest to learn more about the New Beetle, we also interviewed industrial designers and sociologists to capture multiple perspectives about the car.[38]

Target Audience and Positioning

The research that the group conducted revealed polarizing opinions about the car. While many people saw the car as more of a toy, the New Beetle had its fair share of fans. These fans however, were from a wide spectrum of consumer backgrounds—crossing the

[36] Delorenzo, p. 58.
[37] "Beetlemania set to make a comeback with the car," *Plain/Dealer*, Cleveland, Ohio, December 10, 1995, p. 3H.
[38] From Arnold Communication Internal Beetle Case Study.

EXHIBIT 9   (Continued)

boundaries of age, income, and gender. In fact, the target market appeared to encompass both VW's new core audience of 18 to 34 year olds and Baby Boomers. While consumers were demographically diverse, potential buyers did have some common characteristics. Specifically, potential New Beetle drivers embodied qualities such as confidence, individualism, and a desire to be the center of attention. Moreover, they loved to drive and appreciated a spirited design and German engineering.

Interviews with both sets of consumers highlighted the fact that Americans had cherished memories of the original Beetle, and that those memories came welling up at the sight of the New Beetle. Baby Boomers shared their recollections of the car:

- Beetles are repositories of personal history as well as practical transportation.[39]
- I went on my honeymoon in a VW Beetle 20 years ago. "Just Married" was scrawled in shaving cream on the side. And a few years ago, when my wife and I went sailfishing, we found ourselves carting a 7 $1/2$ foot sailfish in the front-end trunk of another Beetle, one of four we've owned.[40]
- My affection for the Beetle can be traced to my college days at the University of Louisville. I think I was attracted [to the car] because I saw them as an underdog, and I like underdogs.[41]

[39] Linda Stahl, "Beetlemania: Volks Folks are going buggy over vintage VWs," *The Courier Journal—Louisville, Kentucky,* December 3, 1994, 04S.

[40] Ibid.

[41] Ibid.

Drivers wanted.

EXHIBIT 9 (Continued)

EXHIBIT 9
(Continued)

While the younger generation did not have past experiences to draw from, the car's strong heritage enabled them to have an emotional connection to the New Beetle:

- My job is very conservative, but that's not really the way I am. Everybody thinks 'Gee this guy is conservative—he works in Finance, he's boring.' But when I get out of work, I'm not that. I mean it's fun, it's a fun car.

- I see myself in it without having to justify it to anybody. I see it for someone who is unique—who knows they will attract attention without being pretentious. There is no sense of snobbishness about it, but it's for someone who is daring enough to step out. . . . Yes, they have confidence.

- The person is not going to make (i.e., define) that car—the car is definitely going to make the person. . . . My clients would laugh at me.

Using product photography and miniature models, designers also offered unique insight into the importance of the shape and design of the car:

Through the research we uncovered people's love of round shapes in our world. Circular shapes represent human forms, such as eyes, faces, and heads. Also, unlike square and triangles, circles are inviting and friendly due to the fact that no sharp edges exist. Finally, circular objects represent a completeness, a wholeness that many people were drawn to. The New Beetle's shape embodied many of these qualities and in doing so, evoked many feelings associated with circles.[42]

What do you want to be seen in? It's about how I present myself to the world. It's not only about how I feel behind the steering wheel but it's also about how people look at me when they pass by when I am sitting at a traffic light. We need to design a car that people will want to be seen in—feel good to be seen in.[43]

[42] From Arnold Communication Internal Beetle Case Study.
[43] From interviews in VW Brand Essence company video.

Finally, the sociologist that was interviewed provided an in-depth understanding of the history and connection that Americans have with the Beetle:

> In the 60s, it took on added meaning that the "Bug" was seen as the counter-culture car. One of the things that emerged from that time was "small is beautiful" and the Beetle was seen as a beautiful car. Today, in American society, on one hand there is this move to standardizing everything and on the other hand, you have this quest for individuality. For many drivers, this car will enable them to express themselves. The Beetle is no longer about being the *people's* car but rather about being a *personal* car.[44]

In addition to the positioning, VW had to determine whether or not to introduce the New Beetle under the existing Volkswagen Drivers Wanted campaign. The team analyzed the affect of the Drivers Wanted campaign on advertising recall, unaided brand awareness, overall brand opinion, and intent to purchase measures. Although an initial review of the data revealed that results were trending positively, the numbers were well below those of competition on several strategic measures (**Exhibit 10**). Advocates of Drivers Wanted argued that the campaign had the creative legs to support the New Beetle launch and would become the consistent theme that brought all the separate VW models together under one umbrella. However, some in the company felt that leveraging the nostalgia surrounding the car demanded a distinctly new and different campaign—one that would be on par with the advertising campaign that made the original Beetle so beloved.

Competition and Pricing

As part of the analysis in determining a target market and product positioning, the VW team also had to assess the New Beetle's pricing and competitive place in the market. In 1997, a total of 8,272,043 cars were sold across four segments: small size, mid-size, large, and luxury. The small size car segment, the second largest segment after mid-size, comprised 27% of the market and had experienced a 5% decline to end 1997 with sales of 2,217,813 cars. While VW had yet to define the New Beetle's competition, the car's size would automatically place it into this segment. Domestic brands, such as Chevrolet's Cavalier, Ford Escort, and Saturn, cumulatively sold over one-third of the segment's cars and would be the New Beetle's immediate competitive set. Japanese car manufacturers Toyota and Nissan were also contenders in the category with their Corolla and Sentra models that combined, held a 15.4% market share (**Exhibit 11**).

Prices for key players in the small-size car segment ranged from a low of $11,035 for a 2-door Saturn coupe to a high of $17,239 for a Sentra SE 4-door sedan (**Exhibit 12**). With a base price tag of $15,200, most New Beetles would probably list out in the $17,000–$18,000 price range with extras like a CD player and sunroof—making it one of the more expensive cars in the small size segment—a description inconsistent with the car's heritage of affordability. In fact, pricing had been a debate since the car began its engineering overhaul and adopted more of the Golf platform. The VW team realized that a premium-price strategy could be a potential issue. If the car was priced too high, consumers might trade-up into a higher priced segment of cars expanding the New Beetle's competitive set. Of course, priced too low, the car might not be attractive enough to dealers due to lower margins and thus fall short of the company's profitability goals.

Dealers

In 1998 there were 600 Volkswagen dealers in the United States, 10% of them exclusive, with both numbers growing. Over the 1980s and 1990s, these dealers had seen the boom and bust cycle of the brand, and while several had dropped the VW line, most dealers had

---

[44] From interviews in VW Brand Essence company video.

EXHIBIT 10   **Summary of Key Marketing Measures vs. Competition**

Source: Allison-Fisher, Inc. Volkswagen Tracking Study.

	Volkswagen Trends—United States								
In Percents(%)	Dec-95	Mar-96	Jun-96	Sep-96	Dec-96	Mar-97	Jun-97	Sep-97	Dec-97
Total ad recall	45	44	44	47	46	45	44	52	53
Overall opinion	49	48	40	45	49	46	46	49	51
Unaided brand awareness	15	16	16	14	15	13	14	13	17
Unaided purchase consideration	4	4	4	5	3	4	4	5	6
	Total Ad Recall—Volkswagen and Key Competitors—United States								
% Seen/Heard Ad	Dec-95	Mar-96	Jun-96	Sep-96	Dec-96	Mar-97	Jun-97	Sep-97	Dec-97
Volkswagen	45	44	44	47	46	45	44	52	53
Nissan	69	74	73	78	82	78	72	82	83
Saturn	85	89	91	91	86	90	85	82	87
Toyota	83	85	88	84	86	85	79	77	89
	Overall Opinion—Volkswagen and Key Competitors—United States								
%Excellent/Good	Dec-95	Mar-96	Jun-96	Sep-96	Dec-96	Mar-97	Jun-97	Sep-97	Dec-97
Volkswagen	49	48	40	45	49	46	46	49	51
Nissan	65	73	68	67	71	67	71	73	74
Saturn	74	76	76	73	69	77	76	74	74
Toyota	84	83	85	84	85	83	86	84	89
	Unaided Brand Awareness—Volkswagen and Key Competitors—U.S.								
% Aware	Dec-95	Mar-96	Jun-96	Sep-96	Dec-96	Mar-97	Jun-97	Sep-97	Dec-97
Volkswagen	15	16	16	14	15	13	14	13	17
Nissan	46	51	44	45	36	46	47	54	53
Saturn	32	27	31	28	23	29	30	29	25
Toyota	78	72	79	74	66	77	75	70	76
	Unaided Purch. Consideration—Volkswagen and Key Competitors—U.S.								
% Considering	Dec-95	Mar-96	Jun-96	Sep-96	Dec-96	Mar-97	Jun-97	Sep-97	Dec-97
Volkswagen	4	4	4	5	3	4	4	5	6
Nissan	21	22	19	19	16	22	21	25	26
Saturn	15	13	15	15	10	17	16	15	21
Toyota	48	40	42	49	46	49	47	46	50

added other brands and correspondingly reduced the amount of time and effort they dedicated to the VW franchise. While the recent results of the Drivers Wanted campaign and the New Passat's successful introduction had encouraged many dealers, the company still needed to prove the true value of the franchise.

To improve relationships with the dealers, Volkswagen had undertaken two organizational efforts. In September 1997, the company had flown its entire base of dealers to the company headquarters in Wolfsburg, Germany.[45] The trip allowed dealers to hear German management's vision for Volkswagen, to visit the plant and technical facilities, and to see the new line-up of Volkswagen cars to be introduced in the United States. In addition, the dealers were included in a company-wide training session at the Disney Institute in early spring 1998, which was designed to help Volkswagen employees understand the value of creating a total brand experience for consumers.

[45] Delorenzo, p. 68.

EXHIBIT 11   1997 Small Car Segment Sales

Source: Adapted from 1998 Ward's Automotive Yearbook, pages 224–225.

	1997 Cars Sold	Percent of Segment	1996 Cars Sold	Percent of Segment	1997 Diff vs. 1996
LOWER SMALL	198,054	8.9%	241,533	10.4%	241,533
UPPER SMALL	1,907,160	86.0%	1,955,056	84.2%	1,955,056
Chevrolet Cavalier	302,161	13.6	277,222	11.9	24,939.00
Dodge Neon	121,854	5.5	139,831	6.0	(17,977.00)
Ford Escort	283,898	12.8	284,644	12.3	(746.00)
Geo Prizm	62,992	2.8	79,288	3.4	(16,296.00)
Honda Civic*	42,190	1.9	11,673	0.5	30,517.00
Hyundai Elantra*	41,303	1.9	39,801	1.7	1,502.00
Isuzu Stylus*	—	0.0	—	0.0	—
Mazda Protege*	53,930	2.4	59,644	2.6	(5,714.00)
Mercury Tracer	43,589	2.0	47,797	2.1	(4,208.00)
Nissan Sentra	122,468	5.5	129,593	5.6	(7,125.00)
Nissan Sentra	—	0.0	—	0.0	—
Plymouth Neon	86,798	3.9	105,472	4.5	(18,674.00)
Pontiac Sunfire	102,160	4.6	95,783	4.1	6,377.00
Saturn	250,810	11.3	278,574	12.0	(27,764.00)
Suburu Impreza 4wd*	24,241	1.1	23,968	1.0	273.00
Suzuki Esteem*	6,968	0.3	6,996	0.3	(28.00)
Toyota Corolla	217,207	9.8	202,417	8.7	14,790.00
Toyota Corolla*	1,254	0.1	6,631	0.3	(5,377.00)
Toyota Tercel	31,651	1.4	56,492	2.4	(24,841.00)
VW Golf	20,702	0.9	24,208	1.0	(3,506.00)
VW Jetta	90,984	4.1	85,022	3.7	5,962.00
SMALL SPECIALITY	112,598	5.1	125,432	5.4	(12,834.00)
TOTAL SMALL CAR	2,217,812	100.0%	2,322,021	100.0%	(104,209.00)
TOTAL SMALL CAR	2,217,812	27%	2,322,021	27%	(104,209.00)
TOTAL MIDDLE CAR	4,050,825	49	4,212,703	49	(161,878.00)
TOTAL LARGE CAR	782,148	9	843,191	10	(61,043.00)
TOTAL LUXURY CA	1,221,257	15	1,147,116	13	74,141.00
TOTAL CARS*	8,272,042	100%	8,525,031	100%	

*Denotes imports.

On the heels of these efforts to build loyalty to the franchise, the launch of the New Beetle would test the company's relationship with its dealers. Most dealers were excited about the new car and encouraged by the number of pre-orders they had received. However, dealers also questioned if this popularity would be sustained or if the New Beetle would become another retro fad with sales quickly tapering off after the initial fanfare.

The Launch

Reaching across her desk, Vanzura picked up the three documents that would be reviewed at her team's strategy meeting. The first, a review of 1997 results, was encouraging and suggested that the Volkswagen brand was well poised for its new product initiatives in 1998 and beyond—the New Beetle, New Jetta, New Golf, and the New Cabrio. From a sales perspective, while a supply issue had once again hampered the company's ability to reach its sales target, efforts to build the brand had paid off generously. In fact, most

EXHIBIT 12
U.S. 1998 Model Car Prices for Top Five Small Car Brands

Source: Adapted from 1999 Ward's Automotive Yearbook, pages 262–270.

Make and Series	Style	Retail Price
Chevrolet		
Cavalier	2-dr coupe	$12,110.00
Cavalier	4-dr sedan	12,310.00
Cavalier RS	2-dr coupe	13,370.00
Cavalier LS	4-dr sedan	13,370.00
Cavalier Z24	2-dr convertible	19,910.00
Cavalier Z24	2-dr coupe	16,210.00
Ford		
Escort LX	4-dr sedan	11,745.00
Escort SE	4-dr sedan	13,045.00
Escort SE	4-dr wagon	14,245.00
Escort ZX2	2-dr coupe	12,995.00
Saturn		
SC1	2-dr coupe	13,035.00
SC2	2-dr coupe	15,295.00
SL	4-dr sedan	11,035.00
SL1	4-dr sedan	11,735.00
SL2	4-dr sedan	13,195.00
SW1	4-dr wagon	12,735.00
SW2	4-dr wagon	14,695.00
Toyota		
Corolla VE	4-dr sedan	12,328.00
Corolla CE	4-dr sedan	14,208.00
Corolla LE	4-dr sedan	15,218.00
Nissan		
Sentra	4-dr sedan	11,989.00
Sentra XE	4-dr sedan	14,189.00
Sentra GXE	4-dr sedan	15,389.00
Sentra GLE	4-dr sedan	16,239.00
Sentra SE	4-dr sedan	17,239.00
Dodge		
Neon Competition	2-dr coupe	11,400.00
Neon Competition	4-dr sedan	11,600.00
Neon Highline	2-dr coupe	11,755.00
Neon Highline	4-dr sedan	11,955.00
Neon R/T	2-dr coupe	13,895.00
Neon R/T	4-dr sedan	14,095.00

quantitative measures had reached their highest levels in 1997. Total advertising recall crossed the 50% mark to 53%, image attributes for the brand had made positive gains, and the Passat's awareness had reached an all-time high in the fourth quarter of 1997.

A report on the recent public relations effort, the second document in the pack, highlighted some of the critical events that had contributed to the motor press's euphoric reception to the New Beetle. This reception had been carefully orchestrated to create an early and overwhelmingly positive consensus among North America's most influential automotive journalists about the "magic" of the New Beetle. In December of 1997, a select group of journalists were invited to Wolfsburg, Germany to meet with management and preview the New Beetle. Similar to the visit by dealers, the visit by the press provided the group with unique insights into the New Beetle's design and development process and offered them a better understanding of Volkswagen's new product line-up. In January 1998, the dramatic unveiling of the New Beetle had stolen the show at the car industry's most important event. And then most recently, journalists had been given an opportunity to drive the New Beetle for at least one day and one night through different communities in the country in order to experience firsthand the outpouring of public excitement about the car. Reading the article that was to appear in the April issue of *Automobile Magazine,* Vanzura realized that the PR efforts had been successful in achieving their objectives. (See excerpts from Jean Jennings article in *Automobile Magazine* that chronicled consumers' reactions to the New Beetle as the car drove from San Francisco to New York City.)

But Vanzura knew that positive press coverage alone would not be enough to sell the New Beetle. The marketing team would have to decide whom to target and how to communicate the car's benefits. Targeting the baby boomers with a value proposition of "indulging in nostalgia" appeared to be the most appropriate strategy for the New Beetle. In addition to their personal history and emotional ties to the Beetle brand, these buyers could also afford the plus $15,000 price tag for the car. But the decision was not that easy. Consumer trends among the Baby Boomers revealed changing preferences to larger cars—sedans, SUVs, and pick-ups. And of course, Volkswagen had shifted its strategy, positioning the brand behind the "driveability of their cars" to target a younger generation of drivers.

Once the positioning for the car had been decided, Vanzura had to maximize the impact of the brand's limited advertising budget. Although the competition had been spending upwards of $100 million in advertising behind the launch of a single car—with 80% of the budget going to television, 15% to print mediums, and 5% to radio and billboards—Vanzura could not spend this much on the New Beetle launch. In fact, she had to contend with something less than 25% of a typical budget—a percentage that could be even smaller with requests to allocate any remaining dollars to supporting the New Passat, which had debuted just five months earlier. If the audience for the car was too broad, would the advertising agency have adequate resources to reach everyone with their messages? A targeted strategy would allow the company to speak to a specific audience more frequently.

Picking up the final document, a proposed media plan, Vanzura wondered if television or print advertising would be more effective in reaching the target market. The advertising agency had explained that building brand awareness among a broader customer base would be best executed with a television campaign. Another option, print advertising, would enable the New Beetle to reach a specific demographic, such as Baby Boomers, more cost effectively. If both mediums were used, Vanzura would have to allocate the dollars. Finally, once these media vehicles were decided, the team would have to identify the specific shows and magazines in which to advertise the car. As the New Beetle was a unique product introduced to the automotive market, it was impossible to utilize standard purchase consumption data as a reference in media planning. Rather, the team had to think about the target audience they wanted to reach and then evaluate each magazine or TV show for the right environment to not only showcase the creative product but also position the brand. Vanzura explained the media buying rationale:[46]

> When we look at where to buy our media, it is important for us to align our target audience strategy, with the creative execution, and the editorial voice of the magazine or television show—thereby creating a synergy between medium and message. Unlike other automotive advertisers, we never buy solely on CPM or coverage.

Looking at the print options, Vanzura was certain that advertising should be purchased in *Car & Driver, Motor Trend,* and *Automobile* magazines. However, with the limited budget, she wondered if a buy in magazines such as *Architectural Digest, Entertainment Weekly,*

[46] Arnold Communications Media Rationale Document.

EXHIBIT 13   New Beetle Magazine Options

Source: Volkswagen company documents.

	Architectural Digest	Spin	Glamour	Entertainment Weekly	Life	Vogue	Sports Illustrated
Page cost	$60,270.00	$35,935.00	$81,580.00	$63,945.00	$71,630.00	$72,230.00	$170,000.00
Circulation	741,452	535,392	2,208,926	1,431,886	1,500,744	1,125,585	3,269,917
Cost per thousand	$81.29	$67.12	36.93	$44.66	$47.73	$64.17	$51.99
Simmons descriptor*	161	406	185	242	172	252	144
J.D. Powers** Driver's Profile	122	NA	108	114	NA	108	116

Note:

*Simmons Descriptor

Index of 161 = Readers of *Architectural Digest* are *61% more likely* than adults ages 18+ *to agree to all of the following descriptions:*

>   Affectionate, Passionate, Loving, Open-minded, Liberal, Sociable, Friendly, Cheerful, Likable,
>   Humorous, Amusing, Inviting, Creative, Inventive, Imaginative, Enjoys taking risks, "Left-of-center"
>   I like to behave as I please without worry, Don't mind standing out in a crowd, Slightly irreverent
>   Very much an individual, Funny, Broad-minded

**J.D. Powers Driver Profile

Index of 122 = Readers of *Architectural Digest* are *22% more likely* than adults ages 18+ *to agree to 2 of the 3 following statements:*

>   Does not like to obey the speed limit
>   Prefers to drive on challenging roadways
>   Views a car as more than transportation from A to B

Spin, Life, Sports Illustrated, Glamour, and *Vogue* would be appropriate. (**Exhibit 13** lists magazines compiled by Arnold as options for the media plan.)

As Vanzura came closer to making these decisions, she remembered a recent article in *Newsweek* that had aptly captured the task at hand:

> We have the opportunity to re-introduce the most loved car in America's history; a car with nostalgia, fond memories, and some of the best advertising this country has ever seen. Yet 1998 is a very different setting, a very different audience, and a very different time. And the New Beetle for all intents and purposes is a very different Beetle.

Vanzura picked up the documents and began walking to her meeting. In the next few hours, Vanzura, Waterhouse, Keyes, and the advertising agency would have to finalize the marketing strategy for the New Beetle. This would be one "Mission Impossible" that the VW Marketing team and the advertising agency would have to accept.

13

Aqualisa Quartz: Simply a Better Shower

Youngme Moon   **Kerry Herman**

Plumbing hasn't changed since Roman times.

—Tim Pestell, Aqualisa national sales manager

Harry Rawlinson (HBS '90) shrugged out of his overcoat and headed to the reception desk of the South Kent County Marriott. "Can you direct me to the breakfast room?" he asked, "I'm meeting some guests from America." The receptionist indicated a hallway lined with photographs of the surrounding region's golf fairways and putting greens. "It's just to the left down there," she said. As he strode down the narrow corridor, Rawlinson, managing director of Aqualisa (see **Exhibit 1**), a U.K. shower manufacturer, felt a surge of energy. He had been looking forward to this opportunity to discuss an HBS case possibility.

In May 2001 Aqualisa had launched the Quartz shower, the first significant product innovation in the U.K. shower market since—well, to Rawlinson's mind—since forever. But here it was early September 2001, and the euphoria surrounding the product's initial launch had long since faded. Rawlinson knew the Quartz was technologically leaps and bounds above other U.K. showers in terms of water pressure, ease of installation, use, and design. But for some reason, it simply wasn't selling.

The U.K. Shower Market

Rawlinson leaned forward as he began to explain his situation. Showers in the United Kingdom were plagued with problems. While everyone had a bathtub, only about 60 percent of U.K. homes had showers. Archaic plumbing, some of it dating to the Victorian era, was

Research Associate Kerry Herman prepared this case under the supervision of Professor Youngme Moon. HBS cases are developed solely as the basis for class discussion. Cases are not intended to serve as endorsements, sources of primary data, or illustrations of effective or ineffective management. Some data have been modified or disguised.

EXHIBIT 1   **The Aqualisa Organizational Chart**

Source: Aqualisa.

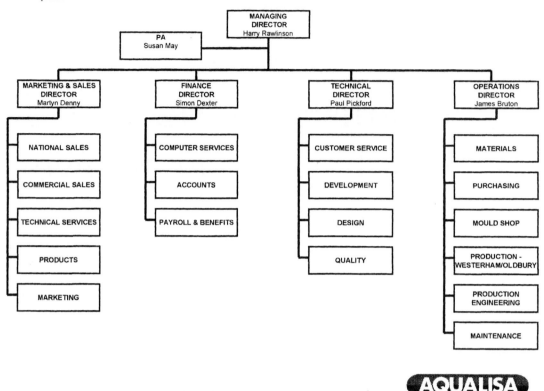

still common in many homes. For the most part this plumbing was gravity fed; a cold water tank or cistern sat somewhere in the roof, while a separate boiler and cylinder were needed to store hot water in a nearby airing cupboard.

Gravity-fed plumbing meant poor-to-low water pressure, about 3–4 liters per minute.[1] Gravity-fed plumbing also created frequent fluctuations in pressure, which caused the temperature to noticeably vary from minute to minute. If the pressure from the cold water pipe decreased momentarily, the flow from the hot water pipe would increase, immediately raising the temperature.

These two problems—low pressure and fluctuations in temperature—were typically addressed through the use of either electric showers or special U.K. shower valves.

1. **Electric showers** used water from the cold water supply. Electrical heating elements in the shower instantaneously heated the water to the required temperature, eliminating the need for a boiler to store hot water. While this made electric showers convenient for small bathrooms, the electrical components were usually mounted in a bulky white box that was visible in the shower stall. In addition, electric showers did nothing to address the poor water flow of many showers in U.K. homes, since the flow was limited by the amount of energy that could be applied to heat the water instantaneously. Aqualisa sold electric showers mostly under a separate brand name, the "Gainsborough" brand. (See **Exhibit 2** for shower sales by type and brand.)

---

[1] Water pressure in the United States, in contrast, is generally at least 18 liters per minute.

EXHIBIT 2   **U.K. Market Share Data: Units Sold (2000)**

Source: Aqualisa.

Brand	Electric Showers	Mixer Showers	Power Showers	Total Units Sold
Triton	479,000	41,000	25,500	545,500
Mira	155,000	200,000	35,000	390,000
Gainsborough	180,000	20,500	3,000	203,500
Aqualisa	6,000	94,000	22,000	122,000
Masco	35,000	50,000	35,000	120,000
Ideal Standard	0	60,000	0	60,000
Heatrae Sadia	40,000	0	0	40,000
Bristan	0	20,000	0	20,000
Grohe	0	20,000	0	20,000
Hansgrohe	0	15,000	0	15,000
Others	205,000	29,500	29,500	264,000
Total Units Sold	**1,100,000**	**550,000**	**150,000**	**1,800,000**

2. **Mixer shower valves** came in two types: manual and thermostatic. Both types blended hot and cold water to create a comfortable temperature, but while thermostatic valves controlled the temperature automatically, manual valves required the user to manually find the right temperature mix. Installing a mixer valve meant excavating the bathroom wall, which was often a two-day job. If a user wanted to boost water pressure, an additional booster pump (typically costing from €350 to €600) could be installed to enhance the flow rate.

   The Aquavalve 609 was the company's core product in the mixer-shower-valve category. At about 60,000 units per year, it was by far Aqualisa's top-selling shower. It was regarded by plumbers as being a high-quality, reliable mixer shower with state-of-the-art technology. It cost about €155 to manufacture and sold (at retail) for €675 to €750. The Aquavalve 609 was thermostatic and could be supplemented by an Aquaforce booster pump to create stronger pressure.

3. **Integral power showers** consisted of a single compact unit that combined a thermostatic mixer valve and a booster pump. Although they provided up to 18 liters of blended water per minute, they had to be mounted in the shower, resulting in the presence of a bulky box on the wall. In addition, these units were generally regarded as being less reliable than a mixer-shower and booster-pump combination. The Aquastream Thermostatic was Aqualisa's primary product in this category. It cost about €175 to produce and sold (at retail) for about €670. At about 20,000 units per year, it was Aqualisa's strongest-selling shower in the power shower category.

Most consumers could readily identify what they disliked about their showers—poor pressure and varying temperature being at the top of the list. But there were other complaints as well. Showers often broke down, or "went wrong," as Rawlinson described. "They break after awhile. The mechanisms get gummed up with lime scale, making the valves stiff and hard to turn; the seals start to leak, or they go out of date." As a result, consumers complained about hard-to-turn valves, leaky seals, and worn out showers. (Almost half the U.K. shower market was comprised of sales of replacement showers—see **Exhibit 3.**) On the other hand, consumers were generally uninformed about showers, and there was little understanding of product options (see **Exhibit 4**). Brand awareness was low; only one company in the market (Triton) had managed to build brand awareness at the consumer level.

EXHIBIT 3
U.K Shower Sales,
by Reason for
Installation

Source: Aqualisa.

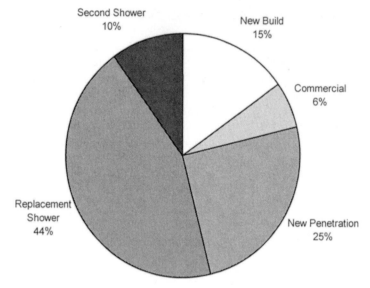

Note: "New penetration" refers to new showers installed in existing bathrooms (where plumbing already exists, e.g., a shower added to a bathtub). "Second shower" refers to installation of a new shower in a location where no plumbing exists.

EXHIBIT 4
Shower Selection for
Mixer Showers

Source: Aqualisa.

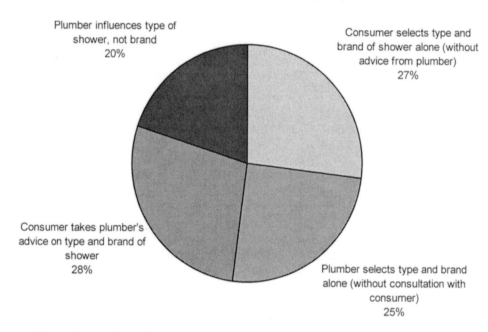

Shower buyers in the United Kingdom tended to fall into one of three pricing segments: premium, standard, and value. Consumers in the premium segment typically shopped in showrooms; they took for granted high performance and service, and for them style determined their selection. Consumers in the standard price range tended to emphasize performance and service; they usually relied on an independent plumber to recommend or select a product for them. Consumers in the value segment were primarily concerned with convenience and price; they liked to avoid solutions that required any excavation and tended to rely on an independent plumber in selecting a product. (See **Figure A** for Aqualisa's core product offerings in the various shower categories.)

In addition, there was a sizeable do-it-yourself (DIY) market in the United Kingdom. Do-it-yourselfers generally shopped at large retail outlets that catered to them (for example, the popular B&Q, which modeled itself after Home Depot in the United States).

FIGURE A **Aqualisa's Core Product Offerings in the Various Shower Categories**[2]

Source: Aqualisa.

Type of Shower		Aqualisa's Core Product Offerings		
		Value	Standard	Premium
Electric Shower	• Does not require hot water supply • Results in bulky box on the wall • Low flow rate	Gainsborough Retail: €95	Gainsborough Retail: €155	Aquastyle Retail: €230
Mixer Shower	• Requires both hot and cold water supply • Requires additional pump to address pressure problems • Installation typically requires excavation of bathroom	Aquavalve Retail: €390	Aquavalve 609 Retail: €715	
Power Shower	• Requires both hot and cold water supply • Results in bulky box on the wall • Regarded as less reliable than a mixer-shower and pump combination	Aquastream Manual Retail: €480	Aquastream Thermostatic Retail: €670	

They were primarily interested in inexpensive models that were easy to install, even though the DIY products were bulky and unattractive. Electric showers were the overwhelming choice in this segment. They could be adapted to all water systems and could be installed in a day; they were particularly popular among landlords and apartment dwellers.

Finally, there was a significant property developer market in the United Kingdom. Most developers did not need to worry about pressure problems because new homes were almost exclusively built with high-pressure systems. Developers faced a different set of issues, preferring reliable, nice-looking products that could work in multiple settings. Developers were also price sensitive; with the exception of luxury builders, most developers did not feel the need to invest in premium valves. Developers usually had relationships with independent plumbers who installed whatever product they selected.

Aqualisa sold to developers under its ShowerMax brand, which was available only through specialist contract outlets. Elements of the Aquavalve technology had been re-designed and re-branded for the ShowerMax product line and optimized for developers' specific needs. Because new homes did not use gravity systems, ShowerMax could deliver a high-pressure shower—with Aquavalve technology—at a significantly lower cost. Rawlinson commented, "Aqualisa's core products are too expensive for them because of extra features aimed at the retail market. Even at a discounted price, they consider Aqualisa too high end. But a cut-down product branded "ShowerMax" just for them, at the right price—they love it."

Rawlinson went on to say:

> Real breakthroughs are pretty rare in the shower market. Innovations are primarily cosmetic. Most of the major manufacturers recycle their product line and relaunch their main products about every four or five years. It refreshes your brand, but market share doesn't really change. At Aqualisa, we've tended to do a relaunch every three to four years. Aesthetically we've changed the look, and we've made incremental technological improvements to boost the performance and quality, but it's basically been the same mechanisms inside. These aren't breakthrough innovations we're talking about.

[2] Aqualisa offered a variety of other specialty shower models in each of these categories. The differences between these showers were primarily stylistic (e.g., contemporary, antique, brass, etc.).

Channels of Distribution

Showers in the United Kingdom were sold through a variety of channels (see **Exhibits 5** and **6**), including trade shops, distributors, showrooms, and DIY outlets.

Trade shops

Trade shops (or plumbers' merchants) carried products across all available brands. Their primary customer was the plumber, who worked for developers, contractors, or directly for consumers. Trade merchants tended to stock whatever there was demand for. The Aqualisa brand was available in 40 percent of trade shops. As Rawlinson put it: "The staff in these outlets don't have the time to learn all the features and benefits of the 45,000 items they offer. They focus on making sure they have the right stock of products that are in demand. Their customers are looking for reliable product availability more than technical advice."

Showrooms

Distributors supplied showrooms, which tended to be more high end. Showroom "consultants" typically led consumers through the process of selecting and designing a bathroom "solution." A shower might be one small part of an overall renovation project. Various shower and bath options were displayed in the showroom, and although no inventory was held on location, these ensembles allowed the consumer a chance to view the product in a pleasant environment. Showrooms preferred to carry high-end product lines and brands (for example, Hansgrohe, a high-end German brand) unavailable in other channels. They also offered installation services. There were about 2,000 showrooms in the United Kingdom; the Aqualisa brand was sold in about 25 percent of them.

EXHIBIT 5
U.K. Shower Market, by Installation Method (Mixer Showers Only)

Source: Aqualisa.

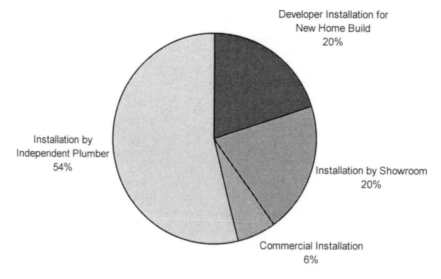

- Developer Installation for New Home Build 20%
- Installation by Independent Plumber 54%
- Installation by Showroom 20%
- Commercial Installation 6%

EXHIBIT 6
U.K. Shower Market, by Product Type and Channel (Total Units Sold, 2000)

Source: Aqualisa.

	Electric Showers	Mixer Showers	Power Showers
Do-It-Yourself sheds	550,000	80,000	20,000
Showrooms	55,000	70,000	20,000
Trade shops	330,000	400,000	110,000
Other (electrical wholesalers)	165,000		
Total Units Sold	**1,100,000**	**550,000**	**150,000**

DIY Sheds

Do-it-yourself retail outlets like B&Q offered discount, mass-market, do-it-yourself products. Electric showers, because they were cheaper and easier to retrofit, led sales in this channel. The Aqualisa brand was unavailable through this channel, but its Gainsborough brand was available in 70 percent of the approximately 3,000 DIY outlets in the United Kingdom.

Plumbers (Installers)

There were about 10,000 master plumbers in the United Kingdom. Plumbers had to undergo several years of training and three years of apprenticeship to become master plumbers. There was a significant shortage of master plumbers in the United Kingdom, and as a result, consumers often had to wait six months before a plumber could take on a new job.

A standard shower installation was usually a two-day job and required significant bathroom excavation.[3] Plumbers—who installed 40 to 50 showers a year—charged about €40 to €80 per hour, plus the cost of excavation and materials (plumbers usually passed the cost of the shower and other materials on to the consumer with a small markup). Because prices to consumers were usually quotes as lump sums, consumers were often unaware of how the costs broke down (labor, materials, excavation, and so on).

For plumbers, unfamiliar products could present unknown performance problems, and a bungled installation often required a second visit, paid for out of the plumber's pocket. For this reason, plumbers generally preferred to install a single shower brand and were extremely reluctant to switch brands. Loyalty to a single brand created expertise in a given brand's installation idiosyncrasies and failure problems. Over time, plumbers also liked to familiarize themselves with the service they could expect from a manufacturer.

As a general rule, plumbers distrusted innovation. For example, in the 1980s some manufacturers had introduced electronic "push-button" controls for temperature settings. Rawlinson recalled: "The mechanisms were poorly designed and didn't work well at all. Ever since that, there's been a great deal of skepticism towards anything that seems technologically newfangled—especially if it involves electronics."

The Development of the Quartz Shower Valve

Historically, Aqualisa's reputation had always been strong in the U.K. shower market; the company was generally recognized as having top quality showers, a premium brand, and great service. Aqualisa's market share ranked it number two in mixing valves and number three in the overall U.K. shower market. (See **Exhibit 7** for additional information on Aqualisa's financials.)

However, when Rawlinson joined the company in 1998, he believed it was vulnerable, for several reasons. First, Rawlinson believed that other companies were catching up to Aqualisa in terms of product quality. Second, Rawlinson feared that the market was beginning to perceive Aqualisa products as being overpriced (see **Exhibit 8**). Third, while Aqualisa's service was still regarded as being "great," actual service had slipped over the past few years. And finally, about ten percent of Aqualisa showers still "went wrong," a percentage that hadn't improved in many years. Rawlinson remembered:

> When I first joined Aqualisa in May of 1998, what I found was a highly profitable company that was quite comfortable with its niche in the market. It had 25 percent net return on sales and was enjoying 5 percent to 10 percent growth in a mature market. Everyone was happy. But I was worried. I knew the current points of difference were eroding and that eventually the market might implode on us. From the start, I firmly believed that the future was to focus on innovation.

[3] Typically, the plumber would either excavate himself, or he would subcontract the work to a plasterer. The price plumbers charged for excavation varied significantly.

EXHIBIT 7
Aqualisa Select Financials 2000 (€ in thousands)

Source: Aqualisa.

Shower sales (electric, mixer, power, and pumps)[a]	€46,212
Other[b]	21,744
Total Sales	**€67,956**
Gross Margins	**€31,824**
Sales	€4,080
Marketing	2,724
Customer service	1,322
Research and development	1,764
Finance, administration & depreciation	4,579
Total Overhead Spend	**€14,469**
Base Profit	**€17,355**

Notes:

[a]Includes all Aqualisa shower lines, including Aquastyle, Aquavalve, and Aquastream. Also includes Aqualisa pumps, as well as a variety of other specialty shower models sold by Aqualisa; these were primarily differentiated by style (e.g., contemporary, antique, brass, etc.). Does not include other brands such as ShowerMax and Gainsborough.

[b]Aqualisa sold a variety of other products, including shower accessories and commercial products.

EXHIBIT 8
Aqualisa: Selected Products and Price Points

Source: Aqualisa.

Model	Segment	Retail Price	MSP	Cost	Margin
Aquastyle	Premium	€230	€155	€95	€60
Aquavalve 609	Standard	€715	€380	€155	€225
Aquavalve Value	Value	€390	€205	€75	€130
Aquastream Thermostatic	Standard	€670	€350	€175	€175
Aquastream Manual	Value	€480	€250	€140	€110
Quartz Standard	**Premium**	**€850**	**€450**	**€175**	**€275**
Quartz Pumped	**Premium**	**€1,080**	**€575**	**€230**	**€345**
Aquaforce 1.0/1.5 Bar	Standard	€445	€230	€125	€105
Aquaforce 2.0/3.0 Bar	Premium	€595	€310	€175	€135

Note: "Retail price" refers to the price charged by the retailer (trade shop, showroom, or DIY outlet) to the customer. "MSP" refers to manufacturer selling price (Aqualisa's price to the channel).

Rawlinson's first priority was to build a research and development (R&D) team:

We brought together a top-notch team of outsiders and insiders to look at the future of showers. We had engineers, R&D, our sales and marketing director, and a market research guy. We did research studies to understand peoples' problems and attitudes to showering. We had a top industrial designer and a bunch of Cambridge scientists who apply technology to industrial applications. We put all these people into a huddle—held brainstorming sessions, with flip charts and felt-tip pens. And we came up with all kinds of things to improve in a shower.

As a result of their market research, Rawlinson realized that the consumer wanted a shower that looked great, delivered good pressure at stable temperatures, was easy to use, and didn't break down. Plumbers wanted a shower that was easy to install, with a guarantee to not break down or require servicing. The team's brainstorming led to some real breakthroughs. Rawlinson noted:

The breakthrough idea was to locate the mechanism that mixes the water remotely—*away* from the shower. All the problems with showers come down to the fact that you have to put a clumsy, mechanical control right where the user doesn't want it—*in* the shower. And that's why you get these big bulky boxes on the shower wall. Or you're constrained to put the mechanism somewhere in the wall behind the shower—equally difficult and costly to install or repair. But locating the mechanism remotely—all of a sudden that opened up all kinds of opportunities because now you didn't necessarily have to excavate.

The problem was, how could a user control a mechanism that was located remotely? And that's when we brought the electronics people in. Of course, that generated a lot of skepticism, because electronics had flopped so terribly in the '80s. But nobody had ever thought of using the electronics to control the valve remotely. And when we came up with the idea, we realized very quickly that it had *huge* potential.

Once the product started to take shape, field tests were next. Rawlinson arranged for about sixty consumer field test sites, installing showers in the homes of sales reps, company personnel, and friends of friends. Feedback from the field tests prompted constant modifications. He recalled:

Consumers told us they wanted maximum pressure. But once we gave them maximum pressure (about 18 liters per minute) consumers felt it was wasteful. So we had to give them the option to run at two-thirds speed—which they liked more than maximum pressure.

With the temperature settings, it was the same thing. We knew from our research that the optimal water temperature was 41° [Celsius]; anything above that would be uncomfortably hot. So we created this temperature control that had an upper limit of 41°. But people hated the fact that it required them to turn the valve all the way to the right, into the "red zone" on the indicator. Even though nobody wanted their water hotter than 41°, they all wanted the *option* of being able to make the temperature hotter. So we reset the maximum to 45°, people set their temperature at 41°, and everyone liked that much better.

After three years of development—during which the company spent €5.8 million—the result was a radically different kind of shower (called Quartz) that cost the company about €175 to €230 to make. By this time, the company had invested in a new state-of-the-art testing facility, had acquired nine patents, and had grown its engineering team from six to twenty. Several additional products were in advanced stages of development, while dozens of other ideas were in the early stages of the new-product development pipeline.

The Quartz: A Breakthrough in Shower Technology

The Quartz came in two versions. The Quartz Standard Shower was designed for installations that already had, or did not need, a pump; the Quartz Pumped Shower included a pump.

To install the Quartz shower, the plumber had to identify a physical space to accommodate the remote processor, which was about the size of a shoe box. The processor contained the thermostatic mixing valve, and when applicable, the pump. The location of the processor could be anywhere within reasonable proximity to the shower—under a cabinet, behind a wall, inside a closet, in the ceiling, wherever. The device could be mounted horizontally, vertically, or on its side, depending on space constraints. The only requirements were that it had to be in a location where cold and hot water could be piped into the processor, and it had to be plugged into a standard power outlet. Once these requirements were met and the processor was in place, a single pipe fed the mixed water from the processor to the showerhead. Because of the flexibility associated with locating the processor remotely, excavation of the bathroom could often be avoided altogether. Instead, a plumber had only to drill a single hole (to accommodate the pipe feeding the mixed water to the showerhead, along with a data cable) into the ceiling above the shower (see **Figure B**).[4]

---

[4] The ease of installation was a big selling point for the Quartz. In fact, it was so easy that the installation guide itself was being used in Quartz's promotional and sales materials.

FIGURE B   **The Quartz Technology**

Source: Aqualisa.

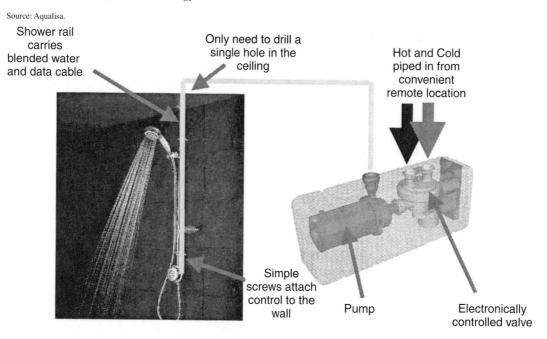

Shower rail carries blended water and data cable

Only need to drill a single hole in the ceiling

Hot and Cold piped in from convenient remote location

Simple screws attach control to the wall

Pump

Electronically controlled valve

The benefits of Quartz were significant. Whereas a traditional shower installation took two days, some plumbers were already reporting an installation time of a half day for the Quartz. Plumbers were finding that the installation was so straightforward they could even send their young apprentices—many with little or no experience—to complete the entire job. Rawlinson had spoken to several plumbers during the field trials, "They raved about it. They said, 'It's just what we want! We need something like this that we can push-fit-connect-you're done. It's not in the wall, and it's very easy to use.'"

For the consumer, the Quartz shower provided efficient and reliable water pressure and temperature. In addition, it featured a "one-touch" control mounted on the shower wall. The easy-to-use push-button control light on the valve flashed red until the desired temperature was reached (see **Figure C**). Rawlinson remembered that this had been another feature with unexpected psychological benefits:

> When consumers turn a traditional shower on, they almost always turn the shower to very hot . . . and then wait for it to warm up. They usually have to stick their hand in the shower a few times until they feel it's hot enough to get in. Once they're in the shower, they immediately start fiddling with the controls again. It's incredibly inefficient and inconvenient.
>
> With our Quartz technology, the temperature control is automatic—there's no more fiddling. You don't have to manipulate anything anymore. Just set the temperature once, and leave it on that setting. When you want to use the shower, just press a button, and you've turned the shower on. When the red light stops flashing, you know the water's at the right temperature. Get in.

During field trials, consumers loved it. "We call it the 'wow' factor," Rawlinson said. "They loved how it looked; it delivered great power, and now it had neat fittings and push-button controls that lit up. Parents loved it because it was safe for their kids to use on their own. The elderly loved it because they didn't have to fight with stiff valves. What wasn't to love?"

FIGURE C
**The Quartz
Thermostatic Control**

Source: Aqualisa.

Rawlinson was already anticipating upcoming product releases. In a few months, Aqualisa would be ready to launch a Body Jet product that fit easily on top of the Quartz control valve, creating several jets of water that sprayed horizontally from the wall onto the body. This feature was popular in spas and health clubs; women particularly liked it because it allowed them to shower without getting their hair wet. The R&D team had also just finished designing a "slave" remote for the Quartz. Rawlinson described it: "Imagine waking up in the morning, rolling over, and pushing a 'remote control' next to your bed that turns your shower on. By the time you stumble in the bathroom, your shower is ready with the water at the right temperature, waiting for you to get in. Because we're dealing with electronics, the wireless technology to do this is almost trivial."

In fact, Rawlinson and the R&D team could spend endless hours coming up with new product ideas; as Rawlinson liked to say, "Once you put a computer in the bathroom, the potential is unlimited!"

To launch the new product, Aqualisa had hit the major shows, like the Bathroom Expo in London in May 2001. At the Expo, the Quartz had been awarded the top prize.[5] Press events had been coordinated with demonstrations. The trade press had raved about the "cleverness" of the product and its "elegant design." One reporter wrote:

> Imagine a shower that takes less than a day to fit, doesn't have flow problems, offers accurate temperature control, is simplicity itself to use and comes in versions to suit all water systems. It sounds too good to be true—but after three years of brainstorming . . . Aqualisa has achieved the apparently impossible with a product that takes a genuinely new look at a set of old problems—and solves them.[6]

Other reviewers had been similarly positive, and the Quartz had been featured on the covers of several prominent trade journals.

Initial Sales Results

Aqualisa had a 20-person sales force that sold to distributors, trade shops, showrooms, developers, and plumbers. Tim Pestell, Aqualisa's national sales manager, described the sales team's priorities: "Our sales force spends about ninety percent of their time on maintaining existing accounts—servicing existing customers: distributors, trade shops,

[5] "Showered with Success," *Bathroom Journal*, June 2001, p. 13.
[6] Ibid.

contractors, showrooms, and developers. Ten percent of their time is spent on developing new customers." Aqualisa's sales force also had long-standing direct relationships with a group of plumbers—"our plumbers" as director of marketing Martyn Denny called them—who were very loyal to the Aqualisa brand.

With the launch of the Quartz, the Aqualisa sales force had contacted its network of plumbers, calling face-to-face to introduce and explain the new product, but few actual sales had resulted. Indeed, despite all the early excitement over the product, and despite being made available in all of Aqualisa's normal channels, very few units had sold in the first four months on the market. Rawlinson worried:

> Our channel partners are sitting there having bought a thousand of these Quartz products, and they've sold 81. The poor product manager is looking pretty stupid at this stage. This is a huge problem for us—pretty soon they're going to write this off as a failure and forget about us. I can see a scenario in six months' time where real sales in the market—currently about 15 units a day—are still down at 30 or 40 units a day. We'll look like a niche product. We've got to sell 100 or 200 a day to break through to the mainstream.

Part of the problem was that plumbers were wary of innovation, particularly any innovation involving electronics. Rawlinson told the story of a personal friend who had to insist that her plumber install a Quartz:

> His initial reaction was negative. He said, "Oh no, I wouldn't put one of these in, Madam. I've had these electronic showers before. They don't work." She insisted and made him put it in. He told her it would take two days. He was done by lunchtime the first day. And he said, "That was so easy. Can I have the brochure?" And now he's got two or three more jobs. So once a plumber puts one in, he's a convert.

Pestell, however, noted that given the conservative nature of most plumbers, "Adoption is a long, slow process. It takes time." In addition, he pointed out:

> Some people at the company think the Quartz will eventually replace our core product—the Aquavalve—and become mainstream. I think it's really a niche product—it's good for homes with children, or for the elderly and the handicapped. It's easy to use, safe and so on, but we can't forget our core products every time we launch something new. The Aquavalve is our bread and butter, and it can go away if no one's watching.

Denny concurred, "How do we pitch our other products alongside Quartz? Right now, if Quartz is mentioned, our salesmen tend to gloss over our other products. In fact, to sell the Quartz, they have to point out *deficiencies* in our existing products. That doesn't really make any sense, does it?"

According to Rawlinson, the only place Quartz seemed to be gaining any traction was in the showrooms:

> Showrooms are traditionally quite a niche market. But I think we've made some penetration into that sector, and we're starting to get working displays around the country. Because you put one of these things in, you press that control button, the little red light comes on: it's sold! Everybody loves it. And where it's gone in—a working display—it's become the leading product in that showroom almost immediately.

A Shift in Marketing Strategy?

The waitress began to clear the coffee cups. Rawlinson absently dusted at the crumbs on the tablecloth as he leaned forward and said:

> Once upon a time Microsoft was a tiny little provider of specialist software. Bill Gates had the vision to see that if you own the operating system on the PC, you can build from there.

One of our presentations calls the Quartz the "Pentium Processor" because we can do so much once we have this kind of control over your bathroom . . . we can use this technology with a shower . . . but in the future we could use it with a bath, the sinks, whatever . . . We're only limited by our creativity.

The question was, how to generate sales momentum? Was the problem that the Quartz was priced too high? Rawlinson wondered whether a discounted price might generate more market enthusiasm for his innovation. Because Quartz was such a breakthrough product, Rawlinson was loath to go this route. On the other hand, Rawlinson *was* willing to rethink his overall marketing strategy for the Quartz. Some of the marketing options he was debating included:

Targeting Consumers Directly

"We have so many problems reaching the plumbers," Rawlinson continued. "So I'm thinking to myself, why not target consumers with this product and try to build a consumer brand? Triton has proven that it can be done. And if there's ever been a breakthrough product to do it with, this is it. I think this is a 'bet the company' kind of product."

The problem with this option was that Rawlinson was finding it tough to justify a high-risk, high-reward strategy when company results were already healthy. As a test, a one-time-only print advertisement campaign was scheduled to run in *The Mail on Sunday* magazine in October (see **Exhibit 9** for copy of the advertisement). But, as Rawlinson noted, "One ad does not a campaign make. I'm not overly optimistic." A large-scale consumer campaign would cost about €3 million to €4 million over two years. With a net income of about €17 million, this would be a very tough sell across the company.

Targeting Do-It-Yourselfers

A second alternative was to target the do-it-yourself market. Rawlinson noted, "The Quartz is so easy to install, you or I could even do it." Aqualisa was currently selling its Gainsborough line to this market. The risk, as Rawlinson pointed out, was that "once you show up in the DIY sheds, you can't climb back out. You have to be careful about associating your premium brand with your discount channel."

On the other hand, the value proposition of the Quartz was so superior to that of the electric showers that dominated this market, perhaps it *was* possible to charge a premium for this product through that channel? In addition, he wondered if Aqualisa could get its partners like B&Q to help push the product, avoiding the need for expensive consumer advertising.

Targeting Developers

A third alternative was to target developers more aggressively. Rawlinson thought aloud, "The plus side is that this could conceivably be a large-volume channel. If we could get a couple of developers on board, we'd sell a lot of showers. In addition, it would force plumbers to get familiar with our product since they would have to install whatever the developers tell them to install." But there were downsides—including the significant time lag before showers would reach consumers through this route. As Rawlinson noted with some urgency, "We've got *at most* a two-year lead on the competition."

Rawlinson also wondered how tough a sell it would be to developers. Developers had already shown a reluctance to spend money on conventional Aqualisa products because they perceived those products to be premium brands; even at a 50 percent discount, the company had been unable to make the sale. And again, given that Quartz was such a breakthrough innovation, Rawlinson was reluctant to discount the price.

EXHIBIT 9 Advertisement for the Quartz Shower

Source: Aqualisa.

What to Do

If his managers were right and this was a niche product, Rawlinson wondered if maybe he should simply lower his expectations. Everything was basically well with the company—but at the same time, he could not help arguing:

> Business school taught me to think strategically, to be a visionary. Everything I learned at HBS tells me this is a breakthrough product. My worry is we'll miss the opportunity and in five years' time, someone else will have got the world market for this technology. We've had a nice, comfortable, contented life in the U.K., and it's hard to get a small company—particularly one that's been so profitable all these years—to be ambitious. But one of the things that a Harvard background gives you is the itch to think big. You see other companies that break out of the pack because they've got the right product and they've got the right vision. So why not this company?

Chapter

14

Documentum, Inc.

Rajiv Lal   Sean Lanagan

After the missed opportunity at Ingres, we saw Documentum as our
chance to build another Oracle.

—Howard Shao, Documentum co-founder and vice president of Engineering

Monday, November 8, 1993, was a tough day for Jeff Miller, the new CEO of Documentum. Miller had been with the Silicon Valley software startup for just four months, but was now about to bet the company's future on an innovative, but unproven, market selection process. This decision would commit the company to a radically different marketing strategy than the one he had pitched to venture capital (VC) investors when he secured funding less than two months earlier. To further raise the stakes, Miller had also promised the VCs that he would grow sales from their current level by over fifty times over the next three years. To this point in his career he had always fulfilled his commitments and he wanted to do so again. Was he making the right decision? As he reflected on his options, the phone rang. One of the sales reps had found a big opportunity at a leading insurance company with the potential to become a million dollar deal. It would be the largest sale in the company's history, but was he willing to do what it would take to win the business?

Background

Documentum was founded on June 11, 1990, by Howard Shao and John Newton, database engineers at Ingres Corporation, one of the leading database software vendors at the time. Shao and Newton believed they could leverage their knowledge of relational databases to develop a new class of software for automating the management of documents across an enterprise. The founders knew that databases were great for managing structured information such as inventory, financial, and manufacturing data that could be neatly stored in the

Sean Lanagan (MBA '02) prepared this case under the supervision of Professor Rajiv Lal. HBS cases are developed solely as the basis for class discussion. Cases are not intended to serve as endorsements, sources of primary data, or illustrations of effective or ineffective management.

rows and columns of a database. But databases were severely limited in their ability to manage unstructured information contained in documents such as product specifications, marketing collateral, training manuals and regulatory submissions. (See **Exhibit 1** for examples of unstructured information.) From their contact with Ingres customers they had learned that the processes that governed the creation, review, distribution, and disposal of these documents were manual, prone to error, and posed a major problem for corporations. Shao and Newton started looking for a way to participate in what they believed would be the next "big thing" in the information management market: managing unstructured information in documents, or as they called it, enterprise document management.

Shao was presented with such an opportunity through Bob Adams and the VC arm of Xerox Corporation. Adams had technology which Xerox had invented to generate the documentation for their 9700 Laser Printer and was looking for someone to develop it into a commercial product and build a company around it. Adams offered Shao the opportunity to be the first employee of the new venture. Xerox would take 80% of the equity in exchange for the technology, free office space in an abandoned Xerox factory, and a $4 million commitment to cover payroll and other expenses. Shao took the deal and brought in his Ingres colleague, Newton.

Rather than jumping into the coding of the system immediately, Shao and Newton focused on learning what the market wanted. As Shao explained,

> We didn't want to create a product that only a vendor could love, so we spent six months talking to companies that were already trying to solve unstructured information management problems to see what we could learn. Xerox connections and prior Ingres relationships got us into insurance companies, aerospace companies, a pharmaceutical company, the Big "8" Consultants, and NASA. We synthesized our learnings from each of these meetings into one comprehensive view of the problem, and as we did that, the market began to resemble what I call the blind men and elephant syndrome. Depending on what technology each of the existing software vendors had developed, they would interpret core customer needs differently: imaging (a trunk), workflow (a foot), configuration control (an ear), and text retrieval (a tail). None of them saw the whole picture or provided a complete solution.[1] Given our customer research, we interpreted the problem as a combination of these point requirements (the whole elephant) and we figured out that we could provide a complete solution by creating a new type of database for managing unstructured information called a document management system. With a vision in place, John Newton and I went through 300 resumes to hire the first five engineers and then began coding.

The Document Management Opportunity

The next step was recruiting a couple of early customers to validate the technology and the market opportunity. The first major lead came through a partner, Frame Technology, which was competing for the Boeing 777 aircraft training manual project. Frame sold publishing software that Boeing's writers used to create complex, multi-chapter manuals. But Boeing also wanted software that would manage these electronic files after they were created, and Frame's chief competitor for the deal, Interleaf, had software that could meet both requirements. Frame asked Documentum to provide the missing piece and help win the business. Shao agreed and flew up to Seattle to pitch his story to a classroom full of Boeing technical writers. In his words:

> I spent the morning explaining the intricacies of our technical architecture, and watched their eyes glaze over. At lunchtime it was obvious I was not connecting and we weren't getting the deal. Then a senior Frame sales rep approached the Boeing opinion leader and asked him to tell us about the problem in his words. I thought, "Wow, what an idea!" The Boeing guy described in painstaking detail how flight training manuals were assembled for pilot trainees.

[1] See **Exhibit 2** for a graphic comparison of vendor offerings.

EXHIBIT 1   **Examples of Unstructured Information**

Source: Documentum.

Documents are ...

Lorem ipsum dolor sit amet, consectuer adipiscing elit, sed siam nonummy nibh euismod tincid unt utlaoreet. Ut wisi enim

Text

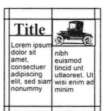

Compound Documents

Graphics

To:	Lorem
From:	Ipeum
Subj:	Dolor sit

Lorem ipsum dolor sit amet, consectuer...

Electronic Mail

Name	Q.1	Q.2	Q.3
Bob	2.3	4.4	6.6
Leslie	4.3	5.6	7.7
Angela	3.3	4.4	6.8
John	1.1	2.1	3.4
Paula	3.6	4.5	6.4

Spreadsheets

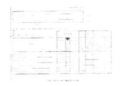

Scanned Images

Multi-Media

Business Critical Documents in the Enterprise

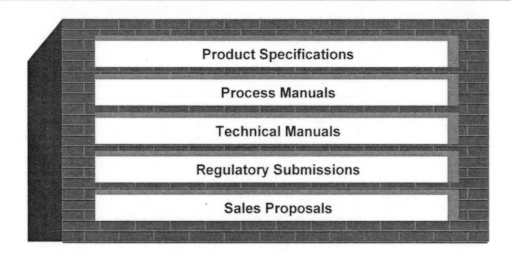

- Product Specifications
- Process Manuals
- Technical Manuals
- Regulatory Submissions
- Sales Proposals

EXHIBIT 2 Solution Comparison

Source: Documentum.

Documentum's Approach Provides a Complete Solution

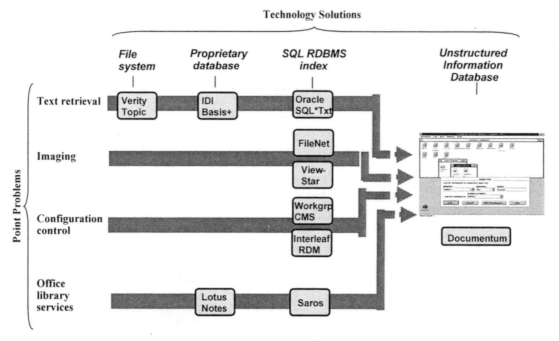

Documentum's Position

The Only Company Delivering the Virtual Document

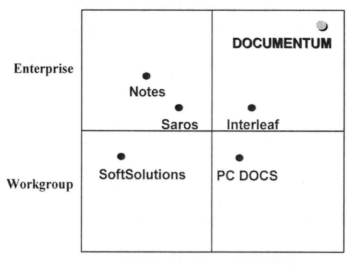

Each aircraft was assembled from thousands of different parts including engines, avionics, etc. and was identified by its tail number. Every training manual had to be tailored to the specific configuration of that airplane, which changed multiple times over the typical aircraft's 30- or 40-year lifecycle. Their current manual process, which consisted of walking around a giant warehouse full of racks and hand-picking the appropriate pre-printed sections, took a highly paid instructor a week to assemble the 6,000-page manual for each course, and there was still a 50% error rate.

After lunch I told the writers, "forget about what you heard before, I understand your problem and here's what I can do to solve it." I painted the vision of a new Documentum system that would assemble a manual at the push of a button as fast as a printer could print. The system would be smart enough to make general or specific updates to manuals and show change marks based on an aircraft's particular tail number. This woke the writers up, put smiles on their faces, and at the end of my pitch, they gave us the deal.

The Boeing situation was special for multiple reasons. The company was building a revolutionary new aircraft, the 777, and needed to completely retool its entire operation. Also, the Boeing tech writers group was known for using innovative technologies—they used Macs in an all IBM shop. On the other hand, Boeing had invested billions of dollars in the 777 project and couldn't afford to risk losing revenue if an unproven software startup failed to deliver on its promises and forced Boeing to launch a product without any documentation. To close the deal, Documentum asked a senior Xerox vice-president to fly to Seattle, meet with Boeing's head of Commercial Aircraft, and commit Xerox to back Documentum up if the training manual project encountered any problems. The visit was not an act of charity, as Xerox was going to sell the high-speed printers for the project, but it was enough to help Documentum close the deal. Almost a year to the day after the original meeting, Documentum delivered the software and Boeing cut a check for $250,000. As Shao reflected, it was not a profitable experience: "We lost our shirts, but Boeing did finance some of our early development, they helped turn our theoretical design into a working solution, and they put us on the document management roadmap."

Documentum tried to build on its success at Boeing by calling on other aerospace manufacturers over the next couple of months, but no one else was retooling operations, and none of the leads panned out. Eventually, they met a pharmaceutical vendor, Syntex, which was in trouble because it had several drugs that were scheduled to come off patent, and didn't have enough new drugs in the approval pipeline to offset the lost revenue. Chip Hay, Documentum's vice president of Industry Development, outlined the business case:

> The New Drug Applications (NDAs) that pharmaceutical companies submit to the FDA are one-quarter million to one-half million-page documents compiled from thousands of reports written by thousands of people over the span of the decade-long research and testing phase. This same information had to be assembled for regulatory submission according to government mandated page numbering, formatting, and indexing schemes that differed country by country. If a regulatory agency made a comment on a particular claim in the submission, the drug companies had to quickly craft a response which tied back to the original report data, before the drug could be approved. The entire submission process was manual. Couriers would pick up completed reports with a cart and wheel them into a large room. When all of the reports were in, clerks wearing rubber thimbles to protect their fingers would flip through the pages, structuring, numbering and indexing the application documents by hand. If they needed to respond to a regulatory comment, the clerks would page though the volumes of documents by hand to find the relevant report data.
>
> It took six months to assemble a single application for a single country. This was costing drug makers millions of dollars a year. A drug is really just a micro-monopoly lasting 17 years from the time a patent is applied for at the beginning of the research phase. With the clock ticking, time spent assembling the applications cut the monopoly time short. If you look at the curve, for every extra day you could keep a pharmaceutical company in the monopoly state, they make an average of $1 million in incremental profits.

The problem seemed to be a natural fit for the Documentum software. Documentum's workflow features would automatically collect all the finished and approved reports and store them in a central document database. Configuration control features would automatically assemble those reports for any regulatory submission scheme. And text retrieval features would enable clerks to find relevant report data instantly to respond to regulators' comments.

Automating this process proved to be more of a challenge. Documentum had to extend some core product functionality and CSC, the system integrator (SI) on the project, spent several hundred hours customizing the Documentum software and developing a publishing program that worked with Documentum to produce the final submission document. CSC also had to spend a lot of time training the clerks to operate the new software solution.

After a year of work, however, the system did go on-line. Using the Documentum software to change a totally manual process to a push-button process, Syntex cut its submission time in half. The first submission alone paid for all of the hardware, software and systems integration costs. Time savings on all of the other country submissions were incremental, but there was another value proposition for the U.S. submissions. When multiple companies submitted applications for the same drug, the FDA only reviewed the first complete application; all others went to the bottom of the priority list. With an average $500 million in up-front investment to develop a drug,[2] plus $1 million per day in opportunity cost, the total costs to pharmaceutical companies of losing the race to submit the first complete NDA were high indeed.

The engagements with Boeing and Syntex allowed Shao and Newton to validate their vision of the document management "elephant" and develop a software program capable of addressing the document management needs of multiple applications in multiple industries. While Boeing and Syntex each had bought software designed for their specific needs, Shao explained how the training manual and NDA applications were almost functionally identical:

> Each report is like a part. The submission requirements for each country are like a tail number and tying FDA comments to the original reports is like tracking changes to a particular aircraft. Sure, you have different file formats, but the basic system is the same—one big document management problem. By generalizing the common set of requirements across multiple applications in different industries, we could build a software product every big company would need to buy, and build a huge company in the process.

The overall market opportunity was big and growing rapidly (see **Table A**). If Documentum could secure even a small piece of this opportunity, it could become a large business.

With a complete product and two satisfied customers, Documentum felt it was headed in the right direction. But the company faced several challenges in the summer of 1993. Documentum would never become profitable at the rate it was acquiring paying customers.

[2] "Bioinformatics," *Business Week,* "The *Business Week* 50 for 2001," September 27, 1993, p. 167.

TABLE A   Documentum Projected Market Share and Revenue (in $ million)

Source: Documentum 1993 Business Plan and InterConsult 1993 Market Study.

	1993	1994	1995	1996	1997
Total available document management market	$1,780	$2,396	$3,048	$3,451	$3,914
Served available market for Documentum's products	$412	$555	$720	$756	$988
As % of total market	23%	23%	24%	22%	25%
Documentum projections:					
Documentum market share	.5%	1.8%	2.8%	5.3%	7.1%
Documentum product revenue	$2	$10	$20	$40	$70

EXHIBIT 3   Documentum Actual and Projected Financials 1992–1996 ($ Millions) as of Q3 1993

Source: Derived from Documentum internal records.

	Actuals		Projections			
	1992	**1993 YTD**	**1993E**	**1994E**	**1995E**	**1996E**
License revenue	$0.364	$0.640	$1.600	$6.400	$16.000	$32.000
Services revenue	0.142	0.160	0.400	1.600	4.000	8.000
Total revenue	0.506	0.800	2.000	8.000	20.000	40.000
Cost of goods sold	0.070	0.313	0.404	1.405	3.545	7.090
Gross profit	0.436	0.487	1.596	6.595	16.455	32.910
Sales and marketing	0.179	1.144	1.546	4.823	9.831	18.800
Research and development	1.661	1.255	1.696	1.946	3.545	6.768
General and administrative	0.226	0.813	1.099	1.340	1.909	3.946
Total operating expenses	2.066	3.212	4.340	8.110	15.285	29.514
Operating income (loss)	(1.630)	(2.725)	(2.744)	(1.515)	1.170	3.396
% Sales						
License revenue	72%	80%	80%	80%	80%	80%
Services revenue	28%	20%	20%	20%	20%	20%
Cost of goods sold	14%	39%	20%	18%	18%	18%
Sales and marketing	35%	143%	77%	60%	49%	47%
Research and development	328%	157%	85%	24%	18%	17%
General and administrative	45%	102%	55%	17%	10%	10%
Operating income (loss)	NM	NM	NM	NM	6%	8%

(**Exhibit 3** shows actual and projected P&L.) The issue was especially acute because the company now had a cash burn rate in excess of $1 million per quarter and the $4 million Xerox lifeline was running out. As Shao recalled, "Xerox expected Documentum to get enough traction in the marketplace to be able to secure additional outside venture funding." To do that in the Silicon Valley of 1993, however, the company needed the right CEO.

The Enterprise Software Business

None of these challenges was unique to Documentum. While the economics of the enterprise software business model were compelling for companies that attracted a critical mass of paying customers and covered their fixed product development and sales costs, doing so required both the right marketing strategy and a sales and marketing organization able to generate the demand needed to reach critical mass quickly and efficiently.

For startups like Documentum that focused on automating the mission-critical business processes of large enterprises, the major obstacle to generating demand was bridging the trust gap they suffered with prospective customers. Enterprise software was typically purchased in conjunction with a companywide initiative to automate a particular core business activity. These projects required significant up-front investments of capital and resources but yielded a sizable return if they were successful. A complete solution would stitch together multiple software applications with systems integration services, and often involved fundamentally re-engineering the way the customer conducted business. They took a long time to roll out and were very risky—failure rates of enterprise software projects were estimated to fall between 15% and 50%, depending on the type of project. Companies that chose to implement technology developed by a startup company faced additional risks, including concerns about the startup's financial viability, product development and testing resources, and execution experience.

Understanding the buying process was the first step in understanding how to bridge the gap. Enterprise software sales typically began with functional line-of-business users who had a business problem they needed to solve with technology. They put this application need on their supporting information technology (IT) department's agenda. IT would then go out and run a formal needs assessment and vendor selection process. If it was an established, core technology infrastructure need, the software solution was often a line item in the IT department's budget. If it was a net new need, the money for the software solution usually came out of the line-of-business unit's budget. In general, this buying process was a complex business decision involving upwards of 15 principals from both IT and the line-of-business units. Enterprise software companies typically relied on direct sales channels because experienced sales reps were well suited to navigate the complex organizations, identify key decision makers and their needs, motivations, and relative power, and then use that information to close deals.

Software marketing strategies typically followed one of two conventions, vertical or horizontal. Vertical strategies addressed specific business activities and sold applications to the line-of-business users that owned the process. For example, McKesson Information Solutions built a large business selling software which helped hospital administrators to automate the process of admitting patients. Horizontal strategies focused on enabling technologies that could be used by multiple departments to automate multiple functional processes. The technology was then sold to IT professionals as a toolkit for building specific vertical applications for line-of-business users. Both vertical and horizontal strategies involved line-of-business users and IT personnel, but the relative influence of each group in the purchasing decision was reversed.

Oracle was the classic example of a company running a successful horizontal marketing strategy. Oracle was Ingres' chief competitor in the relational database business in the late 1980s and early 1990s. Each firm sold their software to help IT departments build applications to manage structured data. When the minicomputer wave hit in the mid 1980s, Oracle used an aggressive, horizontal marketing strategy to attack across a broad front with a consistent story. They rapidly achieved dominant market share over Ingres, though many thought Ingres had better technology. The strategy worked because the IT managers, to whom the database companies were selling, had been using databases for years and already understood what the technology could do. They simply lacked a good database solution that would run on their new minicomputers. Oracle sales reps didn't need to convince prospects that they needed database technology—it was typically already a line item in their IT budgets—they just needed to convince them that Oracle could meet their needs and make their business sponsors happy. Given the technical savvy of their prospects, Oracle did this with horizontal, technology-centric messages.

But document management software was a paradigm-busting product. The business processes it could automate were being done manually then, and no one had a line item in their IT budget for new software to automate the processes. No one had used document management software on an enterprise scale before, no one knew all the things it could do, and no one knew exactly what the optimal product should look like. There were multiple competitors on the scene when Documentum arrived. Each had a slightly different take on the right approach, but all of them had chosen the classic Oracle horizontal strategy and were selling to IT. Almost all of the competitors had more feet on the street, more credibility in the marketplace, and more engineers than Documentum. As a result they were generating more revenue, they were being invited to bid on more deals, and they were building more features into their products. After raising the necessary financing, Documentum's new CEO would have to decide whether to take the competition head-on with a horizontal marketing strategy or out-maneuver them with a new approach.

Jeff Miller and the Venture Capitalists

Documentum hired a leader capable of taking the company to the next level in the summer of 1993. Jeff Miller was a 20-year industry veteran who was plugged into the Silicon Valley tech community. He began his career in marketing at Intel where he launched the 8086 chip and helped drive the infamous "CRUSH Campaign" which secured for Intel the IBM PC as a design win for Intel over Motorola. He went on to run marketing at Adaptec and the largest business unit at Cadence Design before coming to Documentum.

This was a critical time for Documentum. Silicon Valley was littered with startups which had won a couple of initial deals and then sputtered out, winning only a handful of deals over the following years, and never being able to put together the formula to build a big company. In Miller's words:

> Documentum was an engineering-driven company that needed to shift to a market orientation in order to reach the next growth phase. The team had done a fantastic job of validating the technology and the market. Now they needed commercial expertise and money to take the product to the mainstream market. This was going to be the defining moment in my career for better or for worse.

Documentum's initial seed investor and chairman of the board, Bob Adams, had already begun contacting outside VC firms to raise additional capital, so the first order of business was finishing the fund raising process and getting the money in the bank. Getting VC funding was difficult in the best times, but the market conditions of 1993 made it almost impossible. Miller continued:

> VCs invest in three things: a big market, a unique technology, and a good management team (see **Exhibit 4** for the team's background). When I came on board, I did the Sand Hill tour and I found that the VCs generally believed in the team and the technology, but getting them excited about the market was tougher. They're always a tough audience, but I remember one partner stopping me mid-sentence and saying, "I've invested in a few of these document management companies in the past and not a single one has made me a dime, you've got 10 minutes to tell me why you're going to be any different." I told the Boeing and Syntex stories to get them comfortable with the value that customers put on document management, and then got them comfortable with the size of the market opportunity by using the relational database market as an analogue.

Miller's concerted efforts paid off. After several weeks of hard selling, Miller signed a term sheet on October 16, 1993, in the living room of the lead investor in the outside VC round, John Walecka of Brentwood Associates. Miller had secured a $5.8 million round of funding at a pre-money valuation of $8.5 million from a syndicate of A-list venture capitalists that also included Katherine Gould of Merrill, Pickard, Anderson and Eyre, Kevin Hall of Norwest Venture Capital and Mark Stevens of Sequoia Capital. In signing the term sheet, Miller committed to put the company on course to make its numbers.

Selecting the Target Market

With the capital needed to ramp up the business now in hand, Miller set out to lock in the elements of Documentum's marketing strategy so he could put the money to use. The VCs advocated attacking horizontally. Adams was one of the most vocal proponents of the horizontal strategy. As he put it:

> Going after a big market in a big way is risky, but that's where you get the big payoffs. By targeting a niche segment you may lower your risk but it also lowers your upside and leaves

EXHIBIT 4   Management Background as of Q3 1993

Source: Documentum.

Robert V. "Bob" Adams has served as Chairman of the Board of the Company since its inception in 1990. Mr. Adams is the President of Xerox Technology Ventures, a venture capital unit of Xerox Corporation, and has been since February 1989. Mr. Adams is also a director of Tekelec and ENCAD, Inc. Mr. Adams received his M.B.A. from the University of Chicago and a B.S. in Mechanical Engineering from Purdue University.

Richard W. "Chip" Hay, Jr., Ph.D. has served as the Company's Vice President of Industry Development since October 1991. From January 1990 to September 1991, Dr. Hay was Vice President of Marketing at Odesta Systems Corp., a document management software company. From 1987 to 1989, Dr. Hay was Director of Industry Marketing at Ingres. Dr. Hay received his Ph.D. and B.A. from Northwestern University.

Jeffrey A. "Jeff" Miller has served as the Company's President, Chief Executive Officer and member of the Board of Directors since July 1993. From April 1991 to March 1993, Mr. Miller was a division president at Cadence Design Systems, Inc., a supplier of electronic design automation software. From February 1983 to April 1991, Mr. Miller was Vice President and General Manager and Vice President of Marketing of Adaptec, Inc., a supplier of computer input/output controllers. From 1976 to 1983, Mr. Miller held various positions at Intel Corporation, a manufacturer of semiconductor components. Mr. Miller received his M.B.A. and B.S. in Electrical Engineering and Computer Science from the University of Santa Clara,

John E. Newton, a founder of the Company, has served as Director, Product Development of the Company since July 1991. From 1981 to July 1991, Mr. Newton worked in various development and management positions at Ingres including Director of Data Management Development. Mr. Newton received his B.S. in Electrical Engineering and Computer Science from the University of California, Berkeley.

Robert K. "Rob" Reid has served as the Company's Vice President of Marketing since August 1993. From 1988 to August 1993, Mr. Reid was Vice President of Marketing for Octel Communications Corp., a voicemail company. From 1983 to 1988, Mr. Reid was Vice President of Marketing for NBI, Inc., an office systems company. From 1980 to 1983, Mr. Reid was Vice President of Marketing for Zenith Data Systems Corp., a personal computer company. Mr. Reid received his B.S. in Communications from the University of Tennessee.

Howard I. Shao, a founder of the Company, has served as Vice President of Engineering of the Company since June 1990. From 1984 to June 1990, Mr. Shao held a variety of management positions at Ingres Corporation, a relational database company, including Director Product Development. From 1981 to 1984, Mr. Shao was the Manager of Department Database Processor at TTI/Citicorp, a software division of Citicorp. Mr. Shao was a co-founder of Transtech International, a software company. Mr. Shao received his M.B.A. from Pepperdine University and a B.S. in Computer Science from the Massachusetts Institute of Technology.

Marcie L. Stewart has served as the Company's Vice President of Worldwide Sales since October 1992. From 1981 to July 1992, Ms. Stewart held a variety of sales and sales management positions at Ingres, including Vice President of North American field sales. Ms. Stewart received her M.B.A. from the University of Chicago and a B.S. in Business Administration from the University of California, Berkeley.

the big market opportunity open for someone else to steal. Documentum has a chance to dominate the horizontal market for enterprise document management. If Documentum adopts a horizontal marketing strategy that targets companies who want to manage the documents they print with high speed Xerox printers, like Boeing did in its training manual application, they can sell to almost anyone, use thousands of Xerox sales reps to generate leads, and build a multi-million dollar company quickly.

But Miller was considering the novel approach of marketing Documentum's core enabling document management technology vertically as the solution to a single target application. Although he didn't know what the best target would be, he knew how he would select it. In Miller's words:

When you're a small company, you have to leverage your resources more effectively than your larger competitors or they will put you out of business. If you try to go after a broad market you diffuse your resources and your message. Evangelizing a product across a large horizontal market is labor consuming and expensive. So, although it seems counterintuitive to create demand and build a big company by narrowing your focus, it's the best path. The trick is picking a killer application and rallying your troops behind it. I came across an innovative process for doing just that when I worked at Cadence. Unfortunately, we tried to implement it without buy-in from the whole company, and it failed. When I came to Documentum I was determined to implement it across the entire organization from the get-go. The concept was this. You can build traction the quickest with a technology platform product if you pick an industry and an application with a strong value proposition that you can dominate. You build a complete solution using your core product and a partner network and then focus your sales and marketing efforts on winning every deal for that solution to the exclusion of all other business. That doesn't mean you won't take a deal outside of your target if it walks in the door, but you won't do any proactive sales and marketing to find it and you won't make any special changes to the product to win it. It's always scary to ignore opportunities, but you get farther with focus.

Some on his team worried that Documentum might get pigeonholed as the dominant player in a small market. Miller allayed their concerns:

> If we only ever sold a single application, that might be true. But the idea here is to focus your efforts, dominate a segment and then move on to the next most attractive segment that is referenceable from your existing customers and repeat the process. You build a big company by filling in the area under the curve one vertical market at a time, eventually dominating the entire market.

Geoffrey Moore, a well-known Silicon Valley marketing pundit and author, developed a process for identifying the first killer application. Although it had never been explicitly followed in a real business situation, it seemed an effective way to put structure around an inherently unstructured problem. There were four steps in Moore's process:

- **Harvest application proposals from the entire organization**—By having everyone write up an application scenario for the company's technology, managers could systematically pull in the ideas and expertise of the entire organization. The idea was to keep proposals short and punchy, based on experience, not detailed research. Focusing on the person whose problem was being solved and not an impersonal market was key, since strong sales, marketing, and development efforts would follow strong images. (**Exhibit 5** shows five examples from the over 100 scenarios that Documentum employees developed.)

- **Select the most compelling application**—A two-stage scripted process enabled executives to select the most promising application efficiently and build consensus around the decision. Staff members rated every proposal on three key criteria (Economic Buyer, Compelling Reason to Buy, and Whole Product). They discussed their choices and then they rated the top candidates on another layer of attributes and crowned a winner. (See **Exhibit 6** for some of Documentum's analysis, **Exhibit 7** for the rating procedure, and **Exhibit 8** for the calibration.)

- **Communicate the focus to the company**—Closing the loop with all employees and related organizations was an underrated steps. Employee inclusion assured their commitment and understanding of the reasoning behind management's decision. Documentum would hold a company meeting to do this.

- **Make organizational adjustments and execute**—By swiftly making adjustments in sales, marketing, engineering and the partners group to implement the strategy, Miller would begin invading the target market before the window of opportunity closed.

Miller spent $35,000, a sizable amount for a startup with a small marketing budget, to have Geoffrey Moore and his Chasm Group run a weeklong workshop at Documentum. The staff came up with five recommendations from which the most compelling application would be selected.

EXHIBIT 5 Scenarios

Source: The Chasm Group and Documentum.

TITLE: Insurance Policy Documentation   **AUTHOR:** Chip Hay

Scenario Worksheet

PROFILE

Name: John Door   **Employer:** AETNA   **Age:** 35

Location: Conn HQ   **Occupation:** Commercial Insurance Bus. Unit Mgr.   **Salary:** $80K

Key interest or purpose: Provide superior products and customer service at low cost.

BEFORE

Scene or situation: John manages a business unit of an insurance company that writes one-of-a-kind commercial lines policies (e.g. insuring a shopping mall or providing a medical insurance plan to an employer). Each policy is formed by custom combining more or less standardized components—along with a lot of boilerplate to reflect state laws, regulations, etc. Over time the standing policy inevitably changes (new state laws, changes in the shopping mall, etc.) and an accurate record of the policy must be kept so that it can be referenced when claims are filed against it. The commercial lines policies business has the opportunity to grow rapidly and add profits to the insurance company.

Desired outcome: Make a mark in the firm by moving to flexible client/server system that can dramatically increase policy change turnaround, claims processing, and productivity to handle more business.

Attempted approach: 3270 mainframe system to generate policies being shifted to system using PC word processors.

Interfering factors: High cost in time and money to change mainframe system as business changes. PC system is out of control, can't find necessary track changes to policies.

Consequences: Can't keep up with volume or business. Excessive time spent proofing and validating each policy. Lots of errors and re-work. Slow turnaround of policy changes.

AFTER (ASSUME SAME SCENE, SAME DESIRED OUTCOME)

New approach: Client/server system accessible by all offices with dynamic assembly of policies from reusable components. Plan to manage authoring of components. Ability to reconstruct policies as they existed when a claim incident occurred. Policies are continually produced to reflect on-going changes in coverage.

Enabling factors: PC's, networking, document management, flexible assembly and publishing, plan to manage authoring and approval.

Results and rewards: Can handle more policies with fewer people—more follow-on business from improved customer responsiveness. Greater accuracy reduces claim negotiating and unwarranted paybacks.

EXHIBIT 5   (Continued)

TITLE: Aircraft Maintenance Documentation   **AUTHOR:** Chris Lindsay

Scenario Worksheet

PROFILE

Name: Bob Draper   **Employer:** British Airways (BA)   **Age:** 53

Location: Heathrow Airport.   **Occupation:** Ground Crew Training Mgr.   **Salary:** 45K£

Key interest or purpose: To ensure maximum utilization of the BA Fleet by delivering integrated maintenance for each class of BA Aircraft.

BEFORE

Scene or situation: BA buys aircraft and engines and other systems to their specification. Each aircraft has a different history and purpose and maintenance requirements. The use of passenger aircraft is heavily regulated. Costs are increasing and prices are falling.

Desired outcome: Ideally, an aircraft will arrive in the field maintenance depot with all of the required parts available, a trained mechanic qualified to make the necessary repairs, and a full set of specific documentation and sign-off sheets to minimize turn-around time.

Attempted approach: Large quantities of documentation is rewritten by BA from that supplied by the companies, manufacturers, airframe, engines, avionics, etc. BA has more technical authors writing documentation than do BA's suppliers.

Interfering factors: Documentation is delivered on different types of media (paper, tape drive, etc.) The contracts governing the transfer of technical manuals were written many years ago and neither BA nor the suppliers seem to be able to agree on changes to improve matters. The situation will continue for at least the next 15-20 years.

Consequences: The constant revision and updating of documentation is very expensive. Mistakes happen at worst this could cause loss of life at best this could result in more regulations, inspection and cost.

AFTER (ASSUME SAME SCENE, SAME DESIRED OUTCOME)

New approach: Airframe, engine and airline companies able to co-operate with the new Electronic Data Interchange (EDI) type initiative where updates can be distributed electronically across company boundaries.

Enabling factors: The ability to dynamically build airframe and time specific documentation based on design configuration and maintenance/utilization data means that the maintenance shop can be prepared and supplied with parts and people in time when required.

Results and rewards: British Airways is able to maximize aircraft utilization with fewer technical authors, mistakes, and at a significantly lower cost, this can begin to be added to mid-life aircraft as well as new ones.

EXHIBIT 5 (Continued)
TITLE: Pharm NDA   **AUTHOR:** Bill Butler

Scenario Worksheet

PROFILE

Name: Tom Woteki   **Employer:** Merck   **Age:** 45

Location: Blue Bell, PA   **Occupation:** Sr. Director, Research.   **Salary:** $125K

Key interest or purpose: Develop information system infrastructure to improve drugs time to market.

BEFORE

Scene or situation: Tom is working on a re-engineering process and systems for both clinical tests and regulatory submissions processes. This involves everything from desktop system to back-end applications.

Desired outcome: Manage information and documents better! Reduce the time to market and manage the expected increase in volume of data for further submission (2-3x).

Attempted approach: Tom has attempted to manage this effort internally. Two years was wasted re-engineering the processes with little infrastructure. Basically, the process has not moved forward.

Interfering factors: "Merck has launched a thousand ships, all in different directions." The lack of leadership has prevented the different projects from coming together. Lack of internal technical leadership and users are now skeptical.

Consequences: Merck will have to delay a number of submissions over the next few years. Major impact on revenues and profits and stock value.

AFTER (ASSUME SAME SCENE, SAME DESIRED OUTCOME)

New approach: Merck implemented an integrated system which manages information (documents) over the 10 year life of the drug development process and allows for the increase in new submissions.

Enabling factors: The core technology is Documentum information management. Other factors include re-engineering, new networking infrastructure, clinical trail application and integrated publishing software.

Results and rewards: Merck; 1) brings drugs to market sooner; 2) can manage the expected 2-3x increase in volume which results in millions in dollars a day in profit.

- **Insurance Policy Documentation**—The insurance industry was large and served as gateway to the enormous financial services industry. Insurance companies historically made significant investments in technology to automate repetitive, clerical processes and cut overall labor requirements (**Exhibit 9** shows market segment data). Both insurance and financial services companies were clustered around large cities across the globe. As yet, Documentum had neither a customer success story in these industries, nor a systems integration partner in place that understood any key industry problem and could weave together a complete solution. Documentum's technology was a reasonable fit for some applications but other applications were a better fit for high-volume, imaging technology.

EXHIBIT 5   (Continued)
TITLE: Chemical Regulation Management   **AUTHOR:** John N.

Scenario Worksheet

PROFILE

Name: Hans Stohl   **Employer:** Ciba Geigy Agricultural   **Age:** 35

Location: Basel   **Occupation:** Materials Handling Docs Mgr.   **Salary:** $100K

Key interest or purpose: Meet new stringent EC regulations on handling of hazardous materials.

BEFORE

Scene or situation: After the disastrous accident spilling 8 tank cars into the Rhine, EC passes new laws on handling chemicals. Worse situation for CIBA because of they had faulty documentation when the wrong cars were used. Hans' job is on the line.

Desired outcome: Meet new regulations by the end of the year. Disseminate information to operations by QI. No new accidents ever.

Attempted approach: Manual production takes years. Must automate for 20 different product ranges. Must comply with 10 different local, national, and international laws.

Interfering factors: Manual production is too slow. Manual tracking is incomplete and does not comply with law.

Consequences: Ciba Geigy is currently involved in $8B lawsuit. One more can kill the company.

AFTER (ASSUME SAME SCENE, SAME DESIRED OUTCOME)

New approach: Documentum based application allows combination of different parts for submission to different bodies. Workflow insures integrity of information. System is auditable and meet regulations.

Enabling factors: Workflow keeps track of everything and makes sure that deadlines are met. Workflow audit trails document every step.

Results and rewards: No new accidents. Meets new regulations on time. Quick responsiveness helps contain bad press after Rhine disaster.

- **Aircraft Maintenance Documentation**—The aerospace industry was large and served as the gateway into the enormous discrete manufacturing industry. Discrete manufacturers were located throughout the United States and Europe, typically spent heavily on IT, and had professional IT staffs. Although there were similar processes across companies, the industry was extremely fragmented when it came to the specifics. Documentum's product was a good fit but extensive product integration was required for a complete technical solution.

- **Pharmaceutical NDA**—Pharmaceutical companies were clustered in Philadelphia, London and Switzerland, were relatively few in number, had high margins, and routinely made big, innovation-driven investments. They were not unusually big IT spenders for their size, their IT staffs often consisted of scientists, and they were notorious for being conservative in the use of new, unproven technologies. Government regulations ensured that processes were consistent across organizations. The NDA process was very complex, and although it touched thousands of employees, a small number of

EXHIBIT 5   (Continued)
TITLE: Telecom Manufacturing   **AUTHOR:** Marcie

Scenario Worksheet

PROFILE
Name: Nancy Beckwith   **Employer**: Northern Telecom   **Age**: 34

Location: Toronto   **Occupation**: Tech Publications Mgr.   **Salary**: $50K

Key interest or purpose: Develop maintenance manuals for switch upgrades.

BEFORE

Scene or situation: Nancy works with a team of people located in Toronto, Houston and Raleigh. They have five different makes of telecommunications switches. They upgrade their switch software (for each model) twice a year.

Desired outcome: To not hold up the release of the product due to the manual not being ready. And to ship only the manual to customers who want it.

Attempted approach: They have been using low-end document management system. They try to have people in different locations with different managers work on the same documents.

Interfering factors: 10 releases per year of manuals is swamping them. Nancy herself is rewriting chapters that have already been rewritten elsewhere. They have to deliver all the manuals to all of the customers even if the customer doesn't have that feature since they have no organized way to pick and choose.

Consequences: Customers are withholding payment for maintenance because they don't get their switches on time. NT is starting to lose deals because their customers won't give credit references as they want their software upgrades on time. Also, customers want only the documentation required. Instead they get every page of every manual-whether they have that option or not.

AFTER (ASSUME SAME SCENE, SAME DESIRED OUTCOME)

New approach: Nancy now uses Documentum to handle her workflow and composite assembly needs. She also uses Documentum to be able to work with her counterparts in Houston and Raleigh.

Enabling factors: Critical factors: distributed information architecture and configuration control. Nancy and the rest of the team can now easily locate documents no matter where they are. This lessens "re-inventing the wheel" and encourages sharing. Nancy also can print only the parts of the manual a customer needs.

Results and rewards: Customers are paying their maintenance on time. They are now being used as references for other potential customers and they feel they are getting their upgrades on a timely basis—complete with the documentations. Sales are up. Printing costs are down as a result of being able to only print the necessary information.

people drove it on a day-to-day basis. Documentum's product was a good fit, but third-party publishing software was required for a complete technical solution.

- **Chemical Regulation Management**—Chemical companies were clustered in a handful of locations across the world and enjoyed reasonably strong margins. They were not big IT spenders for their size. Government regulations ensured that many processes were consistent across organizations. Documentum's product was a good fit, but third-party

EXHIBIT 6   Scenario Rating Worksheet

Source: The Chasm Group and Documentum.

E.B. = Identifiable, Well-funded Economic Buyer

CRTB = Compellingness of Target Customer's Reason to Buy

WP = Ease with Which Whole Product Can Be Acquired and Assembled

P&A = Strength of Current Relationship with Needed Partners and Allies

WP $ = Attractiveness of Whole Product's Total Price

Dist = Fit with Current Distribution

Comp = Absence of Entrenched Competition

Pos = Fit with Current Company Positioning

BP = Bowling Pin Potential

1. Rate each scenario 1 to 5 (5 = best) for E.B., CRTB, and WP and subtotal.
2. Rank order scenarios based on subtotal, and eliminate low-scoring ones.
3. Rate remaining scenarios 1 to 5 for all remaining categories.
4. Rank order remaining scenarios based on total (includes subtotal).
5. Eliminate low-ranking scenarios again.
6. Group remaining scenarios into "bowling pin" segments.
7. Write marketing strategy strawman for each segment worth pursuing.

Title	E.B.	CRTB	WP	P&A	WP $	Dist	Comp	Pos	BP	Total
Insurance Policy Documentation	4.0	4.5	3.5	2.0	3.5	3.0	2.5	2.0	3.5	28.5
Aircraft Maintenance Documentation	4.0	4.5	4.0	3.5	4.0	3.0	3.5	2.5	4.0	33.0
Pharmaceutical NDA	5.0	5.0	3.5	4.0	3.5	2.0	4.0	2.5	4.0	33.5
Chemical Regulation Management	4.0	5.0	4.0	2.5	3.5	2.5	3.0	2.0	3.5	30.0
Telecom Manufacturing	3.0	4.5	4.0	2.5	3.5	3.0	3.0	2.0	4.0	29.5

251

EXHIBIT 7 Scenario Rating Procedure

Source: The Chasm Group and Documentum.

Scenario Rating Procedure

The scenario rating procedure covers the market development strategy team's efforts to score each candidate scenario in terms of nine factors that measure potential chasm-crossing market segment attractiveness. These factors break out into two sets, as follows:

A. Critical Success Factors: These are the "show-stoppers"—things one cannot change in the near term and which must be rated positively to make a target market segment viable. They include:

- **Economic Buyer:** For a successful chasm crossing, the target market segment should include an economic buyer who is already in place, readily identifiable, likely to want to invest in the type of improvements promised by the scenario, and perhaps most importantly of all, well funded.

- **Compelling Reason to Buy:** Successful chasm-crossing requires customer sponsors who will pull for you against the normal pragmatist resistance to anything new. Such customers need a powerful reason to buy to take this kind of personal risk.

- **Whole Product:** The key to chasm-crossing is to achieve market leadership quickly in the initial target segment. This can only be done by delivering 100% of the whole product requirement right from the outset. If this is not feasible, then a new target must be found.

B. Market Penetration Factors: These are factors which will impact your organization's effectiveness in penetrating its target market segment. Although they are important to your success, you can usually work around problem areas. They include:

- **Partners and Allies:** Delivering the whole product typically requires the support of segment-specific partners and allies. If the company already knows these allies and has good relationships with them, it is a big plus.

- **Whole Product Pricing:** Chasm segments are easiest to develop when the whole product price is several times less than whatever the current approach to the problem entails. Additionally, the ROI must be relatively immediate, typically one year or less to break even.

- **Whole Product Distribution:** To develop the chasm segment quickly requires a distribution channel that already knows the economic buyer and the application of the target end user. If the client company lacks such a channel, then it will have to find one and make it a partner and ally. If no such channel exists, then normally a new target must be selected.

- **Competition:** If the chasm-crossing target is a beachhead, then best strategy says, do not attach a beachhead that has a fortress on it. If the target segment already is well served by an established market leader, then the client must look elsewhere.

- **Positioning:** The impact of positioning on chasm-crossing success is a function of whether the marketplace believes it has a problem worth solving and can readily accept the company as an appropriate source for the market-leading solution.

- **Bowling Pin Potential:** This criterion assesses the leveragability that winning market leadership in the target segment provides as a basis for further market expansion into related marketplaces. This leverage will come either from whole product carryover or word-of-mouth referencing.

---

software for stamping documents either approved or in-review, so that employees using the documents knew their status, was required for a complete technical solution.

- **Telecom Manufacturing**—Telecom companies were spread across the United States and Europe. They had high margins and spent a large percentage of their revenues on innovative IT projects to stay ahead of the competition. Although not strictly regulated by the government, core business processes were fairly consistent across the industry. Documentum's product was a good fit, and only required a small amount of customization to complete the technical solution.

Everyone was satisfied with these choices, despite an underlying unease over whether the application with the highest return might have escaped them all. Miller addressed the concern:

> The key is you don't need the best application; you just need one that's good enough. Most of the benefit comes from deploying your resources against a single market opportunity and dominating it. A powerful chain of references, a higher average sales price, and a lower cost of sales, enable you to win an unfair share of deals and invest in the product at a faster rate

EXHIBIT 8 **Standard Rating Calibration**

Source: The Chasm Group and Documentum.

Standard Rating Calibration
(5 = best, 1 = worst, 3 = neutral)
The following are intended as guidelines for the client team scoring the various scenarios, so that their individual ratings can have a basic level of consistency across the team. Satisfying all of the stated conditions would constitute a 5 rating.

Economic Buyer: There is an existing economic buyer for this scenario and he or she has the authority to make the purchase, is currently making investments to achieve comparable types of benefits, and is typically well funded.

Compelling Reason to Buy: I must have this because (a) it gives me a major improvement on a critical success factor, or (b) it gives me dramatic productivity improvements in an area where I routinely spend a lot of resources. I would buy this even when money is tight.

Whole Product: Working with existing products and service providers, we can readily fulfill all the whole product requirements by the time we introduce the product into the target market.

Partners and Allies: We know all the partners and allies that must actively contribute to the whole products, and we have good working relationships with them.

Whole Product Pricing: The whole product price for our solution is several times less than the cost of the existing market-leading solution which is currently being bought by our target economic buyer, and we expect an ROI such that the buyer can break even on the purchase with a year.

Whole Product Distribution: The target customer we have in mind will want to purchase the whole product from an existing distribution channel which can provide the appropriate added value and with which we already have established a successful distribution relationship.

Competition: The customer is currently purchasing a significantly inferior solution to the problem we address, utilizing products that are late in their product life cycle, from vendors who are taking this market for granted.

Positioning: The problem we solve is already recognized as approaching crisis proportions and falls within the class of problems our company is already known to address.

Bowling Pin Potential: The whole product we must provide for this segment can, with minor modifications, be used to serve a number of other segments, some of which have strong communications ties with the target segment.

---

than the competition. In essence, you get paid to do the best kind of field research, talking with prospects in a focused way, and you end up way ahead of the competition in the end. These advantages are even more pronounced in a paradigm-busting market because you could avoid missionary selling by incubating the market with targeted marketing messages backed by a whole product solution for their key business pain point.

Implementing the Marketing Strategy

Marketing

In figuring out which application to target, Miller encountered implementation issues in every major business function. Rob Reid, Documentum's vice president of Marketing, explained the impact on his organization:

> There were general concerns about the vertical, application-focused strategy. On the surface, it seemed to fly in the face of traditional marketing doctrine. There was no formal, up-front market research to guide our selection of our target market. Given the multi-month engineering investment to build a product and the consequences of picking a market with no money or demand for our product, some felt we were taking an unadvisable risk in using Geoffrey Moore's new process. Worse yet was the looming fear that we would win the battle only to lose the war. While we focused our energies on dominating a specific vertical solution, our competitors might seize the high ground in more profitable segments, expand more quickly, and then leave us surrounded in a hopelessly isolated position from which there was no hope of becoming the market leader.

EXHIBIT 9   **Market Data from the 500 Largest Publicly Traded Corporations Based on Revenue**

Source: Adapted from *InformationWeek,* "*InformationWeek* 500," September 27, 1993.

Industry Segment	Total Companies	FY '92 Revenue ($MM)	Average Net Income Margin	Average Number of Employees	Average Number of IS Employees	Average IS Budget as % of Revenue
Aerospace/Automotive	25	441,421	2.4%	95,132	2,042	3.3%
Banks	34	185,905	9.4	23,430	1,220	4.2
Chemicals	19	119,237	3.8	26,455	881	1.6
Computer/Telecom Hardware & Software	18	161,464	19.6	46,823	3,136	3.5
Computer/Telecom Services	17	208,639	9.0	71,129	7,901	5.8
Consumer Products/Services	26	159,533	5.5	40,835	598	1.8
Electronics	17	168,739	5.9	65,504	1,198	2.5
Energy (Oil & Natural Gas)	35	434,571	2.2	23,682	568	1.2
Financial Services	21	163,454	7.0	25,361	1,126	2.9
Food Processing/Distribution	38	301,359	3.8	50,060	555	0.9
General Manufacturing	21	79,578	2.8	25,691	705	1.6
Heavy Manufacturing	10	46,781	1.8	33,056	1,363	1.8
Health Care Products/Services	11	38,271	4.2	41,325	418	1.9
Insurance	25	149,630	4.1	15,942	1,368	3.0
Broadcasting/Publishing/Media	16	60,825	4.8	20,037	625	2.2
Metals/Mining/Natural Resources	31	129,410	0.2	22,659	348	1.1
Pharmaceuticals	11	70,681	3.4	33,580	964	2.1
Retail (Specialty)	16	70,564	2.0	28,631	359	1.0
Retail (Discount/Apparel)	24	259,234	2.2	96,741	1,190	1.2
Retail (Food/Drug)	30	187,406	1.2	44,681	200	0.8
Transportation/Freight	21	131,001	1.3	54,129	1,737	3.3
Utilities	34	132,736	10.2	12,006	451	1.8
Median	21.0	154,582	3.8%	33,318	922	1.9%
Mean	22.7	168,202	4.9%	40,768	1,316	2.2%

There were concerns about how to secure the reference customers we needed to move into the mainstream market. The first customers of a new software product are invariably technology visionaries who are willing to take a risk with your raw product and wade through technology glitches for the chance to benefit from the technology before others. The sales cycle can be less complex since you often only need to sell the technology to the visionary and they work the system for you, getting the necessary approvals from around the organization to close the deal. They are typically few in number and don't have a lot of money. To grow the business, you need the more pragmatic customers of the mainstream market. They have the money but they are also less willing to give it to a risky technology startup. Without the missionary zeal of the technology visionary, sales cycles can be longer because you often need to sell each of the affected parties on your solution and gain the necessary approvals one-by-one. You need to bridge the trust gap with references they trust: other pragmatists. We didn't have any of those.

Finally, there were concerns about how to spend our scarce human and capital resources. To industry analysts, investment analysts, and the press we were positioning the company and the technology horizontally to pave the way for our future expansion into other markets. But to our prospective customers we would position the company vertically around our target application. Should we go to a huge, horizontal, technology trade show like the Association for Information and Image Management (AIIM) or should we participate in a small vertical show like the Drug Information Association (DIA)? When we do brochures, should we orient them vertically or horizontally?

However, there were potential solutions to all of these issues, as Reid explained:

Maybe calling on 20 customers with a common problem would turn out to be the most effective market research program you could have. With 20 prospects and a good pitch, it might turn out to be a simple numbers game that we could land two or three as initial reference customers. I also wondered whether the focused application strategy would make the traditional marketing job of generating "buzz" any easier. By dominating a smaller market vs. less focused competition, we might be able to loom larger, faster in the minds of our prospects. Word of mouth is your most powerful marketing tool, and with all the activity we would be stirring up with our focused sales and marketing efforts, could we spend less money on formal marketing programs and still be perceived as the market leader?

Sales

Sales faced another set of tradeoffs and implementation issues. Marcie Stewart, Documentum's vice president of Sales, explained:

Before coming to Documentum, I sold relational databases for 11 years. We would sell to anyone that had a dollar and even some that didn't. When I got to Documentum I set up the same type of organization. I hired two ex-database sales reps that knew how to sell enterprise software deals and an ex-Interleaf rep that could teach us about document management. I spread them across the country—San Francisco, Denver, Washington, D.C.—and gave them geographic territories—western, central, and eastern United States. Like database sales, they called on IT departments and sold Documentum as a general-purpose toolkit. The end-business users had only limited involvement in the buying process. And you know, things weren't going that badly, really. We had closed Boeing and Syntex and we had eight other pilot deployments underway.

If we changed from selling Documentum horizontally as a tool to selling it vertically as the solution to a specific high-value application, I wondered how I would have to change my sales organization. With a direct sales model, the geographic location of your sales teams is a key consideration since your reps have to get a lot of customer face time in order to close deals. Would I have to redeploy my guys in new geographic territories? I already had a conversation with one of my best sales reps who said, "I can't move for personal reasons, so if you pick a vertical which has no prospects in my territory, I'm out of here." Even if there were deals to go around, I might have to spend all of my time mediating conflicts over how the existing pipeline should be redistributed rather than selling. Another one of my reps was positioning for this fight when he said, "Marcie, I've spent the last several months building up a pipeline of qualified prospects which I plan to harvest over the next four quarters. If you give any of those accounts to another rep you'll kill my business plan and you'll have to lower my quota."

Some of the choices required an international presence and I didn't have anyone in place much less the budget to build an international sales organization. Moreover, selling an application solution was going to be different than selling a toolkit; the business process owner had to be heavily involved in the buying process. Could my guys successfully transition from selling technology to IT and start selling vertical solutions to business managers, or would I have to find new people? Finally, we had a $3 million revenue target over the next two quarters and had already built the pipeline to hit it. If my reps had no customer references, it would put that number at risk.

Even with these issues, the new strategy also offered sales great potential upside. Stewart elaborated:

Closing these technology-driven toolkit sales was a bear and had to be done one deal at a time. There was little carryover across sales cycles in terms of sales effort and customer reference-ability. As a result, the cycles were long, 12 to 18 months, and our pipeline conversion rate was low. Overall, I wondered how would it affect my guys' sales cycles, the effectiveness of my sales capacity, and my ability to reliably scale the business to meet an ever-growing revenue target?

R&D

The engineering organization faced the schizophrenic challenge of having to support a specific solution for the chosen application while continuing to develop a horizontal platform capable of being taken into successive markets and addressing the larger general document management market. Newton, director of Product Development, articulated the issues:

> Normally in technology companies there is a constant tension between the laundry list of features marketing and sales are asking for and what engineering can deliver with limited resources and time. As a result, the biggest challenge for engineers is getting clarity on which functionality has to be in the final product and what can be dropped if time doesn't allow, which it never does. Most companies manage these product marketing tradeoffs by collecting all of the feature enhancements people are asking for and then prioritizing them by how many people are asking for each one. The output of this logical process is a list that is at most 80% complete for any one customer, but never ends up with a whole product that meets anyone's exact needs.
>
> Would it be easier to prioritize the requirements of one customer over another by using the vertical application approach? By focusing on a list of buyers with a common set of requirements we could pick a list and finish it—that gives you a whole product for that set of buyers. The only question was, in the long-term, could we build this focused solution while making sure that we didn't architect ourselves into a corner and prevent us from entering the next interesting application segment?

Partners

Hay explained Documentum's approach to partnering:

> The goal of partnering is to put together a whole product without having to build it all internally, because companies simply don't have sufficient resources. The partners came in two flavors: technology partners to fill in product holes and systems integrators to stitch together multiple pieces of software and help customers change their business processes. With both sets of partners the key question that the partner organization had to answer was: where do you draw the line between internal development and what the partners supply?

In the Boeing engagement, the key technology partner, Frame, provided the publishing tool to complete the maintenance manual solution. They also introduced Documentum into the deal. Other technology partners for the same engagement included Oracle, which provided the underlying database, and Sun, which provided the Solaris boxes upon which the whole solution ran. Hay wondered, "how will the vertical approach impact the kinds of technology partners Documentum would have to recruit and how the company would support them?"

In the Syntex engagement, CSC filled the role of systems integrator, working with the pharmaceutical company to map out their process, selecting the software and hardware components needed to automate it, installing them and integrating them, and finally training the scientists, submissions personnel, and IT support staff. Unlike the majority of systems integrators who know technology but are generalists when it comes to vertical business processes, the CSC consultants that worked on the Syntex deal had an intimate knowledge of the drug submissions process that was critical to the success of the project. Hay asked, "If we take the vertical approach, how will that impact the kinds of systems integrator partners we need to recruit and how we will have to support them?" The overall Syntex project was scheduled to last three years and cost $14 million, of which Documentum's piece would only be around $1 million. Hay wondered, "How will we deal with the tension between working with systems integrators and making sure that we claim a bigger slice of the pie?"

D-Day: Making the Final Decision

As the next board meeting approached, Miller reflected on the presentation that his management team would have to make. The new process had seemed to work and they had five good choices for their target vertical application. But he wondered whether they had used the right criteria to narrow the list of over 100 choices to just five. Which was the right application to pick? As his staff had reported, implementing the new strategy was also going to present multiple hurdles. Assuming the consensus of his senior executives, could the company marshal the sales, marketing, product development, and partner resources necessary to make the implementation changes it needed to, without losing momentum?

Even if he could answer all of these questions, how would Miller convince the board that the focused vertical rather than the broad horizontal approach had a better chance of realizing the big market opportunity they had invested in less than a month ago? As Walecka had said, "I'm ready to lead this funding round because I believe in the team, the technology, and the opportunity. Documentum has the chance to dominate the rapidly growing document management market and build a billion dollar company in the process."

As Miller thought through these issues, a call came in from Stewart, who announced that one of her sales reps had found a $300,000 opportunity with, Marsh & McLennan, a large New York–based insurance company. The opportunity had the potential to grow into a million dollar deal. However, Marsh & McLennan's CIO, who had heard about Documentum's application-led strategy, would only do the big deal if insurance was selected as Documentum's first target application and if Documentum developed some additional functionality to the product. A million dollar deal would be the largest in the company's history and would enable Documentum to hit 50% of its FY 1993 plan in one shot. But it came with a high price tag and if a good number of the other deals in the pipeline closed, Documentum would make its number without the Marsh & McLennan deal. Miller had an even bigger revenue target next year. Was it shortsighted to take the deal?

He hung up the phone and pondered his decision. It was time to take action. Had he made the right decision to market the multi-purpose Documentum technology vertically? Which was the right vertical application to target? Did the market selection process take into account all of the important parameters in the decision? How could he address the concerns of his senior managers and align Documentum to execute the strategy? What should he do with the Marsh McLennan deal?

Part 4

Communicating Value

Chapter

15

Integrated Marketing Communications

Robert J. Dolan

I. Introduction

"Effective marketing requires an integrated communications plan . . ." because the communication program's role is to foster the consumer's "awareness of the product, knowledge about its features, interest in purchasing, likelihood of trying the product and or purchasing it." Accomplishing the typically multifaceted communications goals means relying not just on one form of communication, but bringing together a number of different modes in a consistent, complementary way.

For example, when General Motors introduced the Saturn as a "different kind of car company" it hired Hal Riney as its agency to coordinate all communications about the new automobile brand. Riney positioned the brand not only through a national advertising campaign, but also through brochures, the "look" and signage of the retail showrooms, local retailer advertiser, and retailer promotions. GM's idea in having a "single source" of all these materials was to ensure that the program elements worked together to position Saturn in the mind of the consumer in a consistent fashion. As part of the introduction, a local automobile dealer wanted to "give away" a Saturn. This would have been at odds with the message being presented in the rest of the campaign. Riney's involvement in all aspects of the program converted the car "give-away" and the negative associations which could go with that to a promotion in which the prize was a trip to Saturn's manufacturing facility in Spring Hill, Tennessee to meet the committed employees and visit the place where their car was born.[1] This promotion fit with the specialness of the new company.

[1] This is described in D. Aaker, *Building Strong Brands,* Free Press, 1996.

Professor Robert J. Dolan prepared this note as the basis for class discussion rather than to illustrate either effective or ineffective handling of an administrative situation.

Similarly, when Southwest Airlines begins service in a new city, a variety of efforts is launched to build consumers' awareness of the new service, to establish Southwest's positioning in their minds, and ultimately induce them to book a flight on Southwest. For example, when Southwest instituted its Baltimore base of operations, the kickoff to the communications program was a joint announcement of the coming event by Southwest's Chairman and Maryland's governor. The announcement event generated wide coverage in the press. As a second public relations event, Southwest took 49 children from Baltimore to Cleveland for a zoo visit—the 49 number being selected to match Southwest's $49 price. Advertising began with direct mail pieces to heavy airline users in the area containing promotional offers and an invitation to join Southwest's frequent-flyer program. Southwest employees then "hit-the-streets" in high traffic areas handing out bags of peanuts to passers-by to emphasize Southwest's "Just Peanut" fares. Traditional newspaper and television advertisements then followed.[2]

As these examples suggest, different types of communications are used for the obvious, simple reason that some types are better than others for specific purposes. For example, television advertising is great for creating awareness of a brand but typically not as powerful as a limited time promotional offer in generating action by the consumer.

In the past, a fair conception of many companys' communications strategy was a media advertising program as the core, flanked by other supporting elements such as promotions. However, this primacy of media advertising is no longer a good general description. For a number of reasons, uses of other communication forms have been growing more quickly than media advertising. More pressure for short-term sales results has swung spending to vehicles like sales promotions, which are more capable of producing quick sales results. Also, the rising power of the trade has led to more communications spending directed to them as opposed to end consumers. Today's marketer has the opportunity and challenge of bringing together a wide variety of possible communication options to achieve the desired consumer impact.

This Note describes major communication vehicles. Section II contrasts personal selling and advertising, discussing media advertising and direct response advertising. Section III covers promotions, of which there are two types: Consumer Promotions and Trade Promotions. A short Section IV describes other communication vehicles rounding out the mix. Section V discusses the process via which elements are brought together to form a cohesive plan. It presents the concept of a "hierarchy-of-effects" model to describe how consumers move through a purchase process and how it can be a useful input to communication program design.

II. Communication Vehicles

A. Introduction

Figure A shows two dimensions along which it is useful to contrast communications options.[3] These dimensions are:

(i) Broadcast vs. Interactive or One-Way vs. Two-Way: The horizontal dimension in **Figure A** is the distinction between situations in which there is outbound communication only vs. one in which there is an interaction between the initiator and receiver of the initial dialog. When Oldsmobile spent almost $2MM for a 30-second ad during the Super Bowl in January 1999, it sent out a message out over the airways to 130 million viewers tuned to Fox TV. Fox TV's technology could not accommodate a reply from the 130 million recipients of the message. It was a simple one-way broadcast of a message.

---

[2] This is described in R. Batra, J. Myers and D. Aaker, *Advertising Management,* Prentice-Hall, 1995.

[3] This two dimensional classification was originally suggested by Professor John Deighton.

FIGURE A   **Characteristics of Communication Options**

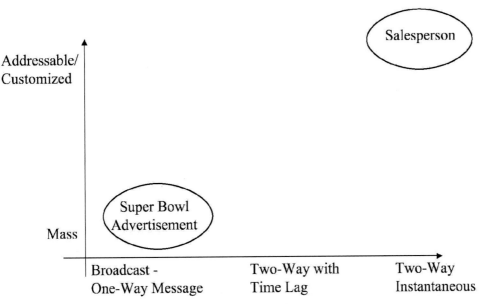

At the other end of the spectrum is communication which is a dialogue, not a monologue. For example, when a prospect visits an Oldsmobile showroom, a salesperson is likely to engage that person. The salesperson delivers a message. The prospect responds. An exchange of some duration typically ensues. If the salesperson's message is persuasive enough, the prospect's ultimate response may well be to buy the Oldsmobile. This type of two-way interaction is instantaneous.

As shown in the middle of the horizontal axis of **Figure A,** other two-way interactions occur with a time lag. For example, a direct mail piece usually solicits a reply by the receiver. That reply however may await the receiver's attention or next trip to the post office.

(ii) Mass vs. Addressable/Customized. The vertical dimension of **Figure A** describes the extent to which the message is able to be varied to meet the particular communication needs of the person receiving it. The Oldsmobile ad on the Super Bowl was not customized, i.e., it was presented to all 130 million people watching in precisely the same way. It is a mass medium.

On the other hand, the salesperson can and should be customizing his or her message to the particular communication needs of the message recipient. A primary advantage and justification for the typically high cost of personal selling is this ability to adjust the message to the situation, e.g., talking about safety features to the family with four children, the cargo carrying capability to the young couple with ski weekends on their minds, and low initial payment leases to the first-time car buyer with no equity in a trade-in.

Figure B fills in this space with some of the more important communication vehicles available. (The positions are generally suggestive rather than absolutes for all situations.) Everything other than Salesperson, anchoring the most northeast position, we can call a form of advertising.

A typical person in the United States is exposed to over 1,500 advertisements per day. Imagine living in a suburb of Boston: your clock radio wakes you with the news that a call to "1-800-54-GIANT" will get your broken windshield fixed; your first sighting of the day as you begin the wake-up routine is the Tom's toothpaste package asserting Tom's "All-Natural" ingredients; the *Boston Globe* snatched from the front doorsteps announces the

FIGURE B **Position of Major Communication Vehicles**

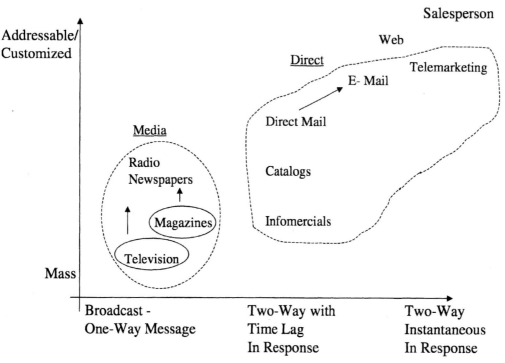

One-Day Sale at Filene's and tells you it's "Two Thumbs Up!" for a Civil Action; driving to work brings Cindy Crawford and her Omega watch into large view on a billboard; arriving at work and logging on to the Internet to check out the late sports scores on ESPN Sportszone produces the banner that "The New Volvo S80 is here. Bigger than a BMW 528*i*"; approaching the door into lunch brings the familiar red circle and the reminder "Coke Always"; after work, picking up the mail brings the offer of a 4.9% interest, no-fee credit card if you act now; looking through the program at your kid's Little League baseball game has a reminder that maybe it's not a Volvo but a "Lexington Toyota" for you; watching the evening news shows you can still "Have it Your Way" at Burger King; just before turning out the light, flipping the last page of Stephen Ambrose's *Undaunted Courage* brings information from the publisher about his upcoming sequel to his bestseller, *D-Day*.

Total advertising spending in the United States recently reached $200 billion annually. Two major types of advertising shown in **Figure B** are media advertising, clustered in the lower left-hand corner, and direct response in the middle. The key distinction is that direct is designed specifically to elicit a purchase action by the consumer whereas media advertising is setting a foundation for that by impacting the consumers' knowledge and attitude.

B. Characteristics of Leading Media Advertising

(i) *Television*—Television is largely a national medium with 70% of the expenditures for national (as opposed to local) coverage in the United States. Television's prime advantage is its ability to reach broad segments of the population at a set time with a "sight-and-sound" message. It can be expensive however in both the production of a high impact sight-and-sound message and also in the payment to the media provider, e.g., the average 30-second prime time ad costs about $185,000; a 30-second ad on Seinfeld cost over $500,000 when that show was at its peak; and a 30-second ad on the final Seinfeld show ran $1.7MM.

A common measure used to summarize the cost of a communication option is the "cost-per-thousand." For example, if a prime-time TV show with a 30-second ad cost of $185,000 drew 10 million households as viewers, we would compute the CPM or "cost-per-thousand" household as:

$$\frac{\$185,000}{10,000,000} \times 1000 = \$18.50 \; CPM.$$

A challenge for television advertisers is that multiple advertisers vie for the consumer's attention on a given show. In a typical hour of prime time programming, more than 15 ads will be featured. In addition to competing with these 14 other ads, an advertiser must compete with other activities for viewers' attention. Ads are frequently "zapped" as viewers use their "clickers" (remote controlled channel changers) to switch to another channel temporarily when a commercial break appears.

The upward arrow shown on Television in **Figure B** is to represent the fact that with the proliferation of cable TV channels, television has increased its addressability/customizability options. Obviously, everyone watching a given show sees the same ad. But, there are now many specialized channels, e.g., The Golf Channel, The Nashville Network (Country Music), which deliver specialized audiences. Ads can be varied by show to match the message to the audience.

(ii) *Newspapers*—In contrast to TV, newspapers are largely a local medium with 90% of dollars in the U.S. placed on local basis. There are about 1,500 daily newspapers in the United States. *The Wall Street Journal* and *USA Today* do attract national advertisers, but most newspaper expenditure is for local presentation of display advertising in the main body of the newspaper or in supplements. A popular type of supplement commonly seen in Sunday papers is the free-standing insert, i.e., a loose sheet, often in color, placed within the paper.

An advantage of newspaper is that most consumers look upon advertising in newspapers positively. Whereas television advertising is deemed an intrusion, newspaper advertising is generally considered informational. Newspapers typically provide broad coverage of the local market as about 70% of adults read a daily newspaper. Newspapers are also flexible in that space need not be reserved far in advance. Noted limitations are: (i) it is a "sight-only" medium with relatively weak reproduction quality (e.g., as compared to magazines) and (ii) the "life" of an ad is typically one day before it is dispatched to the recycling bin or trash with the newspaper.

(iii) *Radio*—Radio is also a largely local medium. Due to the large number of stations available within a market and their distinctive positions, e.g., Rock, Country, Adult Talk, Sports Talk, etc., the audiences are well-segmented. Radio is also relatively low cost and is a good candidate if the marketer is seeking to deliver a message frequently to a well-defined audience.

Limitations are that radio is obviously "sound-only" and ads may easily be tuned out. Also, like television, clutter is an issue as many ads compete for the listener's attention. Most effective radio ads have been creative in capturing the listener's attention and imagination.

(iv) *Magazines*—There has been a sharp increase in the number of magazines published. This has meant a fundamental transformation in the role of magazine advertising. Through the 1950's, leading magazine were similar to television in delivering a broad audience. While some, like *TV Guide,* continue to do this today, a key development has been the emergence of special interest magazines. Magazines like the *Massachusetts Golfer* and *Modern Bride* deliver a very sharply defined audience to the advertiser. This is represented by the upward arrow shown on **Figure B.** Magazines offer the ability to deliver a visually strong message to a well-defined target audience. Magazine ads also have the longest "life" of any medium and also benefit from pass-along readership.

C. Direct Marketing

The second major type of advertising shown in **Figure B** is direct marketing communication. Direct marketing is defined as "an interactive system of marketing which uses one or more advertising media to effect a measurable response and/or transaction."[4] A common characteristic of direct marketing is that a customer file or database records messages sent and whether or not there was a response. Some use the terms "direct marketing" and "database marketing" interchangeably.

A number of direct techniques are used:

(i) *Infomercials* are basically relatively long video presentations of an information-heavy message. Frequently, the infomercial will combine entertainment and information. While infomercials may conjure up images of late-night cable television placement and heavy selling of "miracle" cooking and cutting devices, they can be delivered in other ways as well and present high quality, detailed marketing messages. For example, Chrysler produced the "Chrysler Showcase" a 30-minute infomercial setting out the positioning for the Chrysler 300M, LHS and Concorde models. The car's designers and engineers explain the new product development process behind the new models. The 30-minute version infomercial was on cable-TV and a shorter version on tape delivered via the mail to prospects requesting information from 1-800-CHRYSLER or the company's Web site.[5]

Similarly, Valvoline Oil produced a 30-minute infomercial "Inside Valvoline Racing" that provided an in-depth story of two racing teams. The first goal of the production was to deliver entertainment value, which then provided the right context for product and brand messages.

(ii) *Catalogs,* multi-paged pieces showing merchandise for sale are another common direct technique. Women's apparel and accessories were the largest catalog seller followed by home products, gifts and sporting goods. Many use catalogs to complement a retail presence: e.g., Victoria's Secret, Sharper Image, Brookstone, and J. Crew. A company can have a variety of catalogs, using the customer's purchase history as a guide to which catalogs to send and with what frequency.

Catalogs are a particular form of direct mail which, because of the quality of the production, tend not to be as customized to an individual recipient as a solicitation letter which can be easily and inexpensively customized. *Direct mail* generally includes a letter, a sales brochure, and instructions on how to reply (order) or a reply form. *E-mail,* as shown by its position to the northeast of direct mail in **Figure B** offers more opportunity for customization and quicker exchange of information.

(iii) *Telemarketing* is basically selling-by-phone, rather than in-person. Whereas an in-person sales call might average out to $250 per call, telemarketing expenses typically run in the $5 per call range. A big advantage of telemarketing over direct mail, which in some cases justifies its cost premium, is its immediate two-way nature, allowing the caller to customize the message in accord with the message receiver's initial response.

Technology has been a major force fostering the growth of direct marketing. Computers manage lists of customers and sophisticated statistical techniques help find worthwhile solicitation patterns. 800-numbers and fax machines ease the receipt of orders and widespread credit card use facilitates completing the order. Direct mail still accounts for the majority of direct marketing spending. The primary issue with direct mail is the large number of consumers with a "junk mail" attitude.

The most important recent development for direct marketing is the Web. The Web offers the opportunity to exchange customized messages and responses in an instantaneous way.

[4] W. Wells, J. Burnett, and S. Moriarty, *Advertising: Principles and Practice,* Prentice-Hall, 1998.
[5] This is described in "Infomercial Offers Multiple Use," *Direct Marketing,* September 1998.

A distinctive feature of the Web is its "hyper impulsivity" due to its "closer conjunction of desire, transaction and payment than any other environment." That note describes the potential of the Web as "to be as subtle, as flexible, as pertinent and as persuasive as good communication, with a better memory than the most diligent salesperson . . ." The Web can also serve in a less interactive way, via posting of banner ads without the needed supporting Web Site development for true interactivity. But, its great potential is as a mechanism for bringing the marketing system all together.

III. The Role of Promotion in Integrated Marketing Communications

A. Introduction

Advertising and personal selling generally seek to move a customer through a purchase process by describing reasons to buy. A complementary part of the communications mix is Promotions. In promotions, a specific inducement to generate purchase behavior is offered, e.g., a $1.00 off coupon. Note that a given message to a consumer may include both advertising and promotion components. For example, a page in a magazine may include standard ad copy but then have a coupon at the bottom of the page to be cut out and redeemed at the store. It is important to recognize the two different goals even if the communications are contained in one specific execution.

Promotions can be directed to either the end consumer or the trade. A consumer promotion tries to induce consumer action to "pull" the product through the channel of distribution, while a trade promotion seeks to enlist support to carry an item and/or "push" it through to the end user.

B. Consumer Promotions

There is a wide variety of consumer promotion executions. Major types include:

(i) *Free samples* are especially useful in generating a trial of the product. They can be distributed in the mail, passed out at points of purchase or other high traffic areas, or be made available upon request from a potential buyer.

(ii) Price oriented programs which seek to reduce the consumer's real cost per unit in some way, e.g.,: (a) *cents-off coupons* which can be redeemed at the point-of-purchase, (b) *mail-in refunds* or *rebates* in which the consumer receives the specified amount upon submitting proof-of-purchase. Alternatively, special "pacs" can be offered to improve the value consumers receive: e.g., a "*price pac*" offering the normal size but repriced to provide a savings; a "value" pac offering larger quantity at the usual price; or a "*bonus pac*" offering another unit of the good for free if a certain number are purchased at the usual price, e.g., the "buy-one-get-one free" offer.

(iii) *Premiums*—another item is given away or offered at an attractive price if a certain number of units are purchased, e.g., during Christmas season 1998, Adams offered a free golf bag with the purchase of two of its clubs.

(iv) *Tie-Ins*—similar to premiums, but involves the joint promotion of two items, e.g., buy a Jeep and get two free season's passes to a local ski resort. Typically, the two parties share in the cost of the promotion.

(v) *Continuity Programs*—a reward is given in recognition of continuing relationships, e.g., the frequent flyer programs offered by virtually every airline.

(vi) *Contests/Sweepstakes*—used to generate excitement about product. For example, as part of a large-scale program involving television advertising, free-standing inserts in papers, and point-of-purchase displays, consumers turning in $20 in receipts for Nestle products received certificates for reduced admission to movie theaters and were entered in a drawing for a 5-day "Best of Hollywood Vacation" during the Academy Awards, year 2000.[6] By law, a sweepstakes cannot require the purchase of a product in order to participate, but in many instances participation rates by nonbuyers are low.

The extent of consumer promotions is vast. About 300 billion coupons are distributed annually in the United States. The Sunday newspaper free-standing insert has been the vehicle of distribution for the majority of these coupons. However, as the number of coupons distributed has grown, the percent redeemed has declined, from about 3.5% in the early 1980s to 2.5% in the 1990s. There has been a good deal of research on the impact of coupons on sales and the finding is that while the redemption rates may be low, coupons can have a measurable impact on short-term sales due to their ability to attract new triers and induce brand switching.

C. Trade Promotions

As with consumer promotions, there is a wide variety of trade promotion executions in practice. The objective of each is generally the same however, i.e. to induce the trade member to "push" the brand and through these efforts induce the consumer to buy. More specifically, a trade promotion can serve to induce the trade to:

- Carry an item
- Increase inventory held
- Display/advertise the item
- Lower the price of the item

Common trade promotion vehicles are:

(i) Slotting Allowances—This is a payment used to induce the trade to take on a new item. As the power of retailers has risen, new products, especially those with less certain sales prospects, effectively have to pay to "rent" shelf space from the retailer.

(ii) Cooperative Advertising (Co-op)—the manufacturer agrees to pay a percentage of the trade's advertising cost if the product is featured in advertising in a particular way. For example, restrictions might include that the product be the only one of its type in the ad, be the most prominently featured of any product, and not be advertised at a price below a certain level.

(iii) Floor Planning—the manufacturer basically finances the inventory of the retailer for a given period of time. This is common in expensive seasonal items such as snow blowers. If faced with buying and paying for goods in October and given lots of uncertainty about the timing and extent of demand, a retailer would likely take an amount into his store well less than the amount regarded as optimal by the manufacturer. The deferring of payment until after the selling season induces the trade to order more.

(iv) Temporary Price Cuts—the manufacturer cuts its price to the trade for a fixed period of time, e.g., 10%-off-invoice on all items ordered in March. Often, the trade will require the manufacturer to supply its promotion schedule for the year so buying activities can be planned accordingly. Typically, the manufacturer hopes the "deal" (the price cut) is at least partially "passed through" to the end user by the trade.

(v) Volume Discounts—price is reduced for units above a certain level. A quantity discount is a program whereby the same deal schedule is offered to all. Alternatively, some discounts "kick in" when an account exceeds its own last year's sales volume.

[6] S. Thompson, "Nestle musters up 30-plus brands for Hollywood pegged-sweepstakes," *BRANDWEEK*, January 11, 1999.

(vi) Contests—just as a company may have contests and rewards for its salespeople, e.g., the $1 million club going to Cancun, so too it can generate push by the trade via contests for free gifts or trips.

IV. Rounding Out the Communications Mix

A. Introduction

The five communications options presented to this point are:

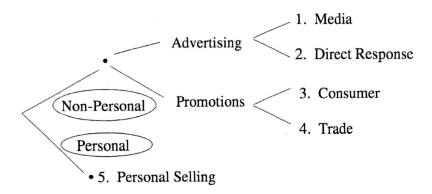

Each of these is under the direct control of the company. Many firms round out their mix with programs not wholly under their control, e.g., Event Marketing/Sponsorships and Publicity and Public Relations. These are not directly under the control of the marketer because another party is involved and to some extent the performance of the other party influences the impact the association will have. For example, if the Boston Celtics and Boston Bruins play poorly, the value of having the Fleet Bank name on the building in which they play decreases. Publicity generally involves a third party who sends its own message about the company.

B. Event Marketing Sponsorships

Sponsorship of events can be a mechanism to gain desirable brand associations. The majority of sponsorships revolve around sports: e.g., the naming of athletic arenas such as the Fleet Center in Boston, RCA Dome in Indianapolis, and the Trans World Dome in St. Louis; ties to on-going events like the Nike Golf tour (for professional golfers just failing to qualify for the PGA Tour), the Virginia Slims Tennis tour and the Winston Cup Series of NASCAR (National Association of Stock Car Racing); as well as specific events like the Bob Hope Chrysler Golf Tournament and the AT&T Rose Bowl Football Game.

Many sponsorships are used to enhance the corporate reputation as a responsible, thoughtful member of the community. Philip Morris, the world's largest cigarette manufacturer, affiliates itself with a number of socially desirable activities such as hunger alleviation and the arts.

While many companies see sponsorships as offering a very high return on their investment, these programs are less controllable than advertising and promotion programs. For example, the Olympics has historically been a prime sponsorship opportunity. However, companies affiliated with the Winter Games of 2002 in Salt Lake City have been rocked by the scandal over bribes paid to obtain the award of the games to the city.

C. Publicity and Public Relations

Communications received from many media sources can influence a consumer's evaluation of a firm and its products. The medium's impact may depend on its perceived impartiality. Advertising is often viewed as biased as compared to the trade press. For example, a favorable review in *Road and Track* or other car enthusiast magazines can be critical in a new car introduction. The manufacturer exerts less control here than in advertising where it specifies the copy, the form and timing of the message's appearance. The marketer can, however, attempt to influence coverage of its product, e.g., by making information available (e.g., Press Releases) or even making the product available for test use to those who would then disseminate information about it to the market.

V. Formulating the Integrated Marketing Communications (IMC) Program

The "Note on Marketing Strategy" set out the 6M's model for communications planning, i.e.,

1. Market—   to whom is the communication to be addressed?
2. Mission—   what is the objective of the communication?
3. Message—   what are the specific points to be communicated?
4. Media—   which vehicles will be used to convey the message?
5. Money—   how much will be spent in the effort?
6. Measurement— how will impact be assessed after the campaign?

A. The First Three M's and the Hierarchy-of-Effects

The Market/Mission/Message part is basically figuring out the strategic and tactical objectives of the communications campaign, i.e., who is being targeted for impact, the desired impact on the target, and the specific message to be delivered.

A useful approach to resolve the first three of the six M's is to analyze the consumer situation in terms of stages in the purchase and consumption process. While the desired end result of all marketing activities, including communications, is typically an exchange (often of dollars for goods/services), there is typically a sequence of steps a consumer goes through leading up to this. A valid communications goal can be to move the customer from one of these early steps to the next. A general model of the steps that a consumer may go through is called the hierarchy-of-effects model. It specifies the following seven steps.

The seven steps fall into three stages: cognitive, affective and behavioral describing the type of response required from consumers to move along in the hierarchy.

In the cognitive stage, the communications job is to put some facts into the mind of the potential consumer. The first step is to make a consumer *aware* of the existence of the product and then build *knowledge* by conveying some information about it. For example, when Adams Golf introduced its Tight-Lies Golf Clubs, it had to first let potential customers know the club line existed and some of its features: e.g., a lower center of gravity and a shallower club face. This cognitive stage sets the foundation for an affective stage wherein the prospect develops a feeling toward the new product.

Adams moved some potential customers from the cognitive stage of just being aware of club features to understanding of benefits delivered and hence "liking" through infomercials which won awards as the best infomercial in the demonstration category in a national competition.

The remaining steps in the affective stage are to move from *liking* to have a *preference* for the product over others and finally a strong intent or *conviction* to buy it. Finally, the process ends with an action, i.e., advancing to the behavioral stage with a *purchase* of the product.

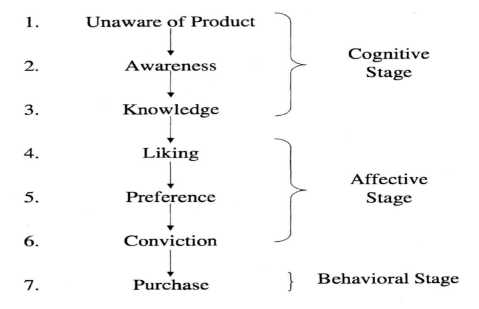

There is no one universally applicable model of the purchase process. For example, if the product was a nondurable, we might be concerned about another act within the behavioral stage, i.e., "repurchase." In some situations, it may be the case that the cognitive → affective → behavioral process (often called a learn → feel → do sequence) is not even descriptive of what is going on. Some researchers have found that the Learn → Feel → Do sequence may well describe a high-involvement purchase; but, Feel → Do → Learn may be an appropriate description in situations where consumers view the purchase of no great consequence and hence are relatively uninvolved in purchase process.

A first step in developing the Integrated Marketing Communications (IMC) plan is to assess the consumer purchase process relevant to the given situation. Note that it is possible that different segments of the market follow different purchase processes. For example, the entry-level buyer of stereo equipment has a different process than the aficionado/high-end purchaser. Once the right description of the process is developed, the next issue is to obtain at least a general sense of the distribution of potential customers over the states of the process at that point in time. For example, General Motors once developed the following stages for a new car model and distribution of target population.

Unaware → Aware → In Buying Class → In Consideration Class → First Choice
  66%   14%   8%   7%   5%

Where:

"In Buying Case" → brand is considered similar to those being actively considered by the person.

"In Consideration Class" → brand is considered favorably by person.

"First Choice" → person would select brand if car purchase were to be made today.

By understanding the distribution of consumers across states, GM had a good understanding of the specific communications job it faced. Additional research showed GM the differences in perceptions/feeling between those in different states and hence what changes had to be brought about in the consumer's mind to move him or her along in the process.[7]

---

[7] This is described in R. Batra, J.G. Myers, and D.A. Aaker, *Advertising Management*.

Communications objectives can be stated in terms of altering the distribution of the target market across the states.

B. The Fourth M: Media

Sections II–IV of this note set out the many communication vehicle options available. With an understanding of the advantages/disadvantages of each and the communication program objectives, one can determine which mix of vehicles is optimal.

For example, in early 1999 M&M/Mars introduced "M&M Crunchy" to join its existing M&M line-up of plain, peanut, and peanut butter candies. The "hierarchy-of-effects" for a new candy item could be:

$$\text{Unaware} \rightarrow \text{Aware} \rightarrow \text{Positive Attitude} \rightarrow \text{Trial} \rightarrow \text{Repeat}$$

In mid-January 1999, some very small percentage of target customers were aware of the coming of M&M Crunchy. It had been covered in the trade press, like *Advertising Age* which projected $60 million spending on communications to support the launch. As is typical of a new product launch, the first task was to move the concentration of target consumers in the "unaware" state along to awareness and positive attitude. Given the broad target market definition and the awareness task, the spot on the Super Bowl chosen by M&M was an ideal vehicle.

M&M/Mars would be hoping to move a prospect through the hierarchy quickly, so even while the awareness building activities were being carried out on television, programs would be put in place to convert the positive attitude to trial in the store. Retail distribution was gained prior to the advertising and special retail displays and trade promotions could be used to gain desired retail "push."

C. The Fifth M: Money

The size of the communications budget is frequently a matter of great debate within companies. Many companies use simple rules-of-thumb, e.g., setting budgets as some percentage of expected or previous year's sales. Others adopt a competitively based benchmark, e.g., "spend to have a share-of-voice (SOV: meaning the percentage of the product category spending attributable to the firm) equal to our share-of-market."

While these guidelines are often used as "reality checks," the right way to approach the budget question is through what is called the "objective and task" method, i.e., figure out what you have to do to attain your objectives and cost it out. Of course, one has to make the business assessment that such expenditures will pay out in the end.

The optimal communications budget is typically a function of:

1. *The Size and Heterogeneity of the Target Audience* to be reached: obviously the larger the audience, the greater the cost typically; but we also have to consider its heterogeneity and accessibility via communication vehicles. For example, it would be less expensive to reach all 1700 MBA students at Harvard Business School than it would be to reach the 100 most technology-oriented students at each of the top 17 MBA programs as identified by *Business Week*.

2. *Nature of Message:* some messages, e.g., the existence of M&M Crunchy in a light blue bag, are easy to get across. Others are more complex; e.g., explaining the details of Tweeter's Automatic Price Protection plan in an impactful way. Many industrial products require intensive communication efforts because new technology must be explained and the user convinced that the new product will interface with his current systems. For this reason, personal selling is often more important in business-to-business situations than in consumer.

3. *Receptivity of the Audience:* if the audience is seeking out information on the product category, the required budget is typically less because there is no need to break through the consumer's mechanism for screening out unwanted messages and then attract attention. For high involvement consumer purchases like automobiles, sporting equipment, and computers, consumers will seek out information in the purchase process. This active information search reduces the burden on the communicator. Alternatively, consider a low interest product category with consumers quite satisfied with current offerings in the category. Here there is the burden of attracting attention and getting a message through when the receiver generally regards such information as unimportant.

4. *Amount of Clutter:* the spending levels of the competition can be a factor in the intensity of the effort needed to get a message through. For example, while a new golf club manufacturer would be aided by consumer search for information, the high level of spending by Callaway on its Big Bertha line represents a burden to overcome. At times, spending has to reach a certain threshold before it "breaks through."

Spending levels vary greatly across industries and even across firms within the same category. On average, game and toy manufacturers spend 16% of sales on advertising; candy companies 12%; food companies 6%; household furniture 4%; motor vehicles 3% and airlines 1.5%. Within industries, one can find very different strategies as one firm might have a low price/low spending strategy while another has a strategy of relatively high price but supported by an appreciable communications budget to convince prospects of the value of the product.

D. The Sixth M: Measurement

An important part of communications planning is to build a mechanism for learning about the effects which the efforts had. This is a critical input to decisions on future spending levels, allocation of the budget across media, and specific communication messages.

Objectives being clearly stated is an important first step. For example, if an objective is to "increase awareness of the three-year warranty on all of our products to 50% of population by June 1," research can be done to see if the goal has been met. Note that "awareness" is not something one can observe in the normal course of business activities. It is a cognitive effect, so we have to do research such as a survey to assess this. As we noted above, another goal may be behavioral, e.g., "get 25% of target population to try the product by June 1." Again, this can be assessed via market research. If a sales goal is specified, e.g., "ship 500,000 cases by June 1" we need only look to company records to assess this.

The trade-off in the type of goals to assess progress against is that behavior/sales is the ultimate goal of the enterprise typically. However, many factors in addition to the communications effort impact sales, e.g., the product quality, price, and activities of competitors. Consequently, separating out the communications program effect is often difficult. Thus, earlier stage measurements of cognitive and affective impacts can be useful adjuncts to the assessment of communications effectiveness and learning about optimal communications methods.

VI. Conclusion

Developing the IMC is a critical part of marketing strategy. A product may in fact offer great value to a target population; but it is that segment's perception of the value that is key. The marketer has a variety of communication vehicles available and the options are expanding with technological developments such as the Internet. A systematic approach in first selecting the target and then understanding the purchase process in detail can lead to an efficient and effective IMC.

Chapter 16

Guru.com

Rajiv Lal   Ann K. Leamon

One day in late February 2000, James Slavet (HBS '99), co-CEO and co-founder of Guru.com, his brother Jon Slavet, also co-CEO and co-founder, and Michelle Cassayre, vice president of marketing, met to review the proposed $12 million off-line brand campaign for their online firm devoted to independent professionals. Marty McDonald, creative director, and Jacquie Arnatt, account director, from Guru.com's advertising agency, DDB in Seattle, Washington, presented three different concepts.

"How did focus groups respond to the different creative treatments?" James asked.

"We don't have time to run them," said Cassayre. "Freeagent.com's brand campaign has been out for a month now. And other competitors are not far behind. We need to get our message out there."

"But there still seem to be a lot of issues that we need to resolve," said James:

> We're in the middle of raising our third round of financing and we've been acquiring customers incredibly cost-effectively with email and direct mail. How can we justify an increase in our marketing acquisition costs? Then there's the audience and the execution—are we targeting the right people? Should we use print or TV? Are we being too touchy-feely with this campaign you're proposing? I really think we need to describe our product, not just evoke some fuzzy feeling.

Guru.com had raised a little under $20 million in two early financing rounds; Jon and James had a third round of $40 million in progress. James continued, "We're spending a lot of money on this campaign at the same time that we're under pressure to keep our customer acquisition costs reasonable. I sure hope this works."

Guru.com competed directly with Freeagent.com, the online division of Opus360, a firm that provided software and services to facilitate the management of a company's project-based workforce. Both operated web-based services that catered to the 25 million independent professionals (IPs) in the United States, by providing a place where IPs could

Ann K. Leamon, Manager of the Center for Case Development, prepared this case under the supervision of Professor Rajiv Lal as the basis for class discussion rather than to illustrate either effective or ineffective handling of an administrative situation.

EXHIBIT 1
Competitors

Source: Company
information.

Type	Competitors
Professional services automation software companies (PSAs)	Opus360 (FreeAgent.com); Niku (iNiku)
Mass full-time online career sites	TMP/Monster.com (Monster Talentmarket)
Other IP project marketplaces	eLance, eWork
Off-line staffing firms	Adecco, Manpower, Aquent, Hall Kinion

find projects and where companies with projects could find IPs (called "gurus" by Guru.com). Both sites also offered back-office support and career advice to IPs, along with tax guidance, discounts on health insurance and other products, and tips on all aspects of running a solo business, from collecting bad debts to maintaining a home office. Guru.com's website had gone live in December 1999 after a five-month preview; Freeagent.com had launched two months before. A number of other competitive web-sites also launched in the same timeframe, including Monster.com's TalentMarket, iNiku (a division of Niku), eLance, and eWork (see **Exhibit 1**).

The Staffing Industry

By the end of the twentieth century, the staffing industry, with an estimated U.S. market size of $85 billion, had changed dramatically. Traditionally, staffing companies had acted as go-betweens, filling companies' needs for flexible and temporary workers that could move into permanent positions. The typical "temp" had been a clerical worker. With the labor shortage of the late 1990s, they had become providers of vital services—qualified employees. One observer commented that the current knowledge-based economy had meant that "the employee has now transcended brand, capital equipment and even technology to become the most valuable corporate asset . . . The most critical determinant of corporate success will be access to human talent."[1]

In the aftermath of the downsizings of the early 1990s, the employment contract changed and so did the nature of the temporary worker. Companies were reluctant to hire large numbers of employees that might have to be let go in a downturn, and wary workers were also reluctant to pledge their lives to a corporation. Since 1983, average job tenures had fallen by 15%, and workers entering the job force in the late 1990s were expected to have between eight and ten employers during their careers.[2] Workers in certain disciplines were in especially high demand; unemployment among "knowledge workers" was estimated at less than 1%.[3] Workers could "job hop" whether as a full-time employee with a short tenure or as a temporary—albeit highly skilled and well-paid—worker.

As a result, corporate expenditures on outsourcing were expected to rise from $51 billion in 1998 to $81 billion in 2003.[4] Between 2000 and 2002, the number of outsourced projects was expected to rise from 20 million to 50 million.[5] Contract work was attractive to workers as well; the ranks of contractors were expected to rise from 21% of the U.S. workforce in 2000 to 41% in 2010.[6]

[1] Judith Scott and Darren Bagwell, "Increasing our Coverage: from Staffing to Human Capital Management," Robert W. Baird & Co., February 17, 2000, p. 2.

[2] Bureau of Labor Statistics, cited in Scott and Bagwell, p. 5.

[3] Forrester Research, cited in Scott and Bagwell, p. 5.

[4] International Data Center.

[5] Bureau of Labor Statistics.

[6] EPIC/MRA.

The Internet offered a uniquely flexible approach to outsourcing. Workers could be miles or continents from the firms whose projects they handled. The revenues of online recruiting firms that specialized in permanent placements were expected to rise from $2 billion in 2000 to $5 billion by 2005. The revenues of talent facilitators, such as Guru.com, which focused on independent professionals, were expected to exceed $2 billion by 2005, from a current level of less than $1 billion.[7]

The Guru Phenomenon

Guru.com supported the 25 million independent professionals (IPs) who performed project-based work as everything from graphic designers and freelance writers to virtual CEOs and computer programmers. Market research showed that the IPs were between 25 and 55, well educated, and content with their decision to be independent (see **Exhibit 2**).

Experts such as Fast Company Editor Dan Pink prophesied the establishment of a "free agent nation." Along with the increased amount of corporate outsourcing, forces contributing to the rise of the independent workforce included the explosion of home computing and telecommunications, and the increasing number of working professionals who wanted to balance their careers with family life or other pursuits. But the freedom that IPs experienced—working for whom they wanted, where they wanted, and on the projects they wanted—came at a price. IPs often experienced a sense of isolation, a workload that was "feast or famine," and the administrative hassles of running a solo business. Said one observer, "Traditionally a lot of people who go into business for themselves fail, not because they're not good at what they do, but because they're bad at business and have trouble dealing with things like 1099 tax forms."[8]

The Internet's IP-focused sites tended toward one of two business models. One model was that of Guru.com and Freeagent.com, which functioned as matching services, where IPs posted their profiles and companies posted projects. IPs could search for projects or for other IPs to help them handle complicated jobs. Companies could search for IPs, obtaining not just a resume but references and pricing information.

Guru.com's service was free to IPs, but companies paid a $125 up-front fee to post each project. Advertisements aimed at the IPs who spent time on the Guru.com site generated additional revenue, as did an online store offering products and services (such as health insurance) to help IPs run their solo businesses. In the works was a product to help IPs

---

[7] Scott and Bagwell, p. 7.

[8] Malcolm Maclachlan in Susan Karlin, "Free me," *Upside,* June 2000, p. 321.

EXHIBIT 2
IP Demographics

Source: Company information.

- Gender: 63% male/37% female overall. Among 45+, 71% male/29% female. Under 35, 58% male/42% female.
- Age: 27% are 25–34, 30% 35–44, 34% 44+.
- Marital status: 53% married, 29% single, 14% divorced. Males: 58% married, 32% single, 10% divorced. Females: 43% married, 37% single, 20% divorced.
- Children at home: 14% one child, 14% two children, 6% three children.
- Education: 24% post graduate degree, 17% some post graduate work, 31% undergraduate degree, 23% some college.
- Personal Income: 30% under $40,000, 31% $40,000–$75,000, 40% over $75,000.
- Household Income: 31% under $55,000, 33% $55,000–$99,0000, 36% over $100,000.
- Technology: Own computer, software, modem, fax, printer, cell phone, pager.
- 51% use the Internet to learn more about their profession, do research, and send email.
- TV viewing: scattered throughout the day, while taking breaks.

manage their back-office time tracking and billing. To extend its reach, Guru.com focused on partnering with relevant and frequently visited sites. Guru.com's distribution partners included Fast Company, Industry Standard, WebHire, DevX, and Macromedia.

Freeagent.com provided project matching and back office support (invoicing and collection services) along with products and services, such as insurance and office equipment. The site reported 170,000 visitors per month and was on track to achieve 86,000 registered users by the end of its first nine months, in March 2000. By the end of its first year, in July 2000, Freeagent.com expected to have 150,000 registered users. While IPs did not have to pay to register, some of the site's other services required a monthly fee.

The other model, adopted by eLance and Monster.com's TalentMarket, used an auction approach, in which employers bid for the services of IPs or IPs bid for a job. Monster Talent Market had 10,000 registered employers bidding for the services of 143,000 IPs in roughly 40,000 live auctions at any one time. Monster.com received a fee up to $1,000 depending on the size of the contract.[9] These models were criticized for their over-emphasis on price. Many experts said that price, while important, was only one component of the decision-making process. In addition, some freelancers complained that the bidding-based model made them feel like commodities.[10]

In general, IPs gave all the online sites mixed reviews. Said one, who had found a $1 million contract online, "I'm not sure [they're] particularly reliable . . . There are a lot of variables in dealing with job hunting. [Others] don't understand the qualifications needed to get the job done." A marketing consultant complained that, of the two on-line jobs for which she was contacted over four months, one was for an engineering/technical position and the other paid far less than her specified rate.[11] Other IPs used online sites to post their resumes but not to look for work.

Companies, too, had a mixed reaction to the sites overall. One company that recruited seven different freelancers online for one position in a three-week timeframe, decided to rely instead on university internships. Some firms complained that candidates registered on freelance sites tended to be of lower quality than those who did not.[12]

Launching Guru.com

James and his older brother Jon had founded Guru.com in early 1999 as James was finishing his MBA at Harvard Business School (HBS). Both brothers had worked in online businesses previously; Jon as the vice president of E! Online and the senior executive for strategic development at Wired Ventures, and James as a member of Drugstore.com's launch team and as the manager of business development at Wired Ventures. Jon explained the genesis of the idea:

> We'd tried to get expert help on projects in our past lives and found it was a real pain. It was entirely hit or miss; you relied on networks of friends and hoped you found a good person for the project. Also, a lot of our friends had left traditional corporate America and gone off on their own, so we knew about the frustrations of working as a guru. With the Net, we figured we had a perfect platform to streamline the contractor-project matching process.

James had direct experience with launching online businesses; during his summer at HBS, he had been the first employee of Drugstore.com and had to decide whether or not to return to school in the fall to complete his degree. He returned to HBS with the set goal of starting his own company upon graduation. He thought of a freelancer service marketplace

---

[9] Karlin.

[10] Karlin.

[11] Karlin.

[12] Karlin.

in January 1999. In March of that year, he, Jon, and Guru.com's third founder, Al Yau (HBS '99), completed the business plan and started raising money. James described the process: "I spent four day weekends in California, pitching investors, interviewing potential employees, and looking for office space. We ran the business out of Jon's living room; that's where we even hired our first employees. In June, we closed on $3 million in angel funding and set up shop."

Although both brothers believed in their concept, they also were aware of their competitors. Jon said:

> I had experience in the ad-supported models of Wired and Hotwired; James knew online retail from his time with Drugstore.com. We both thought that the services exchange model would be very scalable. But we weren't alone; almost every week, someone would mention another company who was doing something related to our business. We had a real scare when one of James' HBS classes featured Jeffrey Taylor [CEO of Monster.com] and he said they'd be doing an auction for IP talent. Then Freeagent put its initial placeholder site up in July. But we went for it—we believed that there was a window of opportunity as the market was coalescing around us. We thought that good execution would make the difference, not necessarily being the first out of the gate.

With the initial round of financing, the brothers put up a preview site.

> It had no functionality—there was some content aimed at IPs and a place for people to pre-register for our service, but we didn't do any project matching at all. We offered free t-shirts to the first 3,000 people who signed up and we got that many people in the first few weeks. It really got people talking and we got a lot of feedback that helped inform our early product development. We had 35,000 people registered off that initial site in the first five months—and that was without the site even doing much. It was really helpful to mention this traction when we were talking to investors. And it supported our notion that this was a viable concept.

The initial Guru.com team was predominantly composed of IPs. Its motto was "Of, by and for gurus." James elaborated, "Our content editor, our lead techie, our designer, even our PR person—they were all gurus. We had two other full-time employees and Al, Jon, and me, the founders."

In November 1999, the team closed their second financing round, raising $16 million from two venture capital firms, Greylock, and August Capital. Guru.com went live on December 10, 1999, with 40 employees, 35,000 registered gurus, and 2,500 registered hiring companies (see **Exhibit 3**). In the first week of operation, 91 new projects were posted. James said, "One of our real concerns was that we might over-promise. We wanted to manage expectations; we never wanted to promise anything that the product couldn't deliver. Gurus are smart and savvy and very attuned to being over-sold through advertising."

By February, Jon and James felt that Guru.com was achieving its mission. Since its official launch, the site had generated significant market activity with more than 250,000 searches per month, 3,760 posted projects with an average project value of $12,000. The growth in pageviews, new hirers, and new projects was close to 17% per week, and in the last week of February, over a million pageviews were served. The founders felt that they had achieved real momentum (see **Exhibit 4**).

Twenty-five percent of projects submitted by hirers had been matched to gurus, translating into 940 project matches and over $11 million in facilitated transactions. Gurus were registering at a rate of 24,000 per month and generating 1.1 million "find work" pageviews. This yielded roughly 44 pageviews per guru per month. Since its inception, visitors to the site had turned an average of 11 pageviews per session. This level of user activity was on the high side of the average for such sites.

Based on a study by Guru.com, the hirers who had used the service were pleased with the experience; almost three-quarters (73%) had rated their experience good or excellent, while only 3% had called it poor or terrible. Of the hirers who had found a guru, 86% had

EXHIBIT 3 **Guru.com Homepage**

Source: Company information.

rated their experience good to excellent. Sixty percent had rated the quality of Guru.com-supplied gurus as good or excellent and only 7% had rated guru quality to be poor or terrible. Each hirer received an average of 17 responses from gurus for each posted project.

While the project matching service often brought gurus to the site, the founders did not want to rely solely on this service in the future. They wanted to increase the usage of other parts of the site, such as the back office support services and the store.

Marketing Guru.com

Michelle Cassayre, vice president of marketing, had come to Guru.com in July 1999 from NetObjects, a maker of website building software, where she had also been vice president of marketing. Prior to that, she had been the director of global advertising at Oracle.

> I knew that if I ever wanted to establish the Guru.com brand, I'd have to prove our member acquisition costs early on. So I set out to track the efficiency of every medium around. My first few months at Guru.com, I tested everything—opt-in email, online ads, the efficiency

EXHIBIT 4 Weekly Performance Metrics

Source: Company information.

Week Starting	Total Pageviews	New Hirers	New Gurus	New Projects	Total Searches	Find Work Pageviews	Unique Work Searches	Find Guru Pageviews	Unique Guru Searches	Unique Users	Unique Sessions
Pre-launch		2,500	35,000								
22-Nov	255,981	115	3,471	NA				32,642		25,915	19,935
29-Nov	267,129	190	5,305	NA				55,800		40,959	31,507
06-Dec	219,686	277	2,981	91		22,693		37,027		35,695	27,458
13-Dec	423,901	416	5,199	138		81,687		44,649		59,682	45,909
20-Dec	355,619	373	3,230	140		76,098		34,335		53,608	41,237
27-Dec	388,252	314	4,087	122		92,394		33,787		55,572	42,748
03-Jan	601,145	461	4,594	139		148,132		53,748		83,104	63,926
10-Jan	592,927	504	4,177	240	60,850	154,189	45,948	50,005	14,902	90,788	69,837
17-Jan	666,929	626	4,437	421	64,349	179,870	49,233	55,224	15,116	86,136	66,258
24-Jan	963,278	724	7,529	394	92,634	264,787	72,778	72,240	19,856	113,537	87,336
31-Jan	897,570	745	5,040	584	81,086	248,705	62,455	74,195	18,631	95,974	73,826
07-Feb	834,409	706	4,708	502	75,349	223,182	57,150	71,071	18,199	93,721	72,093
14-Feb	970,520	745	6,087	440	84,605	270,137	66,848	71,756	17,757	110,466	84,974
21-Feb	1,111,481	833	8,449	549	91,404	309,185	72,372	81,309	19,032	136,111	104,701
Total	8,548,827	9,529	104,294	3,760	550,277	071,059	426,784	767,788	123,493	1,081,268	831,745
Weekly Growth	12%	17%	7%	18%	6%	27%	7%	7%	4%	14%	14%

Notes: "Find Work Pageviews" = the number of pages viewed in a session in which someone looked for work. "Find Guru Pageview" = the number of pageviews during a session when a company looked for a guru. Unique Searches did not equal Unique Sessions because some users simply logged on to read articles.

281

EXHIBIT 5
IP Profile

Source: Company
information.

- Self-assured, optimistic, energetic, active in their spare time.
- Invest wisely, look for discounts, believe that every penny counts, pay off debts.
- Want to be seen as passionate and committed to whatever they are doing; as experts in their professions; in control of work and personal life.
- Define success as "having a feeling of contentment," "achieving personal goals," "doing what you want," "doing what you are good at and getting paid."
- Quotes that inspire gurus:—"I like things to happen, and if they don't happen, I like to make them happen." *Winston Churchill.* "The freedom to make mistakes provides the best environment for creativity." *Unknown.* "The happiness in this life does not consist in the absence but in the mastery of his passions." *Alfred, Lord Tennyson.*

EXHIBIT 6
Guru.com's Brand Platform

Source: Company
information.

For people with these values . . .	independence, freedom, and passion
Who seek these rewards . . .	control, variety, and flexibility
Guru.com with this personality . . .	authentic, quirky, insightful, and passionate
Provides these unique benefits . . .	**relevance, understanding, a true sense of connection**
Because it has these features . . .	project matching, access to products and services, access to community for ideas, advice, and sharing

of banners vs. newsletter sponsorship, print direct mail, referral programs, and back-to-base programs that would enhance our relationship with our existing customers. I wanted to be able to walk into Jon and James' offices and say "By spending X, we can get Y. I can allocate the budget across all the media and get the customers we need, now let me launch the brand campaign." I also wanted to prove how brand marketing could enhance the efficiency of our customer acquisition spending. To create awareness, people need to experience your brand several times, in several mediums. By the time Freeagent.com launched their brand campaign, I had completed my testing. We'd already been working with our ad agency to define our brand personality and establish a profile of the average guru (see **Exhibits 5** and **6**).

"Because we weren't out in the market with brand advertising, we could track about half of our registered visitors," Cassayre continued:

> Direct mail, email, and online banners are very trackable mediums, so we knew exactly how many members we were acquiring per medium and the cost per acquisition by medium. As we launch this campaign, we're hoping to see the percentage of our new customers acquired through trackable sources fall, as people learn about us via offline mediums, because they saw our name on a coffee cup, on a billboard, or attended a Guru event.

Prior to the launch of the brand campaign, Guru.com had spent roughly $500,000 per month on e-mail, online ads and print direct mail. The average cost of acquiring a guru was $15; hirers (companies) were more expensive, often up to $70 each. With gurus signing up at the rate of 6,000 per week, it was very important to attract good projects in order to keep them engaged.

The marketing messages were unique to each group of customers. The message to gurus in an email or direct mail piece was "Guru.com understands the guru workstyle and can meet your needs," and to hirers it was "Guru.com has the expert freelance talent you need for short-term projects."

Other Branding Efforts

Events and public relations had been the bulk of Guru.com's offline marketing soon after the preview site was launched. James explained the strategy:

> We wanted to get our name in the press. It was great free marketing. So we hired a public relations guru. She contacted journalists, suggesting us as the subject of articles, but

concentrating her pitches on the overall trend of the changing workforce and the emerging opportunity to build a business around the freelance workstyle, rather than what we were going to do specifically at Guru.com. Before we really had much of a service going, she had us featured in MSNBC.com, in *Wired,* and the *Industry Standard*. Through her, we defined the movement and positioned ourselves as experts on the new independent workstyle.

Throughout the autumn, Guru.com received significant media attention. In its first six months, the company generated 250 million media impressions, through articles in *Newsweek* and *USA Today,* and a long feature story in *Inc.* magazine, in which a reporter traced Guru.com's venture financing experience.

The firm also contacted the research community, establishing ties with analysts at Forrester and Jupiter. Through these contacts, Guru.com sought to define the IP movement and speak for the category. It hoped to be mentioned anytime the press asked about trends in the IP space. Events were another way to build the brand, as James described:

> I remembered the Harley Davidson case from HBS, where every employee had to attend at least one biker rally a year to see first hand who the customer really was. In the same spirit, we held a series of gatherings in the cities where our gurus lived. It was a way to get our brand and service in front of people but also a way to understand who our customers were and what they wanted. These events also verified our research findings related to the isolation that gurus felt. We would send out an email inviting them to a bar to meet us and other gurus in their city, and within an hour, we'd have 400 responses. Jon and I flew around the country with our marketing team to these guru mixers. We must have met 5,000 gurus. It definitely helped us to build community and brand awareness and to meet our customers.

As part of the their offline event strategy, the company also launched the First Annual Guru Awards. "We thought the Guru Awards would be fun," said James. "It gave us a chance to recognize outstanding gurus, gave gurus a chance to nominate other gurus, and got thousands of new customers to our site. It was a low-cost way to get customers." The total events budget for the year was close to $300,000.

These non-traditional efforts also seemed to work in building the brand. When *E-company magazine* used the phrase, "While not Monster.com or Guru.com, this site. . . ." to review another project-matching web site, James laughed. "I never thought I'd see our site, after so little time, held up as a category leader, or in the same breath as Monster.com."

The Offline Campaign

By February 2000, Guru.com had 105,000 members (hirers and gurus), acquired at an average cost of $34. February's results showed a dramatic increase from January's 77,000 members and a declining average acquisition cost from $51 in January (see **Exhibit 7**). "I still wasn't sure we needed to invest in a big, classic offline brand push. Everything seemed to be going in the right direction," James said.

Examining the data did raise some concerns, however. Only about 10% of the registered members were hirers. During the month of February, almost 2,000 new jobs had been posted, and almost 26,000 new gurus had registered. In addition to the sheer number of potential projects, areas of specialty also needed to be considered (see **Table 1**). Gurus would only stay active on the site for a certain time. If they did not find a project, or if they did not find the content relevant, they would not come back. Guru.com was careful not to promise to provide projects to all visitors. Even if an appropriate project existed, it might be geographically unsuitable—"we have gurus registered from all over the world (see **Exhibit 8**) and if the job is in San Francisco and they have to be on-site, it won't work if you live in Irkutsk."

Even though their Board of Directors had strongly urged them to run a brand campaign, James and Jon knew they had to keep customer acquisition costs down. Cassayre's

EXHIBIT 7 Actual and Projected Acquisitions and Costs

Source: Company information.

	Jan. (A)	Feb. (A)	Mar. (E)	Apr. (E)	May (E)	June (E)	FY 2000 (E)	FY 2001 (E)
Total members[a]	68,958	96,271	145,290	184,000	229,000	278,000	400,000	807,500)
(%guru/%hirer)	(92/8)	(91/9)	(90/10)	(90/10)	(90/10)	(89/11)	(95/5)	(96/4)
New members	18,000	27,313	39,600	38,700	44,340	49,000		
(%guru/%hirer)	(92/8)	(89/11)	(90/10)	(90/10)	(80/10)	(84/16)		
Trackable Acquisition cost[b]	$24	$23	$19	$16	$8	$10		
Total Acquisition cost[c]	$51	$34	$79	$56	$43	$37		
New projects	1,148	1,825	3,066	2,551	2,122	2,821		

[a]January includes 25,000 pre-launch members.
[b]Total spending on trackable media (email, direct mail, banner ads)/# of gurus acquired through those media.
[c]Total marketing spending/total acquisitions.

TABLE 1
Gurus and Projects by Category

Source: Company information.

Category	Number of Projects	Number of Gurus
Creative/Media	496	22,313
Finance/legal	80	2,856
Information	1,253	22,860
Technology Management/Strategy	137	10,250
Marketing/Advertising/Sales	398	7,510
Training/Advice	65	4,539
Web Business and Operations	91	3,209
Web Development and Creative	640	14,054
Other	130	4,748
Total	3,290	92,339

EXHIBIT 8
Domestic and International Membership

Source: Company information.

	Members	Gurus	Hirers
Domestic	75,983	68,689	7,294
—% in top 20 domestic markets	61%	60%	75%
International	11,080	10,079	1,001
—% in top 5 international markets	55%	55%	53%

Top 20 domestic markets: New York, Philadelphia, Detroit, San Francisco Area, Seattle, Phoenix, Los Angeles, Atlanta, Minneapolis, Washington DC, San Diego, Austin, Boston, Houston, Portland, Chicago, Miami, Cleveland, Dallas–Forth Worth, and Denver.
Top Five International Markets: Canada, India, United Kingdom, Australia, and Malaysia.

experience with the performance of various media was helpful here, but even so, the first few months of projected spending for the campaign "made our heads spin," said James:

> But we thought that maybe this would help us get more traction in the market overall. Sometimes, even from the PR we've had, people think we are bigger and more established than we really are, or that we've been around a lot longer. So there might be spin-offs that can't be measured—it might give us more credibility as a strategic partner with other sites or as an investment opportunity.

The Audience

One of the first questions James and Jon had to answer was whether to target the gurus, the hirers, or both. "I thought that we should have a broad-based message," said James:

> We were spending so much money that I thought our advertising campaign should speak to both of our constituencies and say something like, "We understand the needs of gurus and of the people who hire them." Besides, if we placing our ad somewhere like *Wired* magazine, lots of hirers would see it, so why not reach out to them?

Cassayre felt differently:

> It's always important to deliver a message that is relevant to your customer. You can't be all things to all people. More importantly, we needed to develop a campaign that supported our brand foundation: "Guru.com enables and empowers the guru workstyle." And we also wanted to achieve our goal of 400,000 registered gurus by the end of 2000. The scarce resource in this economy is talent, if we have the talent, we'll get the hirers. The gurus are the pollen; the hirers are the bees.

The Message

Another area of discussion was the tone and content of the message. The prevailing tone of offline advertising for online brands tended to be edgy, aimed at the Internet-savvy Generation X.[13] James said:

> Edgy was ok, but I wanted to get our message out there clearly. If we were going to spend that much money, people should walk away knowing EXACTLY what we do. There were too many Internet companies that focus so much on being memorable and edgy that their message was obscure.
>
> If you review our brand platform, you will see that we're selling the notion of empowerment for the independent professional—a very abstract concept. Our creative work needed to come from a place of relevance and understanding. We wanted gurus to see themselves in the images that appear in our ads—and then deliver the message "we know you, and we've got what you need." At the same time, the hirers would know we understand gurus and that we'll provide the best ones.

He also pointed to the nature of the audience:

> Whether gurus or hirers, they're busy and they're smart. They're bombarded by thousands of messages during the course of a day, so they don't have much time or tolerance for advertising and especially advertising that doesn't speak directly to them.

FreeAgent's ads were edgy and irreverent, and poked fun at traditional corporate America. "However," James observed, "we were trying to connect with both, at least to some extent. And we can't say to the hirers that corporations are horrible and we stand for people who don't want anything to do with them."

Most of the gurus used the web extensively in the course of their work, but the older segments, the research showed, were least likely to have searched for projects online. "These tend to be the most established, most experienced, and most accomplished," said DDB's Arnatt. "Just how edgy do we want to make it?"

Another debate centered on whether Guru.com's advertising would position the service as a marketplace or a resource, as Cassayre described:

> We called ourselves the guru marketplace with investors, because that was the most attractive positioning. But that language did not resonate with our gurus—in fact, 85% of our

---

[13] Generation X referred to the 45 million Americans born between 1968 and 1980 whose attitudes had been shaped by divorce, downsizing, video, and heavy marketing. They tended to be savvy about advertising messages, determined to go their own way and make their own decisions. To appeal to this group, marketing messages generally had to have a component of either authenticity or irreverence. (Source: Bill Stoneman, "Beyond rocking the ages," *American Demographics,* May 1998, p. 44.)

customers referred to Guru.com as a resource. The term resource was also a better umbrella for what we provided: project-matching, advice, deals on products and services, and business management tools.

The Medium

The next question involved the medium to use. Arnatt's research had identified television shows and magazines that were popular with gurus: *ER,* the *X-Files, Law and Order, Star Trek, Ally McBeal, Frazier, Friends,* and the Discovery Channel on TV; *Fast Company, Inc, Industry Standard, Fortune, PC Magazine, Wired, Business 2.0, The Economist,* and *Newsweek* for magazines. Although the group was looking at print samples, they could also be shot as TV spots.

While TV, as a visual medium, could create emotional appeal more effectively than could print, it also posed challenges. Arnatt explained:

> TV has a lot of potential but you need to look at a number of variables. We'd need to be sure to educate people about what a guru was and why they should care about Guru.com. We'll also have to be sure we're running our ads when the right people are watching. I've brought a sample rate scheme (see **Exhibit 9**), but because we'd be in the short-term market, we'd probably have to pay more, especially to run something for two or three months.

Print, while less evocative, could relate more information. A solid national print campaign would cost $4 million, leaving $8 million to augment it with radio, billboards, and other methods of generating awareness. In addition, by spreading the ads across a number of publications, Guru.com could access the broad range of specialists who were gurus. Cassayre described other benefits:

> An ad in a magazine gets read by the 500,000 subscribers and then by another million who borrow it, leaf through it on a coffee table in the doctor's office, or read it in the library. Besides, gurus are prolific readers. It's very important to them to stay up to date on their specialty and on the world at large.

The group differed on which magazines should be used. "I really wanted to run in the lifestyle publications," said Cassayre, "*Vanity Fair, Outside, Men's Journal,* even *In Style,* targeting our gurus in their lifestyle environment. But James and Jon wanted to limit our focus more to business publications like *Fast Company, Wired,* and *Industry Standard* (see **Exhibit 10**).

The Internet was only considered briefly for branding. A major advertising presence there would cost roughly $3 million. "It's the most rational of all the media for acquisition, but it's not the most visible and effective for branding," said Cassayre. "Besides, we'd still be running our banners and emails for acquisition programs, so we'd still have a presence there, just not the big branded campaign."

The Ads

Other decisions included the age, gender, ethnicity, and setting of the models in the ads. "There's an increasing concern about ad clutter," said Arnatt. "Everything, TV and print, is cluttered and there's a real backlash. You really have to get creative to stand out."

"We wanted to show the aspirational side of being an independent professional, but it had to be grounded in realism," said DDB's McDonald. "We tried to avoid clichés, such as gurus sitting on mountain tops, but wanted to make it something they'd connect with."

Cassayre said:

> We decided that gurus were EveryPerson—male, female, creative, technical. And we returned to the research to see what would be important to them and what we should depict these people doing. It had to be honest, but also aspirational and inspirational as well.

EXHIBIT 9 **TV Costs and Coverage**

Source: DDB and casewriter.

For One Market:

Market: Seattle (currently the 12th ranked market on population)
Quarter: 2Q (Apr/May/June)
Demo: Sample

Daypart	Cost/Point	Target Rating Points	% of Daypart	Number of Spots	Cost/Spot	Cost/ Daypart
Daytime (10a–4p)	$154	161	15%	48	$ 282	$ 13,536
Primetime (8p–11p)	581	390	36	88	4,727	415,976
Early Morning (5a–9a)	172	119	11	54	379	20,475
Early News (5p–6p)	269	120	11	46	701	32,250
Late News (11p–11:30p)	357	170	16	47	1,649	77,503
Early Fringe (4p–5p)	267	115	11	37	339	12,543
		1,075	100%	320	$1,788	$572,283

Note: Target Rating Points (TRPs) were developed by the A.C. Nielsen Company to measure reach and frequency across a given demographic. Television "families" received a diary in which they noted the programs they watched. From this data, Nielsen compiled rating points that reflected the percentage of the audience watching a given show. A rating of 1,075, adequate but on the low side for a launch, reached 89% of the target demographic an average of 10 times over the five-week ad run. A rating of half that would reach 82% of the target demographic, but only an average of six times over the five weeks.

Dayparts and Representative Shows	Cost per 30-Second Ad	Target Rating Points
Prime—*Ally McBeal*	$8,500	13.0
Prime—Wednesday Movie:	2,200	4.0
Prime—*Who Wants to Be a Millionaire*	8,500	13.5
Daytime—Martha Stewart	400	2.0
Daytime—CBS Soaps	200	1.5
Early News—5–5:30 p.m. News	650	2.5
Early Morning—*Good Morning America*	450	2.5

For Top Five U.S. Markets, Same Demographic, Same Show Profile:

Market	Cost
New York	$1,976,925
Los Angeles	1,622,175
Chicago	1,038,450
Philadelphia	936,863
San Francisco	933,638
	$6,508,050

Arnatt and McDonald had developed five different ad campaigns, which Cassayre and her director of brand marketing had reduced to the three on the table. "What we're trying to convey," she explained, "is that we understand gurus. We know what makes them tick, what they want out of life, why they became gurus in the first place, and what success smells like to them. What do you think?"

The first set of ads walked the reader through a self-test (see **Exhibit 11**). "Are you a guru? Take this simple quiz." "It's engaging," said Arnatt.

The second showed well-known, high-profile gurus going about their projects (see **Exhibit 12**). "It's very authentic," said James.

The last portrayed a wide range of ordinary gurus in their homes, clearly in the midst of a project (see **Exhibit 13**). "This is almost a visual profile," said McDonald. "It's very intimate, almost voyeuristic."

EXHIBIT 10 Selected Print Titles

Source: Company information.

Title	Description	Frequency	Circ.	Readers/ Copy	8-page Est. Cost
AdWeek's Technology Marketing Intelligence	Combination with *AdWeek*, *Brandweek*, and *Media Week*. Targets ad agency executive, brand managers, and people involved in marketing the internet, software, and telecom.	W	84,000	4.85	$158,936
Home Office Computing Inc.	Edited for business owners, telecommuters and people who work from home. Offers business and technology solutions for growing companies. Monster.com has advertised, Freeagent.com has not.	M	504,151	1.9	$197,064
Business Week 2.0	Provides ideas and information for readers to succeed in a changing business environment. 64% tradition business/36% internet. Circulation is small but growing. Competition advertised.	M	660,144	2.6	$295,351
Fast Company	Describes applications of business innovations to your company. Focus on "workstyle." AdAge is magazine of the year. Younger reader, 60% aren't in top management. Competition advertises regularly. Very cluttered.	M	160,000	2.0	$132,198
Wired	Covers changes in business, politics, culture, and society due to technological change. Broad based readership. Competition advertises regularly.	10x/yr.	326,695	3.2	$233,380
Industry Standard	Delivers sophisticated coverage of the people, companies, and business models shaping the economy. Reaches senior level executives. Weekly.	BiM	1,064,766	5.02	$206,551
PC Computing	Addresses business professionals who think strategically about the business benefits of new technology, especially internet.	W	125,000	3.2	$96,390
Internet Week	News and analysis for IS/Network managers. Median age is 39.	M	1,044,252	3.1	$189,114
Interactive Week	News and analysis for IT and business leaders involved in e-commerce and communications. 35% of readers are consultants, 30% manage outsourcing, 41% do not read another tech or business title. Freeagent advertises frequently.	W	215,000	2.52	$168,881
Information Week	Focuses on IT, not web. 10% of readers are computer, network, or non-computer consultants.	W	200,000	2.58	$154,562
PC Week	Delivers breaking news on technology, platforms and trends to over 217,000 IT professionals. 12% consultants.	W	400,000	2.23	$250,461
Communication Arts	Offers product and software reviews and legal advice to designers, art directors and others involved in visual communication. Largest design magazine.	W	400,000	5.57	$288,742
Creativity	Focuses on creative process of advertising in several genres: film, print, video, and graphics.	8x/yr.	73,246	N/A	$57,865
Men's Journal	Redefines success as adventure. Edited for modern, active, achievement-oriented man who wants to achieve balance in his lifestyle.	10x/yr.	23,668	N/A	$46,634
Utne Reader	Keeps readers abreast of new ideas and emerging issues. Each edition presents articles and reviews selected from independently published newsletters, magazines and journals. Covers include politics, international issues, the arts, science, education, economics and psychology.	M	551,635	3.11	$355,499
Vanity Fair	Presents issues, events, and people that define the times. Quality editorial. Broad, upscale reach. 50% more self-employed than average.	BiM	157,493	4.5	$141,494
In Style	Guide to lives and lifestyles of the world's fascinating people and to their personal style. Broad reach.	M	1,064,766	3.3	$540,096
Self	Top women's magazine for lifestyle improvements. Addresses a broad spectrum of life issues from fitness to adventure.	M	1,360,163	3.65	$425,340
		M	400,000	3.45	$297,371

EXHIBIT 11 First Possibility

Source: Company information.

Are you a guru? Take this simple test:

Commuting's a breeze—you just:

a) Hop in your car.

b) Put on your slippers.

289

Exhibit 11 (Continued)

Whenever you need inspiration you take a trip to the:

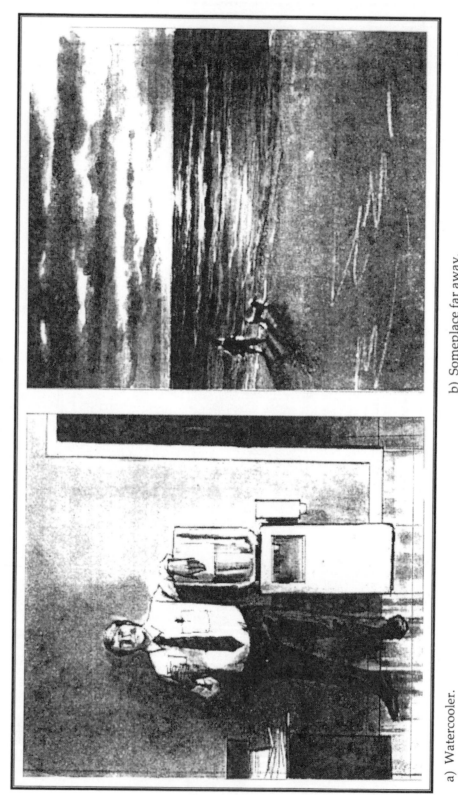

a) Watercooler.

b) Someplace far away.

Exhibit 11 (Continued)

You could use a nice hot cup of coffee, so you:

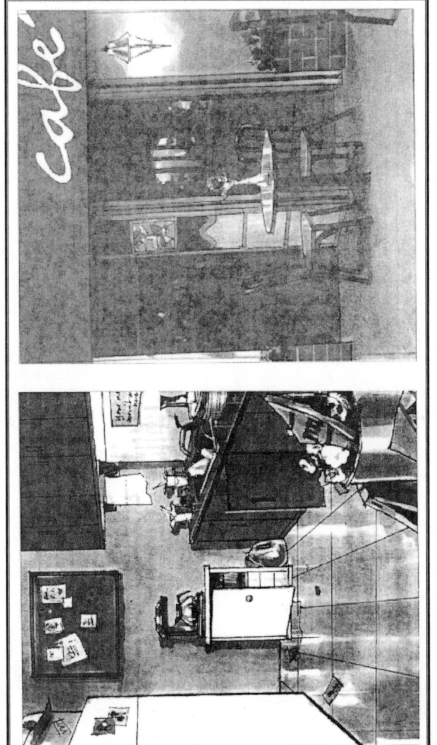

a) Head for the 5th floor kitchen.

b) Take a walk down the street.

How'd you do?

Not everyone makes their living from a conference room or cubicle. If you're your own boss, we're your own network. Visit Guru.com. It's a virtual watercooler for the entire freelance industry. Find gigs, get valuable information, and meet other gurus like yourself.

Guru.com

EXHIBIT 12 **Second Possibility**

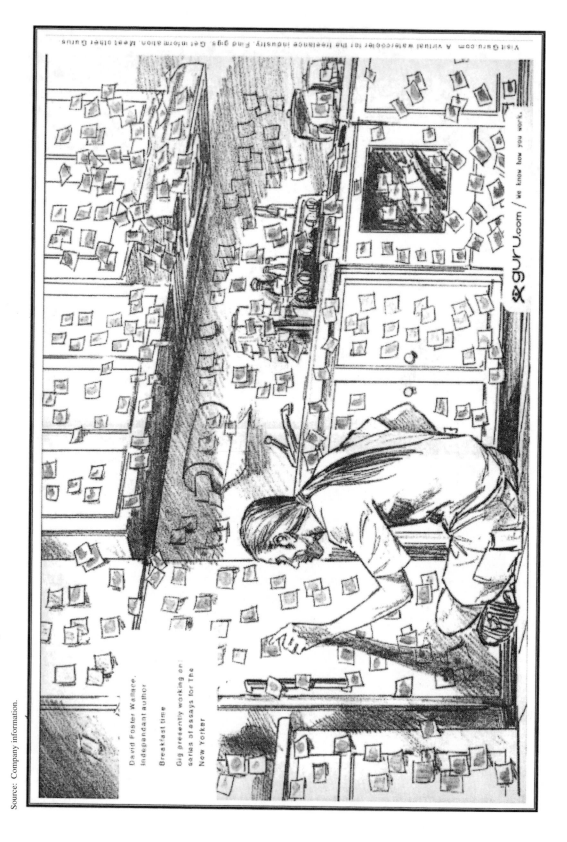

Source: Company information.

EXHIBIT 12 (Continued)

EXHIBIT 12 (Continued)

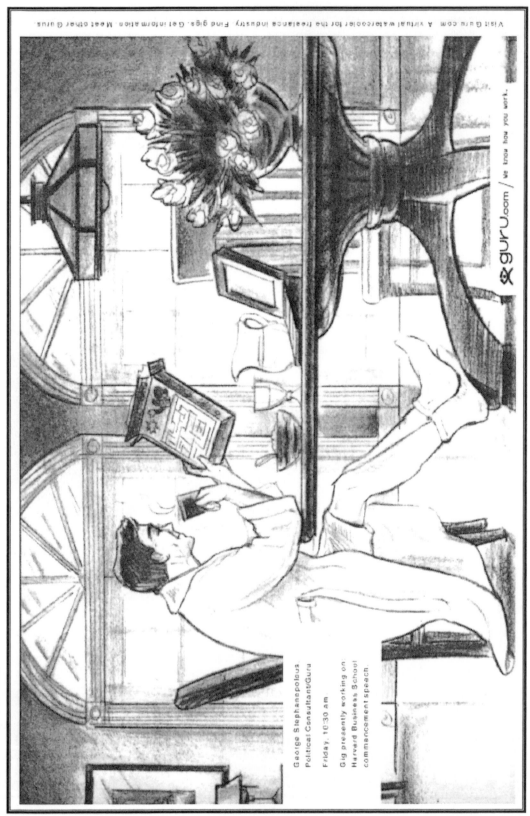

EXHIBIT 12 (Continued)

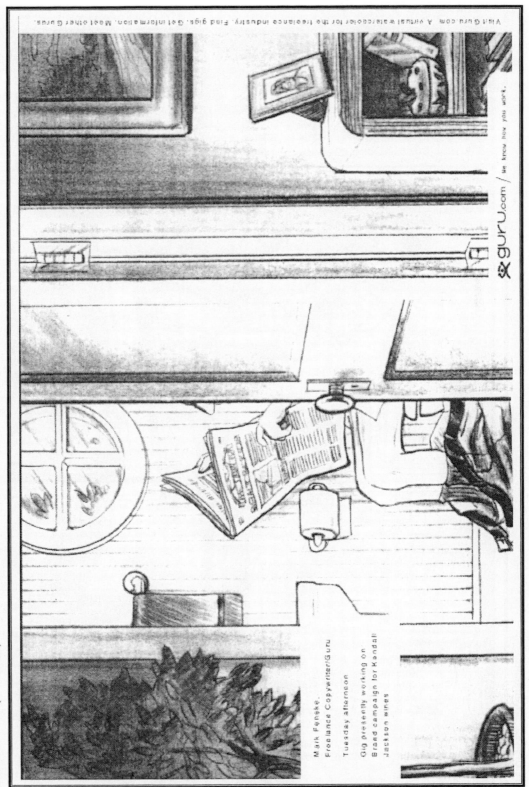

EXHIBIT 12 (Continued)

EXHIBIT 13 Third Possibility

Source: Company information.

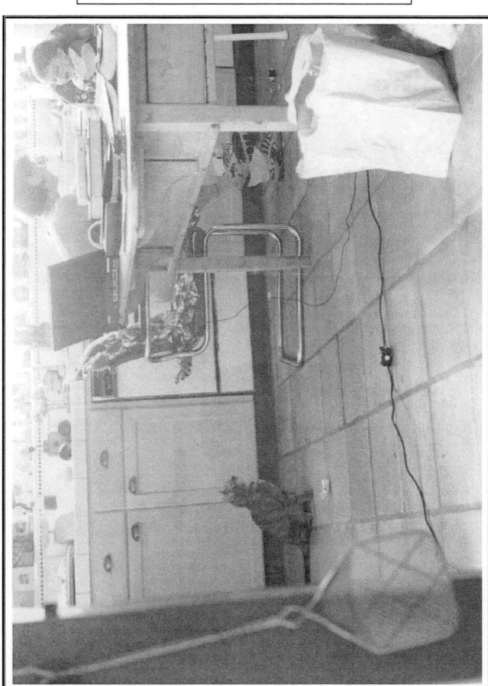

You always know who's picking up the tab. And how to expense it. You're more than an independent professional—you're a guru. Whether you're a virtual CEO, designer, or anything in between, you now have a home on the web. An all-inclusive source for projects, resources like health insurance and tax tips, and a place to connect with other gurus just like you.

Guru.com—Power for the independent professional.

EXHIBIT 13 (Continued)

Go ahead and multitask. As an independent professional, you're an expert in your field, and the master of your day—you're a guru. Whether you're a virtual CEO, designer, or anything in between, you now have a home on the web. A gold mine of projects, resources like health insurance and tax tips, and a place to connect with other gurus just like you.

Guru.com—Power for the independent professional.

EXHIBIT 13 (Continued)

You always know who's picking up the tab. And how to expense it. Whether you're a marketing consultant, an editor, or a web designer, you now have a home on the web. An all-inclusive source for projects, resources, know-how (like tax advice), and a place to connect with other gurus just like you.

Guru.com—Power for the independent professional.

None of the ads said, "Sign up and we'll get you a job." Cassayre felt very strongly on that point. "That would be over-promising, which is always a sure-fire way to get in trouble with your customers."

The Decision

James looked across the table at his brother, [*sic*] McDonald, Arnatt, and Cassayre:

I know I sound like a broken record, but it's so much money. And it's unproven. We've used other methods—remember when we went to MacWorld? That one event cost $10,000 but we registered 2,000 gurus and talked to over 5,000 people. Maybe we should just do more events—I'm talking at Guy Kawasaki's Garage.com bootcamp next week and we'll get a lot of exposure that way.

Jon shook his head. "There's really something to being early to market, as our Board of Directors has said. With the right message, we can solidify our leadership position, we can own the category. And sure, we're going to increase our monthly spend, but think of the spin-off benefits."

Cassayre looked at the brothers and smiled:

I've had this same discussion at every place I've worked. What do we say, whom do we target, how do we reach them, what do we spend. Brand campaigns are hard because we're not selling a thing; we're selling awareness. We've been acquiring customers very efficiently, now it's a strategic shift and it can be hard. But guys, you need to trust me on this one. It's time to take our marketing to the next level. It's time to launch the brand.

Chapter 17

Colgate-Palmolive Company: The Precision Toothbrush

Nathalie Laidler   **John Quelch**

In August 1992, Colgate-Palmolive (CP) was poised to launch a new toothbrush in the United States, tentatively named Colgate Precision. CP's Oral Care Division had been developing this technologically superior toothbrush for over three years but now faced a highly competitive market with substantial new product activity.

Susan Steinberg, Precision product manager, had managed the entire new product development process and now had to recommend positioning, branding, and communication strategies to division general manager Nigel Burton.

Company Background

With 1991 sales of $6.06 billion and a gross profit of $2.76 billion, CP was a global leader in household and personal care products. Total worldwide research and development expenditures for 1991 were $114 million, and media advertising expenditures totaled $428 million.

CP's five-year plan for 1991 to 1995 emphasized new product launches and entry into new geographic markets, along with improved efficiencies in manufacturing and distribution and a continuing focus on core consumer products. In 1991, $243 million was spent to upgrade 25 of CP's 91 manufacturing plants; 275 new products were introduced worldwide; several strategic acquisitions (e.g., of the Mennen men's toiletries company) were

Research Associate Nathalie Laidler prepared this case under the supervision of Professor John Quelch as the basis for class discussion rather than to illustrate either the effective or ineffective handling of an administrative situation. Proprietary data has been disguised.

EXHIBIT 1 Income Statements for Colgate-Palmolive Toothbrushes: 1989–1992

Source: Company records.

	1989		1990		1991		1992E	
Unit sales ('000s)	55,296		63,576		70,560		78,336	
Net sales ($'000s)	43,854	(100%)	57,248	(100%)	77,001	(100%)	91,611	(100%)
Cost of sales	23,988	(55%)	28,190	(49%)	36,827	(48%)	44,846	(49%)
Total fixed overhead	4,429	(11%)	6,304	(11%)	10,007	(13%)	11,423	(12%)
Total advertising								
Media	3,667	(8%)	6,988	(12%)	8,761	(11%)	9,623	(11%)
Consumer promotions	4,541	(10%)	5,893	(10%)	5,286	(7%)	6,978	(8%)
Trade promotions	3,458	(8%)	4,134	(7%)	6,287	(8%)	7,457	(8%)
Operating profit	3,744	(9%)	5,739	(10%)	9,833	(13%)	11,284	(12%)

completed; and manufacturing began in China and Eastern Europe. Reuben Mark, CP's C.E.O since 1984, had been widely praised for his leadership in transforming a "sleepy and inefficient" company into a lean and profitable one. Since 1985, gross margins had climbed from 39% to 45% while annual volume growth since 1986 had averaged 5%. Although international sales remained CP's strong suit, accounting for 64% of sales and 67% of profits in 1991, the company faced tough competition in international markets from Procter & Gamble, Unilever, Nestle's L'Oreal Division, Henkel of Germany, and Kao of Japan.

Colgate-Palmolive's Oral Care Business

In 1991, CP held 43% of the world toothpaste market and 16% of the world toothbrush market. Other oral care products included dental floss and mouth rinses. A team of 170 CP researchers worked on new technologies for oral care products, and in 1991, new products launched in the U.S. market included Colgate Baking Soda toothpaste and the Colgate Angle and Wild Ones toothbrushes.

In 1991, worldwide sales of CP's oral care products increased 12% to $1.3 billion, accounting for 22% of CP's total sales. CP's U.S. toothbrush sales in 1991 reached $77 million, with operating profits of $9.8 million. Toothbrushes represented 19% of CP's U.S. Oral Care Division sales and profits, and CP held the number one position in the U.S. retail toothbrush market with a 23.3% volume share.

Exhibit 1 presents operating statements for CP's U.S. toothbrush business since 1989. CP offered two lines of toothbrushes in 1991—the Colgate Classic and the Colgate Plus. Colgate Classic was positioned in the "value" segment and was CP's original entry in the toothbrush market, while Colgate Plus was positioned as a higher-quality product in the "professional" segment.

The U.S. Toothbrush Market

As early as 3000 B.C., ancient Egyptians used toothbrushes fashioned from twigs. In the twentieth century, a major design advance occurred in 1938 with the launch of Dr. West's Miracle Tuft Toothbrush, the first nylon-bristle brush. In the late 1940s, Oral-B began selling a soft-bristle brush which was better for the gums, and in 1961 Broxodent launched the first electric toothbrush.[1] Until the late 1970s, toothbrushes were widely viewed by consumers as a commodity and were purchased primarily on price. More recently, new

[1] As of 1991, electric toothbrushes were used by only 6% of U.S. households.

EXHIBIT 2
Chronology of Toothbrush Innovations in the U.S.

Source: Company records.

Date	New Product Introductions	Main Feature
1950s	Oral-B Classic	Traditional square head
1977	Johnson & Johnson Reach	First angled handle
1985	Colgate Plus	First diamond-shaped head
1986	Lever Bros. Aim	Slightly longer handle
1988	Johnson & Johnson Prevent	Aids brushing at 45 angle
	Colgate Plus Sensitive Gums	Softer bristles
1989	Pepsodent	"Commodity" brush
	Oral-B Ultra	Improved handle
1990	J&J Neon Reach	Neon-colored handle
	Oral-B Art Series	Cosmetic feature
1991	Colgate Plus Angle Handle	Diamond-shaped & angled handle
	Colgate Plus Wild Ones	Cosmetic feature
	J&J Advanced Reach Design	Rubber-ridged, non-slip handle
	Oral-B Indicator	Bristles change color
	Aquafresh Flex	Flexible handle neck
	Pfizer Plax	Groove for thumb
1992	Crest Complete	Rippled bristles
	Colgate Precision	Triple action bristles

product launches had increased and performance benefits had become increasingly important purchase criteria. (**Exhibit 2** summarizes new product introductions in the category since 1980.)

In 1991, the U.S. Oral Care market was $2.9 billion in retail sales and had grown at an annual rate of 6.1% since 1986. Toothpaste accounted for 46% of this market, mouth rinses 24%, toothbrushes 15.5% ($453 million in retail sales), with dental floss and other products making up the remainder. Dollar sales of toothbrushes had grown at an average rate of 9.3% per annum since 1987, but, in 1992 they increased by 21% in value and 18% in volume, due to the introduction of 47 new products and line extensions during 1991–1992. In the same period, media support increased by 49% and consumer coupon circulation by 48%. Consumers took more interest in the category and increased their purchase frequency. The trade, for whom toothbrushes represented a profitable, high-margin business, responded by increasing in-store promotional support and advertising features. Dollar growth exceeded volume growth due to the emergence of a "super-premium" sub-category of toothbrushes partly offset by downward pressure on average retail prices in mass-merchandiser channels and because of growth in the sales of private label toothbrushes. Unit sales growth in 1993, however, was projected to be slower due to a buildup in household inventories of toothbrushes in 1992 as a result of increased sampling of free brushes through dentists and an abnormally high number of "two-for-one" consumer promotions.

Product Segments

In the 1980s, industry executives divided the toothbrush category into two segments: value and professional. Many consumers traded up to professional, higher-priced toothbrushes with a resulting erosion of the value segment despite growth in private-label sales. The late 1980s saw the emergence of super-premium brushes (priced above $2.00). By 1992, super-premium brushes, with retail prices between $2.29 and $2.89, accounted for 35% of unit volume and 46% of dollar sales. Professional brushes, priced between $1.59 and $2.09, accounted for a corresponding 41% and 42%, and value brushes, priced on average at $1.29, accounted for 24% and 12%.

TABLE A   **Major New Products in the Super-Premium Toothbrush Segment**

Product/Manufacturer	Feature	Benefit	Reason	Tag-line	Launch Date	# SKUs
Oral-B Indicator ORAL-B (GILLETTE)	Indicator Bristles	Tells you when to change toothbrush	Blue band fades halfway. Dental heritage	The brand more dentists use	7/91	4 adult
Reach Advanced Design JOHNSON & JOHNSON	Angled neck; raised rubber ridges on handle	Cleans in even the hardest-to-reach places	Slimmed down, tapered head	Feel the difference	8/91	3 adult
Crest Complete PROCTER & GAMBLE	Rippled bristle design. Handle with rubber grip	Reaches between teeth like a dental tool	Rippled end-rounded bristles	Only Crest could make a brush this complete	8/91 (test) 9/92 (national)	10 adult
Aquafresh Flex SMITHKLINE BEECHAM	Pressure sensitive, flexible neck linking brush and handle	Prevents gum irritation	Flexes as you brush	For gentle dental care	8/91 (Flex) 9/92 (line extension)	6 adult 1 child

In 1992, three players dominated the U.S. toothbrush market overall: Colgate-Palmolive and Johnson & Johnson, whose brushes were positioned in the professional segment; and Oral-B, whose brushes were positioned in the super-premium segment. New entrants in the early 1990s included Procter & Gamble and Smithkline Beecham; both had positioned their new product launches in the super-premium segment. **Table A** profiles the principal new products offered in the super-premium toothbrush segment in 1992.

Toothbrushes differed by bristle type (firm, medium, soft, and extra soft) and by head size (full/adult, compact, and child/youth). Firm-bristle brushes accounted for 8% of toothbrushes sold but were declining at 13% a year. Medium-bristle brushes accounted for 39% and were declining at 4% a year. Soft-bristle brushes held a 48% market share and were growing at 7% per year. Extra-soft-bristle brushes held only a 5% share but were growing even more rapidly. Sixty-nine percent of toothbrushes were sold with adult, full-sized heads, 17% had compact heads, and 13% had child/youth-sized heads.

In the late 1980s, many new toothbrushes were introduced on the basis of aesthetic rather than functional features. The children's segment in particular had seen a variety of new products. For example, in 1988 and 1989 new toothbrushes targeting children featured sparkling handles, Bugs Bunny and other characters, and glow-in-the-dark handles. By 1991, however, new product introductions were again focused on technical performance improvements, such as greater plaque removal and ease of use.

Consumer Behavior

CP's consumer research indicated that consumers of the baby boom generation (adults born in the 1940s, 1950s and early 1960s) were becoming more concerned about the health of their gums as opposed to cavity prevention and were willing to pay a premium for new products addressing this issue. CP estimated that 82% of toothbrush purchases were unplanned, and research showed that consumers were relatively unfamiliar with toothbrush prices. Although consumers were willing to experiment with new toothbrushes, they replaced their brushes on average only once every 7.5 months in 1991 (versus 8.6 months in 1990), while dental professionals recommended replacement every three months. Due to the prevalence of "two-for-one" offers, purchase frequency lagged replacement frequency,

EXHIBIT 3
Brand Decision
Factors for
Consumers

Source: Company records.

Main Reasons for Using a Brand	Percent of Consumers
Fits most comfortably in my mouth	63%
Best for getting at hard-to-reach places	52
The bristles are the right softness	46
The bristles are the right firmness	36
Toothbrush my dentist recommends	35
Important part of my oral care regimen	30

Note: Respondents could check multiple items.

with consumers purchasing toothbrushes once every 11.6 months in 1991 (compared to 12.4 months in 1990 and an expected 9.7 months for 1992).[2] Unlike toothpaste, toothbrushes were not typically shared by members of the same household.

Most consumers agreed that toothbrushes were as important as toothpaste to effective oral hygiene and that the primary role of a toothbrush was to remove food particles; plaque removal and gum stimulation were considered secondary. Proper brushing was seen as key to the prevention of most dental problems. According to CP research, 45% of consumers brushed before breakfast, 57% after breakfast, 28% after lunch, 24% after dinner and 71% before bed. Forty-eight percent of consumers claimed to change their brushes at least every three months; the trigger to purchase a new brush for 70% of them was when their toothbrush-bristles became visibly worn. Eleven percent decided to switch to a new brush after seeing their dentists, and only 3% admitted to purchasing on impulse.[3] Sixty-five percent of consumers had more than one toothbrush, 24% kept a toothbrush at work, and 54% had a special toothbrush for traveling.

Brand choice was based on features, comfort and professional recommendations. **Exhibit 3** summarizes the main reasons why consumers used specific brands. Consumers chose a brush to fit their individual needs: size and shape of the mouth, sensitivity of gums, and personal brushing style. The handle, bristles, and head shape were perceived to be the most important physical features of a toothbrush.

Consumers differed in the intensity of their involvement in oral hygiene. **Table B** summarizes the buying behavior of the three groups. Therapeutic brushers aimed to avoid oral care problems, while cosmetic brushers emphasized preventing bad breath and/or ensuring white teeth. Uninvolved consumers were not motivated by oral care benefits and adjusted their behavior only when confronted by oral hygiene problems.

Competition

Exhibit 4 lists the major brands and product prices for each of the three toothbrush product segments. **Exhibit 5** shows the number and type of stockkeeping units (SKUs) for each major brand, and **Exhibits 6** and **7** summarize market shares over time and by class of trade. Major competitor brands in the super-premium segment included Oral-B, Reach Advanced Design, Crest Complete, and Aquafresh Flex.

Oral-B (owned by Gillette) had been the market leader since the 1960s. In 1991, it held a 23.1% volume market share and a 30.7% value share of U.S retail sales, with 27 SKUs. Oral-B relied heavily on professional endorsements and was known as "the dentist's toothbrush." In July 1991, Oral-B launched the Indicator brush, priced at a 15% premium to its other brushes. The Indicator brush had a patch of blue bristles that faded to white

[2] In 1992, consumers purchased toothbrushes more frequently than in 1991.

[3] Dentists played a significant role, both as a source of information on proper brushing techniques and as a distributor of toothbrushes. At any time, one in four consumers was using a toothbrush given to them by a dentist.

TABLE B
Consumer
Segmentation of
Toothbrush Users

Involved Oral Health Consumers—Therapeutic Brushers (46% of adults)	Involved Oral Health Consumers—Cosmetic Brushers (21% of adults)	Uninvolved Oral Health Consumers (33% of adults)
Differentiate among products. Search out functionally effective products	Search for products that effectively deliver cosmetic benefits	View products as the same. Lack of interest in product category
Buy and use products for themselves	Buy and use products for themselves	Buy and use products for all family members
85% brush at least twice a day, 62% use a professional brush and 54% floss regularly	85% brush twice a day, 81% use mouthwash, 54% use breath fresheners, 69% floss, 54% use a professional brush	20% brush once a day or less, 28% use only regular toothbrushes 54% floss 66% use mouthwash
Major toothbrush brands used are Oral-B Angle and Oral-B Regular followed by Colgate Plus and Reach.	Major toothbrush brands used are Colgate Classic and Oral-B Regular followed by Colgate Plus and Oral-B Angle	Major toothbrush brands used are Colgate Classic and Oral-B Regular followed by Colgate Plus and Reach

EXHIBIT 4
Toothbrush Brand
Prices: 1992

Source: Company records.

	Manufacturer List Price	Manufacturer Net Price	Average Retail Selling Price (Food Channel)
Super-premium			
Oral-B Indicator	$2.13	$1.92	$2.65
Oral-B Regular	1.85	1.78	2.51
Crest Complete	1.67	1.67	2.40
Reach Advanced	1.75	1.66	2.38
Aquafresh Flex	1.85	1.61	2.32
Professional			
Colgate Plus	1.42	1.35	2.00
Reach Regular	1.37	1.30	2.01
Pepsodent Prof.	1.20	1.08	1.88
Value			
Colgate Classic	0.69	0.69	1.22
Pepsodent Regular	0.91	0.48	1.25

Note: Net price was the effective manufacturer's price to retailers after a variety of discounts.

EXHIBIT 5
Principal Toothbrush
Brand Product Lines:
August 1992

Source: Company records.

	Number of Stockkeeping Units	
Brand	Adult	Child/Teen
Colgate	28	8
Oral-B	16	5
Reach	14	4
Crest Complete	10	0
Aquafresh Flex	6	1
Lever	7	2
Plax	2	1
Total	83	21

EXHIBIT 6   **Principal Toothbrush Brand Unit and Dollar Market Shares: 1989–992E**

Source: Company records.

Brand	1989 Vol (%)	1989 $ (%)	1990 Vol (%)	1990 $ (%)	1991 Vol (%)	1991 $ (%)	1992E Vol (%)	1992E $ (%)
COLGATE								
Plus	12.0	12.6	13.7	15.2	16.9	18.5	17.3	18.5
Classic	8.5	6.6	8.1	6.2	6.4	4.9	4.9	2.9
TOTAL	20.5	19.2	21.8	21.4	23.3	23.4	22.2	21.4
ORAL-B								
Oral-B Indicator	0.0	0.0	0.0	0.0	1.0	1.3	3.7	4.9
TOTAL	24.0	31.7	24.5	32.6	23.1	30.7	19.8	26.2
J & J								
Reach	18.1	20.5	18.2	20.0	17.8	20.0	15.2	15.8
Reach Advanced Design	0.0	0.0	0.0	0.0	0.7	0.9	4.0	5.2
Prevent	2.5	2.7	1.6	1.9	0.7	1.1	0.2	0.1
TOTAL	20.6	23.2	19.8	21.9	19.2	22.0	19.4	21.1
LEVER	10.5	10.4	9.8	9.0	7.2	6.6	5.0	4.0
CREST	0.0	0.0	0.0	0.0	0.0	0.0	2.0	2.6
AQUA-FRESH	0.0	0.0	0.0	0.0	0.9	1.1	4.6	5.7
BUTLER	N/A	N/A	N/A	N/A	2.0	2.4	2.0	2.2
PRIVATE LABEL	N/A	N/A	N/A	N/A	11.2	5.9	11.5	6.1

Note: N/A = not available.

EXHIBIT 7
Principal Toothbrush Brand Unit and Dollar Market Shares by Class of Trade: 1991

Source: Company records.

	Food Vol (%)	Food $ (%)	Drug Vol (%)	Drug $ (%)	Mass Vol (%)	Mass $ (%)
COLGATE						
Plus	18.9	21.3	9.6	11.4	29.3	31.4
Classic	7.0	4.8	4.5	3.7	3.9	3.2
TOTAL	25.9	26.1	14.1	15.1	33.2	34.6
ORAL-B						
Oral-B Indicator	0.9	1.1	1.0	1.5	0.7	0.9
TOTAL	20.5	28.2	25.1	34.1	22.4	27.6
J & J						
Reach	22.3	23.8	14.3	16.6	18.3	20.7
Reach Advanced Design	1.2	N/A	0.3	0.4	0.3	0.4
Prevent	0.8	1.2	0.8	0.9	0.5	0.6
TOTAL	23.2	25.0	15.1	17.5	18.8	21.4
LEVER	9.1	8.9	5.8	5.6	6.3	7.4
CREST (TX test market)	5.1	6.5	0.0	0.0	0.0	N/A
AQUA-FRESH	4.9	N/A	0.4	0.5	0.3	0.5
BUTLER	1.3	2.0	3.5	6.6	0.5	0.9
PRIVATE LABEL	10.7	5.5	17.4	10.6	4.4	2.4

when it was time for replacement (usually after two to three months). In 1992, consumer promotions were expected to cost $4.5 million (5% of sales) and include $1.00-off coupons, "buy-one-get-one-free" offers and $2.00 mail-in refunds. Media expenditures for 1992 were estimated at $11.2 million (12.7% of sales). Television commercials would continue to feature "Rob the dentist" using the Oral-B Indicator product. In 1991, Oral-B's operating margin on toothbrushes, after advertising and promotion costs, was estimated to be approximately 20% of factory sales.

In 1992, Oral-B announced that it would restage its dental floss, roll out a new mouthwash, and possibly introduce a specialty toothpaste. Oral-B management stated that "to be a leader in the oral care category, we must compete in all areas of oral care."[4]

Johnson & Johnson (J&J) entered the U.S. toothbrush market in the 1970s with the Reach brand, which, in 1991, comprised 18 SKUs. In 1988, J&J introduced a second product line under the brand name Prevent, a brush with a beveled handle to help consumers brush at a 45% angle—the recommended brushing technique. This product however, was being phased out by 1992. In 1991, J&J ranked third in the U.S. retail toothbrush market with a 19.4% volume share and a 21.8% value share. The Reach line was positioned as the toothbrush that enabled consumers to brush in even the hardest-to-reach places, thereby increasing the efficiency of brushing. New products included Glow Reach (1990) and Advanced Design Reach (1991), which offered tapered heads, angled necks, and unique non-slip handles. Reach Between, scheduled for launch in September of 1992, had an angled neck and rippled bristles that targeted the areas between the teeth. Consumer promotions in 1992 were estimated at $4.6 million (8.6% of sales) and included 60¢ coupons, $1.00 refunds by mail, and "buy-two-get-one-free" offers. Media expenditures were expected to reach $17.1 million (31.7% of sales) with a heavy reliance on television commercials. Johnson & Johnson's expected 1992 operating margin on toothbrushes, after advertising and promotion costs, was 8.4% of factory sales.

Procter & Gamble (P&G) was the most recent entrant in the toothbrush market with Crest Complete, an extension of the company's toothpaste brand name, Crest. Based on successful test markets in Houston and San Antonio from August 1991 to August 1992, P&G was expected to launch Crest Complete nationally in September 1992. The brush had captured a 13% value share in test markets and was expected to reach similar total market share levels in its first year after full launch. The product had long, rippled bristles of different lengths, designed to reach between the teeth. Crest Complete claimed to have "the ability to reach between the teeth up to 37% farther than leading flat brushes." It was expected to be introduced at a manufacturer's list price to retailers of $1.67 and capture a 2.0% volume share and a 2.6% value share of the U.S. retail market by the end of 1992. Consumer promotions already announced included 55 cent coupons and $1.99 refunds on toothbrushes purchased from floor stands. Media expenditures for the last quarter of 1992 were estimated at $6.4 million; television commercials would carry the theme "Teeth aren't flat, so why is your brush."

Smithkline Beecham entered the U.S. toothbrush market in August 1991 with Aquafresh Flex, an extension of the company's toothpaste brand. Aquafresh Flex toothbrushes had flexible handles that allowed for gentle brushing. By the end of 1991, Aquafresh Flex held a 0.9% share by volume and 1.1% by value of the U.S. retail market with six SKUs. In September 1992, the line was expected to expand to include two adult compact heads and one child brush. The 1992 promotion plan, estimated at $4.6 million (25% of sales), included $1.99 mail refunds, "buy-two-get-one-free" offers, toothbrush on-pack with toothpaste, and a self-liquidating premium offer of towels. Media expenditures at $10 million (almost 50% of sales) included television commercials that showed the product brushing a tomato without damaging it, to demonstrate the "flexibility and gentleness" of the brush. Smithkline Beecham was expected to make an operating loss on toothbrushes in 1992.

Other competitors included *Lever, Pfizer,* and *Sunstar.* In 1991, Lever offered three lines of toothbrushes: Aim; Pepsodent Professional with 5 SKUs; and Pepsodent Regular with 4 SKUs. Combined, Lever held a 7.2% volume and 6.6% value share of the U.S. retail market in 1991. Lever's products were sold primarily in the value segment and the

---

[4] *Brandweek,* October 12, 1992.

company did not have a track record of innovation in the category. Pfizer entered the market in June 1991 with its Plax brush, which had a special groove for the thumb; it had captured 1.8% of the retail market by year end. Sunstar, with its Butler brand, held 2% of the retail market in 1992 and 19% of the $45 million in toothbrushes distributed through dentists.

Advertising and Promotion

In the toothpaste category, it was hard to increase primary demand, so new products tended to steal sales from existing products. In the case of toothbrushes, however, increased advertising and promotion enhanced the category's visibility which, in turn, seemed to fuel consumer demand.

As the pace of new product introductions quickened in the late 1980s, the advertising media expenditures needed to launch a new toothbrush rose: Johnson & Johnson spent $8 million in media support to introduce its new Reach brush; Oral-B spent $10 million to launch its Indicator brush; and Procter & Gamble was expected to support its Crest Complete brush with $15 million in media expenditures. Total media spending for the category, primarily on television advertising, was estimated to total $55 million in 1992 and $70 million in 1993. **Exhibit 8** shows media expenditures and shares of voice for the main toothbrush brands. **Exhibit 9** summarizes the main message in each brand's commercials, and **Exhibit 10** summarizes the copy strategy of Colgate Plus's television commercials over time. Advertising and promotion expenditures for Colgate toothbrushes are given in **Exhibit 11.**

EXHIBIT 8
Principal Toothbrush Media Advertising Expenditures and Shares of Voice: 1991–1992E

Source: Company records.

	1991		1992E	
	Media $MM	Share Voice(%)	Media $MM	Share Voice(%)
Colgate Plus	7.0	19	8	15
Reach	15.5	42	17.1	31
Oral-B	10.2	27	11.2	20
Crest Complete	0.4	1	6.4	12
Aquafresh Flex	0.4	1	10	18
Pfizer Plax	2.3	6	2.2	4

EXHIBIT 9   **Television and Advertising Copy Strategies and Executions for Competitor Toothbrush Brands: 1991**

Source: Company records.

Product	Message	Tag-line	Execution
Crest Complete	Has rippled bristles to reach between teeth (37% farther than a flat bristled brush).	"Only Crest could make a brush this complete."	Visual comparison of Crest Complete versus a dental tool.
Aquafresh Flex	Has a flexible neck that is gentle on the gums.	"For gentle dental care"	Spokesperson/demonstration
Advanced Design Reach	Features a new head/handle design.	"Advanced Design Reach"	Visual demonstration of product design with cartoon character.
Oral-B Indicator	Will tell you when to change your toothbrush.	"The brand more dentists use"	Testimonial with demonstration.
Plax	Is especially designed to remove plaque.	"The new Plax, plaque removing toothbrush"	Computer graphic display of product design.

EXHIBIT 10   Colgate Plus Television Advertising; Copy Strategies and Execution: 1985–1992

Source: Company records.

Date	Marketing Situation	Colgate Copy Platform	Execution	Tag-line
1985–1986	First toothbrush with diamond-shaped head. First professional toothbrush from a leading oral care company.	Unique head. Scientific/technical tone. Comfort and efficacy.	Product depicted as a hero.	"Shaped to keep your whole mouth in shape"
1987–1990	Aim enters market, spurring increased competition. Colgate Plus market share suffers.	Diamond-shaped head. Evolution of comfort/ efficacy. Lighter contemporary tone Implied superiority Emphasizes visual differences	"Odd looking" toothbrush character introduced in bathroom setting.	"Odd looking, super-cleaning, comfy feeling toothbrush"
1991	Need to re-energize Colgate advertising copy given long duration of "Odd Looking" campaign.	Diamond shape fits mouth and removes plaque from hard-to-reach places.	The "Odd looking" character in a dental chair. Implied dental recommendation.	"Because your smile was meant to last a lifetime"
1992	Increased competitive activity and consequent need for harder-hitting copy.	Plaque focus. Efficacy message	"Armed to the Teeth" execution where the bristles are soldiers.	"In the fight against plaque, it's a Plus"

EXHIBIT 11   Advertising and Promotion Expenditures for Colgate-Palmolive Toothbrushes: 1989–1992E ($ in thousands)

Source: Company records.

	1989		1990		1991		1992E	
Media[a]	$ 3,667	(31%)	$ 6,988	(41%)	$ 8,761	(43%)	$ 9,623	(40%)
Consumer promotions	4,541	(39%)	5,893	(35%)	5,286	(26%)	6,978	(29%)
Trade promotions	3,485	(30%)	4,134	(24%)	6,287	(31%)	7,457	(31%)
Total advertising and promotion	$11,693	(100%)	$17,015	(100%)	$20,334	(100%)	$24,058	(100%)

[a] Includes: working media expenditures; production and operating costs; and dental professional advertising.

Growing competition also increased the frequency and value of consumer promotion events. In 1992, 8% of all brushes reached consumers either free with toothpaste (as on-pack or mail-in premiums) or free with another toothbrush (buy-one-get-one-free offers). The number of coupon events for toothbrushes increased from 10 in 1990 to 33 in 1992. In the same period, the average toothbrush coupon value increased from $0.25 to $0.75.

Retail advertising features and in-store displays increased toothbrush sales. A typical CP toothbrush display increased sales by 90% over a normal shelf facing. When Colgate toothbrushes were combined with Colgate toothpaste in a single display, toothbrush sales increased by 170%. The importance of point-of-purchase displays and the variety of items, bristle qualities, and handle colors in each manufacturer's line led each to develop a variety of racks and display units for different classes of trade. CP for example, had four display systems: Counter Tops, containing 24 to 36 brushes; Floor Stands, 72 brushes; Sidekicks (used by mass merchandisers), 144 to 288 brushes; and Waterfall displays, 288 to 576 brushes. **Exhibit 12** illustrates these display racks. In 1991, the percentages of special Colgate displays accounted for by each type were 10%, 50%, 25%, and 15% respectively.

EXHIBIT 12   **Colgate Toothbrush Point-of-Sales Display Racks**

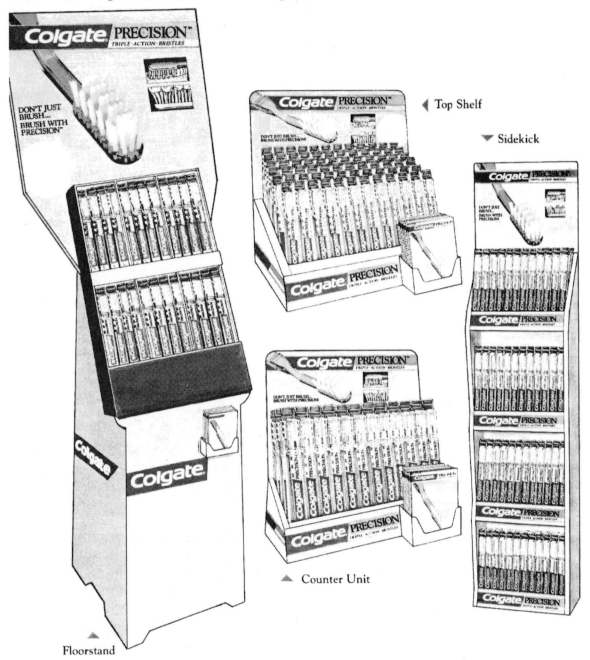

Top Shelf

Sidekick

Counter Unit

Floorstand

The CP toothbrush line held 25% to 40% of the category shelf space in most stores. To maximize retail sales, CP salespeople tried to locate the Colgate line in the middle of the category shelf space, between the Reach and the Oral-B product lines.

Distribution

In 1987, traditional food stores sold 75% of oral care products, but by 1992 they accounted for only 43% of toothbrush sales and 47% of toothpaste sales. Mass merchandisers gained share due to increased in-store promotional support. Partly in response and partly because of the increasing number of SKUs, food stores began to expand shelf space devoted to oral care products. **Exhibit 13** summarizes toothbrush retail distribution trends by volume and value.

Though purchased too infrequently to be used as a traffic builder, toothbrushes provided retailers with an average margin between 25% and 35%, twice that for toothpaste. As a result, many retailers were more receptive to adding new toothbrush products than new varieties of toothpaste. In considering which brands to stock and feature, trade buyers evaluated advertising and promotion support and each manufacturer's track record in the category. Between October 1991 and February 1992, the average number of toothbrush SKUs had increased from 31 to 35 for mass merchandisers, from 27 to 34 for drug stores and from 30 to 35 for food outlets. In September 1992, the average number of brands carried by these three classes of trade were 10, 12, and 8 respectively. Shelf space devoted to toothbrushes had also increased. Kmart for example, had increased per-store shelf space for toothbrushes from 2 to 7.5 feet in two years. Retail sales remained fragmented, with 60% of sales derived from 40% of the SKUs.

In 1992, 22% of all toothbrushes were expected to be distributed to consumers by dentists. With a dedicated sales force, Oral-B dominated this market segment. Manufacturer margins on toothbrush sales through dentists were less than half those achieved through normal retail distribution. **Exhibit 14** summarizes competitors' shares in this segment of the market.

The Precision Marketing Mix

Product Design and Testing

The Precision toothbrush was a technical innovation. In laboratory experiments, researchers used infrared motion analysis to track consumers' brushing movements and consequent levels of plaque removal. With this knowledge and through computer aided design, CP developed a unique brush with bristles of three different lengths and orientations (see **Exhibit 15**). The longer outer bristles cleaned around the gum line, the long inner bristles cleaned between teeth, and the shorter bristles cleaned the teeth surface. The result was a triple-action brushing effect. In initial clinical tests, the brush achieved an average 35% increase in plaque removal, compared with other leading toothbrushes, specifically Reach and Oral-B. At the gum line and between the teeth, the brush was even more effective, achieving double the plaque removal scores of competitor brushes.

In 1989, CP had established a task force comprising executives from R&D and Marketing, dental professionals, and outside consultants. Its mission was to "develop a superior, technical, plaque-removing device." The entire research and development process was managed from start to finish by Steinberg. The task force had five goals:

- Understanding the varying techniques consumers used when brushing their teeth. Researchers later concluded that brushing usually did a good job of removing plaque from teeth surfaces but was often ineffective at removing plaque from the gum line and between the teeth.

EXHIBIT 13 Retail Toothbrush Sales: 1989–1992E

Source: Company records.

	1989		1990		1991		1992E	
	Units MM	$ MM	Units MM	$ MM	Units MM	$ MM	Units MM	$ MM
Food stores	110 (45%)	175 (47%)	107 (44%)	175 (44%)	110 (42%)	192 (42%)	128 (42%)	236 (43%)
Drugstores	77 (32%)	123 (33%)	74 (31%)	131 (33%)	77 (29%)	148 (33%)	88 (29%)	168 (31%)
Mass merchandisers	46 (19%)	61 (17%)	44 (18%)	69 (18%)	54 (21%)	89 (20%)	68 (21%)	114 (21%)
Military	4 (2%)	5 (1%)	5 (2%)	5 (1%)	5 (2%)	5 (1%)	5 (2%)	6 (1%)
Club stores	3 (1%)	4 (1%)	9 (4%)	11 (3%)	12 (5%)	15 (3%)	15 (5%)	19 (3%)
Other	3 (1%)	4 (1%)	3 (1%)	4 (1%)	3 (1%)	4 (1%)	3 (1%)	4 (1%)

EXHIBIT 14
U.S. Professional
Dental Market for
Toothbrushes:
Competitor Market
Shares: 1991–1992E

Source: Company records.

Brand (Parent Co)	1991		1992E	
	$ millions	Market Share (%)	$ millions	Market Share (%)
Oral-B (Gillette)	14.3	34.0	14.3	31.8
Butler (Sunstar)	8.5	20.2	8.5	18.9
Colgate (CP)	6.7	16.1	8.3	18.4
Reach (J&J)	4.0	9.5	4.0	8.9
Pycopy (Block)	3.4	8.1	3.4	7.6
Aquafresh Flex (Beecham)	0.0	0.0	0.4	0.9
Crest Complete (P&G)	0.0	0.0	0.8	1.7
Other	5.1	12.1	5.4	11.9
TOTAL	42.0		45.0	

Note: Aquafresh Flex and Crest Complete were not launched until 1992.

- Testing the between-teeth access of different toothbrush designs. The tests revealed that CP's new design was superior to both Oral-B and Reach in accessing front and back teeth, using either horizontal or vertical brushing.
- Establishing an index to score clinical plaque-removal efficacy at the gum line and between teeth. In tests, a disclosing solution was used to reveal the otherwise colorless plaque, and each tooth was divided into nine specific areas. Presence of plaque was measured on each tooth area; the percentages of tooth areas affected by plaque pre- and post-usage of different brushes were then calculated.
- Creating a bristle configuration and handle design offering maximum plaque-removing efficacy. Three similar designs evolved from the above research, all incorporating bristles of different lengths that would allow freer movement of each individual tuft of bristles and thereby enable different bristle tufts to target different areas of the mouth. Clinical trials established that the new product removed an average 35% more plaque than other leading brushes and therefore helped to reduce the probability of gum disease.
- Determining, through clinical and consumer research, the efficacy and acceptance of the new toothbrush design. Extensive consumer research was carried out over a period of 18 months to test product design and characteristics, marketing concept, and competitive strengths. In addition, dental professional focus groups and product usage tests were conducted to determine the overall acceptance of Precision.

In July 1992, CP senior management decided to launch Precision early in 1993. It was decided that Precision would be priced within the super-premium segment and distributed through the same channels as Colgate Plus. However, the decision on how to position the product and the corresponding branding and communications strategies remained to be finalized.

Positioning

Precision was developed with the objective of creating the best brush possible and as such, becoming a top-of-the range, super-premium product. It could be positioned as a niche product to be targeted at consumers concerned about gum disease. As such, it could command a 15% price premium over Oral-B and would be expected to capture 3% of the U.S. toothbrush market by the end of the first year following its launch. Alternatively, Precision could be positioned as a mainstream brush, with the broader appeal of being the most effective brush available on the market. It was estimated that, as a mainstream product, Precision could capture 10% of the market by the end of the first year. Steinberg developed

EXHIBIT 15   Reproductions of the Colgate Precision Toothbrush

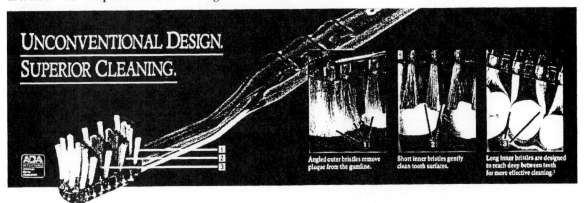

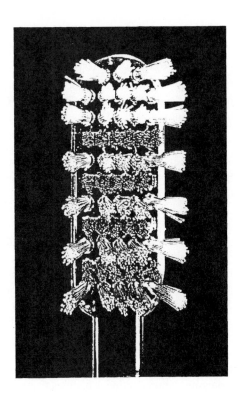

TABLE C
How Unit Volumes
Reach Consumer

	Niche Positioning Strategy	Mainstream Positioning Strategy
# units retail	Year 1 = 8 MM, Year 2 = 15 MM.	Year 1 = 27 MM, Year 2 = 44 MM.
# units consumer promotion sampling	Year 1 & 2 = 2 MM.	Year 1 & 2 = 7 MM.
# units through professionals	Year 1 & 2 = 3 MM.	Year 1 & 2 = 8 MM.

TABLE D

	Investment Cost	Annual Capacity	Depreciation Time
Tufters	$500,000	3 MM units	15 years
Handle molds	$300,000	7 MM units	5 years
Packaging	$150,000	40 MM units	5 years

a marketing mix and financial projections for both scenarios, and this information is summarized in **Table C.** Her assumptions and calculations for the niche and mainstream positioning scenarios were as follows:

Volumes

Steinberg believed that with a niche positioning, Precision retail sales would represent 3% volume share of the toothbrush market in year 1 and 5% in year 2. With a mainstream positioning, these volume shares would be 10% in year 1 and 14.7% in year 2. Total category unit volumes were estimated at 268 million in 1993 and 300 million in 1994. **Table C** outlines how these unit volumes would reach the consumer:

Capacity and Investment Costs

Three types of equipment were required to manufacture the Precision brush: tufters; handle molds; and packaging machinery. **Table D** gives the cost, depreciation period, and annual capacity for each class of equipment.

Production Costs and Pricing

Production was subcontracted to Anchor Brush who also manufactured CP's Plus line of toothbrushes. Production costs included warehousing and transport costs. Under a niche positioning strategy, Steinberg decided that CP would establish a factory list price to the trade of $2.13, a premium over Oral-B regular and at parity with Oral-B Indicator. The mainstream strategy price would be $1.85, at parity with Oral-B regular. In practice however, almost all sales to the trade were made at a discount of approximately 5%. Eighty percent of sales through dental professionals would be priced at $0.79 per unit; the remainder would be sold at $0.95.

Positioning Precision as a mainstream toothbrush raised concerns about the possible cannibalization of Colgate Plus and about pressure on production schedules that had been developed for a niche positioning. Production capacity increases required 10 months' lead time, and switching to a mainstream positioning could result in inadequate supply of product. Some executives argued that unsatisfied demand could create the perception of a "hot" product but others felt that the problems associated with allocating limited supplies among trade customers should be avoided if possible. They argued for an initial niche positioning, which could later be broadened to a mainstream positioning as additional capacity came on line.

The positioning decision had important implications for the appropriate shelf location of Precision. Steinberg believed that the best location for Precision on the retail shelves would be between the Colgate Plus and Oral-B product lines, with the Colgate Classic product

TABLE E
Alternative Positioning Scenarios for Precision

	Precision as a Niche Product	Precision as a Mainstream Product
Planned capacity unit volume	Year 1 = 13 MM units Year 2 = 20 MM units	Year 1 = 42 MM units Year 2 = 59 MM units
Investment in capacity, where year 2 figures are for additional capacity	Year 1 = $3.250 M Year 2 = $1.300 M	Year 1 = $9.400 MM Year 2 = $3.100 MM
Depreciation costs (Derived from **Table D**)	Year 1 = $316,667 Year 2 = $450,000	Year 1 = $ 886,667 Year 2 = $1,270,000
Manufacturer per unit cost: Year 1 and 2	$0.66	$0.64
Manufacturer price	$2.02	$1.76
Suggested retail price	$2.89	$2.49
Advertising—Year 1	$ 5 million	$15 million
Year 2	$ 5 million	$12 million
Consumer Promotions—Year 1	$ 4.6 million	$13 million
Year 2	$ 4 million	$10 million
Trade Promotions—Year 1	$1.6 million	$4.8 million
Year 2	$2.7 million	$ 7 million
# SKUs		
Brushes	4 adult	6 adult/1 child
Colors	6 colors	6 colors

line on the other side of Colgate Plus. She wondered however, if mainstream Precision could be located separately from the other Colgate lines, close to competitive super-premium toothbrushes such as Aquafresh Flex and Crest Complete. If Precision was positioned as a niche product, with 4 SKUs, it was unlikely that any existing SKUs would be dropped. However, positioning Precision as a mainstream product, with 7 SKUs, would probably require dropping one or more existing SKUs such as a slow-moving children's brush from the Plus line.

Steinberg also believed that the positioning decision would impact distribution and percentage of sales by class of trade. Specifically, she reasoned that Precision, positioned as a niche product, would be carried primarily by food and drug stores. Under a mainstream launch scenario, a relatively greater proportion of sales would occur through mass merchandisers and club stores. Steinberg consolidated her best estimate of the cost and price data (see **Table E**). When combined with the unit volume estimates in **Table C,** she hoped to develop a pro-forma income statement to compare the profit implications of the niche versus mainstream positioning strategies. She remained uncertain, however, about cannibalization; anywhere from 35% to 60% of the volumes indicated in **Table C** could come from Colgate Classic and Colgate Plus.

Branding

At the time consumer concept tests were carried out by the task force, name tests were also conducted among those consumers positively disposed towards the concept. Alternative names tested included Colgate Precision, Colgate System III, Colgate Advantage, Colgate 1.2.3, Colgate Contour, Colgate Sensation, and Colgate Probe. The Colgate Precision name was consistently viewed more favorably—it was deemed appropriate by 49% of concept acceptors and appealing by 31%.

CP executives had not yet decided the relative prominence of the Precision and Colgate names on the package and in advertising. They debated whether the brush should be known as "Colgate Precision" or as "Precision by Colgate." Executives who believed that the product represented "big news" in the category argued that the product could stand alone and that the Precision brand name should be emphasized. Stressing *Precision* as opposed to *Colgate* would, it was argued, limit the extent of cannibalization of Colgate Plus. It was estimated, both under the mainstream and niche positioning scenarios, that cannibalization figures for Colgate Plus would increase by 20% if the Colgate brand name was stressed but remain unchanged if the Precision brand name was stressed. On the other hand, CP's stated corporate strategy was to build on the Colgate brand equity.

Communication and Promotion

Once the basic product design was established, four concept tests, conducted among 400 adult professional brush users (Colgate Plus, Reach, and Oral-B users) 18 to 54 years of age, were run during 1990–1991. Consumers were exposed to various product claims in prototype print advertisements and then asked about the likelihood that they would purchase the product (see **Exhibit 16** for copies of the advertisements). The results of these tests are summarized in **Exhibit 17** and indicate that a claim that the toothbrush would prevent gum disease motivated the greatest purchase intent among test consumers. Additional consumer research, including in-home usage tests, revealed that 55% of test consumers found Precision to be very different from their current toothbrushes, and 77% claimed that Precision was much more effective than their current toothbrush.

Precision's unique design could remove more plaque from teeth than the other leading toothbrushes on the market. However, the brush looked unusual and test participants sometimes had mixed first impressions. A further problem was that the benefit of reduced gum disease from extra plaque removal was difficult to translate into a message with broad consumer appeal, since few consumers acknowledged that they might have gum disease. Steinberg believed that Precision was the best brush for people who cared about what they put in their mouths but was still searching for the right superiority claim.

Consumer research revealed that the more test consumers were told about Precision and how it worked, the greater their enthusiasm for the product. Precision created such a unique feel in the mouth when used that consumers often said, "You can really feel it working." Once tried, consumer intent to purchase rose dramatically, and Steinberg therefore concluded that sampling would be critical to Precision's success.

There was considerable debate over the CP toothbrush advertising and promotion budget, which amounted to $24.1 million in 1992, with $9.6 million in advertising and $14.4 million in consumer and trade promotion. Some executives thought the budget should remain level as a percentage of sales in 1993 and be allocated among Classic, Plus, and Precision. Others believed it should be increased substantially to support the Precision launch with no reduction in planned support for Classic and Plus. One proposal consistent with a niche positioning for Precision was to increase total CP category spending by $11.2 million and to allocate this to the Precision launch. However, Steinberg believed that this was not enough to permit Precision to reach its full sales potential. She argued for an 80% increase in CP category spending in 1993, with fully 75% of all advertising dollars assigned to Precision and 25% to Plus. However, the Colgate Plus product manager, John Phillips, argued that Plus was the bread-and-butter of CP's toothbrush line and claimed that his mainstream brand should receive more rather than less support if Precision was launched. He argued that continued support of Plus was essential to defend its market position against competition.

Consumer promotions were planned to induce trial. Steinberg was considering several consumer promotions to back the launch: a free 5 oz. tube of Colgate toothpaste (retail value of $1.89) with the purchase of a Precision brush in strong competitive markets; and a 50%-off offer on any size of Colgate toothpaste (up to a value of $1.00) in conjunction with a 50¢ coupon on the Precision brush in strong Colgate markets. The cost of this promotion was estimated at $4 million and Steinberg believed it should be used as part of the

EXHIBIT 16   **Copies of the Advertisements Used in the Consumer Concept Tests**

PLAQUE REMOVER

Introducing a New Toothbrush from Colgate

This New Toothbrush Removes More Plaque Than The Leading Toothbrushes

Your current toothbrush may not be removing enough sticky bacterial plaque that is harmful to your teeth. This new toothbrush is clinically proven to remove more plaque than the leading toothbrushes because it's designed to clean plaque from those hard-to-reach trouble spots.

It's the unique brush design that allows this toothbrush to remove so much plaque. Short, tightly packed bristles sweep away plaque from the surfaces of your teeth. At the same time, long angled bristles search out and remove plaque between teeth, in crevices, and at the gum line. No other toothbrush is designed to remove plaque like this.

So you can remove more plaque than ever before.

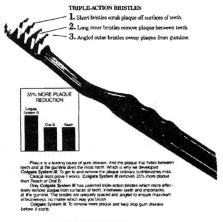

INTRODUCING
THE **Colgate** *SYSTEM III TOOTHBRUSH.*
DESIGNED TO HELP STOP GUM DISEASE BEFORE IT STARTS BECAUSE IT REMOVES MORE PLAQUE–35% MORE THAN REACH OR ORAL B.

"GUM DISEASE ONLY"

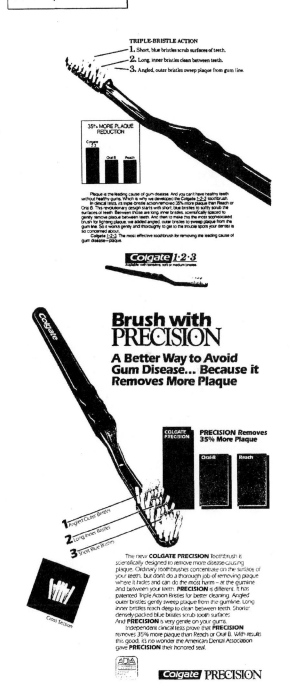

EXHIBIT 17 **Summary of Consumer Concept Test Results**

Source: Company records.

CONCEPT TEST 1.

	Plaque Remover	Healthier Gums	Trouble Spots
Probably Would Buy	69%	68%	66%
Definitely Would Buy	15%	15%	10%

CONCEPT TEST 2.

	35% More Plaque Removal Prevent Gum Disease	35% More Plaque Removal	Prevent Gum Disease	Feel the Difference
Probably Would Buy	80%	71%	74%	68%
Definitely Would Buy	19%	19%	18%	14%

CONCEPT TEST 3.

	Gum Disease/ Replacement	Gum Disease Only	Replacement Message	Trouble Spots
Probably Would Buy	63%	72%	62%	66%
Definitely Would Buy	13%	16%	11%	14%

CONCEPT TEST 4.

	No Price Given Prevent Gum Disease	20% Price Premium to Oral-B Prevent Gum Disease
Probably Would Buy	87%	61%
Definitely Would Buy	29%	19%

Note: "Definitely would buy" is a subset of "probably would buy."

launch program for a mainstream positioning strategy. The Colgate Plus product manager pressed for trade deals to load the trade in advance of the Precision launch. He believed that the trade would be unlikely to support two Colgate brushes at any one time. However, Steinberg believed that the launch of Precision would enable CP to increase its overall share of trade advertising features and special displays in the toothpaste category.

Another important tactic was to use dentists to sample consumers since professional endorsements were believed important to establishing the credibility of a new toothbrush. Steinberg believed that, under the niche scenario, 3 million Precision brushes could be channeled through dental professionals in the first year after the launch, versus 8 million under the mainstream scenario.

Conclusion

Steinberg believed that Precision was more than a niche product or simple line extension and that the proven benefits to consumers represented a technological breakthrough. She wondered how Precision should be positioned, branded, and communicated to consumers, as well as what the advertising and promotion budget should be and how it should be broken down. Steinberg had to develop a marketing mix and profit-and-loss pro forma that would enable Precision to reach its full potential, yet also be acceptable to Burton and her colleagues, particularly the Colgate Plus product manager.

Chapter 18

Launching the BMW Z3 Roadster

Robert J. Dolan   Susan Fournier

January 1996 marked the beginning of Phase II of BMW of North America Inc.'s Z3 roadster introduction. Phase I had centered on the placement of the new $28,750 two-seat convertible in the James Bond hit movie, *GoldenEye,* which premiered several months earlier. While not yet critically evaluated, results of the "out-of-the-box" pre-launch campaign appeared very positive: word-of-mouth concerning the Z3 and the James Bond cross-promotion were favorable, and product orders far exceeded BMW's initial expectations. The challenge now was to design a marketing program that would sustain product excitement until dealer product availability beginning in March. Phase II planning had to be undertaken within the context of other important events in the BMW product family: (1) the April launch of the redesigned 5-Series; and (2) the company's role as "official international automotive sponsor" of the 1996 Atlanta Summer Games, which would begin in earnest with the Olympic Torch Relay 5-Series event in June.

While these other elements of the BMW product family clearly impacted the Z3, the marketing approach and ultimate results for the Z3 would influence the whole BMW operation in the United States. Dr. Helmut Panke, Chairman and CEO of BMW (U.S.) Holding Corp. since 1993, noted that the Z3 was destined to be "the first BMW not made by mythical little creatures in the Bavarian woods. This car will be made in Spartanburg, South Carolina. Some people think BMW means German-made. With the Z3, we must show we can be successful as a global company, manufacturing at strategic locations—even if not in Bavaria. Assembling of cars in the United States requires BMW to replace 'Made in Germany' as a symbol of quality with 'Made by BMW'." As *Brandweek* put it, Panke was "saddled with the task of exporting BMW's mystique from the Bavarian hills to the fields of South Carolina." Industry commentators characterized the Z3 as "the new standard bearer for a line that had relied on German engineering as its point of difference," and wondered whether "the mystique of the BMW brand, so closely interwoven with its Munich parentage, could survive and even thrive after a surgical transplant to South Carolina." Panke and his team were aware of the new era BMW was entering and of the "new and unique" challenges this presented. Meeting the unique challenges was the prime responsibility of Victor Doolan, President of BMW North America.

Project leadership for the Z3 launch in the United States was the job of James McDowell, BMW's Marketing Vice President. The objectives of the roadster launch were two-fold: (1) to use the roadster to motivate and stimulate the dealer network to meet higher standards to qualify for the roadster; and (2) to build an order bank to enable the new Spartanburg plant to build to the specifications of BMW customers. To this point in the Z3 launch, BMW had been quite innovative in addressing their marketing goals, using for example the Bond film placement as a centerpiece of the marketing plan. Now Doolan and McDowell had to put the rest of the program in place to make sure the new "Made in the USA" Z3 was successful, in its own right and for the BMW franchise as a whole.

Background

BMW Business Strategy

BMW was a global company with a significant position in the luxury/performance segment of the U.S. automotive market, having rebounded considerably from setbacks imposed by Lexus, Acura, and Infiniti in the mid-to late-1980s (see **Exhibit 1**). The company reversed the sales decline beginning in 1992 with a program that included a repositioning of the brand from "Yuppie Status Symbol" to the more quality-oriented "Ultimate Driving Machine." At the same time, BMW adjusted model prices as necessary in light of the new competitive situation, improved the dealer network to bring the consumer buying experience in line with evolved expectations for service, and made significant improvements to the product line. All the while, the company's overall business strategy remained the same: To provide the world market with luxury/performance vehicles that were each "the best in its class, with a unique and definitive positioning in the marketplace." While focused on being "the best" rather than the "biggest," BMW wanted to position itself to attain an

EXHIBIT 1
BMW Unit Sales
History (U.S. and
Worldwide)

	U.S. Unit Sales[a] (in thousands)	Worldwide Unit Sales[b] (in thousands)
1984	70.9	434.0
1985	87.9	440.7
1986	96.8	446.1
1987	87.8	461.3
1988	73.3	484.1
1989	64.9	523.0
1990	63.6	525.9
1991	53.3	552.7
1992	66.0	588.7
1993	78.0	534.4
1994	83.8	573.9
1995	94.5	590.1

[a]Source: *Ward's Automotive Yearbook.*
[b]Source: Bayerische Moteren Werke AG BMW, various years.

annual unit sales volume near 100,000 units in the United States as this was a mark that identified major players in the global automotive marketplace and permitted operation at an efficient scale.

Franchise expansion into more youthful targets seemed the most promising way to add incremental sales to the brand. Related recommendations included an updating of the corporate image and a new product development program capable of sustaining that image. As *Adweek*[1] put it: "BMW needs to be perceived as a little less serious and tradition-bound . . . they need to preserve their reputation for driving performance but reposition their German-made cars as being stylish and fun to drive as well."

The BMW Z3 Roadster New Product Initiative

As related by Bert Holland, BMW's Series Manager of the Special Projects Group, the development process that led to the identification of the roadster concept all started in 1992 with the decline of the worldwide motorcycle market. This sparked an internal effort to identify product concepts that were capable of addressing the same feelings, emotions, and fantasies that motorcycles had satisfied. Several alternative platforms on which to execute the "emotional fantasy theme" were developed: race cars, dune buggies, sport utility-vehicles, roadsters. The roadster sportscar concept was adopted because it fit best with the overall BMW positioning of driving excitement, evoked BMW's heritage as a producer of roadsters in years past, embodied the spirit of the company, and captured the essence of the BMW brand. Also, while the concept reflected a niche opportunity, it fit the corporate goal of being the best, not the biggest. No products on the market at the time delivered against this positioning. However, other luxury car import manufacturers (e.g., Porsche, Mercedes) were rumored to have similar concepts under development, so BMW had to move quickly to secure competitive advantage.

The roadster product concept was refined over the next two years. The two-seater convertible Z3 would use the same 1.9 liter 4-cylinder engine as currently used in some 3-series models. The base model would include a six-speaker sound system, power windows and seats, fog lights, cruise control, and air conditioning. Leatherette upholstery would be standard, with upgrades to leather available.

Concept tests revealed high interest across a number of lifestage-defined segment, e.g. Generation Xers interested in unique image statements, men and women in their 40s who expressed a desire "to have that roadster I've been dreaming of all my life," and nostalgic late-Baby Boomers yearning for roadsters of yesteryear. Common across these diverse demographic groups was a "lover of life" mindset and a propensity to seek unique expressions of individuality indicating a target market defined in psychographic versus demographic terms.

Being the first BMW vehicle from the company's new Spartanburg, South Carolina manufacturing plant, and its first 100% "Made in America" offering from the German engineering leader, the Z3 roadster project assumed strategic importance beyond its franchise-expanding mission. Other German manufacturers were already trying to promote skepticism among consumers regarding BMW's impending U.S-manufactured cars. Helmut Panke explained the strategic significance of the Z3:

> Spartanburg is much more than simply escaping Germany's high cost environment. Yes, the plant will cushion BMW against international monetary fluctuations. More importantly, though, Spartanburg demonstrates that we are firmly committed to the U.S. market and rededicated to the performance values that made BMW a cult here in the 1980s. The investment tally at Spartanburg is $600 million dollars and growing. The plant can build 250 to 300 cars a day and production is set up to be flexible so that it can produce several models on the same line in random sequence. The plant currently employs 1,500 people and the plan is to grow to

[1] Source: *Adweek Eastern Edition*, September 11, 1995, p. 7.

2,000 by the end of this decade. This is our first auto plant outside Europe. This is a chance for BMW to take a step away from being a German car manufacturer towards its long-term goal of becoming a truly global brand. Spartanburg can really change what BMW stands for.

Victor Doolan commented on the system-wide implications of the Z3 launch:

Spartanburg offers us the opportunity to develop a new set of relationships in North America. With news of our commitment in Spartanburg, our dealers have gotten serious about this franchise again, and have begun to reinvest in facilities, equipment, and manpower. You can see a complete rejuvenation in enthusiasm for the brand and our products. Dealers are ecstatic about this plant. And that enthusiasm carries into the marketplace.

The Roadster Introductory Marketing Plan

Setting the Preliminary Marketing Platform

In early spring 1994, the launch team led by James McDowell, Vice President of Marketing, articulated a preliminary marketing platform for the Z3 introduction. As one BMW manager put it, the central goal of the launch was "to expand the BMW franchise and further the rejuvenation of the BMW brand by positioning the Z3 squarely in American culture and settling into the hearts and minds of the American public." Managers talked of "weaving the car into the fabric of the American experience," "putting it in the American landscape," "aligning it with everyday experience," and "establishing the vehicle as a cultural icon." According to James McDowell:

The intent was get people to talk about the roadster in the course of normal daily events: in essence, to get the car on people's conversational agenda. The plan was to leverage the excitement and enthusiasm of the core customer base in a way that would draw broader attention and interest to the brand. Management referred to this as "leveraging the buzz."

Given this intent, the launch team focused on "nontraditional" marketing methods believing them more effective than the standard fare of television and print advertising.

The strategic import of the launch dictated the need for something quite different, attention getting. (Bert Holland, Product Advocate)

It's a unique vehicle, so we were looking for unconventional ways to introduce it. (Tom McGurn, Corporate Communications Manager)

By their very nature, nontraditional media are inherently more capable of leveraging the buzz. (James McDowell, Vice President Marketing)

Nontraditional media give you more exposure. (Carol Burrows, Advertising Manager)

Given our psychographic segmentation, nontraditional media are more cost efficient per dollar spent. Traditional media are sold more on demographics. Nontraditional delivers a broader base, something we found especially valuable in light of our goal of getting into the hearts and minds of a large group of publics. (George Neill, Consumer Communications Manager)

BMW also wished to be "multi-media" in its communications strategy. As one executive put it:

We wanted consumers to experience the message in many media, to hear it in many voices. This was a philosophy directly opposed to the repetition philosophy governing traditional advertising thought. This idea operated more along the lines of a "choir" but we recognized that literal ties and threads must be evident across the disparate message elements and that all elements must strengthen and reinforce each other. This would require agencies willing to integrate across each other in an atypical team environment.

In June 1994, requests for proposals were sent to a broad collection of 30 advertising, public relations, and promotional agencies believed capable of mounting an unconventional campaign to achieve company goals. BMW pursued serious discussions with ten of those agencies based on mutual interests and relevant prior experience. Agencies were prepped with a stock footage video expressing the basic concept of the car. They also received input concerning BMW's view of what types of elements qualified as "nontraditional," and preliminary opinions regarding nontraditional marketing tools that might be especially effective. Ideas for a product placement in a premier film, a TV show sponsorship, and a fashion world tie-in ranked among BMW's top choices though agencies were encouraged to come up with their own recommendations.

Based on a review of solicited proposals, seven agencies were invited to make presentations at BMW. Many elements were selected from a proposal by Dick Clark Corporate Productions, a leading Hollywood-based promotional agency known for its experiences in the entertainment industry. These were added to a framework of core events and programs that BMW had developed internally including an aggressive program of dealer facility upgrading, staff training, and the production of 150 pre-production cars for use in pre-selling promotions at the time of the product launch.

A corporate switch from Mullen Advertising to Fallon McElligott was also instituted at this time. Mullen, a small creative shop in Wenham Massachusetts, had been retained in February 1993 to reposition BMW beyond its Yuppie image. Fallon was selected based on their proven experience in integrated and electronic marketing—key skills for a nontraditional launch.

Fixing the First Marketing Element: The *GoldenEye* Product Placement

BMW's predisposition toward movie placements in fact reflected a broader industry trend toward the addition of product placements into the marketing mix.[2] For film producers, manufacturers' branded products added authenticity and realism to settings and aided in character development through the provision of instantly-recognized symbols. Payments and free merchandise also helped defray costs in an increasingly expensive production and marketing environment.[3] Manufacturers who offered their brands for placement sought many rewards beyond exposure and visibility through their Hollywood alliances. The trade press commented on these benefits to corporate partners:

> It's a great way to build brand equity.[4]
>
>   In this increasingly fragmented world, advertisers are forced to go to great lengths to reach their audiences. When we [the viewers] can zap a commercial out and move on, they have to find new ways to reach us. This is a more subtle way for advertisers to reach us.[5]
>
>   In addition to a dollop of glamour, movies give marketers access to two audiences that are hard-to-reach through network TV or print: foreign viewers and young people.[6]

In general, fees for movie placement deals ranged from nothing to several million dollars, with an average fee of $40,000[7] for a highly-visible placement in which the star actor

---

[2] Source: "Planning for a Market Fall," *Brandweek*, July 22, 1996, pp. 32–39.

[3] Source: "Now It's the Cars that Make the Characters Go," *The New York Times*, April 21, 1996, section 2, p. 13.

[4] Source: "Casting Call Goes Out Products Play Major Roles in Movies," *Marketing News*, July 31, 1995, p. 1.

[5] Source: "Movie 4 Sale!," *The Courier-Journal*, May 30, 1996, p. 1C.

[6] Source: "Cue the Soda Can," *Business Week*, June 24, 1996, pp. 64, 66.

[7] Source: "It's a Wrap (But Not Plain): From Budweiser to BMW, Brand Names Are Popping Up More and More On Screen," *The Los Angeles Times*, September 3, 1995, p. 4.

actually used the product (an "impact placement," in industry terms).[8] Many placements were conducted on a quid pro quo basis, however, with manufacturers receiving product visibility in exchange for providing movie producers with product-related cost savings.[9] BMW, as a matter of policy, does not pay for movie placements.

In a newspaper interview, Norm Marshall, a long-standing consultant to BMW, commented on the uncertainty of movie product placement effects:

> Why don't companies have to pay big bucks to get their goods in a picture? In some cases we do. But the counter balance against that is that they can't guarantee anything as they can when you buy an ad. And you never know if it is going to be in the movie or not. And even if it is, you don't know if the movie is going to bomb or not. The reality is, the vast majority of movies are not successful at the box office. So we make choices. Hopefully we are right more than we are wrong.[10]

Exhibit 2 contains examples of some noteworthy movie product placements from 1983 to the present.

BMW entered into deal negotiations with MGM/United Artists on the James Bond *GoldenEye* film in fall 1994. Immediately upon reviewing the script, BMW pegged the opportunity as "a perfect fit" for both parties: MGM sought a partner that could help them revive their 33-year old Bond franchise; BMW sought a premier movie placement capable of reinforcing its brand image. Other firms that contracted with MGM for the *GoldenEye* film included Omega, Perrier, Sharper Image, Yves St. Laurent, and IBM.

Karen Sortito, MGM's Senior Vice President of Promotions, described her first encounter with the Z3:

> We had seen spy photos of the car and it looked great. We all snuck out to BMW's production facility one morning to see the car. It was like an episode of *Get Smart:* we were going through all these doors and they were slamming behind us. They pulled the cover off the car and we all "ooh'ed and aah'ed." Then we took turns sitting in it, just to make sure it was cool enough for Pierce Brosnan, our newest James Bond.[11]

McDowell elaborated on the perceived fit between Bond and the Z3 brand personality:

> BMW was looking for a hero, and a glamorous one at that. The Bond character fit the bill perfectly. He was handsome, sexy, wealthy, resourceful, and adventurous. He was perceived as a man who loves life and is in control of his destiny. He was known for the technology he used. Heck, he was even recognized as a man with a penchant for good, fast cars! The quintessential hero for a quintessential car!

BMW was excited by the strategic significance of the film for MGM and the dollar investment MGM was willing to put behind the re-launch of its cultural icon. Management believed that this level of support and commitment would play well with the dealers. MGM was also talking of the possibility for a multi-movie deal, a prospect that offered continuing leverage potential.

The BMW/MGM agreement was orally sealed in January 1995, and formally signed in July 1995. The basic exchange was simple: MGM got the use of several prototype vehicles for their movie; BMW got placement of the Z3 in *GoldenEye* and obtained worldwide rights to reference that placement in corporate communications through March 1996.

---

[8] Source: "Junior Mints: I'm Gonna Make You a Star," *Forbes*, November 6, 1995, p. 90.

[9] Source: "Product Placement: How It Began, How It's Grown," *St. Louis Dispatch*, April 8, 1995, p. 4D.

[10] Source: "We Ought to Be in Pictures: That's the Rallying Cry as Companies Vie to Get Their Products in Movies and TV," *St. Louis Dispatch*, April 8, 1995, p. 1D.

[11] Source: *Brandweek*, March 11, 1996, p. 21.

EXHIBIT 2 Notable Movie Product Placement Examples

Movie	Product/Brand	Placement/Fee	Placement Detail	Media Comments
E.T. The Extraterrestrial	Reeses Pieces	NA	Candy trial used to coax E.T. out of hiding place	M&Ms' decline of original deal cited as "marketing blunder that ranks with Ford Edsel and New Coke.[a] Reese's pieces sales increased 66%[b]
Risky Business	Rayban	NA	Tom Cruise sports Raybans in his new role as pimp	Rayban sales tripled.[b]
License to Kill	Lark cigarettes	$350,000	Lark as Bond's cigarette brand of choice	"Cigarette placements are tricky. Most companies don't want any part of it anymore because they hear too much negative feedback."[b]
Grand Canyon	Lexus	NA	Lexus breaks down in seedy L.A. neighborhood	NA
Silence of the Lambs	Arby's Roast Beef	NA	Crumbled Arby's wrappers and cups included among decrepit décor of serial murderer's house	"Focus group participants very outspoken about how they would never eat at that restaurant because every time they saw the logo they thought of the killer. I think we can count that as a bad placement."[b]
Forrest Gump	Dr Pepper	NA	Dr Pepper portrayed as Gump's beverage of choice	"If that's not the best placement of '94, I don't know what is."[a]
Dumb and Dumber	Hawaiian Tropic Suntan Lotion	Products and ads for filming	Last 5 minutes of movie show Hawaiian Tropic Girls in Hawaiian Tropic Tour Bus	"Hawaiian Tropic received over 100 placements last year. It's the best kind of advertising there is . . . the fee was small compared to our marketing budget."[c]
Natural Born Killers	Coca-Cola	"Polar bears" and licensing rights	Coke commercial aired as backdrop to violent crime scene	NA
Get Shorty	Oldsmobile Silhouette minivan	Products for filming	Silhouette, touted as "Cadillac of Minivans,"[b] becomes one of film's running gags	Vehicle selected over Ford for side door that opens automatically. Sales down, though dealers liked traffic and word-of-mouth that movie generated.
Waiting to Exhale	Mercedes Benz	NA	Disgruntled wife burns husband's Mercedes	Company was looking for "nice upscale placement," not pleased with the way vehicle depicted.[d]
Twister	Dodge Ram Pickup Truck	5 $25,000 trucks; 20 windshields	Investigative team chases tornadoes in Ram trucks	Ford battled over this "perfect script for a truck" but lost.
Mission: Impossible	Apple PowerBook	$15 million tie-in ad campaign	Laptops prove integral to solving intrigue plot	Apple sales continue long-term sales.
Flipper	Pepsi	$40,000	Shot of crunched-up soda can on dock	Pepsi label digitally added after scene shot with Coke can in response to marketing deal with parent.

[a]Source: "We Ought to Be in Pictures," *St. Louis Post-Dispatch*, April 8, 1995, p. 1D.

[b]Source: It's a Wrap (But Not Plain): From Budweiser to BMW, Brand Names Are Popping Up More and More on Screen," *Los Angeles Times*, September 3, 1995, Calendar Section, p. 4.

[c]Source: "Casting Call Goes Out: Products Needed to Play Major Roles in Movies," *Marketing News*, July 31, 1995, p. 1.

[d]Source: "Now It's the Cars that Make the Characters Go," *New York Times*, April 21, 1996, section 2, p. 13.

To movie industry insiders, the BMW/MGM deal qualified more as a "co-launch" than a traditional movie product placement. The basic marketing agreement between MGM and BMW was that from September through December 1995, the two marketers would jointly promote the Bond actor (Pierce Brosnan), the *GoldenEye* film, and the BMW Z3 roadster. In addition to covering product costs for prototype vehicles, BMW agreed to invest in advertising to support the Z3 as James Bond's new car. MGM, in turn, agreed to support the Z3 in *GoldenEye* movie previews and film trailers.

The Z3 appeared in the movie for only 90 seconds, but was prominent in that it replaced the Aston-Martin, Bond's signature car. "That Aston Martin is such an engrained part of Bond. It's his trademark, really. This marked a first-ever use of the car category in the film series' history," noted Marshall.[12] Bond is presented the Z3 by Q, the legendary R&D engineer at Britain's MI5 Secret Service Agency who says: "Now, pay attention Bond. First your new car. A BMW . . ."[13] The Z3 placement was noted in the marketing press for its "seamless integration" into the storyline, as explained by Entertainment Resources Marketing Association President, Dean Ayers:

> A word that comes up a lot in our work is seamless. Subtly rendered. A blurring of the lines between advertising and entertainment. That's the way placements have to function to be successful. People prefer to see a can of Pepsi or some other familiar brand rather than one that just says "Soda." But nobody wants to pay to see a commercial. You have to pay just the right amount of attention to the product to get this effect.[14]

Acclaim for the seamlessness of the roadster product placement was considered ironic by some in light of the product's limited exposure in the film, as McDowell described:

> A lot of people were surprised that the car was not in the movie for a great amount of time. The car shows up in two segments for a total airtime of 1.5 minutes. It really was intended only as a preview, a teaser. We much rather wanted the car to fit naturally into the film than to look as though someone had forced it into the scene and it was there so long it wore out its welcome.

The *GoldenEye* box office opening was scheduled for November 17, 1995. While the six-month gap between the film launch and Z3 dealership availability presented obvious tactical challenges, the timing fit well with other planned BMW product events and gave the factory the opportunity to build cars to exact customer specifications. The early launch also gave BMW a leg up on the forthcoming Mercedes introduction. By virtue of its timing, the Bond connection became the foundational element around which the remaining Z3 launch plans were formulated.

The Final Pre-Launch Marketing Plan

With the *GoldenEye* placement agreed to in January 1995, the launch team sought to build the other complementary elements of the program that would both pre-sell the Z3 and generate dealer traffic, stimulating interest in other models in the BMW product line. Among the additional elements which would form the launch program for the Z3 were:

1. Neiman Marcus Christmas Catalog offer of a Special Bond Edition Roadster.
2. Featuring the Z3 on BMW's site on the World Wide Web.

[12] Source: "It's a Wrap (But Not Plain): From Budweiser to BMW, Brand Names Are Popping Up More and More On Screen," *The Los Angeles Times,* September 3, 1995, p. 4.

[13] Q is the research and development engineer responsible for design of Bond's state-of-the-art weaponry.

[14] Source: Ibid.

EXHIBIT 3   Timeline of Key Events

Date	Event
1992	Special Project Group founded to lead new product development initiative
1993	Beginning of product clinics to develop roadster concept
May 1993	Spartanburg facility announced. Car(s) to be produced there not specified to public
Spring 1994	Z3 launch team specifies "nontraditional" launch
June 1994	RFP's to 30 agencies for "nontraditional, innovative launch plan"
September 1994	First U.S. made BMWs roll off Spartanburg production line
Fall 1994	Negotiations with MGM begin for *GoldenEye* film
January 1995	BMW/MGM oral agreement (signed six months later)
June 1995	Dealer visits begin
September 11, 1995	Neiman's catalog promotion announced on the *Today Show*
November 1995	Central Park Launch Event, *Tonight Show* appearance, Radio DJ Program, "Go: An American Road Story" Video, and *GoldenEye* premier
March 1996	First cars available at dealers

3. A large-scale public relations event "unveiling" the car in New York's Central Park.

4. An appearance on Jay Leno's *Tonight Show*.

5. The Radio DJ Program.

6. "Go: An American Road Story" Video.

Along with these elements, BMW planned some television and print advertising as well as dealer activities. Each of these programs is described in turn below. A timeline of key program decisions and events is provided in **Exhibit 3.**

1.   Neiman Marcus Catalog Offer

BMW put together a promotion in which a Special Limited Edition Bond Roadster would be available in the Neiman Marcus Christmas Catalog, a publication renowned for its unusual product offerings. On September 11, the catalog insertion and vehicle were featured on the *Today Show*. Originally BMW and Neiman Marcus had set a 20-unit sales goal over the $3\frac{1}{2}$ month Christmas selling period: "the 20-unit number seemed right in light of past experience of the catalog," according to McDowell. In two days, 100 Z3 orders were placed, so BMW agreed to increase the total production to 100 units. By Christmas, Neiman's had received 6000 customers orders or waiting list applications for the 100 cars.

2.   BMW Internet Site

In October, BMW unveiled its new Website. Among the items on the site were *GoldenEye* film segments and the *Today Show* clip featuring the catalog offer. A module developed by the Fallon Agency proved impactful in generating "hits" on the site. This "Build Your Own Roadster" module allowed the site visitor to select exterior, interior, and top colors as well as various options for a Z3. The module then displayed the user "his/her car" from a variety of perspectives, e.g. top up and top down. It also provided the MSRP for the car with options as selected by the user. Hit rates tripled with the addition of this module, from an average of 35,000 hits per day to 125,000. Apple Computer, whose technology was employed to build the module, approached BMW in December for rights to reference the

"Build-Your-Own-Roadster" module in their own corporate advertising. Apple's TV spot aired during the Academy Awards in March 1996. "And we got a full 25 of those 30 seconds," noted McDowell.

3. Press Launch in Central Park

The most prominent PR event was the Central Park Launch in which the Z3 was formally introduced to the public. Over 200 media representatives were on hand as *GoldenEye* character Q detailed the specifications of BMW's "latest invention." The Z3 was revealed amid a splash of special effects precipitated by CEO Panke's entry of "the secret code" that exploded the crate shielding the car. To cap the event, Bond actor Brosnan drove onto the scene in his Atlanta Blue Roadster after completing a circuit through Central Park with a motorcade escort.

On the morning of the press launch the Z3 was also showcased in a segment of the *Today Show* that included an interview with CEO Helmut Panke and test-drives with the show's host.

The Central Park event generated extensive coverage in both broadcast and print, including mention on *Hard Copy, This Morning's Business, The Money Wheel,* and all major network news programs. McDowell added: "There were even cartoons published in the newspapers about how Brosnan was being upstaged by a car!" **Exhibit 4** contains a sample press clipping from the event. **Exhibit 5** contains the cartoon from *Automotive News.*

4. Jay Leno *Tonight Show*

In early November, prior to the *GoldenEye* premier, the Z3 appeared on the *Tonight Show.* BMW had offered Jay Leno the use of a Z3 on his show "should he find it useful in anyway." NBC accepted for Leno without specifying his intent. Leno's writers incorporated the Z3 in a skit where Bond dodged all approaches from NBC Security in crossing the studio lots. In the end, it was a case of mistaken identity since Pierce Brosnan was already in the studio. McDowell commented:

> The unpredictability of the message content was almost unbearable: It was a carefully calculated gamble. We did not know what Leno would say or do, and we would basically not know until the rest of the country knew it as well. We sent one of our guys to sit in the studio audience during filming, and he called us on his cellular to tell us what was going on. But it all worked out very well.

5. Radio DJ Program

Timed coincident with the beginning of TV advertising in early November, the Radio DJ Program featured DJs from leading radio stations in 13 major metro markets. DJs were screened on the basis of disc jockey personality, show content and listener demographics. Qualifying DJs were approached with the opportunity to design a program segment that would somehow incorporate the Z3 into their radio shows or scheduled personal appearances. DJs were encouraged to be innovative in their proposals and to adopt creative license in whatever they did. They were informed that while BMW would suggest potential copy points, they would not censor accepted programs in any way.

EXHIBIT 4   **Sample Press Clipping from the Central Park Z3 Roadster Launch Event**[a]

BMW Roadster meets Bond, James Bond

By Melanie Wells
USA TODAY

NEW YORK — BMW of North America is hitching a ride with Hollywood for the introduction of its new two-seat roadster: Brace yourself for BMW 007.

In *GoldenEye*, the latest James Bond flick from MGM/United Artists, Hollywood's favorite spy exchanges his $135,000 Aston Martin for a BMW Z3 Roadster. The BMW is expected to sell for under $30,000 when it rolls out in the first quarter of 1996.

The link offers the kind of highbrow panache that a low-priced luxury sports car could only find in movieland. David Stolkos of Automotive Marketing Consultants calls the deal a "marketing coup" for the carmaker.

BMW was able to approve the *GoldenEye* script for the studio's use of its car. It's also able to feature the movie's latest Bond, actor Pierce Brosnan, in two TV spots without having to pay a customarily steep celebrity endorsement fee. Why? The actor appears as part of the movie's promotion.

TV commercials break tonight from BMW's new ad agency, Fallon McElligott. Print ads will also feature cuts from *GoldenEye*.

Among the other advertising and promotional plans for the Roadster:

▶ BMW's first-ever cinema commercial — a two-minute spot that will run closer to the time of the Roadster's launch — and an airplane in-

'GOLDENEYE': Ads for BMW Z3 Roadster feature images from new James Bond movie.

flight video, both coordinated by Dick Clark Corporate Productions in Burbank.

▶ A promotional appearance for the car during late night NBC programming, probably on *The Tonight Show*.

▶ Prominent placement during the Olympic Torch Relay, of which BMW is the official "mobility" sponsor. The color of the BMW featured in *GoldenEye* is a new cerulean shade the carmaker calls Atlanta Blue.

BMW vice president of marketing James McDowell says the Roadster's launch will comprise about 15% of the carmaker's 1996 ad budget.

The German automaker spent $64.9 million on all advertising during the first seven months of '95, according to Competitive Media Reporting. The total for 1994: $102.6 million.

[a]© 1995, *USA Today*. Reprinted with permission.

Twenty-five radio stations participated with some interesting programs. A DJ in Atlanta, for example, dressed up in a Santa suit and drove his borrowed Z3 roadster onto the Atlanta Falcon's playing field at half-time of a National Football League game. Another gave away a Z3 roadster during a live radio broadcast in L.A. Baba Shetty, BMW's Media Communications Manager commented on the overall effect:

> The DJ Program was considered the most "at-risk" element of the plan. It was not until the 11th hour. . . only one and a half weeks before d-day . . . that management finally committed to go with it. But it was a great. The DJs granted amazing credibility to our product message. The event was very successful in getting the brand into the conversational milieu. We think it had three times the word-of-mouth effect of other programs. We got over 6,000 spots from the event and we were only promised 3,800.

EXHIBIT 5
Automotive News
Cartoon[a]

[a]© Arkie G. Hudkins, Jr. As seen in *Automotive News,* November 20, 1995. For T. A. Brooks. Reprinted with permission.

6.   "Go: An American Road Story" Video

The BMW Communications Group, in conjunction with Dick Clark Productions, created this story of Faber, an overworked architect who decides to relive a cross-country road trip he took with his Aunt Edna Rose when he was ten years old. Faber drives his Z3 from Savannah to Oregon, retracing his Aunt's steps along the way. The story provides a "celebration of the road focused on the emotional character of the driving experience." The story's original song title, "Feel the Wind in your Soul," captures this theme. The video was made available through BMW's 1-800 number in December, with references to the tape made in corporate advertising.

TV and Print Advertising

In concert with these "nontraditional" activities, BMW considered a possible complementary role for advertising to be produced by their new agency Fallon McElligott. The extent of advertising and the most appropriate media were issues to be considered in light of the "nontraditional" platform. Fallon developed TV and print advertising that, it was ultimately decided, would break nationally on November 1st. While the advertising used "traditional" media of print and television, the launch team felt the nontraditional spirit was maintained. "Even traditional media can be executed in nontraditional ways," noted one BMW executive.

The advertising message was a simple one: James Bond traded in his car for a new BMW. "In essence it was a new Bond in a new world in a new car. Life had evolved and so had Bond," explained Carol Burrows, BMW's Advertising Manager. The tonality of the advertising was bold, witty, and entertaining. The new campaign with its central elements of humor and fantasy provided a sharp departure from traditional BMW advertising, which tended to emphasize performance capabilities in a no-nonsense manner.

The multi-million dollar campaign included two television spots scheduled for placement in popular network shows (*Seinfeld, ER,* and *90210*) and lifestyle cable programming.

EXHIBIT 6   Comparative Launch Advertising Campaign Expenditures[a] and Introductory Year Sales

Product/Brand	Launch Date	Introductory Year Sales[d] (units)	Launch Advertising Support (millions)
Sport Utility Vehicles			
Kia Sportage	January 1995	8,015	30.0
Toyota RAV-4	January 1995	29,815	30.0
Ford Expedition	January 1996	NA	35.0
Acura SLX	November 1995	1,657	40.0
Sedans/Minivans			
Dodge Neon	January 1994	93,300	88.7
Plymouth Breeze	January 1996	NA	45.0
Hyundai Accent	February 1995	50,658	99.9
Ford Contour	September 1994	140,987	55.3
Ford Windstar	March 1994	62,317	57.0
Mazda Millenia	April 1994	29,096	30.0
Nissan Altima	September 1992	69,489	70.9
Oldsmobile Aurora	May 1994	33,206	42.7
Luxury/Performance			
Land Rover Discovery	October 1994	14,085	9.4
Acura RL	January 1996	NA	40.0
Infiniti I-30	May 1995	15,194	35.0
Lexus LX-450	January 1996	NA	20.0
Mercedes C-Class	November 1993	19,351	
Average Launch Budget			$20 million
Average Launch Reach[b] Goal			75–90%
Average Launch Frequency[c] Goal			2.5

[a]Source: Competitive Media Reporting and *Media Week* "SuperBrands 1995."
[b]Note: Reach defined as percent of target audience exposed at least once to advertising in a given period.
[c]Note: Frequency defined as average number of times target audience member is exposed to advertising in a given period.
[d]Note: Sales figures reflect first 12 months after launch date.

National print advertising was placed in business and lifestyle books (*Business Week, Forbes, Fortune, Traveler, Vanity Fair*) as well as auto buff magazines (*Car and Driver, Auto Week, Auto World*). Advertising was scheduled through December, with heavier weight in the initial period to prime excitement for the Bond film. (See **Exhibit 6** for comparative launch advertising expenditures in the industry.)

The resulting advertising was impactful, according to Market Research and Information Manager, William Pettit:

> We attained more mentions of advertising content than ever before. A full 15% of TV viewers demonstrated proven advertising recall. We have not seen a number this high in ten years. This was 50% higher than the 10% proven recall Mercedes was able to generate for their similarly-timed E-class launch advertising, with an estimated launch budget three times as great. This type of data is great because it provides a sort of controlled experiment of a traditional versus nontraditional launch of an entirely new product line.

Dealer Advertising and Promotions

As with all new car launches, generating dealer motivation and cooperation behind the program was critical to success. BMW wanted its dealers to be integrated into the promotion from the outset. Baba Shetty, Media Communications Manager, commented:

> They were not overly enthusiastic when we first told them we wanted them to spend their scarce resources promoting a brand new car that would not be ready for delivery until March of the following year. The Z3 situation provided an important test of BMW's renewed dealer relations. We had to get it right.

Shetty began dealer visits in June 1995 with a presentation emphasizing the strategic value of the launch to BMW, the marketing support levels both BMW and MGM were putting behind the Bond campaign, and the positives of the launch timing vis-à-vis other planned BMW activities. Shetty commented on his dealer road show experience:

> Plan execution was complicated. We had 345 dealers and only 150 cars available for them to display in their showrooms during the promotional period. We had to run the program in three waves, with the vehicles circulating among dealers. Now, that would have been enough in and of itself, but the presentations were about as tough as they get. Some of the dealers just sat there, looking at me in disbelief as I explained this phenomenal opportunity that would not come to fruition until . . . March of 1996. 1 basically told them, "Look. You can go with this and make the most of the opportunity, or you can ignore it. It is your choice. But we are behind it, and MGM is behind it, and we are both behind it 150%." The quality of the promotional materials did the rest.

The dealer promotional package showcased a private screening of the Bond film and car before the box office film opening. Dealers compiled a guest list of 200–400 of their best customers and mailed personalized invitations to the film screening. Dealership owners were on hand at opening night to greet customers and deliver motivating introductory speeches. Some dealers hosted cocktail receptions before or after the show. "007: Licensed to Sell" kits (see **Exhibit 7**) were also created. These included multi-media kiosk videos, a film canister of "spy films" of the product in action, and a mock "BOND 007" license plate. Car toppers, showroom display cars (for a limited loan period), and database-building ideas were also made available to participating dealers. The theater arrangements for the screening events were made courtesy of MGM studios, at the participating dealer's expense. These events attracted great local publicity, appearing in local newspapers, and often reported on metropolitan television and radio.

Frederick Tierney, General Manager of Foreign Motors West, Boston's largest BMW dealership, commented further on dealer reactions to the overall launch plan:

> I had no problems with the overall program or the advertising. It was innovative. It seemed impactful. To be honest, I thought that they were overdoing it. The Z3 was a special interest niche car, it was only shown in the Bond film for a minuscule amount of time, and BMW was going to such elaborate lengths to publicize it. What if they sold too many roadsters with all the hype? How were we going to maintain all this momentum and keep the customers patient? It seemed like a big job ahead for the dealerships.

Success of the Phase I Launch Plan

The final launch plan budget was split 40/60 between what might be labeled "traditional" and "nontraditional" elements. Internally and externally, the MGM/BMW co-launch was declared a success. The Bond film had the largest opening weekend in MGM's history, grossing $26.2 million in ticket sales (see **Exhibit 8** for box office performance data of other notable film placement examples). Marshall estimated that "the advertising, promotion, and associated publicity from the BMW tie-in added millions to *GoldenEye's* earnings."[15] Z3 product reviews were favorable (see **Exhibit 9**). Over 9,000 Z3 product orders were pre-booked by December 1995, as compared with 5,000 projected. The product's unavailability, once viewed as a potential liability, was retrospectively viewed as a great asset. According to James McDowell: "It heightened the excitement value of the message and made people ripe with anticipation for the experience." Dealers agreed, as reflected in comments by Sales Manager Joe Santamaria of Boston's Foreign Motors West BMW dealership:

[15] Source: "Now It's the Cars that Make the Characters Go," *The New York Times,* April 21, 1996, section 2, p. 13.

EXHIBIT 7   **"007: Licensed to Sell" Dealer Promotional Kits**

It was a real shot in the arm for us. Traffic in the dealership was up, and lots of people came in saying, "Hey! That's the car that Bond drives!" Or "I saw that in the movie!" They were placing orders for the car sight unseen. The hype in the movie was excellent.

The net result was that the dealers upgraded to meet the challenge, BMW developed an order bank, the roadster was successfully launched, and a niche was created. Management also noted cost efficiencies gained with the nontraditional launch plan. Management was left with the feeling that the dollars spent were more impactful than they would have been if placed in traditional programs.

We spent about 50% less than the Share-of-Voice/Share-of-Market rule dictates.[16] (Baba Shetty) (See **Exhibit 10**).
    We definitely got higher impact per dollar spent. (George Neill)

[16] Share of voice (SOV) refers to a company's share of total advertising expenditures for all products in a given category. The Share-of-Voice/Share-of-Market rule for ad budget setting declares that all things being equal, the advertising share of voice should be set equal to the company's share of market.

EXHIBIT 8
Box Office Draws for Noteworthy Product Placement Movies[a]

Film	Introductory Year	Opening Week Ticket Sales (in millions of dollars)
Twister	1996	$41.1
Mission: Impossible	1996	56.8
Flipper	1996	4.5
Waiting to Exhale	1995	14.1
GoldenEye	1995	26.2
Get Shorty	1995	12.7
Natural Born Killers	1994	11.2
Dumb and Dumber	1994	16.4
Forrest Gump	1994	24.5
Silence of the Lambs	1991	13.8
Grand Canyon	1991	0.3
License to Kill	1989	8.8
Risky Business	1983	4.3
E.T. The Extra Terrestrial	1982	13.0

[a]Source: *Variety,* various dates.

EXHIBIT 9   Sample Product Reviews from Major Automotive Magazines

Its movie star looks notwithstanding, the Z3 is at its best on sun-blurred country lanes, when the engine is in full, reedy song and your hair is buffeted into bug-laced dreadlocks. This is a great sports car, an enthusiast driver's first wish from the genie. Sexual dynamite on the outside, as intimate as a shared cigarette on the inside, perfectly constructed and effortless fun to drive, the Z3 leaves one wounded with desire. Not bad for a car made in Spartanburg, S.C. (*New York Times,* Automobiles section)

At the start of the day-long press event, I wasn't quite sure that the world really needed another roadster, but by noon I was convinced the BMW Z3 is a vehicle that mankind can't do without. And with the announcement of a $28,750 base price, it's certain that great hordes of Americans will find the Z3 just as irresistible. Z3 fans wishing for more romp in their roadsters will have to wait for the release of versions with the new 2.8 in-line six, which will deliver about another 60 horsepower. But, before you gripe about this machine's lack of tire-burning power, consider this: the 1.9 liter four makes the $28,750 price, putting the Z3 in reach of many more buyers than would a six-powered version, which will be closer to $40,000. *(Motor Trend Magazine)*

I wanted to drive the Z3 to see for myself what all the shouting was about. But I probably would have wanted to put the car through some paces even if it hadn't been the star of the latest Bond movie. There were at least three good reasons for being curious about the Z3. First because it is a Beemer. We all know that the Bavarian factories don't design any junk. The BMW—any BMW—has that good, unmistakable solid feeling of careful German engineering that everyone likes and responds to in a car. The second reason was that it is built in Spartanburg, S.C. The third reason has to do with money. Everyone likes a deal, and the Z3 was priced at just under $30,000 which seemed like a bargain. Word was that Mercedes and Porsche were floored by the price, since they are scheduled to bring out competitive cars in the next year or so but hadn't been planning on giving them away. Maybe, people said, BMW was going to sell the car as a kit . . . you do the final assembly and paint the thing. Well, I got to drive the Z3 and I am here to report, straight out, that BMW isn't selling any kits, and that the car is as exciting as the price. Is the car fun to drive? The answer is: yeah, man. I kept thinking that this was a car that fills a particular niche and fills it just about perfectly. It'll be worth it, believe me. *(Forbes)*

EXHIBIT 10
1995 Unit Sales and Advertising Spending within the U.S. Luxury/Performance Segment

Manufacturer	Total Sales[a] (units)	Media Expenditures[b] (millions)
Acura	$112,137	$197.2
Audi	12,575	25.8
BMW	84,501	87.5
Cadillac	162,672	227.4
Ford/Lincoln	120,191	30.6
Infiniti	51,449	106.7
Jaguar	15,195	34.5
Land Rover	12,045	18.9
Lexus	87,419	202.8
Mercedes	73,002	88.4
Porsche	5,838	10.9
Saab	21,679	31.2
Volvo	81,788	56.5
AVERAGE ADVERTISING EXPENSE PER LUXURY CAR SOLD		**$982**
AVERAGE ADVERTISING EXPENSE FOR ALL CARS SOLD		**$372**

[a]Source: 1995 J.D. Power & Associates.
[b]Source: 1995 LNA Competitive Media Reporting.
Note: Spending includes local dealer and dealer association dollars.

Bill Pettit added a more sober summary: "Bottom line, how do we measure the success of the program? Nothing blew up."

Phase II Launch Strategy

Phase I of the Z3 launch created "a sort of paradigm shift" at BMW. McDowell explained:

> We will probably never return to traditional programs after getting a taste of the power of a plan like this. Sure there are negatives but the impact simply cannot be matched using traditional elements. Usually the risks of new product introduction are so great you find yourself relying on traditional marketing elements for the false sense of security they provide. But that's what it is: a false sense of security. It would have cost at least three times more to do what we did relying solely on traditional media.

This change in philosophy colored January planning meetings in which Phase II Z3 strategies and tactics were to be set. The whole process had been invigorating for the managers involved. But as the January planning progressed, fond memories of Hollywood premiers and rendezvous in Central Park with celebrities were mixed with recognition of the $600 million investment in Spartanburg and the strategic significance of the Z3. As one manager put it, "This is fun. But we better get it right."

Chapter 19

Mountain Dew: Selecting New Creative

Douglas B. Holt

Standing at the front of a PepsiCo conference room, Bill Bruce gestured enthusiastically, pointing to the sketches at his side. Bruce, a copywriter and Executive Creative Director, headed up the creative team on the Mountain Dew account for PepsiCo's advertising agency, BBDO New York. In fact, it was Bruce who devised the famous "Do the Dew" campaign that had catapulted Mountain Dew to the number three position in its category. With his partner, art director Doris Cassar, Bruce had developed ten new creative concepts for Mountain Dew's 2000 advertising to present to PepsiCo management. Gathered in the room to support Bruce and Cassar were BBDO senior executives Jeff Mordos (Chief Operating Officer), Cathy Israelevitz (Senior Account Director), and Ted Sann (Chief Creative Officer). Each of the three executives had over a decade of experience working on Mountain Dew. Representing PepsiCo were Scott Moffitt (Marketing Director, Mountain Dew), Dawn Hudson (Chief Marketing Officer, and a former senior ad agency executive), and Gary Rodkin (Chief Executive Officer, Pepsi Cola North America).

Scott Moffitt scribbled notes as he listened to Bruce speak. Moffitt and the brand managers under him were charged with day-to-day oversight of Mountain Dew marketing. These responsibilities included brand strategy, consumer and sales promotions, packaging, line extensions, product changes, and sponsorships. But for Moffitt and the senior managers above him, the most important decisions of the year were made in conference rooms with BBDO creatives. Each of the ads would cost over a million dollars to produce. But the production costs were minor compared to the $55 million media budget that would be committed to air these spots. Historically, PepsiCo management had learned that selecting the right creative was one of the most critical decisions they made in terms of impact on sales and profits.

Mountain Dew had carried PepsiCo's soft drink revenues during the 1990s as cola brands struggled. But now the *Do the Dew* campaign was entering its eighth year, a long stretch by any consumer goods baseline. Many other brands were now sponsoring the same alternative sports that Mountain Dew had relied upon to boost its image. And teens were gravitating to new activities and new music that Dew's competitors had successfully exploited in their branding activities. Figuring out how to keep the campaign working hard to maintain the brand's relevance with its target consumers had become a chief preoccupation of senior management at both PepsiCo and BBDO. At the same time, key competitors were raising their ad budgets as competition in both the Carbonated Soft Drink (CSD) and non-carbonated drinks categories was heating up, sending Dew sales below targets. Choosing the right ads to maximize the impact of Mountain Dew's relatively small media budget was a make-or-break decision.

PepsiCo and BBDO

PepsiCo was widely considered to be one of the most sophisticated and aggressive marketing companies in the world. In North America, the company had three divisions, each with category-leading brands. Pepsi and Mountain Dew were the number two and three soft drinks. Frito-Lay dominated the salty-snack category with Ruffles, Lay's, Doritos, and Cheetos. And the company had recently acquired Tropicana, the leading juice brand. In 2000, PepsiCo had acquired the SoBe line of teas and "functional" drinks from South Beach Beverages, which it operated as a stand-alone subsidiary.

BBDO was one of the ten largest ad agencies in the world, with worldwide billings of about $15 billion. Of the largest full-service agencies, BBDO was particularly renowned for the quality of their creative work. The roster of the New York office, BBDO New York, included many high-powered clients such as General Electric, Visa, M&M/Mars, Charles Schwab, and FedEx. Their top 10 accounts had been BBDO clients for an average of 32 years. BBDO's relationship with PepsiCo dated to breakthrough campaigns for Pepsi in the 1960s. BBDO took over Mountain Dew from Ogilvy & Mather in 1974 and had held the account ever since. In 1998, PepsiCo hired Uniworld, the largest African-American owned ad agency in the United States, to develop a separate Mountain Dew campaign targeted to African-Americans.

The Carbonated Soft Drinks Category

Similar to most other countries, in the United States soft drink consumption was ubiquitous. And, until recently, soft drinks had meant cola. The retail carbonated soft drinks (CSD) category had long been dominated by the two cola giants, Coke and Pepsi. In the so-called cola wars of the 1960s and 70s, Pepsi directly attacked Coke with taste tests and with advertising designed to make Pepsi the hipper and more stylish "choice of the new generation," implying that Coke was a drink for older and less "with it" people. The soft drink category, and colas in particular, boomed throughout the 1970s and 1980s as people substituted away from coffee to soft drinks as a source of caffeine. The industry also consolidated as once-important brands (RC Cola, Orange Crush, A&W Root Beer) faded into the background. By the 1990s, three companies controlled all of the major national brands: The Coca-Cola Company (Coke, Diet Coke, Sprite), PepsiCo (Pepsi, Diet Pepsi, Mountain Dew), and Cadbury-Schweppes (Dr. Pepper and 7-UP).

CSDs were a promotion intensive category. In most grocery stores, Coke and Pepsi controlled a great deal of shelf space and displays. They had so much clout that their bottlers were able to choose how to stock the shelves and what to display. Impulse purchase displays had become an important source of incremental volume. A substantial and increasing share of volume came from convenience stores, where most purchases were of single servings purchased for immediate consumption. The major brands ran seasonal promotions, such as "under the cap" games in which every tenth bottle had a free bottle giveaway written under the cap. More junior brand managers spent considerable time developing and implementing these promotions.

Product, promotion, packaging, and pricing innovations were constant though usually incremental, quickly diffusing throughout the category. In the last decade, one of the major innovations in the category had been the 20-ounce single serve bottle, usually priced at $.99 and sold as an impulse purchase. The margins on this bottle were higher than the twelve-packs or 2-liter bottles. Also, all of the large brands introduced 24-pack cases sold to heavy users. Brand managers worked to keep package design contemporary. For example, at PepsiCo, both Pepsi and Mountain Dew had substantial make-overs in the 1990s resulting in richer and more vibrant colors and simplified graphics. Other brands, including 7-UP and Sprite also executed similar packaging re-designs.

For most of the twentieth century, PepsiCo and The Coca-Cola Company competed fiercely, each responding in tit-for-tat fashion to the other's successes. Pepsi rolled out lemon-lime Slice in the 1980s to compete against Sprite, but soon withdrew support for that brand. Recently it was rumored that the company was plotting yet another new lemon-lime introduction. In the 1970s, Coca-Cola introduced Mr. Pibb to attack Dr. Pepper and Mello-Yello as a me-too competitor against Mountain Dew. With Mountain Dew's national success in the 1990s, Coca-Cola launched a second frontal assault, introducing another copy-cat brand called Surge. In addition, both companies had launched other new products without much success: Coke had flopped with OK Cola (the cynical retro cola), and Fruitopia (the neo-hippie fruit beverage). PepsiCo had similar problems with the introduction of Crystal Pepsi (the clear crisp cola), though was able to establish Pepsi One as a niche brand.

In the 1990s, cola growth slowed and the "flavor" CSDs did very well. Sprite, Mountain Dew, and Dr. Pepper all enjoyed great success, although 7-UP continued to struggle (See **Exhibit 1**). In 1999, however, all CSD sales suffered as a result of customers' sticker shock to a category-wide 5% retail price increase, and also a trend toward experimentation with noncarbonated drinks and bottled water as substitutes for soft drinks. Sports drinks were led by Gatorade, tea and juice blends by Snapple, Arizona, and SoBe, and the highly caffeinated "energy" drinks by Red Bull. These drinks, sometimes termed "functional" or "alternative," often included a stimulant (caffeine or similar substance) and plant extracts reputed to have medicinal value (ginko, guarana, St. John's Wort, ginseng). Many of these drinks were launched by small companies with grass-roots marketing efforts focused on music and sports sponsorships, on-site promotions, and non-traditional distribution (e.g., sandwich shops for Snapple, record stores for Red Bull). Industry rumors were circulating that Coca-Cola, Anheuser-Busch, PepsiCo, and Cadbury-Schweppes were working aggressively to develop functional drinks to tap into this growing segment.

Advertising and Branding

Over many decades, Coca-Cola had become "America's drink" (and later the preferred drink in many countries around the world) through advertising that conveyed that Coke served as a social elixir. Coke promoted the idea that the drink brought people together in friendship around ideas that people in the nation cared about. From 1995 onward, Coke had struggled as it experimented with a variety of new branding ideas. Pepsi rose to the rank of Coke's loyal opposition in the 1960s with the successful "The Pepsi Generation" ad campaign, in which the brand harnessed the ideas and passions of the 1960s counterculture.

EXHIBIT 1 CSD Sales/Share: (Million Cases/Percent Market)

Source: Maxwell Report.

	1990		1991		1992		1993		1994		1995		1996		1997		1998		1999 (Est.)	
	Sales	Share	Sales	Share	Sales	Share	Sales	Share	Sales	Share	Sales	Share	Sales	Share	Sales	Share	Sales	Share	Sales	Share
Coke	1,565.5	20.1	1,597.9	20.1	1,613.9	20.1	1,680.4	20.2	1,776.7	20.4	1,868.6	20.8	1,929.2	20.8	1,978.2	20.6	2,037.5	20.6	2,018.0	20.3
Pepsi	1,370.0	17.6	1,338.0	16.9	1,327.3	16.5	1,305.9	15.7	1,310.0	15.0	1,344.3	15.0	1,384.6	14.9	1,391.5	14.5	1,399.8	14.2	1,371.8	13.8
Diet Coke	726.9	9.3	741.2	9.3	732.6	9.1	740.6	8.9	767.6	8.8	793.0	8.8	811.4	8.7	819.0	8.5	851.8	8.6	843.0	8.5
Diet Pepsi	490.0	6.3	500.0	6.3	509.5	6.4	491.5	5.9	511.2	5.9	521.4	5.8	541.5	5.8	523.5	5.5	529.7	5.4	503.0	5.1
Sprite	295.0	3.8	313.1	3.9	328.1	4.1	357.6	4.3	396.3	4.5	460.3	5.1	529.8	5.7	598.0	6.2	651.8	6.6	671.5	6.8
Dr Pepper	364.8	4.7	385.3	4.9	414.0	5.2	445.6	5.4	485.1	5.6	515.0	5.7	536.8	5.8	566.8	5.9	599.4	6.1	630.0	6.3
Mountain Dew	300.0	3.9	327.5	4.1	351.1	4.4	387.6	4.7	455.0	5.2	509.6	5.7	535.6	5.8	605.2	6.3	665.1	6.7	705.0	7.1
7-UP	211.5	2.7	207.7	2.6	211.3	2.6	209.9	2.5	221.5	2.5	219.9	2.5	217.7	2.3	216.7	2.3	210.9	2.1	204.9	2.1
Surge															69.0		51.8		26.7	
Mello Yello	42.9		49.5		59.5		64.0		64.6		61.6		59.0		46.6		42.4		41.6	

EXHIBIT 2 **Advertising Spending: Television Media**
(Major CSDs, $MM)

Source: Competitive Media Reports.

	1990	1991	1992	1993	1994	1995	1996	1997	1998	1999	2000 (Est.)
Coke	$157.4	$139.9	$168.1	$131.1	$161.5	$124.7	$199.8	$156.8	$140.4	$167.7	$208.3
Pepsi	129.8	141.3	137.8	144.0	120.6	133.1	98.1	133.1	140.5	165.9	159.6
Mountain Dew	12.9	20.0	25.9	29.1	30.3	38.3	40.4	43.1	50.3	45.0	55.9
Sprite	32.0	36.1	27.5	26.9	36.0	54.6	57.9	60.6	56.2	69.9	87.7
Dr Pepper	32.2	49.3	50.1	52.8	61.5	65.4	67.9	81.0	86.8	102.4	106.8
7-UP	38.8	37.4	23.7	29.4	27.3	23.2	33.1	38.7	27.0	38.7	45.1
Surge	0.0	0.0	0.0	0.0	0.0	0.0	0.0	15.5	21.0	19.6	0.2

More recently, Pepsi used celebrities—particularly musicians such as Michael Jackson, Madonna, Faith Hill, Ricky Martin, and Mary J. Blige—to convey the idea that Pepsi was an expression of youth attitudes. Nonetheless, the Pepsi brand also had struggled to maintain sales in the 1990s.

7-UP was successful in the 1970s branding against the colas as the "uncola" in ads that used a charismatic Jamaican actor to describe the purity and naturalness of 7-UP in a tropical setting. Similarly, the sweet cherry-cola concoction Dr Pepper challenged the audience to "be a Pepper" with well-received dance numbers that encouraged consumers to do their own thing rather than follow the masses in drinking cola. From the late 1980s onward, 7-UP faded as the brand was used as a cash cow with ever-shrinking media investments. Meanwhile, Mountain Dew rose from its regional status to become a major "flavor" brand. The three major flavor brands dominated different geographic areas: Dr Pepper dominated Texas and the rest of the deep South, Mountain Dew dominated rural areas, particularly in the Midwest and Southeast, and Sprite dominated urban-ethnic areas.

Category advertising spending exceeded $650 Million (See **Exhibit 2**). PepsiCo spent substantially less as a percentage of sales than its competitors. Instead, the company relied on exceptional creative to make the advertising work harder for less cost. PepsiCo viewed the creative development process as a key organizational competency, a strategic weapon that was central to their financial success.

Mountain Dew Brand History

Mountain Dew was invented by the Hartman Beverage Company in Knoxville, Tennessee, in the late 1940s. The bright yellow-green drink in the green bottle packed a powerful citrus flavor, more sugar and more caffeine than other soft drinks, and less carbonation so that it could be drunk quickly. The drink became a favorite on the Eastern seaboard, through Kentucky, Tennessee, and eventually spread up through the Great Lakes states (skirting the big cities) and into the Northern Plains of Minnesota and the Dakotas. PepsiCo, amazed by Dew's success in what brand managers would come to call the "NASCAR belt" (the stock car racing circuit that drew rural men as its primary audience), and in need of a "flavor" soft-drink to round out its line-up, purchased Mountain Dew in 1964.

PepsiCo originally assigned Mountain Dew to the Ogilvy & Mather ad agency. The strategy for the new brand extrapolated from Dew's origins and existing packaging. The beverage's heart-pumping caffeine and sugar rush were linked to its backwoods heritage to produce the idea of a comic "hillbilly" character named Willie who drank Mountain Dew to "get high" on the soft drink equivalent of moonshine liquor. The tagline, "Yahoo! Mountain Dew!" was accompanied by "Thar's a bang in ever' bottle."

In 1973 PepsiCo assigned the brand to BBDO, its agency of record for Pepsi. For two decades client and agency worked to expand the brand's reach from America's hinterlands into the suburbs and cities of the major metropolitan areas. The major campaign of the 1970s—"Hello Sunshine"—sought to tie Mountain Dew's distinctive product characteristics to a set of backcountry recreational images. The yellow-green product and strong citrus flavor are represented over and over by the gleaming sun sparkling in beautiful natural settings. The product name is represented in virtually every ad by mountains, dew drops reflecting in the sun, and condensed drops on cans to represent dew. The energizing effects of the caffeine and sugar are toned down and now are a refreshing part of an active outdoor lifestyle. Often the ads featured casual coed athletic activities that always ended in a plunge into a rural pond or creek.

This campaign pulled the Mountain Dew brand into more contemporary terrain, but it was still too rural to get much traction in the suburbs. So in the 1980s, PepsiCo directly targeted suburban teenagers with a new campaign called "Country Cool." The creative idea was to marry the popular athletic endeavors of suburban kids (cool) with Mountain Dew's active rural lifestyle (country), all punctuated by the refreshing Dew plunge. Ads featured male teens performing on skateboards, mountain bikes, and BMX bikes. A new tune was crafted for the occasion: "Being cool you'll find is a state of mind. Your refreshing attitude. Things get hot. Cool is all you got. Dewin' it country cool. So chill on out; when the heat comes on. With a cool, smooth Mountain Dew. Dewin' it Country Cool. Mountain Dew. Dewin' it Country Cool."

BBDO jettisoned the "country" component of the campaign in 1991 to build an entire campaign around athletic stunts. This advertising departed dramatically from anything that BBDO had produced in the previous sixteen years. The spots featured daredevil maneuvers of sports like windsurfing, rollerblading, motocross cycling, and paragliding. The closely framed shots, which put the viewer in the middle of the action, also suggested excitement and energy. The spots were set to aggressive rock music rather than studio jingles. In 1992, a new song called "Get Vertical" is introduced with the lyrics "Ain't no doubt about the power of dew, got the airborne thrust of rocket fuel."

Cultural Trends

PepsiCo and BBDO managers paid close attention to cultural trends. They were particularly focused on track music and sports trends since these activities were so central to youth culture.

Music

Three musical trends dominated the airwaves in the 1990s. Rap music exploded to become the most popular genre in the country. At first, gangsta rap, which flaunted misogynistic and violent lyrics, was said to represent the reality of life in the "hood" (the American ghetto). From 1992 onward, gangsta rap broke out with a lighter sound and slightly less aggressive lyrics, sometimes called gangsta-lite, that made the music much more accessible while maintaining the forbidding connotations. By 1993, media coverage of the travails of celebrity rappers like Snoop Doggy Dog and Tupac Shakur ruled not only the music magazines but *People* and *Newsweek*. Rap music, and the hip-hop lifestyle of which it was a part, permeated teen life. MTV's program *Yo! MTV Raps* and specialty magazines like *The Source* and *Vibe* became mainstream cultural venues. By 1999, rap remained very popular amongst male teens, especially in urban areas, though its Top 40 appeal had subsided somewhat.

At roughly the same time, the alternative rock music scene, which throughout the 1980s existed as a small subcultural scene found mostly on college campuses, also exploded. Two Seattle bands—Nirvana and Pearl Jam—put CDs at the top of the charts with aggressive and emotive music that combined equal parts punk and heavy metal. The media tagged this music "grunge" and anointed Seattle as grunge headquarters. Grunge was marketed heavily by the culture industries—music labels put out dozens of grunge bands, films that displayed the grunge attitude appeared, and fashion runways and J.C. Penny's stores were clogged with flannel shirts and clothes that had the look of the vintage Salvation Army gear that was the uniform of the grunge scene. Grunge faded in its influence in part due to the death of its most talented lead actor when Nirvana's Kurt Cobain committed suicide in 1995.

Later in 1990s, techno music began making significant inroads into American youth culture. Invented in the 1980s as "house music" in low-budget studios of Chicago and Detroit, this beat-driven dance music became the lifeblood of dance parties called "raves" in places like London and the Spanish island of Ibiza. Raves quickly spread throughout continental Europe and beyond. Raves were all-night dancing marathons often set up in warehouses, exotic outdoor locales, and other improvised spaces. Raves attracted young people, mostly teens, who danced for hours at a time, not in pairs, but in free-form groups. The highly rhythmic music and long-winded dancing combined to produce for some fans an ecstatic trance-like state. The music was produced almost entirely by disk jockeys sampling records with tape loops and other electronic tricks. Many sub-genres have since emerged that mix-and-match musical styles from around the world. Part of the scene was a drug called ecstasy, a drug that induces promiscuous affection, sensory overload, and euphoria. And, to keep the energy flowing all night, the dancers demanded energizing drinks. In particular, an enterprising Austrian company marketed Red Bull, a drink that was once an Asian hangover cure, as a rave stimulant. Either straight or mixed with vodka, Red Bull became the rave drink of choice. Raves diffused rather late to the United States, but proved to be most popular in the major metropolitan areas.

Sports

The so-called "alternative sports" took off in the early 1990s. Teen enthusiasts transformed casual hobby activities—mountain biking, skateboarding, paragliding, BMX biking, and in-line skating—into highly technical, creative, and often dangerous sports. Snowboarding became an overnight hit with teens. Bungee jumping was a fad that disappeared quickly. As these sports became increasingly risky and creative, they began to attract spectators. So-called extreme sports—skiing down extremely steep terrain or jumping off tall buildings with a parachute—were covered by ESPN. ESPN also aggressively promoted circuits and tournaments to professionalize these new sports, which culminated in the Extreme Games in 1994, a non-traditional Olympics of sorts. Mountain Dew was one of the founding lead sponsors of the Extreme Games, which later became the X Games. Later, NBC followed with the Gravity Games, and MTV also began to cover these sports. Grunge music, more aggressive styles of rap, and various hybrids were prominent aural expressions of these sports.

GenX Ethos

During the 1990s, teens and young adults evinced a growing cynicism toward the dominant work-oriented values of the previous generation and toward corporations more generally. They found that working hard to get ahead in terms of salary and occupational prestige was harder to swallow in an era of corporate reengineering. Their cynicism also extended to corporations themselves and their marketing efforts. As this cohort became increasingly knowledgeable about how marketing worked and increasingly jaded about why brands were popular, they were not interested in listening to "sales messages" that tried to persuade them into believing a particular brand of soft drink or beer was cool. Instead, these youth adopted a campy interest in non-trendy products, television programs, and music of previous eras. As these odd new tastes became commercialized in programming like Nick-elodeon cable channel's "Nick at Nite" series—which featured less-than-notable program-ming from the 1950s–1970s—"retro" was born.

The Do the Dew Campaign

In 1992, senior management at PepsiCo sensed an opportunity to increase business on Diet Mountain Dew. Diet Mountain Dew's distribution was limited mostly to the rural regions where the brand was strongest, even though regular Dew was now a national brand. Diet Mountain Dew performed very well on product tests versus other diet drinks in the category because the heavy citrus flavor did a better job of masking the undesirable taste of the arti-ficial sweetener. So PepsiCo allocated money for incremental advertising to support an effort to expand Diet Mountain Dew distribution. Bill Bruce, then a junior copywriter working on several brands, was assigned to the project. The strategy statements that guided the initial creative idea and subsequent spots in the campaign are reported in **Exhibit 3.** Bruce came up with the "Do Diet Dew" tag line (which soon evolved into "Do the Dew" to support the entire brand) and several new ideas to embellish what BBDO had begun with the Get Vertical campaign.

The first breakthrough ad of the new campaign, *Done That,* features a hair-raising shot of a guy jumping off the edge of a cliff to take a free-fall toward the narrow canyon's river bottom, set to throbbing grunge music. This was the first ad to feature the "Dew Dudes"—four young guys who are witnessing the daredevil stunts presented in the ad and comment-ing on them. *Done That* became a huge hit, capturing the country's imagination. The ad was widely parodied and the phrase "been there, done that" entered the vernacular. For 1994 and 1995, BBDO produced three carbon-copy "pool-outs"[1] of *Done That.* By 1995, after two years of these ads, consumer interest in the creative was fading fast. According to Jeff Mordos, if the creative hadn't moved to another idea that year, consumer's flagging in-terest and the potential of a revolt by PepsiCo bottlers likely would have forced PepsiCo to develop an entirely new campaign.

For 1995, three of four spots produced relied upon different creative ideas. One of these spots, *Mel Torme,* became the second hit of the campaign. The spot was a parody featuring the aging Vegas lounge singer Mel Torme, tuxedo-clad atop a Vegas hotel crooning "I Get a Kick out of You," with lyrics altered to incorporate Mountain Dew references. He im-presses the Dew Dudes with a base jump of his own. Similar ads followed. In *007,* a teenage James Bond engages in a frenetic pursuit scene with typical Bond stunts, accom-panied by the familiar Bond theme music. The Dew Dudes are not impressed until Bond comes upon a Mountain Dew vending machine. In *Training,* brash tennis star Andre Agassi performs extreme stunts as training exercises, and then plays an extreme game of tennis with the Dew Dudes as his coaches.

In 1997, BBDO came up with two breakthrough spots. The director of Nirvana's classic music video "Smells Like Teen Spirit" was hired to direct *Thank Heaven,* which mimics a music video. The spot stars the lead singer of an alternative rock band called Ruby. She sings a punked-up version of the classic song "Thank Heaven for Little Girls," in which the grunge style suggests the "little girls" of old have been replaced by the feminine brand of aggressiveness presented in the ad. *Jackie Chan* deploys the Hong Kong movie star's patented martial arts with humorous stunts into the campaign's jaded, "seen it already"

---

[1] The noun pool-out is derived from a verb that is particular to the advertising business—"to pool out." The idea is to develop a pool of ads that are all closely related derivations from the same cre-ative idea. Some advertisers feel that pools deliver a more consistent campaign while others feel that the ads become too formulaic when they are so similar. Regardless, there is a great temptation when an ad breaks through and becomes a hit to develop pool-outs to extend the popularity.

EXHIBIT 3 Mountain Dew Brand Communications Strategies (1993–1999)

Source: PepsiCo.

	Objective	Strategy	Target	Executional Direction
1993–94	Increase awareness and trial of Mountain Dew	You can have the most thrilling, exciting, daring experience but it will never compete with the experience of a Mt. Dew	Male teens/young adults	• Distinct campaign with Dew equity consistency • Leverage "full tilt taste" and "rush" as point of difference
1995	Distinguish Mt. Dew within the competitive environment through contemporary communication of the trademark's distinct, historical positioning	You can have the most thrilling, exciting, daring experience but it will never compete with the experience of a Mt. Dew	Bull's eye: 18 yr. old leading edge male Broad: 12–29 year olds	• Shift to a unified trademark focus modeled after "Do Diet Dew" • Explore outdoor settings • Predominant male, mid-20's casting • Preserve balance between "outlandish" and "realistic" actions/sports
1996	Optimize Dew's positioning equity among the target in a highly relevant and contemporary manner	(You can have the most thrilling, exciting, daring experience but . . .) there's nothing more intense than slamming a Mt. Dew	Bull's eye: 18 yr. old leading edge male Broad: 12–29 year olds	• Bring "Do the Dew" trademark campaign to the next level
1997	Optimize Dew's positioning equity among the target in a highly relevant and contemporary manner • Strengthen brand perceptions among AA • Encourage product trial where familiarity is low	(You can have the most thrilling, exciting, daring experience but . . .) there's nothing more intense than slamming a Mt. Dew	Bull's eye: 18 yr. old leading edge male Broad: 12–29 year olds	• Continue "Do the Dew" trademark campaign and encompass the Mt. Dew experience
1998	Build badge value and authentic, true Icon status for Mt. Dew in the world of youth-targeted consumer goods	Associate Mt. Dew with thrilling and exhilarating adventures in a light-hearted manner	Bull's eye: 18 yr. old leading edge male Broad: 12–29 male/female	• Evolve the "Do the Dew" campaign against core target with fresh and relevant copy • Develop ethnically targeted "cross-appeal" spot • Enhance product perception
1999	Optimize relevance of Dew's positioning among the target	Associate Mt. Dew with the exhilarating intensity of life's most exciting, fun adventures	Male Teens (16 yr. old epicenter) • Invite teen girls while continuing as male CSD • Maintain cross-over appeal among 20–39 year olds	• Develop pool of "Do the Dew" executions • Explore other metaphors beyond alternative sports to express "exhilarating intensity" • One execution should have AA/urban relevance • Communicate quenching • Inclusion of water-greenery elements not mandatory

motif. The ad begins in the midst of what seems like a classic chase scene from a Chan film with lots of harrowing action. When Chan faces down his enemy, the Dew Dudes magically appear as Confucian wisemen who assist Chan with cans of Mountain Dew.

Other ads produced were significantly less effective. *Scream,* a high-speed amalgam of extreme sports shots that are organized to answer the lead-in question—"What is a Mountain Dew?"—did not fare well. And *Michael Johnson,* a spot developed to broaden Dew's appeal in the African-American community, did not meet the company's expectations.

By 1998, PepsiCo managers worried that the advertising was becoming too predictable. In particular, they were concerned that the use of alternative sports was becoming less impactful due to oversaturation. Many other brands, including companies like Bagel Bites, AT&T, Gillette Extreme Deodorant, and Slim Jims beef jerky snacks, were now major sponsors of alternative sports. To keep the campaign fresh, they needed to find alternative ways to express Mountain Dew's distinctive features. *Parking Attendant,* produced in 1999, was a solid effort at advancing toward an alternative expression. The spot features a parking attendant who takes liberties when parking a BMW handed off by a stuffy businessman. The kid drives as if in a police chase, flying from one building to another, accompanied by a frenetic surf instrumental that had been featured in Quentin Tarantino's *Pulp Fiction* a few years prior.

Mountain Dew Market Research

Mountain Dew's distinctive demographic profile reflected the brand's historic popularity in the NASCAR belt (see the Brand Development Index Map in **Exhibit 4** and lifestyle analysis in **Exhibit 5a**). And Mountain Dew had much lower penetration of the total population than its major competitors. But its consumers were the most loyal in the category. Mountain Dew had the highest "gatekeeping" rating of all CSDs—it was the drink that mothers tried the hardest to keep out of the stomachs of their children. Periodically, the PepsiCo research department fielded a major study to assess the "health" of the brand, and to direct any fine-tuning. A 1997 "brand fitness" study profiled the status of the Dew brand versus its major competitors (**Exhibit 6a–d**).

PepsiCo monitored both the effectiveness of individual ads, as well as the cumulative impact of advertising on the overall health of the Mountain Dew brand. The contribution made by a single ad toward building brand equity was notoriously challenging to measure. Both quantitative and qualitative research provided data from which managers make useful inferences. But Pepsi managers had yet to find a research method that was accurate enough to rely upon to provide definitive judgments on ad effectiveness. PepsiCo routinely gathered a wide variety of data that hinted at an ad's impact. In addition to formal research, managers monitored "talk value" or "buzz"—the extent to which the ad has been picked up by the mass media. In particular, *The Tonight Show* and David Letterman were useful barometers. Feedback from the Mountain Dew website, unofficial websites, and the brand's 800 number were important gauges as well. In addition, PepsiCo carefully monitored how the salesforce and bottlers responded to the ads, since they were getting direct feedback from their customers. PepsiCo managers used all these data as filters. But, ultimately, the evaluation of advertising rested on managerial judgement. Based on their past experience with the brand and with advertising across many brands, managers made a reasoned evaluation.

However, PepsiCo managers did rely on market research to assess the cumulative impact of advertising on the brand. Because many other factors—especially pricing and retail display activity—had an immediate short-term impact on sales, it was often difficult to draw causal relationships between advertising and sales. But advertising campaigns do directly impact how the brand is perceived. And these perceptions, in turn, drive sales. So PepsiCo

EXHIBIT 4 Mountain Dew Brand Development Index Map

Source: BBDO New York.

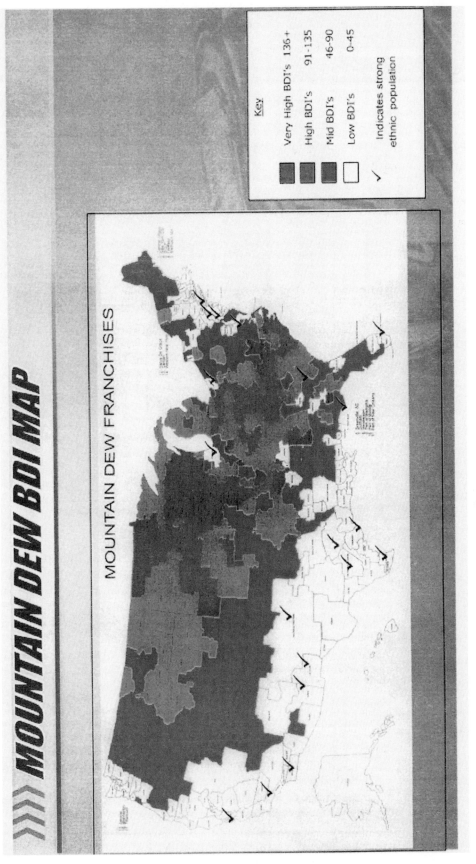

EXHIBIT 5A   **Spectra Lifestyle Analysis**

Source: AC Nielsen Product Library 11/97 to 11/99.

Mountain Dew Consumption Index							
Lifestage							
SPECTRA LIFESTYLE	**18–34 W/Kids**	**18–34 W/O Kids**	**35–54 W/Kids**	**35–54 W/O Kids**	**55–64**	**65+**	**Total Lifestyle**
Upscale Suburbs	82	77	101	56	45	13	64
Traditional Families	118	121	160	79	42	35	96
Mid Upscale Suburbs	101–	111	108	71	64	18	66
Metro Elite	139	85	141	47	47	21	72
Working Class Towns	237	139	242	121	67	42	139
Rural Towns & Farms	225	153	212	141	91	39	140
Mid Urban Melting Pot	148	104	97	52	49	31	74
Downscale Rural	309	142	291	127	87	43	158
Downscale Urban	99	98	107	73	55	32	76
Total Lifestage	171	112	165	83	61	31	100

had assembled a set of what they termed key performance indicators (KPIs), intermediate measures that were directly impacted by advertising and that had been proven to significantly impact sales. Managers tracked KPIs, also referred to as *brand health* measures, both for teens and for 20–39 year olds. But managers were particularly concerned with brand health amongst teens because at this age soft drink consumers often moved from experimenting with a variety of drinks to becoming loyal lifetime drinkers of a single soda. The latest study, conducted in the spring of 1999, reported Mountain Dew's teen KPIs. Dew improved 6 points on "Dew Tastes Better" (to 48% versus a year ago). Unaided brand awareness had dropped 5 points (to 39%). "For someone like me" had increased 5 points (to 53%). And "Dew Drinkers are Cool" increased 5 points (to 64%).

2000 Planning

In 1999, Mountain Dew became the third largest carbonated soft drink at retail, overtaking Diet Coke. However, part of this success in gaining share had to do with the sustained weakness of Pepsi and Coke. In 1999, the problems that the colas were facing seemed to be spreading to Mountain Dew, Sprite, and Dr. Pepper. All of the leading CSDs began to show real weakness as alternative non-carbonated drinks began to attract a great deal of trial, especially amongst teens. While Mountain Dew sales began to lag, all of the "brand health" indicators remained strong. And the advertising continued to significantly outperform competition. In planning for 2000, Moffitt and his senior management were particularly concerned with two dilemmas:

- How to keep the "Do the Dew" campaign working hard to build the brand given that extreme sports were becoming overexposed
- How to respond to the growing threat of non-CSDs, especially Gatorade and the new highly caffeinated and sugary energy drinks like Red Bull

A detailed strategy statement was developed by Moffitt's team at Pepsi-Cola North America, in conjunction with the account team at BBDO New York led by Cathy Israelevitz. This strategy was boiled down to a single sentence to focus the development of new creative: *Symbolize that drinking Mountain Dew is an exhilarating experience.* This document was used to brief Bruce and his creative team (**Exhibit 7**).

EXHIBIT 5B   Lifestyle Glossary

Source: AC Nielsen Product Library 11/97 to 11/99.

Upscale Suburbs
"The American Dream," a nice house in a nice suburban neighborhood. College-educated executives and professionals who index high on travel, eating out, playing golf, going to health clubs, buying imported cars, watching/reading business and news. Low African-American and Hispanic. High income.

Traditional Families
Like Upscale Suburbs, but lower socio-economic level. Mix of lower level administrators and professionals with well-paid blue-collar. Index high on: gardening, DIY home improvement, driving SUVs, camping, classic rock, sports radio. Low African-American and Hispanic. Mid-high income.

Mid/Upscale Suburbs
Live in first-generation suburbs that are now part of the urban fringe. Lower income than Traditional Families, but more college-educated and white collar. Index high on: baseball fans, casino gambling, using internet, attending live theatre, reading science and technology, listening/watching news. Low African-American and Hispanic. Mid-high income.

Metro Elite
Younger and more urban, college-educated, ethnically diverse. Very attuned to new fashions. Geographically mobile. Index high on: health clubs, bars and night clubs, fashion magazines, VH-1, music, film, computers. Middle income.

Working Class Towns
Well paid blue collar families living in suburbs of smaller cities. Index high on: auto racing, fishing, hunting, country music, camping, televised sports. Own trucks or minivans. Low African-American and Hispanic. Middle income.

Rural Towns & Farms
Small towns mostly in the middle of the country, dominated by blue-collar and agricultural work. Index high on: rodeos, fishing, woodworking, chewing tobacco, wrestling, camping, country music, TV movies, USA and TNN channels. Don't read magazines and newspapers. Low African-American. Lower income.

Mid Urban Melting Pot
Urban multi-ethnic neighborhoods. Old European ethnic enclaves and new Asian immigrants, mixed with African-American and Hispanic neighborhoods. Index high on: menthol cigarettes, dance music, boxing, pro basketball, lottery, Home Shopping Network, heavy TV viewing, urban contemporary radio. Lower income, low college, service industries.

Downscale Rural
Poor rural areas in Appalachia, throughout the South, and the Plains States. This socially conservative and religious area is sometimes called "the bible belt:" While indexing high African-American, these are very segregated neighborhoods with little racial mixing. Lowest on education, occupation, income, housing. Index high on: trucks, chewing tobacco, belonging to veteran's club, target shooting, tractor pulls, country music, fishing and hunting, daytime drama TV programs.

Downscale Urban
Same socioeconomic profile as Downscale Rural but very different cultural profile, more similar to Mid-Urban Melting Pot. Mostly African-American and Hispanic urban neighborhoods.

Super Bowl

In addition to these strategic issues, Moffitt had to consider carefully where these ads would be broadcast. Mountain Dew's national media plan focused on a younger audience. Typical buys would include MTV, *The Simpsons*, and ESPN during alternative sports broadcasts. However, with its long run of sales increases in the 1990s, Mountain Dew was becoming less of a niche brand. Partly in recognition of this expanding customer base and partly to celebrate within the company Dew's arrival as the third most popular CSD, top management decided to feature Mountain Dew rather than Pepsi during the Super Bowl.

The Super Bowl had for decades been a hugely influential event for advertisers. The game drew the biggest audience of the year and the ads received an amazing amount of attention. In recent years, the frenzy around the advertising had grown disproportionately to the game itself. The media paid almost as much attention to the ads shown as to the teams and players. The networks interviewed the advertisers and the stars of the ads, and even replayed the ads on their programs. So a Super Bowl ad now had a huge ripple effect in free public relations. In addition, the Super Bowl was an extremely important contest for

EXHIBIT 6A
Brand Imagery—
Mountain Dew

Source: BBDO New York.

Product Imagery

User Imagery (54%)

Psychographic Imagery

*Too sweet
Most entertaining ads
Fun to drink
Intense experience
Lots of flavor

When need energy boost
In mood for something different
*At a sporting event

Adventurous
Wild
Active
Daring
*Courageous
Exciting
Free-spirited
Rebellious
Spontaneous
Athletic
Youthful
Cool
Hip
*Out-going

EXHIBIT 6B **Brand Imagery—Surge**

Source: BBDO New York.

Product Imagery

User Imagery (49%)

Psychographic Imagery

*Can't relate to ads
*Low quality product
*Not always available
Unique
Intense experience
*Tastes artificial

When need energy boost
In mood for something
    different

Wild
Rebellious
Daring
Adventurous
Active
Up-to-date
Athletic
*Trendy
Youthful
*Leading-edge
Exciting
Spontaneous
Individualistic
*Powerful
Hip
In style

EXHIBIT 6C   **Brand Imagery—7 UP**

Source: BBDO New York.

Product Imagery

*Least fattening
 Lowest calories
 Low in sodium
*Too little flavor
*Not sweet enough
*Not filling
*Healthy/good for you
 Most refreshing

User Imagery (48%)

Psychographic Imagery

Sensitive
Relaxed
Peaceful
*Healthy
Feminine
Kind
*Nurturing

(Nice)
(Loyal)
(Cooperative)

EXHIBIT 6D   **Brand Imagery—Sprite**

Source: BBDO New York.

Product Imagery

Lowest calories
Most refreshing
*Thirst quenching
*Goes down easy
Low in sodium

 In a nice restaurant
*After exercise/sports

(In the evening)
(In the morning)

User Imagery (56%)

Psychographic Imagery

Feminine
Sensitive
Peaceful
*Nice
Relaxed
Free-spirited
*Cooperative
*Friendly
*Happy
Kind

(Innovative)

EXHIBIT 7
**Mountain Dew
FY 2000 Brand
Communications
Strategy**

Source: PepsiCo.

Objective: Expand appeal of Mountain Dew to new users while reinforcing it among current users
Positioning: To 18 year old males, who embrace excitement, adventure and fun, Mountain Dew is the great tasting carbonated soft drink that exhilarates like no other because it is energizing, thirst-quenching, and has a one-of-a-kind citrus flavor.
Communication Strategy: Symbolize that drinking Mountain Dew is an exhilarating experience.
Target: Male Teens—18 year-old epicenter

- Ensure appeal amongst 20–39 year olds (current users)
- Drive universal appeal (white, African-American, Hispanic, and other ethnic)

Product Benefits	Emotional Benefits	Personality
Energizing	Exhilaration	Irreverent
Quenching	Excitement	Daring
Great Taste		Fun

advertisers and especially for ad agencies. To "win" the Super Bowl (to be voted the top ad in the *USA Today* Ad Meter poll reported in the newspaper the following day) was a prestigious honor within the industry. Finally, Super Bowl ads provided a powerful sales tool to motivate retailers and distributors. PepsiCo and other grocery products advertisers used their annual Super Bowl advertising to sell in retail displays.

Super Bowl advertising, as a result, had become a distinctive genre within advertising. The demographically diverse audience demanded advertising with hooks that were easily understood. Insider humor did not work. While MTV ads could talk in a colloquial language to teens, Super Bowl ads could not afford this luxury. Second, the heated competition to win the affection of the audience had led to "big" productions that would stand out against an ever-more impressive set of competitors.

The New Creative

Bruce and Cassar had just finished presenting ten new ad concepts for PepsiCo to evaluate. For each concept, PepsiCo managers were given a "storyboard"—a script and a set of rough pencil sketches that depicted the most important scenes. Bruce and Cassar talked through each storyboard to help the client imagine how the ad would look if it were produced. The storyboard served as the skeletal outline of the ad. The creatives put flesh on these bones by describing in detail the characters, the action, how the scene is depicted, and the music. Of the ten new concepts, Moffitt and his senior managers hoped to select three ads to produce. The two best ads would run on the Super Bowl and then all three ads would be broadcast throughout 2000. It was already October, so there was barely enough time to produce the ads presented to get them on the Super Bowl. Asking Bruce to try again was not an option. The ten initial concepts were quickly whittled down to five finalists.

1) *Labor of Love.* A humorous spot about the birth of a Dew drinker. The doctor in the delivery room calls out "code green" and retreats to catch with a baseball mitt the baby as it shoots out of its mother like a cannon.

2) *Cheetah.* One of the Dew Dudes chases down a cheetah on a mountain bike. The cheetah, running on the African plain, has stolen his Dew and he wants it back. He tackles the cat, pulls the can out of the cat's stomach, but finds that it's empty and full of holes.

3) *Dew or Die.* The Dew Dudes are called in to foil the plot of an evil villain who is threatening to blow up the planet. Performing daredevil maneuvers down a mountain, they get sidetracked in a ski lodge with some girls, but accidentally save the world anyway, powered by a spilt can of Dew.

4) *Mock Opera*. A parody of the Queen song *Bohemian Rhapsody* sung by the Dew Dudes who mock the cover of the original Queen album. The ad portrays the story of the altered lyrics: alternative sports action in which the athletes just miss cans of Dew as they shoot by.

5) *Showstopper*. A take-off on an extravagantly choreographed production number that mimics a Buzby Berkeley musical/dance film from the 1930s. The dancers are silver-clad BMX riders and skateboarders who perform for the Dew Dudes posing as directors.

PepsiCo viewed the evaluation of new creative as the most challenging aspect of brand management. Unlike decisions on new product ideas, consumer promotions, or product improvements, there was no market research or marketplace data to guide the decision. Junior managers typically did not sit in the agency presentations as they were not yet seasoned enough to judge creative work. PepsiCo believed that managers first had to gain knowledge of how advertising worked to build brands through years of seasoning and tutorials on several of the company's brands. So Scott Moffitt was the most junior person in the room. The skills and judgment that he demonstrated would be key to moving up the ladder at PepsiCo.

Bill Bruce finished presenting his last storyboard and scanned the room to lock eyes with the PepsiCo executives who would be deciding the fate of his ideas. Scott Moffitt didn't return the gaze. Instead he looked anxiously at his superiors, knowing that the spotlight would next focus on him. This was his chance to prove himself not only to PepsiCo senior management, but also to BBDO. BBDO's senior managers had become influential advisors, whom PepsiCo's top marketing executives routinely relied upon to help guide branding decisions. With six years of experience under his belt, this was Moffitt's chance to earn their respect as a contributing member to these critical discussions. Moffitt was eager to make a strong impression with nuanced and well-reasoned evaluations. Following longstanding protocol in packaged goods companies, the junior manager at the table gets the first crack at evaluating the creative. Moffitt cleared his throat, complimented Bruce on the high quality of the new work he had presented, and began his evaluation.

# Part 5

Going to Market

Chapter 20

Going to Market

Robert J. Dolan

The marketing channel is the set of mechanisms or network via which a firm "goes to market." **Figure A** shows four major classes of functions this network typically serves. The channel first has to generate demand for a product/service, then fulfill that demand and provide for after-the-sale service. Finally, the channel often serves a useful function in transmitting feedback from the customer base back to the manufacturer.

When we think about "going to market" we have to consider what each of the functions will specifically entail, and who will do them—the manufacturer or a chosen partner such as a distributor or retailer. Very different "go to market" systems can be found in the marketplace. For example:

- Knoll Furniture, a leading maker of high-end office furniture systems, uses its own salesforce to generate demand from large accounts. Demand fulfillment takes place through a dealer network.

- Avon Products generated $5 billion in sales in 1997 selling through 2.6 million sales representatives worldwide. Selling mostly cosmetics and fragrances, these reps are independent agents, not employees of Avon, who work part-time selling to female customers on a door-to-door basis.

- Tupperware follows a similar direct selling model for its food storage containers, utilizing 950,000 independent Tupperware "consultants" worldwide. These consultants sell via the "party plan" in which potential customers gather at the home of a hostess for refreshments, product demonstration, and product ordering.

- The Gap, Inc. designs all its own products which it sells through over 2,000 company-owned retail stores. It recently moved into electronic retailing opening the "Gap Online" store at www.gap.com. It outsources manufacturing, purchasing from 1200 suppliers, but manages the "going-to-market" phase entirely itself.

FIGURE A
Market Channel
Tasks

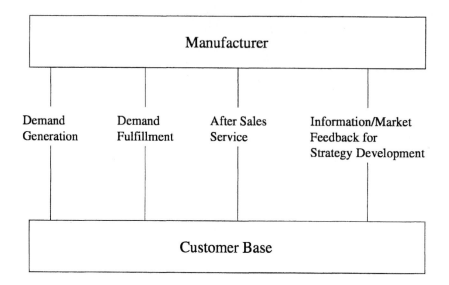

- BMW, on the other hand, goes-to-market through partners, about 300 franchised deal-ers selling its automobiles in the United States. The dealers and BMW share responsi-bility for demand generation. BMW designs and implements national advertising. Dealers provide for product display and convenient testing by customers. Dealers fulfill demand, delivering vehicles to customers, and provide local after-the-sale service.
- Compaq Computer sells primarily through third-party resellers. A systems integrator may obtain a Compaq computer and package it with other equipment to sell a system to a customer. Like the Gap, Compaq has recently added a direct on-line selling capability.

Due to differences in the market situation, these manufacturers have seen fit to "go-to-market" in different ways.

The go-to-market approach may vary even within firm for different customer segments. The firm may choose "multiple channels." The Gap's set up of electronic store on the Web is an example of this strategy. The not-time-pressured customer who enjoys shopping vis-its the company store at the mall; while the time-pressured shopper visits the on-line store. A given individual may find a different channel more efficient depending on the buying oc-casion, e.g., a new sweater meriting a store visit, a simple blue jean replenishment order for a known size and style being best handled "on the Web."

This note expands on the treatment of "Marketing Channels" in the Note on Marketing Strategy. As noted there, and suggested by these examples, the two key issues in "going to market" are (i) designing the network, i.e., who is on the team and what do we want each to do, and (ii) managing the network. In the short-term, this means figuring out how do we mo-tivate each team member to do the desired tasks. In the longer term, it means how do we evolve and hold the system together in light of new products, evolution of the customer base (e.g., formation of buying groups) and new communication technologies such as the Internet.

Channel Design

Not too long ago, the most common approach to channel design was a very simple one. It was made simple by two assumptions which are no longer tenable. The first was that you should reach all your customers the same way. The thinking was that "dual distribution" schemes were unworkable, e.g., selling to some customers via a company salesforce and to others via a distributor was asking for trouble; similarly having your own retail store on the streets of Manhattan and relying on retailers for coverage of less densely populated areas was a route to continual conflict. The second assumption was that if you signed up a channel partner between yourself and the end user you basically did a "baton pass" of the entire marketing job to that intermediary. A manufacturer using a distributor shipped product to that distribution and the distributor was responsible for generating leads, qualifying customers, conducting the selling process, closing the sale and delivering the product.

Now, however, the fragmentation of most firms' customer base has ruled out the "one-size fits all" channel strategy. For example, the boom in working at home has created a home office furniture business which those traditionally supplying large corporations find too significant to ignore. And, it's obvious you shouldn't sell to American Express and one of its cardholders in the same way. New customers have different information needs from the installed base. At the same time, the options for reaching customers have expanded. Quick delivery of a product in response to a customer used to necessitate a distributor holding stock in local areas. Now, the same can be provided by a single inventory point and a contract with Federal Express.

Instead of a one-size-fits all, baton-pass mentality we need to break up "the market" into segments and "the marketing job" into its component pieces, having the concept that different mechanisms could be the best way of accomplishing certain tasks for certain segments.

The first step in channel design is to ask: (1a) what segments of the market should be considered and then (1b) *for each segment individually* ask what tasks need to be performed and what are the feasible options for doing them? Moriarty and Moran[1] set out a process for designing "hybrid systems" in which different tasks are accomplished by different players.

In their example, they break demand generation down into four subtasks:

1. Lead generation
2. Lead qualification
3. Pre-sale activity persuading target customer
4. Closing the sale

Their terminology for the two other key channel tasks is:

5. Post-sale service
6. On-going account management

Using these basic tasks as a guide, one should develop a more specific set for each segment. For example, consider an office furniture manufacturer. As step 1a, he elects to serve both the "at home" segment and the large corporate segment. Research shows the following about the tasks needed to be accomplished in "obtaining and maintaining" the "at home" buyer.

Moriarty and Moran suggest using "The Hybrid Grid" to support decision-making on how tasks should be accomplished. The grid, as shown **Figure B,** is a map of the tasks to be accomplished as the columns and the ways of possibly accomplishing the task as the rows. Each column has one "X" placed in it to show the mechanism via which the task moving the customer through the purchase process may be effected.

At the start of the process, one should think expansively about the possible matrix rows, i.e., the options for providing for specific task accomplishment. For our furniture seller, for example, task #4 "Demonstrate Products" may initially suggest the need for a customer visit to retail outlet. But, with new technology, perhaps an adequate "demonstration" could be done virtually on the Web. Or, if convinced of the power of an in-home demonstration, one could induce it by offering free delivery and return if the product is not satisfactory.

[1] Rowland T. Moriarty and Ursula Moran, "Managing Hybrid Marketing Systems," *Harvard Business Review,* November–December 1990.

| Preliminary | 1. | Attract Attention as Potential Supplier |
| | 2. | Position Company as Ergonomic Experts and One-Stop Shop for All Needs (desk, chair, files, etc.) |

Present the Offering	3.	Describe Available Products
	4.	Demonstrate Products
	5.	Communicate Prices

Sale-to-Install	6.	Accept Order. Provide means of Tracking Order Status
	7.	Provide Rapid Delivery ("at home" buyer typically does not pre-plan)
	8.	Enable Easy Assembly/Installation

Post/Sale	9.	Manage Warranty Service Issues
	10.	Sell Accessories
	11.	Extend Credit

FIGURE B
The Hybrid Grid

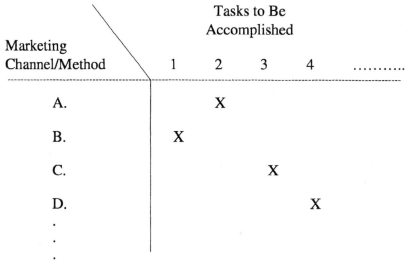

Imagine that the best plan for accomplishing the eleven at home buyer tasks are as follows:

Tasks 1–2:	Advertising in Mass Magazines
Tasks 3 and 5:	Website Preferred; Catalog for Those without Web Access
Task 4:	Free In-Home Trial
Task 6:	Limit Variety Available to Allow Delivery from Inventory and Use Federal Express or Other Express Shipper
Task 7, 8, 9:	Company Telemarketing/800 Number
Task 10:	Direct Mail (Using Addresses From Shipping Data)
Task 11:	MasterCard/Visa

In this model, the firm did not "pass the baton" of its marketing job to another entity. Rather it kept 9 of the 11 functions itself, and outsourced two: task 6 to Federal Express and task 11 to the credit card companies.

Obviously, the approach for our furniture maker to serve a large corporate account moving into a new headquarters building would be quite different. The economics of a large order allow for different selling techniques, but more fundamentally the tasks which need to be accomplished are different, e.g., they might be:

1. Get on Short List for This Job (any account of this size would already be aware of company and its positioning vis-à-vis competitors)
2. Present the Product Line
3. Demonstrate Company Ability to Customize a Solution to Client's Needs
4. Work with Client's Architect/Designer to Specify Furniture Solution, including Mock-up of Furniture at Customer Location
5. Negotiate Price/Terms
6. Facilitate Disposal of Old Furniture
7. Accept Order
8. Work with Other Vendors to Develop Installation Plan
9. Respond to Changes Made to Order from Time of Order to Delivery
10. Deliver and Install Systems
11. Maintain Systems
12. Sell Accessories and Additional Systems
13. Upgrade as New Products Are Introduced
14. Extend Credit

Again, the Hybrid Grid should be used to specify the possible mechanisms to accomplishing these tasks. This helps to show key handoffs and cooperations. For example, step 2 may be best achieved by a visit to the local dealer showroom. Then steps 3–7 are to be accomplished by the company salesperson without any dealer input.

This example we have worked through is typical in the sense that the different segments have very different marketing systems set up to serve them. In the case here, the at-home buyer and large corporation are so different that the systems are unlikely to come into conflict with one another. They could, if the firm made the mistake of offering a lower price on an item on its Website for the "at home" buyer than it offered to the customer buying large quantities of the same item. But generally, this example's two segments seem to be distinct enough that the manner of servicing one would have little impact on the other. Such is not always the case however. Once the tentative assessments have been made at the segment level, they have to be rolled up into a system view for potential channel conflicts.

As an example, **Figure C** depicts a marketing system in which the manufacturer has a multiple channel strategy, i.e., it "goes to market" through its own salesforce calling on large accounts and uses distributors to call on smaller accounts. Potential Conflict area #1 is that between the company salesforce and distributors. A distributor may regard a potential account as rightfully his to serve and resent the loss in margin opportunity due to the company's serving the large customers directly.

A specific example of this type of conflict in channels was Compaq's November 1998 decision to sell computers directly to small business customers via the Internet. The new Prosigna line was offered via the Compaq DirectPlus on-line service. Compaq was already selling through 44,000 dealers and described the addition of the direct channel for the segment as a melding of traditional sales channels and the Internet, offering customers a choice. However, one commentator noted "Customer choice is great, but can they really continue this highwire tension between channel sales and the direct model."[2]

---

[2] R. Guth, "Compaq Goes After Direct-Sales Model," *Infoworld,* November 16, 1998.

FIGURE C
Three Types of
Channel Conflict

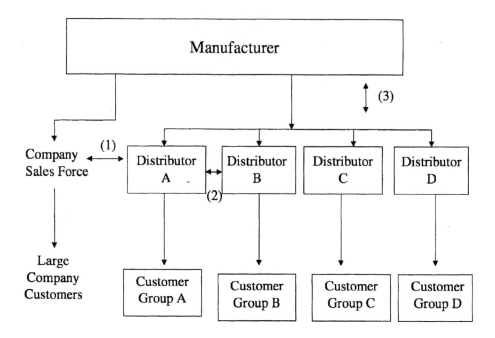

In the Compaq case, the potential conflict stemmed from a change in the marketing channel. Dealers felt an entitlement to the customers and that Compaq was now bypassing them
and reaching customers directly. Conflict issues of type #1 can arise even at the set-up of a
marketing channel from scratch. Often a firm perceives two segments in the market: a price
sensitive one and a service sensitive one. In an attempt to serve the price sensitive segment,
it distributes through "no frills" channels which keep costs low by performing little market
education and compete on price. The service-sensitive segment is to be served in a higher
cost, more service intensive channel. Conflicts arise when there is "leakage" between the
segments. For example, a customer gets his/her education needs met in a specialty store,
then goes to buy at a discount outlet or mail-order. Some service customers will not desert
their channel, but use the price they come to see in the "no-frills" channel as a negotiating
device with the full-service provider.

Conflict area #2 shown in Figure C is between the same type of entities in the channel
structure, here two distributors. In the figure, we show the manufacturer has chosen to have
four independent distributors. This is the company's answer to the question of channel
breadth, i.e., how intensely to cover the market at a particular stage in the channel. We saw
real world examples above.

For example, Tupperware had to figure out how many sales "consultants" it should have
running parties. Too few would not generate enough sales for the company; too many
would have individuals competing directly for too small a business potential. The Gap set
its strategy of owning its own retail stores and then had to decide how many of each type it
would have. Even in the same product category, firms can choose different intensity levels.
For example, when Nissan set up distribution for its new Infiniti automobile, it chose to
limit the number of dealers to just over 100 despite the fact that BMW and Mercedes each
had over 350 each in the United States. The basic alternatives with respect to channel
breadth or intensity of market coverage are:

1. Exclusive distribution
2. Selective distribution
3. Intensive distribution

In exclusive distribution, the manufacturer establishes only one reseller in each region to carry the product. Yamaha pianos are an example of this policy. Exclusivity is granted by the manufacturer in the hope that it will induce strong selling support by the reseller. The cost is that, with an exclusive policy, the consumer must be willing to seek out the one outlet in his or her area carrying the brand.

The middle ground between exclusivity and seeking the maximum coverage possible is selective distribution. In selective distribution, there is more than one but a limited number of resellers in each market. Selective distribution is practiced by many higher-end clothing manufacturers, such as Perry Ellis and Bally. The purposive limiting of the number of outlets is intended to increase the support the reseller provides the brand over the case of intensive distribution. Having more than one outlet is intended to increase shopping convenience over exclusive distribution.

Finally, many manufacturers try to place their products with as many resellers as possible. For some markets, it is believed that "share of space" (i.e., retail shelf space) delivers "share of market," and, thus, the objective is to be as widely and intensively distributed as possible. Gillette razor blades, Kodak film, and Budweiser beer are examples of intensive distribution at the retail level.

Note that it is not necessarily the case that the more outlets the product is in, the better off the manufacturer is. Moving from exclusive to intensive trades off reseller support in return for easier availability of goods for the consumer.

As is usually the case in marketing, an analysis of consumer behavior is the primary input into the resolution of the channel breadth issue. Consider three examples:

1. *Shaving cream*: Shaving cream is a frequent purchase for the majority of adult males. The acquisition of a new can is a routine and unexciting event. Since the buyer most likely thinks there are a number of acceptable shaving creams, the manufacturer sees convenient availablity as critical.

2. *Television set*: A television set is a relatively infrequent purchase of considerably greater expense than shaving cream. When the decision is made to buy a television set, several members of the family get involved—checking *Consumer Reports* and newspaper ads, shopping around, and generally gathering information appropriate to the importance of the decision. Since consumers do shop around, rather than just visit the most convenient outlet and buy there, there is no need for the manufacturer to be in every outlet. In fact, being in every outlet would likely be a mistake if the family relied on the retail salesperson for information. Intensive distribution is justified for the shaving cream because the only retail support required is shelf space. However, when strong point-of-purchase personal selling is required, going beyond selective distribution would jeopardize the required support.

3. *Automobile*: For some makes, the consumer behavior may be like that just described for television sets. However, for a specialty item, such as a Porsche Boxster, it is likely that the purchaser has a very strong brand preference even before the acquisition process begins. Thus, convenience of outlet is not a consideration, and the buyer will go just about anywhere to get the brand he or she insists on. Since the car is purchased infrequently and is an extremely important purchase, the buyer can behave this way. In this event, the permissibility of relatively inconvenient outlets indicates exclusive distribution. (Note that some provision may have to be made for less than exclusively distributed warranty servicing of the car.)

These examples illustrate a categorization of goods frequently used in marketing. Our shaving cream, television, and exotic car represent a "convenience good," a "shopping good," and a "specialty good," respectively. Of course, no item can be definitely classified as any one of these three types for all consumers. However, the following is a useful guideline:

Convenience good ⟶ Intensive distribution
Shopping good ⟶ Selective distribution
Specialty good ⟶ Exclusive distribution

Turning back to the conflicts of Figure C, whereas the first two types of conflict shown are horizontal, the third is vertical, i.e., between successive levels in the marketing system. Channel members are interdependent in the sense that their joint efforts determine the level of sales achieved for the product. Consequently, there is a natural incentive to cooperate. However, there is also an inherent stimulus to conflict. Each party would like to see the other "do more" to improve the sales situation. A distributor wishes the manufacturer would spend more on national advertising to set the stage better for the distributors' sales-force as it calls on customers. The manufacturer wishes that the distributor would invest in better training for the salesforce and outfit them with the state-of-the-art selling tools.

Researchers[3] have identified the major sources of conflict as parties' differences in:

1. Goals
2. Understanding of proper scope of activities
3. Perceptions of reality

An obvious difference in goals between a manufacturer and a distributor is each is focused on its own sales not the other's. The manufacturer may see an opportunity to expand its sales by opening up a new channel like the Internet. The distributor sees this as cannibalizing sales it would otherwise make. A distributor typically incorporates the manufacturer's product with lines from other manufacturers. To suit the distributor's purpose, the line may take on a strategic role that does not serve the best interests of the manufacturer.

These conflicts are natural occurrences between two business entities each trying to serve its stakeholders. Contracts can be set up to mitigate goal incompatibility problems. These might specifically address what each party will contribute to the joint effort, how the effort will be monitored, and the division of the system profits contingent upon inputs each party provided.

The second related major source of conflict is differences in understanding about the scope of activity, viz. (a) the functions which each party will carry out and (b) the target population for whom they will perform these functions. For example, a distributor may see it as the company's job to open new accounts which are then turned over to the distributor for service; meanwhile, the company expects the distributor salesforce to be "cold calling" and can't understand why the customer list is not seeing new additions each month.

A second key scope issue is the population served, defined either geographically or by account type. This is basically the issue of "who owns the account?" If a copier manufacturer serves the City of Boston direct (through its own salesforce) but has a distributor for outlying districts (e.g., Cambridge) whose account is Harvard Business School, physically located in Boston but part of Harvard University based in Cambridge? The hybrid grid model described earlier can be a useful mechanism for getting all channel partners to understand how the overall system is designed to work and their role in it.

The third source of conflict is simple different perceptions of the reality of a situation. For example, the distributor with its salesforce "on-the-street" everyday may see the performance gap that has developed between the manufacturer's product and those of competitors in the eyes of customers. But, the manufacturer still believes it is delivering

---

[3] L.W. Stern, A.I. El-Ansary, and A.T. Coughlan, *Marketing Channels,* 5th ed., Prentice-Hall, 1996.

superior quality. As another example, the manufacturer, tracking unit sales, sees a downward trend while the distributor sees a rapidly declining overall market in which it has more than held market share for the manufacturer.

Effective channel management requires recognition of these potential threats to the system's working as it should. Some issues can be avoided by carefully drawing up a specific understanding about roles, duties, performance measurement, and payoffs. The key is to have all members see the interdependence of system members and to arrange communications and contracts so that each party perceives a "fair" return to their value added to the system.

Summary

Marketing system design issues are critical and can be a source of competitive advantage. Some companies are, in fact, defined more by their marketing system than their products. For example, the innovation and phenomenal success of L'Eggs pantyhose was not so much in the product as in the distribution through supermarkets and drugstores with efficient display racks.

A marketing system also needs to be examined for its adaptability to new market opportunities and new technologies. Because channels involve complex legal relationships, they can be difficult to adjust and flexibility should be a criterion in judging a proposed structure.

21

Ring Medical

V. Kasturi Rangan   Christopher Fay

On Wednesday, May 4, 1988, Paul Ruggieri, president and CEO of Ring Group, a wholly owned subsidiary of Scanvest Ring, Norway, faced two highly challenging issues as he prepared for the May 5 board meeting. Ruggieri strongly believed that the HCS-100 product, for which he had nominal responsibility, could well represent the single major opportunity for Ring Group to turn a profit for the first time since 1984. (See **Exhibit 1** for Ring Group financial statements.) Moreover, the HCS-100 would enable Ring Group, headquartered in Great Neck, New York, to break its dependence on mature products and markets and position the company for future growth. Before this might happen, however, board members would have to (1) resolve how the organizational responsibilities for the HCS-100 product should be divided, and (2) approve a marketing plan of action.

Currently, the HCS-100 product was housed at Ring Medical, a division of Ring Group (see **Exhibit 2** for an organization chart). From its inception in July 1986 until recently, Ring Medical had operated autonomously, headquartered in Billerica, Massachusetts. In January 1988, Ed Owens, formerly in charge of product development, was promoted to head Ring Medical, reporting directly to Paul Ruggieri. The entire management team at Ring Medical—and especially Ed Owens and Dave Forster (technical director), the two men credited with designing, engineering, and launching the HCS-100 product—strongly wanted their autonomy to continue. Reporting up through Ring Group would destroy the entrepreneurial spirit of their group, they argued.

Much was expected of Ring Medical's development and launch period initiated in October/November of 1987. An average of two to three units a month was expected to be sold, yielding total revenues of approximately $150,000 per month at average gross margins of nearly 50%. As of April 1988, however, only 5 systems had been sold versus a budgeted annual sales volume of over 30. Revenues totaled about 15% of the targeted annual amount of over $1.7 million. Management's attention focused on the HCS-100's sales and distribution system.

Christopher Fay, MBA 1988, prepared this case under the supervision of Associate Professor V. Kasturi Rangan as the basis for class discussion rather than to illustrate either effective or ineffective handling of an administrative situation.

EXHIBIT 1
**Ring Group
Statements of Income
and Retained
Earnings**

	1987	1986	1985	1984
Net sales	$3,265,194	$2,103,552	$2,363,468	$2,953,590
Cost of sales	2,049,763	1,341,233	1,313,959	1,717,108
Gross profit	1,215,431	762,319	1,049,509	1,236,482
Selling, general and administrative expenses	2,804,306	2,289,033	1,571,457	1,335,162
Operating profit (loss)	(1,588,875)	(1,526,714)	(521,948)	(98,680)
Income (loss) from foreign currency transactions	(85,698)	(101,639)	(59,203)	96,145
Interest expense	(45,496)	(206,421)	2,048	7,005
Other income	20,032	11,296	(32,839)	(3,935)
	(111,162)	(296,764)	(89,994)	99,215
Extraordinary gain[a]	—	1,352,870		
Net income (loss)	(1,700,037)	(470,608)	(611,942)	535
Retained earnings (deficit), beginning of year	(1,260,169)	(789,561)	(163,531)	(164,066)
Retained earnings (deficit), end of year	$(2,960,206)	$(1,260,169)	$(775,473)	$(163,531)

[a]Trade payables forgiven by Scanvest Ring.

The company had recruited eight manufacturers' reps who were offered a 20% commission rate on sales for each installed system. In the six to seven months that the manufacturers' rep network had been operational, only one system had been sold by any rep; the other four systems had been sold by Ed Owens. Both Owens and Forster were critical of the efforts of national sales manager Charlie Witteck, who was located in Great Neck, New York. "Either the rep concept is lousy, or Charlie Witteck is not doing his job," argued Forster. Matters came to a head in April 1988 when Witteck, touring the Massachusetts area for a trade show, refused to visit the division headquarters at Billerica. He instead reported back to Paul Ruggieri at Great Neck that "a problem with our HCS-100 sales effort is the utter lack of consistency in product policy, pricing, and customer support from Billerica. Without sorting out these problems, it would be futile to expect our reps to work miracles in the field."

To date, Scanvest Ring had spent in excess of $700,000 on the HCS-100 effort, and its CEO Helge Midttun and other board members were hesitant to invest further in a project that had so far shown lackluster results. Ring Group was the only subsidiary of Scanvest Ring not located in Scandinavia. Its board had recently been quite forthright in announcing a strategy of focus on Scandinavian markets, both to shareholders and management. The historical tendency of tolerating its U.S.-based "problem child" was not likely to continue.

Helge Midttun had a general philosophy of separating new and mature products in Scanvest Ring's efforts in Norway. Indeed, there had been a marked tone of approval in Midttun's voice as he described the vibrant, upbeat culture—complete with a background of Beatles music—he witnessed on his last visit to Ring Medical. Ruggieri felt that the key to any course of action regarding the organization of the HCS-100 product effort was consistency—not only across all aspects of marketing management but also with Ring Group's current strategy and operation.

Ring Group of North America, Inc.

Ring Group of North America, Inc. was established in 1971 as a wholly owned subsidiary of Scanvest Ring a.s., one of Scandinavia's largest information technology companies, with 1987 profits of $12.7 million on sales of $138 million. (See **Exhibit 3** for Scanvest Ring financial statements.) Ring Group's charter was to develop U.S. markets for selected

EXHIBIT 2 Ring Group, Inc., Organization Chart, Effective 2/23/88

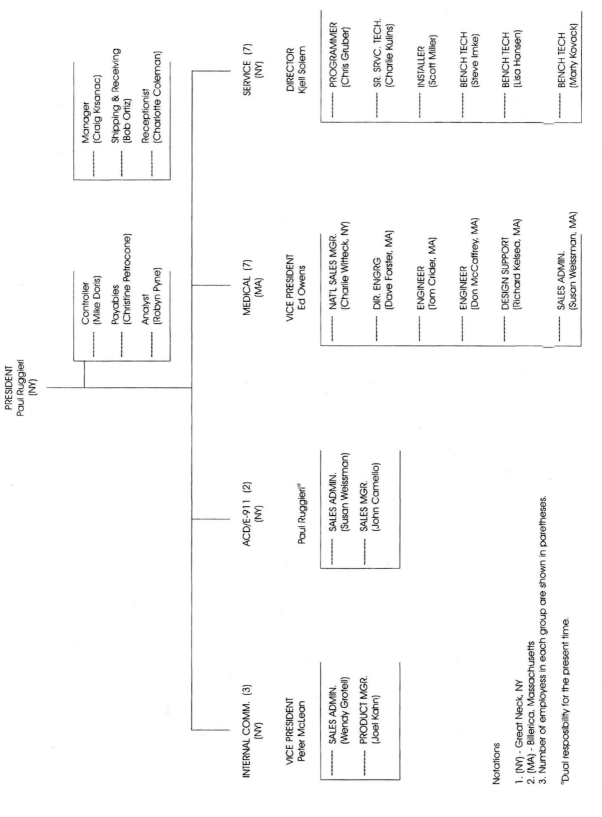

PRESIDENT
Paul Ruggieri
(NY)

Controller
(Mike Doris)

Payables
(Christine Petrocone)

Analyst
(Robyn Pyne)

Manager
(Craig Krsanac)

Shipping & Receiving
(Bob Ortiz)

Receptionist
(Charlotte Coleman)

SERVICE (7)
(NY)

DIRECTOR
Kjell Solem

PROGRAMMER
(Chris Gruber)

SR. SRVC. TECH.
(Charlie Kulins)

INSTALLER
(Scott Miller)

BENCH TECH
(Steve Imke)

BENCH TECH
(Lisa Hansen)

BENCH TECH
(Marty Kovack)

MEDICAL (7)
(MA)

VICE PRESIDENT
Ed Owens

NAT'L SALES MGR.
(Charlie Witteck, NY)

DIR. ENGRG
(Dave Forster, MA)

ENGINEER
(Tom Crider, MA)

ENGINEER
(Don McCaffrey, MA)

DESIGN SUPPORT
(Richard Kelsea, MA)

SALES ADMIN.
(Susan Weissman, MA)

ACD/E-911 (2)
(NY)

Paul Ruggieri[a]

SALES ADMIN.
(Susan Weissman)

SALES MGR.
(John Camello)

INTERNAL COMM. (3)
(NY)

VICE PRESIDENT
Peter McLean

SALES ADMIN.
(Wendy Grotell)

PRODUCT MGR.
(Joel Kahn)

Notations

1. (NY) - Great Neck, NY
2. (MA) - Billerica, Massachusetts
3. Number of employess in each group are shown in parentheses.

[a]Dual resposibility for the present time.

371

EXHIBIT 3 Scanvest Ring Income Statement (in '000 Kronas)

	1978	1979	1980	1981	1982	1983	1984	1985	1986	1987
Sales	27,548	55,065	92,582	131,675	183,156	647,123	957,991	1,133,405	705,097	860,361
Cost of goods sold	9,574	23,294	40,040	50,272	68,228	260,445	413,076	439,398	272,346	342,021
Wages and other personnel expenses	8,197	15,735	22,897	35,074	52,716	220,343	307,596	373,398	221,061	271,256
Other operating expenses	6,322	9,089	13,575	21,677	31,892	110,315	162,285	282,438	112,808	148,583
Ordinary depreciation	659	1,790	2,065	2,482	3,029	11,080	17,060	30,676	22,785	22,701
Bad debts	—	—	201	2	201	1,260	4,732	19,104	7,658	2,271
Changes in stocks	—	—	—	—	—	(5,081)	(12,553)	4,533	466	(1,366)
Total operating expenses	24,752	49,908	78,778	109,507	156,066	598,362	892,196	1,149,547	637,124	785,466
Operating profit (loss)	2,796	5,157	13,804	22,168	27,090	48,761	(65,795)	(16,142)	67,883	74,895
Net financial items	105	1,393	2,794	5,236	12,990	14,428	9,069	41,756	16,694	(4,121)
Profit (loss) ordinary activities	2,691	3,764	11,010	16,932	14,100	34,333	56,726	(57,898)	51,189	79,016
Net extraordinary items	—	528	—	1,500	1,542	967	2,430	102,001	9,811	24,952
Profit (loss) before year-end allocations	2,691	3,236	11,010	15,432	12,558	33,366	54,296	(159,899)	41,378	54,064
Year-end allocations	2,442	2,596	9,007	12,893	10,752	28,886	60,176	(36,786)	3,991	21,734
Net profit (loss)	249	640	2,003	2,539	1,806	4,480	(5,880)	(123,113)	37,387	32,330
Ordinary result	2,368	2,995	8,880	14,148	12,102	29,789	51,889	(55,061)	50,177	77,407
Earnings per share (unadjusted)	4,736	922	1,076	1,715	112.06	22.22	4.96	(4.71)	4.28	6.45
Earnings per share (adjusted)	0.51	0.55	1.70	2.75	1.91	2.64	4.46	—	4.28	6.45
Average number of shares	500	3,250	8,250	8,250	108,000	1,340,564	10,453,940	11,687,410	11,716,643	12,008,310

Note: The 1987 exchange rate was $ = K6.2.

Scanvest Ring products. Its preeminent business base quickly came to be selling and servicing a "hands free" duplex intercom system. Intercom sales topped $2 million in 1987, giving Ring Group in excess of 20% of the estimated market. While this market, composed mainly of hospitals, was considered mature, new markets for the latest generation intercom products had been identified. An intercom system had recently been sold to the brokerage division of a leading New York investment bank. An average configuration of the latest generation intercom system, the Tridex, sold for about $10,000 and contained 20 extensions (see **Exhibit 4**). Some larger systems had over 300 extensions. All system functions were controlled by a microprocessor which is not shown in the exhibit.

Approximately 60% of intercom sales in 1987 were made to end-users through five or six manufacturers' reps, under the direction of Peter McLean, vice president of the Internal Communications Division of Ring Group. Direct sales earned a gross margin of 50% to 60%. Nearly 60 national distributors constituted an additional branch of the intercom distribution effort, accounting for about 35% of sales, with a contribution margin of roughly 35%. Most of these distributors were audio contractors, who merely bid on products such as intercom systems and, therefore, did not carry inventory. Bids were submitted from 60 to 90 days in advance of approval and delivery. Ring Group maintained the appropriate inventory to serve this demand. OEM (original equipment manufacturers) arrangements represented the final channel for the intercom product. Sales to OEMs, such as the Contel Executone Group, had a margin of less than 20%. OEMs generally sold the intercom product under a private label.

The second major family of products handled by Ring Group consisted of a variety of telephone switches known as Automatic Call Distributors (ACD).[1] An ACD switch could distribute a large volume of incoming phone calls evenly across internal operators. This feature made the ACD attractive to such users as airlines, car rental agencies, and "catalog houses," who relied on high-volume telephone response. The ACD market, with an estimated size of $600 million in 1988 and $1 billion in 1990, had attracted a range of competitors, from companies such as Northern Telecom, AT&T, and Rockwell, to much smaller firms, such as Redcom and Suma-Four. Ring Group sold a customized version of the ACD, known as E-911 to several cities, towns, and municipal counties. E-911 service enabled citizens to dial "911" on any telephone to report an emergency requiring medical, fire, or police assistance. The system was so configured that the call receiver was able to locate the call source automatically.

The E-911 and other ACD products were sold directly by Ruggieri and a field sales representative. Seven manufacturer representatives, coordinated by a sales administrator, also sold ACD products. Currently, there was no sales coverage in the western region of the United States. The E-911 and ACD products had a long sales cycle: from 6 to 18 months from initial contact to installation. While the decision maker for the E-911 product—the city, town, or county officials—generally endeavored to become well acquainted with Ring Group people and products, a crucial influence for basic ACD products was often a local telephone company that configured, installed, and maintained the system of which Ring Group equipment was a part. ACD products ranged in price from under $100,000 to over $5 million, depending on size and complexity. A typical Ring ACD is pictured in **Exhibit 5.**

In addition to the intercom and switch product lines, Ring Group marketed peripheral and other ancillary telephony equipment with a less concerted effort. Product design and assembly were the concern of Norwegian management. All products were manufactured by

---

[1] An ACD was a variety of a general class of telephone switch called Private Branch Exchange (PBX). A PBX functioned to connect incoming telephone lines, or trunks, to internal telephone extensions at the site of a telephone user. PBXs ranged widely in capacity and expense, according to the total number of trunks and extensions serviceable (trunks and extensions were collectively referred to as "ports"). For a user who received many more incoming calls than made outgoing calls, a PBX, or an ACD, was often needed. An ACD that relied on digital technology was referred to as a Digital Call Distributor, or DCD.

EXHIBIT 4   **Intercom System**

A TRIDEX STATION FOR ANY LOCATION

The TRIDEX system is designed to function efficiently in all ambient conditions – quiet offices, noisy industrial areas, or for example, hospitals where discreet, low-level sound is often a necessity.

Lifting the TRIDEX unit automatically gives the user a confidential handset – an essential feature in the medical profession, in banks and in other fields where discretion is needed.

Other models: Singlebutton keyboards, flushmounted stations, industrial stations, sub-stations restricted to receive calls, remote microphone units – in fact a full range of stations to answer the needs of any organisation. Reserve your telephone for essential external services and use TRIDEX for efficient internal communication.

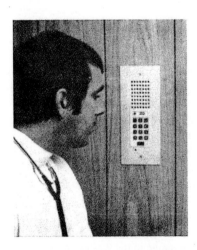

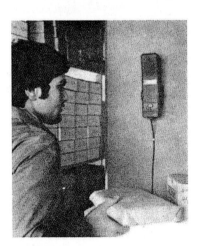

RING

RING GROUP, INC.
230 Community Drive, Great Neck, New York 11021
(516) 487-0250 / (800) 645-9690

Kitron, a Scanvest Ring manufacturing subsidiary based in Norway; after the manufacturing stage, switches, intercoms and other products were sent to Brekke, the Norway-based Scanvest Ring distribution division. Brekke paid a transfer price to the manufacturing division at a level above cost, but below Norway market price. Brekke then added a margin of 20% to 30% and distributed product to the Norway market, Ring Group, and other international markets.

EXHIBIT 5　**ACD Switch**

DCD 600: DIGITAL CALL DISTRIBUTOR

The Ring Digital Call Distributor (DCD) 600 is a technologically advanced digital automatic call distributor that operates in today's predominantly analog environment. Yet it can be configured to operate equally well in tomorrow's digital environment.

By automatically routing incoming calls, queueing calls, recording traffic loads, providing printed hard-copy statistics and real-time, on-screen management information, the DCD 600 solves the problems of handling large numbers of incoming calls. And it does it efficiently, effectively and reliably.

In addition to a wide array of standard features, the DCD 600 offers a number of optional features to meet specialized operating needs and requirements.

Ring Group management cited two sources of frustration in its operating relationship with Scanvest Ring. First Ruggieri estimated that a Ring ACD was priced from 50% to 80% above U.S. competition. "While the relatively high Norwegian labor costs account for some of Ring's cost disadvantage, Kitron's practice of channeling product through Brekke substantially adds to our procurement costs," he added. In effect, Ruggieri felt his hands were somewhat tied as he tried to show Scanvest Ring a reasonable profit.

A second source of frustration for Ring Group management was Scanvest Ring's general unwillingness to allow Ring Group to make revisions to, or otherwise customize, Scanvest Ring products. According to Ruggieri, Scanvest Ring maintained that the benefits from modification of completed product designs were outweighed by the R&D and manufacturing cost advantages that Scanvest Ring would enjoy through product standardization. Ruggieri suspected that Scanvest Ring's near-monopoly position in Norway accounted substantially for its unwavering adherence to this policy. "Because the Norwegian market is essentially uncontested, competitive product features are either not demanded by Norwegian customers, or at the very least, such features are not required for success in Norway," Ruggieri thought.

Helge Midttun disagreed. Scanvest Ring had grown in leaps and bounds from 1982 to 1985 through a series of acquisitions and opening of several foreign subsidiaries in Europe. The company's profit performance, however, plummeted. On taking over as CEO in 1986, Helge Midttun consciously chose a strategy of focusing on the two core businesses of telecommunications and information systems. While telecommunications products and markets were mature, information systems technology and markets were new and rapidly growing. Through strategies of cost reduction, product line rationalization, and focus on Scandinavian markets, Scanvest Ring management had achieved a turnaround (see **Exhibit 3**). Scanvest Ring had divested all its foreign holdings; Ring Group was the lone foreign subsidiary.

It was in the context of this unique relationship to its corporate parent that Ruggieri would have to address the pressing issues relating to the budding HCS-100 effort.

Ring Medical

In the spring of 1986, Charlie Witteck, a sales representative then working for Telphi, Inc., approached Paul Ruggieri with what both men saw as a terrific opportunity for Ring Group. Witteck's firm had developed a computerized internal communications system for the hospital market. The product would both enhance the quality and reduce the cost of communication between physicians, patients, hospital administrators, and others connected to the hospital's community.[2] Because of the proprietary nature of the product's operating system, as well as a shortage of cash, the product seemed doomed to failure if left in the hands of Telphi. Encouraged that Ring's engineering expertise and experience in selling, when combined with the Telphi product, could add up to success, Ruggieri convinced Scanvest Ring to acquire the intellectual property rights to the Telphi product. In July of 1986, Scanvest Ring paid $25,000 to complete that acquisition. The new division, Ring Medical, was to be operated independently from Ring Group for legal and financial reasons. Scanvest Ring was to make an initial cash contribution of $200,000, and if certain goals were met, an additional $500,000 for working capital in the form of a loan.

[2] Operating System is the building block (or language) which enables a computer to configure and run application programs. Telphi's software was based on its proprietary operating system. By 1988, AT&T's UNIX operating system was fast emerging as the industry standard for the size range of computers discussed in this case.

Former Telphi vice president of sales and marketing, Ed Owens, 50, was hired with overall responsibility for product and market development, operating out of Billerica, Massachusetts. Owens had had offers from four companies for Telphi's intellectual property rights. It was apparent to bidders that the real "intellectual" value was that of Ed Owens, and an acquisition of Telphi would be incomplete without him. Of all the offers he received, the one from Ring Group was most attractive. Charlie Witteck, 60, also a former Telphi employee, was initially hired by Ring Group at Great Neck, New York, to assist in ACD sales, but in March 1987 was appointed national sales manager for Ring Medical.

Dave Forster, 25, left an engineering position at Northern Telecom to become director of engineering at Ring Medical in Billerica. A promising young engineer with strong interest in management, Forster too was not without ample career options. His confidence in the Telphi product was strong testimony to its potential value.

The HCS-100

In the broadest sense, the HCS-100 served to improve the cost effectiveness and quality of communication between various participants in a hospital's operations, including physicians, patients, administrators and maintenance workers. The HCS-100 was an assembly of telephone and computer hardware and software, all of which were available "off the shelf," with the exception of the Digital Call Distributor (DCD). The DCD employed in the HCS-100 was the DCD-601, manufactured by the Norwegian Scanvest Ring subsidiary, Kitron.

In addition to the DCD-601, the HCS-100 was made up of a 32-bit minicomputer manufactured by Convergent Technologies. The computer used a Relational Data Base Management System (RDBMS), based on the widely standardized UNIX operating system. The fourth major component of the HCS-100 was a terminal and customized keyboard, manufactured by Wyse Technologies. An emergency manual backup system, touchscreen, and other interconnecting software for the HCS-100 were developed by Ring Medical.

DCD-601

Of the four main building blocks of the HCS-100, the DCD-601 was considered to be of greatest strategic importance. It was one of only a handful of DCDs made that was architecturally suitable for U.S. telephony equipment and sufficiently economical for an HCS-100-type product. Only two U.S.-based firms manufactured such a switch, Redcom, in Rochester, NY and Suma-Four, in Manchester, New Hampshire. The remaining firms were based in Europe, and none of their switches were of suitable construction for U.S. telephony hardware. Ed Owens was convinced that to modify a foreign-made DCD for application in the U.S. would be grossly uneconomical. He and Dave Forster also felt that it would be uneconomical for a North American manufacturer of large DCDs, such as AT&T, Rockwell, or Northern Telecom, to custom-engineer a DCD either for a would-be Ring Medical competitor or for the DCD maker's own entry into the HCS-100's target market. "The current hospital market is simply too specialized and small for large players to exploit economically," argued Ed Owens.

HCS-100 Modules

The arrangement of the HCS-100's four key building blocks in addition to the specific software determined the function that the system would perform. There were six general, distinct functions for which the HCS-100 could be configured as modules. Ring Medical intended to offer modules independently or in any combination. (See **Exhibit 6** for a schematic diagram of a full HCS-100 system, and a listing of the offerings of each module.) A fully configured system with all modules was priced at about $70,000.

EXHIBIT 6   HCS-100

*Our integrated HCS-100 system means **substantial** savings, over time, for the health care organization that is planning ahead.*

After implementing one module, you can add others at minimal cost—certainly much less than the cost of purchasing them from separate vendors.

And the modules you add will interact with each other to increase staff efficiency—giving you further reductions in operating costs and an increasingly effective communications system.

- **a portable printer** available for the physician's convenience. It will reduce the number of check-in calls and enable operators to provide a higher standard of service to the physician's private patients.

- **a physician registry** that allows physicians to view their messages on any touch terminal screen.

- **printouts** that can be made at the hospital and picked up by the physician or distributed through the internal mail system.

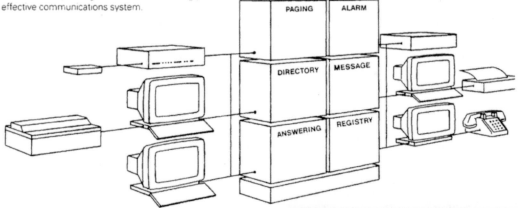

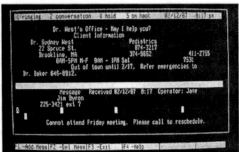

You also get more value for each dollar you invest because our systems are designed *specifically* for the health care environment. We know that no two health care institutions are alike, so we've built a variety of options into our systems so they can be customized to meet your specific needs—at *no* additional cost.

Physicians' Telephone Answering Message Service:

With a RING HCS-100 system, you can offer physicians in your area a personalized and professional answering/message service tailored to their specific needs.

When a call is forwarded from a physician's office, RING HCS-100 automatically displays the physician's account data, a personalized answering phrase, and message pad.

To reduce call-handling time, several standard message phrases can be accessed at the touch of a single key. And, on completion of the call, the system automatically "stamps" the message with the operator's initials, date, and time.

To further increase efficiency—while still providing a high quality service—the system incorporates several message delivery options, including:

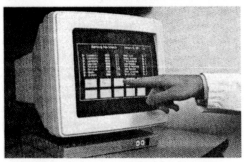

This touch-activated color terminal makes it easier for physicians to register their status. When it is used in conjunction with our Physicians' Telephone Answering Service/Message Center, physicians will be encouraged to sign in because the screen will display their messages and provide access to other important information. (They also have the option of registering from a telephone inside or outside the hospital.) Physicians using the registry to retrieve messages will not have to bother the answering service operator with a check-in call.

EXHIBIT 6   (Continued)

If a message is urgent, RING's HCS-100 complete call-out and patching capability allows the operator to reach the physician directly—or to patch the call through to the emergency room or the on-call physician.

And to ensure continuity of service, operators can key in reminders that will alert the next shift to wake-up calls or to unanswered pages that need to be repeated.

SUMMARY OF KEY FEATURES

- PBX interfaces
- supports both DID and secretarial lines
- speed dialing
- remote printing
- call out and patching
- statistical reports
- message printout at client offices
- automatic "no message" indication at check-in
- automatic display of account data
- automatic time stamping
- timed reminders
- customized message prompts
- billing package for your personal computer
- single key message input
- automatic call distribution
- color display terminal

Registry

RING's HCS-100 physician Registry system does a better job of keeping track of physicians and other key staff members—while giving them instant access to important messages and to each others' whereabouts.

Physicians are encouraged to "sign in" because the system is engineered for touch access and rapid delivery of messages and hospital bulletins geared to the physicians' needs. For added convenience, the system has a telephone interface with stored voice instructions so a change in status can be registered from any Touch Tone® phone.

Key information available through the Registry:

- department bulletins
- patient roster
- in-house staff
- operating room schedules
- meeting announcements
- messages from answering service or message center

The Registry system helps switchboard personnel handle calls more efficiently. The RING HCS-100 terminal will display the status and location of any physician—so that operators can easily determine whether to page, take a message, or refer the caller to someone else.

The Registry display can be customized to fit the different categories you use (e.g., "in and available," "in and not available," "in delivery room," etc.). And information is labeled with the time of the last update or sign-in so users can see if the physician's status is current. The system can also be set up to automatically delete information that hasn't been updated in the last twenty-four hours.

Paging

RING's HCS-100 Paging system, consisting of one or more encoders, will interface with your existing transmitter control equipment. Paging can be initiated from any designated terminal on the system, or with the proper access code, from any Touch Tone® telephone. This dial access feature allows a high percentage of pages to be initiated without involving the operator. The system supports multiple/mixed coding formats so your tone, tone and voice, numeric and

RING helps you strengthen ties with physicians by offering a medically-oriented, cost efficient answering service/message center.

alphanumeric display pagers need not be replaced. An optional voice storage module will provide added efficiency if you do a lot of voice paging.

In addition, for flexibility in group paging, individuals can belong to multiple groups—with mixed pager types included in a single group.

For convenience, and in compliance with F.C.C. regulations, station identification is automatically broadcast. To provide the documentation you need, all pages are logged and the log may be printed at any time.

Directory

A computerized Directory system dramatically reduces operators' call handling time by enabling them to find information in less than two seconds—and to respond to callers' requests more professionally and accurately.

The Directory may contain more than 100,000 records in ten customized files, which may include, for example:

- staff directory
- patient directory
- corporate directory
- on-call schedules
- physician directory
- volunteer directory
- benefactors directory

In addition, printed directories can be produced on the premises at no additional expense. Updates are easy, and those staff who need the critical information have it at their fingertips.

Alarm Monitor

Engineered to *supplement* existing alarm systems, the RING HCS-100 alarm system reduces emergency response time.

When a security, fire, electrical, mechanical, or environmental problem occurs, operators are alerted instantly via a message on the screen and an audible tone.

With the touch of a button, they receive both the problem location and precise instructions—pre-written by your own staff. They are told whom to notify, under what circumstances (including pertinent telephone and pager numbers), and any follow-up action they should take—from beginning full-scale hospital evacuation to transmitting lifesaving information to fire, police, or repair personnel.

Touch Tone is a registered trademark for AT&T.

Telephone Answering Service (TAS)

The TAS, priced at about $55,000, allowed for efficient handling of physicians' phone calls dialed to their private offices during hours when the office was unattended. The office attendant programmed the office phone to forward calls to a special number that dialed the HCS-100 system at the physician's hospital. By virtue of a special kind of trunk, known as a Direct Inward Dialing (DID) trunk, the HCS-100 system recognized from which doctor's office the call had been forwarded. The HCS-100 terminal screen then immediately displayed a file of information on the physician. This information included how the physician would like the phone answered, how the physician could be reached, and special instructions for handling emergency calls. The operator was then able to carry on a normal conversation with the caller, providing information according to instructions the physician had "filed" in the TAS, and simultaneously type a message into the physician's TAS file. The physician could then easily access message information without directly contacting the operator by checking a registry terminal, printer, or FAX machine located at the physician's home or office at the hospital. Messages could also be transmitted to physicians' digital pagers.

Ring Medical management was confident that the HCS-100 TAS was both superior to competing products and preferable to alternative solutions, largely because of its flexibility in screen design. The hospital was not constrained to a standard series of screens but could request custom-designed screens. The HCS-100 software was so adapted that Ring Medical could provide this at nominal cost. No current Ring Medical competitor had this degree of flexibility. A hospital-run TAS such as the HCS-100 was also expected to offer a more professional service to physicians than would a "mom and pop" answering service. The hospital TAS operator would answer calls exclusively for physicians affiliated with one hospital. The TAS operator was therefore expected to be more informed and of greater assistance to a caller than would a third-party answering-service operator who handled calls for a number of physicians affiliated with a variety of hospitals.

Target Market

Ring Medical managers claimed that the primary reason for choosing hospitals as a target market for the HCS-100 was based on fundamental facts and characteristics about the hospital business. Changes in hospital reimbursement procedures introduced in April 1983 and new forms of competition from groups like HMOs (Health Maintenance Organizations) were forcing hospitals to operate more efficiently and cut costs. An HCS-100-type system was believed to be a useful tool in that regard. Nearly 7,000 U.S. hospitals spent over $1.4 billion on telecommunications equipment in 1987. Other potential markets existed for an HCS-100-type product, however, and a number of Ring Medical competitors had made inroads into the commercial telephone answering market.

Ring Medical's preliminary strategy was to target large and medium hospitals (see **Exhibit 7**). Of all U.S. hospitals, only 5% had an automated telephone answering system. Under Ring Medical's current pricing scheme, the roughly 95% of unpenetrated medium and large hospitals represented a market of some $260 million (see **Exhibit 7**). Internal company estimates projected that at least half of these hospitals would be "upgraded" to offer an automated TAS service within the next five years.

Customer buying behavior was complex in the hospital industry. Many hospitals were part of multihospital buying groups, and purchase negotiations were often centralized. Equipment buy, however, tended to be more decentralized, and the hospital administrator invariably was involved. While large hospitals often included many managers and clinical people in their decision-making units (DMUs), small hospitals tended to have smaller DMUs. Purchasing an HCS-100 product would typically involve the administrator and the telecommunications manager in hospitals, although others might participate, depending on the module configuration.

EXHIBIT 7
Ring Medical's
Target Market

Product:

Hospital Communication System (HCS). System unit price $70,000 with six integrated modules:

Directory	Telephone Answering	Message
Alarm/Security	Registry	Paging

U.S. Hospital and Health Care Market (Source: American Hospital Association):

Present Number: 6,988 hospital sites in U.S.
(size 6–99 beds) 3,239 small sites
(size 100–399 beds) 2,847 medium sites
(size over 400 beds) 902 large sites

Market Potential:

% with automated Telephone Answering Systems: Less than 5% penetrated.
% to be upgraded: 50% estimated medium and large sites.
2,847 + 902 = 3,749 sites with over 100 beds.
3,749 sites × $70,000 per site = $262 million.
% to be upgraded: 50% estimated = $131 million.

Competition

Ring Medical had five principal competitors, of which only one, A.I.S., focused exclusively on the hospital market. Ring's product offerings and those of its five competitors are shown in **Exhibit 8.**

A.I.S. Waltham

A.I.S., privately held, was established in 1981, employed 40 people, and had estimated 1986 sales of $3 MM. A.I.S. was a designer and marketer of an integrated hospital communication system; all software, paging and voice board designs were proprietary. All hardware was based on Data General Computers. Five of the six HCS-100 modules were offered; no Premise Alarm module was offered. Distribution was direct to hospitals and also via telecommunications distributors. Direct sales effort covered New England, New York, and Chicago. Ring management estimated 80 A.I.S. installations.

A.I.S. relied on the PBX switch already installed for other telecommunications devices at the hospital as the basic building block for its systems. Ring management considered this to be a severe disadvantage. While an HCS-100 switch was independent of the hospital telephone switch and therefore operational even when the main switch failed, an A.I.S. system was totally dependent on the PBX. A second benefit of an independent TAS switch was that data on incoming and outgoing TAS-related calls were tracked separately from other call traffic. This meant a hospital using an A.I.S. system would be forced to charge a flat fee for subscription, while the user of the HCS-100 could opt for a fee based on usage.

Progress of the HCS-100 Effort

Ring Medical's efforts to date could be summarized in three phases. The first phase, commencing in July 1986, pertained mainly to legal and administrative issues in connection with the formation of the company. Phase two, initiated in January 1987, was considered remarkable: in just six months, the company was able to develop and sell its first system to Yale University Medical Center, under the assurance of comprehensive service (referred to as a Beta test site). While the Yale system was being installed, the company geared itself to commercializing the product concept. Research and product development was still considered a priority issue. By late September 1987 the company was ready to enter the

EXHIBIT 8 **Ring Medical's Hospital Communication Competitors and Their Product Offerings**

HCS-100 System Features*	A.I.S.	AMTELCO	CANDELA	STARTEL	MULTITONE
1. Telephone Answering	RA	X	X	X	X
2. Message Storage/retrieval	RA	X	X	X	X
3. Directory	RA	RA	RA	RA	RA
4. Touch Screen Registry	O	O	O	O	O
5. Dial Access Registry	X	O	O	O	O
6. Remote Alarm Monitoring	X	X	X	X	X
7. Premise Alarm Monitoring	O	O	O	O	O
8. Paging Encoder	X	O	O	O	O
System Price ($1,000)	$80–$100	$50–150	$30–75	$50–150	$70–$100
Annual Revenue	$3-5M	$12M	$11M	$10M	$5-8M

RA = Ring Competitive Advantage   O = Feature not offered   X = No Ring Competitive Advantage

*Feature Descriptions:

1. System interconnects to Bell Network and PBXs to provide automatic display of account information and all standard call-handling functions.
2. Computer storage, retrieval, and counting of text messages.
3. Allows databases to be created, modified, displayed and printed in different formats.
4. Provides facility for physicians and staff to register location and availability status via touch-sensitive terminal screens. Terminals also provide access to a wide variety of information, including messages.
5. Provide facility for physicians and staff to register location and availability status via Touch Tone telephone.
6. System will display alarm-response instructions when alarm condition occurs in physician's office. The alarm sensor triggers an auto-dialer to call a specific number that will be answered by the system.
7. Provides hard-wire interface to on-premise hospital alarm systems. Senses alarm conditions through dry contact closure and automatically displays notification and response instructions.
8. Allows pages to be initiated from any designated system terminal. Accommodates all common paper types and coding formats.

product-launch and commercialization phase. After long arguments, members of Ring Medical's management team agreed that a manufacturers' representative network was the best way to reach the customer. Ring Medical needed to preserve its internal capital for product development, and manufacturers' reps cost the company nothing in terms of fixed cost. A 20% commission would be paid on orders generated. There were at least 100 manufacturers' reps in the industry selling a wide array of telecommuncations products. However, since the company was headquartered at Massachusetts, the New England area (consisting of Vermont, Maine, New Hampshire, Massachusetts, Connecticut and Rhode Island) was reserved as headquarters sales territory, to be sold and developed directly by Ed Owens. In addition to the Yale system, four more systems were sold in the launch phase. A brief description of the sales process for each of the five systems is provided below:

1) Yale University Medical Center, 829 beds, sold June 1987.

Ed Owens contacted Cathy Johnson, director of telecommunications at Yale, in February 1987. Owens already knew Johnson, for he had sold her a product much like Ring Medical's Directory module while he was at Telphi. The Telphi Directory product was essentially useless to Yale, primarily because the operating system was proprietary and could not be supported. Aware of Johnson's dismay with her purchase, Owens suggested that he "replace" the Telphi Directory with a Ring Medical Directory. Additionally, he would "sell" Johnson a Message module. The price of the entire package was $58,000. Johnson was free to return the system for a complete refund if not satisfied.

Between the time of initial contact in February 1987 and closure of the sale in June, Owens and Forster devoted an estimated 60 hours each to the Yale account, making three presentations. In addition to Johnson, Doris Cousins, chief PBX operator, and a couple of consultants attended the presentations. The buyers' primary concerns were the system's reliability and Ring Medical's reputation and history. While the consultants' and PBX operator's input seemed important to Johnson, she alone was responsible for the decision to buy.

2) St. Anthony's Hospital, Ohio, 404 beds, sold November 1987.

This account was sold by Judy Petty, a manufacturer's representative. Petty first became acquainted with the St. Anthony's director of telecommunications while she was employed by Tascom, a Ring Medical competitor, as a salesperson. Petty left Tascom expressly to be a manufacturer representative and largely to be able to carry the Ring Medical line. Her strong confidence in the superiority of the HCS-100 was encouraging to Ed Owens.

After brief training, conducted by Ed Owens, Petty was assigned the Midwest sales territory and issued a modem and terminal—standard equipment for all of Ring Medical's reps. These sales aids allowed Petty to access a "canned" demonstration package at the Billerica headquarters, which provided the decision makers with a very realistic display of the various HCS-100 modules.

The key decision makers at St. Anthony's were the director of telecommunications and the administrative VP. Petty noted that the sales process was very difficult, for the DMU was quite familiar with competitive offerings. After five months, a TAS and Registry were sold. St. Anthony's paid $73,000 for the package.

3) Winchester Hospital, 223 beds, sold February 1988.

After a nine-month sales effort, Ed Owens sold a TAS and Registry to this Massachusetts hospital. Like the Yale sale, this was a "replacement" of a formerly installed Telphi unit as well as an additional Ring Medical "sale." The price was $54,000.

Like that of St. Anthony's, Winchester's was a highly competitive sales process. Five players were known to have bid for the business. Although the hospital DMU comprised the director of telecommunications, vice president-finance, and the PBX operator, the decision to buy the HCS-100 was largely influenced by Nancy Aldrich, a prominent industry consultant, with the consulting firm TMC. Aldrich, with over 150 client hospitals, deemed HCS-100 the most technologically advanced product available.

4) Danbury Hospital, 366 beds, sold April 1988.

This Connecticut-based account was closed by Ed Owens after one presentation. The time from contact to close was two months, primarily due to the hospital's budgeting and capital appropriations process. A TAS module was purchased for $40,000.

The director of telecommunications contacted Owens by reference of Cathy Johnson at Yale, and also on the advice of a representative of Homisco, a value-added reseller which had recently sold the hospital a computerized accounting system to track and bill outgoing long distance calls. Owens knew the president of Homisco from past business dealings and had apprised him of the HCS-100 package. Because both the HCS-100 and Homisco's key products were based on the same UNIX operating system, Homisco considered the products complementary and mutually beneficial to each company's sales efforts. Danbury had been in the market for a TAS-type product, and Owens's assessment was that the DMU was generally well informed as to the available products and technologies.

5) Dow Jones, 32 users.

Ed Owens contacted Norm Smith, director of telecommunications for Dow Jones Corporation, to interest him in replacing Dow's existing directory product. One remote demonstration in Dow's corporate offices in Princeton, N.J., and one visit to Ring Medical's office by Stephanie Matthews, a communications manager under Smith, convinced Dow to replace its Telphi computer with Ring's UNIX-based Convergent computer and HCS-100 Directory System.

Since Dow was an OEM user of Wyse terminals, it was able to retain the 20 existing operator position terminals for use with the Ring system. The Directory module was purchased for $30,000 (utilizing existing Dow Jones terminal hardware, as explained above).

Marketing Challenges

Organizational issues apart, there were two distinct marketing challenges that the HCS-100 product launch faced. The first was the question of product policy; the second issue concerned channels of distribution.

Product Policy

For most hospitals, a TAS represented an incremental investment, a new addition, as opposed to an expenditure to replace an existing activity with new technology. Thus, the question was whether the HCS-100 should be positioned as a source-efficiency (i.e., cost reduction), or a source-effectiveness (i.e., quality enhancement) system.

In addition to eliminating a physician's need for a separate answering service, TAS was considered a potential source of hospital revenue, as physicians could be charged for system use. Management estimated that an average physician spent $100 monthly on an answering service. A physician TAS subscriber should therefore be expected to pay at least this amount. For a TAS capable of servicing 65 physicians, the incremental operating expenses incurred by a hospital would be salary and benefits for one full-time equivalent HCS-100 attendant (estimated to be $30,000 to $35,000 annually), plus one-time costs of added telephone company-supplied hardware and Ring Medical-supplied servicing fees of about $10,000. With a basic TAS price of $55,000, the decision maker could readily calculate a satisfactory pay-back period as well as impressive contribution levels.

Beyond the "hard dollar" revenue from physician fees, Ed Owens and Dave Forster were particularly convinced that potentially larger "soft dollar" revenues would accrue to the hospital offering a TAS. Physicians were ultimately responsible for "filling beds" in the fixed-cost-intensive hospital. Any measures a hospital's administration took to make its hospital more desirable for physicians should be rewarded by greater utilization. The TAS was seen as a significant hospital enhancement.

Ruggieri, Owens, and Forster were in agreement that the HCS-100 should be positioned as the unequivocal "high end" hospital internal communications system for large- and medium-size hospitals. Relative to the competition, the HCS-100 was considered to have both the "cutting edge" and most dependable hardware, and the greatest number of module offerings. The current thinking was to couple a clear quality edge (i.e., "high end") with a low relative price point. As **Exhibit 8** shows, the HCS-100 was priced well below chief rival A.I.S., and at parity with, or moderately below, all other competitors.

Another issue concerned line extension into add-on products. Owens anticipated extremely attractive margins from add-on sales, consisting of service, spare parts, additional modules, and new generation software. On an installed base of 24 hospitals, add-on sales alone could account for an additional $1 million in gross margins (see **Exhibit 9**). The critical question, however, was how should Ring Medical organize its sales and distribution efforts now to position itself to take advantage of an add-on market to be developed later.

EXHIBIT 9   Projected Add-on Sales

Installed Customer Hospital Base Worksheet 3/10/88	Initial Sale	2nd Year Add-on Sale Spare Parts (A)	2nd Year Add-on Sale Modules (B)	2nd Year Add-on Sale Service (C)	2nd Year Total Add-on Potential (A,B,C)	3rd Year 1 Module & Service (B,C,D)	4th Year 1 Module & Service (B,C,D)	5th Year Module & Service (B,C,D)	4 Yr Total Add-on Potential (A,B,C,D)
Assumptions									
Yale Univ. Med Cntr	$58,000	$9,000	$6,000	$6,000	$21,000	$12,600	$13,860	$15,246	$62,706
St. Anthony's Med Cntr	73,000	9,000	6,000	6,000	21,000	12,600	13,860	15,246	62,706
Winchester Hospital	54,000	9,000	6,000	4,000	19,000	12,600	13,860	15,246	60,706
Danbury Med Cntr	40,000	9,000	10,000	6,000	25,000	12,600	13,860	15,246	66,706
Total Sales—4 Hospitals	—	36,000	28,000	22,000	86,000	50,400	55,440	60,984	252,824
Est. gross margin %		50%	80%	70%		75%	75%	75%	
Est. gross margin $		18,000	22,400	15,400	55,800	37,800	41,580	45,738	180,918
Installed Base of 24	Add-on Sales								
Hospital Customers		216,000	168,000	132,000	516,000	302,400	332,640	365,904	1,516,944
Est. gross margin in $		108,000	134,400	92,400	334,800	226,800	249,480	274,428	1,085,508
Installed Base of 48	Add-on Sale	432,000	336,000	264,000	1,032,000	604,800	665,280	731,808	3,033,888
Est. gross margin in $		216,000	268,800	184,800	669,600	453,600	498,960	548,856	2,171,016
Installed Base of 96	Add-on Sale	864,000	672,000	528,000	2,064,000	1,209,600	1,330,560	1,463,616	6,067,776
Est. gross margin in $		432,000	537,600	369,600	1,339,200	907,200	997,920	1,097,712	4,342,032

Assumptions

A—Hardware sales of spare parts package @ $9,000 @ 50% margin
B—Add-on sale of 1 new software feature module and moderate system expansion @ $6,000 @ 80% margin
C—Annual service revenue and software upgrade @ $500/month @ 70% margin
D—Estimated 10% price increase per year in 3rd, 4th, 5th years

Projected five-year market share of system sales and installed base
1988—24 projects sold
1989—40 projects sold
1990—60 projects sold
1991—80 projects sold
1992—100 projects sold
Total 5-year sales—304

Hospital Profile of Installed Base	Location State	Number of Beds	Number of Admits	Annual Expenses (in $000)	Number of Personnel
Yale Med Cntr.	CONN	829	31,004	$187,744	3,715
St. Anthony's Med Cntr.	OHIO	404	11,867	$ 57,548	1,220
Winchester Hospital	MASS	223	7,848	$ 29,133	666
Danbury Hospital	CONN	366	16,460	$ 87,551	1,742

EXHIBIT 10   **Manufacturers' Reps**

Rep	Prior Selling Experience	Region	Age
Ms. Petty	Telephony (TAS com)	Ohio, Kentucky, Pennsylvania	40
Mr. Dunne	Contel Executone	Maryland, Washington, D.C. Delaware, Eastern Pennsylvania	64
Mr. Kline	Data and Telephony Systems	Florida	65
Mr. Hirsch	Data and Telephony Systems	New York, New Jersey, Connecticut	50
Mr. Mawn	Hospital Intercoms	Georgia, Alabama, South Carolina, Tennessee	50
Mr. McCadden	Northern Telecom Sales	New York, Long Island	55
Mr. Schmidt	Contel Executone	Colorado, Nevada	55
Mr. Smith	Computer and Oil Industry Sales	Texas	55

Channels of Distribution

While there was strong consensus that gaining access to the complex decision-making unit at large and medium hospitals posed a significant challenge, there was disagreement about the most appropriate channels of distribution. Three fairly distinct schools of thought prevailed.

The first approach centered on the aggressive deployment of manufacturers' representatives and was most embraced by Charlie Witteck, national sales manager. At 60, Witteck had logged more "time in the field" than any other Ring Medical manager. He was confident in his ability to understand the type of people in the hospital buying environment and therefore to know what sort of people should be deployed to sell in that environment. "In short, they must be seasoned. Young salespeople simply do not have the aplomb or personal bearing for the job," Witteck had argued. In keeping with this philosophy, he had recruited eight manufacturers' reps in November 1987. Their backgrounds and assigned territories are presented in **Exhibit 10.**

On the organization of the marketing effort, Witteck felt that the time had come for the bright, young enthusiastic product development team in Massachusetts to turn the sales responsibility for HCS-100 over to the more stable, seasoned New York management team. He had often expressed his opinion:

> Even though you'd think this thing would sell itself—it's so damn good—it requires a great deal of patience and maturity. You can't just go to the PBX operator; she has no authority. The telecommunications director, on the other hand, has authority, but she has no motivation to invest in something for the sake of cutting costs, let alone creating a new function and source of profit for the hospital. For concerns like these, you need to find the appropriate hospital administrator, maybe a vice president of finance. But chances are that person knows nothing about telecommunications. . . . Sometimes, you even have to get the MIS people involved, or perhaps outside consultants.

According to Witteck, one had to endure the mire of bureaucracy presented by the target hospital's organization and successfully bring all relevant parties together so that they could see the tremendous worth of the HCS-100. To Witteck, this challenge would be most effectively met by representatives "who've been around a while." The obvious choice of distribution strategy entailed a complement of able manufacturer reps, reporting to an administrator at the New York Ring Group headquarters. Witteck further supported the manufacturer rep scheme by arguing that "we simply do not have the resources to deploy a direct sales force. No matter what you do, each salesperson will end up costing the company at least $60,000 to $75,000."

Ed Owens and Dave Forster, on the other hand, saw a direct sales force as a necessity that had to be afforded. Their view was that

> with a decision-making unit of this complexity, and a product with such a high price tag, you've got to have dedicated field salespeople. Sure, the manufacturer's rep might make

a pretty penny, but if he or she gets frustrated with the process, attention can easily be shifted to other products, for other companies. We also need to have assurance that these people in the field are well trained. Training can make all the difference, and with the manufacturer's rep, you've got no control.

Owens further argued that the direct sales force should report to a sales director at the Ring Medical headquarters at Billerica. Well aware of the intensive effort by design and service personnel in the Billerica office over the last two years, Owens was concerned at the loss of momentum, lack of coordination, and general shock to the entrepreneurial culture in Billerica that would surely result if the sales effort were not administered from his office. Moreover, "nearly everything else is handled from here in Massachusetts, why not sales as well?" Owens asked.

Paul Ruggieri disagreed. Ruggieri was compelled by a number of reasons to believe that the HCS-100 product launch would run much more smoothly if many important functional tasks were administered from Ring Group's Great Neck, N.Y., headquarters. Service was a prime example. From his experience with users of other Ring Group products, Ruggieri felt strongly that a well-staffed service center, complete with a warehouse of spare parts, was immediately needed in New York. Ruggieri also envisioned a network of similar dedicated service centers in due course, strategically located all over the country. In addition, other support functions would clearly be less costly and executed more efficiently, Ruggieri thought, if handled out of Ring Group headquarters. At least in the near term, services such as warehousing, shipping, and secretarial support could be absorbed by excess capacity in New York.

Reacting to Paul Ruggieri's concerns about service, Ed Owens commented:

> We entirely agree that without satisfactory post-installation service, the technological edge of the HCS-100 will be for naught. Presently, we have two full-time software engineers devoted fully to service. Most of it has taken the form of answering questions and removing program "bugs" via a modem. But we really don't need a full-fledged field service operation. That's where Paul is wrong. He's used to selling mature hardware-oriented systems; a large part of HCS-100 is the software. All we need to do is make a phone call, and then via modem fix the problem from here. In addition, Dave Forster spends a substantial portion of his time in the field performing services that cannot be accomplished otherwise.

"On-site service will not be required," added Owens, "because most hospitals anyway have a sophisticated maintenance crew to handle their various complex hardware. On-site inventory of critical parts and telephone instructions should more than suffice to handle emergencies."

Dave Forster noted that the servicing process tends to spur creativity and enhance the product development process. "Let's not forget," he said, "we are dealing with a high-tech product in a new market. It would be foolish for the product development people to be separated from customers' problems."

Perhaps more compelling than the economies from shared overhead functions, however, was the ability to coordinate Ring Medical activities with other Ring Group activities to achieve strategic goals. This could happen only if the operations were housed in New York, Ruggieri argued:

> Why restrict the HCS-100 to hospitals? There are a number of good opportunities out there that make sense. I am making inroads into several of these with other products we've got here. Take the business market, for instance. It's huge by comparison to hospitals, and what's more, we just sold an intercom system to a major corporate client. The way I see it, we've got some mature markets which we have been chasing with hardware-intensive product. The HCS-100 is different; the money there is in the software, especially the add-on sales. It's a product that would make a great fit for us here as we try to transition from hardware to the software side.

EXHIBIT 11
1988 Ring Group
Budget ($000)

Gross Sales	Total
Commercial ACD	$ 600
911	1,100
Intercomm Dealer	1,300
Intercom Direct	400
Contel	500
Schools	200
Medical (HCS-100)	1,720
Total Gross	**$ 5,820**
Returns and Allowances	6
Total Net	**$ 5,814**
Cost of Sales	
ACD	$ 811
Intercomm	1,572
Medical	640
Total Cost of Sales	**$ 3,023**
Operating Expense	
ACD	$ 206
Intercomm	374
Medical	885
Technical Services	335
Shipping and Receiving	37
General and Administration	677
Total Operating Expense	**$ 2,514**
NET INCOME	**$ 277**

While Ruggieri acknowledged that the engineers and other staff in Billerica had done a great job of bringing the HCS-100 to its current market-ready state, he was of the opinion that it was time to make a change. He was not enamored of the manufacturer's rep distribution option, which seemed most consistent with a New York–based sales administration. Ruggieri advocated a third distribution strategy altogether—a network of telecommunications distributors, such as Introlink, a West Coast–based reseller with experience in telecommunication products, and a reasonable clientele of health-care customers.

Ruggieri had spoken with Introlink in the past about selling Ring intercoms to West Coast hospitals, where Ring Group was not represented. The distributor would take responsibility for marketing the HCS-100. A few issues would still have to be resolved with this option. Would Ring allow Introlink to carry the HCS-100 under its own brand name, if demanded? What would their margins be? How could Ring ensure uniform pricing levels across the nation if Introlink had free rein in the West Coast, while Ring's own sales force of manufacturers' reps sold on the East Coast?

Decisions

As Ruggieri recalled the views of Witteck, Owens, and Forster, he thumbed through the latest revision of the 1988 Ring Group budget he had sent to Scanvest Ring (see **Exhibit 11**). He knew that in contrast to the sanguine projections for HCS-100 sales, he would tomorrow confirm that a scant five systems had been sold. A quick look at the budget would also indicate to board members that cash generated from Ring Group operations would not sustain operating and other expenses projected for Ring Medical. His audience would be cautious, if not skeptical, from the start. His answers to the interdependent organizational and marketing plan issues would have to be airtight.

22

HP Consumer Products Business Organization: Distributing Printers via the Internet

Kirthi Kalyanam   Rajiv Lal   Edith D. Prescott

In spring 1998, Pradeep Jotwani, vice-president and general manager of the Consumer Products Business Organization of the Hewlett Packard Company (HP), was contemplating the increasing success of eCommerce and its implications for his division. The consumer products group had started selling refurbished printers through an Internet outlet center in December 1997, but Jotwani was now considering a move to sell new printers directly to consumers via this new eChannel. If he were to make such a move, he wondered which products to sell online at what prices, and how to communicate this strategy to the channel partners without damaging the existing distribution structure. Jotwani commented:

> Channel inflections are very challenging. The last time we faced a similar situation was when we had to transform ourselves from being a predominantly business-to-business company that sold printers through value added resellers [VARs] to a consumer products company that had to reach consumers through the retail channel. Even then there were the doubters, but

Research Associate Edith D. Prescott prepared this case under the supervision of Professors Kirthi Kalyanam of Santa Clara University and Rajiv Lal as the basis for class discussion rather than to illustrate either effective or ineffective handling of an administrative situation. Parts of this case were based upon the material presented in, "Hewlett Packard Consumer Products Business Organization: Distribution through E*Commerce Channels," by Kirthi Kalyanam and Shelby McIntyre of Santa Clara University, 1998–1999. Shen Li, General Manager of HP Shopping Village, also provided helpful input in the preparation of this case. Some of the information in this case has been disguised for confidentiality.

not only did we make the transition successfully, but we also emerged stronger. The challenge today is to decide on the level of strategic emphasis on Internet distribution so that we emerge stronger after the transition, rather than just defending our position.

The decision is complicated by several factors. Companies like Dell have shown that the direct model can work quite well. However, all of our current sales are through retailers and any direct selling efforts may lead to conflict with our retail partners.[1]

HP History

Bill Hewlett and Dave Packard founded HP in 1939 in a Palo Alto garage. One of HP's first clients, Walt Disney Studios, purchased eight audio oscillators to develop a new sound system for the movie "Fantasia." In the 1940s, the needs of WWII created a demand for HP's electronic instruments. HP also began signing with sales representatives to market products throughout the United States. During the 1950s, the company mastered the internal effects of growth, defining corporate objectives and developing a path toward globalization. By 1962, HP was ranked number 460 in the *Fortune* 500. The company enjoyed growth in the test and measurement segment and introduced itself to related fields, such as medical electronics and analytical instrumentation.

Innovation continued in the 1970s with the release of the first scientific handheld calculator, the HP 35, which made the slide rule obsolete. The 1980s were critical to HP's success, as it became a major force in the computer industry and printer market. Both the ThinkJet (inkjet) and the LaserJet printers were introduced in 1984. In 1985, HP's net revenue was $6.5 billion and the company had 85,000 employees.[2]

With the continuous release of computers, peripherals, and related products in the 1990s, HP became known as one of the few organizations that was able to marry measurement, computing, and communication. This success translated into HP's number 16 ranking on the Fortune 500 list by 1997. Net revenue for HP was then $42.9 billion and employees totaled 121,900, up from $38.4 billion and 112,000 in 1996. For the same period, net earnings rose from $2.6 billion to $3.1 billion. Despite these increases, 1997 was the first time since 1992 that revenues increased by less than 20%. Lew Platt, the president and CEO since 1992, blamed HP's inability to control operating expenses, lower demand, and the strength of the dollar as compared to other currencies.[3]

In 1998, HP grouped its products into five general categories: Computer Products, Service & Support; Test & Measurement Products & Service; Medical Electronic Equipment & Service; Electronic Components; and Chemical Analysis & Service.

Computer Products, Service & Support

In 1997, this segment of operations made up 83% of HP's total revenue and included computers ranging from palmtops to supercomputers, plus peripherals and services.[4] Though HP was well known for its technological innovation and product quality, marketing was the key to HP's success. The company had always considered the needs of its customers and partners; it had not only met their requirements, but had also grown with them as their needs became more demanding and involved. HP knew that the success of its customers and partners was directly correlated with its own.

HP had shown its ability to respond to demanding needs when it introduced its first computer in 1966, which was used to collect and examine data originating from HP

---

[1] This section was drawn from "Hewlett Packard Consumer Products Business Organization: Distribution through E*Commerce Channels" by Kirthi Kalyanam and Shelby McIntyre, 1998–1999, p. 1.

[2] Hewlett Packard Web Site. August 24, 1999. http://www.hp.com.

[3] Hewlett Packard 1997 Annual Report, p. 2.

[4] Ibid., p. 55.

electronic instruments. Expansion into business computing occurred in the 1970s with the HP 3000. HP introduced its first personal computer (PC) in 1980 and later released a family of computer systems in 1986 that were based upon RISC architecture. In 1991 HP unveiled the 11-ounce 95LX palmtop PC, the three-pound OmniBook 300 in 1993, and the HP Pavilion PC in 1995.[5] HP was the fastest-growing PC company in the world by 1997, ending the year as the number four PC manufacturer worldwide. The top four companies, Compaq, IBM, Dell, and HP, had a combined market share of 38% (and increasing) of the PC market. Compaq held the number one position with a 13.5% market share.[6]

Just as it had been a significant player in the PC market, HP led the printer industry. This was despite the fact that HP was not associated with printers as of the early 1980s. Instead, Epson, Diablo, and Qume led the way with their dot-matrix and daisy-wheel printers. Then, in 1984, HP released its ThinkJet, which was based on the thermal inkjet technology the company had developed in its own labs in the 1970s.[7] Laser printers were also released in 1984 and changed the industry dramatically. These printers generated eight pages per minute (ppm), had 300 dot-per-inch (dpi) resolution, and cost $3,495. The technology later improved to 1200 dpi and 24 ppm. HP released the first network printer, LaserJet IIISi, in 1991, allowing printers to be connected directly to LANs. HP then introduced the first desktop color laser, Color LaserJet, in 1994. Companies were slow to acquire this color technology, however, and vendors had difficulty finding the appropriate price points.[8] In 1997 and 1998, demand for HP products was soaring and the company had leading market shares in both the InkJet and LaserJet segments. HP was also a leader in the printer supply business, which contributed $5 billion to its total sales of $42.9 billion in 1997.[9]

HP management was credited with making two vital decisions that led to the success of the LaserJet series. First was the move to sell via the reseller channel. David Packard said in his 1995 book, *The HP Way:*

> The importance to distribute LaserJets through resellers cannot be overemphasized. It was a critical final piece of the overall strategy. It established a fundamental channel strength for HP that has been a competitive advantage over the past ten years.[10]

The second marketing decision was in the naming of the product. The LaserJet was nearly called the 2686 because the engineers were simply going to use the standard numerical naming sequence. Jim Hall, one of the original engineers on the LaserJet project said:

> There wasn't a jet in it, and we thought we'd be laughed off the street.[11]

The Printer Industry

As with all hot new technology, printer prices eventually came down which resulted in lower dollar growth rates for printer manufacturers. Nevertheless, significant enthusiasm remained for new releases of technologically superior printers, fueled partly by the emerging trends in printer usage. One such trend beginning in 1997 was the "distribute-then-print" model for information flow within companies. These models enabled a document created in one

---

[5] Hewlett Packard Web Site. August 24, 1999. http://www.hp.com.

[6] Stephen C. Dube, "Computer Industry Commentary," *Wasserstein Perella Securities, Inc. Equity Research,* (May 18, 1998): p. 1.

[7] Kirthi Kalyanam and Shelby McIntyre, "Hewlett Packard Consumer Products Business Organization: Distribution through E*Commerce Channels," 1998–1999, p. 2.

[8] Kelly Damore, "Laser Printers," *Computer Reseller News,* June 1, 1997, p. 80.

[9] Norm Alster, "Is Printer Ink Replacement a License to Print Money?" *Investor's Business Daily,* May 28, 1998, p. 8.

[10] Kelly Damore, "HP LaserJet Milestone," *Computer Reseller News,* May 10, 1997, p. 195.

[11] Ibid.

location to be distributed electronically to users in multiple locations, where it would be printed out individually.

In 1997, revenues of printer manufacturers were $8 billion for the U.S. and $22 billion worldwide. These numbers included all InkJet, Laser, and multifunction peripherals for personal and home/small office use. As home PCs became more prevalent in the 1990s, printer demand rose dramatically. By 1998, InkJet models accounted for 70% of all units sold.

The printer supply business obviously benefited from this surge in printer sales. Printer supplies, including toner cartridges, were an annuity to the retailer and manufacturer once a printer was purchased. They were very profitable and the strategy was analogous to the razor blade scenario—sell the razor cheap and then charge premium prices for the blades.

InkJet Printers (All Speeds)

Most people opted for InkJet printers due to their versatility and low cost. For $150, a consumer could buy even a color InkJet that produced exceptionally good results. In spring 1998, HP had a 55% market share in this segment, up from 49% in December 1997. HP's InkJet sales were expected to improve further with the release of the 2000C in June 1998, which incorporated its new Modular Ink Delivery System (MIDS). Canon's market share was 19% and declining, while Epson's share had increased to 18% due to its aggressive marketing and affordable products. Lexmark's market share, which had nearly doubled to 6% since 1997, was attributed to its low-end $99 ColorJet 1000 and its new $249 model 5700.

Laser Printers (11 ppm and Higher)

LaserJet printers could handle high volumes of text documents, had superior quality and speed, and could be used on a network. By 1998 black-and-white laser technology was mature and recent advances had focused on performance and price. A black-and-white laser jet printer giving eight ppm, for example, could be purchased for about $300. Color laser technology was a different story. Although prices had dropped significantly, the price points still began at $3,000.[12] In spring 1998, HP led this segment with an impressive 85% market share, primarily due to the overwhelming adoption of the LaserJet 4000 family. Lexmark was the closest second holding an 8% market share.

Multifunction Printers (MFP)

MFPs, machines that could print, copy, fax, and scan, were introduced in 1993 but did not catch on until 1997. Some units could perform color scanning and copying, and could shrink and enlarge originals. To do all the same tasks with independent machines would cost about twice as much and obviously take up more office space. Another bonus was that they were easier to install than stand-alone machines because separate device drivers were not needed. These machines were criticized, however, for being competent in all functions, but doing none exceptionally well. Because they were slower, they were also unsuitable for high-volume printing. Furthermore, they were not designed to connect to networks—although such connections were technologically possible. And, finally, it was risky to rely on only one device because if one function failed, the whole system went down.[13] The release of new MFPs was directly correlated with the technology updates for InkJets and LaserJets because MFPs had either one or the other capability as its underlying function.

The pace of technology and life cycles of products varied between InkJets and Laser printers. For InkJets, the core technology was the printer cartridge, which affected speed and quality. The life cycle of an InkJet printer was between one and two years and the difference depended on whether the InkJet was targeted to personal or business use. InkJets with longer life cycles were intended for the business customer and were more expensive.

---

[12] Susan Breidenbach, "Printed Matters," *Forbes,* fall 1998, pp. 38–40.
[13] Susan Breidenbach, "The Swiss Army Printer," *Forbes,* fall 1998, pp. 46–48.

For laser printers, key technologies were printer cartridges, toners, photoreceptors, paper handling, optics, and scanners. The life cycle for a Laser printer, which targeted business users, was two-to-three years. The speed of technological change could also be measured by the volume of new SKUs being introduced each year by all manufacturers. By December 1997, for example, 52 Laser and 84 InkJet SKUs were distributed through the reseller channel, the majority of which were introduced during the prior twelve months.

Consumer Buying Patterns

The At-Home Market

By February 1997, 91% of people with home computers also owned a printer. Some households had more than one printer with an even split between color and black-and-white models. InkJets were the most common, particularly among color printers. The typical head-of-household in a home with a printer had an average annual income of $60K and children living at home.[14]

The home market could be divided into "first-time" and "repeat" buyers. In general, first-time buyers shopped for about one month, focusing on quality, speed, after-sales service and support, availability, brand, and price. These buyers usually went through the normal phases of awareness, consideration, and purchase behaviors. During the first two phases people visited web sites and physical stores, talked to friends, and read *Consumer Reports*. Most had a preconception of which brand and SKUs to buy before entering a store, but only 65%–70% of the time would a shopper find a particular SKU in a high-volume retailer. Once in the store, shoppers could be influenced by in-store demonstrations of other printer brands. Manufacturer guarantees were an important buying factor because consumers believed that retailers had poor after-sales support and repair services.[15]

First-time buyers also tended to purchase a PC, monitor, and printer as a bundle, which accounted for 20% of all printers sold. Because the PC was the most expensive of these items, it was the focus of the buying decision.

In contrast, repeat buyers tended to buy a printer as a single purchase.[16] Often they were motivated by the need to update previously owned technology (the quality, speed, or color of their printer). Other motivations were the printing needs associated with their growing fascination with digital cameras, scanners, and Internet distribution as well as the emerging needs of their children. For example, a two- or three-PC home might have needed a second printer, or a child off to college might have needed a new and smaller printer for the dorm room. In effect, repeat buyers came in two flavors. When they were simply upgrading their existing technology or buying additional units similar to the original, they had shorter shopping periods and were more likely to buy "sight-unseen." Mail order was a popular channel for these buyers and accounted for 8% of all printer sales. When they were introducing themselves to a new printer category, however, repeat buyers became like first-time buyers, but were more informed. Repeat buyers were also the larger of the two segments.

The Home Office Market

Individuals with home offices became important to the printer market in the 1990s. These individuals were primarily telecommuting, moonlighting, or were self-employed. Their preference for using a home office ranged from a better quality of life to tax deductions and

[14] "1997 Digital Imaging Survey—Printer Ownership & Usage #11073," *Investext*, February 1,1997, Ch. 5.

[15] Kirthi Kalyanam and Shelby McIntyre, "Hewlett Packard Consumer Products Business Organization: Distribution through E*Commerce Channels," 1998–1999, p. 3.

[16] Ibid.

convenience. In 1997, it was estimated that 52 million Americans worked from home and 11 million telecommuted from a home office at least once a month.[17] The changing demands of the work place were expected to sustain this trend.

The all-in-one peripherals, or MFP, were the most popular product for the home office. As previously mentioned, these machines printed, copied, scanned, and faxed, and were particularly useful when minimizing costs and saving space were paramount. Buying patterns for this segment were even more deliberate than in the at-home category because these people tended to know exactly what they needed and had specific price points in mind.

Channels of Distribution

Although HP sold printers to consumers through seven channel types, the first three listed below accounted for bulk of the sales.

1. Computer Product Superstores. CompUSA was an example of this type of retailer. It carried a broad and deep assortment of PCs, peripherals, and computer-related products. Store employees were generally knowledgeable enough to respond to customers' questions. This type of superstore was known as a category specialist, focusing on PCs.
2. Consumer Electronic Superstores. Circuit City was an example of this type of retailer. Computers and related products were only one of many types of consumer electronics offered. Salespeople, who often worked on commission, tended to encourage customers to buy more expensive products.
3. Office Product Superstores. Staples was an example of this type of retailer. Computers and related products were only one of many types of products offered. The sales mix included printers, copiers, fax machines, telephones, office furniture, and related supplies. Both small offices and home offices (SOHO) were the primary target markets of these stores. Sales help in these stores was as good as in other self-service stores.

The remaining channel types were corporate account dealers, indirect mail-order companies, mass merchants, and department stores.[18] An example of a corporate account dealer was Inacom, which did not have a physical store and derived at least 50% of its revenue from its outbound corporate account sales force. MicroWarehouse was an example of a mail-order company. It generated more than 75% of its revenue from catalogue advertising and/or the Internet. Delivery of goods to consumers was almost always by US mail or UPS. Mass merchants, such as Wal-Mart, and department stores, such as Sears, focused on the at-home market and stocked a limited selection of computers and computer-related products.

Retail Account Management

HP had a solid reputation with its primary retail accounts and was reinforced by all of the services that HP provided. Large retail accounts represented 90% of HP's printer sales (in units). The company used an account team to do business directly with each account. These teams worked with their assigned retailers on many fronts. For example, they helped coordinate co-marketing efforts, which included cooperative advertising and in-store displays, and provided merchandise development funds. These funds, which subsidized retail promotions to consumers, amounted to 2%–3% of sales in computer-related product categories.

[17] Debra Cash, "There's No Office Like Home," *Inc. Web Site,* August 26, 1999. http://www.inc.com.
[18] This section was drawn from "Hewlett Packard Consumer Products Business Organization: Distribution through E*Commerce Channels" by Kirthi Kalyanam and Shelby McIntyre, 1998–1999.

Manufacturer's Advertised Price (MAP) policies were common practice in the industry. MAP clauses were typically inserted into the cooperative advertising contracts. These clauses stipulated that the manufacturer would not reimburse the reseller for cooperative ads that involved a price below a specified level. As a result, there was little variation in advertised retail prices across channels for the fast-moving SKUs. Other segments of assistance were category management, which aided the retailer in understanding trends, and detailing. Detailers tended to work for a third party but were paid for and scheduled by HP. They performed functions such as making sure that the appropriate type of paper was being used in the printers displayed on the shop floor and that the signage was adequate. HP teams also helped manage logistics and inventory for its major accounts.[19] The cost of all of these support services to HP was 1.5% of sales, in addition to the cost of cooperative advertising funds. Finally, HP provided price protection for inventory that became obsolete on the retail shelf, and this resulted in a payoff of 1%–2% of sales to the retailer.

HP retailers were responsible for a number of value-added functions. These included breaking bulk orders and shipping merchandise to individual retail stores, sales assistance, advertising, after-sales customer service and support, credit/collections from consumers, and returns processing.[20] Most importantly, retailers enabled shoppers to see the physical products, get a sense for their speed, and judge the quality of their output.

HP also did business with smaller retail chains, such as TOPS. HP, however, used distributors to reach such customers, rather than going direct. These distributors could sell only to HP authorized retailers. The authorization process included an evaluation of the history of the retailer, its operating practices, and the management team.[21]

Retailer Prices and Profitability

Average retail prices for printers had declined steadily and were $299 for the most popular InkJet printer and $999 for the most popular LaserJet printer in 1998. Both retail and manufacturer printer margins had declined over the past five years. On average, printers accounted for 5%–10% of a retailer's sales volume, with retail margins at 8%–14% and net margins in the low single digits. This was a result of all the services the retailer provided plus the cost of six weeks of inventory in the retail channel and the payment terms to the manufacturer set at 30 days. Moreover, since the popular HP products were advertised frequently by retailers (in the weekly fliers), net margins on HP products were even less than those on competing products.

The printer supply business was profitable for both the retailers and the manufacturer (with net margin in the teens). InkJet cartridges retailed between $22 and $30 and LaserJet cartridges averaged $60 per unit. Office product superstores received the bulk of this business, whereas consumer electronic superstores received a disproportionately lower share of the supply market. Maintaining an adequate selection was challenging because, with so many different SKUs, customers had problems matching their printer models with the corresponding printers' supplies. InkJet cartridges had to be replaced, on average, once or twice a year versus LaserJet cartridges which had to be replaced approximately once a year. Consumers were expected to use about 3–7 cartridges before updating their printers. Together, InkJet and Laser cartridges represented a total U.S. market of $7 billion in sales in 1997.[22]

[19] Ibid.

[20] Kirthi Kalyanam and Shelby McIntyre, "Hewlett Packard Consumer Products Business Organization: Distribution through E*Commerce Channels," 1998–1999, p. 7.

[21] This section was drawn from "Hewlett Packard Consumer Products Business Organization: Distribution through E*Commerce Channels" by Kirthi Kalyanam and Shelby McIntyre, 1998–1999.

[22] Norm Alster, "Is Printer Ink Replacement a License to Print Money?" *Investor's Business Daily*, May 28, 1998, pp. 8–9.

Retail Disruption and the Internet

The goals of retailing were always to get the right product in the right place at the right price and at the right time. The Internet created the ideal platform for retailers to excel in offering a wide selection of products (more than in any bricks and mortar company), 24 hours a day, at lower prices, and significant time savings. The Internet, in general, was proving to be an unstoppable force and was changing the way everyone worked and played. One hundred years ago British economist Alfred Marshall said:

> The full importance of an epoch-making idea is often not perceived in the generation in which it is made. A new discovery is seldom fully effective for practical purposes until many minor improvements and subsidiary discoveries have gathered themselves around it.[23]

Who could have imagined, for example, the way the automobile would affect urban design, shopping, and courtship? Or how electricity would enable women to move into the workplace with the creation of the washing machine and vacuum cleaner?

As Irving Wladawsky-Berger, IBM's general manager of the Internet Division, said:

> It's going to be huge. It's going to permeate everything. It's going to be a ubiquitous channel for doing commerce.[24]

eChannels for Computer Products

In spring 1998, two basic types of eChannels existed. First were traditional resellers like CompUSA, Office Depot, and Wal-Mart, which were using their brand leverage from their brick and mortar base and applying it to the web. These companies had existing infrastructure costs and needed to balance strategies between in-store and on-line goals.

Second were the new virtual stores that existed only on the Internet. An example was Value America (VA), which was founded in 1997 and offered a large selection of technology, office, and consumer merchandise. Considered an eTailer mall, VA sold only leading branded products (no private labels or knockoffs) at a discount. VA used a membership structure, just as Costco did, to give customers even deeper discounts—usually 5%. There was no charge for membership, but that was sure to change in the future. One key for VA was the establishment of relationships with over 1,000 brands. VA advertised these brands in exchange for cooperative advertising payments. VA abided by MAP and also received product presentation fees to aid in overhead costs. Another unique aspect was VA's use of non-Internet advertising methods, such as newspapers, to drive sales.

VA kept no inventory and would send product orders directly to distributors or manufacturers. Although VA offered a variety of products, the majority of sales came from computers. As of Q1 1998, the majority of sales were from products supplied by IBM, with the largest other sources from HP, Compaq, and Toshiba. Analysts expected VA to break even by 2002 and to become a major eCommerce destination.[25]

Internet Retailing

Convenience shopping dates back to the success of the Sears catalogue mail-order business in 1906, when 2,000 workers were hired to handle the 900 sack-loads of daily orders.[26] These web-retailing roots were transformed into 46 million Internet users in 1997, and this

---

[23] "When Companies Connect," *Economist,* June 26, 1999, p. 19.

[24] Marc Songini, "IBM's Internet Division Crafts Company Vision," *Network World,* August 18, 1997, pp. 23–24.

[25] Keith E. Benjamin and Laura Cooks Levitan, "Value America-E-Tailing Research," *BankBoston Robertson Stephens Research Report,* May 4, 1999.

[26] Robert Gray, "Delivering the Goods," *Marketing,* May 21, 1998, p. 26.

number was expected to grow to 150 million by 2000. Internet use reached this benchmark in only five years, as opposed to radio, TV, and cable which took 38, 13, and 10 years, respectively.[27] Reasons for this rapid adoption included consumers' growing dissatisfaction with the level of service and lack of knowledgeable salespeople offered by the conventional channels. Another reason was the increasing acceptance of the indirect mail-order channel, meaning that shoppers were becoming comfortable purchasing goods "sight-unseen." In fact the mail-order channel accounted for 8% of customers in spring 1998.

One example of Internet retail success was Amazon.com, which achieved a 100% growth rate in every quarter of 1996. Growing at a rate of over 70% in each of the first two quarters of 1997, Amazon sales had reached $148 million by the close of that year. This company, however, did not post a profit—which was standard in this emerging eBusiness category. Based upon this fact, Internet businesses were valued according to their prospect for future growth and their number of new customers, not their profitability.[28] In addition, the most critical aspect of pure-play Internet companies was the expense of acquiring a new customer. This tended to be very high in the early brand-awareness-building stages, but was expected to decrease later as economies of scale came into reach.

The largest wake-up call was by Dell Computer, as it set the standard in the direct-order selling model. As of early 1998, Dell was selling $3 million a day worth of computers, software, and related accessories on the Internet, with the intent to transfer as much as half of its $12 billion revenues to the Internet within three years.[29,30] The Dell model became the standard of industry efficiency because the whole process from order to shipping took 36 hours. Incoming components were pulled through the production process and ordered on a just-in-time (JIT) basis. This allowed Dell to have only about 13 days of inventory, versus 75 to 100 days in an ordinary indirect model.[31] An industry insider remarked:

> While machines from Compaq or IBM can languish on dealer shelves for two months, Dell doesn't start ordering components and assembling computers until an order is booked. That may sound like no biggie, but the price of PC parts can fall rapidly in just a few months. By ordering right before assembly, [Michael] Dell figures his parts, on average, are 60 days newer than those in an IBM or Compaq machine sold at the same time. That can translate into a 6% profit advantage in components alone.[32]

Online retail sales were $600 million in 1996 and over $2 billion in 1997. The most popular products and services in 1997 were computer hardware, travel, brokerage, books, and software (see **Exhibit 1**). With an estimated 150 million users by 2000, the sales figure was expected to reach $21–$56 billion that year and $115 billion by 2005. As impressive as this seemed, 1997 Internet sales represented approximately a few days of business for Wal-Mart and barely a dent in the $2.5 trillion of overall retail sales. Demographic trends supported these online sales and user predictions. The combination of two-income families and the expanding workweek, for example, had shaved leisure time from 26 hours per week to 19. A 1997 survey by Kurt Salmon Associates also found that 52% of people wanted to reduce their shopping time. In addition, Deloitte & Touche research discovered that 50% of Americans considered shopping an "unpleasant chore" and of this group, 55% under age 34 felt that way.[33]

[27] Kirthi Kalyanam and Shelby McIntyre, "Hewlett Packard Consumer Products Business Organization: Distribution through E*Commerce Channels," 1998–1999, p. 7.

[28] Ibid., p. 8.

[29] James Kim, "Dell: Built-to-Order Success Rivals Rush to Imitate Direct Sell," *USA Today,* June 30, 1997, p. 1B.

[30] "Dell Online," HBS No. 598-116, p. 1.

[31] Ibid., p. 4.

[32] Gary McWilliams, "Whirlwind on the Web, " *Business Week,* April 7, 1997.

[33] Joel Kotkin, "The Mother of all Malls," *Forbes,* April 6, 1998, pp. 60–65.

EXHIBIT 1
eTailing Growth by
Category (millions)

Source: Technology Research,
BancBoston Robertson
Stephens, February 12, 1999,
p. 22.

Category	1997	1998E
Travel	$804	$2,183
Online brokerage	696	1,498
Computer hardware	866	2,432
Computer software	139	385
Books	254	925
Gifts/flowers	77	214
Apparel	53	171
Food/drink	46	120
Music	37	188
Automobile	40	206
Other sales	80	240
Total	$3,092	$8,562

Potential threats to Internet retailing came from mass merchandisers like Wal-Mart or from manufacturers themselves. Wal-Mart's strong brand awareness, state-of-the-art information technology and distribution systems, and superior channel muscle were expected to pose a formidable challenge to existing web retailers. For manufacturers, it seemed natural to want to eliminate the "middleman" and sell directly to consumers online, but they hesitated for fear of angering their channel partners. K-Swiss, for example, would be hurt by the loss of its partner Foot Locker, which accounted for about one-fifth of its annual sales.[34] Even some retailers posed a threat as they introduced private label products that competed directly with national brands.

Going direct was not only about increased gross margins. In addition to possible channel disruption, obstacles included: the large investment for developing and maintaining a solid web site; security and bandwidth issues; uncertain return on investment; competitors having easy access to information; higher rates of product return; and customer-incurred shipping charges (which averaged $12–$14 for two-day delivery and $22–$30 for overnight delivery of an HP printer, for example).

Strategic Options

HP believed that its market share neither reflected the company's comparative advantages, nor accounted for consumers' awareness and preferences for its products. The company also believed that the retailers could have provided better in-store support for HP products. This stemmed from high sales personnel turnover and low product knowledge.

HP management was also assessing the position of its Internet outlet center that sold refurbished products at reduced prices, as well as the associated printer supplies and accessories. The outlet store was established for two reasons. One was to enable the company to sell open-box returned products, recovery of which was a significant problem prior to the establishment of the online store. (Previously HP would break down returned products for spare service parts.) The second was to use it to learn the mechanics of Internet direct selling and as a means of recognizing the increasing number of Internet shoppers.[35] HP believed there would be little channel conflict by focusing on refurbished products. Reflecting on this experience, Shen Li, the HP North American channel marketing manager commented:

[34] Ibid.

[35] M2 Presswire, "HP Opens Web Outlet Center to Sell Refurbished Consumer Products," January 8, 1998.

We get a continuous stream of information regarding the supply chain (sales, inventory, etc.), advertising response (banner ads and site referrals), and customer behavior (page views, site path, shopping time of the day, day of the week, phone versus Internet orders, shopping basket, etc.). In some ways it is overwhelming to get information with this level of depth and in a real-time manner. Synthesizing this information is like trying to drink from a fire hose.[36]

HP management considered its options:

1. **Wait and See**—HP could continue selling refurbished printers through its Internet outlet center, which would maintain channel relationships and profits. Competitors were not selling directly on the Internet at this time; thus HP would be taking a risk by being the first to use that channel. If competitors took a direct route, HP could benefit from possible retail retaliation. Alternatively, if competitors became successful on the Internet, HP could join the new channel at a more mature stage.[37]

2. **Participate through Online Retailers**—Some traditional retailers, such as CompUSA, were selling via online stores by mid-1997. HP was already selling to the brick and mortar stores, so it seemed reasonable to expand with them on the web. The problem was that these stores were moving slowly in the eCommerce arena, as opposed to the nimble eTailers like Value America. Also worth noting were computer manufacturers such as Dell and Gateway, who were leaders in direct sales. These companies had had low printer sales in the past, but were beginning to see the advantage as the printer drivers could be pre-loaded into their machines.[38]

3. **Expand the Offerings Online**—Going direct would enable HP to interact with its customers, build relationships, and strengthen the HP brand. Although there was first-mover risk, there was also potential benefit as evidenced by the success of Amazon.com. If this course were taken, a business plan would have to outline the products and prices to be offered online. A budget would also be needed to allow for development and maintenance of the web site, including marketing and advertising allowances. Amazon, for example, spent $40 million of its $150 million revenue on marketing and advertising expenses in 1997. A general minimum investment was $500K to develop a web site. A popular advertising method was banner ads, which were priced around $35 per thousand impressions and had a click-through rate of 0.5%–2.5%.[39] Associated with the click-through rate was the visit-to-buy rate of 1%–2%. In addition, the cost of acquiring a new customer had to be considered. This customer acquisition cost was approximately $25 for companies such as Amazon, eBay, and OnSale, whereas it was about $200 for companies such as E*Trade, CDNow, and Preview Travel.

---

[36] This section was drawn from "Hewlett Packard Consumer Products Business Organization: Distribution through E*Commerce Channels" by Kirthi Kalyanam and Shelby McIntyre, 1998–1999.

[37] Ibid.

[38] Ibid.

[39] Ibid.

Chapter

23

Goodyear: The Aquatred Launch

John A. Quelch   Bruce Isaacson

In January 1992, Barry Robbins, Goodyear's vice president of marketing for North American Tires, was contemplating the upcoming launch of the Aquatred, a new tire providing improved driving traction under wet conditions. The Aquatred would be positioned in the U.S. market as a replacement tire for passenger cars. Over recent years, the replacement tire market had matured and new channels had gained share, so Robbins needed to make sure Goodyear had the right product and the right timing to generate support from the company's traditional base of independent dealers. Despite a long and close relationship with those independent dealers, Goodyear was also weighing the risks and benefits of expanding the company's distribution channels. If new outlets were added, Robbins would also have to assess whether the new channel would sell the Aquatred.

The Tire Industry in the United States

From the early 1900s through the early 1970s, the U.S. tire industry was dominated by five companies: Goodyear, Firestone, Uniroyal, BF Goodrich, and General Tire. All five were based in Akron, Ohio, and were run by executives who socialized together at the same country club. The five companies had competed in a U.S. market characterized by not only consistent growth in revenues and profits but also a complete absence of foreign competition. In the 1970s and 1980s, the U.S. tire industry experienced three important changes. The first was the emergence of the radial tire to replace the older "bias" and "bias-belted"

Doctoral Candidate Bruce Isaacson prepared this case under the supervision of Professor John Quelch as the basis for class discussion rather than to illustrate either effective or ineffective handling of an administrative situation.

TABLE A
Trends in Passenger Tire Sales, 1975–1991 (in millions of tires)

Source: *Modern Tire Dealer.*

	1991	1986	1981	1976
Replacement	152	144	123	137
OEM	43	54	37	50
Total	195	198	160	187

tire constructions.[1] Compared with the older constructions, radials offered superior tread-wear, handling, and gas mileage, but had a stiffer ride. While bias and bias-belted tires lasted under 20,000 miles, by the early 1980s radials lasted over 40,000 miles. Between 1975 and 1991, radials' share of unit sales in the U.S. passenger tire market increased from 32% to over 95%, and virtually all new cars were equipped with radial tires. Converting factories to produce radials required major investments, but many U.S. tire manufacturers had hesitated, hoping that consumers would continue to prefer the softer ride of bias-belted tires.

The second major change was increased foreign competition. Some companies, such as Michelin of France, used expertise in radial production as a lever into the U.S. market. Other tire manufacturers gained access by equipping new cars exported from their home country. Imported passenger tires represented 8% of unit sales in the U.S. passenger tire market (both original equipment and replacement) in 1972, 12% in 1982, and 22% in 1990.

The third major change was in the nature of demand from consumers and car makers. In the 1970s, the price of oil had risen, causing consumers to drive less. Producing one tire typically required seven gallons of oil or derivative products, so the cost of manufacturing tires also increased. Automobile sales shifted towards cars that were smaller, lighter, and had front-wheel drive; these cars placed less wear on tires. Coupled with the radial's longer life, this meant that consumers replaced tires less frequently.

These changes had four major impacts. First, demand for passenger tires grew sluggishly during the 1980s (see **Table A**). While the average life of a new tire rose from 28,600 miles in 1980 to 37,300 miles in 1990, annual miles traveled per passenger car in the United States grew only slowly, rising from 9,100 miles in 1980 to 10,600 miles in 1990.

Second, new tire prices in the U.S. market declined. The median retail price of a typical passenger tire (size P195/75R14) in the United States dropped more than 25% from 1980 to 1990. By 1991, the average retail price of all passenger tires was $75.00. Third, tire-producing capacity outstripped demand. U.S. tire-making capacity rose 12% between 1987 and 1990; capacity utilization fell from 87% to 76% during the same period. Despite plant closings and layoffs, analysts expected the overcapacity to last through the mid-1990s.

Fourth, the industry's difficult economic conditions, coupled with the tire manufacturers' slow response, resulted in a number of mergers and acquisitions. In 1986, Goodrich and Uniroyal spun off their tire divisions to form the Uniroyal-Goodrich Tire Company, which was sold to Michelin in 1990. In 1987, General Tire was sold to Continental, a German tire manufacturer, while Pirelli, an Italian company, bought the Armstrong Tire Company, and Sumimoto Rubber Industries of Japan acquired Dunlop. In 1988, Firestone was sold to Bridgestone, a Japanese company. By 1991, Goodyear was the only major U.S. tire manufacturer that had not been acquired.

Company Background

Since the early days of the tire industry, The Goodyear Rubber and Tire Company had been known as "The Gorilla" for its dominance of the world tire industry. In 1991, Goodyear operated 41 plants in the United States, 43 plants in 25 other countries, six rubber plantations, and more than 2,000 distribution outlets worldwide. In fiscal year 1991, Goodyear earned

[1] In the radial tire, layers of rubberized material extended from side to side across the tire, perpendicular to the direction of travel. An additional layer or "belt," typically steel, was placed underneath the tread.

net income of less than one percent on total revenues of $10.91 billion; the company had approximately 105,000 employees. Goodyear ranked third in worldwide sales of new tires (see **Table B**).

Exhibit 1 lists the brand shares of U.S. retail sales for the largest tire manufacturers from 1975 to 1990. During this period, Michelin achieved large share gains in both the replacement and OEM markets. Unlike other U.S. tire manufacturers, Goodyear had made large investments (over $1.5 billion) during the late 1970s to convert its factories to produce radials. The company also had a strong track record in launching innovative products. In 1977, Goodyear introduced the Tiempo, the first all-season radial. All-season radials did not have to be replaced with snow tires during winter months; their unit sales grew from 2% of U.S. replacement passenger tires in 1978 to 71% in 1991. In 1981, Goodyear successfully launched the Eagle, the first radial tire offering high-speed traction for sports cars. On a typical radial, the cost of goods sold was 60% of the manufacturer's selling price, but the Eagle provided Goodyear and its dealers with higher percentage profit margins than standard radials.

TABLE B
World Leaders in New Tire Sales, 1991 (in billions of U.S. dollars)

Source: *Modern Tire Dealer.*

Michelin/Uniroyal/Goodrich	$10.4
Bridgestone/Firestone	9.8
Goodyear/Kelly-Springfield	8.5
Continental/General	3.9
Pirelli/Armstrong	3.7
Sumimoto/Dunlop	3.5

EXHIBIT 1
Brand Shares of Unit Sales in the U.S. Passenger Tire Market

Source: *Modern Tire Dealer.*

	1975	1980	1985	1990	1991
Replacement Market (includes larger brands only)					
Goodyear	14.0%	14.0%	15.5%	15.0%	15.0%
Michelin	2.5	7.0	8.0	8.5	8.5
Firestone	10.5	10.0	9.5	8.0	7.5
Sears	10.0	10.0	9.0	6.5	5.5
General	2.0	3.0	2.5	4.0	4.5
BF Goodrich	4.0	5.0	4.5	4.0	3.5
Bridgestone	0.0	2.0	2.0	3.0	3.5
Cooper	1.0	1.5	2.5	3.0	3.5
Kelly	3.0[a]	4.0	3.0	3.0	3.0
Uniroyal	3.5	3.5	3.0	3.0	2.5
Dunlop	2.5	2.5	2.5	2.5	2.0
Pirelli	0.0	0.0	1.0	2.0	2.0
Montgomery Ward	4.5	3.5	2.0	2.0	1.5
Other[b]	42.5	34.0	35.0	35.5	37.5
OEM Market					
Goodyear	35%	28%	32%	36%	38%
Michelin	2	5	11	16	16
Firestone	24	22	22	17	17
General	11	11	13	12	11
Uniroyal	20	24	22	17	13
BF Goodrich[c]	8	0	0	0	0
Dunlop	0	10	0	1	3
Bridgestone	0	0	0	1	2

[a]Estimates.
[b]Other included a variety of smaller brands, some of which were exclusively private label.
[c]BF Goodrich was sold to Uniroyal, and eventually to Michelin.

In the early and mid-1980s, Goodyear diversified, making large investments in pipelines for natural gas and oil transmission. In 1986, Sir James Goldsmith attempted to take over Goodyear and was bought out by management after a highly emotional takeover battle which greatly increased Goodyear's debt. Although 13% of the company's work force was furloughed between 1987 and 1991, in 1991 Goodyear was still spending $1 million per day on interest payments, and earnings were sluggish (**see Table C**).

In June of 1991, Stanley G. Gault, retired chairman of Rubbermaid, became chairman of Goodyear. Gault had been a member of Goodyear's board of directors, and many hoped that he would bring the same marketing flair and new product skills that he had shown at Rubbermaid. Gault stated his goal at Goodyear:

> . . . to create a market-driven organization. That means to serve the customer and the ultimate user. People are wrong to think of tires as a commodity—that a tire is a tire is a tire. . . . Customers want safety—they want that car to stop. They want reliability.[2]

Gault installed his own management team, sold off assets that were not directly related to the tire business, and placed an increased priority on new product development.

The Market for Passenger Tires

The market for passenger tires could be segmented three ways. One segmentation was based on the distinction between performance and broad-line tires. Performance tires were wider than broad-line tires, were more expensive, and provided better traction. Although performance tires could be replaced with broad-line tires, consumers rarely made this substitution because of the resulting decrease in handling and performance. **Exhibit 2** shows Goodyear's tire lines for both segments, demonstrating the substantial price differential between them. **Exhibit 3** shows the differences among Goodyear's broad-line tires. In the U.S. passenger tire market, performance tires represented 25% of Goodyear's unit sales, 30% of dollar sales, and an even higher percentage of profits.

[2] Source: *Fortune,* July 15, 1991.

TABLE C
Sales and Income for Goodyear and Subsidiaries, 1987–1991

Source: Annual reports.

	1987	1988	1989	1990	1991
Net sales (in millions)	$9,905.2	$10,810.4	$10,869.3	$11,272.5	$10,906.8
Net income (loss)	770.9	350.1	206.8	(38.3)	96.6
Net income (loss) per share	12.73[a]	6.11	3.58	(0.66)	1.61

[a]Includes income of $257.0 million, or $4.24 per share, for discontinued operations.

EXHIBIT 2
Goodyear Tire Lines with Typical Suggested Per-Tire Retail Prices

Source: Company records.

Performance Radials		All Season Radials		Light Truck Tire	
Eagle GS-C	$280	Aquatred	$90[a]	Wrangler	$120
Eagle VR/ZR	255	Invicta GS	80	Workhorse RIB	70
Eagle GT+4	140	Invicta GL	65	Workhorse M&S	80
Eagle GA	120	Arriva	60		
Eagle ST	100	Tiempo	50		
Eagle M&S	215	Corsa GT	40		

[a]Suggested retail price in Aquatred test market.
Note: All tires varied in price according to tire size.

EXHIBIT 3 Goodyear's Broad-Line Tires

AQUATRED

Improved Wet Road Stopping, Quiet All-Season Performance.

Aquachannel, deep connecting grooves pump water out of the way fast

Exclusive new compound gives road-hugging traction and longer life

Careful tread placement offers a smoother, quieter ride

Sleek sidewall design to complement today's automotive designs

INVICTA GS

Luxury Handling, Smooth, Quiet Ride, All-Season Performance

A smooth, quiet ride enhances the pleasure of driving a vehicle

Unique crisscross tread elements plus deep, effective shoulder grooves produce outstanding year-round traction

A noticeable dexterity in cornering, braking, and handling, the result of carefully selected tread rubber compounds

Impressive long term mileage capability for both front and rear wheel drive vehicles

ARRIVA

Great Traction In Any Weather

All season tread design for year round traction

Aggressive tread design features more gripping edges for improved snow traction

Easy rolling, long wearing tread compound

Dependable wet/dry traction for year-round performance

INVICTA GL

Advanced Rib, All Season Tread Design

All season traction from segmented tread lugs and open shoulder grooves

Long, even wear, quiet ride, excellent fuel economy from advanced tread rib pattern

Precision handling from natural molded shape

TIEMPO

Steel Belted Strength, All Season Traction

Flexible sidewalls deliver a smooth, comfortable ride

Steel belted radial construction delivers strength, tread wear, and fuel efficiency

Tread designed to dissipate heat for tire durability

CORSA GT

Great Handling And Mileage For Small Cars

All season traction designed tread

Center rib tread design and special tread rubber compound deliver long, even tread wear

Wraparound shoulder and tread lug design produce outstanding year-round traction

The market could also be segmented based on replacement and OEM tires. Replacement tires were sold to individual consumers, while OEM tires were sold to car manufacturers. Car makers used volume purchases to negotiate substantial discounts on tires. In 1991, U.S. replacement tire sales were estimated at $8.6 billion (see **Table D**). In the United States, Goodyear's passenger tire division derived 65% of its revenues from replacement tires and 35% from OEM tires. Division revenues were $1.98 billion on sales of 39.1 million tires.

A third segmentation scheme was along brand classifications, which included major brands, minor brands, and private label. Major brands, which carried the name of a major tire manufacturer, accounted for 36% of unit sales in the replacement passenger tire market. Major brands had the highest recognition among consumers and included Goodyear, Firestone, Michelin, Bridgestone, Pirelli, and Goodrich. Minor brands represented 24% of unit sales and included tires made by smaller manufacturers as well as tires made by major manufacturers but sold under a different name. Minor brands included Sears, Dunlop, General, Kelly (a Goodyear subsidiary), Uniroyal, Cooper, Yokohama, and Toyo. Although minor, these brands were often well-recognized by consumers and included high-priced niche brands.

Sales of private label tires constituted the remaining 40% of the market. Many small manufacturers specialized in private label tires, while some larger manufacturers used excess capacity to service the private label market. Most private label tires carried names exclusive to a particular retailer, but others were available to any retailer. Private label manufacturers typically had only one distributor per territory, which gave the distributor some flexibility in pricing. In 1991, private label tires constituted 80% of the sales of Goodyear's wholly owned Kelly-Springfield subsidiary; the remaining 20% were sold under the Kelly brand.

The average retail selling price of a private label tire was 18% lower than the price of a comparable branded tire. Although sales of private label tires had grown, their average life remained lower than the life of a branded tire (see **Table E**).

Many of the attributes important to consumers when purchasing a tire were not apparent upon visual inspection. To certify product quality, some retailers added warranties to their tires. These warranties were paid for by the retailer and would typically guarantee the tire for 60,000 miles, with the value of the guarantee decreasing on a pro-rata basis over the life of the tire. Retailer warranties were particularly common on sales of private label tires.

In past years, Goodyear had produced two lines of private label tires: the All American and the Concorde. The Goodyear brand was not placed on these tires, providing Goodyear's independent dealers with low-priced lines to compete with other types of outlets. In 1991, Robbins replaced the All American and the Concorde with Goodyear-branded tires at comparable prices because market research showed that the nonbranded lines

TABLE D
The U.S. Market for Passenger Tires, 1991

Source: *Modern Tire Dealer.*

	Dollars (in millions)			Units (in millions)		
	Replacement	OEM	Total	Replacement	OEM	Total
Industry	$8,600	N/A[a]	N/A	152.0	43.0	195.0
Goodyear	1,290	$695	$1,985	22.8	16.3	39.1

[a]Indicates data were not available.

TABLE E
Average Tire Life (miles)

Source: Company records.

	All Tires	Branded Tires	Private Label
1991	38,600	39,700	37,000
1986	33,100	34,500	30,900
1981	28,600	29,100	28,500

cannibalized sales of branded tires. Although the sales of these two lines were relatively small, some analysts felt that discontinuing the All American and Concorde increased incentives for Goodyear's independent dealers to sell tires made by other manufacturers. Some independent dealers believed that consumers wanted to choose from a range of tires, and favored offering private brands to provide consumers with a reference point, which they argued would increase the sales of Goodyear tires.

Consumers in the Replacement Passenger Tire Market

Consumer Behavior

Most consumers viewed tires as a "grudge purchase"—an expensive necessity to keep a vehicle in driving condition. The average time between purchases of tires was 2.5 years, but over half of all tire-buying consumers made their purchase the same day they became aware of their need for tires. Most tires were bought in pairs: 42% of consumer purchases involved two tires, 40% involved four tires, 16% involved one tire, and only 2% involved three tires. Purchases of sets of four tires accounted for 60% of all units sold.

Goodyear regularly surveyed car owners, asking about performance attributes considered when purchasing tires. The five most important tire attributes, in order from higher to lesser importance, were tread life, wet traction, handling, snow traction, and dry traction. Goodyear also regularly surveyed car owners concerning the criteria they used to select a tire retailer. The seven most important criteria, again in order from higher to lesser importance, were as follows:

1. Price
2. Offers fast service
3. Can trust personnel
4. Store is attractive
5. Offers mileage warranty
6. Brand selection
7. Maintains convenient hours

A 1989 Goodyear survey had shown that with no other information available, consumers expected Goodyear's broad-line tires to be priced within a six-dollar range from the most expensive to the least expensive. The research also demonstrated that Goodyear's point-of-sale displays did little to alter consumers' expectations of retail prices.

Consumer Segments

Goodyear used research about consumers' shopping behavior to segment tire buyers into four categories (see **Exhibit 4**):

1. **Price-constrained buyers** Price-constrained buyers bought the best brand they could afford within their budget. They had little loyalty to any specific outlet or brand and tended to shop around for tires before purchasing.
2. **Value-oriented buyers** Value-oriented buyers searched for their preferred brand at the best price. They were predisposed to major brands, shopped around extensively, and had little loyalty to any specific outlet.
3. **Quality buyers** Consumers in this segment were loyal to outlet and brand, tended to be upscale, and shopped for only a brief time before purchasing. The segment could be divided into two subsegments. *Prestige buyers* wanted to own the best tires on the market, while *comfortable conservatives* tended to develop a strong, lasting relationship with a

EXHIBIT 4
Major Consumer Segments for Replacement Passenger Tires

Source: Company records.

	Percent of Consumers	Percent of Sales Represented by		
		Major Brands	Minor Brands	Private Brands
Price-constrained buyers	22%	30%	35%	35%
Value-oriented buyers	18	54	29	17
Quality buyers	23	51	28	21
Commodity buyers	37	18	37	45
All tire buyers	100	33	33	34

TABLE F
Distribution Channels (percent of U.S. passenger tire replacement sales in units)

Source: *Modern Tire Dealer.*

Type of Outlet	1976	1981	1986	1991
Oil companies	9%	5%	3%	2%
Large retailers	24	20	16	19
Manufacturer-owned outlets	11	10	13	12
Independent dealers	56	65	68	67

specific outlet. Comfortable conservatives would often buy the brand recommended by their favorite outlet; major brands accounted for 38% of their purchases, versus 65% of purchases made by prestige buyers.

4. **Commodity buyers** Commodity buyers valued price and outlet and could be divided into two sub-segments. Typically, *bargain hunters* were young, with little brand preference, low retailer loyalty, and a tendency to shop around extensively. *Trusting patrons* viewed brand as unimportant and tended to buy lower-priced tires at a preferred retailer. Trusting patrons made their purchase decision relatively quickly, without extensive shopping.

In 1992, 45% of tire buyers were price oriented when shopping for tires; 22% were brand oriented, and 33% believed the outlet was most important. By contrast, in 1985, 48% were price oriented, 26% were brand oriented, and 26% were outlet oriented. Over the past four years, the percent of consumers classified as quality oriented declined by four percent, while commodity buyers increased four percent.

Wholesale and Retail Channels for Replacement Tires

Tire manufacturers sold replacement tires to wholesalers. Wholesalers resold the tires to a variety of retailers and dealers, who then sold the tires to consumers. This section describes both wholesale and retail distribution channels for replacement passenger tires.

Wholesale Distribution Channels

The U.S. replacement passenger tire market depended on the four wholesale channels listed in **Table F.**

The majority of tires wholesaled to oil companies were resold through franchised or company-owned gas stations or service stations. Wholesaling by oil companies had declined in recent years, reflecting increased competition at the retail level.

Large retailers, including mass merchandisers and warehouse clubs, bought tires directly from the manufacturers to resell in their stores. Independent dealers had increased their share of distribution in recent years. Like other tire makers, Goodyear sold passenger tires to three kinds of independent dealers. Dealers who were strictly wholesalers, with no retail operations, accounted for 10% of Goodyear's factory sales to independent dealers and resold their tires to car dealers, service stations, small independent dealers, and other secondary outlets. Another 40% went to dealers who both sold tires at retail and resold tires to other dealers or to secondary outlets. The remaining 50% went to dealers who bought tires to resell in their own retail outlets and did not resell to other outlets. This breakdown was typical of the industry.

Retail Distribution Channels

Six major retail channels competed for market share in the U.S. replacement passenger tire market. (**Exhibit 5** shows each channel's market share, relative prices, and reliance on private label tires.) The six channels can be described as follows:

1. **Garages/service stations:** These were typically small, neighborhood outlets offering gasoline, tires, and auto services. Their share of the tire market had declined in recent years in favor of lower-cost, higher-volume outlets. Garages and service stations sold private label tires as well as branded tires to combat price pressure from larger outlets.

2. **Warehouse clubs:** Warehouse clubs operated large stores carrying categories as diverse as food, clothing, electronics, tires, and hardware. Sam's, the largest of the warehouse clubs, had 208 outlets, while PACE had 87 outlets, Price Club had 77 outlets, and Costco had 75 outlets. Warehouse clubs offered a limited brand selection, with the selection changing according to the deals their buyers could strike with vendors. Also, warehouse clubs offered minimal in-store service other than installation. For example, in some warehouse clubs, consumers had to select tires from sales floor racks, cart the tires to the cash register, and bring the tires around the outside of the store to service bays for installation. Although warehouse clubs were a relatively new retail format, they were growing quickly due to their low prices. Some independent dealers felt that warehouse clubs offered tires at cost to increase store traffic, generating profits from tire installation and sales of other merchandise.

EXHIBIT 5
Share of Retail Sales of Replacement Passenger Tires by Channel (U.S. market only)

Source: Company records.

Channel Share of Retail Sales	1976	1981	1986	1991
Garages/service stations	18%	11%	8%	6%
Warehouse clubs	0	0	2	6
Mass merchandisers	28	24	16	12
Manufacturer-owned outlets	11	10	11	9
Small independent tire dealers	36	47	46	40
Large independent tire chains	4	2	12	23
Other	3	6	5	4
Total	100%	100%	100%	100%

	Relative Price Index, 1991	Sales of Private Label Tires as a Percent of Retail Sales Dollars, 1991
Garages/service stations	110%	57%
Warehouse clubs	80	8
Mass merchandisers	97	34
Manufacturer-owned outlets	107	16
Small independent tire dealers	100	36
Large independent tire chains	90	54
Other	N/A	59

Note: Relative price index indicates typical retail prices for the same tire in each channel. Retail prices in "other" category varied according to the specific outlet.

3. **Mass merchandisers:** Mass merchandisers were retail chains that sold tires, performed auto services, and carried other types of merchandise. The largest mass merchandisers had many outlets. Kmart sold tires in 990 outlets, Sears in 850 outlets, Wal-Mart in 425 outlets, and Montgomery Ward in 335 outlets. Mass merchandisers typically maintained a very wide brand selection. For example, Sears sold Michelin, Goodrich, Pirelli, Bridgestone, Yokohama, and its own Roadhandler brand; while Montgomery Ward sold Kelly, Goodrich, Michelin, Bridgestone, General, and its own RoadTamer brand.

4. **Manufacturer-owned outlets:** These outlets, owned and operated by the tire manufacturers, typically sold only one brand of tires and offered a range of auto services.

5. **Small independent tire dealers:** Small independent tire dealers operated one or two outlets, where they sold and installed tires and also offered auto services. Many small independent tire dealers started as single-brand outlets but over time added additional brands. Both small dealers and large independent tire chains derived an increasing portion of their revenues from private label tires.

6. **Large independent tire chains:** Also known as "multibrand discounters," large independent tire chains typically had 30–100 outlets concentrated within a geographic region. Examples of this type of outlet included Tire America, National Tire Warehouse, and Discount Tire. These chains carried major brands of tires as well as private label, and tended to be low-priced, high-volume operations. In recent years, large independent tire chains gained share, often by acquiring smaller independent dealers.

7. **Other:** Half the sales in the "other" category were accounted for by full-service auto supply stores such as Western Auto, Auto Palace, or Pep Boys. These stores sold tires at low prices as traffic builders and were resented by independent dealers as a consistent source of low-priced competition.

In most markets, consumers could choose among these types of channels. As one independent dealer noted, "The tire manufacturer is not only our supplier but also our competitor through manufacturer-owned outlets. On top of that, we compete with the warehouse clubs, mass merchandisers, corner station, and who knows who else."

Goodyear's Distribution Structure

Goodyear did not sell tires in garages/service stations, warehouse clubs, or mass merchandisers; instead, the company relied on three types of outlets. Goodyear's 4,400 *independent dealers* accounted for 50% of sales revenues, while the 1,047 *manufacturer-owned outlets* generated 27% of sales, and the 600 *franchised dealers* accounted for another 8% of sales. (The remaining 15% of sales were primarily to government agencies.) Goodyear was also testing a new retail format, *Just Tires*.

Manufacturer-owned outlets could be opened or closed at the discretion of the manufacturer. During the 1970s, Goodyear opened as many as 200 outlets per year. By 1983, the company owned 1,300 outlets in the United States, but became concerned about the associated demands for capital and management attention. Despite Goodyear's efforts to site company-owned outlets in locations that would minimize competition with its independent dealers, complaints were common. Over time, Goodyear placed increasing emphasis on franchising new outlets and also converted some company-owned outlets into franchised and independent dealerships.

New owners were franchised by Goodyear for three years and then became independent. During the three years, Goodyear provided training in operations, finance, and other aspects of the business. The number of franchised dealers was kept at 600 by adding new outlets as older franchisees became independent.

Goodyear had 4,400 independent dealers, but only about 2,500 were considered active dealers in that they generated a consistent level of sales, maintained the major Goodyear retail displays, and offered the full line of Goodyear tires. A typical independent outlet required the owner to invest $100,000 and generated annual revenues of $1,000,000. Goodyear's independent outlets sold an average of 15.5 tires/day, including both Goodyear and other brands of tires, although most Goodyear dealers derived the majority of their sales from Goodyear tires. The average selling price of all tires sold by Goodyear's independent dealers was $75 per tire. Retail margins for independent dealers averaged 28% on Goodyear tires, 25% for dealers carrying other major brands, and 20% for private label tires. Average wholesale margins were 18% for private label tires and 14% for Goodyear tires.[3]

Although Goodyear claimed not to want its tires sold in low-priced outlets such as warehouse clubs, mass merchandisers, and auto supply stores, those outlets sporadically obtained Goodyear tires. The price-based ads and frequent discounting from those outlets angered Goodyear's independent dealers. One owner of two independent tire outlets said, "The mass merchandisers are eating up the distribution of our product. It could drive me out of the tire business."[4] Industry observers felt that tires were diverted to those outlets by the large independent dealers who acted solely as wholesalers. As one analyst said, "There's a lot of big wholesalers who will sell to anybody."

Goodyear's options to stop the diversion were limited by legal restrictions which prohibited manufacturers from dictating either retail selling prices or to whom their tires could be resold. However, in December 1990, Goodyear sued two automotive chains: Tire America and Western Auto Supply. Both were owned by Sears, and neither was an authorized Goodyear dealer. The suits charged that the Sears units were advertising Goodyear tires without maintaining enough inventory to meet demand. Consumers drawn to the store were allegedly switched to other brands in a "bait and switch" tactic. Goodyear also maintained that the chains were not authorized to use the Goodyear trademark in their advertising.

Just Tires was a new retail format under test by Goodyear. Modeled after "quick lube" stores which offered fast oil changes without an appointment, *Just Tires* stores sold and installed tires but did not offer any other products or services. *Just Tires* stores provided consumers with guarantees covering speed and quality of installation.

Although there was some overlap, most outlets that sold Goodyear tires did not sell Kelly-Springfield tires. Kelly-Springfield had no company-owned outlets and sold primarily through mass merchandisers, independent tire dealers, and gas/service stations.

Promotions

It was estimated that three-fourths of all Goodyear tires sold in independent or company-owned outlets were sold on promotion, at an average discount of 25%. This discount was offered to the consumer in a number of ways, such as one free tire with the purchase of three tires, one tire for half price with the purchase of another tire at full price, or 25% off the price of selected tires. For both independent and company-owned dealers, promotions were organized around "core events"—six 3-week periods spread throughout the year during which Goodyear dealers could buy merchandise at a discount. Goodyear supported core events with radio, television, and print advertising announcing special prices on specific tire lines. Every spring, Goodyear offered dealers "spring dating," which provided extended financing on tire orders. Experiments with everyday low pricing in the tire industry had been unsuccessful because price competition among dealers undermined attempts to set consistently low but fair prices. As one dealer explained, "Consumers expect to buy their tires on sale. We have created a price-conscious monster."

---

[3] These margins are estimated from several sources and may vary by region or time period.

[4] *Wall Street Journal*, June 24, 1991, p. B1.

Goodyear's Independent Dealers

Goodyear operated separate sales organizations to service company-owned outlets and independent dealers. The company-owned outlets were grouped into 42 districts, each with 20 to 23 stores. There was one district manager per district, plus one store manager per store. Another sales organization called on independent dealers and was organized into 28 districts, each with a district manager and an average of three area sales managers.

Besides providing tires, Goodyear supported its independent dealers with a variety of services, including the following:

Expertise and training on issues such as financing, architecture, wholesaling, operations, and merchandising.

Certified Auto Service, which allowed dealers to attend training classes and become certified in auto services.

The Goodyear Business Management System, a computer system to help dealers with inventory and accounting.

National and regional advertising to support dealer sales.

Research on market trends, such as information on the popularity of each tire, by size, in a given market.

Goodyear serviced independent dealers through the area sales manager, who made sure that dealer orders were placed properly, provided information about market trends, offered advice on operations, and handled complaints. Visits from area sales managers were very important to dealers. As one area sales manager noted, "You never get to the dealer enough. You could spend all day there and then the next day the guy would say, 'Gee, I have this problem today. Too bad you weren't around.'"

Most dealer complaints involved relatively minor billing problems, although complaints about competition from other channels or the location of company-owned outlets were also common. Issues that could not be handled by the area sales manager were referred to the district manager. Complaints common to many dealers were taken up by the dealer council.

Goodyear had established ten regional councils to represent the views of Goodyear's independent dealers. Each regional council elected one dealer to Goodyear's national dealer council for passenger tires. Goodyear's top marketing and sales executives attended council meetings to answer questions, address complaints, or hear suggestions. Council meetings typically covered issues such as market trends in a region or city, new product development, advertising schedules, the availability of particular tires, or Goodyear's overall strategy. Due to antitrust laws, the council could not discuss the selling practices of specific dealers, the brands sold by specific dealers, competition from Goodyear-owned outlets, or retail prices.

The services Goodyear provided its dealers were not free. The cost of these services was built into Goodyear's prices. Discounts were available for dealers who paid upon receipt of merchandise, ordered in full trailer loads, or purchased under occasional promotional programs. Also, various allowances applied. A *wholesale allowance* applied on all approved wholesale sales to any authorized Goodyear dealer within a specific territory. (The wholesale allowance helped Goodyear limit competition among wholesalers.) A *merchandising allowance* of 1.5% was credited on all dealer sales; these credits could be used to obtain point-of-sale materials such as brochures, signs, and displays. Independent dealers also earned *advertising accruals* equal to 4% of tire purchases. The accruals could be used for local advertising, which Goodyear split evenly with the dealers provided no other brands were mentioned in the ad and the ad focused on tires rather than auto services.

Not all of these services were popular with every dealer. For example, some of Goodyear's largest dealers would have preferred to buy their tires at the lowest possible "net" price and develop their own advertising and promotion programs. However, smaller dealers had neither the staff nor the expertise to develop their own programs, and Goodyear was concerned that, without coordinated programs, some dealers would stop advertising and simply reap the benefits of other dealers' efforts.

Independent Dealers in the Tire Industry

In the 1970s, most major tire companies had maintained networks of company-owned dealers. By 1991, tire manufacturers owned fewer of their distribution outlets, as independent dealers typically offered more choice than the single-brand selection offered at most company-owned stores and required less capital and attention from the manufacturer. Some tire companies believed that expanding independent dealer networks would grow sales faster than company-owned outlets. The expectation was that increasing the number of independent dealers would expand brand availability and increase market share. During the 1980s, both Uniroyal and General Tire sold or closed all of their company-owned outlets.

In 1992, Michelin had fewer than 125 company-owned outlets, but Michelin tires were available through 7,000 independent dealers. Most of Michelin's independent dealers were multibrand outlets and sold Michelin as the prestige brand in their product offerings. Michelin tires were also available in 95% of the 600 warehouse clubs in the United States, mass merchandisers such as Montgomery Ward and Sears, and a variety of gas and service stations. Michelin, Uniroyal, and Goodrich had recently combined their sales forces to allow their salespeople to sell all three brands.

Firestone was an exception to the trend toward independent distribution. During the mid-1980s, many of Firestone's independent dealers switched to other manufacturers; some felt that the company had stopped supporting its dealers and its products in order to maximize short-term financial results. In 1991, there were 1,550 company-owned Firestone outlets, which also carried Bridgestone tires. Firestone's presence in independent dealers, mass merchandisers, and warehouse clubs was minimal. Also in 1991, General Tire decided to exit the retail store business entirely and instead rely on independent dealers.

While manufacturer-owned outlets were part of the manufacturer's management hierarchy, independent dealers had more autonomy. For example, tire manufacturers could suggest retail prices, but by law independent dealers were free to set their own prices. Some manufacturers felt that independent dealers' focus on price had contributed to the decline in retail tire prices.

Independent dealers also set their own inventory policies. For many years Goodyear had protected its dealers by not selling Goodyear-branded tires in other outlets; in exchange, Goodyear dealers did not carry other brands. In 1989, 70% of Goodyear's independent dealers carried only Goodyear tires, while 30% stocked other brands. Typically, the other brands were not aggressively merchandised but used only as lower-priced alternatives to Goodyear. By 1991, estimates suggested that 50% of Goodyear's independent dealers sold only Goodyear tires, while the other 50% stocked at least one other brand. Among the latter, some aggressively merchandised other brands but Goodyear tires still generated 90% of the revenues for most independent dealers.

Independent dealers' concern for protecting their interests led the National Tire Dealers and Retreaders Association (NTDRA) to pass a bill of rights in 1992 (see **Exhibit 6**). NTDRA president Robert Gatzke said, "[T]his bill of rights clearly identifies certain rights which independent tire dealers have a right to expect from their tire suppliers."[5] The bill

[5] Source: *Tire Business*, June 1992.

EXHIBIT 6   **Tire Dealers' Bill of Rights**

Source: Adapted from *Tire Business*.

"Tire dealers as independent business people have earned the right to the respect of all other facets of the tire, retreading, and auto service industries since it has long been established that they fulfill the role as the most important channel of tire distribution. . . .

Tire dealers expect to give loyalty to, and receive loyalty from their manufacturers; to be treated like valued customers; and to be encouraged to sell to end users without direct competition from their manufacturers. Independent tire dealers have a right to the uninhibited exercise of their ability to increase their market share with the cooperation of their manufacturers. . . .

Tire dealers have a right to expect reasonable and timely communications from, and where appropriate, consultation with their manufacturers on actions taken by the manufacturers which directly affect independent tire dealers and their customers. . . .

Independent tire dealers have the right to expect their manufacturers to pay careful attention to supply and demand, pursuing neither to excess, and to keep the dealer supplied in a timely fashion with high quality products which will allow the dealer to sell and serve the customer properly. . . .

Independent dealers have a right to a level playing field including the availability of tire lines, pricing, terms, and programs equal to those offered to wholesale clubs, discounters, company-owned stores, mass merchandisers, chains, and other forms of competition. . . .

Tire manufacturers should recognize the need for profits, not only for themselves, but also for the independent tire dealer who performs the major distribution function for them. . . .

Independent tire dealers have a right to the timely, proper, and uniform issuance of credits for advertising, national account sales, return goods, adjustments, and any other money due. . . .

Independent tire dealers . . . have a right to expect that the manufacturer will use the network of independent tire dealers as the first step for expansion, increasing the dealers' market share; and that commitments made are commitments kept."

demanded that manufacturers respect the independent dealers' importance, consult independent dealers on key decisions, avoid placing company-owned outlets in competition with independent dealers, supply tires to independent dealers in a timely manner, and grant dealers the same pricing and programs given to high-volume outlets such as wholesale clubs and multibrand discounters.

Auto Services

Auto services were a $50 billion market in 1991. Auto services included jobs such as oil changes, tune-ups, and front-end alignments, as well as repairs to parts such as brakes or transmissions. Revenues from auto services included parts and labor and were differentiated from tire sales. The price of services varied by outlet and job, but $60 was typical. Garages and service stations had a 40% share of auto service revenues, while new car dealers had a 29% share. Specialty outlets focusing on parts such as mufflers or brakes had a 15% share, followed by tire dealers with an 8% share, and mass merchandisers with an 8% share.

Monthly auto service sales for independent tire dealers averaged $38,100 per outlet. Most tire dealers changed oil, performed alignments, replaced shocks, fixed exhaust systems, and did minor engine work. Independent dealers derived, on average, 48% of their revenues from auto services in 1991, up from 26% in 1980. On average, 20% of service revenues came from tire-related work. Margins for independent dealers were 50% on service labor and 20%-25% on parts installed; 70% of service revenues were earned from labor, with the remaining 30% earned from parts. Revenues from tire installation were considered auto services and averaged the following:

Mount and balance new tires:	$8.00 per tire
Place a valve on new tires:	$2.50 per tire
Scrap charge to dispose of old tires:	$2.00 per tire

The average number of tires installed per day at a typical independent dealer increased 13% from 1983 to 1991, but the average service dollars per outlet grew 92% during the same period. Not all dealers were pleased with their reliance on service revenues. As one dealer said, "To me it's an indictment of the industry that we cannot support ourselves on tire sales. We have to have that service to survive." Tires were an expensive purchase for most consumers, and independent dealers worried about the "sticker shock" resulting from service charges increasing the bill to the consumer.

Competition

Goodyear regularly surveyed car owners to monitor their image of the major tire brands (see **Exhibit 7**). In 1991, Goodyear and Michelin were virtually even, but Michelin's image was stronger among value-oriented and quality buyers, while Goodyear had a stronger image among price-constrained buyers and commodity buyers. The percentage of consumers who did not know what brand of tire they planned to buy next rose to 53% in 1992 from 36% in 1982.

Exhibit 8 presents a brand-switching matrix, showing loyalty by brand among consumers replacing passenger tires. Michelin owners were the most loyal, followed by Goodyear owners, but significant proportions of consumers who owned major brands replaced their tires with private label brands. Goodyear typically spent 9%–11% of sales on advertising and promotion, with 60% being spent on promotion. Among U.S. tire marketers, Goodyear's share of voice in television and magazine advertising was about 60%.

EXHIBIT 7   **Brand Image of Major Tire Manufacturers, 1991**

Source: Company records.

A survey of broad-line tire owners asked what brand of tires the owners intended to buy the next time they needed tires. Results are reported below for the five major brands and for the four major consumer segments.

Intent to Buy for Major Consumer Segments

	All Buyers	Price Constrained Buyers	Value-Oriented Buyers	Quality Buyers	Commodity Buyers
Goodyear	13%	16%	17%	18%	10%
Michelin	13	9	24	22	6
Other	19	18	20	25	16
Uncommitted	55	57	39	35	68

EXHIBIT 8
Switching Among Tire Brands, 1991

Source: Company records.

Brand Replaced	Brand Bought						
	Bridgestone	Firestone	Goodyear	Michelin	Minor Brands	Private Label	Total
Bridgestone	29%	4%	8%	8%	7%	43%	100%
Firestone	2	27	11	6	7	45	100
Goodyear	2	5	39	5	9	38	100
Michelin	3	3	7	44	6	36	100
Minor brands	2	4	10	7	32	42	100
Private label	2	5	8	5	7	70	100

Note: The above chart can be read as follows: Four percent of car owners with Bridgestone tires bought Firestone tires to replace the Bridgestone.

Goodyear's competitors were planning a wide range of campaigns for 1992. Both Bridgestone and Michelin were planning to introduce new tires with 80,000-mile warranties, while Uniroyal was introducing a new tire for light trucks. Under Michelin's ownership, BF Goodrich was focusing on the high performance market, while Goodyear's Kelly-Springfield subsidiary used advertising primarily to announce the low price of its tires.

The Aquatred Tire

In 1989, Goodyear started the NEWEX project, to develop a new and exciting replacement market tire that would have a tangible, perceptible difference over existing models. Howard MacDonald, marketing manager for Passenger Tires, said, "We were looking for something that appearancewise was different—something that a customer would walk into a showroom and tell from a distance that it was different."[6] The Aquatred was developed after comparing 10 different designs on performance and consumer preference. The deep groove down the center of the tire was dubbed the "Aquachannel." According to Goodyear, the Aquatred's tread design channeled water out from under the tire, reducing hydroplaning and improving traction in wet conditions.[7] Performance tests showed that in wet conditions, cars equipped with Aquatreds traveling at 55 miles per hour stopped in as much as two-car-lengths-less distance than similar cars equipped with conventional all-season radials. When 50% worn, the Aquatred maintained the same wet traction as a new all-season tire.

Goodyear planned to sell the Aquatred with a 60,000-mile warranty and to position the tire at the top of the broad-line segment. The last tire to promise increased wet traction to the broad-line segment was the Uniroyal Rain Tire, introduced in the early 1970s. The Aquatred was patented, but patent protection on tread designs was difficult to enforce. Continental Tire was known to be working on its own antihydroplaning tire, to be called the Aqua Contact, which could be launched in early 1993.

The Aquatred was test-marketed in a large, representative, metropolitan area. A Goodyear survey from the test market compared purchase behavior for Aquatred buyers with purchase behavior for buyers of the Invicta GS, Goodyear's most expensive broad-line tire (see **Exhibit 9**). Compared with buyers of the Invicta GS, Aquatred buyers were more likely to replace competitors' tires, searched more extensively for information prior to purchase, were more likely to drive imported cars, and more often came to Goodyear outlets specifically for the Aquatred. **Exhibit 10** presents data gathered by a "mystery shopper," a Goodyear employee who shopped for tires at independent dealers without identifying his or her affiliation with Goodyear. Despite the uniformity of the company's literature and policies, there was variation in the presentation and pricing of the Aquatred by dealers in the test market.

In another survey, Goodyear asked drivers of cars equipped with either the Aquatred or the Invicta GS to rate their tires' traction on wet roads. Owners of each tire responded as follows:

Response	Aquatred Drivers	Invicta GS Drivers
1 (Poor traction)	5	3
2	5	5
3 (Average)	30	27
4	80	81
5 (Excellent)	180	184
Total responses:	300	300

[6] Source: *Modern Tire Dealer,* March 1992.

[7] Hydroplaning occurs in wet conditions due to a layer of water forming between the tire and road, causing a momentary loss of traction.

EXHIBIT 9
Aquatred Test
Market Data

Source: Company records.

	Buyers of the . . .	
	Aquatred	**Invicta GS**
What brand of tire was replaced?		
Goodyear	38%	51%
Michelin	17	15
Other	25	16
Don't know	20	18
Steps in information search:		
Checked newspaper ads	33%	23%
Telephoned outlets	21	14
Shopped other dealers	20	12
Primary shopping orientation:		
Store	36%	44%
Brand	56	47
Price	8	9
Purchase decision segments		
Price-constrained Buyers	6%	6%
Value-oriented Buyers	23	13
Quality Buyers	61	64
Commodity Buyers	10	17
Bought four tires	91%	54%
Reasons for buying tires at Goodyear (multiple answers allowed)		
Past experience	36%	49%
Want Goodyear brand	33	33
Want Aquatreds	25	N/A
Convenience	11	18
Familiar with personnel	11	12
Advertising	9	N/A
On sale/good price	8	13
Recommended by a friend	4	4
Always go to that dealer	4	9
Other	26	20
Vehicle make:		
Domestic	74%	94%
Import	26	6
What features or benefits did the salesperson tell you about the Aquatred? (multiple answers allowed)		
Has 60,000 mile warranty	41%	10%
Great wet traction	33	38
Didn't tell me about them	13	42
Won't hydroplane	16	9
Other	29	18

EXHIBIT 10
Results of Mystery Shopping in Aquatred Test Market

Source: Company records.

A male mystery shopper visited nine independent Goodyear outlets in the Aquatred test market during October 1991. The mystery shopper told the staff in each outlet that his wife needed tires for her Plymouth Voyager. In the sales presentations that followed:

Eight of the nine salespersons mentioned the Aquatred during their presentations. Of those eight, five began their presentation with the Aquatred and three finished with the Aquatred.

Three salespeople made specific claims concerning the Aquatred's superior performance in wet traction. One claimed the Aquatred was 15% better than other tires; another claimed 20%–25%; and a third claimed up to 35% better traction with the Aquatred.

Goodyear's suggested retail prices for the Aquatred were $89.95 with a black sidewall, and $93.95 with a white sidewall. Prices quoted by six outlets were as follows:

Store Number	Price with Black Sidewall	Price with White Sidewall
1	$79.95	$79.95
2	81.95	81.95
3	80.00	83.00
4	85.00	85.00
5	85.00	88.00
6	100.00	100.00

The Launch of the Aquatred

A storyboard for a proposed Aquatred television advertisement is presented in **Exhibit 11.** Due to the long buying cycles of auto manufacturers, the Aquatred would not be available as original equipment, so all sales of the Aquatred would come through the replacement market. It was estimated that a full-scale launch would cost Goodyear about $21 million.

Managers at Goodyear still had two concerns about the launch. First, did Goodyear have the right product for the dealers and for the consumer? Michelin and Bridgestone both planned to launch new tires with 80,000-mile warranties in 1992 backed by heavy advertising. Would Goodyear's dealers be receptive to a high-priced tire when the industry seemed to be turning toward long-life warranties and low-cost private labels? One dealer had said,

> I would be much more interested in a tire that went 80,000 miles than one that channels the rain out of the way. Even a 35,000-mile tire at a decent price point would be better. The Aquatred is a boutique tire, but where do we make our money as a dealer? Middle-of-the-road products.

Second was the channel itself. Goodyear management debated whether distribution should be expanded, and if so, what specific channels or retailers should be added. Expanding distribution could boost sales and prevent Goodyear OEM tires from being replaced by other brands in the replacement market. However, selling tires in lower-service outlets could erode the value of the Goodyear brand, cannibalize sales of existing outlets, and might cause dealers to take on additional lines of tires. Stanley Gault, Goodyear's new chairman, had expanded distribution at Rubbermaid, and many Goodyear dealers were concerned that he would do the same at Goodyear. As one dealer said, "Today, you can go to any store and get a Rubbermaid product, and the prices on Rubbermaid have dropped accordingly. We feel that Goodyear tires should not be that way."

If the decision was made to launch the Aquatred, there would be a variety of launch-related issues to settle. For example, Robbins was concerned about the timing. Goodyear had made commitments for commercial time during the Winter Olympics in January of

EXHIBIT 11   **Proposed Aquatred Advertisement**

GOOD/YEAR

"TIRES OF THE FUTURE" :30

AQUATRED

GTBM 8863

(MUSIC UNDER)
ANNCR: (VO) You're about to see

how Goodyear is changing all-season driving

right before your eyes.

Introducing Aquatred...

only from Goodyear.

(MUSIC)

Aquatred's advanced design

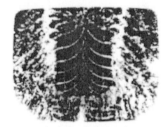

channels water out of your way

for dependable

all-season traction,

especially in the rain

when you may need it most.

Aquatred.

The newest reason why we say the best tires in the world

have Goodyear written all over them.

1992 and could use this time to introduce the Aquatred. Launching during the Olympics might spark sales of the Aquatred, but the initial inventory of Aquatreds had been made to fit domestic cars, as opposed to the smaller sizes for imported cars. Molds to produce other sizes would not be available until several months after the Olympics.

Given the wide range of tires sold by Goodyear, dealers would need advice regarding which customers would be likely to switch to Aquatreds. In the test markets, some dealers had tried to sell Aquatreds only to customers who drove newer cars or looked affluent. And if distribution was expanded, Goodyear would need to decide whether the new channel would receive the Aquatred.

In addition, Goodyear had to finalize pricing and promotional policies for the Aquatred. Goodyear hoped to price the Aquatred at a 10% premium over the Invicta GS, but the successful launch of the Tiempo in 1977 was partly attributed to a low retail price. Independent dealers in test markets had consistently asked for price promotions on the Aquatred. Robbins had turned down all such requests, but given the growing problem of tires diverted to unauthorized dealers, it was not clear that the tire could be kept out of channels that were prone to discounting and promotions.

Plans for the national launch were proceeding during an important period in Goodyear's history. Any change in distribution strategy would affect the launch, but the launch and the associated marketing programs would affect Goodyear's dealers. Stanley Gault was upbeat and saw the Aquatred as a product to revitalize Goodyear. Robbins, armed with consumer research, wanted to be sure that the consumer and the channel would agree.

Chapter 24

Merrill Lynch: Integrated Choice

V. Kasturi Rangan   Marie Bell

We have put together the widest range of choice for our clients. Merrill Lynch can say to either you, your children, or your grandchildren, "How do you want to approach the market?" No matter how you respond, we will have a market offering to fit your needs.

—*David Komansky, Chairman & CEO, Merrill Lynch*
  The Wall Street Week, *October 15, 1999*

We have moved forward like a bullet train and it is our competitors that are scrambling not to get run over.

—*John L. Steffens, Vice Chairman & Head of U.S. Private Client, Merrill Lynch*

John L. (Launny) Steffens, vice chairman[1] and head of Merrill Lynch's U.S. Private Client Group, sat in his New Jersey office taking a brief moment to contemplate the frigid January landscape. Time, always at a premium in the retail brokerage business, was in especially short supply these days. Six months earlier, Merrill Lynch had stunned the financial services community by unveiling a new vision for the business. While it had been expected that the company, the market leader in full-service brokerage but under attack from discount and electronic traders, would make some kind of an "online move," the scope of the new offering and its pricing levels had raised the bar beyond anyone's expectations.

---

[1] During the course of writing this case Launny Steffens was promoted to chairman, U.S. Private Client.

Professor V. Kasturi Rangan and Research Associate Marie Bell prepared this case as the basis for class discussion rather than to illustrate either effective or ineffective handling of an administrative situation.

Merrill Lynch envisioned itself as a one-stop source of financial services where clients self-selected the range of products and services they wanted. Called Integrated Choice, the new product and service offering was based on its customers' desire to choose—the products they wanted, the level of advice they wanted, and the way they wanted to transact their business. For those clients that wanted advice, Merrill Lynch would continue to offer the services of its nearly 14,000 Financial Consultants. The do-it-yourself (also called self-directed) investor who liked to trade online could do so with or without the advice of one of Merrill Lynch's Financial Consultants or the need to go to another firm.

As seen in **Figure A** below, with Integrated Choice, Merrill Lynch clients were offered a continuum of products from the fully self-directed (ML Direct) to the fully delegated (discretionary). Based on their individual needs and preferences, clients could opt for single or multiple accounts.

Clients who wished to invest online without the advice and guidance of a Financial Consultant could do so by opening a Merrill Lynch Direct account. ML Direct, a brand new offering from Merrill Lynch, offered online trading for as little as $29.95 per equity trade. Additionally, clients could purchase a range of fixed-income products through a Merrill Lynch Direct Service Associate and participate in initial public offerings through the online IPO Center. In addition to online trading, Merrill Lynch Direct clients had free access to proprietary, award-winning Merrill Lynch research, plus a wide range of other premier sources of information. Further, clients could access special discounts and bonus reward points through the Cash Management Account (CMA) Visa Signature card and Merrill Lynch's eShopping site, and manage their bills through the company's electronic bill payment service.

Next in the range of do-it-yourself products was Investor Services. Clients could access a Merrill Lynch representative 24 hours per day, seven days a week, for information, advice, and transactions via a toll-free telephone number. Utilizing fully licensed and trained representatives who were salaried rather than commissioned, Investor Services was also proactive with representatives contacting clients at designated intervals to service any client needs. Although Investor Services was initially designed in 1997 to serve clients with assets of about $100,000 or less at Merrill Lynch, experience showed that some clients with substantially larger assets preferred to be served this way. In 1999, Investor Services

FIGURE A   **Integrated Choice**

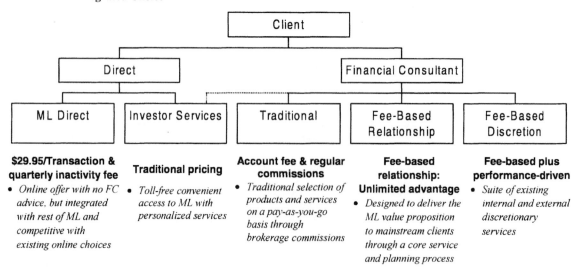

serviced nearly 200,000[2] clients who reported an increase in customer satisfaction. Investor Services clients had the option of selecting either fee-based pricing (% of assets) or traditional commission-based pricing ($ per trade).

There was a range of options available to clients who desired a relationship founded on advice from a Financial Consultant, the traditional brokerage relationship with a Financial Consultant being one. Clients opting for this paid on a fee-for-service basis based on the existing commission structures. These clients continued to receive a host of other services, such as a cash management account (CMA), checking facilities, and a Visa credit card. An annual fee of $100 was levied for such services. Nearly half of Merrill Lynch's 5 million private clients had this type of account.

Another choice was to establish an Unlimited Advantage account. For an annual fee, charged as a % of assets, starting at a minimum of $1,500, clients received personalized service from a Financial Consultant, a Financial Foundation (Merrill Lynch's comprehensive personal financial plan), virtually unlimited trading (by telephone, person-to-person, or online), cash management, check and bill payment capabilities, a Visa Signature credit card and rewards program, and an array of other financial services benefits and products. Although clients received advice from their Financial Consultants, they could also execute transactions independently through Merrill Lynch Online or an automated touch-tone phone service. While Merrill Lynch had offered asset-priced products for individual investors as part of its traditional offering, the scope of Unlimited Advantage and its value proposition were vastly different; for example, for the first time Merrill Lynch's clients could tap into virtually unlimited online trading.

Clients who wanted decisions made with the advice of a financial-services professional but wanted to minimize their involvement with investment decision making could use Merrill Lynch's discretionary services, assigning portfolio management responsibilities to a professional money manager or, in some cases, a specially designated financial consultant. Merrill Lynch had access to hundreds of independent professional money managers, who for a fee would manage the client's portfolio. Such customers received customized asset-based pricing. About 100,000 of Merrill Lynch's clients chose this kind of service.

Not wanting to limit client choice, Merrill Lynch clients had the option of maintaining more than one type of account with Merrill Lynch. Thus clients could have some of their money in ML Direct and the rest in Unlimited Advantage or a traditional account, and further they could choose whether to let their financial consultant view their ML Direct account.

Merrill Lynch clients received more than just flexibility in defining their relationships with their brokers. No matter which option they chose, clients gained access to a range of exclusive Merrill Lynch products and services. First in these services was access to proprietary Merrill Lynch analyst research, considered among the best in the industry, and produced by a staff of nearly 600 research analysts. Further, Merrill Lynch had created an extensive electronic shopping site with access to over 400 retailers from Barnes & Noble.com to Toys'R'Us.com that offered special promotions to Merrill Lynch customers.

(**Exhibit 1** provides a more detailed summary of Merrill Lynch's product and service choices.)

Merrill Lynch announced its new direction on June 1, 1999, and products were rolled out over the next six months. Unlimited Advantage came to market on July 12, followed by Merrill Lynch's expanded online shopping site on November 5. Then, on December 1, Merrill Lynch Direct was successfully launched. While there had been initial speculation about the company's motives and ability to offer clients flexibility, with each successful new product rollout, both clients and industry observers became more and more confident in Merrill Lynch's strategy and determination to succeed.

---

[2] Charles Gasparino, "Wall Street has less and less time for small investors," *The Wall Street Journal,* October 5, 1999, p. C1.

EXHIBIT 1 **Merrill Lynch's Integrated Choice Products and Services**

Products: "By mouse, by phone, by human being"	
Merrill Lynch Direct	➤ $29.95 per trade for online equity trades
	➤ Self-directed investment channel
	➤ Access to Merrill Lynch's award winning research
	➤ Thousands of mutual funds from more than 90 fund families
	➤ Participate in e-IPOs
	➤ Cash management services, including checking and Visa card
	➤ Tools and resources of Merrill Lynch Online
Investor Services	➤ Personalized client service from teams of registered Investor Service Consultants (ISCs)
	➤ 24 × 7 on-demand access to account information, financial guidance, and most ML products/services via an 800-telephone number
	➤ Scheduled, proactive follow-up from ISCs to help clients understand their current financial situation, plan for the future, and invest with confidence
	➤ Access to Merrill Lynch's award-winning research
	➤ Tools and resources of Merrill Lynch Online and other automated features
Traditional Relationship	➤ Personalized services from a Financial Consultant
	➤ Financial Foundation report with periodic updates
	➤ Cash management, checking, and bill payment capabilities
	➤ CMA Visa Signature card and rewards program
	➤ Mortgage, insurance and trust services
	➤ Access Merrill Lynch's award winning research
	➤ Tools and resources of Merrill Lynch Online
Unlimited Advantage "One fee equals total access."	➤ Personalized services from a Financial Consultant
	➤ Virtually unlimited trading by telephone, person-to-person, or online for most investors in most securities
	➤ Financial Foundation report with periodic updates
	➤ Cash management, checking, and bill payment capabilities
	➤ CMA Visa Signature card and rewards program
	➤ Reduced origination fee on eligible home financing
	➤ Cost benefits on insurance and trust services
	➤ Access to Merrill Lynch's award winning research
	➤ Tools and resources of Merrill Lynch OnLine 2000
	Pricing: Simple annual fee, minimum fee $1,500
	First million: 1% equity/mutual funds, .3% fixed income/cash equivalents
	Next 4 million: .75% equity/mutual funds, .25% fixed income/cash equivalents
	Next 5 million: .50% equity/mutual funds, .20% fixed income/cash equivalents
	Over 10 million: customized pricing
	Fee-Based Discretionary Services
Fee-Based Discretionary Services	➤ Money management by a professional money manager
	➤ Products included: ML Consults, Mutual Fund Advisor, Strategic Portfolio Advisor, Strategy Power, Personal Investment Advisory
	➤ Range of services specific to each product. All included: discretionary portfolio management, services from a Financial Consultant, Financial Foundation report, custody services, client profiling; in addition to product specific services
	➤ Pricing as a % of assets based on asset size and specific product
Unique Services:	
Global Investor Network	➤ Merrill Lynch exclusive "financial plug-in" offers daily global research commentary
	➤ Exclusive access to Merrill Lynch daily research call
	➤ Video and audio market coverage from around the world
	➤ Syndication onto portals

EXHIBIT 1   (Continued)

Ecommerce	➤ Convenient online shopping
	➤ 4 million products, several hundred merchants
	➤ Select merchant discounts
	➤ Triple reward points using CMA Visa Signature card
	➤ Online rewards, redemption, and point balances
	➤ Access to Merrill Lynch Online Business Center
	➤ Auctions through uBid
Visa Signature Points	The CMA Visa Signature Rewards program is the only high end travel rewards program linked to an investment account. Program offered unrestricted travel on any airline, anytime, with no blackouts and restrictions. Points can also be used for hotel stays, car rentals, restaurant, and retail certificates as well as a wide range of premium, special events
Bullhorn	➤ Free e-mail notification service on a variety of topics

TABLE A
Wealth Management Revenues (worldwide)

Source: Company documents.

($ in millions)	1996	1997	1998
Net Revenues	**$7,984**	**$9,505**	**$11,331**
Brokerage and Lending	$5,435	$6,328	$6,989
Asset Management and Portfolio Service	$2,431	$3,002	$4,202
Other	$118	$175	$140
Net Earnings	**$855**	**$1,056**	**$1,346**

Armed with its expanded strategic insight, U.S. Private Client was bullish on itself and established "choice" goals for 2005; specifically, it had set a target of being the Money Manager of Choice (with 20% of affluent relationships and $5 trillion in assets), the Advisor of Choice with 17,500 Financial Consultants with high performance goals, the Bank of Choice with $100 billion in deposits, and the Credit Card of Choice with billions in VISA Signature transactions. Additionally, the company sought to be the portal of choice with 2 million clients on Merrill Lynch Online/Merrill Lynch Direct. As of 1998, Merrill Lynch had about 15% market share of affluent relationships, about $1.5 trillion in assets, and $6 billion in customer deposits. Clearly Merrill Lynch was re-defining what full service meant in the industry—but there was much work to be done.

Merrill Lynch's U.S. Private Client

Company Background

Founded by Charles E. Merrill in 1914 with a belief that the financial markets should be accessible to everyone, Merrill Lynch was often credited with bringing Wall Street to Main Street. In its modern form, Merrill Lynch's income was derived from operations in two main business segments: Wealth Management Group with 1998 revenues of $11,331 million and the Corporate and Institutional Client group (CICG) with revenues of $6,522 million. As seen in **Table A** below, Wealth Management had two broad product categories: brokerage and lending (e.g., securities transactions on behalf of clients, secured lendings, and asset allocation activities) and asset management and portfolio services. CICG's principal products included trading, underwriting, and strategic services. U.S. Private Client was part of the Wealth Management group.

Central to Merrill Lynch's Wealth Management strategy was asset gathering from millions of individual investors and small- and medium-sized businesses. Over the last 10 years, client assets had increased at a 16% compound annual rate to nearly $1,500 billion at the end of 1998. Included in these assets were $500 billion managed by the company's Asset Management Group. Thus for example, if a Merrill Lynch client invested in a Merrill Lynch mutual fund, the brokerage transaction fee (in this case the "load") would show up as brokerage fee and the fee for management of the fund would show up as asset management fee. If, however, the client bought an outside security, then the only revenue source would be the brokerage transaction fee. U.S. Private Client managed nearly 80% of all assets, the rest coming from international operations. Approximately 66% of Merrill Lynch's Private Client assets were represented by equities (such as stocks and mutual funds), 22% by debt (fixed income vehicles) and 12% by cash. (See **Exhibit 2** for Merrill Lynch's financial statements. **Exhibit 3** summarizes historical growth of client assets from 1991–1998 for Merrill Lynch and selected competitors.)

U.S. Private Client—All Things to Some People

U.S. Private Client served individuals, small businesses, and employee benefit plans, using a planning-based approach to provide cash, asset, liability, and transition management services. Through nearly 14,000 Financial Consultants in approximately 750 offices throughout the United States, Merrill Lynch provided one of the widest arrays of financial services and products, sound advice, and effective execution. These Financial Consultants had strong relationships with 5 million households, ranging from high net worth individuals to young "next generation" clients (about 3 million clients), and with small- to mid-sized businesses and regional financial institutions (about 2 million clients).

Much of Merrill Lynch's strategy in the 1990s was based upon a visionary white paper written by Launny Steffens in the early 1980s. In that document, he described "Why Becoming All Things to Some People" was so important,

> All of our research has pointed toward a strategy of segmenting our client base, better identifying our target client groups, and then developing broader and stronger relationships with our key clients. It is obvious that the biggest payoff to Merrill Lynch does not lie in expanding our client base randomly across the entire spectrum of American households. Instead, the real profit potential rests with our ability to target and meet the financial needs of current and prospective affluent "A" individuals and small businesses that already provide the bulk of income to the financial services industry. Hence the goal is to become "All Things to Some People,". . . Thus the key to attracting such individuals to Merrill Lynch is to provide them with comprehensive, innovative solutions to their financial problems. We must package products like CMA to provide day-to-day convenience along with truly sophisticated financial planning and advice. The relationship between the client and the [financial consultant] is the central issue here, and must be the focus of our efforts.

Financial Consultants worked with clients in managing their assets. The Cash Management Account (CMA), which Merrill Lynch pioneered for individuals in 1977, and the Working Capital Management Account for businesses were important tools for delivering a wide range of client services, including effecting trades in stocks, bonds, and other securities in financial markets around the world. For example, with the CMA account Merrill Lynch clients could hold cash and write checks outside their bank accounts, and yet earn money market fund interest rates, which were higher than what they could get from bank deposits. Merrill Lynch also made available its investment research and offered various advisory programs, including fully discretionary accounts like Merrill Lynch Consults and Mutual Fund Advisor, which offered Merrill Lynch as well as other investment advisory services.

Merrill Lynch Financial Consultants[3] were considered some of the best in the industry. A Financial Consultant's first two years were spent primarily in training and initial prospecting

---

[3] Even though we broadly refer to all members of Merrill Lynch's salesforce as Financial Consultants, in reality, depending on their experience and productivity they were designated as Senior FC, Assistant VP, VP, First VP, or Senior VP.

EXHIBIT 2   Income Statement 1995–1998

Merrill Lynch & Co., Inc.

Consolidated Annual Earnings - Restated					(in millions)
	Year Ended Last Friday in December				
	1994	1995	1996	1997	1998
Revenues					
Interest and dividends	$9,608	$12,449	$13,125	$17,299	$19,314
Interest expense	8,614	11,445	12,092	16,243	18,306
Net interest and dividend profit	994	1,004	1,033	1,056	1,008
Commissions	3,060	3,308	4,085	4,995	5,799
Principal transactions	2,406	2,601	3,531	3,827	2,651
Investment banking	1,273	1,343	2,022	2,876	3,264
Asset management and portfolio service fees	1,872	2,030	2,431	3,002	4,202
Other	354	329	519	500	623
Net Revenues	9,959	10,615	13,621	16,256	17,547
Non-Interest Expenses					
Compensation and benefits	5,165	5,478	7,012	8,333	9,199
Communications and technology	722	814	1,010	1,255	1,749
Occupancy and related depreciation	637	671	742	736	867
Advertising and market development	387	408	527	613	688
Brokerage, clearing, and exchange fees	355	377	433	525	683
Professional fees	259	312	385	520	552
Goodwill amortization	5	19	50	65	226
Provision for costs related to staff reductions	-	-	-	-	430
Other	682	700	834	1,098	1,057
Total Non-Interest Expenses	8,212	8,779	10,993	13,145	15,451
Earnings Before Income Taxes and Dividends on Preferred Securities Issued by Subsidiaries	1,747	1,836	2,628	3,111	2,096
Income tax expense	717	710	980	1,129	713
Dividends on preferred securities issued by subsidiaries	-	-	-	47	124
Net Earnings	$1,030	$1,126	$1,648	$1,935	$1,259
Preferred stock dividends	13	48	46	39	39
Net Earnings Applicable to Common Stockholders	$1,017	$1,078	$1,602	$1,896	$1,220
Cash Basis Net Earnings prior to After-Tax Staff Reduction Provision	$1,035	$1,145	$1,698	$2,000	$1,773

Per Common Share Data

	Year Ended Last Friday in December				
	1994	1995	1996	1997	1998
Basic	$2.55	$2.98	$4.63	$5.57	$3.43
Diluted	2.37	2.68	4.08	4.79	3.00
Dividends paid	0.445	0.505	0.58	0.75	0.92
Book value	14.48	16.25	19.24	23.63	26.89

Note: Amounts have been restated from that originally reported to reflect the August 26, 1998 merger with Midland Walwyn Inc.,
   which has been accounted for as a pooling-of-interests, as well as reclassifications to conform to the current presentation.
   1994 amounts are unaudited. Share data reflect the effect of a second quarter 1997 two-for-one common stock split.

EXHIBIT 2 (Continued)

Merrill Lynch & Co., Inc.

Consolidated Balance Sheets - Restated

(dollars in millions)	December 30, 1994	December 29, 1995	December 27, 1996	December 26, 1997	December 25, 1998
Assets					
Cash and cash equivalents	$4,457	$6,106	$6,331	$12,073	$12,530
Cash and securities segregated for regulatory purposes or deposited with clearing organizations	2,817	2,408	2,692	5,357	6,590
Receivables under resale agreements and securities borrowed transactions	65,452	65,744	85,071	107,443	87,713
Marketable investment securities	2,326	2,365	2,180	3,309	4,605
Trading assets, at fair value					
Equities and convertible debentures	6,355	10,938	13,374	24,031	25,318
Contractual agreements	9,519	11,833	13,465	21,205	21,979
Corporate debt and preferred stock	14,698	17,727	24,507	32,537	21,166
U.S. Government and agencies	8,197	6,672	9,308	9,848	15,421
Non-U.S. governments and agencies	6,845	7,133	8,068	10,221	7,474
Mortgages, mortgage-backed, and asset-backed	5,224	3,749	5,189	7,312	7,023
Other	2,577	3,019	2,779	2,937	3,358
	53,415	61,071	76,690	108,091	101,739
Securities received as collateral, net of securities pledged as collateral	-	-	-	-	6,106
Total	53,415	61,071	76,690	108,091	107,845
Securities pledged as collateral	-	-	-	-	8,184
Other receivables					
Customers *(net of allowance for doubtful accounts of $43 in 1994, $36 in 1995, $39 in 1996, $50 in 1997, and $48 in 1998)*	14,526	15,349	19,177	27,319	29,559
Brokers and dealers	7,330	9,357	6,314	5,182	8,872
Interest and other	4,443	4,800	5,345	8,185	9,278
Total	26,299	29,506	30,836	40,686	47,709
Investments of insurance subsidiaries	5,719	5,619	5,107	4,833	4,485
Loans, notes, and mortgages *(net of allowance for loan losses of $181 in 1994, $131 in 1995, $117 in 1996, $130 in 1997, and $124 in 1998)*	1,609	2,183	3,334	4,310	7,687
Other investments	888	964	1,126	1,829	2,590
Equipment and facilities *(net of accumulated depreciation and amortization of $1,897 in 1994, $2,277 in 1995, $2,566 in 1996, $2,955 in 1997, and $3,482 in 1998)*	1,607	1,621	1,680	2,099	2,761
Goodwill *(net of accumulated amortization of $10 in 1994, $26 in 1995, $71 in 1996, $131 in 1997, and $338 in 1998)*	21	551	633	5,467	5,364
Other assets	1,310	1,314	1,586	1,483	1,741
Total Assets	**$165,920**	**$179,452**	**$217,266**	**$296,980**	**$299,804**

Note: Amounts have been restated from that originally reported to reflect the August 26, 1998 merger with Midland Walwyn Inc., which has been accounted for as a pooling-of-interests, as well as reclassifications to conform to the current presentation. 1994 and 1995 amounts are unaudited.

for clients. During this period the firm supported the Financial Consultant's salary, but thereafter compensation was based on a complex formula that included commissions on traditional transactions (about 50% of brokerage commissions), client assets, and cash balances. Roughly 65% of a Financial Consultant's compensation came from brokerage fees, 25% on assets and asset growth, and the rest from performance against targeted marketing programs. As a client's assets grew with Merrill Lynch, Financial Consultants directed their clients through a financial planning program, where clients filled out a detailed questionnaire, often with the help of the Financial Consultant, which was then processed at Merrill Lynch's centralized Financial Planning Resource Center in New Jersey. The outcome of the analysis, typically a substantial document with considerable detail, was sent back to the Financial Consultant who sat down face-to-face with the client to explain its implications and to

EXHIBIT 3   Client Asset Growth 1991–1998 ($ billions)

Source: Adapted from *Financial Services Retail Brokerage*, "The Bumpy Ride to Bigger, Better, Cheaper, Faster," Morgan Stanley Dean Witter, October 12, 1999.

	1991	1992	1993	1994	1995	1996	1997	1998
U.S. household financial assets	$16,450	$17,294	$18,403	$19,081	$21,697	$24,039	$27,300	$30,633
Deposits	2,889	2,911	2,845	2,806	2,916	3,034	3,210	3,400
Total Securities Assets[a]	5,232	5,692	6,256	6,420	7,695	8,715	9,923	11,465
Merrill Lynch								
U.S. Private Client Assets	$422.2	$463.7	$527.4	$537.0	$664.8	$791.5	$979.0	$1,164.0
Assets under Mgt.[b]	123.6	138.5	161.0	163.8	196.4	234.1	446.4	501.0
% of Client Assets	29.3%	29.9%	30.5%	30.5%	29.5%	29.6%	45.6%	43.0%
American Express Financial Advisors								
Total Assets Owned or Mgd.[c]	$65.8	$83.3	$99.7	$105.5	$129.5	$149.4	$181.8	$212.4
Assets Managed	38.1	51.4	62.4	65.3	81.2	96.7	113.6	133.8
% of Total Assets	57.9%	61.7%	62.5%	61.9%	62.7%	64.7%	62.5%	63.0%
Paine Webber								
Assets under Control	$93.2	$118.0	$139.1	$142.7	$216.3	$244.7	$297.1	$352.0
Assets under Mgt. & Admin.	33.6	35.2	38.9	34.4	43.7	44.8	48.9	58.5
% of Assets under Control	36.1%	29.8%	28.0%	24.1%	20.2%	18.3%	16.5%	16.6%
Charles Schwab								
Total Client Assets	$47.5	$65.6	$95.8	$122.6	$181.7	$253.0	$354.0	$491.1
Mutual Fund Assets under Mgt.	14.6	22.9	40.7	54.3	81.7	93.0	160.4	210.6

[a]Corporate equities, fixed income, mutual funds, money market funds, and free credit balances.
[b]Reflects the acquisition of Mercury Asset Management in 1997.
[c]Includes administered assets as of 1997 and 1998.

redirect their savings, investments, insurance, estate planning and other such financial matters. Merrill Lynch Financial Consultants were considered very entrepreneurial and built their businesses through mailings, seminars, client referrals, cold calling and word-of-mouth. There was no set rule on how they gained clients, some focusing on doctors, some on ethnic groups, some on personal relationships in neighborhoods, and so on.

In the industry brokers usually earned about $100,000–$175,000 per year, but average compensation at Merrill Lynch was much higher, estimated at $300,000,[4] with some earning in excess of $1 million. Recognizing the value of Financial Consultants in their relationships with clients, Merrill provided its experienced Financial Consultants some latitude in pricing its products. For example, they could discount brokerage transactions by as much as half the brokerage fee. Turnover was high with 20%–40% of new hires leaving the organization within three years. Some who left the firm failed to meet Merrill Lynch's performance and quality targets, while others found the work unappealing long-term. The firm prided itself on the very high standards it set for its Financial Consultants. On occasion Merrill Lynch lost highly productive Financial Consultants to competitors, but at this level the churn rate of experienced Financial Consultants was at about the industry average of 5%, which was very creditable given the large size of Merrill Lynch's salesforce. The strong stock market (see **Exhibit 4** for a chart of market performance from 1970 to 1999) and the caliber of Merrill Lynch Financial Consultants made them a target for competitive firms anxious to hire proven high producers, with some "Wall Street securities firms offering upfront hiring packages of more than 100% of top brokers' commissions and fees for the past 12 months in order to persuade brokers to change firms."[5] Merrill Lynch's Financial

[4] Charles Gasparino, "Wall Street is rocked by Merrill's online move," *The Wall Street Journal,* June 2, 1999, p. C1.

[5] Randall Smith, "Wall Street still spends big to court top stockbrokers," *The Wall Street Journal,* July 14, 1999, p. C1.

EXHIBIT 4
Dow Jones Industrial Average Performance 1970–1999

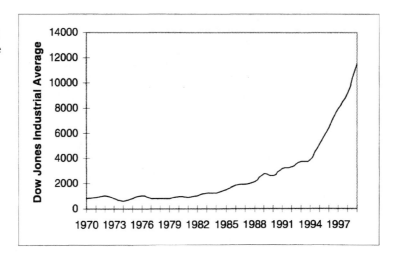

Consultants were housed in 750 offices, reported to a manager who in turn reported to 180 Regional Vice Presidents, who reported to 25 District Managers and ultimately to two National Sales Directors.

Merrill Lynch actively used technology to enhance client service and leverage its Financial Consultants. Initiatives included Trusted Global Advisor (TGA), a technology platform for Financial Consultants which enabled them to view their clients' assets and transaction history online, thus making them more effective in advising their clients.

Merrill Lynch also served clients' diverse liability management needs. Through Merrill Lynch Credit Corporation (MLCC), Financial Consultants offered their clients a broad selection of first mortgage loans, home equity, and securities-based lines of credit and commercial real estate financing. The company was increasingly active in transition management. Its Insurance Group offered both fixed and variable annuities and variable life insurance products designed for retirement and estate planning. Through the Merrill Lynch Trust Company, the firm offered clients numerous trust and estate planning services designed to minimize estate taxes while preserving income in retirement. In addition, Merrill Lynch Group Employee Services provided 401(k) administration and investment services.

Trends and Competition

Consolidation and New Entry

In the 1990s the change in the financial service industry was driven by two factors: deregulation and technology. In the 1930s, in response to bank failures during the depression, the United States government had passed the Securities Exchange Act and the Glass-Steagall Banking Act, which prohibited banks from acting as brokers or securities dealers. As a result, U.S. investment firms were traditionally totally separate from other financial services firms such as banking and insurance. In 1977, Merrill Lynch launched its innovative CMA account which successfully challenged banks for their cash deposits. To remain competitive, banks responded by lobbying for changes to the banking act. Beginning with Congress overturning Regulation Q that had capped interest rates, there had been slow but steady erosion of those boundaries through the 1980s and 1990s. With changes to the Glass-Steagall Act, banks saw securities brokerage as a way to diversify their revenue sources and in an up-market earn increased returns. For example, the Section 20 Provision to the Glass-Steagall Act that limited banked involvement in securities underwriting was first relaxed in 1987 to permit banks to earn up to 5% of their revenues from securities underwriting. The limit was raised to 10% in 1989 and 25% in 1996. In order to gain a share of the business, several banks had acquired underwriters, such as the U.S. Bancorp acquisition of Piper Jaffray in May 1998. Banks were not alone in their encroachment into securities brokerage. Others such as American Express, a major player in the credit card market, had made significant inroads into financial planning and online securities trading.

Still other firms enabled by technology had become aggressive players in multiple financial services products. For example, E*Trade, a pioneer in electronic securities trading, had established a virtual banking operation, a full-service bank without any branch offices. The roles of still other types of Internet-based companies continued to evolve. Firms like Yahoo! and America OnLine were being used by both traditional players and new entrants to gain access to customers. Some suggested that in the future these firms themselves could become direct competitors. Microsoft's attempted acquisition in 1995 of Intuit, a software firm that provided easy-to-use financial services software for the consumer, and other such trends were early indicators of how the industry might eventually evolve.

Deregulation and technological advances created opportunities for the development of one-stop financial services, furthering the consolidation trend among major financial service providers. One of the most significant consolidations was the $73 billion merger of Citicorp and Travellers and the creation of Citigroup. The post-merger entity, Citigroup, could now offer Citicorp credit cards to Salomon Smith Barney investors; the stock-selling services of Salomon Smith Barney to Citicorp banking clients; and Citibank customers could now buy insurance products from Travellers. A similar merger between Dean Witter and Morgan Stanley created another brokerage powerhouse committed to the one-stop shopping concept. These consolidations were occurring in an already concentrated industry where the top 10 firms accounted for 50.4% of revenues. The 15 next-largest firms accounted for 23.6% of industry revenue, with the remaining 7,760 firms contributing only 26% of industry revenues in 1997. (**Exhibit 5** details the number of registered reps and locations for major retail brokerage firms.) Indeed several industry experts believed that in the future the financial services industry would evolve toward the European model, characterized by the dominance of a select few comprehensive firms that offered multiple services.

Discount Brokers

The retail brokerage industry, until the mid 1970s, consisted primarily of full-service firms. As their name implied, full-service firms engaged in all aspects of the investment process from initial decision through execution and follow-up. Using the broker as the client

EXHIBIT 5
Top 15 U. S. Brokerage Firms by Number of Retail Registered Representatives

Source: *Securities Industry Yearbook*, 1999–2000.

	Number of Retail RRs	Number of Institutional RRs	Total Locations
Merrill Lynch & Co	17,400	800	895
Morgan Stanley Dean Witter	11,238	2,000	494
Salomon Smith Barney Holdings	10,803	884	490
Paine Webber Group	6,951		303
Prudential Securities	6,473	229	273
A. G. Edwards, Inc.	6,392	70	630
The Charles Schwab Corporation	5,209		294
Fidelity Brokerage	4,995	476	96
Edward Jones	4,685		4,484
Waterhouse Investor Services Inc.	1,901		153
EVEREN Securities Inc.	1,820	69	171
American Express Financial Advisors Inc.	1,576		3,677
Dain Rauscher Corporation	1,188	111	103
Legg Mason	1,176	81	121
US Bancorp Piper Jaffray Inc.	1,110	80	117

contact point, full-service firms recommended investment opportunities, provided research reports, executed trades, offered customer service support, and issued monthly reporting statements. The discount brokerage industry emerged after the deregulation of commissions in May 1975 when several brokers, most notably Charles Schwab, entered the industry and reduced commissions to almost half of the standard full service firm's commissions and began to steal share. Discounters benefited from an increased flow of financial information (newspapers, financial-related cable television, and magazines) that created confident, educated investors.

Electronic Trading

A third segment developed in the late 1990s when a group of electronic brokerage firms dramatically reduced costs beyond the discounters by leveraging technology not only in the back office but also in their interface with the customer. These electronic firms typically did not have any branch offices and relied on purely electronic order entry. Like the discount brokers, electronic traders advertised heavily (approximately 50% of revenues) to attract customers, with recent industry estimates suggesting that customer acquisition costs had climbed to $250 per client. But, the margins for electronic brokers being thin, Ameritrade, an e-trader that performed basic trades for as little as $8 per trade, charged extra for each additional service.

By 1999 nearly 31% of all retail trades were conducted online, with expectations that this would increase to two-thirds by 2003. Initially, firms such as E*Trade and AmeriTrade were discounted as upstarts attracting low margin clients. Soon, however, the electronic channel became legitimized when leading discounters such as Charles Schwab began trading online and large numbers of investors converted accounts to the online channel. As more and more clients traded online there was increased pressure on margins. For example, while a full-service broker might charge $200 to execute a trade, a discounter such as Charles Schwab was charging $29.95, and a pure electronic trader might be charging $8. In such an environment, many industry observers expected the industry to transition from a fee-based execution business (where investors paid brokerage firms on a per-trade basis) to an asset management business (where investors paid brokerage firms a fixed fee of assets held at the firm). (**Exhibit 6** provides projections for online trading.)

From its inception Charles Schwab embodied the brash upstart discount brokerage firm. In the 1970s, this pre-eminent discount broker determined that it would not sell advice on which securities to buy and sell, but rather focus on providing informed investors with

EXHIBIT 6
Projected Growth of Online Investing

Source: Forrester Research, March 1999.

	1999 (E)	2000 (E)	2001 (E)	2002 (E)
Deep discount				
Household millions	1.4	1.5	1.6	1.8
Accounts millions	3.0	3.4	3.8	4.5
Average account size	$30,600	$33,500	$36,900	$40,600
Assets billions	$91.91	$112.67	$140.65	$183.10
Middle tier				
Household millions	1.6	2.1	2.9	4.0
Accounts millions	2.3	3.3	4.9	7.5
Average account size	$93,000	$98,200	$110,400	$124,400
Assets billions	$214.98	$321.20	$544.38	$928.51
Full service				
Household millions	0.1	0.2	0.3	0.9
Accounts millions	0.1	0.3	0.5	1.7
Average account size	$750,000	$500,000	$400,000	$325,000
Assets billions	$67.37	$130.31	$221.91	$537.12

convenient, low-priced access to securities trading. Unlike full-service brokers, Schwab's brokers did not have a four-year degree and earned significantly less than their counterparts in full-service firms (about $50,000 in discount firms compared to over $100,000 in full-service firms). This fueled Schwab's discount model leading to significantly lower compensation and benefit costs (approximately 40%–45% for discounters versus 52%–57% for full-service brokers).[6]

While its aggressive advertising was clearly visible to the investing public, its investments in technology and innovative product offerings were less overt, but no less important. One of Schwab's product innovations was the development of Schwab Mutual Fund OneSource. This no-load mutual fund (with Schwab and non-Schwab products) generated revenue by charging fund providers at 25 to 35 basis point fees for listing the fund in the "supermarket" and providing shareholder servicing. Further, Charles Schwab was one of the first non-etraders to embrace the Internet, first as a separate operating unit and then folding it into Schwab's main operations. Indeed several industry sources suggested that the growth in the number of online accounts and online trading was mostly due to effective conversion of traditional discount brokerage accounts to online accounts. For example, Schwab saw its online account share of its total account base jump from 5% in 1994 to 60% in 1999.

As Schwab grew and its clients became more affluent, it found that more and more of its clients wanted access to information to make their investment decisions. The median Schwab customer was 45 years old, with $95,000 average income, and about $100,000 in assets. Recognizing this need, Schwab began to reposition itself as a "full-service discount broker." It added research to its product offerings and made arrangements to offer its customers initial public offerings from firms such as CreditSuisse First Boston and J. P. Morgan. Then Schwab developed analytic tools for asset allocation, stock selection, and financial planning to proxy the sophisticated tools possessed by the full-service brokers. Schwab also introduced Signature Service where customers with assets more than $100,000 were able to receive advice through a team of brokers who were paid on salary rather than commissions.

Schwab identified three customer segments. The first was the 3 million "self-directed" investors that were high-tech in orientation, seeking low-cost products and services available through direct distribution channels such as the Internet. Relying extensively on technology rather than human relationships, these investors were more likely to be clients of discount or online brokers. Another group, "delegators" (12 million households), were primarily concerned with having a relationship to guide them through their investments. Not surprisingly these affluent investors were more likely to be clients of full-service brokerage firms. To attract this segment, Schwab had developed affiliations with some 5,600 independent financial advisors (called Registered Independent Advisors) that used Schwab to execute transactions on behalf of their clients; these relationships were estimated to account for 30% of Schwab's client assets. Schwab's largest segment was 22 million "validators" that used both technology and relationships in making investment decisions. These customers preferred to make their own investment decisions but wanted a relationship with a professional capable of providing a second opinion. Schwab used a call center to provide for these clients.

Schwab's recent advertising emphasized the affluent customer, suggesting that it was time for customers "to trade up to Schwab." Many industry observers also perceived Schwab's purchase of U.S. Trust (that managed $86 billion in assets mostly for clients with investable assets of $2 million and up) in January 2000 as a means of furthering its initiatives with high-net-worth investors.

Until the late 1990s, for the most part firms competed against other firms within their segment as well as focusing on key competitors in other segments. For example, Merrill Lynch would compete against other full-service brokers such as Prudential Securities and

---

[6] Estimate based on annual reports.

EXHIBIT 7
Account Size,
Number of Trades,
and Commission
Rates by Segment

Source: *Financial Services Retail Brokerage*, "The Bumpy Ride to Bigger, Better, Cheaper, Faster, Morgan Stanley Dean Witter, October 12, 1999.
Note: This table divides the industry into three segments: discount (e.g., E*Trade), mid-tier (e.g., Schwab) and full service (e.g., Merrill Lynch).

	1998	1999(E)	2000(E)	2001(E)	2002(E)	2003(E)
Discount (e.g., E*Trade)						
Account size	$26,812	$28,957	$31,274	$33,775	$36,477	$39,396
Avg. # of trades	21.3	23.5	21.7	19.8	18.9	17.9
Avg. commission rate	$13.34	$13.27	$12.16	$11.09	$10.05	$9.05
Mid-tier (e.g., Schwab)						
Account size	75,000	84,000	94,080	104,429	114,872	126,359
Avg. # of trades	6.1	8.1	8.3	7.9	7.7	7.2
Avg. commission rate	$48.84	$39.06	$29.04	$24.37	$21.03	$18.79
Full Service (e.g., Merrill Lynch)						
Account size	178,085	185,944	187,098	191,007	196,907	204,497
Avg. # of trades	4.0	3.8	3.9	4.2	4.4	4.7
Avg. commission rate	$105.00	$99.75	$80.45	$62.88	$50.38	$41.57

Morgan Stanley Dean Witter, while maintaining an awareness of the activities of discount brokerage leader Charles Schwab. Moreover, brokerage firms like Merrill Lynch competed with banks by drawing away their affluent customers' deposit accounts, which formed the entry point for many customers' use of securities firms. Facilitated by advances in technology, the differentiation between the segments began to blur and there was increased competition between the segments for the affluent individual investor. (**Exhibit 7** shows projections for average client account balances, number of trades, and commission rates for brokerage segments).

Conversely, while Schwab was targeting full-service firms' clients, full-service firms were becoming increasingly interested in discount brokers' higher-net-worth clients. Indeed, full-service firms had begun to focus more and more on Charles Schwab as a significant competitor, effectively turning the tables from "predator to prey."[7] One Merrill Lynch executive noted:

> In the past we viewed Schwab solely as a discount firm, believing that once its clients reached a certain level of affluence, about half a million dollars or so, that they would need more sophisticated analysis and advice and transition to a full-service firm, and indeed much research shows that at that stage most investors seek expert financial advice. However, with the blurring of competitive lines between full-service and discounters, we are on the offensive and actively seeking to take affluent clients from Schwab.

Merrill Lynch Continues to Lead

Although competitive forces pummeled the industry, Merrill Lynch commanded the largest share of household assets. (See **Exhibit 8** for a summary of client assets for key competitors.) As traditional competitive lines blurred, U.S. Private Client expanded its competitive set beyond traditional full-service firms. It paid special attention to two groups: competitors who posed clear threats to Merrill Lynch through their use of open architecture or the breadth and integration of their product lines; and a second class of competitors who posed a competitive threat because of their proven ability to re-shape the industry through innovations. (See **Exhibit 9.**)

[7] Rebecca Buckman, "Schwab, once a predator, is now prey," *The Wall Street Journal*, December 8, 1999.

EXHIBIT 8
Client Assets—
Selected Firms
($ billions)

Source: MDS&A company
earnings releases. Comparisons
are August to August.

	1998	1999
Merrill Lynch	1,057	1,222
Salomon Smith Barney[a]	724	852
Charles Schwab	390	595
Morgan Stanley Dean Witter	392	529
Goldman Sachs	293	413
PaineWebber[a]	329	384
American Express Financial Advisors[a]	202	232

[a]June to June comparisons.

EXHIBIT 9
U.S. Private Client
Competitors

Source: Company records.

Competitors	Rationale
Top Tier Competitors	
American Express	Building retail client base by using like financial planners and accountants
Bank of America/NationsBank	Largest bank in the United States
Charles Schwab	Innovator in discount brokerage. Moving beyond self-service model to aggressively compete for certain full-service clients
Citigroup	Pursuing universal financial service model. Global scale and presence.
Fidelity Investments	Leading mutual fund 401(k) provider in the United States. Noted for exceptional performance of funds.
Morgan Stanley Dean Witter	Full-service provider noted for integration of its operations and execution of the "Merrill Lynch" strategy. Aggressively competes for brokers.
Other Industry Shapers	
A. G. Edwards	Leader in customer satisfaction among full-service companies
E*Trade	State-of-the-art technology. Marking strides toward building a virtual universal financial services company.
First Union	State-of-the-art technology to support cash management and identify cross-selling opportunities
Goldman Sachs	The "gold standard" for the delivery of products and services to high-net-worth clients
KeyCorp	Creative use of strategic alliances to build an extensive product line
USAA	Leader in back-office technology and customer service
Vanguard	Mutual fund leader noted for indexing, low expenses, and self-help philosophy

Target Market

Various players sought relationships with the approximately 45 million households that defined the prospective U.S. investor market. This target market included 35 million households that currently used a full-service, discount, mutual fund company, financial planning firm, or investment firm with services on the Internet, excluding assets held in an employer sponsored plan. A further 10 million households who were not using investment firms but had household incomes of $75K or more or investable assets of over $100K were also considered targets. Industry research indicated that, as a client, a typical customer generated about $2,500–$3,000 in revenues for the financial services industry, with about 50% of that

EXHIBIT 10
Merrill Lynch Client Profile

Source: Company survey data based on a stratified random sample of 704 Priority clients, 504 Near Priority clients and 500 Low Asset clients.

	Total Merrill Lynch Clients	Merrill Lynch Priority Clients
1999 Demographic Profile		
Age (median)	53 years	63 years
% male	51%	53%
% retired	37%	62%
% self or spouse currently own a business	16%	16%
% with college degree or more	58%	63%
% married	67%	69%
Financial Profile		
1998 annual income (median)	$63K	$80K
Total household investable assets	$120K	$500K
% of household investable assets held at ML (median)	50%	75%
Work-related savings (e.g., 401 (k)) (median)	$50K	$120K
Years with Merrill Lynch (median)	10 years	15 years
# of total trades across firms used in the last 12 months (median)	3 trades	6 trades
Planning and Technology		
% with written financial plan	27%	42%
% use PC at home or work	68%	60%
% access Internet	54%	47%

amount from mortgages/home equity loans. Mutual funds, equities, individual retirement accounts, and insurance/annuities for 8%–10% each, and the remainder came from other products such as bonds and money market funds.

Several segmentation studies had been conducted by the industry, with investors generally falling into one of three segments. The first segment comprised those active, do-it-yourself investors that preferred to manage their own investment portfolio. Younger, technologically savvy, and predominantly male, these investors were focused on growth. They were more likely to have a discount or electronic brokerage account than a relationship with a full-service firm. The next group of investors sought advice in creating and managing their investment portfolio. The range of advice varied, with some investors wanting an expert's review of their own decisions and others relying on the advice of an investment professional to shape their portfolio. Generally more risk averse and conservative in their portfolios, many in this group were women and retirees who wanted the financial planning and security of dealing with a professional advisor. Well over half of these investors had a relationship with a full-service firm, but increasingly many also had accounts with discount or electronic brokerage firms. The final group of investors, slightly older and predominantly male, did not get involved in their personal finances, preferring to delegate those activities to a financial professional. These investors often had relationships with full-service firms and mutual fund companies.

For its part, similar to many full-service firms, Merrill Lynch targeted the affluent individuals with investable assets of at least $100,000. Priority Clients with at least $250,000 in assets at Merrill Lynch were a key group of customers. On average they were about 60 years old, with assets of $650K, and traded about 6 times per year. (See **Exhibit 10** for a profile of Merrill Lynch's clients.) Premier Priority Clients represented a generally higher level of affluence (greater than $1 million in assets) and a generally greater use of products across product categories. They usually had at least $100K in each of three products—assets, liabilities, and transition (insurance and 401(k)) with Merrill Lynch. Premier Plus Clients were wealthy individuals with even higher levels of investable assets that, given their asset bases, often required very specialized financial products and services.

TABLE B
Households by Client Segment

Source: Adapted from company records.

Households (000s)	Existing Merrill Lynch Private Clients	Potential U.S. Market
Premier Plus	25	266
Premier Priority Clients	150	8,864
Priority Clients	825	10,495
Other Household Relationships	2,500	94,577
Group Employee Services Relationships	2,000	27,000

Overall clients with more than $1 million in household assets accounted for about 5% of client households, but represented about 60% of assets. The top 15% of private client households represented three-quarters of assets. **Table B** summarizes U.S. Private Client households by client segment.

Merrill Lynch Transforms Its Business Strategy

In early 1998, U.S. Private Client's Executive Committee established eight initiatives for further exploration. Of these initiatives, Launny Steffens believed that Technology and Pricing were the most pressing. On the technology side, the Internet, which had initially been no more than a "gnat," was attracting increasing attention. In May 1998, Jupiter Communications reported that nearly 12% of U.S. households with incomes above $75,000 (i.e., 4.6 million households) conducted online financial transactions. By 2000 that number was projected to increase up to 31%. More important, trends also suggested that the affluent were considering adopting the Internet not only as an information portal but also as a medium for executing the transaction. Pricing was a related but separate issue. When Schwab had integrated its online operations in 1997, it had priced its fees at $29.95 per trade; pure electronic traders were charging much less. Equally interesting had been the success of Merrill Lynch's fee-based products—Asset Power and Merrill Lynch Financial Advantage (MLFA)—that had grown to about $20 billion in client assets without significant marketing support.

Without any pre-conceived bias toward change, Steffens established separate taskforces to analyze these issues. In June 1998, a taskforce led by Madeline (Maddy) Weinstein, Senior V.P. and Director of U.S. Private Client (USPC) Business Innovation Group, was established with a mandate to look into the online phenomena. It was only natural for Maddy Weinstein to head the technology taskforce because, according to Launny Steffens, "Maddy was the visionary in getting the senior management to focus on the Internet long before it was a pervasive force. Her technology perspective was a big asset." In August 1998, Steffens charged another taskforce, led by Allen Jones, Senior V.P., Private Client Marketing, with the pricing question. Having spent a number of years in the field organization, Jones had a strong empathy for the clients and the value that Merrill Lynch provided them. Steffens recalled, "My job as a leader is to determine where the world is going and how to get there first. Then I think about the implications for the business. The taskforces were the means of taking that step."

The Online Taskforce

In August 1998 Maddy Weinstein brought in Bob Brewster, a 19-year veteran of Private Client who had spent 15 years in the sales organization, to head the online taskforce. "Our job was to investigate whether online offered a new opportunity to enhance Private Client's service to its clients," recalled Brewster. Immediately, Brewster and his team (composed of "borrowed" internal strategists and outside consultants) set to work delving into industry trends, client behavior, and the industry economics. Additionally they went online on competitor systems, trading E*Trade and Schwab and "speaking with everyone possible in the industry." The taskforce traveled extensively to hear directly from brokers and customers nationwide. Close to 2,000 pages of research data were collected. Even for Merrill Lynch, a company that systematically and frequently collected its clients' preferences and buying behavior, this was a massive effort. Reflecting on the process, Brewster stated, "The meetings were open, honest, contentious, and very productive. It didn't matter who was right, what mattered was what was right." He continued, "Looking back, Maddy Weinstein was right to bring me in as an outsider to headquarters and not give me a staff. I could look at the situation objectively, without being bound to a particular group of stakeholders."

The leaders of the pricing and the online taskforces were members of each other's taskforce. The outside consultants were connected as well. This cross-membership ensured that data were actively shared between the two groups. Brewster recalled:

> The recommendations of the online taskforce were unanimous. It was clear to us that there had been a rapid, significant change in investor attitudes toward electronic trading. We were seeing increasing pressure on margins, existing clients were opening online accounts with our competitors, and we were failing to attract newer customers at a fast enough rate. It was clear that we had to act.

While the online taskforce was solidly behind its recommendation, its work had only really begun. It needed to convince Merrill Lynch, one of the world's most successful firms, that it needed to change its business model. Utilizing the extensive amount of ongoing client feedback and quantitative data about the industry, the process began with a presentation to Launny Steffens. While acknowledging the validity of the data from Brewster's team, he remained cautious about changing a highly successful business paradigm. He, like much of Private Client senior management, had originally come from the field and thus was acutely aware of the value of the best-trained salesforce in the industry and the strength of its customer relationships. However, 10 days later, Steffens and other members of the team flew to the Silicon Valley where they met with both Financial Consultants and clients to continue the dialogue about the online environment. When clients were asked at the focus group "How many of you have online trading?" two-thirds of participants raised their hands. About the same proportion of the Financial Consultants at the later meeting also urged Merrill Lynch to go online.

That trip was followed by a second trip to Austin, Texas, where, once again, Steffens listened closely to clients explain their wants and needs. One client with a 20-year relationship with Merrill Lynch told Steffens that he used a separate online account for his frequent trades and among the stocks he traded was Merrill Lynch itself. Additionally, Steffens received approximately 10 email messages a day from brokers concerned about the Internet threat. After weighting factors on all sides, on the way back to New York Steffens told his colleagues, "I'm convinced. We have to do a dot.com business." With that decision made, Private Client began to make strides in getting a product to market.

Beginning in November 1998, the company began offering free access to its global stock research over the Internet for a four-month trial period. Many perceived this step as a watershed event for two reasons. First, Merrill Lynch was putting one of its most valued assets, its analyst reports, on the Web. Second, it proved that Merrill Lynch had "got the Internet" and was doing business differently—well before its full-service competitors understood the deeper impact of the Internet. Visitors to the website were able to create a "watch" list of stocks and pull up full text research reports on over 1,500 companies covered by Merrill Lynch analysts across the globe, with Merrill Lynch then passing on leads to its Financial Consultants. Then, on December 28, 1998, Schwab's $25.5 billion market capitalization overtook Merrill Lynch's $25.4 billion. Schwab had increased its assets by 39% in 1998, while Merrill Lynch's grew only 18%. It was the moment "when Merrill got religion."[8] William Henkel, First Vice President, Senior Director, Client Marketing and Strategy, recalled, "That was an enormously difficult day for us. Here we were, with over a trillion dollars in client assets, to less than $500 billion for Schwab, and yet, our market cap was equal. That was a powerful market signal."

The Pricing Taskforce

Concurrent with the online taskforce, Allen Jones had formed the pricing taskforce under the leadership of Jeff Bennett, First Vice President, Director, Strategic Pricing, who had managed Unlimited Advantage's predecessor products, Asset Power and Merrill Lynch Financial Advantage. Asset Power, a fee-based program that charged 2% of assets under management, was launched in 1993. In 1997 Financial Advantage was launched with a 1.5% fee, about $300–$500 in inclusive services and up to 17 free trades for an entry account. The product grew to $3 billion in its first year, growing to $8 billion by the second year. Both products, however, had met resistance from Financial Consultants reluctant to trade off commission revenue streams in favor of more in-depth client relationships and asset growth. As of 1998, Merrill Lynch's various fee-based products had attracted about $100 billion in client investments. About $20 billion was from Financial Advantage and Asset Power, with the remaining $80 billion from other fee-based products (such as ML Consults, Mutual Fund Advisor, Strategy Power, Strategic Portfolio Advisor, and Personal Investment Advisory).

The role of the pricing taskforce was to thoroughly evaluate all aspects of the product/ price equation. As Allen Jones remarked, "For years we viewed the value proposition as the three Ps: Planning, Performance, and Personal Service. Price was considered an issue only in the absence of value. Our challenge was to make the case that in the emerging new economy, price is an integral component of our offer, which we redefined as: Relationship (based on trust), Performance (against client's goals), Service (beyond expectations), and Price (appropriate to client benefit). We decided to aggressively compete on each of these components, including price." Like its online counterpart, the pricing taskforce worked with consultants, conducted focus groups with Financial Consultants and clients (among very high net worth clients with over $25 million in assets, as well as clients with $250,000 to $1 million in assets), and conducted competitive comparisons. Jeff Bennett summarized the findings:

> It became very clear to us that our pricing structure was not aligned with how we delivered value to our clients. The execution component in the value chain had become a commodity and we were putting a premium price on the execution of that commodity. For example, sometimes the best advice our Financial Consultants can give is not to trade. But when there was no trade we didn't get paid anything. It was like charging for the grocery bag, but not the groceries inside.

Looking outside the traditional brokerage firm, the taskforce also noted the rise of the RIAs (Registered Independent Advisors) that had been growing 40% per year, based on a price model that charged 1% of assets plus the costs of execution. Economic models were built to try to pinpoint the optimal pricing strategy. Within the traditional model, prices had been falling steadily, from 120 basis points (1.2% of assets) to approximately 80 basis points (0.8% of assets) within three to four years, and was expected to further fall to 50 basis points by 2003. Moreover, Merrill Lynch priced its asset-based products at above 100 basis points, which was on par with other full-service brokers charging 150 to 200 basis points. For many at Merrill Lynch, especially senior managers like Allen Jones, the taskforce research reinforced their drive to transform the business from "brokerage" to "asset gathering,"—only the company would now have to accelerate in that direction.

[8] Leah Nathans Spiro, "Merrill's Battle," *Business Week,* November 15, 1999, p. 259.

An Integrated Offer of Choice

As work progressed on both fronts, in February 1999, Merrill Lynch acquired D.E. Shaw Financial Technology, the developer of a real-time online trading system. This acquisition gave Merrill Lynch a cadre of developers, supplementing the existing technology team, to build a custom online trading system for the brokerage. Another program, Microsoft's COM (Component Object Model), was being used to link the front-end system to Merrill Lynch's back-end systems. Additionally, while the front-end systems were to be based on clustered NT servers, Internet Information Server Web servers, and applications developed with Microsoft's Back office wares, Merrill Lynch also developed in-house "middleware" that would link those systems to its mainframes. As for communications, Merrill was also well into the deployment of an ATM backbone based on Cisco hardware and bandwidth from AT&T.

On March 4, 1999, Merrill Lynch became one of the first full-service firms to offer online trading. This move, however, was on a limited basis to 55,000 of its fee-based (MLFA and Asset Power) clients rather than commission clients. Indeed, in an attempt to offer online trading without undercutting their brokers' commission schedules, full-service firms such as Morgan Stanley Dean Witter and Paine Webber also planned to switch online customers from commission-based transactions to asset management fees (a percentage charge based on account size that covered a pre-set number of trades per year). For example, Paine Webber planned to charge $2,250 per year for a $100,000 account with up to 52 trades per year. On a per-trade basis this was significantly higher than discount brokers or online trading companies ($43.27 per trade versus $29.95 or $8.00). The full-service firm maintained that customers received value such as customer profiling, planning, asset allocation, and research as well as trade execution.

While some within Merrill Lynch advocated the formation of an independent wholly owned online firm, Steffens was determined to keep all of Merrill Lynch's product offerings under the same brand. He recalled:

> Morgan Stanley set up its online brokerage operations as a separate business called Discover Brokerage. When it first started advertising the Discover name, it was huge and the only affiliation with Morgan Stanley was a very small line at the bottom of the ad. As we watched, the Morgan Stanley name became bigger and bigger. They spent tens of millions of dollars trying to build the Discover Brokerage brand without much success. It is difficult to build a no-name into a brand; many online start-ups have paid the price.

In March, Steffens made an eight-hour presentation to the 18-person Merrill Lynch & Co. Executive Committee, providing the outline of an Internet strategy that integrated the work of the Online and Pricing task forces. Steffens argued that "Merrill Lynch had to offer an online-only account or it would lose too many assets, not to mention the next generation of investors."[9]

Steffens advocated a transformation in Merrill Lynch's entire product-service portfolio. One significant change was the "Unlimited Advantage" service. Priced at 1% of assets or less depending on the asset mix, with a declining percentage as assets grew, the account was designed to be the best price/value equation in the industry. As shown in **Exhibit 1,** for an average Merrill Lynch client with a little over $200,000 in assets (66% in securities and 34% in fixed income), the fee would net out to $0.66 \times 1\% + .34 \times .3\% = .77\%$. Competitively, Merrill believed that it exceeded Prudential Securities offerings and was a better value than Schwab's outside advisor system, where customers could pay up to two percentage point on assets, plus commission on each trade. Jeff Bennett commented:

> Unlimited Advantage creates a "win/win" relationship between the Financial Consultant and the client. If the client's assets grow, the Financial Consultant's compensation grows. It

[9] Leah Nathans Spiro, "Merrill's Battle," *Business Week,* November 15, 1999, p. 260.

effectively eliminates any suspicion that the broker's advice is based on the broker's desire to trade stock and earn a commission.

The second major change was the Merrill Lynch Direct channel that would offer customers online purchasing of equities, no load and load mutual funds and telephone orders for fixed-income and other products at a basic charge of $29.95 a trade. Merrill Lynch research and a suite of portfolio management, cash management, and e-commerce services was also slated for online delivery. Additionally, the traditional broker relationships continued to be available to both new and existing clients.

The new strategy was perceived as high risk both internally and externally. An important challenge was the risk to the firm's revenue by effectively setting a fee ceiling at 1% of assets. Mitigating this factor was a long-standing strategic commitment to move toward operating like a major bank, beginning with the 1977 introduction of the CMA account. Anticipating the 1999 passage of Financial Service Modernization and the repeal of the Glass-Steagall Banking Act, Merrill's internal economic analysis showed that linking the Unlimited Advantage service to a Money Market Deposit Account (MMDA) would yield significant revenue to the firm. CMA accounts were currently linked to a Money Market Fund, but regulation prevented these balances from being invested in any instruments with average maturity exceeding 90 days. Merrill Lynch, however, could be more aggressive with MMDA deposits, thus delivering higher returns for its clients and a better spread than it was able to earn with the Money Market Funds. Consequently, although MLUA exposed the firm to the possibility of adverse selection (because some clients could lower their cost without bringing in new assets), the MMDA strategy would minimize this risk. Merrill Lynch decided to apply this innovative idea to all its accounts, not just MLUA, and this delayed the rollout date to June of 2000 so that all clients could be properly notified and the strategy explained to FCs.

During the planning phase, the internal code-name for the direct trading program was Rubicon and indeed the decision was a paradigm shift for the firm. After the announcement observers speculated on the impact of online trading on Merrill Lynch's revenue—how much new business would be generated versus how much would be lost due to the much lower commission structure. Adverse selection was an issue, as it was possible under the new scenario for a customer to keep the minimum balance in the brokerage account and use that advice to trade through the ML Direct Account. Internal models had indicated that a potential $400 million of earnings could be at stake. Moreover, while Merrill Lynch could be insulated while the market remained hot and online trading surged, many wondered what would happen if the bulls turned to bears and individual investors cut back on their trading. Conversely, while some were wondering if Merrill Lynch had made the right decision, others were concerned that they hadn't made it soon enough. "Merrill Lynch had created a highly successful business model," William Henkel astutely noted.

> One of the most difficult decisions for senior management is distinguishing short-term bumps from long-term trends. As a market leader with $1.5 trillion in assets at risk, there needs to be a compelling reason to change, especially to change so profoundly and irrevocably. But once we reached our epiphany we moved dramatically—at Internet speed. We seized the initiative, and now people are reacting to us. After all, leadership is that difficult balance involved in trading off what is enduring for what is transient.

For Launny Steffens, Integrated Choice was not a revolutionary, but rather an evolutionary, step in a process begun several years earlier. He explained:

> Our fundamental business model of a universal financial services company has been the same for the past 15 years; we've just added two new rooms to our house. We began with a belief in asset gathering. At first our salesforce was incredulous but then began to see that

once assets were at Merrill Lynch, we could help our clients with their full range of needs, be it managing their cash, investment decisions, liabilities, or the structure and disposition of assets over time. That led to our emphasis on financial planning and building a relationship with clients that allowed them to meet their goals. ML Direct, Unlimited Advantage, and electronic commerce are just additional ways to help clients increase their assets and meet their financial goals.

The Rubber Meets the Road

By early 1999, it was clear that the recommendations of the online taskforce and the pricing taskforce were beginning to converge into an integrated model of choice where clients would choose from a suite of traditional and online products according to what best suited their needs. The firm was speeding ahead, with a goal of announcing its Integrated Choice offer on July 1, 1999. However, that was not to be. Business reporters got wind of Merrill Lynch's plans. On the Friday just before the Memorial Day long weekend at the end of May, reporters from *The Wall Street Journal* contacted Merrill regarding a report they were preparing on Merrill Lynch's impending online initiative.

Buying time until the following Tuesday, Merrill Lynch scrambled to put implementation plans in place. Merrill Lynch had not planned to announce until July, and its online product was not due for launch until the 4th quarter. Only a very small group of senior field sales people on the Advisory Council to Management (ACTM) was privy to the company's new strategic directions. It was paramount, therefore, that Merrill Lynch's salesforce hear about the announcement from its senior management rather than the newspapers. Over the holiday weekend, presentations were pulled together and action plans put in place. When employees came in on Tuesday morning, monitors were informing them of the announcement and further explanations were offered in employee meetings scheduled throughout the day. Launny Steffens went on the company's satellite broadcasting system to address its Financial Consultants. On June 1, 1999, Merrill Lynch made it official. The reaction of the market was immediate. While some in the business press saw it as a reactive move to stave off further intrusion into its client base, others in the business press and analysts were showering praise on Merrill Lynch's new strategy.

Merrill Lynch's move to a $29.95 trade price point seems almost designed to be something of a Schwab killer . . . In our view, it is clearly a better value than Schwab's existing offering . . . [Schwab's] Registered Investment Advisors average 194 bps vs. Merrill Unlimited Advantage at 85 bps!

—*Steve Galbraith (Sanford Bernstein)*[10]

Further proof that Merrill Lynch had moved boldly in the right direction occurred in October 1999 when Morgan Stanley Dean Witter announced its new "iChoice" service with a range of products very similar to those in Merrill Lynch's Integrated Choice offering. Online trading was available for $29.95. Morgan Stanley offered a combination of human advice and online capabilities for fees ranging from 2.25% of assets to 0.2%, with fees decreasing as assets rose.

In making Integrated Choice a reality, however, Merrill Lynch faced several key challenges. The first was technology. Despite an annual IT budget of more than $2 billion and 6,000 IT people and 2,220 outside contractors, several hundred of whom were dedicated to

[10] Steve Galbraith is a leading industry analyst. Quotation from Merrill Lynch documents, combining remarks from Berstein Research Call, October 8, 1999, and October 18, 1999.

the online project, bringing Merrill Lynch Direct to market effective December 1999 was a daunting challenge. Failure to deliver would be risky. A June 1 announcement of services to be available six months later had given competitors (several of whom already offered more deeply discounted trading) time to counter Merrill Lynch's strategy even before it was fully implemented. Additionally, while the company seemed to have made the requisite technology investments, several firms wondered how Merrill Lynch's systems would react to the surges associated with online volumes, noting, "Merrill will have to work hard to convince those people that they should return to their father's stockbroker—particularly one like Merrill whose computer systems haven't yet been seriously tested by big surges in online trading."[11]

In addition to the technical hurdles in offering online trading, Merrill Lynch also needed to bring its Financial Consultants (as well as other internal Merrill Lynch people) and clients on board. While the Financial Consultants had been told about Integrated Choice, they still needed to be sold. Unlike the upstart e-traders, Merrill Lynch's salesforce had been successful with the traditional business model and they were relative neophytes to the Internet and its potential. It took a combination of increasing online trading and flight of client assets from the field to create the need for change. As one observer noted:

> The firm had to wait until its brokers had accepted that the online world was here to stay. If Merrill had rolled out online trading in July 1999, 75% of its brokers would not have supported it. And Merrill stood the risk of having brokers and the assets they manage walk out. Because of the bull market for brokers and the practice of Wall Street firms paying multimillion-dollar signing bonuses, a successful Merrill broker could—and would—change jobs in a heartbeat.[12]

For many, the initial reaction to Integrated Choice was that their personal incomes, dependent on trading commissions, would be dramatically reduced, and with that reaction there was a risk that Financial Consultants would be lured to other firms. As Jeff Bennett pointed out, "The Financial Consultants had been insulated from many of the changes in the market. With the strongest market in memory, trading volumes were effectively shielding softening in commission rates."

To address this problem, Merrill Lynch executives launched a "full court press" with its Financial Consultants. While in the longer term Merrill Lynch expected that compensation would rise, particularly among Financial Consultants that executed the Private Client planning-based strategy and converted clients to the Unlimited Advantage, in the short term some Financial Consultants could experience a near term decline in compensation (of 10%–15%). Key elements of a new plan were a "compensation bridge" for Financial Consultants for at least one year on assets converted to Unlimited Advantage and incentives for transitioning clients. Allen Jones remarked:

> Throughout the course of several weeks we met with all of the Financial Consultants, taking special care with our highest producers. We explained Integrated Choice and what it could mean for the Financial Consultants' income in the future as well as what the firm was doing to help mitigate short-term transitions. All in all we were successful—only losing a few of our top people. To manage the process, we sent each regional office the projected impact on the compensation package of their top Financial Consultants, so that the office managers could better manage the affected people.

In addition to programs specifically targeted to Financial Consultants, Merrill Lynch had planned an extensive series of internal communications. The primary audience for these communications was the Financial Consultant and branch management; the secondary

[11] Rebecca Buckman, "Ambitious plan could result in lower fees," *The Wall St. Journal*, June 1, 1999, p. C1.

[12] Leah Nathans Spiro, "Merrill's Battle," *Business Week*, November 15, 1999.

audience was the broader pool of Merrill Lynch domestic employees. The communications had three phases. The first, "Building the new Merrill Lynch," was focused on creating understanding, awareness, and excitement for the new business model. One component of this phase was a revamped National Sales website, designed to be the main source of detailed information for Financial Consultants about key initiatives. The second phase, "From Wall Street to Main Street to My Street," continued with employee education efforts, primarily through an Employee Channel delivered via Merrill Lynch's Intranet (WorldNet). The employee channel contained information on the new business model, incorporated programs, and provided a vehicle for two-way communication. The third communication phase, "Ongoing Communications," continued employee education efforts by providing information on how new events related to the business model. In conjunction with these efforts "town hall" and business unit meetings and senior management "walk-arounds" were held to build employee excitement and commitment. All of these efforts were in addition to the many, many personal visits by senior management to speak directly to Financial Consultants.

Perhaps the most important constituency that needed to understand and be converted to Integrated Choice was Merrill Lynch's clients. To reach out to its customers, the firm launched an extensive communication program that encompassed traditional media (television and print), as well as Internet-based media. Additionally, Merrill Lynch planned direct mail programs with messages included in clients' statements.

Next Steps

Launny Steffens knew that there was much work to be done. At every opportunity he sought to remind his managers, exhorting:

> As you may recall, this time last year I summarized our position with a Will Rogers quote, "Even if you're on the right track, if you're sitting there, you'll get run over." Well, it seems everyone took those words to heart, because we certainly did not just sit there in 1999. As we look forward to keep this momentum going, three things will be critical in 2000. First, implementation. Second, implementation. Third, implementation. I think you get the point. We must live up to our promise and deliver seamless financial services.

No one was more aware of the need to execute than Launny Steffens himself. High on his agenda were three issues. First, motivating the Financial Consultant community. There was a critical need to get Merrill Lynch's biggest asset, the Financial Consultants, converted from merely accepting the suite of Integrated Choice offerings to actively promoting the products—meeting with clients to identify the product that best matched client needs, preparing a financial plan with the client, and ultimately bringing a larger and larger share of that client's assets under the Merrill Lynch product umbrella. Rolled into this issue were a number of questions. How to position the ML Direct product to the general public? Further, how much to advertise? What should the role of the Financial Consultant be in attracting such customers?

A second issue was client transition and seamless service. Once clients met with their Financial Consultant and decided on the optimal relationship for the client, Merrill Lynch needed a process for clients to be made aware of other products and services that might be appropriate. As one Merrill Lynch executive explained:

> Today a younger client with assets of, say, about $75,000, might be best served through ML Direct. However, as his or her assets and income grow, they may well want more advice and a relationship with a Financial Consultant, perhaps using the Unlimited Advantage account or a traditional account. We need to establish a process so that we reach out to that client at the right time. Right now we've got discrete product offerings, but we need proactive efforts to help clients make the best choices.

Allen Jones wondered whether the customers received the kind of information they needed to assess the value of their brokerage firm. As of now most of Merrill's clients received a consolidated statement of their assets and their valuations at the end of each month, in addition to the transactions information which was mailed as and when they were effected. A year-end account summary for tax purposes was also provided. "We need to include metrics that would differentiate our service," stated Jones.

The third issue concerned the future role of the Financial Consultant. At present, Financial Consultants, often with the help of an administrative assistant (called Client Associates), performed all facets of servicing the client relationship. This included a range of services from brokerage transactions, arranging financial planning, to administrative needs such as having checks certified for clients. Many at Merrill Lynch believed that there needed to be an evolution of the role, especially with its ambitious goal to be a full-service provider in all respects. Some suggested that the enhanced Financial Consultant might continue to manage the relationship, but expand access to specialists (such as estate planning) that was already available, in addition to delegating more and more of the administrative tasks. Indeed, the entire structure of the selling operation would have to be carefully transformed to match the reality of the business situation.

While Integrated Choice was launched, its success was not yet guaranteed. As one industry observer noted:

The next nine months will prove to be a defining period in MER's history. The stakes are obviously quite high—if the company successfully reinvents itself where needed, MER's market cap could rise over 50%.[13]

—*Steve Galbraith (Sanford Bernstein)*

---

[13] First Call, November 19, 1999.

Chapter 25

Avon.com (A)

David B. Godes

As Len Edwards, president and general manager of Avon.com, sat in the backstage Green Room at the Venetian Hotel Conference Center in Las Vegas on a hot evening in July 2000, he went over in his mind the many things he would be presenting to the thousands of Avon sales representatives gathered for the annual convention. In minutes, he would describe to them the details behind Avon.com, the company's long-awaited online effort, which would be launched in September. They would, of course, not know all that had gone into the building of the strategy. He and his team had spent months and millions of dollars on the project in an effort to ensure they were doing things the right way. Had they made the right decisions in the end? Time would tell, but the choices were not easy ones. Which of the company's thousands of products should be sold online? How would they promote the site? Most important, what was the best way to leverage their 500,000 sales representatives in building Avon.com? Avon had been the original pioneer of direct selling and was still the industry's leader. Everyone felt that they probably should not stray too far from this tradition. On the other hand, the Web seemed to offer unlimited potential to reach directly the millions of women who were not being reached by the sales representatives.

Avon was the world's largest direct seller[1] of beauty products and fifth-largest beauty company overall with annual sales of over $5 billion (see **Exhibit 1** for aggregate financial information, **Exhibit 2** for a breakdown of sales by region, and **Exhibit 3** for a breakdown by product line). The U.S. beauty industry, however, was a mature one; annual growth rates between 2% and 4% were expected for the foreseeable future. In 1999, Avon's products were sold through a network of about 2.8 million sales representatives worldwide, nearly 500,000 of whom were in the United States (see **Exhibit 4** for the growth of the sales force).

[1] "Direct selling" generally refers to a context in which manufacturers sell directly to consumers, bypassing middlemen. It is generally reserved for manufacturers of consumer products.

Professor David B. Godes prepared this case. HBS cases are developed solely as the basis for class discussion. Cases are not intended to serve as endorsements, sources of primary data, or illustrations of effective or ineffective management.

EXHIBIT 1
Avon Products
Operating Profit,
1997–1999 (numbers
in millions)

Source: Avon Products Annual
Report, 1999.

Years ended December 31	1999	1998	1997
Net sales	$5,289.1	$5,212.7	$5,079.4
Costs, expenses, and other:			
Cost of sales	2,031.5	2,053.0	2,051.0
Marketing, distribution, and administrative expenses[a]	2,603.0	2,570.0	2,490.6
Special charges	105.2	116.5	—
Operating profit	549.4	473.2	537.8

[a]Includes cost of Avon representatives.

EXHIBIT 2
Avon Sales by
Region, 1997–1999
(numbers in millions)

Source: Avon Products Annual
Report, 1999.

Years ended December 31	1999		1998		1997	
	Net Sales	Operating Profit	Net Sales	Operating Profit	Net Sales	Operating Profit
North America						
U.S.	$1,809.3	$329.3	$1,774.0	$302.8	$1,696.7	$261.8
Other	274.0	44.7	287.6	40.2	275.4	35.1
Total	2,083.3	374.0	2,061.6	343.0	1,972.1	296.9
International:						
Latin America	1,607.7	353.6	1,665.1	344.4	1,513.3	280.0
Europe	878.0	126.2	862.7	102.2	811.6	85.4
Pacific	720.1	102.1	623.3	62.5	782.4	67.0
Total	3,205.8	581.9	3,151.1	509.1	3,107.3	432.4
Total from operations	$5,289.1	$955.9	$5,212.7	$852.1	$5,079.4	$729.3

EXHIBIT 3
Sales by Product
Line, 1997–1999

Source: Avon Products Annual
Report, 1999.

Products	1999	1998	1997	1996	1995	1994
Cosmetics, fragrance, and toiletries	3,226	3,176	3,094	2,947	2,797	2,604
Gift and decorative	1,052	1,060	1,050	934	781	769
Jewelry and accessories	455	4,089	370	377	414	413
Apparel	556	568	566	556	501	580

EXHIBIT 4
Growth in Sales
Force, 1994–2000

Source: Avon Products Annual
Report, 1999.

	Total	U.S.
FY ended 94	1,745	415
95	1,900	440
96	2,000	445
97	2,300	440
98	2,600	445
99	2,800	445
00	3,000	445

History of Avon

In the late 19th century, David McConnell launched what would become the direct-selling industry, almost by accident. As a book salesman, he was interested in getting people to listen to his sales pitch. He devised an idea by which he offered housewives a gift of small bottles of perfume if they would listen to him describe his books. It was not long before he realized that the perfume was more popular than the books. So, in 1886 he launched the California Perfume Company. Based on his background, it was natural for him to attempt initially to distribute the products door to door.

Mrs. P.F.E. Albee in Winchester, New Hampshire, was the first "Avon lady" hired by McConnell. Within six months, he had hired 100 more. Twelve years later, there were over 5,000 Avon ladies selling perfume direct to the consumer. While the name of the company was not changed to Avon until 1939, many of Avon's hallmark business practices, still in use in 1999, were begun in the 1930s. In 1932, Avon instituted the three-week sales cycle (later changed to a two-week cycle). Moreover, the company's broad product line was already taking shape, reaching over 100 products by 1939. It had already diversified out of perfume into other low-cost home and beauty products, as well as personal care items such as toothbrushes.

In the 1950s, Avon began mass advertising of its products with the well-known "Ding Dong, Avon Calling" campaign. This period also saw Avon expand into overseas markets including those of Europe and South America. Overseas markets would hereafter be extremely important for the company. Avon went public in 1964. In the 1970s, women began entering the workforce on a large scale. This had a negative effect not only on Avon but also on the entire direct-selling industry, for two reasons. First, if women were not home during the day, the calls of the representatives would go unanswered. Moreover, a career as an Avon representative no longer represented as unique an opportunity for women as it had in years past.

Many thought that this shift of women into the workforce would spell the end of direct selling as an institution. Avon's initial response to this was to attempt to use the direct-selling business as a "cash cow" to diversify into other businesses. It purchased such well-known brands as Tiffany and Giorgio Beverly Hills, as well as other less-related businesses including Foster Medical, a medical equipment maker; Retirement Inns of America; and Mediplex Group. This strategy produced disastrous results. Each of these divisions was subsequently sold by Avon as it returned to its roots as a direct seller of beauty products. One key strategic change that accompanied this "back-to-basics" move was a change in emphasis on the locus of the sale. Previously, nearly all of Avon's sales took place in one-to-one meetings in the home. However, by the late 1980s Chairman James Preston began encouraging representatives with other jobs to sell the products at work. By 1988, these at-work sales accounted for 25% to 30% of all Avon's sales.[2]

In the mid-1990s, Avon experimented with direct mail. Brochures were sent directly to consumers, who could then purchase from Avon without having to work through a representative. To ensure that the representatives did not feel threatened by this plan, Avon paid them a commission on any sales made in their area, even if the customer was new to Avon. The commission was 20%, about half of what they were normally paid.[3] Customers paid for the cost of shipping the product to their home. The direct-mail experiment was a failure. A subsequent analysis showed that one main reason for the lack of success was that the order sizes tended to be too small to meet Avon's required profit margins.

[2] "For James Preston, It's Still Avon Calling," *The Wall Street Journal,* December 9, 1988.
[3] "Catalogs Help Avon Get a Foot in the Door," *The Wall Street Journal,* February 28, 1992.

In 1999, Andrea Jung was named Avon's first female CEO. Jung had previously been the company's president and head of marketing. Her stated goal as CEO was to lead a "thoughtful transformation" of Avon. Her specific thrusts were:

- strengthening and enhancing Avon's beauty image around the world
- leveraging the equity of the Avon brand into new markets
- building new products and new channels
- accelerating top-line growth
- enhancing the experience of the Avon representatives

Avon Products in 1999

Products

Avon's well-known beauty products—including lipstick, cosmetics, and nail care—made up the core of its product line. The "Avon Color" brand was the leading cosmetics brand in the world. Avon's U.S. products were designed to appeal to the mass market of roughly 25 million U.S. women aged 25–50 with average to below-average household incomes. The products were positioned to deliver high quality and highly innovative products at an outstanding value. As **Table A** shows, Avon's products were priced at or below the levels charged by other mass market beauty companies selling through traditional retail channels.

Avon also had a history of success with its line of fragrance products. Per unit, Avon sold more perfume than any company in the world. Beginning in the late 1990s, the company also launched an effort to enhance its position in personal care products. These products—such as those for hair and skin care—made up almost 50% of the global cosmetics, fragrance, and toiletries (CFT) market, but Avon had traditionally not been a major player. Jung planned significant increases in the research and development budget to solidify, or improve, Avon's position in nearly all CFT product lines.

Sales Force

In 1999, Avon had nearly 500,000 sales representatives in the United States, which represented almost 5% of all Americans employed in direct selling. The profile of the Avon representative was fairly typical of the direct-selling industry. As Avon.com's director of channel integration, Vicki Banchak-Crowell, noted, "From a sales force perspective, Avon's not that different from other direct sellers. Just about all of our U.S. representatives are women, they tend to be in their 30s and 40s and very often sell Avon products as a second job. In fact, the average representative probably spends less than 10 or 15 hours a week selling."

All Avon representatives were independent contractors and not employees of the company. However, Avon employed an extensive sales management hierarchy to recruit, train, and advise them. (See **Exhibit 5** for a picture of the corporate sales organization.) The recruiting function was of particular importance to the company. Like all direct-selling companies, Avon experienced a nearly 100% turnover of its sales force each year.[4]

[4] Of course, this did not mean that every representative left every year. It meant that if the average number of representatives selling Avon in a year was 500,000, then Avon needed to recruit 500,000 new representatives that year just to maintain the size of its sales force.

TABLE A
Avon Products'
Competitive Price
Position

Source: Company records.

Product	Avon	Other Mass (Revlon, e.g.)	Prestige (Lancôme, e.g.)
Lipstick	$ 3–$ 7	$ 6–$ 9	$12–$16
Nail polish	$ 2–$ 4	$ 3–$ 5	$ 8–$12
Anti-aging treatment	$16–$24	$13–$22	$30–$60
Fragrance	$ 20	$ 20	$ 45

EXHIBIT 5
Avon's Sales
Organization

Source: Company records.

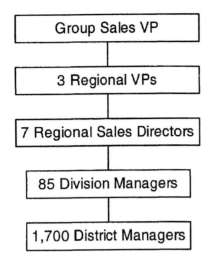

```
┌─────────────────────────────┐
│      Group Sales VP         │
└─────────────────────────────┘
              │
┌─────────────────────────────┐
│      3 Regional VPs         │
└─────────────────────────────┘
              │
┌─────────────────────────────┐
│  7 Regional Sales Directors │
└─────────────────────────────┘
              │
┌─────────────────────────────┐
│    85 Division Managers     │
└─────────────────────────────┘
              │
┌─────────────────────────────┐
│  1,700 District Managers    │
└─────────────────────────────┘
```

Avon was different from the prototypical direct seller in two ways, however: how their representatives were organized, and how they sold. Again, Banchak-Crowell:

> We part ranks from some other direct sellers in that we don't focus our attention solely on network marketing.[5] Most of our representatives are organized into a single level, which frees up their time for selling versus recruiting efforts, although we do encourage and reward recruiting participation within our recognition programs. Of course, this just means that our management team needs to do more recruiting than they do at the network marketing companies. Also, our representatives, while they have the opportunity to utilize a "party plan," as a rule most don't sell in this manner. The picture some people have of a group of women sitting around in someone's family room being pressured into buying lipstick is not what Avon's about. Our representatives tend to sell in one-on-one meetings either at work, over coffee after work or at home where the benefits of the Avon products can really be explained and understood.

As a comparison, about 80% of direct sellers in the United States were organized on a multilevel structure. In these organizations, it was not uncommon for representatives to earn more from the sales of their recruitees than from sales they made on their own. Also, about 50% of direct sellers used a party-plan approach, either exclusively or in conjunction with person-to-person selling.

Selling Process

As independent contractors, Avon's representatives were free to pursue the selling approach that best matched their style. Thus, while the image of Avon had been built around women going door to door selling their products to strangers, this was seldom seen in 1999. According to Edwards:

> It's hard to describe a single "typical" Avon representative. In fact, there are really a couple of different prototypes. On one hand, we have the career Avon representative, our Presidents Club members. These women sell our products full time. They tend to have very long customer lists and have been selling Avon products for a long time. They probably make up about 20% of the representatives. We also have a *lot* of women who sell our products part time. They might have gotten into it because they loved the products but their representative moved or left the business. By becoming a representative, she gets the product at a discount

[5] In a typical network marketing organization, one can earn money in two ways, either via his or her own product sales or by recruiting other people to sell the product and earning commission on *their* sales.

and ensures that her friends at work have access to Avon products. This latter group, though, has a lot of turnover. Selling is not an easy job. A lot of new representatives find out pretty quickly that selling just isn't for them.

This high turnover had another important impact: it created a lot of "stranded customers." These were customers who had previously purchased Avon products from a representative who quit or moved. The company estimated that there were approximately 5 million U.S. customers who fit into this category. Since the representatives were independent contractors and thus "owned" their customer list, the company had very little detailed information on who the end customer was.

Partially in an effort to increase the proportion of women who might consider Avon as a career, the company launched several special programs. The Leadership program allowed a representative to earn additional money by encouraging other women to become Avon sales representatives. This program was somewhat different from those of many other direct-selling organizations in that Avon required a level of personal sales in addition to the sales from those they recruited to ensure eligibility for bonuses. As a result, leadership representatives still spent a great deal of time selling. In 1999, there were 12,000 leadership representatives.

Another program under development in 1999 was the Beauty Advisor program. These representatives would go through special training in order to help them advise their customers on selecting and applying the right beauty and personal care products. This was important because the products looked and performed differently on women of different ages, ethnicities, and skin types. In addition to product and application training, this program incorporated consultative selling skills critical to the success of the advisor. Both of these programs had been designed to expand a representative's earning opportunity and support her efforts to grow her business.

Campaigns

The timing of the selling cycle was dictated by Avon's "campaign" calendar. Each year, Avon ran 26 two-week selling campaigns. For each campaign, the company produced a 150-plus page full-color brochure featuring the products available for sale (see **Exhibit 6** for sample pages). Each brochure contained a core set of products—including, for example, the "Avon Color" line of beauty products—that was featured in every edition of the brochure along with seasonal items of interest (back-to-school items, holiday gifts, summer clothing). In addition to the standard beauty and personal care items, each brochure contained items in other categories including jewelry, toys, collectibles, and clothing.

On average, each active Avon representative participated in 12 of these campaigns per year. "Participation" implied that she purchased a set of brochures, distributed them to her customers, and placed an order. On average, a representative had about 15 customers on her list, though some representatives had upwards of 200 or more. Brochures were sold to representatives on a sliding scale, from $0.56 per brochure in quantities of 10 to $0.19 per brochure for quantities of 100 or more. These fees just covered Avon's cost of designing, producing, and distributing the brochures. An Avon representative received a discount of, on average, 30% to 40% off the retail price of the product listed in the brochure. This discount could sometimes reach 50%. This represented her earnings on the sale.

Selling

The most common way for an Avon representative to find a new customer was through her existing customers. For example, a satisfied customer might mention the name of her representative to a friend who, in turn, might also become a customer. As Banchak-Crowell explained, Avon representatives were also trained to be proactive in their networking:

> The typical Avon representative starting out on day one will call on the circle of people closest to her . . . her friends, relatives, coworkers. These people are certainly not guaranteed

EXHIBIT 6 Sample Pages from Avon Catalog

Source: Avon Company Catalog, Campaign 27, 2000, pp. 5 and 6.

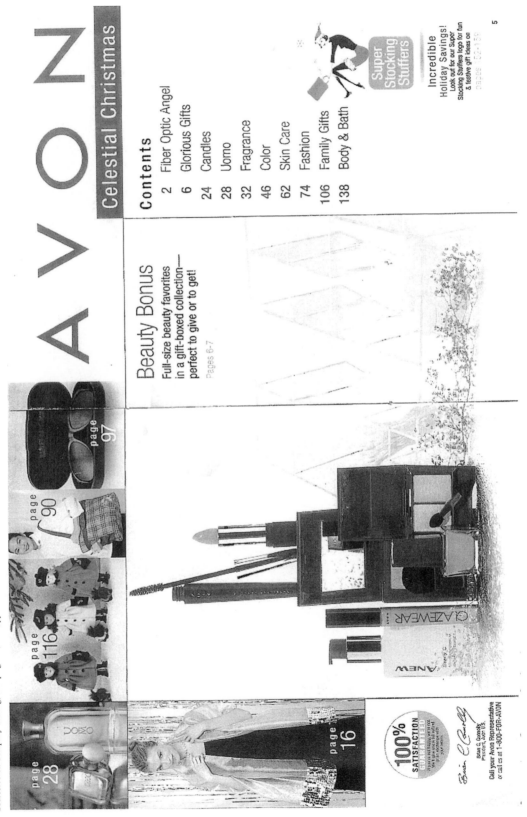

AVON

Celestial Christmas

Contents

Beauty Bonus

Full-size beauty favorites
in a gift-boxed collection—
perfect to give or to get!

Pages 6-7

Incredible
Holiday Savings!
Look out for our Super
Stocking Stuffers logo for fun
& festive gift ideas on

Super Stocking Stuffers

100% SATISFACTION GUARANTEED

Brian C. Connolly
Brian G. Connolly
President, Avon U.S.

Call your Avon Representative
or call us at 1-800-FOR-AVON

453

EXHIBIT 6 (Continued)

Source: Avon Company Catalog, Campaign 27, 2000, pp. 6 and 7.

EXHIBIT 6 (Continued)

Source: Avon Company Catalog, Campaign 27, 2000, pp. 50 and 51.

sales, but they're at least willing to give her a minute of their time to hear what she has to say. Some of them will buy something, and this has two impacts. First, it gives the representative the confidence to keep going. Second, given the quality of our products, this is likely to create a satisfied customer, which in turn creates opportunities for the representative to ask, "Is there anybody else you know that might be interested in this product?" This chain of referrals is really the magic of direct selling.

While Avon still assigned "territories" to some representatives—particularly those in rural areas—most were free to sell to friends, relatives, and colleagues wherever they lived or worked. There were many ways for a representative to distribute the most recent brochure, Banchak-Crowell said:

> Most brochures are distributed in one of three ways. First, many of them are simply handed out by the representative. She might have a core set of customers at work, say, that she makes sure will see the latest copy of the brochure. Also, many representatives have customers that don't live or work right around the corner, and so they mail them out. This is really common for the representatives with bigger customer lists. Finally, a lot of representatives buy extra copies of the brochure and leave them in conspicuous places. For example, I know of a representative who has a sister that owns a hair salon. Her sister lets her put a stack of brochures on the counter, and she's found a few new customers this way. This can get sort of expensive for the average representative but if well thought out can be quite effective.

Logistics

After collecting orders from her customers over the course of the two-week period, the representative aggregated the purchases and placed an order with Avon. To do so, she filled out the 35-page purchase order (see **Exhibit 7** for an example). It was also not uncommon for a representative to order extra quantities of popular items in order to keep an inventory for quick delivery. On average, each customer on a representative's list ordered $20 worth of products per campaign. Avon's costs to process the order were about $4. Of this $4, about $1 covered the processing of the order itself (opening the envelope, feeding it through the automated reader, handling errors, etc.), while shipping the products to the representative accounted for the rest. This did not include the cost of delivering the order via UPS or Fedex to the representative, which was borne by the representative.

The representative generally received the shipment of products about five days after submitting her order to Avon. The shipment arrived in several large boxes, and it was the representative's responsibility to sort the inventory into customer orders and to deliver the items. This delivery generally took place in person, either at the customer's home or work. Some representatives also mailed products to their customers, particularly those who did not live nearby. Avon provided a 100% satisfaction guarantee for both consumers and representatives. If a customer was dissatisfied with a product, the representative was responsible for returning the item to Avon for a refund.

Marketing

In the 1980s, Avon was the target of several hostile takeover attempts. They were all unsuccessful, but they pointed to the attractiveness and power of the Avon brand name. As shown in **Figure A,** surveys done by the company supported this view of the strength of the brand. These results indicated that the majority of U.S. women in their target market believed that Avon products were worth considering for purchase.

Avon's message to customers and representatives was that Avon was the "company for women." Avon's goal was to be perceived as the company that listened to, and truly cared about, the lives of women worldwide. Primary in meeting this goal was the mission of the

EXHIBIT 7   **Sample Page from Avon Purchase Order**

Source: Company information.

Page 5   Campaign 27/2000   Page 5

Column A (Qty. A)

#	Code	Item
1	010-820	Soft Musk
2	011-239	Timeless
3	010-854	Vanilla Soft Musk
4		**PAGES 42/43**
5		COLOGNE SPRAYS
6	106-925	Candid
7	036-971	Fantasque
8	011-679	Night Magic
9	011-650	Odyssey
10	012-307	Sweet Honesty
11	194-708	Topaze
12		VINTAGE COLOGNE SPRAYS
13	052-420	Charisma
14	052-674	Cotillion
15	052-598	Hawaiian White Ginger
16	052-621	Honeysuckle
17	052-435	Occur!
18	052-401	Tasha
19		**PAGES 44/45**
20		BLACK SUEDE
21	083-342	After Shave
22	083-251	Cologne Spray
23	180-470	Deodorant Talc
24	083-950	Shower Soap-on-a-Rope
25		FRIKTION
26	130-201	After Shave
27	080-491	Body Talc
28	107-960	Cologne Spray
29	234-960	Exfoliating Body Bar
30		MESMERIZE FOR MEN
31	137-502	After Shave
32	137-498	Cologne Spray
33	176-835	Deodorant Body Talc
34	060-186	Soap-on-Ja-Rope
35		WILD COUNTRY
36	086-447	After Shave
37	149-502	Cologne
38	056-938	Deodorant Body Talc
39	086-580	Soap-On-A-Rope

Column B (Qty. B)

#	Code	Item
1		**PAGES 46/47**
2		PARTY PERFECT MAKEOVER KIT
3	268-805	Gold
4	268-810	Silver
5		**PAGES 48/49**
6		Order the exact quantity you want (including FREE units).
7		NAIL EXPERTS
8	030-514	Advanced Micro-Cuticle Vanishing Complex
10	168-500	Even Out Base Coat
11	053-025	Liquid Silk Wrap
12	166-603	Speed Dry Top Shine
13	053-154	Strong Results Complex
14	037-629	Tough Enough Base/Top Coat
15		SPEED DRY NAIL ENAMEL
16	067-764	Adoring Rose
17	068-445	Amethyst Shimmer
18	068-369	Brown Pearl
19	068-316	Cafe Au Lait
20	068-684	Carnelia
21	067-889	Cappuccino
22	068-995	Carnival
23	068-392	Creamy Coral
24	067-669	Crystal Calm
25	068-187	Delicate Mauve
26	068-206	Dreamy
27	067-711	Earthly Taupe
28	067-855	Fiesty
29	068-340	Iced Coffee
30	067-860	Innocent Violet
31	068-210	Juicy Plum
32	068-005	Melon
33	068-230	Mocha
34	068-263	Pearly Queen
35	067-908	Petal
36	068-225	Pink Delight
37	068-851	Pink Pearls
38	068-407	Red Red
39	068-737	Red Wine
40	069-069	Rose

Column C (Qty. C)

#	Code	Item
1		**Brochure**
3	067-927	Siren
4	068-282	Smoke
5	068-278	Snowflake
6	069-040	Strawberry
7	067-635	Tranquil
8		**PAGES 50/51**
9		Order Glazewear Liquid Lip Color and Ultra Color Rich Renewable Lipstick on Purchase Order pages 6.
11		Order Split Second Brush Stick and True Color Powder Blush on Purchase Order pages 7.
13		Order Nailwear Nail Enamel on Purchase Order pages 6 & 7.
14		RETRACTABLE
15	181-223	Lip Brush
16		**PAGES 52/53**
17		BEYOND COLOR TRIPLE BENEFIT EYESHADOW
19	034-653	Blue Sky
20	031-984	Cappuccino
21	034-672	Heather
22	031-965	Lace
23	034-539	Limestone
24	031-999	Mink
25	035-152	Petal
26	034-725	Plum Satin
27	034-869	Quartz
28	031-946	Sunbeam
29	034-395	Taffeta
30	032-039	Tiger's Eye
31	032-043	Twilight
32		EYEWRITER LIQUID EYELINER
33	103-380	Beaming Bronze
34	086-959	Black
35	124-578	Clean Slate
36	103-376	Plum Pizzazz
37	103-429	Sparkle Night
38		INCREDIBLE LENGTHS MASCARA
39	006-946	Black
40	007-191	Brown/Black

FIGURE A
Percent of Target Market That Would Buy Avon

Source: Company survey.

Would not buy Avon	12%
Would buy from Avon but not through a rep	18%
Would buy from Avon through a rep	70%

company to provide exciting and lucrative career opportunities for women. Further, Avon had established and supported numerous foundations focused on the health and welfare of women, including the Avon Products Foundation and the Avon Worldwide Fund for Women's Health. The latter had raised nearly $100 million by year-end 1999. The company was probably best known in this regard for its passionate support for the battle against breast cancer. In 1998, it launched the annual Avon Breast Cancer 3-Day Walk, which by 1999 had raised over $20 million to combat the disease. Jung had committed to contributing $250 million to breast cancer awareness by 2003.

Relative to sales, Avon spent very little on traditional advertising. While worldwide sales in 1999 were $5.3 billion, the company allocated just $45 million to advertising and about $12 million to sampling. While U.S. sales were $1.8 billion, Avon spent about $38 million on advertising and $6 million on sampling.

Avon.com

The Early Days: 1997

Avon was one of the first direct-selling companies to venture online. In 1997, it launched Avon.com, which was developed on a budget of less than $400,000. This initial approach to the Web was limited in several ways. First, it was commerce only; there was little community-building or "how-to" information that might have supported Avon's brand positioning. Further, the site provided for direct-to-consumer sales only; there was no role for the representative. Finally, Avon.com sold only beauty products. Other products—which made up about 40% of the company's revenues—were not made available online. This limited functionality was due largely to the fact that Avon viewed the site more as a test of a potential new channel than as a new profit opportunity. For this reason, the company did little advertising of the site and, thus, Avon.com never accounted for a significant sales volume.

Avon.com Take II

By late 1998, it was clear that the Web offered many more opportunities than the company was taking advantage of. Edwards was hired to be president and general manager of Avon.com and charged with the task of formulating the company's Web strategy. Edwards had been with Avon for 17 years and had successfully launched several new business lines for the company. Edwards explained the challenge that he faced: "With the tradition and brand equity of Avon, there were so many directions that we could take with the Web. Did we want to be Eve.com or iVillage, both or neither? The answer was not obvious, but we had to place our bets. There was a sense that we had to act fast."

The Eve.com strategy would be to build a commerce-only site, as Avon.com had largely been since 1997. Eve.com, like Sephora, was a fairly traditional online retailer that carried a variety of high-end cosmetic and fragrance brands. Similarly, in the mass market, companies such as drugstore.com and CVS.com offered brands that one could typically find on the shelves of a local drugstore, including Revlon and L'Oreal. Pursuing this strategy would mean that Avon.com would remain the only well-known branded product being sold online directly from the manufacturer. Still, this seemed like it might fit well with Avon's direct-selling tradition.

On the other hand, the iVillage model was an appealing one. It, like Oxygen.com and women.com, had quickly built massive and active online communities of women. In this role, the sites acted as information exchanges in which women engaged in often deep discussions on a range of topics. This approach was also exciting to Stephen King, vice president of e-commerce:

> The idea of an online community really meshes well with our view of Avon as the "company for women." Since Avon started, the company has been about building relationships, and it seems natural that we would embrace the power of the Web to help women forge relationships beyond their geographic confines. We could easily envision strong communities evolving at both the customer level and at the representative level. Remember, we've got half a million U.S. representatives at any one time. Three in four have access to a computer, and two in three have access to the Web. That could be quite a community.

Edwards felt strongly that the first phase of the project had to be data collection. Thus, he hired a well-known e-commerce consulting firm to help him think through the strategy. He also invited experts in e-commerce from such noncompeting firms as AOL, Yahoo!, and Microsoft to visit Avon and give their opinions on how it should approach the Web. Finally, he held a series of focus groups with representatives in order to get their feedback. In all, he spent about nine months collecting the information that he felt was necessary to come to the right decision.

Edwards's Dilemma

After having collected all of the data, the time had come for Edwards and his team to make a recommendation to the board of directors. There were many issues to resolve. The two major decisions related to how Avon would utilize the Web in its business-to-consumer (B2C) and business-to-business (B2B) relationships.

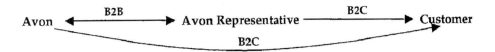

B2C

What, if any, role should the representatives play in Avon.com? While many dot-coms seemed to espouse the view that the New Economy meant that "all the rules had changed," King preferred not to ignore completely the realities of the company's business:

> On the surface, the economics are hard to argue with. We pay 30% to 40% of the retail price to the representative. However, it's not like she isn't working for that money. She finds the prospects, helps them select a product, delivers the product to the customer, and handles any problems after the sale. Could we do all of that for less than $6 or $8 on a $20 lipstick order? I'm not sure.

The decision about how the Avon representative would be integrated into Avon.com, if at all, was not an either-or one. At one extreme, as with the original Avon.com, the site might be a consumer-only venture. At the other extreme, it could copy what some other direct sellers had done and not sell directly to the public at all. In this case, the company might use Avon.com as a content or community site. In between, of course, lay an infinite set of possible configurations.

The role of the representatives, however, was just the first step. Once that had been decided, Edwards had to make recommendations regarding the details behind the strategy.

Commissions Should a representative be paid if her customer bought from Avon.com? If so, how should this commission compare with the standard commission? What should this depend on?

Marketing How would Avon drive people to the Avon.com site? Should it count on the representatives to do it?

Product Which products should it sell on Avon.com? Should it make all of the products in the brochure available or just a subset? Should there be any products that were sold *only* on Avon.com?

Shipping Should the company ship products directly to the customer or maintain for now the traditional method of aggregating the representative's purchases and allowing her to deliver them?

B2B

It seemed to Edwards that the Web ought to be able to help Avon strengthen its relationship with its representatives. Moreover, there was a sense that the "right" way to do things would be to make it easy for representatives to place their orders online rather than filling out the archaic purchase orders with No. 2 pencils. This capability would not come cheaply, however. According to the consultant hired to advise Avon on the project, fully functional online ordering with a seamless link to the legacy inventory and purchasing systems would cost in excess of $60 million over three to five years. This was not necessarily an onerous investment for a company the size of Avon, but Edwards had to convince Jung and the rest of the board that it would be worth it. After all, it would cost only about $3 million to $5 million to simply update the 1997 version of Avon.com to make it a state-of-the-art online store. Moreover, the sheer complexity of the project—integrating it with all of the other existing systems, for example—made the B2B approach a much-riskier proposition.

Part 6

Capturing Value

Chapter 26

Pricing: A Value-Based Approach

Robert J. Dolan

A firm's marketing program is directed to creating value for its customers. Understanding customers' wants is the foundation for building the marketing mix consisting of:

- A product meeting the wants;
- An information program conveying the value of the product to customers;
- A distribution program making the product readily available.

Each part of this value creation process obviously costs money. Pricing's role in the marketing mix is to tap into the value created and generate revenues to: (i) fund the current value creation activities, (ii) support research activities for future products and, for most organizations, (iii) generate a profit from the firm's activities.

A complete pricing program has many components. For example, consider U.S. Pioneer's pricing of its DVD player, model DV-525:

- A unit price to dealers/distributors had to be set
- Accompanying terms and conditions specified, e.g.
    - any quantity discounts
    - when payment was due
    - any discounts for payment in that time interval
    - whether price included shipping or not

Professor Robert J. Dolan prepared this note as the basis for class discussion.

- The Manufacturer's Suggested Retail Price (MSRP) was set at $425.00
- For Christmas season 1999, a $50 consumer rebate was offered for this model
- Terms and conditions set for the rebate.[1]

Thus, in addition to setting the unit price to dealers for the DV-525, Pioneer's pricing policy also included decisions on: (i) terms and conditions governing the sale, (ii) how to "position" the product in its DVD line via the $425 MSRP, (iii) a "sale" offered to consumers for a limited time, (iv) the form that "sale" would take (a direct-to-customer mail in rebate), (v) restrictions on where the "sale" would be available.

Pricing decisions have a broad scope and a highly levered effect on net income. Consider the impact of being able to increase average price received from customers by 1% while still holding unit sales volume. This could be done for example by finding 10% of customers for whom the product was "underpriced" by 10% or 20% for whom it was "underpriced" by 5% and raising prices accordingly. How much would that impact net income? Given a cost structure typical of a large corporation, a 1% boost in price realization yields a net income gain of 12%.[2] Thus, "getting pricing right" is a big deal. However, pricing is often an afterthought in corporate strategy. If:

$$Profits = [Price - Cost]*Unit\ Sales$$

there is often more emphasis on the Cost and Unit Sales parts of the profit equation than Price. Price is seen as "determined by the market" or "something we really don't have much control over." Marketers with this reactive attitude typically miss great profit opportunities.

This note covers some of the important fundamentals behind "pricing right." The three major sections of this note address:

- Determining Customer Value and Sensitivity to Pricing
- Customizing Price to the Value Delivered
- Integrating Price with the Other Mix Elements

The note closes by consideration of important legal and ethical issues.

Determining Customer Value and Sensitivity to Pricing

Pricing should be driven primarily by the value of the product to the customer. There are a number of ways in which this value can be estimated. This value analysis should be complemented by an analysis of just how important price is in the customer's decision making process. This price sensitivity varies markedly across situations.

Consider, for example, an interventional cardiologist preparing to do surgery on a heart patient with an artery blockage. The best solution is to insert a "stent" into the artery to hold back the plaque against the artery walls allowing blood to flow freely again through the artery. There are three major stent suppliers in the market—how important is the price of the stent to the doctor in choosing which one to insert?

Not very. Because this is a life-or-death situation for the patient, product performance is the key. Second, the doctor is a very knowledgeable, sophisticated decision maker, aware of stent features and the advantages/disadvantages of each for various types of blockages.

---

[1] The rebate only applied to bricks-and-mortar retail purchases and at the two Pioneer authorized internet sellers (Crutchfield and Circuit City).

[2] See R.J. Dolan and H. Simon, *Power Pricing,* Free Press, 1997, p. 4 for specific firm examples and discussion.

Third, he or she may have more experience inserting one type of stent or another and would prefer not to shift away from the "usual brand" if it is appropriate for the situation. Finally, perhaps the fact that the doctor is not the one paying for the stent would be an added factor in depressing the sensitivity to price.

Much of this may seem pretty intuitive or common sense. But, a systematic approach can be helpful in judging price sensitivity and seeing how it may even be influenced by marketing efforts. Five major areas to be considered are now discussed in turn.

1. Product Category Factors

Price sensitivity tends to be lower in low cost product categories, e.g., a 10% price differential may not be a big deal when the issue is choosing among hammers in the $5 price range, but a bigger deal when considering $1500 personal computers. Three factors should be considered:

A. Absolute Dollar Cost.

B. Dollar Cost to be a "regular user" of the product. This accounts for purchase frequency. For example, a "no-name" golf ball may cost $2.00 and a Titleist $3.00. But a retired individual playing golf 200 times per year on a water-hazard-filled course may see it as a decision on a yearly supply of three balls per day making it a $1200 versus $1800 decision not a $2.00 versus $3.00 decision.

C. Dollar Cost of item as a percentage of total cost. Particularly in business-to-business situations, it is important to understand the proportion of the total cost represented by the item. The lower the percentage, the lower will be the price sensitivity. Dolan and Simon[3] give the example of a chemical whose use accounted for 50% of the cost of producing heat insulation and 5% of the cost of producing polyesters. A 10% price increase for the chemical would increase the heating insulation manufacturer's total cost by 5%; polyester producer's by only .5%. The polyester producer was less sensitive to any price increases.

2. Who Pays?

Somethings the user of the product pays for; sometimes not (as demonstrated by the interventional cardiologist example). Situations vary from ones wherein the decision maker pays no portion to the cost, to shared cost situations (e.g., the decider pays some percentage of the cost), to cases where the decision maker bears full responsibility. To the extent that the decider is responsible for the costs, the great is the price sensitivity.

3. Competitive Factors

A number of competitive factors influence price sensitivity. Price sensitivity is higher to the extent that:

A. The decision maker does not perceive significant differences in alternative products

B. (A slight variation of #1)—the more knowledge a decision maker is about alternative products and their prices (a corollary of this is that price sensitivity is higher when such information is easy to obtain).

C. It is easy to compare products and their price schedules. Some comparisons are apples-to-apples, e.g., two life insurance policies paying $1 million if the holder dies. Easy comparison on product features highlights price. Price sensitivity is dampened when products are not easily compared (e.g., two disability policies varying in number of days after disability that payments begin, maximum number of days of coverage, and type of

[3] R.J. Dolan and H. Simon, *Power Pricing,* Free Press, 1997, p. 130.

injury/certification required to qualify). Price sensitivity is also dampened when price is hard to compare, viz. price schedules are stated differently, e.g., one vendor is 10¢ per unit consumed in the month, another is 8¢ per unit plus a $10 per month fee.

D. It is easy for the decision maker to switch products. Difficulty in switching can arise for psychological reasons (e.g., a perception of risk and the desire to stick with the familiar brand) or functional ones (e.g., other systems have been set up anticipating being used in tandem with this particular item, loyalty programs such as frequent flyer miles, or investments in training).

4. References Prices

In some situations, the consumer develops a "reference price" which forms the foundation from which the suitability of actual prices is judged. The reference price may be function of: (i) what is seen as "fair" (based perhaps on some estimate of the cost of production), (ii) a competitor's price for a similar item, (iii) the price last paid for the item, and (iv) what others are paying for the item. Reference prices are subjective formulations in the consumer's mind and thus are possibly influenced by many factors including the firm's marketing program. Price sensitivity is greater to the extent that price moves above this "reference" value.

5. Price/Quality Relationships

In some categories, particularly ones in which product quality is difficult to judge by inspection before purchase (e.g., perfume, consulting services), price can be used as cue to product quality. Price being used in this way dampens price sensitivity.

There is no formula to blend these various considerations together but a systematic consideration of these, which may individually point in different directions, helps assess overall sensitivity.

Assessing a Product's Value to Customers

Once price sensitivity is understood, regardless of the summary judgment on how great or small it is, it is important to develop an understanding of the product's value to customers. The major methods of assessing this value, whose applicability varies by situation, are:

- Judgments based on an understanding of the buyer's cost structure.
- Surveys in which customers are asked either directly or indirectly about value.

1. Cost Structure Studies

In a cost structure study, one assesses the "true economic value" (TEV) of a product to a customer by understanding the competitive alternatives, the price and performance of those alternatives, and the buyer's costs.

TEV has two major components:

$$TEV = \text{Cost of the Alternative} + \text{Value of Performance Differential}$$

If the buyer has several alternatives, the calculation has to be relative to the "best" alternative. For example, what is the value of a flight on the Delta Shuttle to a busy advertising agency executive needing to get from Boston to New York? One could calculate the TEV relative to going on the bus; but, this leads to an irrelevant number, as the "best" alternative is the U.S. Air Shuttle, flying essentially the same departure every hour schedule as Delta from the same airport. In this case, the "Value of the Performance Differential" is likely to be very small, as there is little product differentiation. Hence, in this situation, the executive's TEV for Delta would be very close to U.S. Air's price.

This approach is more useful when there is a performance differential to be considered. A product may be superior to the reference alternative in some dimensions, but inferior in others. For example, consider a "reference product" and "new product" with the following characteristics:

	Reference	New
Operating Cost/Hour	$10	$15
Probability of System Crash	20% over one year	1% over one year
Price	$75,000	To be determined

The "New" product has higher operating cost per hour but a significantly lower probability of System Crash.

Consider a customer obtaining a one year useful life of the system and operating it 2500 hours over that time. To assess the TEV of "New" to this potential customer one needs to estimate the cost of a system crash. If this was $100,000 (and both "Reference" and "New" agree to bear the cost of any crash after the first one in the year):

$$\text{TEV} = \text{Price of Reference} + \text{System Crash Savings} - \text{Added Operating Cost}$$
$$= \$75,000 + [.2(100,000) - .01(100,000)]$$
$$\quad - \{[2500 \text{ hours} \times \$15/\text{hour}] - [2500 \text{ hours} \times \$10/\text{hour}]\}$$
$$= \$75,000 + \$19,000 - \$12,500$$
$$= \$81,500$$

While this is the *true* economic value, it may not be the economic value the customer *perceives*. For example, if the customer perceived the cost of a system crash to be only $50,000, the perceived value of "New" would be seen to be $72,000. In many situations, marketing's job is to make the perceived value approach true economic value. This is done by customer education. For example, in this case, "New" would have established the cost of a system crash in the customer's mind and also provide compelling evidence that its probability of failure was only 1% as compared to Reference's 20%. TEV's is important because it usually sets an upper bound to what a customer will pay. It can be the case that the customer perceived the value to be greater than the TEV, e.g., if in the above example the customer perceived the cost of the system crash to be $250,000. The common case though is that marketing's task is to educate the customer to push perceived value up to TEV.

2. Customer Surveys

A second way to assess customer value relies on survey methods. Two fundamentally different methods are commonly used to obtain price response data from customers:

A. Directly ask for reaction to certain prices, price changes, or price differentials.

B. Infer the response from an analysis of data on customers' expressed preference for one product over another.

Direct Price Response Surveys

In a direct response survey, the respondent is typically asked a question such as:

• What is the likelihood you would buy this product at a price of $25?

• At what price would you definitely buy this product?

- How much would you be willing to pay for this product?
- How much of this product would you by at a price of 99¢?
- At which price difference would you switch from product A to product B?

Eastman Kodak Company used this method to set price for a new line of cameras. Respondents were provided a description of a new generation of cameras, presented prices of $150, $80, and $40 and asked to indicate their purchase intention on a seven-point scale, from "Definitely Not Buy" to "Definitely Would Buy." Results were:

Purchase Intention for Camera

	Stated Price of Camera		
	$150	**$80**	**$40**
1. Definitely Would Buy	4%	5%	15%
2.	—	—	2%
3. Probably Would Buy	7%	14%	30%
4.	1%	2%	4%
5. Probably Not Buy	22%	34%	18%
6.	2%	2%	1%
7. Definitely Not Buy	65%	54%	30%

The fact that 47% of people responded at the "probably would buy" level or higher for the $40 price (as opposed to only 19% for the $80 price) was instrumental in Kodak's introducing the line at a suggested retail price of $39.95.

The direct questioning method is simple, easily understood, and inexpensive, but has important limitations for some situations. It can:

- Induce unrealistically high price consciousness in respondents.
- Suffer from bias in that respondents may be reluctant to admit that they cannot afford a premium product or that they "buy cheap." Under these circumstances, they would overstate their willingness to pay.

Preference-Based Inference: Conjoint Measurement

Conjoint measurement is a relatively new but powerful procedure which has been widely applied for both consumer and industrial products and services to overcome some of the limitations of the direct questioning method. It has been used in the pricing and design of many products ranging from computer hardware and software to hotels, clothing, automobiles, and information services.

Its superiority stems from the fact that the questions posed to respondents replicate the realistic scenario of a customer facing an array of competitive alternatives with different features and prices and having to choose among them. For example, in the camera situation a consumer might be asked which is preferred "A" or "B" where features were:

	Camera A	Camera B
Image Size	3 × 5 inch	4 × 6 inch
Camera Weight	1.2 lbs.	1.8 lbs.
Built-In Flash	No	Yes
Price	$75	$100

A series of this type of preference questions for different product profiles yields the input data to a statistical method whose output is the customer's tradeoff of price versus product features.

Customizing Price to Value Delivered

Upon adopting the perspective of pricing-to-value, one quickly realizes that in many cases the value varies markedly across individuals. For example, the value of the latest innovation in golf club technology is more highly valued by someone trying to make a living on the professional tour than it is by even the serious amateur. A number of factors cause value variation across potential customers, e.g.

- The simple matter of taste—some people think Godiva Chocolates are the greatest; others would just as soon have a Hershey bar.
- Knowledge/availability of substitutes—those with access to and knowledge of the availability of the Boston Globe newspaper "on-line" may value home delivery of the "hard copy" less.
- Prices/"deals" made available by substitute providers—one hotel's "50% off for senior citizens" rate on weekends creates value variation by age group for rooms at the hotel adjacent to it. It generally viewed as substitutes, the adjacent hotel's value will be less for those able to access the "special deal" of the competitor.
- Importance of performance differentials to the user—the experienced computer user values speed and storage capacity more than the novice user.
- Ability-to-pay—the executive, retiring after an Internet IPO, simply has more capacity to pay for a high-definition television set than a true television fan of lesser economic means.
- Intensity of use—convenience features on a cell phone are more highly valued by a person using the device regularly as compared to those in "emergency use only" mode.

Since value can vary greatly across customers, part of the pricing program must consider the advisability of customizing prices to the values, i.e., getting those who value the product more highly to pay more for it.

The four primary methods of customizing prices are:

A. **Product line sorting:** This entails offering "high-end" products with many features for the high value customer and more basic models for lower value. For example, most new automobiles come from "stripped" to "loaded" and customers placing high value on the options simply select that option. Generally, the higher featured items yield greater margins.

B. **Controlled availability:** This involves making different prices available only to certain groups. For example, a direct mail operation can vary the prices in the catalog sent into a home depending on past purchasing history. Online sellers have the same ability to "address" prices to individuals. Delivering money-off coupons to selected households for redemption at the point-of-purchase is another method for selective pricing.

C. **Price based on buyer characteristics:** Here, one looks for some characteristic of buyers which correlates with willingness-to-pay. For example, common buyer characteristics observed are:

- Age—children and "senior citizens" discounts
- Institution type—end user versus reseller

D. **Price based on transaction characteristics:** Price is tied to the particular features of the transaction, e.g., when the airline ticket was bought, quantity discounts schemes in which the number of units of material bought impacts price.

Integrating Price with Other Mix Elements

A key to effective pricing is to have pricing's value *extraction* "in synch" with the value *creation* process of the other elements of the marketing mix. For example, when Glaxo introduced its ulcer medication Zantac at a substantial price premium to market incumbent Tagamet, it was still able to become the market leader because the product was superior and Glaxo invested in the marketing effort necessary to communicate that superiority to consumers. In other words, the core product itself established a TEV and Glaxo's marketing effort pushed the customers' perceived value up to TEV. In turn, the high margins generated by the premium pricing funded that marketing effort.

The pricing/marketing spending choices can often be captured in the following 2 × 2 matrix:

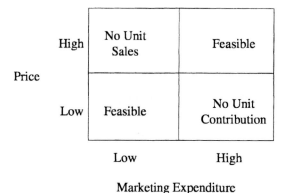

Marketing Expenditure

As shown, two strategies are feasible. The company can follow a low marketing expenditure and low price (relative to TEV) strategy. The product must speak for itself in establishing value; but, because of the low price, the hurdle to purchase is not high. Similarly, it can follow the Zantac "high/high" strategy: investing in marketing to boost perceived value but pricing to capture the perceived value thereby created, attaining the margins necessary to fund marketing effort.

Conversely, the other price/expenditure combinations are not feasible in the long-term. High price/low marketing fails because the perceived values do not get pushed high enough to justify the price; consequently, unit sales are low. Low/price high marketing, on the other hand, generates sales but at unattractive margins.

Legal/Ethical Issues

Pricing is an area which can raise a number of legal and ethical issues whose resolution requires full consideration of the specific context.[4] Only several can be covered in this brief note. Since consideration of price customization has been advocated in this note, it is important to state that it is not illegal to charge different prices for the same product.

[4] See "Ethical Issues in Pricing" by G.K. Ortmeyer in C. Smith and J. Quelch, *Ethics in Marketing,* Irwin, 1993 and Chapter 14, "The Law and Ethics" in T. Nagle and R. Holden, *The Strategy and Tactics of Pricing,* Prentice-Hall, 1995.

Some, however, view the practice as "unfair" or "unethical." Some studies have, for example, shown that poor people, lacking mobility and access to alternative sources, pay higher prices for groceries in local supermarkets. Others have criticized the pricing of pharmaceuticals particularly of life-saving variety, such as AIDS drugs. In some cases, the criticism has been about how high prices are in a market (e.g., United States) versus a neighboring region (e.g., Canada). In others, the criticism has been about too much price similarity across markets, advocating instead very low prices in countries with low per capita incomes and overall low ability to pay.

Legal questions arise whenever pricing actions including price customization are seen as potentially having the impact of reducing competition. Pricing actions with potentially anticompetitive effects include:

- Predatory pricing—price "low" for a time to drive a competitor from the marketplace
- Pricing fixing—setting prices in a cooperative agreement with competitors
- Price maintenance—requiring that distributors/retailers of goods sell only at a specified price level. One may *suggest* reseller prices (as noted for Pioneer at the beginning of this note), but may not *require* that such prices be maintained.
- Price customization—charging competing resellers of a product different amounts so as to reduce one's ability to compete (this has been alleged by mom-and-pop pharmacies as drugs are sold to big chains at lower prices).

A company can be charged by the government and/or sued by customers or competitors for anticompetitive acts. The situation is not easy to navigate, e.g., one observer noted ". . . when pricing tactics are illegal is not always clear. The laws themselves are vague."[5] This means that pricing practices need to be subjected to both investigation from an ethical perspective and informed legal review within the company before being implemented.

[5] T. Nagle and R. Holden, ibid., p. 386.

27

Pricing and Market Making on the Internet

Robert J. Dolan   Youngme Moon

Introduction

The emergence of the Internet raises important price management issues. Many observers see the Internet creating downward pressure on price levels. Potential buyers can speedily search the net, perhaps employing shopping agents to check prices. These low consumer search costs will lead to greater price competition and ultimately lower prices and better value for customers. Some have proclaimed that the Internet economy means "inflation is dead—dead as a doornail" or even "an era of negative inflation."[1]

The specter of price pressure and resulting slashing of margins has cooled many's enthusiasm for e-commerce. They perceive doing business on the Internet to be a necessary evil. Thus, an important question is whether lower prices and margins are the inevitable conclusion of doing business on the Internet—in all situations, in some, and can the seller do anything about it? In addition, there is a second, more general issue. The same technology behind customer search power enables other important phenomena driving how the e-commerce market operates, e.g., the Internet:

- Facilitates a buyer's acquisition of quality information for various goods.
- Enables suppliers to update prices dynamically in response to observed demand.

[1] W.A. Sahlman, "The New Economy Is Stronger Than You Think," *Harvard Business Review,* November–December 1999, pp. 99–107 and J.N. Sheth and R.S. Sisodia, "Consumer Behavior In the Future," in *Electronic Marketing and the Consumer,* R.A. Peterson, ed., SAGE Publications, 1997.

Professor Robert J. Dolan and Professor Youngme Moon prepared this note as the basis for class discussion rather than to illustrate either effective or ineffective handling of an administrative situation.

- Allows a seller to create a meaningful market of potential buyers with price being the outcome of an auction process rather than prespecified by the seller.
- Permits a prospective buyer to specify in detail the product's requirements and put fulfillment out to bid to an organized market of potential sellers.

These impacts may be more fundamental than any effect of more customer price information. They change how exchanges between buyers and sellers take place. The how of a transaction, i.e., the connecting a buyer and a seller has many forms.

For example, consider a couple buying a new home:

- During a break in the home hunting trip, they walk into a McDonald's, see 99¢ as the *posted price* for a hamburger and decide whether to buy it or not.
- Finally finding a desirable house, they hear the seller's $695,000 "asking price" and begin to *negotiate* downward from that price.
- Having bought the house, they go off to an Estate *Auction* to bid on needed furniture.
- Needing to move some personal belongings to the new home, they contact several moving companies *requesting proposals*. The companies submit *bids* for meeting the couple's requirements.
- Needing to come up with a down-payment for the house, they instruct their broker to sell 500 of their shares of IBM stock on the New York Stock *Exchange*.

The couple has thus transacted through five different market mechanisms. These same five market mechanisms can be found in business-to-business situations in the real world and also on the Internet. The Internet makes certain ways of transacting more broadly feasible. As shown in **Figure 1,** the mechanisms are of three fundamentally different types. Type I is the set price mechanism. Within this, there are two subclasses. First is the I(a)

FIGURE 1   **Three Types of Marketing Making Mechanisms**

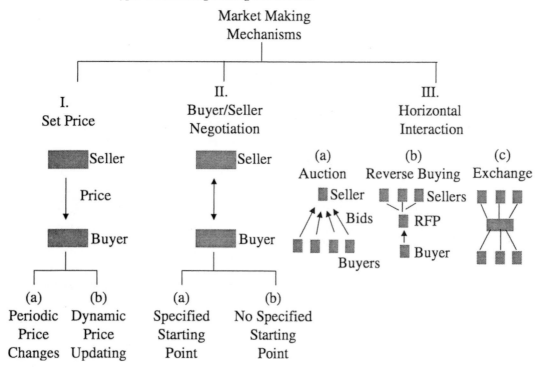

situation shown where prices are updated only periodically, like at McDonald's. A second subclass is shown as I(b) wherein the set of "take it or leave it prices" is updated continually, e.g., as the airlines do. Type II is the negotiated price mechanism. In a negotiated price situation, there can be either: II(a) a specified starting point for the negotiation (e.g., the seller's asking price on a house, the dealer's "list price" on a new car) or not, II(b). Type III is a class of mechanism which relies on competition across buyers and sellers to produce prices. Here there are three subclasses.

In an auction system, III(a), the seller does not specify a price, but, rather provides an item which buyers compete for the right to buy in a bidding process. III(b) is "reverse buying" where the customer takes the lead in organizing the pricing process. An example of this is when the buyer develops a Request for Proposal on an item or service and price is determined via a competition involving a bidding process among potential sellers. This is termed a "Reverse Auction." Finally, in III(c), there is a coming together of multiple buyers and multiple sellers and a price determined by the interaction on an exchange to "clear the market."

One impact of the interactive nature of the Internet is that market mechanisms of type III can be very efficiently organized. For example, the owner of a 1955 Coca-Cola sign could not really conduct a nationwide auction for that single item pre-Internet. The Internet, and sites such as eBay, make this possible. Generally, the Internet makes the choice of market mechanism a salient question in many situations. The challenge of managing price on the Internet is not only how to set price in an era wherein the consumer has more information; but also, how to select the most advantageous combination of market making mechanisms via which to transact exchanges.

This note describes the operation of each of the three market mechanisms on the Internet. We describe the rationale for each, examine the determinants of economic efficiency, and assess pressure—upward or downward—on prices. The goal is to provide insight to guide price management, not only in a set price situation but also to illuminate when an alternative market mechanism is desirable. Throughout the note, reference will be made to currently operating sites of interest.

Type I: The Set Price Mechanism

Are Set Prices Lower on the Internet?

In the "set price" scenario (see Figure 1, Type I), the seller simply sets a fixed price, and the buyer is expected to either accept or reject that price. Negotiation is not an option; the seller's attitude is "take it or leave it." This mechanism has some advantages, viz. (i) low transaction costs (no haggling, for example), and (ii) perception of fairness (since every buyer must pay the same price).

Numerous Internet retailers, including Amazon.com and eToys.com, have adopted fixed pricing mechanisms. These leading Internet retailers are often perceived as having *lower* fixed prices than their real-world counterparts. Indeed, as mentioned above, the conventional wisdom is that the Internet tends to drive prices down, primarily because online consumers have easier access to accurate information about the market.

In traditional retail markets, buyer ignorance is often a source of profit for companies. Firms set prices with reasonable confidence that the majority of buyers is unlikely to spend a large amount of time and effort comparison shopping. But on the Internet, several factors have begun to bite into this "ignorance premium." For one thing, potential buyers no longer have to physically travel from store to store in search of the best deal; rather, they can comparison shop a number of websites from the comfort of their own computer. In addition, a number of Internet search tools have made online comparison shopping even more efficient.

These search agents (also called "bots" or "spiders") can theoretically compare prices and features across every available retailer on the Internet. Of course, none of the existing tools are currently capable of searching the entire Web universe, and several online merchants have even succeeded in "blocking" search agents from mining their sites for data. Nonetheless, these search agents are becoming increasingly sophisticated. Some of the more popular tools include:

- **Third-party price comparison sites.** Price comparison sites like MySimon.com, Compare.Net, and DealTime.com perform automatic price and feature comparisons in a matter of seconds. Potential buyers simply visit the site, indicate the item of interest, and the search agent scans product and pricing information from a list of hundreds of online sellers stocking the item. Many of these sites charge merchants a fee to be part of their searches. Other sites, such as MySimon.com, earn a commission every time a buyer accesses a merchant site and ultimately buys an item, through the search.

- **Third-party price comparison agents.** Imagine someone infiltrating the checkout line at an OfficeMax, peeking into people's shopping baskets, and telling them exactly how much money they could be saving on the same products at Staples. Several companies including ClickTheButton, DealPilot, and R U Sure have developed a new breed of online search agents that do exactly that: Offer shoppers better deals on whatever merchandise they happen to be viewing on a Web page. Once a user has downloaded software from one of these agent services, the software is activated anytime the user's Web browser is open. A consumer viewing a book on, say, Amazon.com, is then automatically given price comparison information on the same book from competing retailers.

- **Retailer price comparison agents.** Some online merchants have become so resigned to the prospect of comparison shopping that they offer their customers a comparative pricing feature *within* their own websites, as a means of building customer trust. Online computer merchant NECX, for example, offers buyers a "Price Comparison" feature. Click on the price comparison, and the buyer finds the competitors' price of the item being considered at NECX. In some cases, these competitive prices are lower than NECX's and for those shoppers wishing to take their business to one of these competitors, NECX even provides a direct link.

Classic economic theory predicts that if electronic tools allow consumers to comparison shop more easily, the end result will be greater price competition and ultimately, downward price pressure. A number of high-profile, "zero margin" Internet businesses seem to be bearing this prediction out. For example, Buy.com pioneered the strategy of selling products at or below cost to lure customers, aiming to make money eventually by selling advertising on its website. Its proprietary software works 24 hours a day to gather millions of prices for books, CDs, computer hardware and software, and other products from hundreds of competitors. In order to circumvent attempts to "block" its gathering of price information from competitors' sites, Buy.com enlists hundreds of individual, anonymous accounts from Internet Service Providers to conduct its price comparison searches. All of this technology is designed to sniff out the cheapest bargains online and help the company deliver on its advertising promise to have "the lowest prices on earth."

Critics have described Buy.com's business model as "selling dollar bills for 99 cents," and in one year, the cost to Buy.com of the products it sold actually *exceeded* the amount of sales it generated by several million dollars. But the company's phenomenal growth spawned a host of zero-margin imitators. Onsale.com, the Internet auction company, recently launched an AtCost model built around a similar pricing strategy. Free-PC made a splash in 1998 by "giving away" computers to consumers who agreed to view advertisements every time they used their computer.

But despite these rather conspicuous examples, there is to date no conclusive evidence that prices on the Internet are lower per se than prices in conventional outlets. In fact, the results of studies conducted on Internet pricing have yielded mixed results.[2]

Some of the most popular online retailers do *not* offer the lowest prices. Clearly, merchants are able to leverage other dynamics—such as branding and trust, a quality shopping "experience," and customer lock-in—to maintain healthy margins on products.

Branding and Trust

Branding and trust may take on added importance in electronic markets for several reasons. First, buyers are often purchasing from sellers they have not seen and whose physical location is either unknown to the buyer or quite distant. Second, most online transactions are not instantaneous; they typically involve a delayed exchange of money and goods. Buyers usually have to submit their payment and then trust that they will receive their goods in a timely fashion. Third, a significant percentage of buyers may be purchasing goods online for the first time; this may lead to heightened concerns about being "ripped off." Assurances from credit card companies about protection offered to buyers may reduce some of these concerns. However, for all of these reasons, online consumers may still be willing to pay a premium to purchase a product from a retailer they are familiar with, rather than risk dealing with an unknown seller.

Conversations with managers from price comparison sites support this view. These managers point out that many of the shoppers using their sites to compare prices end up purchasing items from branded retailers such as Amazon.com, even when they are given information about dozens of other retailers offering lower prices.[3] In fact, Amazon.com reportedly gets two-thirds of its business from returning shoppers. And some online companies feel so strongly about the importance of building consumer confidence, they are refusing to compete on price alone. For example, although NECX raised eyebrows when it began offering the built-in price comparison tool that seemed to encourage its customers to shop elsewhere, it argues that the feature reinforces consumer trust. As proof, it claims a 30% *increase* in business since launching the feature.

The Shopping Experience

As in the brick-and-mortar world, online retailers offering similar products and prices may differ significantly across a variety of other dimensions. Some websites are simply easier to navigate than others, for example. The most sophisticated shopping sites offer a number of features that contribute to the shopping experience, such as:

- superior product information;
- sophisticated search tools;
- extensive product reviews from experts and other customers;
- product samples (e.g., music clips, book chapters)
- product recommendation tools;
- convenient check-out services.

All of these features contribute to the creation of a particular shopping environment that affects the likelihood that customers will enjoy shopping at the site. Firms that successfully leverage these features may be able to charge a price premium.

[2] Smith, M.D., Bailer, J., and Brynjolfsson, E., "Understanding Digital Markets: Review and Assessment," forthcoming in *Understanding the Digital Economy* (E. Brynjolfsson and B. Kahin, eds.), MIT Press.

[3] "Call your agent for online shopping," *Information Week,* December 7, 1998.

Lock-in

Lock-in refers to mechanisms that increase customers' switching costs. Sometimes lock-in occurs simply as a result of familiarity with a particular website. Rather than incur the switching costs associated with learning how to navigate a new website, customers may choose to pay a higher price to avoid this inconvenience. In other cases, firms explicitly attempt to increase lock-in by creating additional incentives for repeat customers. Frequent buyer programs, such as that marketed by Netcentives, are a good example of this. Other, less obvious, mechanisms include personalization features such as individualized shopping lists, customized interfaces, and "one-click" ordering accounts.

One company that has managed lock-in particularly well is Dell Online. While first-time visitors are greeted with Dell's standard website, for its most valuable corporate customers Dell has developed hundreds of *customer-specific* webpages. These Dell Premier Pages not only display specific computer configurations that have been pre-approved by the customer's firm, but they display prices that reflect negotiated discounts. Detailed account purchasing reports and inventory analyses are also customized for these customers. As a result, Dell's Premier Pages have become management control tools for its customers, who use the customized webpages as a means of enforcing product standards and increasing internal efficiencies. Dell's prices may not be the lowest in the industry, but the company has succeeded in creating extremely high switching costs for its most valuable customers.

Dynamic Pricing

Figure 1 describes another set price mechanism in which posted prices are continually updated (Type Ib). Of course, dynamic pricing is not new. Airlines, for example, often have dozens of different fares paid by passengers on a given flight. These fares depend on a number of variables, including how early customers booked their flights, inventory of available seats at the time of booking, what restrictions they were willing to accept, their travel history, etc. The hotel and car rental industries have followed suit, adopting the airline industry's yield management principles. Grocery stores also employ dynamic pricing using "smart" cash registers. These cash registers automatically offer customers discounts (e.g., cents-off coupons) depending on their purchases. Even soft drink companies are experimenting with vending machines that charge different prices depending on the weather (the hotter the temperature, the higher the price).[4]

On the Internet, the opportunities for dynamic pricing are even greater, for at least two reasons:

- **Customer Information.** While the Internet has made it easier for customers to collect information about products and prices, it has also made it easier for *sellers* to gather information about *customers*. This information can be used to more accurately determine how much individual customers are willing to pay for certain goods.
- **Lower Menu Costs.** Menu costs refer to the costs associated with making price changes. For example, every time a traditional catalog retailer decides to change prices, it must incur the costs associated with reprinting its catalog. On the Internet, lower menu costs increase the likelihood that retailers will change prices more frequently.

Add to these factors the fact that technology has made it easier for online retailers to check the prices of their competitors, and the end result is that online prices tend to be more dynamic than prices in conventional settings. As one online computer merchant has advertised:

---

[4] *Revenue Management*, R.G. Cross, Broadway Books, 1997 discusses the broad applicability of yield management/dynamic pricing techniques across industries.

When you shop at eCOST.com, you don't have to wonder if you're getting a great value on what you need. . . To make sure we are offering you the best price at all times, we update our prices at least once a day, and more often as needed. . . When you visit eCOST.com, you can be sure you are getting the latest information available.

—eCOST.com website

Dynamic pricing can be implemented in a variety of ways. Firms can simply update prices frequently, as in the eCOST.com example. Firms can also engage in various forms of price customization, where different customers are charged different prices, as in the airline example.

On the Internet, price customization has many forms:

- Online retailers can track the clickstreams of customers, instantaneously making special offers based on online activity.
- Other retailers rely on their extensive customer databases to "micromarket" customized offers to customers based on their past purchase behavior, often using personalized email.
- A smaller number, such as Dell's Premier Pages, enact price customization by establishing different "storefronts" that reflect variable pricing schemes.
- Others use price comparison technology to develop instantaneous "price-matching" systems. When a customer visits the website directly, he sees the prices which have been regularly posted. However, if the customer uses a third-party search tool to compare prices among a number of competitors, the prices automatically drop. As a result, customers that access the website via the price comparison tool get a lower price than customers who access the website directly.

This movement to price customization is pursued widely and when well implemented can offset the added customer information on prices. The ultimate form of price customization is customization directly to the buyer's willingness-to-pay. That is pursued on the Internet via auctions which will be addressed fully later in this note.

Type II: The Buyer/Seller Negotiated Price Mechanism

Negotiations, big and small, are commonplace in the real world. Agents negotiate the price of star athletes' services with teams. A buyer haggles over the $2.00 asking price for a set of six chipped saucers at a Saturday morning yardsale. Some buyers like the negotiation or bargaining process, perceiving it as a route to a "good deal." Others detest it. This latter segment has grown large enough that it has prompted the institution of the option of "no haggle" pricing in some historically negotiation situations. For example, General Motors institutionalized "no haggling" for its Saturn model and many dealers of other vehicles have adopted "Saturn pricing" either on a full-time basis or for special sales events.

However, a supplier's expressing a willingness to negotiate can attract certain customer groups. It can also offer an additional way in which the seller can customize the price to the individual buyer.

Historically, the negotiation mechanism has had some disadvantages compared to Type I: Set Price. For example, in a negotiation situation:

(i)   it typically takes longer to complete the transaction;
(ii) the price aspect of the transaction can become highlighted dominating the buyer-seller interaction and squeezing out presentation of the product features and value;
(iii) for negotiation to be effective, the customer contact person must have some degree of pricing authority.

The Internet provides an efficient mechanism for buyer/seller(s) interaction alleviating each of these problems. For instance, to overcome disadvantage (iii), the seller can develop an intelligent agent to simulate the process of person-to-person negotiation. Several general purpose and many special purpose negotiation sites have operated on the Internet.

For example, NexTag.com was a site of market mechanism type II(a)—negotiation with a specified starting price. To illustrate the process, consider a customer wishing to buy a Palm V. To start, NexTag produces the "seller price" from a number of vendors. In one buying experience at the site, there were ten potential sellers sorted by "seller price" ranging from $288.98 to $437.12. Entering a ship-to zip code added the supplier's shipping and tax to yield a comparison of out-of-pocket or "Total Price." If the price from any seller was acceptable, the customer just purchased the item. (We have just reverted to a Type I mechanism.) However, if no price was acceptable, Step 2 was to "Enter Your Own Total Price" and select the suppliers to whom this information or counteroffer was conveyed. At this point, the buyer is under no obligation; e.g., the buyer could enter $275.00 but is not obligated to buy the product if a supplier accepted that price. The process could then follow the real world negotiation process. Sellers respond to the "total price" offered by the buyer. Some seller responses were automated, viz. as the NexTag site put it, "If a seller's systems has been fully integrated with NexTag.com, you may see an immediate response to your offer . . ." Sellers could send a message along with their price counteroffer. As in the real world, the seller's response could be more complex than just a price offer; it could be for a substitute item (e.g., a Palm III not a V) or include other goods (e.g., hold on price but throw in software). NexTag provided a "price history" of completed transactions for the item to help the buyer in the negotiation. This "price history" also served to indicate to the buyer what a reasonable offer might be, to help keep the system from being clogged with fruitless bargain hunting.

This transition of the negotiation process to the Internet overcomes many of the disadvantages of negotiations in the real world. From a customer's point of view, negotiation can be done with multiple suppliers at once. Because response is immediate in many cases, the transaction can still close quickly even with multi-supplier negotiation. The customer is always in control and not subject to unwanted persuasion attempts such as many have encountered trying to end a real world negotiation about a car purchase. The advantage to the seller is that the dialog about price provides information about the buyer which can be used to customize prices.

Other sites offered variations on the theme. For example, Make Us An Offer offered "Real-Time Online Haggling" hosted by an animated "artificially intelligent sales agent" named Chester. It positioned itself as a solution to the delayed respond time of other sites such as the auction site eBay, as bid responses are delivered "within seconds." Hagglezone "where everything is negotiable" featured six hagglers with "unique personalities, moods and tendencies." A buyer chose the haggler to deal with. Hagglezone emphased the fun/entertainment aspects of buying. Its television ad campaign humorously showed a women attempting to haggle in a traditionally set price format (a supermarket) as the customer behind her became upset given the time involved in completing the transaction.

Some special purpose sites simulated face-to-face negotiations for a particular product category. For example, Adoutlet brought together media buyers and sellers displaying available inventory, e.g., a one-page ad for a particular issue of Mac World at its "rate card" price. The buyer then made an offer which the seller responded to with "accept, reject, or hold" (hold meaning the seller wants to wait and see if other offers come in or not). If not accepted, the potential buyer was free to make another offer.

Buying-Power Based "Negotiations"

A common negotiation tactic in the real world is to stress the size of the order at issue or even increase the quantity of goods to be purchased as a mechanism to get the price down, e.g., "I'll take both the white and blue set of chipped dishes if you give them to me for

$1.50 each." Even this "buying power" tactic has an analog on the Internet. Sites such as Accompany and Mercata aggregate the demand from different customers, who are unknown to one another, to use in "negotiating" lower prices. Accompany called itself the "Get It Together Network." Rather than truly negotiating lower prices as buyers come together, Accompany had pre-determined a set of quantity discount schedules with its "Supplier Partners." These discount schedules were provided to buyers at the site. For example, for the Palm V on December 1, 1999 at 1:40 P.M., the price schedule off the Manufacturer's Suggested Retail Price of $399.00 was:

Number of Buyers	Price
0–5	$304.95
6–10	$297.95
11–20	$290.95
21–50	$279.95
51–126	$267.95

At that point in time, 74 buyers had already signed up so that "tier 5," the last price tier of $267.95, was already hit. Consequently, a new buyer arriving at the site could join the 74 already committed to the item knowing that $267.95 would be the price paid. In contrast, when buyer #8 signed on, only "tier 2" had been reached so he or she agreed to pay up to $297.95 but with the prospect of the price declining as more users signed on for the deal. This is precisely what happened, driving the price for all buyers down to $267.95 per unit (in contrast to a $299.99 price the same day at egghead.com).

The Internet creates situations in which this Type II mechanism is feasible. Some buyers prefer the option to "haggle." Sellers have the ability to automate the process on their side via intelligent agents, yielding more price customization opportunity. Thus, for at least some segment of the market, this mechanism will likely be operative as the market mechanism itself provides value to buyers.

Type III: Auctions and Exchanges

Figure 1 displays three types of pricing mechanisms involving *horizontal* interactions between buyers and sellers. In Type II, negotiations, it was one-on-one vertical negotiation between entities at different levels of the marketing system that drove prices. In these three cases, competition across buyers and/or sellers produces prices that can be highly variable across transactions. In the case of the "classic auction" model (Type IIIa), competition across buyers leads to a price. In the case of the "reverse buying" model (Type IIIb), competition across sellers leads to a price. And in the case of "exchanges" (Type IIIc), multiple buyers and multiple sellers interact to set prices.

III(a): Classic Auctions
In the classic auction a vendor puts items up for sale and would-be buyers are invited to bid in competition with each other. Bidding can take a number of forms, e.g., sealed bid or open. Most common is the ascending price format wherein the highest bidder "wins" the item. As more potential buyers become involved, there is upward pressure on prices.

Classic auctions differ from other pricing mechanisms in several fundamental ways. In contrast to "take it or leave it" pricing, classic auctions involve a flexible pricing scheme in which prices are *tailor-made for each transaction*. Moreover, in a fixed price system, the item can sit unsold. In an auction the price moves to a level where the item is sold. And in contrast to negotiated selling in which a seller bargains with an individual buyer, classic auctions bring buyers together in *competition* with one another. They are basically demand aggregation models that function to deliver the best price for the seller, given the market demand the seller has been able to assemble.

Classic auctions have existed for hundreds of years, typically in situations where the value of the product is (i) difficult to determine, (ii) a matter of private taste and opinion, or (iii) highly variable depending on market conditions. For example, the world-famous auction houses of Sotheby's and Christie's both date back to the 1700's and specialize in the sale of antiques, artwork, and other fine collectibles—products whose value is almost impossible to determine prior to the actual sale.

Until a few years ago, classic auctions—while the predominant mode in certain industries (e.g., the famous Dutch Fresh Flower Auctions, the Thoroughbred Horse Auctions in Kentucky)—tended to be a niche phenomenon. They also tended to be concentrated in highly specialized agricultural and commodities markets. The interactive nature of the Internet has changed all of that; indeed, auctions constitute some of the most popular sites on the Web. Their popularity has largely been driven by the fact that the Internet increases the economic efficiencies associated with auction models. More specifically, for suppliers the Internet has not only lowered the search costs associated with finding a critical mass of buyers in the market, but it has also lowered the costs associated with making inventory available to buyers on an immediate basis. For buyers, the Internet has lowered the costs associated with accessing hard-to-find items, and finding other buyers who share common interests.

The Internet Lowers the Search Costs for Sellers Looking for Buyers

In traditional markets, sellers face significant hurdles associated with "finding" a critical mass of buyers in a large, unorganized open market. In order to access these potential buyers, they often have no choice but to incur significant marketing costs. In some cases, geographical dispersion precludes the efficient organization of potential buyers altogether. An auction can be risky because it is not clear that at any one time the market of potential buyers can be brought together.

The Internet, however, has produced a number of "market-makers" that have been able to pool together significant numbers of potential buyers without having to deal with physical search and travel costs. These market makers set up the infrastructure which individual sellers can plug into.

Indeed, in the Web universe, several factors make it easy to transform "niche" market segments into "mainstream" market segments. First, the global reach of the network provides a much greater pool of potential buyers to draw from. Second, reduced search costs make it easier to identify small pockets of people with highly-specialized needs. Finally, reduced communication costs make it easier to establish and sustain relationships with these segments.

The end result is a situation in which firms are discovering that there is significant value associated with simply aggregating demand among these market segments. Some of the busiest sites on the Web are those fulfilling this market-making function, in three settings: the consumer-to-consumer, business-to-consumer, or business-to-business context.

The Internet Lowers the Costs Associated with Making Inventory Available to Buyers Immediately

When it comes to excess merchandise—such as surplus, refurbished, or closeout computer merchandise—the need to liquidate inventory has traditionally been a problem for suppliers. Internet auctions, however, allow suppliers to make this inventory available to buyers on an immediate, and continually updated, basis. When sellers make errors forecasting demand for perishable inventory, instantaneous auctions mitigate the costs associated with such errors.

Of course, sellers who choose to dispose of surplus goods via auction must accept the uncertainty associated with dynamic pricing. However, for many sellers, this uncertainty is easily worth the cost-savings associated with quick inventory turnover: online auctions generally move goods much more quickly than direct sales, catalogs, or off-line auctions. In addition, firms that use auction mechanisms to liquidate surplus goods are able to bypass liquidation brokers who tend to pay fire sale prices. As a result, auctions—particularly business-to-consumer auctions—are becoming an increasingly common mechanism by which firms adjust inventory levels.

For Buyers, the Internet Lowers the Costs Associated with Accessing Hard-to-Find Items

In the past, buyers searching for hard-to-find items had very restricted choices, regardless of whether those items consisted of collectibles and memorabilia, or closeout computer hardware. In the former case, hobbyists were left to either scan local classified listings or make the rounds among a few, scattered dealers who specialized in such merchandise. In the latter case, bargain-hunters typically had to choose from the limited supply of surplus goods carried by their local computer retailer. In both cases, even when buyers were able to find what they were looking for, prices tended to be non-negotiable.

Internet auctions have significantly increased the options available to buyers in the market for hard-to-find items. Indeed, the online classic auction houses not only aggregate demand for sellers, they aggregate *supply* for buyers. In this sense, they have become convenient "one-stop shopping" sources for buyers in this market. A collector looking for a rare Beanie Baby now has a myriad of online auction choices; similarly, a home-office worker looking for a deal on a 17" computer monitor can now bid on dozens of such monitors online. Moreover, buyer choices are not limited to the big auction firms. Niche auction companies have sprung up all over the Web, covering every product category imaginable.

The Interactive Nature of the Internet Facilitates the Creation of Buying Communities

While the economic efficiencies afforded by Internet auctions have no doubt played a large role in their popularity, it is impossible to overlook another factor that has contributed to their success: Auctions are "fun." Indeed, online auctions owe at least some of their popularity to the fact that they have become choice destinations for bargain-hunters who derive significant pleasure from the "thrill of the hunt." In this regard, it is important to reiterate that classic auctions do not necessarily lead to bargain prices; on the contrary, the competitive dynamic tends to push prices upward (the "winner," after all, is typically the individual willing to pay the highest price).

Classic auctions on the Internet also have had a distinctly social component that most successful auction sites not only recognize, but promote. They provide an online forum where buyers and sellers can become acquainted, discuss topics of common interest, and exchange information about one another. A typical example: Members of the eBay community who met while trading in the Elvis category have forged such strong relationships that they now gather to make annual pilgrimages to Graceland together. As Meg Whitman, eBay's CEO explains, this community-building dynamic is impossible to replicate off-line:

> Whereas so many of the Internet companies in existence had borrowed something that existed off-line and translated it into an online version, [eBay] is actually the creation of something that could not be done in the real world.[5]

Types of Classic Auctions

Classic auction firms on the Internet can be roughly categorized into three groups: consumer-to-consumer sites that conduct auctions in which both the sellers and the buyers are individuals; business-to-consumer sites that conduct auctions for businesses wishing to sell products to consumers; and business-to-business sites that conduct auctions in which both the sellers and the buyers are businesses.

[5] From *eBay, Inc.,* HBS case #700-007.

Consumer-to-Consumer Auctions

In 1999, the total consumer-to-consumer auction market on the Internet was estimated to be about $2.3 billion (sales), and expected to grow to $6.4 billion by 2003.[6] And while most activity in this category was in collectibles, antiques, memorabilia, and second-hand goods, the amount of variety was growing.

Typically, a firm acted as an electronic intermediary, connecting sellers with a pool of buyers. This intermediary generated the bulk of its revenues from seller fees, complemented by some advertising and buyer fees. eBay was the runaway leader in this category. In late 1999, it had over 7 million registered users who at any given time found up to 3 million items at auction, ranging from placemats to cars to homes. eBay collected a modest fee from sellers in exchange for listing an item, ranging from $0.25 to $2. It also collected a seller's fee, i.e., a percentage of the sale ranging from 1.25% to 5%. From the seller perspective, the fees were a bargain compared to the $50 it would typically have cost them to post a traditional classified ad for a week. And from the company perspective, the commissions may seem tiny, but they add up: eBay had net revenues of $225 million, and net income of $11 million, for 1999.

One of the biggest challenges facing consumer-to-consumer auction businesses was fraud. Because firms served only as intermediaries, they exerted little direct control over the sellers posting items. The most common complaint came from buyers who paid for merchandise, only to have the seller disappear without delivering the goods. eBay, however, has implemented some elegant (albeit imperfect) ways to address some of these potential hazards. On its site, regular sellers establish a "reputation" for reliable delivery and quality through a ratings system based on comments from previous buyers who have transacted with the seller. Bidders can not only browse through these comments and ratings, but they can also add their own feedback, based on their experience. Extensive chatboards also let eBay-ers share tips and gossip. In effect, the company relies on the users themselves to establish trust between buyers and sellers. Its fraud rate is subsequently very low: 25 out of every million transactions. Note that this reputation-building system not only promotes "community," but it increases the switching costs for both buyers and sellers.

eBay faced many competitors including Yahoo! auctions and Auction Universe. And, recognizing an opportunity to leverage its already existing customer base, Amazon.com jumped into the auction business in the spring of 1999. Traditional, off-line auction houses were also entering the fray.

Business-to-Consumer Auctions

In 1999, the total business-to-consumer auction market on the Internet was estimated to be about $0.4 billion (sales), but was expected to grow to $12.6 billion by 2003, overtaking the consumer-to-consumer category.[7] While many sites in this category began by specializing in computer hardware and other technology-related items, a number have since expanded to offer everything from travel packages to sporting goods items.

In some cases, firms in this category do not own the goods up for auction; rather, they conduct auctions on behalf of vendors in exchange for a seller's fee. In other cases, they take title to the goods and handle shipment to customers.

Onsale (later merged with Egghead.com) was the first business-to-consumer auction site on the Internet. Other sites that fall into this category include uBid, BidOnline, and WebAuction. Niche sites also became popular. For example, Millionaire.com was founded by Robb Report founder Robert White to target the high-end market by connecting buyers of luxury items such as antiques, fine art, yachts, watches, wine and jewelry with dealers and galleries.

---

[6] Source: Forrester Research.

[7] Source: Forrester Research.

Even investment banks got into the on-line auction business. Many initial public offerings display classic signs that shares are being sold too cheaply and to the wrong people (i.e., not to those who value them the most highly). As a result, there is often a sharp rise in price on the first day's trading, and a huge volume of shares changes hands. W. R. Hambrecht instituted OpenIpo, an auction process to sell initial public offerings of shares more efficiently. Investors submitted secret bids; the price was set at the highest level at which all available shares could be sold, and allocated at that price to everybody who bid that amount or more. This extended the buying group from business to individual consumers.

Business-to-Business Auctions

Business-to-business auctions were expected to eventually make up most of the volume of the online auction market. In fact, many auction firms that started out as business-to-consumer firms (e.g., Onsale, uBid) found that an increasing percentage of their revenues being generated by business customers.

In general, business-to-business auctions involve fundamentally different dynamics than consumer auctions. They typically involve larger amounts of money, firms are not seeking entertainment, and firms tend to be wary of jeopardizing long-term strategic relationships.

AdAuction.com was an example of an business-to-business auction site. The company provided a venue for companies to buy and sell advertising space for all sorts of media: online, broadcast, and print. Sellers had to fulfill certain criteria to qualify for participation in the auctions, which provided the opportunity to sell excess ad inventory to over 6,000 registered media buyers. TradeOut was a business-to-business liquidator auction with products ranging from a lot of 2,000 Duncan Yo-Yo's to 70 tons of Borosilicate Glass Tubing. Its developer was inspired in his design by reading eBay's prospectus. eBay invested in TradeOut in November 1999.

Entering the Classic Auction Market

In all of the classic auction categories, barriers to entry are relatively low, and competitors can launch new sites at a relatively low cost using commercially available software. However, the biggest hurdles involve building a potential bidder and seller base. Success literally breeds success; the large bidder base draws the suppliers which enhance the site's appeal to bidders. For smaller players seeking to enter the market, breaking this self-reinforcing cycle can pose quite a problem.

But several firms arose to offer smaller players an alternative. These firms focused on helping other firms get into the auction business by using network synergies to quickly build a large bidder and seller base. FairMarket, a leader in this category, created an auction network that connected a number of smaller auction sites hosted by some of the leading portals and vendors on the Web, including Microsoft (MSN), Excite, Lycos, AltaVista, Dell, CompUSA, Cyberian Outpost, MicroWarehouse, and Boston.com. Each individual site was connected to a single massive database of merchandise. A computer listed from Dell at www.dellaucion.com, for example, automatically appeared on all the auction sites in the FairMarket network. Besides developing the network, FairMarket provided a number of other services to its members: It hosted the servers, and created the software and user interface for member auction sites. It also provided customer service, including fraud protection and security features. In 1999, the company had a combined reach of 50 million users (compared to eBay's audience of 7 million).

III(b): Reverse Buying

The term "reverse" buying refers to the fact that in these mechanisms there is a flip in the usual role of buyer and seller. Usually, the seller indicates what is for sale and buyers search around for what they want. In reverse buying, the buyer is more proactive—specifying what it is that will be purchased; then, suppliers' bids indicate the price of fulfilling the specified demand. In some situations, this happens in a true reverse auction process, as sellers perceive themselves in active competition with one another. In other cases, a service will identify potential sellers and their posted prices for buyers, but without anything approximating a bidding process among sellers.

Reverse Auctions

In a reverse auction, a buyer communicates a need to a set of potential suppliers and suppliers bid on fulfilling that demand. The reverse auction has been a staple of purchasing in business-to-business situations for many years, often under the name of competitive bidding.[8] The process entails the buyer drafting a Request-for-Proposal (RFP) or Request for Quotation (RFQ) specifying what is to be purchased. This request is transmitted to qualified sellers. In some cases, drafting the RFP/RFQ and then identifying and communicating to potential suppliers is easy. For example, when the Tennessee Valley Authority needed electrical generation equipment in the 1950's, it knew only three suppliers, Allis-Chalmers, Westinghouse and General Electric were qualified to supply its needs. The products to be bought were well-known commodities, easy to specify. Similarly, in current times, a U.S. government agency making a bulk buy of PC's would need only contact a few firms and these firms would be well known to them. In other situations, the "making of the market" by bringing in a more complete set of potential suppliers is a major task.

Supplier bidding can be of two general types:

(i) sealed bidding, in which each qualified supplier submits one secret bid and the buyer chooses on the basis of bids submitted in that round

(ii) open bidding, in which sellers interact in real time just as buyers do in a classic auction, except the bidding goes down over time and the lowest supplier price wins

The Internet's interactive communication capability broadens the feasibility of economically efficient reverse auctions. The Web expands the scope of sellers participating. This creates an overall downward pressure on prices. Online analogs of business-to-business competitive bidding situations emerged on the Web. Need2Buy, for example, was a special purpose site at which a buyer could engage in a ready-made reverse auction for electronic components. These components were tightly specified by industry standards so the buyer needs were easily expressed, e.g., part number 74L5240AN meant the same thing to everyone in the industry. The process worked as follows: The buyer submits the RFQ to the system and indicates his choice of the Sealed Bid or Open Bidding format. The Need2Buy expert system searches the database to find vendors carrying the requested product. The buyer may delete vendors unacceptable to it. Accepted vendors then receive an e-mail inviting bids on the RFQ. In an open-bid system, vendors are informed of the lowest bid and invited to rebid if not the lowest. The buyer reviews the final bids, which could include quantity available and delivery date in addition to price, and decides how to proceed, following up with sellers via e-mail, fax, or telephone as desired.

FreeMarkets attracted lots of attention as a firm creating effective Competitive Bidding Events for industrial buyers. In contrast to some vendors selling just reverse auction software enabling buyers to construct their own auctions, FreeMarkets' approach was to provide the total package of services necessary for an effective reverse auction process. It recognized that, in many situations, preparation of the RFQ is a non-trivial task. As stated on the company's Website, ". . . products are often technically complex and custom-made. That's why we work with several members of each clients organization to specify their needs

---

[8] See for example, Chapter 9 "Competitive Bidding" in B.C. Ames and J.D. Hlavacek, *Managerial Marketing for Industrial Firms,* Random House, 1984.

in detail and communicate them to buyers." FreeMarkets' staff worked to have auction bidders (suppliers) "present and prepared" at the bidding event. At the bidding event, FreeMarkets' BidWare proprietary software was used by suppliers from many geographic locations to submit real time bids. FreeMarkets online auctions covered over $1.5 billion in purchase orders from January 1998 to June 1999. Major clients included General Motors, Quaker Oats, and AlliedSignal. A November 1999, *Wall Street Journal* ad of FreeMarkets described its work for United Technologies Corporation (UTC) in its acquisition of specialty metals. In one bidding day, 14 bidders submitted 318 bids covering about $20 million in UTC requirements, saving UTC 22% in the process. In general, the company estimated that its process saves individual buyers between 2 and 25%.

The Internet makes possible the more efficient organization of reverse auctions—bringing in the maximum number of qualified suppliers, well-informed on the requirements. The real-time bidding process also helps the buyers. Overall, the net result is downward pressure on prices.

Emerging Business-to-Consumer Reverse Buying Models

Business-to-Consumer reverse buying services were less well developed as of late 1999, and less truly auctions, but several types of mechanisms were in operation. For example, as described on its website, imandi was the place "Where Customers Rule"—"Connecting You with Thousands of Merchants Competing to Serve You." imandi trademarked the phrase "we're turning shopping on its head." As the site put it, "our aim is to put an end to fixed pricing on the Web." Originally set up for the acquisition of services from a fragmented supplier base of painters, carpenters, etc., the scope expanded to include collectibles. An individual buyer effectively entered an RFQ, i.e., what it wished to purchase. imandi searched its database of merchants (168,000 of them as of December 1999) to provide a list of local and national merchants believed capable of supplying the desired product. The buyer eliminated any undesired suppliers. imandi transmitted the RFQ to the remainder who submitted price quotes. imandi had 40,000 registered users in December 1999 compared to 7 million for eBay.

Similar services were offered by MyGeek and Respond. Basically, these operations functioned as buying services broadcasting a buyer's RFP to potential suppliers who respond via e-mail. The customer could then choose the seller to transact with or not buy at all. Respond was able to accommodate a situation in which the buyer was only able to describe the item sought in generic terms, e.g., "an inexpensive two-bedroom condominium rental on a beach." Buyers remained anonymous to potential sellers and could choose to follow up or not on e-mailed offers sent to Respond.com for their attention.

The Priceline-type Variant

A particularly high-profile variant in the reverse buying genre was Priceline, with the marketing proposition (as noted on the Website and in advertising) "Name Your Own Price and Save!" It was hyped as the ultimate in consumer-driven commerce.[9] In some respects, however, the service represents the sacrifice of customer power in favor of solving a vendor's problem of selling off excess inventory.

Priceline's initial product category was airline seats. This process had a buyer naming a price he or she was willing to pay for a roundtrip flight between points A and B. The customer specified only the day of departure and day of return. Then, supplier databases were searched to see the minimum revenue an airline cooperating with Priceline was willing to take to fly someone from A to B and back on those days.

---

[9] This has been noted in the popular press, e.g., see "The hype is big, really big at Priceline," by Peter Elkind, *Fortune,* September 6, 1999.

Restrictions included the following:

- The buyer could not specify a preferred carrier, nor even exclude a carrier which was undesirable to them;
- The buyer could not specify times of travel and must take anything the system found between 6 A.M. and 10 P.M.;
- When the buyer named an "offer" price, he or she was obligated to pay that price if the departure/return days were met.

Note that the database of vendors' minimum revenue requirement for fulfilling the demand could show numbers significantly lower than the willingness-to-pay expressed by the buyer. (To induce consumers to express high willingness-to-pay, requests could be made only once a week.) The buyer was charged the expressed willingness-to-pay price, generating margin for Priceline.

As described by Priceline on its Website, ". . . we collect consumer demand. . . By requiring customers to be flexible with respect to brands, sellers and/or product features, we enable sellers to generate incremental revenue without disrupting their existing distribution channels or retail pricing structures."

Priceline has extended the service to additional product categories: hotel rooms in 1100 cities, home financing, and new cars.

Expedia offered similar services for air travel and hotel rooms. Expedia described the service as "It's all about helping you get the price you want—YOURS! If Hotel Matcher finds a hotel that meets your criteria and price, we'll automatically select that hotel on your behalf and charge a pre-paid, nonrefundable reservation to your credit card."

Rationale for Reverse Buying Models

As an Internet-based analog to familiar real world competitive bidding, reverse auctions on the Internet have the potential to reduce acquisition costs significantly in many situations. For complex products, an integrated approach as proposed by FreeMarkets is necessary. Their work with very sophisticated purchasing organizations has already proven the value of developing the worldwide seller pool and providing the tools for real-time bidding which promotes competition. For commodity products, simple systems can be effective in expanding the seller base to promote lower prices for buyers.

The economic rationale for reverse buying of the Priceline and Expedia variety is less clear. These systems seem less a reverse buying mechanism with great customer power (as these companies have touted) than a way to create a new product—the unbranded, unknown airline seat or hotel room. In an age of increased buyer information, here the buyer works with markedly *less* information and cannot withdraw from the deal when the actual product definition is known. It offers "guaranteed demand" to suppliers and lots of flexibility in exactly how to meet it. It degrades the quality of the product supplied to the consumer and presents downward pressure on price as compared to a regular transaction.

III(c): Exchanges

Exchanges are electronic marketplaces where a group of buyers and a group of sellers interact to trade and set prices for transactions. The familiar exchanges would be the stock exchanges and currency exchanges around the world. The early electronic product exchanges of the Internet were typically organized around a particular industry. For example:

Metal Site: has 18 sellers of metals interacting with many buyers. It also is designed to be a comprehensive industry resource providing information on factors influencing industry supply and demand.

Fast Parts: an exchange, patterned after the NASDAQ, to serve the electronics manufacturing and assembly industries. The site has also added an auction facility.

ESteel: for the steel industry, facilitates negotiations between buyers and sellers rather than an auction model.

ChemConnect: Internet's largest chemical and plastics exchange. The exchange evolved out of an online suppliers directory.

The general process at an exchange is conceptually that for each item, a dynamically updated list of "offers to buy" and "offers to sell" is maintained. These buys/sells are matched up through a process. The process on ChemConnect's World Chemical Exchange is exemplary. A buyer arriving at the site with a need to procure something began by querying the system to see currently posted Product Offerings. The system showed available offers to sell including price, quantity available, and expiration time of the offers. (Product offering submitters may post an expiration time of between 15 minutes and 7 days when the offer is posted.) The buyer also saw any bids already made for a given Product Offering.

The buyer then selected among the Product Offerings posted and submitted a bid. The exchange member who posted the Product Offer could then negotiate with the buyer on his bid via an e-mail process. An offering firm could accept bids on any terms it wished and the buyer could modify the bid at any time to reflect current market conditions.

If the current list of Product Offerings did not include the item the buyer was seeking or if the offers were in any way undesirable, he could post a Product Request. The system first showed other buyers' Product Requests posted for the same item (if any) and any offers made against those Product Requests. The prospective buyer's Product Request typically included an indication of the price the buyer was willing to pay, quantity desired and any other important terms-and-conditions of sale. Sellers submitted offers against the Product Request which could then be accepted, rejected or negotiated by the buyer.

At ChemConnect, all negotiations had to be anonymous, i.e., neither buyer nor seller could reveal their identity in the negotiation process. The outcome of the negotiation was to be a product of the forces of market supply and demand. A seller coming to the exchange behaved in a mirror-image fashion to buyers—typically first checking Product Requests posted by potential buyers then perhaps posting Product Offers, interacting with buyers as described above. No access fees were charged to either buyers or sellers. Both the buyer and seller paid a fee for completed transactions.

A major advantage of these organized exchanges is that they bring together buyers and sellers on a global scale. The impact of this on average price paid is not clear. A buyer benefits by having access to all sellers on the exchange—not just those with whom he is familiar or in geographic proximity. For an individual transaction conducted at a given point in time, this expanding of the potential supplier pool should drive the price paid down. On the other hand, the exchange also opens up a host of new potential buyers to sellers. A seller needing to sell quickly will sell at a less distressed price than if his potential set were restricted to local, known buyers. A real benefit to both buyers and sellers is a reduction in the variability of prices across transactions. Prices on the exchanges are the product of marketwide economic forces impacting all buyers and sellers—not specific, highly variable and relatively unpredictable local conditions.

Summary

As the description above shows, the Internet has already changed the way many markets are organized and consequently the mechanisms via which prices are set. Figure 1 set out three distinct market making mechanisms and, for the sake of clarity in exposition, discussed each separately. However, some sites already in effect offer a combination of these market mechanisms, from which the buyer can choose. For example:

Set Price and Negotiation Combination: As noted in the NexTag discussion (under the Negotiation heading above) the process begins by searching sites and bringing back the set prices of alternative suppliers. If any of these set prices is acceptable, the buyer can select one and conduct the transaction in that way without invoking the negotiation capability of NexTag.

Set Price and Auction Combination: Some sites offer a capability wherein a seller conducting an auction can specify a "Quick Buy" price. Any buyer willing to pay the "Quick Buy" price in order to save time can click on it, effectively buying under a set price mechanism.

Negotiation and Exchange Combination: While some exchanges, such as Chem-Connect discussed above, require anonymous exchanges between buyers and sellers, others such as e-Steel allow the buyer to restrict the set of sellers to whom requirements are made known. By restricting the seller set to one or two potential vendors, the market mechanism becomes more negotiation than open market exchange.

To summarize the impact of the Internet on pricing by saying that increased price information availability to buyers will drive prices down is like saying "the effect of global warming is that it's hotter at the beach in July." As usual, the answer to seemingly simple question "will prices go up or down?" is the not so simple "it depends." Markets will be more efficient and different forms of market mechanisms will operate. As noted above, different price effects will be found.

A great deal depends on the nature of the product. Certainly, commodity products will experience increased price pressure due to more buyer information about prices. As discussed at the outset of this note, the information of the Internet cuts into the "ignorance premium." However, even for commodities, the Internet can increase some realized prices. In an inefficient information market, some commodities bring a price of zero—unsold advertising time is used for a public service announcement, empty seats fly into the air, and a truck delivering an order in Boston from New York returns to New York empty. While the Internet will not increase airline industry load factors to 100% or put an end to truckers returning to home base empty, it can create a market for the commodities which would have gone unsold even though buyers were willing to pay more than sellers required as a price. National Transportation Exchange (NTE) created such a service for shippers planning to evolve it into a system where individual drivers will respond to buyer RFP's in real time from the road via wireless Internet access devices.[10]

In contrast to the general price pressure befalling commodity products, the Internet can be a boon to price realization for those with a differentiated product. While the Internet can convey to consumers a more full understanding of competitive products and prices, it can also provide another communication vehicle via which to create the perception of value in the consumer's mind. For example, the Bose site provides detailed information on the Bose Wave Radio/CD including "The Technology Inside" in supporting the premium $499.00 price; the Gap site includes current television commercials and communicates the benefits of Gap's integration of online and real world presence for consumers; and the BMW site lets a buyer build a custom car. More customized information can be delivered in response to either consumers' explicit requests or their observed behavior.

In short, the Internet offers expanded opportunities for avoiding the commodity trap. More consumer information can mean more information about how sellers are the same and increase the emphasis on price. Alternatively, it can mean more appreciation of how sellers and products are different, decreasing the emphasis on price.

---

[10] "The Rise of the Infomediary," *The Economist,* June 26, 1999.

The Internet is a disaster for those with a commodity selling mentality. For them, the story of increasing consumer power over sellers resulting in price pressure and margin erosion will come true. The more sophisticated will see the possibility of new market mechanisms for transacting with customers and take advantage of the opportunity to differentiate themselves not only by giving consumers products they want to buy but also by giving them choices about how they can buy them. For these marketers, the Internet will not be a story of buyer triumph over sellers through information but rather a mutually beneficial success story built on taking advantage of more efficient communication and the opportunity for a more intimate, personalized relationship.

Chapter 28

Coca-Cola's New Vending Machine (A): Pricing to Capture Value, or Not?

Charles King III   Das Narayandas

On December 17, 1999, *The Wall Street Journal* ran a front page story headlined "*Tone Deaf:* Ivester Has All Skills of a CEO but One: Ear for Political Nuance." The article detailed how Coca-Cola Chairman and Chief Executive Officer M. Douglas Ivester's handling of one flap after another cost him the Coke Board's confidence, eventually leading him to abruptly announce that he would step down from his position in April 2000.

One of the many events highlighted concerned Ivester's comments about Coke's new vending machine technology. The article reported:

> A few months later came another public relations gaffe. Asked by a Brazilian newsmagazine about Coke's testing of vending machines that could change prices according to the weather, Mr. Ivester gave a theoretical response that came across as both a defense of the technology and a confirmation that it would hit the streets. "Coca-Cola is a product whose utility varies from moment to moment," he said. "In a final summer championship, when people meet in a stadium to have fun, the utility of a cold Coca-Cola is very high. So it is fair that it should be more expensive. The machine will simply make this process automatic."

Professors Charles King III and Das Narayandas prepared this case using publicly available sources as the basis for class discussion rather than to illustrate either effective or ineffective handling of an administrative situation.

EXHIBIT 1 Text of the Article That Appeared in *The New York Times* on October 28, 1999

Coke Tests Vending Unit That Can Hike Prices in Hot Weather

by Constance L. Hays

[T]aking full advantage of the law of supply and demand, Coca-Cola Co. has quietly begun testing a vending machine that can automatically raise prices for its drinks in hot weather.

"This technology is something the Coca-Cola Co. has been looking at for more than a year," said Rob Baskin, a company spokesman, adding that it had not yet been placed in any consumer market.

The potential was heralded, though, by the company's chairman and chief executive in an interview earlier this month with a Brazilian newsmagazine. Chairman M. Douglas Ivester described how desire for a cold drink can increase during a sports championship final held in the summer heat. "So, it is fair that it should be more expensive," Ivester was quoted as saying in the magazine, *Veja*. "The machine will simply make this process automatic."

The process appears to be done simply through a temperature sensor and a computer chip, not any breakthrough technology, though Coca-Cola refused to provide any details Wednesday.

While the concept might seem unfair to a thirsty person, it essentially extends to another industry what has become the practice for airlines and other companies that sell products and services to consumers. The falling price of computer chips and the increasing ease of connecting to the Internet has made it practical for companies to pair daily and hourly fluctuations in demand with fluctuations in price—even if the product is a can of soda that sells for just 75 cents.

The potential for other types of innovations is great. Other modifications under discussion at Coca-Cola, Baskin said, include adjusting prices based on demand at a specific machine. "What could you do to boost sales at off-hours?" he asked. "You might be able to lower the price. It might be discounted at a vending machine in a building during the evening or when there's less traffic."

Vending machines have become an increasingly important source of profits for Coca-Cola and its archrival, Pepsico. Over the last three years, the soft-drink giants have watched their earnings erode as they waged a price war in supermarkets. Vending machines have remained largely untouched by the discounting. Now, Coca-Cola aims to tweak what has been a golden goose to extract even more profits.

"There are a number of initiatives under way in Japan, the United States and in other parts of the world where the technology in vending is rapidly improving, not only from a temperature-scanning capability but also to understand when a machine is out of stock," said Andrew Conway, a beverage analyst for Morgan Stanley. "The increase in the rate of technology breakthrough in vending is pretty dramatic."

Bill Hurley, a spokesman for the National Automatic Merchandising Association in Washington, added: "You are only limited by your creativity, since electronic components are becoming more and more versatile."

Machines are already in place that can accept credit cards and debit cards for payment. In Australia and in North Carolina, Coke bottlers use machines to relay, via wireless signal or telephone, information about which drinks are selling and at what rates in a particular location. The technology is known as intelligent vending, Baskin said, and the information gathered and relayed by Internet helps salespeople to figure out which drinks will sell best in which locations.

"It all feeds into their strategy of micro-marketing and understanding the local consumer," Conway said. "If you can understand brand preferences by geography, that has implications for other places with similar geography."

Coca-Cola and its bottlers have invested heavily in vending machines, refrigerated display cases, coolers and other equipment to sell their drinks cold. Over the last five years, Coca-Cola Enterprises, Coke's biggest bottler, has spent more than $1.8 billion on such equipment. In support, Coca-Cola has spent millions more on employees who monitor and service the equipment. In 1998 alone, it spent $324 million on such support to its biggest bottler.

And last week, Coke's chief marketing officer unveiled the company's plan to pump more sales of its flagship soft drink, Coca-Cola Classic. The program includes a pronounced emphasis on Coke served cold.

Sales of soft drinks from vending machines have risen steadily over the last few years, though most sales still take place in supermarkets. Last year, about 11.9 percent of soft-drink sales worldwide came from vending machines, said John Sicher, the editor of *Beverage Digest*, an industry newsletter. In the United States, about 1.2 billion cases of soft drinks were sold through vending machines.

In Japan, some vending machines already adjust their prices based on the temperature outside, using wireless modems, said Gad Elmoznino, director of the Trisignal division of Eicon Technology, a Montreal-based modem maker. "They are going to be using more and more communications in these machines to do interactive price setting," he said.

Industry reactions to the heat-sensitive Coke machine ranged from enthusiastic to sanctimonious. "It's another reason to move to Sweden," one beverage industry executive sniffed. "What's next? A machine that X-rays people's pockets to find out how much change they have and raises the price accordingly?"

EXHIBIT 1   (Continued)

"Bill Pecoriello, a stock analyst with Sanford C. Bernstein, applauded the move to increase profits in the vending-machine business. "This is already the most profitable channel for the beverage companies, so any effort to get higher profits when demand is higher obviously can enhance the profitability of the system further," he said.

He pointed to a possible downside as well. "You don't want to have a price war in this channel, where you have discounting over a holiday weekend, for example," he said. "Once the capability is out there to vary the pricing, you can take the price down."

A Pepsi spokesman said no similar innovation was being tested at the No. 2 soft-drink company. "We believe that machines that raise prices in hot weather exploit consumers who live in warm climates," declared the spokesman, Jeff Brown. "At Pepsi, we are focused on innovations that make it easier for consumers to buy a soft drink, not harder."

EXHIBIT 2   **On October 28, 1999, the Coca-Cola Company Posted the Following Press Release on Its Corporate Website**

Source: Coca-Cola Company Website: http://www.coke.com.

STATEMENT ON VENDING MACHINE TECHNOLOGY

ATLANTA, October 28, 1999 · Contrary to some erroneous press reports, The Coca-Cola Company is not introducing vending machines that raise the price of soft drinks in hot weather.

We are exploring innovative technology and communication systems that can actually improve product availability, promotional activity, and even offer consumers an interactive experience when they purchase a soft drink from a vending machine.

Our commitment for 113 years has been to putting our products within an arm's reach of desire. Offering the products that people want at affordable prices is precisely why Coca-Cola is the favorite soft drink of people in nearly 200 countries around the world.

The new technologies we're exploring will only enhance our ability to deliver on that promise.

EXHIBIT 3 **Text of the Article That Appeared in *The Philadelphia Inquirer* on October 31, 1999**

Source: Reprinted with permission of *The Philadelphia Inquirer.*

Have a Coke, and Big Brother is sure to smile

by Jeff Brown

Now for the latest evidence that the world is going to hell in a handbasket: The Coca Cola Co., seeking new ways to make thirst pay, is working on a weather-sensing vending machine that will raise prices when it's hot. Isn't that immoral? I mean, if a man crawls in from the desert dying of thirst, would you demand a C-note for a glass of water?

No, but a Coke . . . that's different. It's just an indulgence. So what's wrong with charging what the market will bear—more when it's hot, less when it's cold?

In fact, computer chips may soon enable vending machines to constantly adjust prices according to any number of factors that cause momentary fluctuations in supply and demand, not just weather.

So, some busy fall evening in the not-too-distant future, you sidle up to a well-lit Coke machine in South Philly. The box has no buttons, does not display any prices. A spotlight shines on your face as sensors zoom in on your vital signs. A head-high video screen flickers on.

The machine sees you're in jeans, not a suit, so it scans its library of personalities, skipping the erudite Englishman and the slinky French model. It displays the good-natured face of Sylvester Stallone.

"Yo!" the Coke machine calls. "What can I do ya for?" Sly smiles, thinking of his royalty, perhaps.

"A Coke Classic, please."

"No problem. Four bucks."

"Whoa! They're 50 cents at the supermarket."

The machine pauses while its accent analyzer determines you aren't from the neighborhood.

"You see a supermarket around here?" it says. "Four dollars."

You decide to bluff. "Look, the machine around the corner gave me a Pepsi for half that."

"When?"

"A couple of hours ago."

"Yeah, it's rush hour now. You won't get a two-dollar soda anywhere." The head on the screen shakes from side to side sympathetically. Then the red and white machine goes silent, letting you sweat. This is going to be tougher than you'd thought. You pull out your Palm Pilot X, link to the Internet, and go to sodamachines.com.

"There are 14 soda machines within four blocks," you report, holding up the Palm Pilot for the machine to see. "You're telling me I can't beat four dollars?"

The Coke machine tallies the 90 seconds it has expended on this negotiation. Its motion sensor detects two customers moving around impatiently behind you. Its atomic clock reports that rush hour is winding down.

"Okay, three dollars," it offers, peeved.

"No way." You stuff your wallet into your pants and step back.

The Coke machine focuses an infrared scanner on your lips, calibrating your thirst. It counts its inventory and finds a surplus of Diet Coke. Its hard drive whirs for a second.

"I'll give you a Coke Lite for $2.50," it offers resentfully.

"Terrible aftertaste," you say.

"With a bag of nuts."

"Nah."

"Look, pal, if you're not buyin' move along."

Traffic is getting lighter. The two people behind you give up and leave.

"All right," the box grumbles.

You deposit two dollars, get your can, and turn to go.

"How about those peanuts?" the machine asks hopefully. "Fifty cents."

"I'm allergic," you answer.

The machine pauses a nanosecond while electrons zip around its circuits. It's a week day. Rush hour. Statistics suggest you work nearby. You'll be back. The machine activates its customer relations software.

"Have a nice evening, bud," it calls as you turn away, the face smiling widely.

"Hey!" it calls. "I'm a soft touch today. Just got my circuits cleaned. Don't expect a deal like this next time!"

As you disappear around the corner, the machine counts its remaining cans, assesses the odds of making a sale this late in the day, and looks at how it's doing on its sales goal—a little behind. It cranks up the volume on its Rocky voice and calls out to the nearly empty street.

"Coke Classic! Get your Coke Classic here!"

"Only a dollar!"

EXHIBIT 4   **Excerpts from an Article That Appeared on the About.com Web-site on November 3, 1999**

Mean Vending Machines

by John S. Irons

This past weekend the news wires were all buzzing about the latest idea to come from the world of soft drinks. Coca-Cola is apparently considering creating a new kind of vending machine that would test the outside temperature and adjust the price of a can of soda upwards when it is warmer outside. Here's some of the typical reactions to the idea:

- "a cynical ploy to exploit the thirst of faithful customers" (*San Francisco Chronicle*)
- "lunk-headed idea" (*Honolulu Star-Bulletin*)
- "Soda jerks" (*Miami Herald*)
- "latest evidence that the world is going to hell in a handbasket" (*Philadelphia Inquirer*)
- "ticks me off" (*Edmonton Sun*)

What did they think the Coca-Cola company was doing anyway? Selflessly providing the world with a glorious beverage to further the goals of all mankind? Why should all these people be suddenly offended by a company trying to maximize profits?

"Price discrimination" is the term economists use to describe the practice of selling the same good to different groups of buyers at different prices. In the Coke case, the groups of buyers are segmented by the outside temperature (i.e., Jill when it is hot outside vs. Jill when it is cold). If possible, a company would like to charge a high price to those who place a high value on the good, while charging less to those that do not.

So, are you personally offended by Coke's plan to charge more for soda's when it is warm outside? Well, you had better get over it pretty quickly, there is already plenty of price discrimination out there, and there is MUCH more to come.

Rampant Price Discrimination

Price discrimination is quite common. Ever wonder why hardcover books are produced first and are so much more expensive than paperback books? Or, why it is so much cheaper to buy airline tickets far in advance? Or, why there are student discounts? Or, why matinee prices are cheaper for movies? Ever tried to buy a soda from a vending machine at a hotel or at a movie theater?

All these examples are attempts by sellers to charge different people different prices for the same good.

Much of the price discrimination in the economy may in fact be quite hidden. How do you know that the Crate and Barrel catalogue you just received has the same price for you as for someone living in another zip code? Those with a 90210 zip code see higher prices on their catalogues.

Why is the Vending Machine different?

In principle, the temperature sensitive vending machine is no different from any other form of price discrimination.

Although, I do think the idea that the process is automatic generates some additional discomfort—it is the idea that technology can effectively gauge our buying interests. The heat sensitive machine is a small step toward applying machine "intelligence" to profit maximization.

If you think that the vending machine idea is worrisome, just wait—the internet will be the most sophisticated price discriminator the world has ever seen. Smart vending machines will be the least of your worries. Online vendors such as Amazon.com may know quite a lot about you—your past purchasing habits, your internet preferences, your zip code, etc.,—and they may want to use this information to adjust prices. Did you buy a Stephen King book last month? Maybe you'd like to buy another, more expensive, Grisham novel this month with a smaller "discount" chosen just for you.

The internet is much better than the "real world" at price discrimination, because it is so much easier to change prices. In fact they can set a price just for you. It's hard to imagine a traditional store doing this ("Hey, here comes John. Quick, raise the price of the new Krugman Book"). But for an on-line e-commerce store, this is feasible and, with a clever programmer on the payroll, quite easy.

Not all bad: Discrimination means increased efficiency. Actually, price discrimination can actually increase the overall efficiency of a market.

A loss of economic efficiency may occur when a company has some ability to set prices and there is no discrimination. The seller must pick a price that balances their desire to charge a high price to those that really want a product, with their desire to sell a higher overall quantity to those that are not willing to pay very much for it. Because of this, there are trades which would benefit both buyer and seller that do not happen—the resulting price is "too high" and the total quantity traded is "too low."

EXHIBIT 4 (Continued)

> By identifying individual groups of consumers, a seller can provide an additional unit at a lower price to someone who before would have been priced out of the market. The company would now be willing to do this since they would not have to sacrifice profits by lowering prices for the high-demand group.
>
> In the Coke case, some consumers—those who drink Cokes on hot days—will be worse off since they must pay a higher price, while some consumers—those who drink Coke on cold days—will be better off since they will receive a lower price. The Coca-Cola company, of course, will be better off. The sum total will be positive (pick your favorite Introduction to Economics textbook to see why).
>
> Would you really be as offended if it was described as a discount on cold days?
>
> So, if you are still stewing about the potential of higher Coke prices, I suggest you stock up the refrigerator and put some of that retirement money into Coca-Cola stock.

A Coke spokesman says the remarks were taken out of context. Though the company had tested the technology in a lab, it never had an intention of introducing it, the spokesman says, and [Coke] bottlers confirm this. Nevertheless, the CEO's answer created a flap, seeming to cast the company as one that wasn't customer-friendly.

The article also pointed out that:

To Mr. Ivester, the accountant, the concept [of changing prices based on the ambient temperature] was just the law of supply and demand in action. To the board, the ensuing flap was Murphy's Law at work.

For a consumer-product company that, in the words of a person close to the board, "is a giant image machine," the pummeling of Coke's image was increasingly intolerable.

Earlier, on October 28, 1999, *The New York Times (NYT)* had reported that Coke was testing vending machines that could raise prices in hot weather (see **Exhibit 1**). The *NYT* story precipitated an immediate response from the Coca-Cola Company (see **Exhibit 2** for the company press release posted on the firm's web-site on the same day), triggered a lampoon in *The Philadelphia Inquirer* on October 31, 1999 (see **Exhibit 3**), and generated national and international controversy (see **Exhibit 4**).

Chapter 29

Tweeter etc.

John Gourville   George Wu   James Evans

On August 16, 1996, Sandy Bloomberg, founder and CEO of Tweeter etc., reflected on the recent history of his small, upscale New England retailer of consumer electronics. Tweeter had grown from a 13-store chain with $35 million in annual sales in 1991 to a 21-store chain with $82 million in annual sales in 1996. Bloomberg had always attributed part of this growth to Tweeter's "Automatic Price Protection" policy, which had been implemented in 1993. Under Automatic Price Protection (APP), Tweeter monitored local newspaper ads and automatically mailed a refund check to a consumer if an item purchased at Tweeter during the past 30 days was advertised for a lower price by a competitor.

Two recent developments in the marketplace gave Bloomberg reason to reflect on APP, however. First, on May 16, 1996, Tweeter ventured outside its traditional New England base and purchased a controlling interest in Bryn Mawr Stereo, another small, high-end consumer electronics chain based in suburban Philadelphia. One year earlier, Bryn Mawr had adopted Tweeter's "Automatic Price Protection" policy, but up to the time of Tweeter's purchase, had failed to see any significant impact on sales. Second, on June 16, 1996, Nobody Beats the Wiz ("The Wiz") opened a 50,000 square foot electronics retail outlet in suburban Boston, the second of ten outlets planned for the New England market and the first in Greater Boston. The Wiz, a nationally recognized New Jersey-based discount retailer, threatened to change the playing field in the already highly competitive New England audio and video consumer electronics market.

Three years earlier, Tweeter's introduction of APP had received national press coverage in *The Wall Street Journal* (see **Exhibit 1**). Now, Bryn Mawr's seeming lack of success with the policy gave Bloomberg cause to question the impact of APP. Moreover, whatever its past impact, Bloomberg wondered how effective the policy would be in a market increasingly dominated by large discount retailers such as The Wiz.

Professors John Gourville and George Wu prepared this case with research assistance from James Evans as the basis for class discussion rather than to illustrate either effective or ineffective handling of an administrative situation. Some nonpublic data have been disguised.

EXHIBIT 1
The Wall Street Journal Article, August 17, 1993

> # *Tweeter's Customers Told: 'Your Check Is in the Mail'*
>
> * * *
>
> ### New England Retailer Says Its Computers Shop the Ads Of Rivals to Ensure Refunds

By WILLIAM M. BULKELEY
Staff Reporter of THE WALL STREET JOURNAL

Tweeter etc., a New England stereo and television retailer, is going a step beyond its rivals by promising to automatically mail customers a refund check anytime a competitor advertises a lower price.

Most companies in the competitive electronics field will give refunds to customers who buy a product, then see it advertised for less and bring in the ad within 30 days. Tweeter says it will save customers the trouble of monitoring ads and returning to the store.

"In electronics, everyone has a low-price guarantee. But then, it's try and catch them," said Jeffrey Stone, president of Tweeter. "This time, the check really is in the mail."

Nothing Under $50

Based in Canton, Mass., Tweeter, a unit of closely held New England Audio Co., sets some limits. It said it will monitor one or two daily newspapers in each of its markets. Any time a competitor within 25 miles of one of its stores advertises a lower price, the "automatic price protection" program goes into effect. Radio, television and direct mail ads don't count. And the guarantee applies only to items over $50.

When Tweeter's competitive marketing staffers see a rival's ad quoting a price, they enter it in Tweeter's computer. A program then checks to see if anybody has bought that item from Tweeter for a higher price in the past 30 days. If so, the computer spits out a check for the difference.

Edgar Dworsky, Massachusetts assistant attorney general for consumer protection, said: "It's a brilliant idea. The problem with price protection guarantees has been that it's the consumer's burden to find a lower price somewhere else. Tweeter's going to do the watching for you. I just hope they don't lose their shirts."

Volume Discounts Available

Tweeter, with $40 million a year in sales at 14 stores, is a medium-sized player in the increasingly competitive New England market. It sells name-brand stereos, televisions, car radios and car phones. It doesn't compete at the very low end of the market. However, Tweeter says that because it is part of the Progressive Retailers Organization Inc., a Palm Springs, Calif., buying group, it can get the same volume discounts available to national chains.

Mr. Stone of Tweeter estimates that the company mails $3,000 to $4,000 a month in refund checks to sharp-eyed customers. He says the amount could double under the new program.

Retail consultants say the total may be far higher. "I'd guess 5%" of customers actually check competitors' ads, says Robert Kahn, a retail consultant in Lafayette, Calif. But he says, "This will build customers because somebody who gets a check will say something exceptional about Tweeter to his friends."

Banking on 'Incremental Sales'

That's what Tweeter is counting on. "A few incremental sales will more than pay for the program," said Sandy Bloomberg, chief executive and founder of Tweeter.

Tweeter officials said the company worked to build a high-price, high-quality image during the 1980s. But focus group research showed it needed to reverse that image for the '90s. "People used to boast about how much they paid for something. Now they boast about how much they saved on it," said Mr. Stone.

The Consumer Electronics Industry

The United States Market

In 1995, consumer electronics was a $30 billion industry in the United States, as measured by manufacturer sales (see **Exhibit 2**). The previous ten years had seen the market grow at a 5.6% compound annual rate, with future growth projected to be strong through 1998. While industry data on retail sales was unavailable, it was widely believed that retail margins averaged about 30% across product categories.

EXHIBIT 2   Annual Domestic and Import Manufacturer Sales of Consumer Electronics in the United States by Category[a] (in millions of dollars)

Sources: *U.S. Consumer Electronics Sales & Forecasts 1991–1996;* Consumer Electronics Manufacturers Associations, January 1996.

		1990	1991	1992	1993	1994	1995	1996 (est.)
Video:								
Direct view color TV		$ 6,247	$ 6,035	$ 6,651	$ 7,376	$ 7,285	$ 6,969	$ 7,100
Projection TV		626	683	714	841	1,117	1,398	1,720
Monochrome TV		132	92	79	73	70	65	62
TV/VCR combo		178	265	375	599	710	729	816
VCRs		2,504	2,525	2,996	2,912	2,933	2,859	2,716
Camcorders		2,269	2,013	1,841	1,958	1,985	2,160	2,183
Laserdisc players		72	81	93	123	123	105	92
Home satellite		421	370	379	408	900	1,265	1,479
	Sub-Total	$12,449	$12,064	$13,128	$14,290	$15,123	$15,550	$16,168
Audio:								
Rack systems		$ 804	$ 667	$ 614	$ 545	$ 595	$ 537	$ 507
Compact systems		466	597	756	919	1,108	1,242	1,335
Separate components		1,935	1,805	1,586	1,635	1,686	1,940	2,100
Portable equipment		1,645	1,780	2,096	2,187	2,495	2,749	2,724
Home radios		360	310	324	307	306	298	298
	Sub-Total	$5,210	$5,159	$5,376	$5,593	$6,190	$6,766	$6,964
Mobile Electronics:								
Car stereo equipment[b]		1,192	1,232	1,467	1,604	1,898	1,935	1,975
Cellular telephones		1,133	962	1,146	1,257	1,275	1,431	1,620
	Sub-Total	$2,325	$2,194	$2,613	$2,861	$3,173	$3,366	$3,595
Blank Media:		$1,638	$1,661	$1,568	$1,486	$1,436	$1,413	$1,442
Accessories & Batteries:		$2,167	$2,145	$2,253	$2,974	$3,286	$3,475	$3,745
	Total	$23,789	$23,223	$24,938	$27,204	$29,208	$30,570	$31,914

[a]Excludes home office equipment (e.g., telephones, fax machines, personal computers), and electronic gaming equipment.
[b]Excludes factory installed car stereo equipment.

At the retail level, consumer electronics were distributed through a variety of channels, including specialty electronics stores (e.g., Tweeter), electronics/appliance superstores (e.g., Circuit City), mass merchants (e.g., Wal-Mart), warehouse clubs (e.g., Sam's Club), department stores (e.g., Macy's) and mail order houses (e.g., Sound City). **Exhibit 3** provides an overview of these channels. **Exhibit 4** shows the distribution of sales across channels for select categories of consumer electronics.

The New England Market

With a population of 13.2 million, New England represented 5% of the U.S. consumer electronics market. In 1996, there were 8 retailers in this region with market shares in excess of 2% (see **Exhibit 5**). By far the two largest were Lechmere (35% share) and Circuit City (19%).

For decades, Lechmere had been the region's most popular retailer of consumer electronics and home appliances, growing to 28 stores (averaging 50,000 square feet) throughout New England and northern New York by 1995. Selling televisions and stereos since the 1960s, Lechmere had become, for many New Englanders, the only place to consider when buying video and audio equipment. Historically, such attitudes had been reinforced with well-informed salespeople, good customer service and fair pricing on a wide variety of entry and middle-level products. In 1994, Lechmere was purchased for $200 million by Montgomery Ward, a privately owned, national mass merchant with approximately $6 billion

EXHIBIT 3   Channels of Distribution for Consumer Electronics

Source: *Consumer Reports*, February, 1996, pp. 18–27.

Specialty Stores and Boutiques

Characterized by good to excellent customer service, high salesperson knowledge and moderate selling pressure. Medium- to high-end product lines, especially in terms of audio components (e.g., Sony, …). Limited use of promotional sales. Typically smaller in size with good facilities (e.g., sound-proof listening rooms). Examples include Tweeter, Cambridge Sound Works, and Bryn Mawr Stereo.

Electronic/Appliance Superstores

Hectic, high-volume selling machines. Moderate to good customer service, varied salesperson knowledge, and strong selling pressure. Carry a wide selection of all the major product lines (e.g., Sony, Pioneer, JVC, …). Heavy use of promotional sales. Large, open facilities with listening rooms common, but not a certainty. Examples include Circuit City, Best Buy, Nobody Beats the Wiz and Lechmere.

Department Stores

Poor to moderate customer service, limited salesperson knowledge and low to moderate selling pressure. Carry a more limited product line, mainly entry and middle level products. Prone to promotional sales. Examples include Sears and Macy's.

Mass Merchants

Little to no customer service, little salesperson knowledge and little selling pressure. Limited product line, geared toward "value" brands, such as Sound Design and Yorx. Unlikely to find audio components at these stores. Examples include Wal-mart and K-Mart.

Warehouse Clubs

No customer service and no selling pressure. Price, not service or ambiance, is the reason people shop at warehouse clubs. Product selection is varied and limited and selection changes all the time. On occasion, good values on good quality equipment can be found. Examples include Costco and Sam's Club.

Mail Order Houses

Advertise in stereo and video magazines as well as via their own catalogs. No service and no selling pressure. No ability to sample equipment. Prices are sometimes attractive, but shipping can be expensive. Returns are difficult. Examples include Crutchfield and Sound City.

EXHIBIT 4   1995 Market Share by Channel for Select Consumer Electronics Categories

Source: *Dealerscope Merchandising*, July 1996, pp. 46–50.

	Direct View Color TV's	Video Camcorders	Portable Audio[a]	Audio Components	Blank Media[b]
Specialty stores/Electronic superstores	49.0%	46.0%	37.0%	64.0%	17.0%
Mass merchants/Warehouse clubs	25.0	25.0	32.0	14.0	45.0
Department stores	6.5	7.5	17.0	6.5	16.0
Mail order houses	3.0	6.5	5.0	3.5	2.0
Other	15.0	15.0	9.0	12.0	20.0
Total	100.0%	100.0%	100.0%	100.0%	100.0%

[a]Portable Audio includes Walkman and Discman-type portable systems.
[b]Blank Media includes bland audio cassettes, VCR cassettes and Camcorder cassettes.

in annual sales. While Lechmere stores continued to operate under the Lechmere name, many consumers believed that the level of customer service and salesperson knowledge had decreased appreciably under Montgomery Ward's control.

In contrast to the regional legacy of Lechmere, Circuit City, the nation's largest consumer electronics retailer, only arrived to the New England market in early 1993. However, their New England presence quickly grew to 15 full-sized stores (approximately 30,000

EXHIBIT 5
New England Market Share—1992 to 1996[a]

Source: Company records; Based on research conducted by WCVB-TV, Boston, MA.

	1992	1994	1996
Lechmere	33.0%	36.0%	35.6%
Circuit City	0.0	7.4	18.6
Sears	7.8	7.4	8.7
Radio Shack	4.9	5.8	3.9
Wal-Mart	n/a[b]	n/a[b]	3.9
Tweeter	2.8	2.7	3.6
Bradlee's	2.2	2.5	2.4
Service Merchandise	4.1	3.0	2.1
Fretter	5.0	4.9	1.7
BJ's Wholesale Club	2.5	2.3	1.2
K-Mart	0.6	0.4	1.2
Costco	n/a[b]	0.7	0.6
Jordan Marsh	1.3	0.4	0.6
Cambridge Sound Works	n/a[b]	n/a[b]	0.6
Other	35.8	26.5	15.3

[a]Based on an annual telephone survey of approximately 1,000 adults in the New England market in response to the question, "In the past 2 years, at which store did you make your LAST purchase of home electronics equipment?"

[b]Market share not reported separately, but included in "Other."

square feet) and 6 smaller "Circuit City Express" stores (approximately 3,000 square feet). With a reputation for knowledgeable salespeople and good service, Circuit City topped $5.5 billion in sales across more than 350 stores nationwide in 1995. Although Circuit City's offerings included personal computers, medium to large home appliances, audio tapes and compact discs, approximately 60% of their total sales were derived from the sale of video and audio equipment.

At the other end of the spectrum was Cambridge Soundworks, with less than a 1% share of the New England market. Founded in 1988, Cambridge Soundworks specialized in the design, manufacture and sale of their exclusive line of medium to high-end stereo and home theater speakers. Accounting for 69% of their total revenues in 1995, these speakers regularly received positive reviews in the audio and consumer electronic magazines and were often rated as a good value for their $200 to $600 per set price tags. The bulk of Cambridge Soundworks' remaining sales consisted of popular brand-name audio electronics, such as receivers by Harman Kardon and CD players by Sony, which complemented the sale of their private label speakers. While still only a niche player in the region, Cambridge Soundworks had grown appreciably in recent years, with revenues increasing from $14.3 million in 1993 to $26.9 million in 1995. Having traditionally relied on catalog sales (67% of total sales in 1993), much of this growth was due to the opening of a series of small retail outlets in 1994 and 1995. By the end of 1995, Cambridge Soundworks had 23 retail locations throughout New England (15 stores) and Northern California (8 stores), and revenues were divided between catalog (32%), wholesale (13%) and retail sales (55%).

Tweeter etc. Company History

The Formative Years: 1972 to the Mid-1980s

The competitive environment was quite different when Tweeter first arrived upon the consumer electronics scene in 1972. In the early-1970s, 21-year old Sandy Bloomberg had been working at Audio Lab, a hi-fi repair shop and components dealer located in Harvard Square in Cambridge, Massachusetts. While at Audio Lab, Bloomberg became entranced

EXHIBIT 6
Tweeter Store
Openings

Source: Company records.

1972	Commonwealth Avenue, Boston, MA
1973	Harvard Square, MA
1974	Newton, MA
1976	Burlington, MA
1977	Framingham, MA
1979	Dedham, MA; Warwick, RI
1982	Peabody, MA
1984	Hyannis, MA
1985	Waterford, CT; Hanover, MA
1986	Danbury, CT; Seekonk, MA
1990	Newington, CT
1993	Avon, CT
1994	Manchester, CT; Salem, NH
1995	Boylston Street, Boston, MA; Milford, CT
1996	Holyoke, MA; Nashua, NH

by high quality audio components.[1] At that time, the high-end stereo market was only just developing in the United States, with few consumers beyond the hobbyists and avid audiophiles even aware of the increasingly high quality of stereo components available to the general public. In 1972, Bloomberg traveled to Europe where he witnessed and was encouraged by a more mainstream acceptance of high-end stereo components. Shortly afterward, Bloomberg opened his first Tweeter etc. in the storefront of his cousin's industrial music business located near Boston University.

Within a few years of Tweeter's founding, the U.S. stereo components market tripled and the Boston market became littered with a number of small independent retailers, of which Tweeter was only one. At the time, there were two major stereo retailers in the Boston—Tech Hi-fi, started in 1963 by two MIT dropouts, and Lechmere. Tweeter avoided direct confrontation with either retailer by initially focusing on the student market, serving their more sophisticated tastes for higher quality stereo components. Bloomberg's business philosophy was built on a commitment to value, quality, and service.

By 1979, Tweeter had expanded to six stores in the Boston area and one in Rhode Island (see **Exhibit 6** for a chronology of Tweeter's expansion). These stores averaged 6,000 square feet in space, although some, such as the Harvard Square store at 2,000 square feet, were significantly smaller. At about this time, Tweeter expanded its product line to take on high-end video equipment, principally in the form of color televisions.

Much as Bloomberg had anticipated, the general population's knowledge of and demand for high-end stereo and video equipment continued to grow through the mid-1980s. This growth was aided by strong regional and national economies and by the introduction of new technologies (e.g., Video Cassette Recorders [VCRs], Compact Disc [CD] Players). These conditions helped to solidify Tweeter's positioning at the high-end of the audio and video market.

By the end of 1986, Tweeter had grown to 13 stores throughout eastern Massachusetts and Rhode Island and by the late-1980s, Tweeter's share of the New England consumer electronics market had grown to almost 2% overall, and close to 5% in the Boston area.

---

[1] Stereo components are separate audio devices that can be combined to form a single stereo system. For example, a component system might consist of a receiver, a CD player, a cassette deck, and one or two pairs of speakers, all separately purchased to obtain the best of what each manufacturer has to offer. Typically, component systems are more flexible (components can be added or upgraded with ease) and capable of higher quality sound than "rack systems" or "compact systems," which offer prepackaged componentry.

During this period, Tweeter continued to be recognized as a retailer of high quality, high-end audio components and video equipment, with knowledgeable salespeople who offered high levels of customer service. Two of their advertising slogans during this period were, "We don't carry all the brands, only the ones that count" and "Some hi-fi salesman can sell you anything, and often do." Tweeter customers generally perceived that they were paying a premium price for the products they purchased, but were receiving the best customer service in the region for that premium.

The Shake-out Years: Mid-1980s to 1993

The euphoria of the mid-1980s was short lived, however, as three factors contributed to an overall decline in the New England electronics market in the late-1980s and early-1990s.

First, the market growth of the mid-1980s led to new competitive entrants, especially at the lower end of the retail market. In 1985, for instance, two Michigan-based chains, Fretter Superstores and Highland Superstores, both warehouse-like electronics chains, opened four stores each in the Boston area. Second, by the late-1980s, household penetration for color televisions, VCRs and many other home electronics had grown appreciably, thereby limiting future growth in those product categories. Third, the once growing U.S. economy came to a screeching halt in 1987 and 1988, with New England among those geographic regions hardest hit.

These factors combined to have two major consequences. First, not all retailers survived. The first to falter was Tech Hi-fi, which found itself financially overextended just as competition was heating up. In 1985, it declared bankruptcy and closed its 11 Massachusetts stores. The demise of Tech Hi-fi was followed six years later by Highland Superstores (10 New England stores) and in 1995 by Fretter (15 stores), both of whom also suffered from being financially overextended.

The second major result of the increasingly competitive environment of the late-1980s was increased price promotion. Traditionally, the New England electronics market had been characterized by four major "Sale" periods during which retailers discounted certain products to draw consumers into their stores—a Presidents' Day Sale in mid-February, a Father's Day Sale in June, a "Back to School" Sale in early-September, and a "Wrap it up Early" or "Pre-Holiday" Sale in mid-November. For the remainder of the year, product prices remained relatively steady, with only limited advertised price discounting.

Beginning in 1988, however, as the Boston economy bottomed out and consumer electronics sales growth flattened, Lechmere initiated an ongoing series of weekend "Sale" campaigns in which they would cut prices on select items on Friday, Saturday and Sunday. In order to retain their market shares, Tweeter and most other major retailers followed suit. As a result, the weekend "Sale" became a commonplace event, and consumers began to expect price discounts when purchasing audio and video equipment. In some cases, sales people would even tell customers not to buy on Wednesday, but rather to wait until Saturday when the desired item would be 20% off. During this period, it was not uncommon for 60% to 80% of a retailer's sales to occur on Saturday and Sunday.

As consumers increasingly focused on price in their purchasing process, Tweeter's profitability suffered. Noah Herschman, Tweeter's vice president of Marketing, described the problem in the following fashion:

> The consumers just wanted price, price, price. But, we didn't carry entry-level products, like a $139 VCR or a $399 camcorder. We carried the middle and high-end stuff. So people would look at our ads and they would look at Lechmere's ads. Lechmere would advertise a $139 VCR, and we would advertise a $199 VCR. They'd have a $399 camcorder, and we'd have a $599 camcorder. Even though their middle and high-end equipment sold for the same price as ours, we seemed to be more expensive to the inexperienced consumer. Our print advertising was actually driving people away—doing more damage to our business than if we never ran it.

EXHIBIT 7   Tweeter etc. Income Statement: FY 1990 to FY 1996[a]

Source: Company records.

	FY 1990	FY 1991	FY 1992	FY 1993	FY 1994	FY 1995	FY 1996 (est.)[b]
Gross revenues	$39,500	$35,660	$41,140	$43,714	$55,164	$70,305	$82,400
Cost of goods sold	26,228	23,586	27,209	28,485	35,739	45,299	52,300
Total gross margin	$13,272	$ 12,074	$13,931	$15,229	$19,425	$25,006	$30,100
Total expenses	15,146	14,085	13,894	15,890	18,038	22,304	26,500
Net income	($1,874)	($2,011)	$ 37	($661)	$ 1,387	$ 2,702	$ 3,600

[a]Fiscal Years are from October 1 of the previous year through September 30 of the year indicated.
[b]Figures for FY 1996 are based on midyear projections and do not include the purchase of Bryn Mawr Stereo and Video.

In response to the profitability downturn, Tweeter attempted to compete on price as well as product quality and customer service. For instance, Tweeter began to carry Sherwood audio components, an entry-level brand comparable in price to the low-end offerings of Lechmere, Fretter and others. In addition, Tweeter began to stock the lower-end models of brands it had been carrying only at the middle and high-end, such as Sony. Nevertheless, the majority of Tweeter's product line was still in the middle to high-end and included brands such as Denon, Alpine, Kenwood, Klipsch and Boston Acoustics.

To further aid in this price-based competition, Tweeter joined the Progressive Retailers Organization in 1988, a buying consortium founded in 1986 that consisted of small high-end consumer electronics retailers throughout the United States which combined for over $1 billion in annual sales. As a result, Tweeter was able to obtain prices from manufacturers that were comparable with those obtained by its larger competitors.

Despite these efforts, the public perception of Tweeter remained unchanged. Customers continued to view Tweeter as more specialized and more expensive than Lechmere and the other New England retailers. While most consumers still recognized the high level of service Tweeter provided, many believed that such service came at the expense of higher prices, something they were increasingly less willing to accept. As a result, Tweeter's sales and profitability began to deteriorate starting in the early-1990s (see **Exhibit 7**). Tweeter's plight was exacerbated by Circuit City's entrance into the New England market in the spring of 1993. Circuit City's media-blitz advertising and fierce price competition further focused consumers attention on price as the primary determinant of product choice.

A Change in Strategy: August 16, 1993

Frustrated by Tweeter's financial performance, Sandy Bloomberg, Jeff Stone (Tweeter's recently hired president and COO), Noah Herschman and the rest of the Tweeter management hashed out possible competitive responses at a management retreat in the spring of 1993.

In preparation for this retreat, Tweeter had conducted a number of focus groups in the months leading up to the retreat. Herschman boiled down the results of these focus groups into the two sets of insights.

First, individuals shopping for consumer electronics in the New England area displayed the following general characteristics and behavior:

- On average, consumers actively thought about purchasing a new product one to two months before actually making the purchase.

- On average, consumers visited two to three retailers prior to purchasing a desired product. The factors most cited by consumers in their selection of stores to visit include newspaper advertisements (cited by 70% of consumers), past experience with the store (50%) and recommendations of friends and family (40%).
- Eight out of ten consumers checked newspaper advertisements for product availability and price information when in the market for consumer electronic equipment. Virtually all of these consumers delayed purchase until they saw the desired product or class of product advertised in a newspaper circular.

Second, individuals who were familiar with or considered purchasing at Tweeter displayed the following specific characteristics and behavior:

- Four out of five consumers viewed Tweeter as being more expensive than the major competitors in the market (i.e., Lechmere, Fretter). However, most of these consumers reported that if price were not an issue, they would prefer to purchase their desired product from Tweeter.
- Of all consumers who visited Tweeter in search of a product, 60% also visited Lechmere, 45% also visited Fretter and 20% also visited Sears in the course of their product search.
- One in three consumers specifically came to Tweeter to figure out what to buy and then went to Lechmere or Fretter, believing they could get a better price there.

These focus groups also allowed Tweeter to characterize four types of electronics consumers in the New England market: the "entry-level customer," the "price biter," the "convenience customer," and the "quality/service customer":

> **Entry-Level Customers** The *entry-level customer* was interested in buying the cheapest item in a given category and was relatively indifferent to product quality and customer service.
>
> **The Price Biter** The *price biter* was very cognizant of price, but was also concerned with product quality and customer service. Price biters were more focused on getting the "absolute best deal" than on getting the "absolute lowest price" in a particular category.
>
> **The Convenience Customer** For the *convenience customer,* price, service and product quality were of secondary importance to shopping convenience. A convenience customer tended to shop in a store such as Lechmere or Sears because it was familiar and/or because they could purchase products in many different categories (e.g., luggage, jewelry, camera equipment, housewares, etc.) on the same shopping trip.
>
> **The Quality/Service Customer** For the *quality/service customer,* high levels of product quality and customer service were of primary concern and price, while still important, was of secondary concern. Some retailers referred to these consumers as "BBCOs"—"Buy the Best and Cry Once."

Herschman estimated that while this final group represented only 10% of the total New England customer base, it accounted for 70% of Tweeter's clientele. **Exhibit 8** provides Herschman's estimates for the distribution of customers for Tweeter as well as for the other major competitors in the New England market.

Armed with these insights, Bloomberg and his team used the spring management retreat to completely revamp the marketing strategy for Tweeter etc. This new strategy was announced to the public on August 16, 1993, and was referred to by Herschman as a "three-pronged attack" to restore price credibility at Tweeter.

EXHIBIT 8
Makeup of Customer Bases across New England Retailers

Source: Tweeter company estimates.

Customer Segment	Total Market	Tweeter	Lechmere	Circuit City
Entry Level	50%[a]	5%[b]	40%	35%
Price-Biter	15%	20%	10%	35%
Convenience	25%	5%	40%	15%
Quality/Service	10%	70%	10%	15%
	100%	100%	100%	100%

[a]To be read, 50% of all New England consumer electronics customers are Entry-level customers.
[b]To be read, 5% of all Tweeter customers are Entry-level customers.

Abandonment of the "Sale"

First, in a radical departure from the practices of its competitors and from their own historic behavior, Tweeter eliminated the use of the "Sale" to build store traffic and promote consumer spending. Herschman explained:

> We were getting killed by the big players—Lechmere, Circuit City and Fretter. Every weekend, everyone was having a sale, but on different makes and models of product. This made it almost impossible to compare prices across retailers. This worked in favor of the big stores, who were already perceived as low priced, but it was killing us. Even though we were competitively priced, because of our high-price image, no one was listening. And even more frustrating was the fact that our increasing reliance on the weekend "Sale" drew attention away from our unique selling proposition—high quality products and great customer service.

Thus, as part of Tweeter's new strategy, Sandy Bloomberg and Jeff Stone decided to do away with the weekend "Sale" and move to an "Every Day Fair Pricing" strategy. They vowed to set Tweeter's prices competitively and to look to policies other than the "Sale" to communicate its price competitiveness to potential customers.

Automatic Price Protection

As the primary means to communicate their price competitiveness, Tweeter instituted "Automatic Price Protection" as the second prong of their "three-pronged" strategy. "Price Protection" or "Price Guarantees" were an oft-used retailing tactic intended to assure customers that they were receiving the best price available on any given product. In its typical form, if a consumer purchased a product at one store and later found it for a lower price at another store, the consumer could return to the first store with proof of that lower price and get reimbursed for the difference. Typically, these price protection policies were in effect for 30 days from the time of purchase and promised to refund 100% of the price difference, although some retailers promise refunds of 110%, 150% or even 200% of the price difference.

Over the years, this form of price protection had led to some interesting battles amongst retailers. In New York City, for instance, the consumer electronics retailer Crazy Eddie advertised "We will not be undersold. Our prices are the lowest—guaranteed. Our prices are insane." At the same time, its primary competitor, Newmark and Lewis, advertised a "Lifetime low-price guarantee" which promised to rebate 200% of the price difference if a consumer found a lower price at any time during the life of the product. Both stores declared bankruptcy in the 1980s.

As of 1993, most of the major consumer electronics retailers in New England practiced some form of price protection. For instance, Lechmere, Circuit City and Fretter all offered a 110% refund for a period of 30 days. In contrast, Tweeter offered a 100% refund for 30 days. Jeff Stone, president of Tweeter, estimated that Tweeter refunded $3,000 to $4,000 per month to its customers under this price protection strategy. One industry expert estimated that across all price protection programs, only about 5% of consumers entitled to a rebate actually followed through and redeemed that rebate.[2] Often cited reasons for this low rebate redemption included the effort needed to physically track newspaper ads and to travel back to the retailer to obtain the refund.

On August 16, 1993, Tweeter took price protection one step further. Under Automatic Price Protection, Tweeter took it upon itself to track the local newspapers and send out rebates. If a consumer purchased an item at Tweeter and it was advertised for less in a major local newspaper within 30 days, Tweeter automatically mailed that consumer a check for the difference. Tweeter's APP covered individual items priced at $50 or more and applied to price differences of $2 and greater (see **Exhibit 9** for Tweeter's advertised explanation of their policy). In addition to APP, Tweeter retained and extended their former price protection policy to 60 days and renamed it "Regular Price Protection."

Operationally, APP was administered by a specialized department at Tweeter's corporate headquarters in Canton, Massachusetts. A staff member would physically check every issue of eight major newspapers in the New England area for price advertisements from Tweeter's competitors. These papers included *The Boston Globe, The Boston Herald, The Cape Cod Times, The Danbury News Times, The Hartford Courant, The New Haven Register, The New London Day* and *The Providence Journal*. If any product carried by Tweeter was advertised by a competitor, the price and model number of that product and the date of the advertisement were entered into the Tweeter database. This information was then cross matched against Tweeter sales data to check for purchases of that product at a higher price within the past thirty days. If any such purchase was found, the computer generated a check for the difference and automatically mailed it to the purchaser within five days.

A Change in the Marketing Mix

The third prong of Tweeter's "three-pronged" strategy to restore price credibility was a shift in their marketing mix away from print advertising and toward television and radio advertising as well as direct mail and product catalogs.

Over the years, Tweeter's marketing budget had typically run at about 8% of gross sales. Under their old "Sale" based promotional strategy, the vast majority of this marketing budget was dedicated to newspaper advertising in the form of weekly "Sale" announcements. In FY 1993, for example, 80% of their $3.1 million marketing budget was spent on newspaper advertising, with the remaining 20% split between radio advertising, direct mail, market research and in-store promotions.

With the elimination of their Sale-based strategy, the Tweeter marketing mix changed significantly (see **Exhibit 10**). Most noticeably, the choice of media and message shifted from newspaper advertising which focused on "Sale" prices to radio and television advertising which focused on Tweeter's price competitiveness and Automatic Price Protection policy.

In conjunction, Tweeter instituted a direct marketing campaign which revolved around a 50- to 100-page seasonal "Buyer's Guide," which provided product descriptions and prices for all of Tweeter's major products. Produced four times per year, by 1996 this guide was mailed to approximately 325,000 individuals. Herschman estimated that of these 325,000 recipients, 270,000 had made a purchase at Tweeter within the past 18 months. It was believed that 90% of those who purchased some item at Tweeter ended up on this catalog mailing list for at least a period of two years. Buyer's Guides were also made available to consumers at each of Tweeter's retail locations as well as at various musical events sponsored by Tweeter, such as the summer outdoor concert series at Great Woods in Mansfield, Massachusetts.

---

[2] *The Wall Street Journal,* August 17, 1993, p. B6.

EXHIBIT 9   Tweeter Automatic Price Protection

Source: Company records.

Only Tweeter **Automatically** Mails You A Check For The Difference!

If you buy something at Tweeter and it's advertised for less in a major local newspaper within 30 days, we'll <u>automatically</u> mail you a check for the difference!

It's been more than two full years since we introduced Automatic Price Protection.^{SM} And to date, Tweeter remains the only retailer in the country (world?) to provide such a service.

Needless to say, customers who have received APP^{SM} checks in the mail have been delighted by the fact that they didn't have to shop around for a better price. INSTEAD, TWEETER DID THE PRICE SHOPPING FOR THEM <u>AFTER</u> THE SALE!

Here's How APP™

Step 1

Staff members in the Automatic Price Protection Department go through each consumer electronics ad in every edition of the major local newspaper. When we find an item advertised that Tweeter sells, we record the model#, price, and date of the ad in our computer.

Step 2

Our Management Information Department then finds every customer who purchased that item from Tweeter within the 30-day period preceding the ad.

Step 3

The names and addresses of customers who paid more than the advertised prices are separated and spooled.

Step 4

Checks are cut for the difference between what the customer paid and the price advertised. They are mailed within five days.

Common Myths about Automatic Price Protection^{sm}

Myth: That APP doesn't work because most retailers have model numbers that are unique to them, so we can't compare prices.

Reality: The truth is, that Tweeter has no unique model numbers. In fact, we share all of our TV, VCR, Camcorder, and Portable Audio models with the other big retailers like Lechmere, Circuit City, and the Wiz. And we share most of our Car Stereo models, and many of our Home Stereo models with them as well.

Myth: That Tweeter only mails out checks for large amounts and that small price protection amounts are omitted.

Reality: Tweeter mails out APP checks for amounts of $2 and over.

Myth: That Tweeter only Price Protects items that are high-priced.

Reality: Tweeter Price Protects items priced $50 and over.

Myth: That the APP checks Tweeter mails out are only redeemable for merchandise at Tweeter.

Reality: The APP refunds that Tweeter mails out are bonafide checks. You can cash them anywhere.

EXHIBIT 10
Tweeter Marketing Mix

Source: Company records.

	FY 1993		FY 1996	
	$ (000s)	As % of Sales	$(000s)	As % of Sales
Print	$2,500	7.1%	$ 300	0.3%
Television	0	0.0	1,150	1.4
Radio	375	1.1	2,750	3.3
Direct mail[a]	125	0.3	1,000	1.2
Music series[b]	0	0.0	225	0.3
Pre-openings[c]	0	0.0	275	0.3
Other[d]	125	0.3	1,000	1.2
Total	$3,125	8.9%	$6,700	8.0%

[a]Includes quarterly buyers guides and other one-time only direct mail campaigns.
[b]Includes sponsorship of Great Woods Concert Series.
[c]Includes promotional efforts related to new store openings.
[d]Includes marketing research, public relations and cellular telephone promotions.

EXHIBIT 11
Tweeter Product Mix: 1996

Source: Company records.

Product Category	% of Dollar Sales
Video:	
TV's 40" and under	14%
TV's over 40"	10
Video cassette recorders (VCRs)	6
Camcorders	4
Direct satellite systems (DSS)	1
Sub-Total	35%
Audio:	
Speakers	14%
Receivers	9
CD players	7
Personal portable	4
Tape decks	2
Other audio electronics[a]	5
Sub-Total	41%
Car Stereo:	14%
Other: [b]	10%
Total	100%

[a]Includes amplifiers, preamplifiers, boom boxes and compact systems.
[b]Includes cellular phones, cables, bland tapes, warranties and labor.

August 1996

By most accounts, Tweeter's shift in strategy had a positive effect on financial performance. Sales almost doubled in the three years since the institution of the new strategy, from $43.7 million in FY 1993 to a projected $82.3 million in FY 1996. A breakdown of 1996 sales across major product categories, by percentage, is shown in **Exhibit 11.** Part of this recent growth could be attributed to an increase in sales per store, with same-store sales increasing by 50% between 1993 and 1996, and part could be attributed to an increase in the number of stores from 14 to 21 over the same period.

The Impact of Automatic Price Protection

Immediately after the announcement of Tweeter's new strategy, the media response to APP was extremely positive, with articles in *The Wall Street Journal*, *The Boston Globe* and *The Boston Herald* all extolling the virtues of the Tweeter's unique price guarantee. There were a few skeptics, however:

> . . . most suppliers sell retailers products that are not available elsewhere in the market. Thus, there is little chance that many items will qualify for the refunds.[3]
>
> . . . the impact will be more one of perception than of massive price refunds, in part because Tweeter's moderate to high-end products don't overlap with many other retailers.[4]

Other observers disagreed. Edgar Dworsky, the Massachusetts assistant attorney general for consumer protection commented:

> It's a brilliant idea. The problem with price protection guarantees has been that it's the consumer's burden to find a lower price somewhere else. Tweeter's going to do the watching for you. I just hope they don't lose their shirts.[5]

By the end of 1995, Tweeter had mailed a total of 29,526 APP checks totaling over $780,000 (see **Exhibit 12**). It was not clear to Sandy Bloomberg what to make of this number, however. For instance, if Tweeter's prices were competitive, why were they sending out any checks?

An added concern for Bloomberg and his management team was whether Tweeter's message of price competitiveness was reaching potential customers. While routine price comparisons suggested that Tweeter was competitive on price relative to its major competitors (**Exhibit 13**), some recent surveys indicated that many customers still perceived Tweeter as being more expensive (see **Exhibit 14**). In addition, few consumers seemed to understand the essence of APP and most were unaware of that it was Tweeter who offered it (see **Exhibit 14**). In looking at this data, Herschman noted the difference in customer attitudes between those who were aware of Tweeter's APP policy and those who were not.

The Purchase of Bryn Mawr Stereo and Video

APP was only one of the things on the mind of Tweeter management in spring and summer of 1996. On May 16, after several years of friendly discussions, Tweeter finalized the purchase of Bryn Mawr Stereo and Video, a privately-owned consumer electronics chain headquartered outside of Philadelphia, in King of Prussia, Pennsylvania. Using a similar high-end, high-service strategy as Tweeter, Bryn Mawr had grown to approximately $35 million in annual sales over 13 stores located in eastern Pennsylvania, New Jersey, Delaware and Maryland. Tweeter planned to retain the Bryn Mawr name to capitalize on its brand recognition, while merging management across the two chains.

Not surprisingly, Bryn Mawr faced many of the same competitive challenges as Tweeter. Long known for its high-end merchandise and superior service quality, many consumers held the perception that Bryn Mawr was not price competitive with the large electronic superstores operating in the Mid-Atlantic region, such as Circuit City, Best Buy and Nobody Beats the Wiz. To fight this perception, at Bloomberg's urging, Bryn Mawr adopted Tweeter's Automatic Price Protection in September of 1995. Unlike Tweeter, however, Bryn Mawr failed to see any appreciable increase in sales through the time of their purchase by Tweeter. While some at Tweeter attributed this shortcoming to Bryn Mawr's less aggressive campaign to advertise APP and its features, it gave others cause to question the role of APP in building sales.

---

[3] *The Boston Globe,* August 17, 1993, p. 35.

[4] *The Boston Herald,* August 17, 1993, p. 1.

[5] *The Wall Street Journal,* August 17, 1993, p. B6.

EXHIBIT 12
Automatic Price Protection Rebates by Month (in dollars)

Source: Company records.

		Number of Checks		$ Value of Checks	
		Month	Cumulative	Month	Cumulative
1993	August	89	89	$ 1,816	$ 1,816
	September	268	356	5,105	6,921
	October	549	905	15,718	22,639
	November	843	1,748	25,595	48,234
	December	1,571	3,319	31,229	79,463
1994	January	433	3,751	10,295	89,758
	February	341	4,093	9,188	98,945
	March	403	4,495	12,410	111,355
	April	475	4,970	10,600	121,955
	May	591	5,561	13,714	135,669
	June	690	6,251	14,331	150,000
	July	483	6,734	11,350	161,350
	August	529	7,263	12,014	173,364
	September	581	7,844	9,354	182,718
	October	681	8,525	14,949	197,666
	November	1,594	10,119	39,003	236,669
	December	4,249	14,368	104,260	340,929
1995	January	1,528	15,895	36,389	377,318
	February	849	16,744	17,751	395,069
	March	850	17,594	20,154	415,223
	April	561	18,155	12,656	427,879
	May	610	18,765	12,636	440,515
	June	1,108	19,873	25,583	466,098
	July	160	20,033	3,236	469,334
	August	675	20,708	16,614	485,948
	September	628	21,335	16,498	502,445
	October	1,078	22,413	27,881	530,326
	November	2,403	24,815	72,038	602,364
	December	4,711	29,526	181,499	783,863

Nobody Beats the Wiz

Another issue that concerned Tweeter management in the summer of 1996 was the recent entry of Nobody Beats the Wiz into the local market. On June 16th, The Wiz opened a sleek new 50,000-square-foot retail outlet in Saugus, Massachusetts, their first store in the Greater Boston area and their second in Massachusetts. In total, The Wiz had plans to open ten stores in the New England market over the next several years. Lon Rebackin, vice president of real estate for The Wiz, noted:

> This is a priority market for us. In the short term and the long term, we will be a player in New England.[6]

A privately held company with over $900 million in sales in 1994, the Wiz was the third largest consumer electronics retailer chain in the United States, offering a wide selection of audio and video electronics, as well as personal computer hardware and software. The Wiz operated a total of over 50 stores in New York, New Jersey, Connecticut, Pennsylvania and most recently, Massachusetts.

The Wiz was known for its monstrous marketing campaigns touting rock bottom prices, a strategy they had used with great effectiveness in the New York metropolitan market. These campaigns often included noted sports stars as football's Joe Namath and basketball's

[6] *The Boston Globe,* June 7, 1996, p. 38.

EXHIBIT 13 Product Line and Price Comparisons across Major New England Retailers—27" Color Televisions

Source: Comparison of products and prices in the week of September 16, 1996.

Model	Lechmere	Circuit City	Wiz	Tweeter
GE-27GT600	320 (Sale)			
GE-27GT616	280 (Ad)			
Hitachi-27CX1B		450		
Hitachi-27CX5B	480 (Sale)	500 (Ad)		
Hitachi-27CXSB		440		
JVC-AV27720	450	430		
Magnavox-TP2770	500			
Magnavox-TP2782C	500	450		
Magnavox-TS2743			400	
Magnavox-TS2752C	350 (Sale)			
Magnavox-TS2753C	370	350 (Ad)		
Magnavox-TS2775C		380 (Sale)		
Magnavox-TS2779			400 (Ad)	
Mitsubishi-CS27205	500 (Ad)		479	500
Mitsubishi-CS27305	670		598	600
Mitsubishi-CS27407	920		850	850
Panasonic-CT27G11	400 (Sale)	430	430	480
Panasonic-CT27G21	430 (Sale)	480	497	
Panasonic-CT27SF12	650 (Sale)	630		650
Panasonic-CT27SF21	700 (Sale)			
Panasonic-CT27SF22	700 (Sale)			
Panasonic-CT27SF23	750		750	750
Panasonic-CT27SF33	900			
ProScan-PS27108		600 (Ad)	548	600

Model	Lechmere	Circuit City	Wiz	Tweeter
ProScan-PS27113		630 (Sale)	578	
ProScan-PS27123				750
ProScan-PS27160		870		
RCA-F27204BC	530 (Ad)			
RCA-F27240WT	350 (Sale)		380	
RCA-F27638BC				400
RCA-F2767SBC	430 (Sale)	450	395 (Ad)	
RCA-F2767BC	330 (Ad)			
Sharp-27GS60			330 (Ad)	
Sharp-27HS120				550
Sony-KV27S20	500 (Ad)	500		
Sony-KV27S25	550 (Sale)	550	550	
Sony-KV27V20	590	550 (Sale)	550	550
Sony-KV27V25				650
Sony-KV27V35	840		750	750
Sony-KV27V55	800		750	
Sony-KV27XBR45	900 (Sale)		970	1000
Toshiba-CF27E30	400 (Ad)			
Toshiba-CF27F50	470 (Sale)		497	
Toshiba-CF27F55	500 (Ad)	500		
Zenith-SM2789BT		500		
Zenith-SR2787DT	650 (Sale)			
Zenith-SR2787DT	550 (Sale)			
Zenith-SY2772DT	480	450 (Ad)		
Zenith-SY2773DT				

Notes: (Ad) indicates a price advertised in the local paper; (Sale) indicates an unadvertised, in-store markdown.

EXHIBIT 13 (Continued)   **Product Line and Price Comparisons across Major New England Retailers—Multiple CD Players**

Source: Comparison of products and prices in the week of September 16, 1996.

Model	Lechmere	Circuit City	Wiz	Tweeter
Adcom-GCD700				700
Admiral-MWDK1	90 (Sale)			
Denon-DCM360				330
Denon-DCM460				400
Fisher-DAC503			158	
Fisher-DAC6005		300 (Sale)	219 (Ad)	
Harmon-Kar.-FL8300	120 (Ad)		299 (Ad)	
JVC-XLF108BK		120		
JVC-XLF152BK		180 (Sale)	180	
JVC-XLF252BK		200 (Ad)	180 (Sale)	
JVC-XLM418BK			220 (Sale)	
Kenwood-DPJ1070		300 (Ad)		300
Kenwood-DPJ2071		500		
Kenwood-DPR3080	200	170	199	180
Kenwood-DPR4070		180 (Ad)	188	
Kenwood-DPR4080	220		230	200
Kenwood-DPR5080		220		300
Kenwood-DPR6080				
Onkyo-DXC320	350			
Onkyo-DXC330	270	300	280	
Onkyo-DXC530	330			
Onkyo-DXC606	400 (Sale)			
Pioneer-PD65				800
Pioneer-PDF59				300
Pioneer-PDF79				400
Pioneer-PDF109				800
Pioneer-PDF505	220	200 (Ad)	200	
Pioneer-PDF605	200 (Sale)	240	220	
Pioneer-PDF705		300 (Ad)		
Pioneer-PDF901		180		
Sony-CDPC425				
Sony-CDPC445				350
Sony-CDPC545	200 (Ad)		279	550
Sony-CDPCA7ES				200
Sony-CDPCA8ES				
Sony-CDPCE405		200 (Sale)	200	
Sony-CDPCE505		250	270	
Sony-CDPCX153	350 (Ad)	300	377	350
Sony-CDPCX200		350 (Sale)		450
Sony-CDPCX270				
Sony-CDPXE500	160			160
Technics-SLMC400	230 (Ad)		299 (Ad)	
Technics-SLMC50	150 (Sale)		248 (Ad)	
Technics-SLPD687		170 (Sale)		
Technics-SLPD787			168	
Technics-SLPD887	170 (Ad)	140	168 (Sale)	
Yamaha-CDC555			230 (Ad)	220
Yamaha-CDC755				350
Yamaha-CDC845				450

Notes: (Ad) indicates a price advertised in the local paper; (Sale) indicates an unadvertised, in-store markdown.

EXHIBIT 13 (Continued)   Product Line and Price Comparisons across Major New England Retailers—Camcorders

Source: Comparison of products and prices in the week of September 16, 1996.

Model	Lechmere	Circuit City	Wiz	Tweeter
Canon-ES80		470		
Canon-ES90		560		
Canon-ES100		500		
Canon-ES200		600	598	
Canon-ES900		800	898	
Hitachi-VM1900A		500		
Hitachi-VM2900A		600		
Hitachi-VMH710A		800		
Hitachi-VMH720A		800 (Ad)		
Hitachi-VMH825LA		1200		
JVC-GRAX310			498 (Ad)	
JVC-GRAX350		550 (Ad)	648	
JVC-GRAX410U	500	550 (Ad)	498 (Ad)	
JVC-GRAX510U	500			
JVC-GRAX710U	600 (Ad)	630 (Sale)	648	
JVC-GRAX810U		700 (Sale)		
JVC-GRAX910U	730 (Ad)	800	798	
JVC-GRAX1010U		900		
Panasonic-PVA206	550 (Ad)	570	528 (Ad)	
Panasonic-PVA306	600 (Sale)	680		
Panasonic-PVD406	800	800	800	700
Panasonic-PVD506	900	900 (Ad)	900	800
Panasonic-PVL606	1000 (Ad)	1000 (Sale)	998 (Ad)	900
Panasonic-PVIQ295			600	1000
Panasonic-PVIQ305		600		
Panasonic-PVIQ475		630 (Sale)		
Panasonic-PVIQ505			798	
RCA-CC431	500 (Ad)			
RCA-CC436	600			
RCA-CC616	700 (Sale)			

Model	Lechmere	Circuit City	Wiz	Tweeter
RCA-PRO800	300 (Ad)	300 (Ad)	370	
RCA-PRO844		500		
RCA-PRO847		600		
RCA-PROV712		600 (Ad)	648 (Ad)	
RCA-PROV714		850 (Ad)	798 (Sale)	
RCA-PROV949HB		800 (Ad)		
Sharp-VLE37U	600 (Ad)	580		
Sharp-VLE39U	600 (Sale)		700	
Sharp-VLE47U	800 (Ad)	850	998	
Sharp-VLL65U	450 (Ad)			
Sony-CCDFX730		900 (Sale)		500
Sony-CCDTR44	500 (Ad)	500 (Ad)		
Sony-CCDTR54		500 (Ad)		
Sony-CCDTR64	600 (Ad)	600 (Ad)	598	
Sony-CCDTR74	650	650 (Sale)	648	650
Sony-CCDTR78			650	
Sony-CCDTR82	650 (Ad)			
Sony-CCDTR83	850 (Ad)			
Sony-CCDTR84	770	750 (Sale)	700	700
Sony-CCDTR88			748	
Sony-CCDTR94	800	800 (Ad)	800 (Sale)	800
Sony-CCDTR600	1150 (Sale)	1100 (Ad)		
Sony-CCDTR910				1300
Sony-CCDTRV11	700 (Ad)	700 (Ad)	698 (Sale)	700
Sony-CCDTRV21	900 (Ad)	900 (Ad)	898	900
Sony-CCDTRV29		1000 (Ad)		
Sony-CCDTRV30		800	998	
Sony-CCDTRV40	1190 (Sale)	1100	1198	
Sony-CCDTRV41	1200	1200 (Ad)		1200
Sony-CCDTRV81	1500 (Ad)	1500 (Ad)		1500

Notes: (Ad) indicates a price advertised in the local paper; (Sale) indicates an unadvertised, in-store markdown.

EXHIBIT 13 (Continued)   **Product Line and Price Comparisons across Major New England Retailers—Full-Sized Speakers**

Source: Comparison of products and prices in the week of September 16, 1996.

Model	Lechmere	Circuit City	Wiz	Tweeter
Advent-ADVAmber			299	
Advent-ADVHeritage			350	
Advent-ADVLaureate			250	
BOSE-100		75		
BOSE-151		120		
BOSE-201 Series 1VB	100 (Ad)	100 (Ad)		
BOSE-301 Series 1VB	160 (Ad)	159 (Ad)		
Compact Reference-CR6				200
Compact Reference-CR7				260
Compact Reference-CR8				340
Compact Reference-CR9				420
Infinity-REF20001		100		
Infinity-REF20003		160		
Infinity-REF20004		200		
Infinity-REF20005		280 (Ad)		
Infinity-REF20006		350		
Infinity-RS20002C	280			
Infinity-RS20003C	330			
Infinity-RS200SL	300			
Infinity-RS225BL	220			
Infinity-RS325	200 (Sale)			
Infinity-RS625	250			
JBL-ARC30		130		
JBL-ARC50		170 (Sale)		
JBL-CM42		130		
JBL-L1		260 (Ad)		
JBL-L3		400		
JBL-L5		500		
KEF-Q10				250
KEF-Q30				400

Model	Lechmere	Circuit City	Wiz	Tweeter
KEF-Q50				600
KEF-Q70				900
Klipsch-Heritage				1000
Klipsch-KG.5			198 (Ad)	200
Klipsch-KG1.5				300
Klipsch-KG2.5				400
Klipsch-KG3.5V				500
Klipsch-KG4.5V				600
Klipsch-KG5.5V				800
Klipsch-KLPKSS3			800	
Klipsch-Series				1300
Lerwin-VS80	130			
Lerwin-VS100	180			
Lerwin-VS120	200			
Lerwin-VS150	370			
Lerwin -CVEAT10BK			230	550
Lerwin -CVEAT12BK			250	500
Lerwin -CVEAT1SBK			400	
Lynnfield -VR20				1400
Lynnfield -VR30				200
Lynnfield -VR40				
Mirage-M90IS				450
Mirage-M290IS				600
Mirage-M5901				700
Mirage-M8901				1200
Mirage-M10901				
Mission -731	180			
Mission -732	300			
Mission -735	450			
Polk-M3IIB			250	
Polk-S8B			200	

Notes: (Ad) indicates a price advertised in the local paper; (Sale) indicates an unadvertised, in-store markdown.

EXHIBIT 14   1995 Customer Survey Data[a]

Source: Company records; based on research conducted by WCVB-TV, Boston, MA.

Q1: Home electronic stores are offering price protection plans. What is AUTOMATIC PRICE PROTECTION?

Response	% of Responders (n = 1,286)
Buy item/Receive a refund by mail*	17.8%
Guaranteed lowest price*	14.2
Buy item/Pickup refund check	9.7
Item covered under warranty	8.9
Buy item/Pickup refund check + 10%	4.4
Other	4.4
Don't know	40.6

Q2: Automatic Price Protection is after you buy an item, if the store sees the item advertised for less, the store mails you a check. Which one store sells home electronics and offers the Automatic Price Protection plan?

Response	% of Responders (n = 1,286)
Tweeter etc.	22.1%
Circuit City	13.4
Lechmere	10.3
Fretter	5.8
Radio Shack	1.2
Sears	1.0
Other	4.6
Don't Know	37.9
None	3.9

Q3: Compared to the big chains, like Lechmere and Circuit City, do you think that Tweeter's prices are . . .

Tweeter Prices are . . .	% of Responders (n = 1,286)	Aware of Tweeter's APP Policy (n = 284)	Unaware of Tweeter's APP Policy (n = 1,002)
Lower	4.7%	5.1%	4.6%
About the same	25.3	36.1	22.2
Higher	16.0	14.5	16.4
Don't know	54.0	44.3	56.8

*Considered a correct response to the question.

[a]Data are based on a random telephone survey conducted in the Greater Boston area.

Julius Irving. In addition, The Wiz was generally recognized as offering intensive customer service. They also offered 110% price protection for 30 days on all items except camcorders and cellular telephones.

Publicly, the competitive reaction to the entry of The Wiz was understated. Harlan Platt, a professor of finance at Northeastern University commented:

> They're marvelous at creating the perception that they're giving customers the best deal of all. But the New England consumer is more worldly and wise. I wouldn't be surprised to see The Wiz withdraw and seek greener pastures.[7]

In commenting for Tweeter, Noah Herschman claimed:

> It's a great time to be in Boston when The Wiz comes in. They only generate interest in the product category. But the people we sell to are enthusiastic about what we have. Our niche is more the personal touch.[8]

[7] *The Boston Globe*, March 1, 1996, p. 65.

[8] Ibid.

Privately, however, Tweeter's management was concerned that the entry of The Wiz could lead to a new round of price wars, much like those of the late 1980s and early 1990s. Bloomberg could not help but wonder whether APP would continue to be an effective policy under those circumstances.

The Future

Having reviewed the events of the recent past, Sandy Bloomberg found himself back where he had started. He had always believed that Automatic Price Protection had played a major role in Tweeter's growth, but now Bryn Mawr gave him reason to question that belief. Even if he could attribute Tweeter's recent success to APP, however, the entry of The Wiz had the potential to reshape the competitive playing field in the increasingly crowded New England market. Sandy wondered what role Automatic Price Protection would play in Tweeter's future competitive positioning.

Chapter 30

DHL Worldwide Express

John A. Quelch   Greg Conley

In July 1991, in Jakarta, Indonesia, the shouts of the kaki lima (street vendors) outside did little to soothe Ali Sarrafzadeh's concerns. Sarrafzadeh, DHL's Worldwide sales and marketing manager, had spent the previous three days chairing the Worldwide Pricing Committee workshop at DHL's annual directors' meeting. On the following day, he was to present his recommendations on pricing to the conference's 300 attendees.

Some of the statements made during the workshop meetings were still ringing in his head:

> If I have P&L [profit and loss] responsibility for my region, then I better be able to set my own prices. If not, how am I supposed to impact profits? By managing my travel and entertainment account?
>
> *—Jurgsen Beckenbauer*
> *Regional Director—Central Europe*

> Many of our large multinational customers have come to us and told us that they want a consistent worldwide pricing structure. . . . If we don't offer worldwide prices and our competitors do, are we going to lose some of our largest accounts?
>
> *—Christine Platine*
> *Account Manager, Brussels headquarters*

If our pricing structures were consistent across regions, it would be much easier to consolidate regional reports. With better reporting, we could gain valuable information about our costs. . . . The simpler our pricing structure, the easier it is to manage hardware and software around the world.

> —*Adelina Rossi*
> *VP Systems, Brussels headquarters*

We are the only company which services some regions of Africa. Thus, we charge premium prices in these markets. If we are forced to charge the same rates as in other regions, we will only lose profits. Sales will not grow with lower prices.

> —*Aziz Milla, Country Manager—*
> *Cameroon, Africa*

Our prices have always been 20%–40% higher than the competition's prices. We can command these premium prices by continuing to give more value to our customers. . . . Our pricing must not encourage "cherry picking." We don't want customers to just ship with us on routes that are difficult to serve, such as those to and from Africa.

> —*Bobby Jones, Regional Director—USA*

Sarrafzadeh wanted to make recommendations on pricing strategy, structure, and decision making. On strategy, he viewed his options as recommending either a price leadership strategy or a market response strategy. The former meant DHL would charge premium prices and aim to deliver superior value-added services in all markets. The latter meant DHL would set prices independently in each country, according to customer usage patterns and competitive pressures.

If the principle of standardized worldwide pricing was pursued, what were the pricing structure implications? For example, should DHL charge a weekly or monthly handling fee (a set fee in return for automatically visiting a customer each business day) in all countries? Should the same price be charged for shipments between any two cities, regardless of which was the origin and which the destination?

Regarding pricing structure, Sarrafzadeh had to address several additional questions. Should DHL have different pricing schedules for documents and parcels? Should DHL set different prices for different industries? For example, should prices be different for banking and manufacturing customers? Should DHL offer special prices to multinational corporations seeking to cut deals with individual shippers to handle all their express document and parcel delivery needs worldwide?

Another issue was the DHL discount program. Sarrafzadeh had to decide whether DHL should continue to offer volume discounts. If so, should they be based on units, weight, or revenue?

In addition, Sarrafzadeh wanted to recommend who should hold primary price setting responsibility. He considered his three options to be a centralized, decentralized, or hybrid approach. A decentralized approach would continue the present policy in which country/region managers set all prices and headquarters offered counsel and support. Under a centralized approach, a headquarters management committee would set all prices around the world. Country managers would be responsible for collecting data and making suggestions to headquarters. A third option was to establish multiple pricing committees, each including managers from both headquarters and the regions and each responsible for setting prices for one or more specific industries.

Company Background and Organization

DHL legally comprised two companies: DHL Airways and DHL International. DHL Airways was based in San Francisco and managed all U.S. operations. DHL International was based in Brussels and managed all operations outside the United States. Each company was the exclusive delivery agent of the other. Revenues for 1990 were split: $600 million for DHL Airways, and $1,400 million for DHL International. One DHL executive commented, "The main reason DHL is involved in domestic shipping within the United States is to lower the costs and increase the reliability of our international shipments. If not for our domestic business, we would be at the mercy of the domestic airlines bringing our packages to the international gateways." In 1990, DHL accounted for only 3% of intra-U.S. air express shipments but 20% of overseas shipments from the United States.

DHL was the world's leading international express delivery network. It was privately held and headquartered in Brussels, Belgium. The company was formed in San Francisco in September 1969 by Adrian Dalsey, Larry Hillblom, and Robert Lynn. The three were involved in shipping and discovered that, by forwarding the shipping documents by air with an on-board courier, they could significantly reduce the turnaround time of ships in port. DHL grew rapidly and, by 1990, serviced 189 countries. In 1990, revenues were approximately $2 billion. Profits before taxes were 4%–6% of revenues. (**Exhibit 1** summarizes the growth of DHL operations from 1973 to 1990; **Exhibit 2** displays DHL's revenues by industry.)

DHL used a hub system to transport shipments around the world. In 1991 the company operated 12 hubs (as shown in **Exhibit 3**). Within Europe, the United States, and the Middle East, DHL generally used owned or leased aircraft to carry its shipments, while on most intercontinental routes it used scheduled airlines. In 1991, approximately 65% of DHL

EXHIBIT 1
DHL Operations Statistics, 1973–1990

	1973	1978	1983	1990
Shipments	2,000,000	5,400,000	12,400,000	60,000,000
Customers	30,500	35,000	250,000	900,000
Personnel	400	6,500	11,300	25,000
Countries served	20	65	120	189
Hubs	0	2	5	12
Flights/day	14	303	792	1,466
Aircraft	0	5	27	150
Vehicles	300	2,235	5,940	7,209

Note: Shipments included both documents and parcels. Hubs were major shipment sorting centers. Aircraft and vehicle data included both owned and leased equipment.

EXHIBIT 2
DHL Worldwide Revenues by Industry, January–June 1991

Conglomerates	10%
High technology	8
Import-export	8
Banking	7
Transport	7
Heavy engineering	6
Chemicals	5
Precision manufacturing	5
Professional services	4
Foodstuffs	4
Textiles/leather	4
Other	32

EXHIBIT 3   **DHL Hub System**

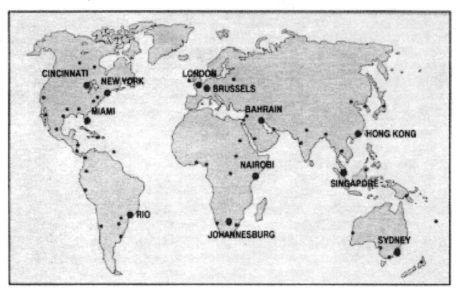

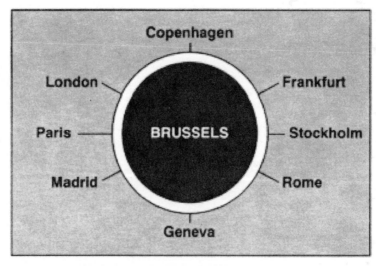

shipments were sent via scheduled airlines and 35% via owned or leased aircraft. The other leading shippers also utilized scheduled airlines but to a lesser extent than DHL. Federal Express relied on its own fleet of planes to transport all its shipments. Pierre Madec, DHL's operations director, noted:

> FedEx has a dedicated airfleet which ties up capital and limits the flexibility of its operation: express packages are forced to wait until the FedEx plane's takeoff slot, which at major international airports frequently does not tie in with the end-of-the-day courier pickups. By using a variety of scheduled international carriers, DHL is able to optimize its transport network to minimize delivery times.

DHL was organized into nine geographic regions. Region managers oversaw the relevant country managers and/or DHL agents in their regions and held profit and loss responsibility for performance within their territories. Revenues and profits were recognized at the location where a shipment originated. Only 70 people worked at DHL's world headquarters in Brussels. The main functions of the worldwide marketing services group, of which Sarrafzadeh was a member, were business development, information transfer, communication of best practice ideas, and sales coordination among the country operating units.

Of DHL's 60 million shipments in 1990, 50 million were cross-border shipments. DHL's worldwide mission statement, included in its 1990 annual report, read:

> DHL will become the acknowledged global leader in the express delivery of documents and packages. Leadership will be achieved by establishing the industry standards of excellence for quality of service and by maintaining the lowest cost position relative to our service commitment in all markets of the world.

DHL management believed that achievement of this mission required the following:

- Absolute dedication to understanding and fulfilling DHL's customers' needs with the appropriate mix of service, products, and price for each customer.
- Ensuring the long-term success of the business through profitable growth and reinvestment of earnings.
- An environment that rewards achievement, enthusiasm, and team spirit, and which offers each person in DHL superior opportunities for personal development and growth.
- A state-of-the-art worldwide information network for customer billing, tracking, tracing and management information/communications.
- Allocation of resources consistent with the recognition that DHL is one worldwide business.
- A professional organization able to maintain local initiative and local decision making while working together within a centrally managed network.

DHL's annual report also stated: "The evolution of our business into new services, markets or products will be completely driven by our single-minded commitment to anticipating and meeting the changing needs of our customers."

The International Air Express Industry

Total revenues for the international air express industry were approximately $3.4 billion in 1989 and $4.3 billion in 1990. The air express industry offered two main products: document delivery and parcel delivery. Industry revenues were split roughly 75:25 between parcels and documents. In 1989, the parcel sector grew 40%, while the document sector grew 15%. The growth of parcel and document express delivery was at the expense of the air cargo market and other traditional modes of shipping.

TABLE A
Worldwide International (Cross-Border) Air Express 1992 Estimated Revenue Growth Rates

Market	1992 Estimated Growth Rate
Europe	28%
Asia/Pacific	30
United States	25
Rest of the world	9
Total	25%

Note: Growth rates are for time-sensitive documents/packages under 30 kilograms.

The growth of the air express industry was expected to continue. One optimistic forecast for 1992 is presented in **Table A.** Other observers were concerned that shipping capacity would expand faster than shipments, particularly if economic growth slowed.

Acknowledging continuing progress toward completion of the European market integration program by the end of 1992, an article on the air express industry in Europe in *Forbes* (April, 1991) noted:

> The express-delivery business in Europe is booming. . . . Measured by revenues, the European express-delivery business is growing at a 28% compound annual rate. Big European companies are stocking products and parts in central locations and moving them by overnight express, instead of running warehouses in each country.

Competitors

Air express companies serviced a geographic region either by using their own personnel or by hiring agents. Building a comprehensive international network of owned operations and/or reliable agents required considerable time and investment and, therefore, acted as a significant barrier to entry.

DHL's principal competitors in door-to-door international air express delivery were Federal Express, TNT, and UPS. **(Exhibit 4** provides operational data for the top four competitors; **Table B** summarizes their 1988 market shares.)

Founded in 1973, FedEx focused for many years on the U.S. domestic market. During the late 1980s, the company began to expand internationally through acquisitions and competitive pricing, sometimes undercutting DHL published prices by as much as 50%. Between 1987 and 1991, FedEx invested over $1 billion in 14 acquisitions in nine countries: the United Kingdom, Holland, West Germany, Italy, Japan, Australia, United Arab Emirates, Canada, and the United States. FedEx also entered the international air freight business through the acquisition of Tiger International (Flying Tigers), which expanded further FedEx's global reach in document as well as parcel delivery, particularly in Asia. However, the challenge of integrating so many acquisitions meant that FedEx's international operations lost $43 million in 1989 and $194 million in 1990. Nevertheless, with 45% of the U.S. air express market, 7% of the European market, and leadership in value-added services based on information systems technology, FedEx remained a formidable competitor.

Thomas Nationwide Transport (TNT) was a publicly owned Australian transport group which had historically concentrated on air express delivery of documents. TNT focused mainly on Europe and had a low profile in North America. To participate in the North American market, TNT held a 15% stake in an American shipper—Airborne Freight Corporation. This stake could be increased to a maximum holding of only 25% under U.S. aviation laws.

EXHIBIT 4
Major Air Express Competitors, 1988

	DHL	FedEx	TNT	UPS
International Air Express revenues (in $ millions)	$1,200	$200	$500	$100
International Air Express employees	23,000	5,000	10,000	3,000
Countries covered	184	118	184	175
Total service outlets	1,427	1,135	800	1,700
Service outlets outside United States	1,207	278	750	465
Ratio of Owned:Agent country operations	2.00:1	0.53:1	0.77:1	0.36:1
Owned aircraft	49	38	17	3
Years of international experience	20	5	17	3
Document: Parcel revenues	65:35	20:80[a]	50:50	20:80

[a]After FedEx's 1989 acquisition of Tiger International, Inc., its document:parcel revenue ratio remained relatively unchanged as Tiger concentrated on heavy air freight. However, post-acquisition, document and parcel combined revenues represented a smaller portion of total revenues.

TABLE B
International Air Express Market Shares by $ Revenue (1988)

Company	Market Share (%)
DHL	44%
FedEx	7
TNT	18
UPS	4
Others	27
Total	100%

During the late 1980s, TNT began to target heavier shipments and bulk consolidations to fuel its growth.

United Parcel Service (UPS) was a privately held U.S. company, most of whose equity was owned by its employees. UPS had traditionally been known as a parcel shipper that emphasized everyday low prices rather than the fastest delivery. Unlike DHL, UPS sometimes held a package back to consolidate several shipments to the same destination in the interest of saving on costs. UPS had historically tried to avoid offering discounts from its published prices.

UPS's 1990 annual report proclaimed the company's strategy as follows:

UPS will achieve worldwide leadership in package distribution by developing and delivering solutions that best meet our customers' distribution needs at competitive rates. To do so, we will build upon our extensive and efficient distribution network, the legacy and dedication of our people to operational and service excellence and our commitment to anticipate and respond rapidly to changing market conditions and requirements.

In addition to the industry giants, there were many small shipping forwarders which concentrated on a specific geographic area or industry sector. In the late 1980s, many of these small companies were acquired by larger firms trying to increase their market shares. National post offices were also competitors in air express, but they could not offer the same service and reliability because they were not integrated across borders (that is, no national post office could control the shipment of a package from one country to another). One industry executive commented: "When we have internal competitive discussions on international business, the post offices just don't come up."

Finally, the regular airlines were minor competitors in door-to-door express delivery. British Airways operated a wholesale airport-to-door courier service called Speedbird in cooperation with smaller couriers that did not have international networks. Swissair serviced

50 countries through its Skyracer service in cooperation with local agents. In the heavy cargo sector, most airlines were allied with freight forwarders who consolidated cargo from different sources and booked space in aircraft. These alliances represented significant competition as DHL expanded into delivery of heavier shipments. Some airlines were reluctant to upset their freight forwarder customers by dealing with integrated shippers such as DHL.

Competition in the air express industry, aggravated by excess capacity, had resulted in intense price competition during the late 1980s.[1] DHL's chairman and CEO L. Patrick Lupo estimated that prices had dropped, on average, 5% each year from 1985 to 1990, with extreme price drops in some markets. For example, in Great Britain, DHL's list prices for shipments to the United States fell approximately 40% from 1987 to 1990. Some of the price reductions were offset, in part, by rising volume and productivity, yet Lupo noted, "There's no question that margins have been squeezed."

DHL Services

DHL offered two services: Worldwide Document Express (DOX) and Worldwide Parcel Express (WPX). DOX offered document delivery to locations around the world within the DHL network. DOX was DHL's first product and featured door-to-door service at an all-inclusive price for nondutiable/nondeclarable items. Typical items handled by DOX included interoffice correspondence, computer printouts, and contracts. The number of documents sent to and from each DHL location was, in most cases, evenly balanced.

WPX was a parcel transport service for nondocument items that had a commercial value or needed to be declared to customs authorities. Like DOX, WPX offered door-to-door service at an all-inclusive price that covered DHL's handling of both the exporting and importing of the shipment. Typical items handled by WPX included prototype samples, spare parts, diskettes, and videotapes.

DHL imposed size, weight, and content restrictions for all parcels. The size of a package could not exceed 175 centimeters in exterior dimensions (length + width + height), and the gross weight could not exceed 50 kilograms. Further, DHL would not ship various items such as firearms, hazardous material, jewelry, and pornographic material.

Table C compares DHL's parcel and document businesses for 1990.

DHL offered numerous value-added services, including computerized tracking (LASERNET), 24-hour customer service every day of the year, and proof of delivery service. Customers could also tap the assistance of specialized industry consultants based in DHL regional offices. Such value added services could enhance customer loyalty and increase DHL's share of a customer's international shipping requirements. However, such services were expensive to provide and customers using them were often not always charged extra, particularly since those services were also offered by key competitors such as FedEx.

---

[1] DHL planes flew, on average, 85% full in 1990. FedEx and UPS planes on international routes were thought to be achieving only 60% capacity utilization.

TABLE C
DHL's Document and Parcel Businesses, 1990

	Total Revenues	Revenues Growth (1989–90)	Total Shipments	Total Weight	Gross Profits
Document	60%	+14%	70%	50%	53%
Parcel	40%	+28%	30%	50%	47%

DHL had 20 years of experience in dealing with customs procedures and, by 1990, was electronically linked into an international customs network. All shipments were bar coded, which facilitated computerized sorting and tracking. Thanks to a direct computer link between DHL and customs authorities in 5 European countries, customs clearance could occur while shipments were en route. In addition, DHL's staff included licensed customs brokers in 80 countries.

DHL had been cautious about differentiating itself on the basis of speed of service, and arrival times were not guaranteed. However, DHL executives believed that their extensive network meant that they could deliver packages faster than their competitors. Hence, in 1991, DHL commissioned an independent research company to send on the same day five documents and five dutiable packages from three U.S. origin cities via each of five air express companies to 21 international destinations (three cities in each of seven regions). **Exhibit 5** reports the percentages of first place deliveries (i.e., fastest deliveries) achieved by each competitor in each region. DHL had the highest percentage of first place results in six of the seven regions. The research also indicated that DHL was consistently able to deliver more dutiable items through customs in time for earliest business district delivery (before 10:30 A.M.) than any of its rivals. A similar intra-European study found that DHL also achieved the highest percentage of first place deliveries on packages shipped between cities within Europe.

DHL also commissioned the independent research company to ascertain how it was rated by customers against its key competitors. **Table D** reports the ratings on the two attributes considered by customers to be the most important in choosing an international air express service.

The study also asked the customer sample which air express carrier they would turn to first when sending both a document and a parcel to destinations in each of four geographic regions. Results are presented in **Exhibit 6.** The results of a comparative study of unaided brand awareness for the major international air express companies are summarized in **Exhibit 7.**

EXHIBIT 5
Shipment Delivery Speed Tracking Study: Fastest Delivery, 1991

	DHL	TNT	FedEx	UPS	Airborne
Western Europe	39%	34%	4%	26%	NA
Eastern Europe	42	16	14	28	1%
Southeast Asia	34	16	18	6	27
Far East	56	11	21	3	9
Middle East	70	6	16	2	7
South America	28	10	32	9	21
Africa	62	9	13	10	7
All documents	55	15	13	13	6
All parcels	40	14	21	11	14

Notes: To be read, for example: Of the packages shipped on the five carriers to Western Europe, 39% of the packages that arrived first at their destination were shipped by DHL.
Some rows do not sum to 100% due to ties.

TABLE D
Ratings of Air Express Carriers

Source: Triangle Management Services Ltd. and IRB International Research, 1991.

	DHL	TNT	FedEx	UPS
Reliability	8.4	7.7	7.8	8.1
Value for money	8.0	7.3	7.5	8.0

Note: Respondents rated each carrier on a ten point scale (10 = high).

EXHIBIT 6

Sample Customers' First Choice of Air Express Carrier by Final Destination, 1991

Source: Triangle Management Services Ltd., and IRB International Research, 1991.

	DHL	TNT	FedEx	UPS
Documents				
Europe	32%	7%	8%	5%
North America	38	10	10	4
Middle East	35	14	6	5
Australia	38	10	7	5
Other	40	14	6	6
Parcels				
Europe	28%	5%	7%	7%
North America	32	7	12	8
Middle East	33	13	6	7
Australia	27	9	10	9
Other	32	10	4	9

EXHIBIT 7

Sample Customers' Unaided Brand Awareness for International Carriers of Documents and Parcels, 1991

Source: Company records.

	DHL	TNT	FedEx	UPS
Documents				
All countries	87%	50%	23%	16%
France	77	27	20	20
Germany	90	71	25	20
Italy	91	45	19	15
United Kingdom	85	67	37	22
Parcels				
All countries	72%	58%	28%	29%
France	58	40	14	10
Germany	67	76	28	46
Italy	75	62	23	27
United Kingdom	72	58	43	35

Customers

In the early years of air express, banks and finance houses were the major customers. For financial institutions, delays in delivery of checks and promissory notes could cause considerable financial losses. During the 1970s, most air express shipments were "emergency" in nature. Examples included an urgent contract, a check or note that sealed a financial transaction, a computer tape, a replacement part, and a mining sample which had to be studied before drilling could begin. During the 1980s, many customers began to use air express more systematically. For example, companies which operated "just-in-time" inventory systems began to use express delivery services to deliver components.

In 1990, DHL had 900,000 accounts, of which the top 250 accounts represented 10% of revenues and 15% of shipments. DHL had only about 10 global contracts with customers (representing 1% of revenues), as few multinational corporation (MNC) headquarters had expressed interest in negotiating such agreements. Like DHL, most MNCs were decentralized. However, DHL did have many regional agreements with MNCs as well as contracts in individual country markets.

Exhibit 8 shows how DHL segmented its U.S. customers in 1990 by level of monthly billings and provides profile information on each segment. Tony Messuri, DHL New England area sales manager, noted:

EXHIBIT 8 Profile of DHL's U.S.A. Customer Base (1990)

Source: Company records.

Customer Segment: Level of Monthly Billing, International	Percent of Total Accounts	Percent Typical Sales	Percent DHL Profits	Percent Using Discount[a]	Penetration[b]	Only DHL[c]
$ 0–$ 2,000	15%	5%	45%	10–35%	70%	95%
$ 2,001–$ 5,000	40	15	20	30–40	70	80
$ 5,001–$15,000	35	30	25	40–50	60	60
$15,001+	10	50	10	45–60	35	35
	100%	100%	100%			

[a]The exact discount was negotiated between DHL and the account. Percentages represent discounts off the published DHL tariff.
[b]Penetration means the percentage of all accounts in the segment that used DHL for at least some of their international shipping needs.
[c]To be read, percent of DHL customers who use only DHL for international shipping.

There are two principal types of customers. First, there are the people who know where they're shipping. They know where their international offices are located and will ask overseas offices for feedback about shippers. These customers select a carrier that's well-received and well-respected by their own customers, both internal and external.

Second, there are customers who cannot forecast where their future shipments will be going. They are more price sensitive but they can't give us enough information to enable us to set their discounts properly on the basis of anticipated volume. We are at more risk here of making a poor pricing decision. Sometimes a few months after we and the customer agree on a price and discount, the customer will conclude that it's overpaying, then seek more discounts from us or switch shippers.

Customers are very service sensitive. The small customers tend to switch shippers more readily. Often it only depends on which company's sales rep visited most recently.

The parcel market was typically more price sensitive than the document market. For most companies, the total cost of shipping parcels was a much larger line item than the total cost of shipping documents. Further, the decision-making unit was often different for the two services. The decision on how to ship a document was frequently made by an individual manager or secretary. As one shipper stated, "Documents go out the front door, whereas parcels go out the back door." Parcels were shipped from the loading dock by the traffic manager who could typically select from a list of carriers approved by the purchasing department. In some companies, parcel shipment decisions were being consolidated, often under the vice president of logistics. As one European auto parts supplier stated: "We view parts delivery as a key component of our customer service."

As a result, many customers split their air express business among several firms. For example, all documents might be shipped via DHL, while parcels might be assigned to another carrier. Alternatively, the customer's business might be split by geographic region; a multinational company might assign its North American business to Federal Express and its intercontinental shipments to DHL. For the sake of convenience and price leverage, most large customers were increasingly inclined to concentrate their air express shipments worldwide with two or three preferred suppliers.

Pricing

Evolution of Pricing Policy

As DHL expanded service into new countries throughout the 1970s and 1980s, it developed many different pricing strategies and structures. DHL country managers had almost total control of pricing. They typically set prices based on four factors: what the market could bear, prices charged by competition (which was often initially the national post office), DHL's initial entry pricing in other countries, and DHL's then-current pricing around the world.

DHL's prices were historically 20% to 40% higher than those of competitors. (**Exhibit 9** provides sample prices for DHL, TNT, FedEx, and UPS.) In most countries, DHL published a tariff book which was updated yearly. Competitors who followed DHL into new markets often patterned their pricing structures after DHL's.

DHL had developed a sophisticated, proprietary software package called PRISM to analyze profitability. A PRISM staff officer at each regional office advised and trained country operating units on use of the software. The program could calculate profitability by route or by customer in a given country. However, PRISM could not consolidate the profits of a given customer across countries. (**Exhibit 10** provides a fuller description of PRISM.) All profitability analyses had to be based on average costs due to the variability in costs associated with transporting a shipment. For example, a package from Perth, Australia, to Tucson, Arizona, might be consolidated seven to eight times in transit and travel on five to six planes. Further, every package from Perth to Tucson did not necessarily travel the same route. (**Exhibit 11** shows the revenues and costs associated with two sample lanes to illustrate the significant impact of geographical differences on costs and profitability.)

EXHIBIT 9
Sample Published List Prices on Selected Routes (1990)

Service	DHL	TNT	FedEx	UPS
1 kilogram document London–New York	$51	$47	$50	$44
2 kilogram document Brussels–Hong Kong	131	143	118	97
2 kilogram parcel Singapore–Sydney	120	120	39	34

EXHIBIT 10 **Development and Description of PRISM**

Source: Company records.

DHL local management was judged on revenue and controllable costs. The contribution of each local operation was calculated by subtracting local costs from revenue. This measure of performance did not, however, consider the costs to other country operations of delivery and whether the selling price was sufficient to cover the cost of pickup, line haul, hub transfer, delivery, and headquarters overhead and management costs.

In 1987, all countries and regions analyzed their costs and provided DHL headquarters with detailed delivery, pickup, hub, and line haul costs. Using these data, headquarters developed the PRISM (Pricing Implementation Strategy Model) software package. The inputs to the model were cost data along with competitive price information. PRISM costs were based on historical data which had been consolidated and averaged.

Country organizations were provided with the PRISM software which enabled them to analyze their profitability at the country, customer segment, and individual customer levels. The methodology was refined further to take into account the scale economies large shippers provided to DHL.

PRISM was used for the following purposes:

• Analyzing the profit impacts of possible tariff adjustments, taking into account the competitive intensity of the route.

• Identifying low- or negative-margin customers whose yields should be managed upwards.

• Settling price strategy for different customer segments.

Country and regional managers were still measured on local contribution (local revenues minus local costs). They were, however, encouraged to analyze profitability by account when developing their annual budgets and use PRISM when considering price revisions. The level of use of PRISM varied by region and country.

EXHIBIT 11
Revenue and Cost Lane Examples: DOX and WPX

	DOX (Document)	WPX (Parcel)
U.K. to United States (1990)		
Revenue	$5,723,000	$2,342,000
Outbound cost	2,392,915	667,712
Hub cost	596,608	490,436
Line haul[a]	1,121,882	647,915
Delivery	1,376,953	386,049
Margin	234,642	149,888
Margin %	4.1	6.4
Shipments	231,139	68,580
Revenue/shipment	$24.76	$34.15
Belgium to Hong Kong (1990)		
Revenue	$13,800,000	$6,660,000
Outbound cost	6,341,100	1,837,733
Hub cost	1,138,146	1,181,400
Line haul	2,926,662	1,767,733
Delivery	2,276,292	1,180,134
Margin	1,117,800	693,000
Margin %	8.1	10.5
Shipments	456,802	109,544
Revenue/shipment	$30.21	$60.25

[a]Line haul refers to the air segment of the shipment.

TABLE E
DHL Sample Prices, 1990

From London	First ½ Kilo	Each Additional ½ Kilo
Document:		
to New York	£24.50	£1.60
to Switzerland	£26.00	£2.20
to Japan	£26.50	£2.50
Parcel:		
to New York	£27.00	£1.60
to Switzerland	£32.00	£2.20
to Japan	£34.00	£2.50

PRISM was not used extensively by all DHL offices. As one country manager put it: "We and the customer both want a simple pricing structure. PRISM just provides more information, adds to complexity, and takes time away from selling."

Base Prices and Options

DHL's base prices were calculated according to product (service), weight, origin, and destination. Prices were often higher for parcels than for documents of equivalent weight due to extra costs for customs clearance, handling, packaging, and additional paperwork. FedEx charged the same for parcels and documents. Shipment weights were computed in pounds in the United States and in kilograms in all other countries. Moreover, weight breaks varied among countries. For example, in Hong Kong breaks were every half kilogram, and in Spain, every two kilograms. Some DHL executives believed that, for the sake of simplicity, DHL's weight breaks should be the same worldwide. (**Table E** gives examples of base prices on routes from London.)

Pricing Structures

In all country markets served, DHL followed one of three pricing approaches: monthly handling fee, frequency discount, and loaded half-kilo.

Under the first approach, DHL charged a flat monthly fee to customers who wanted to be included on its regular pickup route. DHL automatically visited such customers once each business day without the customer having to contact DHL for pickup. The purpose was to motivate customer usage of DHL's services and encourage customers to process all their shipments through DHL. Customers who elected not to be on DHL's regular route could either call for shipment pickup or drop off a shipment at a DHL office. Customers who called for pickup were charged a nominal pickup fee. Under the monthly fee structure, customers did not receive volume discounts.

Sarrafzadeh summarized his views on the problems with this approach:

> The monthly fee can work but only if it is properly marketed. Because it does not relate to a unit of value, customers resent it and salespeople can't defend it. As a result, it has often proved hard to raise the monthly fees as fast as the per-shipment charges.

In some markets, including Great Britain, DHL offered a frequency discount structure under which a discount was provided based on number of units shipped. The more often a customer used DHL during a given month, the cheaper the unit shipment cost.

The frequency discount was based on the total number of documents and parcels shipped. For example, if a customer purchased 10 document and 20 parcel shipments in a given month, it received a discount of £10 per shipment. Under the frequency discount structure, a customer did not pay a standard monthly route fee and DHL visited the account only upon request.

The per-shipment frequency discount was retroactive and was computed for each customer at the end of the calendar month. Conversely, FedEx's discounts were based on forecast demand rather than past performance and on revenues rather than unit shipments. FedEx monitored a new account's actual shipments for six months before the account qualified for a discount and then adjusted the discount upward or downward based on quarterly shipment data and shipment density.[2]

Sarrafzadeh noted:

> Once you publish your frequency discounts, they're no longer discounts. They're expected. Though they may sometimes attract the small routine shipper, it's easy for competitors to discover what the discounts are and undercut them. Better to publish only the book prices and apply discounts as needed on a case-by-case basis.

The loaded half-kilo structure used in the United States resembled the frequency discount structure, except that discounts were based on total weight shipped during a given month rather than on the number of shipments.

Price Negotiations

The largest customers sought one- or two-year deals with shippers to handle their transport needs. Typically, when a current agreement was nearing its end, the customer put its business up for bid and solicited proposals from interested shippers. Proposals incorporated the following information: transit times, overhead rate structures, rates for specified countries, tracking capabilities, sample tracking reports, sample annual activity report, and a list of international stations (indicating which were company-owned versus run by agents). Most bid

---

[2] Shipment density referred to the number of items picked up per stop. The more items collected per stop, the lower the pickup cost per unit. DHL's information systems did not permit it to award discounts based on shipment density.

requests were made by the purchasing manager, yet the decision-making unit was often a committee comprising managers from the traffic, sales and marketing, customer service, and purchasing departments. The decision was complicated because the major shippers were organized into different regions and lanes, thereby hindering direct comparisons among proposals. Sophisticated accounts typically calculated the bottom-line cost of each proposal, while unsophisticated accounts based their decisions on comparisons on a few "reference prices" (e.g., New York–London).

The average term of shipping agreements was two years, with almost all ranging between one and three years. Fifteen percent of DHL agreements involved formal contracts, while the other 85% were "handshake" agreements. Some customers tried to renegotiate prices in the middle of an agreement, though most *Fortune* 2000 companies abided by their deals.

DHL sales reps had significant flexibility when negotiating proposals. For example, the rep could tailor discount rates by lane such that an account would obtain large discounts on its most frequently used routes. DHL senior management typically gave only general direction to sales reps on negotiating discounts. For example, senior management might advise, "Hold price on Asia, yet you can give some on the United States and Europe." Most proposals associated a monthly minimum level of billings (adjusted, if necessary, for seasonality of the business) with the offer of any discounts.

DHL sales reps could negotiate discounts from book prices up to 35%. District sales managers could approve discounts up to 50%, while discounts above 50% required the approval of a regional sales director. Further, discounts over 60% required approval from the vice president of sales. For all discounts over 35%, a sales rep had to submit a Preferred Status Account (PSA) report, which included a detailed analysis of the profitability of the account. As shown in **Exhibit 12,** the PSA used a computer model to calculate fixed and variable costs, net profits by geographic lane and product line, and overall contribution margins. When deciding on the discount, management considered not only the financial implications of the discount but also competitive and capacity factors.

Tony Messuri, DHL New England area sales manager, stated:

> It is good to have pricing flexibility. Managers at most companies are just looking for justification to use us. But they and DHL upper managers both know that we're not the only game in town. . . . We can sit down with a customer and build our own rate table leaving the book prices aside. We can customize the table to the customer's needs. This customization really helps negotiations.

Sales and Advertising

DHL had a single sales force which sold both document and parcel services. Sales reps were organized geographically and were evaluated primarily on monthly sales. Typically, sales reps had separate monthly sales objectives for international, domestic, and total sales and received a bonus whenever they exceeded any one of the three. Sales managers were evaluated against profit as well as revenue objectives.

When a new account called for a pickup, that account was assigned an account number the next day and was called upon by a DHL sales rep within a week.[3] At large companies, sales reps targeted the traffic, shipping and receiving, and purchasing departments, while at small companies, they focused their efforts on line managers such as the vice president of marketing or vice president of International.

[3] In the United States, prospective accounts with less than $500 in annual express shipment expenditures were handled by DHL's telemarketing center in Phoenix.

EXHIBIT 12
Sample DHL
Preferred Status
Account Report

PSA Analysis for:	Plasmo Systems
No. of Pickup Sites:	1
Stops per Month:	20
Origin Station:	Boston
Model Date:	1/31/90
Costs Date:	4/7/89

Margin by Lane (Note: not all lanes included)

Service	Lane	Revenue	Pickup Costs	Ship Costs	Weight Costs	Net Profit	% Profit
DOC	A Europe	45.89	3.12	24.02	7.62	11.13	24.3%
DOC	B Europe	48.02	3.12	28.72	7.66	8.70	18.0
DOC	C Europe	31.99	3.12	24.59	4.94	−0.66	−2.1
DOC	D Europe	23.17	3.12	20.46	2.34	−2.75	−11.9
DOC	E Latin Am	38.01	3.12	20.92	4.32	9.65	25.4
DOC	F MidEast	40.79	3.12	22.08	7.26	8.33	20.4
DOC	G Caribbn	31.32	3.12	21.29	3.76	3.15	10.1
WPX	A Europe	44.95	3.12	38.61	4.44	−1.22	−2.7
WPX	B Europe	73.25	3.12	47.36	5.49	17.28	23.6
WPX	D Canada	25.49	3.12	29.24	3.51	−10.38	−40.7

Margin by Product Line

Service	Revenue	Pickup Cost	Ship Cost	Weight Cost	Net Profit	% Profit
DOC	743	46	535	90	72	9.7%
WPX	214	12	196	21	−15	−7.0

Fixed/Variable Cost Report

Service	Revenue	Variable Cost	Gross Margin	Fixed Cost	U.S. Cost	Int'l Cost	Net Profit	% Profit
DOC	743	476	267	195	494	177	72	9.7%
WPX	214	173	41	56	180	49	−15	−7.0

Prior to 1984, DHL headquarters developed global advertising campaigns which the regions and countries could adopt or not as they saw fit. After 1984, each country operation could contract with its own local advertising agency. Headquarters approval of locally developed commercials was not required, though standard guidelines on presentation of the DHL name and logo had to be followed worldwide. In addition, headquarters marketing staff disseminated to all DHL offices commercials that had worked especially well in a particular market that might be worth extending to others.

DHL spent roughly 4% of worldwide sales on advertising. In 1990, DHL launched a new advertising campaign in the United States based on the slogan: "Faster to More of the World." This campaign, inspired by the fighter pilot movie "Top Gun," featured flying DHL delivery vans. (See **Exhibit 13.**) In the United States, the objectives of DHL's advertising campaign were threefold. First, DHL wanted to raise brand awareness. Second, DHL aimed to explain that shipping overseas required different capabilities from shipping within the continental United States. Third, DHL sought to convince consumers that DHL was the best at shipping overseas because of its experience, network, worldwide scope, and people.

DHL advertising in Europe used the slogan: "You know it's arrived the moment it's sent." (See **Exhibit 14.**)

EXHIBIT 13   Portion of a Sample U.S.A. Advertising Flying Van

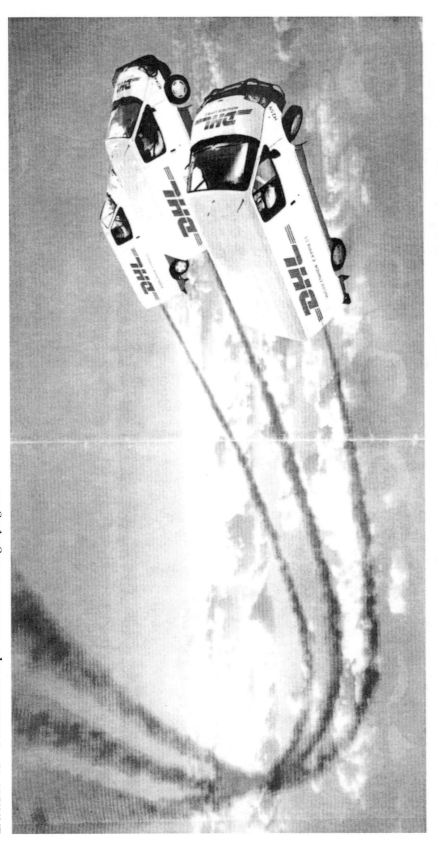

Our business took off 21 years ago, and we're flying higher than ever.

It's significant that the letters DHL stand for the names of three people (Dalsey, Hillblom and Lynn).

Significant, because it took their personal entrepreneurial vision to recognise a business need, and their personal energy to get the solution off the ground.

Today, however, it's even more significant that the letters DHL stand for over 23,700 names: the highly trained, highly motivated employees

DHL is as international as the United Nations. Our network spans 186 countries, states, territories and protectorates.

And from Ouagadougou to Wagga Wagga, Jakarta to Jeddah, there is not likely to be any city or town that you might wish to send something to, that does not feature on our list of 70,000 destinations served.

Most of all, however, the letters DHL have come to stand for two key words which mean so

If you're a major company you cannot afford anything less than total reliability when you air express your important documents and packages.

And as the world's largest international air express company, it is DHL's mission to provide it. Which we do.

It may be that your own company has an equally impressive growth story to tell. But old or new, large or small, please consider this.

and wouldn't you be better able to concentrate on your own job, if you allowed DHL to apply its expertise to your international air express needs?

537

EXHIBIT 14 Part of a Sample Advertisement: Europe

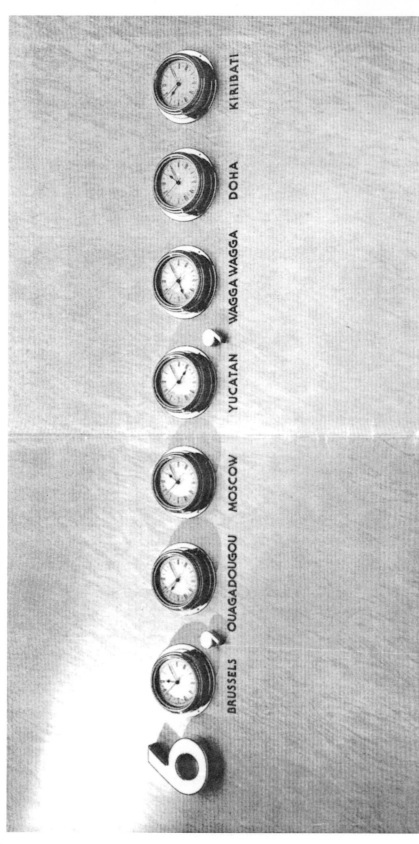

Sixty million deliveries a year around the world and around the clock.

London to Ouagadougou, Wagga Wagga.
Yucatan, Kiribati — wherever. Take it from us that,
with 70,000 cities and towns on our list, your air
express destination is not likely to faze us.

Every 58 seconds, a plane takes off
somewhere in the world carrying some of those
60,000,000 shipments.

190 of those planes are our own. Plus over
7,200 vehicles. Plus more owned-and-operated
service centres in more countries than any of

Plus, above all, over 25,000 DHL employees.
Trained in over 100 languages. But trained in the
same company philosophy.

To think globally and act locally. To apply our
global and group resources to each customer's
advantage. To go that further mile which shows a
customer that we're not just going through the
motions — we care.

That care is demonstrated by the fact that we
never use agents. We believe that if you want a

So if your concern is on-time delivery of your
important documents and packages, you are
unlikely to do better with any other operator.

But where you *definitely* will not be able
to do better is with the total reliability which
DHL provides.

From oil wells in Alaska to clinics in Africa,
farms in South America to factories in China,
people turn to DHL when they have to be sure.
In some places, indeed, DHL is just about the

So please consider the implications of this for
you and your business.

After all, such total reliability is hard to find
these days.

Conclusion

As he pondered DHL's pricing options, Sarrafzadeh recalled the old adage: "The value of a thing is the price it will bring." Perhaps DHL's profits would be maximized if each country manager simply charged each customer "whatever the market could bear." However, from a headquarter's perspective, Sarrafzadeh believed a degree of order and consistency was necessary in DHL's pricing strategy, structure, and decision-making process. In particular, he wondered how pricing policy could enhance customer relationships, help to retain customers, and minimize their tendency to split their shipments among several air express carriers. Further penetration of existing accounts where DHL carriers were already making pickups and deliveries would, he was convinced, result in increased profits.

Part 7

Branding

Chapter

31

Brands and Branding

Douglas B. Holt

Branding has become one of the most important aspects of business strategy. Yet it is also one of the most misunderstood. Branding is sometimes considered to be merely an advertising function. And many managers and business writers hold the view that branding is about the management of product image, a supplementary task that can be isolated from the main business of product management. This note provides an alternative perspective, arguing that:

- Branding is a strategic point of view, not a select set of activities.
- Branding is central to creating customer value, not just images.
- Branding is a key tool for creating and maintaining competitive advantage.
- Brands are cultures that circulate in society as conventional stories.
- Effective brand strategies must address the four distinct components of brand value.
- Brand strategies must be "engineered" into the marketing mix.

This note develops a set of concepts and frameworks to guide the design of brand strategies.

From Value Proposition to the Brand

Marketing strategies begin with the *value proposition*: the various types and amounts of value that the firm wants customers to receive from the market offering. The value proposition is value as perceived by the firm, value that the firm seeks to "build" into the product.[1] In marketing, the value proposition is sometimes referred to as the positioning

---

[1] To simplify the exposition, I use the term "product" generically to refer to all types of market offerings—products, services, events, knowledge, etc.—and to include augmented aspects of the product (such as the service outputs delivered by the marketing channel).

Professor Douglas B. Holt prepared this note as the basis for class discussion.

statement.[2] Common wisdom in business often assumes that product value as measured by the firm and product value as experienced by the customer are identical. If the firm builds a better product, customers will experience it as such. Marketing makes a crucial break with this assumption. Marketing emphasizes that customer value is perceptual, never objective fact. Value is shaped by the subjective understandings of customers, which often have little to do with what the firm considers to be the "objective" qualities of the product. The brand is the product as it is experienced and valued in everyday social life. The verb "to brand" refers to all of the activities that shape customer perceptions, particularly the firm's activities. Branding, then, is a *management perspective* that focuses on shaping the perceived value of the product as found in society.

Brand Cultures

Think of the brand as the *culture of the product*. We can borrow from the disciplines of anthropology, history, and sociology to understand products as *cultural artifacts*. Products acquire meanings—connotations—as they circulate in society. Over time, these meanings become conventional, widely accepted as "truths" about the product. At this point, the product has acquired a culture.

Consider a new product that has just been introduced by a new company. While the product has a name and a trademarked logo, and perhaps other unique design features—all aspects that we intuitively think of as "the brand"—in fact the brand does not yet exist. Names and logos and designs are the material markers of the brand. But, because the product does not yet have a history, these markers are "empty." They are devoid of meaning. Now think of famous brands. They have markers also: a name (McDonald's, IBM), a logo (the Nike "swoosh," the Traveler's umbrella), a distinctive product design feature (Harley's engine sound), or any other design element that is uniquely associated with the product. What is different is that these markers have been filled with customer experiences, with advertisements, with films and sporting events that used the brand as a prop, with magazines and newspaper articles that evaluate the brand, with conversations with friends and colleagues that mention the brand. Over time, ideas about the product accumulate and "fill up" the brand markers with meaning. A brand culture is formed. Let us consider how this happens.

Four Authors

Brand cultures accumulate as various "authors" create stories that involve the brand. Brands have four primary types of authors: companies, popular culture, influencers, and customers.

Companies The firm shapes the brand through all of its product-related activities that "touch" customers. All elements of the marketing mix—product, communication, channels, and pricing policies—can potentially "tell stories" about the product. We will take up the firm's authoring role in considerable detail below.

[2] The traditional positioning statement has three important weaknesses that this note seeks to correct. First, positioning statements are devoid of strategic focus. Second, positioning statements fail to recognize that the brand has a history, a *brand culture,* as developed below. The branding goal for an existing brand must be to move the brand from Point A to Point B. The strategy should recognize this. Finally, positioning statements do not isolate the four distinct components of brand value (below) and the relationships between these components. As a result, positioning statements can lead to vague brand strategies that fail to direct marketing actions.

Popular culture Products are a prominent part of the world in which we live. As such, they are frequently used as props in films, television, books, magazines, on the Internet, across all mass media. These representations can have a powerful influence on brands. Popular culture can comment on brands directly—as when a talk show host like David Letterman spoofs an advertisement or when a product becomes a news story, such as when Firestone tires were recalled. Alternatively, brands can be used as props in entertainment products such as films—as with Reese's Pieces in *E.T.* and Pepsi in *Wayne's World.* For nearly a century, companies have sought to manage how their brands are presented in the media, through public relations efforts and paid sponsorships.

Customers Customers help to author the brand culture as they consume the product. As they interact with the product, customers create consumption stories involving the product, which they often share with friends.

Influencers In many categories, noncustomers' opinions are influential. Think of trade magazine reviews, the opinions offered by mavens and connoisseurs during work and leisure gatherings, and the opinions offered by retail salespeople.

Of course, the stories circulated by these four authors interact, often in complex ways. Customers watch ads and listen to influencers as they use the product. The media monitor how customers use the product and consider this in how they represent the product. In fact, the quantity and complexity of these interactions mean that isolating the influence of each author is usually quite difficult.

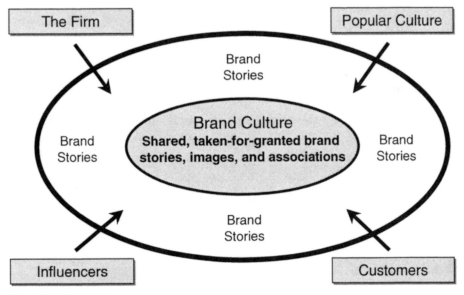

Source: Casewriter.

Stories, Images, and Associations

The cultural materials circulated by these authors come in three forms: stories, images, and associations. Stories and images are the more potent sources of brand culture. Brand stories and images have plots and characters, and they rely heavily upon metaphor to communicate and spur our imaginations. Think of brand associations as the residue of these stories and images. We may forget the specifics of a product story but still attribute some characteristics to the brand ("it's for old people," "often falls apart," etc.).

As these stories, images, and associations collide in everyday social life, conventions eventually form. A common story emerges as a consensus view (or, often enough, a few different common stories, each of which constitutes a customer segment for the brand). At this point the brand has become established as a cultural artifact. Marketers often think of branding at the individual level as perceptions of individual consumers. But what makes branding so powerful is the collective nature of these perceptions, the fact that the stories/images/associations have become conventional and so are continually reinforced because they are treated as "facts" in everyday interactions.[3]

A Perceptual Frame Structuring Product Experiences

It is common in marketing to think of the brand as an image, as the "frosting on the cake" above and beyond the "actual" value delivered by the product. This intuition distorts how brands create value. Rather, a brand culture acts as *a perceptual frame* through which customers understand, value, and experience the product. Customers never experience products objectively. Rather, the brand culture acts as a frame, shaping how their senses (see, hear, touch, feel, smell) experience the product. Brand cultures can have a powerful influence on sensory appeal (e.g., how products taste), on the emotions one feels when consuming, and on the remembered satisfactions of the experience.

Brands and Competitive Advantage

Branding is a potent means to establish competitive advantage. The brand culture concept helps us see why this is so. Brand cultures are "sticky." Once they have accepted them as conventional wisdom, people are usually reluctant to abandon the conventions of the brand culture. Unless they have product experiences or encounter brand stories that profoundly contradict conventions, people are usually happy to maintain the taken-for-granted understandings of the brand. In addition to the stickiness of taken-for-granted understandings, there are two reasons for this durability.

Psychological research demonstrates that brand cultures are durable because people are cognitive misers. Because we are so overloaded with information—far more information than we can reasonably digest even if we wanted to—we rely upon a variety of heuristics to simplify the world. We seek ways to minimize the amount of thinking and searching that we must do to make good decisions. Brand cultures work as one such heuristic. Once we determine that the conventional wisdom of a brand culture "works" for us (e.g., a detergent whose conventional brand story is that it performs great in all temperatures seems to do so), we are not interested in seeking out new information that would contradict this assumption. The heuristic provided by the brand works well, so we go on using it.

Sociological research demonstrates another reason why brand cultures are durable. Brand cultures are shared by many people and expressed in a variety of contexts (talk, product experiences, ads, and so on). Brand cultures are maintained as the brand's stories, images, and associations pulse through these networks. Hence, it is quite difficult for an individual to opt out of the conventional wisdom of a brand culture and assign the brand alternative meanings. Just as brand cultures are formed collectively, to decommission a brand is also a collective decision. Because of this network effect, brand meanings maintain a tenacious hold until a critical mass of customers and influencers join together to transform conventions.

---

[3] Of course, individuals' experiences with brands are more complicated. People routinely overlay brand cultures with their own personalized stories, images, and associations. These many "stray" stories that individuals weave into their consumption can add to and alter the conventions of the brand culture. However, as marketers are usually interested in aggregations of customers, these idiosyncratic meanings have little managerial relevance unless they aggregate to transform conventions.

Powerful brand cultures provide competitive advantage not only with respect to consumers but also in negotiations with channel partners. A strong brand culture gives the firm considerable leverage in configuring channel policies and provides leverage in negotiating with retailers.

The Four Components of Brand Value

Brand cultures can greatly enhance customer value. If we conduct a thought experiment, we can imagine the value of a brand as the difference between what a consumer will pay for a branded product (a product experienced through the lens of its brand culture) and a physically identical product without the culture. This difference can be decomposed into four dimensions, which, together, constitute the value added by the brand. The four components each have a strong base of research in academic disciplines that inform marketing. Each of these four components accumulates through the stories, images, and associations of the brand culture.

Reputation Value: Brand Cultures Shape Perceived Product Quality

From an economic point of view, brands serve as containers of reputation. Products have tangible features that deliver on utilitarian goals: flights are on time, fabrics clean easily, tools never break down. Customers take on risk when they purchase products, particularly products that will be used into the future and products for which quality cannot be reliably evaluated upon inspection before purchase. Sometimes the risk is huge: for consumers, consider the purchase of an automobile or an HMO policy; for business to business (B2B), consider the purchase of a mission-critical software program. Customers, to varying degrees, get added value from products that lower the risks of future performance failures. So when there is risk inherent in a product, customers are usually willing to pay to reduce risk. The brand operates as a signaling mechanism to increase customers' confidence that the product will provide excellent quality and reliability on important functions. The history of product experiences—both successes and failures—is spread in stories and aggregates to form part of the brand culture.

Relationship Value: Brand Cultures Shape Relationship Perceptions

Brands also communicate that the firm producing the product can be trusted to act as a long-term partner that will flexibly respond to future customer needs. For many products, especially in B2B and in services, customer uses and needs cannot be fully anticipated (and so built into a contract) at the time of purchase. For these products, research in economic sociology has demonstrated that a significant aspect of product value is the perception that the firm will respond as desired to uncontracted future contingencies. The brand is, once again, the material marker that "contains" stories conveying that the firm can be trusted to deliver on these future contingencies. Relationship value accumulates as particular stories, images, and associations that circulate around the product become conventional, taken for granted. For example, if a story that "IBM consultants would rather miss their own wedding than fail to respond immediately to IT failures" becomes a widely accepted part of IBM's brand culture, social value increases. Customers assume, *a priori,* without any particular evidence, that IBM will go the extra mile to make sure that its IT solutions always function as desired.

Experiential Value: Brand Cultures Frame Consumer Experiences

From a psychological perspective, the brand acts as a perceptual frame that highlights particular benefits delivered by the product. This framing guides consumers in choosing products and also shapes their product experiences. The heuristic value of the brand provides for considerable savings in search costs and in the need to continually process information to make effective choices. Hence, firms often seek to brand their products as particularly effective in delivering on a single benefit desired by customers. A classic example comes from Procter & Gamble's lineup of detergent brands, each of which is framed to consumers as designed to solve a particular cleaning problem (all-temperature cleaning, removing tough stains, etc.).

Experiential framing relies upon consumers who are cognitive misers, uninterested in investigating the technical supporting evidence for how brands are framed. As a result, branding efforts that frame benefits can sometimes tread in a gray area between adding customer value and manipulating customers' uses of heuristic thinking. For example, Winston cigarettes were effectively reframed by removing a few chemicals used in processing the tobacco and then pronouncing via advertising that the cigarettes were "100% natural." While the removal of the chemicals used to process the tobacco did nothing to the cigarette's carcinogenic properties, the framing of the brand as 100% natural made a dangerous product seem a little less dangerous, and sales shot up. Similarly, consider how Intel's "Intel Inside" campaign was able to create the perception that CPUs were the most important component of the computer and also that there were significant differences in performance and reliability across chips.

Symbolic Value: Brand Cultures Express Values and Identities

Brands also act as symbols that express values and identities. Historically, humans have depended upon their material culture (clothes, homes, craft goods, public monuments, religious icons) to serve as concrete markers of values and identities. In contemporary market economies, consumer goods now dominate in serving this function (hence the term "consumer culture"). In particular, brands have become powerful markers to express statuses, lifestyles, politics, and a variety of aspirational social identities. Consider, for instance, how Nike became a powerful marker for American ideals of achievement and perseverance in the 1990s. Or how Apple became a symbol for the rebellious, creative, libertarian values associated with New Economy professionals. When symbolic value becomes conventionalized in a brand culture, it often exerts a powerful halo effects on the other dimensions of brand value. For example, when Budweiser's *Lizards* ad campaign created powerful symbolic value for the brand, Bud drinkers reported that the beer tasted better.

Customers get three types of symbolic value from brands: they viscerally experience desired values and identities when they consume the brand (what anthropologists call *ritual action*); they use the brand symbol to create social distinction, to make status claims; and they use the brand symbol to forge solidarity and identification with others. On rare occasions, brands serve as the center of communities. This extreme case of the solidarity effect has been considerably overstated and glamorized in marketing circles of late. Imitating Harley-Davidson is not a good idea for the vast majority of brands.

Most brand cultures are made up of several, or even all, of these four components (consider, for example, an Apple computer). However, often one component will be the primary driver, accounting for the brand's success versus competitors. The relative importance

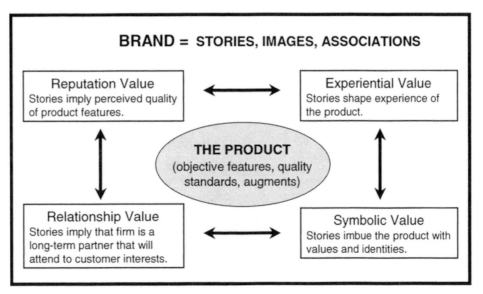

Source: Casewriter.

of each component will vary by society, product category, segment, and brand. While it is useful to break up brand value into these four discrete parts for strategic purposes, customers rarely experience the brand in this way. Rather, the components are overlapping and interdependent inferences that customers draw from the brand culture. The most successful brand cultures, then, offer a single coherent story where the components work together in a synergistic fashion so that the whole is greater than the sum of the parts.

Designing Brand Strategy

Brand strategy is a key part of the overall marketing strategy. Brand strategies deliver on business goals by enhancing the brand culture. Because brands, business contexts, and corporate goals vary so much, there are no universal rules for designing brand strategies. Rather, a systematic four-step process can be used to tailor strategies to respond appropriately to the specifics of the context:

Step 1: Identify Goals That Branding Can Address

Brand strategies are appropriate when the business goal can be achieved by enhancing perceived product value. Identify the key business goals for the product and ask: *Is this goal amenable to branding?* Not all goals demand a branding solution. While branding is often a central component of an effective marketing strategy, there are a number of business issues for which branding is not particularly relevant. If a product is trapped in a weak position in a value chain, there is little that branding can do to resolve such a difficulty. Since branding requires changing shared conventions, it is necessarily a long-term project. And, so, branding is not usually a good tool to achieve short-term sales goals. Conversely, it is also important to consider whether nonbranding strategies (e.g., lowering cost to serve, pursuing price discrimination with promotions) have unintended consequences on branding.

Step 2: Map the Existing Brand Culture

Evaluate the existing brand culture across the four components of brand value (and for influencers as well if relevant). This evaluation requires designing and collecting market research that is attuned to the four different components of brand culture. Also consider the firm's current brand strategy, noting where it diverges from the brand culture.

	Brand Culture		Current Brand Strategy
	Customers/Prospects	Influencers	
BRAND STORY			
Reputation Inferences			
Relationship Inferences			
Experience Inferences			
Symbolism Inferences			

Source: Casewriter.

Step 3: Analyze Competition and Environment to Identify Branding Opportunities

Competitive Benchmarking

One important driver of brand strategy is to deliver superior brand value versus primary competitors. Competitive superiority in brand value requires benchmarking against competitors' brands. Map competitors' brand cultures as you do your own (Step 2). Given the strengths of the brand and the firm, identify opportunities to improve the brand culture versus those of key competitors, and identify opportunities to shore up any erosion that could allow competitors to make inroads.

Environmental Shifts

There is a danger, though, in branding exclusively with an eye on competitors. The most significant advances in brand value come from identifying opportunities in the environment (consumers, technology, infrastructure, etc.) that competitors have not yet acted on and designing the brand strategy to take advantage of these opportunities. For example, new product technologies can provide significant opportunities to enhance reputation, emerging information and process technologies (e.g., the Internet, customer relationship management) can allow for improvements in relationship value, changing customer preferences can create opportunities for different experiential framing, and shifts in society and culture create opportunities to deliver new symbolism. Changes in the category life cycle are important to consider as well.

The relative importance of the four components often shifts over time. For a new category, where consumers have little product experience and technologies are unproven, quality and relationship values will be of primary concern. As the category matures and competitors become proficient at delivering basic product values, experience framing and symbolism often become considerably more important.

Step 4: Design the Strategy

A brand strategy describes the movement from the existing to the desired brand culture and the logic for its taking this path. A strategy document should map the current brand culture, outline the most promising opportunities to enhance the brand culture considering both environment shifts and competitive benchmarking, and finally detail the desired brand culture.

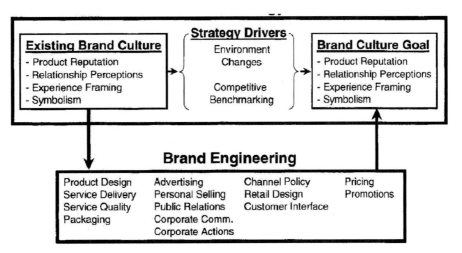

Source: Casewriter.

Implementation: Engineering the Brand

Ultimately, a strategy is only as good as the care and creativity taken in implementation. This is particularly true of brand strategies, where implementation requires coherent "engineering" of the desired brand culture across all relevant aspects of the marketing mix. A brand strategy requires an action plan that specifies which marketing mix elements will be used, how they will be used, and how they will be integrated to achieve a consistent branding effort. Every firm activity that engages prospective customers is a potential branding tool. Branding is not limited to communications. Rather, all elements of the marketing mix contribute to branding (and also destroy brand value if they are not managed properly). And, of course, each marketing mix element must also serve purposes other than branding (for instance, meeting next quarter's sales objectives). Therefore, managers must always balance branding objectives against other marketing goals.

Product Policy/Service Delivery

Brands are not mere images. Rather, they are multisensory prisms that are "built into" products. Often the most critical and challenging branding task is how to design the product in a way that optimizes brand value. Thinking of product design as a branding issue is a relatively novel approach that has emerged only recently in design-intensive industries (autos, computers, consumer electronics, appliances, etc.). Product policy becomes a branding question when we ask: how can we use product design to enhance brand value? Rather than design products to achieve internal technical hurdles, engineering the brand into the product requires a reverse logic: what designs will best influence customers' perceptions of value?

Packaging

Packaging also conveys stories, images, and associations about the product inside, creating meaning. Consider how department stores wrap and bag products, how the packaging of perfumes and other beauty products influences brand stories, or, similarly, the various "extras" that you are often given when you buy a new car.

Advertising

Advertising has long been a powerful tool for building brand cultures because it is a storytelling medium. Advertising is used not just to convey information but to shape how the audience thinks about the product by embedding the product in dramatic fictions and using imaginative metaphors to provoke the audience to think differently about the product.

Public Relations/Corporate Communications

Representations of the product in popular culture and discussion of the product by influencers can have a powerful impact on the brand culture. Therefore, public relations efforts that seek to manage these indirect branding efforts are often important.

Pricing/Promotions

While we usually think of pricing decisions primarily as an economic calculus concerned with extracting value, pricing can also have powerful branding effects. For example, pricing policies can express either a transactional view (maximizing profits from a current purchase) or a relational view (treating customers as long-term partners). Similarly, pricing policies that customers perceive as "gouging," perhaps price discrimination mechanisms that seem to take advantage of customers, can lead to stories of an inconsiderate and self-centered company, which would destroy relationship value.

Personal Selling

We usually consider salespeople as conduits rather than creators of brand value. They convince clients and prospects of the value proposition with effective salesmanship. But, master salespeople are often master storytellers who can have a powerful impact on the brand culture.

Channels/Retail

For products sold by partners in a market channel, the customer-facing parts of the channel can have a powerful impact on the brand culture. In fashion, for example, the retail brand, retail design, store merchandising, and salesperson interactions can all have a significant impact on the brand culture. Consider the storytelling power of Starbucks outlets or of Nike's flagship stores.

Other Corporate Actions

Even corporate actions that seem furthest removed from marketing can have powerful branding effects: CEOs' discussions with Wall Street can be reported in the press. Firm policies that seem to be "backstage" and so out of the branding limelight can blow up into news stories. Consider, for example, how recent labor strife in General Motors' Saturn division impacted that brand's culture. Or consider that Nike's response to criticisms about its labor policies in outsourced Asian factories had such a negative impact on Nike's brand culture that the firm was forced to redesign its production policies.

When devising brand strategies, it is easy to fall into the trap of repeating popular formulas that seem to have worked well in the past. Imitation is rampant in marketing. But following historical patterns as formulas, especially without acknowledging changes in environment and competition, can lead to mediocre and anachronistic plans. The most powerful plans are often those that locate creative new ways to brand.

The most powerful branding levers in the marketing mix often change over time. For example, consider the rapid changes in how branding works in the American pharmaceutical industry. Until recently, doctors had vast influence over the reputations of drugs. Companies focused their efforts on influencing the stories that doctors told their patients. Now that medical advice flows freely on the Internet, through sites like WebMD, consumers have dramatically changed their decision-making processes. So, many companies have shifted part of their branding efforts to focus directly on consumers, often in the form of television advertising. Companies that anticipate the impact of these sorts of institutional shifts on brand strategy have a considerable advantage over those that simply follow rote formulas until they no longer work.

Evaluating the Brand

How do managers know if their brand strategies are working? Managers use four primary measures to "read" the brand's health and evaluate marketing effectiveness.

Behaviors

When the brand increases in value, one expects—all other factors being unchanged—that customers will purchase the brand more regularly and will be less likely to switch away from the brand. Thus, one way to measure the strength of a brand is to measure behavioral loyalty. Measurements of loyalty behaviors alone can be misleading, though, because so many factors influence purchase behavior. So marketers commonly look at additional indicators.

Attitudes

Valued brands tend to share certain consumer attitudes: they are well known among the relevant customers for delivering particular benefits, they are associated with influential users, and they are personally relevant. Attitudinal measures are gathered from traditional market research as well as other informal feedback mechanisms (Web sites, customer centers, retailers) to make benchmarked comparisons on attitudinal strength.

Relationships

When brand value is high, customers tend to rely heavily on the brand in their daily life and, so, develop deep relationships with the brand. Like a personal relationship, people come to depend on the brand, enact norms of reciprocity, and exhibit strong emotions and feelings about the brand. Hence, measures of relationship strength can provide accurate indicators of brand value.[4]

Equity

The ultimate measure of brand value is the brand's reservation price (the price at which consumers are indifferent between the brand and competitive offerings). If the demand curve shifts outward, all other factors being equal, the brand is more valued by customers. Successful branding allows firms to charge more for their products or to sell more at the existing price, or some combination thereof. The future stream of earnings produced by this shifting of the demand curve attributed to branding is called *brand equity*. For many companies, branding has a tremendous impact on profits. Thus, brands are some of the most important assets owned by the corporation. For example, 80% of both Nike's and Apple Computer's market capitalization has been attributed to brand equity. Brand equity measures are in their infancy. Current measures offer very rough heuristics that improve only modestly over previous financial measures of "goodwill." As research progresses in this area, more accurate measures will emerge.

Branding and Ethics

Branding is one of the most powerful tools in the marketing arsenal. So brandishing this tool comes with a responsibility to use it ethically. Recently, branding has come under significant criticism, particularly in Naomi Klein's popular book *No Logo* (Picador, 2001). Klein argues that firms use branding in an imperialist manner, feeding on consumers' base desires while ignoring issues of social welfare. Such critiques have a long history across the globe. Beneath such criticism is the question of power. Branding is a form of rhetoric—an

---

[4] See Susan Fournier, "Consumers and their Brands," *Journal of Consumer Research,* 1998.

instrument to persuade people to think differently. Branding can create considerable value. But it can also be used in an exploitative manner. For branding to be a benevolent activity, four conditions need to hold:

- Firms and consumers are equipped with equal information about the product.
- Firms and consumers have equivalent sophistication in understanding how branding works.
- Consumers are not heavily reliant upon heuristic decision making.
- The authors of the branding effort are revealed.

When these conditions do not hold, there is potential for abuse. For example:

- Branding products with information asymmetries
- Stealth branding
- Branding to populations lacking rhetorical literacy, such as children

In such conditions, managers must vigilantly watch over the ethics of their branding policies, assuring the activities create value rather than take advantage of customer weaknesses.

32

Charles Schwab Corp.: Introducing a New Brand

Rajiv Lal   David Kiron

On May 12, 2001, at 3:45 P.M., Jack Calhoun (MBA '92), Schwab's Sr. Vice President of Advertising and Brand Management was making sure that everything was ready for his 4:00 P.M. presentation. Calhoun was recommending a fall advertising campaign to David Pottruck, co-CEO, and the company's founder, Chairman, and co-CEO, Charles Schwab.[1] After nine months of planning the new brand strategy, the time for planning its implementation had arrived. Calhoun was aware of the strategic importance of the marketing campaign to the company, whose stock price had dropped 35% in the past year. As Calhoun reviewed the advertising campaigns for one last time, he wondered how Pottruck and Schwab would react to the fundamental question that had been on everyone's mind: Do we have the right tone and correct approach for the new marketplace?

Schwab's stock price decline was a significant reversal of its success in previous years. Between 1997 and 2000, Schwab's profits had doubled. For a brief period, Schwab, one of the nation's largest financial services firms, had a larger market capitalization than Merrill Lynch, with only 30% of the brokerage giant's revenues.[2] Morningstar named Schwab and

---

[1] The term "Charles Schwab" is used in the text to refer to company founder, Charles Schwab. The term "Schwab" is used to refer to the corporate entity.

[2] In December 1999, Schwab had a market cap of $33.9 billion compared to Merrill Lynch's $31.3 billion.

Research Associate David Kiron, Ph. D., prepared this case at the Global Research Group under the supervision of Professor Rajiv Lal. HBS cases are developed solely as the basis for class discussion. Cases are not intended to serve as endorsements, sources of primary data, or illustrations of effective or ineffective management.

Pottruck as CEO of the year 2000. In January 2001, *Forbes* magazine named Schwab "Company of the Year." However, as 2001 unfolded, the Nasdaq crashed and Schwab's on-line trading volumes fell sharply. As a result, commissions plummeted, earnings dropped, client asset value diminished, and Schwab's stock price steadily declined. Calhoun explained that the advertising campaign was a key component of Schwab's response:

> In 1999 and early 2000, when Internet trading reached its highest levels, we had to invest more in our IT infrastructure, and in hiring more people to keep up with demand. But when trading fell, revenues dropped, and the company was left with little return on these investments. We weren't the only ones in this situation, and now all of the major brokerages are looking beyond their traditional business practices to adapt to emerging client preferences.
>
> Today we face two major challenges. The first concerns client retention. The larger brokerage houses are looking to gain market share in our profitable emerging affluent segment, (investors with between $250,000 and $1,000,000 in assets). For investors with assets below $250,000, all brokerages are pushing their smaller accounts to automated channels. Online brokerages are also looking to take market share from us. Some, like E*Trade, are moving beyond online and building a physical presence, opening offices in Target stores around the country. We need to hold onto our own customers, as a growing percentage of our revenues and profits come directly from client assets housed at the company.
>
> This brings me to the second major challenge: how do we attract new clients that are a good match with our firm's future? So far we've done a good job of bringing in new client assets, even though many investors still don't seem to know what we are best at. We are still known as a discount brokerage, but the fact is we provide many of the same services as full-commission brokerages. Investors who go to these "full commission" brokerages are typically wealthier and older than our clients, and they tend to want different levels of advice, which we offer, but are not known for offering. The challenge is to do a better job of establishing our brand in the affluent market. Will we need to create a separate brand, as Toyota did with Lexus, or can we work within our current brand position? How should we pursue the affluent sector? Should we even go up market at all?
>
> As a company with a strong history of innovation, technological expertise, and investor empowerment, Schwab has several different assets to leverage as we position our brand in this changing market. My group has developed two advertising campaigns that promote Schwab's ability to advise investors with our people and our objective advice. (See **Exhibit 1.**) Each campaign is expected to connect with customers and potential customers of full-commission brokerages (FCBs). We estimate that FCBs hold 60% of all investable assets. The question is: have we chosen the correct approach to the FCB market segment?

Context

In 2001, the securities brokerage industry was divided into two segments. Full-commission brokers (FCBs) such as Merrill Lynch offered customers a comprehensive range of investment products and services. Online brokerages, such as E*Trade, Datek and Ameritrade, focused primarily on cut-rate, online trade execution. Schwab, a unique combination of the two groups, offered an array of products and access to investment advice through non-commissioned branch representatives and third party advisors.

Several trends were increasing competition among all brokerages. In April 2001, Nasdaq began quoting stocks in penny increments rather than fractions of a dollar (1/8 or 1/16). This so-called "decimalization" diminished trade-related revenue, an important source of earnings for all brokerage firms. Brokerages were also increasing spending on their respective marketing efforts (see **Exhibit 2**). FCBs, in particular, were moving their message up market, targeting high net worth (HNW) individuals, who had at least one million dollars in investable assets. The HNW market segment controlled 50% of all investable assets in the United States. Finally, brokerages in all categories were beginning to

EXHIBIT 1A Advertising Story Boards: "Manager"

Source: Company documents, 2001.

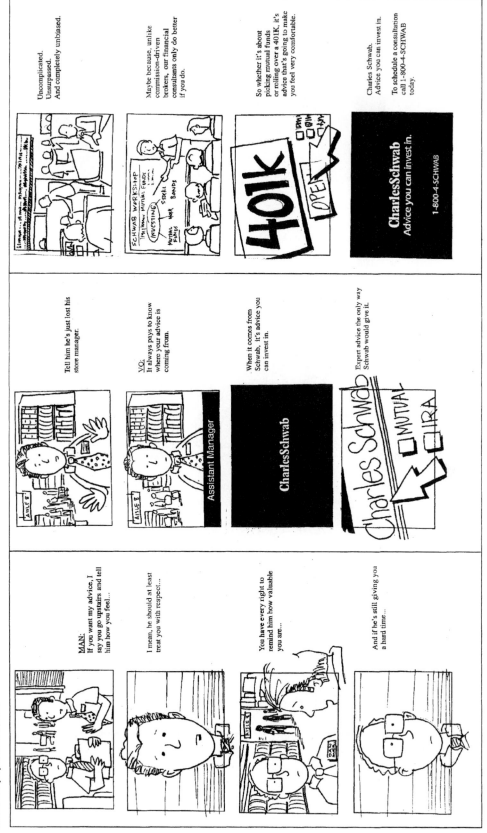

558

EXHIBIT 1B Advertising Story Boards: Grandmother

Source: Company documents, 2001.

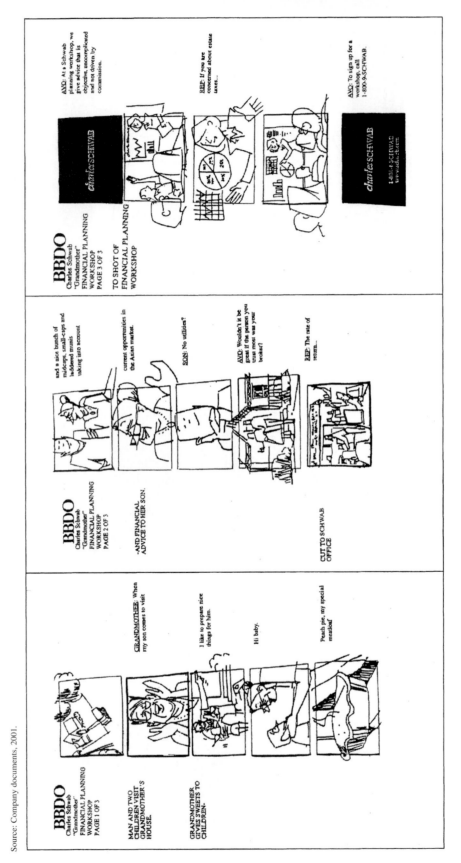

EXHIBIT 2
Financial Services Firms—Advertising Spending

Source: Competitive Media Reporting, 2001.

	11-Media ($000)				
	1996	**1997**	**1998**	**1999**	**2000**
Ameritrade	2,866.7	28,393.8	15,941.4	105,932.2	160,947.1
Charles Schwab Corp	62,245.4	90,813.5	97,117.5	183,568.9	235,399.6
Datek	301.1	18,400.8	8,734.5	36,166.5	109,292.5
E*Trade	5,670.3	89,873.9	41,421.6	130,188.0	72,499.2
FMR Corp (Fidelity)	85,968.6	66,347.0	87,027.8	164,060.5	178,600.9
Merrill Lynch	64,726.8	40,447.4	50,965.5	103,934.8	120,528.2
Morgan Stanley	39,115.1	29,382.8	79,255.3	157,507.6	151,595.2
Salomon Smith Barney	21,536.6	28,393.8	33,632.5	43,238.0	70,831.0

offer a similar mix of products and services. For example, Schwab was renowned for its independent third-party advisor network, with more than 70% of market share, but by 2001, Merrill Lynch was seeking to develop its own network of fee-based third-party advisors, a departure from its reliance on its own commissioned broker service.

Full-Commission Brokers (FCB)

FCBs had four main revenue streams: commissions, principal transactions, investment banking, and asset management and portfolio service fees. (See **Exhibit 3.**) FCBs served individual and large institutional investors, such as universities. FCBs also served the business community, assisting in mergers and acquisitions, and performing underwriting services, e.g., initial public offerings. FCBs offered their retail clients personalized financial plans and convenient one-stop shopping for a wide range of products and services. These included zero-coupon bonds, precious metals, foreign debt securities, futures, commodities, along with mortgages, credit cards, insurance, 401(k) plans, margin loans, and asset management accounts. With an account size of $400,000, the average FCB customer was in his mid-50s, and received asset management and trade execution services.

FCBs had more clients within the HNW segment than any other type of brokerage. In 2000, the $8.8 trillion North American HNW market was composed of 2.5 million individuals.[3] Analysts believed that this market would grow to $13 trillion by 2005. HNW clients demanded superior service, individualized portfolio management, greater diversity of products and specialized services, such as trust, property and tax management.

Online Brokers

Online companies were divided between the pure plays, such as E*Trade and Ameritrade, and the online business units of larger brokerage houses. According to Meridien research, Schwab and Fidelity captured about 68% of the online assets under management (38% and 30% respectively).[4] The average account at online trading companies such as E*Trade and Ameritrade was roughly $11,000 in 2001. With a do-it-yourself mentality, the typical online trader bought and sold stocks frequently and was more interested in price and speed than in research tools or advice.

In 2001, online companies were scrambling to make up for lost revenues that came with lower trading volumes. The pure plays derived a majority of their revenues through trade commissions, though in 2001, they were looking to become less dependent on this revenue stream. By the end of the first quarter 2001, the online trading population had declined by

[3] Information in this paragraph is based on "J.J. Hughes, "Brokerage and Asset Management Research: The Charles Schwab Corporation," *Robertson Stephens,* June 13, 2001.

[4] Lynnette Khalfani, Getting Personal: Pros and Cons of Account Aggregation," *Dow Jones Newswires,* March 27, 2001.

EXHIBIT 3
Full Commission Brokerage Revenue Streams*

Source: Robert P. Napoli, Jeffrey Harte, Laura E. Kaster, "The Silver Lining is recurring revenue," ABN AMRO (Analyst reports), Ocotober 1, 2001.

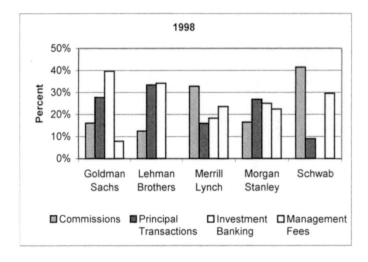

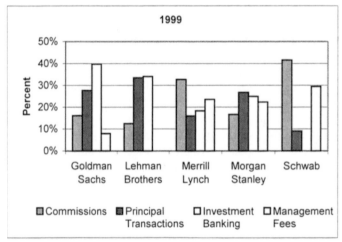

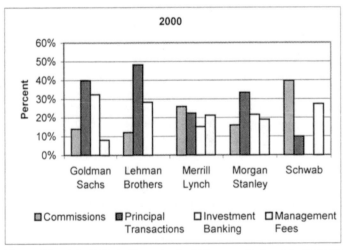

*The terms "Commissions" "Principal Transactions," and "Management Fees" are defined in Exhibit 4.

20% from the same quarter a year before. Online brokerage firms introduced novel products and features to attract skittish individual investors. Ameritrade offered pre-market trading (between 8 and 9:15) through an ECN and a new portfolio management tool. E*Trade offered advice in a joint venture with Ernst & Young. Datek offered certain clients the ability to trade in increments as low as 1/10 of a cent, a competitive advantage among active traders.[5]

Company Background

In 1975, Charles Schwab launched the world's first discount brokerage firm, following the abolition of fixed rate brokerage commissions. Its mission was to empower the individual investor by offering unbiased products and services at discounted prices. With Schwab, investors could buy and sell stocks without paying the high priced asset management fees and trading commissions demanded by full-commission brokerages. Unlike full-commission brokerage firms, which managed investment portfolios, sold proprietary products, recommended stocks, and sold (at a premium) proprietary research, Schwab offered investors access to independent investment advisors and inexpensive trading. Initially, Schwab attracted market savvy customers who felt "burned" by traditional full-commission brokers. By 1982, the company had gained a more mainstream following, and was well known for its concern for individual investors, its use of technology, and efficient service for a reasonable price.

Schwab avoided a potential conflict of interest inherent in the traditional full-commission brokerage business—where broker's pay was based on commissions from trade volumes rather than customer portfolio return. Schwab paid its brokers a salary plus a job performance bonus that was determined by several team-based measures, including business development and client satisfaction.

In 1983, BankAmerica bought Schwab for $57 million. However, a four-year clash between the entrepreneurial culture at Schwab and the more conservative culture at Bank of America persuaded Charles Schwab to lead a management-led buyout of the firm. In 1987, Schwab went public. The IPO valued the firm at $450 million.[6]

After going public, Schwab grew quickly. Between 1988 and 1997, Schwab's client assets and revenues grew at compound annual growth rates of 37% and 29%, respectively.[7] In the same period, Schwab's roster of full-time equivalent employees jumped almost sixfold.[8] By December 1997, Schwab had a market value of almost $11 billion.

Schwab's growth was due to several factors. Foremost among these was the expansion of its branch network, which numbered 360 domestic branch offices in 47 states in mid-2000.[9] With 70% of the U.S. population within 10 miles of a Schwab branch, and plenty of television advertising, new accounts flocked to Schwab.[10] Each branch office was equipped and staffed to open customer accounts, assist in order executions, answer general investment questions, track customer portfolios, and provide information about the stock market. Routine operations (e.g., quotes, balances, positions, trades) eventually migrated to telephone

---

[5] Consider a seller who is willing to sell a security for a tenth of a penny (but not an entire penny) less than his or her asking price. A buyer who was able to offer the asking price less 1/10 of a penny would hold an advantage over a different buyer who did not want to pay the full asking price but was unable to bid 1/10 of a penny less than the asking price.

[6] The paragraph and the next were adapted from HBS Case: 9-300-024, "Charles Schwab Corporation (A)."

[7] Client assets grew from $18 to $354 billion over this period. Revenues grew from $267 million to $2.3 billion.

[8] From 2,200 to 12,700 full time equivalents.

[9] Louise Lee, "When You're Number 1, You Try Harder," *Business Week,* September 18, 2000, p. 88.

[10] Company estimates.

and online service channels, leaving branches with more time to focus on opening accounts, assisting customers with more complex transactions, and providing customers with investment coaching.[11]

Internet trading also contributed to Schwab's growth. In 1985, Schwab began offering online trading (through a dial-up network) well before others realized the potential of the Internet for this market. However, by 1996, industry observers were viewing Internet trading as a threat to Schwab. As one noted: "What Schwab did to the full-service firms, Lombard and E*Trade will do to Schwab and the full-service firms."[12] The observers erred, however. Thanks to heavy investments in technology, its early success online, and the self-directed nature of its clients, Schwab established itself as a market leader, despite charging twice as much as some online trading firms. By December 1997, Schwab had 25% of all online accounts (1.2 million).[13] By 1998, Schwab led the market in active online accounts (1.9 million, about a 40% market share); online customer assets (more than $120 billion, nearly a 70% share), and online trades (more than 63,000 daily, about a 31% share). Of the total universe of online commissions, 57% went to Schwab.

When Schwab made its move into Internet trading, branches continued to play an important role in new account generation. Schwab estimated that more than 80% of all accounts opened in a branch.[14] Calhoun explained, "Customers want to kick the tires before opening an account. They want to see that there's a *real* building with *real* people who look reputable before handing over a check." Pottruck added:

> Our branches distinguish us from the other online brokerages. Our customers have higher average-balances than customers of the pure online brokerages, and that's in part due to our branch system.[15] People aren't going to put a $500,000 check in the mail; they just don't do that. New customers that come into our branches want to hand a real person their money, look that person in the eye, and know something about how that person is going to serve them. They want to have a sense of the company's commitment to them, and our branch personnel provide that.

Schwab's entry into the mutual fund market also had a dramatic impact on its growth. In 1992, as investor interest in mutual funds soared, Schwab introduced its OneSource product—the industry's first no-transaction-fee mutual fund "supermarket." OneSource gave customers access to hundreds of no-load mutual funds from dozens of fund families and simplified investor record keeping by consolidating mutual fund account information in a single Schwab statement. Instead of charging a transaction fee, Schwab earned a 25-basis-point fee on assets-under-management from participating funds, in return for marketing, distribution, and accounting services. In less than five years, OneSource garnered the number three position among direct mutual fund distributors, behind industry heavyweights Fidelity and Vanguard. While Schwab's margins on its mutual fund business were lower than the commission rate it generated on trades, the volume increase from mutual fund products more than made up for the lower margins. As Pottruck noted: "In the beginning, OneSource was not a very profitable product for us, but it brought a lot of business, which on the whole was quite profitable."[16] By 2001, OneSource was the biggest distributor of third-party mutual funds in the United States.

---

[11] In 1991, 40% of all trades were made at branches, by the end of 1997 that figure had dropped to 5%, resulting in a 50% reduction in the cost of processing trades. The source of this information is, again, HBS Case: 9-300-024, "Charles Schwab Corporation (A)."

[12] "With the World Wide Web, Who Needs Wall Street?" *Business Week,* April 29, 1996, p. 120.

[13] Includes all of Schwab's online trading products.

[14] The paragraph and the next were adapted from HBS Case: 9-300-024, "Charles Schwab Corporation (A)."

[15] Referring to online brokerages that did not have branch offices.

[16] "Cyber-Schwab," *Forbes,* May 5, 1997, p. 42.

Schwab in 2001

The Business

Schwab was organized into four lines of business. (See **Exhibit 4** for revenue contributions of each.) **Retail Investor** included domestic and international retail operations. Schwab was focusing its new product development on products and services for individuals with investable assets of $100,000 and up. Through its extensive branch office network, call centers and online trading system, Schwab aimed to provide "optimal" combinations of technology/touch and advice/low cost execution. In 2000, this segment accounted for 63% of both net revenue and operating profits.

Schwab Institutional provided custodial, trading, and support services to more than 5,800 independent financial advisors (IFAs), as well as services to 401(k) plan sponsors and third-party administrators. In 1996, Schwab began a referral program called AdvisorSource that sent advice-seeking investors to a select group of 423 advisors (roughly 7% of all affiliated advice firms). These advisors paid Schwab a nominal annual fee to

EXHIBIT 4
Schwab's Revenue by Segment and Activity ($ in millions)

Source: 2000 Annual Report.

	1998	1999	2000	YTD'01
Revenues				
Retail investor	$1,936	$2,762	$3,645	$1,319
Institutional investor	461	632	861	434
Capital markets	339	551	639	185
U.S. Trust	442	542	643	333
Total Revenue	$3,178	$4,486	$5,788	$2,271
Revenue Mix				
Retail investor	61%	62%	63%	58%
Institutional investor	15	14	15	19
Capital markets	11	12	11	8
U.S. Trust	14	12	11	15
Total Revenue Mix	100%	100%	100%	100%
Revenue by Activity				
Commissions[1]	41%	42%	39.%	
Principal transactions[2]	10	11	10	
Asset mgmt. & admin. fees[3]	29	27	27	
Net interest revenue[4]	18	18	21	
Other	2	2	3	
Total Revenue by Activity	100%	100%	100%	

[1]Commissions: Schwab earned commission revenue by executing trades for the Individual and Institutional Investor segments. These revenues were affected by the number of client accounts that trade, the average number of commission–generating trades per account, and the average commission per trade.

[2]Principal Transactions: These revenues were primarily comprised of net gains from market-making activities in Nasdaq and other securities activity through the Capital Markets segment. Factors that influenced these revenues included volume of client trades, market price volatility, average revenue per share traded and changes in regulations and industry practices. As a market maker in Nasdaq and in other securities, Capital Markets generally executed client trades as principal.

[3]Asset management and administration fees: These included mutual fund service fees, as well as fees for other asset-based financial services provided to individual and institutional clients. Schwab earned mutual fund fees for record keeping and shareholder services provided to third-party funds, and for transfer agency services, shareholder services, administration and investment management provided to its proprietary funds. These fees were based on the daily balances of client assets invested in third-party funds and on the average daily net assets of Schwab's proprietary funds. Mutual fund service fees are earned primarily through the Individual Investor and Institutional Investor segments. Financial service fees were based on the value and composition of assets under management and are earned primarily through the U.S. Trust segment, as well as the Individual and Institutional segments.

[4]Net interest revenue: This was the difference between interest earned on assets (mainly marginal loans to clients, investments required to be segregated for clients, securities available for sale and private banking loans) and interest paid on liabilities (mainly brokerage client cash balances and banking deposits). Net interest revenue was affected by changes in the volume and mix of these assets and liabilities, as well as by fluctuations in interest rates and hedging strategies.

EXHIBIT 5 **Schwab Client Assets and Accounts**

Source: Justin J. Hughes and Melissa M. Kerin, "The Charles Schwab Corporation," Robertson Stephens (analyst report), June 13, 2001.

Figure A   Top 10 Holders of $17 Trillion in U.S. Investable Assets

	Market Share	2000 Market Share Growth
Merrill Lynch	8%	2%
Citigroup	7	3
Fidelity	5	(4)
Schwab	5	21
Prudential	4	7
Morgan Stanley	4	11
Vanguard	3	11
Bank of America	3	7
Mellon Bank	3	16
State Street	3	7

Figure B   Schwab Total Client Assets ($ in billions)

	1995	1996	1997	1998	1999	2000	2001E
Total client assets ($ in billions)	$243.7	$324.1	$437.2	$594.3	$846.0	$871.7	$978.4
Net new client assets ($ in billions)	$38.3	$54.1	$68.9	$79.1	$106.9	$171.3	$110.9
Customer accounts (thousands)	3,400	4,100	4,800	5,600	6,600	7,500	7,800

obtain referrals.[17] AdvisorSource clients (whose asset levels ranged from $100,000 and up) paid the advisors an asset-based fee for advice and investment management services. By 2001, Schwab had referred about 75,000 investors and $10.5 billion in assets to investment professionals through AdvisorSource.[18] The entire IFA network housed more than 25% of all Schwab assets. Most advisors who used Schwab's back-end support also used Schwab to conduct trades for their clients. The advisors paid a negotiated trading fee for each trade execution. In 2000, this segment represented 15% of net revenues and 21% of operating profits.

U.S. Trust, an affiliate of the Schwab brokerage firm, provided investment, fiduciary, and private banking services for high net worth individuals and institutions. In 2000, Schwab purchased U.S. Trust a respected wealth management firm to enhance its ability to serve the HNW market. In 2000, this segment delivered 11% of net revenues and 11% of operating profits.

Capital Markets provided trade-execution services for Nasdaq, listed and other securitites to broker-dealers and institutional clients. Virtually all of Schwab's Nasdaq orders were routed through this segment. In 2000, this segment contributed 11% of net revenues and 7% of operating profits.

Schwab Clients

By 2001, Schwab had 7.7 million active client accounts and $858 billion in total client assets, making Schwab the fourth largest brokerage (in terms of client assets). (See **Exhibit 5, figure A.**) The typical Schwab client account averaged $110,000 in investable assets.

[17] AdvisorSource IFAs acquired clients through several channels, including word-of-mouth and advertising. IFAs earned revenues primarily from asset-based fees, commissions, margin loans, and trade execution services. IFA businesses ranged in size from two person shops that had several clients with assets in the low million dollar range to larger shops that offered select services to dozens or several hundred clients with combined assets over a billion dollars.

[18] Josh Friedman, "Schwab sets its sights on greener turf brokerages," *Los Angeles Times,* June 10, 2001.

EXHIBIT 6
Relative Client
Asset Growth
($ in millions)

Source: Robert P. Napoli, Jeffrey Harte, Laura E. Kaster, "The Silver Lining is recurring revenue," ABN AMRO (Analyst reports), Ocotober 1, 2001.

	1996	1997	1998	1999	2000	CAGR
American Express	154	182	212	263	274	15.5%
Charles Schwab	324	437	594	846	872	28.1%
Merrill Lynch	860	1,229	1,446	1,696	1,681	18.2%

Despite the market downturn, Schwab continued to attract new client assets and accounts (see **Exhibit 5, figure B**), offsetting a then ongoing decline in Schwab's average commission per trade and lower trade volumes. In fact, Schwab was growing client accounts at a much faster rate than its competitors. (See **Exhibit 6.**)

Calhoun explained that the typical Schwab client had changed over time:

> Originally (in the 1970s), there was only one type of Schwab client—a 45-year-old, self-directed male who knew how to invest in the stock market. They just came to us to place the cheap trade, which we did fast and accurately. Accordingly, we segmented our clients based on their behavior and asset levels. The classic investor had assets under $100,000 and traded less than 11 times a year. Active traders had less than $100,000 in investable assets, but traded more than 48 times a year. The affluent segment had more than $100,000, but traded less than 48 times a year. Classic investors were the most numerous account type; affluent investors held the most assets, and active traders delivered the most revenue.
>
> But now our customer base is much more heterogeneous, ranging from the novice investor with very strong needs for education to the affluent investor, who has much more complex needs in areas of wealth management. The transition to customers with different sets of needs and interests forced us to think about our customers in a much more segmented way. Now, we segment our customer base according to the level of investment advice they need and want. See **Graphic A.**

Schwab's client segmentation approach was to get the right mix of products and service for every client. For self-directed clients who wanted limited interactions with brokers, Schwab provided a host of online products and branch office services. For validator-clients who wanted to check in with an advisor before making an investment decision and to retain control over their investments, Schwab provided numerous products and services, access to which depended on client asset level (see **Exhibit 7**). For delegator clients who wanted others to manage their investments, Schwab offered access to mutual funds (managed by third parties), to independent advisors, to whom clients could be referred, and to U.S. Trust to whom wealthy clients with specific wealth management needs could be referred, as appropriate.

- **Self-directed investors.** This do-it-yourself group represented Schwab's original client base. These individuals wanted minimal support for their investment decisions, but wanted the best tools to help them invest and manage their money better. These investors, regardless of asset level, used Schwab's online service and its branch offices to take care of their investment needs. This group made up the majority of Schwab client accounts.

- **Validators.** This group used both technology and relationships in making investment decisions. These investors liked to have a sounding board or second opinion. In large part, they controlled their assets, but wanted someone they could call and say, "here's what I'm thinking."

- **Delegators.** This group wanted investment managers to actively manage their investments. In the past, Schwab served the affluent delegator segment through its IFA network. Schwab could also refer its most affluent delegator-clients to U.S. Trust. This group had the fewest accounts at Schwab, though the number was growing.

GRAPHIC A   **Schwab Client Segmentation**

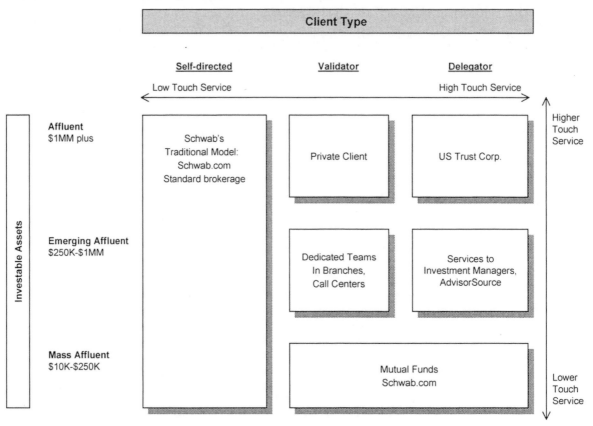

Schwab managers anticipated significant growth in the validator category. (See **Exhibit 8a and 8b**.) According to Pottruck, "The big cycle we're seeing now is more wealth moving toward Baby Boomers. This is a market we have served well, integrating technology and people to serve a generation that wants to maintain control but also needs some help and advice." However, as Calhoun noted, "In the past we lost some of our largest asset accounts because we did not offer FCB style one-on-one relationships to wealthy investors. But now we have several products that serve this category. The newest offering is our Private Client service, which is available at a select group of branch offices, and caters to clients with at least one million dollars in assets. These offer personal brokers, non-commissioned of course, and portfolio management services for an asset-based fee."

Schwab's effort to offer clients access to advice through its Private Client offices differed in several ways from its effort to offer clients access to independent advisors through AdvisorSource. One difference was that Private Client branch offices were Schwab-owned and staffed. AdvisorSource advisors did not work for Schwab, and were not considered Schwab staff. Another difference was that Private Client investors were more involved in managing their investment portfolio than investors working with AdvisorSource advisors. The Schwab Private Client investor was assigned a personal broker, with whom the investor created an investment plan. The AdvisorSource client delegated daily investment portfolio decisions to the IFA, an independent advisor that had agreed to serve Schwab referrals on an asset-fee basis.

EXHIBIT 7   Signature Service (Private Client) Product Offerings

Source: Company (website). http://www.schwab.com/SchwabNOW/navigation/mainFrameSet/0,4528,516,00.html. Accessed November 26, 2001.

Getting Started	**Accounts & Services**	Investments	Mutual Funds	Quotes and Research	Smart Investor

Why Schwab | Accounts/Features | Signature Services | Active Trader | Retirement | Other Services | International

Signature Services Overview

Schwab Signature Services

Schwab Signature Gold

Schwab Signature Platinum

Active Trader Services

Complete Program Benefits Listing

Comparison Chart

Site Map | Demo | Help

SCHWAB *signature* SERVICES™ | COMPARISON CHART

		signature SERVICES	signature GOLD	signature PLATINUM
Expanded Access	Fast Access via a Dedicated Toll-Free Number	✓	✓	✓
	Bond Investor Service	✓	✓	✓
	Global Investing Service	✓	✓	✓
	Schwab Signature Services Web Site	✓	✓	✓
	Velocity™ Trading Software	✓	✓	✓
	Priority Service from Experienced Investment Specialists		✓	✓
	Specialized Trading Services		✓	✓
	Direct Access to a Schwab Signature Platinum Team			✓
	Access to Structured Products Group			✓
Enhanced Research	Online Research from respected third-party providers	✓	✓	✓
	Unlimited, Free Real-Time Quotes and Research Online	✓	✓	✓
	Quarterly Portfolio Profile Report Online	✓	✓	✓
	Exclusive Signature Alerts	✓	✓	✓
	Market Updates via E-mail		✓	✓
	Up to 25 Free Research Reports per Month via Mail or Fax		✓	✓
	Free, Unlimited Research via the Web, Fax, and Mail			✓
Exclusive Benefits	Schwab AdvisorSource™	✓	✓	✓
	Schwab's Estate Planning Hotline	✓	✓	✓
	On Investing™ Magazine	✓	✓	✓
	Schwab Access™ Account	✓	✓	✓
	Discounted Trading			✓
	Privileges Extended to Family Members			✓
	Participation in Initial Public Offerings			✓
	Active Trader Commissions as Low as $14.95			✓
	Real-Time Streaming Quotes			✓
Requirements	Minimum net asset level at Schwab:	$100K	$500K	$1M
	OR Commissionable trades per year	12 +	24 +	48 +
	plus a minimum net asset level of:	$10K	$25K	$50K

Open an Account Now ▶

Or call 1 800 435-8804

EXHIBIT 8A

Source: Company document, 2001.

% of U.S. Investors describing themselves as

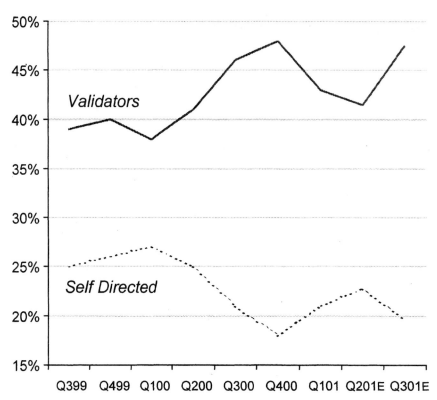

Validators

Self Directed

"E" means estimated.

One of the challenges facing Schwab was to identify where to send clients with a given set of assets and desire for advice. According to Calhoun,

> We're looking for a way to "vector" investors when they walk into our branches. Do we serve them at Schwab or do we vector them to U.S. Trust or refer them to an AdvisorSource advisor? How much of their portfolio do they want to manage by themselves? We want the client to have what is right for him or her and hopefully, when some life event happens, such as an inheritance, we want that money to be placed with us. To attract these accounts, we advertise our advice services, workshops, and new products. For most people we have not been on their radar for doing expert financial advice. In past years, we haven't tried to break free of this image of us as a discounter. Now we must, in order to be successful.

Schwab was concerned that members of its network of IFAs might feel threatened by its advice offerings. At a meeting of network members, Pottruck said, "We're not going to steal your clients."[19] But to many advisors these words were unnecessary. One participant said, "I don't know why they keep bringing it up. I was at a table of advisors, and everyone agreed that they can't hurt us."[20]

[19] Brooke Southall, "Addresses problems head-on at sparsely attended conference: Schwab music on quiet dance floor," *Investment News,* October 15, 2001.

[20] Ibid.

EXHIBIT 8B
Anticipated Growth in Several Client Asset Ranges

The cube at the top reflects the distribution of assets among investors in several different categories in 2001. The cube at the bottom reflects the expected distribution of assets in the same categories by 2006. The number of households with more than 10 million in investable assets was expected to increase 25% by 2006. The number of households with between one and ten million dollars in investable assets was expected to increase 40% by 2006. The number of households with between $100,000 and $1,000,000 in investable assets was expected to increase 20% by 2006.

Source: Company document, 2001.

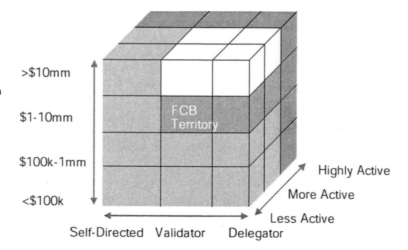

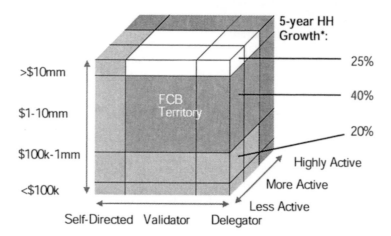

Positioning the Schwab Brand

In the late 1990s, branding became increasingly important to financial services companies.[21] Indeed, according to Schwab's own research, more than 50% of all affluent households in the U.S. deemed a firm's brand "extremely" or "very important" when considering a business to handle their money. Calhoun argued that Schwab's new brand position needed to be as strong and as successfully focused as other well-known brands, such as Disney, Visa or Volvo. (See **Exhibit 9.**)

The overall project objective was to develop a brand position that was long term, compatible with Schwab's brand heritage, and unique. To achieve these goals, the marketing team argued that the positioning needed to be viable in different market conditions, support all the products in the Schwab portfolio, and create an emotional connection with customers. Once a position was agreed upon, they would work to execute the strategy in marketing communication, advertising, web, and direct mail.

[21] Pam Varela, "Are your members loyal to your brand?" *Credit Union Executive,* September 1, 1998.

EXHIBIT 9
Examples of Well-Positioned Brands

Source: Company document, 2001.

 = Magic

VISA = Acceptance

 = Performance

 = Safety

Present Brand Identity

Schwab's brand position was: "Schwab can give me everything I need to be a smart investor." But as the marketing team began its research, they soon discovered that this position, which had successfully created brand awareness of Schwab among potential customers in the previous market, was not as effective when the targeted investors began seeking advice in greater numbers. The team's quantitative research indicated that affluent, non-Schwab investors had a strong awareness of the Schwab brand (see **Exhibit 10**). In terms of brand personality, Schwab was viewed as more innovative, down-to-earth, easy to deal with, and more open-minded, when compared to Fidelity, Merrill Lynch, and Smith Barney brokerage. However, relative to this group of competitors, Schwab could have done better on such attributes as "prestigious" and "respectful." This group did not consider Schwab to be uniquely "best" at any attribute they considered important to a financial service brand (see **Exhibit 11**). The marketing team concluded that the lack of knowledge about Schwab was "widespread."

The marketing team's qualitative research indicated that Schwab loyalists had a better understanding of Schwab, but did not believe that Schwab had (at the time of the case) the ability to deliver expert market advice. Schwab loyalists were independent and wanted to make informed decisions and to have the final say about their investment choices. However, they also wanted support, advice, and education to be available to them when they needed it, precisely so that they could maintain control over their investments and make good decisions. They wanted to educate themselves about the market. According to Calhoun, "they don't want to hand over their financial decisions to someone else. Their ideal investment situation was one in which they could get the support, advice, and education

EXHIBIT 10
Quantitative Data*

Source: Company documents, 2001.

	Schwab	Merrill Lynch	Fidelity	Morgan Stanley/Dean Witter	Salomon Smith Barney	Vanguard	E*Trade
Unaided brand awareness	5	5	5	4	3	3	3
New account consideration[a]	5	5	3	4	3	N/A	3
Mutual funds[b]	3	3	5	N/A	2	4	N/A
Online trading[c]	5	1	2	1	1	N/A	5

*These numbers have been disguised and are set on a scale of 1–5, where 5 is the highest score. "Highest score" corresponds to the highest numbers of responses to the questions below. Survey respondents were affluent customers who held assets at other brokerage firms.
[a]"Which brokerage firm or firms would you be most likely to consider opening an account with?"
[b]"When thinking about mutual funds, firms, where you can buy or sell mutual funds what names come to mind?"
[c]"When thinking about investment or financial services companies, where you can buy or sell stocks, bonds or mutual funds by computer, what names come to mind?"

EXHIBIT 11   Comparison of Brand Attributes[1]

Source: Company documents, 2001.

	Schwab	Fidelity	Merrill Lynch	Smith Barney	E*Trade
Welcomes small and beginning investors	X				X
Produces superior investment return		X			
Is a good place for mutual funds		X			
Good place for online investing					X
Better value than the rest	X				X
Is a good place for invest for retirement		X			
Timely and comprehensive research			X	X	
Trusted source of unbiased guidance	X		X		
Educates its customers		X	X		
Builds personal rapport with customers			X	X	
Gives customers feedback			X	X	
Offers a good value					X
Offers low commissions					X
Good reputation		X	X	X	
Access to independent investment managers	X		X	X	
Provides tools to help with investment decisions		X	X		
Doesn't suit your needs			X		X
Gives conceptual/directional advice				X	
Accessibility	X				X
Personal service			X	X	
State-of-the-art website					X
Recommends specific investments			X	X	

[1]The "X's" represent companies that scored high on a particular attribute.

when they wanted it, but they wanted to be left alone at other times. They wanted a stream-lined advice experience that did not disrupt other important activities." However, Schwab's own research found that many of its most loyal customers had come to Schwab, not for advice but for discount brokerage trading.

Calhoun summed up the differences between non-Schwab investors and Schwab loyalists: "People who know Schwab truly know Schwab. But people who do not know Schwab, know virtually nothing about Schwab. Until now, we had not really done much to challenge the widespread perception of Schwab as 'only a discount brokerage.' That is changing now." Another manager added:

Most investors seem to lack a strong image of Schwab beyond its stability and democratic orientation. This means that they know little about how Schwab does business with investors, little about the products Schwab offers, and little about what makes Schwab distinctive. Communications and public relations need to develop a clear, cohesive message and a strong image that speak to the consumer and give them knowledge of what Schwab can offer them.

Target Audience

The marketing team found that FCBs were vulnerable in the (then) current and future market. FCB customers did not believe that FCBs were delivering on their promise of trustworthiness and reliability. More specifically, FCB clients were experiencing a growing sense of dissatisfaction. This conclusion was based on a series of focus groups and interviews. Part of this effort involved an internal corporate audit, which included an in-depth interview with Charles Schwab, who was heavily involved in the brand development process, interviews with employees at Schwab headquarters, and interviews with Schwab employees in branch offices. The effort to develop qualitative data also included:

Mini-groups: This research involved 21 focus groups with 4–5 participants each. Three groups were conducted with discount on-line brokerage customers, 3 groups with full-commission brokerage customers, 8 groups with Schwab rejecters, 3 groups with current Schwab customers, 2 with new Schwab customers, and 2 with Schwab "loyalists"—long-term Schwab customers with real enthusiasm for the company.

Investor Interviews: Included 14 in-depth interviews. Some recruits were from the mini-groups; the remainder was a mix of HNW individuals and small investors. These interviews were comprised of 4 discount on-line brokerage customers, 4 full-commission brokerage customers, 2 Schwab rejecters, 2 new Schwab customers, and 2 Schwab "loyalists."

Investment Club: The team also attended, observed, and interviewed members of an Atlanta investment club, whose members were all full-commission brokerage clients.

From these interviews, the marketing team discerned that a substantial group of non-Schwab investors wanted a firm that delivered good value, produced superior investment returns, and had a good reputation. But they also wanted their brokerage firm to be a trusted place where they could buy mutual funds and invest for their retirement. Members of this group tended to be dissatisfied with their broker relationships, but were reluctant to move their accounts elsewhere. When these investors did decide to move their accounts, doing so took a long time. Other investors avoided the problem of moving their account by simply opening a new account somewhere else without transferring the former account. The team identified several factors that fed into this "inertia."

Low Expectations: Some investors felt that they couldn't do any better than their broker. Several investors said that they would need a lot of money to get the kind of attention and support they would like to have. These investors felt that they might as well stay with their broker.

"Maybe It's Me": Some investors felt that their own lack of knowledge or resources prevented them from getting more out of their broker relationship. They felt that if they knew more, or had more money to invest, they would have more influence and control in the relationship. Several felt that they didn't know the norms of relationships with brokers, and so were not able to "talk the talk" or find a way to get what they wanted. As a result, this group of investor felt they wouldn't be better off elsewhere, and that moving the account would unfairly place blame on the broker.

Leaving the Court a Loser: Some investors resisted leaving their broker relationship when they had suffered recent financial losses. They didn't want to move from a weak position, and possibly incur further losses.

A Fear of Being Judged: Some investors resisted leaving their broker relationship because they were afraid of being scolded or looked down upon for past investment decisions. Continuing with an unsatisfactory relationship was less embarrassing than displaying one's unsatisfactory investment history to someone new.

The marketing team concluded that dissatisfied full-commission brokerage customers who wanted to move all or some of their funds elsewhere constituted a ripe market opportunity for Schwab. The question became how to reach these groups.

The New Brand Position

Overcoming investor inertia was possible, Schwab managers decided, if they could leverage Schwab's brand assets. One manager said:

> Our qualitative research shows that investors who resonate with Schwab are investors who are not passive, and they want their lives to be rich and interesting. The idea of just putting money in some recommended place and letting it sit is not compelling to them. They want to be more involved, and they want the money to make a difference in their lives. Schwab's message needs to be not just about getting one's finances in order, but also about building oneself and one's life. This message also needs to capture these investors' confidence in themselves, their ability to learn what they need to, and their ability to make good decisions for themselves. We need to offer dissatisfied investors at the big FCBs what they want, even if they are not "big fish."
>
> Investors who know about investing are not attracted to messages that offer to educate beginners, and beginners are not attracted to messages that make them feel ignorant or stupid. Even those who know very little or feel overwhelmed by the category think they are smart people, and do not want to be treated otherwise. Schwab's message needs to make clear that people, resources, advice and support are available to the extent that investors need them, but that investors can choose their level of independence.

The marketing team recognized that the message needed to fit the following context: Schwab was interested in building client assets, the market was volatile, demographics were changing, investor confidence was low—even among the most market savvy, and full commission brokerages were going after a similar target audience. With these considerations in mind, the team evaluated several positioning options (see **Exhibit 12**).

EXHIBIT 12 Positioning Options

Source: Company documents, 2001.

Relevant	Schwab Equity	Superiority vs. Discount	Superiority vs. FCB		Not uniquely ownable	Stretch for Schwab	FCB Superiority	Difficult to Communicate
✓	Potential	✓		Advice	✓	✓	✓	✓
	Potential		✓	Unbiased Advice				✓
✓	✓	✓	✓	Mentor/Educator	✓			
✓	✓		✓	Technology Leader	✓			
✓	✓		✓	Access	✓			
✓			✓	Convenience	✓			
✓				Performance	✓			✓
		✓		Prestige		✓	✓	

EXHIBIT 13 Media Messages from Other Brokerages

Source: Company documents, 2001.

Competitor	Key Message	Tagline:
Fidelity	No matter what your financial need, you have the full support of Fidelity to successfully guide you.	"See yourself succeeding."
Merrill Lynch	Merrill Lynch's Financial Advisors help simplify your life by managing your finances, so you can get back to living yours.	"A simple fee. A simpler life."
Morgan Stanley	Morgan Stanley has the expertise, knowledge, and research to help guide investors.	"Well connected."
E*Trade	The #1 online place for investors to take control of their investments.	"It's your money."
Datek	Datek is the best place for online trading, because they were built specifically for online trading.	"Datek Online. Built to trade."
Salomon Smith Barney	SSB has the expertise to help investors make the best investment choice that is right for them.	"See how we earn it."
CSFBdirect	CSFBdirect provides you with resources and information to keep up with the market.	"People who know, know CSFBdirect."
Ameritrade	Provides the cheapest and easiest way to manage all of your financial accounts, in one convenient place.	"It's how you get somewhere on Wall Street."

Moving Forward

Calhoun began the meeting by discussing the conceptual support for the positioning strategy, which had received backing from Chuck Schwab and Dave Pottruck on previous occasions. Schwab's advertising firm, BBDO, then sketched the two advertising campaigns, presenting several advertising storyboards that could be shown on television in the fall. Calhoun emphasized that the brokerage space was crowded with similar images and messages (see **Exhibit 13**), and that it was a tremendous challenge to identify a distinctive niche for Schwab. As Calhoun finished the presentation, he told the group that the campaign would, in Chuck's words, get the company to where "the puck is going to be." But when the presentation ended, and the pause continued, Calhoun wondered whether Schwab would get to "the puck" before any of the other brokerages.

33

Heineken N.V.: Global Branding and Advertising

John A. Quelch

In January 1994, senior managers at Heineken headquarters in Amsterdam were reviewing two research projects commissioned to clarify Heineken's brand identity and the implications for television advertising. Project Comet defined five components of Heineken's global brand identity and explored how they should be expressed in Heineken brand communications. Project Mosa, which involved a different team of executives, identified the expressions of taste and friendship that had the most appeal and explored how they should be expressed in Heineken television advertising worldwide.

Heineken's senior managers were interested in assessing whether or not the conclusions of the two studies were mutually consistent. They also wished to determine how far they should or could standardize Heineken's brand image and advertising worldwide.

Company Background

The Heineken brewery was founded in Amsterdam in 1863 by Gerard Adriaan Heineken. He was quoted as saying: "I will leave no stone unturned in attempting to continuously supply beer of the highest quality." The strain of yeast which continued through the 1990s to give Heineken beer its special taste was developed in 1886. Heineken beer won a gold medal at the 1889 Paris World's Fair and, by 1893, was one of the largest selling beers in the Netherlands.

One hundred years later, in 1993, Heineken N.V. recorded net sales of 9,049 million guilders and a trading profit of 798 million guilders. Beer accounted for 82% of sales, the remainder being derived from soft drinks, spirits and wine. The geographical breakdowns of sales (in litres) for Heineken and the worldwide beer industry were as follows:

	Heineken 1993 Sales %	% Change vs. 1992	Total 1993 Beer Sales %
Netherlands	24	} (1.6)	} 38
Rest of Europe	47		
America	13	5.3	38
Asia/Australasia	8	23.7	19
Africa	6	(1.5)	5

In 1993, sales of beer brewed under Heineken's supervision reached 5.6 billion litres, second in the world only to Anheuser-Busch with 10 billion litres. World beer production in 1993 totaled 120 billion litres.

Sales of the Heineken brand were 1.52 billion litres in 1993. The company's other brands with some international distribution were Amstel (formerly made by the second-largest Dutch brewery, acquired by Heineken in 1968) which sold 630 million litres; Buckler, a nonalcoholic beer, which sold 90 million litres; and Murphy's Stout, recently acquired and sold principally in Ireland and the United Kingdom. As a result of acquisitions, Heineken also oversaw the brewing of many local and regional beer brands marketed by its subsidiaries, such as Bir Bintang, the leading Indonesian brand.

International Presence

The Heineken brand had long been available in markets outside the Netherlands. In 1937, Heineken granted its first license to a foreign brewer to produce Heineken beer according to the original formula. While licensing agreements also aimed to specify how the Heineken brand should be marketed, Heineken could not influence how a licensee marketed its own brands. In management's view, some licensees did not maintain a sufficient price premium for the Heineken brand over their own national brands. By the 1980s, Heineken was seeking majority equity stakes in its existing and prospective partners to ensure tighter control over production and marketing. The ideal national brewer partner, from Heineken's point of view, was one that did not have international ambitions for its domestic brands.

By 1993, Heineken's worldwide brewing interests were as follows:

	Wholly Owned Subsidiaries	Majority Equity Stakes	Minority Equity Stakes	Licensees
Europe	3	5	0	2
American	0	4	10	2
Asia/Australasia	0	2	8	2
Africa	0	4	10	2

In Europe, for example, Heineken owned outright its operations in the Netherlands, France, and Ireland. It held majority interests in breweries in Greece, Hungary, Italy, Spain, and

Switzerland and licensed production to breweries in Norway and the United Kingdom (Whitbread). Heineken was not bottled in the large United States market, but was the number one imported beer. In Germany, the heaviest beer-consuming country in Europe (144 litres per capita), national brands still dominated the market and Heineken was available only through imports.

In the early 1990s, the brewing industry was becoming increasingly global as the leading brewers scrambled to acquire equity stakes and sign joint ventures with national breweries. This trend was especially evident in the emerging markets where population expansion and increased per-capita consumption promised faster growth than in the developed world. In Europe, in particular, overcapacity and minimal population growth resulted in price competition, margin pressures, and efforts to segment further the market with no- or low-alcohol beers, specialty flavored beers, and "dry" beers.

Despite the increasing globalization of the industry, there remained substantial differences in per-capita beer consumption, consumer preferences and behaviors, and the mix of competitors from one market to another. For example, annual per capita consumption ranged from 132 liters in Ireland and 88 liters in the U.S.A. to 56 liters in Japan and 30 liters in Argentina. Heineken executives believed that the beer market in each country followed an evolutionary cycle and that, at any time, different countries were at different stages of market development. **Exhibit 1** depicts the beer market development cycle while **Exhibit 2** notes Heineken's principal marketing objectives in selected markets.

At the end of 1993, the Heineken brand held a 24% volume share in the Netherlands, several share points ahead of its main competitor, Grolsch. As the market leader, Heineken was viewed as a mainstream brand. Sales volume was declining and the brand image needed some revitalization. Outside the Netherlands, however, Heineken had consistently been marketed as a premium brand. In some markets, such as the United States and Hong Kong, Heineken had successfully established a distinct image for the brand. The image was sometimes narrowly drawn such that Heineken was seen as appropriate solely for special occasions when making a social statement was important rather than for daily consumption. In other markets, such as in Latin America, Heineken was viewed as just one among many European imported beers. But across all markets, the Heineken brand was acknowledged as a lighter beer of superior quality presented in attractive packaging.

Comparative data on the Heineken brand's market position in seven European countries are presented in **Exhibit 3.** Premium brands accounted for around 25% of beer volume in 1993 and around 30% of measured media beer advertising. Heineken was the most heavily advertised premium brand in Europe and worldwide. Over 90% of Heineken advertising took the form of television commercials.

Project Comet

Managers at Heineken headquarters were concerned that Heineken's brand image was not being consistently projected in the brand's communications around the world. Two television advertising executions were used in multiple country markets in 1991, but, particularly in the larger markets, local Heineken managers had the resources to develop their own commercials and justified their decisions to do so on grounds of unique competitive conditions, industry structures, and/or consumption behaviors.

Project Comet was established in 1991 by Heineken's international marketing manager to recommend how to enhance Heineken's competitive advantage by more consistently

578

EXHIBIT 1   Beer Market Evolution for Selected Countries and Regions

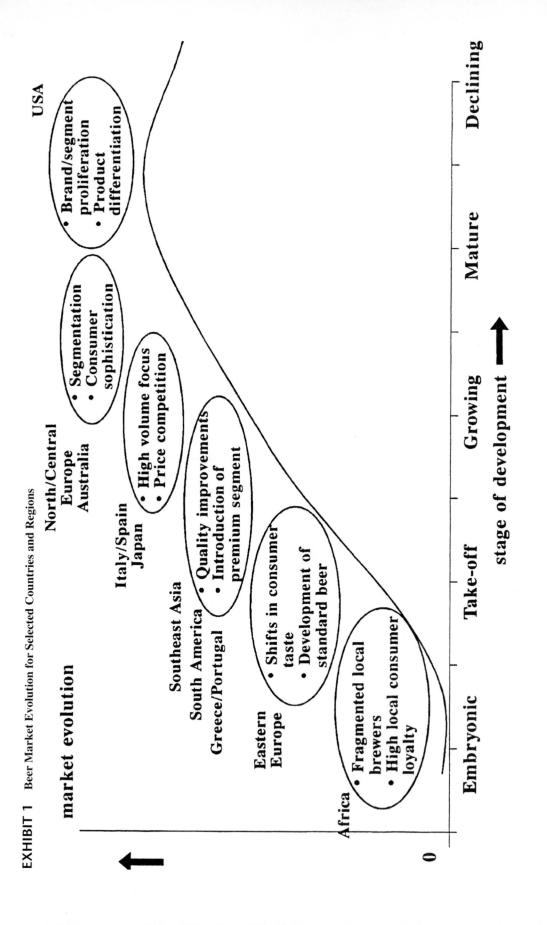

EXHIBIT 2   Key Heineken Marketing Objectives in Eight Countries

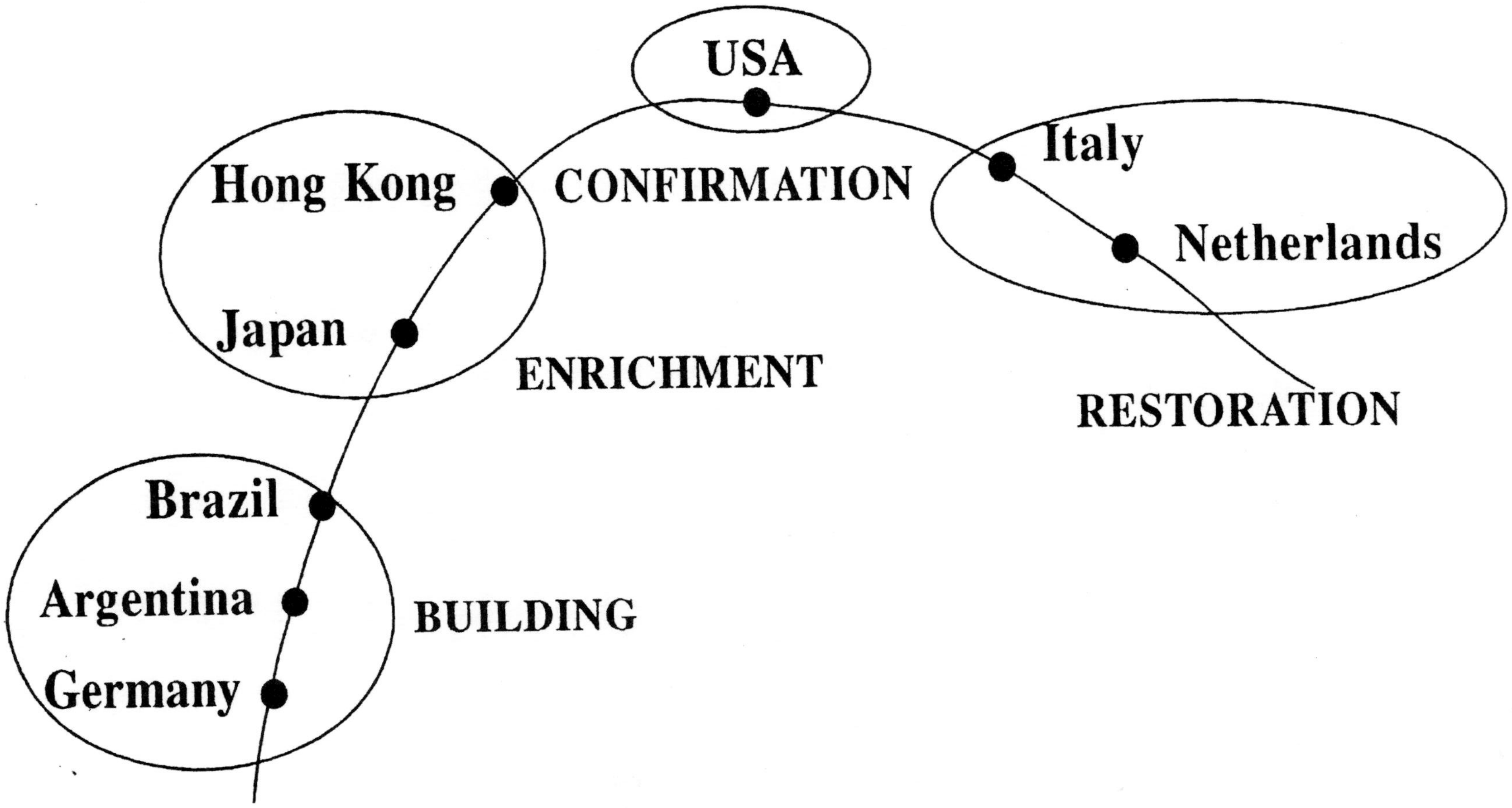

579

EXHIBIT 3 **Comparative Heineken Usage Data for Seven European Markets**

	Netherlands	France	Greece	Ireland	Italy	Spain	United Kingdom
Main brand usage[a]	17	14	44	25	7	5	11
Trial/awareness ratio	92	89	99	91	86	66	90
Regular/total usage ratio	46	40	54	42	28	25	41
Monthly brand penetration[b]	60	48	79	57	53	63	60
Market share position[c]	1	2	1	2	3	7	7
Advertising share of voice position[d]	1	2	4	5	4	6	6
Per capita beer consumption (litres)[e]	90	41	40	123	24	71	103

[a]Percentage of beer drinkers naming Heineken as their main brand.
[b]Percentage of beer drinkers who had consumed a Heineken in the previous month.
[c]Overall market share position. In most markets, Heineken was the largest-selling brand in the premium segment.
[d]Overall SOV position among beer brands advertised. In *all* markets except the United Kingdom, Heineken SOV ranked first or second in the premium segment.
[e]Based on consumption of *all* beer, not just Heineken.

projecting the brand as "the world's leading premium beer." The project team concluded that Heineken's desired brand image was "good taste":

- Because of Heineken's flavor, its roots, commitment to and pride in brewing a high-quality lager.
- Because Heineken is a symbol of premiumness, taste, and tradition around the world.

The team believed that no other brand in the world could claim superior good taste with as much credibility as Heineken.

The brand's good taste image would be built on five core brand values:

- Taste
- Premiumness
- Tradition
- Winning spirit
- Friendship

Taste and premiumness were regarded as the price of entry. They had to be communicated in advertising messages but would not, in themselves, be enough to differentiate Heineken from its competition. A unique, differentiated image would depend on effective communication of the other three core brand values. Project team members acknowledge the challenge of communicating all five values in each advertisement. However, they thought that all five could be reflected in one way or another through the locations, situations, relationships, casting, lighting, style, and tone used in each commercial.

The team detailed how each of the core brand values should be portrayed in Heineken brand commercials:

Taste The product should be shown in slow-pouring shots where its golden color, sparkling texture and refreshing coolness would celebrate its taste. Actors should be portrayed genuinely enjoying Heineken with no gulps or "knocking it back." The slogan used should be competitive but not comparative.

Premiumness The production quality of every execution should be at the level of excellence to be expected of a premium brand. In some geographies, Heineken's premiumness might be a unique reason for purchase; in such cases, this attribute could be presented as part of the brand promise.

Tradition The genuine aura of the brand should be especially evident in the casting and tone of voice of each commercial. Heineken should be the preferred brand of people who believed in true values and whose brand choices reflected their personal value set.

Winning spirit Tone of voice was thought to be especially important in conveying this value "because winners are confident and relaxed, take a quiet pride in everything they do and do not shout."

Friendship Heineken should not be portrayed as a solitary beer or a "mass-gathering" drink. The Heineken group should be a few (even two) people who clearly enjoy their relationship. The "Heineken moment" should show people as themselves, content, relaxed with each other and confident. Interactions should be sincere, self-confident, warm and balanced, displaying mutual respect and free from game-playing.

The project team next tried to develop guidelines for the visual images—the people, the relationships and the settings—to be included in Heineken commercials.

The Project Comet report concluded as follows:

> All of our advertising must be consistent with these guidelines. We also need impactful advertising. Heineken advertising is therefore never *safe*. It should always be leading edge and state of the art, taking calculated risks and initiatives to achieve the desired effects.

Project Mosa

In late 1993, Heineken's international advertising manager commissioned focus groups in eight countries[1] to understand (a) what male beer drinkers meant by taste and friendship in relation to premium beer drinking and (b) which expressions of taste and friendship could be used by the Heineken brand in advertising. The project team identified in advance the following expressions of taste which "appealed to the head" and expressions of friendship which "appealed to the heart":

Taste (Head)	Friendship (Heart)
Brand vision	Trust
Quality	Sports
Brewing skills	True friends
Tradition	You can count on Heineken as a friend
Availability	Respect

Boards with visual and message stimuli depicting each of these expressions were used in the focus groups to elicit reactions. Examples of these boards are presented in **Exhibits 4** and **5.** Eight focus groups were run in each country, four with 21–27 year olds and four with 28–35 year olds. Four groups in each country explored taste cues, four explored friendship cues.

Members of the focus groups dealing with taste were asked to identify which of several factors they perceived as strong or weak indicators of beer taste. These responses are summarized in **Exhibit 6.** Members of the other four focus groups dealing with friendship discussed the different social occasions when a standard versus a premium beer would be appropriate. On this issue, there was substantial agreement across national markets. The conclusions are summarized in **Exhibit 7.**

---

[1] The countries were Netherlands, Italy, and Germany in Europe; USA, Argentina and Brazil in the Americas; and Japan and Hong Kong in Asia.

EXHIBIT 4   **Sample Project Mosa Concept Boards: Taste Expressions**

"I consider a bad bottle of Heineken a personal insult"

Alfred H. Heineken
Chairman

Heineken. The clear beer for the purest taste.

EXHIBIT 5   **Sample Project Mosa Concept Boards: Friendship Expressions**

Nevada, USA.

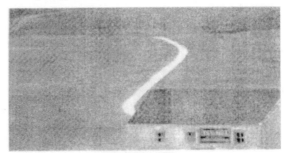

Yorkshire, UK.

Cameroon, West Africa.

Papeete, Tahiti.

Wherever you are, you can always count on Heineken

Heineken. When true friends get together.

EXHIBIT 6
Indications of Beer Taste: Summary of Focus Group Responses

	Netherlands	Germany	Italy	USA	Average 8 Countries
Manufacturing					
Ingredients	−	+	−	−	−
Water quality	+	+	−	−	0
Scale of plant	+	+	−	+	+
Product					
Taste experience	+	+	+	+	+
Balanced taste	+	+	+	+	+
Aftertaste	−	−	+	+	0
Freshness	+	−	−	+	0
Foam	+	+	0	+	+
Drinkability	+	+	−	−	+
Day after	+	+	−	−	0
Marketing					
Price	−	+	−	+	0
Advertising	+	−	+	+	+
Packaging	−	+	+	+	+

Note: A minus sign (−) indicates the factor is an unimportant or negative indicator of quality.

EXHIBIT 7
Standard vs. Premium Beer: Summary of Focus Group Responses

	Standard	Premium
Company	• nuclear family • large groups • your wife • colleagues	• intimate friends • smaller groups • girlfriend • boss
Occasions and Moments	• after work • at meals • at home • watching TV • thirst-quenching • (popular) bars • beach • to party • daytime • after sports • sport events	• meeting people • fancy meals • away from home • new encounters • savouring • traveling • intimate moments and places • elegant parties • nighttime • entertaining • disco/nightclub
Role of Beer	• social participation • thirst-quencher • alcohol effect • problem solver	• ego enhancement/self-esteem • a treat • a communication tool • signal function

EXHIBIT 8
Taste Expressions:
Overall Heineken
Suitability

	Netherlands	Germany	Italy	USA	Average 8 Countries
Brand Vision	−	+	+	−	−
Quality					
Two years Amsterdam training	+	+	+	+	+
24 quality checks	+	+	+	+	+
Bottles returned to Amsterdam	+	+	+	+	+
Brewing Skills					
100% malt	0	+	0	+	0
Smooth taste	−	+	+	+	0
Pure taste	+	−	+	+	0
Matured longer	−	0	−	−	−
Tradition					
Family since 1863	−	+	−	+	0
Original recipe	+	+	0	+	+
Where beer was born	+	+	+	+	+
Availability					
More bars/more countries	+	0	−	0	0

EXHIBIT 9
Friendship
Expressions: Overall
Heineken Suitability

	Netherlands	Germany	Italy	USA	Average 8 Countries
Friendship					
Cat and dog	0	0	+	−	0
Rugby (sport)	+	0	+	−	0
True friends	+	+	0	+	+
Always count on Heineken	+	+	+	+	+
Respect	−	−	−	−	−

Participants in the focus groups were then exposed to a variety of advertising boards for Heineken, each of them highlighting a particular attribute. Those in the focus groups dealing with taste were exposed to twelve boards while those in the friendship focus groups were exposed to ten. The objective was to elicit consumer reactions to both the visual and message claims presented on each board and to establish each claim's relevance to and overall suitability for promoting the Heineken brand. The overall suitability rankings, first for the four focus groups concentrating on taste cues and, second, for the focus groups concentrating on friendship cues, are presented in **Exhibits 8** and **9.**

Chapter 34

UNICEF

John Quelch   Nathalie Laidler

In September 2002, Marjorie Newman-Williams, director of communications, was about to present the results of a United Nations Children's Fund (UNICEF) rebranding exercise to the 47th Annual Meeting of National Committees for UNICEF. The rebranding effort flowed from the desire to ensure that the UNICEF identity reflected its evolving mission. As Newman-Williams said, "UNICEF's public image and awareness is very different from who we are, and who we want to be." The rebranding process had taken over two years, and Newman-Williams described it "as a challenge in an organization that had little understanding of the importance of branding and not much stomach for it." She expanded:

> Four forces drove the branding effort. First, UNICEF's internal shift towards a rights-based organization, increasingly appreciating the importance of advocacy as a strategy to achieve its goals. Second, an increasingly challenging external donor environment, combining a decline in multilateralism and an increase in restricted funds. Third, market research conducted at national levels, which showed that the UNICEF image did not match with whom we thought we were. Fourth, a need to provide greater clarity and consistency in our communication strategy. The objective was to refresh and revitalize UNICEF's image and reputation, uncover what UNICEF stands for, and find a way to express this individuality in a clear and focused way and reflect it in everything we do as an organization. We started the rebranding process in 1999, and I think we are very close to implementation now.

United Nations Children's Fund

UNICEF was mandated by the United Nations General Assembly to advocate for the protection of children's rights and was guided by the Convention on the Rights of the Child. UNICEF's stated mission was to "reduce childhood death and illness, protect children in the midst of war and natural disaster, promote education for girls and boys alike, and strive to build a world in which all children live with dignity and security."

Professor John Quelch and Research Associate Nathalie Laidler prepared this case. HBS cases are developed solely as the basis for class discussion. Cases are not intended to serve as endorsements, sources of primary data, or illustrations of effective or ineffective management.

In 2002, UNICEF worked in 162 countries and territories and had 6,000 staff people, 14% of whom worked at headquarter locations. In 2001, total income was over $1.2 billion, with governments and intergovernmental organizations accounting for 64% of contributions. An additional 33% was derived from the private sector (individuals, foundations, businesses, and nongovernmental organizations), mostly through National Committees, with the remaining 3% coming from other sources.

History

Founded in December 1946, UNICEF (the United Nations International Children's Emergency Fund) was established to help children after World War II in Europe. In 1950, its task was expanded to help children living in poverty in developing countries, and in October 1953, UNICEF became a permanent part of the United Nations system. Its name was changed to the United Nations Children's Fund, although it maintained the acronym UNICEF.

In 1953 Danny Kaye became UNICEF's "ambassador," and his film, *Assignment Children,* was seen by more than 100 million people. In 1959, the U.N. General Assembly adopted the Declaration of the Rights of the Child, focusing on children's rights to education, health care, and nutrition. As of 1962, UNICEF began to support teacher training and provide classroom supplies in the newly independent African countries. By 1965, education made up 43% of the organization's assistance to Africa. In 1965, UNICEF was awarded the Nobel Peace Prize, and in 1983 the organization launched a drive to save the lives of millions of children through programs focusing on oral rehydration, immunization, breast-feeding, and good nutrition.

In 1987, UNICEF's study, Adjustment with a Human Face, prompted global debate on how to protect women and children from the negative effects of economic reform, and in 1989, the U.N. General Assembly adopted the Convention on the Rights of the Child. In 1990, the World Summit for Children set 10-year goals for children's health, nutrition, and education, and in 1996 UNICEF supported a study, "The Impact of Armed Conflict on Children," raising awareness of war's effect on children. In 2001, the Global Movement for Children and the Say Yes for Children campaigns mobilized millions of children and adults around the world, and on May 10, 2002, the Special Session of the General Assembly on Children released its official outcome document, "A World Fit for Children."

Over the past five decades, UNICEF had evolved from an organization focused on providing supplies and services to a rights-based organization that combined field support and services with broader advocacy work. Newman-Williams explained:

> In the 1950s and 1960s, UNICEF was a supply and logistics organization that could provide a steady supply of goods in turbulent times, and to troubled and hard-to-access regions. In the 1970s, a tug of war developed between advocacy programs and supply operations, and in the 1980s and 1990s, the concept of children having rights really started taking hold. In the 1990s, UNICEF began to realize that the organization could do more to bring about the sustainable change it hoped to achieve, and we therefore gave greater emphasis to advocacy work. Today, the supply and service programs in the field buy us a seat at the national policymaking table, to address broader issues of children's rights. There is some debate internally as to whether we are going too far, and it is true that, unless we can show tangible results for children, our credibility is at stake.

Mission and Objectives

Mandated by the U.N. General Assembly to advocate for the protection of children's rights, help meet children's basic needs, and establish opportunities for children to reach their full potential, UNICEF was guided by the Convention on the Rights of the Child, an international human rights treaty ratified in 2002 by 191 countries, with the notable exception of the United States. The United States refused to sign any multilateral agreement that conceded power to any authority other than itself. (See **Exhibit 1** for UNICEF's mission statement.)

EXHIBIT 1   **UNICEF's Mission Statement, 2002**

Source: UNICEF Annual Report, 2002.

UNICEF is mandated by the United Nations General Assembly to advocate for the protection of children's rights, to help meet their basic needs and to expand their opportunities to reach their full potential.

UNICEF is guided by the Convention on the Rights of the Child and strives to establish children's rights as enduring ethical principles and international standards of behavior towards children.

UNICEF insists that the survival, protection and development of children are universal development imperatives that are integral to human progress.

UNICEF mobilizes political will and material resources to help countries, particularly developing countries, ensure a "first call for children" and to build their capacity to form appropriate policies and deliver services for children and their families.

UNICEF is committed to ensuring special protection for the most disadvantaged children—victims of war, disasters, extreme poverty, all forms of violence and exploitation and those with disabilities.

UNICEF responds in emergencies to protect the rights of children. In coordination with United Nations partners and humanitarian agencies, UNICEF makes its unique facilities for rapid response available to its partners to relieve the suffering of children and those who provide their care.

UNICEF is non-partisan and its cooperation is free of discrimination. In everything it does, the most disadvantaged children and the countries in greatest need have priority.

UNICEF aims, through its country programs, to promote the equal rights of women and girls and to support their full participation in the political, social and economic development of their communities.

UNICEF works with all its partners towards the attainment of the sustainable human development goals adopted by the world community and the realization of the vision of peace and social progress enshrined in the Charter of the United Nations.

UNICEF cooperated with 162 countries and territories, in partnership with governments, which focused on nine key areas: child protection; education; health; HIV/AIDS; nutrition; water and environmental sanitation; early childhood development; gender concerns; and emergency aid. Providing essential supplies for children was a core component of UNICEF programs. In 2001, UNICEF provided nearly $600 million worth of supplies including vaccines, essential drugs, food, medical equipment, education supplies, transport, and IT equipment.

UNICEF's medium-term strategic plan (MTSP) for the period 2002–2005 combined a results-based management approach and a human rights-based approach and was developed to serve three functions: (1) outline the role and contribution of UNICEF to the "A World Fit for Children" document (see **Exhibit 2** for key elements of the document), (2) describe UNICEF's organizational priorities and objectives, and (3) serve as a framework of accountability for UNICEF and its stakeholders. (See **Exhibit 3** for UNICEF's financial forecast in the MTSP.)

The MTSP also established the following five organizational priorities, for each of which both service and advocacy activities were identified: girls education, integrated early childhood development, immunization "plus," HIV/AIDS, and child protection. In 2001, UNICEF spent just over $1 billion on direct program assistance, broken down into the above-mentioned priorities as follows: 15% for girls education, 36% for integrated early childhood development, 24% for immunization "plus," 7% for HIV/AIDS, 14% for child protection, and 4% for other programs. Key to its effort to promote these organizational priorities, UNICEF planned to use information, communication, and advocacy to influence the actions of others. UNICEF's MTSP stated clearly:

We will put children at the heart of every agenda and ensure that the voice of children is heard. We will expose disparities, confront discrimination and end violations of children's rights. We will continually develop our knowledge and expertise to create, deliver and inspire solutions. We will maximize the resources devoted to children, both by acting directly and by building powerful alliances to force action and change.

EXHIBIT 2 **Key Elements of "A World Fit for Children"**

"A World Fit for Children" was a document, adopted by the U.N. General Assembly at the 27th special session in May 2002, that comprised a declaration and a plan of action.

DECLARATION

We reaffirm our obligation to take action to promote and protect the rights of each child—every human being below the age of 18 years including adolescents. We are determined to respect the dignity and to secure the well-being of all children.

We hereby call on all members of society to join us in a global movement that will help build a world fit for children through upholding our commitments to the following principles and objectives:

1. Put children first.
2. Eradicate poverty: invest in children.
3. Leave no child behind.
4. Care for every child.
5. Educate every child.
6. Protect children from harm and exploitation.
7. Protect children from war.
8. Combat HIV/AIDS.
9. Listen to children and ensure their participation.
10. Protect the earth for children.

PLAN OF ACTION

1. Promote healthy lives . . . through access to primary health care systems, adequate water and sanitation systems.
2. Provide quality education . . . ensure that all children have access to and complete primary education that is free, compulsory and of good quality.
3. Protect against abuse, exploitation and violence.
   - General protection
   - Protection from armed conflict
   - Combating child labor
   - Elimination of trafficking and sexual exploitation of children
4. Combat HIV/AIDS.
5. Mobilize resources.

The majority of UNICEF's top management believed that two factors made UNICEF unique:

1. UNICEF was mandated by the United Nations and had global agreement by governments of its strategy and frameworks. "We are a multilateral agency that works at all levels," said Anupama Rao Singh, one of the deputy directors of headquarters' (HQ's) program division. "Our success is that we have privileged access and relationships with local governments."

2. UNICEF was firmly anchored in the developing countries it operated in, and the organization's rigorous approach and integrity allowed it to be a player in all countries. "This is our core competence," commented Cecilia Lotse, director of HQ's program funding office. "Even if our environment changes, UNICEF must maintain its competitive advantage in the field." Omar Abdi, deputy director of HQ's program division, expanded on this idea: "The strength of UNICEF is in the field. Programs are decentralized and developed at the local level. The difference between UNICEF and NGOs [nongovernmental organizations] is that we have lengthy track records in many countries and unique access to a range of partners."

EXHIBIT 3
Financial Forecasts
for UNICEF's MTSP

Source: UNICEF MTSP,
November 7, 2002.

Millions US$	2001	2002	2003	2004	2005
INCOME					
Regular Resources	$ 545	$ 588	$ 629	$ 673	$ 720
Governments	340	343	355	362	370
Private Sector	170	210	195	205	215
Other	35	35	35	35	35
Other Resources	423	420	420	420	420
Governments	283	280	280	280	280
Private Sector	140	140	140	140	140
Other	0	0	0	0	0
Emergencies	192	190	190	190	190
TOTAL INCOME	1,160	1,198	1,195	1,212	1,230
EXPENDITURES					
Program Assistance	900	925	925	932	942
Program Support	230	243	252	260	268
TOTAL EXPENDITURES	1,130	1,168	1,177	1,192	1,210
Income less Expenditures	30	30	18	20	20
Movements noncash assets/liabilities	30	8	−9	−9	−9
Year-end cash balance					
Convertible currencies	479	517	526	537	548
Nonconvertible currencies	8	8	8	8	8
TOTAL CASH BALANCE	$ 487	$ 525	$ 534	$ 545	$ 556

Increasing Focus on Advocacy

UNICEF's advocacy work was both national and global in scope. National advocacy work was considered an inherent part of the field programs. "These two missions are different sides of the same coin," said Philip O'Brien, regional director for the CEE/CIS[1] region. "For example, in Albania our field programs and analysis resulted in policy changes at the national level." Global advocacy work was based on extensive data and research gathered by the field offices and compiled by UNICEF's research arm in Florence, resulting in major studies with a global impact. For example, "Adjustment with a Human Face," which was fairly controversial when published, and "Children on the Frontline" were both part of UNICEF's global advocacy work.

Being an international organization financed in large part by voluntary contributions from individual governments did, however, create a certain conflict for UNICEF's advocacy work. "We have a responsibility to be the world advocate for children," explained O'Brien, "but there is a tension inherent with any government that is a major partner. We can never become an organization like Human Rights Watch because we are an intergovernmental body. We can have the same message, but we will say it in a different way." "We might be criticized for not speaking out against certain governments," added Abdi, "but we have the kind of access that most other organizations do not have, and we use that special privilege to challenge governments behind the scenes when we feel it is necessary."

Organizational Structure

In 2002, UNICEF was a subsidiary body of the General Assembly, reporting through the U.N. Economic and Social Council, and an integral part of the United Nations. It maintained its own staff and facilities and was financed by its own sources, received as voluntary

[1] CEE = European Economic Community. CIS = Commonwealth of Independent States (former U.S.S.R.).

contributions from governments, intergovernmental agencies, NGOs, and individuals. UNICEF was governed by a 36-member executive board, members of which were elected by the Economic and Social Council and served a three-year term.

UNICEF comprised an HQ in New York, eight regional offices, 126 country offices worldwide, offices in Tokyo and Brussels that supported fund-raising, a research center based in Florence, and a supply operation based in Copenhagen. Thirty-seven National Committees, mostly based in industrialized countries, raised funds and spread awareness about the organization's mission and work. (See **Exhibit 4** for UNICEF's organizational chart.)

The role of HQ was to provide overall strategic direction and guidance and lead the development of the global UNICEF perspective by integrating the experiences and contributions of all parts of the UNICEF system.

Seven regional offices provided guidance, support, oversight, and coordination to the country field offices, and one regional office (Europe) served as the focal point for relations with the National Committees for UNICEF. Regional offices also provided technical support to the field, and each region had a management team that met twice a year to develop regional strategies and share best practices.

The field offices supported the planning, implementation, and monitoring of country programs in collaboration with national governments. In recent years, UNICEF had pushed for increased financial decentralization, giving field offices more accountability and responsibility for their budgets. From the broad strategies developed in the MTSP, countries developed their operational plans and, every year, annual work plans were submitted, along with country reports, to both the regional offices and HQ. The program division was responsible for defining the criteria for unrestricted country allocations and establishing the planning ceilings for programs in field offices. Country ceilings were determined by three criteria: child mortality, per capita income, and absolute number of children under the age of five. These unrestricted funds were used to support a five-year program in each country.

National Committees

The National Committees' main task was to raise funds from private donations, but they also played a role in advocacy, communication, and education. National Committees were separate legal entities and NGOs that had a standard agreement with UNICEF, similar to that of a franchise, enabling them to use the UNICEF logo. In exchange, they were required to provide, on average, 75% of their gross revenues to UNICEF, although some variations existed, with countries such as Japan and Germany providing 85% and 90%, respectively, and smaller eastern European countries around 25%. (See **Exhibit 5** for details of contributions from National Committees.)

Each National Committee had a board of directors drawn from civil society, with line management reporting to these boards. "The caliber of the board is vital," commented Steve Woodhouse, director of the Geneva regional office. "There is a direct correlation between the success of a National Committee and the strength of its board." UNICEF HQ maintained the power to close down a National Committee by withdrawing recognition and use of the logo. This had occurred several times in the past.

Funding

UNICEF derived its income entirely from voluntary contributions from two main sources: governments and intergovernmental organizations, and nongovernmental private sector groups and individuals. In 2001, the former accounted for 64% of UNICEF's total income of $1.2 billion and the latter for 33%. Regular resources (core funds) were unrestricted funds used to support country programs and finance the management and administration of UNICEF; other funds were resources restricted for special projects. (See **Exhibit 6** for a breakdown of UNICEF income by major donor country.) In 2001, regular resources made

EXHIBIT 4 UNICEF Organizational Chart, 2002

Source: UNICEF Communications Division.

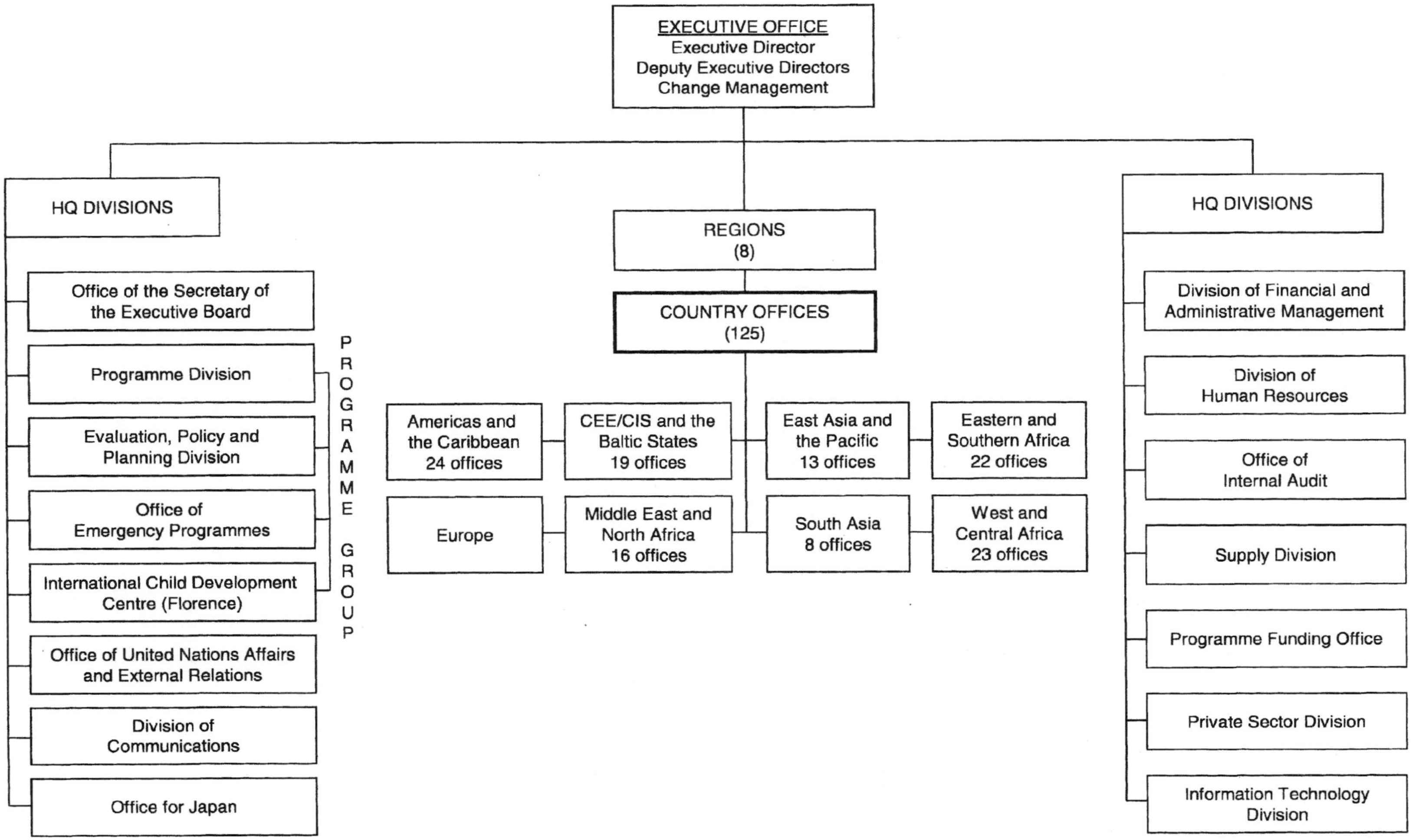

EXECUTIVE OFFICE
Executive Director
Deputy Executive Directors
Change Management

HQ DIVISIONS

- Division of Financial and Administrative Management
- Division of Human Resources
- Office of Internal Audit
- Supply Division
- Programme Funding Office
- Private Sector Division
- Information Technology Division

REGIONS
(8)

COUNTRY OFFICES
(125)

- Eastern and Southern Africa 22 offices
- West and Central Africa 23 offices
- East Asia and the Pacific 13 offices
- South Asia 8 offices
- CEE/CIS and the Baltic States 19 offices
- Middle East and North Africa 16 offices
- Americas and the Caribbean 24 offices
- Europe

HQ DIVISIONS

PROGRAMME GROUP

- Office of the Secretary of the Executive Board
- Programme Division
- Evaluation, Policy and Planning Division
- Office of Emergency Programmes
- International Child Development Centre (Florence)
- Office of United Nations Affairs and External Relations
- Division of Communications
- Office for Japan

EXHIBIT 5
National Committee
Contributions, 1998

Source: UNICEF internal
documents.

National Committee	Proceeds to UNICEF ($000s)	Performance Index[a]	Fund-raising as % of Total Proceeds
San Marino	$ 82	9.11	N.A.
Netherlands	41,060	7.05	87%
Luxembourg	1,849	6.82	51
Slovenia	1,296	4.60	22
Hong Kong	6,573	4.22	93
Switzerland	15,856	3.51	67
Spain	22,581	2.73	53
Greece	4,258	2.40	49
Portugal	3,316	2.12	39
Belgium	7,630	1.96	69
Estonia	106	1.54	0
Germany	47,362	1.42	68
France	30,597	1.38	58
Italy	22,092	1.33	52
Finland	2,218	1.21	50
Austria	6,589	1.20	54
Bulgaria	164	1.17	0
Japan	76,490	1.10	82
Slovakia	310	1.09	23
Ireland	855	0.91	76
United Kingdom	15,025	0.85	89
Austria	2,629	0.80	61
Denmark	2,019	0.76	24
Lithuania	90	0.75	0
Canada	5,569	0.64	0
Sweden	2,051	0.61	51
Norway	1,196	0.52	7
Hungary	304	0.46	5
Rep. Korea	2,738	0.39	74
New Zealand	308	0.36	100
Czech Republic	270	0.35	17
Turkey	971	0.33	4
Latvia	26	0.31	0
Poland	529	0.26	3
United States	21,600	0.19	70
Israel	NA	9.11	0
Andorra	NA	NA	NA

[a]National Committees with a performance index over 1.0 generate above-average proceeds for their countries, controlling for both population size and GNP per capita.

up 45% of contributions and had been shrinking as a percentage of total contributions (down from 55% in 1999), causing some concern within the organization. Ellen Yaffe, UNICEF's chief financial officer, summarized as follows:

> UNICEF's key challenge is the decline in core income. Further declines seem likely, and this will restrict our ability to manage long-term projects and maintain operational field offices. If our field capabilities are eroded because the unrestricted funds, which are used to maintain these offices and our field staff, decline, then our ability to manage the growing restricted funds will also be jeopardized, and our business model will have to change. If we essentially become a contractor for donors of restricted funds, which by the way are much more cumbersome to manage, our relationship with local governments will also change, and we may not have the same ability to conduct our advocacy work.

EXHIBIT 6   **Sources of UNICEF 2002 Income by Major Donor Country**

Source: UNICEF Annual Report, 2002.

Country	Government Regular (US$000s)	Per Capita Contribution ($)	Government Other (US$000s)	National Committee Regular (US$000s)	Per Capita Contribution ($)	National Committee Other (US$000s)	TOTAL (US$000s)
Australia	$ 2,625	$0.14	$ 6,853	$ 64	$0.003	$ 2,463	$ 12,006
Belgium	3,131	0.31	6,652	2,841	0.28	2,056	14,681
Canada	8,599	0.28	29,626	461	0.02	5,273	43,951
Denmark	22,456	4.22	8,250	1,625	0.31	408	32,739
Finland	10,480	2.03	3,276	2,101	0.41	1,834	17,691
France	6,631	0.11	1,732	18,156	0.31	7,370	33,889
Germany	3,870	0.05	610	28,620	0.35	30,411	63,616
Italy	11,621	0.20	24,758	21,352	0.37	6,749	64,480
Japan	25,596	0.20	72,007	66,332	0.52	21,648	185,592
Netherlands	31,744	2.00	37,062	24,928	1.57	8,241	101,975
Norway	34,510	7.72	29,805	835	0.19	90	65,240
Spain	1,606	0.04	140	12,923	0.32	9,740	24,409
Sweden	29,748	3.36	30,358	1,306	0.15	1,078	62,490
Switzerland	9,551	1.33	1,759	7,103	0.99	3,256	21,715
United Kingdom	24,638	0.41	49,244	8,093	0.14	14,465	96,440
United States	109,758	0.39	106,619	9,463	0.03	36,560	262,456

Private Sector Funds

In 2001, National Committees contributed 33% of UNICEF's total income, with fund-raising as the prime income driver as compared to the more established greeting card sector. The larger committees had over a million regular supporters. Although net revenues from greeting cards in 1991 still represented 80% of private sector funds, in 2001, they represented less than 20%. A fairly wide variation existed among countries, with the poorer countries still deriving a higher proportion of revenues from greeting card sales. In 2002, the private sector division at HQ had 200 dedicated staff focused on product development and sourcing of greeting cards, marketing, and fund-raising support.

Many National Committees oversaw highly professional fund-raising organizations, often relying heavily on direct mailings. National Committees assured 80% of fund-raising costs, and activities were by and large decentralized. HQ provided know-how, guidelines, and support as well as investment funds to promising fund-raising or marketing projects. "Being able to provide seed capital for certain projects gives us some leverage with the National Committees," explained Rudolf Deutekom, director of the private sector division.

UNICEF's typical donor was a female 45 to 65 years old. In 2002, UNICEF fund-raising efforts in addition to direct mail focused on committed giving and legacy development. "Part of our big challenge," added Deutekom, "is that most of our volunteers are now over 50 years old. Even though we have great brand awareness, if we continue to reach out through our traditional constituencies, we will have a hard time changing our image or attracting new donors."

In 2002, UNICEF and its National Committees were facing increased competition, particularly from child sponsorship organizations such as Save the Children and World Vision. In Canada, for example, World Vision had raised $200 million in 2001, whereas UNICEF had raised only $25 million. "We are often viewed as being part of the United Nations," commented Deutekom, "rich and not cost conscious."

EXHIBIT 7   UNICEF's Key Corporate Partnerships in 2001

Source: UNICEF Annual Report, 2002, and published sources.

Program	Description	Impact
Change for Good on International Airlines	For over a decade passengers have donated change.	In 2001, the program raised $37.4 million.
Procter and Gamble	"Clean up for kids"/trick or treat for UNICEF	$550,000
Pier 1	Largest seller of UNICEF cards	$1.5 million in 2001 in the U.S.
MobiNil (Egypt)	Three-day promotional sale of mobile phones	Percentage of proceeds to UNICEF
MasterCard	Use of credit card at defined times	Percentage of proceeds to UNICEF
Ta-Ta (Uruguay supermarket chain)	Fund-raising campaign at check-out	One peso per customer at checkout
Amway	Purchase of UNICEF Christmas cards	0.5 million cards in 2001 ($200,000)
Aeon (Japan)	Promotions, customer and employee campaigns	$845,000 (2001)
Diners Club International	Affinity card in Ecuador	$100,000 (2001)
Esselunga (supermarket chain in Italy)	Matched donations of customers	$220,000 (2001)
Fater (JV between Angelini and P&G)	Promotion linked to the sale of Pampers	$120,000 (2001)
FTSE International	FTSE4Good Index/license fees	$500,000 (by end 2001)
IKEA	Code of conduct and financial support	
Manchester United (football club)	"United for UNICEF"	$1.5 million (2001)

An important part of the private sector division's work was the management of corporate partnerships and alliances. Through the National Committees, UNICEF had, over the past 20 years, built ties with corporations and businesses throughout the world (see **Exhibit 7** for an overview of UNICEF's key corporate partnerships in 2002). "The key is to tap into the logistical resources of a partner," said Deutekom, "and use an indirect approach to cobranding, more of an association of brands in fact. The best partnerships are with insurance or financial services companies because they represent a low risk for UNICEF. Other good partnerships involve promotional projects, where point-of-sale materials make a reference to UNICEF and we get a percentage of proceeds." A coordination committee, made up of top executives at HQ, reviewed all major international proposals, and in August 2002, UNICEF had screened over 850 companies in three years and approved close to 200 while typically managing 120 alliances at any point in time. (See **Exhibit 8** for results of the corporate partnerships and alliances program.)

UNICEF had developed selection guidelines for the National Committees based on two guiding principles: find the best ally, and find the best alliance. Two steps were taken to determine whether a corporation was the best ally for UNICEF. First, UNICEF had to undertake research and conduct due diligence on the potential ally. Second, UNICEF evaluated the potential partner against UNICEF's mission, mandate, and brand values. The best alliance involved a strong corporate fit with UNICEF's values, program, advocacy, and fundraising goals. Certain sectors were considered unacceptable: armaments and weapons makers, toy manufacturers selling replica weapons, alcohol and tobacco companies, companies employing child labor, and companies involved in pornography. Any companies that violated U.N. sanctions, or those found in violation of environmental laws, were also excluded. In addition, UNICEF never endorsed products, goods, or services and would not grant sector exclusivity to any company.

In 2002, UNICEF entered into a partnership with McDonald's in North America that, apart from a significant cash donation, consisted of the distribution, through McDonald's

EXHIBIT 8
Review of UNICEF's Corporate Partnership and Alliance Program

Source: Internal documents.

7/98 through 8/02 Worldwide	Number	US$ Million (estimated total benefits to UNICEF)
Number of proposals reviewed	222	$64
Number of proposals approved	193	57
Number of proposals declined	15	4
Number of proposals in process	14	3

Number of Proposals Submitted for Review 7/98 through 8/02	By National Committees	By Field Offices
1998	5	18
1999	9	31
2000	15	40
2001	20	42
2002	24	19

Approved Alliances by Type, 2001	US$000s	Approved Alliances by Industry Sector	US$000s
Customer fund-raising	$5,600	Banking and finance	$1,630
Events and sponsorship	4,050	Soaps, cosmetics	720
Promotional licensing	3,100	Telecommunications	510
On-product promotional licensing	400	Diversified financials	500
Employee fund-raising	150	Food and drug chains	430
Cash donation	90	Other retail	310
Licensed-product royalties	20	Media	220
		Beverage	220
		Pharmaceuticals	200
		Food	150
		Health care	120
		Automotive	100
		Other	100

franchises, of trick-or-treat "Change for UNICEF" collection boxes. The partnership was driven by the U.S. National Committee, which had a strong ongoing relationship with McDonald's but had the potential for fund-raising in other countries. Once approved, global partnerships were open to all countries, but given resistance from some National Committees, particularly in Europe, HQ allowed an opt-out to the McDonald's partnership, which most National Committees chose to take. In order to publicize the partnership, McDonald's published a photograph of the secretary-general of the United Nations and the executive director of UNICEF with the CEO of McDonald's. The media and the NGO community reacted negatively. Deutekom summarized the impact and next steps for UNICEF as follows:

> Corporate partnerships will continue to grow, but the McDonald's experience will slow us down and make us more stringent in our requirements. Going forward, we will be even more careful about any partnership that suggests UNICEF is endorsing a product or a service. Note, however, that in spite of its growth potential and visible role, corporate alliances still only represent about 10% of all funding. Our main source of revenue, therefore, is still heavily secured through and by individual donors, i.e., the general public.

Key Challenges Facing UNICEF

Positioning the Organization

Some top UNICEF executives worried that the increasing rights-based focus of the organization would stretch UNICEF's capabilities too thin and possibly dilute the organization's impact. Specifically, prior programs focused on children in the first five years of life, but in

2002, programs covered children from birth through adolescence. In addition, two human rights principles promised to extend UNICEF's potential scope. Rights were considered universal, so the focus of programs could no longer be solely on developing nations. In addition, rights were considered indivisible, which brought into play a whole spectrum of rights (the right to access to health, education, safety, and so on). "In the past," said Abdi, "our reputation was built on immunization and education programs, and our impact was clearly measurable. In the advocacy arena, how do we measure and communicate our results?"

Other executives highlighted UNICEF's unique position and role. UNICEF was in essence part NGO and also part of the U.N. system. The organization differed from NGOs in that its mandate came from the United Nations, giving UNICEF a unique legitimacy with member governments and access to discuss sensitive issues such as the reform of national legal systems for protecting children's rights. The disadvantages, however, were that states and governments were very protective of sovereignty and resistant to change. "Consensus building takes time and is challenging" said Singh. "Right now, there is a sense of cynicism towards the U.N. system, although UNICEF has an advantage in that we focus on children, which is less contentious than other issues."

Global Funds

In 2002, there was a continued shift toward an increasing number of bilateral development agreements, with developing countries increasingly wanting to drive their own development agendas. This drove the creation of "global funds" for specific sectors and areas, and donors were asked to participate directly with these global funds. The global funds were, by definition, restricted, and the question for many UNICEF executives was how would UNICEF adapt to these changes. Lotse explained, "UNICEF ends up acting like a conduit or channel for these earmarked funds. We are asked to help at the local level to play a management role, but we want to be more than a consultant." Yaffe expanded on this idea: "For example, in one country, the World Bank might like the program UNICEF was doing in the area of education, and they would give money to the government's global education fund. The government would then turn around and give the money to UNICEF to manage, effectively becoming UNICEF's boss."

The rise in global funds was therefore directly linked to the decrease in general, or unrestricted, funds. Yaffe worried that the decrease in unrestricted funds would reduce income predictability and affect existing field operations. Singh was also concerned: "Because of our work we have a presence on the ground at the community level which represents experiential learning that has been built over time. The concern is that we may not have the same comparative advantage if we don't have funds to maintain this presence."

Rebranding UNICEF

UNICEF Brand Image and Research

Research interviews conducted between 1999 and 2002, both externally and internally, revealed the following trends. Externally, while the UNICEF image was positive, the organization appeared distant, institutional, cold, and rigid. Like other bureaucracies, UNICEF was seen as a necessary but cumbersome institution that had a role but no longer projected leadership and hope. UNICEF was regarded as worthy but inefficient, important but not current. The communications team felt that the UNICEF brand was living off the past and not providing a vision for the future.

UNICEF had changed its logo and emblem twice in the past: once in 1960, following the adoption by the United Nations of the Declaration of the Rights of the Child, and once in 1985/1986 to celebrate UNICEF's 40th anniversary. (See **Exhibit 9** for a pictorial history

EXHIBIT 9 **Pictorial History of UNICEF Logo**

Source: UNICEF Communications Division.

1960

1985

1946

599

of the UNICEF logo.) In 2002, UNICEF and its National Committees were using a wide variety of different logos, emblems, and straplines in different countries. (See **Exhibit 10** for an overview of some of the different logos and straplines being used in 2002.) "It is very important for UNICEF to have just one look," explained Kjersti Gjestvang, secretary general of the Norwegian National Committee. "At this point, each National Committee has done its own branding exercise and developed a slightly different approach, but that dilutes our brand, and we need to get behind a single image."

In 1999, Censydiam Worldwide conducted market research on UNICEF's logo and positioning in four countries: Japan, Germany, France, and Italy. The common public perception was that UNICEF was a well-structured, competent organization that took care of children in poor countries in the areas of health, food, housing, and clothing and focused on the long term. UNICEF's vocation was clear, but many people were confused about how and where UNICEF realized its objectives. UNICEF appeared too abstract, vague, and uncontrollable. The link with the United Nations gave an impression of solidity, trust, and credibility but also caused UNICEF to seem distant and bureaucratic. Hardly anyone knew that UNICEF stood for United Nations Children's Fund, but most had the impression that UNICEF was centrally organized with a strong link to the United Nations. There was no awareness that each country had its own National Committee. The term "committee" was also perceived as creating distance and associated with more administration. The term "fund," however, was found to imply raising money and came across as more friendly and flexible.

Spontaneous recognition of the logo was generally vague. Aspects that were remembered included the blue color, the mother and child symbol, and sometimes the globe. The logo was felt by some to project a message of warmth and care. To others, it depicted UNICEF as stable and reliable but also strict. The logo came across as authoritative without being dominant but was also considered old-fashioned. There was a general preference for small letters rather than capital letters.

In 1999, UNICEF conducted a survey in Norway and found that, although UNICEF's brand recognition (prompted awareness) was high, only 13% of the Norwegian adult population knew that UNICEF worked with children, whereas 24% were able to spontaneously mention UNICEF as one of the organizations selling greeting cards. In the same survey, respondents were also asked to rate issues people were facing in developing countries (such as hunger, health, education, etc.) in terms of importance. In 1999, only 46% of respondents rated the lack of education as a very important issue, compared with 84% for hunger, 81% for children in need, 77% for war, and 63% for HIV/AIDS. UNICEF was seen as a leader in education and, consequently, Gjestvang focused communication efforts on education. A new survey conducted in 2001 revealed that UNICEF's spontaneous brand awareness had increased significantly to 36% versus 15% in 1999, and that 21% of the Norwegian population now recognized that UNICEF worked for children. Funds raised over this period went from 10 million krone ($1.3 million) in 1999 to 27 million krone ($3.5 million) in 2002.

In 2001, UNICEF Canada also conducted a brand audit, which revealed that all child-focused organizations were struggling for consumer donations and most consumers did not easily differentiate between them. UNICEF Canada's communication materials were found to be informative but too ponderous, with no unified UNICEF look or tagline and no communication piece that spoke directly to donors. Internally, employees and volunteers felt that UNICEF should be known as the advocate for children and that the image needed to become more modern, aggressive, and proactive. UNICEF's name was well known, but its work was not. In donor focus groups, participants were unclear as to the purpose of UNICEF and what differentiated it from the major child-focused NGOs. The concept of children's rights was not well understood. UNICEF was perceived by some as a "fat cat"

EXHIBIT 10 Overview of Different Logos and Straplines Used in 2002

Source: UNICEF Communications Division.

EXHIBIT 11
UNICEF Perceived Strengths and Weaknesses

Source: Summarized from UNICEF internal interviews and workshops.

Perceived Strengths

- Reputation and track record
- Being global
- Focused on children
- Unique mandate from governments
- Powerful international force via U.N. agency status
- No political or religious affiliations
- Dedicated staff
- Intellectual leadership
- Field program (action, not just words)
- Decentralization
- Logo

Perceived Weaknesses

- Task too big to deal with
- Bureaucracy
- Rift between HQ and field/National Committees
- Elephant (slow and inflexible)
- Old-fashioned (aging in style, image, supporter base)
- Too diplomatic
- Lack of public faith in the U.N. system
- Internally poor communicator (no shared direction)
- Externally poor communicator (messages too complex and academic)
- Competition with clearer, sharper messages

and funded by the United Nations. The current brand footprint was found to be traditional, unassuming, and principled, but the ideal brand footprint needed to be confident, effective, and compassionate.

Internal Branding Workshops and Focus Groups

Phase One

In July 2000, over 100 questionnaires and face-to-face interviews were conducted by the advertising agency TBWA across the entire UNICEF organization. The interviews generated insights into staff perceptions of UNICEF's strengths and weaknesses. (UNICEF's perceived strengths and weaknesses resulting from these interviews are summarized in **Exhibit 11.**)

In August 2000, TBWA helped UNICEF design a branding workshop with 15 key UNICEF individuals from the field, HQ, and the National Committees, split into two groups, to explore the brand essence. Internal discussions about the difference between a child-rights organization and a child charity were initially very important. "Some people believed that people who are starving don't worry about dignity," said Newman-Williams. "Others responded that the thing people in refugee camps worry about the most is their dignity." The first day of the workshop, two groups worked in parallel to develop a series of working definitions of UNICEF's vision, mission, and positioning, outlined below:

- *Vision:* To be the passionate driving force that builds, with children, a better world in which every child's right to dignity, security, and self-fulfillment is achieved.
- *Mission:* We will put children at the heart of every agenda and ensure that the voice of children is heard worldwide. We will expose disparities, confront discrimination, and work to end violations of children's rights. We will continually develop our knowledge

and expertise to create, deliver, and inspire solutions. We will maximize the resources devoted to children both by acting directly and by building powerful alliances to force action and change.

- *Positioning:* For people who want to make a lasting difference, UNICEF is the champion of rights for all the world's children, with the authority, knowledge, and resources to get things done.

The second day, the two groups worked toward a brand profile for UNICEF made up of rational and emotional values. TBWA defined rational values as those appealing to the consumer's head ("gives consumers something to buy") and emotional values as those appealing to the heart ("gives consumers something to buy into"). The agreed profile of the combined groups was as follows:

- Rational values: principled, leading, credible, influential, innovative, "gets things done"
- Emotional values: passionate, courageous, inspirational, visionary, loving, admired

The two groups were also asked to develop a brand essence that "encapsulates how consumers connect with the brand, represents the core—heart, sole, spirit, DNA—of the brand, and illustrates how UNICEF would want consumers to think and feel about the brand." TBWA cautioned that the brand essence was not "a reflection of current consumer attitudes, short term in its approach, just brand personality and character or an advertising proposition." Four components were used to build the brand essence: form, personality, differentiation, and authority. (The resulting brand essence is presented in **Exhibit 12.**)

Follow-up work with TBWA combined this brand essence with the above definitions of vision, mission, positioning, and rational and emotional values and resulted in the UNICEF brand model depicted in **Exhibit 13.** The brand model was seen as central to the MTSP, communication strategy, and all future communication plans, including those for fund-raising.

In June 2001, UNICEF's division of communications summarized the results of the branding exercise in an internal presentation as follows:

> What do we mean by the UNICEF brand? We mean the organization, its reputation and everything it does and stands for. Everything we do contributes to building the UNICEF brand and builds trust in the organization. Whatever the nature of the interaction with UNICEF, a common personality should be evident, a sort of DNA that runs through everything we do: in our policies, programs and operations, in our relationship with donors, partners and suppliers and in the way we recruit, manage and develop our staff.

Phase Two

In November 2001, the brand agency Wolff Olins was retained to develop UNICEF's information architecture and the organization's key message. It proposed a communication framework consisting of three elements—issue, action, and impact—and a UNICEF identity that included guidelines on imagery, voice, layout grids, color palate, typeface, a new strapline, and a modified logo. (See **Exhibit 14** for proposed new logo emblem, strapline, and color scheme compared with those of the existing identity.)

As part of the new brand toolkit, which combined all the elements of the proposed new identity, a number of changes were proposed:

- Initially, it was suggested that the mother and child emblem be removed, but this was later changed to suggesting that the emblem and logo be separated.
- The proposed strapline was "For every child, health, education, equality, protection. Advance Humanity."
- The central "I" in the UNICEF logo should be made more dominant.
- UNICEF should adopt a more vibrant cyan blue color.

EXHIBIT 12 UNICEF Brand Essence, 2001

Source: UNICEF Communications Division.

UNICEF Brand Essence

Personality

'Gets things done'
Courageous
Inspirational
Passionate
Engaging
Visionary

Form

The world's children's
rights organisation -
100% funded by
voluntary donations to
implement its mandate
from the UN to act for all
the world's children

Change the world with children

(By acting with and on behalf of children, ensuring that they have a voice and that their
rights are fulfilled, we will help build a better world)

Source of Authority

Unique mandate from all nations to act for
children and their rights, *but only exists
because it earns its support (100% voluntary
funded)*

Results / what we've done
(both via direct delivery of programs
and by influencing others eg. CRC)

Expertise (breadth and depth)

Household name, known and
trusted

Differentiation

Unique status - mandated by
the UN to act for children but 100% funded
by voluntary donations

Truly global - present
everywhere, acting for all children, all rights
around the world

Unrivalled leverage and results
- unique ability to mobilize all
actors via unmatched access,
influence and innovation:
resulting ability to turn one
dollar
into 10, and produce
lasting
results

EXHIBIT 13 UNICEF Brand Model, 2001

Source: UNICEF Communications Division.

Brand Model for UNICEF

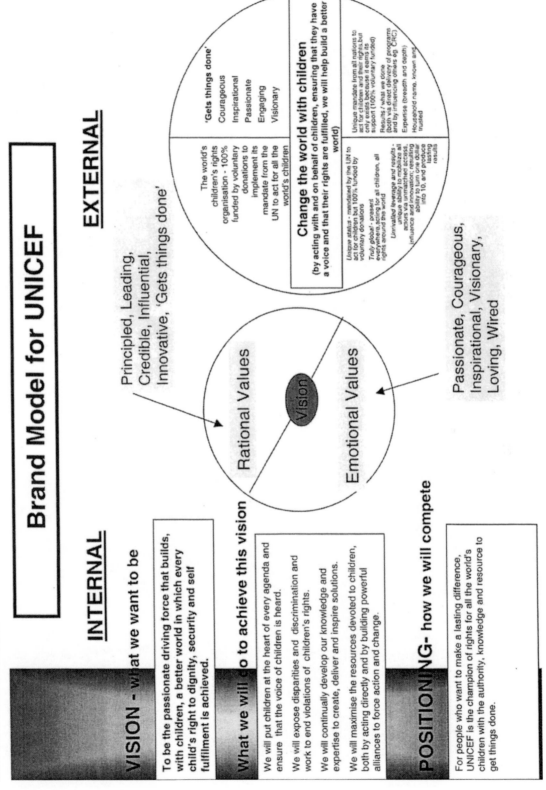

INTERNAL

VISION – what we want to be

To be the passionate driving force that builds, with children, a better world in which every child's right to dignity, security and self fulfilment is achieved.

What we will do to achieve this vision

We will put children at the heart of every agenda and ensure that the voice of children is heard.

We will expose disparities and discrimination and work to end violations of children's rights.

We will continually develop our knowledge and expertise to create, deliver and inspire solutions.

We will maximise the resources devoted to children, both by acting directly and by building powerful alliances to force action and change.

POSITIONING – how we will compete

For people who want to make a lasting difference, UNICEF is the champion of rights for all the world's children with the authority, knowledge and resource to get things done.

EXTERNAL

Principled, Leading, Credible, Influential, Innovative, 'Gets things done'

Passionate, Courageous, Inspirational, Visionary, Loving, Wired

Rational Values

Emotional Values

Vision

'Gets things done'
Courageous
Inspirational
Passionate
Engaging
Visionary

The world's children's rights organisation - 100% funded by voluntary donations to implement its mandate from the UN to act for all the world's children

Change the world with children
(by acting with and on behalf of children, ensuring that they have a voice and that their rights are fulfilled, we will help build a better world)

Unique status - mandated by the UN to act for children but 100% funded by voluntary donations

Truly global - present everywhere, acting for all children, all rights around the world

Unrivalled leverage and results - unique ability to mobilize all actors via unmatched access, influence and innovation; resulting ability to turn one dollar into 10, and produce lasting results

Unique mandate from all nations to act for children and their rights, but only exists because it earns its support (100% voluntary funded)

Results / what we done (both via direct delivery of programs and by influencing others eg. CRC)

Expertise (breadth and depth)

Household name, known and trusted

605

EXHIBIT 14 Proposed New Logo Emblem and Color Scheme

Source: UNICEF Communications Division.

Reactions to the Rebranding Process and Toolkit

Overall, the first phase of the rebranding exercise was well received internally. Most executives recognized the need for revitalizing the brand and believed that the development of the brand essence and brand model had been worthwhile. Abdi commented, "Brand is important in the field because of increasing clutter. Being able to differentiate the brand can really help you get attention from customers, governments, and populations." "As we move towards a rights-based approach, the organization needs a sense of common values and ethics," commented Singh. "The values dimension of the brand model could be a great unifying force for UNICEF, but the challenge seems to be internal communication. We need everyone down the line to understand the brand essence." Gjestvang added, "The brand essence was excellent, and I recently saw a version of it in a recruitment slide, so I think it has been well adopted by the entire UNICEF organization."

Many executives felt that the second phase of the branding exercise had not been fully understood within UNICEF and that too much focus was being placed on the logo and the emblem. The suggested changes presented in the brand toolkit stimulated widespread comment, the last part of the "Advance Humanity" strapline and the issue of separating the logo from the mother and child emblem prompting the strongest reactions. "The second consultant that was used," explained Jacques Hintzy, president of the French National Committee, "did not take into account the excellent work that was done before on the brand model. The strapline was perceived as pretentious, and abandoning the mother and child symbol met with a lot of resistance. The process to date has been successful, it is now just the design phase that is a problem. It is an execution issue rather than a philosophical concern."

"The National Committees felt that their views had not been taken into account in the second phase," explained Woodhouse. "Separating the signature from the emblem particularly caused grave concern, and the strapline was considered too long." Abdi said, "When I was a child growing up in Mogadishu, there was an area in the city known as UNICEF. It was associated with services that were delivered there, and the symbol was the sign that everyone recognized, particularly if they couldn't read. The explicit link to the U.N. through the mother and child symbol is critical." Some felt that the strapline had too much of a U.S. focus and would not work in other cultures. Others thought that there was nothing unique about "Advance Humanity" and that the general public would not link it especially to UNICEF. Still others felt that "equality" was not easily measurable and was more of an aspirational goal. Gjestvang expanded on the second phase of the brand exercise: "In the development of the toolkit, the feedback from the field and National Committees was not taken into account, I felt more like a hostage than a participant. I am concerned about the strapline because if we say that we advance humanity, it sounds like bragging, and we will put off potential partners."

Newman-Williams acknowledged the above arguments but urged that in certain moments in UNICEF's history the organization had gone against the tide and advanced its mission:

> "Advance Humanity" is another example. Our donor base is bolder on these issues than we think they are. UNICEF executives have a low tolerance for external consultants and tend to become nervous when confronted by unfamiliar marketing speak. The risk is that the central purpose gets lost. The process has been challenging, there have been a lot of different opinions and influences. And the logo redesign is a real stretch for everyone, especially the National Committees.

In early 2002, the National Committees had raised concerns about the logo to the executive board, and it had become a highly political issue. "This organization operates on consensus," added Newman-Williams, "and ultimately you're changing the way the organization behaves. Implementation will be the critical part of the whole rebranding process."

EXHIBIT 15

List of Attendees of 47th Annual Meeting of National Committees, September 2–4, 2002

Source: UNICEF Communications Division.

National Committees	Participant	Title
Andorra	Mr. Marc Vila Amigo	President
Australia	Ms. Gaye Phillips	Executive Director
Austria	Dr. Martha Kyrle	President
	Dr. Gudrun Berger	Executive Director
Belgium	Mr. Marc Van Boven	Chairman
Bulgaria	Mr. Zdravko Popov	President
	Ms. Jetchka Karaslavova	Executive Director
Canada	Ms. Laura Ludwin	Chairperson
	Mr. David Agnew	President and CEO
Czech Republic	Ms. Pavla Gomba	Executive Director
Denmark	Mr. Ole Kyed	Chairperson
	Mr. Steen Andersen	Executive Director
Estonia	Ms. Elle Kull	President
	Mr. Toomas Palu	Executive Director
Finland	Ms. Astrid Thors	President of the Board
	Mr. Kalle Justander	Senior Adviser, Member of the Board
France	Mr. Jacques Hintzy	President
	Mr. Gilles Paillard	Executive Director
Germany	Mr. Reinhard Schlagintweit	Chairman
	Dr. Deitrich Garlichs	Executive Director
Greece	Ms. Joanna Manganara	Executive Board Member
	Mr. Ilias Liberis	Information, EDev. & Fund-raising Officer
Hong Kong	Mr. Robert Fung	Chairman
	Mr. Matthew Mo	Executive Director
	Ms. Teresa Wong	General Manager, Fund-raising
Hungary	Ms. Edit Kecskeméti	Executive Director
Ireland	Mr. William Early	Chairman
	Dr. Chris Horn	Incoming Chairman
	Ms. Maura Quinn	Executive Director
Israel	Ms. Evi Adams	Board Member & BFHI Coordinator
Italy	Dr. Giovanni Micali	President
	Mr. Giacomo Guerrera	Vice President
	Mr. Roberto Salvan	Executive Director
Japan	Mr. Yoshihisa Togo	Executive Director
South Korea	Ms. Dong-Eun Park	Executive Director
Latvia	Ms. Ilze Doskina	Executive Director
Lithuania	Mr. Jaunius Pusvaskis	Executive Director
New Zealand	Mr. Dennis McKinlay	Executive Director
Norway	Ms. Kjersti Gjestvang	Executive Director
Poland	Mr. Marek Pietkiewicz	Executive Director
Portugal	Mr. Manuel Pina	President
	Ms. Madalena Marçal Grilo	Executive Director
Slovakia	Ms. Veronika Lehotska	President
	Mr. Miroslav Kana	Executive Director
Slovenia	Ms. Andreja Crnak-Meglic	President
	Ms. Maja Vojnovic	Executive Director
	Ms. Zora Tomic	Member of the Executive Board
	Ms. Barbara Volcic-Lombergar	Member of the Executive Board
Spain	Mr. Francisco Gonzalez-Bueno	President
	Ms. Consuelo Crespo	First Vice President
	Mr. Jaime Gonez-Pineda	General Treasurer
	Mr. Victor Soler-Sala	Adviser for International Affairs

EXHIBIT 15
(Continued)

National Committees	Participant	Title
Sweden	Mr. Kent Harstedt	Chairperson
	Mr. Ingvar Hjärtsjö	Secretary-General
Switzerland	Mr. Wolfgang Wörnhard	President
	Ms. Elsbeth Müller	Executive Director
Turkey	Ms. Ayse Sevinc Soysal	Executive Director
United Kingdom	Sir John Waite	Chairman
	Mr. David Bull	Executive Director
	Ms. Anita Tiessen	Deputy Executive Director, Programme
	Mr. William Cottle	Deputy Executive Director, Finance & Services
United States	Mr. Anthony Lake	Vice Chair, Board of Directors
	Mr. Charles Lyons	President
<u>UNICEF Office</u>		
New York Headquarters	Ms. Carol Bellamy	Executive Director
	Ms. Marjorie Newman-Williams	Director, Division of Communications
	Ms. Cecilia Lotse	Director, Programme Funding Office
Geneva Regional Office	Mr. Stephen Woodhouse	Regional Director
	Ms. Janet Nelson	Deputy Regional Director
	Mr. Hans Olsen	Chief, Communications Section
	Mr. Ken Maskall	Senior Programme Officer
	Ms. Katharina Borchardt	Planning Officer
	Mr. Jean Metenier	Planning Officer
	Mr. Eduardo Rodriguez	Planning Officer
	Ms. Valérie Pascal-Billebaud	Assistant Project Officer
Private Sector Division, Geneva	Mr. Rudolf Deutekom	Director
	Mr. Prom Chopra	Deputy Director, Operation & Finance
	Mr. Per Stenbeck	Deputy Director, Fund-raising
	Mr. Sergio Furman	Marketing Officer
	Mr. Roger Keczkes	Marketing Officer
	Ms. Helene Reymann	Marketing Officer
	Mr. John Winston	Brand Manager
Private Sector Div., New York	Mr. Alejandro Palacios	Chief, International Accounts
India Office	Ms. Maria Calivis	Representative
Support Staff	Mr. Oktavijan Aran	Fund-raising & Sales Assistant
	Ms. Ana Beauclair	Senior Secretary

Three UNICEFs

Some executives felt that there were three distinct groups within UNICEF: the HQ staff, the National Committees, and the field offices. UNICEF had three corresponding roles as a child-rights organization, a fund-raiser in developed countries, and an implementer of field programs in developing countries. Considered the bolder and more long-term focused part of UNICEF, HQ staff was sometimes thought to be wrapped up in ideology, with concepts that were too cerebral to be understood by the general public. The National Committees and field offices were thought to be slower to embrace change and more short term in perspective. The older National Committees were considered part of the old guard and were thought to be particularly resistant to change. "These three UNICEFs each see the brand in different ways," commented Deutekom. "Their roles are all slightly different and so are their messages and target audiences."

Testing the New Brand Identity

In August 2002, the Sofres market research company was retained to evaluate the new brand identity. Consumer focus groups were carried out in France and the United States and exploration of the current logo revealed that the emblem was critical. The laurel leaves were thought by some to be old-fashioned or to represent wheat. The logo was well liked for its lower-case font. Without the emblem, the logo was found to be cold, rigid, and bureaucratic. The descriptor (United Nations Children's Fund) evoked limited recall but did bring into focus the link to the United Nations and the organization's target: children.

Initial reactions to the new brand identity as a whole were that the changes were not noticed much. The new brand identity seemed to function but did not bring any real changes or evolution. The cyan blue color and larger "I" were noticed the most, but the meaning of the larger "I" was not decoded by most. It appeared that the descriptor became slightly more prominent alongside the new logo. Different degrees of modernity were associated with the three elements, with the logo perceived as young and dynamic but the emblem perceived as outdated. An analysis of the strapline: "For every child, health, education, equality and protection. Advance Humanity" revealed that "Advance Humanity" was considered pretentious and overpromising. In addition, the word "equality" seemed to some to be unachievable.

Recommendations from the study included: keep the logo with the large "I"; always accompany the logo with the emblem but renew the emblem, perhaps by removing the laurel leaves; keep the descriptor unchanged; and consider returning to original dark blue rather than cyan. As for the strapline, the details of the first sentence could be preserved (without reference to equality), but the second sentence needed to be modified.

Conclusion

Newman-Williams was at a crossroads. Should she move ahead with the implementation of the brand toolkit as it stood, with the new color scheme, the larger "I," the unmodified emblem, and the proposed strapline? Or should she attempt to adapt and modify some of the elements of the toolkit, and, if so, which ones? Newman-Williams wondered how long further modifications would take and doubted that she would be able to satisfy everyone. She believed that the second sentence of the strapline, "Advance Humanity," truly symbolized the new UNICEF and felt strongly that it should remain unchanged. As she prepared for her presentation to the heads of the National Committees and key HQ directors (see **Exhibit 15** for a list of attendees), she wondered what questions would be asked and how she would answer them.

Chapter 35

Steinway & Sons: Buying a Legend (A)

John T. Gourville   Joseph B. Lassiter

On April 19, 1995, Dana Messina (HBS '87) opened his *New York Times* to see the headline "Steinway & Sons is Sold for $100 Million." One day earlier, he and Kyle Kirkland (Stanford MBA '88), had finalized their purchase of the legendary piano maker by the Selmer Company, a maker of band instruments that the two men had purchased controlling interest in two years earlier.

In scanning the *New York Times* article (see **Exhibit 1**), Dana Messina read that " . . . people familiar with Steinway and the piano industry's problems . . . were amazed that the company fetched [$100 million]." One critic of the deal went so far as to claim that the $100 million price was "an extraordinary number, and does not seem rational."

Reading this, Messina could not help but wonder what he and Kirkland had just gotten themselves into. First, there were almost no synergies between Selmer and Steinway. Second, the unit sale of Steinway grand pianos had slipped from 3,576 in 1990 to 2,698 in 1994. Third, Yamaha, a Japanese piano powerhouse, continued its efforts to challenge Steinway as the maker of the world's finest concert grand piano. Finally, Messina questioned Steinway's recent introduction of a mid-priced line of pianos, marketed under the name Boston Piano. Manufactured under contract by a Japanese competitor and with a price tag less than half that of a comparably sized Steinway, Boston Piano represented a significant departure from the handcrafted pianos that made Steinway famous.

At the same time, Messina was excited by the possibilities. First and foremost, Steinway was the pre-eminent brand name in the music business and the producer of the highest quality grand pianos in the world. For over 100 years, Steinway was the piano of choice for

Professors John T. Gourville and Joseph B. Lassiter, III prepared this case as the basis for class discussion rather than to illustrate either effective or ineffective handling of an administrative situation. This case borrows some Steinway historical information from an earlier case entitled "Steinway & Sons" (682-025) by Professor David Garvin.

EXHIBIT 1   The *New York Times* Article, April 19, 1995

Steinway & Sons Is Sold for $100 Million

By KENNETH N. GILPIN

Steinway & Sons, the piano manufacturer that has been a New York institution since its founding by Heinrich E. Steinway in 1853, was sold yesterday for $100 million to the Selmer Company, a maker of musical instruments.

A private company that is probably most famous for its Selmer saxophone, an instrument used by both amateur and professional musicians including President Clinton and Kenny G, Selmer is controlled by two young former Drexel Burnham Lambert investment bankers who purchased their stake in the company in 1993.

Under the terms of the transaction, Selmer and Steinway will continue to operate as independent entities, with no changes in management, plant locations, marketing strategy or total employment. Each company employs about 1,000 people.

"We are very excited," said Dana Messina, who along with his partner, Kyle Kirkland, controls Selmer. "We think it is quite an honor to become part of the team with Steinway."

Steinway has been producing concert grand and baby grand pianos for many of the world's most accomplished pianists from its factory in Long Island City, Queens, since shortly after the turn of the century. The sale marks the third time in its illustrious history that Steinway has changed hands.

In 1972, Henry Z. Steinway, the founder's great-grandson, sold the company to CBS for an undisclosed price, ending family control. Then in 1985, a group of investors led by John P. Birmingham and his brother Robert M. Birmingham, bought Steinway for a price rumored to be in excess of $50 million.

Without disclosing what his group paid for the company, he said the $100 million sale price "beats inflation by a little bit" over what was paid a decade ago.

In an interview, John Birmingham said "personal reasons" prompted the group to seek a buyer for Steinway about four months ago.

Still, people familiar with Steinway and the piano industry's problems, said they were amazed the company fetched that much.

Over the last 10 years, critics have been quick to fault Steinway for what they say is a decline in the quality of its new pianos, which currently sell for as much as $75,800. In addition, the company has had to fight what some contend is a decline in demand, as well as compete with a huge supply of older Steinway pianos.

The $100 million price is "an extraordinary number, and does not seem rational," said D.W. Fostle, author of "Steinway Saga," a book about the company to be released by Scribner's on May 1.

According to Mr. Fostle, sales of upright pianos in the United States have fallen since 1988 by more than 40 percent, and show few signs of coming back.

Competing with the huge pool of surviving Steinways is another serious problem.

"It's as if every Ford build since 1903 is still on the road and is as good as a Lincoln Continental," Mr. Fostle said. "There is no way to get rid of those pianos."

In the interview, Mr. Birmingham acknowledged that the piano market in the United States was mature, and that the company's biggest competition was from "our own used pianos." But he said the quality problems had been solved.

In coming years, Mr. Birmingham said the company was likely to find demand from aging baby boomers, as well as foreign markets.

Steinway employs about 500 people in the United States. The company also has a manufacturing plant in Hamburg, Germany. Last year the company had sales of a little more than $100 million.

Selmer, based in Elkhart, Ind., recorded earnings of a little less than $3 million on revenue of $101.1 million last year.

the world's greatest artists including Rubinstein, Rachmaninoff and Horowitz. Second, economic conditions were improving in the U.S. and Europe, Steinway's two largest markets. Third, Steinway had yet to take full advantage of a growing Asian market. Finally, Steinway was a company that would be fun to own. As Kirkland recalled, "who would have believed that a couple of 33-year-old investment bankers could end up one owning one of the greatest names in all of music."

The Steinway Purchase—April 18, 1995

On April 18, 1995, the Selmer Company agreed to purchase Steinway & Sons for $101.5 million, which it planned to finance through the sale of $105 million in 11% notes due in 2005. At the time of the purchase, Selmer was the leading manufacturer of band and orchestral instruments in the United States. In 1993, it had been purchased for $95 million by Messina and Kirkland, two investment bankers who began their careers at Drexel Burnham Lambert. Messina describes their 1993 leveraged buyout of the Selmer Company as follows:

> Selmer was not in good shape. Its parent company, Integrated Resources, was in bankruptcy, many long-time customers were shopping elsewhere, and Selmer revenues had dropped from $86 million to $80 million between 1989 and 1990. At the same time, however, Selmer had a great history and reputation. One of its flagship products, the $1000 Vincent Bach trumpet, had a 70% market share and 50% gross profit margin. On top of that, sales of musical instruments tended to closely follow the birth rate, plus 11 years. With U.S. births up an average of 8% every five years since 1980, the 1990s looked very promising for the sale of Selmer instruments.
>
> Our challenge was putting the deal together. Kyle and I only had $250,000 between us. But our days at Drexel had taught us how to structure deals without much money. We got Cardinal Capital Management to take on $4.5 million in long term debt. We sold $60 million in junk bonds and $4.5 million of preferred stock to SunAmerica, John Hancock and Alliance Capital. And we secured a $30 million bank loan. Together, these lenders ended up with 68% of the company. Another 9% of the company went to Selmer's management team and the remaining equity stayed with us. So for our $250,000, Kyle and I ended up with 23% of the company.

By 1994, Selmer had revenues of $100 million on the sale of 130,000 instruments (see **Exhibit 2** for Selmer financials). The company's brand names included Selmer, Bach, Glaesel, and Ludwig. Each was highly regarded, with Selmer saxophones, Bach trumpets, and Ludwig snare drums considered among the finest instruments in the world. In 1994,

EXHIBIT 2   Selmer Financial Information (Prior to Acquisition of Steinway)

Source: Selmer company records.

	Fiscal Year Ended December 31, (All Dollars in Thousands)				
	1990	**1991**	**1992**	**1993***	**1994**
Income Statement Data:					
Net sales	$79,798	$83,232	$85,895	$91,510	$101,114
Gross profit	24,900	27,139	29,458	28,193	31,925
Operating income (loss)	6,725	7,993	9,233	3,880	12,472
Net income (loss)	(1,325)	766	2,343	(1,704)	2,922
Other Financial Data:					
EBITDA	$12,208	$13,128	$14,437	$13,119	$ 16,638
Interest Expense	7,923	7,165	6,797	7,100	7,752
Depreciation & amortization	4,625	4,715	4,385	3,903	3,198
Capital Expenditures	812	744	720	879	1,112
Margins:					
Gross profit	31.2%	32.6%	34.3%	30.8%	31.6%
EBITDA	15.3%	15.8%	16.8%	14.3%	16.5%
Balance Sheet Data:					
Current assets	$59,507	$54,671	$55,712	$56,736	$ 56,265
Total assets	94,984	85,649	82,785	88,970	85,524
Current liabilities	10,119	8,870	9,519	10,174	13,388
Long-term debt	68,961	60,374	55,024	71,369	62,057
Stockholder equity	13,798	14,537	16,626	4,226	7,253

*Selmer sold to Messina & Kirkland on August 11, 1993.

Selmer held a domestic market share of 34% in student band instruments and 45% in professional band instruments. Student instruments, which sold for an average price of $500, accounted for 75% of Selmer's unit sales and 50% of revenues. Professional instruments, which sold for an average price of $1,500, accounted for the rest. Overall, 85% of Selmer sales were in the United States.

In 1994, Steinway & Sons also had sales of $100 million (see **Exhibit 3** for pre-purchase financials), derived from the sale of 2,698 Steinway grand pianos, 600 Steinway vertical (or "upright") pianos, and 2,300 Boston pianos. As shown in **Exhibit 4,** the 2,698 Steinway grands sold in 1994 represented a 25% decrease relative to 1990. The Steinway vertical and grand pianos were manufactured in two factories located in Long Island City, New York and Hamburg, Germany. The Boston Pianos, introduced by Steinway in 1992, were designed by Steinway and manufactured under contract by a Japanese piano company named Kawai.

Steinway and Boston pianos were sold through a network of 93 dealers in North and South America and 92 dealers in Europe, Africa and Asia. In 1994, roughly 85% of all Steinway and Boston pianos were sold through these independent dealers, with Steinway's 15 largest dealers accounting for 28% of unit sales. The remaining 15% of pianos were sold through four company-owned retail locations in New York, London, Berlin, and Hamburg. Overall, 58% of all Steinway sales were in the United States (**Exhibit 5** shows Steinway's top ten American markets in 1994), followed by Germany (8.6%), Japan (7.3%), England (6.1%) and Switzerland (2.9%). The typical buyer of a Steinway piano was over 45 years old, had an annual income in excess of $100,000, and had a serious interest in music. The typical buyer of a Boston piano was 5 to 10 years younger and was slightly less affluent.

EXHIBIT 3 Steinway & Sons Financial Information (Prior to Acquisition by Selmer)

Source: Steinway company records.

	Fiscal Year Ended June 30, (All Dollars in Thousands)				
	1990	1991	1992	1993	1994
Income Statement Data:					
Net sales	$92,037	$98,816	$89,240	$89,714	$101,896
Gross profit	33,673	35,586	30,759	26,139	31,636
Operating income (loss)	10,096	9,124	4,556	1,919	8,795
Net income (loss)*	3,077	2,753	(2,930)	(3,009)	2,487
Other Financial Data:					
EBITDA	$13,500	$13,535	$ 9,591	$ 6,067	$ 13,068
Interest Expense	3,448	3,186	3,307	4,390	3,842
Depreciation & amortization	1,669	2,099	2,675	2,695	2,664
Capital Expenditures	2,451	1,889	1,936	1,237	1,145
Margins:					
Gross profit	36.6%	36.0%	34.5%	29.1%	31.0%
EBITDA	14.7%	13.7%	10.7%	6.8%	12.8%
Balance Sheet Data:					
Current assets	$68,306	$70,120	$73,300	$56,259	$58,760
Total assets	85,701	87,832	91,784	72,677	76,019
Current liabilities	30,327	32,078	45,602	31,896	32,969
Long-term debt	31,921	29,395	28,715	26,934	25,379
Redeemable equity	3,614	4,227	1,471	1,000	270
Stockholder equity	9,066	10,606	3,690	767	4,935

*From continuing operations, before extraordinary items.

EXHIBIT 4   Unit Sales of Steinway Grand Pianos—1965 to 1994

Source: Steinway company records.

1965–1979				1980–1994			
Calendar Year	U.S. Grands	Hamburg Grands	Total Grands	Calendar Year	U.S. Grands	Hamburg Grands	Total Grands
1965	1,659	1,259	2,918	1980	1,897	1,349	3,246
1966	1,770	1,056	2,826	1981	2,041	1,394	3,435
1967	1,603	1,043	2,646	1982	1,677	1,141	2,818
1968	1,932	1,250	3,182	1983	2,036	1,263	3,299
1969	1,806	1,163	2,969	1984	1,876	1,340	3,216
1970	1,470	1,142	2,612	1985	1,337	1,291	2,628
1971	1,540	1,173	2,713	1986	1,763	1,369	3,132
1972	1,809	1,212	3,021	1987	2,144	1,237	3,381
1973	1,919	1,131	3,050	1988	2,144	1,283	3,427
1974	2,001	937	2,938	1989	2,096	1,385	3,481
1975	1,875	1,160	3,035	1990	2,117	1,459	3,576
1976	1,908	1,241	3,149	1991	1,550	1,438	2,988
1977	1,590	1,372	2,962	1992	1,344	917	2,261
1978	1,819	1,334	3,153	1993	1,631	887	2,518
1979	1,815	1,357	3,172	1994	1,720	978	2,698
30-Year Average					1,796	1,219	3,015

EXHIBIT 5
Steinway's Top Ten American Markets in 1994

Source: Steinway company records.

Market	Wholesale Dollar Sales (000's)
New York City	$6,007
Los Angeles	2,643
Baltimore/Washington D.C./Virginia	2,250
Dallas	1,642
Phoenix	1,438
Boston	1,144
San Francisco	1,078
Salt Lake City	848
Minneapolis/St. Paul	793
Detroit	605

Steinway's New York retail store provided the unofficial benchmark that Steinway's independent dealers used to guide their pricing. While Steinway could not dictate retail prices to its dealers, dealers rarely discounted prices relative to New York. In 1995, Steinway grands were priced from $26,400 to over $70,000, Steinway verticals were priced from $11,900 to over $17,000, and Boston pianos were priced from $6,395 to over $30,000. The 1995 retail prices of Steinway and Boston pianos are provided in **Exhibit 6.** At these prices, Steinway dealers earned the best margins in the business on both Steinway and Boston pianos.

Following the purchase of Steinway & Sons, Kirkland and Messina formed Steinway Musical Instruments, Inc., with Steinway & Sons and Selmer as wholly owned subsidiaries. Within this newly formed company, Kirkland was named Chairman of the Board and Messina was named Chief Executive Officer. **Exhibit 7** provides post-purchase financials for Steinway Musical Instruments, Inc.

EXHIBIT 6
Prices of Steinway and Boston pianos in 1995*

Source: Steinway company records.

Steinway Pianos		Boston Pianos	
Model	**Retail Price**	**Model**	**Retail Price**
Verticals (height):		Verticals (height):	
1098 (46 $\frac{1}{2}$")	$11,900	109C (43")	$ 6,395
4510 (45")	12,900	118C (45")	6,895
K-52 (52")	15,800	118E (46")	7,295
		125E (49")	8,295
		132E (52")	9,995
Grands (length):			
S (5' 1")	$26,400		
M (5' 7")	30,500	Grands (Length):	
L (5' 10 $\frac{1}{2}$")	34,500	163 (5' 4")	$16,690
B (6' 10 $\frac{1}{2}$")	44,900	178 (5' 10")	18,990
D (8' 11 $\frac{3}{4}$")	68,800	193 (6' 4")	24,390
		218 (7' 2")	30,990

*All retail prices represent pianos with traditional ebony finishes.

EXHIBIT 7
Steinway Musical Instruments, Inc. Financial Information Post-Acquisition

Source: Steinway company records.

	Three Months Ended March 31, 1995 (All Dollars in Thousands)			
	Selmer	**Steinway**	**Adjustments due to Merger**	**Post-Merger Pro Forma**
Income Statement Data:				
Net sales	$31,880	$28,240		$ 60,120
Gross profit	10,147	9,893		20,040
Operating income	4,681	3,380	$ (154)	7,907
Other Financial Data:				
EBITDA	$ 5,613	$ 4,432		$ 10,045
Interest Expense	1,608	830	$ 1,822	4,260
Depreciation & Amortization	819	731	454	2,004
Capital Expenditures	679	650		1,329
Margins:				
Gross profit	31.8%	35.0%		33.3%
EBITDA	17.6%	15.7%		16.7%
Balance Sheet Data:				
Current assets	$55,287	$61,459	$ 7,210	$123,956
Total assets	84,601	79,445	78,634	242,680
Current liabilities	14,909	29,034	(7,081)	36,862
Long-term debt	57,605	24,982	85,823	168,410
Redeemable equity		510	(510)	
Stockholder equity	9,261	9,696	(9,696)	9,261

The Piano Industry

Pianos came in two types—grand pianos, in which the strings were mounted horizontally, and vertical pianos, in which the strings were mounted vertically (see **Exhibit 8**). Grand pianos were larger and more expensive than verticals and generally possessed a louder and more resonant tone. In 1994, about 540,000 vertical and 60,000 grand pianos were sold worldwide. These pianos were sold into two major markets. The home (or private) market

EXHIBIT 8   **A Typical Vertical Piano and Grand Piano**

accounted for 90% of vertical piano sales and 80% of grand piano sales. The institutional market, which included sales to universities, music institutes, hotels, and performance halls accounted for the rest.

Satisfying demand at the apex of the institutional market was the concert grand piano, measuring 9 feet in length, costing over $50,000 and reserved almost exclusively for performing artists of the highest caliber. In 1994, fewer than 500 concert grand pianos were manufactured worldwide, with Steinway leading the way at 350 concert grands produced and sold. Baldwin, Bösendorfer, Yamaha, Kawai, Young Chang and Fazioli combined to manufacture another 100 concert grands. However, industry experts believed that many of these 100 concert grands were given to performance halls and music institutes, thereby generating no direct revenues.

Industry Trends

In recent years, four major trends impacted the piano industry. The first involved a sustained downturn in the piano industry, with global sales dropping by 40% since 1980. In the United States, piano sales dropped even farther, from 233,000 units in 1980 to less than 100,000 units in 1994, as reflected in **Exhibit 9.** The reasons for this downturn were complex. Some argued that it was merely part of the natural cycle of piano sales. Others credited it to the rise of the computer as a home entertainment device. Still others pointed to the growing popularity of increasingly sophisticated, low-priced electronic keyboards, noting that by the mid-1980s, many times more electronic keyboards were being sold than conventional pianos. Further contributing to this downturn, the industry was hurt by the global recession of the early 1990s.

The second major trend in the industry was the consolidation of the piano manufacturing industries in the United States and Europe. In the United States, for instance, where there were several hundred piano makers at the turn of the century, there were only eight piano makers by 1992.

The third major trend was the emergence of several Asian manufacturers. In particular, four Asian companies combined for 75% of global sales by the 1990s. These included two Japanese companies, Yamaha (~200,000 units) and Kawai (~100,000 units), and two South Korean companies, Young Chang and Samick (~75,000 to 100,000 units each). The impact

EXHIBIT 9
Vertical and Grand Piano Sales in the United States—1980 to 1995

Source: Piano Manufacturers Association International.

	Vertical Pianos		Grand Pianos	
Year	Unit Sales	Dollar Sales	Unit Sales	Dollar Sales
1980	215,000	N/A	18,000	N/A
1981	211,067	N/A	19,933	N/A
1982	182,417	N/A	20,583	N/A
1983	176,660	N/A	20,340	N/A
1984	153,788	N/A	26,212	N/A
1985	123,659	N/A	27,641	N/A
1986	133,155	N/A	33,400	N/A
1987	142,964	$395,375	32,029	$287,350
1988	109,348	$264,185	32,349	$304,598
1989	97,691	$257,220	28,626	$276,699
1990	84,186	$224,443	27,742	$277,420
1991	79,086	$210,843	27,855	$287,826
1992	73,513	$203,336	29,369	$312,369
1993	72,108	$245,400	27,613	$320,800
1994	60,779	$258,100	28,999	$347,100
1995 est.	70,000	$278,000	28,000	$372,000

EXHIBIT 10
The Worldwide Market for Vertical and Grand Pianos in 1994

Source: Steinway company records.

Unit Sales by Country			
Vertical Pianos		**Grand Pianos**	
South Korea	140,000	Americas	30,000
East Europe/Russia	101,000	Japan	12,300
China	80,000	Germany/Switzerland	3,500
Japan	78,000	South Korea	2,500
United States	60,000	Italy	1,200
Europe	50,000	United Kingdom	900
Other Asia	17,000	Taiwan	900
Taiwan	12,000	Australia	900
Brazil	2,000	France	900
		Spain	600
		Other	6,300
Total	540,000	Total	60,000

of these manufacturers on the United States piano market was quite noticeable. Starting from a near zero share in 1950, Asian imports achieved a 35% unit share of the vertical pianos market and an 80% unit share of the grand piano market by 1994.

The fourth major trend in the piano industry was the opening of new and potentially large markets. Whereas the traditional piano markets in the world were the United States and Western Europe, countries such as Japan, South Korea and China now represented huge opportunities for the world's piano makers. **Exhibit 10** offers an estimate of the world's top piano markets in the 1990's.

Competition

Steinway viewed only a handful of piano manufacturers as potential competitors. These included Baldwin, Yamaha and Kawai, which were high-volume producers of both vertical and grand pianos. It also included Bösendorfer and Fazioli, which were low volume producers of primarily high-end grand pianos. **Exhibit 11** provides 1995 retail piano prices for each of these firms.

Baldwin

By 1995, the Baldwin Piano and Organ Company was the sole remaining large-scale producer of vertical and grand pianos in the United States. More importantly to Steinway, it was the only other American manufacturer of high-quality grand pianos. Founded in 1862, Baldwin sold its pianos under the Baldwin and Wurlitzer brand names through a network of 700 dealers. In 1994, Baldwin sold about 20,000 pianos domestically and abroad, generating revenues of $122 million.

Historically, Baldwin offered a full line of pianos. These ranged from relatively inexpensive verticals and small grand pianos, manufactured in highly automated production facilities, all the way to handcrafted concert grand pianos which were well respected by trained musicians. Over the years, Baldwin concert grands were the pianos of choice for artists such as Dave Brubeck, Stephen Sondheim and Leonard Bernstein, as well as the "official" piano of organizations such as the Boston, Chicago, and Philadelphia orchestras.

Yamaha

The 100-year old Yamaha Corporation, a $4.0 billion diversified multinational,[1] was the largest producer of pianos in the world. With $1.0 billion in piano sales, it held a 35% share

---

[1] The Yamaha Corporation produced musical instruments of all kinds, as well household and industrial products. The financially independent $6B Yamaha Motor Company produced motorcycles, boats, and jet skis.

EXHIBIT 11   Approximate Prices of the Pianos of the Major Manufacturers in 1995*

Source: Ancott Associates, Music Product Directory, Acoustic Piano Edition, Spring/Summer 1995.

Baldwin Pianos		Bösendorfer Pianos		Fazioli Pianos	
Model	**Retail Price**	**Model**	**Retail Price**	**Model**	**Retail Price**
Verticals (height):		Verticals:		Grands:	
650 (40")	$3,690	130 (52")	$39,580	F156 (5' 2")	$58,700
243HP (45")	4,770			F183 (6')	64,700
6000 (52")	8,590	Grands:		F212 (6'11")	74,700
		170 (5' 8")	$74,780	F228 (7' 6")	85,100
		200 (6' 7")	90,180	F278 (9' 2")	106,000
Grands (Length):		213 (7')	102,380		
M (5' 2")	$18,732	225 (7' 4")	109,980		
R (5' 8")	20,242	275 (9')	140,780		
L (6' 3")	22,052	290 (9' 6")	169,380		
SF10 (7')	32,694				
SD10 (9')	54,174				

Kawai Pianos		Yamaha Pianos	
Model	**Retail Price**	**Model**	**Retail Price**
Verticals (height):		Verticals (height):	
502-S (42")	$3,770	M1F (44")	$4,790
UST-8C (46")	4,650	P2E (45")	5,290
US-6X (52")	8,650	U1S (48")	6,590
		U3S (52")	8,790
Grands (Length):			
GM-1 (4' 9")	$10,590		
GE-1 (5' 1")	11,670	Grands (Length):	
KG-1A (5' 4")	15,090	C1 (5' 3")	$15,090
KG-2A (5' 10")	16,790	C2 (5' 8")	17,190
GS-40 (6' 1")	22,150	C3 (6')	18,990
GS-60 (6' 9")	24,530	C5 (6' 7")	24,590
GS-70 (7' 5")	28,490	C6 (6' 11")	27,590
GS-100 (9' 1")	59,990	C7 (7' 6")	31,390
		CFIIIS (9')	87,990

* For reasons of comparison, all retail prices represent pianos with traditional ebony finishes.

of the world market and a 50% share of the Japanese market. In 1994, it produced 175,000 pianos (down from 240,000 in 1980), half of which were sold in Japan. Most were vertical pianos (90%) or small grand pianos (10%), all of which were produced using highly automated, assembly-line techniques.

In addition to its mass-produced pianos, Yamaha also produced a limited number of concert grand pianos using traditional craft methods. The goal of this effort was to produce the best grand piano in the world, as was made clear as early as 1966, when Yamaha announced that, "We have now succeeded in manufacturing a test model of what we believe to be the world's finest concert grand piano."[2] This test piano resulted in the Yamaha Conservatory CF concert grand, introduced in 1967 to relatively favorable reviews. While many questioned whether the CF was up to Steinway standards, it represented a clear departure from Yamaha's assembly line pianos. From the beginning, Yamaha made no secret of its interest in emulating, and eventually surpassing, Steinway:

> We are chasing hard, we want to catch up with Steinway. Oh, but it's unfair to compare the two, like comparing Rolls Royce with Toyotas. That makes us nervous; Steinway too, no doubt.[3]

[2] Richard K. Lieberman, *Steinway & Sons,* Yale University Press, 1995.

[3] "On Yamaha's Assembly Line," *New York Times,* February 22, 1981.

In chasing Steinway, Yamaha's overarching strategy for its concert grands was continuous improvement. First, the firm used noticeably higher quality raw materials in its concert grand pianos than it used in its other pianos, often claiming that the lumber for its concert grands came from the same mills supplying Steinway. Second, its engineers regularly purchased and disassembled Steinway concert grands in an effort to duplicate the techniques of Steinway. It was once remarked by a Steinway executive, "If a quiz on Steinway pianos were given to Yamaha and Steinway engineers, I am not sure who would score better." Third, Yamaha's production process was automated wherever possible, with partially completed pianos transported through the factory on moving assembly lines. Fourth, Yamaha employed a high degree of vertical integration, as evidenced by the fact that they were one of the very few piano makers to cast its own iron plates (the inner core of the piano, to which the strings are attached). Finally, worker discretion was kept to a minimum and the entire operation was designed to ensure a consistent product.

To promote its concert grand pianos, in 1987, Yamaha launched an "Artist Program" that was nearly a direct copy of Steinway's "Concert and Artist Program." In particular, Yamaha enticed several well-known pianists to adopt the Yamaha Conservatory CF as their instrument of choice and supplied those artists with pianos as they performed around the world. The best known of these artists included Sviatoslav Richter and Andre Watts. While Yamaha's "Artist Program" never really challenged Steinway's leadership and was discontinued during the early 1990s, Yamaha continued to heavily invest in the promotion of its concert grand pianos.

In addition to its efforts in courting the professional concert artists, Yamaha actively marketed its pianos to major universities, such as Stanford and Michigan, and to music institutes and conservatories. These organizations would often obtain dozens of pianos in a single instance, with brand choice being driven by product quality, prompt delivery and competitive pricing. Quite often, manufacturers would "loan" pianos to these organizations to expose budding artists to their brand.

Kawai

Following in the footsteps of Yamaha was the 70-year old Kawai Corporation of Japan, which produced about 90,000 vertical pianos and 10,000 small grand pianos per year. As with Yamaha, these pianos were manufactured on highly automated assembly lines. For promotional reasons, Kawai also focused efforts on making a high-quality concert grand piano. However, while Kawai was known to produce good quality verticals and small grand pianos, it had not yet impressed the critics with its concert grands, as reflected in the following concert review:

> Concertgoers goggled last night when they looked at the Meany Theater stage and discovered not a Steinway, not a Bösendorfer, but a Kawai grand piano awaiting the evening's recitalist, Awadagin Pratt. . . . It wasn't a good choice. The Kawai has a nice, resonant base, and the instrument sounds fine at low volumes. But it lacks depth and sounds tinny in the middle register, where most of the playing takes place, and even Pratt's considerable talents couldn't make this instrument sing.[4]

Bösendorfer and Fazioli

In contrast to the high-volume strategies of the Asian manufacturers, Bösendorfer of Austria and Fazioli of Italy had taken a different approach. Both focused almost exclusively on very small volumes of top-quality grand pianos. In 1994, for instance, Bösendorfer produced 400 grand pianos while Fazioli produced 60 grand pianos. As with Steinway, both of these companies employed traditional handcraft production techniques that had

[4] *The Seattle Times,* January 21, 1999.

remained substantially unchanged for the past 100 years. In turn, both brands of grand piano are widely recognized as being among the highest quality in the industry, as reflected in the following industry reviews:[5]

> [Bösendorfer] has been one of the most distinguished and sought after instruments for a period of over 160 years. . . . [It] remains an honored and respected instrument, sought after by classical and popular musicians alike.
>
> [Fazioli's] models . . . are considered on par with the best-known current international names. . . . it seems the Italian piano industry has finally been able to produce a concert instrument with its own individual personality and worldwide marketability.

New Piano Distribution

For most manufacturers, the primary vehicle for piano distribution was through the independent dealer. In the United States, for instance, over 95% of all new pianos were sold through a network of about 1,000 independent acoustic piano dealers. Typically, these dealers would carry a primary piano brand, such as Steinway or Yamaha, as well as three or four other brands to fill out their portfolio. For instance, a dealer that specializes in Yamaha might also carry Bösendorfer at the high end and Samick as its entry-level brand. Similarly, a Steinway dealer might also carry Kawai (or, increasingly, Boston) as its mid-tier brand and Young Chang as its entry-level brand.

Typically, these independent dealers purchased pianos directly from the manufacturers and sold those pianos at margins that varied across brands. Entry level pianos, such as Samick and Young Chang, typically would command retail margins around 25%, while higher end pianos, such as Steinway, Bösendorfer and Fazioli, typically would command retail margins approaching 45%. On average, an independent dealer would turn its inventory two to three times per year.

The Used Piano Market

The market for new pianos also was impacted by an active market for used pianos. With many brands of piano lasting 40 or more years, over 40 million pianos were believed to exist around the world. By one estimate, for every new piano sold in the United States, 10 used pianos also changed hands. While most of these exchanges were private (e.g., private sales or generational gifts), there also was an active commercial market for used pianos. In 1994, for instance, domestic dealers of new pianos sold about 25,000 used pianos that they had obtained as trade-ins on the purchase of new pianos. Another 50,000 used pianos were sold by second-hand dealers that specialized in used pianos.

At Steinway, management believed that a used Steinway represented a serious threat to the sale of a new Steinway. This was partly due to the fine reputation that both new and used Steinways possessed. It also was due to the extremely long life that characterized a properly maintained Steinway piano—70 to 80 years without a major restoration and many years longer with one. In the 1960s, when asked how long a Steinway piano would last, Henry Steinway only half-jokingly replied, "Steinway & Sons is only 120 years old, so we don't know yet." As a result of these factors, for every new Steinway piano sold, about five used Steinways also changed hands. While the prices for these used Steinways varied greatly, a well maintained 20-year old Steinway grand could be expected to sell for 75% of the price of a new Steinway grand of the same type.

Steinway & Sons—Company Background

For 140 years, Steinway & Sons has been recognized as a leader in the market for high-quality grand pianos. Established in New York City in 1853 by Henry Engelhard Steinway, a German immigrant, the firm quickly prospered because of its technical excellence. A year

[5] Robert Palmieri, *Encyclopedia of the Piano,* Garland Publishing, New York, 1994.

after its founding, the company had won a gold medal at the Metropolitan Fair in Washington D.C., for one of its square pianos. The next year, it introduced the cross-stringing technique in a piano with a cast-iron frame, an innovation that is now universal in all grand pianos. Based on these advances, orders grew rapidly, and in 1860, a new and larger factory was constructed on Fourth (now Park) Avenue in New York. Reportedly, the site was chosen because "the Harlem and New Haven Railroad cars passed directly in front making thousands of people acquainted with the name Steinway."

This promotional flair continued with the 1866 opening of Steinway Hall, which served as New York City's major concert facility for many years. The firm also engaged in artist management, bringing to the United States such piano virtuosos as Anton Rubinstein and Ignace Jan Paderewski for their first American performances.

Succeeding generations of Steinways guided the company by following the advice of its founder to "build the best piano possible and sell it at the lowest price consistent with quality." Technical excellence continued to be emphasized, with the firm taking out over 120 patents in piano making over the years. To facilitate this mission, Steinway purchased 400 acres of land in Long Island City, New York in 1871 to serve as the company's worldwide headquarters. Over the years, the area would be developed as Steinway Village, a largely self-contained company town complete with its own kindergarten, park, library, and streetcar line. Few vestiges of the village remain, although the factory is still Steinway's sole U.S. production facility. Steinway also built a new factory in 1880 in Hamburg, Germany, to service the international trade. That factory also remains in use.

Milestones in the company's history include the construction of a specially designed piano, Steinway's 100,000th, presented to the White House in 1903; the construction of a second grand piano, Steinway's 300,000th, presented to the White House in 1938; the firm's survival during World War II when piano making was deemed unessential to the war effort; and Steinway's rapid postwar recovery and return to piano-making eminence. In 1988, Steinway produced its 500,000th piano.

The Steinway Tradition

Steinway pianos have long been received enthusiastically by knowledgeable musicians. By one estimate, in any given year, over 90% of all classical music concerts featuring a piano soloist are performed on a Steinway concert grand. Major music schools and conservatories showed a similar fondness for Steinways—with schools such as Juilliard, Oberlin and Indiana University each owning in excess of 100 Steinways. In addition to these professional and institutional markets, Steinway sold to affluent individuals who had a serious interest in music. In fact, approximately 90% of all Steinway pianos sold in the United States in 1994 were sold to individuals.

The reasons for this enthusiasm have changed little over time as Steinway has followed the same basic principles throughout its history. All Steinways are still assembled by craft methods, with limited use of assembly-line techniques. In fact, it was estimated that a Steinway grand piano took two years to manufacture (one year for the piano's lumber to dry and one year to physically make and assemble the piano components) and contained over 12,000 individual parts. **Exhibit 12** provides an overview of the process by which a Steinway grand is manufactured. As a consequence of this age-old manufacturing process, volumes remained small, with Long Island City producing about 1,800 grand pianos and Hamburg producing about 1,200 grand pianos in any given year.

Skilled labor was employed throughout the production process, with Steinway workers averaging 15 years with the company and with many workers representing second or third generation Steinway employees. In addition, Steinway used the highest grade of over seven species of lumber and nine exotic veneers.[6] For example, Steinway relied on its own wood

---

[6] At the same time, Steinway was conscious of its environmental responsibility, with efforts that included financial support of the "Hardwood Forestry Fund."

EXHIBIT 12   The Making of a Steinway Grand Piano

Two years are required to make a Steinway grand—one year to dry the lumber and one year for the actual manufacturing. In turn, the manufacturing process at Steinway could be divided into two six-month components—traditional woodworking operations used to produce parts and, thereafter, the assembly of those parts into the finished piano. Upon completion, it was estimated that more than 12,000 individual parts went into a Steinway grand piano.

Wood-drying operations   In order to minimize expansion and contraction, the wood used in a Steinway piano required a moisture (water) content of about 6%. However, lumber typically arrived to the factory with a moisture content of 45% to 50% and sometimes as high as 80%. To reduce the moisture content to 25%, the lumber was air-dried outside in the factory yard for many months. To then reduce the moisture content to 6%, the lumber spent several weeks in large drying kilns, cavernous rooms where computer-controlled temperatures reached 160° F. Sufficient time was a critical element in this process, for Steinway believed that slow and natural drying was necessary to ensure the best sound-producing qualities of the wood were retained.

Parts-making operations   After drying, the parts-making operations began. The first of these operations involved bending of the piano rim (the curved side giving a grand piano its familiar shape). These rims were formed of multiple layers of specially-selected maple that were manually forced into a unified shape, held in presses for several hours, and then seasoned for 10 weeks before being joined to other wooden parts. During this time, the sounding board (a specially tapered spruce panel placed inside the rim to amplify the sound made when a string was struck) and many other case parts were being cut and prepared. The final critical operation with parts making involved the fabrication of the 88 individual piano action sets that existed inside a piano. Piano actions were the intricate mechanical assemblies, made almost completely of wood (and some felt) that transmitted finger pressure on the piano keys into the force that propelled the hammers that struck the strings.

The action was a particularly important part of a piano, for it was this mechanical linkage that gave Steinways their distinctive feel. Actions were constructed of a large number of small, wooden parts containing fine metal components and small pieces of felt and leather. Although the firm had experimented with plastic parts and recognized certain advantages, consumer resistance—the perception that Steinway employed only traditional materials—had prevented their widespread adoption.

Within any of the parts making operations, the company's approach was to find the tasks for which handcrafting was not required, and then to utilize automatic machinery for those operations. In 1990, for example, Steinway introduced an English-made hydraulic hammer press that replaced the 13 hand presses that had been in use since the turn of the century. Similarly, action component machining centers that performed many functions were currently being installed to improve quality and reduce the total number of single-function machines that had previously been used.

Piano-making operations   Bellying—so called because workers both concentrated on the heart of the piano (the marriage of piano plate, soundboard, and rim) and also performed many of these tasks while leaning their stomachs against the rim of the piano—was generally considered the starting point of the piano-making operations. At this stage, precise and careful fitting of the soundboard and iron plate was considered extremely important for final tonal quality. Because of individual variations in material and the high degree of precision required, bellying often took considerable skill and required several hours per piano. The fitting of an iron plate generally required 2 hours per piano, while the complete fitting of a soundboard required 5 to 6 hours.

After the bellying operations, pianos were strung. Stringing had been an extremely tedious job that required three hours per piano and involved the insertion of each string into a tuning pin and the subsequent hammering down of those pins using a hand mallet. During the 1980s, Steinway mechanized most of this operation by employing special hydraulic equipment to turn and press fit each tuning pin, realizing greater ease and precision than had been possible by hand.

Once strung, pianos were moved to the grand finishing department. At this stage—roughly akin to final assembly—the remaining major components of the piano were installed and regulated to produce a working instrument. Actions and keyboards were individually fit to each instrument to accommodate differences in materials and tolerances. The installation of these components normally took 2 or 3 hours.

Pianos were also "broken in" in grand finishing using special "pounding machines." After keys were weighted for touch, regulated, and rough-tuned, each piano was brought to a pounding machine (an electrically driven device with plungers that struck all 88 keys at the rate of 10,000 cycles per hour) which simulated continual playing. This was done so that tuners and tone regulators were able to work with "played in" instruments not subject to drifting off-key. Pounding machines also were used occasionally for reliability testing to determine an instrument's durability.

Next, the instruments were moved to tone regulating. It was here that the pianos were voiced for Steinway sound. Unlike tuning, which involved the loosening and tightening of strings, voicing required the careful softening or hardening of the felt which surrounded the hammers that struck the strings to produce tone. This operation was one of extreme delicacy and was performed by only a small handful of tone regulators. The tone regulators at Steinway were widely considered to be among the most skilled artisans in the factory. Their voicing of a concert grand could take as much as 20 to 30 hours. All tone regulators at Steinway had worked for the company in various other positions before reaching their present posts, and several had more than 20 years with the firm.

Finally, after tone regulation, all pianos were brought to the rubbing and polishing department. There the wood cases were polished, the keys were cleaned, and the pianos were inspected one last time before packing and shipment.

technologists to aid in the purchase of million of dollars worth of wood annually, including rosewood from India, mahogany from South America, and Sitka spruce from Alaska. Yet, after the wood was seasoned, the firm still discarded half of some kinds of lumber because standards had not been met.

This attention to detail contributed to the legendary sound and durability of a Steinway. Concert pianists generally cited the instrument's even voicing (the evenness of character and timbre in each of the 88 notes of the keyboard), the duration of its tone, and the sweetness of its registers (the roundness and softness of tone throughout the piano's entire range) as especially significant.

At the same time, no two Steinway grand pianos sounded the same. Each piano possessed its own distinct personality, which was influenced by the guiding hands of Steinway's tone regulators. Given small differences in construction, the sound of each piano would have different nuances. In turn, the tone regulator would work with these nuances to make the most of each piano. One tone regulator tried to capture this process as follows:

> Sometimes you get a piano that is nice and even and mellow . . . , and you will disturb it too much if you try to make it brilliant. . . . It gives you the feeling that it's better the way it is. How could I give you an example? Say I would like to take a picture of a something, a person, and I would like to have a lot of light in there—full light. And I don't have it. Yet with a subdued light, the object shows certain qualities, certain mysteries. . . . And you don't want to disturb that, risk it, by exposing it to light.[7]

Much of the Steinway mystique rested on the Steinway Concert D, the nine-foot-long grand piano used in performing halls. Its use by performing artists was assisted by Steinway's Concert and Artist Program, which maintained a "bank" of pianos for use by about 850 "Steinway Artists."[8] Across 160 cities, some 330 pianos valued at over $17 million were dedicated to this program. Once a performer had achieved sufficient stature to be considered eligible by the company, he or she was offered the opportunity to use Steinways for all performances, their only expense being the cost of transporting the piano to the recital hall and tuning it to that performer's requirements. A performer could visit dealers in any of the cities involved, try out the concert grands available there—ranging from one piano in out-of-the-way places to over 40 in New York City—and request that a specific piano be made available on a particular date. Steinway would then handle the logistics. **Table A** provides a list of some of the more famous Steinway Artists over the years.

Because of the concert bank, long-standing relationships often developed between individual performers and specific pianos. Artists considered each piano subtly different in tone and feel. Moreover, pianos were specially adjusted and tuned to suit the individual performer's temperament and style. Steinway provided master piano technicians to perform these tasks. In return for these services, Steinway was granted exclusive use of the artists' names for publicity purposes. In addition, concert pianists served as informal testers of the

[7] Building a Steinway, *The Atlantic Monthly*, 1982.
[8] These Steinway Artists were not paid to endorse Steinway pianos.

TABLE A
A Partial List of Immortal "Steinway Artists"

Source: Steinway company records.

Irving Berlin	Josef Hofmann	Sergei Prokofiev	Artur Schnabel
Duke Ellington	Vladimir Horowitz	Sergei Rachmaninoff	John Philip Sousa
George Gershwin	Franz Liszt	Gioachino Rossini	Igor Stravinsky
Glenn Gould	Ignace Jan Paderewski	Anton Rubinstein	Arturo Toscanini
Edvard Grieg	Cole Porter	Arthur Rubinstein	Richard Wagner

company's pianos, as reflected in the following comment by a Steinway family member in 1980 and as was still true in 1995,

> We use the concert pianist as a proving ground. They know it. Part of this association with performing artists is the fact that we say, "Look, we are trying to make a better piano for you guys, will you try this one?" . . . There's no real scientific laboratory way you could take an experimental action, put it in a piano and test it, and say, "This is 89.27 percent better than the other" or something. I want Gary Graffman to try the thing.[9]

Steinway & Sons—1972 to 1995

Its stable legacy notwithstanding, the recent past has been somewhat turbulent for Steinway & Sons, with the watershed event being the sale of Steinway to the CBS Musical Instruments Division in 1972. After 120-years of family control, it was decided that Steinway could no longer survive as a closely held family operation.

The factors leading up to the sale of Steinway in 1972 were primarily financial. After four generations of family control, ownership of the company was spread among many family members. Some were intimately involved in the day-to-day operations of the company, but others were non-active partners who were mostly interested in income and were unwilling to invest in capital improvements. However, by the early 1970s, Steinway's return on capital was only about 5%. As noted by one family member, "We could get as much in a government bond as we can from this."[10]

The CBS Years 1972–1985

As Steinway was wrestling with its family management problems, CBS (of television fame) was assembling a Musical Instruments Division. Over time, this division would grow to include Fender guitars, Rodgers organs, Squire strings, Leslie speakers, Rhodes electric pianos, and Lyon & Healy harps. All were considered to be among the finest instruments in their field.

Given these efforts, Steinway seemed like a natural fit. After several rounds of negotiation, Steinway was sold to CBS for about $21 million in CBS stock. As part of the deal, CBS agreed to retain Henry Steinway as president of Steinway for at least five years, reportedly to ease the transition of Steinway to a corporate-owned operation and to ensure a continued focus on production quality.

In spite of these early promises, however, results under CBS were mixed. On the positive side, CBS did invest in Steinway's aging Long Island City and Hamburg facilities. Whereas the Steinway family had never invested more than $150,000 per year in capital improvements, CBS invested several million dollars in the first few years after purchasing the company.

Looking for a reasonable return upon its investments, however, CBS sought to increase revenues and decrease manufacturing costs. In particular, CBS took steps to increase piano production—steps that were not well received by traditionalists. To sell the additional pianos being produced, CBS also grew the Steinway dealer network. In the Americas, for instance, CBS increased the number of independent dealers carrying Steinway pianos from 110 to 153. It did this by adding dealers in cities that had previously been considered too small to adequately support a Steinway dealership and by accepting dealers who carried Yamaha pianos as their primary product line.

The net effects of these actions were two-fold. First, sales volumes and profits increased relative to the early 1970s. Second, critics began to question the quality of the Steinway

[9] "Conversation with John Steinway," *The Boston Monthly,* April 1980.
[10] Richard K. Lieberman, *Steinway & Sons,* Yale University Press, 1995.

pianos being produced and of the dealer network supporting those pianos. The impact on consumer perceptions was clear, as reflected in the following assessment:

> . . . [the] word going around in music lovers' circles was that Steinway is not what it used to be before CBS. [At the same time], the business in repairing used Steinways was booming. Even the Juilliard School was opting to repair used Steinways. The work was being done by ex-Steinway employees in their own shops, plus current Steinway employees at night and on the weekends.[11]

These concerns about quality were further fueled by a steady turnover in Steinway management. After his promised five years were up, Henry Steinway retired as president. In his place, CBS delved into its Musical Instruments Division to appoint a series of presidents, each of whom ran into problems of one sort or another. Henry Steinway was replaced by Robert Bull (May 1977–January 1979), who was replaced by Peter Perez (January 1979–May 1982), who was replaced by Lloyd Meyer (May 1982–September 1985). With the appointment of Lloyd Meyer, CBS had named more presidents to Steinway & Sons than the company had had since the turn of the century. And with each new president, critics further questioned the quality of the Steinway pianos being turned out.

CBS's management of Steinway came to a close in 1985. In November 1984, despite being moderately profitable, CBS announced plans to sell its Musical Instruments companies and to focus its efforts on broadcasting. Ten months later, CBS sold Steinway & Sons to a group of Boston investors headed up by two brothers—John and Robert Birmingham. It was believed the investors paid $50 million—$1 million of their own capital and $49 million borrowed from several commercial banks. Thus, after 13 years of corporate management, Steinway was again taken private.

The Birmingham Years 1985–1995

The Birmingham brothers were not obvious candidates to purchase Steinway. Their family had made its money in the fuel oil distribution business in New England and the two brothers had taken jobs in corporate America—John as a trial lawyer and Robert as a businessman. Neither played the piano nor had any previous experience in running a musical instruments company.

In spite of their lack of industry experience, the Birmingham's set out to reestablish Steinway as the maker of the highest quality piano in the world. Aiding them in this effort was Bruce Stevens, a minority partner in the Steinway purchase, who was appointed CEO and President of Steinway. Prior to coming to Steinway, Stevens had worked for Polaroid Corporation for 18 years, where he had risen to Director of Marketing for Polaroid's international business.

The First Six Months

One of the first tasks Stevens faced was assuring Steinway's employees, dealers, and customers that the new owners were committed to quality. This task was made that much more difficult by the ten months it took CBS to sell Steinway & Sons. In those ten months, rumors ran rampant as to who would buy the company and what they would do with it. Employee morale plummeted in the face of the uncertainty and dealers became reluctant to take shipment of new pianos from a lame-duck owner. The situation had deteriorated to the point where 740 finished pianos, boxed and ready for shipment, languished in Steinway's Long Island factory.

Having inherited these woes, Stevens and the management team decided to unbox each of those 740 pianos prior to shipment and to re-tune and re-voice each one—an undertaking that took almost three months. Further, Stevens personally visited many of the top Steinway

---

[11] Richard K. Lieberman, *Steinway & Sons,* Yale University Press, 1995.

dealers around the world, hearing their concerns and explaining his plans for the company. To his surprise, Stevens learned that CBS management had rarely (if ever) visited dealers in such a fashion. He felt these visits helped build a "sense of responsiveness" on the part of the new management team.

Manufacturing

Changes also were made to upgrade and modernize the manufacturing facilities. This included the purchase of new machinery and the introduction of statistical process control in the production of the piano actions (the intricate mechanical assemblies, made almost completely of wood, which transmitted pressure on the keys to hammers that struck the strings). It also included the careful documentation of the entire piano manufacturing process, something that had not existed prior to the mid-1980s. In reflecting back on these efforts, Stevens notes:

> Given our highly leveraged purchase of Steinway, money for capital improvements was scarce. But what limited dollars we did have, we spent on the manufacturing process. Our number one goal was to eliminate any question of product quality.

The Dealer Network

Feeling that Steinway's dealer network was overextended and unfocused, Stevens also focused efforts on distribution. Early on, he promoted Frank Mazurco to the position of Executive Vice President with responsibilities for sales and marketing. Mazurco quickly set out to reduce the size of the dealer network, only keeping dealers who were fully committed to Steinway as their primary product line. In the Americas, for example, Steinway reduced the number of independent Steinway dealers from 153 to 93 between 1985 and 1995. In large cities that were deemed strategically important to Steinway, this involved the replacement of over 20 underperforming dealers. In smaller cities that could not support a full-scale Steinway dealership, it involved the termination of 60 dealers.

Second, for its remaining dealers, Steinway developed a "Partnership Program" which included; (1) formal sales training programs, (2) formal technical support programs, (3) promotional events planning, (4) coordinated advertising and public relations, (5) institutional sales programs, (6) concert and artist activities, and (7) extensive merchandising support. As an example of Steinway's merchandising support, Steinway aided dealers in the creation of a separate "Steinway Showroom" within the dealer's retail space. These rooms were designed to showcase Steinway pianos in a quality environment, increasing sales for both the dealer and for Steinway.

The Defection of Andre Watts   The importance of a high-quality dealer network became painfully obvious to the Steinway management team in early 1988 with the defection of a prominent "Steinway Artist." In a televised Lincoln Center performance to commemorate the 25th anniversary of his debut with the New York Philharmonic, Andre Watts had chosen a Yamaha concert grand. Reportedly, Watts was dissatisfied with the service he had received from certain Steinway dealers and was frustrated by what he felt was a lack of attention to his requests. He made this clear in a 1988 interview in which he justified terminating his relationship with Steinway and endorsing Yamaha as his piano of choice:

> I sit in my house and practice and prepare a program. And I start to go on the road and the instruments I encounter start taking away, start stealing parts of what I've built up, what I've developed . . . this doesn't work, that doesn't work, you can't get this fixed. When you call back to New York, you may find out, very cordially, . . . "that it's an independent dealer, we don't have any control over that person, I'm sorry." After a while, if there is something better, I don't see why not.[12]

Others would claim that the primary reason for Watts' defection was financial. Whereas Steinway charged for piano delivery and in-hall tuning, Yamaha waved these fees for its

---

[12] *The MacNeil/Lehrer News Hour*, April 1, 1988.

concert artists. For a performer such as Watts, who played about 150 concerts per year, the resulting annual savings came close to $100,000. Regardless of the reason for Watts' departure, however, Yamaha had attracted a high-profile artist to endorse its concert grand pianos and this endorsement came at the expense of Steinway.

The Product Line

Finally, Steinway began to expand its product offerings. This involved the introduction of the Boston Piano line in 1992, the launch of the Steinway Limited Edition pianos in 1993, and the launch of the Crown Jewel Collection of Steinway pianos in 1994.

The Boston Piano   Steinway's first new product introduction was a mid-priced piano under the brand name "Boston." This new product concept was the brainchild of Steinway's Robert Dove, who refined the concept and was subsequently given responsibility for the worldwide launch and marketing of the Boston line. For Steinway & Sons, the introduction of the Boston piano line represented a significant break with tradition, as suggested by the following assessment:

> In 1992 the Birminghams did something that Steinway & Sons had resisted throughout its history. They introduced a mid-priced piano. Every time the idea had been raised before, it had been rejected because Steinway wanted to stay in the exclusive niche, selling only a top-of-the-line prestige piano. The Birminghams believed that they could retain the high end of the market while providing a lower priced [instrument] for "customers who were not yet ready to acquire a Steinway." They named their new piano after their hometown of Boston.[13]

Importantly, the Boston piano line was "designed by Steinway & Sons," but manufactured in Japan by Kawai. The intent was to produce a line of pianos that sold for about half the price of a comparably sized Steinway and to sell that line exclusively through Steinway dealers. In the process, the line would provide dealers with a high-margin product in the mid-market price range and allow Steinway to capture sales that might otherwise have gone to Yamaha. It was believed that Kawai agreed to manufacture the pianos to make use of idle capacity.

In 1995, the Boston piano line consisted of eight models of vertical and grand pianos that ranged in price from $6,395 to $29,990. By 1994, Boston piano revenues had grown to $16.9 million on the sale of 2,300 units, up from $2.7 million on the sale of 600 units in 1992.

Steinway Limited Editions   Steinway's second new product introduction was its Limited Edition Collection. To celebrate 140 years of piano making, Steinway introduced a specially designed 140th Anniversary Limited Edition Piano in 1993. Limited to 140 grand pianos, each in a mahogany finish, these pianos sold at a 25% premium to the traditional ebony Steinways. Within hours of being made available, Steinway dealers had purchased all 140 pianos. Based on this success, Steinway decided to introduce a limited edition piano every two years. Its 1995 limited edition, numbering 146 grand pianos, was entitled "Instrument of the Immortals" and was engraved with the names of the 73 immortal "Steinway Artists." It also sold out to dealers within hours of being made available.

The Crown Jewel Collection   Steinway's third new product introduction was its Crown Jewel Collection. Through 1993, over 90% of the pianos sold by Steinway were finished in classic ebony, with the remaining 10% finished in walnut or mahogany. In 1994, Steinway sought to shift these proportions with the introduction of the Crown Jewel Collection—otherwise traditional Steinway pianos that were finished in exotic woods, such as east indian rosewood, kewazinga bubinga, african pommele and macassar ebony. These pianos sold at 20% to 30% price premiums to the traditional ebony Steinway. In spite of these price premiums, by 1995, the Crown Jewel Collection represented almost 30% of Steinway unit sales.

[13] Richard K. Lieberman, *Steinway & Sons,* Yale University Press, 1995.

The Purchase by Messina & Kirkland—April 18, 1995

In spite of the positive changes made by Stevens and his management team, by the mid-1990s, the running of Steinway was constrained by limited financial resources. With the company still highly leveraged, there was a constant lack of working capital. Stevens described the situation as follows:

> Making Steinway pianos is capital intensive. Between lumber, semi-finished pianos and finished pianos, there is over $75 million in inventory at any given moment. Yet we were financed on a shoestring, constantly banging up against our credit line, so that even a $200,000 expenditure had to be negotiated with the banks. This was especially true during the summer when we would experience our seasonal downturn in demand. Costs would stay constant, revenues would decrease, and we'd be left scrambling for funds. Rather than focusing on the making and selling of pianos, we'd be dealing with bankers and lawyers. It got to the point where it was really tough coming to work in the summer.

Finally, in late-1994, for personal reasons, the Birminghams decided to sell the company. Made aware of the sale by an investment banking firm, Kyle Kirkland and Dana Messina became intrigued. By 1995, their small firm, Kirkland Messina, had purchased controlling interest in Selmer (in 1993), a meat processing company (in 1992), and a paper company (in 1993). In Steinway, they saw a well-run company that could benefit from their financial expertise. In addition, as frustrated musicians, they saw a company that sparked their imagination. The decision to bid on Steinway was not without risks, however, as noted by Messina:

> When we purchased Selmer in 1993, we had little to lose. We put in $250,000 of our own money, which represented the bulk of our assets, and we came away with 23% of the company. By the time Steinway became available, that 23% was worth over $10 million. So while many people saw the buying of Selmer and the buying of Steinway as being similar, we had a lot more to lose in Steinway.

Nonetheless, on the strong insistence of Kirkland (the piano player among the two), they were one of 64 groups to bid for Steinway. And with a first round bid of $75 million, they were one of ten groups invited to give a second bid. Subsequent rounds saw the number of bidders drop from 10 to 4 to 1, with Kirkland Messina increasing their bid from $75 million to $90 million to $100 million. Messina noted that their final bid of $100 million was not the highest received by the Birminghams. However, combined with their successful track record with Selmer, it was sufficient to win Kirkland Messina the bidding war.

Moving Forward

Upon completing the purchase of Steinway, the questions facing Messina and Kirkland quickly became one of building a business. In particular, they needed to decide whether Steinway would continue its high-end, niche strategy of being the world's pre-eminent maker of high quality vertical and grand pianos? Alternatively, might it make more sense to forego this long-standing strategy to pursue some bolder, more aggressive plan? Within these larger questions, the two partners needed to decide what to do with the recently introduced line of Boston Pianos. First, did it make sense for Steinway to sell a mid-priced line of vertical and grand pianos? Second, if it did make sense, might there be other ways to leverage the Steinway brand name to further enhance revenues? Finally, what role should Messina and Kirkland play in the running of Steinway? It was one thing to own the company; it was something else to run it effectively.

Managing Customers for Profits

Part

8

Chapter

36

Note on Customer Management

Das Narayandas

Marketing is the process whereby an enterprise creates value by meeting the needs of its targeted customers. A firm is thus defined not only by the products it sells, but also by the customers it serves. Despite the fact that customers are at the heart of any enterprise, not all firms manage individual customers. Without such an emphasis, vendors will find it difficult to manage changes in vendor-customer alignment that result from changes in the nature of vendors' current customer relationships or their choice to serve other customers.

In the Black and Decker case we saw how *increased emphasis on a sub-set of its customer portfolio can affect a firm's relationship with other customers currently served.* Throughout the 1980s, Black and Decker achieved phenomenal growth in sales and profits as it expanded its relationship with the DIY (Do-it-Yourself) customer base. Acquisition of the GE Spacemaker product line enabled it to offer these customers kitchen and bathroom appliances as well as power tools. But, as the firm moved from the garage into the kitchen and bathroom, its traditional tradesman customer began to have trouble identifying with the Black and Decker brand. As this customer segment grew faster than other segments in the 1990s, the firm had to reformulate its approach to its original customer base.

Customers' needs and the value they perceive in vendors' offerings are subject to change over time. For example, products in the early stages of their life cycle are often viewed as specialties, involving the participation of customer engineering and R&D staff in their design and application-specific customization. Owing to the value added and technical orientation of those at their end, customers tend to be less price sensitive. But as a product matures and becomes a commodity, customers' engineers give way to buyers in their purchasing departments who are less interested in modifying product specifications than in managing price with the vendor. Unless the vendor evolves its customer management

Professor Das Narayandas prepared this note.

strategy, misalignment between its customer management efforts and customers' expectations and needs will amplify resulting in customer dissatisfaction and possible defection and reduced prices and profitability for the vendor.

A firm's customer management strategy can also be affected by technological and environmental changes. The recent explosion in inexpensive and rich customer information and customer interaction opportunities has enabled marketers to shift from a transactional approach that emphasizes individual exchanges to the management of customer relationships over time. Firms can now leverage customer-level information to develop strategies to manage relationships and individual interactions with each and every one of their customers. But markets and industries need to temper their enthusiasm for building long-term relationships with all customers. Recently there have several reports about Mobil's successful launch of its Speedpass™, whereby customers can pay for gasoline purchases by simply waving a wand in front of the pump. Although this might be deemed a significant value added by most customers, for others concerns about sharing a great deal of personal information with a gasoline vendor might far outweigh the benefit of quicker payments at the gas pumps. Depending on their resistance level to the firm's efforts, it might not make economic sense for Mobil to expend effort and convince the latter type of customers to ever use the Speedpass™. In fact, Mobil might find its interests to be better served by learning the art of managing a spectrum of customers from those who prefer anonymity to buy just gasoline to those that are willing to share personal information in exchange for the convenience of waving a wand at the pump to buy not just gasoline, but also other products stocked in the stations' food marts.

The Customer Management Process

The foregoing examples suggest that firms need to have a clear cut, well-defined approach to managing their customer relationships. Typically, the customer management process entails:

- selecting the portfolio of customers to serve and developing a corresponding portfolio of customer management strategies, and
- monitoring the health of customer relationships over time in order to link their customer management effort to economic reward, i.e., customer profitability. How well a firm monitors the health of customer relationships will determine the degree to which it is able to quantify the costs and benefits associated with customer relationship, which, in turn, will influence its decision about which customers to continue to serve.

Selecting Customers

Marketing strategy has always emphasized the importance of market selection. With a lot at stake, including enormous investments of resources, firms spend significant amounts of time in defining the businesses they are in. Customer selection requires the same discipline since every customer can have a significant impact on a vendor's profits.

The familiar phrase "known by the company one keeps" is very apropos to customers. Firms need to be mindful that their choice of customers defines their skill set over time (*Whom we serve affects who we are*) and, in turn, their abilities affect their choice of customers (*Who we are affects whom we can serve*).

Through a rash of opportunistic customer selection decisions, Fabtek landed in an anomalous situation of operating unprofitably at full capacity with dissatisfied customers that were complaining about project delays. Recollecting the case details, Refco, Fabtek's largest customer, represented an opportunity to produce in much larger volumes a product similar in design to past orders, and put Fabtek at risk of becoming too dependent on a single customer relationship. The second opportunity, an order from Pierce-Pike, which had done business primarily with Fabtek's competitors, represented the culmination of a four-year sales effort by Fabtek's head of sales. An order from Worldwide Paper for a line of proprietary products that could potentially be developed into a standard product line presented an opportunity for Fabtek to shift from custom orders and a job-shop environment to standardized orders manufactured on a production line. The final opportunity, an order from Kathco for titanium electrodes, was a "one-shot" deal that would not tax Fabtek's specialist titanium welding capability, its current resource constraint. That Fabtek's capacity and capabilities affect the orders it can satisfactorily serve highlights the point that *"who we are affects whom we can serve,"* and the fact that each order was likely to pull Fabtek in a different direction calls to mind the dictum *"who we serve affects who we are."*

Recognition of the interplay between customer choice and skill set leads to an appreciation for the following:

- Customers are not orders;
- Different customers play different roles and need to be managed differently.

Customer Selection Is Different from Order Selection

In the real world customers typically turn up at vendors' doorsteps in the form of orders. But customer selection is not the same as order selection. Customer choice is based on a firm's long-term strategic vision and affects its skill set (*What business are we in?*). Order selection affects vendor capacity and tends to be decided on the basis of resource constraints (*Where are the bottlenecks? What are the shortfalls? What can we do in the short-term?*).

If not managed appropriately, this disconnect, can occasion inter-functional conflict between marketing and manufacturing with marketing loading up the plant with wrong orders in the ill-informed pursuit of the right set of customers and manufacturing trying to establish discipline at order-level without considering the long-term implications of its decisions on customer choice. This exact conflict led to Fabtek's unenviable circumstance of losing money while operating at capacity.

Customers and Orders

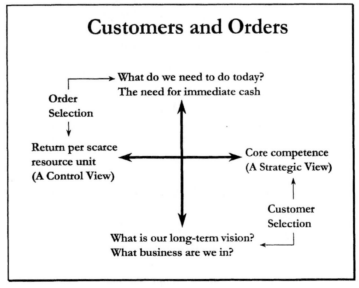

Source: Author.

The disconnect between orders and customers complicates matters for vendors that would prefer to receive good orders from good customers and avoid bad orders from bad customers. But as often firms need to decide on bad orders from good customers and good orders from bad customers. The logic put forward for accepting a bad order from a good customer is for the vendor to preserve its relationship with a good customer. Yet, firms might be better off avoiding the bad orders that do not fit with their skill set.

Taking a good order from a bad customer could be viewed as an opportunity to gouge a customer in the short run. Vendors of commodity products like DRAM chips that are subject to spikes and troughs in demand and supply sometimes opportunistically raise their prices when selling to customers that they would not traditionally have served. Yet, firms need to be careful of the long-term reputation effects of such a gouging strategy.

Different Customers Play Different Roles and Need to Be Managed Differently

The second important issue related to the selection decision is the fact that customers in vendors' portfolios play different roles and need to be managed differently. In every vendor's customer portfolio, there are different customer types. Coke, for example, can segment cola drinkers into those that are loyal to Coke (or Pepsi) and those that switch across brands. Here the different customer types are defined by individual customers' orientation towards the various cola brands. Given a market share protection orientation, Coke could view its loyal customers as a source of predictable revenues and consider it vital to ensure the longevity of such a revenue stream. In such a case, Coke would want to reward its loyal customers periodically for the favorable behavior (regular purchase of only Coke products) by selectively offering such customers a price break. Fabtek's dilemma with the Refco, its largest customer is based on the same issue of managing a loyal customer. It is also possible for a firm to potentially view its relationships with its loyal customers to be very strong and to extract some of the equity it has created by raising prices charged to such customers.

It is important to note that the definition of loyalty can vary depending on the circumstances. For example, Hunter defined its loyal customers (the Gold accounts) as customers that purchased a minimum amount of each of the categories sold by the firm. The rationale behind such a definition was that the firm believed it could build deeper and sustainable relationships with customers that purchased all product categories. Harrah's defined customer loyalty based on volume and frequency of usage given that heavy users accounted for a significant portion of its sales and profits. It was critical for Harrah's to not only identify such customers, but to also design and deliver superior and customized products and services that would bring these customers back to the firm.

The variety of approaches that Coke, Hunter, and Harrah's could use to manage relationships with their loyal customers highlights the fact that beyond the customer selection decision, it is also important for the vendor firm to design appropriate relationship management strategies. When should the firm take a long-term view of the relationship? How should it customize its products and services to serve its special customers (and at a more general level, its various customer types)? When would it be preferable to adopt a transactional view?

Developing Customer Management Strategies to Maximize Customer Profitability

The process of designing appropriate customer management strategies that enhance customer value and maximize customer profitability begins with an understanding of customer needs and behavior. Specifically, a firm needs to identify underlying dimensions that explain differences in needs and behavior of the customer portfolio it serves (or plans to serve). The decisions to be made go beyond designing individual products and managing the product line, to include the associated marketing effort (including pricing, communications, and go-to-market strategies). The next step is to anticipate how customers' needs are expected to evolve and regularly update customer management strategies.

Hunter and Harrah's highlight different approaches to maximizing customer profitability. By definition, profits are the difference between customer response (sales revenues) and the vendor's costs-to-serve the customer. Profits can therefore be increased either by increasing revenues or decreasing selling effort. Harrah's is an example of the former and Hunter an example of the latter.

Harrah's focused on managing its sales and marketing effort to provide customized programs that increased its customers' usage levels. The emphasis in this case was more on top-line growth rather than the management of costs-to-serve individual customers, i.e., customer profitability was enhanced through revenue increases leading to top-line growth rather than the management of costs incurred in serving the customers.

The opposite was true with Hunter. Here, the market conditions forced the firm to accept the fact that revenues were expected to decline over time. Rather than trying to swim against the tide, Hunter's approach was built around managing costs given the trend in revenues. This was achieved by appropriate reductions of the various elements of the firm's customer management effort including direct sales calls, mailings, and telephone contact. It is important to note that the firm reduced its customer management effort without negatively affecting the revenue stream and therefore maximized current and future customer profitability.

While their approaches to maximizing customer profitability were different, the two firms were similar in the way they monitored the health of their customer relationships using a combination of actual customer behaviors (for example, revenues generated) and customer attitudes and intent (for example, satisfaction surveys). By having a finger on the pulse of the relationship, each firm was able to make appropriate changes in the way it managed its customer relationships and maximized customer profitability.

Potential Issues in Managing Individual Customer Profitability

Choices among investment opportunities typically rely on evaluations of anticipated return on investments (ROI) and associated risks. The same logic must be applied to investments in customer management strategies. To accurately calculate customer profitability and remove inefficiencies in current customer management efforts firms need information about the impact of individual actions on the revenue generated and costs incurred in a customer relationship. Linking specific elements of the customer management effort with the customer revenue stream enables firms to isolate and remove inefficiencies in the customer management effort.

In addition to the lack of precision in measuring costs incurred in serving individual customers, the lag between vendor effort and customer response, coupled with the cumulative effect of vendor actions on customer response, can thwart attempts to isolate cause-effect relationships between different elements of vendor effort and corresponding customer responses. The best option under these circumstances is to calculate an overall ROI for total customer management effort during a specified period of time using a simplified, albeit reasonable, approach, namely, by taking the difference between the net present value (NPV) of a customer's purchases and anticipated costs of serving the customer divided by the costs. Vendors can use such information to decide whether or not to remain in a given customer relationship and whether to change the nature and level of their customer management effort. Although sophistication of NPV models makes them excellent tools for valuing customers, the value of the models reflects the accuracy of the data inputs.

Chapter 37

Fabtek (A)

Benson P. Shapiro   Rowland T. Moriarty   Craig E. Cline

In mid-June 1991, the senior management of Fabtek's Fabrication Division was grappling with a problem unprecedented in the company's 15-year history. Because of an acute shortage of capacity and increasing customer dissatisfaction with late deliveries, the company's marketing vice president, Amy Vitali, and the Fabrication Division's vice president of operations, Rob Lightfoot, had to agree on which of four potential orders the company should accept and how it should bid on them. Each of the orders represented a different customer situation, mix of labor and materials, and mix of manufacturing talents, so a direct comparison among them was difficult. Stanley Ho, Fabtek's president, had advised them to work it out themselves, but reminded them that a quick decision was necessary "if we're going to be able to fit *any* of them into our shop schedule."

Fabrication Division

Early History

The Fabrication Division was the second-largest industrial fabricator of titanium in the United States. Corporate and sales offices for the company, as well as its primary fabricating facility, were located in Philadelphia.

Fabtek was one of the first companies to provide titanium products for industrial use. Before the mid-1970s, titanium had been used almost exclusively in the aerospace industry because of its light weight and high strength. It wasn't until the price dropped (from $20 per pound for some alloys used in aerospace to $5 per pound for industrial titanium sheet and plate) and its corrosion resistance was demonstrated, however, that titanium became competitive for some applications with stainless steel, copper and nickel alloys, brick-lined steel, fiberglass, and other products used to counter corrosion. Even in 1991, titanium won the industrial applications battle only if (1) it could outlast competitive metals to such an extent that it was less expensive overall or (2) it was the only industrial metal that could do

Professor Benson P. Shapiro, Professor Rowland T. Moriarty, and Research Assistant Craig E. Cline prepared this case as the basis for class discussion rather than to illustrate either effective or ineffective handling of an administrative situation. All industry and company data have been disguised.

the job. Nevertheless, Ho was enthusiastic about titanium's potential and estimated that its industrial use would grow by 15% to 20% per year during the foreseeable future.

Growth

From its inception, Fabtek's principal business was fabrication of titanium equipment for industrial corrosion-resistant applications. The company had little involvement in the aerospace industry. Over time it added technical staff, participated in industry symposia, sponsored technical papers, and studied developing titanium markets. Active consulting and field services, such as field repairs and corrosion analysis, developed from these efforts.

In addition to the fabricating business, Fabtek sold titanium metal and specialty hardware (pipe fittings, bolts, nuts, pipe flanges) to the industrial market. The two organizations shared a common raw materials inventory. The corporation also purchased titanium in ingot and semifinished form and converted it (using steel mills that rented time on their machinery on a price-per-pound basis) to finished product forms, such as bars or plates. As business expanded, these activities were separated into a materials profit center that included metal trading, warehousing, and conversion.

In 1986 and again in 1988 capacity expansions were made in Philadelphia and efforts toward geographic expansion followed. During the 1980s a subsidiary was formed in Montreal, a branch was opened in Texas to serve the petrochemical markets, and a small, bankrupt titanium wire mill was acquired. In addition, a small subsidiary was formed in Brazil to take advantage of the rapid expansion of basic industries, such as pulp, occurring there. (**Exhibit 1** provides corporate financial data.)

Organization

Operations was headed by Rob Lightfoot (who previously had been involved in Fabtek's marketing area). It consisted of two engineers who evaluated customer product designs to

EXHIBIT 1
Corporate Financial Summary, 1988–1990

	1990	1989	1988
Net sales	$31,155,402	$26,317,527	$23,137,485
Expenses			
Cost of sales and engineering	26,351,184	22,077,768	18,604,803
SG&A	4,587,780	3,089,676	2,141,031
Interest, net	529,023	301,479	228,462
	$31,467,987	$25,468,923	$20,974,296
Income (loss) before provision (credit) for taxes on income and minority interest in subsidiary	(312,585)	848,604	2,163,189
Taxes on income	(179,400)	417,600	1,017,300
Net income before minority interest in subsidiary	$ (133,185)	$ 431,004	$ 1,145,889
Minority interest in subsidiary	(11,145)	22,791	0
Net income	$ (144,330)	$ 453,795	$ 1,145,889
Financial Position			
Current assets	22,170,168	13,502,616	13,072,680
Working capital	641,322	976,062	1,997,385
Property and equipment, net	2,129,571	1,510,308	848,172
Inventories[a]			
Raw materials	6,496,350	5,215,398	4,832,166
Work-in-progress	8,898,744	4,282,422	4,909,455
Long-term debt	535,278	831,000	822,000
Stockholders' equity	2,654,223	2,798,553	2,326,758

[a]Inventory is stated at the lower of cost (substantially on a first-in, first-out basis) or market.

determine the best manufacturing processes; two drafting people; two estimators who calculated the cost of manufacture for pricing; and several administrative and clerical people. In addition, Operations' shop, which was nonunion, had 78 employees in three sections: fabrication, welding, and the machine shop. Additional fabrication capacity was available in the Texas and Montreal facilities, but these were primarily intended to serve their respective regional markets and were operating at full capacity through 1991.

Fabtek's marketing organization was headed by Amy Vitali; it included two regional managers located in Philadelphia and Texas, the titanium metal sales group, and a customer service function. In addition, the company was represented by several manufacturers' representatives who operated both in the United States and abroad.[1] (**Exhibit 2** shows the organization chart.)

Markets and Customers

Fabtek had over 90 significant customers in 11 markets:

1. General chemicals—pressure vessels, tanks, heat exchangers, shafts and mixers, pumps, valves, piping, blowers, anodes for chlorine.
2. Pulp and paper—bleaching equipment, chemical preparation vessels, piping.
3. Basic metals—cathodes for copper, vessels for hydrometallurgy.
4. Petroleum—heat exchangers for refineries, down-hole equipment, hot-oil coolers for production.
5. Pollution—heat exchangers, vessels, and pipe for municipal waste oxidation; air scrubbers, blowers.
6. Fibers—chemical equipment for various polymer intermediate products.
7. Water desalinization—heat exchangers, tubing, piping.
8. Marine activities—high-voltage undersea electrical connectors, diver rescue chambers, research submarine components.
9. Electric power generation—tubes for surface condensers.
10. Food—corrosion-resistant equipment for pickle solutions.
11. High-performance toys—12-meter sailboat parts, race cars, golf clubs.

The majority of Fabtek's customers were located within a 500-mile radius of Philadelphia, but the firm also shipped worldwide. Customer orders ranged from $75 to $6 million, with $150,000 being typical. Approximately 20% of Fabtek's customers provided 80% of its business.

Close business and personal relationships existed between the Fabtek staff and certain customers who gave Fabtek a considerable percentage of their titanium business. One customer, Refco, typically represented 15% to 20% of sales each year. Two other companies accounted for 10% to 15% of sales on a fairly regular basis. In early 1990, Fabtek's management established a corporate policy of allowing a maximum of 20% of its business to reside with one customer and 30% to be in one market area.

Competition

Fabtek had five major competitors, none of which was located in the immediate area. The largest was in Ohio and had annual sales of $49.5 million. The others were scattered across the country and had annual sales of between $6 million and $30 million in competitive

---

[1] A manufacturers' representative was an independent company or salesperson who sold products of related but noncompeting companies for commissions on the sales.

EXHIBIT 2 Fabtek's Organization Chart

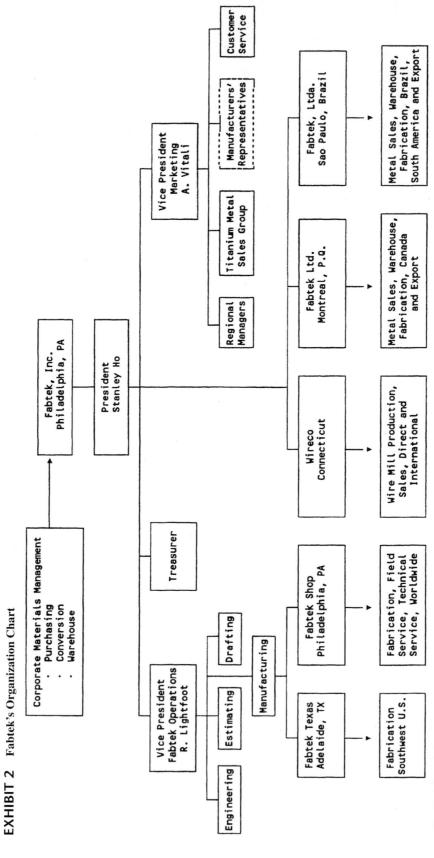

Note: The intimate ties between the Fabricating Division's Operations and the rest of the company make it impossible to separate the Fabtek organization from that of the Fabrication Division.

titanium work, with $18 million being average. Fabtek had an estimated 16% share of a total industrial titanium fabrication market of just under $150 million. It had a reputation for a higher quality, but also a higher price, than most of its competitors.

Forecasts

Fabtek's sales and equity had grown steadily from 1985 to 1988, but 1989 sales were disappointing. In 1990, despite record sales of $31.2 million, the company experienced its first net loss. Management felt that the 1989 and 1990 results were more a consequence of erratic pricing and unstable market conditions than internal problems. The titanium industry had been operating at a significantly lower level than in 1987 and 1988. Capital spending on process equipment, refinery expansion, pulp and paper projects, and chemical construction had been well below anticipated levels in 1990 and was not expected to increase significantly in 1991.

Manufacturing Process

Although titanium had several fabricating peculiarities that required special skills, some operations—such as shearing, machine work, and forming—closely paralleled those used in precision fabrication of certain stainless steels.[2] In fact, the company often was able to subcontract excess machine work to local precision machine shops. Heat treatment, thermal cutting, and especially welding were generally considered the most difficult operations. Because titanium was a "reactive" metal, it was easily embrittled by increases in its gas content (primarily oxygen and nitrogen, but also most other elements). Melting titanium, such as in welding, or heating it above 1,200°F, caused it to react instantly with air, absorbing oxygen and nitrogen and becoming brittle and useless. Consequently, cleanliness and special inert-gas welding techniques were required to produce good welds.

Fabtek used its strong competence in welding as a major selling point. One executive noted, "We feel that our expertise lies in high-quality welding. Over 80% of our jobs involve welding." This reputation for outstanding welding was supported routinely by radiographic, ultrasonic, and liquid penetration inspection of each weld.

The company had 33 welders who were graded from A to D, according to their ability to handle difficult work. In addition, Fabtek had several automatic welding machines. Finally, various helpers and trainees assisted the welders. (Shop capacity is shown in **Exhibit 3.**)

Costs

Generally a product's cost had five components, with manufacturing overhead averaging about 200% of direct labor cost:

Component	Range	Average
Raw material	30–65%	45%
Direct labor	5–20	9
Manufacturing overhead	10–40	18
Subcontracting	10–15	12
General and administrative costs and profit	10–25	16

The company's objective was to have cost of goods average 80%, with 85% the upper limit.

[2] Shearing was cutting titanium sheets to a specified size. Machining used lathes, mills, drills, and other chip-forming high-precision tools to obtain close tolerances. Forming, done on plate or bar rolls or on a press brake, bent the item to its ultimate shape.

EXHIBIT 3
Fabtek's Operations'
Shop Capacity

	Number of People		
	Day Shift	Night Shift	Total
Welding			
Welder A	7	3	10
Welder B	3	1	4
Welder C	5	6	11
Welder D	6	2	8
Trainee	2	—	2
Helper	7	7	14
Auto A	1	1	2
Auto B	—	—	—
Auto C	2	2	4
Auto trainee	1	—	1
			56
Fabrication			
Layout mechanic	2		2
Mechanic	2		2
Fab A	1		1
Fab B	1		1
Trainee	4		4
Helper	3		3
			13
Machine Shop[a]			
Machinist 1st Class	3	—	3
Machinist 2nd Class	1	—	1
Operator A	1	—	1
Operator B	2	1	3
Trainee	1	—	1
			9

[a]Additional machine capacity could be obtained through subcontracting.

Existing Situation

Shop backlog had reached a critical level in June 1991 (see **Exhibit 4**). This was the first time the company's booking exceeded its capacity by a significant margin. Delivery history for the past several months had been, in the word of one Operations executive, "horrendous." Although routine orders were going out on time, most major or complex jobs were late. Delivery times had increased from an average of 8–10 weeks in 1987 to 16–60 weeks, depending on complexity and size, in 1990. Another Operations executive added, "The main reason many customers are still coming back to us is our quality. There also aren't many other people who fabricate titanium."

According to a third Operations official, one factor underlying Fabtek's capacity problem was the difficulty the company had hiring and training qualified welders.

The labor market around Philadelphia and our need for highly skilled workers make it difficult to find new people, especially because we can't offer much higher than average pay. The competition's shops are generally located in less expensive areas, and we must be careful to keep our labor costs competitive. Even hiring a new welder as part of our regular work force is difficult. If we're lucky, we can find one or two a month. Then it takes between two months and two years to train them to be A level, depending on whether they were welders before. For many jobs the welders must also qualify under the ASME Boiler Code, which is expensive but necessary for A and B level welders. This situation is even more critical because the majority of our jobs require A and B level welding.

EXHIBIT 4 Fabtek's Shop Schedule as of June 1991

	June 1991			July 1991			August 1991			September 1991		
	W[a]	M[a]	F[a]	W	M	F	W	M	F	W	M	F
Backlog	7,200	1,670	2,350	6,800	1,040	2,050	4,200	900	1,050	4,200	1,100	1,050
Capacity	6,920	1,560	2,250	6,920	1,560	2,250	6,920	1,560	2,250	6,920	1,560	2,250
Difference	(280)	(110)	(100)	120	520	200	2,720	660	1,200	2,720	460	1,200
Cumulative	(280)	(110)	(100)	(160)	410	100	2,560	1,070	1,300	5,280	1,530	2,500

	October 1991			November 1991			December 1991			January 1992		
	W	M	F	W	M	F	W	M	F	W	M	F
Backlog	5,000	1,350	1,500	4,120	1,300	1,070	4,700	700	800	5,000	400	1,350
Capacity	6,920	1,560	2,250	6,920	1,560	2,250	6,920	1,560	2,250	6,920	1,560	2,250
Difference	1,920	210	750	2,800	260	1,180	2,220	860	1,450	1,920	1,160	900
Cumulative	7,200	1,740	3,250	10,000	2,000	4,430	12,220	2,860	5,880	14,140	4,020	6,780

	February 1992			March 1992			April 1992			May 1992			Total		
	W	M	F	W	M	F	W	M	F	W	M	F	W	M	F
Backlog	4,050	560	1,150	4,220	660	1,500	4,300	750	1,350	4,300	640	1,020	58,090	11,070	16,240
Capacity	6,920	1,560	2,250	6,920	1,560	2,250	6,920	1,560	2,250	6,920	1,560	2,250	83,040	18,720	27,000
Difference	2,870	1,000	1,100	2,700	900	750	2,620	810	900	2,620	920	1,230	24,950	7,650	10,760
Cumulative	17,010	5,020	7,880	19,710	5,920	8,630	22,330	6,730	9,530	24,950	7,650	10,760	24,950	7,650	10,760

Notes:

Welding and fabrication helpers and trainees were each counted as 50% of a regular welder or fabricator for planning purposes.

Data assume each welder, machinist, and fabricator works 2,080 hours per year.

[a]W = Welders

M = Machinists

F = Fabricators

This official felt, however, that the major underlying factor was Fabtek's lack of reliable information on the shop's actual capacity at any given moment.

> In the past, Marketing would ask us if we had capacity available for a job before they quoted on it. But in recent months late material deliveries and problems on two major jobs have swelled our backlog, which has extended delivery dates on existing jobs. These fill the capacity Marketing thought would be open for the jobs we had just bid, thereby pushing ahead *their* delivery dates. Consequently, Marketing no longer believes our capacity forecasts; they simply go ahead and book the order for the longest delivery they can get away with, which, of course, adds to our capacity problem. It's a vicious cycle.

Lightfoot concurred with his subordinates; he felt Marketing only recently had become realistic about the capacity limit and thus willing to work with Operations to improve the company's delivery schedule. He observed:

> We started Fabtek because we were excited by what we could do in the industrial market. In fact, Stanley Ho has made it our basic operating philosophy "to make money by moving titanium." It's been fun, and that's largely what kept us going—until now. At present we are faced with declining profits and a delivery crisis. Something has to be done, and perhaps being more selective in taking orders will do it.

From an Operations standpoint, he felt several criteria could make an order attractive:

1. The job is technically challenging.
2. The job fits with Fabtek's high-quality image and capabilities.
3. The company's engineering expertise is utilized.
4. The job is long-run and repetitive.
5. The company has experience with similar products.
6. Specifications and job scope are clear.
7. For larger orders, progress payments can be negotiated (payments made on labor and material as applied, over the course of the contract, rather than all at the end).
8. Overall contribution before S,G&A (sales, general and administrative expenses) is near 20% of the product's price.

Marketing

Fabtek's fabrication and titanium metal sales were under the direction of Amy Vitali in Marketing. She spent an estimated 60% of her time on fabrication sales and the remainder on metal sales. Similarly, the two regional sales managers each devoted 10% of their time to fabrication sales, and a manufacturers' representative in California handled both fabricated products and titanium metal sales. Generally, however, Fabtek relied on advertising in trade publications, participation in industry symposia, and trade shows for fabrication sales. Also, Ho, Lightfoot, Vitali, and other staff people who had close relationships with customers usually handled their accounts personally. Lightfoot, for example, had close ties with certain Refco officials and thus handled all but the smallest details of this account. As one executive observed, "Most of the management people here have two or three job functions, and almost anyone can make a sale."

Bidding Process

One of the principal tasks of the people in Marketing and Sales was to make sure that Fabtek was on the bid lists of potential customers. Once a request for a quote was received, Marketing sent it to Operations for estimating (to obtain a quote as well as an estimated delivery date). Marketing then modified the quote to reflect market conditions and corporate goals.

The company had a bid success rate of 15%. Vitali felt this percentage was somewhat low compared with the industry average, but pointed out that only one of seven requests for quotes was "solid." She thought a more serious problem was the price competitiveness that had recently gripped the market, forcing Fabtek to play pricing games.

> Our aggressive posture has been a reaction to forces in the market more than a philosophy. As the titanium market stabilizes, which I'm sure it will eventually do, we will be better able to formulate an effective rather than a freewheeling, reactive strategy about taking orders. This is a serious concern of mine, because we haven't been able to maintain market share in the last year. We've got to pick our shots better—but we can only become more selective if we get the opportunity to call the shots.

Possible Changes

Vitali felt that the company had to become more selective about the high-risk custom jobs it took; she was also in favor of diversifying Fabtek's business among customers and markets. "We have an excellent relationship with Refco, but what do we do if they represent 30% to 40% of our business and then suddenly stop sending us orders?" She believed Fabtek would eventually move away from custom fabrication and become more involved in developing proprietary products. She also felt that the company had to determine its costs more accurately. "We've got to target our markets better to be sure we are using our resources to their maximum potential." To do this, she felt that Marketing had to get better information out of Fabtek's Operations concerning costs and capacity availability.

Vitali's preferred criteria for taking an order were as follows:

1. The job is similar to what Fabtek had built before.
2. The design is simple and the cost estimate reliable.
3. The job has good payment terms (progress payments on labor and material as applied).
4. The market area has potential for further development.
5. The job allows adequate delivery time.
6. Price is not the primary factor in the customer's decision.

The Four Prospective Fabrication Orders

In mid-June 1991 Vitali and Lightfoot met to decide whether to accept each of the prospective orders: Refco, Pierce-Pike, Worldwide Paper, and Kathco. Prices were fixed for the larger two orders but still had to be determined for the smaller two. In addition, both Vitali and Lightfoot had been uneasy about the entire bidding process and wondered if it should be changed. Lightfoot, for example, thought perhaps the company should expect a greater markup on labor than on materials. He went on to explain that the material cost estimates tended to be much more reliable than the labor estimates. He mused:

> I think that we should be paid more for the greater uncertainty of the labor estimates. Overruns on costs—almost solely labor costs—were a prime reason for our poor 1990 profit performance. Right now our bidding procedure makes no differentiation between labor and materials. Maybe the customer should pay for some of the uncertainty in labor costs through a higher markup.

Exhibit 5 shows cost estimates and **Exhibit 6** the projected shop load for each order.

Refco

Refco, Fabtek's largest single customer, was one of the world's leading engineering contractors. Refco and its competitors (for example, Bechtel, Brown and Root, and others) designed and constructed large projects around the world. Like most contractors, Refco specialized—concentrating on petroleum refineries and petrochemical plants.

EXHIBIT 5   Cost Estimates for the Four Prospective Orders

	Refco (petroleum refining)		Pierce-Pike (wastewater treatment)		Worldwide Paper (paper)	Kathco (electrodes)
Selling price	$6,000,000		$3,900,000		≈$2,400,000??	≈$1,500,000??
Material	2,100,000	(35%)	2,250,000	(58%)	1,080,000	960,000
Labor						
Welding	600,000		105,000		132,000	
Machining	156,000		18,000		15,000	30,000
Fabrication	99,000		42,000		45,000	60,000
Total labor	$ 855,000	(14%)	$ 165,000	(4%)	$ 192,000	$ 90,000
Factory overhead	1,710,000	(29)	330,000	(8)	384,000	180,000
Subcontracting	300,000	(5)	390,000	(10)	450,000	—
Total factory cost	$4,965,000	(83%)	$3,135,000	(80%)	$2,106,000	$1,230,000
Contribution (before SG&A)[a]	$1,035,000	(17%)	$ 765,000	(20%)	≈$294,000??	≈$270,000??

[a]Sales, general and administrative expenses.

Note: "≈" means approximately.

Several years earlier Refco had developed a specialized piece of machinery to perform certain refinery operations under demanding pressure, temperature, and corrosion conditions. Refco had supplied many of the units in stainless steel, but corrosion failures and increasing corrosive process requirements caused a gradual shift to titanium. The units, nicknamed *Whoppers* because of their large size and hamburger shape, had to be made to exact tolerances and with great care in welding. Fabtek had worked closely with Refco in developing the design. From time to time, Refco also had come to Fabtek for other titanium pieces—usually large process vessels, such as reactors, requiring a good deal of welding and fabrication. As far as Fabtek's management could ascertain, Fabtek was the only outside titanium fabricator in the world that Refco used. On the other hand, Refco did some in-house fabrication of superalloys and titanium at its large Rotterdam manufacturing facility.

As an engineering contractor, Refco had a trained staff of field welders and welding supervisors; however, they did little titanium work because of the unique properties of the metal. Industry rumors that Refco would set up a fabricating facility for superalloys and titanium had been circulating for the past four years. According to Lightfoot (who, among Fabtek's managers, knew Refco best), Refco's executives were totally unwilling to discuss this possibility except with "Cheshire cat-like smiles." Lightfoot believed Refco was unhappy about Fabtek's long delivery schedule and occasional late deliveries and doubted its ability to handle very large requirements expected in the future.

In May 1991, Refco had come to Fabtek with a request for production of an above-size Whopper, which soon became known as a *Super Whopper*. The purchasing/subcontracting specialists at Refco stated that they were willing to pay $6 million. Refco had offered to pay for 80% of direct "material and labor as applied" in four installments. Thus, each time 25% of the work was done, Fabtek would receive 20% of the cost of materials and direct labor. Thirty days after delivery Fabtek would be paid for the completed piece. (Refco always paid its bills on time.)

To be completed on time, the Super Whopper would have to enter production at Fabtek in June. It was certain that the first progress payment, and perhaps the second, would come in Fabtek's 1991 fiscal year, which ended in October.

In 1990, Refco had purchased $4.5 million worth of products from Fabtek. Not counting the Super Whopper order, its 1991 purchases from Fabtek were expected to be $6 million (out of Fabtek's projected $36 million in sales).

EXHIBIT 6   Projected Shop Load for the Four Prospective Orders

	Refco			Pierce-Pike			Worldwide Paper			Kathco		
	W[a]	M[a]	F[a]	W	M	F	W	M	F	W	M	F
1991												
June	100	100	—	50	50	—	—	—	—	—	—	—
July	1,500	600	—	1,400	100	—	1,000	200	—	—	400	1,800
August	2,000	700	—	1,150	100	50	1,000	300	400	—	600	800
September	1,800	200	—	1,000	50	150	1,000	200	500	—	200	900
October	1,900	100	500	1,200	50	250	2,000	130	1,000	—	200	700
November	2,000	200	500	1,000	100	300	1,000	—	600	—	200	700
December	2,000	700	1,000	600	300	350	1,000	—	—	—	100	—
1992												
January	2,000	800	1,000	500	250	500	650	—	450	—	—	—
February	2,000	600	1,000	—	—	500	—	—	—	—	—	—
March	2,500	600	1,000	—	—	500	—	—	—	—	—	—
April	2,500	800	500	—	—	150	—	—	—	—	—	—
May	2,500	500	500	—	—	—	—	—	—	—	—	—
Post-May	12,000	2,800	500	—	—	—	—	—	—	—	—	—
Total	34,800	8,700	6,500	6,900	1,000	2,750	7,650	830	2,950	—	1,700	4,900

[a] W = Welders
M = Machinists
F = Fabricators

Pierce-Pike

For almost four years Vitali had been pursuing business with Pierce-Pike, a company that specialized in constructing proprietary wastewater treatment plants. Pierce-Pike was the subsidiary of a large chemical company and had developed a strong position in a rapidly growing market. Until early April 1991, it had shown no interest in giving business to Fabtek. All its work was shared by Fabtek's largest competitor and its number-four competitor in the market.

In April, Vitali had received a request for proposal on a pressurized reactor from Pierce-Pike. She was ecstatic; it represented a partial victory, or at least some interest, following a long battle. After some difficult pricing decisions, Vitali quoted $3.9 million on the job, although she had some concern about whether Fabtek could do the job in the hours estimated. The reactor involved some unusual fabrication with which Fabtek was inexperienced. On the other hand, both Vitali and Lightfoot had decided it was important to develop this capability.

On June 13, Fabtek received the order, which it could refuse. Its original quote had contained a note indicating that Fabtek might not have enough capacity to fill the order. Vitali believed Pierce-Pike's two existing sources had capacity available, but she had heard that Pierce-Pike was unhappy with the quality of both, especially the larger one. Also, Pierce-Pike was willing to make progress payments only on raw material.

Worldwide Paper

Worldwide Paper was a large integrated producer of pulp, paper, and fabricated paper products. In the late 1980s, its process development laboratory had tested a new piece of equipment made entirely of titanium. The scale-up to pilot plant and small production units had gone smoothly. Now, Worldwide was putting its first full-sized production unit out for bid. Although earlier units had been made of less-corrosion-resistant materials, this one was to be made of titanium. From Vitali's point of view, this order had a particularly interesting facet:

> For some time we have been anxious to develop a line of proprietary items. It would ease our management task and enable us to train employees on standard work, which is less demanding than custom work. It would smooth our work flow and enable us to begin to develop a sales force. Right now we don't have a standard product line, so we can't have a regular sales force.
>
> Worldwide is willing to license this item to its manufacturer. If we get the bid, we can then develop it into a standard product line. There is little opportunity for customization in the primary part of the unit, so it could be a standard product.

Lightfoot was equally excited about acquiring or developing a standard product line. In addition, he saw the opportunity to add a new capability to Fabtek's operation:

> The $450,000 subcontracting involved is for special heat treatment. It is going to cost us that much because we have to move very large parts between our plant and the subcontractor. Furthermore, this subcontractor is really taking advantage of us, because they are one of the very few facilities that can do this type of heat treating. If we made the piece as a standard product line—even at a relatively low volume—we could develop the heat-treating competence in-house with a payback of a matter of months, including the transportation savings.

Vitali suspected that the cost estimators had been very conservative in their calculations. She could not be sure of the prices that competitors would offer, but she believed the $2.4 million range to be about right. She stated, "Someone will come in lower—probably in the $2.1 million range. A couple may be at $2.25 million. But we have the quality to command some sort of premium over our competitors."

This order offered no progress payments but required a penalty of 0.1% of the contract price for each working day that the complete order was late. There was no incentive for early delivery.

Kathco

The fourth order was fairly straightforward. Kathco was a metal refinery that manufactured its own titanium electrodes for purifying manganese. In the spring and summer of 1991 its sales were high. During 1991 the company had a new electrode production facility under construction. Construction was delayed, so Kathco had an important shortfall in its electrode availability.

Kathco had solicited bids from only Fabtek and one competitor because it knew the companies well. Fabtek had a good relationship with Kathco. But this order was clearly a "one-shot deal": Once Kathco's plant was operating, it could supply all of Kathco's needs.

Other Considerations

Fabtek also made money by buying, warehousing, and selling titanium. The added volume from any one of these orders would affect all metal purchases. The total effect was difficult to predict because of changes in the metal suppliers' strategy and pricing, but it was generally considered good for the company. As a rule, net profit varied from nothing to about 4% of material cost estimates. Gross profit was a little higher but varied substantially.

The shop capacity estimates considered only the availability of labor on a straight-time, two-shift basis (that is, during normal working hours). It was possible to have people work overtime, although some resented it—especially in the summer. Overtime was expensive (150% of regular labor rates) and usually resulted in lower productivity and quality. Over the short run, however, it was the only feasible way to increase capacity. Skilled third-shift personnel were unlikely to be available, at least in the near future. More important, Fabtek's limited facility size might make overtime or a third shift impractical, because there would be no room to store work in process.

Chapter

38

Hunter Business Group: *TeamTBA*

Das Narayandas   Elizabeth Caputo

Sometimes you have a secondary product line that is moving in a direction different from that of the firm . . . You think that everything is OK, that it is just an incremental business, but in fact, it becomes more like an anchor. . . .

—*Vic Hunter, Chairman and CEO, Hunter Business Group*

Such was the dilemma that Star Oil faced during the summer of 1992. Its tire, battery, and accessory (TBA) business, the "ugly stepchild" of its gasoline station services division, was now unprofitable and consuming valuable field resources. Its downward trend in profitability had led to a growing sentiment within the firm toward abandoning Star's branded TBA business. Yet, a recent survey of the firm's service stations produced a surprise finding. Customers who had their cars serviced at the 2,200 U.S. gasoline service stations[1] selling Star-branded TBA products bought four times more gasoline than those who bought only gasoline there. This suggested that Star's branded TBA products played a strategic role in boosting Star's gasoline sales. The decision to exit the TBA business, therefore, no longer appeared easy. In the face of increasing competition, Star could not afford an erosion of customer loyalty that might damage its well-known brand. However, the unprofitable

---

[1] Gasoline service stations typically had one or more service bays in addition to multiple self-serve and full service gasoline pumps. Based on the availability of labor, these establishments offered a range of services from simple maintenance jobs (replacement of tires/batteries/wiper blades/engine oil/transmission oil/windshield washer liquid) to more complex repairs (repairing brake-pads/ mufflers/ struts, tuning engines, etc.).

Research Associate Elizabeth Caputo (MBA '99) prepared this case under the supervision of Professor Das Narayandas. This case was developed from published sources. HBS cases are developed solely as the basis for class discussion. Cases are not intended to serve as endorsements, sources of primary data, or illustrations of effective or ineffective management.

nature of the business was unacceptable to the firm's top management. Star executives sought a way to retain the branded TBA business and restore profitability. At this point Star turned to the Hunter Business Group (HBG) for assistance.

Hunter Business Group

The Hunter Business Group (HBG) specialized in reorganizing the sales and marketing efforts of large and small firms, in industries ranging from computers and biomedical supplies to office supplies and auto parts. Vic Hunter (an alumnus of the Harvard Business School), the company's President and CEO, had founded HBG in 1981 after amassing a wealth of direct marketing and sales management experience. Hunter believed that strategic use of direct marketing technologies could revolutionize the face of business-to-business (B2B) marketing. Seeing direct marketing as more than just a technique, Hunter expressed his vision:

> Our goal is to facilitate the *transformation of change* within our clients' businesses. We believe that direct marketing is a *highly personal* form of marketing that respects and recognizes the unique needs of each customer. A properly designed and maintained database allows communications to be derived from specific information attached to a given customer account. When a seller's communications provide genuine value to a customer, direct marketing programs result in solid relationships, high retention rates and increased profitability.

HBG achieved these objectives by stepping beyond traditional approaches to sales and marketing to find new ways to increase brand penetration and customer satisfaction, while cutting sales and marketing expense. Consequently, HBG had become widely recognized as a "Statue of Liberty," both for fatigued and impoverished divisions of large companies and for healthy firms looking to revolutionize their sales and marketing efforts. Over the years, HBG had built a highly diversified client base, including IBM, Du Pont, Hallmark Cards, 3M, Monsanto, and BellSouth.

When presented with the details of Star's dilemma, Hunter found it an ideal match for HBG's unique expertise. In fact, based on his experience, he was confident that HBG could turn around the TBA division and make it profitable within a year. Of course, this required fundamentally altering the way Star's gas station operators approached their business. It also meant that Star's sales reps would need to redefine the way they managed dealer relationships, using HBG's integrated direct marketing model to maximize their sales and marketing effectiveness.

Direct Marketing and HBG's Customer Contact Matrix

Direct marketing had long held a mixed reputation. In the consumer arena, for example, manufacturers and service providers saw it as the lowest-cost approach for promoting to attractive customer segments by using databases and linked, automated telephone and mailing systems. For many consumers this meant endless dinnertime phone calls offering low-rate credit cards, long-distance rate deals, and other kinds of "come-ons."

In the arena of business marketing, however, direct marketing techniques had not been fully explored until the 1980s. In this domain, telemarketing methods were often put to more careful use, supplementing rather than replacing expensive face-to-face sales calls. Hunter defined direct marketing as "an interactive marketing system that employs *integrated,* organized contacts to effect a measurable customer response." The effectiveness of integrating mail, telephone, and field contacts, he believed, would always be greater than that resulting from using each medium independently (**Exhibit 1**).

EXHIBIT 1 Costs by Contact Type for Star *TeamTBA* (1993)

Source: Hunter Business Group, Inc.

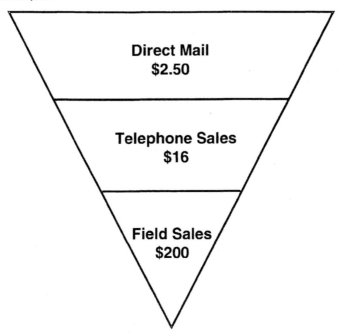

- The dollar values above represent the costs per a single, completed contact with a prospective Star dealer.
- Telemarketing is best used as part of a total marketing and sales program.
- Cost per contact is not contiguous from medium to medium.
- Lower-cost contacts must leverage higher-cost contacts.

Central to the HBG approach was the use of an economic model—a customer contact matrix—developed by Hunter. The foundation for the model (**Electronic Exhibit 1, Exhibit 4**) rested upon the research of the service management group at the Harvard Business School.[2] This group developed groundbreaking methods to measure customer loyalty and adjust customer contact frequency based on current and future revenues. Therefore, even in a dying industry like typewriters where sales had gone down 20% in one year, there would be stability and sustainability as long as selling expenses declined more rapidly than revenues.

The Evolution of Gasoline Service Stations and the Branded TBA Market

The concept of the modern-day gasoline service station evolved during the 1950s with the advent of the U.S. Interstate system. In order to differentiate themselves in a highly competitive gasoline market, service stations began providing "under the hood" checks during fill-ups and replaced worn-out tires, batteries, and other accessories with their own

[2] James L. Heskett; Earl W. Sasser Jr.; and, Leonard A. Schlesinger, *The Service Profit Chain: How Leading Companies Link Profit and Growth to Loyalty, Satisfaction and Value* (New York: Free Press, 1997).

branded products.[3] Station operators discovered that offering these "expert/advisory" services gave them an opportunity to strengthen their bonds with customers. Many also discovered that their customers often were willing to pay a premium for branded TBA products. By the 1970s, it was common for major gasoline retailers, including Amoco, Shell, and Star (all of which had very strong brand images) to offer their own branded TBA products and services. These stations used their branded components to maintain a competitive edge in retail gasoline sales. In addition to providing a point of differentiation and margins of more than 20%, branded TBA products could often represent half or more of a service station's overall contribution while accounting for only a small portion [of] its revenues.

Although gasoline retailers like Star dominated the TBA market during the 1960s and 1970s, the market's high margins soon attracted the attention of specialty competitors that included high-volume/low-price service models (Kmart, Wal-Mart), specialty service chains, (NTB, Jiffy Lube), and independent dealers. These firms aggressively entered the TBA market in the 1980s and gained significant share at the expense of traditional players like Star, who encountered market share declines as high as 70% versus 1960s levels. This trend continued in the 1980s with the closing of nearly 72,000 service stations throughout the decade—an additional 35% decline. By 1990, 80% of repairs on the nation's 190 million automobiles were made, almost equally, by car dealerships, private garages, specialty repair shops, and gasoline service station dealers. The "do-it-yourself" market made up the remaining 20%.

The Star Oil Account

The branded TBA business was not new to HBG. The firm had recently ended an eight-year relationship with Amoco, a global gasoline retailer like Star. Amoco had partnered with HBG to increase lagging TBA sales at its nearly 6,000 service stations (hereafter referred to as *dealers*). Despite the implementation of a highly successful, integrated, direct marketing program at Amoco, the HBG partnership was discontinued in 1991 when Amoco decided to outsource its entire branded TBA business to the National Automotive Parts Association Supply Company (NAPA).

When Star approached HBG soon thereafter, Vic Hunter was delighted. Star recognized the importance of the TBA business in supporting its ubiquitous, industry-dominant logo. To Hunter, the importance Star's management ascribed to preserving this brand image suggested its long-term commitment to the TBA business—something he had found lacking in the Amoco relationship.

Nonetheless, with revenues having fallen over 20% in the past twelve months, Star managers were finding it difficult to justify maintaining the TBA division despite its importance in supporting the brand. Hunter described the situation:

> In 1991–92 Star was losing money. They were unsure how much but knew the amount was substantial. On a variable cost basis, the small part that they could track, the loss was about $8 million. Further, the TBA division had become unattractive not only from the financial standpoint, but also from that of human resources. TBA was not an exciting place to be. Yet, a significant amount of Star's brand equity rested in its TBA product lines. Strong customer relationships had been built around these products throughout the marketplace.
>
> I was convinced that the integrated approach we had used at Amoco would also work well at Star. Consequently, we told them we would turn their business around within a year. We also promised that we would design a sales and marketing program to maintain their brand image and increase dealer satisfaction while simultaneously reducing sales and marketing

[3] Gasoline retailers like Star had traditionally sold branded TBA products through their gasoline service station dealers.

expenses. Their reaction was "yes, but what about the dealer/employee relationships? We have seasoned people who were hired to work for Star forever and you're telling us that you can do things better and with a significantly lower budget?" Star's managers were clearly skeptical about our ability to deliver on our promises, but their only alternative was to give us a chance.

TeamTBA

HBG began by establishing an entirely new company to address the Star business. It was named *TeamTBA*. The company operated out of HBG's Milwaukee headquarters under the leadership of Julie Kowalski, a member of HBG's management team. The initial agreement between the firms stated that HBG would license the Star brand, and independently manage a direct marketing operation that would include marketing, sales, manufacturing, and product design. Star would receive no compensation on sales below $20 million per year, but was entitled to 2% of *TeamTBA* revenues exceeding that. Additionally, Star would retain control over the product—HBG would need to obtain Star's approval before making changes to current TBA products. This included dropping existing products, changing vendors, and introducing new products and services. Star also wanted *TeamTBA* to live up to its word and reduce operating costs by fifty percent in the first year. Star retained the right to terminate the agreement if this condition was not met.

TeamTBA began operations by creating an extensive branded TBA dealer database. Prior to 1992, Star had maintained dealer profile databases by product line. However, like other firms in this industry, it maintained this information entirely on paper. Rebecca Nguyen, HBG's Information System Manager at the time, recalled:

> When we began work with Star, all service station (hereafter referred to as *dealer*) information was stored on paper and much of it was incomplete. We used that information to create a master that would then be updated as our salespeople called on the various dealers and collected current information. It took us more than six months to gather all the pertinent information. By September 1992, our dealer master database had grown to include all 2,200 dealers.

TeamTBA organized its sales and marketing effort around sales teams, each consisting of a field sales representative (FSR), an internal telesales representative (TSR), and a customer service representative (CSR). In contrast to Star's field sales force of 84 reps, *TeamTBA* began with just 18 sales people (16 HBD employees or new hires and two former Star field sales representatives). Hunter explained:

> It is not that we did not want to hire Star's reps. In fact, we gave them an option to join us. However, most stayed on at Star to focus on gasoline sales, or left because they lacked confidence in our approach. Some felt the transition would be too difficult to handle.

TeamTBA's FSRs were assigned sales territories and teamed with a headquarters-based TSR. This partnership formed the field customer interface (**Exhibit 2**). FSRs were to advise dealers on how to better manage and grow their service bay operations, thereby stimulating demand for TBA products. Also, internal TSRs would proactively initiate contacts with station owners, in close collaboration with FSRs, to solicit orders, conduct and coordinate predefined sales strategies, and maintain/update customer profiles in the dealer master database. Inbound CSRs, also located at headquarters, would augment the process by providing order status, order processing support, and immediate customer problem resolution. Weekly conference calls (between the FSR and the TSR) would be conducted to share information about recent dealer contacts and to develop future contact strategies.

EXHIBIT 2 *TeamTBA* Process Chart

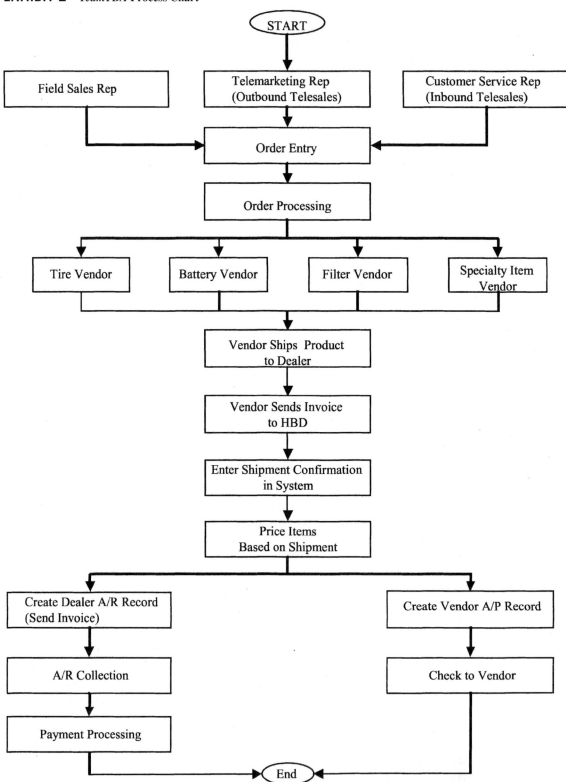

These calls would also be taped so that management could ensure that the sales teams were working effectively to develop value-added, integrated, contact plans. Further, contact and coordination with the existing Star gasoline sales force would be part of the overall contact plan and the responsibility of the FSRs.

Marketing and promotional resources were to be provided through a Marketing Coordinator located centrally. This coordinator was responsible for overseeing production and distribution of key marketing elements by working with Star (as required) and with outside vendors. An initial 1993 Promotion Calendar had already been created to guide these efforts.

Accounting resources had been established to handle order entry, vendor invoice processing, accounts receivable, financial analysis and reporting, pricing analysis, sales analysis, and auditing of intra-company transactions.

Information Systems was charged with maintaining and enhancing software and hardware resources, developing new systems to support the business process, training and communicating with all system users, managing a "help desk" function, and managing the EDI process with vendors.

Vendor negotiations and relationship management were the responsibilities of the general manager. Hunter explained:

> We took a radically different approach with vendors. To begin with, in each category we short-listed those vendors we thought capable of meeting our quality standards. Based on their experience, most of these vendors came to the negotiating table expecting to talk price and play "hardball." They were surprised when we refused to talk about price. Not that price was unimportant, we were more interested in hearing what these vendors had to offer in terms of added value that would help us differentiate *TeamTBA* products in the eyes of our dealers and the end consumers. We were looking for partners, not suppliers. We offered long-term, single-source contracts to these vendors in return for their commitment to customize existing products and to develop new ones for us. Interestingly, several vendors walked away from the table because they were unprepared to do business this way. Those that remained were committed to making *TeamTBA* a success.

By December 1992, *TeamTBA* had selected Kelly Springfield as its main tire vendor, Delco-Remy for batteries, and Champion for filters—each a well-known manufacturer in its industry. A vendor decision on chemicals was to be made before the end of December. All TBA products, regardless of vendor, would be labeled and marketed under the Star brand name.

In order to ensure a smooth transition, *TeamTBA* had assumed some of Star's telemarketing, order processing, and customer service responsibilities in August 1992. By the end of December of that year, *TeamTBA*'s field sales representatives were in place, and the new sales plan was launched at the beginning of January 1993.

Using the Star Customer Contact Matrix

Understanding and applying Hunter's customer contact matrix was the backbone of *TeamTBA*'s customer (gasoline service station) management strategy. The process began by projecting revenues for 1993 (**Exhibit 3**). Hunter forecasted revenues at $20 million—a significant reduction from the 1991 and 1992 levels. *TeamTBA* made this downward projection based on their belief that the earlier Star TBA revenues had been overreported. Further, a large portion of the TBA volume had resulted from Star reps "pushing" TBA products. Finally, the negative impact of the Persian Gulf War was expected to hit the industry that year. Assuming reduced product costs (now budgeted at 80% of revenues) as a result of stronger relationship management and the consolidation of suppliers, *TeamTBA* projected a gross margin of $4 million for 1993. With this in mind, *TeamTBA* began to think about a reasonable estimate for direct marketing expense.

EXHIBIT 3   Star Financial Information, 1991–1992 (actual); 1993–1994 (projected); in millions

Source: Hunter Business Group, Inc.

	1991	As % of 1991 Revenues	1992	As % of 1992 Revenues	1993 (*TeamTBA* Projection)	As % of 1993 Revenues	1994 (*TeamTBA* Projection)	As % of 1994 Revenues
Revenue	$36.7		$39.4		$20.0		$16.0	
Product Costs	32.3	88.0	33.6	85.3	16.0	80.0	12.8	80.0
Gross Margin	4.4	12.0	5.8	14.7	4.0	20.0	3.2	20.0
Operating Costs	11.3	30.8	14.0	35.5	3.55	17.75	2.84	17.75
Operating Income	(6.9)	(18.8)	(8.2)	(20.8)	.45	2.25	.36	2.25

Star wanted *TeamTBA* to honor Hunter's verbal commitment that his team could implement their program successfully while reducing operating costs by 50% of the expected 1993 revenues. This meant that HBG's projected operating costs had to be reduced from 35.5% to 17.75% as a percentage of revenues, or to $3.55 million. **"Operating costs,"** as noted in **Exhibit 3,** comprised two expenses: the **direct marketing and sales expense** (which included mail, phone, and field operations, salaries) and **fixed operating expense** (which included rent, salaries for internal office support, database management, and miscellaneous costs associated with *TeamTBA's* Milwaukee headquarters). HBG's experience suggested that fixed expenses would run between 40–45% of operating costs, or about $1.5 million. Consequently, the team established a baseline of $2 million for direct marketing and sales expense.

Exhibit 4 illustrates the cost and corresponding frequency of contacts by medium—mail ($2.50 per contact), phone ($16 per contact), and face-to-face meetings ($200 per contact)—and shows the number of active dealers by sales volume grade. *TeamTBA* knew from experience that as the amount of sales visits fell, the frequency of phone and mail contacts would need to go up. The question for *TeamTBA,* however, was whether or not this could be done more effectively given their $2 million budget. The next step was to determine the optimal combination of mail, phone, and field contacts within the budget, yet still meet the new sales target.

Dealers graded by purchase volume: Dealers were sorted into buckets based on their TBA purchase volumes. The buckets were labeled "AA" (more than $30,000), "A"($20,000–$30,000), "B" ($10,000–$20,000), "C"($5,000–$10,000) and "D" (less than $5,000). Using past purchase data, *TeamTBA* established the average dollar sales for each grade, as shown in the table.

Number of dealers: It was HBG's standard industry practice to sort customer accounts (dealers in this case) according to a 5/15/25/25/30 rule, designating the "top 20%" accounts as AA and A respectively. Thus, regardless of industry, the percentage of accounts allocated to each grade always remained constant.

Sales revenue: HBG's customer contact matrix usually extended the "20/80" rule across industries—the AA and A accounts typically generated 80% of the overall sales revenues. However, this was not the case with TBA, where the AA and A dealers only accounted for about one-half of all sales revenue.

Average field calls per dealer account: Field calls were the most expensive yet most effective component of the program, and therefore were the starting point for decisions on the allocation of marketing efforts. As Julie Kowalski, head of *TeamTBA,* described:

Profit for *TeamTBA* needed to be considered for each grade. For a dealer account in the D grade, bringing in around $1,650 of revenue and $330 of margin, a single field contact costing $200 would be ineffective and unprofitable, hence the zero demarcation in the model. In contrast, AA accounts might justify as many as 24 visits a year, or $4,800 in field expense.

EXHIBIT 4 Customer Contact Matrix

Source: Hunter Business Group, Inc.

Customer Grade Target Customers	Dollar Sales Range	Actual Avg Sales Revenue per Account	# of Accounts	Sales Revenue	Avg Mail Contacts per Account	Total Mail Contacts	Mail Cost Avg Cost per Contact $2.50	Avg Phone Calls per Account	Total Phone Calls	Phone Cost Avg Cost per Contact $16.00	Avg Field Calls per Account	Total Field Sales Calls	Field Sales Cost Avg Cost per Contact $200	Total Cost	Expense to Revenue Ratio
AA (5%)	>$30,000	$50,000	88	$4,400,000	72	6,336	$15,840	48	4,224	$67,584	24	2,112	$422,400	$505,824	11.50%
A (15%)	$20,000–$30,000	$25,000	264	$6,600,000	72	19,008	$47,520	24	6,336	$101,376	12	3,168	$633,600	$782,496	11.86%
B (25%)	$10,000–$20,000	$12,000	440	$5,280,000	48	21,120	$52,800	18	7,920	$126,720	4	1,760	$352,000	$531,520	10.07%
C (25%)	$5,000–$10,000	$6,500	440	$2,860,000	24	10,560	$26,400	12	5,280	$84,480	0	0	$0	$110,880	3.88%
D (30%)	<$5,000	$1,650	528	$871,200	12	6,336	$15,840	6	3,168	$50,688	0	0	$0	$66,528	7.64%
Total			1,760	$20,011,200		63,360	$158,400		26,928	$430,848		7,040	$1,408,000	$1,997,248	9.98%

EXHIBIT 5
TeamTBA **Direct Marketing Salesforce Salary Information (1993)**

Employee Category	Number of Employees	Fully Burdened Salary	Total Salary Cost to HBG	Total Contact Cost for HBG	% of Total Contact Cost Attributed to Employee Salary
Field Sales	18	$70,000	$1,260,000	$1,408,000	89%
Telesales	6	56,000	336,000	430,848	76
Mail	1.5	36,000	54,000	158,400	34
TOTAL	**25**		**$1,650,000**	**$1,997,248**	

Average mail contacts per dealer account: The number of times a dealer would be contacted by mail was determined by HBG's experience. Virtually all direct mail solicitation was performed at least monthly; thus, even for C and D accounts, 12 contacts per year were reasonable. For higher-level accounts more frequent mailings (including targeted offerings and marketing calendars) were added (72, 48, 24, and 12).

Average phone calls per dealer account: Telephone contact frequency was also based on HBG's experience. *TeamTBA* believed that every dealer should be contacted at least every two months. As with mail contacts for higher volume dealers, more frequent phone contacts were planned.

TeamTBA planned to adjust the number of mail, phone, and field contacts to reflect changes in incoming revenue throughout the program.

"Gold" Accounts

In order for the *TeamTBA* approach to be successful, sales teams had to provide incentives to dealers: not only so dealers would purchase larger volumes of Star products, but more importantly so they would purchase a *wider assortment* of these products. To do this, *TeamTBA* established the "Gold Account" program. A Gold Account was defined as a dealer who purchased $17,000 or more from *TeamTBA* during a given year. This $17,000 had to include at least 25 batteries ($1,250), 50 tires ($2,500), $250 in filters, and $250 in chemicals every 90 days. This translated to sales of $4,250 per quarter, or $17,000 annually. Kowalski explained:

> The heart of our methodology is to identify dealers who take a proactive approach to TBA products. Based on experience, we found that the easiest way to identify such accounts is to look at their purchase patterns. A dealer who routinely orders a certain amount of product in each category is presumably committed to selling those product categories. We are therefore interested not just in volume, but also the breadth of products purchased.

Based on this definition, an AA account that purchased $50,000 of "product" consisting only of tires would not receive Gold Account recognition. But, a B account purchasing an $18,000 combination of filters, batteries, tires, and chemicals would achieve Gold Account status due to the combination of products purchased. Consequently, Gold Accounts were not limited to AA accounts and included some in each of the AA, A, and B accounts.

Using Star information from the end of 1992, *TeamTBA* discovered that of 2,200 stations, only 14 qualified for Gold status. Vic Hunter remarked: "What looked like a very strong brand because 80% of dealers purchased Star-branded products, proved to be poor brand foundation with weak market penetration. We were very disappointed."

TeamTBA encouraged its sales teams to increase the number of Gold Accounts by offering them $100 bonuses for each net addition to the number of Gold Accounts in their territory. **Exhibit 6** shows the dramatic increase in the number of Gold accounts during 1993,

EXHIBIT 6
Number of Gold Accounts—Year One (1993)

Source: Hunter Business Group, Inc.

Month	Gold Accounts
January	—
February	14
March	46
April	55
May	87
June	116
July	105
August	122
September	136
October	145
November	154

the first year of the program. Hunter credited the surge to active management of customer needs. Unlike the past, when TBA representatives "pushed" products onto dealers, *TeamTBA* representatives now showed dealers how to sell TBA products more efficiently. Hunter explained:

> We helped dealers learn to market. Under the new model, our representative would notice, for instance, when a station had not purchased filters for a given time period. The *TeamTBA* rep would then demonstrate how offering a discounted oil change with every 50 gallons of gas purchased would increase the dealer's revenues.

TeamTBA Results

A few months after *TeamTBA* started operations it conducted a satisfaction survey of the 2,200 dealers (**Exhibit 7**). The survey results were encouraging and surprising. First, in all but one category dealer satisfaction had risen after *TeamTBA* had taken over the business. Second, and perhaps more striking, was the seemingly counterintuitive increase in territory sales manager (TSM) contact frequency, despite *TeamTBA* decreasing its number of field representatives from 83 (Star) to 18 (*TeamTBA*), and decreasing its frequency of direct personal contact by 70%. Hunter clarified this point:

> Classic marketing suggests that if I [the Star rep] call dealers less frequently, I get less business. . .we went from 83 to 18 field reps—this should have spelled disaster. The survey showed that dealers' perceptions of the frequency of face-to-face contacts had actually risen. This is not as counterintuitive as it seems at first. People don't differentiate between contact media. They differentiate based on the frequency of "valued communications." If you generate valued communications by phone and through the mail that are seamlessly integrated with field activities, the overall perception is that face-to-face contact frequency has increased. Previously, a Star representative, for instance, would ordinarily visit a retailer or owner in San Antonio, 50 times a year. Now, (with the *TeamTBA* model) field visits were reduced to 12 times a year, but when a dealer was asked the question "How many times does a TBA rep visit you?," they responded that the frequency had increased 17% (59 visits), much higher than it actually was (12 visits).

The survey results demonstrated the effectiveness of Hunter's integrated marketing approach. In fact, by contacting dealers through a variety of media, *TeamTBA* had actually increased the number of contacts by 600%. Hunter concluded:

> Star's main problem had been a lack of understanding about what dealers really needed—it was not face-to-face contact from field representatives. Before *TeamTBA,* Star reps had focused on the politics of the relationship between Star and its dealers, rather than focusing

EXHIBIT 7 *TeamTBA* **Customer Survey**

Source: Hunter Business Group, Inc.

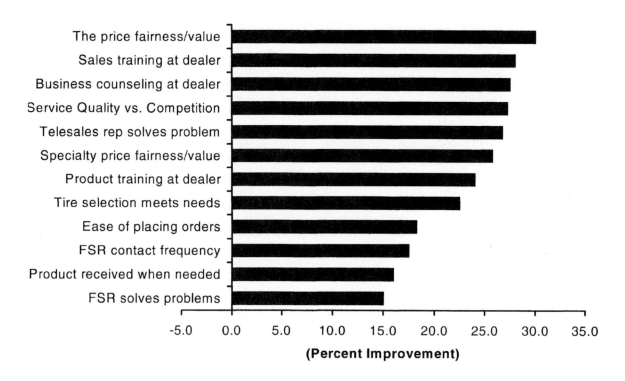

Change in Star Dealer Satisfaction
Key Factor from Survey, 1993

(Percent Improvement)

on tires, batteries, and accessories. Dealers saw their relationship as confrontational at best, involving prolonged meetings that accomplished little. Meetings typically had concluded with dealers buying Star's products based on a sense of obligation, or to gain access to co-op marketing funds.

Within the new business approach, the starting point was a dealer specific plan based on information recorded in the dealer master database. Next, a phone conversation between the *TeamTBA* telesales rep and the dealer would ensue to confirm the dealer's needs. More research would then be done before the first field visit. Following the visit, another four or five phone/mail contacts would be made before the next field trip. As Hunter described:

> When a Team member makes an initial phone contact, they say something like "I would like to talk to you about the battery program. What are some of the problems that you encounter that are not currently being addressed. . .? And, by the way, Vic Hunter will be in your area next week. Would you like him to come in and show you our line?" If the dealer expressed an interest, the field rep would call on the dealer personally, discussing any unmet needs or other issues. Dealers then feel better about buying our products because their needs are addressed and value is being exchanged.

Other Survey Results

Several other dealer responses piqued HBG's interest. For instance, the survey confirmed the impression that a majority of the dealers carried branded TBA products. However, tires and batteries—which generated a significant portion of *TeamTBA* revenues—were being sold by only a small percentage of accounts. Secondly, it appeared that dealers' perceived value of the Star brand varied with the type of products they purchased. For example, across all dealers in the survey, 65% considered the Star brand to be of equal or greater importance than price. Yet, among those who also sold tires, this number rose to 80%. Finally, dealers reflected in their responses their reluctance "to throw out the TBA baby with the bath water." 80% of respondents reported that service bay repairs were highly important to their overall business, with an additional 16% describing such services as having average or above average importance.

Early Successes

Within six months of the *TeamTBA* launch, the program looked like a great success. The number of active Star accounts (those accounts having purchased within the previous 30 days) had increased 24%. Even more impressive was the significant increase in the number of Gold Accounts, which had exceeded 100 by June. Jim Jaskoske, chairman of Star's National Dealer Council, wrote a letter to council members reporting on a *TeamTBA* sales training meeting that he had attended in mid-1993:

> I can assure you that *TeamTBA*'s only objective is to help us earn a profit. Their only business is selling Star branded TBA products. We can look forward to competitive pricing, point-of-sale materials, award programs, quantity discounts, and the fastest possible delivery service.

Hunter was delighted that the results of the dealer satisfaction survey seemed to prove the merits of his firm's customer contact matrix. Even though face-to-face contact had decreased by 70% or more in many cases, dealers were more satisfied with the sales interactions they had under the *TeamTBA* program than they ever had been. Over 85% of respondents in the survey considered *TeamTBA* to offer equal or better service than that of Star, and nearly 30% found that service to be "much better" than previous service offerings. Nearly 40% of dealers reported that the Star brand added a 15% premium to the prices they were able to charge.

Through 1993, the good news continued for *TeamTBA,* as cumulative first year sales passed the target of $20 million. While this represented about half of the revenue generated a year earlier, the cost of sales had plummeted, thereby meeting the initial goal of attaining profitability for the *TeamTBA* program.

However, one concern was beginning to grow. By the beginning of 1994, it looked as though the number of active accounts and total sales volume had begun to level off. Further, Star had launched a program to convert franchised service stations at major intersections (usually *TeamTBA*'s best customers) into convenience stores with no service facilities. The number of service stations with service bays was also expected to fall from 2,200 to 1,700 in the next year or two.

Planning for the Journey Ahead

As she reviewed the situation for the coming year, Julie Kowalski made an assumption that there would be 1,500 active accounts. Based on the data and projections she had before her, she also expected the average sales volume within each account grade to decline, and that *TeamTBA*'s sales revenues would drop to around $16 million in 1994. Along with Vic Hunter and the rest of the management team, she set out to develop a plan that would allow product costs and margins as a percentage of revenues to remain constant for the next year, leaving *TeamTBA* with an expected operating income of $360,000 for 1994. Based on this, Kowalski began evaluating her options, knowing that *TeamTBA*'s strategy could take any of several approaches.

As one approach, Kowalski could assume that *TeamTBA*'s fixed costs would remain constant at $1.5 million. This meant that they would not shut down any facilities, abandon any territories, or scale back operational expenses associated with running the TBA program. By freezing these fixed costs, *TeamTBA* would have only $1.34 million to spend on direct marketing and sales efforts. They would thus have to reduce sales and marketing expenditures by $660,000 from 1993 in order to meet their $360,000 profitability target.

This scenario raised several obstacles. First, there was the salesforce question. At present, the cost of salaries for the *TeamTBA* salesforce exceeded $1.6 million (**Exhibit 5**). It appeared impossible, then, to meet the new profitability target without drastically cutting back the sales and marketing force—whether in mail, telesales, or field sales. Indeed, Kowalski even wondered if there was any merit to eliminating the field sales force entirely and establishing *TeamTBA* as a premier telesales operation. Just looking at the original matrix, she recognized that such a move could eliminate $1.4 million in costs.

Kowalski knew that making such a move could create a serious morale problem within the team, so she weighed the expected cost recovery against the likely adverse reactions among the remaining *TeamTBA* salesforce and the Star dealers who were their valued customers. She also knew that the fruits of such cost recovery would be partially consumed in the investments required to expand telemarketing capacity.

A second strategy would be to maintain the fixed component of *TeamTBA*'s operating expenses at a constant *percentage of revenue,* or 40–45%. This would equal $1.28 million, given Kowalski's projection of $2.84 million for total 1994 operating costs. Such a move, however, would leave only $1.56 million for sales and marketing costs—a figure that included salary expense. Consequently, a certain number of jobs would still have to be cut.

A third alternative strategy would be a hybrid approach. This scenario involved reducing fixed costs as well as sales and marketing costs by 20%, consistent with the 20% decline in revenues from 1993. *TeamTBA* could do this in a variety of ways. They could make wholesale changes in the frequency of contacts by mail, phone, or field; they could try to increase the number of Gold Accounts and make an effort to boost sales volume among the highest performers, while decreasing or terminating contacts among C and D accounts; or they could experiment with a combination of the two: adjusting contact frequency and encouraging more dealers to "step up" to the Gold Account level.

There were several questions that needed to be addressed with this hybrid approach. Would reducing the number of contacts hasten the decline in revenues? Was it possible for *TeamTBA* to improve its effectiveness over 1993 levels by developing Gold accounts? Was the team capable of getting these dealers to buy more TBA products? After all, TBA products were not their primary source of revenues. Was this asking for too much from the dealers?

Amidst all this, Hunter, Kowalski, and the management team were debating whether this was the time to change their sales compensation structure from trying to maximize revenue to maximizing contribution margin. Hunter explained: "By educating the sales force on the costs of TBA products and the types of purchasing arrangements that would be most conducive to *maximizing contribution margin,* we could get them to make more autonomous decisions on how to manage individual dealer accounts. This would align their efforts with our goal of managing the sales-to-expense ratio." Would this move be counterproductive as well?

In the face of all the questions associated with each of the options, Hunter and Kowalski needed to come up with a plan to counter the forthcoming decline in revenues.

Chapter 39

Harrah's Entertainment Inc.

Rajiv Lal   Patricia Martone Carrolo

The results are impressive enough that other casino companies are copying some of Harrah's more discernible methods. Wall Street analysts are also beginning to see Harrah's—long a dowdy also-ran in the flashy casino business—as gaining an edge on its rivals. Harrah's stock price has risen quickly in recent weeks as investors have received news of the marketing results. And the company's earnings have more than doubled in the past year.

—Wall Street Journal, *May 4, 2000*[1]

Philip G. Satre, Chairman and Chief Executive Officer of Harrah's Entertainment Inc., read with satisfaction the *Wall Street Journal* article about Harrah's. The story discussed the company's marketing success in targeting low rollers, the 100% growth in stock price and profits in the year to December 1999, and the revenue growth of 50% which significantly outpaced the industry (see **Exhibit 1**).

The $100 million investment in information technology seemed to be paying off.

---

[1] Christina Binkley, "Lucky Numbers: Casino Chain Mines Data on Its Gamblers, and Strikes Pay Dirt— 'Secret Recipe' Lets Harrah's Target Its Low-Rollers at the Individual Level—A Free-Meal 'Intervention'," *The Wall Street Journal,* May 4, 2000.

Dean's Research Fellow Patricia Martone Carrolo and Professor Rajiv Lal prepared this case. We would also like to thank Professors Walter Salmon and Alvin Silk for their contributions to this effort. HBS cases are developed solely as the basis for class discussion. Cases are not intended to serve as endorsements, sources of primary data, or illustrations of effective or ineffective management. Certain names and financial data have been disguised.

EXHIBIT 1   Consolidated Statements of Income (in thousands, except per share amounts)

Source: Harrah's Entertainment Inc.

	Year Ended December 31		
	1999	1998	1997
Revenues			
Casino*	$2,424,237	$1,660,313	$1,338,003
Food and beverage	425,808	231,568	196,765
Rooms	253,629	153,538	128,354
Management fees	75,890	64,753	24,566
Other	131,403	78,320	78,954
Less: Casino promotional allowances	(286,539)	(184,477)	(147,432)
Total revenues	$3,024,428	$2,004,015	$1,619,210
Operating expenses			
Direct			
Casino	$1,254,557	$ 868,622	$ 685,942
Food and beverage	218,580	116,641	103,604
Rooms	66,818	41,871	39,719
Depreciation of buildings, riverboats and equipment	188,199	130,128	103,670
Development costs	6,538	8,989	10,524
Write-downs, reserves and recoveries	2,235	7,474	13,806
Project opening costs	2,276	8,103	17,631
Other	690,404	467,999	383,791
Total operating expenses	$2,429,607	$1,649,827	$1,358,687
Operating profit	594,821	354,188	260,523
Net income	$ 208,470	$ 102,024	$ 99,388

*A breakdown of Casino revenues by regions is as follows:
Western region—$730.1 million, Central region—$970.9 million and Eastern region—$723.3 million.

EXHIBIT 2A   Glossary of Terms in Exhibits 2B–2F

Source: Harrah's Entertainment Inc.

# of Guests—The number of guests in a particular month. The largest quantity typically indicates selection month.
Hotel %—% of guests who stayed in the hotel.
Red %—% of guests redeeming ANY offer in a month.
# of Trips—Trips (can be multiple consecutive days) captured on the Casino Management System. The Harrah's loyalty card had to be used to capture this information.
# of Days—The number of individual days a customer visited Harrah's during a month.
Theo(theoretical) Win—On average what we would expect the profitability of the customers to be based on their play in the **month**.
Observed Win—Actual profitability for the casino for the **month**.
Complimentary (Comp) Amount—Comp dollars provided to customers in the month (and does not include cost of the offer redeemed).
Complimentary (Comp) %—Comp dollar amount as a percentage of theoretical win.

But that day Satre was more interested in the marketing activities that had contributed to these results (see **Exhibits 2A–2F**). He asked Gary Loveman, then Chief Operating Officer, and his team of "propeller heads" two questions. He wanted to know "how much" these marketing efforts had contributed to Harrah's overall performance, and if these marketing results were a one-shot event or could be achieved year after year, especially as the competition introduced similar programs.

EXHIBIT 2B **New Business Program Analysis**

Source: Harrah's Entertainment Inc.

Sign-up Month	New Customers		1 Month After Signup		2 Months After Signup		3 Months After Signup	
	Customers	Theoretical	Customers	Theoretical	Customers	Theoretical	Customers	Theoretical
1-Apr-99	1022	$31,992	125	$10,857	103	$10,478	85	$10,093
1-May-99	837	44,673	133	10,772	134	15,799	102	10,950
1-Jun-99	825	46,291	135	13,231	128	10,941	91	12,823
1-Jul-99	808	45,725	162	24,712	137	23,229	109	26,629
1-Aug-99	742	43,423	164	17,494	103	11,122	97	11,817
1-Sep-99	760	42,257	141	20,102	118	15,744	104	18,995
1-Oct-99	990	54,935	178	26,086	151	24,168	148	16,080
1-Nov-99	1064	63,687	225	28,657	182	23,824	142	21,988
1-Dec-99	772	41,494	143	15,906	149	16,517	94	13,229
1-Jan-00	986	$46,502	206	$20,041	193	$22,123	92	$12,476

Customers

	1st Month	2nd Month	3rd Month	1st–3rd
1-Apr-99	12%	10%	8%	31%
1-May-99	16	16	12	44
1-Jun-99	16	16	11	43
1-Jul-99	20	17	13	50
1-Aug-99	22	14	13	49
1-Sep-99	19	16	14	48
1-Oct-99	18	15	15	48
1-Nov-99	21	17	13	52
1-Dec-99	19	19	12	50
1-Jan-00	21%	20%	9%	50%

Revenues

	1st Month	2nd Month	3rd Month	1st–3rd
1-Apr-99	34%	33%	32%	98%
1-May-99	24	35	25	84
1-Jun-99	29	24	28	80
1-Jul-99	54	51	58	163
1-Aug-99	40	26	27	93
1-Sep-99	48	37	45	130
1-Oct-99	47	44	29	121
1-Nov-99	45	37	35	117
1-Dec-99	38	40	32	110
1-Dec-99	43%	48%	27%	118%

Note: The first two columns report the number of new customers signed up in a particular month and the predicted worth of these customers. Offers, of varying type and value, were sent to each new customer that played at Harrah's, and were redeemable one month, two months and three months after their first visit. The following columns report the number of customers who came back to Harrah's in the subsequent months and predicted worth of these customers. For example, in April 1999, 1,022 new customers came to Harrah's. In May, 125 customers of these 1,022 customers returned to Harrah's and their predicted worth was $10,857 compared to $31,992, the predicted worth of the 1,022 customers who signed up in April. Similarly, 103 of the customers who signed up in April returned in June, and 85 returned in July, with no demonstrable change in predicted worth for the pool. Each month brought a new vintage of customers signing up.

669

EXHIBIT 2C Loyalty Program (Frequency Upside)—Offer Behavior Change by Offer and Month

Source: Harrah's Entertainment Inc.

Offer	Report Period	# of Guests	Hotel %	Red %	# of Trips	Trips per Guest	# of Days	Days per Trip	Hours	Hours per Day	Theo Win	Observed Win	Comp Amt.	Comp %	Avg. Theo Win per Trip	Avg. Theo Win per Day	Avg. Theo Win per Hour
PRE	Jan-99	21*	24%	5%	20	1.0	34	1.7	109	3.2	$7,770	$12,745	$1,361	18%	$389	$229	$71
	Feb-99	28	18	11	28	1.0	50	1.8	166	3.3	11,957	15,436	2,434	20	427	239	72
	Mar-99	30	17	10	28	0.9	41	1.5	148	3.6	6,596	(1,432)	799	12	236	161	45
	Apr-99	40	23	18	40	1.0	61	1.5	173	2.8	5,051	6,100	845	17	126	83	29
	May-99	36	14	8	36	1.0	64	1.8	218	3.4	9,000	5,838	1,585	18	250	141	41
	Jun-99	**953**	**29**	**22**	**978**	**1.0**	**1,709**	**1.7**	**6,496**	**3.8**	**267,907**	**270,836**	**42,514**	**16**	**274**	**157**	**41**
POST	Jul-99	133*	25	31	153	1.2	252	1.6	987	3.9	74,275	95,263	12,558	17	485	295	75
	Aug-99	146	26	44	172	1.2	286	1.7	870	3.0	43,240	51,900	8,987	21	251	151	50
	Sep-99	166	40	58	188	1.1	362	1.9	1,270	3.5	70,824	94,739	16,110	23	377	196	56
	Oct-99	152	42	53	178	1.2	319	1.8	1,286	4.0	58,354	87,082	12,300	21	328	183	45
	Nov-99	102	52	55	111	1.1	198	1.8	761	3.8	29,095	50,920	7,151	25	262	147	38
	Dec-99	83	42	41	98	1.2	167	1.7	554	3.3	23,187	38,983	4,304	19	237	139	42
Total		1,890	31%	32%	2,030	1.1	3,543	1.7	13,037	3.7	$607,256	$728,410	$110,948	18%	$299	$171	$47

*To be read as, of the 953 customers who received an offer in June, 21 customers had patronized the casino in January and 133 customers patronized the casino in July.

Note: Harrah's identified a list of potentially loyal customers who could increase the number of trips that they made to Harrah's. An offer was sent to a total of 953 customers in June, redeemable in July, August, and September. Each offer consisted of three individual offers—one for each month, at an average incremental cost to Harrah's of $40 per each redeemed offer. The type and level of offer was similar in value and type to what the customer had historically received. The offer was different for customers of different perceived worth to Harrah's but was predominately cash and food based. **Exhibit 2C** tracks the behavior of this pool of 953 customers before and after the offer was sent in June. While, on average, only 30 of these 953 customers were visiting Harrah's between January and May, the number jumped to an average of 150 per month during the subsequent months. The theoretical win from these customers also increased accompanied with the increase in offer redemptions. Harrah's calculated the profitability of these programs by comparing the incremental theoretical wins to the incremental cost of the program.

EXHIBIT 2D Loyalty Program (Budget Upside)—Offer Behavior Change by Offer and Month

Source: Harrah's Entertainment Inc.

Report Period	# of Guests	Hotel %	Red %	# of Trips	Trips per Guest	Days	Days per Trip	Hours	Hours per Day	Theo Win	Observed W/(L)	Comp. Amt.	Comp. %	Avg. Trip	Avg. Day	Avg. Hour
Jun-99	235	0%	37%	368	1.6	401	1.1	767	1.9	$13,544	$18,011	$88	1%	$37	$34	$18
Jul-99	241	0	33	374	1.6	405	1.1	878	2.2	16,931	15,699	182	1	45	42	19
Aug-99	284	0	26	427	1.5	474	1.1	1,015	2.1	18,710	22,042	233	1	44	39	18
Sep-99	302	0	26	528	1.7	611	1.2	1,247	2.0	23,520	20,004	603	3	45	38	19
Oct-99	578	0	40	1,028	1.8	1,135	1.1	2,109	1.9	28,905	31,918	534	2	28	25	14
Nov-99	267	0	50	577	2.2	649	1.1	1,193	1.8	23,646	39,205	318	1	41	36	20
Dec-99	291	0	75	721	2.5	830	1.2	1,528	1.8	32,105	63,248	668	2	45	39	21
Jan-00	250	0	62	583	2.3	686	1.2	1,228	1.8	27,370	30,952	617	2	60	40	22
Feb-00	247	0	63	581	2.4	679	1.2	1,237	1.8	36,885	39,060	1,550	4	63	54	30
Mar-00	288	0	67	717	2.5	852	1.2	1,529	1.8	43,318	59,028	1,927	4	60	51	28
	3,802	0%	44%	7,025	1.8	7,897	1.1	15,443	2.0	$327,763	$447,149	$8,214	3%	$47	$42	$21

Note: **Exhibit 2D** tracks a group of customers with an upside budget potential. In October, 578 customers were selected and mailed offers that were redeemable in November, December, and January. In January, these customers were evaluated again as high budget upside and sent additional offers intended to capture a larger share of budget in February, March, and April. Each offer consisted of one coupon per month.

The offers provided an unconditional cash incentive for visiting and a larger play-based incentive to increase play. For example, a customer would receive $5 for visiting and $20 for playing to a $200 level of theoretical wins, $30 for playing to a $300 level, and so forth. The value of the unconditional offer was typically less than they had previously received via direct mail; however, the conditional part was significantly greater—resulting in a direct mail piece that was only slightly more costly to Harrah's, about $15 compared to $10 in the past.

EXHIBIT 2E   Retention Program—Offer Behavior Change by Offer and Month

Source: Harrah's Entertainment Inc.

Offer	Report Period	# of Guests	Hotel %	Red %	# of Trips	Trips per Guest	# of Days	Days per Trip	Hours	Hours per Day	Theo Win	Observed W/(L)	Comp. Amt.	Comp. %	Avg. Theo Win per Trip	Avg. Win per Day	Avg. Win per Hour
	Jul-98	5,980	0%	14%	8,695	1.5	11,079	1.3	27,882	2.5	$1,603,196	$1,691,024	$312,370	19%	$184	$145	$57
	Aug-98	5,041	0	13	7,284	1.4	9,330	1.3	22,962	2.5	1,325,049	1,366,126	209,748	16	182	142	58
	Sept-98	3,098	0	17	4,369	1.4	5,416	1.2	12,791	2.4	705,836	1,008,256	106,832	15	162	130	55
	Oct-98	1,444	1	21	2,272	1.6	2,661	1.2	6,303	2.4	354,198	483,471	55,006	16	156	133	56
	Nov-98	326	2	16	478	1.5	553	1.2	1,213	2.2	63,140	94,869	9,242	15	132	114	52
	Dec-98	10	10	0	14	1.4	16	1.1	25	1.6	1,293	1,729	54	4	92	81	51
	Jan-99	362	4	14	366	1.0	441	1.2	1,086	2.5	60,999	68,786	9,089	15	167	138	58
	Feb-99	3,578	0	22	4,140	1.2	5,325	1.3	12,676	2.4	661,868	803,336	105,703	16	160	124	53
	Mar-99	4,592	0	24	5,659	1.2	7,114	1.3	16,967	2.4	900,992	1,048,778	130,620	14	159	127	53
	Apr-99	4,052	0	22	5,166	1.3	6,597	1.3	16,488	2.5	911,712	1,040,968	123,737	14	176	138	55
	May-99	3,576	0	22	4,637	1.3	5,850	1.3	15,134	2.6	810,873	967,491	114,451	14	175	139	54
	Jun-99	3,325	0	23	4,492	1.4	5,710	1.3	14,113	2.5	806,390	863,057	108,807	13	180	141	57
	Jul-99	3,934	0	21	5,606	1.4	7,074	1.3	18,357	2.6	1,160,901	1,099,528	179,247	15	207	164	63
	Aug-99	3,769	0	20	5,277	1.4	6,827	1.3	17,713	2.6	1,047,831	1,293,718	169,202	16	199	153	59
	Sep-99	3,197	1	20	4,476	1.4	5,737	1.3	15,139	2.6	922,912	1,031,069	124,268	13	206	161	61
	Oct-99	2,882	1	22	3,982	1.4	5,057	1.3	13,743	2.7	760,428	918,241	105,493	14	191	150	65
	Nov-99	2,589	1	21	3,455	1.3	4,397	1.3	11,750	2.7	635,578	815,021	91,749	14	184	145	54
	Dec-99	2,151	1	21	2,834	1.3	3,597	1.3	10,144	2.8	595,359	562,899	71,643	12	210	168	59
Total		53,906	0%	20%	73,202	1.4	92,781	1.3	234,484	2.5	$13,328,555	$15,163,367	$2,027,261	15%	$182	$144	$57

Note: The report shown in **Exhibit 2E** summarizes the visitation patterns for a group of customers whose patronage was declining in the second half of 1998. These customers had significantly reduced their aggregate frequency to Harrah's casinos. Based on their historical pattern of behavior, Harrah's had expected to see them in December but hadn't.

In order to reinvigorate relationships with these customers, Harrah's sent a direct mail offer to approximately 8,000 customers in January of 1999 that was redeemable in February, March and April. One cash coupon was sent per month, with the amount varying by customer worth. If these customers returned to Harrah's, they were put into the loyalty-marketing program and managed according to their upside potential. The program seemed to be working even though the cost of the offer had gone up from $30 to $40.

EXHIBIT 2F Consolidation of Play (Theoretical Win) by Customer

Source: Harrah's Entertainment Inc.

Customer IDs	Q1	Q2	Q3	Q4	1998	Q1	Q2	Q3	Q4	1999	Attrition	New	Change
1	$800	$700	$300	$—	$1,800	$800	$900	$900	$200	$2,800	0	0	$1,000
2	—	—	—	60	120	120	60	80	—	200	0	1	70
3	—	60	—	60	120	80	—	—	50	190	0	0	—
4	—	—	—	—	—	—	—	80	—	80	1	1	—
5	—	60	40	60	160	150	70	80	—	300	0	0	(100)
6	—	60	120	220	400	40	—	50	70	160	0	0	120
7	—	40	—	—	40	60	—	80	70	160	0	0	120
8	80	80	—	—	160	—	60	—	80	280	0	0	4,300
9	—	1,200	2,000	500	3,700	—	2,500	1,500	4,000	8,000	0	0	80
10	—	60	—	—	60	20	50	20	50	140	0	0	220
11	80	—	40	80	200	120	80	220	—	420	0	0	80
12	—	40	40	40	120	50	50	50	50	200	0	0	—
13	—	—	—	—	—	—	—	—	150	150	0	1	900
14	800	1,500	1,200	800	4,300	1,100	1,500	1,200	1,400	5,200	0	0	1,980
15	7,000	2,500	—	—	9,500	5,000	6,000	—	480	11,480	0	0	—
16	—	—	—	—	—	—	60	70	70	200	0	1	1,200
17	—	—	—	—	—	—	40	40	—	80	0	1	20
18	300	400	500	500	1,700	900	900	700	400	2,900	0	0	20
19	40	40	—	—	80	50	50	—	—	100	0	0	40
20	50	—	—	50	100	40	40	40	—	120	0	0	(720)
21	—	30	30	—	60	40	30	30	—	100	0	0	(120)
22	400	600	—	—	1,000	—	—	280	—	280	0	0	200
23	—	1,000	—	—	1,000	—	600	280	—	880	0	0	1,100
24	50	—	—	—	50	100	—	—	150	250	0	0	—
25	2,000	2,000	2,200	1,500	7,700	2,100	2,200	3,000	1,500	8,800	0	1	—
26	—	—	—	—	—	60	—	—	—	60	0	1	20
27	30	—	30	50	110	—	—	—	—	—	1	0	—
28	40	40	50	—	130	20	40	—	—	100	1	0	—
29	40	40	—	—	80	—	40	—	40	—	0	0	20
30	—	—	60	60	120	—	—	—	—	210	1	0	—
31	100	—	80	—	180	40	40	80	90	130	0	0	30
32	—	60	30	—	90	—	—	50	40	160	0	0	40
33	30	—	—	100	130	60	50	50	—	160	0	0	30
34	—	—	4,000	2,000	6,000	3,500	—	1,000	—	4,500	0	0	(1,500)

(Continued)

Customer IDs	Q1	Q2	Q3	Q4	1998	Q1	Q2	Q3	Q4	1999	Attrition	New	Change
35	50	70	—	200	320	—	—	—	—	—	1	0	—
36	—	—	200	—	200	—	—	600	—	600	0	0	400
37	60	—	40	—	100	40	40	60	80	220	0	0	120
38	—	—	200	—	200	—	240	100	90	430	0	0	230
39	50	—	60	—	110	60	260	40	—	260	0	0	150
40	—	—	—	40	40	60	60	—	—	160	0	0	120
41	120	—	—	—	120	—	—	—	—	—	1	0	—
42	—	—	200	—	200	150	100	80	—	330	0	0	130
43	40	40	60	—	140	—	—	70	60	130	0	0	(10)
44	—	—	—	—	—	70	60	80	60	270	0	1	270
45	400	400	400	500	1,700	800	800	700	500	2,800	0	0	1,100
46	—	40	—	40	80	—	60	70	—	130	0	0	50
47	—	50	—	—	50	40	—	40	260	340	0	0	290
48	—	—	—	—	—	—	—	—	120	120	0	1	120
49	—	—	70	—	70	—	140	70	60	270	0	0	200
50	—	—	—	—	—	—	3,000	1,500	70	4,570	0	1	4,570
51	40	40	—	—	80	70	70	50	70	190	0	0	110
52	60	120	—	—	180	70	70	50	80	230	0	0	50
53	120	60	30	60	240	—	150	—	50	180	0	0	110
54	40	—	—	—	70	40	50	50	40	250	0	0	150
55	40	60	60	—	100	50	60	90	50	120	0	0	60
56	—	—	—	60	60	40	50	—	70	240	0	0	90
57	50	50	—	100	150	80	60	70	70	130	0	0	30
58	60	40	—	70	100	60	—	—	50	60	0	0	(10)
59	—	—	—	70	70	60	—	—	—	180	0	0	110
60	70	70	—	30	70	50	50	—	70	180	0	0	70
61	40	40	—	60	110	880	30	50	50	180	0	0	110
62	50	50	—	—	100	40	500	400	600	2,380	0	0	2,280
63	20	—	40	—	80	50	50	50	70	210	0	0	130
64	30	—	—	80	70	—	—	—	—	—	1	0	—
65	—	—	200	—	—	—	200	200	200	600	0	1	600
66	60	120	120	—	380	70	80	50	100	300	0	0	(80)
67	60	—	—	80	180	220	60	—	220	500	0	0	320
68	150	—	60	80	230	100	140	200	80	520	0	0	290
69	20	120	—	40	80	50	—	80	—	130	0	0	50
70	—	—	—	—	200	200	50	220	—	420	0	0	220
71	40	—	40	—	120	80	50	—	150	280	0	0	160

	1	2	3	4	5	6	7	8	9	10	11	12	13
72	70	0	0	170	50	50	40	30	100	—	60	40	—
73	(20)	0	0	80	—	—	80	—	100	30	—	70	—
74	—	1	0	300	—	150	—	150	—	50	—	40	60
75	150	0	0	300	80	60	100	60	150	800	700	400	800
76	(900)	0	1	1,800	—	300	800	700	2,700	—	100	50	40
77	—	1	0	—	—	—	—	—	190	—	—	—	—
78	260	0	0	150	180	70	—	80	—	—	—	—	400
79	1,720	0	0	660	—	1,400	480	—	400	600	—	400	400
80	(100)	1	0	3,120	—	—	1,500	220	1,400	—	—	—	400
81	—	1	0	300	300	80	—	—	400	—	—	—	—
82	—	0	0	310	70	50	80	80	—	—	600	40	—
83	(80)	0	1	130	—	—	—	80	600	40	—	—	—
84	240	0	0	520	—	320	520	—	80	—	200	500	400
85	—	0	0	320	—	—	—	—	200	—	—	200	70
86	900	1	0	—	600	600	700	500	1,500	600	400	3,300	—
87	(170)	0	1	2,400	2,000	500	—	1,500	670	—	2,200	—	400
88	900	0	0	500	780	1,500	1,400	—	5,500	30	400	—	60
89	(20)	0	0	6,400	—	—	50	50	800	1,000	—	600	1,000
90	10	0	0	780	—	—	260	320	90	—	—	—	—
91	—	0	0	100	—	1,100	—	—	1,000	—	400	—	—
92	(420)	0	0	580	—	—	260	100	1,400	1,000	400	—	40
93	(300)	0	0	1,100	—	—	50	40	1,000	60	200	20	—
94	—	0	0	—	—	—	260	—	200	—	50	600	50
95	240	0	0	440	80	—	50	40	50	—	30	—	—
96	100	0	0	150	60	—	—	200	1,000	1,000	600	200	200
97	—	0	0	—	—	—	200	—	110	60	190	176	176
98	70	0	1	160	120	1,100	—	40	90	115	45	47	52
99	500	0	0	1,300	—	—	—	200	800	36	3,300	3,300	7,000
100	90	0	0	200	—	—	200	—	656	2,000	4,000	—	—
Average				885	165	221	282	219	656	115	190	176	176
Actives				88	52	61	61	60	86	36	45	47	52
Max				11,480	4,000	3,000	6,000	5,000	9,500	2,000	4,000	3,300	7,000
Min				—	—	—	—	—	—	—	—	—	—
Total				88,470	16,340	22,080	28,200	21,850	65,620	11,530	18,840	17,620	17,630

Gambling in the United States

The United States had a long and complicated relationship with gambling. Early religious settlers felt that it was immoral. Yet the limited entertainment options of the frontier meant that gaming parlors co-existed, often uneasily, with churches.

During the 1950s, Benjamin "Bugsy" Siegel, a known gangster, saw an opportunity to elude California's strict ban on gambling and also quench its citizens' thirst for gaming. Siegel traveled to Nevada, since the state had tolerated gambling in the 1930s during the construction of the Hoover Dam, and built a luxury Caribbean-style hotel and casino called the Flamingo in Las Vegas. To attract gamblers, Las Vegas began offering inexpensive hotel rooms, food, free drinks, and well-known entertainers. Performers such as Frank Sinatra and Elvis Presley played to full houses there.

In 1978 casinos spread to Atlantic City and then to states like Colorado, Louisiana, and South Dakota. The early 1980s saw casino resorts become more popular for guests and businesses alike, and casino growth was poised to increase dramatically by decade's end. Casino gambling was approved in Iowa, Illinois, Mississippi, Missouri, and on many Native American reservations. In 1989 Iowa became the first state to allow gambling on riverboat casinos.

Also in the late 1980s, Stephen Wynn almost single-handedly changed Las Vegas by taking gambling to the next level when he built the Mirage resort. The casino resort had a shark tank, a wild animal haven, and an artificial erupting volcano. Others soon followed suit. Old casinos such as the Sands, the Hacienda, and the New Frontier were demolished. New casinos like the Luxor—a glass version of the Great Pyramid with copies of Egyptian monuments and statues of the pharaohs—were built to attract tourists looking for entertainment.

Although many new casinos were introduced in various cities in the early to late 1990s, by 1999, Nevada and Atlantic City still claimed over 40% of the $31 billion in total gambling revenue in the United States (see **Exhibit 3**).

Las Vegas, the largest U.S. gaming market, was a unique destination city and, during the late 1990s, became a mecca for national conventions and "must-see" mega resorts. Vacationers could easily spend a week visiting all of the major casinos and other attractions in Las Vegas, or simply sit poolside, go to a show or shop, and enjoy fine dining. Wynn's $1.6 billion Bellagio Hotel, inspired by Italy's Lake Como region, opened in October 1998 with an 8.5-acre lake and 1,400 fountains.[2] According to data compiled by the Las Vegas Convention and Visitors Authority (LVCVA), the average Las Vegas visitor in 2000 was expected to spend $1,329 during a 3.7 day stay—50 percent on gambling, 20.6 percent on lodging, and the remainder on meals, shopping, transportation, shows and sightseeing.

[2] Tom Graves, "Standard & Poor's Industry Surveys—Lodging and Gaming," August 17, 2000.

EXHIBIT 3
Total Gaming Revenue in the United States, 1995–1999 ($ in millions)

Source: Gaming Commissions and Merrill Lynch estimates.

	1995	1996	1997	1998	1999
Traditional					
Total Nevada	$ 7,366.4	$ 7,420.2	$ 7,802.7	$ 8,064.1	$ 9,020.5
Las Vegas Strip	3,607.4	3,579.6	3,809.4	3,812.4	4,488.5
Atlantic City	3,747.6	3,814.6	3,905.8	4,032.2	4,164.2
Total	$11,113.9	$11,234.8	$11,708.5	$12,096.3	$13,184.7
Riverboats	$ 4,732.0	$ 5,549.2	$ 6,437.9	$ 7,299.6	$ 8,332.2
Native American	$ 4,175.9	$ 4,731.3	$ 5,779.3	$ 7,890.9	$ 8,426.3
Other	$ 430.3	$ 639.0	$ 772.9	$ 873.9	$ 1,199.8
Total United States	$20,452.1	$22,154.4	$24,698.6	$28,160.7	$31,143.0

Note: Other includes Colorado, Delaware, Detroit, and South Dakota.

Unlike Las Vegas, Atlantic City was more of a "day tripper's" destination. Approximately 30% of its visitors arrived by charter bus and generally stayed for less than a day. The winter cold made the Boardwalk less appealing to tour group business.[3] In 1999, there were 12 hotel/casinos, of which 10 were located on or near the famous Atlantic City Boardwalk. Only one new casino had been built in Atlantic City since 1987: the Taj Mahal, opened in 1990.[4]

The geographic expansion of legalized and state supervised gambling broadened the industry's customer base. People who had never seen the bright lights of Las Vegas nor strolled the Boardwalk in Atlantic City were being lured to riverboats in states like Iowa and Louisiana, land-based casinos in Detroit and New Orleans, and casinos on Native American land in various states. By 1999, riverboat-type casinos were operating in six states, and Native American–owned facilities were in business in over 12 states.[5]

Company Background

The man who industrialized gambling, William Fisk Harrah—26-year-old charmer, pathological car lover, and bingo entrepreneur—arrived in Reno, Nevada, in May 1937 and commenced his casino operations.[6] In 1939, Harrah opened a bingo parlor in the two-block gambling heart of Reno, Nevada, which had legalized gambling eight years earlier. In 1942, Harrah opened a casino, equipping it with blackjack, a dice table, and 20 slot machines.[7] In 1946, the company, by now called Harrah's, expanded and added roulette to the card and dice tables and began serving liquor. The spotless, glass-fronted, plush carpeted casino was a sharp contrast to the rough frontier-type betting parlors of the time.

In 1955, Harrah bought a dingy casino on the southern shore of Lake Tahoe, and four years later, he relocated the casino across the highway to create the world's largest single structure devoted to gambling. The new casino had a 10-acre parking lot and an 850-seat theater-restaurant that drew star entertainers. Next, Harrah constructed the highest building in Reno—a 24-story hotel across the street from his casino, and then, in 1973, he opened an 18-story hotel in Lake Tahoe. Every room came with a view of the lake and a marble-finished bathroom.

By 2000, Harrah's Entertainment, Inc. was well-known in the gaming industry and operated casinos in more markets than any other casino company. Harrah's had 21 casinos in 17 different cities, including operations in all five major traditional casino markets (Las Vegas, Lake Tahoe, Laughlin, Reno, and Atlantic City). The company also owned or operated casinos in Joliet and Metropolis, Illinois; East Chicago, Indiana; Vicksburg and Tunica, Mississippi; Shreveport, Lake Charles, and New Orleans, Louisiana; and Kansas City and St. Louis, Missouri. In addition, Harrah's managed a number of Native American casinos located in Arizona, North Carolina, and Kansas.[8] In summary, Harrah's operated land-based, dockside, riverboat, and Indian casino facilities in all of the traditional and most of the new U.S. casino entertainment jurisdictions (see **Graphic A**).

[3] Brian Maher and Jennifer Smith, "Credit Lyonnais Securities (USA) Inc.—Gaming Industry Highlights," March 6, 2001.

[4] Tom Graves, "Standard & Poor's Industry Surveys—Lodging and Gaming," August 17, 2000.

[5] Ibid.

[6] Leon Mandel, *William Fisk Harrah, The Life and Times of a Gambling Magnate,* Garden City, NY: Doubleday & Co., 1982, p. 1.

[7] Harrah's Entertainment Inc.

[8] Jason Ader, Mark Falcone, and Eric Hausler, "Outside the Box: Exploring Important Investor Issues—Harrah's Entertainment, Inc.—Reaping the Benefits of Total Rewards," Bear Stearns Equity Research, November 10, 2000.

GRAPHIC A **Harrah's Operations, early 2000[9]**

Source: Harrah's.

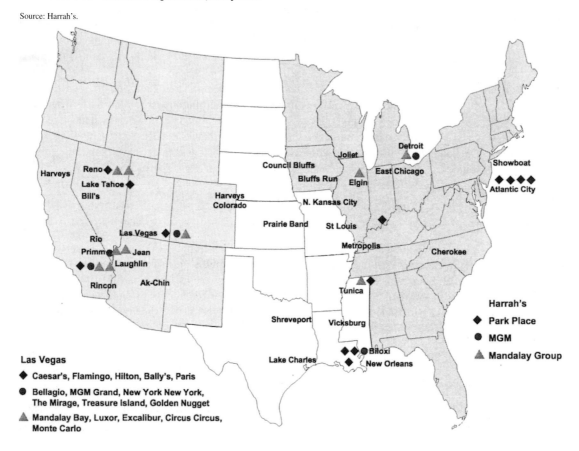

Las Vegas

◆ Caesar's, Flamingo, Hilton, Bally's, Paris

● Bellagio, MGM Grand, New York New York,
The Mirage, Treasure Island, Golden Nugget

▲ Mandalay Bay, Luxor, Excalibur, Circus Circus,
Monte Carlo

Early Strategy

Satre, who joined Harrah's in 1980 as Vice President, General Counsel, and Secretary before becoming CEO in 1984, reflected on his first moves:

> Initially I focused on people more than anything else and I thought that was a sustainable competitive position at that time. The strategy seemed to be working in the early 1990s as Harrah's led the way to take advantage of legalized gambling in many states beyond Nevada and New Jersey. These new markets provided Harrah's with explosive growth and a highly profitable business.
>
> I also started a program to communicate with customers who won over a certain amount in our jackpots. I asked them which other casinos they had visited and planned to visit. I was amazed at the amount of cross-market visitation from these customers and yet we received only a small fraction of their gaming dollars when they visited Las Vegas and Atlantic City. At the same time, we were developing rewards programs based on tracking cards (akin to frequent shopper cards) at each of our different properties. The rewards took totally different forms at each property because each property was pretty autonomous.

Satre frequently talked with John Boushy, then the head of marketing/IT, about how much better it would be if customers could use the same loyalty card at every Harrah's location.

[9] Rio and Showboat were Harrah's properties.

That way Harrah's would know more about customer play at each property. Harrah's first investment toward this goal was the Winner's Information Network, a national database. The plan was to follow up with both a common card and common analytical tools for making decisions that were based on the data from tracking customers' play.

Customer Loyalty as a Core Competency

By the mid 1990s, competitors had entered the new markets with better and flashier properties. The Mirage in Las Vegas had set a new standard and began to spawn imitators. With no new jurisdictions planning to legalize gambling, Harrah's was facing the formidable task of growing the business in a limited market. Satre realized that the people strategy was not sufficient to grow patronage and play at existing casinos:

> I remember reading *The Discipline of Market Leaders,* which I shared with the management of the company. The book's fundamental thrust was that you could become a leader based on one of three competencies: innovations of product, cost structure, or relationships/customer intimacy.
>
> We saw MGM and Mirage trying to innovate—creating highly themed environments that had lots of new experiences for their customers. Whether it was the theme park at the MGM or the dolphin tank and the tigers at Mirage. . . . In the early '90s, these companies were put up on a mantel as the companies to show where the industry was headed. Anyone who came to Las Vegas would say, "you guys [Harrah's] are living in the past." I told them that this would be great if you were starting from scratch, but if you were a 50-year-old company, the capital costs of making "must-see" properties would be enormous.
>
> While there was great temptation to go down that path because it was exciting to try to design and build, we ultimately decided against it: customer loyalty was really our competency and we decided that we could become an industry leader based on that skill.

But by early 1998, the company's performance was not meeting Satre's expectations. He realized that Harrah's did not have the marketing horsepower to implement the strategy across all properties in a consistent manner. The company had excellent technology and great operations but not effective marketing. He expressed his concerns to Sergio Zyman, then Chief Marketing Officer at the Coca-Cola Company and a noted authority on consumer marketing whom he knew through the Coca-Cola/Harrah's strategic alliance. Satre recalled:

> I went to see Sergio to get references for people that I might hire into a marketing job. He was a quick study, and said, "You are heading in the wrong direction. You don't need a marketing executive. How is your marketing executive going to implement in a company that has a history of autonomous operations and marketing is so tied to your operations strategy? You need a COO who is a marketer—who can implement your marketing, but make sure it goes through all the properties, and that there is no hiccup or interruption between the corporate strategy and what is implemented at the property level."

A New Approach

Satre turned to Gary Loveman to fill this void. At the time Loveman was on the HBS faculty in the service management area and had worked with Harrah's as a consultant for five years. Satre felt that Loveman would help the company move "from an operations-driven company that viewed each property as a 'standalone business,' to a marketing-driven company with a focus on our target customers and what it took to build their loyalty to the Harrah's brand."

The board supported Satre's recommendation to hire Loveman as Harrah's COO. He joined Harrah's in 1998 bringing his atypical range of experience. Loveman described his challenge at Harrah's in the following way:

> In 1998, we were sitting on all this transactional data but not using it effectively. The statistic that jumped out and bit me was that for customers who visited Harrah's once a year or more, we got 36 cents out of their gaming dollar. Hence, they were visiting our competitors and showing remarkably little loyalty to Harrah's. That was the principal anomaly around which we organized everything else, and since then it has been an all-inclusive effort to envelop customers with reasons to be loyal.
>
> The Total Gold program, launched in Fall 1997, was intended to increase customer loyalty in a variety of ways, and it was supported by a lot of other marketing interventions that all had the same mission. They all intended, for example, to attract a 60-year-old lady from Memphis, Tennessee, on a Friday night, as she and her husband were thinking about where to go in Tunica, Mississippi, where Harrah's is one of 11 casino alternatives. We wanted people to think "Harrah's, Harrah's, Harrah's" in the same way that they went to the same hairdresser, cobbler and auto mechanic. All of our tools were a means to that end.

To achieve this goal, Loveman launched three major initiatives: changing the organization structure, building the Harrah's brand, delivering extraordinary service, and exploiting relationship marketing opportunities.

A New Organization Structure

His first priority was to build a new organizational structure. Harrah's division presidents and their subordinates in brand operations, information technology, and marketing services, started reporting to Loveman instead of to the CEO (see **Exhibit 4**). This emphasized that customers belonged to Harrah's and not simply to one of its casinos. Loveman explained:

> Changing the organizational structure was a major accomplishment in light of the fact that historically, as with all our competitors today, each property was like a fiefdom, managed by feudal lords with occasional interruptions from the king or the queen who passed through town. Each property had its own P&L and its own resource stream, and the notion that you would take a customer and encourage them to do their gaming at other properties was not common practice. It required a lot of leadership from my boss and the people who ran these businesses to adopt this strategy and encourage customers to spend their money at Harrah's locations broadly rather than simply at their property.

Brand and Service

Next, because Harrah's had little meaningful brand differentiation in the casino industry, Loveman set out to develop a brand that had a gaming orientation and was centered on what the research told them was the most profound emotion of gaming—the feelings of anticipation and exuberance. He explained:

> People go to a casino because it makes them feel "exuberantly alive." That is what they are buying. They don't believe that they are going to win on average, but when they win, they have a ball. With every bet, gamblers anticipate the possibility of winning. Many described the adrenaline rush, the high, the pounding of their hearts and the tingling in their bodies that they feel when they were gambling. With every bet, they hoped to be able to sustain the level of fantasy that gambling provided. One gambler stated: "When you look up and you see that it's a hit and that you're going to get paid off, it's a tingling from my toes on up to the top of my head that comes into my body. That's what makes me want to put more money into the machines."

EXHIBIT 4 Harrah's Entertainment, Inc. Operations

Source: Harrah's Entertainment Inc.

Office of the President
& Chief Operating Office
Gary Loveman

Sr. Vice President Marketing — Rich Mirman

Director Customer Assurance — John Bruns

Division President New Orleans & Rio — Jay Sevigny
- SVP & GM New Orleans — Joe Hasson
- SVP & GM Rio — Cary Rehm
- VP Marketing — Michael Weaver

Division President Western Division — Carlos Tolosa
- SVP & GM Ak-Chin — Janet Beronio
- SVP & GM Lake Tahoe — Gary Selesner
- GM Bill's — Pete Bonner
- SVP & GM Las Vegas — Tom Jenkin
- Acting GM Laughlin — Bill Keena
- SVP & GM Reno — Michael Silbering
- VP Marketing — Ginny Shanks

Sr. Vice President Brand Ops. & I.T. — John Boushy

Division President Eastern Division — Tim Wilmott
- SVP & GM Atlantic City — Dave Jonas
- VP & GM Cherokee — Jerry Egelus
- SVP & GM E. Chicago — Joe Domenico
- SVP & GM Joliet — Michael St. Pierre
- SVP & GM Showboat — Tom O'Donnell
- VP Marketing — Gaye Guilo

Executive Assistant — Karen Spacek

Division President Central Division — Anthony Sanfilippo
- SVP & GM No. Kansas City — Bill Noble
- VP & GM Prairie Band — Patrick Browne
- SVP & GM Shreveport — Tom Roberts
- SVP & GM St. Louis — Vern Jennings
- VP & GM Tunica — TBD
- VP & GM Vicksburg — TBD
- VP Marketing — Jeff Hook

681

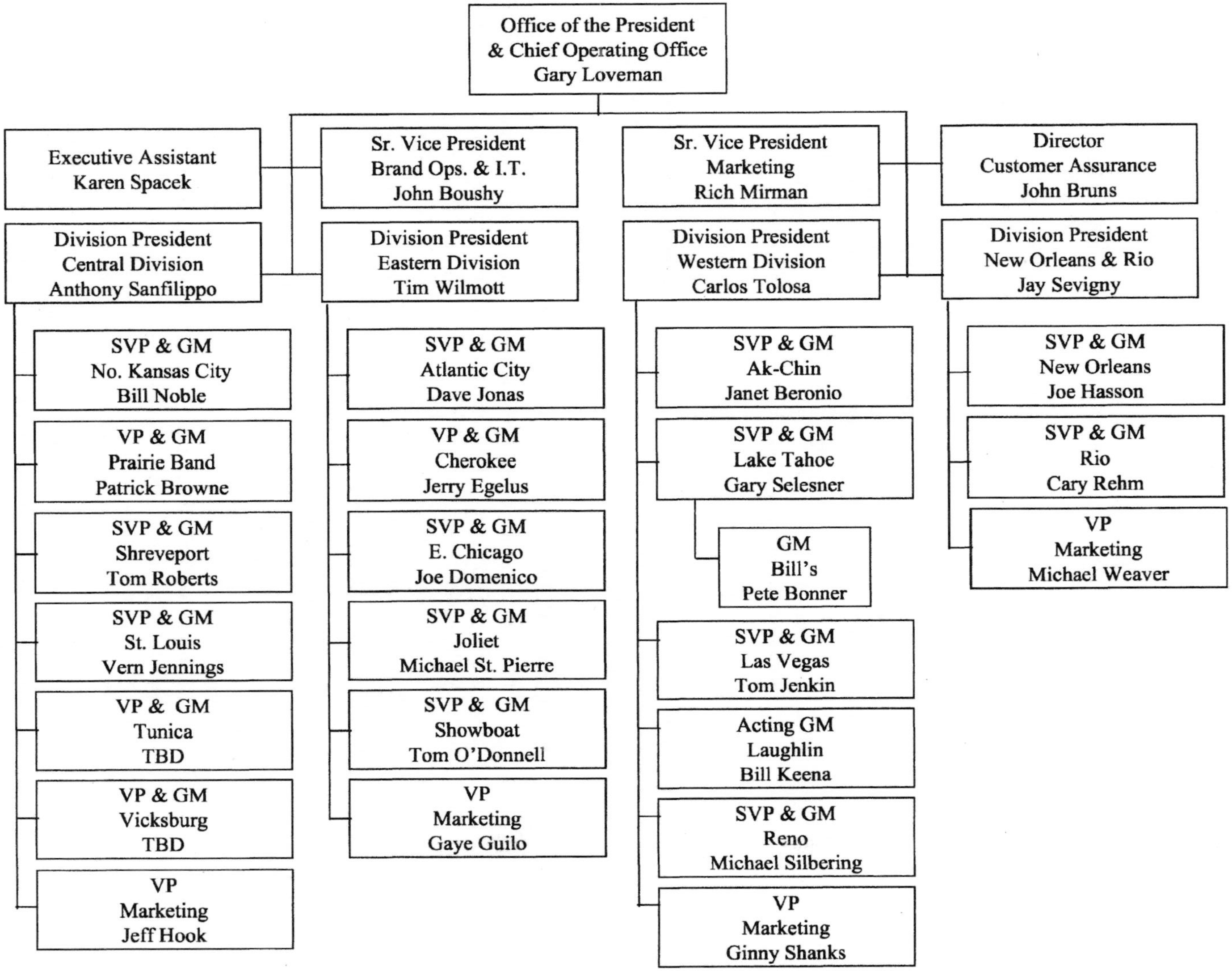

Harrah's research showed casino entertainment provides consumers a momentary escape from the problems and pressures of their daily lives. Gaming customers share the "exuberantly alive" feeling that risk-taking affords the likes of mountain climbers and skydivers, though casinos provide a far safer playing field. "So we focused all of our advertising around the feeling of exuberance," explained a Harrah's manager. Since Loveman's arrival, Harrah's spent $15–20 million per year in advertising to communicate the feeling of anticipation to the general audience.

Improving service was also important to the brand image. Harrah's was known for having the "friendliest employees." However, Loveman believed that the service was good but not distinguished. He recognized the need for better service on his very first night on the casino floor.

> I stopped and asked a gentleman who was playing a slot machine, "How are you doing tonight, sir?" and he said "Shitty." It dawned on me that my parents had not taken me through the "How are you—shitty" dialogue. I did not know what to say. The same experience was repeated more than once that night and I found myself not wanting to ask that question any more. But that is the world my employees live in every day. Providing service in this environment is tricky because most guests end up losing while playing in a casino. We had not trained our people to deal with these kinds of situations. We wanted to deliver a world class service experience that would transcend this issue.

Finally, Harrah's put in place a variety of interventions at the employee level—service process design, reward and recognition, measurement of executives—in as pervasive a fashion as possible to make service demonstrably better. Harrah's thereafter won the award for "best service" from *Casino Player,* the magazine of choice in the casino industry, for three years in a row.

Customer Relationship Management

The third and the most important initiative was to implement marketing tools and programs across all Harrah's properties. Loveman disbanded the existing marketing function and rebuilt it with people who preferred slide rules to mock-ups. Richard Mirman, a former University of Chicago math whiz, left Booz Allen & Hamilton to join the new team as Senior Vice President of Relationship Marketing. Under Mirman marketing became a very quantitative undertaking. Loveman explained:

> Customer Relationship Management (CRM) at Harrah's consists of two elements: Database Marketing (DBM) and the Total Gold program. The Total Gold program motivates customers to consolidate their play, and the data collected through the program allows us to execute direct marketing strategies that increase the efficiency and effectiveness of our marketing dollars.
>
> The big innovation by Mirman and his group of "propeller heads" (David Norton, vice president of Loyalty Marketing and Dave Kowal, vice president of Loyalty Capabilities and Revenue Management) was development of quantitative models to accurately *predict* "customer worth"—the theoretical amount the house expects to win, over the long term, from a customer based on his level of play (see **Table A**). Historically, the casino industry had determined customers worth based only on observed play. Our ability to accurately predict play enabled us to begin building relationships with customers based on their future worth, rather than on their past behavior.

While it was simpler to make this prediction for a slot machine player, it was significantly more complicated for table game play. The transactional data collected ever since the launch of the Total Gold card in 1997 was used to build these models and forecast customer worth. Mirman called it Harrah's secret recipe.

TABLE A
Theoretical Win

Source: Harrah's.

Theoretical Win from a Customer per day = A * B * N * H
A = the house advantage on a game (e.g., 6% hold on slot machines)[10]
B = the average bet (e.g., $1)
N = the number of bets per hour (a good slot machine player can pull the lever almost 15 times per minute)
H = the number of hours played per day.

Database Marketing (DBM)

DBM changed the way Harrah's invested in its customers. Consider the case of Ms. Maranees, reported in the *Wall Street Journal* article, who received invitations to two tournaments, along with vouchers for $200, all courtesy of Harrah's Entertainment Inc. According to Loveman:

> These decisions were made using the decision science tools to predict customer worth rather than relying on observed worth from her first visit to the casino. While she would be considered a lousy customer based on her short visit to Harrah's, with the help of the information generated from one visit and one visit alone, Harrah's concluded otherwise by submitting her profile to the database. She was probably a great customer, but a great customer of Harrah's competitors. It makes sense to invest in converting her to a Harrah's customer. In the past, she would not have shown up on the radar screen.

Proactive Marketing: Opportunity-based Customer Segmentation—As soon as players used their Total Gold cards, Harrah's began to track their play preferences, betting patterns, where they liked to eat in the casino and whether they stayed the night, how often they visited, how much and how long they played. Combined with the basic information contained on the application card, which included birth date and home address, Harrah's could begin to develop a sophisticated customer profile. Harrah's estimated that 26% of players provided 82% of revenues, with avid players spending approximately $2,000 annually.[11] These "avid experienced players" that tended to play in multiple markets became Harrah's target customers.

Using this detailed information for every customer, Harrah's predicted potential customer playing behavior at Harrah's properties. Harrah's compared observed to predicted behavior and identified opportunity segments based on a disparity between predicted and observed values. As shown in **Graphic B,** there were three key opportunity segments for Harrah's as well as a segment where re-investment could be rationalized. Harrah's used customized marketing to achieve specific objectives such as driving incremental frequency, budget, or both. (See **Exhibit 5** for an overview of the potential messages and types of offers that Harrah's sent to customers. **Exhibit 6** provides a typical letter to a customer.)

Marketing Experiments—Harrah's quantitative approach also made it possible to conduct "marketing experiments" and track customers over time. This helped Harrah's discover the right marketing instrument, for the right behavior modification, for the right customer. As an example, Harrah's chose two similar groups of frequent slot players from Jackson, Mississippi. Members of the control group were offered a typical casino-marketing package worth $125—a free room, two steak meals and $30 of free chips at the casino. Members of the test group were offered $60 in chips. The more modest offer generated far

[10] The hold referred to the theoretical amounts a particular machine retains for the house over an extended period. In this case, the machine would theoretically return to the player $94 for every $100 played. Persistent players would eventually lose all their money.

[11] Jason Ader, Mark Falcone, and Eric Hausler, "Outside the Box: Exploring Important Investor Issues—Harrah's Entertainment, Inc.—Reaping the Benefits of Total Rewards," Bear Stearns Equity Research, November 10, 2000, p. 5.

GRAPHIC B **Opportunity-Based Customer Segmentation**

Source: Harrah's.

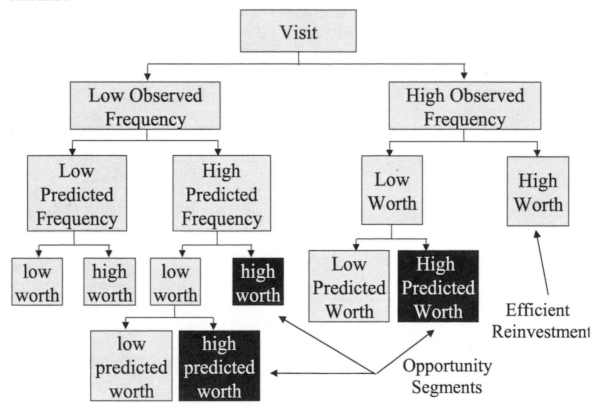

more gambling, suggesting that Harrah's had been wasting money giving customers free rooms.[12] Harrah's tracked the gambling behavior of the customers in the test and control group over the next several months to conclude that the "less attractive" promotion was indeed more profitable. Using such techniques, Harrah's eradicated the practice of "same day cash" at most of its properties—the process by which casinos returned a portion of a customer's bet each day with the hope that the customer would play it. Loveman explained:

> As we were looking for incremental business, we thought that giving people things today had no effect on their decisions when they were ready to go gambling again. We used the test and control methodology to gradually ramp back "same day cash" from 5% to zero. We saved half of it and gave back the rest to customers as incentives for the next visit. My operators were convinced that they would have screaming customers. By tracking customers over time, we could show the operators that they could eliminate "same day cash" without adversely affecting their business. Today, "same day cash" does not exist anywhere except to a very modest degree at Harrah's Nevada destination properties. Our industry has it everywhere and they advertise against us. The piece that is critical for us is to get our internal folks to recognize that we need to do things that drive incremental revenues.

Harrah's believed it had developed a customer centric approach to direct marketing. There were three key phases to a customer relationship. The first phase, "new business," was focused exclusively on customers new to the brand or to the property. Harrah's goal with its new business program was to encourage customers to take a second and third trip.

[12] Binkley, op cit.

EXHIBIT 5 Segment Communication Program

Source: Harrah's Entertainment Inc.

Segment Number	Segment Description	Reinvestment	Hotel Coupon	Goal of Contract	Redemption Window	Letter Tone	Letter Messages
1	Local, lodger		no, maybe too high worth only	probably don't mail			note: do not want locals in hotel as there is no incremental value generated
2	Local, nonlodger		no	probably don't mail			note: do not want locals in hotel as there is no incremental value generated
3	New, lodger	normal to high	yes	get back for second trip	longer	introductory	welcome, explain Total Rewards
4	New, nonlodger	highest	yes	get back for a second trip as a lodger	longer	introductory	welcome, explain Total Rewards, want in the hotel, explain why our hotel is the best
5	Existing, 1 trip in last 12 months, lodger	normal	yes	thanks	longer	friendly	thanks, make sure you stay with us on your next trip
6	Existing, 1 trip in last 12 months, nonlodger	higher	yes	thanks	longer	friendly	thanks, want in the hotel, reinforce the hotel as the place to stay
7	Existing, 2+ trips in last 12 months, lodger	normal	yes	thanks	longer	appreciative	thank our best guests
8	Existing, 2+ trips in last 12 months, nonlodger	higher	yes	thanks	longer	appreciative	Thank our best guests, want in the hotel (these guests likely to stay with competitors or be day trip guests)

685

EXHIBIT 6   **Sample Letter to Loyal Customers (Low Actual and High Predicted Frequency)**

Source: Harrah's Entertainment Inc.

Dear Steve,

All of us want you to know how much we appreciate your recent Harrah's visit. It's always gratifying when good, loyal customers like you keep coming back. But the bottom line is, WE WANT YOU TO BRING ALL YOUR PLAY TO HARRAH'S. That way, you'll earn even bigger rewards, more often . . . just by playing at Harrah's. To thank you again for your recent play we've enclosed these valuable rewards. Why settle for less anywhere else?

It may be cold outside, but the action and winning are hotter than ever inside. But don't take our word for it. [Ask Veronica Hale of Goldsby, Oklahoma. She just won $42,468 playing Harrah's one dollar Red, White and Blue slot machine.] At Harrah's you're always a winner when you use your Total [Gold] card. The more you use it, the more you can count on receiving exclusive discounts, comps for meals and hotel stays, even CASH REWARDS near the middle of each month. Right now, you can count on enjoying special happenings like these:

Offer:

Offer:

Remember, nobody rewards loyal players better or bigger than Harrah's. So doesn't it just make good sense to bring even more of your play to Harrah's? After all, the more you play using your Harrah's card, the more it pays. And the sooner you can move up to Harrah's next level of exclusive rewards and recognition. Make the most of your play. Come back to Harrah's now!

Best of Luck Always

Name
Vice President and General Manager

P.S.: With all that Harrah's has to offer, just imagine how much greater your rewards could be if you only play Harrah's.

The second phase, "loyalty," was focused on customers known for at least six months or three trips. Harrah's goal with its loyalty program was to extend continuously the relationship. The final phase, "retention," was focused on customers who had broken their historical visitation pattern. Harrah's goal with its retention program was to reinvigorate customers who had demonstrated signs of attrition. By using IT and decision science tools, Harrah's developed a variety of direct marketing programs to establish relationships with new customers, strengthen relationships with loyal customers, and reinvigorate relationships with customers who had shown signs of attrition.

Results from Data Base Marketing—Loveman and his team focused on results from the following programs:

• New Business Program

The New Business Program was designed to improve the effectiveness at converting new Total Gold members into loyal customers. The program used predicted customer worth (theoretical wins) to make more effective investment decisions at the customer level—thus allowing the particular offer to be more competitive with what the customer was currently receiving from their existing scenario of choice. This resulted in a more effective and more profitable new business program. **Exhibit 2B** illustrates the impact of such a program at a property.

• Loyalty Program—Frequency Upside

This program was designed to identify customers that, Harrah's predicted, were only giving Harrah's a small share of their total spending in a particular market. Harrah's capabilities enabled property marketers to develop programs that offered incentives for these customers to visit Harrah's properties more frequently—i.e., switch a trip from a competitor to Harrah's. **Exhibit 2C** tracks the behavior of a pool of 953 customers before and after the offer was sent in June. Harrah's calculated the profitability of these programs by comparing the incremental theoretical wins to the incremental cost of the program.

- Loyalty Program—Budget Upside

Harrah's also identified customers with budget upside—customers who were only giving a small share of their gaming budget to Harrah's on each trip. In most cases, a customer's allocation of budget was directly related to the order in which they visited casinos on a particular trip—the first stop received the largest share, the second received the second largest and so on. Therefore, the objective of this program was to encourage the customer to visit Harrah's first and thereby capture the majority of the single casino trips. **Exhibit 2D** tracks a group of customers with an upside budget potential. Harrah's was less sure if this program was working.

- Retention Program

The objective of Harrah's Retention Program was to reinvigorate customers who had broken their historical visitation pattern or had demonstrated other signs of attrition. Harrah's tested a variety of offers with customer segments to determine how much to reinvest in retaining loyal guests. The report shown in **Exhibit 2E** summarizes the visitation patterns for a group of customers whose patronage was declining in the second half of 1998. These customers had significantly reduced their aggregate frequency to Harrah's casinos. Based on their historical pattern of behavior, Harrah's had expected to see them in December but hadn't. The effects of the program are evident from tracking the behavior of 8,000 customers who received a direct mail offer in January 1999.

Having worked on the system for more than two years, Mirman and his team recognized that the full potential of these ideas would be realized only if these capabilities could be used at the local property level. Therefore, they made significant efforts in educating the local property managers and their marketing teams about the potential and effective use of these Data Base Marketing capabilities. Mirman and his group had to contend with the fact that marketing efforts at a property were ultimately the responsibility of the property manager and decided on how the Data Base Marketing efforts were integrated with their knowledge of the local market.

Mirman and his team accomplished these goals using a technology platform that was designed to track and manage transactions in casinos. However, it was generally acknowledged that execution of marketing programs based on the most current customer information was possible but required further investments.

The Total Rewards Program

The Total Gold program was designed to facilitate and encourage the cross-market visitation patterns of Harrah's customers. Through market research, Harrah's realized that a significant share of business was lost when Harrah's loyal customers visited destination markets like Las Vegas, but did not stay or play at a Harrah's during their visit. Harrah's estimated that more than a $100 million of lost revenue was generated by Harrah's customers in Las Vegas alone. The Total Program was intended to capture this lost business by making it easier for customers to earn and redeem rewards seamlessly at any of Harrah's properties across the country.

To execute Total Gold, Harrah's designed a completely integrated information technology network that linked all their properties together. The network enabled customer level information, like customer gaming theoretical value, to be shared in real time across the various casinos. This technology was then patented so as to bar Harrah's competitors from replicating what Phil Satre believed to be the company's future.

As a result of Total Gold, cross-market revenues (i.e., revenue generated from a customer in a market other than the one they signed up for) have grown significantly—from 13% in 1997 to 23% in 2000. At the Harrah's Las Vegas property alone, cross-market revenue now generates nearly 50% of the property's total revenue. Mirman says, "our cross-marketing effort is what enables our Las Vegas property to compete against properties like the Belaggio and the Venetian (multi-billion dollar properties that are right next door to Harrah's Las Vegas). Mirage Resorts spent $1.8 billion to develop Bellagio to attract customers, we developed a distribution strategy that invites customers to our properties. A subtle but powerful difference."

In July 1999, Mirman and his team revamped the program and called it Total Rewards. The motivation behind the change was the realization that even in local markets, Harrah's was only capturing a small share of the customer's gaming budget. The intention was to develop Total Gold into more of a loyalty program that would complement the direct mail strategy described earlier. Mirman added,

> Total Gold was a revolutionary technological innovation, but it lacked a number of the marketing fundamentals necessary to make it a true loyalty program. A loyalty program gives customers the incentive to establish a set of goals and then provides them with a very clear criteria for how to achieve them. Airlines have done a very good job at giving customers the incentive to aspire to earn free travel. Frequent flyer members have been trained to consolidate their travel on a particular airline until they have flown 25,000 miles and earn a free ticket. We wanted our customers to think about earning a complimentary steak dinner or a membership to our tiered card program.

The program is designed to encourage customer loyalty or consolidation of play both within a particular trip and across multiple trips or over the course of a calendar year. To promote the consolidation of play over the course of a trip, The Total Reward program provides a Reward Menu that translates reward credits to the various complimentary offerings. This menu enables customers to understand exactly what compliments are available and exactly what level of play is necessary to earn them. For the annual incentives to drive more frequency, Harrah's added two additional tier levels to the program. Total Rewards became a tiered customer loyalty program, consisting of Total Gold (no minimum customer worth), Total Platinum (theoretical customer worth $1,500 annually), and Total Diamond (theoretical customer worth $5,000 annually). The two programs, represented by different colored plastic cards, have accumulating benefits that are highly valued by the customers. The criteria to earn a membership into the program is based on a customer's annual accumulation of reward credits.

According to Mirman, there was also an emotional component to the Total Rewards program. "We want customers to think . . . I want to go to Harrah's because they know me and they reward me like they know me, and if I went somewhere else they would not."[13] Even though Harrah's knew everything about the customers' gaming behavior, customers were not concerned about privacy issues because they perceived the rewards and mail offers to be valuable to their specific needs. The company awarded three billion points during its first year of Total Rewards and had 16 million members in late 1999. Total Rewards seemed to be having an impact on play consolidation based on the theoretical worths described in **Exhibit 2F,** for a sample of 100 customers.

Signing Up Customers

To encourage sign-ups and play, Harrah's held give-away events for all cardholders at each property. Harrah's gave away houses, cars, million dollar prizes, trips (to great vacation destinations), jewelry, and the like. All one had to do to participate was to enroll in the Total Reward program and play. Customers knew that all these goodies came from the play being recorded.

---

[13] Richard H. Levey, "Destination Anywhere. Harrah's Entertainment Inc.'s Marketing Strategy," *Direct,* 1999.

Competition

Harrah's competed with numerous casinos and casino hotels of varying quality and size. Park Place Entertainment Corporation, with revenues of $2.5 billion, was the industry leader in 1998. A spin-off of Hilton Hotels, it owned 18 casinos and 23,000 hotel rooms, including Paris Las Vegas, Caesars, the Flamingo, Bally Entertainment Casinos, and Hilton Casinos. Park Place's gambling operations included resorts in Las Vegas, Atlantic City, New Orleans, and Biloxi, Mississippi, as well as Australia and Canada. The company seeks to maintain geographic diversity to reduce regional risk and provide more stable income streams. It strives to cluster properties in key locations to control operating expenses, reduce overhead and enhance revenue through cross-marketing. Acquisitions are an integral part of the company's overall strategy and a diverse customer base is served through a variety of properties such as Caesars for the high end market to the Flamingo for the value segment.

With $1.52 billion in revenues, Mirage Resorts mainly operated casinos in Las Vegas, but the company also had operations and tropical theme parks in Mississippi, New Jersey, and Argentina. Some of its better-known properties were the Mirage, Treasure Island, the Golden Nugget, and the Bellagio. Mirage is the leader in the Las Vegas strip gaming market targeting the upper-middle and premium segments of the market. It controlled approximately 60% of the high-roller market. Its strategy has been to develop high profile "must see" attractions. "We don't think of Mirage Resorts in terms of concrete and marble, games and shows, payrolls and budgets. We strive to create great resorts, each accommodating guests with a distinctive signature of charisma and style."[14] Mirage invests handsomely in its properties because "the presentation assumes that our guests appreciate and warrant fine quality, authenticity, and moments of unexpected, yet delightful grandeur."[15]

In 1998, Circus Enterprises, Inc. had revenues of $1.47 billion and owned about 10 casino resorts, including Circus Circus, the Edgewater, Excalibur, and Luxor. The company had casinos in Nevada, Mississippi, and Illinois. The strategy of the company is well stated in its 1999 annual report. "In Las Vegas, we are designing, piece by piece, spectacle by spectacle, the most ambitious, fully integrated gaming resort complex in the world—a fantasy of castles, glass pyramids, golden skyscrapers and more. One day we will own or control close to 20,000 hotel rooms along a single, continuous mile in the world's leading entertainment destination."[16] The most recent project, Mandalay Bay, was inaugurated on March 2, 1999. The property's attractions include, an 11-acre tropical lagoon featuring a sand-and-surf beach, a three-quarter-mile lazy river ride, a 30,000-square-foot spa and other entertainment attractions.

Trump Hotels & Casino Resorts, Inc. was also among the leaders in the gambling industry with several casinos such as Trump Plaza, Taj Mahal and Trump Marina, all in Atlantic City, and a riverboat casino on Lake Michigan. Owned by Donald Trump, the casinos had revenues of about $1.4 billion. With no growth in revenues, and $133 million loss on top of the losses in the previous two years, 1999 was not a good year for the company. Donald Trump, chairman, took on the additional responsibility of Acting President and CEO. His stated goal for the company was "to increase profitability by targeting better margin business coupled with a relentless pursuit of cost controls and efficient operations without diminishing the Trump experience our valued customers expect when they visit our properties."[17] The company had a major presence in Atlantic City. With the largest poker

---

[14] Mirage Resorts annual report, 1998.

[15] Mirage Resorts annual report, 1999.

[16] Circus Circus annual report, 1999.

[17] Trump Hotel and Casino annual report, 1999.

room in Atlantic City, the Taj Mahal is a "must-see" property in the Trump portfolio. The Trump Plaza targets the lucrative high-end drive-in slot customer and The Trump Marina is geared towards younger affluent customers but does not exclude its traditional base, middle and upper-middle market segments.

As part of its integrated marketing strategy, the Trump card was an important tool in its portfolio. Gamers were encouraged to register and use their cards at slot machines and table games to earn rewards based on their level of play. The computer systems kept records of cardholders playing preferences, frequency and denomination of play and the amount of gaming revenues produced. The management at the casino provided complimentary benefits to patrons with a demonstrated propensity to wager. A gamer's propensity to wager was determined by their gaming behavior at casinos in Atlantic City. It was important that a patron's gaming activity, net of rewards, was profitable to the casinos. The information collected though the Trump card was also used in sending direct mail offers to customers expected to provide revenues based on their past behavior and were offered more attentive service on the casino floor.[18]

Finally, on the East Coast, Harrah's competed with the largest Native American casino. The Foxwoods Resort and Casino, run by the Mashantucket Pequot tribe in Connecticut, grossed about $1 billion a year. Harrah's faced only local competition in many of the remaining markets.

The Gamble

As Satre stared out the window at the new construction that was taking place at the hotel next door, he tapped his fingers on the dense exhibits and thought about the term "Pavlovian marketing," once used by Mirman to describe these efforts. He hoped the reinvigoration campaign begun with Loveman's hiring would work, because Harrah's needed customer loyalty to stave off the onslaught of entertainment options from the competition. "The farther we get ahead and the more tests we run," Loveman had argued, "the more we learn. The more we understand our customers, the more substantial are the switching costs that we put into place, and the farther ahead we are of our competitors' efforts. That is why we are running as fast as we can."

---

[18] Paragraph excerpted from Trump Hotel and Casino's annual report, 1999.

Part 9

Sustaining Value

40

Sustaining Value

Robert Dolan

Introduction

Marketing is the "process via which a firm creates value for its chosen customers." How successful this process is depends on the relationship between value created and the cost of the value creation activities. If, as shown in **Figure A,** the value created far exceeds the firm's cost, a highly profitable pricing opportunity exists. The ratio of value to cost creates a wide "profitable pricing band." A price in this band partitions it into "consumer surplus" and "firm margin" components as shown in **Figure A.** Callaway Golf Company enjoyed such a situation in 1997. It produced golf clubs which satisfied the founder's vision of being "pleasingly different from the competition." It had industry leading sales of $843 million; and cost of goods sold was only 47% of these revenues. Often a firm creates a situation such as shown in **Figure A,** i.e., at a particular point in time it has created high customer value at relatively low cost. However, as the "Note on Marketing Strategy" points out, achieving such a position is not a guarantee of success; rather "to remain a viable concern, the firm must *sustain* this process of creating and capturing value over time" (emphasis mine). Callaway could not sustain the peak it reached in 1997 as 1998 sales dropped to less than $700 million and cost of goods sold increased to 58% of revenues. Selling expenses also increased. The net result was that the company suffered a loss in 1998. The case study quoted an "industry insider" as saying "the biggest problem in golf is coming up with Act II." Act I, the first stage of industry evolution had been profitable, but increased competition presented new challenges going forward.

Professor Robert Dolan prepared this note as the basis for class discussion rather than to illustrate either effective or ineffective handling of an administrative situation.

FIGURE A **High Value-to-Cost Relationship**

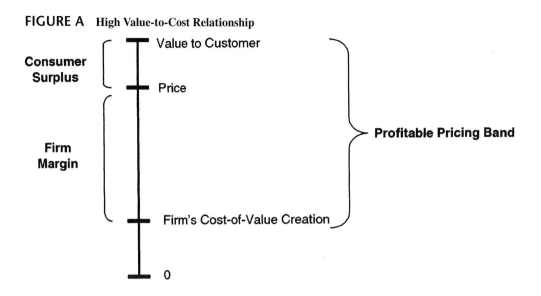

Act II's are more necessary now than ever. Nintendo had a great Act I in the game player business; only to be unseated by Sony with its PlayStation. IBM led the personal computer business; only to be unseated by the likes of Compaq, Dell, and Gateway. Even in less technologically driven industries, Act I's seem not to last very long these days. The notions of a "steady-state" and "equilibrium" may survive in economics textbooks but real markets today are typically not well described by these terms. The simple fact is that things change; and, a firm has to focus on how it will sustain the value creation/value capture process as things change. This note has two major objectives:

1. To set out systematically what are the things that change and how those changes end a firm's Act I. This describes the major market evolutions which a firm must monitor, understand and incorporate into strategy development.
2. To suggest the actions a firm can take to sustain the value create/value capture process over time. In other words, it sets out how to come up with a good Act II, III, etc., avoiding a situation where the passage of time and new developments bring declining perceived value by customers, collapsing margins, and declining sales.

Forces behind Market Evolution

The five major areas of analysis underlying marketing decision making described in the "Note on Marketing Strategy" also provide a useful framework for setting out the major forces of market evolution. Each of the "5 C's"—customer, company, competition, collaborators, and context—change over time. Changes in each are capable of bringing down the curtain on Act I; anticipating and shaping (insofar as possible) these changes facilitate sustaining the value create/capture process in successive acts. We now discuss each in turn.

A. Customers

Customers evolve over time in five major ways.

Factor 1: Defining Requirements Differently

The fit of a product to a customer's wants is the determinant of the product's value to that customer. However, as Slywotzky argues in his book, *Value Migration:* "Customer priorities—the issues that are most important to them, including and going beyond the product or service offered—have a natural tendency to change. . . ."[1] This means that the value of the product changes. If the fit has been optimized to the then-existing priorities, the value typically goes down as the priorities follow their natural tendency to change rather than remain fixed.

Why do priorities change? A key factor is the customer's experience with the product itself. For example, in selecting a packaging material for shipments, a retail store's primary purchase considerations were price and assurance that the shipped item did not break. These priorities led to the use of polystyrene "peanuts" for shipment of semi-rugged items. It was only after the shipping room consistently became messy, with the little "peanuts" all over the floor, that the criterion of a "clean solution" gained any significance in the purchase process. Experience with the product category helps the consumer understand their preferences and needs better. This leads to shifts in the importance of various product attributes in the purchase process.

New uses for a product can surface over time. In the pre-Internet era, most home-PC buyers were focused on the number-crunching power of machines. Modem speed was not a big concern for many. As the Internet era arrived, connectivity became the key over computational speed and attribute importances shifted dramatically.

Factor 2: Getting Smarter about Options

Factor 1 dealt with the consumer becoming smarter about his own wants. Factor 2 is the consumer getting smarter about alternative ways of meeting those wants. At a given point in time, a product can be highly valued due to the customer's ignorance of viable alternatives. As the customer becomes better informed, the value of the product declines because it is now evaluated against a stronger competitive field.

Factor 3: Shifting Locus of Purchasing Authority

In a decision-making unit with multiple players, the power of individual parties can shift over time. This is different from Factor 1 in that the priorities of individual members may remain unchanged, but the decision-making process of the unit works quite differently due to shifting power. For example, it is common that in early stages of using a new technology, performance requirements are key as sophisticated end users hold a great deal of power in the decision-making process. Over time, as performance uncertainty declines, the power of the purchasing department increases and the focus in customer decision making shifts to price. Just as in Factor 1, when the priorities of an individual change, the net result of this power shift is an effective change in the priorities of the decision-making unit.

Factor 4: Changing Ability to Pay

In addition to a value and corresponding willingness-to-pay element, consideration should be given to changes in customer's ability to pay. As Slywotzky puts it, "Changes in customer wealth create new priorities. . . ."[2] The effect of increased ability-to-pay is not necessarily obvious. Increasing consumer wealth is not necessarily good for a product. For example, part of the demand for a PlayStation-type game player with a price of several hundred dollars could be fueled by the lack of disposable income for a personal computer in the home. As disposable income rose and brought a PC into the home, the incremental value of a PlayStation would decline. The ability-to-pay effect must be carefully thought through as an increase in customer wealth will raise the product's value to the customer in some situations and lower it in others. The same applies to a decrease in customer wealth.

---

[1] A.J. Slywotzky, *Value Migration* (Boston: Harvard Business School Press, 1996).
[2] Ibid., p. 252.

Factor 5: Exiting the Marketing

The process of sustaining value differs depending upon the durability of the product in question. Consider the very different challenges facing Coca-Cola and Dell. Every day the consumer wakes up with the need for a daily supply of liquids. Even though he or she drank 100 ounces of liquid yesterday, another 100 is needed today. In a sense, potential demand for Coke replenishes itself overnight. In contrast, if the consumer bought a new Dell computer yesterday, he or she is out-of-the-market today and is likely to be so for the next couple of years.

The Dell purchase destroyed (at least temporarily) some of the future demand for Dell computers. Similarly, if someone buys a Big Bertha driver from Callaway, it's unlikely he will show up the next day to buy another—no matter how much he liked it. The same is true for a Sony PlayStation. Whereas the marketer of a nondurable is concerned with sustaining the value with the same customers, the durable goods marketer must move to new customers as its sales effectively put buyers on-the-sidelines of the market for a long period of time.

B. Competitors

Actions by competition may be the most significant threat to the value a company has created with customers. The most important actions to track are product modifications, new product introductions, and pricing moves. While there is lots of discussion of the benefits of being "first-to-market," a follower strategy has proven successful in many situations. Levitt originally set out the value of "Innovative Imitation" in the *Harvard Business Review* in 1966 and Schnaars' book, *Managing Imitation Strategies,* puts forth the proposition that imitation is a "more prevalent road to business growth and profits" than innovation.[3] In a similar vein, McGrath[4] has set out the benefits of a "fast-follower strategy" in which a "follower firm" deliberately waits for the pioneer firm to enter the market. The "follower firm" closely observes the reaction of the market to the pioneer's offering, thereby gaining a deeper understanding of user wants.

In-kind competitors can respond to another firm's successful Act I with three types of offerings:

(i) The basic "me-too-product"—there may be small differences from the firm's product, but the basic intent is just to get a share-of-the-pie which the firm's product has shown existed at a certain price point.

(ii) The low-cost "knock-off"—here the competitor uses the cost advantage of not being the pioneer to offer low prices. A pioneer typically incurs both market development and research and development expenses to commercialize a product. Perhaps aided by reverse engineering of the pioneer's product, the follower develops its product with much lower investment. This is basically what PC-clone manufacturers did to IBM after IBM's successful market entry in 1981.[5]

(iii) The "innovative imitation"—a truly better product, perhaps incorporating some technology which was not available to the pioneer. Smith-Kline's Tagamet was the first anti-ulcer medication to reach the market. Smith-Kline incurred the marketing expense of convincing the medical community that a pill was a viable alternative to surgery, and Tagamet became the best-selling drug in the world. However, years later, Glaxo bought Zantac to market with superior performance characteristics. Zantac soon took over market-share leadership from Tagamet.

[3] T. Levitt, "Innovative Imitation," *Harvard Business Review,* September–October 1996; and S.P. Schnaars, *Managing Imitation Strategies* (Detroit: The Free Press, 1994).

[4] M. McGrath, *Product Strategy for High-Technology Companies* (New York: McGraw-Hill, 1995).

[5] Ibid., pp. 55–56 and 149.

Competitors naturally have much more of an interest in seeing a very successful Act I come to an end than the firm enjoying it does. For example, in the early 1980s, Eastman Kodak enjoyed over 70% market share and 70% gross margins in the conventional film business and would just like to have that situation persist as long as possible. Fuji, on the other hand, would like to change things a bit. While a distant second to Kodak in market share, the 55% margins it enjoyed meant Fuji was not interested in instantaneously destroying the market either though. A player with no stake in the enormously profitable film business thus had more of an incentive than either of the two conventional film giants in developing a next-generation picture-taking technology not using conventional film. Thus, the firm must be alert not only to moves by in-kind competitors, but also from potential cross-category competitors who might meet the same basic consumer need in a fundamentally different way.

Finally, the value a firm has created with a customer can be damaged by pricing actions by competitors. The price at which a viable competitor sells is a component of the value-in-use judgment a customer either explicitly or implicitly makes. Thus, a price decrease by a competitor (motivated either by a desire to gain market share or the more short-term goal of clearing out excess inventory) triggers a decease [*sic*] in the value of a firm's product.

C. Collaborators

Both upstream suppliers and downstream distributors can bring about changes in the value placed on a firm's product. One mechanism for this is for the collaborators to become more competitors than collaborators. For example, Sony supplied BARCO with key tube technology for its overhead projectors. While Sony sold its own projectors to the low end of the market, it initially left BARCO and other "niche" suppliers the high end of the market.[6] However, Sony then entered the high end to exploit its latest advances in its tube technology. Similarly, major distributors can become competitors via the sourcing of product to be sold under its own name. For example, major drug chains and retailers such as CVS and Wal-Mart compete with Kodak in the film business, selling film sourced from suppliers such as 3M and Polaroid under the "house's" brand name.

D. Company

Over time, the company could lose its ability to sustain its value creation activities for internal rather than external reasons, as many firms in the high-technology arena are experiencing. Key employees in engineering, manufacturing or marketing may be drawn away to competitors as the company's success in Act I draws attention and people develop an appreciation for the management talent. Success in Act I can lead to an arrogance that distances the company from customers and key collaborators and erodes value over time.

E. Context

Context refers to the environment in which the interaction of the other 4 C's takes place. The two most important factors to consider here are the regulatory/legal setting and technological changes.

The regulatory/legal realm is critical in determining which products may even be on the market. Callaway Golf clubs must conform to United States Golf Association (USGA) specifications or else demand would be severely limited.[7] More stringent is the Food and Drug Administration (FDA) approval necessary for the sale of drugs and medical devices. FDA action can result in products being recalled from the market. Finally, patent laws can

---

[6] See HBS case No. 591-133.

[7] Legally, a vendor can sell clubs or balls not meeting USGA specifications. However, players in any tournaments, even amateurs in local country club competitions, play under the rules of the USGA so the equipment would not be used even in such play.

restrict what products may be offered when. Expiration of a patent typically brings in "generic" manufacturers in attractive drug markets and other fields. Companies must monitor how the changing regulatory/legal landscape impacts both its own and competitors' ability to supply product.

The underlying enabling technologies for either making the product or marketing it can change dramatically over time. A new chip may offer the possibility of a new feature set for a game machine. The Internet impacted the value of many firms' products by providing an effective route to the market for competitors previously blocked from competing effectively by clogged distribution channels.

All of these possible routes to upsetting the value created show that a value proposition fixed at a moment in time is unlikely to last for long. Thus, as noted by John Nesheim, in *High Tech Start Up*,[8] the two key questions to be answered in a business plan presented to venture capitalists are:

1. What is the competitive advantage?
2. What is the plan to sustain that competitive advantage over time?

Likewise, McGrath[9] cites "sustainable competitive advantage" as a key ingredient in a successful product strategy. The following section sets out the major routes to sustaining the value proposition over time.

Sustaining the Value Creation/Capture Process

The three major strategies for sustaining the value creation/capture process are:

1. Prevent competitors from eroding value by keeping the value creation process proprietary.
2. Introduce new products which adapt to or better anticipate the changes in the C's just discussed.
3. Build brand equity.

These strategies are not typically substitutes, but rather complements to one another. We now discuss each in turn.

Strategy 1: Proprietary Process

A sustainable advantage can derive from a process which is proprietary and can be protected. Building this sustainability has to be part of the design phase of the product. For example, IBM's inability to sustain its position in personal computers can be traced to its decision to base its product on outsourced materials, viz. an Intel microprocessor and Microsoft's operating system. IBM could not control competitor's access to these underlying technologies and competitors were easily able to replicate the essentials of IBM's offering.[10]

The two major paths to consider for protecting a proprietary process or product are: (i) to keep it a trade secret and (ii) to apply for a patent.

The law does offer protection of the misappropriation of "trade secrets." Defining if something is or is not a "trade secret" is typically nontrivial, however. Stern and Eovaldi[11]

---

[8] J. Nesheim, *High Tech Start Up* (Detroit: The Free Press, 2000).

[9] See McGrath, op. cit.

[10] See McGrath, op. cit., for details.

[11] L.W. Stern and T.C. Eovaldi, *Legal Aspects of Marketing Strategy* (Englewood Cliffs, N.J.: Prentice-Hall, 1984).

provide a list of questions to which a "yes" answer increases the likelihood that something would be judged a "trade secret" in legal proceedings:

1. Is the information known only within the firm and not by competitors?
2. Does only a small select group of employees have access to the information?
3. Does the firm employ measures to protect the information from disclosure?
4. Has the firm expended efforts in developing the information?
5. Would acquisition or duplication of the information by others be difficult and costly?
6. Is the information valuable to the firm and its competitors?

Some examples of trade secrets are design drawings, customer lists and manufacturing processes. Reverse engineering is a legal activity—so a competitor is free to learn whatever it can about the design or manufacturing process behind an item by procuring one and systematically pulling it apart.

In October 1996, the passage of the Economic Espionage Act greatly increased the penalty of theft of trade secrets—making it a felony. Contracts in which an employee agrees not to disclose a trade secret or use it if he or she should leave the company are enforced.

Some regard a patent as the ideal way to protect a proprietary process or product.[12] The U.S. Patent and Trademark Office (PTO) can grant a patent to a person who "invents or discovers any new and useful process, machine, manufacture, or composition of matter, or any new and useful improvement thereof. . . ."[13] The patent typically runs for 20 years from the date of application and grants to the patentee "the right to exclude others from making, using, offering for sale, or selling" the patented invention in the United States or "importing" the invention into the United States. Currently, the Patent Office receives about 200,000 patent applications per year, a large number coming from e-commerce ventures.

A possible downside of patenting a product or process is that the invention must be fully disclosed in the patent application and such information becomes public if the application is granted. The application must include everything required for "someone skilled in the act" to practice the invention. Consequently, it is possible that a competitor could review the patent and be stimulated by it to a new idea which becomes the source of a new product which does not violate the patent.

Strategy 2: New Product Introductions

In 1988, Callaway Golf brought an innovation to market, the S2H2 woods. It followed this three years later with the Big Bertha line; four years after that with Great Big Berthas; and finally, two years after that the Biggest Big Bertha Titanium Driver. Thus, the technology went through four generations in a decade as Callaway sought to stay a step ahead of competitors who were introducing their own products aimed at the high-performance/premium-price segment developed by Callaway.

The length of the typical product life cycle has generally decreased over time, especially in technology-intensive industries. For example, a particular model of personal computer now typically has only a 3–4 month time on the market before it is replaced with a higher-performing or lower-priced item. A key to sustaining the value creation/value capture process in such an environment is an efficient new product development process. An efficient process has two key characteristics:

1. Superior speed to market
2. Management of the cannibalization phenomenon.

---

[12] The book, *Rembrandts in the Attic* by Rivette and Kline (Boston: Harvard Business School Press, 2000), describes patent policy in detail.

[13] U.S. Patent and Trademark office website, www.uspto.gov.

Having a process which yields superior speed to market yields two benefits to a firm. First, its products embody the latest technology. Second, in an environment where consumer priorities are evolving, there is less time lag between beginning product development based on observed and predicted customer priorities and getting a product to market. Thus, the offering when it "hits the market" is more likely to be in tune with market wants.

Cannibalization is a key phenomenon to manage since generally one will be obsoleting one's own products. McGrath[14] judged cannibalization to be one of the most poorly managed aspects of product development in high-technology situations, viz. "Cannibalization is perhaps the most misunderstood or more overlooked product strategy in high-technology companies."

The key is to find the right timing, i.e., achieving the right balance between not cannibalizing one's own products too early and not waiting so long that a competitor's line takes business away. The cannibalization issue is particularly significant when the economics of the new product are not as favorable to the firm as the earlier generations.

For example, United Airlines was the leading "full-service" airline in the United States. Over time, the price-oriented leisure segment became more significant as evidenced by the share gained by low-price/no-frills suppliers such as Southwest. United debated the timing of entering this segment with its own low-frills service which would yield lower margins. A key question was how many people who would have otherwise flown with the "full-service" United would now "trade-down" to the "no-frills" United. A simple representation of the kind of economic analysis to be done in deciding whether or not to offer the "no-frills" service is as follows. First, estimate the sales and margins which would occur if the new no-frills service were not introduced.

Let:

f = predicted unit sales of full service if "no frills" is not introduced.

M = per unit margin for the "full-service" product.

Now estimate:

n = predicted unit sales of a "no-frills" service if introduced

L = per unit margin for the "no-frills" product.

C = % of "no-frills" sales derived from cannibalizing full-service sales.

Introducing the no-frills service is profitable only if:

$$\underbrace{M*f}_{\substack{\text{margin if}\\\text{"no frills"}\\\text{not introduced}}} \leq M*[f - \underbrace{C*n]}_{\substack{\text{full}\\\text{service}\\\text{units}\\\text{cannibalized}\\\text{by no}\\\text{frills}}} + \underbrace{L*n}_{\substack{\text{margin}\\\text{from}\\\text{no}\\\text{frills}}}$$

The left-hand side of the inequality is the expected profit if no frills is not introduced. The right-hand side is the adjusted profit for full service, taking into account the $C*n$ units of values lost to no frills, plus the profit from no frills. (This assumes no fixed cost in introducing the no-frills service). Simplifying the inequality a bit, we see that introducing no frills is profitable if:

$$C \leq \frac{L}{M}$$

---

[14] See McGrath, op. cit., p. 176.

So, if C (the rate of cannibalization) is low, meaning that almost all the sales of the introduced "no-frills" product represent incremental business to the firm rather than cannibalization of the "full-service" item, the no-frills margin, L, can be a small relative to the full-service margin, M. As the estimate of C increases, the disparity between "no-frills" and "full-service" margins has to be less if "no frills" is to be economically justified. This is just a simplified presentation to show the nature of the considerations. In reality, the fixed costs of introducing no frills need to be considered as well as the possibility of changing the full-service price (and consequently M) if no frills is introduced, and long-term competitive impacts.

The economic impact of successive generations need not be negative. For example, successive generations of Callaway woods may well have meant increasing rather than decreasing unit margins to the firm. Here, cannibalization is not a compelling issue. The drive is to stay a step ahead of the competition in delivering customer value. In this drive, technology sometimes reaches a natural limit and the major opportunities for delivering superior value to customers lies not in the product itself but in the "augmented product," i.e., aspects such as delivery, warranty, assurance which surround a product. For example, with everyone basically getting computer chips from the same sources, how can a PC manufacturer be continually differentiated from competitors over time? Dell found a way—its build-to-order system allowing custom design of PCs and quick delivery. Dell secured patents on its process to protect this advantage.

Strategy 3: Brand Equity

As noted by Keller,[15] brand equity makes the firm "less vulnerable to competitive marketing actions." Brand equity signals a tie between the product/company and the consumer. Keller's choice of words is important—brand equity makes the firm not "invulnerable" but only "less vulnerable." Thus, he is in concert with Callaway Golf's view as stated in the case study, that brand is important but "as soon as a manufacturer comes out with a golf club that's better than ours, the brand won't save us—it will only give us some time to react." Still, brand equity is a foundation on which efforts to stay in tune with consumers' wants better than competitors can be built.

In summary, the ability to create value at a given moment in time is not the basis of a business. The consumer "C" naturally changes over time—not deliberately to destroy the value a firm created but just naturally. The competitor "C" is more destructively oriented. In a competitive battle, the value ascension of one firm inevitably means the destruction of another's value position. Thus, in sustaining value, there are three complementary avenues to work. First, ensure the proprietary nature of your value creation process as long as possible through careful guarding of business processes and products, employing trade secrets and patents as appropriate. Firms today need an intellectual property strategy. Second, build the brand to keep customer relations strong. Third, continually be on a path of product improvement, not fearing but understanding the economics of obsoleting your own products.

---

[15] K. Keller, *Strategic Brand Management* (Englewood Cliffs, N.J.: Prentice-Hall, 1998).

41

Koç Holding: Arçelik White Goods

John Quelch   Robin Root

In February, 1997, the top management team of Arçelik, the major appliance subsidiary of Koç Holding, Turkey's largest industrial conglomerate, assembled in Cologne, Germany, for the biannual Domotechnica, the world's largest major appliances trade show. The team was led by Hasan Subasi, president of Koç Holding's durables business unit, and Mehmet Ali Berkman, general manager of the Arçelik white goods operation, which accounted for two-thirds of the durables business unit's turnover.[1]

The Arçelik stand was in a prime location in Building 14; nearby were the booths of Bosch, Siemens and Whirlpool. The Arçelik stand displayed 236 products carrying the Beko brand name, 35% of them refrigerators and freezers, 25% washing machines, 20% ovens and 15% dishwashers.[2] Several innovative products were on display including washing machines that were more water and energy efficient than competitive products, as well as refrigerators made from materials that were 80% recyclable and incorporating special insulation panels for greater operational efficiency. In 1996, Arçelik's Beko brand had received a Green Dove award from the European Community (EC) for attention to the environment in design and production.[3]

---

[1] "White goods" was a term used to describe major kitchen appliances. The corresponding term, "brown goods," described major household appliances used outside the kitchen, such as televisions and stereo systems.

[2] Most Arçelik products sold outside Turkey carried the Beko brand name.

[3] The European Community comprised, in 1997, 15 member countries with a combined population of around 350 million.

The trade show exhibit, costing $1 million to organize, reflected Arçelik's determination to become a major player in the global white goods industry. Yet there was still debate in the company regarding how much emphasis to place on international sales; which geographical markets to concentrate on; and whether to focus on supplying appliances on an OEM basis, building the company's own Beko brand, or both.[4]

Country and Company Background

Turkey

In 1997, Turkey, a country of 63 million people, was positioned at the historical crossroads between East and West, communism and capitalism, Islam and Christianity. Turkey bordered Eastern Europe, the Caucasus, the Balkans, North Africa and Middle East—all regions in various states of political and economic flux in the 1990s. In this context, successive Turkish governments promoted domestic and foreign policies that would nurture its still modest private sector yet promote the pursuit of global competitiveness so that Turkey would be a credible candidate for entry into the EC.

The establishment of the Republic of Turkey by Mustafa Kemal Ataturk as a secular nation state in 1923 marked the end of 600 years of sultan rule. Ataturk aimed to move Turkey quickly into the ranks of industrialized Western nations by anchoring the republic's constitution in a parliamentary democracy. From the start, a strict division between religion (Islam) and government was constitutionally guaranteed and backed by the Turkish military. To build the economy, Ataturk set up temporary state-run enterprises that would later be turned over to private sector management. Privatization, however, did not get fully underway until the mid-1980s, when the government also formally established the Istanbul Stock Exchange.

During the 1980s, the Turkish government established the convertibility of the Turkish lira, and promoted exports to improve its balance of payments. Turkey's rapid growth and relative economic stability, while the envy of other developing countries, was long overlooked by Western governments who focused instead on its strategic role as a NATO firewall against Soviet expansion. The possibility of membership in the EC changed the business mentality within Turkey. Large family-run industrial conglomerates, the engines of Turkish modernization, started to emphasize professional management and to apply global manufacturing standards.

In 1990, the growth in Turkey's gross national product reached an all-time high of 9.2 percent, sparking the interest of investors from Europe and North America. After a slowdown to 0.9% growth in 1991, the Turkish government stimulated consumer demand and increased public investment; the economy grew 5.9% in 1992 and 7.5% in 1993. A major recession in 1994 which saw 5.0% negative growth was followed by 7.3% growth in 1995 and 7.1% in 1996. Despite the political uncertainties that accompanied Turkey's first Islamist government, sustained GNP growth of 8% was forecast for 1997. The country was, however, afflicted by high inflation (80% in 1996 and 75% forecast for 1997), high interest rates, depreciation of the lira, and a deepening budget deficit. Data on the Turkish economy between 1992 and 1996 are presented in **Exhibit 1.**

Koç Holding

Vehbi Koç began his business in 1917 with a $100 investment from his father, who was a shopkeeper. Seven decades later, he left behind one of the world's largest private fortunes and the most advanced industrial conglomerate in Turkey, Koç Holding, which was established

---

[4] An OEM (original equipment manufacturer) sold products to other manufacturers, distributors or retailers; these products typically carried brand names specified by the purchasing companies.

EXHIBIT 1
Turkish Economic
Data: 1992–1996

Source: Bank of America WIS
Country Outlooks, November
1996; Union Bank of
Switzerland New Horizon
Economies, August 1995;
Union Bank of Switzerland
New Horizon Economies,
April 1997; Statistical Yearbook
of Turkey, 1996.

	1992	1993	1994	1995	1996
GDP growth rate (%)	6.4	8.1	−5.4	7.3	7.1
GDP per capita (US$ at PPP¹ rates)	4,991	5,562	5,271	5,411	5,634
Inflation	70%	66%	106%	94%	80%
Exchange rate (lira/US$)	8,555	14,458	38,418	59,501	81,995

¹Purchasing Power Parity (PPP) refers to the rates of currency conversion that equalize the purchasing power of different currencies. The GDP and PPP per capita in Istanbul were thought to be double the national average.

in 1963. Until the death of Vehbi Koç in early 1996, at age 95, Koç Holding had been the only company on the *Fortune* 500 list of international businesses to still be owned and operated by its founder.

The legacy bequeathed by Vehbi Koç was as philosophical as it was financial. Shortly after Ataturk established the Republic of Turkey in 1923, Mr. Koç became the first Turk to challenge the trading power of the Republic's Greek, Armenian and Jewish minorities. By age 22, he had discerned that the higher living standard enjoyed by these groups was a function of their dominance in commerce—a vocation which most Turks had been discouraged from entering. Mr. Koç went on to become one of the first Turkish businessmen to realize the benefits of foreign partnerships. In the late 1930s, he became a sales agent for companies such as Burroughs, Mobil Oil and Ford, and in 1948 he built his first factory to manufacture light bulbs with General Electric. Half a century later, Koç Holding controlled close to 100 companies in nearly every sector of the Turkish economy, the total output of which accounted for approximately one-tenth of the country's GNP.

As a testament to the passions and principles he cultivated over his seven-decade reign, the Koç patriarch circulated a letter among his three grandsons just three months before he passed away in 1996. In it, he exhorted them to rise to the challenge faced by most third-generation managers in family businesses, namely, to single-mindedly focus on enhancing further the company's financial and social value.

In 1996, the 36,000 employees of Koç Holding generated $12 billion in revenues. Koç was a major player in the automotive industry, household appliances, consumer goods, energy, mining, construction, international trade, finance, tourism, and services sectors. The company grew three times faster than the Turkish economy between 1985–1995. Its corporate logo, a red ram's head (Koç means ram in Turkish), was visible on street corners, shops and office buildings throughout Turkey. Koç Holding had a nationwide distribution network of 9,400 dealers, and 23 overseas offices responsible for achieving $884 million in foreign exchange earnings. As the leading taxpayer in Turkey, Koç Holding initiated and underwrote numerous philanthropic projects in the areas of education, health, cultural heritage, and environmental conservation.

Arçelik

Arçelik was established in 1955 to produce metal office furniture.[5] In 1959, the company began manufacturing washing machines. Arçelik subsequently began manufacturing refrigerators, dishwashers, air conditioners and vacuum cleaners in five Turkish factories. Unit sales across these five categories reached 2,110,000 in 1995, making Arçelik the sixth largest European manufacturer of household appliances and the only significant white goods manufacturer between Italy and India. In addition, Arçelik sourced other appliances including ovens, televisions, water heaters and space heaters from affiliated Koç companies.

[5] Arçelik (pronounced arch-e-lick) is a Turkish word meaning clean steel.

EXHIBIT 2
Arçelik's Sales and
Earnings: 1990–1996

Sources: Company records.

$U.S. million	1990	1991	1992	1993	1994	1995	1996
Sales	765	1,001	1,060	1,150	859	982	1,241
EBIT	98	134	159	148	147	144	172
Net Earnings	72	91	86	97	39	60	84

EXHIBIT 3
Key Dates in
Arçelik's History

Sources: Company records.

Year	Event
1955	Arçelik is founded.
1959	Arçelik produces Turkey's first washing machine.
1960	Arçelik produces Turkey's first refrigerator.
1965	JV with General Electric to produce electric motors and compressors.
	Bekoteknik is founded to operate in the "brown goods" electronics industry.
1966	Arçelik produces vacuum cleaners.
1974	Bekoteknik manufactures TV sets.
	Arçelik produces Turkey's first automatic washing machine.
1975	Arçelik receives General Electric technology licenses for white goods.
1977	Ardem joins the Koç group to produce kitchen ranges.
1980	Arçelik exports refrigerators.
1985	Arçelik licenses washing machine technology (2 models) from Bosch-Siemens. (Production ceased in 1994.)
1986	Arçelik licenses dishwasher technology (1 model) from Bosch-Siemens. No exports are permitted. (Still in production in 1996.)
1989	Arçelik establishes its Beko sales office in the United Kingdom.
1991	Bekoteknik and Arçelik receive ISO 9001 certification.
	Research and development center is established.
	Arçelik launches first toll-free customer call center in Turkey.
1993	Arçelik opens a new dishwasher plant in Ankara.
1994	Bekoteknik receives the EU Green Dove Award.
1996	Arçelik agrees to supply 100,000 OEM dishwashers to Whirlpool each year for five years.
	Çayirova, Eskirsehir and Ankara plants receive ISO 14000 certification.

Unit sales of these products reached 900,000 in 1995. Arçelik owned 63% of Ardem, a Koç company that made cooking appliances, and 23% of Bekoteknik, which made televisions and other consumer electronic products. To round out its product line, Arçelik sourced small household appliances such as irons from other companies outside the Koç Group. By 1996, Arçelik was the largest company within Koç Holding. Sales and earnings data for 1990–1996 are reported in **Exhibit 2.** Key dates in Arçelik's history are summarized in **Exhibit 3.**

Arçelik manufacturing capacity, actual production and unit sales for 1992–1996 in the three most important white goods categories are summarized in **Exhibit 4.** Arçelik's unit market shares in Turkey in 1996 were 57% in refrigerators, 60% in washing machines and 70% in dishwashers. Competitive market share and market size data for each category of white goods are presented in **Exhibits 5** and **6.** Refrigerators accounted for 38% of Arçelik sales (by value), washing machines for 32%, dishwashers for 10%, and ovens for 15%.

EXHIBIT 4
Arçelik Capacity,
Production and Sales
by Major Appliance:
1992–1996 ('000)

Source: Company records.

	Capacity	Production	Change	Capacity Utilization
Refrigerators				
1992	1,050	569.2	2.7%	54%
1993	1,050	709.6	24.6	67
1994	1,050	630.4	−11.1	60
1995	1,050	900.6	42.8	85
1996	1,050	990.8	10.1	94
Washing Machines				
1992	760	551.8	−7.2	72
1993	800	653.7	18.4	81
1994	800	500.4	−23.4	62
1995	900	625.6	25.0	70
1996	1,100	750.8	20.0	68
Dishwashers				
1992	200	180.0	36.9	90
1993	300	244.5	35.8	81
1994	300	217.3	−11.1	72
1995	300	205.3	−5.5	68
1996	500	301.6	46.9	60

EXHIBIT 5   **Turkish Market Share and Unit Sales for White Goods[1]**

Source: Company records.

	Refrigerators		Washing Machines		Dishwashers		Ovens	
	1995	1996	1995	1996	1995	1996	1995	1996
Koç	54.6%	56.5%	64.2%	59.7%	75.8%	70.4%	68.0%	67.6%
Peg	38.2	30.9	23.5	23.5	17.0	20.5	25.9	23.0
Merloni	4.3	4.1	4.0	5.5	1.9	2.6	—	—
Others	2.9	8.5	8.3	11.3	5.3	6.5	6.1	9.4
Unit Sales[1]	868,197	1,039,519	856,890	1,135,669	263,570	331,030	446,591	509,493

[1]Unit sales include imports so Arçelik market shares reported here are lower than the company's share of domestic production.

EXHIBIT 6
Brand Share
Breakdowns for Two
Principal White
Goods Marketers
in Turkey: 1996

Source: Company records.

	Refrigerators	Washing Machines	Dishwashers	Ovens
Koç Group				
Arçelik	39.2%	39.9%	53.7%	44.4%
Beko	17.3	19.8	16.7	22.9
Peg Group				
AEG	8.3	5.6	2.4	5.1
Profilo	18.9	10.6	2.8	13.1
Bosch	3.3	6.1	13.7	4.5
Siemens	0.4	1.2	1.6	0.4

In 1988, the Turkish government agreed to a phased program of tariff reductions with the European Community. With respect to white goods, Turkish tariffs on imports from the EC, which ranged between 40% and 55%, would be reduced to zero between 1992 and January 1996, according to the schedule shown in **Exhibit 7.** A 5% Turkish tariff on imported components from the EC would also be removed. As a result, exports into Turkey of

EXHIBIT 7
Turkish Tariff Reduction Program for White Goods Imports from the European Community: 1992–1996

Source: Company records.

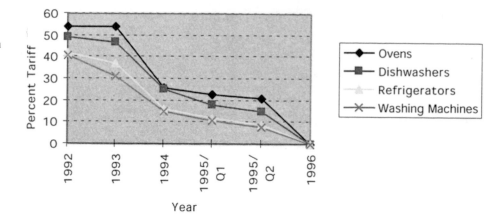

Western European appliances would become progressively more price competitive (not least because white goods plants in Europe were operating at only 65% capacity utilization) and possibly challenge Arçelik's dominance of the Turkish market.

In preparation for the removal of import tariffs, Arçelik invested heavily in upgrading its manufacturing quality and productivity to world class standards. Between 1991 and 1996, capital expenditures totaled $247 million, approximately 6% of sales. By 1995, all Arçelik plants had received ISO 9001 quality certification. Through the incorporation of just-in-time and flexible manufacturing systems, Arçelik reduced raw material and labor costs, thereby increasing the productivity of its refrigerator production by 43% between 1990 and 1995. The corresponding increases for washing machines and dishwashers were 50% and 20%. Arçelik had no manufacturing plants outside of Turkey.

In addition, Arçelik also invested heavily in R&D. During the 1970s and 1980s, Arçelik licensed technology from General Electric and Bosch-Siemens. Arçelik paid unit royalties but was only permitted to sell its production in Turkey. Over time, Arçelik developed its own appliance designs, often at lower cost than the licensed technologies. Starting in 1989, Arçelik transformed itself from a manufacturer that used licensed technologies to one of the leaders in white goods research and development. The company sponsored master's theses at Turkish engineering schools on subjects relevant to its research agenda, and secured World Bank funding to research how to eliminate CFCs from refrigerators. Between 1990 and 1995, $69 million or 1.5% of sales was allocated by Arçelik to R&D. The fruits of these investments were evident in the innovative technology-based features on display in the Arçelik booth at Domotechnica in 1997.

In the area of human resources, Arçelik prided itself on lean management with only four levels in the organization. The work force was highly educated and many Arçelik managers had attended business schools in North America and Europe.

White Goods Marketing in Turkey

Demand

As of 1996, 99% of Turkey's 13 million households owned refrigerators, the same percentage as in the EC. The corresponding percentages for other major appliances were 47% for automatic washing machines (90%), 15% for dishwashers (31%) and 56% for ovens (70%).

Demand for white goods in Turkey was influenced by the pace of household formations and urbanization, interest rates, retail price levels and the rate of economic growth. Sensitivity analyses estimating the effects of changes in some of these variables on unit sales of

EXHIBIT 8

Impact of Changes in Interest Rates, Consumer Prices and GNP per Capita on Arçelik Sales and Profits

Source: Adapted from a Schroeders investment report, 1996.

Change in Arçelik's	Interest Rates Increase by 10%	Consumer Prices Increase by 10%	GNP per Capita Increase by 10%
Refrigerator unit sales	−12.5%	−12.7%	+1.3%
Washing machine unit sales	−8.1	−7.1	+4.3
Dishwasher unit sales	−10.4	−10.1	+21.6
Total sales revenues	−6.9	−8.1	+3.7
Total profits	−13.3	−14.1	+11.5

EXHIBIT 9

Change in White Goods Retail Unit Sales in Turkey

Source: Adapted from a Schroeders investment report, 1996.

	January–April 1995	January–April 1996
Refrigerators	−8.6%	+17.8%
Washing machines	−36	+68
Dishwashers	−40	+56
Ovens	−15	+4.5

appliances in Turkey are presented in **Exhibit 8.** Consumer purchases of appliances increased dramatically in the first half of 1996 as shown in **Exhibit 9.** Arçelik sales increased 21% in this period. Mr. Berkman commented:

> Domestic demand is strong and will remain so. Annual population growth is 1.7% and the number of households increases by 2.5% each year. Around 50% of the population is under 30 and an increasing percentage (currently 63%) live in cities and towns which makes it easier for us to reach them.

Imports satisfied some of the increase in domestic demand, reaching 3% of white goods sales in Turkey in 1993. When, in 1994, the Turkish lira devalued sharply and the economy went into recession, imports of white goods declined while exports increased. In January, 1996, with the import tariffs cut to zero and the economy strengthening, imports increased. For example, between January and July of 1996, 20% of dishwashers sold in Turkey were imported. Analysts estimated the sustainable import penetration rate at 5% for refrigerators, 10% for washing machines and 15% for dishwashers.

Competition

Arçelik's principal white goods competitor was Peg Profilo. Facing increasing competition, Peg Profilo had been sold to Bosch-Siemens of Germany in 1995. Peg Profilo sold its products under the Profilo and AEG brand names.[6] Imports of premium-priced Bosch and Siemens appliances began in 1996. Although penetration was limited to date, Arçelik managers noted heavy advertising behind the Bosch name aimed at challenging Arçelik's dominance of the premium end of the white goods market. Several Bosch shops were opened to supplement the existing network of Peg Profilo dealers. There was some evidence of strained relations as Bosch-Siemens tried to impose formal contracts on dealers used to the handshake-style agreements of Peg Profilo.

Profilo's market shares in 1996 were 31% in refrigerators, 24% in washing machines, 23% in ovens, and 20% in dishwashers. Profilo capacity utilization was only 60%. Arçelik managers expected that Profilo would become more competitive in washing machines and dishwashers (in which the firm had not invested in new production technology) as a result

[6] AEG was an Electrolux brand sold under license in Turkey by Peg Profilo. After the Bosch-Siemens acquisition, little effort was put into promoting the AEG brand.

of the acquisition. Units carrying the Profilo name could be imported from Bosch-Siemens' efficient German or low-cost Spanish plants. In addition, Profilo refrigerators, which were more up-to-date, were expected to be exported through Bosch-Siemens' overseas network.

The number three competitor, Merloni, was a joint venture between the Italian consumer durables producer and Pekel, the Turkish white goods company owned by Vestel, which was originally owned by Polly Peck International. Merloni had obtained majority control of the refrigerator factory in 1993. Arçelik managers believed that Merloni competed for market share with Peg Profilo's brand more than with the Arçelik and Beko brands.

Consumer Behavior

Relative to per capita income, the penetration of white goods in Turkish households was high. This was attributed to the desire of Turkish consumers to buy prestigious durables for their homes and to sustained marketing efforts on behalf of the Arçelik and Beko brands.

When buying a new or replacement appliance, 50% of consumers were believed to shop only one store; the remainder shopped around. Replacement purchasers were invariably triggered by the breakdown of an existing appliance and were therefore especially unlikely to shop around. High inflation also encouraged consumers to shorten their decision making processes. In 1996, wage increases were outpacing inflation so demand for white goods was especially strong.

A consumer's perceived risk and brand sensitivity varied according to the white goods being purchased. As explained by Arçelik's marketing manager:

> Refrigerators are nothing more than boxes and consumers are familiar with them. There's little that can go wrong. Dishwashers, on the other hand, are more complex appliances and first-time dishwasher purchasers are more risk averse.

Arçelik Marketing in Turkey

Brand Building

Arçelik sold white goods under two brand names, Arçelik and Beko. A third brand, Aygaz, that Arçelik had inherited through the acquisition of an oven manufacturer, was discontinued in 1995 and its product line absorbed into the Beko brand family.

In 1996, there were 33 million Koç white goods appliances in use in 13 million Turkish households. Arçelik was a trusted brand. However, some older consumers did not remember fondly the product quality of Arçelik's early appliances sold in the 1960s; to them, the quality of Turkish-made products was still doubtful. Though the product lines of both brands were similar, except for external design differences, Beko brand managers claimed their brand had a more "high tech" image that appealed to younger consumers. The strong penetration of Beko in brown goods (25% market share) was believed to reinforce this perception. Beko was also marketed in Turkey as a "world brand"; Beko retailers capitalized on the brand's penetration of export markets as a signal of quality to Turkish consumers.

In 1996, Arçelik and Beko advertising and promotion budgets accounted for 2% and 4%, respectively, of both brands' sales. Advertising included both television and print advertising. The print component included some cooperative advertising with the cost shared between Arçelik and its retailers on a 50/50 basis. Promotions included "trade-in" offers designed to accelerate consumers' repurchase cycles.

Pricing

Arçelik's product lines covered a full range of price points; the most expensive, fully featured item in a product line was typically double the price of the least expensive. With an inflation rate of 80% in 1996, Arçelik prices were increased that year by 9% every two months. Reductions in unit manufacturing costs, stemming from improved productivity

EXHIBIT 10

Comparative Index of Retail Prices for Turkish White Goods Brands: 1996

Source: Company records.

Brand Name	Refrigerators	Washing Machines	Dishwashers	Ovens
Arçelik (Arçelik)	100	94	58	42
AEG (Peg)	91	89	64	38
Bosch (Peg)	112.5	102	87	—
Miele (import)	123	—	—	—
G.E. (import)	320	—	—	—
Westinghouse (import)	147.5	—	—	—
Electrolux (import)	116	127	90	—

EXHIBIT 11

Arçelik Cost and Price Structure in Turkey

Source: Company records.

Cost Structure	
Retail selling price[1]	125
Wholesale price[2]	112
Advertising and promotion	3
Selling and distribution	5
Factory price	100
Variable costs	58
Direct materials	51
Direct labor	4
Variable overhead	3
Research and development	4
Depreciation	10
General and administrative expenses	15
Operating profit (before interest and taxes)	13

[1]The price at which exclusive Arçelik retailers sold to the end consumer excluding value added tax. Retailers generally made 5–6% pretax profit.
[2]The price at which Atilim, Koç's captive marketing company, sold the product to the exclusive retail network in Turkey.

and declines in world plastic and stainless steel prices, enabled Arçelik to take price increases below the rate of inflation. Doing so helped Arçelik retain market share.

Arçelik white goods were priced consistently nationwide. They were the highest priced among domestically manufactured white goods but retailed at prices lower than imported models. **Exhibit 10** compares white goods retail prices (including 23% value added tax) across a variety of brands.

As shown in **Exhibit 11,** Arçelik's average operating profit before interest and taxes was 13%. Arçelik's operating profit on exports was considerably lower. While registering strong profits on refrigerators, Arçelik unit margins on washing machines and dishwashers in 1996 were lower than competitors' margins due to depreciation charges associated with Arçelik's heavy investments in plant modernization and the fact that several lines were still ramping up to efficient volumes of production.

Distribution and Sales

Ninety-five percent of white goods were sold to individual consumers through retail stores; only 5% were sold by manufacturers direct to building contractors. Single brand retailers accounted for 60% of retail unit sales of white goods in Turkey; the remaining 40% were sold through multibrand outlets. In addition to traditional appliance specialty stores, new channels such as Carrefour and Metro hypermarkets were opening in greater Istanbul. Selected Beko products (but no Arçelik products) were sold through these outlets. Around 28% of Turkish white goods were sold in Istanbul.

Arçelik delivered products to the Turkish market through exclusive retailers. There were 1,650 outlets carrying only the Arçelik brand, of which 700 accounted for 70% of sales.

Another 1,050 outlets carried only Beko products. Beko also reached consumers through a further 2,500 to 3,000 non-exclusive outlets, which accounted for 30% of Beko sales. Arçelik was not available in any multibrand outlets. Arçelik typically added 100 new outlets per year and discontinued 30. New outlets included existing multibrand appliance dealers who applied to become Arçelik dealers, stores established by the sons of existing Arçelik dealers, and stores started by sufficiently well-capitalized entrepreneurs. New outlets had to be established in new residential areas and in areas where appliance demand increased with disposable income. According to Arçelik's national sales manager:

> Being the Arçelik dealer in a community is a much sought after position of importance. We have many applicants to choose from. Our dealers are loyal because our brand pull results in inventory turns three times faster than for our nearest competitor. As a result, our unit margins at retail can be narrower.

The product mix varied according to the size of each store and the demographics of the neighborhood in which it was located. An Arçelik store manager commented:

> Consumer demand for appliances is strong. People are switching from semiautomatic to automatic washing machines. First-time purchases of dishwashers are strong. Consumers living in apartments often have big families and need large refrigerators.

One hundred salespeople visited the Arçelik dealers, typically once every two weeks. Beko sold through 150 salespeople. Salesforce turnover was a modest 5% per year.

A strong Arçelik retailer might carry $100,000 worth of inventory in the store and $500,000 in a warehouse, all on 100 day payment terms from the manufacturer. Typically, 15 sales would be made each day including 6 washing machines, 4 refrigerators and 2 dishwashers. An average dealer might make 5 sales per day and hold $50,000 in floor inventory.

Ninety percent of Arçelik white goods were sold to consumers on credit installment plans of between three and fifteen months. In addition to factory-sourced finance, a newly established Koç finance company also offered credit, often at interest rates slightly below the rate of inflation.[7] Each Arçelik dealer was liable for payment on the units sold on installment. The bad debt rate was less than 1%. Arçelik's competitors such as Bosch were obliged to offer the same terms. Carrefour stores in the major cities could only offer their consumers bank credit at rates significantly higher than Arçelik.

Service

With the average white goods appliance in use for twelve years, the quality and availability of after-sales service was important to Turkish consumers in influencing other brand purchase decisions. Service for Arçelik and Beko white goods was provided by 500 authorized dealers who serviced only these two brands. Another 450 dealers serviced the brown goods of the two brands. There was no joint ownership of sales outlets and service dealers, though informal ties were common. Forty percent of service dealer revenues was generated by installations of newly purchased appliances; delivery and installment costs were included in the retail prices. The service organization was especially challenged when there was a surge in consumer sales, as in 1996.

International Expansion

Opportunistic exports of Arçelik white goods began in the 1980s through Koç Holding's export company, principally to the geographically neighboring markets of the Middle East and North Africa. Arçelik models did not have to be adapted to local requirements. In 1983,

---

[7] Securitizing receivables and installment loans through Koç Finans reduced Arçelik's working capital needs and, therefore, its average cost of capital.

TABLE A
Value of Arçelik
Exports, by
Destination: 1996

Destination	Percentage	Destination	Percentage
United Kingdom	28%	North Africa	17%
France	18	Eastern Europe and Central Asia	6
Other European Union	14	Other	17

TABLE B
Arçelik White Goods
Exports and Mix:
1996

	Export Units	% Beko	% OEM
Refrigerators	430,000	70	30
Washing machines	55,000	50	50

an export department was established within Arçelik. One of its tasks was to develop bid proposals on foreign government tenders and for foreign contract builders of low income housing. In 1988, Arçelik's export department contracted to supply refrigerators on an OEM basis to Sears Roebuck for distribution in the Caribbean and Latin America under the Kenmore name. Though Arçelik's exports were a modest percentage of total sales during the 1980s, Arçelik was the largest exporter among Koç Holding companies.

In 1988, the Turkish government's tariff reduction agreement with the European Community prompted an increased interest in exports. Mr. Berkman explained:

> We needed to find out more about our likely future competitors. One way to do so was to sell Arçelik products in the tough developed markets. The Americas were too far away, in terms of both transportation costs, product adaptation requirements (for 110 volt current), and our ability to understand consumers. Western Europe was much closer. We thought we would learn a great deal by competing against the best in the world on their home turf and better prepare ourselves to defend our domestic market share against the likes of Bosch and Siemens.

As of 1996, almost half of the 990,000 Arçelik and Beko refrigerators produced were exported. In that year, 7.6% of Arçelik's total sales (by value) were exports, up from 2.4% in 1991. A breakdown of exports by destination is presented in **Table A.** Arçelik exported to the countries listed in **Exhibit 12,** which reports 1996 unit sales of refrigerators and washing machines by market. Arçelik's most successful European market was the U.K., where it had achieved 8% market penetration. In the Middle East and North Africa, Arçelik had achieved almost 20% market share in Tunisia. The firm held between 1% and 4% market share in most of the other product-markets listed in **Exhibit 12.**

In 1996, Arçelik exports of white goods were principally refrigerators and washing machines, as shown in **Table B.** Technology licensing agreements precluded exports of most dishwashers. In 1996, Arçelik's refrigerator plants were operating at full capacity. By 1998, an extra 350,000 units of capacity was expected to come on stream. Management expected to double exports of washing machines in 1997 without any addition of capacity. Dishwasher exports were expected to increase to 110,000 units in 1997 when Arçelik was to supply the first of five annual installments of at least 100,000 OEM units to Whirlpool for distribution in Europe. This was the first time Arçelik had agreed to an OEM contract with a global competitor; Arçelik was not permitted to sell similar models in Europe under its own brand names.

Arçelik in Western Europe

Starting in 1989, Arçelik opened sales offices in the United Kingdom, then France, then Germany, reasoning that, in these larger European markets, there might be more opportunity for a new brand to establish a sufficient volume of sales to be viable. At the same time,

EXHIBIT 12
Total Refrigerator
and Washing
Machine Unit Sales
in Arçelik Export
Markets: 1996

Source: Company records.

	Refrigerators 1996 Unit Sales	Automatic Washing Machines 1996 Unit Sales
European Community		
France	2,500,000	1,600,000
Germany	3,600,000	2,600,000
United Kingdom	2,500,000	1,400,000
Benelux	1,200,000	600,000
Denmark	200,000	130,000
Spain/Portugal	2,000,000	1,300,000
Greece	NA	NA
Middle East & North Africa (MENA)		
Egypt	500,000	250,000
Lebanon	100,000	40,000
Syria	200,000	100,000
Iraq	400,000	200,000
Iran	1,000,000	250,000
Tunisia	120,000	25,000
Algeria	250,000	30,000
Morocco	110,000	20,000
Eastern & Central Europe, & Central Asia		
Albania	NA	NA
Romania	300,000	150,000
Bulgaria	130,000	70,000
Russia	2,200,000	600,000
Malta	NA	NA
Turkmenistan	100,000	15,000
Uzbekistan	100,000	15,000
Kazakstan	100,000	15,000
Azerbaijan	NA	NA
Ukraine	300,000	50,000

the export effort to other markets continued. In all export markets, Arçelik focused on building the Beko name (since it was easier to pronounce than Arçelik in a wide variety of languages).

United Kingdom

A sales office was established in the U.K. in 1989. The U.K. market was selected for this initial effort because it was price sensitive and not dominated by domestic brands. By 1997, there were 1 million Beko appliances in use in the U.K., two-thirds of which were refrigerators and one-third televisions. Sales of 300,000 Beko refrigerators were expected in 1997, of which two-thirds would be tabletop height refrigerators and one third full-size refrigerators.[8]

In addition to refrigerators, Beko was beginning to sell dishwashers, washing machines and ovens. Management had focused from the outset on building the Beko brand; only 10,000 of the units sold in 1996 were marketed on an OEM basis.

Melvyn Goodship, managing director, explained Beko's success in the U.K.:

> We exploited an underserved niche for tabletop refrigerators. Our factories in Turkey had spare capacity in the early nineties, so could promptly fill our orders and deliver consistent

[8] In contrast, the market as a whole comprised 60% full-size refrigerators and 40% tabletop height refrigerators.

product quality. At first, we were accused of dumping but lower priced brands from Eastern and Central European countries are now criticized for that. Through patience and persistence, we have built our brand reputation and distribution.

By 1996, Beko had penetrated the three principal specialty appliance chains in the U.K.—Curry's, Comet and Iceland. Beko appliances were also sold through the principal mail order catalogs—Empire and Littlewoods. Management believed Beko appliances were available through 65% of selling points in the U.K. Beko maintained a warehouse in the U.K. to serve its retail accounts.

In 1996, the Beko brand was supported by £600,000 of advertising, including £100,000 to launch Beko washing machines and £150,000 of cooperative advertising.[9]

The retail price of a typical Beko tabletop refrigerator was £150 including 17.5% value added tax and a 25% distribution margin. Comparable refrigerators of other brands would retail at £300 for Bosch, £200 for Hotpoint (the U.K. market share leader) and £160 for Indesit (an Italian manufacturer). Cheap brands of inconsistent quality from Eastern and Central European countries could be found for £120. Manufacturer prices of branded products were so competitive that large retailers saw no need to assume the inventory risk of contracting for OEM production.

France

Arçelik opened a French sales office in 1993. By 1996, annual sales were up to 75,000 units. However, according to the French sales manager:

> The French market is in a recession and is cluttered with competitors. It is hard for us to break into new accounts. 1997 will be a crucial year.

The French white goods market was highly competitive. Fifteen trade accounts controlled 75% of consumer sales. Thirty percent of white goods unit sales carried store brand names. Appliance specialty stores accounted for 45% of unit sales, hypermarkets for 30%, and mail order companies and department stores for 25%. There were no dominant national brands. The long-standing French brands, Thomson and Brandt, each accounting for 20% of unit sales were, by 1997, owned by Italian manufacturers.

Arçelik pursued a two brand strategy in France. Management believed that, if the Beko brand was launched at a low price, it would be impossible to raise it later. The Beko brand was therefore positioned and priced similarly to the mainstream Candy brand from Italy. The Beko brand accounted for 25% of the company's unit sales in France in 1996. Other Koç or OEM brands were priced lower than Beko to attract volume orders.

Of 75,000 units sold in France in 1996, 68,000 were refrigerators and 7,000 were washing machines and ovens. Of the 75,000, 15% were sold to kitchenette manufacturers and 15% were sold on an OEM basis to Frigidaire. Seventy percent of the remaining units were shipped to hypermarkets, notably LeClerc (the third largest hypermarket chain in France), and 30% to appliance specialty stores. The French sales office had not yet been able to break into any department stores or mail order accounts. A two year test, involving tele-marketing Beko white goods to high street retailers, was currently underway. The only advertising for Beko in France appeared in the LeClerc catalog.

Germany

Arçelik opened a German sales office within an existing company called Interbrucke GmbH in 1994 under a general manager who had previously been an importer of Beko televisions.

---

[9] In 1996, one U.S. dollar was equivalent to 80,000 Turkish lira (June, 1996); one British pound was equivalent to $U.S 1.60; and one German mark was equivalent to $U.S. 0.65.

Well-known, premium-priced German brands such as Bosch, Siemens, AEG and Miele held a 60% unit market share of white goods. The remaining 40% was divided among numerous lower-priced Italian and East European manufacturers, none of whom held more than a 4% share.

About 60% of white goods were sold through traditional appliance retailers, almost all of whom were members of retail buying groups or served through regional wholesalers. Twenty percent of white goods were sold through mail order firms like Quelle, usually at prices below those in the specialty retailers. Of the remaining units, 10% were sold through mass merchandisers, 5% through hypermarkets, and 5% through traditional department stores.

In 1996, Beko sold 30,000 refrigerators in Germany, up from 10,000 in 1995, and 20,000 washing machines, up from 5,000 in the preceding year. Unit sales of refrigerators and washing machines in Germany in 1996 were 3,600,000 and 2,600,000 respectively. Management predicted sales of 70,000 and 30,000 for the two Beko lines in 1997. To date, 80% of Beko sales had been made to retail buying groups and regional wholesalers; the remaining 20% had been made to the manufacturers of prepackaged kitchenettes which were sold to home builders. By the end of 1996, Beko white goods were being bought by 12 accounts, in all cases on an OEM basis.

Beko white goods were imported from Turkey and stored in a rented warehouse in Germany. The average retail price of a Beko refrigerator was DM 399. Comparable Bosch and Siemens refrigerators sold for DM 499 to DM 599.

Beko had no resources for a consumer advertising campaign, though some funds were available to buy advertising space in retailer catalogs.

The general manager commented on Beko's prospects in Germany as follows:

> The German economy is weak right now and population growth is flat. Demand for appliances is soft but fairly predictable. Consumers and, therefore, distributors are more price sensitive, especially in the former East Germany. This plays to our strength as a value brand. More retailers than ever before are scrambling to sell appliances, so that's putting further pressure on margins.
>
> In this price sensitive climate, I believe Beko's prospects are good. Germany is Turkey's largest trading partner. The challenge is to develop relationships with the big customers and persuade them to switch to Beko. If we can build unit volume by supplying OEM (or private label) product to these customers, we may be able to make enough money to invest in building the Beko brand.

Assessing Progress

Progress in Western Europe was slower than some executives expected, leading them to question the strategy. A senior manager at headquarters in Istanbul commented:

> We should not focus on breaking into Western Europe where growth is limited and where five companies control 75% of unit sales of white goods. Instead, we should focus on the emerging markets of Russia and Central Asia where foreign brand names are not yet entrenched in consumers' minds. We are geographically well-positioned to supply these markets. The fact that our products are made in Turkey will be a plus in those markets whereas, in Western Europe, we have to avoid mentioning it.

However, others supported the emphasis on Western Europe:

> The former communist markets of East and Central Europe will be important but, right now, they are too volatile. Tariff rates change overnight and we have no tariff advantage over Japanese and Korean competitors in these markets like we do in Western Europe. We would have to make risky investments in local manufacturing and distribution; finding the right local partners and sufficiently skilled workers would be difficult. I would rather focus on Western Europe for the moment. The markets are tough to crack and our unit margins are lower than in Turkey but at least our goods enter duty free and demand is predictable.

Conclusion

In between hosting visitors to their Domotechnica booth in Cologne, Arçelik's managers continued to discuss informally whether or not they were placing the correct emphasis on international markets, and whether their brand-building and market selection strategies were appropriate. Some of the comments at the booth included:

In 1996, we showed we could hold our own in the Turkish market against the top brands in the world. In fact, our market share in refrigerators actually increased. This means we can now push our international exports more aggressively.

Wait a minute. Capacity is tight. If the Turkish market continues to grow at the current rate, we'll need most of our planned capacity for 1997 to meet domestic demand. And we know that we make at least twice as much unit margin if we sell an appliance in Turkey than if we export it.

The current rate of economic growth is not sustainable. The government, in anticipation of a general election, is pumping money into the economy. The economy will probably slow down, maybe even go into recession in 1997. I don't think we'll have a capacity problem.

We've got to emphasize building the Beko brand worldwide. We'll never make big money on OEM business, whether we are making to order for other manufacturers—who are, in fact, our competitors—or for retail chains. Special orders add to complexity costs in our plants and we lose our R&D edge when we simply follow the customers' blueprints. Occasionally, you can build up a long-term relationship with an OEM customer through consistent on-time deliveries but, more often than not, OEM orders are one-shot deals through which the customer is trying to exert leverage on his or her other suppliers or cover against a strike threat.

I'm not so sure. Selling OEM production is more profitable than selling the equivalent number of Beko branded units. Marketing costs per unit are lower and we don't have to invest in pull advertising support through our national distributors.

You don't understand. We're making products of outstanding quality these days. Because Turkey's reputation for quality manufactures is not well-established, we've had to work doubly hard to achieve recognition. We shouldn't be wasting any more time doing OEM production of lower-priced, simple models when we have the quality to take on the best in the world at the premium end of the white goods market.

42

KONE: The MonoSpace® Launch in Germany

Gordon Swartz   Das Narayandas

In November 1996 Raimo Hätälä, director of KONE Aufzug's new elevator business, was in the midst of planning the launch of his firm's latest product. The interim financial report he had just received in the mail confirmed that region-wide construction slumps and low differentiation among competitive offerings had led to significant price competition and margin erosion in the industry. KONE's operating income for the first eight months of 1996 was 6.0% of turnover, which compared with 6.7% for the same period in 1995. The report also projected that, absent significant changes, after-tax income for 1996 would be zero and worsen in the future.

To pull the firm out of the commodity rut Hätälä and other KONE managers were looking to the company's newest, revolutionary product, MonoSpace. Although news of the MonoSpace product had initially led him to exclaim to his colleagues, "With this, we can conquer the German market!," early test market and product launch results had given Hätälä cause for concern.

What, Hätälä wondered, was the size of the MonoSpace opportunity in Germany? How should he price and position MonoSpace? To what extent might MonoSpace cannibalize sales of KONE's existing low-rise elevators? What would be needed to ensure a successful launch? With more questions than answers before him, Hätälä began to review his options.

The Elevator Industry

Significant restructuring and consolidation in the late 1970s and 1980s found the worldwide elevator industry dominated in the early 1990s by five companies: Otis of the United States; Schindler of Switzerland; KONE of Finland; Mitsubishi Electric of Japan; and Thyssen of Germany (see **Exhibit 1** for more details on each competitor). Although they competed globally, these companies generally remained strongest in their domestic or regional markets. Toshiba and Hitachi of Japan and Goldstar of Korea were important competitors in the fast growing Asian market.

Numbers and types of elevators sold varied dramatically across the globe (see **Table A**), reflecting factors such as urbanization, population density, and government support for public housing.

EXHIBIT 1   **Brief Descriptions of KONE's Major Global Competitors**

Otis

Founded in 1853, Otis, a wholly owned subsidiary of the United Technologies Corporation, was the global market share leader in the manufacture, sales, and service of elevators. In 1995 it sold more than 30,000 elevators and had 730,000 under maintenance contract. Otis employed 68,000 people worldwide in 17 production units and more than 600 sales offices in 45 countries. Revenues for 1995 were $5.3 billion, up 14% from $4.6 billion in 1994, and operating profits $511 million, up 21% from $421 million in 1994. Industry analysts attributed this increased profitability to aggressive and wide-reaching process re-engineering in the early 1990s (Otis had closed factories and reduced headcount). The company invested approximately 1.6% of annual revenues in R&D.

Otis was dominant in Europe, the United States, and Canada, with market share in these regions close to 30%. Its market share in Asia was approximately 20%. The company's aggressive, new-market entry strategy had made it the first foreign elevator company in the emerging markets of Asia and Eastern Europe.

Schindler

The Swiss engineering firm Schindler was ranked second in global elevator sales. Manufacture and sale of elevators and escalators accounted for 87% of the Schindler Group's 1995 revenues. Service accounted for 60% of these revenues, reflecting the company's shift during the 1990s from equipment sales to service. Although Schindler's total revenues had been flat in 1994 and 1995, approximately SFr 4.7 billion ($4.0 billion) in both years, its 1995 after tax profits of SFr 78 million ($67 million) were only one-half those of 1994. Most of Schindler's 20 production sites in 15 European countries had been converted from manufacturing to assembly. The company also operated more than 30 sales, maintenance, and installation facilities in 23 countries.

Schindler's expressed strategy was to expand its position in elevators and escalators and achieve an equal market split among its operations in Europe, America, and Asia/Pacific (the latter market requiring an aggressive growth plan). Schindler's profit strategy was to maintain its margins over volume and, to that end, avoid price wars.

Mitsubishi Electric

In 1995, 60 years after it began producing elevators, Mitsubishi Electric was Japan's leading elevator manufacturer, controlling more than 36% of the Japanese market. Turnover in 1995 was ¥2752 billion ($27.8 billion), operating profit ¥177 billion ($1.8 billion). Revenue broke down among the company's five divisions as follows: Consumer Products, 22%; Data Processing, 21%; Semiconductors, 20%; Industrial Equipment and Automation, 18%; and Heavy Electrical, including elevators, escalators, conveyors, and transformers, 24%. Particularly aggressive in Asia, Mitsubishi was the market leader in many Asian markets. In 1996 it opened a new Asian factory, doubled production in two existing Asian factories, and launched two joint ventures.

Thyssen

Thyssen Aufzüge, the world's fifth largest elevator manufacturer, was owned by Thyssen AG (1995 net sales of DM 10.1 billion ($7.1 billion)). Thyssen Aufzüge's 1995 revenues were DM 2.2 billion ($1.5 billion), up 5.2% from 1994. A decentralized operation, its subsidiaries exercised considerable autonomy over product ranges and sources. Thyssen Aufzüge manufactured only its most strategic components, outsourcing all others. Strong in Europe, with greater than 15% market share in 1995, but weak in North and South America, with a mere 2%, the company was investing heavily in Asia, having established manufacturing facilities in China and sales offices in China and Korea.

TABLE A   **Estimated Demand by Region for 1996 (units)**

Source: Company records.

	Residential Low-rise	Other Low-rise	Mid-rise	High-rise	Total
Europe, Middle East, and Africa	65,000	8,500	4,000	500	78,000
North and South America	18,000	10,500	10,000	1,500	40,000
Asia and Australia	50,000	10,000	20,000	10,000	90,000
Total	133,000	29,000	34,000	12,000	208,000
Current Total Elevator Installed Base					>5,000,000

The elevator industry business was traditionally split into two sectors: new equipment and service that accounted for approximately $9 billion and $13 billion in global sales in 1995.

The traditional separation of product and service had generated interesting competitive dynamics in the elevator industry. Competition for new elevator installations was fierce leading to new elevator equipment often being sold at or below cost by the large competitors. Competition for elevator service contracts, on the other hand, was traditionally more orderly. Equipment suppliers usually had an advantage in winning contracts to service their installed bases. By tacit agreement, elevator companies maintained high margins on annual service contracts that were roughly equal to 5% of the purchase price of an elevator.

Low entry barriers due to the relatively simple electro-mechanical technology, steady demand and high margins in the service market had recently attracted many new competitors. These included small, local service-only providers that often enjoyed an advantage over the big manufacturers in terms of price, proximity and speed to service, important factors in the award of service contracts. Despite this trend, the large equipment suppliers had continued to do well given that approximately 80% of service contracts still flowed automatically from new equipment sales. However, there was some doubt that this situation would last for very long given the current economic environment.

Elevator Technology

Elevator technology varied dramatically with respect to travel height, traveling speed, ride comfort, machine room requirements, drive system, controls, cabin size, interior finishing, and price. Selecting an appropriate elevator technology often involved making multiple trade-offs that were all related to the type of drive system used to lift the elevator cabin.

Drive Mechanisms

The primary elevator drive technologies were: gearless (high speed) or geared (medium speed) traction (also called or "rope"); and hydraulic. Sales by type, subject to significant variations by region and country, were 10% for gearless, 30% for geared traction, and 60% for hydraulic. *Gearless traction* elevators, used primarily in commercial buildings, employed large, low-speed electric motors connected directly to drive pulleys to deliver the greatest ride comfort, travel height, and speed (2–12 meters per second). They were generally the only option for high-rise buildings (more than 20 floors). Being gearless, wear and tear and replacement costs were less than for geared traction elevators. *Geared traction* elevators, which employed a reduction gear between the motor and the drive pulley to move the cabin, provided moderate ride comfort, low to moderate travel height, and low to moderate speed (1.0–2.0 meters per second). Their speed was inadequate for high-rise buildings. Used only in low-rise buildings (less than 6 floors), *hydraulic* elevators offered minimal ride comfort, limited travel height, low speed (<0.6 meter per second), and could be priced as much as 50% below substitutable geared traction elevators. Each hydraulic elevator needed 200+ liters of oil that some elevator consultants considered to be a potential fire or environmental hazard.

Based on their performance characteristics and cost/benefit analysis, hydraulic elevators were suitable only for low-rise applications, gearless elevators for high-rise. Geared traction elevators had the widest application, primarily in mid- and low-rise, but occasionally in high-rise, buildings.

Machine Room Requirements

The appendage-like shape of machine rooms, an inevitable component of elevator construction, made them difficult and costly to integrate into many buildings. They either occupied potentially useable building space in the basement or sat atop the shaft, rising above and marring the roofline. (**Exhibit 2** depicts the various machine room configurations.) In general, the taller the building the larger the larger the required machine room.

Gearless elevator machine rooms, always located on the roof above the shaft, ranged in size from 11 to 15 square meters per elevator. Geared traction elevator machine rooms averaged 11 square meters per elevator and offered three fixed placement options. The most common and least expensive, on top of the shaft (termed PT). The next most common location, on the lowest floor next to the shaft (termed PU), was generally more expensive because of more complex roping arrangements. The PU design was usually selected only if the machine room could not be placed on top of the building. The most expensive and least common selection, slightly above the top floor and to the side of the shaft (termed PS), involved the most elaborate roping arrangements. Hydraulic elevator machine rooms (termed PH), which averaged 5 square meters, could be placed on the lowest floor within 10 meters of the shaft.

Total elevator cost was roughly half equipment and installation and half construction of the shaft and machine room. The geared traction elevator machine room typically represented approximately one-quarter of total elevator cost, hydraulic slightly less.

The Elevator Purchasing Decision

The complexity of elevator purchase decisions varied with building type and design. Generally, the taller, costlier and more complex a building, and thus the elevator system, the larger the number of people involved in the decision and factors to be considered. Selection of a high-rise commercial building elevator system, for example, might involve the property developer, building owner, construction contractor, architect, elevator consultant, and major tenants.

Prioritization of features and properties varied among individual participants, even within a class. Owners' decisions, for example, reflected their post-construction purpose. Owner/developers who intended to sell a building upon completion, tended to be most concerned about up-front costs. Owner/landlords were likely to care more about life-time costs, but, unless they could command a premium from their tenants, little about ride comfort and aesthetics. Owner/tenants, being involved throughout an elevator's life cycle, usually considered most factors.

A low-rise residential elevator purchase decision might involve from one to as many as five parties, the latter typically being property owner, construction company manager, architect, construction company purchasing agent, and building service manager.

KONE

KONE (pronounced *kô'-ne* and meaning "machine" in Finnish) was established in 1910. Originally focused on the repair and sale of rebuilt electrical motors, it expanded its business activities over the years to include the manufacture and sale of steel, maritime equipment, cranes, wood handling systems, and clinical chemistry analyzers. By 1995 KONE

EXHIBIT 2 Elevator Machine Room Configurations

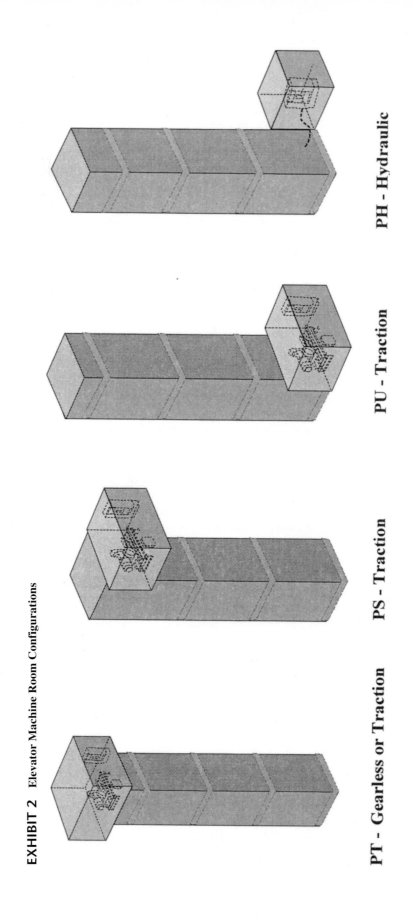

PT - Gearless or Traction   PS - Traction   PU - Traction   PH - Hydraulic

723

had divested its non-elevator businesses and become, through a series of 19 acquisitions, the world's third largest elevator company, behind Otis and Schindler.

KONE's elevator business was organized as two divisions: New Equipment, called V1; and Services, called V2. In 1995 KONE generated revenues of $2.2 billion from sales of 16,500 new units and service contracts for 425,000 units. V1 accounted for 38%, V2 for 62%, of these revenues. Within V2, maintenance contracts accounted for 78% of revenues, modernization of existing elevators for 22%. (**Exhibit 3** presents KONE's organizational chart. **Exhibit 4** summarizes the financials.)

KONE manufactured and sold a broad line of equipment, including standardized low-rise passenger elevators, medium-rise elevator systems, high-rise elevator systems, scenic elevators, hospital elevators, freight elevators, escalators and autowalks, and elevator components (see **Exhibit 5** for examples of KONE products). Low-rise elevators accounted for approximately 75% of KONE's equipment sales, mid-rise and high-rise elevators for 15% and 10%, respectively. In 1995 KONE spent approximately 1.5% of revenues on new product development.

With 90% of its sales outside Finland, KONE operated two headquarters, one in Helsinki and the other in Brussels. Sales by market in 1995 were: 53% EU; 4% rest of Europe; 29% North America; 10% Asia and Australia and 4% other countries.

KONE Aufzug

KONE Aufzug, which operated in Germany, continental Europe's largest elevator market, generated revenues of DM 216 million and profits of DM 12 million in 1995. The size of the German market and the volume of KONE's sales of Europe made KONE Aufzug's financial performance central to KONE's overall success (See **Table B** for KONE Aufzug's summary financials.)

KONE Aufzug was organized as a matrix of business divisions and geographical regions. The business divisions included V1 (new elevators), V2 (service), finance, and personnel; the three regions were North, South, and East. There were 25 local sales branches within the three regions. Each salesperson reported to a branch manager who, in turn, reported to both the regional director and the business division directors.

In 1996 KONE Aufzug employed 23 full-time and 20 half-time salespeople in V1 sales. Full-time salespeople averaged four to five half-day sales calls per week and spent the remainder of their time preparing proposals, answering queries from current and potential customers, and prospecting. The half-time salespeople divided their time equally between V1 sales and their other responsibilities; 13 were also branch managers and seven also worked as V2 salespeople. When describing their selling activities, branch managers were quick to remark that "Thyssen's, Otis', and Schindler's sales forces each outnumber us by four or five to one."

Forty-eight percent of 1995 sales were residential. Of these, 92% were PH; 6% PT; and 2% PU. Average prices for KONE's standard 4-floor, low-rise, residential, volume-range elevator were: DM 60,000 for hydraulic PH, DM 75,000 for traction type PT; DM 80,000

TABLE B **KONE Aufzug** **Summary Financials** **(figures in DM** **1,000s)**	1993	1994	1995
V1 revenue	88,003	87,876	86,852
V1 profit	−4,328 (4.9%)	−1,886 (2.2%)	−6,300 (7.3%)
V2 revenue	114,718	116,762	118,628
V2 profit	17,140 (14.9%)	18,140 (15.5%)	19,086 (16.1%)
Total revenue	202,594	203,614	215,931
Total profit	15,254	11,840	12,087

EXHIBIT 3   **KONE Organization Chart**

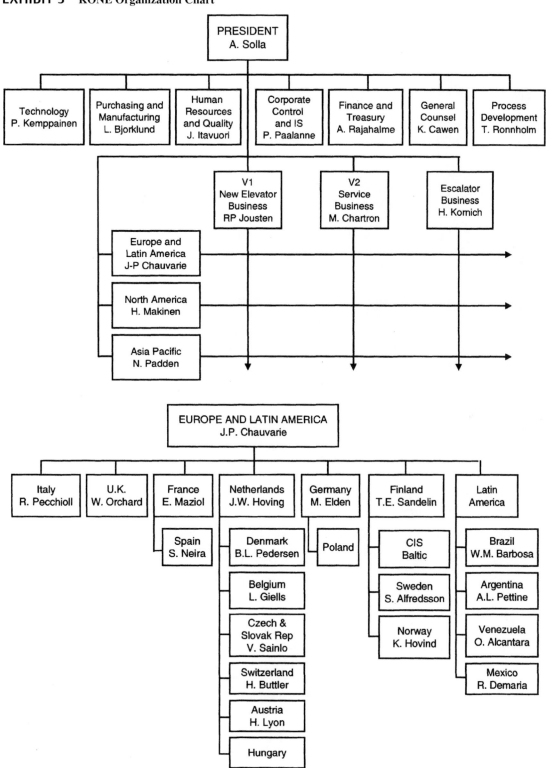

EXHIBIT 4 **KONE Five-year Financial Summary**

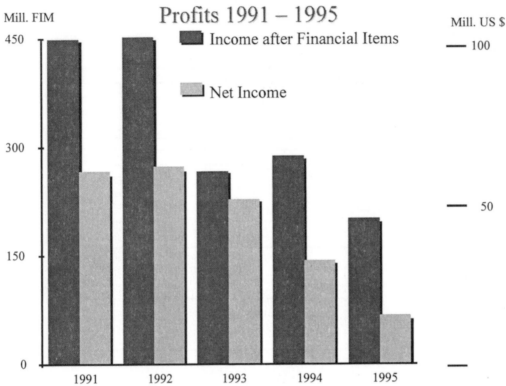

for traction type PU; and DM 120,000–DM 200,000 for traction type PS.[1] KONE's losses on new equipment sales averaged approximately 8% of sales for hydraulic, and roughly 5% of sales for traction elevators.

Evolution of KONE MonoSpace

A commercially viable, machine-room-less elevator had long been a compelling notion to elevator manufacturers, as it would yield significant additional usable space for revenue-generating purposes, and greater architectural freedom. In 1992 Otis Japan introduced a prototype machine-room-less elevator based on a linear induction motor, but its price premium exceeded its construction cost savings and revenue-generating possibilities and it was not a commercial success.

Building on the induction motor concept, a KONE R&D team in 1993 redesigned the motor geometry and used new materials to develop extremely thin, lightweight permanent magnets that eliminated the need for bulky, expensive components. Unlike comparable geared traction systems, that required a gearbox, KONE's new machine, the "EcoDisc," controlled speed by varying the frequency of alternating current supplied to the motor, as was commonly done in modern high-speed gearless elevators. The EcoDisc thus offered ride comfort comparable to that of a gearless drive system. The need for a machine room was eliminated by placing the EcoDisc machine at the top of the shaft between one of the guide rails and the shaft wall; the entire elevator was thus said to occupy a "Mono"Space. The EcoDisc and MonoSpace are depicted in **Exhibit 6.**

[1] Average 1995 DM/$ exchange rate was DM 1.43/$1.00.

EXHIBIT 5   Product Examples

EXHIBIT 6 KONE's MonoSpace and EcoDisc

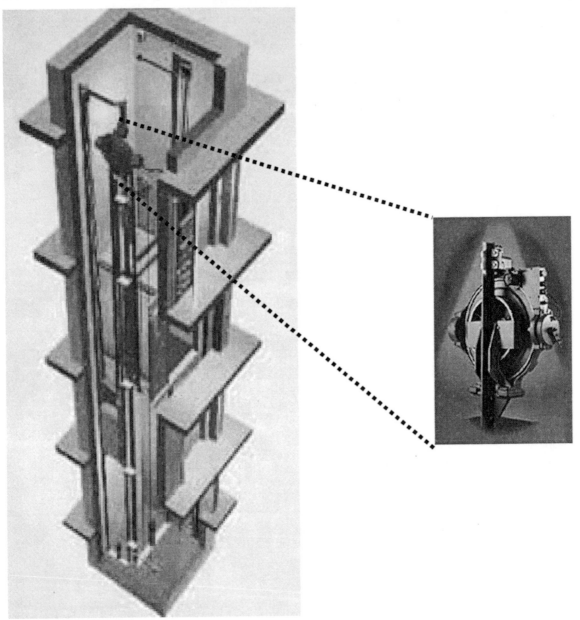

The EcoDisc power unit also was extremely energy efficient, consuming only half the energy of comparable geared traction, and one-third of the energy required by comparable a hydraulic system. This and lower peak current translated into less expensive electrical wiring and fuses. Moreover, unlike hydraulic elevators the MonoSpace required no oil, eliminating potential fire and environmental hazards. Its installation time was approximately 190 hours, 60 hours less than for the simplest traditional elevator. (**Exhibit 7** compares the different drive systems.)

Theoretically, the EcoDisc was applicable to elevators across KONE's existing product line. But as elevator load and speed increased so did the size of the machine, being eventually too large to fit within the shaft. With current EcoDisc technology a 16-person cabin

EXHIBIT 7
A Comparison of Hydraulic, Traction, and EcoDisc Drive Units

Source: Company records.

Feature	Hydraulic	Traction	EcoDisc
Speed (mtrs/s)	0.63	1.0	1.0
Load (kg)	630	630	630
Motor size (kW)	11	5.5	3.5
Main fuse size (amp)	50	35	15
Energy consumption (kWy)	7,200	5,000	3,000
Thermal loss (kW)	4.3	3.0	1.0
Oil requirements (Liters)	200	3.5	0
Weight (kg)	650	430	190
Machine room (m³)	5	12	0

Note: kWy—kilo-watt years is a standard measure for comparing energy consumption of equipment.

required a machine room. Consequently, based on the most common cabin sizes KONE engineers had developed MonoSpace systems for 8-person and 13-person elevators with operating speeds of one meter per second that could be used in buildings of 12 floors or less. Concurrently, they were working to extend the capabilities of the EcoDisc machine and the MonoSpace product line.

The MonoSpace Experience in Europe

KONE had targeted MonoSpace directly at Europe's largest new-equipment market segment, low-rise residential elevators. By the time Hätälä began developing a launch plan for Germany, MonoSpace had been test marketed in the Netherlands and officially launched, with varying degrees of initial success, in the Netherlands, France, and the United Kingdom. KONE managers selected the Netherlands because the market was dominated by low-rise elevators, KONE was the market leader, and the country's regulatory authorities, being relatively progressive, were likely to view the MonoSpace as a new elevator solution rather than one not in compliance with existing codes.[2]

Market Launches

Although construction was relatively stagnant in the three countries in which the MonoSpace was first officially launched, residential building accounted for roughly half of all construction activity (see **Table C** for more details on market size and KONE's market share in each country market). Approximately 90% of the units sold in France and 70% of those sold in the United Kingdom and the Netherlands were low-rise elevators.

The U.K. market was unique in being dominated by one-star (low-quality construction) and five-star (high-quality construction) buildings with little in between, driving demand for top-of-the-line and rock-bottom elevators. Many low-quality residential elevators were installed in the United Kingdom simply to meet regulatory requirements for access, particularly for elderly and handicapped persons. The preponderance of two- and three-star (medium-quality) buildings in France and the Netherlands drove broad demand for mid-range, mid-quality elevators.

Sixty to seventy percent of all elevators sold in the Netherlands were geared traction, a consequence of an anomalous market situation that had led to geared traction type elevators being about 15% less expensive than hydraulic elevators. With substitutable, low-rise

[2] Because existing elevator codes had been written for installations with machine rooms, the MonoSpace, by definition, was not in compliance. Efforts were underway to promote EU standards, but the difficulty of modifying regulations varied dramatically from country to country. For example, because elevator regulations were part of Italy's constitution, to change them to allow a "machine-room-less" elevator would require an act of the Italian Parliament.

TABLE C
Unit Sales and
Market Shares
in 1995

Source: KONE's Director of
Marketing Communications.

	Units	KONE	Otis	Schindler	Thyssen	Others
France	7,000	14%	41%	20%	18%	7%
United Kingdom	3,300	20%	30%	10%	10%	30%
Netherlands	2,100	40%	19%	13%	6%	24%

TABLE D
Price Levels for
KONE Low-Rise
Elevators, 1996[a]

	PH (Hydraulic)	PT (Traction)	PU (Traction)	MonoSpace
Netherlands	DG 65,000	DG 62,000	DG 68,000	DG 69,000
France	?	FF 150,000	?	FF 180,000
United Kingdom	£ 15,800	£ 30,000	?	£ 30,750

[a]Average 1995 currency exchange rates were: DG 1.60/$1.00, FF 5.0/$1.00, and £ 0.65/$1.00.

geared traction elevators costing nearly twice as much as hydraulic elevators in the United Kingdom, hydraulic elevators accounted for 90%, geared traction elevators only 10%, of low-rise sales in that market. The French market was in between, with 80% of low-rise elevators hydraulic and the remaining 20% geared traction.

Pricing

Given KONE's differentiation and brand building objectives, the MonoSpace was generally priced in line with equivalent (and more expensive) geared traction elevators. Managers at KONE's Brussels headquarters suggested that the MonoSpace be priced above existing prices if KONE held less than 15% market share and in line with existing price levels if KONE otherwise (see **Table D**).

The premiums exacted on the MonoSpace in the Netherlands and France equaled approximately one-half the cost of constructing a machine room. KONE branch managers reasoned that one-half the savings of *not* building a machine room would accrue to either the owner or construction company, motivating them to specify the MonoSpace. In France the MonoSpace's energy costs would be FF5,000 per year less than that of a comparable traction elevator, effectively repaying a FF30,000 premium in six years. The price in the United Kingdom was dictated primarily by the £15,000 transfer price to KONE U.K., which put it near the PT price.

Market Strategies

KONE viewed formal launches and articles in national and local specialist building and architectural journals as but a preamble to face-to-face, relationship-based selling, the activity it most relied upon to drive sales. To foster initial market acceptance, the MonoSpace was touted as a new drive system all other elements of which were identical to other KONE low-rise elevators. The style and scope of KONE's marketing activities varied according to the MonoSpace's projected sales success in the respective markets.

The Netherlands

The MonoSpace was marketed in the Netherlands primarily through individual customer meetings. Approximately 3,500 architects, construction companies, owners, and consultants were invited via mailings to compare in one-on-one presentations a working MonoSpace with hydraulic and geared traction lifts. More than 100 such presentations were made within the first year of MonoSpace sales. MonoSpace-related articles published at the rate of approximately one per month subsequent to the launch each generated from 40 to 60 inquiries. Building specifications for the MonoSpace, supplied on disk to enable contractors and architects to "drop" this section into a building's plans, were due to be approved and included on the official Netherlands Building Design CD ROM, a resource used for most Dutch building designs.

France

Letters announcing the MonoSpace to KONE's 22,000 existing French customers requested that they watch a television program that was to include a feature on the elevator. Concurrently, a MonoSpace advertisement was placed in a specialist building newspaper. The main market launch took the form of a series of breakfast meetings held in large cities across the country to which each office invited 20–30 guests, primarily architects, developers, building owners, owners or managers of smaller construction companies, and safety officials. Approximately 20 such breakfasts were held during the first three months of sales. KONE salespeople also made individual on-site presentations at each of the country's six largest construction companies.

The United Kingdom

Given the price sensitivity of the U.K. low-rise market, the MonoSpace was launched "to remind people that KONE is a technology leader." The underlying technology rather than low-rise elevator application was emphasized in a series of three presentations made at London's Science Museum. Five hundred construction companies, developers, quantity surveyors, consultants, and architects were invited; of 220 who accepted, 80 attended at least one presentation.

Sales Results

KONE's Netherlands managers projected that MonoSpace would account for 70% of sales, and 100% of the low-rise segment, within three years. MonoSpace reached the 70% target within the first 10 months of official sales and, within one year, controlled 62% of the Netherlands low-rise market (up from 52% the year before) and 43% of the overall Netherlands market (up from 40%). KONE Netherlands was in the odd position of worrying about having gained too much market share and upsetting the market. "We didn't want to conquer the world with this," observed the Netherlands general manager,

> we just wanted to maintain market share and get higher profits. We didn't want to scare the competition, because there is no way for us to eliminate an Otis or a Schindler. We'll have to live with these competitors forever. . . . Otis could buy KONE for cash . . . and can afford to drop its prices to the point that MonoSpace benefits—not having a machine room, energy savings, and so on—become meaningless.

Sales in France and the United Kingdom contrasted with the success in the Netherlands. Against a first year sales target for MonoSpace of 70% of KONE's annual residential sales (approximately 300 units), only 40 units had been sold in the first three months. In the United Kingdom no units had been sold one month after launch.

Customer Reactions and Learning Points

Notable among customers' generally extremely positive reactions to the MonoSpace were the oft heard "At last there is something new in the elevator industry" and "Why didn't you come up with this earlier?" Some aspects of the MonoSpace were more positively received than expected, others generated unanticipated worries. (**Exhibit 8** presents a summary of learning points.)

Competitor Reactions

Although minor spoiling tactics were encountered, KONE's director of V1 sales remarked that "the competition's reaction was one of stunned silence for the most part." One competitor offered to pay for the machine rooms if customers bought its elevators; another

EXHIBIT 8 **Learning Points from European Marketing**

Sales messages Construction companies, perhaps owing to their emphasis on initial price, proved the hardest sell. Most of the aspects expected to appeal to construction companies—elimination of the need for a machine room and for scaffolding or a crane and simplified installation processes—either were consequent to there being no machine to be built, a savings that usually accrued to the owner, or were benefits shared by the entire range of low-rise elevators.

Netherlands builders stood to save DG 7,000–DG 8,000 if a machine room already in the budget was not built. Otherwise the builder's savings would be nil. With the low-rise range builders rarely needed scaffolding and used a crane only if it was already on-site. Although less coordination needed between elevator installer and general builders, such process savings were generally not valued in the Netherlands. One-half day saved in the middle of a building process that took a year was considered inconsequential by construction companies that reasoned that their workers might spend that half day playing cards anyway. In France, however, where union regulations dictated a high degree of coordination among workers and weekly meetings of the *métier* heads, any process compression was valued. The situation was much the same in the United Kingdom.

KONE found that, aggregated, savings from using lower risers, some time/process savings, could amount to 5% for a construction company.

Appeal of energy savings The MonoSpace's energy savings were not expected to be an important selling point in the Netherlands. Energy suppliers, in particular, however, found that the low-energy consuming MonoSpace didn't dim lights as geared traction or hydraulic elevators sometimes did as a consequence of the power surge required for take-off. The electrical fuses required by the MonoSpace were also much less costly: DG 60 per year for MonoSpace versus DG 1600 per year for hydraulic elevator fuses or DG 800 per year for geared traction elevator fuses. KONE Netherlands found that energy suppliers, an influence group it initially had not targeted, were consequently recommending MonoSpace.

Warning label Its drive unit and controller being located in the shaft on the top floor, the MonoSpace could not be used in buildings with penthouses (public access was necessary). Because its temperature had to be maintained at between 5°C and 40°C, it was also not suitable for outdoor use. KONE Netherlands discovered that architects had begun designing all their buildings, including those with penthouses and outdoor elevators, for the MonoSpace, that is, sans machine rooms. To avoid repercussions, all publicity for the MonoSpace carried a "warning" explaining these two limitations.

Construction company surcharge KONE discovered that in both France and the Netherlands some construction companies had retained the machine room savings by exacting a surcharge from the owner/developers. Consequently, all future literature directed to construction companies omitted the cost savings from eliminating the machine room and lower running costs of the MonoSpace.

Single supplier worries In all three countries, and particularly in the United Kingdom, customers worried that leaving the machine room out of building designs would leave them open to price gouging [*sic*]. Absent other machine-room-less suppliers, customers feared they had to pay whatever KONE asked. KONE countered by emphasizing its interest in long-term partnerships and preserving its reputation.

Example installations Customers wanted to see an installed MonoSpace before buying and few were willing to be "guinea pigs." This problem was addressed in the Netherlands by installing a working MonoSpace in KONE's Netherlands headquarters.

competitor told customers that there was no provision for ventilation with the MonoSpace, which was true, thermal losses being so low that there was no need for ventilation. In France some competitor salespeople told customers that KONE had received approval for only 10 MonoSpace elevator installations, which also was true; government authorities were to review the initial 10 installations and, if they proved acceptable, grant complete approval, standard procedure for the approval of any new technology in France.

Preparing for the German MonoSpace Launch

Pricing for the MonoSpace elevator in Germany had not been set, but production costs were estimated to be about the same as for a comparable hydraulic elevator.

The German Elevator Market

The German construction industry had undergone a cycle of boom and bust since the 1988 reunification of East and West. With the boom in construction the new elevator market grew from 8,000 units in 1988 to a high of 15,500 units in 1995, when the construction

TABLE E
German Elevator
Industry: 1995
Market Shares

| | New Elevator Market | | Lifts in Service | Total Turnover |
	Value	Units	Units	Value
Schindler	17.7%	19.4%	13.3%	21.1%
Otis	13.8	11.6	11.3	19.4
Thyssen	15.4	12.9	12.4	18.1
KONE	8.5	9.2	4.9	6.7
Haushahn	6.5	5.8	6.4	5.6
Schmitt & Sohn	5.4	5.8	3.3	4.4
Others	32.7	35.5	48.2	25.0

boom ended abruptly. Demand for new elevator equipment was now expected to shrink by 15% by the year 2000. The German elevator market was dominated by residential construction. The proportion of elevator units installed in residential buildings in 1995, 74%, was not expected to change significantly over the following five years. In 1995 hydraulic elevators accounted for approximately 60% of the German low-rise elevator market, geared traction elevators making up the rest. Two-thirds of the geared traction units were of the more expensive PU type. Demand for new commercial space, on the other hand, was dampened by significant over capacity.

Competition

The Majors

The six major players in the German elevator market were Schindler, Otis, Thyssen, KONE, Haushahn, and Schmitt & Sohn (see **Table E**). All operated throughout Germany and each maintained 24-hour service networks and new elevator sales and installation branches and manufacturing facilities both in Germany and abroad.

The Mid-size Players

Approximately 30 mid-size players, with new equipment sales ranging from 100 to 300 elevators per year, operated regionally, although some of these produced a few key components (e.g., cars), most outsourced manufacturing.

The "Cowboys"

Small, local companies, termed "cowboys," that usually operated within a single city numbered about 150. Most, lacking internal manufacturing capabilities, were focused on the purchase and assembly of components and installation and local service.

Market Performance

With the abrupt end of Germany's construction boom, new elevator prices fell between 5% and 7% in 1994 and 1995. Many small and some mid-size players responded by abandoning or sharply curtailing efforts to sell new elevator equipment in favor of focusing on service, exerting additional price pressure there as well. Amongst the majors, Schindler's reported losses were approximately 11%, Otis' 13%, of turnover. Further, Schindler had focused during this period on gaining share and become the clear market leader in hydraulic elevators. Otis' professed objective, to eliminate losses in the new elevator business, had caused it to lose market share.

Low-Rise Elevator Customers

Property developers, general contractors, and architects were among those involved in purchase decisions in Germany's low-rise elevator market. Property developers were principally concerned with the overall cost of developing a new building or renovating an existing property and factors that affected the investment value of their properties, including construction quality, timeliness of completion, and operating costs. Because choice of elevator was viewed as having little impact on overall construction costs, KONE and other elevator companies, perceiving property developers to rarely be involved in the decision, seldom communicated directly with them.

For buildings of all types, the general contractors responsible for construction and renovation according to property developers' and architects' plans exerted the greatest influence on elevator purchase. Although the four largest German contractors controlled approximately 20%, the construction market was highly fragmented, with nearly 20,000 small contractors vying for contracts.

Property developers consistently used the bid process, typically inviting bids from three or four, to pressure contractors for price reductions. In turn, contractors often used a competitive bidding process to procure specialized building systems such as steelwork, elevators, and HVAC (heating, ventilation, and air conditioning) systems. Occasionally, a two-stage bidding process was employed whereby contractors would invite "preliminary" bids, as from elevator suppliers, and incorporate a low-price offering into their overall construction bid, then, after the construction contract had been awarded, re-open the process and ask suppliers to resubmit bids. If the property developer and contractor had negotiated an overall price reduction, the contractor would try to pass on similar price reductions to the system suppliers.

Residential buildings were usually built by smaller contractors who, possessing little technical knowledge, often relied on architects to select elevators. Although architects generally did not make the elevator selection for the mid-size hotels and offices that larger contractors usually built, for which the higher end "residential" elevators were typically used, they almost universally selected elevators' cosmetic options (e.g., side- or middle-opening door, interior paneling material and colors, and so forth). KONE managers believed that in the German residential market the final elevator purchase decision was made by the general contractor 50% of the time, by the architect 40% of the time, and by a property developer 10% of the time.

KONE Aufzug's Selling Process

KONE Aufzug's selling process for new equipment had become well established over the years. In most cases (96% of purchases) customers initiated contact by sending elevator specifications and a request for bid to a local KONE branch. KONE being one of the major players, virtually all the customers included the firm in the shortlist of vendors to whom they sent out the request for bid. Thus, KONE had access to the entire demand for elevators in the German market.

Customer inquiries were followed by a visit from a KONE Aufzug salesperson to the customer contact, usually the construction company manager or architect. The salesperson reviewed the architect's drawings, design specifications, and any special requirements and would detail elevator options in the form of a sketch or CAD drawing.

In general, contractors wanted, at the lowest possible price, elevators that fit planned shaft dimensions and required no changes to architectural drawings. Purchase decisions were also influenced by the quality and relevance of the information the customer received, level of service, design of the bid document, and the customer's general impression of the salesperson. Observed one KONE branch manager: "The customer must feel that this salesperson alone is the expert in meeting the customer's needs." Once elevator specifications had been negotiated, a contractor's purchasing manager became the main point of contact and discussion shifted to payment terms and price. From start to finish, the procurement process ran 8–15 months.

EXHIBIT 9   Details on the Marketing Kit and Summary of Marketing Resources

The marketing kit developed by KONE's Brussels headquarters included the following components:

- A press kit featuring a CD-ROM and web site.
- A MonoSpace concept brochure to supplement existing low-rise line literature.
- Two PowerPoint sales presentations, one directed at builders, architects, and owners, the other a technical presentation for consultants and training purposes.
- A 13-minute MonoSpace videotape.
- Trade press releases directed at architects, builders, and property owners/managers.
- Building and planning guides that included dimensional sketches and a front-line CAD rendering of the MonoSpace.
- MonoSpace architectural specifications.
- A total elevator cost comparison form.
- A trade media advertisement on CD-ROM; a set of posters; a sample direct mail piece; a miniature static MonoSpace model.
- A sampling of promotional gifts such as pens and mouse pads.

The marketing resources available for the MonoSpace launch in Germany included the following:

Advertisements, which appeared mainly in elevator newspapers and journals (national) and architectural newspapers and journals (local and some national), were used primarily by small and mid-size companies. Large elevator companies seldom advertised. Single ads were most common, campaign rare.

Direct mail was targeted by large companies to architects, investors, and general contractors.

Launch events preceded new product introductions. All the large players had used "road shows" between 1993 and 1995. Customers were invited to local hotels for seminars and refreshments and received follow-up telephone calls.

Exhibitions were used mainly by component companies.

Customer visits supported by sales collateral were elevator companies' most common means of communication. Most literature had a technical slant, reflecting the average German customer's technical orientation.

Public relations activities were centered around press releases and press conferences. Otis and Schindler appeared regularly in the national and local press. Other companies generally received notice only in local papers or when something out of the ordinary occurred.

Launch Options

Direct mail—KONE's direct mail experience was limited. Ready-to-mail/fax response cards had achieved response rates of three to four per thousand. A mailing of 30,000 fax response cards, including list purchase and printing, cost DM 60,000.

Road show—The cost of 12 road shows—including two presentations per day, hotel space, catering, travel costs, equipment (portable model eco-disc and car), but excluding internal expenses (e.g., employees' time)—was roughly DM 350,000.

Sales visit—A sales visit usually required 1/2 day of a salesperson's time. Cost of materials and salesperson's time was roughly DM 500.

Video—Dubbing the video into German would cost DM 20,000, each video copy DM 5.

Telemarketing—One two-to three-minute telephone call to 30,000 people would cost approximately DM 100,000.

Seminar—For an audience of about 70, hotel space, catering, and the printing and mailing of invitations would cost approximately DM 10,000.

Exhibition/Trade show—To appear for three days at "The Konstructor," a large, annual construction industry trade show held in Germany, would cost about DM 300,000. Previously, KONE had found that cost too high relative to the response it had elicited.

Trade press and journal advertising—Germany hosted approximately 25 architectural journals and about 12 building and construction journals.

- A black and white, one-page advertisement in a free monthly journal with a circulation of 25,000 would cost about DM 3,000.
- A black and white, one-page advertisement in a weekly journal priced DM 3.50 with a circulation of 17,000 would cost DM 2,300.
- A black and white, one-page advertisement in a weekly journal with a circulation of 31,000 cost DM 2,700.
- A black and white, one-page advertisement in a monthly journal with circulation 18,000 cost DM 1,600.

EXHIBIT 10 European Market Segments by Value

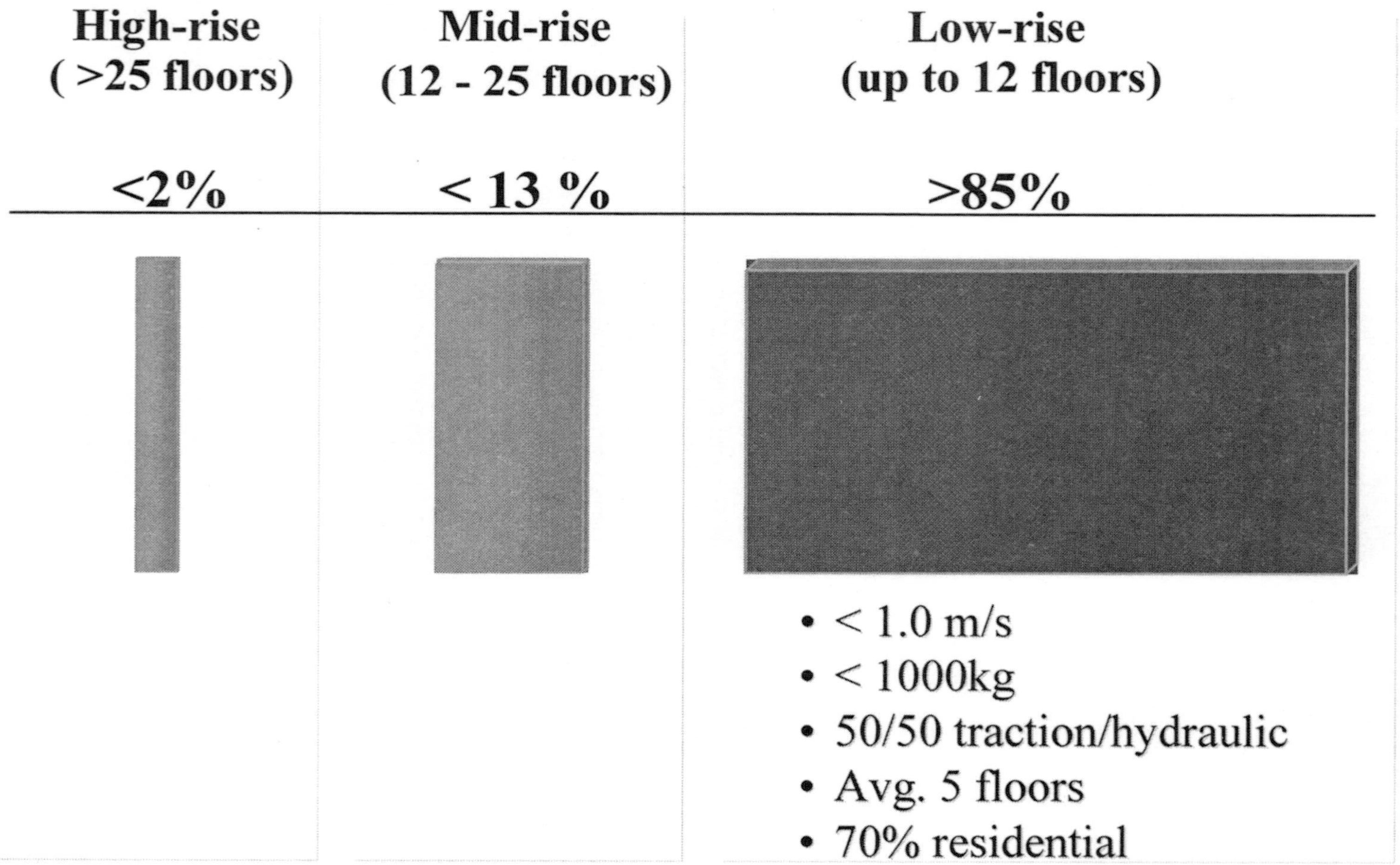

High-rise
(>25 floors)
<2%

Mid-rise
(12 - 25 floors)
<13 %

Low-rise
(up to 12 floors)
>85%

- < 1.0 m/s
- < 1000kg
- 50/50 traction/hydraulic
- Avg. 5 floors
- 70% residential

Regulatory Approval

Regulatory approval of KONE's new technology was a precondition of the launch of MonoSpace in Germany. To gain regulatory approval, KONE Aufzug approached, in April 1995, the Hanover branch of Technischer Überwachungsverein (TÜV), the governmental body responsible for testing and approving all electrical and mechanical items to be sold in Germany. TÜV also employed 300 inspectors who checked and approved installed elevators. Each German state had its own affiliated TÜV branch, which had to independently approve items to be sold within the state. By January 1996 the MonoSpace had been approved in all German states, but efforts to educate TÜV officials continued. In May 1996 KONE Aufzug invited 50 senior TÜV officials to Frankfurt to view the first MonoSpace pilot installation.

Launch Decisions

Hätälä's pre-launch planning included establishing MonoSpace pilot installations in buildings across KONE Aufzug's three regions. In November 1995 four hydraulic elevator customers were given the option of converting their existing orders to MonoSpace. They were told that they would receive a new, improved drive unit at the previously agreed hydraulic elevator price, but, as the machine rooms for these buildings had already been designed and constructed, not that the MonoSpace technology eliminated the need for a machine room. Between January 1996 and June 1996 two salespeople were charged to arrange 30 more pilot installations. All pilot customers were given the option of switching from geared traction elevators to MonoSpace at no additional cost. The benefits of eliminating the machine room and reduced energy consumption, and the manner in which the roping worked, with an emphasis on feasibility and reliability, were carefully explained. All prospective pilot customers were, however, asked to "keep quiet about the technology."

Having consolidated his knowledge of the German market and lessons gained in the Netherlands, France, and the United Kingdom, Hätälä was concentrating on selecting the best marketing resources. He had at his disposal a marketing kit that had been developed by KONE's Brussels headquarters included [*sic*] the following components (**Exhibit 9** provides details of the marketing kit components and a summary of marketing resources).

Hätälä knew that German elevator companies, particularly KONE's larger competitors, relied on a broad range of marketing communications that included advertising, direct mail, customer and launch events, exhibitions, customer visits, and public relations. He wondered which of these were most appropriate for the launch of MonoSpace.

As he pondered these details, Hätälä recognized that immediate, favorable results from the German launch were vital to KONE. Yet, he had to keep in mind that the pricing and product positioning strategies he set for MonoSpace in Germany would have significant impact on the long-term prospects for KONE. With a lot at stake, he had little room for error.

Chapter 43

H-E-B Own Brands

V. Kasturi Rangan   Marie Bell

Rob Price, a 1997 graduate of a leading Business School, moved through the aisles of an H-E-B supermarket shortly after being named vice president of Own Brand in early 2000. He noted many of the strengths that had made H-E-B a leader in its markets. The supermarket was clean, the store associates were friendly, the shelves were well stocked with a broad assortment of merchandise, and the meat and produce departments featured appetizing fresh products. Above all else, H-E-B was delivering on its promise of everyday low prices.

As Rob scrutinized the shelves, he paid close attention to his own area of responsibility, the private label portfolio. H-E-B's Own Brands included 3,000 items concentrated into two principal brand families: H-E-B Brand and Hill Country Fare. Rob Price commented:

> H-E-B's Own Brands are key to the company's ongoing success. Currently our Own Brand products account for 19% of sales and generate gross margins 50% higher than national brands. More importantly, if we manage our Own Brand product portfolio well we can deepen our relationships with customers. Our chairman, Charles Butt, is passionate about our Own Brand business reaching its economic and strategic potential.

Indeed, because Own Brand products often carried the H-E-B label (and, implicitly, the Butt family's name) Charles Butt took Own Brands' product quality and performance seriously. He recalled:

> When I first took responsibility for this business almost 30 years ago, H-E-B was a predominantly private label company. Recognizing the customer drawing power of national brands, I took steps to consciously build a strong national brand presence. Today, we need to find the appropriate balance between our Own Brands and the national brands. I know Own Brands are important, but I'm not sure whether the European model of over 40% share is right for us, and neither is a store controlled by the national brands. I would like to target 30% of sales within the next five years.

Research Associate Marie Bell prepared this case under the supervision of Professor V. Kasturi Rangan. HBS cases are developed solely as the basis for class discussion. Cases are not intended to serve as endorsements, sources of primary data, or illustrations of effective or ineffective management.

Rob Price   8/24/00
Rob —
   quess what
MoRe oN GLacia!
ARe we getting
Full CReDIT
(Through inStoRe
MateRial,
advertising, Label
design etc) FoR
This Being PremIUM
spring wATeR
FroM CANADA ?
—THANKS for your
Leadership —
                    Charles

Given Charles Butt's deep interest in Own Brands, he often queried department managers directly about Own Brand strategy and tactics. For example, Butt took interest in H-E-B Brand Glacia spring water, a product launched shortly after Rob Price took charge of the Own Brand department. Rob Price received the following note in August 2000:

Bottled water was an important category to H-E-B, generating $36 million in sales in 2000. Category sales were growing 20% annually. Despite the fact that water was a basic commodity, the marketing and sale of water was complex. Water was segmented both by source (imported spring, domestic spring, and purified) as well as by size (single serve, multi-pack, and gallons).

The sales leader in H-E-B's market in the bottled water category was Ozarka, a Texas spring water. The leading imported spring water was Evian, from France. Recently the purified drinking water niche was growing dramatically, fueling demand for Coca Cola's Dasani and PepsiCo's Aquafina, among others. Purified water was chemically processed municipal water.

Glacia (see **Figure A** below) was launched in 2000 after three years of research and product development. Glacia was positioned as Evian-quality water. The product was bottled at the source at a spring in Feversham, Canada. Importing this product from Canada made shipping substantially more expensive than for domestic spring water. While it was formulated against Evian, Glacia was shelved next to Ozarka, priced below Ozarka, and packaged in all the same key sizes as Ozarka. **Table B** provides a summary of Glacia's relative price positioning and the unit economics of the popular six-pack half-liter variety.

FIGURE A
Glacia Water

TABLE B
Economics of Six-pack Half-liters

Source: Company records.

Brand	Cost per Unit	Price per Unit	Gross Margin Percent	Profit per Unit
Ozarka	$ 1.46	$ 1.86	21.5%	$ .40
Glacia	1.23	1.79	31.3	.56
Evian	4.23	5.49	23.0	1.26
Aquafina	1.90	2.39	20.5	.49

Rob Price interpreted Charles Butt's note as a question regarding the positioning of Glacia with respect to others in the category. The note reinforced the chairman's desire to advance the company's reputation by linking the store name to premium products.

Industry Background

Grocery was one of the oldest and most competitive businesses in the United States. In 1999, approximately 31,500 supermarkets generated $365.4 billion in sales. Of the 31,500 supermarkets, 64% were affiliated with a chain and 36% operated independently. Approximately $292 billion (80%) of industry revenues were generated by chain supermarkets and $73.4 billion (20%) by independents. Among chain supermarkets, annual sales per store averaged $11.6 million in 1999, up from $11.3 million in 1998. The average chain supermarket had 28,310 square feet of selling space and averaged annual sales per square foot of about $410.[1] Overall, profit margins were extremely thin, with gross margins of 20%–35% and operating margins of only 3%–6% of sales. Estimates suggested that net income levels ranged from 0%–3% of sales. Comparisons of same-stores sales indicated only 1%–3% growth for the industry from 1999 to 2000. H-E-B was long recognized as an innovative leader in the industry and achieved sales per store and sales per square foot performance significantly above national averages. Because of H-E-B's steadfast commitment to consumer value, its gross margins were consistent with its every day low price (EDLP) strategy; however, because of its superb operation it was able to earn operating and net margins that were above industry averages.

The 1990s saw supermarket chain consolidation. Kroger's acquisition of Fred Meyer for $13.5 billion and Albertson's $11.8 billion acquisition of American Stores created national scale for two of America's largest chains, but also created the challenge of harmonizing multiple brands, systems, and overlapping trade areas. Safeway was also an active buyer of strong regional operators. In 1999, for example, Safeway purchased Randalls Food Stores (with 127 stores in Houston, Austin, and Dallas) for $1.8 billion.

Large European grocery players led international retail consolidation. Ahold, Tengelmann, Delhaize, and Aldi all had significant holdings in the United States.[2] Two of the largest international players, Tesco and Carrefour, had yet to enter the U.S. market. The Europeans were recognized for their strong visual merchandising, sophisticated supply chain management, and successful private label programs. In fact, Switzerland, the United Kingdom, Germany, France, Belgium, and the Netherlands all had higher private label penetration than did the United States.

The other significant development of the 1990s was Wal-Mart's move into food retailing.[3] In 1992, after several years of experimentation, Wal-Mart amalgamated its discount mass merchandise store format and a grocery store under one roof, creating its "supercenter" format. Supercenters averaged 100,000 to 200,000 square feet and contained not only the 36 general merchandise departments found in a traditional Wal-Mart discount store, but also traditional grocery products such as frozen foods, bakery, fresh produce, meat and dairy. Most supercenters had separate entrances for the grocery and the general merchandise sections of the store but operated a single bank of check-out stands serving the entire operation. Wal-Mart supercenters were open 24 hours a day and employed upwards of 500 people. A high-performing store could generate more than $75 million in annual

---

[1] As national statistics, these averages represent a variety of format types, ranging from small rural units to large regional superstores.

[2] Ahold owned the Stop & Shop, Giant, Bi-Lo, and Tops Market supermarkets. Delhaize owned Food Lion, Kash n' Karry, and Hannaford. Tengelmann owned 53% of the Great Atlantic & Pacific Tea.

[3] Information concerning Wal-Mart has been substantively derived from its Annual Reports and 10Ks.

EXHIBIT 1
Wal-Mart Income
Statement and
Selected Statistics
($ millions)

Source: Annual Report,
Wal-Mart Stores, Inc.

	1997	1998	1999	2000
Net revenue	119,299	139,208	166,809	193,295
Cost of sales (FIFO)	93,438	108,725	129,664	150,255
Gross profit	25,861	30,483	37,145	43,040
SG&A expense	19,358	22,363	27,040	31,550
Operating income	6,503	8,120	10,105	11,490
Net income	3,526	4,430	5,575	6,295
Gross margin (FIFO)	20.79%	21.20%	21.36%	22.50%
SG&A margin	16.41	16.25	16.39	16.50
Operating margin	5.51	5.90	6.13	6.00
Net margin	2.99	3.22	3.38	3.29
Traditional Wal-Mart stores	1,921	1,869	1,801	1,736
Supercenters				
New supercenters[a]	97	123	157	167
Total # of supercenters	441	564	721	888
Avg. sq. foot/store (000s)	182	181	181	183

[a]Includes conversions or relocations of Wal-Mart discount stores to Wal-Mart superstores.

revenue. Customers were drawn to Wal-Mart's supercenters not only by the one-stop shopping experience, but also by Wal-Mart's reputation for low prices. Leveraging its vaunted merchandising strength and international buying power, Wal-Mart consistently claimed to offer the lowest prices in its trading area.

By year end 2000, Wal-Mart operated 888 supercenters in the United States and expected to contribute 50% of sales and earnings growth from 2001–2005.[4] (See **Exhibit 1** for Wal-Mart's income statement.) To support its supercenter expansion, Wal-Mart invested heavily in distribution, opening four full-size dry groceries and two fresh produce distribution centers in the United States. Two of these centers were proximate to H-E-B markets. Wal-Mart's supercenter success inspired similar efforts by other large discount-store operators. By 2001, Target had 30 supercenters and Kmart had 104 supercenters.

In addition to its supercenter stores, Wal-Mart was testing the Neighborhood Market format in select cities (including Dallas and Houston). These 40,000–52,000-square-foot stores offered a narrowly focused grocery store, an in-store pharmacy with a drive-through, extensive health and beauty care items, and a narrow range of deli and bakery products. Neighborhood Markets held true to Wal-Mart's corporate reputation for low price.

Wal-Mart used its national volume-purchasing power and supply-chain leadership to negotiate fiercely with its vendors. This strategy supported Wal-Mart's low prices. Since H-E-B had grown its business in an area characterized by low household incomes, the company was particularly sensitive about its price reputation. H-E-B recognized that it was in a business made up largely of commodities undifferentiated to the customer. In light of this reality and Wal-Mart's stand on prices, H-E-B paid special attention to maintaining its EDLP reputation. Charles Butt remarked:

> When an 800-pound gorilla comes into your backyard, you sit up and take notice. Wal-Mart is an excellent organization and a fierce competitor. Sam Walton, whom I knew well, was a merchant genius and revolutionized retailing in this country. We recognize that to continue our successful growth, we must price very closely with Wal-Mart. Given their purchasing power, this is a challenging assignment but early on we were realistic about them being the principal competitor in the retail food field for the foreseeable future.

[4] Wal-Mart had the largest number of supercenters in Texas (112), followed by Florida (57), Missouri (46) and Georgia (45).

We are also keenly interested in those aspects of our business that allow us to differentiate ourselves. These include wide selection, outstanding baked goods, produce, flowers, meats and seafood. Customer-focused service and our growing Own Brand assortment are also vital elements.

Wal-Mart carried a smaller variety of both national brand and private-label products than did H-E-B. The "grocery-side" of a typical Wal-Mart supercenter carried about 25K–35K SKUs, about 70%–75% of H-E-B's assortment. A key distinction between the companies' assortment strategies lay in their different views of the importance of premium private-label products. Charles Butt sought to create innovative products under the H-E-B brand that were tailored to the tastes of South Texans. In contrast, Wal-Mart primarily offered private label products that were less expensive alternatives to existing brands. Bob Anderson, Wal-Mart's vice president of Private Label, indicated his company's skepticism about premium private-label products in a trade magazine interview. He said, "I'm a little concerned about all these premium [private label] programs. I think you risk diluting the customer's impression of your [own] brands. If you have 500 or 800 premium items, how can everything truly be premium?"[5]

Wal-Mart's Own Brand private-label products were concentrated mostly in its Great Value Brand. The company's limited assortment of higher-quality items was under the Sam's Choice Brand. Wal-Mart also offered exclusive brands such as White Cloud toilet tissue, Parent's Choice diapers, and No Boundaries cosmetics that were not explicitly identified as private-label goods.

The pasta sauce category offered an example of the companies' different private label strategies. Wal-Mart offered five national brands and the Great Value line. A typical H-E-B store offered the same national brands, along with seven specialty brands. In addition, the store carried H-E-B Brand products to compete against premium players like Classico and Five Brothers, and Hill Country Fare was merchandised next to economy brands like Ragu and Prego.

H. E. Butt Grocery Company

The H. E. Butt Grocery Company, headquartered in San Antonio, Texas, was the 11th largest grocery chain in the United States. (**Exhibit 2** summarizes the top 20 grocery chains in the *United States.*) Florence Butt founded the company in Kerrville, Texas, in 1905 with a $60 investment. Fifteen years later, the Butts' youngest son Howard took over the family business. After four failures, Butt opened a successful second store in the border town of Del Rio, Texas, in 1927. Howard Butt's motto was "He profits most who serves best," and he passed on that belief to his youngest son Charles, who became president of the company in 1971. In 2001, as sales approached $9 billion and the chain surpassed 275 stores, H-E-B remained privately held by the Butt family, and Charles Butt stayed actively involved in corporate strategy. Charles Butt took a strong, public role as a cheerleader for the company's employees (called "partners") and as ambassador to the communities served by H-E-B. The company routinely donated more than 5% of its pre-tax income to charity, with particular focus on education and hunger relief.

Charles Butt was committed to maintaining H-E-B's entrepreneurial spirit without detracting from the focus on the detail needed to succeed in the grocery business. He noted, "Grocery retailing needs to focus on the pennies, leveraging that small margin over a large volume of fresh and exciting offerings." He felt strongly that the key to success was to imbue each H-E-B store manager with that philosophy. "The store manager is the key person who

[5] *PL Buyer Magazine,* October 2000 (www.privatelabelbuyer.com).

EXHIBIT 2   Top 20 Largest Supermarket Chains

Source: *Supermarket Business,* April 15, 2001, Company Records.

Company Name	# of Stores ($2M+ sales)	2000 Sales (millions)	Sq. Ft. Selling Area (000s)	# of Check outs	FTE Store Employees	Major Trading Areas (# of stores)	Store Formats
Kroger	2,366	43,120	100,653	26,581	220,925	Pacific (645) East North Central (481) Mountain (364)	Conventional (2,224) Supercenter (142)
Albertson's	1,715	31,461	67,048	17,228	139,537	Pacific (612) Mountain (295) West South Central (283)	Conventional (1,715)
Safeway	1,482	28,829	51,854	14,025	111,103	Pacific (839) Mountain (260) South Atlantic (129)	Conventional (1,482)
Wal-Mart	908	22,947	54,735	25,309	237,786	West South Central (236) South Atlantic (236) East South Central (151)	Supercenter (890) Conventional (18)
Ahold USA	974	20,022	39,769	12,398	90,923	South Atlantic (422) Mid Atlantic (255) New England (202)	Conventional (970) Limited Selection (4)
Delhaize America	1,435	15,042	39,346	12,044	67,103	South Atlantic (1,216) East South Central (102) New England (82)	Conventional (1,435)
Winn Dixie	1,081	13,731	40,714	11,490	87,136	South Atlantic (740) East South Central (173) West South Central (150)	Conventional (1,081)
Publix	645	13,021	25,382	7,213	65,926	South Atlantic (641) East South Central (4)	Conventional (645)
Great A&P Tea	553	8,075	16,492	6,107	44,888	Mid-Atlantic (276) East North Central (140) South Atlantic (67)	Conventional (552) Limited Selection (1)
H-E-B	270	7,900	10,274	3,396	32,323	West South Central (270)	Conventional (270)
Supervalu	539	7,197	16,357	5,240	35,920	South Atlantic (177) East North Central (133) Mid-Atlantic (67)	Conventional (305) Limited Selection (213) Supercenter (21)
Shaw's	165	4,001	6,806	2,197	16,261	New England (165)	Conventional (165)
Pathmark	138	3,807	5,799	2,193	17,262	Mid-Atlantic (134) South Atlantic (4)	Conventional (138)
Defense Commissary Agency	190	3,607	5,076	2,364	11,418	South Atlantic (56) Pacific (42) West South Central (22)	Military (190)
Meijer	144	3,545	6,968	4,248	49,171	East North Central (136) East South Central (8)	Supercenter (144)
Hy-Vee	184	3,383	7,503	2,493	26,545	West North Central (173) East South Central (11)	Conventional (184)
Fleming Cos.	200	3,120	7,427	2,029	14,308	Mountain (66) West North Central (59)	Conventional (200)
Raley's Supermarkets	149	2,982	6,360	1,674	11,626	Pacific (110) Mountain (39)	Conventional (149)
Giant Eagle	120	2,856	5,592	1,512	15,004	East North Central (75) Mid-Atlantic (44)	Conventional (120)
Aldi	697	2,522	6,696	2,952	12,254	East North Central (315) West North Central (104) Pacific (102)	Limited Selection (697)

Data based on Trade Dimensions database of 32,358 supermarkets selling a minimum of $2 million apiece per year. Stores under $2 million not included. For supercenters, Trade Dimensions estimated the square footage of items typically sold in the traditional supermarket format and the equivalent square footage and sales volume was entered into the calculations for the listing.

can blend service and attention to detail, a leader for the floor people, whose values become the store's values. If the store leadership does its job, then every partner contributes to giving every customer an experience that integrates outstanding customer service and great prices."

Despite H-E-B's regional concentration, it was regarded as a world-class competitor. At Charles Butt's urging, company leaders traveled worldwide seeking new ideas and best practices. Executives explored multiple segments of retail in locations as diverse as London, Milan, Warsaw, Seoul, and Bangkok. These visits led to new products, formats, and supply chain strategies. The team also sought new ideas to make the company a more exciting and fulfilling place for partners.

This search for new ideas complemented H-E-B's reliance on a stable leadership team steeped in H-E-B's legacy of service and value. Long tenures were common in senior management. Company employees' badges prominently indicated years of service. Fully Clingman served as H-E-B's president and COO for the last seven years of his 26-year career at H-E-B. Reporting to Clingman were the Central Market, Mexico, and U.S. Retail Divisions as well as Human Resources and Information Systems. The president of the U.S. Retail Division, Harvey Mabry, had authority over Store Operations, Marketing, Distribution, Manufacturing, and Own Brand. Marketing at H-E-B included Procurement, Advertising, and Pricing. Mabry had been with H-E-B for 40 years.

H-E-B Strategy

H-E-B's "Bold Promise" is shown in **Exhibit 3.** This document was visible in conference rooms and on screen savers throughout the company. It expressed the company's vision of "partners taking a stand together to build the greatest retailing company." This vision was supported by the pillars of providing an exceptional shopping experience, great employees, financial strength, and community impact.

A senior leader at H-E-B characterized the company's strategy as "refusing to choose between low cost and differentiation." H-E-B jealously protected its EDLP reputation. Each week, senior leaders reviewed H-E-B's prices against those of its competitors. In addition, monthly tracking studies were conducted to evaluate customer perceptions of H-E-B's prices. At the same time, Charles Butt insisted that his team not sacrifice service, variety, and freshness. Rob Price commented, "Delivering a combination of exceptional shopping experiences and low prices has resulted in extraordinary sales growth and store productivity. This provides cash flow, which funds additional investment in the customer experience and lower prices. This 'virtuous cycle' only breaks down when we lose our reputation for price or quality."

Cost containment initiatives included H-E-B's commitment to internal manufacturing. H-E-B's meat processing plant prepared 50 million pounds of meat per year. Two dairy plants shipped 110 million gallons of milk annually and produced the H-E-B brand yogurt, cottage cheese, and sour cream. Other manufacturing operations produced ice cream, bread, tortillas, snack foods, and cakes and pastries. About 30% of Own Brand sales were in self-manufactured goods. H-E-B had high hurdle rates for its investment decisions, expecting a rate of return in excess of 18% for new plant construction and 10%–15% return for capital improvements within existing facilities. Despite these high targets, the market potential had proven itself. H-E-B estimated that it had invested well over $100 million in its internal manufacturing capabilities.

Concurrently, H-E-B had implemented innovations to improve the customer experience. The company had rolled out automated replenishment in some categories, which provided better in-stock conditions and freed up shelf space for additional variety. Some stores were fitted with self-checkout technology, which increased throughput at the front end. Convenience services like drive-through pharmacies and on-premise gas stations were commonplace.

EXHIBIT 3 H-E-B's Bold Promise

Source: Company records.

H-E-B **bold promise**

H-E-B Partners taking a stand together to build the greatest retailing company.

customers

Together we will provide each and every Customer a shopping experience that meets their individual expectations through:

- Great people.
- Best service.
- Freshest, safest products.
- Great products for today and tomorrow.
- Low prices with best value.

great people

Together we will attract, develop, and retain Great People by:

- Acting with integrity and trusting each other.
- Respecting diversity.
- Providing opportunities for great pay and benefits.
- Ensuring a safe work environment.
- Guaranteeing the freedom to communicate openly.
- Recognizing and acknowledging each other's contributions.
- Creating a flexible environment to meet individual and business scheduling needs.

sales growth

Together we will maximize Sales Growth while meeting profit goals.

- Always look for what is missing and what is next.
- Turn our ideas into action quickly.
- Maximize each store's unique potential.
- Work continuously to lower costs.
- Include Customers in our fun and celebration.

communities

Together we will make our Communities better.

- Earn community trust and respect through our individual and collective actions.
- Share our time and resources with our neighbors.
- Take action in times of crisis.

EACH AND EVERY PERSON COUNTS

EXHIBIT 4   **H-E-B's Geographic Coverage**

Source: Adapted from company records.

Stores

H-E-B operated 271 stores in Texas, 16 stores in Mexico, and 1 store in Louisiana. (**Exhibit 4** provides an outline of the H-E-B's geographic coverage.) The areas served in Texas included Houston, San Antonio, Austin, the Rio Grande Valley, the Gulf Coast and Midland/Odessa. In south and central Texas, H-E-B had a market share in excess of 60%. H-E-B continued to expand with the population in Texas, the second-fastest growing state in the United States. H-E-B's expansion strategy was to maximize share in contiguous markets that could be served by the company's existing distribution system. This approach made Dallas, Houston, and Northern Mexico particularly important sources of growth.

Company research indicated that 90% of the households within its core market area visited an H-E-B store at least monthly. H-E-B had three different formats in the United States: traditional supermarkets (182 stores and 77% of sales), Pantry stores (86 stores and 16% of sales), Central Markets (4 stores and 2% of sales). H-E-B's Mexico stores (16 stores and 5% of sales) were similar to its U.S. supermarkets, with a larger space commitment to general merchandise and perishables. **Exhibit 5** summarizes store counts for H-E-B and its competitors in key markets.

Source: JP Morgan Securities
document—Shapiro and
Associates, October 2000;
Shelby Report, June (2000)
Houston Metro data only;
company records.

EXHIBIT 5
H-E-B Markets—
Market Share and
Store Counts

Market	Company	Market Share %	Store Count
San Antonio	H-E-B	67	43
	Albertson's	18	23
	Handy Andy	7	20
	Comm.Px/Bx	2	3
	Wal-Mart	2	8 Conventional
			3 Supercenters
	Super Kmart	1	3
	Other	4	17
Austin	H-E-B	62	36
	Albertson's	13	15
	Randall's	10	12
	Sam's Club	2	2
	Wal-Mart	2	4 Supercenters
	Whole Foods	1	1
	Fiesta	1	1
	Other	9	6
Corpus Christi	H-E-B	77	29
	Wal-Mart	9	9 Conventional
			5 Supercenters
	Albertson's	5	3
	Super Kmart	2	3
	Other	7	15
Waco	H-E-B	54	6
	Wal-Mart	17	1 Supercenter
	Winn Dixie	6	1
	Albertson's	5	1
	Brookshire	5	1
	Super Kmart	2	1
	Other	10	3
Texas Border	H-E-B	69	38
	Wal-Mart	12	8 Conventional
			8 Supercenters
	Albertson's	10	8
	Super Kmart	2	4
	Other	7	39
Houston	Kroger	26	98
	Randall's	18	46
	H-E-B	12	84
	Fiesta	10	35
	Albertson's	9	45
	Wal-Mart	6	25 Conventional
			7 Supercenters
	Other	19	>100

H-E-B Supermarkets

The average H-E-B store was 55,000 square feet with approximately 50,000 SKUs. New
H-E-B stores were about 45,000 square feet in smaller markets and 80,000–90,000 square
feet in larger markets. Typically, smaller market stores had 10–15 check-out lanes and employed about 200 people. H-E-B's larger stores typically provided more than 400 parking
spaces, operated a minimum of 20 check-out lanes and employed in excess of 350 people.

Development costs for new stores were $8 million–$15 million (including land, building, equipment and inventory) and were projected to achieve weekly sales volumes of $12–$15 per square foot of selling space.

The H-E-B supermarket format was similar to that found throughout the United States, with produce, meat, dairy, deli and bakery products on the outer perimeter flanking aisles of shelf stable, frozen foods and health and beauty. Most H-E-B stores offered one-hour photo finishing, large beer and wine departments, floral departments, coffee shops, bakeries, and pharmacies. Information regarding key store categories is summarized in **Table C** below.

H-E-B supermarkets averaged approximately $700,000 to $1 million in sales per week. (**Exhibit 6** provides additional information regarding the major categories within the store.) H-E-B was able to achieve such high performance by tailoring its assortment to its local

TABLE C
H-E-B Sales Composition (Excluding Mexico and Central Market)

Source: Company records.

Department	% of Sales	# of SKUs	% of Store Space
Grocery	46%	22,000	40
Meat and Seafood	16	2,500	12
Health and Beauty / General Merchandise	15	35,000	22
Pharmacy	9	3,250	2
Produce	7	1,000	12
Gasoline	3	3	Pad site on property
Deli	2	2,000	6
Bakery	2	1,000	6

EXHIBIT 6   **H-E-B Categories**

Source: Adapted from company records.

Category	Representative Products	Category Gross Margin	Own Brand Share of Category Sales (average = 19%)	Share of Total Own Brand Sales
Grocery perishables	Milk, eggs, ice cream, frozen vegetables	Above average	Above average	29%
Commercial bakery	Sandwich bread, tortillas, bagels, English muffins	Above average	Above average	5
Expandable consumption	Salty snacks, cookies, crackers, soft drinks	Below average	Below average	7
Basic ingredients	Baking, canned goods, coffee, cooking oil	Below average	Above average	8
Shelf stable commodities	Soup, water, cereal, pickles, pasta sauce	Below average	Below average	8
Household items	Detergent, cleansers, bar soap	Below average	Above average	8
Home, hardware & garden	Batteries, candy, charcoal, school supplies, lawn and garden	Above average	Below average	2
Deli	Hot foods, heat and eat, luncheon meats	Above average	Below average	2
Drug, health & beauty	Diapers, first aid, cosmetics, eye and dental care, vitamins	Above average	Below average	6
Meat & seafood	Lunch meats, bacon, meats, fresh and frozen seafood, fully cooked meats, poultry, processed cheese	Above average	Above average	25

markets and by a powerful combination of everyday low prices and exciting special events. One such innovation was the Meal Deal that ran every other week. The Meal Deal offered a central item surrounded by complementary products that together made an easy meal. For example, one Meal Deal featured H-E-B Brand King Ranch-style frozen chicken entrée at $5.49, a free pack of H-E-B Brand soda, a free Mrs. Smith cobbler, and a free package of Pillsbury frozen biscuits.[6] H-E-B generally used one of its leading Own Brand products as the focal item and obtained complementary product at reduced cost from the national brands.

H-E-B Pantry Foods

H-E-B also operated 86 Pantry Stores with a low cost, low price format. The smaller Pantry Stores were 25,000–30,000 square feet and averaged $270,000 in sales per week. The small stores were originally developed in 1988 to facilitate a quick entry into the Houston market. However, in the late 1990s, the small formats were limiting H-E-B's ability to offer the full assortment sought by customers. H-E-B planned to transition many Pantry stores to full-sized H-E-B supermarkets as large as 87,000 square feet.

H-E-B Central Market

H-E-B operated two Central Market stores in Austin and one in San Antonio. Central Market stores were 60,000 square foot stores with a focus on premium products. The store created lavish displays of premium quality merchandise. Customers entered the store through elaborate produce departments, with more than 600 items abundantly displayed. Rather than pre-cutting and packaging meat in plastic wrap, the meat and fish departments merchandised their products behind glass showcases reminiscent of traditional butcher shops. Central Markets stores also featured extensive "ready-to-eat" and "ready-to-heat" products. Targeting food enthusiasts, the stores had a very large wine and beer selection, self-service pasta and olive bars, international cheeses and full aisles of vinegar, oils, and salsas.

While a typical H-E-B supermarket drew from a one-to-five-mile radius, each Central Market was a destination shopping experience targeted to draw shoppers within a 50-mile radius. Central Market proved effective in transforming H-E-B's reputation in key trade areas. As one executive noted, "In Austin, H-E-B was known more for price than freshness. When Central Market came in 1994, it elevated H-E-B's reputation in that upscale community."

H-E-B Mexico

H-E-B began operations in Mexico in 1997, with most of its stores located in the Monterrey area. Monterrey was the third-largest metropolitan area in Mexico, with a population of 3.5 million. H-E-B's reputation in northern Mexico for low prices, excellent variety (particularly in product imported from the United States and in Own Brands), and fresh perishables led to very successful stores. H-E-B believed that Mexico was one of its highest growth opportunities. It had created a full management infrastructure for the region and planned on opening an additional 8–12 stores in the next two to three years.

H-E-B's Own Brands

Early in the 1990s, H-E-B signaled a new commitment to its private label with the assignment of Stephen Butt as the company's first dedicated Own Brand vice president. At that time, the company had 28 different private labels on the shelf. Senior management commissioned a review of internal capabilities and a worldwide benchmarking effort. H-E-B participated in an extensive executive exchange program with U.K.-based Sainsbury, a highly regarded grocery retailer with a particularly strong own brand reputation. H-E-B

---

[6] Example taken from "*H-E-B a passion for new frontiers*," *Supermarket Business,* December 15, 2000.

emulated many aspects of Sainsbury's Own Brand strategy. H-E-B established teams dedicated to brand management, quality assurance, consumer research, and package design. These functions collaborated on product development with a new process that incorporated best practices from consumer package goods companies.

The Own Brand team consolidated the existing labels into three brands that would be more clearly positioned versus the national brands. **Figure D** provides a representation of the positioning proposed in the early 1990s. The H-E-B Brand offered products that equaled or exceeded national brand quality. Where possible, H-E-B Brand products would provide customers with a "point of difference." The next tier of products was Hill Country Fare. This tier served to compete against other store brands and approach national brand quality. Targeted toward the price-conscious shopper, the quality of Hill Country Fare products was intended to be "good" but not "cheap." The third tier, generics, were products of reasonable quality with some acceptable quality variation. These would be the lowest-price products available in the market. Own Brand products were typically priced 10%–30% below competing brands, while still allowing H-E-B to make positive gross profit.

In 2001, H-E-B's Own Brands grew to $1.4 billion in sales. The total gross margin of $450 million earned by Own Brand represented a disproportionately high percentage of H-E-B's total profitability. **Table E** shows a comparison of overall and Own Brand profitability for selected categories. Own Brand's share of sales (excluding gasoline and

FIGURE D
Own Brand
Positioning

Source: Company records.

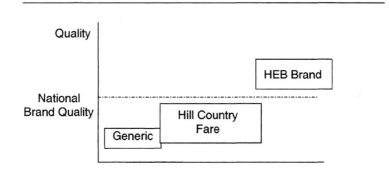

TABLE E
1999 Profitability
Analysis for Selected
Categories (based on
fully burdened costs)[a]

Source: Company records.

Category	Fully Burdened Category Profit	Own Brand Profit Percentage
Flour/Meal	−1%	−1%
Syrup	1	16
Baby formula	−4	10
Soft drinks	−13	−2
Frozen meals	9	18
Tortillas	20	24
Milk products	18	19
Pasta sauce	7	7
Canned vegetables	−6	−8
Frozen vegetables	10	11
Ice cream	12	12
Water	7	−5
Sports drinks	3	3
Baking mixes	1	−6

[a]Fully burdened costs reflected an estimate of all costs associated with the product including the base product cost and other associated costs such as stocking shelves, inventory carrying costs, etc.

pharmacy) was 19%, putting H-E-B in the top tier of private label performers in the industry. As a comparison, Safeway and Kroger reported 22%–25% share from their private label products. At H-E-B, most categories had Own Brand products, but the share of sales these products achieved varied widely. In cold cereals, the share was 13%. In contrast, Own Brand milk enjoyed a 90% share.

H-E-B had three major objectives for its Own Brand product lines: improved profitability, sales growth, and deeper customer relationships. Own Brand products typically provided better margin than national brand alternatives. This was because branded manufacturers' investments in advertising and trade promotion boosted the cost of their products to H-E-B, reducing their retail profitability. Own Brand products did not require the same level of investment since H-E-B's overall marketing activities created awareness and demand for Own Brand products. An additional cost advantage came from H-E-B's captive manufacturing of highly profitable products. Internal manufacture allowed H-E-B to capture both retail and wholesale profitability. Finally, successful Own Brand products influenced some branded manufacturers to provide additional funding and reductions in cost to remain competitive on the shelf.

H-E-B sought to generate sales gains by using Own Brand products to increase the frequency of customers' shopping trips and the size of the basket per trip. Purchase frequency was primarily driven by demand for core commodities like milk, bread, and eggs. These categories were dominated by Own Brand. Ensuring their quality and value influenced customers' selection of H-E-B as their store of choice. H-E-B's unique Own Brand products further influenced customer patronage. Once in the store, customers were exposed to attractively packaged and abundantly merchandised Own Brand expandable consumption categories like chips and cookies as well as products such as ice cream and fully cooked meats particularly formulated for the Southwestern palate. The price and quality of these products contributed to enlarging customers' total shopping basket. Additionally, to further generate sales, Own Brands selectively promoted and advertised key products, spending approximately $10 million annually on Own Brand advertising and promotion.

Charles Butt felt the most important objective of the Own Brands product line was to deepen customer relationships. Low prices on Own Brand products reinforced the company's image as the leader for great value. Own Brand's food safety standards enhanced H-E-B's quality reputation. More qualitatively, H-E-B employees took pride in the innovative Own Brand products. This pride was reflected in their interactions with customers.

Own Brands: A Mixed Bag

The Own Brand strategy conceived in the early 1990s was in need of a review in 2000. A 1999 customer study indicated that customers perceived H-E-B's Own Brand products as generally lower quality than national brands. Consumers also saw no distinction between the H-E-B and Hill Country Fare brands. Product research revealed that in some categories, including diapers and feminine hygiene, the H-E-B brand products did not meet national brand performance. This violated the original standards set for the tier. To help get a handle on the dynamics in the Own Brand segment, Rob Price delved deeply into a number of product categories. An overview of select categories is outlined in **Table F** and the descriptions below. **Exhibit 7** shows some of the products on the shelf as they appear to the customer.

Ice Cream

H-E-B Creamy Creations Ice Cream had a 40% share of the Premium Ice Cream category three years after launch. Creamy Creations was priced 25% less than the market's leading brand, Blue Bell. Research found that Creamy Creations equaled or exceeded Blue Bell's taste scores. Occasionally H-E-B offered limited edition flavors that featured ingredients

TABLE F   Sampling of Own Brand in Selected Product Categories

Source: Company records.

Ice Cream	H-E-B	Hill Country Fare	Leading Brands Blue Bell, Dreyers
Price	$3.97	$2.69	$4.69
Sales (millions)			
1998	$4,606	$3,897	$22,214
1999	$15,155	$4,805	$21,874
2000	$18,272	$5,037	$22,551
Gross Margin	25%	37%	21%

Beef Brisket	H-E-B (Fully Cooked)	Hill Country Fare	Leading Brand (Raw)
Price	$2.99 -$4.99 / lb.	NA	$.98 – $2.79 / lb.
Sales (millions)			
1998	$4,809	NA	$10,258
1999	$8,510	NA	$10,351
2000	$7,804	NA	$10,599
Gross Margin	21%	NA	-10%

Pasta Sauce	H-E-B	Hill Country Fare	Leading Brands Ragu, Classico
Price	$1.79	$.99	$1.28 – $2.38
Sales (millions)			
1998	$649	$465	$8,102
1999	$708	$481	$8,204
2000	$656	$580	$8,333
Gross Margin	18%	6%	17%

Flour	H-E-B	Hill Country Fare	Leading Brands Gold Medal, Pillsbury
Price	$.99	$.87	$.98 - $1.17
Sales (millions)			
1998	$609	$864	$2,201
1999	$657	$847	$2,020
2000	$661	$840	$1,743
Gross Margin	18%	21%	7%

Canned Vegetables	H-E-B	Hill Country Fare	Leading Brands Green Giant, Del Monte
Price	$.44 - $.50	$.33 - $.40	$.50 -$.57
Sales (millions)			
1998	$649	$9,850	$3,663
1999	$547	$10,519	$3,543
2000	$423	$10,719	$2,701
Gross Margin	18%	13%	14%

Frozen Vegetables	H-E-B	Hill Country Fare	Leading Brands Birdseye, Green Giant
Price	NA	$.78 - $.98	$.98 - $1.19
Sales (millions)			
1998	NA	$2,277	$1,512
1999	NA	$2,305	$1,427
2000	NA	$2,454	$1,411
Gross Margin	NA	35%	24%

EXHIBIT 7 **Selected Products—Shelf Displays**

EXHIBIT 7   (Continued)

such as locally grown strawberries. Creamy Creations was supported by television and radio advertising as well as extensive display. H-E-B also carried Hill Country Fare ice cream, which was comparable to other retailers' private label ice creams.

Fully Cooked Meats

Fueled by the creativity of the meat procurement team, H-E-B had commercialized local favorites like chicken fried steak, fajitas, and brisket in ready-to-heat form. The products were rigorously tested to meet restaurant quality. In addition, they were formulated to reduce preparation time to the bare minimum. In the case of H-E-B Fully Cooked Brisket, the customer saved over 10 hours of marinating and cooking time. Extensive sampling and advertising supported the Fully Cooked products. Fully Cooked meats were rarely discounted, since competitors did not offer comparable products.

Pasta Sauce

The Hill Country Fare brand was positioned against national entry brands such as Ragu and Prego, while the H-E-B brand competed against more premium sauces such as Classico and Five Brothers.

Flour

H-E-B stocked both H-E-B Brand and Hill Country Fare flour in addition to multiple national brands. Both Own Brand products were "hard winter wheat." H-E-B Brand flour was distinguished from Hill Country Fare by a higher "ash content" which was an advantage when baking cakes. Rob Price was not certain if customers were aware of the difference or considered such factors in selecting between flour alternatives.

Canned Vgetables

H-E-B offered both the H-E-B brand and Hill Country Fare canned vegetables. H-E-B stores carried 276 SKUs in 27 types of vegetables, creating 1,500 individual facings for the product. The H-E-B brand technical specification was "extra fancy" while Hill Country Fare was "fancy." Rob Price noted that in addition to variability within these different specifications, when a bumper crop of "extra fancy" created oversupply, the excess would be canned as Hill Country Fare.

Frozen Vegetables

Hill Country Fare frozen vegetables were solid performers. The Own Brand offering contained basic varieties, with quality that was equal to existing alternatives. The price was significantly lower than Green Giant and Birdseye. Hill Country Fare frozen vegetables were held as the lowest price in the category. The H-E-B Brand was not offered in the frozen vegetable category.

As Rob Price began to review the Own Brand strategy, he became more aware of how decisions in many parts of the organization influenced the success of H-E-B Own Brands. The product quality, packaging, pricing, placement, and promotion provided cues to shoppers about what the H-E-B and Hill Country Fare brands represented. Frequently these elements were managed harmoniously, leading to strong performance for a given product. At times, however, competitive pressure and differences in incentives made alignment difficult.

One area central to the success of Own Brand was Procurement, the department responsible for sourcing all products for H-E-B's stores. Procurement was charged with achieving the lowest cost of goods for the right assortment of items. In addition, this group was accountable for securing vendor funds (called procurement revenue) from national brands. Vendors paid procurement revenue for ad space in circulars and displays in stores. On an annual basis the procurement group sold 80% of the end-caps (end-of-aisle displays) to its vendors, where a strong product could double its unit volume during the promotional period. The store managers retained the remaining 20% of the display ends for their local merchandising. With extremely thin operating margins, procurement income was an important revenue source, not just for H-E-B, but also for other grocery store chains. Industrywide it was estimated to range from 5–10% of sales in packaged goods.

The Procurement Group's Business Development Managers (BDM) directed negotiations, ordering, advertising, displays, and events. While the meat and produce departments managed their own pricing, grocery and drug BDMs relied on an independent pricing department. BDMs were compensated on salary plus bonus based equally on category sales, gross margin, and procurement revenue. In their negotiations, BDMs were constantly balancing variables such as order quantities, shelf space, and promotional dollars to achieve the highest bonusable results. For example, if a national brand wanted to promote a particular product, the BDM might negotiate additional shelf space, special pricing, and a payment from the national brand for promotional activities in exchange for guaranteed volumes. Duncan McNaughton, VP of Grocery Procurement, commented on the complexity of growing Own Brands in this context,

> There is a constant challenge in balancing Own Brands and national brands in the store. Own Brands are critical to our financial health and differentiation. However, if Own Brands dominate, we may lose the interest of the national brands. The economics of Own Brands are complex. Own Brands generate good margins but they do not have procurement revenue associated with them, which is a consideration for the Business Development Manager as he or she manages total category profitability.
>
> In addition, Own Brand products are handled exclusively through our own distribution channels. Many competing national brands have direct store delivery and labor at the store. In these categories, which include chips, ice cream and soft drinks, gross margin does not tell the whole story. For example, Frito-Lay orders the goods, stocks the shelves, and takes back unsaleable product. With Own Brands, H-E-B has to handle all of those tasks, which eats into the profitability.

Another area that impacted Own Brands was pricing. Unique for the grocery industry, an independent seven-person team was responsible for grocery and drugstore pricing at H-E-B. H-E-B believed that taking pricing out of the Business Development Manager's control led to BDMs having greater focus on reducing cost of goods and product merchandising. The pricing group's goal was to deliver on H-E-B's promise of everyday low prices.

As competition rose in H-E-B's trade areas, the competitive pricing process became increasingly complex. Jim McTighe, director of Pricing, outlined the challenge for Own Brands,

> Consider a hypothetical case in canned vegetables. We sell Del Monte canned corn for 2 for $1. Assume Green Giant offers a cost reduction that enables us to reduce their price temporarily to $.39. Green Giant is $.39, our H-E-B brand is $.35, and Hill Country Fare is $.33. What happens if a competitor like Wal-Mart prices Del Monte at 3 for a $1.00?
>
> Then H-E-B is in an awkward position. If we match the competitor's price on Del Monte, then Green Giant becomes the highest priced product on the shelf. This would be unfortunate, given their support of our low cost positioning. Moreover, our Own Brand would be higher priced than Del Monte. If we don't match the competitor's price on Del Monte, then we risk the perception that we have failed to honor our everyday low price stand.

The Glacia Question

Charles Butt's note about Glacia prompted Rob Price to commission customer research. The results suggested that Butt's intuition was correct. When prompted without packaging, only 19% of Glacia consumers were aware the product was bottled in Canada. Sixty-four percent believed it was from Texas. Even when prompted with packaging (which incorporated a red maple leaf and the phrases "Product of Canada" and "Natural Canadian Spring Water"), only 74% of customers recognized Canada as the source.

TABLE G
Dollar Share of Single-Serve Bottled Water—Pre and Post Launch of H-E-B Glacia

Source: Company records.

Brand	Before Launch	After Launch
Domestic spring water (includes Ozarka)	73%	52%
Imported spring water		
Glacia	0	22
Other (includes Evian)	12	6
Purified drinking water	15	20

Before taking any new action, the Own Brand team reviewed the original research upon which the launch of Glacia had been based. Original concept testing suggested that sourcing from Canada appealed greatly to users of imported drinking water. In fact, Evian users indicated preference for Canada over France, Evian's source. The water from Glacia's spring performed equally to Evian in blind taste tests. It appeared that heavy emphasis on Canada would make Glacia the water of choice for Evian users.

Canada was much less appealing to a broader base of water drinkers. Only one in five bottled-water drinkers perceived any advantage from imported water. Ozarka users indicated that their preference for Texas water was 44% higher than for Canadian water. In blind taste tests, consumers rated Glacia at parity to Ozarka.

Rob Price also sought Duncan McNaughton's input. McNaughton acknowledged Glacia's strong performance and its contributions to gross margin. (**Table G** outlines the role of Glacia in the category.) McNaughton urged consideration of the procurement revenue derived from national brands, which did not show up as gross margin but nonetheless contributed to company earnings. Additionally, national brand promotions had an important role in driving overall store traffic. These events were often funded by special vendor allowances. A typical promotion of the Ozarka six-pack half-liter would be priced at 2 for $3.

Careful review of the research and the economics of the water category did not suggest a clear course of action. One alternative was to target Glacia against Evian more directly. This would require moving the product closer to Evian on the shelf and increasing the price above that of Ozarka. The brand would not need to be changed, but the Canada message would need to be more clearly emphasized. This path would provide an opportunity to launch a Hill Country Fare product in a lower tier. It was not clear if the Hill Country Fare product should be spring water or purified water.

Another alternative would be to reposition Glacia as domestic spring water. Placement and pricing would remain intact. However, significant time and expense would be spent on product development and package redesign. Scarce advertising resources would also be consumed re-launching the new product. The Own Brand team would need to determine if the H-E-B brand or the Hill Country Fare brand was the appropriate brand for this re-staged product. This approach also left open the question of how to approach the purified water market.

Rob Price needed to make a specific recommendation on Glacia within the broader context of a powerful overall Own Brand strategy. The Own Brand team had frequently heard the following questions from Charles Butt and other senior company leaders:

- How should Own Brands respond to competitive price promotions? When should H-E-B follow? What about national brand promotions?
- Specifically, what is the role of H-E-B and Hill Country Fare as the two Own Brand labels? How should these be positioned with respect to the other brands in the category?
- What is the role of Own Brand in H-E-B's overall corporate strategy? Why is it important? Should it be scaled up? Or dialed down? If so, in what products or in what product categories?

Chapter 44

Zucamor S.A.: Global Competition in Argentina

V. Kasturi Rangan

"Oh, please, don't get Gustavo started," pleaded Norm Nelson to the group gathered at the bar. "This Harvard-educated economist will give us a long lecture," he joked, as Gustavo Herrero, Osvaldo Zucchini, and others responded with laughter. There was a lot of mirth at Union Camp's "International Senior Managers" meeting at Wayne, New Jersey, called for by Norm Nelson, division vice president.

Gustavo Herrero, the object of the joke, was the managing director of Zucamor in Argentina. Zucamor was the only overseas venture of Union Camp, a $4.0 billion (in sales) integrated U.S.-based paper and container producer, in which Union Camp had only a minority stake (30%); normally it fully owned or had a majority stake in its foreign holdings. But Zucamor's three local shareholding families retained 70% of the equity. Zucamor was unique in other respects, too. For example, its marketing director Osvaldo Zucchini was one of the principals, in fact, the chairman of the board of directors. In his role as marketing director, he reported to Gustavo Herrero, who was a professional manager with no equity.

With the collapse of worldwide paper prices in 1996, accompanied by aggressive foreign entry, Zucamor's operating profits had taken a dramatic tumble. But it remained one of the few paper companies in Argentina that even made a profit. By the middle of 1997, there were several strategic questions facing Herrero and his team of managers. They had to decide how much to push the "value-enhancement" concept as a way of serving customers. This had to be balanced, however, by persuasive internal data, which showed that

Zucamor's sales volumes had gained when prices were lowered. No matter which option Zucamor's management took, the fundamental goal was to improve the profitability of its operations, which had slumped from $7.6 million in 1995 to $2.24 million in 1996.

"Don't believe it," said Gustavo Herrero, in a measured and well-moderated voice, "when economists tell you that businesses will prosper in open economies with free inflows and outflows of capital. Don't believe a word of it. Take it from me—globalization is a nanosecond phenomenon and when it happens, it is painful for local companies that are not quick on their feet," he paused. With Gustavo's gesticulating right hand frozen in mid-air, his international colleagues around him all raised their cocktail glasses in unison to loud chantings of "Sí! Sí! Gustavo. Speech, we want a speech."

Background

Zucamor was founded in 1951 by four friends, Dante Zucchini, Bautista and Marceliano Campo,[1] and Luis Morra. In 1990, the first-generation owners and founders decided to retire simultaneously and make way for the next generation, represented by Osvaldo and Nestor Zucchini, Alberto Morra, Marcelo Campo, and his brother-in-law Hugo Anitori, all in the 35- to 45-year age group.

Each of the new generation owners had held significant functional responsibility for an aspect of the company's operations, but decided that under their new regime it would be best to remove themselves from the day-to-day operations and govern the company from their position on the Board. Their first attempt to professionalize the company got off to a moderate start and, yet, the experience did not prove to be totally successful. Two years later, they decided to hire Gustavo Herrero, 43-year-old managing director of a woolen textile mill, as their chief executive. About 10 years before coming to Zucamor, Herrero had managed an integrated packaging company, and he and Osvaldo Zucchini had met each other then. Herrero was known to Osvaldo as someone who would not hesitate to make tough decisions and controlling costs was a priority concern for Zucamor.

In 1992, at the time of the transition to the new management, the company's sales were about $36 million, with a reported operating loss of about $1.4 million. The change in leadership and management at Zucamor coincided with a new political and economic climate in the country. See **Exhibit 1** for a brief history.

The new administration under President Carlos Menem (elected in 1989 and re-elected in 1995 as well) broke with the past. Restrictive trade and investment barriers were lifted and nonproductive and non self-sustaining public sector companies were privatized. Financial accounts were placed on a current basis by linking the Argentine peso to the U.S. dollar under the Convertibility Law. The intransigent Argentine system of 50 years was replaced by a largely open regime. Carlos Menem's government, anchored by Harvard Ph.D. Finance Minister Domingo Cavallo, engineered a three-pronged reform program for the economy:

The first pillar of the program was state reform. A fiscal equilibrium program forced through an all-inclusive privatization program, a sharp cutback in public employment and expenditure, the elimination of nearly all subsidies to public enterprises, a comprehensive pension reform, and improved tax collection coupled with the elimination of taxes that distorted economic incentives. Balanced budgets were submitted to Congress for timely review.

The second pillar of the program was the re-creation of a market economy through the elimination of controls on prices, wages, interest rates, foreign exchange rates, and capital flows, as well as the removal of hidden subsidies. A broad deregulation effort swept away numerous regulations that impeded the operations of free markets.

[1] Marceliano Campo sold his share to the other partners in the late 1980s.

EXHIBIT 1   **Argentina—A Brief History[a]**

With an estimated population of 34 million people in 1994, and a per-capita income of $8,159 (GDP: $280 billion), Argentina was considered an upper-middle-income country. Some 87 percent of Argentines lived in urban areas; more than 12 million lived in the Buenos Aires metropolitan area.

Argentina developed an economy based on the exchange of agricultural commodities for foreign capital and manufactured goods. At the beginning of the century, it was run primarily by and for the landowning aristocracy and porteño (Buenos Aires) business interests. However, this commodity-based economy was at the mercy of volatile international market prices and dependent on the nations which bought Argentina's low-value produce and in return sold Argentina expensive, value-added products.

In 1946, following 15 years of military influenced or direct military governments, free elections were held, resulting in the election of Juan Domingo Perón as president. Under Perón, labor took on a significant role in society, many industries were nationalized, and foreign investment and participation in the economy was restricted in an effort to allow Argentina to develop a self-sufficient industry. However, development was inefficient and Argentine goods became uncompetitive in world markets. The country incurred massive debt to support its various projects.

By 1955, deteriorating economic conditions led to a backlash among the middle class, students, and elements of the clergy, business, and military. Perón fled the country following a military coup. If Perón had erred by catering too much to the demands of labor, the military pushed the pendulum too far in the opposite direction, offending not only leftists but also students, business interests, and Argentina's large middle class. Greater military repression triggered more intense public discontent and gave rise to armed guerrilla opposition movements during the late 1960s. It was not until 17 years later that democracy returned to Argentina. Perón returned from exile, and was re-elected in 1973, but passed away before his term ran out. His wife/vice president Isabel was ousted, by the military, in 1976. Finally, the Christian Democrats, under Raul Alfonsin, won the elections in 1983 and then in 1989, Perónists won power again with Carlos Menem at the helm.

[a]Much of this section has been taken from *Argentina Business: The Portable Encyclopedia for Doing Business with Argentina* (San Rafael, Calif.: World Trade Press,1996).

The third pillar of the program was investment and trade liberalization. The regulations on foreign direct investment were liberalized: First, registration requirements were eliminated; second, foreign investors had full access to local credit markets; third, prior approval was required only in cases where special laws applied (such as defense); and fourth, there was no waiting period for the repatriation of profits and capital.

Few countries have had a worse experience with inflation than Argentina. Between 1980 and 1988, consumer price rises were in the triple-digit range every year except 1986, when they fell to 86%. Argentine inflation reached a high of 4,924% in 1989, dropped to 1,344% in 1990, and then fell precipitously to 3.9% in 1994. Despite the financial turmoil caused by the liquidity crisis in Mexico and the devaluation of its peso, in late 1994, Argentina showed no change in inflation. Financial stability was there to stay, and inflation firmly in control.

Zucamor Takes a New Direction

One of Herrero's first decisions after taking over in November 1992 was to persuade each of the owners to accept a significant line responsibility within the operation. Thus, Osvaldo Zucchini became its marketing chief, Marcelo Campo took on the finance and administrative functions, Alberto Morra became its technical director, Nestor Zucchini agreed to oversee the company's business development effort, and Hugo Anitori became purchasing director (see **Exhibit 2** for organization chart).

Shortly thereafter, Herrero began to streamline and regularize many business practices to be in tune with the new regulatory and economic environment. For example, he eliminated the procedure of paying labor out-of-contract. They were all brought in as regular employees and their wages were paid "on the books." Zucamor, like many companies in Argentina at that time, paid a considerable portion (20% of wages) outside-the-books. Because the social security and pension benefits were often more than 100% of the basic wages, paying "off-the-books" saved the company a significant amount of labor costs. But in order to manage the payments, the company also had to generate an equivalent amount of revenue outside-the-books.

EXHIBIT 2 Zucamor Organization Chart

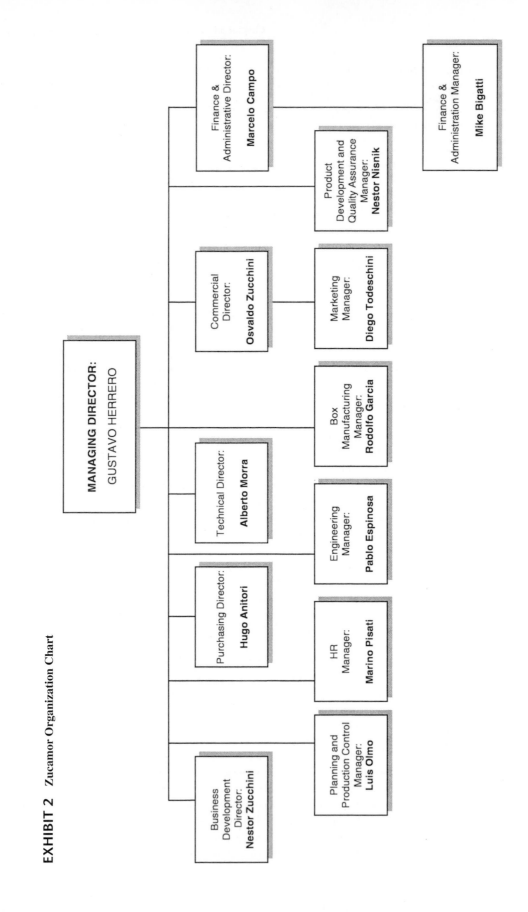

All in all, this ended up in lower reported earnings and tax payments. Herrero put a stop to this practice because he thought it was morally wrong to evade social costs, particularly when the Government, conscious of this widespread behavior in the economy, had come out with a regularization program (*Blanqueo Laboral*), which allowed firms to straighten out their practices.

Herrero knew that all this would increase the costs of production by close to $1 million a year, so he set in motion a program to improve quality, productivity, and plant utilization. Managers and workers were provided bonuses and incentives linked to productivity gains. The managers' bonus, SBG (*Sistema de Bonus Gerencial*—Management Bonus System), was a group quarterly incentive based on achieving objectives, and the workers' bonus, PCP (*Programa de Calidad Productiva*—Productive Quality Program), was based on qualitative and quantitative productivity parameters and was paid out monthly, based on a bimonthly moving average. By April 1993, these schemes were fully in place and Zucamor's productivity was beginning to pick up.

Notwithstanding the production improvements, Herrero and the shareholders were all convinced that the only way to survive and grow in the newly liberalized market environment would be to become a world-class manufacturer, and that would involve seeking partnerships with global players. Herrero recalled:

> Once I had the owners' blessings, I simply picked up the phone and dialed the directory assistance operator in New Jersey asking for the Union Camp number. Why Union Camp? Why not International Paper or Inland or Stone? Only because rumors were floating that Union Camp was actively looking around for a partner in Argentina. Well, I made contact with their vice president for international operations and that's how I first met Norm Nelson.

But Union Camp had already signed a "letter of intent" with another local company, and so Zucamor looked for an alternate suitor and signed a similar "letter of intent" agreement with a South African paper company. Herrero recalled the early days of the partnership.

> Norm and I had really hit it off very well and I struck a similar chord with Union Camp's Chairman and CEO, Craig McClelland. Both of us were educated at the Harvard Business School and had memories to share. But Union Camp was committed elsewhere. Fortunately for us at Zucamor, Union Camp's agreement with the other company started coming apart at the due diligence stage. When Norm Nelson called me to say they wanted to talk to us, we, in turn, were deep into assessing another potential partner's interest. In the end, it all worked out because the South African company's parent was not that interested in our idea.

Marcelo Campo and I visited three U.S. paper companies—Union Camp and two others that had shown interest. We asked each of them five questions:

- What was their expectation regarding equity control and management of their investment?
- What was the ballpark figure for investment they had in mind?
- Was the fact that Zucamor owned its own recycled paper mill an obstacle?
- What was their strategy? Was it low cost? Valued-added?
- Were they thinking of making the investment "in kind" or was it to be a cash transaction?

> It became clear that Union Camp was the right partner. We began exchanging information in mid-December 1993, signed a letter of intent on March 15, 1994, and closed the deal on August 22, 1994. It was lightning fast.

Union Camp was a leading manufacturer of paper, packaging, chemicals, and wood products. With annual sales of nearly $3.0 billion in 1993, and nearly 19,000 employees, Union Camp ranked among the top 200 U.S. industrial companies. See **Exhibit 3** for Union Camp's revenue and balance sheet information. In 1993, the company's four paper and paper board plants produced a total of 1.92 million tons of paper products of which its 29 converting

EXHIBIT 3 Union Camp: Key Financial Information

Source: Annual Report.

	1987	1988	1989	1990	1991	1992	1993	1994	1995	1996
Net sales	$2,361,684	$2,660,918	$2,761,337	$2,839,704	$2,967,138	$3,064,358	$3,120,421	$3,395,825	$4,211,709	$4,013,197
Income from operations	398,053	504,630	500,684	388,217	285,420	192,278	230,926	284,286	841,389	252,539
Net income	207,483	295,146	299,400	229,591	124,790	76,233	50,043	113,510	451,073	85,308
Working capital	458,065	443,244	354,233	216,756	145,074	124,002	1,346	67,209	413,704	354,241
Total assets	2,919,115	3,094,414	3,413,862	4,403,354	4,697,714	4,745,197	4,685,033	4,776,578	4,838,343	5,096,307
Long-term debt	632,706	627,928	690,149	1,221,597	1,348,157	1,289,706	1,244,907	1,252,249	1,151,536	1,252,475
Stockholders' equity	1,452,017	1,559,327	1,754,524	1,910,643	1,936,256	1,881,878	1,815,848	1,836,321	2,121,692	2,093,594

Note: 1996 includes a $46.9 million special charge relating to restructuring costs and asset writedowns.

plants used 1.0 million tons for making corrugated containers and folding cartons. In addition, the company also produced another 265,000 tons of kraft paper for conversion in nine flexible packaging plants. The 1993 paper mill capacity in the United States was about 90 million tons, of which approximately 15 million tons was used for making medium and liner, the type of paper used in corrugated box making. The box market was about 30 billion square meters. The company's $23 million investment in Zucamor was split: a small part went to the owners, but most of it to Zucamor as new capital for effecting manufacturing improvements and paying off expensive local debt.

Union Camp had long been a leading exporter of kraft linerboard to world markets and by the mid-1980s had undertaken a strategy to expand its corrugated box manufacturing investments in select world markets. The strategy to grow packaging operations in international markets was consistent with Union Camp's overall strategy, which was based on the belief that its cash flow should be focused first on generating higher returns followed by investment for growth, and without necessarily serving as an outlet for linerboard from Union Camp mills. The U.S. consumption of corrugated paper was 96 kgs per capita in comparison to Argentine consumption at 12 kgs per capita. Moreover, with U.S. paper and box-making capacity usually outstripping demand, the industry was subject to pricing cycles and corresponding fluctuations in profitability.

According to division VP Norm Nelson:

We had been in Europe for a long time; over 25 years in Spain, but we had not entered Latin America and Asia, where the opportunities for growth were attractive. In Latin America, Chile stabilized first and reformed its economy, so we entered there. Brazil was saturated with many strong local players, so we sought Argentina next. It was a systematic market entry process.

Craig McClelland in his chairman's report (1994 Union Camp Annual Report) explained the company's globalization strategy:

A key strategic element is to build on our international presence especially in Latin America and the Pacific rim.

We've been a major linerboard exporter for 40 years. We also have long experience in operating offshore container plants, with six facilities in Ireland, Spain, Chile, the Canary Islands and Puerto Rico, plus recent equity investment in an Argentine containerboard and corrugated box manufacturer. We intend to expand linerboard exports and add more corrugated plants outside the U.S. to strengthen this growing and profitable segment of our packaging group.

In the Far East, we're setting up a business development office in Hong Kong to help us further penetrate the markets in Asia. Our aim is to expand our foothold through greater market presence in high-end reprographic paper and packaging—servicing the expanding needs of those high growth markets.

Zucamor, Capacity and Performance

Zucamor was a vertically integrated corrugated box manufacturer. It made its own paper from recycled raw material (wastepaper); it then converted the paper to corrugated sheets by sandwiching a wavy middle layer called "medium" or "fluting" in between external layers called "liners." This operation was done by a corrugating machine. Finally, the corrugated sheets were converted to boxes. Depending on customers' specific needs (such as, where to have the handling slots in the box), customized die-cuts were used in slotting machines, which customized the box types. Similarly, depending upon the customers' desired printing requirements on the box, customized printing plates were used in the final printing (see **Exhibit 4** for a process flow diagram).

EXHIBIT 4   **Paper and Boxmaking Process: Line Diagram**

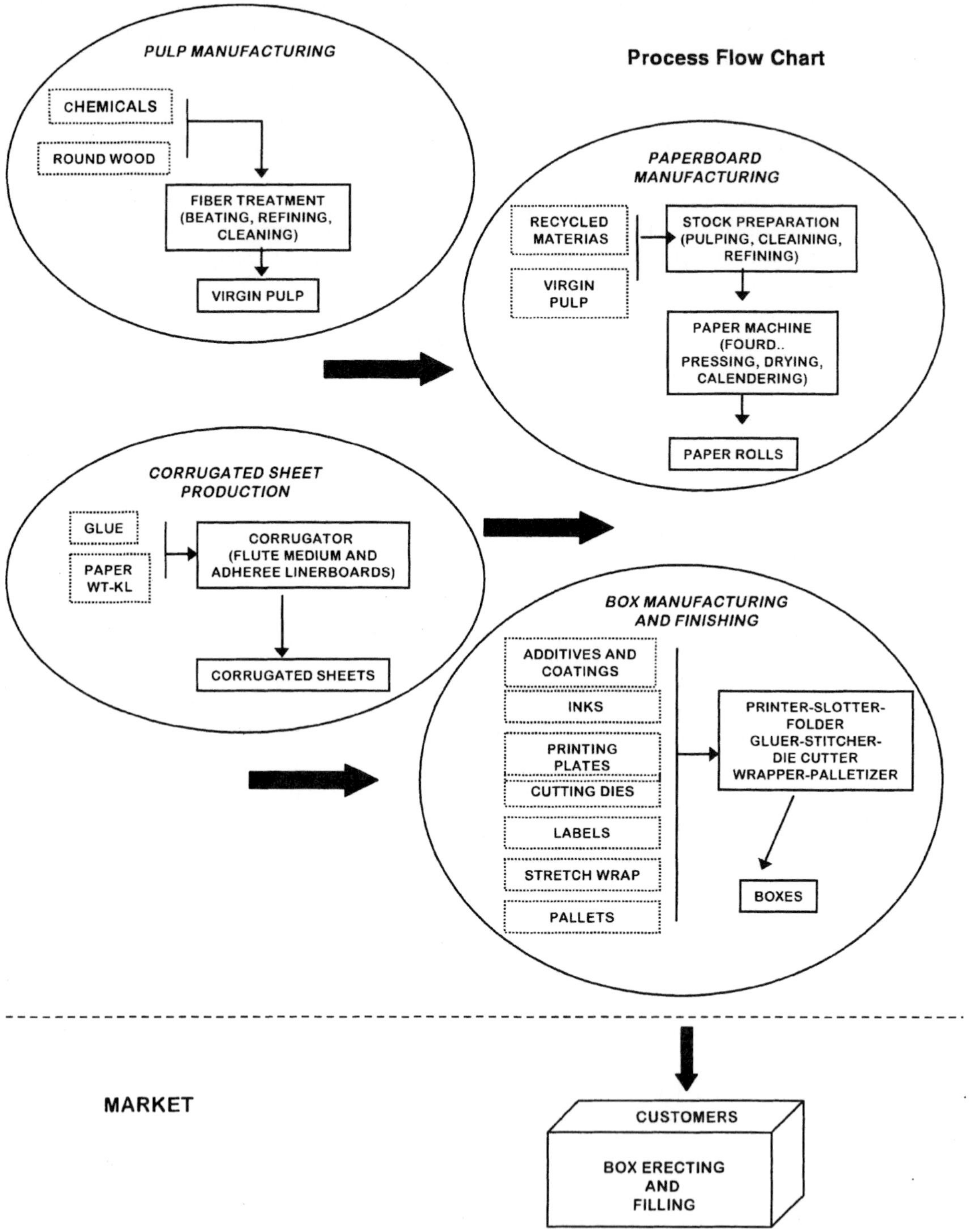

Process Flow Chart

PULP MANUFACTURING

CHEMICALS

ROUND WOOD

FIBER TREATMENT (BEATING, REFINING, CLEANING)

VIRGIN PULP

PAPERBOARD MANUFACTURING

RECYCLED MATERIAS

VIRGIN PULP

STOCK PREPARATION (PULPING, CLEAINING, REFINING)

PAPER MACHINE (FOURD.. PRESSING, DRYING, CALENDERING)

PAPER ROLLS

CORRUGATED SHEET PRODUCTION

GLUE

PAPER WT-KL

CORRUGATOR (FLUTE MEDIUM AND ADHEREE LINERBOARDS)

CORRUGATED SHEETS

BOX MANUFACTURING AND FINISHING

ADDITIVES AND COATINGS

INKS

PRINTING PLATES

CUTTING DIES

LABELS

STRETCH WRAP

PALLETS

PRINTER-SLOTTER-FOLDER GLUER-STITCHER-DIE CUTTER WRAPPER-PALLETIZER

BOXES

MARKET

CUSTOMERS

BOX ERECTING AND FILLING

The two distinctive aspects of the operation, papermaking and boxmaking, were characterized by very different scale economies. Paper output was usually measured in "weight"—in this case, metric tons; and box output in "area"—square meters. A papermaking plant was capital intensive, while boxmaking was labor intensive. A 300,000 metric ton/year paper mill cost about $500 million to set up—in comparison to a $25 million investment for a 60 million square meter/year box plant. Plant sizes below this threshold were increasingly uneconomical.[2] An approximate rule of thumb equated 1 metric ton (i.e., 2,200 lbs.) with 2,000 square meters of corrugated box. Ultimately, of course, the conversion was based on the grade of medium and liner used for box making.

Zucamor had an integrated paper and boxmaking capability at Ranelagh, just 20 miles south of Buenos Aires. It had two more boxmaking plants, one at Cuyo near the Chilean border at the heart of Argentina's wine country, and the other at Hurlingham, 20 miles west of Buenos Aires (see **Exhibit 5** for Zucamor's paper and box shipment volumes). All three factories combined, Zucamor had about 120 million square meters of boxmaking capacity. The Ranelagh mill was unique in that it used 100% recycled fiber as raw material. In the highly inflationary shortage environment (pre-1989), the strategy of owning a factory making paper based on recycled material was very helpful in keeping the prices of linerboard and medium at a predictable lower level. After Argentina's economic liberalization in 1990, however, many local box plants were able to import virgin fiber kraft linerboard from paper-rich Brazil and from the United States for about the same price as (or even less than) Zucamor's recycled liner. Compared to recycled paper, virgin paper had longer fiber length and therefore displayed higher strength for an equivalent gauge of liner.

Argentina consumed about 421,275 metric tons of medium and liners in 1995, of which Zucamor supplied 60,000 metric tons for a 15% market share in the country. Of the domestic paper producers, Zucamor's share was even higher because about 100,000 tons of consumption were from imported sources. The bulk of Zucamor's paper production (about 50,000 metric tons) was consumed by its own box plants. It sold about 10,000 tons to other box manufacturers. Zucamor also bought about 10,000 tons of kraft linerboard for making special grades of boxes, mainly from Papel Misionero, a government owned paper plant. Of the six paper companies in Argentina, only the government-owned Papel Misionero produced kraft liner (i.e., from virgin fiber); the other five, like Zucamor, produced test liner (i.e., from recycled fiber).

Herrero explained the transition to higher productivity:

> We systematically and ruthlessly approached our operating task with the dual objective of increasing throughput and quality at the same time. This led to a series of initiatives that were pursued with key support from Union Camp's resources. By June 1995, all three of our box plants were certified under ISO 9001. The next two years brought achievements in other areas of operations. Product quality and service claims were brought down from nearly 10% of shipments to 1%. We cut machine set-up time by more than half, from 25 minutes to 10 minutes, even as we compressed the average run size from 10,000 square meters to 5,000 square meters. On-time delivery performance increased from 70% to 90%. Absenteeism went down, productivity went up and labor cost per square meter produced was halved.

These tremendous gains in productivity led to impressive gains in market share and operating income (see **Exhibits 6A** and **6B** for Zucamor financials).

Globalization with a Vengeance

The largest corrugated boxmaker in Argentina was Cartocor with about 21% market share. Cartocor was wholly owned by Arcor, a local producer of packaged food (such as candies, crackers, and preserves). Cartocor was the broadest player and served a complete range of markets in the industrial and agricultural segments. Zucamor, on the other hand, only catered to the industrial segment which comprised 80% of the market. Zucamor considered the agricultural segment too seasonal and risky to play in. Zucamor was second with 12%

---

[2] 1 metric ton—1,000 kilos. Given Zucamor's product mix, .58 kilos of pulp made 1 square meter of linerboard.

EXHIBIT 5A

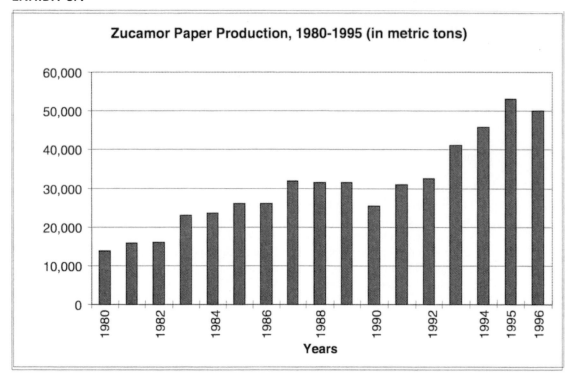

Zucamor Paper Production, 1980-1995 (in metric tons)

EXHIBIT 5B

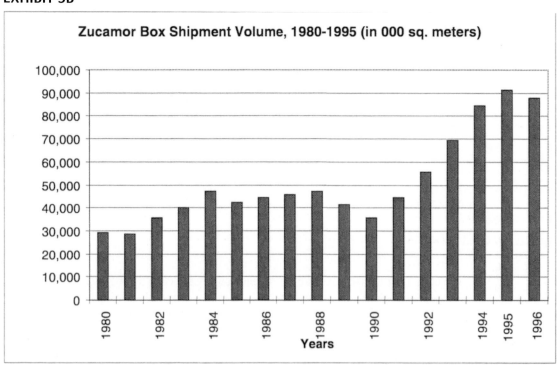

Zucamor Box Shipment Volume, 1980-1995 (in 000 sq. meters)

EXHIBIT 6A Zucamor: Financial History

Balance Sheet (in US$)

ASSETS	12/31/96	12/31/95	12/31/94
Current			
Cash & bank	2,147,936.79	2,098,939.99	2,663,778.04
Investments	311,320.72	3,012,345.33	139,138.36
Accounts receivable	12,599,660.81	14,082,967.91	15,042,873.99
Other credits	6,844,294.13	6,269,534.49	5,539,314.54
Inventories	10,151,113.82	11,869,930.40	9,289,767.13
Other assets	2,176,560.39	2,231,880.83	0.00
Total current assets	34,230,886.68	39,563,598.95	32,674,872.06
Noncurrent			
Investments	65,137.37	57,119.86	175,446.70
Other assets	0.00	0.00	2,867,033.55
Fixed assets	72,318,146.61	69,542,102.65	68,827,694.31
Intangible assets	516.34	516.34	516.44
Total noncurrent assets	72,383,800.32	69,599,738.85	71,870,691.00
Total assets	106,614,686.98	109,163,337.80	104,545,563.06

LIABILITIES	12/31/96	12/31/95	12/31/94
Current			
Accounts payable	4,742,504.30	6,226,974.79	7,044,897.36
Financial debt	4,807,054.53	1,216,718.67	2,118,104.96
Payroll and social security benefits	1,264,208.58	1,527,580.98	1,298,498.73
Taxes payable	1,015,355.22	3,823,751.08	2,094,668.64
Total current liabilities	11,829,122.63	12,795,025.52	12,556,169.69
Noncurrent			
Taxes payable	734,214.00	700,953.00	3,809,035.73
Other liabilities	0.00	0.00	0.00
Long-term debt	6,006,775.00	1,494,158.61	1,571,946.38
Total noncurrent liabilities	6,740,989.00	2,195,111.61	5,380,982.11
Total liabilities	18,570,111.63	14,990,137.13	17,937,151.80
Minority interest	111.36	103.31	86.93
Net worth	88,044,463.99	94,173,097.36	86,608,324.32
Total liabilities and net worth	106,614,686.98	109,163,337.80	104,545,563.05

DIVIDEND DISTRIBUTION	12/31/96	12/31/95	12/31/94
	8,363,810.36	0.00	0.00

EXHIBIT 6B **Zucamor Income Statement (in US$)**

	1996	1995	1994	1993
Net sales	60,813,737.51	75,076,430.47	66,166,231.79	47,395,423.25
Cost of goods sold	(46,200,534.92)	(52,750,752.69)	(49,823,922.66)	(37,692,034.93)
Gross income	14,613,202.59	22,325,677.78	16,342,309.13	9,703,388.32
Selling expenses	(7,076,347.60)	(6,696,067.44)	(5,273,457.89)	(3,593,517.91)
Administrative expenses	(4,224,026.66)	(4,587,622.04)	(4,487,455.76)	(2,254,11.62)
Other expenses	(722,129.39)	(987,308.38)	(722,155.98)	(1,491,634.65)
Total SG&A/other	(12,022,503.65)	(12,270,997.86)	(10,483,069.63)	(7,339,364.18)
Operating profit	2,590,698.94	10,054,679.92	5,859,239.50	2,364,024.14
Permanent investments result	0	0	0	0
Other income	787,513.49	931,408.43	893,807.91	1,298,552.40
Extraordinary income	88,278.00	1,569,553.02	11,611.25	59,811.18
Financial expenses & holding gains (includes results from exposure to inflation)	(241,839.28)	(1,256,418.30)	(1,930,271.43)	(1,240,929.52)
Minority interest income	(11.01)	(9.05)	(3.79)	21.69
Profit before income tax	3,224,640.14	11,299,214.02	4,834,383.45	2,481,479.89
Income tax provision	(989,463.15)	(3,706,414.57)	(1,177,241.14)	0
Net income	2,235,176.99	7,592,799.45	3,657,142.31	2,481,479.89

market share in box sales (this was less than its 15% share of paper because it sold some paper in the open market), followed by Inland Argentina, Stone-Cartonex, FACCA, and Asindus-Smurfit, each with a 3% to 7% share. Inland Argentina was 100% owned by Inland Container, a $3.4 billion integrated U.S. paper- and boxmaker (entered in 1994); Stone-Cartonex was 51% owned by another large U.S. box manufacturer, Stone Container (entered in 1996); and Asindus-Smurfit was 80% owned by a large Irish box manufacturer, Jefferson Smurfit, a $3.6 billion global paper and box manufacturer (entered in 1996).

The top six players served about 44% of the market. The other 56% plus was catered to by nearly a hundred small boxmakers, many with sales as low as $1 million. Only four box manufacturers were integrated (i.e., produced their own paper) in Argentina—Zucamor, Stone-Cartonex, Asindus Smurfit and, to a much lesser extent, Cartocor.

"Given the competitive nature of the container business in North America, we should have expected this foreign invasion," offered Marcelo Campo, "but we were very surprised by its speed and intensity," he added. As shown in **Exhibit 7,** U.S. paper and container prices had started to climb up in 1994, and the larger players now had the cash for making offshore investments. Unlike the previous boom periods when domestic capacity expansion fueled excessive supply over demand in the down cycle, this time around manufacturers looked for offshore expansions. Gustavo explained, "sheltered markets like Argentina became attractive because of the price umbrella they offered. But unlike previous price expansions, the U.S. recovery was short lived, soon putting even more pressure on overseas investments to outperform domestic operations."

Even as the Argentine economy opened up to post steady GNP gains, competition among the box manufacturers was quite intensive, especially for the larger, growth-oriented accounts. Meanwhile, in 1997, Cartocor had completed a state-of-the-art 100-million-square-meter capacity corrugated container plant near Buenos Aires, creating additional corrugated capacity in an industry that was already in an overcapacity situation. Zucamor's managers considered Cartocor as the most formidable competitor. First of all, because it was only partially integrated it was able to buy paper in the open market for box conversion. Good quality paper from Brazil at cheap prices was abundantly available.

EXHIBIT 7   **U.S. Linerboard (Paper) Price vs. Fibre Box Price (quarterly prices in $US per metric ton)**

Source: Zucamor records.

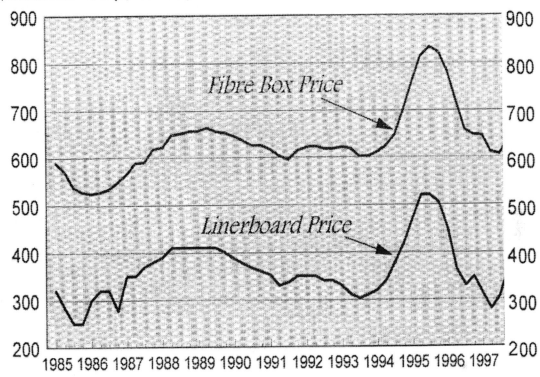

Moreover, Cartocor's boxmaking lines were considered very modern and efficient, with good product development and design capability. It operated with a very lean marketing and sales overhead structure. For example, the company covered the entire Buenos Aires market with three sales people. All this combined with captive consumption at its own packaged food operations gave Cartocor clear cost leadership in the Argentine market. In contrast, Inland Argentina and Stone-Cartonex were rumored to be encountering some difficulties. Even though their equipment and the quality of the boxes they made were considered quite good, both these competitors resorted to aggressive competitive pricing and provided only moderate service levels.

According to a Zucamor executive:

> For some reason, two of our multi-national competitors concentrated on the sale of produce boxes (fruits and vegetables), and on Tetrapack trays for the wine industry, which are two of the most competitive segments in our business. Both are fairly standard, so they are actually tradable across borders. The little business they captured in the regular consumer market was opportunistic; long runs, low margins, with price being the main buying attribute.

After Cartocor, Zucamor managers thought that Smurfit could turn out to be the most formidable competitor. One of them explained:

> Jefferson Smurfit entered the market in 1997. They acquired a small, integrated local company that made paper and boxes. Even though the plant was poorly equipped, it had cornered the business of a couple of large customers, from which it made its living with probably

handsome profits, given their low overhead. Smurfit has been re-equipping the firm since they bought it, and can be a fearsome contender. It will depend on whether they can develop the service skills that the more sophisticated markets require.

As compared to the top-tier players, the small and medium boxmakers provided their customers with fast response and short runs. Even though their equipment and efficiency was not exactly top class, they managed to retain customer loyalty, and according to Herrero, "they are not subject to the same accounting principles and business standards that larger national players are used to."

Customers

From Zucamor's viewpoint, the market could generally be divided into three types of customers by their buying behavior. Category 1 and 2 customers, who were the larger customers, accounted for about 47% of the market volume, and the small customers for the rest. Large suppliers like Zucamor supplied 44% of the market's requirements.

Among the large customers, some were very professional in their purchasing practices and strongly emphasized quality, often supplying custom specifications for their box design. A number of the multinational companies such as P&G and Unilever and domestic manufacturers like Molinos would fall into this category. They expected high service levels and would not tolerate overruns or underruns. Zucamor's sales division labeled them Category 1 customers. Other medium to large customers with similar requirements but at a slightly lower intensity were classified as Category 2 customers. Many of these customers along with almost all the Category 1 customers supplied to the aggressive retail industry in Argentina, characterized by the likes of global giants like Carrefour and Walmart. Finally, the smaller customers who were somewhat less professional in their purchasing patterns were classified as Category 3 customers. They were known to buy on relationship.

Table A provides an estimate of how sales volume was distributed among the large, and medium and small boxmakers.

Of Zucamor's sales volume, 41% went to Category 1 customers, 32% to Category 2 customers, and 27% to Category 3 customers.

Zucamor's customer list had about 484 accounts, of which the top 5 (with annual purchases exceeding $3 million) accounted for 25% of sales, the top 16 (with purchases exceeding $1 million) for 50% of sales, and the top 51 (with purchases exceeding $.5 million) for 75% of sales. An internal survey of customers' buying preferences revealed that about half its customers bought on quality and service; another 40% included price as one of the buying attributes; only about 10% bought purely on price.

Exhibit 8 provides an analysis of the company's top 51 customers and their volume and purchasing characteristics.

TABLE A
Corrugated Box Suppliers

	Large Suppliers	Medium and Small Suppliers	Total
Category 1	14%	4%	18%
Category 2	22	7	29
Category 3	8	45	53
Total	44%	56%	100%

TABLE B
Development of the Value Proposition

Quantitative Attributes	Qualitative Attributes	General
Replenishment	Vertical integration	Teamwork
On-time delivery	Packaging training	ISO exposure
Space reduction		CTR experience
Waste reduction (elimination?)		UCC know-how
Administrative cost reduction		Global network
Less claims/less downtime		Value analysis
Faster/better response		Environmental
Practices		
Quality certification		Customer satisfaction program
Logistics skills		
Design capability		

Value-Enhancement

The senior management of the company, with leadership from Union Camp, was then engaged in a major cycle time reduction (CTR) program in the factory, and again with Union Camp's support, was adopting similar principles to reengineer the customer value chain. According to Marketing Director Osvaldo Zucchini:

> With the technical help of Union Camp, we were squeezing out all these costs in the plant, so we attempted to extend those ideas to customers as well. After two days of intense brainstorming we arrived at the *Paquete Zucamor* (Zucamor Package). The *Paquete* identified our sources of differentiable advantage along three dimensions—quantitative, qualitative and general (See **Table B** above.)
>
> We started by writing down the various elements that we felt entailed value to our customers (the "what"). We then qualified them in two categories: those that translated into specific cost reductions, and those that entailed intentions of goodwill on our part. Within those that implied reductions of cost (or addition of value), we identified "quantitative" attributes and "qualitative" ones. Finally, we covered the entire list, and we decided to leave out from our immediate value proposition certain elements where we felt we were not sufficiently equipped to deliver value to our customers. It was agreed that we should interpret the list of "ingredients," but the "recipe" should be custom-made for each account, depending on their needs and on their perception of value.

The two-day meeting also considered the question of which accounts to go after with the Zucamor package. According to Herrero:

> We started by identifying those that had already expressed interest in the concept. We then matched their fit with our strategic objectives, their receptivity to letting us explore the value chain and the incidence of packaging costs in their overall product cost.
>
> The team made a list of criteria to drive account selection for the value package:

1. Strategic long-term accounts
   a. Growth potential of firm and the business segment it participates in
   b. Their segment leadership and financial performance
   c. Our contribution margin
   d. Credit risk
   e. Professionalism in their management
   f. Competitive presence in their supply
2. Receptivity to our value proposition
3. Incidence of packaging cost on end product

EXHIBIT 8 Customer Analysis by Buying Attribute (1996)

	Segment	Category	Sq. Meters	Quality	Service	Price	Percent Share of Total	Customer Share (%)	Cartocor	Inland	Other Large Competitors	Small Competitors	Import
1.	Food Oils	I	5,521,250	X	X	X	7.45	60%	X			X	
2.	Beverages	II	3,864,715	X	X		4.64	80	X				
3.	Cleaning products	I	2,675,677	X	X		4.45	70	X				
4.	Beverages	I	3,272,197	X	X	X	4.40	25		X		X	
5.	Beverages	I	2,738,431	X	X		3.35	75	X				
6.	Foods	I	1,197,014	X	X		3.03	100					
7.	Foods	I	2,222,440	X	X	X	3.00	60	X			X	
8.	Glass/ceramics	II	1,993,759		X		2.75	80		X	X		
9.	Beverages	I	1,467,806	X	X		2.63	70				X	
10.	Beverages	II	1,902,484	X	X		2.14	80				X	
11.	Beverages	II	1,036,870			X	1.94	0	X			X	
12.	Meat packers	II	1,028,587	X	X		1.91	60				X	X
13.	Cleaning products	I	1,207,456	X	X		1.82	70			X	X	
14.	Tobacco	I	1,181,681	X	X		1.64	80			X	X	
15.	Beverages	II	696,690	X	X	X	1.28	60		X	X	X	
16.	Food oils	II	774,531	X		X	1.28	20	X				
17.	Meat packers	II	654,831		X		1.26	70					
18.	Foods	II	832,337	X		X	1.21	50		X	X	X	
19.	Milk Ind.	II	792,620	X	X		1.20	75				X	
20.	Foods	I	725,519	X	X		1.20	75		X	X		
21.	Cleaning products	I	862,741	X		X	1.08	5	X			X	
22.	Cleaning products	I	757,381			X	1.06	20				X	X
23.	Beverages	II	657,363			X	0.94	25	X	X	X		X
24.	Meat packers	II	641,177	X	X		0.91	50				X	X
25.	Foods	III	675,889		X	X	0.90	20		X		X	X
26.	Beverages	II	665,948	X	X		0.82	20		X	X	X	
27.	Milk Ind.	I	435,179	X	X		0.80	10	X			X	
28.	Cleaning products	I	430,579	X	X		0.79	75	X			X	
29.	Foods	I	799,446	X		X	0.75	50	X			X	

Source: Zucamor records.

#	Category	I	II	III											
30.	Beverages		II		578,240	X	X		0.73	100					
31.	Foods		II		500,160	X		X	0.73	50	X			X	
32.	Foods		II		384,069	X	X	X	0.72	80				X	
33.	Cosmetics		II		492,447	X	X		0.67	100					
34.	Beverages		II		440,029	X	X		0.66	100					
35.	Iron & Steel			III	332,434	X	X		0.65	80	X			X	
36.	Foods	I			500,963	X		X	0.65	50	X			X	
37.	Beverages		II		394,209	X	X	X	0.57	60	X				
38.	Foods		II		345,823	X	X		0.45	25	X			X	
39.	Beverages			III	341,275	X	X	X	0.43	90	X				
40.	Beverages		II		426,223	X	X	X	0.41	40	X	X			
41.	Iron & Steel			III	191,557	X	X		0.39	100					
42.	Beverages			III	441,296	X	X		0.39	100					
43.	Food oils			III	287,095		4	X	0.37	50	X	X			
44.	Chemicals/Refinery	I			182,736	X	X	X	0.33	100					
45.	Beverages			III	259,318			X	0.33	100					
46.	Beverages			III	209,414			X	0.31	50					
47.	Meat packers		II		181,042			X	0.30	20				X	
48.	Foods			III	207,327	X	X	X	0.30	90		X			
49.	Foods	I			189,104	X		X	0.27	5	X			X	
50.	Beverages		II		169,896	X	X	X	0.24	60	X				
51.	Chemicals/Refinery	I			94,883	X	X	X	0.19	0	X				
	Total	19	23	9	49,115,348	38	36	28	71.10		20	13	3	27	4

775

In choosing which accounts to go after, Herrero highlighted the need for customers' top management commitment and assurance that the customer would not shift allegiance after the development work was completed. He recalled:

> It was horrible at a Canadian food manufacturer. We worked through their packaging line and spotted many interesting ways to redesign their box so that it would lead to productivity gains at their end. Finally, after all the work was done, they simply turned around and placed the box order with one of our competitors who was willing to come in at a lower price.

Since then, Zucamor had been considerably more careful in its relationship building efforts with strategic accounts. At Avon, for instance, a study of their packaging line revealed significant scope for productivity improvements; there was also room for improving the integrity of the box. Following Zucamor's recommendations, Avon agreed to invest half a million dollars to revamp the picking line; Zucamor staffed and managed its operations. One full-time supervisor and four operators (two per shift) were hired and paid by Zucamor to operate Avon's final packaging step.

According to Avon's purchasing team (consisting of the purchasing manager and the engineering manager, both of whom had been on the job for over 10 years):

> This is a true partnership. We don't order boxes anymore. Once the parameters of the size and price have been established, Zucamor's supervisor on our shopfloor gets the needed quantity of boxes in, or stores them here, or does whatever it takes to operate a smooth finishing line. We simply pay for the actual quantity of boxes used. We don't pay for any defect, any inventories, or any transportation.

Nestor Nisnik, Zucamor's product development manager, commented on the evolution of this partnership:

> We were told by Avon of persistent pilferage problems of rather expensive cosmetics en route to their salesforce. We took a look at their box design and packing line and were able to come up with recommendations that will perhaps save them $300,000 in packaging and labor costs per year. This is a considerable savings on Avon's nearly $300 million turnover in Argentina. In turn, we were rewarded with a sole-source contract. We beat out Cartocor, who was a second source for Avon. Of course, Cartocor cannot offer our level of value engineering.

Diego Todeschini offered this note of caution:

> Zucamor has only recently rolled out its value analysis concept. The initial success is varied. For every successful account like Avon, we have corresponding accounts like Nabisco that are tough to crack. We need to understand why. Sometimes we don't even have to go all the way to demonstrate shopfloor productivity gains. At YPF (Argentina's recently privatized oil company), we have been able to get a sole-source arrangement for their motor oil shipments [in boxes] to retailers because they have faith in our logistics and JIT systems. But we have to get more customers on board to our value concept. We have the largest salesforce in the industry; they are most experienced with good relationships with their customers. We need to tap into this unique strength.
>
> Besides, we must thoroughly review our cost structure. In spite of our progress, we continue to have higher overhead than all our competitors. Even if we choose not to be the low cost producers, we cannot afford to run with steeper costs. Prices may continue to drop, and our break-even point is too high.

Zucamor's marketing and sales organization had 10 salespeople, of whom 7 were direct employees and 3 were agents who carried nothing but the Zucamor line. The agents were paid on a straight commission basis. Because of the concentration of customers, nearly 60% to 70% of the salesforce was located in the Buenos Aires province. They had been with the organization an average of seven years and were considered knowledgeable and had good relationships with their customers. Each salesperson on average called on about 50 accounts.

EXHIBIT 9   **Zucamor: Fibre Box Volume and Prices**

Source: Zucamor records.

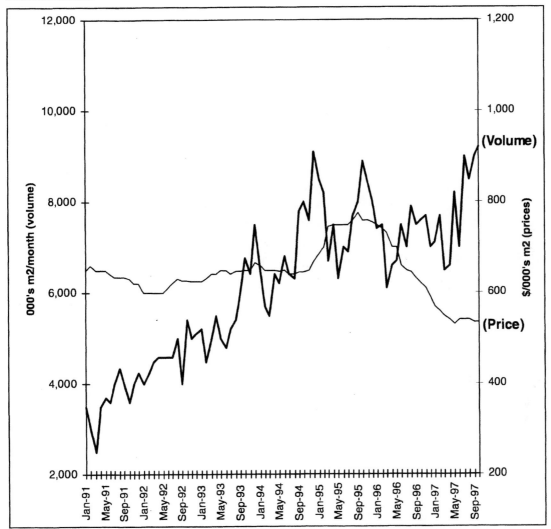

Three customer service representatives handled customer complaints and followed up on order status. The product development and quality assurance function with another three supporting staff usually handled customers' specific requests for design and customization.

But even as Zucamor's marketing team attempted to refine its Value Engineering Concept, internal analysis revealed a strong correlation between price and volume (see **Exhibit 9**). Some Zucamor managers wondered if they might be better served by simply attempting to gain share by keeping prices and costs at lower levels. This might involve product line rationalization, and an internal analysis revealed that the bulk of sales and contributions came from only 13 grades (see **Table C** below).

Exhibits 10A and **10B** provide further details on the margin contribution of Zucamor's product portfolio. In general, the thinking in the company was that much gain would not be achieved by tinkering with product mix and grades, especially when major strategic directions remained unresolved.

EXHIBIT 10A

Source: Zucamor documents.

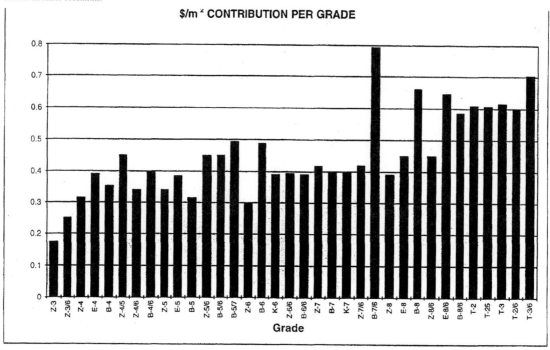

EXHIBIT 10B

Source: Zucamor documents.

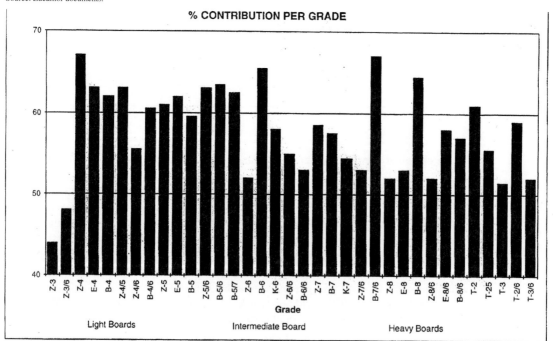

TABLE C
Contribution and
Volume of the Top
13 Grades

	Grades of Paper Used in Box	$ Contribution (% of total)	Volume (square meter) (% of total)
1	Z-6	13%	30%
2	Z-4	12	24
3	B-5	12	21
4	Z-5	6	6
5	Z-8	7	5
6	Z-7	7	3
7	Z-6/6	6	2
8	Z-4/6	5	1
9	B-4	5	1
10	E-8	6	1
11	B-5/6	6	1
12	B-4/6	3	1
13	Z-7/6	3	<1

Actions

Gustavo Herrero pondered his options: value enhancement versus volume gain (through competitive pricing). At times, he was convinced that the two were interrelated and intertwined and that the only way to sustain a competitive advantage in the marketplace was to pursue both. At other times, the two options seemed incompatible. At the end of the day, the only thing that mattered was to restore Zucamor's historical earnings performance. As an integrated producer of corrugated boxes, would mill production requirements and expected efficiencies be a dominant factor? Would value enhancement and cost cutting efforts be compatible?

Chapter 45

Dell—New Horizons

V. Kasturi Rangan   Marie Bell

Dell entered the 21st century as the most successful company in the PC industry. Founded in 1984, the company had achieved phenomenal records in sales and profit growth. Dell surpassed the $1 billion in sales mark in 1992, the $10 billion mark in 1997, and for fiscal 2000 (year ending January 2000), it surpassed the $25 billion mark. Dell's revenues and earnings grew by over 30% year after year, and the company reported a return on invested capital of 243% for 2000. Riding a wave of hyper-growth in the personal computer (PC) industry, Dell's market capitalization exceeded $200 billion in December 1998, and *Fortune* magazine listed it as America's third-most admired company.

The PC industry juggernaut continued to grow through 2000. As growth rates climbed to over 30%, PC companies were left scrambling to keep up with demand. At Dell, new product groups and customer segments were formed to manage exploding opportunities, and new employees were hired in record numbers. In the fourth quarter of 2000, the growth came to a screeching halt. Rather than managing a market growing at 30%, for the first time in the PC industry's history, growth actually declined by a whopping 10%. Industry analysts were unsure as to whether this was an aberration or a harbinger of things to come. The PC industry's hyper-growth in 1999 and 2000 was driven by several factors. Primary among these was the enormous business investment in technology infrastructure to prepare for Y2K. The explosion of the Internet was also a boon to tech companies. Not only were there thousands of new companies that needed a technology platform to get up and running, but the competition from dot.coms spurred bricks and mortar companies to invest in Internet infrastructure as well. Finally there was the flood of service providers that came into existence in order to service the technology needs of Internet companies. Perhaps the best barometer of all this heightened demand for technology infrastructure was the NASDAQ stock index, which rose from 1,835 in March 1998 to a high of 5,132 in March 2000. And then the bubble burst as the NASDAQ plummeted to a low of 1,619 in April 2001.

FIGURE A **Market Capitalization and Stock Prices, Selected Firms (March 1997–September 2001)**

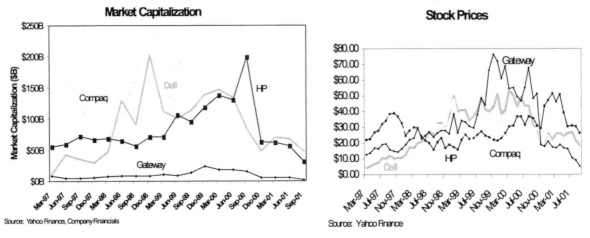

Source: Yahoo Finance, Company Financials

Source: Yahoo Finance

Dell, along with its rivals, saw a slump in stock price and market capitalization. (See **Figure A.**) As the market cooled, Dell, a company that had hired 16,000 people over the prior two years, announced its first ever reduction in work force. More cuts were possible. This was in spite of Dell's record $32 billion in fiscal 2001 sales (year ending January 2001) and a new high on return on invested capital of 355%. (**Exhibits 1** and **2** provide relevant balance sheet and profit and loss statement information. **Exhibit 3** summarizes selected financials for significant computer hardware vendors.)

Dell responded to early signs of a potential slowdown as it had done many times before—aggressively moving on price. *The Wall Street Journal* reported:

> In the past, computer prices have fallen steadily as they became cheaper to make, yet that simply fueled higher demand. But recent price cuts have been much steeper than anything seen before, and combined with a slowdown in demand, could result in a first-ever decline in PC revenues in the United States. . . .
>
> At the heart of the industry's troubles is a stunning slowdown in revenue growth. Recession fears have certainly hurt sales. But consumers and some companies also are holding onto their computers longer, in part because the powerful machines already provide more than enough heft for most computer tasks thrown at them. Combine that with an increasingly saturated U.S. market, where 53% of homes already have a PC and most businesses are computerized, and that means fewer buyers. . . .
>
> Dell Co-President Kevin B. Rollins insists that Dell can continue its aggressive pricing and remain profitable. "We believe we are the lowest-cost producer," he says. "We can do better than our competition in a tough environment."[1]

In spite of the slowdown and Dell's significantly reduced growth targets for 2001–2002, the company's top management of CEO Michael Dell and President and COO Kevin Rollins remained supremely confident of Dell's future success.[2]

[1] Gary McWilliams, "E-business: Price wars squeeze PC makers," *Wall Street Journal,* March 26, 2001, B1.

[2] Morton Topfer also acted as Advisor to the CEO. Michael Dell had brought in the experienced Morton Topfer from Motorola as vice-chairman in 1994 in an effort to broaden Dell's leadership and to position Dell as a *Fortune* 500 company. Kevin Rollins, who had worked with Dell as a senior partner at Bain and Company, joined Dell as vice chairman in 1997. The trio of Dell, Topfer, and Rollins were credited with much of Dell's success in the 1990s. With Morton Topfer's retirement in 2000, James Vanderslice joined Dell as co-vice chairman after 33 years at IBM, most recently as senior vice-president of IBM's Technology Group. In August 2001, Dell announced that Vanderslice was moving to a senior advisory role as vice-chairman in advance of his retirement the following year.

EXHIBIT 1
Dell Computer Corporate—Balance Sheet (yr. ending Jan. 31 of that year)

Sources: Company records.

Balance Sheet ($ millions)	1997	1998	1999	2000	2001
Assets					
Cash and equivalents	115	320	1,726	3,809	4,910
Other short term investments	1,237	1,524	923	323	528
Accounts receivable	903	1,486	2,094	2,608	2,895
Inventory	251	233	273	391	400
Other current assets	241	349	791	550	758
Total current assets	2,747	3,912	5,807	7,681	9,491
Long term investments	—	—	532	2,721	2,418
Property, Plant & Equipment	374	509	775	1,140	
Accum. Depreciation and amortization	(139)	(167)	(252)	(375)	
Property, Plant & Equipment other	—	—	—	—	
Property, Plant & Equipment (net)	235	342	523	765	996
Goodwill/Intangibles	—	—	15	304	
Other Long term Assets	11	14	—	—	530
TOTAL ASSETS	2,993	4,268	6,877	11,471	13,435
Liabilities					
Accounts Payable	1,040	1,643	2,397	3,538	4,286
Short term Debt	—	—	—	—	—
Current long term debt and CLOs	—	—	—	—	—
Other Current Liabilities	618	1,054	1,298	1,654	2,257
Total Current Liabilities	1,658	2,697	3,695	5,192	6,543
Long term Debt	18	17	512	508	509
Other Long term Liabilities	511	261	349	463	761
Total Liabilities	2,187	2,975	4,556	6,163	7,813
Shareholders' Equity	806	1,293	2,321	5,308	5,622
Total Liabilities and Shareholders' Equity	2,993	4,268	6,877	11,471	13,435

Some in the industry, however, believed that the hyper expansionary phase of the industry's growth was over, and that the players would have to adjust their strategies to reflect the commodity nature of the environment. In response to such pessimism, Kevin Rollins offered:

> Well that's what they said in the 1990s—that PCs were becoming a commodity and that we would have to adjust our expectations downward. But the beauty of our model is that commodities fall right into our sweet spot. Industry gross margins have dropped from about 50% in the early 1990s to about 25% today and at that level the business is not profitable for many of our competitors, yet we continue to show profit growth. We just need to continue to catch products as they move to the commodity phase and apply our low-cost direct model.

In addition to continually improving its position in PCs, the Dell company's leadership was aggressively pursuing a multi-pronged growth strategy: product opportunities that encompassed high-growth categories (storage and servers), opportunities in the service side of the business, and a geographic opportunity to expand all products and services in international markets. Dell believed that with these opportunities, coupled with over $7.9 billion in cash on its balance sheet, its future was bright.

EXHIBIT 2   **Financial Performance of Dell Computer Corporation ($ in millions) (Yr. End. Jan. 31 of that year)**

Sources: Company records.

Income Statement	1987	1992	1993	1994	1995	1996	1997	1998	1999	2000	2001
Net sales ($ in millions)	69.5	889.9	2,013.9	2,873.2	3,475.3	5,296	7,759	12,327	18,243	25,265	31,888
United States		648.1	1,459.6	2,037.2	2,400.0	3,474	5,279	8,531	12,420	17,879	22,871
Europe		241.9	553.0	781.9	952.9	1,478	2,004	2,956	4,675	5,590	6,399
Other international			1.3	54.0	122.4	344	476	840	1,149	1,796	2,618
Cost of sales	53.6	607.8	1,564.5	2,440.4	2,737.3	4,229	6,093	9,605	14,137	20,047	25,445
Gross profit	15.9	282.2	449.5	432.8	738.0	1,067	1,666	2,722	4,106	5,198	6,443
Operating expenses:											
SGA	10.3	182.2	268.0	422.9	423.4	595	826	1,202	1,788	2,387	3,193
R&D	1.5	33.1	42.4	48.9	65.4	95	126	204	272	568	482
Special Charges											105
Total operating expenses	11.7	215.3	310.3	471.8	488.8	690	952	1,406	2,069	2,955	3,780
Operating income	4.1	66.9	139.1	−39.0	249.3	377	714	1,316	2,046	2,263	2,663
Net income	2.2	50.9	101.6	−35.8	149.2	272	531	944	1,460	1,666	2,177
% of Net sales											
Net sales	100.0	100.0	100.0	100.0	100.0	100.0	100.0	100.0	100.0	100.0	100.0
United States		72.8	72.5	70.9	69.1	66.0	68.0	69.2	68.0	70.7	71.6
International—Europe		27.2	27.5	27.2	27.4	28.0	26.0	23.9	25.6	22.1	20.1
International—others		0.0	0.1	1.9	3.5	6.0	6.0	7.1	6.4	7.2	8.3
Cost of sales	76.9	68.3	77.7	84.9	78.8	79.9	78.5	77.9	77.5	79.3	79.8
Gross profit	23.1	31.7	22.3	15.1	21.2	20.1	21.5	22.1	22.5	20.7	20.2
Operating Expenses											
Marketing and sales	14.8	20.5	13.3	14.7	12.2	11.3	10.7	9.8	9.8	9.4	10.0
R&D	2.3	3.7	2.1	1.7	1.9	1.8	1.6	1.6	1.5	2.3	1.5
Special Charges											.3
Total operating expenses	17.1	24.2	15.4	16.4	14.1	13.1	12.3	11.4	11.3	11.7	11.8
Operating income	6.0	7.5	6.9	−1.3	7.1	7.2	9.2	10.7	11.2	9.0	8.4
Net income	3.1	5.7	5.0	−1.3	4.0	5.1	6.8	7.7	8.0	6.6	6.8

Other Significant Dell Operating Statistics

	1997	1998	1999	2000	2001
Employees	10,350	16,200	24,400	36,500	40,000
Days supply of inventory	13	7	6	6	5
Return on invested capital	85%	186%	195%	243%	355%
Avg. total revenue per unit	$2,700	$2,600	2,350	$2,250	$2,050

EXHIBIT 3
Selected 2000
Financial Statistics
($ in millions)

Sources: Company Financial
Statements.

International Business Machines	1999	2000	2001 YTD
Total Revenues	$87,548	88,396	63,040
Personal systems revenue	$16,118	$16,250	$9,072
Personal systems pre-tax income	−$360	−$148	−$136
Enterprise systems revenue	$11,503	$11,340	$9,669
Enterprise systems pre-tax income	$1,832	$2,092	$1,111

Notes: IBM changed the definition of its segments between 2000 & 2001. For 1999 & 2000, Personal Systems included PCs and PC servers. Enterprise Systems included Unix & mainframe servers and all storage. For 2001, Personal Systems included PCs and printing systems, and Enterprise Systems included PC servers in addition to Unix and mainframe servers, and all storage. 2001 YTD includes first three fiscal quarters (January–September 2001). In addition to revenue from Personal Systems and Enterprise Systems, IBM, in 2000, earned significant revenues from the following segments: Technology Hardware that included peripheral equipment for use in general-purpose computer systems and components such as semiconductors and hard disk drives ($10 billion), Global Services ($33 billion), and Software ($12 billion), Global Financing ($3 billion) and Enterprise Investments ($1 billion).

Compaq Computer Corp.	1999	2000	2001 YTD
Total Revenues	$38,525	$42,383	$25,126
Access Group (PCs) revenue	$18,179	$20,722	$11,453
Access Group (PCs) operating income	−$186	$459	−$485
Enterprise Computing revenue	$12,974	$14,316	$7,995
Enterprise Computing operating income	$1,201	$2,140	$102

Notes: Compaq's Access Group consists of PCs and handheld devices sold to consumers and businesses. Compaq's Enterprise Computing Group consists of Intel servers, high-end servers, and storage. 2001 YTD includes first three fiscal quarters (January–September 2001). Compaq garnered approximately $7 billion in additional service revenues.

Hewlett-Packard	FY 1999	FY 2000	FY 2001 YTD
Total Revenues	$42,370	$48,782	$33,702
Computing Systems Group revenue	$17,814	$21,095	$13,539
Computing Systems Group operating income	$850	$960	−$327

Notes: Hewlett-Packard's Computing Systems Group consists of PCs, Intel-based workstations and servers, Unix-based workstations and servers, and storage. Hewlett-Packard's fiscal year ends in October. 2001 YTD includes first three fiscal quarters (November 2000–July 2001). Other segments that contributed significant revenues for HP were Imaging and Printing ($20 billion) and IT Services ($7 billion).

Gateway	FY 1999	FY 2000	FY 2001 YTD
Total Revenue	$8,965	$9,601	$4,944
Operating income	$596	$511	−$128

Notes: Includes all company revenues and operating income on a pro-forma basis, excluding one-time charges. 2001 YTD includes first three fiscal quarters (January–September 2001).

Dell	FY 1999	FY 2000	FY 2001 YTD
Total Revenues	$25,265	$31,888	$23,107
Operating income	$2,263	$2,663	$1,195

Notes: Includes all company revenues and operating income on a pro-forma basis, excluding one-time charges. 2001 YTD includes first three fiscal quarters (February–November 2001).

The Dell Way[3]

Starting in 1977, there were several waves of entries by firms into the personal computer market. The first wave was between 1977 and 1978, with the entry of Apple as the clear technology leader. Apple offered a unique operating system, with an intuitive and easy graphic user interface (GUI) that enabled applications to be driven by a simple point-and-click menu system rather than typing commands. This ease-of-use attracted many first-time users in the consumer market and made Apple particularly strong in the educational and hobbyist market. Apple, sensing the user-based advantage, refused to license its technology, betting on its proprietary system.

Industry giant IBM entered the PC market in 1981. IBM's entry legitimized the PC in the minds of business customers. Maintaining a premium-priced position, IBM used its sales force to sell PCs to large corporate customers and retail channels to reach small-and-medium-sized businesses. IBM's decision to use an open architecture (that essentially allowed for the development of IBM clones) created an environment that allowed new manufacturers to enter the market and meet unsatisfied demand. Compaq, founded in 1982, was one such manufacturer. Unlike IBM, Compaq was a new player to the industry and lacked a sales infrastructure to get its products to market. Faced with this challenge, Compaq recruited retail dealers and value-added resellers (VARs) by promising them full rein of the market including the large-volume corporate accounts. More efficient and focused than IBM, Compaq soon rose to the top of the PC market. (See **Table A** below.) With the expansion of the open system architecture promoted by Microsoft's operating system software, Apple found it increasingly difficult to gain share. First, because many software publishers preferred to write software for the larger PC environment, and second, operating systems upgrades to match the rapidly evolving capability of hardware were quite expensive (nearly a $500 million effort).

Dell, like Compaq, was a company that had been created as a result of the PC's open architecture. In 1983, Michael Dell, an 18-year-old freshman at the University of Texas at Austin, spent his evenings and weekends pre-formatting hard disks for IBM-compatible PC upgrades. A year later, he dropped out of college to attend to his burgeoning business, which had grown from nothing to $6 million in 1985 by simply upgrading IBM compatibles for local area businesses. In 1985, Dell shifted his company's focus to assembling its own brand of PCs—PC's Limited—that were available on a Build-to-Order basis, and the business grew dramatically, with $70 million in sales at the end of 1985. By 1990, sales had grown even further to over $500 million and with it, Dell's reputation as a national supplier

[3] Some parts of this section have been drawn and adapted from HBS case No. 596-058, "Dell Computer Corporation," and HBS case No. 598-116, "Dell Online."

TABLE A
U.S. Market Share (%) of Vendors—Personal Computer (Desktop and Portable) Units

Source: Company Records based on IDC database.

	1985	1994	1999	2001 YTD September
IBM	37%	8.6%	7.2%	5.9%
Compaq	4	13.4	15.6	12.7
Apple	18	11.6	4.5	4.2
Dell	—	4.2	16.5	24.6
Gateway	—	5.4	9.1	8.3
HP	—	2.2	8.8	9.8
Others	41	54.6	38.8	34.4
Total Units	8 million	18.5 million	46.9 million	30.4 million

of desktop and portable computers based on the most recent Intel processors. Nearly all of Dell's sales were to business customers, splitting up almost evenly between the large corporate accounts and medium and small businesses. Even though Dell was labeled a "mail order company," revenue from individual consumers was less than 5% of sales. In ferocious price wars with its Texas rival, Compaq, Dell steadily gained a footing in the lucrative corporate market. Many of Dell's corporate customers not only valued the ability to customize their PC configurations to meet the unique needs of users but also liked being able to deal with the manufacturer directly and to receive Dell's attractive pricing that was the result of its direct model.

Dell's success continued through 1992, until in 1993 it faced an operating loss for the first time in its history, despite a 40% increase in sales. The problem, Dell quickly discovered, stemmed in part from its entry into retail channels. In an attempt to broaden its penetration of the consumer market, in 1992 Dell had struck agreements with retailers like CompUSA and Sam's Club. But the 15% gross margins that retailers needed left Dell with a 5% net loss instead of the 5% net profit it had achieved through the direct channel. Dell's problems were then exacerbated when quality problems arose with its laptops. In the late 1980s, Dell, along with several desktop manufacturers had seen the portable market as a logical extension of their desktop business. Unfortunately many of them, including Dell, had not realized that the component supply and quality for laptops had not yet reached a level of robustness and technological stability for an assembler like Dell to exploit successfully.

Dell acted decisively. By late 1993, Michael Dell realized that the retail channel didn't fit the Dell model because it did not leverage one of its major attributes: the ability to custom-configure its products. Dell exited the retail channel and resolved to re-enter the laptop market only when that product's quality matched or exceeded the quality of the Dell desktop.

From the mid-1990s Dell experienced ever-increasing sales and profits driven both by the demand for PCs and Dell's superior ability to execute. By the early 1990s, businesses had fully embraced the PC, and were more willing to trade off better pricing for less custom support. *Fortune* 2000 customers had developed the internal expertise to specify PC requirements and, employing a direct sales force to sell its products, Dell's direct model became the means of delivering a high-quality PC in a very cost-efficient manner. By 1999, Dell was the leading seller of PCs in the United States, having surpassed early leaders IBM and Compaq. The company had developed a reputation for effectively entering a product market where core proprietary elements had become standardized and undercutting existing players based on price. Michael Dell had coined the phrase "virtual integration" to express Dell's strategy of choosing best in class providers like Intel and Microsoft, for each component, and leveraging their scale investment in R&D.

A powerful example of success for the Dell model was workstations. These high-end desktop computers designed to run complex applications were originally dominated by products based on UNIX operating systems. In 1996, they began transitioning to standards-based Windows NT powered workstations. Dell entered the market in 1997 with a Windows product priced below anything else in the market. At the time of Dell's entry into workstations the market had been skeptical of Dell's ability to compete successfully in this complex product category. Kevin Rollins explained, "When we went into workstations, everyone expected Dell to fail. We were told that the product was too complex for our direct model. But we proved them wrong."

The same pattern repeated in 1996 when Dell entered the high-margin server market by offering a more powerful Pentium Pro server at the price point of a less powerful Pentium product. By November of that same year, the company had expanded from a single processor server to a dual processor model, and by February 1997 had a four-way offering as well.[4]

---

[4] Generally the greater the number of processors, the more powerful and complex the product.

By 1999, Dell emerged as the second-largest Wintel server (i.e., servers based on Intel processors and Microsoft Windows operating systems) producer in the United States, and in the first quarter of 2001, took the first place position in the United States from Compaq.

By 2000, Dell had exhibited an uncanny ability to reach out into the market and identify the next high-margin technology product that could be driven to scale with lower priced products driven by its direct model. Michael Dell remarked: "High margins are a sort of paradox. You look at a business and say, 'Gee, you've got high margins and that's good. But in this case it's not good. Because if you have high margins, that means you have this big, soft underbelly. That's what we live for. That's what we consider to be fun.'"[5]

The Dell Direct Model

The Dell Direct Model was the engine of Dell's success. Easy to describe, but difficult to duplicate, the Dell Direct model was about low cost, direct customer relationships and virtual integration. It was a high velocity, efficient distribution system characterized by build-to-order manufacturing, and products and services targeted at specific market segments. Dell serviced the North American market from its plants in Austin, Texas, and Nashville, Tennessee. To support its global business, Dell had manufacturing facilities in Limerick, Ireland, and Penang, Malaysia, and two new sites in Porto Alegre, Brazil, and Xiamen, China, that came online in 2000.

From its earliest days, Dell was a build-to-order computer manufacturer. Orders would come to the factory from two major streams: (1) inbound calls from consumers and small business customers who'd seen a Dell catalog or print ad referring them to a specific toll-free telephone number, and (2) orders placed by Dell "inside sales reps" on behalf of large accounts. This method for taking orders allowed Dell to sell richer configured systems and achieve a higher ARU, or average revenue per unit, despite the fact that its gross margins and pricing were the lowest in the industry. The phone sales reps typically sold all Dell products, although over time the various business units added sales specialists for server and workstation products, as well as third-party peripherals such as printers.

Once Dell received an order at its factory, the order was electronically broken down into a list of parts required for the computer. When the specification sheet was generated, an electronic bar code linked the system back to its original order number. This identification number not only allowed the customer to check on order status, but also became the basis for problem solving if required after the customer took delivery.

After the parts spec sheet was generated, the assembly of the computer began. First, the motherboard was configured with the ordered microprocessor and the required amount of RAM. Then the other optional parts (disk drives, CD ROMs, etc.) were assembled into a bin, with workers pulling the needed parts from stock. The bin was forwarded to a five-person production cell equipped with computers that provided instant, detailed access to information regarding part configurations and setup. Dell found that the high-volume cell production lines improved the plant's capacity and also more easily integrated DellPlus components (the company's custom configuration program) components allowing for even greater customization for customers. After all the options had been installed in the manufacturing cell per the spec sheet, the system was sent to the software loading zone, where the appropriate software, including operating system software, application software, and diagnostic software, were loaded into the hard disk of the system. After all the software was loaded, the system was sent to a "burn-in" area where it was powered and tested for four to eight hours before being packed into a box and sent to the packaging area. There, the completed system was boxed, along with peripherals such as a keyboard, mouse, mouse pad, and the manuals and floppy disks for all the installed software.

---

[5] *Fortune,* October 16, 2000, p. 100.

The entire purchase process from order receipt to product shipping required only about 36 hours. Indeed, at Dell's Optiplex factory in Austin, 84% of orders were built and shipped within eight hours. Incoming parts were pulled through the system and ordered on a just-in-time basis. Dell's model was one of continuous improvement, making it difficult for its competitors to emulate. For example, in the mid-1990s Dell's direct model operated on 13 days of inventory, versus the 75 to 100 days in the typical indirect model. At the close of fiscal 2000, Dell had six days of inventory with its build-to-order process, compared with 20 to 70 days for most of its major competitors. Dell's ability to operate on a just-in-time basis was facilitated by its suppliers, who warehoused the bulk of their components within 15 minutes from the Dell factory. Dell had been able to reach these agreements by reducing the number of primary suppliers, from about 200 in 1992 to about 25 in 2000. Shipping was contracted out, with multiple shippers delivering the systems anywhere in North or South America.

Post shipment, a customer had several service options: the customer could go online to dell.com to access technical support, or call Dell over the telephone. The phone service model was a major innovation in the PC industry and allowed Dell to handle over 75% of service calls either online or over the phone, with fewer than 25% of calls requiring the dispatch of a tech support person.

If the problem required onsite repair, one of Dell's major service partners (such as Unisys, Wang, Techtronics, or IBM Global Services) sent technicians to solve the problem, generally within a 24-to-48-hour window. In many product categories Dell set the standard for customer service. For example, the industry average downtime for a PC was 16 hours, but only 8 hours for a Dell PC. For servers, the industry average downtime was 5 hours compared to 1 hour for a Dell server. Dell's service procedures resulted in satisfied customers. A March 2001 *Fortune* and Trilogy survey of senior officers of *Fortune* 1000 companies ranked Dell first in managing customer relations.[6] Dell's service also delivered significant economic benefits given the cost of servicing a customer over the telephone was $14 to $18 compared to an on site visit by a field engineer which cost between $250 and $300. Indeed, Dell's operating costs were the lowest in the industry at about 11.5% in 2000. Gateway with 16% and Compaq and Hewlett Packard at 22% were significantly higher.

To address the needs of its most independent customers, as well as those who had a close partnership with a regional service provider, Dell created a program called Premier Access. This program provided subscribing customers with special training and certification, and allowed them to bypass the first level of phone support and go directly to the higher-level technical assistance. This offering was attractive to large corporations who had their own onsite IT staffs capable of handling routine problems, as well as those who chose not to use a designated Dell service provider but still wanted manufacturer training and support and access to spare parts.

Integrating the Internet

In late 1995, well before the Internet was considered hot, Michael Dell saw its potential to provide the ultimate extension of the Dell direct model. He established a small team of about nine people and began delivering online technical support and order status information. Next the team designed an online retail store, using in-house programmers to build a "configurator" to translate the build-to-order model to an online environment. The configurator performed the role traditionally played by the telephone sales rep—guiding the customer through the configuration of the PC by offering several different options (size of hard drive, amount of memory, peripherals, etc.). By July 1996, Dell's online revenues were beginning to ramp.

[6] "Trilogy-*Fortune* CRM Survey: High Satisfaction with Customer Relationship—Particularly Key in Tight Times," *Business Wire,* April 4, 2001.

In addition to the www.dell.com site for transactional customers, Dell offered customer-specific sites called "Premier Pages." These Premier Pages were accessible only by authorized employees of the specific customer, and provided innovations such as paperless purchase orders, approved product configurations, pricing, real-time order tracking, purchase history and account team information. Starting with its largest customers in 1997, by the end of 1999 Dell had more than 40,000 Premier Pages up and running. As one Dell executive noted, "The Premier Pages have become an extension of the account management team. On the relationship side of the business, customers don't want our sales people in their offices every day, but the Premier Pages give us that daily presence. Customers can conduct commerce via the Premier Pages, notably with fewer errors involved." Premier Pages were also helpful from a service perspective in two ways. First, individual employees of corporate customers could access the Premier Pages and gain access to answers for basic service issues. Second, corporate MIS managers responsible for computer support went online via their Premier Pages to access information regarding higher order service questions. In fact, in many instances it proved to be a convenient way to manage and monitor corporate IT budgets.

The online model strengthened Dell's efficiencies on both the transaction and relationship sides of the business. On the transaction side, the productivity of the average Dell sales rep increased by as much as 50% when the customer first went to the online channel to do the preliminary configuration. On the relationship side, where the typical external sales rep had spent about 40% of his or her time on face-to-face customer contact with customers and 60% on administrative matters before the Internet, they now spent 60% of their time with customers and 40% dealing with administrative matters.

The online model proved exceptionally successful. By 2000, sales generated through the Internet reached approximately 50% of revenues and averaged $40 million per day. With its Internet-enabled strategy, Dell achieved increased penetration among consumers, a challenging market to serve profitably for Dell and its competitors. Dell's consumer market share in the United States grew from 2.3% in 1997 to 6.6% in 2000.

Dell also used the Internet to develop a collaborative planning methodology with its key suppliers. Modeled along the lines of its premier pages with customers, each of Dell's suppliers accessed a Dell Internet Portal site that enabled them to see the order flow and pipeline inventory of their components. Suppliers' input of cost forecasts helped Dell's sales management price accordingly.

Segmentation at Dell: The U.S. Market

Recognizing that large corporations had very different product and service needs from small businesses or government customers, Dell set out to optimize its approximately 7,500 worldwide sales and support reps for each different customer segment.

For Dell, the primary differentiation was between a relationship and a transactional customer. Transactional customers were consumers or small businesses that tended to make one purchase at a time, and did not require a designated sales representative assigned to them. Relationship customers were large enough to have ongoing technology purchase requirements and expected continuity in their interactions with Dell. By 2000, Dell had created nine market segments in the United States (see **Table B**), which were organized into three business divisions: Relationship, Small and Medium Business, and Consumer Business. Although sales teams were entirely segmented by business, Dell continued to manage functions like technical support on a shared basis, allowing them to leverage scale where it improved cost and performance. Technical support, in fact, was organized primarily on a product basis, with separate call queues for desktops, notebooks, servers, and storage.

TABLE B
Dell's Market
Segmentation

Market Segment	Buying Process
Relationship Business	
Global	Relationship
Enterprise (>18,000 employees)	Relationship
Large corporate accounts (3,500–18,000 employees)	Relationship
Federal government	Mixed
Education	Mixed
State & local government	Mixed
Small and Medium Business	
Preferred Account Division (400–3,500 employees)	Relationship
Business Systems Division (2–400 employees)	Mixed
Consumer Business	Transactional

Relationship Business

Relationship business represented about 60% of Dell's U.S. revenues and included the Global, Enterprise, and Large Corporate Accounts (LCA) representing the *Fortune* 500 companies, as well as "public accounts," government and education, which accounted for nearly a third of the relationship business. Global, Enterprise, and Large Corporate Account customers all had dedicated account teams that included program managers and technical support, as well as sales personnel. "Relationship" customers thought of computer purchasing as a multi-dimensional process, regardless of whether they were purchasing 5 or 500 computers. The information sources they depended upon in making decisions included industry analysts, conferences, trials and testing, and referrals from other large customers. Dell's major competitors in the Relationship segment were Compaq, IBM, HP, and other leading brands who traditionally sold to the customers through VARs (value added resellers), but were increasingly attempting to "go direct" in order to lower their cost structure.

Joe Marengi, senior vice president, Dell Americas, commented:

> In this business you are only as good as your last customer relationship. On the relationship side, especially in the global and enterprise accounts, execution is exceptionally important. Dell is executing very large orders with thousands of pieces of equipment that need to be deployed globally and on a timely basis. For example, we recently worked with a partner to provide 20,000 units to a remote sales force. We needed to have the right equipment there, at the right time, with the right installations. It sounds simple but required incredible logistics to execute. What makes it work is not only our systems, but also our culture of personal accountability. You could say we run paranoid.

In the case of Relationship buyers, payment was usually effected through corporate purchase orders or lease agreements, resulting in a longer payment cycle than Dell achieved in its transactional business, which was mostly credit-card based.

Small and Medium Businesses

Much of Dell's growth in the 1990s came from the small- and medium-sized businesses, which by 2001, accounted for roughly 30% of Dell's U.S. revenue. Dell segmented the over 10 million potential customers into Preferred Accounts (PAD), companies with 400 to 3,500 employees, and the Business Systems Division (BSD) for companies with 10 to 400 employees. Like the education and government segments, both PAD and BSD supported their customers with a hybrid relationship/transactional model. Dell had relationships with nearly 25,000 PAD customers and nearly a million BSD customers.

Both the PAD and BSD groups had created an impressive customer relationship management system that included custom premier pages for all relationship customers, and a detailed customer profile with buying criteria, service needs, competitive presence, and sales history. This sales history was updated every time a Dell rep interacted with a customer. The customer profile not only identified key people associated with the account, but classified them as influencers, gatekeepers, or financial decision makers. To further prioritize client sales, Dell used the same "RAD" model (retain, acquire, develop) developed for large accounts. Based on the status of the account and its purchasing potential, the phone sales account rep could schedule an onsite visit with one of the division's field sales reps. The results of these efforts were impressive. Dell used direct mail and catalog mailings to "make the phone ring," though about half of the orders to the group came through the online channel. David Lockett, vice president of BSD Sales, remarked:

> For most companies reaching the small business segment is a hazard. But based on the application of the Dell Direct model to the front end of this business, we have proven that it can be penetrated and meaningful relationships developed. We really know the customer and we know our products—that's why we can sell even complex products like servers over the phone.

Consumer Business

By early 2001, the consumer business accounted for about 5% of Dell's revenue worldwide, and close to 10% within the United States. Consumers were notoriously fickle, and tended to buy from the company that offered the lowest price, although service was also important. Dell marketed to consumers by highlighting overall product performance, specifications, features, bundles, reviews, and awards. The transactional customer consulted information sources such as reviews, editorials, advertising, as well as word of mouth in the buying process, relying on previous brand experience only as an indicator.

Dell's main competitors in this segment were Gateway—which also sold direct—and Compaq and Hewlett Packard—who sold through the retail channel. Private label or "white box" companies were also a consistent factor in the consumer market. One Dell executive summarized, "On the transactional side of the business, you need to 'acquire' the customer every time they buy a system; the only difference is that they're much more educated the second time than the first."

Traditionally, Dell had not targeted first-time PC buyers, because these customers required significant handholding in technical support and were therefore less profitable than the more knowledgeable buyers. A senior Dell executive added, "Consumers at retail don't know what they are looking for, other than price. We, on the other hand, like to sell to the educated consumer."

Consumers were given the option of paying for their purchase using a credit card or being charged in full on delivery. The ability to generate cash from its orders was another example of Dell's process velocity. In its transaction business, Dell converted the average sale to cash in less than 24 hours by tapping credit cards and electronic payment. By comparison, Compaq, which sold primarily through dealers, took 35 days and Gateway, 16.4 days.

Strategic Opportunities

Although competitors had been threatening for years to duplicate the efficiencies of the direct model, they had made no lasting progress against this goal. Michael Dell and Kevin Rollins were committed to maintaining rapid growth. They agreed that success in the future required "doing the same things we have been doing for a long time. Picking our spots to focus our engines, and driving the organization behind them."[7]

[7] "System Upgrade . . . " *Wall Street Journal,* Aug. 31, 2000, A1.

TABLE C **PCs and Notebooks—Market Share (% Units)**

Source: Company records.

Top Five	1997 Desktops		1997 Portables		YTD Sept. 2001 Desktops		YTD Sept. 2001 Portables	
	U.S.	Worldwide	U.S.	Worldwide	U.S.	Worldwide	U.S.	Worldwide
Dell	9.8	6.0	6.8	4.7	24.6	13.3	24.8	13.9
Compaq	17.1	13.9	13.8	11.5	13.1	11.6	11.3	10.3
IBM	7.4	8.0	13.3	12.0	4.2	5.4	11.6	10.9
HP	7.6	6.2	1.8	1.3	10.8	7.8	6.4	4.7
Gateway	8.2	3.7	2.8	1.5	9.3	3.6	4.8	2.0
Apple	4.3	3.2	3.3	3.0	3.9	2.6	5.5	3.4
Total Industry (000s of units)	24,823	65,435	6,000	14,186	23,518	68,048	6,914	20,031

At the same time, they were evaluating alternative strategies for accelerating Dell's entry into new product categories such as high-end servers, external storage and enterprise services. Product growth, however, was only one of three avenues for Dell's growth, the other two being service revenues and international expansion. Kevin Rollins was particularly keen to bring Dell's international revenues up to the U.S. benchmark.

Product Growth

Personal Computers

In 2000, worldwide PC sales were $217 billion, of which $87 billion was in the United States.[8] Accounting for almost 75% of Dell's revenues, laptops and desktops remained core product categories for Dell. As seen in **Table C** above, Dell was the market share leader in PCs and notebooks in the United States. Compaq led on a global basis until the end of the first quarter of 2001 when Dell overtook it.[9] By 2001, while Dell's performance in PCs had never been stronger, analysts questioned its sustainability. The economic downturn had some industry observers predicting the rate of growth in desktop revenue would slow to about 5% versus the 15% in 2000, while the growth rate of notebooks and other portables was projected to fall to about 15% from 25%.

As the technology sector and broader economy began to slow toward the end of 2000, Dell responded with aggressive price cuts in an effort to maintain revenue and grow share. "Amid a slowdown that is crunching its own profits, the world's No. 1 PC maker is employing ferocious high-tech tactics to grab an ever larger share of the PC market,"[10] claimed a *Wall Street Journal* article. This pricing strategy helped insulate Dell from the full effects of the macro economy, while competitors such as Compaq and HP were severely impacted in financial performance (see **Exhibit 3**).

Workstations

In 2000, the workstation market was about $9.2 billion, down 9.7% from the 1999 level of $10.2 billion worldwide. Originally pioneered by Sun Microsystems based on a Unix platform in the late 1980s, workstations were high-powered desktop computers designed to handle data-intensive scientific and engineering applications, or graphic analysis (such as CAD).

[8] Data supplied by IDC Technology Market group.

[9] IDC press release, from IDC.com

[10] *Wall Street Journal,* June 8, 2001.

TABLE D
Workstations—U.S.
and Total Market
Share Windows
NT and Total
Workstations (%)

Source: Company records
from IDC data.

	1997 U.S.	1997 Worldwide	2001 Jan–June U.S.	2001 Jan–June Worldwide
Windows NT Workstation				
Dell	8.6	7.0	55.4	43.9
HP	45.5	44.3	10.0	12.0
Compaq/Digital	29.0	32.6	11.6	17.6
IBM	10.6	9.2	14.1	13.9
Other	6.3	6.9	8.9	12.5
Avg. Selling Price	$5,348	$5,773	$3,340	$3,436
Units	195,227	354,367	245,891	511,585
All Workstations				
Dell	3.7	2.7	36.8	29.6
Sun	29.9	30.6	24.1	20.8
HP	28.8	28.3	10.3	12.5
IBM	10.2	11.3	12.6	13.0
Compaq/Digital	15.5	16.1	7.7	11.8
SGI	9.0	8.5	1.9	2.2
Other	2.7	2.6	6.6	10.1
Avg. Selling Price	$10,780	$11,424	$4,632	$4,976
Units	448,063	926,097	370,441	760,025

Unix-based proprietary systems dominated the workstation market until the mid-1990s when Windows-based open systems offered a powerful and less expensive alternative. Dell entered the workstation market in mid-1997, behind competitors such as HP, Compaq, and IBM. Yet by 2000, Dell was the U.S. and worldwide market leader in Windows NT workstations (see **Table D**). In addition, worldwide shipments of Windows-based workstations continued to grow at a faster rate than UNIX workstations.

Servers

Driven by the lower cost of ownership provided by open platforms, as well as increasing availability of applications, companies were steadily migrating their higher-end computing from mainframe computers to servers.

In 2000, the worldwide server market totaled $69 billion—a 7% increase from 1999. Like the workstation market, the server market was divided into proprietary (CISC/RISC) servers and open architecture servers (SIAS or Standard Intel Architecture Servers), with the proprietary systems accounting for $42 billion in revenues (615K units at an average retail selling price of $67K) and SIAS systems accounting for $27 billion (4.1 million units at an average retail selling price of $6.6K). Dell entered the server market in 1996, and by 1999 servers accounted for almost 12% of sales. Unlike its competitors who offered both proprietary and SIAS servers, Dell competed only in the open standards arena. In the late 1990s, SIAS servers enjoyed annual growth in excess of 30%, as companies began to invest heavily in internet infrastructure. This growth rate was expected to slow with the economic downturn and demise of dot.coms.

Exhibit 4 provides a brief overview of Dell's server range. The overall server market was segmented into high-end servers, midrange servers, and entry-level servers. Dell participated primarily in the entry-level server market, with two-thirds of its server sales in that segment. **Table E** provides a summary of U.S. market share in the midrange and entry-server segments.

EXHIBIT 4   **Storage and Server Products in Dell's End-to-End Enterprise Offering**

Sources: Company records.

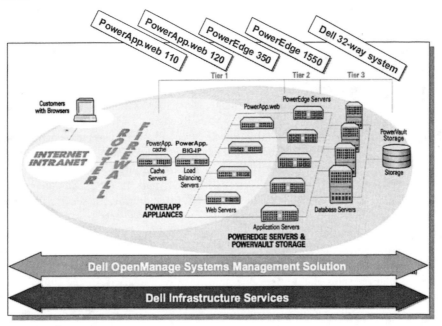

Consistent with its distribution strategy, Dell sold its servers through its direct sales force to larger relationship clients and through telephone and online channels to smaller business clients. Dell had designed a three-tier architecture to help guide customers through their total enterprise computing needs with Dell's server and storage product lines at the heart of the system. At **Tier 1** the most basic level, companies needed servers to perform basic functions such as load balancing and caching. For these functions Dell sold its PowerApp appliance servers. At the next level of complexity **(Tier 2)** companies that required servers to perform higher order functions such as web hosting might be sold either a PowerApp appliance server or an entry-level general purpose PowerEdge server. **Tier 3**, the most sophisticated and mission critical applications (such as maintaining databases or server farms) required Dell's most powerful general purpose server configurations. In addition to servers functioning in the Internet space, Dell sold servers for a variety of other purposes, such as the basic print servers within workgroups or departments of large companies.

TABLE E   **Computer Servers[a]—U.S. Market Share (units %)**

Source: Dell Sourced IDC data.

Mid-Range Servers	1997	1999	Jan–June 2001	Entry-Level Servers	1997	1999	Jan–June 2001
Compaq	0.7%	8.8%	13.8%	Compaq	28.4%	27.5%	24.0
IBM	27.8	16.6	18.1	IBM	15.0	10.0	9.9
HP	23.1	23.9	25.1	HP	12.5	9.5	7.2
Sun	21.8	34.5	38.0	Dell	9.7	17.1	25.5
				Sun	5.3	5.5	6.4
Average retail price	$189,205	$151,500	$181,867		$11,636	$7,726	$6,089
Total units	31,824	39,622	11,062	Total units	820,668	1,463,134	1,183,948

[a] Mid-range servers are servers sold between $100,000 to $999,999. Entry-level servers are servers sold under $100,000.

Storage

Until the 1990s, data storage was typically sold inside the server in the form of multiple internal disk drives. This storage configuration was referred to as Direct Attach Storage or DAS. In the late 1990s, companies like EMC began to sell storage that was external to the server. External storage offered customers greater manageability and reliability (mostly provided by special software) as well as potential for storage consolidation.

EMC Corporation was a small, financially strapped Massachusetts disk drive company that decided in the early 1990s to scrap all of its product lines to focus on external storage systems for IBM mainframes at a time when "IBM sold huge, old-fashioned disk drive systems." Led by hard charging CEO Mike Ruettgers, EMC entered the market from the bottom by using technically inferior RAID (redundant array of inexpensive disks) technology to couple together a dozen or more smaller, cheaper, standardized disk drives in a single box. These early Symmetrix systems quickly ate into IBM's storage market share, with IBM's share falling from 58% to 33% in four years. In 1995, EMC introduced a *heterogeneous* storage unit that could work with different types of servers (from mainframes to Unix workstations). Equally important to EMC's success was the concurrent realization that the proprietary software to manage these storage-filing systems had higher profit margins than the hardware itself.

As Internet infrastructure drove massive demand for increased storage capacity, EMC achieved sales of almost $9 billion in 2000. As a focused storage company, EMC invested heavily in storage-related research and development and customer service. EMC had earned a 99% customer retention rate and 80% of sales were to existing customers. EMC prided itself on its service and technology. Despite its high-growth profile, EMC like Dell was not exempt from the slowdown that faced technology companies in early 2001. By October 2001, its stock had fallen under $12 per share, down from a 52-week high of $104.93. (See **Exhibit 5** for EMC's balance sheet and selected financial information.)

By 2000, external storage was a $32 billion market, growing at 23% per year. Although Dell was the sixth-largest overall storage provider worldwide with revenue of more than $1 billion in sales, its market share in external storage was still very small. There were two alternative architectures for external storage, SAN (EMC's primary platform) and NAS (pioneered by start-up Network Appliance). NAS was easier to install than SAN and attached directly to the network. SAN required connections to the switches and servers and had a heavier software component as well. **Exhibit 6** provides more detail on these storage architectures with pricing for a Dell NAS product. In 2000, DAS (Direct Access Storage) still represented nearly 70% of the volume in the industry, but by 2005 NAS and SAN were projected to take two-thirds of the market. DAS was the simplest of the three technologies. As the name implies, it was linked to the server directly.

EXHIBIT 5 **EMC Selected Consolidated Financial Data ($ in millions, except share data)**

Source: Company financials.

	1996	1997	1998	1999	2000
Revenues	$3,616	$4,487	$5,436	$6,715	$8,872
Operating income	539	716	834	1,241	2,256
Net income	420	587	654	1,010	1,782
Net income per weighted avg. share (basic)	$0.22	$0.29	$0.32	$0.46	$0.79
Year-end stock price (unadjusted for splits)	$33.125	$27.438	$85.00	$109.25	$66.50
Weighted avg. shares (basic)	1,878	2,002	2,030	2,061	2,164
Working capital	$1,597	$2,582	$2,825	$2,922	$3,986
Total assets	$3,178	$4,627	$5,627	$7,173	$10,628
Stockholders equity	$1,978	$2,900	$3,728	$4,951	$8,177

While EMC dominated the external storage market, other competitors were coming on strong, and Dell believed this was an ideal opportunity for its model. A senior Dell executive remarked:

> As the market for storage system expands over the next several years, there will be significant opportunity to grow Dell's business through the same core strategies that have driven success in other areas of our company. Dell is coming in at a moderate price point at the bottom of the market. We aren't attacking EMC at the top end—we don't have that capability. There is sufficient growth in the market for several profitable players including Dell.

The Table in **Exhibit 6** provides an illustrative price comparison for Dell versus competitors for a low-end product.

EXHIBIT 6   Storage Architectures

Sources: Company records.

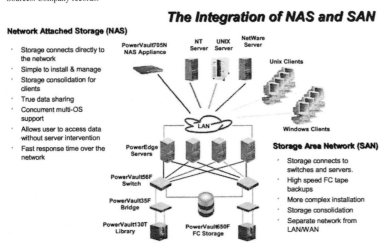

The Integration of NAS and SAN

Representative Product Comparison—Power Vault 735N			
	Dell PowerVault 735N	**Compaq TaskSmart N2400**	**Network Appliance F740**	**Sun N8200**
Capacity	1.4 TB	2.0 TB	1.0 TB	0.8 TB
Availability/ Disaster Tolerance	• Redundant hot swap power, cooling & drives. • -Snapshot • Phone-home alert	• Redundant hot swap power, cooling & drives. • -Snapshot • Phone-home alert • Cluster support	• Redundant hot swap power, cooling & drives. • -Snapshot • Phone-home alert • Cluster support • Mirroring	• Redundant hot swap power, cooling & drives. • -Snapshot • Phone-home alert • Cluster support
Rackability	130 GB/U	133 GB/U	52 GB/U	40 GB/U
OS Platforms	• Windows, Unix, Linux, Netware, MacOS	• Windows, Unix, Linux	• Windows, Unix, Linux	• Windows, Unix, Linux
Entry Pricing	• $9,999: 1 proc, 144GB–$0.07/MB • $11,999: 2 proc, 144GB–$0.08/MB	• $34, 710: 2 proc, 72GB–$0.21/MB	• $79,900: proc, 126GB (CIFS, NFS)–$0.61/MB	• $53,800: 1 proc, 200GB–$0.27/MB

Kevin Rollins noted:

> A small business is not going to buy a big, huge EMC [storage system]. It's too expensive, and they don't need it. They'll go buy a little storage solution. What about a medium-sized business? They'll need something else. So we'll sell and target the storage solutions we have for each of these customers. We'll take apart the [storage] market and target rifle shot at every one until we get big enough that the competition can't deal with us anymore.[11]

Despite this internal optimism, industry analysts expressed concerns about Dell's ability to win big in the high-end server and external storage markets. Dell's R&D budget was well below that of its primary competitors, and some enterprise customers still questioned Dell's ability to support mission-critical environments. One observer noted:

> The bad news is, Dell is getting shut out of the big enterprise accounts. They don't have the robust products they need to get into the data centers. Frankly, they're not getting a lot of help from Microsoft and Intel in terms of getting the quality of stuff customers are looking for. The flip side is the small-business market is pretty big and pretty untapped.[12]

While another commented:

> I don't think Dell understands what it's up against. PC companies think the business is done when they put stamps on the box. But selling a server is just the beginning of a long relationship. It's about reliability, serviceability, availability, and manageability.

In response to these kinds of concerns, Dell launched its own in-house services capabilities to install complex solutions. Called the Controlled Deployment Team or CDT, this group of Dell field engineers offered an alternative to the network of Dell Service Providers (DSPs). As one Dell executive remarked, "Having Dell's own people on site is all part of deploying a solution rather than installing a piece of hardware." Where possible the system engineers were brought into the sales process early to better understand the customer's objectives for its server and storage solutions because, as one Dell executive noted, "Customer satisfaction is about getting the system to work in the customer's environment and having it do what the customer wants it to do."

Dell also announced in November 2001 a marketing alliance with EMC under which Dell would become a major sales channel for EMC's CLARiiON line of products, which it had previously acquired as part of Data General. This partnership combined a leading mid-range SAN product line with Dell's powerful direct sales force in medium and small business and government accounts, where EMC's share was low, as well as large corporate accounts. Response from both customers and investors was positive.

Service Portfolio Growth

With 2000 revenues of approximately $2.0 billion, services were an increasingly important part of Dell's portfolio. Within the United States, associated services revenues accounted for 12.4% of server revenues, 9.8% of notebook revenues, 8.4% of desktop revenues, and 6.9% of workstation revenues. Dell believed that a key opportunity for the company lay in further expanding Dell's services offerings to include technical consulting and software migration as well as installation and break/fix services. Based on the growth of its services business, Dell forecast revenues of $3 billion to $5 billion by 2002.

Dell had begun to apply its commoditization model to the services business, taking the time needed to install a Dell "commerce server" to less than one hour, compared with the seven hours needed to install a similar competitor's server. Dell achieved this service time reduction by offering key applications that were already validated, and preloaded software

---

[11] "Can Michael Dell Escape the Box," *Fortune,* October 16, 2000.

[12] "Dell's New Storage Devices Aimed at Small Business," *Austin American Statesman,* August 30, 2000.

and hardware bundles to speed deployment of the application. With two different service levels (gold and silver), Dell offered various levels of support and pricing according to the type of product and customer (high-end workgroup, low-end enterprise, and high-end enterprise). A high-end enterprise service package would cost about $8,000 for Dell's gold level customers and $3,500 for Dell's silver level customers, compared to about $12,000 and $6,000, respectively, for comparable Compaq service packages. Dell's packages offered customers improved efficiency with customers experiencing a 19% reduction in logistics costs and a 21% decrease in technical support costs. Dell resolved 72% of problems remotely (twice the industry average), thereby leveraging Dell's installed technical services capabilities.

International Market Growth

By 2000, Dell generated $7.4 billion, about 25% of its total revenue outside the U.S. market. Because Dell's market share outside the United States was about half what it was inside the United States, Michael Dell consistently highlighted the potential for international expansion (**Exhibit 7** provides market share in key global regions.)

In all major markets, Dell used its direct model. In smaller markets, where the market potential had yet to be proven or infrastructure issues presented logistical challenges, Dell used a network of distributors to sell and service its products. (**Exhibit 8** provides an overview of where Dell used its direct model and where it operated through distributors.)

Dell had created three regions outside the United States: Americas International (that comprised Canada, Mexico, South and Central America), EMEA (Europe, Middle East and Africa), and APCC/Japan (covering Asia Pacific, China, Australia, India, and Japan).

EMEA

Like many U.S. companies, Dell began its global expansion in Europe, opening a U.K. sales office in 1987. In 1988, it created a wholly owned subsidiary in Germany and added one country each year after that. By 1992, Dell had operations in all of the major Western European countries and had ventured into Poland and Czechoslovakia as well. To support its European business, Dell built a manufacturing site in Limerick, Ireland, in 1990, and customer support centers in the Netherlands and Bray, Ireland. In a number of countries in the Middle East and Africa, where market potential was modest, foreign ownership limited by government, or tariff barriers prohibitive, Dell worked through a distributor network. Within EMEA, Dell participated in the Consumer/SOHO (small office home office), medium business, corporate, global, and government segments.

As Dell's international business grew, the application of the model improved. For example, in Europe Dell originally developed a call center for each country but later migrated to four regional call centers. It had become apparent that with multi-lingual capabilities, a northern European call center could handle the Scandinavian region, another regional center could handle calls from France, Italy, and Spain, etc. Worldwide service partners such as Unisys provided a cohesive service offering especially attractive to Dell's Global Accounts. As one Dell executive explained, "It wasn't so much that the global accounts didn't want a patchwork of local providers, but they really needed the service data collection that a global firm could provide."

APCC/Japan

In 1993, Dell launched direct businesses in both Japan and Australia, and established distributor relationships in China and Thailand. By 1995, Dell's APCC and Japan revenue justified building a manufacturing facility in Penang, Malaysia. Over the next several years, Dell launched direct models in Hong Kong, China, New Zealand, Taiwan, South Korea, and India.

EXHIBIT 7
Leading Vendor
Market Share
(%, units in 000s)

Source: Company records
(IDC) W Europe does not
align with Dell's EMEA
segment. IDC does not
include Eastern Europe
in this segment.

Region: Western Europe	1996	1998	2000
Compaq	14.9	18.3	16.9
Fujitsu Siemens	8.4	11.3	11.2
Dell	4.4	8.4	9.8
Hewlett Packard	5.3	6.9	8.3
IBM	9.3	9.1	7.9
NEC	4.5	5.2	5.6
Toshiba	3.3	3.8	4.6
Acer	2.7	2.8	4.2
Apple	4.2	2.8	3.1
Gateway	1.6	1.0	1.3
Units	**16,698**	**23,638**	**29,741**

Region: Asia/Pacific	1996	1998	2000
Legend	1.6	5.3	10.4
IBM	7.3	8.0	7.6
Samsung	6.4	4.3	7.4
Compaq	9.2	8.4	6.4
Hewlett Packard	3.4	5.3	4.9
Acer	6.1	4.6	4.3
Dell	1.3	2.6	3.7
Trigem	4.1	2.2	3.6
Founder	0.0	1.4	3.3
Units	**9,083**	**10,630**	**19,976**

Region: Japan	1996	1998	2000
NEC	33.2	27.2	21.7
Fujitsu Siemens	21.9	23.1	20.4
IBM	11.4	10.4	9.8
Sony	0.0	3.8	8.8
Toshiba	6.3	7.0	6.2
Compaq	3.7	4.3	4.9
Sotec	0.0	0.2	4.8
Dell	1.6	3.1	4.2
Hitachi	3.9	5.3	4.0
Apple	10.4	5.1	3.9
Gateway	0.6	2.2	2.1
Hewlett Packard	0.4	1.0	1.6
Units	**8,099**	**7,925**	**14,129**

Region: Latin America	1996	1998	2000
Compaq	14.0	13.8	19.2
IBM	11.4	8.0	6.0
Hewlett Packard	5.0	5.2	5.5
Acer	10.1	5.1	4.9
Dell	1.1	2.0	3.3
Toshiba	0.4	1.4	1.8
Apple	3.1	1.3	1.4
Units	**3,462**	**5,118**	**7,761**

Region: Rest of the World	1996	1998	2000
Compaq	7.6	8.7	9.3
IBM	7.0	8.0	5.4
Hewlett Packard	3.1	3.8	4.1
Acer	3.6	2.0	3.6
Dell	1.7	2.4	3.6
Units	**4,174**	**5,454**	**7,594**

EXHIBIT 8   **Dell Worldwide Manufacturing and Sales Sites**

Sources: Company records.

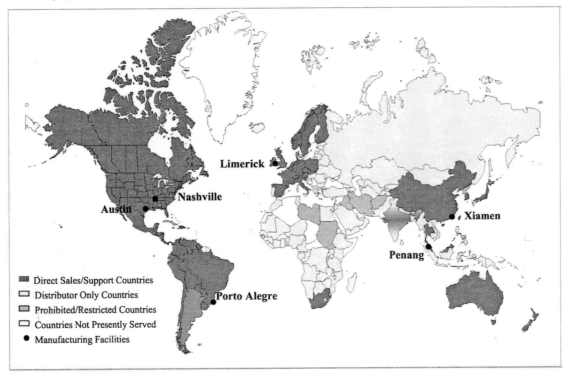

By 2000, Dell had added a second Asia manufacturing site in Xiamen, China, and four technical support offices in Penang, Sydney, Seoul, and Tokyo. Louise O'Brien, vice president of Corporate Strategy at Dell, who had launched Dell's Global Enterprise Account Program in 1997, commented on Dell's international market expansion:

> We have successfully leveraged our global customer relationships to gain scale in new international markets. For example, we were pulled into India by customers like P&G and Exxon. They demanded local support, and so we were able to start out with a base of global business that could then be expanded into local companies. In globalization as in many parts of the Dell model, we evolved in response to what our customers told us they needed us to do.

South/Central America

In November 1999, Dell opened its Latin America manufacturing facility in Porto de Alegre, Brazil, signaling a significant commitment to the Latin American market. As early as 1992 Dell had developed a direct model in Mexico but it wasn't until the late 1990s that Dell began to put emphasis on Latin America. In 1997 Dell introduced the direct model in Chile and opened its first South American sales office in Santiago. Within Latin America, Dell competed in the Consumer/SOHO, global, and corporate market segments. Again, where necessary Dell adapted to meet market conditions. For example, a Dell executive noted, "In Latin America with a smaller customer base, we started with just two basic market segments (transaction and relationship) rather than the nine-plus sales segments we have in the United States."

As Kevin Rollins considered the international markets, he remarked:

What we've seen especially in the international markets is that if you can get to the number one or number two in the market, you grow at a much faster rate than the rest of the pack. It is a question of relevance. If you are relevant in the market you can get the growth you need. As we look at the international markets we need to consider the markets that are key to unlocking the region: Germany in Europe, China in Asia, Brazil in South America. We need to look at these markets, understand how they work, and set our direct model to work.

New Horizons

Kevin Rollins summed up Dell's traditional approach to strategy:

We have a well-crafted Dell-Direct Model that provides value to customers, keeps our costs low and provides lofty returns for shareholders. We have to aggressively pursue growth and share gains. There is no secret to our strategy. It is all in the execution, and we believe that we have the confidence and capabilities to keep it going.

Many at Dell had argued that with its superb Direct model, the corporation should be able to take a larger bite out of the server and storage market. They pointed out that there was much room for growth on the international front as well. It was the view of this group that while the 25% to 30% growth rates of the past may not be attainable in the future, a company like Dell could handsomely grow margins even at a somewhat lower sales growth.

Other senior managers, however, questioned whether continued superior execution would be able to generate sufficient growth. For the first time, Dell's leaders began to ponder the pros and cons for Dell of strategic acquisitions.[13] It was likely that such a strategy could provide incremental growth, but at what cost to Dell's strong internal culture and focus on execution? How would it fit Dell principles of low cost, superior customer value, and virtual integration?

---

[13] On September 4, 2001, Hewlett Packard (HP) and Compaq announced a merger agreement to create an $87 billion technology leader. Under the terms of the proposed deal valued at $25 billion, HP shareholders would own 64% of the merged company, with Compaq shareholders owning 36%. The merged company was expected to hold the leading position in servers, PCs, and handhelds, and imaging and printing as well as strong positions in IT services, storage, and management software. In 1998, Compaq had purchased Digital Equipment Corporation for $9.6 billion to gain entry into the high-end computing markets dominated by IBM and HP. After some uncertainty regarding shareholder approval of the merger, in part driven by a lack of public support from HP's founding families, the merger was narrowly approved in March 2002.

Index